PSYCHOLOGY Fifth Edition

John P. Dworetzky
Western Washington University

West Publishing Company
Minneapolis/St. Paul   New York   Los Angeles   San Francisco

Copy Editor:	Pat Lewis
Composition:	Parkwood Composition Service
Cover Artwork:	*Umbrellas in the Rain*, 1898–99
	Maurice Brazil Prendergast
	Charles Henry Hayden Fund
	Courtesy of Museum of Fine Arts, Boston

West's Commitment to the Environment   In 1906, West Publishing Company began recycling materials left over from the production of books. This began a tradition of efficient and responsible use of resources. Today, up to 95 percent of our legal books and 70 percent of our college and school texts are printed on recycled, acid-free stock. West also recycles nearly 22 million pounds of scrap paper annually—the equivalent of 181,717 trees. Since the 1960s, West has devised ways to capture and recycle waste inks, solvents, oils, and vapors created in the printing process. We also recycle plastics of all kinds, wood, glass, corrugated cardboard, and batteries, and have eliminated the use of Styrofoam book packaging. We at West are proud of the longevity and the scope of our commitment to the environment.

Production, Prepress, Printing and Binding by West Publishing Company.

Library of Congress Cataloging-in-Publication Data
Dworetzky, John.
        Psychology / John Dworetzky.—5th ed.
            p.   cm.
        Includes bibliographical references and indexes.
ISBN 0-314-02478-6 (alk. paper)
1. Psychology.   I. Title.
BF121.D96   1994
150—dc20
                                                    93-41549
                                                    CIP

To Harold Jensen
Still Riding the High Country at 90

Contents in Brief

Contents

Chapter 1

An Introduction to Psychology   1

Chapter 2

The Biological Bases of Thought and Behavior 35

Chapter 3

Lifespan Development I: Infancy, Childhood and Adolescence 79

Chapter 4

Lifespan Development II: Adulthood and Aging   119

Chapter 5

Sensation   159

Chapter 6

Perception   199

Chapter 7

States of Consciousness   235

Chapter 8

Learning and Conditioning   273

Chapter 9

Memory   311

Chapter 10

Thought and Language   345

Chapter 11

Motivation and Human Sexuality 381

Chapter 12

Emotion   415

Chapter 13

Intelligence and Creativity   441

Chapter 14

Personality   471

Chapter 15

Stress, Health, and Coping   499

Chapter 16

Abnormal Behavior   527

Chapter 17

Therapy   571

Chapter 18

Social Psychology   609

Chapter 19

Gender, Attraction, and Intimacy   647

Appendix A

Applied Psychology   A-1

Appendix B

Statistics   A-21

Appendix C

How to Locate and Read Research Articles in Psychology   A-35

Appendix D

Using the Computer for Psychological Research   A-39

Appendix E

Ethics and Psychological Research   A-41

Preface

Psychology is the study of ourselves, our behavior, our thoughts, our feelings, our lives. We have learned much about human behavior, and we are learning more. Someday, perhaps in the not too distant future, psychologists might be able to apply their knowledge to help reshape the world. Perhaps this power will come from our increasing knowledge of the brain and its chemistry, or from our understanding of aggression and war, or perhaps from a greater comprehension of the factors that motivate us or control our feelings. This textbook contains an introduction to the research and knowledge that psychologists and others have accumulated.

While the text has been designed as an introduction to psychology for undergraduates, it has a strong emphasis on reporting the most recent and important research. The text material is extensive and sometimes detailed, but great efforts have been taken to write every aspect in a way that is clear and easy for a beginner in psychology to understand. This does not mean that the material has been made simple, but that it is understandable. For this, I thank the many students who have given me invaluable feedback in the more than 50 introductory psychology classes that I have taught.

The text is comprehensive, but, like all introductory textbooks, it presents selective rather than inclusive research. Within the text are focus sections in which a particular discussion appears in depth. These sections focus on applications, controversies, gender differences, ethnic diversity, and possible effects that research might have on our future. Every chapter begins with a prologue that helps to introduce the chapter.

Most chapters also include a feature known as the enduring question. The Enduring Question section of any chapter addresses important philosophical questions or issues that have been of lasting concern to psychologists. For example, the enduring question addressed in chapter 1, asks, "Where is the mind within the brain?" This, in turn, leads to a discussion of the mind-body problem, a problem about human consciousness that has fascinated philosophers for centuries and continues to influence psychology to this day. By examining psychology's "enduring questions" students are given an uncommon opportunity to see the big issues that often helped shape and drive psychological research placed side by side with the more traditional material found in introductory textbooks.

Also within each chapter, following a particularly complex or difficult section, is a pedagogical aid known as a concept review. Within the concept review difficult material is addressed once again, but from a different angle or perspective, which helps to make the concept easier to grasp or understand.

Furthermore, a running glossary is provided in the margins. Whenever a new important term is presented, it appears in boldface. Even though it may be defined in text, it is also defined in the marginal glossary to help students review and reinforce their learning. This aid emphasizes important terms so that readers may become more familiar with them. Every boldface term also appears in the glossary at the back of the book.

At the end of each chapter are a chapter summary and suggestions for further reading. The suggestions for further reading have been chosen with care, and provide students who are interested in pursuing a particular area more information at a suitable introductory level.

Throughout the text, each important piece of research is referenced. These references generally appear at the end of the sentence to which they pertain and are shown parenthetically. The original sources of the research and statements are listed in full in the reference section at the back of the text so that students may examine particular research in greater detail.

Five appendices are also included. Appendix A describes and discusses major areas in applied psychology. These areas include industrial/organizational psychology, environmental psychology, sports psychology, consumer psychology and educational psychology. Appendix B provides the students with a brief introduction to the statistics used in psychological research. Appendix C describes a typical research article, lists sources of psychological research, and identifies selected journals that contain articles in psychology. Appendix D describes how to use a computer to search the psychological literature and Appendix E describes the ethical guidelines used by psychologists in their work.

In addition, there are a number of important supplements to this textbook. A study guide for *Psychology* has been prepared by two of my colleagues, Richard D. Rees and Stephen S. Cooper, to assist students in making full use of the textbook. An instructor's manual, containing suggestions for class and lecture, has been developed by Elizabeth Lynch of Glendale College, Arizona, and myself. It includes a comprehensive test bank, along with film suggestions, a capsule summary for each chapter, and behavioral objectives.

No work of this size could ever be accomplished alone, and I owe a great debt to many others. I wish to express my gratitude once again to those colleagues who helped me with the previous editions of *Psychology* and whose ideas and comments are a continuing influence:

J. Whorton Allen
Utah State University

Ellen B. Barker
Bloomsburg State College

Ronald K. Barrett
Loyola Marymount University

D. Thompson Bond
Thomas Nelson Community
  College

Ann Brandt
Glendale Community College
Glendale, Arizona

Arthur Brody
Lehigh University

James Butler
James Madison University

Roy E. Cain
Pan American University
Eidenburg, Texas

William H. Calhoun
The University of Tennessee
Knoxville, Tennessee

Dennis Coon
Santa Barbara City College

Ernest J. Doleys
DePaul University, Illinois

Jack E. Edwards
Illinois Institute of Technology

Donald Elman
Kent State University

Robert B. Graham
East Carolina State University

Michael Grelle
Central Missouri State University

Charles G. Halcomb
Texas Tech University

Robert O. Hansson
University of Tulsa

A. Christine Harris
Chaffey College

Bruce H. Hinrichs
Lakewood Community College
White Bear Lake, Minnesota

Courtland Holdgrafer
Santa Ana College

Ellen C. Huft
Glendale College

Lela Joscelyn
Mount Mary College
Milwaukee, Wisconsin

Khalil A. Khavari
The University of Wisconsin,
    Milwaukee
Milwaukee, Wisconsin

Maria Krasnec
University of Idaho

Brian M. Kruger
Wright State University

Barbara Hansen Lemme
College of DuPage, Illinois

Max W. Lewis
University Western Washington

Svenn Linkskold
Ohio University

Wesley C. Lynch
Montana State University

Raul C. Martinez
Adams State College
Alamosa, Colorado

Charles F. Matter
University of Wisconsin,
    Green Bay
Green Bay, Wisconsin

Spencer A. McWilliams
University of Arizona

Inger Olsen
Vancouver Community College

Gayle H. Olson
University of New Orleans

Robert R. Pagano
University of Pittsburgh

John N. Park
Mankato State University

Robert J. Pellegrini
San Jose State University

Janet D. Proctor
Auburn University

Linda Sandham Quinn
Penn State, Wilkes-Barre Campus
Lehman, Pennsylvania

Duane Reeder
Glendale College

Robert P. Robison
Everett Community College

Robyn Rogers
Southwest Texas State University
San Marcos, Texas

Susan A. Schodahl
San Bernardino Valley College

Lee Springer
Glendale College

Laura A. Stephenson
Washburn University of Topeka,
    Kansas

Barbara Streitfeld
University of Hartford,
    Connecticut

Robert Tilley
Amarillo College

Joe M. Tinnin
Richland College

Donald L. Tollefson
Canisius College

Marcia L. Weinstein
Salem State College

David Wilson
Texas A & M University

Warner Wilson
Wright State University

Carol Woodward
California State University

Rudolph L. Zlody
College of Holy Cross,
    Massachusetts

I would also like to express my thanks to the following members of the academic community who reviewed the chapters included in this fifth edition, and who provided comments, suggestions, and critiques.

William Calhoun
Western Washington University

Roger Fouts
Central Washington University

Charles Hontz
University of North Dakota

Jim Hail McLennan
Community College

Deborah McDonald
New Mexico State University

Michele Manber
Bellevue Community College

Daniel Montello
North Dakota State University

Laurence Miller
Western Washington University

Buddy Grah
Austin Peay State University

Carol Pandey
Los Angeles Pierce College

Michael Rodman
Middlesex Community College

I am especially grateful to Dr. Nancy Davis for her help with chapter four of this text concerning lifespan development. Her input can be felt throughout the chapter.

I also wish to thank all of my colleagues at Western Washington University and Glendale College for their comments, especially Professors Stephen Cooper and Richard Rees for their advice, collaboration and friendship.

I am especially grateful to Bill Stryker for the excellent design of this textbook, and for his great speed, talent, and encouragement. I also wish to thank Pat Lewis for her extremely fast and competent copy editing, and Parkwood Composition Service for their skillful typesetting. Finally, I wish to thank my friend and editor, Clyde Perlee, Jr., editor-in-chief of West's College Division, for his skill, ideas, and encouragement. As always, without his friendship and support, this book could never have been written.

John P. Dworetzky

PSYCHOLOGY   Fifth Edition

Chapter One

An Introduction to Psychology

PROLOGUE

WHAT IS PSYCHOLOGY?

What is the best way to motivate students to learn?

When is it safe to release someone from prison who has been previously violent?

What causes some people to become depressed?

What is the best way to discipline children?

Is intelligence mostly inherited, or is it mostly acquired through experience?

Why do some people smoke, overeat, or drink to excess when they know that it is bad for their health?

What are the best ways to negotiate peace and avoid war?

The world would be a different and better place if we had the answers to just these few questions and yet, there are many more questions, perhaps equally important, that we could ask about people.

Psychology is the field of study that deals with these kinds of questions. The term psychology means the study of the mind. In modern usage, **psychology** *is defined more broadly as the science of behavior and mental processes. These behaviors and mental processes include our thoughts, feelings, and actions.*

Psychologists often conduct research in an effort to get at the answers to the kinds of questions just posed. To do such scientific research, it is necessary to approach problems with an open mind, to make careful observations, and to have a desire to get to the bottom of things. If you feel that these qualities describe you, then you may well be on your way to becoming a psychological researcher.

In many ways, psychological research is like detective work. Some researchers even carry this searching philosophy into their private lives, enjoying the hunt for knowledge whenever and wherever they can. One such person was Clark Hull (1884–1952). Early in his career, Hull earned a reputation for his rigorously controlled experiments on smoking and hypnosis.

There is an interesting story about Hull that shows just how passionate and rigorous his curiosity was. One day Hull surprised his colleagues by announcing that he planned to attend a seance in an effort to contact his dead sister. Hull pointed out that many prominent citizens believed that a particular medium really had the power to reach the spirit world. So why not try? At the time seances were very popular. Many people believed in them and in the spirit world. So Hull was displaying an important characteristic of any good researcher; he was keeping an open mind.

At the seance, Hull took a seat and joined hands with the medium and other members of the group. He explained what he wanted, and the medium said she would do her best. Like a good researcher, Hull carefully watched what happened next.

The lights dimmed and the medium appeared to enter a trance. She called on the spirit world, and suddenly a different voice seemed to come from her throat. "Clark, Clark, it's your sister," the voice said. Hull asked his sister how she was and what the spirit world was like. His sister said that her spirit was at rest and that all was well. She added that someday they would be together and that until then she would keep a protective watch over him. She told him not to worry, that she was all right. Hull began to ask specific questions, but suddenly the lights came on again and the medium awoke from her trance. "I'm sorry," she said, "I can only maintain contact for a short time; the strain is too great." Hull was smiling. The medium said, "But I see you were pleased to talk to your sister." As he stood up to leave, Hull's smile became a grin. "I never had a sister," he said.

I suppose you might argue that that was an odd way to spend an evening, but Hull obviously had fun doing it. While all serious efforts to uncover why we feel, think, and act the way we do require the same kind of skill, curiosity, openness, and ingenuity that Hull brought to the seance, setting up an investigation and carrying it through can also be fun. As you read this book, I can promise you one thing about psychology, it's interesting. I will even hazard a guess that you won't be able to get through a single chapter without saying to yourself any number of times, "That's amazing."

Finally, through your experience with this book, I hope that you will come to acquire a new understanding of yourself and those around you. So welcome to "psychology." I trust that you will find it as exciting and as interesting as I have.

IN THIS CHAPTER, you will read about some of the contributions that researchers like Clark Hull made in the early days of psychology. You will also see how researchers study a problem "scientifically." We will even conduct a psychological experiment together using the techniques psychologists use. Finally, we will look at the limits to our understanding of human thought and behavior.

WHAT IS PSYCHOLOGY?

◆ A group of people who have volunteered for a psychology experiment are shown a very sad movie. Some of them start to cry. The researcher says, "That's okay, go ahead and cry, let it all out." Then, she and her assistants quickly collect the subjects' tears in little glass containers for later chemical analysis to see just what, in fact, her subjects were "letting out." She is wondering if tears serve some purpose. Perhaps tears contain some substance that the body must rid itself of to overcome or compensate for sadness. If so, the substance might be an important chemical affecting our emotions.

◆ A researcher working for NASA asks astronauts to respond to emergency lights on a control board as quickly as possible. When green and red lights are flashed suddenly in the periphery of their vision, the astronauts have trouble telling the lights apart. When the researcher substitutes yellow and blue lights for the red and green ones, the astronauts' errors decrease significantly.

◆ In a laboratory, an investigator stays awake all night observing sleeping subjects who are attached to sensors and measuring devices. By watching the sensors, she can tell when the sleepers begin to dream, when they become restless, or when sleep disturbances start. She is trying to find patterns that may help to explain why some people have difficulty sleeping.

◆ At a large metropolitan zoo, a scientist places a series of small steel rails along the ground throughout the mountain lion compound. From time to time, a mechanical rabbit runs along one of the rails starting from a tunnel. When a lion catches a rabbit, meat is automatically dispensed from a hopper at the far end of the enclosure. The scientist structures the situation so that the lions quickly learn what to do. The curator of the zoo notes that the big cats are healthier and more active now that they are getting exercise and "hunting game."

◆ An investigator observes a three-month-old infant who is watching a rolling ball. The moment the ball rolls behind a couch, the infant loses all interest in the ball and acts as if it no longer exists. The investigator repeats the process with an older infant. When the ball disappears, the older infant leans to one side and tries to see where the ball went. The investigator wonders whether the younger infant simply doesn't yet understand that objects still exist even though they are out of sight.

◆ A therapist in a city hospital interviews a young female patient who wants to go home. Five weeks earlier the woman had suffered a deep depression and had tried take her own life. The therapist interviews her carefully, calling on all his skill to make a decision that will represent his best professional judgment. He doesn't want to detain her without cause, but he also doesn't want her to return to a situation she cannot handle.

◆ An investigator leaves self-addressed unsealed envelopes containing money in church pews all over the city just before the congregations assemble. She leaves similar envelopes in nonreligious halls just before meetings begin. The envelopes are secretly marked so that they can be distinguished later. The investigator then waits at home to see whether people attending church are more likely to return the money they have found than are people attending a nonreligious meeting.

All the professionals in these examples have one thing in common. Whether studying the chemistry of emotion, an astronaut reacting to an emergency, a sleeping person, a hungry mountain lion, a three-month-old baby, a depressed woman in a hospital, or churchgoers' honesty, each of these researchers is studying some aspect of psychology.

PSYCHOLOGY
The science of behavior and mental processes.

PSYCHIATRIST
A medical doctor who has completed specialized training in the field of mental health, such as a psychiatric residency.

Look at the table of contents in this text and you will begin to appreciate how diversified and encompassing psychology is. If you were to become a psychologist, as your career developed you might spend your entire time working within an area described by just one of these chapters, perhaps by just one paragraph within one chapter! One nice thing about having so many topics from which to choose is that those of you who are considering careers in psychology are almost assured of finding something to do that really interests you.

Areas of Specialization

Psychology includes many areas of specialization (see Figure 1.1). The field offers something for everybody. In the following paragraphs, we will describe a few of the different kinds of psychologists and their interests:

◆ *Experimental psychologists,* like many psychologists, rely on scientific methods and experiments to examine behavior. Their research often is conducted in a laboratory. They investigate areas such as sensation, perception, learning, memory, and motivation in humans and other animals. Their emphasis is on basic research, that is, knowledge for its own sake without much consideration as to its possible application.

◆ *Neuropsychological* and *psychobiological psychologists* are interested in biological factors and their effects on behavior. Both neuropsychological and psychobiological psychologists study the brain, nervous system, genes, and drugs in relation to behavior. Neuropsychological psychologists, however, often work hand in hand with physicians to treat disorders related to the nervous system.

◆ *Developmental psychologists* study the way in which behaviors develop and change during a lifespan. Often their emphasis is on childhood. Special areas of interest include the development of language, social attachments, emotions, thinking, and perception.

PSYCHOLOGY THROUGH THE AGES

AT AGE 20: As an undergraduate I majored in psychology.

AT AGE 25: As a graduate student I focused on neuropsychology.

AT AGE 30: I did a postdoc in psychoneuroimmunology.

AT AGE 35: I branched off into psychoneuroimmunoendocrinology.

AT AGE 40: I've been examining the psychoneuroimmuno-endocrinological aspects of cardiovascular disease.

Cartoon by Jane Zich

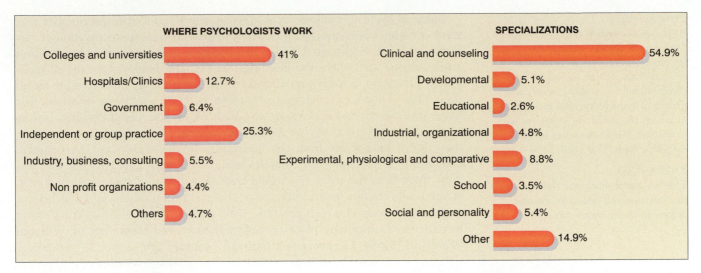

WHERE PSYCHOLOGISTS WORK

Colleges and universities — 41%
Hospitals/Clinics — 12.7%
Government — 6.4%
Independent or group practice — 25.3%
Industry, business, consulting — 5.5%
Non profit organizations — 4.4%
Others — 4.7%

SPECIALIZATIONS

Clinical and counseling — 54.9%
Developmental — 5.1%
Educational — 2.6%
Industrial, organizational — 4.8%
Experimental, physiological and comparative — 8.8%
School — 3.5%
Social and personality — 5.4%
Other — 14.9%

◆ **FIGURE 1.1**

*Places of work and specializations of people in psychology. Data were obtained by using a stratified random sample of members of the American Psychological Association employed full-time as psychologists. (*SOURCE: *After Pion, 1991.)*

◆ *Cognitive psychologists* study internal mental processes, which include thinking, memory, concept formation, perception, and processing of information. To the cognitive psychologist, behavior is composed of mental events, internal representations, desires, beliefs, and thoughts.

◆ *Social psychologists* use scientific techniques to examine the effects that people have on one another. They are interested in topics such as cooperation, aggression, affection, and group pressure.

◆ *Industrial* or *organizational psychologists* generally work with businesses. They are concerned with improving working conditions, raising production rates, and developing decision-making abilities. Many of these I/O psychologists, as they are called, began their work as experimental psychologists and then became consultants for business or industry.

◆ *Educational psychologists* study educational systems, methods of teaching, curricula, and other factors influencing the learning process. Their goals are to improve education and to make learning easier and more efficient.

◆ *Clinical psychologists* focus their efforts on understanding, diagnosing, and treating abnormal or deviant behaviors. Efforts are being made to change the law to allow clinical psychologists to prescribe drugs after further training. As the law currently stands, however, prescribing drugs for mental health is still the province of physicians.

A physician who receives three to five years of specialized training in medicine and mental disorders following medical school is called a **psychiatrist** and has an M.D. degree. Clinical psychologists, like most psychologists, typically have a Ph.D. as their advanced degree.

◆ *Counseling psychologists* were traditionally trained to help individuals solve personal, academic, or vocational problems that did not stem from serious mental disorders. However, counseling and clinical psychologists often have similar training, and the distinction between the two has become practically nonexistent (Fitzgerald & Osipow, 1986).*

*The names enclosed in parentheses are a reference. References are often given after statements made in this text. Their function is to inform you about the sources used to obtain information in case you wish to know more than is provided directly by the text. The reference also contains the underlying research that supports the statement. In this case, take a moment to turn to the References section at the back of the book. Look up "Fitzgerald and Osipow, 1986" to see the original sources of this information. If you wish to know more about the subject, all you need do is to go to a library and find the May 1986 issue of *American Psychologist*—there you can read everything you're ever likely to want to know about the distinctions between counseling and clinical psychologists (of which there are currently very few).

PHILOSOPHY
In the most general terms, philosophy is "the search for the truth." It encompasses two major branches: epistemology, which includes efforts to comprehend the origins, limits, and nature of knowledge; and metaphysics, in which the reality of existence is examined. Minor branches include esthetics, logic, and ethics.

PHYSIOLOGY
The biological discipline that examines the functions of cells, tissues, and organs in living organisms.

Some of these specialized areas may be new to you, and the number may seem a little overwhelming. When I was first introduced to psychology, for instance, I felt as though I had walked into a strange town where I didn't know anyone and where the buildings, streets, and landmarks were all unfamiliar. Of course, a town isn't strange to the people who have lived there all their lives. They can remember when this building was built, or when that street was named, and they know who lives where and which children belong to which parents. It's easy for long-time residents to make sense of a place; they saw it take shape from the beginning. In the same way, the complex community of psychological interests would be more familiar to you had you been there from the start. You would know why certain "structures" had been created, why certain "roads" were more important than others, and which ideas were the offspring of which psychological families. If you want to know about modern psychology, the place to begin, then, is the laboratory of Wilhelm Wundt in Leipzig, Germany, a little over a century ago.

THE BEGINNINGS OF PSYCHOLOGY

Psychology was born of two parents, **philosophy** and **physiology.** For centuries, philosophers had asked questions about human nature, about our emotions, thoughts, and behavior. They had tried to deduce answers to their questions by applying logic and commonsense reasoning. This method achieved some success. For example, people knew that water would not flow through something solid, nevertheless, they observed that perspiration came through the skin. Based on this observation, philosophers deduced that skin must have holes in it—thereby recognizing the existence of pores centuries before such structures could actually be seen with a microscope. Philosophers did not always make accurate deductions, however. For instance, the great philosopher Aristotle (384–322 B.C.) believed that thinking occurred in the heart, while the brain served only to help cool the blood. (Aristotle based his deductions on the observations that strongly felt emotions were often sensed in the chest and that the convolutions of the brain would provide a greater surface from which heat could radiate—not bad, I suppose, for an educated guess. Then again, we all have days when our brains don't seem to be doing much except radiating heat, but that's probably not what Aristotle meant.) Also in error was the famous physician Hippocrates (ca. 460–377 B.C.), who believed that all emotions resulted from different combinations or levels of four bodily fluids or "humors." These were black bile, yellow bile, blood, and phlegm—interesting, and in some ways predating our modern knowledge of hormones, but still basically wrong. Although such errors were common, Aristotle's and Hippocrates' ideas about the body and behavior were accepted as fact for almost 2,000 years before they were finally challenged by physiologists' experiments during the last few centuries.

Physiologists were especially influential in providing a new understanding of the brain and the nervous system and the ways in which these structures affect behavior. For example, at one time it was commonly believed that a person's muscular responses occurred the instant that he or she summoned them. By a series of careful scientific experiments, however, physiologists were able to demonstrate that nerve impulses take time to travel from their place of origin in the brain or spinal cord to the muscles. You can discover this for yourself if you assemble about 30 people in a line that forms a complete circle. If time permits, it's fun to do in class. Simply ask each person to place a hand on the shoulder of the one in front. Then tell the group: "As soon as you feel your shoulder squeezed, squeeze the shoulder of the person in front of you. Do this as fast as you can." Someone with a stopwatch then starts the process and stops the watch when he feels his own shoulder squeezed by the person behind him. The nerve impulse has now made the complete circle. Now do the process again, only this time, ask each person to place a hand on the ankle of the one in front. With the extra distance of ankle to shoulder for everyone in the line, the nerve impulse will take longer to make the circle than it did before!

Many of the founders of psychology were trained in both philosophy and physiology. In fact, it was the blending of the questions asked by the philosophers with the careful scientific experimentation of the physiologists that led to the field of study we call psychology.

It may surprise you to learn that psychology hasn't always been concerned with the pursuits commonly associated with it such as mental illness, animal behavior, unconscious thoughts, dreams, IQ tests, personality, or childhood. At the beginning, its objective was to systematically analyze immediate conscious experience, that is, to analyze the thoughts or experiences one was aware of having in reaction to whatever was going on at any given moment.

Careful analysis of conscious experience began when a German physician named Wilhelm Wundt (1832–1920), acting on his persistent curiosity concerning matters of the human mind, started his psychological laboratory in 1879. One of the first questions that attracted his interest was the speed of human thought and whether this differed from person to person. While considering this question, Wundt took the bold step of applying the scientific methodology of physiologists to the study of the mind. He built a device he called a thought meter (see Figure 1.2) and began the first truly psychological experiment.

The thought meter worked as follows. The pendulum (B in Figure 1.2) swung back and forth. As it did so, the needle (S) attached horizontally to the pendulum would strike the bells (g). The observer's job was to note the exact position of the pendulum when he heard the bell. By adjusting the length of the needle beforehand, Wundt could predetermine the time between bell "dings" and the position of the pendulum at each ding. Wundt discovered that most observers disagreed with the actual time and position by as much as ⅕ second. Wundt's own observations were off by about ⅛ second. Wundt believed that what he had measured was the time of the swiftest thought; that is, the time it took for the person to think about looking at the pendulum from the moment that he heard the bell.* This, Wundt argued, clearly showed that not everyone thought at the same speed!

The very idea that anyone might try to measure the speed of a thought was astounding. Wundt had opened a new area, the scientific investigation of mental processes. He then attempted to build a theory by investigating conscious acts of will and the way in which such acts were related.

Although Wundt's works are of historical interest and he got psychology off to a good start, modern researchers have actually found most of Wundt's discoveries to be of limited scientific value. While developing his theories, Wundt often contradicted himself or failed to consider important aspects of his own work. For example, modern researchers now understand that Wundt's thought meter measures not only the speed of thinking but also attention, the speed of muscular responses, and motivation—all now considered under the general heading *reaction time*. Still, all psychology owes Wundt a debt of gratitude for doing something no one had done before—setting up a psychological laboratory in which the mind was subjected to scientific scrutiny and measurement.

*The time it takes for the sound of the bell to reach the observer's ears is negligible (about 1/1000 second).

Wilhelm Wundt, the father of experimental psychology (1832–1920).

◆ **FIGURE 1.2**

The "thought meter" used by Wilhelm Wundt in his early psychological experiments. (SOURCE: Wundt, 1862, p. 264.)

STRUCTURALISM
The school of psychological thought founded by Edward Titchener that is concerned with reducing experience to its basic parts, determining the laws by which the parts are synthesized, and investigating the structure and content of mental states by introspection.

INTROSPECTION
The method introduced by structural psychologists, in which the subject describes his or her own conscious experiences.

DIFFERENT APPROACHES TO THE STUDY OF PSYCHOLOGY

Structuralism

Edward B. Titchener (1867–1927) was an Englishman who taught for many years at Cornell University in New York. Titchener was a dynamic and flamboyant speaker who attracted a large following, some have argued, through little more than his own theatrical personality (he sometimes lectured wearing a red-lined cape that swirled about dramatically as he gestured). He cast himself in the role of Wundt's primary representative and interpreter in the English-speaking world.

Titchener wrote and lectured extensively about Wundt's theories. Since many people in the English-speaking world were interested in Wundt's works but couldn't read German, they turned to Titchener for an explanation. Unfortunately, Titchener liked to add and change ideas as he went along, still claiming that he was merely expounding Wundt's theories (Janik & Toulmin, 1973; Blumenthal, 1980). Titchener argued incorrectly that Wundt was trying to discover an exact structure or blueprint of the mind by reducing experience to its elemental components. Curiously, what then developed was a philosophical approach to the study of psychology known as **structuralism,** attributed to Wundt but mostly based on Titchener's ideas and interpretations.

However based on misinterpretation it may have been, structuralism was interesting in its own right. It relied on a self-observation technique known as **introspection.** Trained self-observers, or introspectionists, tried to break down the content of their own conscious experience into all of its component parts. Only persons skilled in the techniques of introspection could, it was argued, provide an objective description of an experience, because only they were trained to describe their immediate perception of an event without adding biased conclusions drawn from expectations or knowledge.

The structural approach taken by Titchener might have remained a powerful force in psychology had it not been for a few critical flaws. The worst of these was the introspective method itself. Have you ever applied introspection to your own conscious experience? For instance, have you ever tried to stop in the middle of a daydream and carefully examine your exact thoughts or sensations? Observing what you are experiencing *changes* the experience. Psychologists began to discover that the very act of introspection altered many of the conscious experiences they wanted to isolate and examine. It was like trying to grab a handful of water. Even more devastating was the discovery that different researchers independently using the introspective method were getting different results. Nothing could be done to resolve the problem of a disagreement between trained observers. After all, each was describing a personal experience that no one but that individual could measure or verify. Who could say which observer was correct?

By the 1930s, researchers had begun to abandon structuralism as a way of learning about the mind. By that time, other approaches were yielding more satisfactory results: psychologists working with animals were obtaining exciting results without introspection; European psychoanalysts were examining the influence of unconscious mental processes on maladaptive behavior; and many American psychologists were simply more interested in searching for practical solutions to everyday problems than analyzing conscious experience.

Still, all psychology owes a debt to the structural approach for three reasons. First, it provided psychology with a strong scientific and research impetus. Second, it gave the introspective method a thorough test, which was worthwhile because now we understand the limitations to this seemingly straight-

Edward B. Titchener (1867–1927).

forward approach. Third, it provided a body of work against which new schools of psychological thought could react.

From what has been said up to this point, it might appear that psychology developed solely from the German scientific tradition, but that is not wholly correct (Buxton, 1985). Along with Wundt's influence, many other ideas and forces were at work during those early days. These schools of philosophical thought included **British empiricism,** whose advocates argued that all mental thought and activity were the direct result of a person's experiences; French psychiatry, which was making interesting headway using hypnosis (see Chapter 7) to probe the mind; Russian physiology, which, under the guidance of Ivan Pavlov (see Chapter 8), was breaking new ground in the understanding of learning; and evolutionary theory as espoused by the British naturalist Charles Darwin.

Functionalism

Functionalism was the first American approach to the study of psychology. In sharp contrast to structuralism, this approach was simply an assortment of ideas loosely connected by a common thread. Some have argued that the founder of this approach (if it can even be said to have had a founder) was John Dewey (1859–1952) a prominent American philosopher and educator, while others look to William James (1842–1910) and his work as the clearest embodiment of the approach. James is still regarded by many people as the greatest American psychologist. He received an M.D. from Harvard and was a professor of anatomy. Again, we see with Dewey, the philosopher, and James, the anatomist, the two roots of psychology.

James became interested in psychological inquiry in 1875 and published his famous two-volume work, *Principles of Psychology,* in 1890. Like his famous literary younger brother Henry James, William was also a skilled writer. His works still make fascinating reading. Although James wasn't an experimentalist, he had a way of synthesizing psychological principles brilliantly and of getting to the heart of difficult problems. He rejected the structuralist idea that the conscious mind had a permanent structure, or blueprint. To him, conscious experience was more like a river that was always changing and flowing. He coined the famous term **stream of consciousness** to express this property.

James was greatly influenced by the work of Charles Darwin (1809–1882), who stated that, through the process of **natural selection,** characteristics in animals that served a valuable function would be favored and carried over from one generation to the next. For example, Darwin argued that sex was pleasurable because only those species that found it so would have survived; a species that didn't like sex would not last more than a generation. Physical characteristics as well—such as eyes, ears, hands, paws, and claws—had all been favored by natural selection because they served a useful function. With this in mind, James concluded that human consciousness must also have a *function*, or why else would it have evolved? He believed that the conscious mind enabled people to make rational choices, which in turn enabled them to survive generation after generation. James considered consciousness to be like "an organ added for the sake of steering a nervous system grown too complex to regulate itself" (James, 1890, p. 144).

Because of this philosophical emphasis, other functionalists who followed in this tradition were concerned with *why* a thought or behavior occurred, rather than with *what* a thought or behavior was. This is the major distinction between functionalism and structuralism, and it opened the door to many new areas of psychological study by a number of important individuals.

G. Stanley Hall (1844–1924) was perhaps James's most illustrious student. Hall was the first person to receive a Ph.D. in psychology; he was also the

BRITISH EMPIRICISM
A theory put forth by British philosophers during the seventeenth and eighteenth centuries (most notably, by Locke, Berkeley, and Hume) arguing that all knowledge and understanding come only from learning and experience (e.g., the mind is a blank slate on which experience writes our nature). In light of our modern understanding of inheritance, the idea of a *tabula rasa* or blank state is no longer considered to be plausible.

FUNCTIONALISM
The school of psychological thought founded by William James, which proposed that the function, not the structure, of conscious experience should be studied.

STREAM OF CONSCIOUSNESS
A term coined by William James to describe the idea that conscious experience is like a river, always changing and flowing, rather than a permanent fixture.

NATURAL SELECTION
The process, suggested by Charles Darwin, by which the individuals of a species who are best adapted to their environment have a better chance of passing their genes on to the next generation than do those who are less well adapted.

William James (1842–1910).

PSYCHOANALYSIS
A therapy through which one seeks to bring unconscious desires into consciousness and make it possible to resolve conflicts, which usually date back to early childhood experiences. Psychoanalysis is also the school of psychological thought founded by Sigmund Freud; a theory that offers an explanation of unconscious mental processes.

FREE ASSOCIATION
A method used in psychoanalytic therapy in which the patient is asked to say whatever comes to mind, no matter how trivial, inconsequential, or unrelated to the matter being discussed. Freud believed that the first thing to come to mind was often a clue to what the unconscious was trying to conceal.

founder of the American Psychological Association. Hall's interest in the development of human beings during childhood, adolescence, and adulthood and his systematic investigations of changes during the lifespan marked the beginnings of developmental psychology.

John Dewey (1859–1952) pursued his interest in the problem-solving ability of the conscious mind as a factor in our species's survival (Dewey, 1910). Dewey's interest in problem solving and in ways of improving teaching contributed to the establishment of another new discipline, educational psychology. Also, because animals are capable of learning and because their behavior too serves a purpose or function, the study of animal psychology was born. Industrial psychology also came into being when researchers began making time-motion studies of the value and function of each movement of workers on assembly lines, with the goal of improving efficiency by eliminating wasteful motions. All these psychologies, although quite different from one another, shared the functional philosophy.

Functionalism is no longer a distinct psychological approach if, indeed, it ever was. Even at its peak early in this century, it was a diversified and informal system, a collection of new fields that were linked by the common idea that the mind's function was more important than its structure. Today, the areas of psychology to which functionalism gave birth have matured to become fields in their own right.

Psychoanalysis

Psychoanalysis probably has been the most widely publicized psychological system, especially among nonpsychologists. Psychoanalytic theory was developed by a Viennese physician, Sigmund Freud (1856–1939). From its beginning in 1895, psychoanalysis created a storm of controversy. Some of its principles and concepts were so shocking that many people regarded them as entirely new. Nevertheless, like all important ideas, it had its antecedents (Sulloway, 1979).

Psychoanalytic theory traces its roots to neurology and medicine. Its goal was to understand human behavior. Freud presented, as one of the major tenets of psychoanalysis, the concept of the unconscious mind. He argued that the mind is like an iceberg in that most of it is hidden beneath the surface. He stated that human beings are controlled primarily by drives and urges hidden within the unconscious, not by rational and conscious processes. To some critics, this was the last of three great blows to human pride. The first was dealt when Copernicus demonstrated that Earth was not the center of the universe; the second came when Darwin's work implied that humans had evolved from lower species. Now Freud was arguing that we were not even the conscious masters of our own actions!

Freud believed that abnormal behavior and, for that matter, all aspects of personality, could be explained by analyzing the motives and drives of the unconscious. Like the functionalists, Freud had been influenced by Darwin, and he maintained that the unconscious served a function—it kept unacceptable thoughts or desires repressed or hidden from the conscious mind. Because of this, he argued, the unconscious mind was reluctant to give up its knowledge, so special techniques were needed to probe its secrets.

Among the techniques Freud used were hypnosis, **free association** (in which the patient is asked to say whatever comes to mind, regardless of how foolish it may seem), dream interpretation, and analysis of slips of the tongue. In the last technique, for example, a psychoanalyst might conclude that the patient was exhibiting a repressed sexual desire if she answered the question "What is your religion?" by stating, "I'm a prostitute, eh, I mean Protestant!" Freud believed that analysis could help resolve unconscious conflicts and correct arrested personality development or abnormal behavior.

Psychoanalysis, however, has been severely criticized for its lack of scientific control and careful experimentation (Rosenzweig, 1985). Many modern psychologists, although agreeing that psychoanalysis is interesting, argue that as a psychology it is unscientific:

The unfortunate truth is that the analysts' statements are so general that they can explain whatever behavior occurs. A genuine scientific explanation cannot do this. (Marx & Hillix, 1963, p. 231)

Others point out that psychoanalysis relies on techniques that have never been validated. For instance, although it may come as a surprise to you, no one has ever found a way to determine whether dreams have important meanings or whether, in fact, they mean anything at all. Yet many conclusions drawn by psychoanalysts rest heavily on dream interpretation.

At the same time, the importance of psychoanalysis cannot be denied. Freud's work made a great contribution to psychology because the interest it stimulated in many previously neglected areas—the workings of the unconscious mind, sexuality, emotionality, abnormal behavior, conflict, childhood—proved fruitful.

Behaviorism and S-R Psychology

Early in this century, an American psychologist, John B. Watson (1878–1958), helped to develop **behaviorism,** a system of psychology he believed to be far more objective than any other. Watson had been trained as a functional psychologist and was especially interested in the purpose and functions of animal behavior. Like most psychologists who investigated humans, researchers who studied animal subjects were careful to be scientific in their work. They objectively observed and recorded everything they could. But to Watson's way of thinking, human psychology still had a serious fault: There was no way to observe the conscious mind objectively. If you wanted to know what people thought, you had to ask them. They alone could tell you. To Watson, this was introspectionism again. He thought that if a purely objective experimental science of psychology was to be developed, psychologists must reject all subjective methods and rely solely on what could be observed and recorded objectively. In Watson's view, psychology had

made a false start under Wundt . . . because it would not bury its past. It tried to hang on to tradition with one hand and push forward as a science with the other. Before progress could be made in astronomy, it had to bury astrology [the belief that the positions of the stars and planets control our lives]; neurology had to bury phrenology [the study of personality by measuring the skull and the shape of bumps on the head]; and chemistry had to bury alchemy [a mystical "science" that had as its centerpiece the effort to change lead into gold]. But the social sciences, psychology, sociology, political science, and economics, will not bury their "medicine men." (Watson, 1929, p. 3)

Before Watson's time, the Russian physiologist Ivan Sechenov had noted that all human behavior might be reduced to the study of muscular movement. In 1863, Sechenov stated,

A child laughing at the sight of a toy, a young girl trembling at the first thought of love . . . Newton discovering and writing down the laws of the universe—everywhere the final act is muscular movement. (Sechenov, 1863/1965)*

*When a reference contains two dates, as in this instance, the first is the publication date of the original article, while the second is the publication date of the English translation.

BEHAVIORISM
The school of psychology that views learning as the most important aspect of an organism's development. Behaviorists objectively measure behavior and the way in which stimulus-response relationships are formed.

John B. Watson, the father of behaviorism (1878–1958).

S-R PSYCHOLOGY
The school of psychology that views the stimulus-response connection as the foundation of behavior. The goal of S-R psychology is to discover the functional relationships between stimuli and responses.

GESTALT PSYCHOLOGY
The school of psychological thought that emphasizes that wholes are more than the sum of their parts. Gestalt psychologists study forms and patterns and contend that stimuli are perceived as whole images rather than as parts built into images.

PHI PHENOMENON
Specifically, a perceptual illusion brought about by observing two lights placed side by side in a darkened room and flashed alternately. The resulting perception is of one light moving back and forth. Also, often applied to any circumstance in which stationary objects presented in succession appear to be moving, such as occurs when we view a motion picture.

Watson built on this idea, taking the tremendous philosophical step of rejecting the study of conscious thought and mental activity because they were not directly observable! Instead, he emphasized observable environmental stimuli (for example, a loud noise, the sight of a candy bar, praise from a friend) and the observable behaviors or muscular responses that occurred in the presence of such stimuli. Of course, Watson also rejected the ideas of psychoanalysis as these too, he argued, dealt with unobservable events, such as dreams (observable only to the dreamer) or the actions of a supposed unconscious mind. For this reason, behaviorism was also referred to as "black-box" psychology because its earlier proponents considered the mind to be like a mysterious black box whose contents could never be examined objectively.

Under Watson, behaviorism became one of the more influential and controversial schools of psychology and was greatly championed in later years by B. F. Skinner (1904–1990). In the tradition of the behaviorists, Skinner argued strongly right up until his death a few years ago that psychology could never be a science of the mind and that the "mind" was not an appropriate object of study (Skinner, 1990).

A branch of behaviorism known as **S-R psychology** (for stimulus-response) remains an important force in modern psychology. S-R psychology has been of great value in demonstrating that much of our behavior is the product of our immediate environment and of our past experiences. S-R psychologists have shown that the associations we experience—the pleasant or unpleasant consequences following our actions—and our observations of the actions of those around us, called social learning, often determine our responses. Through behavioral technology, problems such as aggression, phobias, shyness, and poor study habits often can be corrected.

The behaviorists are owed a debt of gratitude for emphasizing the need to define terms carefully, to conduct controlled experiments, and in general to make psychology more of a science. Ironically, this effort has provoked some of the strongest criticism of behaviorism and S-R psychology. It has been argued that by ignoring the mind or concentrating on reactions to stimuli, researchers using this approach often ignore important but unobservable aspects of human behavior, such as emotion, thought, and unconscious processes, and that they discredit feelings or ideas that do not readily lend themselves to controlled experimentation.

Gestalt Psychology

At about the same time that behaviorism was becoming an important force in American psychology, a different reaction to structuralism was developing in Germany, the Gestalt view. To understand the view of **Gestalt psychology,** it is helpful to consider how a motion-picture projector works. Structuralists, who wished to break down conscious experience into its simplest elements, had a difficult time when they tried to explain how a series of still pictures, shown one after another, could seem to move (which is, of course, how a "motion" picture works). The structuralists reasoned that if sensations are elemental, then each picture should appear as a separate sensation—especially to a trained introspectionist. But that's not what happens. Even a trained introspectionist viewing a movie sees a single picture that appears to be moving. This kind of false perception of motion is known as the **phi phenomenon.**

In 1912, Max Wertheimer (1880–1943) presented a paper in which he argued that the phi phenomenon needed no explanation. Rather, it was a real phenomenon in its own right, and any attempt to reduce it to simpler sensations would destroy it. At first glance, this argument may not seem revolutionary, but it was. It rejected a fundamental tenet of structuralism—that we can break down all experience into elemental parts in order to understand it better. Wertheimer, along with his most famous students, Wolfgang Kohler (1887–1967) and Kurt Koffka (1886–1941), argued that the whole experience (in German, the *Gestalt*) was not just the sum of its parts; it was more, it was itself. For example, the color white is created by an equal mixture of red, green, and blue. (Although at first this may be difficult to believe, if you take a disk that has been divided like a pie into three equal parts, one part fire-engine red, another part forest green, and the third part royal blue, and spin it at high speed, the disk will appear snow white!) Gestalt psychologists emphasized that the experience of white is more than the sum of its parts. Certainly, it is red plus green plus blue, but it is also itself; it is white. Experiencing red, then experiencing green, and finally experiencing blue is obviously not the same as experiencing white. The experience of "whiteness" cannot be broken down into its elemental parts without destroying the experience.

The Gestalt psychologists weren't the first people to rebel against the idea of reducing consciousness to its supposed constituent parts. Some 22 years before the beginning of Gestalt psychology, William James, whose brilliant mind seems to have been everywhere at once, stated,

> The traditional psychologist (structuralist) talks like one who would say a river consists of nothing but pailsful, spoonsful, quartpotsful, barrelsful, and other molded forms of water. Even were the pails and the pots all actually standing in the same stream, still between them the free water would continue to flow. (James, 1890, p. 279)

Had James pursued this line of reasoning a little farther, he might have added the founding of Gestalt psychology to his long list of accomplishments!

Gestalt psychologists argued that conscious sensations can be examined, but that the whole experience must be taken for what it is. Moreover, the use of specially trained self-observers is unnecessary. To the Gestaltists, the laws of psychology are the laws of *systems*, not of parts, and there is little value in breaking down experiences mechanistically.

The Gestalt philosophy is still prevalent throughout modern psychology. It is now well appreciated that many experiences must be analyzed and understood as whole entities and cannot necessarily be broken down into constituent parts.

Phenomenology

Phenomenology is an interesting approach developed by the German philosopher Edmund Husserl (1859–1938). In essence, he advanced the philosophical position that since reality could only be perceived as a subjective experience, all reality, therefore, *was* subjective. In other words, nothing can ever be any more real than our perception of it. Taken to the extreme, the argument can be made that there is no reality and that, in fact, nothing is "real," there is only our subjective experience. Husserl, however, did not reject the idea of reality or the scientific investigation of it, but rather emphasized focusing on our perceptions and private experiences rather than on the physical events surrounding us. Building on this conceptual tactic, psychologists Abraham Maslow (1908–1970), and later Carl Rogers (1902–1987), helped to build a psychological approach referred to as **humanistic psychology.**

Humanistic psychologists' understanding of behavior is different from that of psychoanalysts or behaviorists. Humanists do not believe that behavior is governed in an important way either by unconscious drives and motives or by external stimuli and rewards in the environment. Instead, their focus, centered in the phenomenological perspective, looks inward toward one's subjective experience. They argue that people are free agents, have free will, are conscious and creative, and are born with an inner motivation to fulfill their potential. Maslow referred to such fulfillment as **self-actualization.** The humanists view self-actualization as a lifelong process rather than as a goal that a person even-

PHENOMENOLOGY
The approach developed by the German philosopher Edmund Husserl (1859–1938) which stated, in essence, that reality can only be perceived as a subjective experience and that all reality, therefore, was subjective.

HUMANISTIC PSYCHOLOGY
A school of psychology that emphasizes the uniqueness of the individual and the search for self-actualization.

SELF-ACTUALIZATION
Abraham Maslow's term for the process in which an individual constantly strives to realize his or her full potential.

Abraham Maslow (1908–1970).

tually reaches. The influence of the Gestalt view is also evident—humanists strongly believe that human beings cannot be understood piecemeal; rather, the whole person must always be taken into account if we are to achieve a reasonable understanding of behavior. Furthermore, in keeping with phenomenology, if we wish to consider the whole person, we can understand behavior only by examining each individual's unique self-perception. In this view, the world is different for all of us, because we all perceive it differently and because each of us, as a whole, is unique—*there is no shared reality*.

Some humanistic psychologists, such as Maslow, developed a concept of personality and motivation based on these ideas. Others, such as Carl Rogers, devised therapies to help people develop their individual potential. These aspects of humanistic psychology are examined in greater detail in Chapters 11 and 17. Like psychoanalysis, humanistic psychology has been criticized for more often being based on speculations than on evidence obtained from scientific experiments.

The Biological Approach

Learning, remembering, thinking, feeling, perceiving, in fact, all of our abilities and actions, are rooted in our biology. Physiologists and physicians have been interested in the human brain for centuries. But the brain is so complicated that for most of that time even its basic functions remained mysterious and beyond the reach of our understanding.

With few exceptions, most of our early knowledge of how the brain works came from the study of head injuries. During the First World War in particular, improvements in medical care meant that a significant number of brain-damaged people were able to survive their injuries and become objects of study. The biological approach to the study of psychology has expanded rapidly in the last few decades, however, owing to the development of new techniques and instruments that have enabled us to pry loose some of the brain's secrets. And, as we enter the next century, even newer and more sophisticated methods hold the promise of revealing far more than we currently know.

Through the use of modern techniques, we are continuing to look inside the brain and observe how it acts under different circumstances, learning which parts perform which functions, and even seeing how it communicates and talks with itself. We are also beginning to unravel the genetic code and starting to understand in a deeper way how inheritance can influence behavior.

Many researchers believe that unraveling the mysteries of the brain and genetics will give us a profound understanding that will dwarf all previous attempts to explain the mind and behavior. In fact, neurobiology is now considered so basic to our overall understanding of psychology, that we will start our exploration into human thoughts and behavior in Chapter 2 by looking at what this approach has uncovered. Some of the things you will read about would have seemed implausible only a few years ago.

Cognitive Psychology

Cognition generally refers to thinking, remembering, and perceiving. Although Wilhelm Wundt was interested in mental phenomena, he believed that advanced processes, such as thinking, were so dependent on culture and language that they could not easily be studied. As a result, Wundt limited his investigations to "simpler" matters, such as the perception of objects, until the very end of his career. Consequently, until about the time of the Second World War, studies that focused on what are now considered to be the traditional topics of cognitive psychology, namely, attention, pattern recognition, memory, language, reading and writing, reasoning, and problem solving (Best, 1989).

At that time, a psychologist named Donald Broadbent became interested in a problem that fighter pilots were having. During combat, pilots discovered that they could not read all of their gauges and instruments without taking their eyes off the action for a dangerously long time. Broadbent discovered that the pilots had learned to compensate for this difficulty by using some gauges more than others or by taking shortcuts to get the vital information they needed. To Broadbent, this meant that human beings were much more than passive receivers of environmental stimuli; they actively gathered and interacted with the information in their environments. Human beings were active information processors. This concept is the keystone of cognitive psychology.

Behaviorists continued to criticize strongly those who studied areas such as thought or perception, because such things could not be directly observed. Nevertheless, cognitive psychology came of age and flourished owing to two events: first, behaviorists were finding some interesting phenomena that seemed impossible to explain without resorting to the concept of thought, and second, scientists were developing computers that held the promise of eventually being able to think.

This second point has had the greatest influence on the upsurge of cognitive psychology. We know what is inside a machine, because we put it there. It is not, as John Watson called the human brain, "a black box forever mysterious." As computer technology developed, we made computers that could actually "see," "reason," and, to a limited degree, even learn from experience. As part of the effort to find better ways to make computers, the cognitive processes of human beings have attracted special interest. In what ways are they like the machine's processes? How are humans different? Can machines be made to work more like the human brain? These questions have led to many interesting efforts to understand the human thought process and to the development of many ingenious ways to measure it, albeit indirectly. In Chapter 10, you will have a chance to explore the history and advances in this interesting area of psychology.

AN ENDURING QUESTION: THE MIND-BODY PROBLEM

Now that you have had a chance to read a little bit about the different approaches to psychology, you may have noticed that many of the differences between these approaches center on how to treat the concept of "mind." For instance, should the mind be the focus of study as cognitive psychologists argue, or, as the behaviorists stressed, should it be ignored? Should it be examined piecemeal as the structuralists suggested, or taken as a whole, or gestalt? Should it be seen in terms of cells and nerves as the neurobiologists suggest, or taken for a subjective entity as the humanists argue? In fact, what is the mind and where is it?

This last question, "What is the mind and where is it?" is one of the oldest in philosophy and is considered to be the most challenging question in all of psychology—perhaps the most challenging question in all of human experience. Since *psychology* is literally "the study of the mind" (*psyche* is the Greek word for *mind*), you might think that psychologists could tell you what the mind is, or at least where it is. But we cannot. And, the problems we encounter when we try are the sort that tend to leave those making the attempt sitting alone in a corner babbling to themselves. Daring the prospect that such an effort might have a similar effect on you and me, let's take a moment to search for the mind or at least attempt to figure out what it is.

MIND-BODY PROBLEM
A classical issue concerning what is mental and what is physical. In some instances, it has been argued that the mind is purely physical (see the materialist hypothesis). In other instances, it has been argued that the mind is not physical, but functions in parallel with the physical body (see the dualist hypothesis). The issue remains unresolved.

MATERIALIST HYPOTHESIS
The argument that the mind is purely physical and, as such, is subject to the laws of physical nature. This position denies the existence of a spirit, soul, or mind other than what could be created from the physical or biological.

THE DUALIST HYPOTHESIS
The argument that the mind is separate from the body and not physical in nature. In this view, the mind is often thought of as functioning in parallel with, but unconnected to, the physical body.

AN ENDURING QUESTION, CONTINUED

Somewhere—probably among the cells, or combinations of cells, of your brain—is your mind. Call it your spirit, your soul, your "youness," your consciousness, whatever, we all feel it—the sense of being alive, looking out of our eyes, hearing with our ears, thinking things over with our "inner voice." But what exactly is "you"? Visual images enter your eyes and travel about your brain, but where are you in there? Where is the conscious person who *sees* the image? Where is the "ghost in the machine" as philosophers used to ask? This has come to be known as the **mind-body problem,** and solving it, if it can be solved, will be one of the greatest accomplishments in all of human history.

With our modern understanding of anatomy and biology, most scientists today argue that conscious experience, the sense of residing somewhere inside your body, is an interesting illusion created by the interaction of the brain's different parts in much the same way as the illusion of white light is generated by the equal mixing of red, green, and blue light. This position is known as the **materialist hypothesis.**

And yet, certain problems remain. Consider the following: You are sitting in a chair. Now pretend that I have a machine that can create an exact copy of you, right down to the last atom or electron. Zap!—the copy appears in a chair next to you. It, of course, looks just like you. It has all of your memories. In fact, its "last" memory is of sitting where you are, and it is very surprised to find that it has "moved." It is you, and yet it isn't, because you aren't in that body (at least, I don't think that you would be!). But if you aren't in that body, why aren't you? Is someone else in there? If so, who? If your bodies are exactly the *same* in every way, why is there this *difference* between you? Maybe you are not your duplicate and your duplicate is not you because you each have a different spirit, a spirit that is not made of anything physical that the machine could copy. In fact, the Greek word *psyche,* which we have mentioned means "mind," actually denotes a spiritual as well as a physical presence. This view is called the **dualist hypothesis.** Although it was popular among the ancient Greeks, this position is currently unpopular among scientists, probably because the idea of nonmaterial spirits sounds too much like ghosts and phantoms to suit the tastes of anyone engaged in "hard" science and also because there is, so far, absolutely no respectable evidence to support the existence of any such energy, force, or entity. And yet, who would be living in that exact copy of you?

One the other hand, if there is no spirit and the materialist position is correct and the mind is an illusion created by the interaction of the parts of the brain, might this mean that someday we could build machines that, through the interaction of their parts, would develop conscious awareness? Arthur C. Clark certainly thought so when he wrote, in his book *2001,* of a computer that fought for its "life" when it discovered that scientists were planning to unplug it. Who knows, perhaps one day in the distant future, a case will come before the court in which a computer claiming conscious awareness will ask for equal protection under the law. I suppose at that point we could hand the mind-body problem over to the lawyers (whom, some argue, deserve it).

Whatever the answer may be, it is certain that something about conscious existence is very, very peculiar. What conscious awareness actually turns out to be may well be beyond our wildest dreams or anyone's science fiction. Maybe someday we will know. ◆

Modern Trends and the Emergence of Scientific Psychology

Psychology continues to be influenced by new ideas and philosophical forces. Some of the original systems of psychology, too, have matured and changed. For example, behaviorism and cognitive psychology have both expanded and, to a certain extent, even merged (Kleinginna & Kleinginna, 1988; Mahoney, 1989). Both have given birth to clinical therapies, social and other learning theories, and theories of motivation. Psychoanalysis has become more diversified but still includes many of Freud's original therapeutic treatments.

Although hundreds of pages could be written about the different psychological groups, subgroups, and offshoots, this does not mean that psychology has become a loose amalgam of splinter groups, all going in different directions. All psychologists who rely on the special techniques of the **scientific method** are, philosophically, sharing the same view: They are scientific psychologists. That one might be a psychobiological psychologist studying a hormone's effects on behavior, another a cognitive psychologist studying memory, and yet another a school psychologist testing a child's academic ability is not important. If they are using or relying on scientific methods, they share a common ground. To help you understand the power and importance of these scientific methods and why they must be used, let's take some time to explore them and even conduct a psychological experiment.

❧ RESEARCH METHODS

All scientific research is based on systematic and objective methods of observing, recording, and describing events. Table 1.1 outlines the six dimensions of psychological research. All the research discussed in this text (and, for that matter, all psychological research) can be categorized in terms of one or the other dimension in these pairs. If you become familiar with these dimensions, it will be easier for you to understand the research described in the following chapters.

Experimental Methods

The scientific **experiment** is one of the most powerful research tools that psychologists possess. Perhaps the best way to learn how to conduct an experiment—and how not to conduct one—is to try it yourself.

For the next few pages, let's work on an experiment together. First, we need an issue that is testable. Some issues are not currently testable, such as the following:

- ◆ Will psychology still be taught 500 years from now?
- ◆ How did prehistoric people raise children?
- ◆ How much did Thomas Jefferson's liver weigh?
- ◆ Is there life on Neptune?

Tests cannot currently be devised for these questions because no one today has access to concrete observable information about them. For example, we would need samples from Neptune, child-rearing advice carved in stone by prehistoric people, a time machine, or an autopsy report from Jefferson's physician before we could explore these subjects. Instead, let's examine an issue that can be tested: What is the relationship between violence on television programs and aggressive behavior in children who view these programs?

Sigmund Freud believed that the desire to be violent was instinctive and that viewing violence might satisfy an instinctive urge, acting as a release or a **catharsis.** As a result, watcing violence would reduce the viewer's desire to be violent. On the other hand, the contemporary psychologist Albert Bandura has developed a **social learning theory** (which stems from behaviorism) that

---

SCIENTIFIC METHOD
The principles and processes used to conduct scientific investigations, including formation of hypotheses, observation, and experimentation.

EXPERIMENT
A test made to demonstrate the validity of a hypothesis or to determine the predictability of a theory. Variables are manipulated and changes are contrasted with a control that has not been exposed to the variable of interest.

CATHARSIS
In psychoanalytic theory, elimination of a conflict by bringing it to consciousness and allowing it to express itself; in general, any emotional releases resulting from a buildup of internal tensions.

SOCIAL LEARNING THEORY
A theory developed by Albert Bandura that stresses learning by observing and imitating others. Social learning is sometimes called observational learning or vicarious conditioning.

HYPOTHESIS
Any statement or assumption that serves as a possible, but tentative, explanation of certain observations. A hypothesis is always formulated in a way that makes it amenable to empirical test.

contradicts Freud's catharsis prediction. Bandura predicts that viewing violence will increase the probability that the viewer will imitate the violence. Clearly, we have a disagreement—and one that can be tested. When researchers like Bandura make such a prediction, they are, in technical terms, generating a **hypothesis.** Simply put, a hypothesis is an educated guess stated in terms that can be tested.

To begin our experiment, we need some children and some violent programs. We need some observers to watch the children's behavior and to record

---

TABLE 1.1 ◆ DIMENSIONS OF RESEARCH

DIMENSION OF RESEARCH	DESCRIPTION
Descriptive versus Explanatory	Descriptive research describes only what has occurred, while explanatory research attempts to explain how or why something has occurred; that is, what caused it. Descriptive research often is a good way to begin, as it is generally less subject to error. A caveman giving a description of what occurred during a thunderstorm might say, "There was a bright flash of light followed by a terrible loud rumble," and he would be accurate. The same caveman attempting an explanation might state, "Great God Zog throw rock at sky." Not only is he inaccurate, but, as is the case with all make-believe cavemen, his grammar is poor. (Real cavemen, on the other hand, may have had good grammar—but more about Noam Chomsky's theories in Chapter 10.) Of course, descriptions can be inaccurate, too. The more objective they are, however, the more accurate they are likely to be; for example, you can count objectively the people standing in a given room and not be likely to make an error. The more subjective descriptions become, the more they are open to misinterpretation; for example, how many people on the street would you describe as "happy"? The description of someone as happy is open to personal interpretation and is more likely to be inaccurate. For this reason, psychological researchers often begin with objective descriptions and then, through careful experimental research, examine cause-effect relationships in the hope that they eventually will explain how and why the events they have described occurred. In other words, they hope to arrive at a good explanation through scientific experimentation.
Naturalistic versus Manipulative	When conducting naturalistic research, researchers refrain from interacting with the subjects of their observations. This research is often carried out in a natural setting. Researchers conducting naturalistic research keep careful, detailed records of their observations. During manipulative research, however, researchers purposely manipulate the treatments to observe how these manipulations affect the subjects. Manipulative research is often carefully controlled in a laboratory setting, allowing the limits and parameters of each studied behavior to be observed.
Historical versus Ahistorical	If research is fundamentally dependent on the subject's past experience or on past events, it is considered historical research; if not, it is called ahistorical. For example, a study concerned with the effects of a particular therapy for abused children would be historical, because a previous history of child abuse would be an important factor. In contrast, a study concerned with the effects of brightly colored blocks on an infant's vocalizations would be ahistorical, because the researchers would have no particular interest in the infant's previous experience or history.
Theoretical versus Serendipitous	Research designed to investigate a particular theory is called theoretical research, while research designed simply to investigate phenomena without regard to theoretical speculations is called serendipitous.
Basic versus Applied	Basic research advances knowledge; applied research advances technology. Once the basic knowledge has been gathered, applied research is concerned with assembling it for a particular purpose. The Apollo program to send astronauts to the moon is a good example of applied research—most of the basic knowledge about rockets, aerodynamics, and space had been gathered before the program's inception. The search for a cancer cure, however, is more typically an example of basic research. No one is certain of the fundamental causes of cancer, so our basic knowledge of biology must be expanded before the next major application of technology can occur. For this reason, basic research is the foundation on which applied research can be built. Although at first glance basic research may appear to have no value because it has no obvious application (What do you want to know that for?), it is the lifeblood of all science, and there are thousands of examples of important advances being made due to an earlier discovery that, at the time, seemed useless or pointless.
Single-Subject versus Group	In single-subject research, the thoughts or actions of only one subject at a time are of interest; in group research, the researcher looks at group averages and is not concerned with whether those averages accurately reflect the patterns of any given individual within the group.

what happens when the children are exposed to the shows. We also need informed consent in writing from the parents of all the children.*

SELECTING SUBJECTS.   In selecting the children, we probably should choose children of many ages and backgrounds, because it is always risky to generalize beyond a particular **sample.** If you conduct a study on little boys, for instance, you must be very cautious about applying your findings to little girls. (And, unless you have a sound reason for doing so, you shouldn't even attempt such a generalization.) Psychologists, like all scientists, should not go beyond their data unless they specifically state that they are speculating.

Now that we've assembled the children, let's show them some of those violent Saturday-morning cartoons and see what happens. But first we must solve a problem: How can we tell which cartoons are violent? Moreover, after showing the cartoons, how will we decide whether the children are being aggressive? We will need to define our terms very carefully.

DEFINING TERMS.   In France, there used to be a platinum-iridium rod that was kept inside a sealed glass case that had been emptied of air. By agreement, the rod was said to be exactly one meter in length. Whenever a physicist needed to be certain that her meter stick was one meter long, she could compare it with the rod. The rod was the *standard.* Nowadays, physicists use an even more precise standard for the length. The point is that everyone agrees on the definition of a meter—but do we all agree on what aggression is? Is an effective salesperson aggressive? Are all murderers aggressive? Are successful football players aggressive? Obviously, aggression has come to mean many different things, and before we can study it, and perhaps conclude that watching TV violence does or does not cause aggression, we must be able to define it. If aggression means something different to everyone who reads our findings, we will have succeeded only in confusing the issue.

If a tree falls in the forest and no one is there to hear it fall, does it make a noise? You may have heard this famous philosophical question before, but do you know the answer? There is one. It depends totally on how you *define* noise. If you define noise as the *production* of sound waves, the answer to the question is yes. If you define noise as the *perception* of sound waves, the answer is no. The only reason such a question can cause an argument in the first place is that people are often unaware that they are using different definitions when discussing the issue.

How shall we define aggression to avoid confusion in our experiment? One definition might be "any act committed with the intention of damaging property or injuring another person." Since this description fits most people's idea of aggression, let's try it. We might have some problems with this definition, however, because intentions cannot be directly observed. Perhaps we could devise a more exact definition, one with less chance for observational error. For instance, I once saw a similar experiment in which children were placed in a room filled with balloons after watching violent shows. In this instance, aggression was defined operationally by how many balloons the children popped. While this was easy to measure, many found it unsatisfactory as a measure of aggression because balloon popping seemed far removed from most people's idea of what the term "aggression" meant. So, for our purposes let's go ahead with "any act committed with the intention of damaging property or injuring another person" despite its possible limitations. As you can see,

*When conducting experiments or research, it is important to keep in mind ethical concerns that may arise. The American Psychological Association has published guidelines for research with animal and human subjects as well as a code of conduct for all psychologists. Appendix E includes a point-by-point description of both the code and guidelines as well as some actual examples of unethical conduct or research.

SAMPLE
A group of subjects who are representative of the population about which an inference is made.

OPERATIONAL DEFINITION
A definition derived from a set of clearly stated operations; for example, human strength = the amount of weight that a person can lift from the floor to a height of 1 foot in 5 seconds. Although such definitions are exact and work well in scientific studies, they are sometimes considered limited because they may not include everyone's understanding of the construct being defined.

INTEROBSERVER RELIABILITY
The degree of disagreement or agreement between two or more observers who simultaneously observe a single event.

CONTROL
Deliberate arrangement of experimental or research conditions so that observed effects can be directly traced to a known variable. This is often accomplished by exposing two like groups to identical conditions with the exception that one group is exposed to the variable being tested.

just coming up with a good operational definition for your terms can be difficult.

We now have what is known as an **operational definition.** We also need an operational definition of "violent cartoons." One common operational definition is "any act performed by a cartoon character that would be likely to result in injury if it had been carried out by real people." Once we have operationally defined both terms, we can begin the experiment. Your job will be to watch a particular child after the child has viewed a violent cartoon. You will note whether aggression occurs and, if so, how often. Can you be trusted to be accurate in your observations?

INTEROBSERVER RELIABILITY.   As we noted, our definition may allow too much subjectivity. If this is the case, you might consider an event to be an aggressive act according to our definition, whereas another observer applying the same definition to the same event might not record an aggressive act. This could be a serious problem, because different observers would describe the same behavior as both aggressive and nonaggressive. To avoid this problem, we will use two or more people who will independently observe the same child over the same period of time. We can then compare their observations. If they are in fairly good agreement, we can conclude that we have a reliable means of observing and recording the behavior in question. This technique yields a measure of what is known as **interobserver reliability.** If our interobserver reliability turns out to be low, we will have to define aggression more carefully.

THE CONTROL.   Now that we will use interobserver reliability to ensure that we agree on definitions of aggression and violent cartoons, shall we show a violent cartoon to the children and observe their behavior? If the children are aggressive after viewing the cartoon, how will we know that the violence in the cartoon provoked the aggression? For that matter, how can we be sure that the children wouldn't have been even more aggressive had they not watched the cartoon? If you ask, "Who won the soccer game?" and all someone tells you is that one team scored five times, you won't know whether that team won or lost. To know, you need the other team's score as a comparison. It's the same with an experiment. You need a comparison, in this case, a similar group of children who do not see the violent cartoon. This second group of children is the **control.** In fact, it is the use of a control that defines an experiment.

The best way to obtain a second group of children who are similar to the first is simply to divide the original group of children in half. Then, in all probability, the two groups will be alike. You must divide the groups randomly, however. *Random* assignment of subjects to experimental and control groups means that each child has an *equal* chance of being placed in either group. For example, you might assign each child to an experimental or control group by flipping a coin.

The control and experimental groups *must be treated in exactly the same way* except for the one thing you wish to measure, in this case, watching TV violence. If you show the control group no cartoon at all, you fail to control for the effects of simply watching a cartoon. Thus, while the experimental group is watching a violent cartoon, the control group should see a nonviolent cartoon. Ideally, it should be exactly the same cartoon without the violent acts. In this way, the effect of violence is isolated from all other effects. Everything that happens to the experimental group is *controlled for* if the same thing happens to the control group. In our case, everything is controlled except viewing violence, which happens only to the experimental group. If the amount of aggression observed in both groups of children is similar before they see the cartoon but different afterward, we have isolated the effect of watching violence and probably nothing else. In this way, psychologists are able to separate variables and to observe their effects one at a time. A *variable* is any characteristic that may vary, as opposed to a constant, such as the speed of light, which does not vary. Examples of variables include a person's height and weight, the outside temperature or barometric pressure, the miles per gallon obtained by a car, the rainfall in Rangoon, the number of teeth in an audience, or the number of scoops of ice cream dropped on the sidewalks of Detroit each day by consequently upset children.

To repeat, since both groups shared all the variables but one, and since both groups were similar to each other at the beginning of the experiment, any increased difference between the groups at the end of the experiment can be attributed to the one variable the groups did not share. Remember, variables shared by both groups are controlled. Or, putting it another way, if it starts to rain on the experimental group, your experiment will not be disrupted as long as it starts to rain on the control group, too. The variable that is manipulated, in our case, how much and what kind of TV violence we showed, is called the **independent variable.** The variable that may be influenced by the manipulations, in our case, the amount of aggression, is called the **dependent variable.***

OBSERVER AND SUBJECT BIAS. Before continuing the experiment, we need to examine other problems that might arise. Among these are observer and subject bias. In our experiment, we have used a control group and an experimental group and have treated them in the same manner except for

*If you have trouble recalling which variable is which, just think of freedom and independence. The variable that the experimenter is free to manipulate is the independent variable. Also, the behavior of the subject *depends* on what the experiment does to him or her.

INDEPENDENT VARIABLE
In an experiment, any variable that is manipulated so that its effects on the dependent variable may be observed.

DEPENDENT VARIABLE
In an experiment, the variable that may be affected by changes in the independent variable.

Most children who watch violent television programs behave more aggressively after viewing them.

OBSERVER BIAS
An error in observation caused by the expectations of the observer.

SUBJECT BIAS
Unwanted changes in a subject's behavior owing to her knowledge about the experiment or awareness of being observed.

DOUBLE-BLIND CONTROLLED EXPERIMENT
A research technique in which neither the subjects nor the observers know which subjects have been exposed to the independent variable. It is used for controlling biases that may be introduced by either the subjects or the observers.

REPLICATION
Repeating an experiment to establish the reproducibility of the results.

EXPANSION
An enlargement or extension of initial research efforts.

showing violence to the latter. Still, you and the others observing the children might be susceptible to an **observer bias.** For example, suppose that all of you are scornful of Freud's theories and certain that Bandura's predictions are accurate. You might all be hoping to see more aggression in the experimental group. Although working independently, you might all consider certain behavior aggressive if it is exhibited by a child from the experimental group, whereas you might consider the same behavior nonaggressive if you observed it in a child from the control group. In this way, your observations could be badly biased even though interobserver reliability might remain high in that you all agree.

Even careful observers can't always avoid such mistakes, since it is very hard not to see what you expect to see. For years, sly professors have sent students to observe "bright" rats and "dull" rats running mazes in psychology labs. Even the most careful students tend to report that the bright rats do better than the dull ones, although the rats have been labeled bright or dull simply by the flip of a coin.

The subjects in experiments can also be biased. **Subject bias** may occur whenever subjects are aware that they are being observed or that particular results are expected from them. In such instances, they too may change their behavior.

Fortunately, we can easily avoid these kinds of biases in our experiment; the observers simply must not know whether the children they are watching are from the experimental or the control group (someone else can keep track of that). This will prevent the observers from unconsciously leaning toward one group or the other, because they won't know which is which. Because the children, too, are unaware of which group they are in, subject bias is eliminated. Our study can now be called a **double-blind controlled experiment,** that is, neither the subjects nor the observers know who is in which group—they are both "blind" to that knowledge. Double-blind controlled experiments are extremely effective as research tools, since they allow researchers to examine variables one at a time while eliminating the effects of human biases.

THE RESULTS OF OUR EXPERIMENT.   Once we have observed the levels of aggression in the children from both groups, we will statistically analyze the data to determine whether there is a significant difference in observed aggression between the control and the experimental groups.* Let's assume that the results of our hypothetical experiment are similar to those obtained by researchers who have conducted actual experiments examining the effects of TV violence on children. Like them, we find through the use of our statistics that the experimental group is significantly more aggressive (Eron, Huesmann, Brice, Fischer, & Mermelstein, 1983; Huesmann, Lagerspetz, & Eron, 1984). Our conclusion (and notice how very limited and specific we have to be) is that "viewing cartoon violence increases the probability of immediate postviewing aggression in grade-school children." In addition, we may note that Albert Bandura's theory fits our observations well, while Sigmund Freud's does not. After we have carried our experiment a bit further, we may even have enough "hard data" to suggest that cartoon violence in children's television programs should be toned down or eliminated.

REPLICATION AND EXPANSION.   At the finish of our double-blind controlled experiment, we might want to consider two other valuable procedures, **replication** and **expansion.** An old rule in research states, "If it hasn't hap-

*Appendix B outlines the kinds of statistical analyses psychologists use to determine whether the differences between groups are, in fact, statistically significant and explains how that significance is determined. In this instance, we used inferential statistics, also described in that appendix.

pened twice, it hasn't happened."* For this reason, it would be a good idea to have other researchers, perhaps at another institution, replicate (duplicate) our study to see whether they obtain the same results. If they did, we would feel more confident about our own findings. Such confirmation is important, since our particular sample of children may have been unusual in some way or an important event, unknown to us, may have interfered with the treatment or testing. To be honest, not enough replication is conducted in psychology. Although it lacks the glamour of original research, replicating published studies provides a valuable service. It has been estimated that as many as 3 percent of all the findings published in the psychology literature are not real; that is, they are due to statistical quirks or to faults in research methodology. The only way to weed out these errors is to conduct the studies again and then discover that they "fail to replicate."

We may also wish to expand our research. For instance, what would happen if we used live actors instead of cartoons? Would adults become more aggressive in the way that children do? How long does the increased aggression last? Obviously, the answer obtained in an experiment can generate many new questions, all of which may be worth pursuing.

Recalling the division of research methods given in Table 1.1, we can define the dimensions of our own experiment as follows:

◆ *Explanatory:* We concluded that watching violence was *why* aggression occurred.
◆ *Manipulative:* We altered the situation so that the children were exposed to the variable that we wanted them to see.
◆ *Ahistorical:* We were not concerned about the children's history, that is their backgrounds or particular childhoods.
◆ *Theoretical:* We were deciding between Freud's and Bandura's theoretical predictions.
◆ *Basic:* We were advancing our knowledge rather than attempting to change the technology of the cartoon industry (although that may eventually be a result of our research).
◆ *Group:* We worked with groups of children instead of concentrating on a single subject.

SINGLE-SUBJECT EXPERIMENTS.   You may wonder about the practicability of conducting an experiment with only one subject, since you would have no obvious control group. But it can be done. In a **single-subject experiment,** we use time as a control and compare the subject's behavior at two different times. This basis of comparison makes the procedure experimental. To conduct such an experiment, we create a certain condition and note the response, then we observe whether the response continues as long as the condition is maintained. Examine Figure 1.3, the record of an experiment to find the effect of a drug on memory. Since time has been used as a control, we can feel confident that the drug has indeed reduced the subject's ability to recall a list of items. First, the drug was administered and the subject's recall ability declined (condition A). Then, the effect of the drug wore off and recall improved (condition B). To be sure that this result was not just a coincidence, the drug was administered a second time, and once again the ability to recall decreased (a return to condition A). Since recall ability again diminished when the drug was given, the experimenters could assert with more confidence that the drug was

SINGLE-SUBJECT EXPERIMENT
An experiment in which only one subject participates. Time is normally used as the control; that is, the subject's behavior changes over time in relation to the presentation and withdrawal of the independent variable.

---

*This only means that studies sometimes have confounding variables associated with them that were not apparent when the study was first conducted. Naturally, sometimes the results are so clear that twice isn't necessary. For example, Americans didn't have to go back to the moon a second time before they were sure that they had really succeeded.

CONCEPT REVIEW ◆ THE EXPERIMENT

The Concept Review summarizes the concepts concerning psychological experiments that you have learned so far.

Selecting Subjects

Obtain a sample of subjects who will adequately represent the entire population to which you intend to generalize your findings.

Defining Terms

Set up operational definitions that will help to eliminate confusion about what the findings are and what they represent; also helps to remove subjectivity, which may lead to bias.

Measuring Interobserver Reliability

Use this procedure to ensure that independent observers agree about what they are observing. Low reliability implies that the phenomenon being observed is defined too subjectively.

Setting Up the Control

Provide a comparison measure with which the experimental group may be compared by controlling for all variables to which the experimental group is exposed, except the variable under study.

Use the Double-Blind Method

This will help to eliminate the effects of subject and observer bias.

Perform Statistical Analysis

Determine whether there is a significant difference between the control group and experimental group measures at the end of the experiment.

Replicate the Experiment

This will provide further support for the findings and help to ensure that the findings are valid.

causing a recall deficiency. By giving the drug, withholding it, and giving it again, the researchers were seemingly controlling the subject's ability to recall. This is called an **A-B-A single-subject experimental design.** If you wish, it can be taken a step further by measuring recall once more after the drug has worn off. An A-B-A-B design will thus be created, demonstrating once again the expected behavioral change in the B condition and lending support to the conviction that a **cause-effect relationship** exists between the administration

◆ **FIGURE 1.3**

Example of an A-B-A single-subject experimental design. The purpose of this experiment was to test a drug's effect on immediate recall (memory) by introducing and withholding the drug. In condition A, the drug is active; in condition B, it has worn off.

of the drug and the subsequent decline in recall ability. Be cautious, however, about assuming that what you have discovered about one subject will explain the behavior of any other subject; it may not.

Nonexperimental Methods

THE CORRELATIONAL METHOD.   A **correlation** is defined as a relationship between two variables such that when one variable systematically increases, the other will systematically alter as well (either increase or decrease). For example, there is a fairly strong correlation between IQ and health. The more intelligent one tends to be, the fewer health problems one tends to have and vise versa. These data are correlational, and although we may speculate as to why (for example, intelligent people may be more likely to see a doctor or are better informed about how to care for themselves), we really can't be certain of the *cause* for the effect without experimental evidence.

Still, the knowledge we get from correlations can give us power. For example, by the late 1800s army physicians were aware that the best way to stop a malaria outbreak was to move everyone to high, dry ground. Although at the time these physicians were unaware that the disease was carried by mosquitoes, they knew that malaria was well *correlated* with altitude and moisture. Without knowing the cause of the disease, they were still able to predict the chances of an outbreak and, in some cases, prevent it by moving people to safer locations.

Sometimes psychologists are unable to conduct experiments because they have no control over the variables they wish to examine, or sometimes such experiments would simply be unethical to conduct. For example, if we wish to measure the effect of abusive parenting on children's grades in school, we can't very well divide children randomly into two groups and then ask the parents of one group to please abuse their children so we can see what happens to their grades. The correlation method may be the only reasonable way to gather evidence concerning such relationships.

Sometimes experiments cannot be conducted because, like the army doctors in the malaria example, psychologists may not know on which variables to focus their study. Under these circumstances, they may also be forced to rely on correlational data. But such data are still valuable because they allow us to make predictions. Frequently, too, correlations are scientists' first clue on the path to an important discovery. As you can imagine, doctors soon wondered what it was about damp, warm lowlands that related to malaria.

Nevertheless, when dealing with a correlation you should not assume that a cause-effect relationship exists simply because two variables vary together. For example, if you were to tell me that ice-cream sales in Detroit had increased, I would be able to predict that the number of drownings had also increased—and I'd be correct. But this does not mean that eating ice cream makes you drown or, conversely, that seeing people drown makes you want ice cream. Either of these would be an example of cause and effect. The reason for the correlation between ice cream and drowning is, of course, that in summer both swimming and ice-cream sales increase. Although no one is likely to make such a cause-effect connection, the difference between a correlation and an apparent cause-effect relationship is not always so clear.

NATURALISTIC OBSERVATIONS.   We noted in Table 1.1 that researchers conducting **naturalistic observations** refrain from interacting directly with the subjects they are observing. Naturalistic observations can be carried out in an informal or a structured way. The more informal the observations, however, the greater the chance that bias or inaccuracy will affect the results. Part of

A-B-A SINGLE-SUBJECT EXPERIMENTAL DESIGN
An experimental design in which time is used as a control and only one subject is monitored. The independent variable is given in condition A and withdrawn in condition B. The dependent variable is the subject's behavior over time as the independent variable is presented, withdrawn, and finally presented again.

CAUSE-EFFECT RELATIONSHIP
A relationship in which one act regularly brings about a particular result.

CORRELATION
A relationship between two variables such that when one variable systematically increases or decreases, the other will systematically alter as well.

NATURALISTIC OBSERVATIONS
Observations in which researchers refrain from directly interacting with the organisms being observed.

CASE STUDY
An intensive study of a single case, with available data, test results, and opinions about that individual.

◆ FIGURE 1.4

Harlow's illustrations of the case of Phineas Gage: (a) Comparison of the relative sizes of the tamping iron and Gage's skull. (b) View depicting the trajectory of the iron through Gage's cranium. (c) Upward view of the cranium showing the location and diameter of the hole. (SOURCE: From Harlow, 1868.)

our experiment with children and TV violence could have been a naturalistic study. Suppose we had simply wanted to observe aggression in a group of children. If we had just watched the children, perhaps from behind one-way glass, and had carefully recorded incidents of aggression, we would have been performing a naturalistic observation. But once we decided to manipulate variables by showing violent and nonviolent cartoons to randomly chosen experimental and control groups, our study became a manipulative experiment.

Naturalistic observation is most often used to investigate behavior in the natural environment outside the laboratory. Technically, a *natural environment* is defined as any environment that the researcher has not purposely manipulated for reasons of experiment, though the term is often used to mean a natural setting, one in which things are going on much as they would be regardless of the presence of the experimenter. The incidence of aggression among gorillas in their natural habitat, the amount of overt affection displayed in a college cafeteria, or the number of vehicles on a particular road that exceed the speed limit could all be subjects for naturalistic observation. When collecting data of this kind, observers should be as unobtrusive as possible in order not to change the behavior of the subjects being observed. As you might imagine, information about the incidence of highway speeding might not be too accurate if you collected it from inside a marked, clearly visible police car.

CASE STUDIES. In a **case study,** researchers report or analyze the behavior, emotions, beliefs, or life history of a single individual in more depth than is usually possible with groups of subjects. The rigorous controls common to the single-subject experimental design are not applied in case studies. Like correlational and naturalistic observations, case studies are not experimental. Still, careful observation of a subject and scrupulous recording of what is observed can yield valuable information.

Sometimes, a case study is the only option available because, for one reason or another, it is impossible for a psychologist to conduct an experiment or to observe a correlation in order to gather data. It would not be ethically proper, for example, to remove part of a healthy individual's brain just to see what would happen afterward. Sometimes, however, such information becomes available through a case study, as in the classic case of Phineas Gage. In 1848, Gage was working as the foreman for a railroad crew where part of his job was to tamp dynamite with a 13-pound steel rod into holes bored into rock. One unfortunate day, the dynamite charge detonated while Gage was tamping it with the rod. The explosion sent the rod through Gage's face and out the top of his skull (see Figure 1.4), taking with it the front matter of his brain. Incredibly, he survived, but not without undergoing some profound personality changes. As Dr. J. M. Harlow, who reported this case study, stated:

His physical health is good, and I am inclined to say that he has recovered. Has no pain in head, but says it has a queer feeling which he is not able to describe. Applied for his situation as foreman, but is undecided whether to work or travel. His contractors, who regarded him as the most efficient and capable foreman in their employ previous to his injury, considered the change in his mind so marked that they could not give him his place again. The equilibrium or balance, so to speak, between his intellectual faculties and animal propensities, seems to have been destroyed. He is fitful, irreverent, indulging at times in the grossest profanity (which was not previously his custom), manifesting but little deference for his fellows, impatient of restraint or advice when it conflicts with his desires, at times pertinaciously obstinate, yet capricious and vacillating, devising many plans of future operations, which are no sooner arranged than they are abandoned in turn for others ... his mind is radically changed, so decidedly that his friends and acquaintances said he was "no longer Gage." (1868, pp. 339–40)

Although such case studies provide valuable data, no single case can stand alone as the basis for a solid conclusion. In the Gage case, for instance, it is impossible to know without further scientific evidence whether Gage's personality changes were due to the loss of brain matter or to the severe shock and facial disfigurement he had suffered. But by combining this study with others in which similar injuries have been recorded, a picture may emerge. For instance, there are many similarities between the changes in Gage's behavior and the changes in the behavior of others who have suffered similar injuries to the frontal regions of their brain. James Brady, former President Reagan's press secretary is the most recent well known example. Brady was shot in the frontal lobe of the brain during an attempted assassination of the president in 1981, and his emotional control and behavior changed drastically following the incident. These case studies, taken collectively, strongly indicate that the front portion of the brain plays an important role in the control and processing of emotion. Such information was not readily obtainable until the collected findings of numerous case studies became available.

SURVEYS.   Another important technique relied upon by psychologists is the **survey.** A survey may include such techniques as conducting interviews or administering questionnaires. Among the best-known national surveys are the Gallup and Roper political polls, the Nielsen television survey, and the U.S. census. Surveys, however, can be difficult to conduct properly or interpret. Like all investigative techniques, they are subject to a number of problems. For instance, when people answer questions, they often report what they wish were true or recall events differently from the way they actually happened. As an example, when married couples are asked to report how often they engage in sexual relations per month, they have a tendency to, shall we say, overestimate.

The way in which questions are worded can also influence the results of a survey. For example, subjects who viewed a traffic accident were more likely to answer "yes" to the question "Did you see *the* broken headlight?" than they were to the question "Did you see *a* broken headlight?" Also, surveys often are susceptible to sampling error. The classic case is the 1936 political poll in which a random sample was picked from the telephone book and asked, "For whom will you vote in the presidential election, Landon or Roosevelt?" The majority chose Landon, and the pollsters predicted Landon the winner. Unfortunately for the pollsters and the newspapers that relied on them, in 1936 only more affluent people had telephones—and Roosevelt won easily because he had practically everybody else's vote.

TESTING.   Some psychological tests, like IQ tests and the Rorschach inkblot test, are so familiar to the public that people can hardly think of psychology without also bringing the tests to mind. Psychologists have hundreds of tests available to them to help in their investigations. Tests can be valuable research instruments. Psychologists use them to measure many aptitudes and abilities. Tests also may make it possible to measure various characteristics of people by testing large groups of individuals at one time. For this reason, group tests have an important place in education, business, the military, and industry. Tests may also be administered individually, often for the purpose of clinical, intellectual, or personality assessment.

Test construction and use are not simple matters, however. Psychological tests must be given only by people who are trained to understand their limits and value. Unfortunately, the general public has come to believe that many psychological tests are far more authoritative and accurate than they really are and, perhaps, put too much trust in them. In Chapters 13 and 14, we will

SURVEY
A method of collecting data through the use of interviews or questionnaires.

Psychological tests may be administered to individuals one-on-one. This may often be done for purposes of assessing personality, intelligence, or mental disorders.

CHAOS THEORY
The theory that states that predictions for most systems are limited because initial states are subject to deviations that are too small to measure, but can, nevertheless, lead to pronounced effects. In other words, a certain amount of chaos will accompany each prediction, lessening the accuracy of the prediction over time.

examine some of the problems encountered in developing and interpreting tests, as well as the benefits that can be derived from their proper use.

All the efforts of scientific psychology are aimed at a common goal: to understand, to predict, and to bring under control the behaviors that people wish to change. Many psychologists hope eventually to isolate and understand the variables that have the most important effects on our feelings, thoughts, and behavior. Such knowledge would provide us with a better understanding of ourselves and of other people.

THE LIMITS OF PSYCHOLOGICAL UNDERSTANDING

At first glance, it might seem that we could acquire a complete understanding of human beings by just conducting experiments until we have enough knowledge about behavior to allow us to make very accurate predictions about how people will behave in any given set of circumstances. After all, this kind of experimental approach has served physics well. Physicists have studied the fundamental particles and forces, seen how they interact under different conditions, and then made assessments about how these particles and forces may be controlled and manipulated. The development of computers, atomic power, television, and space travel bear witness to the physicists' success.

Psychology, however, is more the study of extremely complex systems (behaving organisms, especially human beings) than the study of fundamental particles or forces. Consequently, a psychologist studying variables in a tightly controlled environment may not always obtain results that apply readily to a "real" world of complex interacting systems. In this sense, psychology has more in common with meteorology (the study of weather) than it does with physics. As an example, consider a meteorologist studying the formation of storms in the laboratory. In the same way that an experimental psychologist might, she explores how different variables such as air pressure, humidity, and wind interact under carefully controlled conditions. Although this experimental exploration in the laboratory may provide a rough understanding of how real storms develop, it's never going to give her the power to predict, with extreme accuracy, the exact behavior of a real storm. For the physicist, one electron appears to be just like any other (so far, anyway!), but a storm is an evolving system with many parts, and we can pretty much assume that *no two storms are ever going to be exactly alike*. For a similar reason—that no two people are ever going to be exactly alike—our knowledge derived from experiments will be somewhat limited when applied to the real world. We simply don't know how thoroughly we will ever be able to understand human behavior.

One area of philosophy and mathematics that is addressing this problem is called **chaos theory** (Pool, 1989). As an example of chaos theory, consider the efforts of scientists to predict where a hurricane will strike the eastern United States a few days before the storm is due to come ashore. Until the storm is very close to shore, the prediction is extremely difficult because the smallest change in the storm when it is far out to sea may translate into a difference of hundreds of miles by the time it reaches shore (see Figure 1.5). The same is true for humans. The slightest change in your life today may send you off on a different path that will show up as a major difference years from now. For this reason, to make *long-term* predictions about complex systems like people or storms, we would need to understand the tiniest interactions of all the variables right at the start (because tiny changes, over the long term, can lead to big differences). But, we know now that even at the tiniest level, predictions cannot be perfect, because physicists have shown that the actions of subatomic particles are, in fact, not exact, but chaotic and can only be

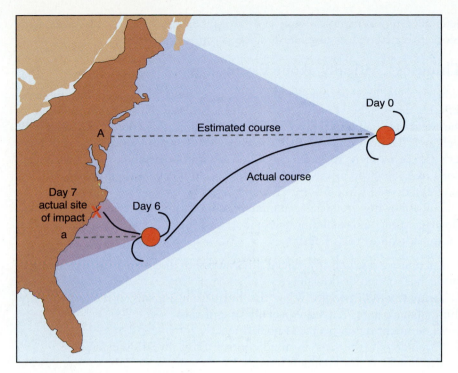

◆ FIGURE 1.5

In the initial state, a hurricane seven days from shore is expected to strike point A. In this chaos model, an undetectable change in barometric pressure and temperature sets off a snowball effect that causes the storm's path to shift in an ever-increasing arc. Seven days later, the storm wil come ashore 600 miles south of where it was predicted to strike seven days earlier. No amount of experimentation or research could have helped to narrow the range of error inherent in the prediction made seven days beforehand (shaded area). The same effect occurs between days 6 and 7, but with less error because a shorter time frame is involved.

understood in terms of probability. This subatomic chaos, which appears to be an indisputable part of nature, was not originally thought to be very relevant to large systems like storms or people. But, because the smallest of changes can have huge consequences later, researchers now believe that even when studying people, the underlying chaos of matter does fundamentally limit our ability to predict behavior, especially over the long term.

Of course, even if our experimental evidence is eventually found to have boundaries that cannot be transcended, it is still valuable because it often provides us with *enough* information to yield an understanding that is sufficient for most purposes.

🧬 FOR CRITICAL THOUGHT AND ANALYSIS

1. As far as we can tell, there is a fundamental limit to human knowledge; research has shown that we can never be absolutely certain of anything.* Science must, therefore, become an investigation of probabilities. But if scientists can never be absolutely certain of their results, why shouldn't someone's opinion be considered just as valid as findings derived from scientific research?
2. Textbooks such as this and research literature very rarely state that "A proves B" or that "one thing is proof of another." Instead, authors commonly say that "A suggests B" or that "this is an indication of that." Why do you think they do that? How is this similar to jurors who are instructed to find the

---

*Except, perhaps, that we can never be absolutely certain of anything.

ETHICS
The study of the general nature of morals and of the specific moral choices to be made by the individual in professional relationships with others.

defendant innocent unless guilt can be established *beyond a reasonable doubt* (notice that here, too, absolute proof is not mentioned)?

Thinking Critically about Psychology

Now that you have become familiar with psychological research and the many different approaches that researchers take, you may be finding that some of the ideas you had about psychology before taking this course are undergoing a change. To help you assimilate these new ways of thinking about psychology, let's take a moment to look at some of the misunderstandings or misconceptions often held by members of the public and compare them with what you have discovered while reading this chapter.

The following are some common misconceptions concerning psychology. How has your understanding of some or all of these been changed by what you have read in this chapter?

1. Laboratory research is artificial, and anything discovered by such manipulation has limited or no value.
2. Animals aren't people. What you learn from animals won't tell you anything about people. This is especially true of rats.
3. Experimenting on people is not ethical.
4. Psychology is the same as mind control. Basically, it's dangerous.
5. Psychology is just common sense.
6. Psychologists analyze all the people they meet. They can see right through you and discover your most inner thoughts.
7. Psychology is all about dreams and sex.

Let's look at each misconception in turn and see how it stands up against what you have read so far about psychology. According to the first statement, laboratory research is of little real value because it is artificial and relies on manipulation rather than dealing with the "real world," which is natural. But now that you know the distinctions between manipulative and naturalistic research, you can see that both approaches have merit. You also know that a laboratory isn't just some building where researchers walk around in white coats recording data; rather, it can be any place in which variables are being manipulated under controlled conditions. And, although naturalistic research is very valuable, without manipulative "laboratory" research, we can never hope to isolate individual variables and their separate effects.

The second point contends that we can't learn anything about human thoughts, feelings, or behavior from animals because they are not people. As you know from reading about behaviorism, Watson, Skinner, and others were able to learn many *general principles* from the behavior of animals that applied to people as well. Skinner even called his first book *The Behavior of Organisms* even though most of the research reported in the book was conducted on rats. By calling it *The Behavior of Organisms* instead of *The Behavior of Rats*, Skinner was stressing that rats have many things in common with people and other animals. Furthermore, examining the *differences* between various animal species and humans can help us learn what makes humans special.

The third point, that it is not ethical to experiment on people, is covered in Appendix E, which concerns the ethical principles of psychologists. There you will read that experimentation can be **ethical** when maximum efforts are made to place the well-being of the subjects first and to make sure that dignity, safety, and confidentiality are maintained.

The fourth point, that psychology is mind control and dangerous, may be a more important issue someday, but as you can probably tell, psychology is a young science and there is very little indication that we have such powers as yet. Still, given the way psychological techniques are used in political campaigns to make candidates seem more attractive, "dangerous" may not be a wholly inappropriate word to apply to such techniques, considering how they might be misused.

Even so, the use of psychological techniques to get others to do one's bidding are notoriously ineffective. Reports of a hypnotist making someone do whatever he wishes or a movie manager boosting sales by subliminally flashing BUY POPCORN on the movie screen have been greatly exaggerated. In fact, neither is possible. Frankly, if we knew how to control minds that effectively, advertisers would pay us fortunes to do so. It would also probably be unethical for psychologists to work with advertisers if we had such power. But psychologists are not power masters. We are pretty much like everyone else and tend to have our hands full just trying to manage and control our own lives. However, the use and possible abuse of psychological power as the field grows and develops do bear watching.

The fifth point refers to common sense. But take a moment and think of the embodiments of common sense—proverbs. Let's consider some. For example, *Absence makes the heart grow fonder.* But isn't it also true that *Out of sight, out of mind?* How about *Two heads are better than one?* But, then again, don't *Too many chefs spoil the broth?* Okay, how about *All comes to him who waits?* But then again, *He who hesitates is lost!* How about *A penny saved is a penny earned?* But, of course, *You can't take it with you!* No wonder common sense seems to work well, it has all the bases covered!

While common sense may have its uses on a day-to-day basis, it has also been proven wrong in many notorious instances. The Earth is not the center of the universe. The world is not flat. Both are examples of "common sense." Similarly, many commonsense ideas have been disproved by psychological research. Look at just ten of the thousands of "commonsense" ideas (all of which were commonly believed at the turn of the last century), and you can begin to see the value of psychological research. All of the following were overturned by our modern understanding of psychology:

1. African-Americans are unable to comprehend complex tasks.
2. Babies are born blind.
3. Women are too emotional to be entrusted with important decisions.
4. Intelligence is something that you are born with—you either have it, or you don't.
5. Sleep is a time of physical rest and calm.
6. Only humans are capable of thought.
7. Genius is next to insanity.
8. Masturbation is abnormal and will lead to illness and even death.
9. Spare the rod, spoil the child.
10. Rote memorization is the best way to learn.

All of these once common beliefs have been shown to be false through psychological research.

Another commonly held belief is that psychologists "analyze" people they meet and in some way learn secret things about them. In fact, only yesterday while I was with a group of new acquaintances, someone mentioned that I was a psychologist. One woman in the group immediately said, "Oh, I hope I didn't say anything." Of course, what she meant was that she hoped she hadn't given me enough information with which to analyze her. The fact remains that in spite of all of our tests, our honed clinical skills, and our knowledge of psychology, if we really wish to know something about a particular person, nothing beats simply asking him or her (Shrauger & Osberg, 1981).

In a similar vein, people still commonly think of psychology as focusing mainly on dreams and sex. From your reading, you now know that this is owing to the theories of Sigmund Freud. Dream interpretation, as you recall, is an important part of that theory and so is erotic attachment and desire. But you will also recall that no one knows if dreams really mean anything, and that psychologists study all behaviors, thoughts, and feelings, of which sex plays a relatively small part.

So perhaps, then, you are beginning to reshape your own impression of psychology after having read only this first chapter. By the time you have completed this book, you will have a good grasp of this new and emerging field.

❧ SUMMARY

◆ Psychology is the science of behavior and mental processes.

◆ There are many different areas of specialization or interest within psychology. Among them are experimental, neuropsychological, psychobiological, developmental, social, clinical, industrial, organizational, educational, and counseling psychology.

◆ Psychology was born of two parents, philosophy and physiology. The union of the philosophers' questions and the physiologists' careful scientific analysis led to psychological research, which began in a laboratory in Leipzig, Germany, in 1879.

◆ The first experimental psychology laboratory was started by Wilhelm Wundt, who was interested in analyzing the mind. Edward Titchener's subsequent reanalysis of Wundt's work, which became known as structuralism, relied on the technique of introspection. Introspection failed to gain popularity, and by the 1930s structuralism was being abandoned.

◆ Functionalism was the first completely American psychology. Functionalists, including John Dewey and William James, were influenced by Charles Darwin and his views of evolution. In general, functionalists believed that human consciousness and behavior must serve a function. Functionalism gave birth to many modern areas of psychological interest.

◆ Early in this century, an American psychologist, John B. Watson, developed an objective system of psychology he called behaviorism. An offshoot of behaviorism, S-R psychology, remains an important force in modern psychology and has been of great value in demonstrating that much of our behavior is determined by our immediate environment or previous history of learning.

◆ At about the same time that behaviorism was becoming the dominant force in American psychology, a different reaction to structuralism was developing in Germany—the Gestalt view. Gestalt psychologists argue that conscious sensations can be examined but that the whole experience must be taken for what it is.

◆ Psychoanalytic theory was developed by a Viennese physician, Sigmund Freud. It did not develop as a reaction against structuralism but rather had its roots in neurology and medicine. Psychoanalysis has been severely criticized for its lack of scientific control and careful experimentation.

◆ Humanistic psychologists' understanding of behavior is different from that of psychoanalysts and behaviorists and stems from the philosophical approach know as phenomenology. Humanists do not believe that people are governed by stimuli or unconscious motives and drives. Rather, they believe that people have free will and a need to achieve self-actualization.

◆ The biological approach to the study of psychology has expanded rapidly in the last few decades. It concerns itself with the investigation of the brain, nervous system, genetic inheritance, and biology of the organism as they pertain to behavior and mental processes.

◆ Cognitive psychology is the study of internal mental processes, which include thinking, memory, concept formation, and the processing of information.

◆ All scientific research relies on systematic and objective methods of observing, recording, and describing events. The scientific experiment is one of the most powerful tools that psychologists possess.

◆ Ethical considerations in the conduct of research are required to protect the subject from possible abuse or harm.

◆ A good experiment makes use of proper procedures for selecting subjects, defining terms, maintaining control, and eliminating biases.

◆ Single-subject experiments use time to allow the subject to serve as her own control.

◆ Data from correlations are valuable because they allow us to make predictions. However, cause-effect relationships cannot be assumed merely because a correlation exists.

◆ In naturalistic observations, researchers refrain from directly interacting with the subjects they are observing. Naturalistic observation is most often used to investigate behavior in natural environments, in which the researcher refrains from manipulation.

◆ Other research tools used by psychologists include case studies, surveys, and testing.

◆ All the work in scientific psychology is aimed at a common goal: to predict, to explain, and eventually to control behavior. Psychological research is limited, however, because it is the study of changing complex systems.

✺ SUGGESTIONS FOR FURTHER READING

1. American Psychological Association. (1986). *Careers in psychology*. Washington, D.C.: American Psychological Association. Describes possible career choices in psychology.
2. Greening, T. (1987). *Politics and innocence: A humanistic debate*. New York: Saybrook Publishing. A collection of essays on the past and future of the humanistic movement in psychology. Contains some interesting debates among humanists about the meaning of their movement.
3. Hilgard, E. R. (1987). *Psychology in America: A historical survey*. San Diego: Harcourt Brace. A general survey of the history of psychology in America by an eminent modern psychologist.
4. Parrott III, L. (1993). *How to write psychology papers*. New York: Harper & Row College. A comprehensive review for the college student of how to research, collect, and write about topics in psychology.
5. Pryzwansky, W. B., & Wendt, R. N. (1987). *Psychology as a profession: Foundations of practice*. New York: Pergamon Press. A book designed for the professional psychologist that outlines the future of the profession. Includes sections on ethics, the impact of the legal system, and emerging trends in professional areas.
6. Rieber, R. W., & Salzinger, K. (Eds.). (1980). *Psychology: Theoretical-historical perspectives*. New York: Academic Press. Discusses the theoretical roots of psychology and those who began the discipline. Helps clear up some of the myths about the early psychologists.
7. Shaughnessy, J. J. & Zechmeister, E. B. (1993). *Research methods in psychology*. New York: McGraw Hill. A thorough compendium of the methods psychologists use when conducting scientific research.
8. Wilson, C. (1993). *Research methods in psychology: An introductory laboratory manual*. Dubuque, Iowa: Kendall-Hunt. A how to manual for the college student with step by step descriptions of research methods used by psychologists. Includes exercises for students to complete.

Chapter Two

The Biological Bases of Thought and Behavior

PROLOGUE

TALKING BACK

Nothing we know of is more complex than the human brain. Within just three and one-half pounds of living material lie all of our thoughts, feelings, hopes, and dreams.

How complex is the human brain? To give you a hint, imagine that you are looking at a glass slide under a microscope. On the slide is a tiny speck, a piece of brain no larger than the period at the end of this sentence. As you focus the viewfinder, you see that the piece of brain resembles a small translucent blob. Within that blob are thousands of extremely tiny, black, spiderlike specks with long streaks emanating from them (see Figure 2.1). The spiderlike specks and streaks appear to meander in a chaotic, tangled pattern.

What you are seeing are individual nerve cells. In the human brain, these nerve cells number in the tens of billions. Almost every one of these cells has a long streaklike projection emanating from its body down which it can send messages to literally thousands of other nerve cells. In return, it can receive messages from thousands more.

As you continue to look into the microscope, you notice that in the background there seems to be a black haze, caused by the microscope's inability to accommodate the whole depth of the speck at one focus setting. As you turn the focus knob, the nerve cells you were looking at become blurred and the haze that was in the background becomes clear, revealing more nerve cells. Beneath are even more nerve cells, thousands of them, with millions of connections among them—all of this in one small speck of brain. Exploring the brain at this microscopic level in the hope of tracing all of the connections made by these nerve cells is far beyond the present capacity of our science. As you can see, the experience of viewing just one small speck can be overwhelming in its complexity.

Even professionals familiar with the brain and its workings sometimes find themselves overcome by a sense of awe. Consider the story of a neurosurgeon I know who was once mapping the brain of a patient. Brain map-

CONTENTS

◆ FIGURE 2.1

Within one small speck of brain, there are millions of neurons and billions of neural connections.

ping is a technique neurosurgeons use to make certain that they don't cut through or destroy a vital area of the brain during surgery.

The surgeon had used a local anesthetic while opening the skull and exposing the brain, so the patient was alert and awake throughout the brain-mapping procedure, but felt no pain. The surgeon then touched different places on the surface of the brain with a small electrode through which a tiny current was passed. This current caused the nerve cells on the surface of the brain to activate, or "fire." When this happened, the patient reported what he sensed. For example, when one point on his brain was stimulated, the patient reported feeling a tingling on his gums; at another point, he reported a ringing in his ears; at yet another point, the little finger on his left hand twitched.

The surgeon then placed tiny numbered paper tags directly on the brain at each point identified and recorded the function of the point. (The tags, of course, were sterile and removed when the surgery was over). In this way, she knew which areas were vital and could avoid cutting through them while she was removing a tumor or carrying out other procedures required by the surgery.

During this brain mapping, in the midst of discussing with her patient the various sensations that the electric probe was causing, the surgeon stopped for a second and stood there staring at her patient's brain. After the surgery, which had gone well, the resident who had assisted asked what she had been thinking about during that brief moment. "You know," the surgeon said, "I've done this procedure hundreds of times, but for some reason it suddenly occurred to me that I was talking to a body organ and it was answering back! I mean, no one expects to have a chat with a liver or a spleen. I guess for a moment it just didn't seem possible that this lump of blood and protein could be carrying on a conversation with me about what it was feeling while I was touching it. It took me a second to snap back and think of my patient as a person again, someone who was like me, and not look at his brain that way. But isn't it truly amazing when you stop to think about it?"

IN THIS CHAPTER, we will examine two of the three major areas of interest among psychologists who study the biological bases of behavior. These are neurology (the study of the brain and nervous system) and endocrinology (the study of glands and their secretions, such as hormones). The third area of interest, behavioral genetics (the study of how inheritance influences behavior), is covered in detail in Chapter 3. As you read through this chapter, you will find out how your endocrine and nervous systems affect your behavior, and you will have a chance to learn about your brain. Your brain already knows a great deal, so why not give it a chance to learn something about itself?

🧬 WHY PSYCHOLOGISTS STUDY THE NERVOUS SYSTEM AND THE BRAIN

All human thought, feeling, or action is related in one way or another to the functioning of the nervous system, of which the brain is the central part. Many neuropsychological and psychobiological psychologists, those psychologists who study the biological bases of psychology (see Chapter 1), believe that knowledge of the brain and nervous system will eventually be so complete that the physiological approach will be the predominant means of understanding, predicting, and controlling all behavior. They may be right, but there is a problem with this approach. The problem lies in the staggering complexity of the human brain and nervous system, which makes nuclear physics seem too simple for words. For this reason, many psychologists argue that even thinking about abandoning nonneurobiological approaches to the understanding of psychology is premature and that complete answers from the neurobiological level may be centuries away, assuming that we can ever find them. But the work to uncover the secrets of the brain and our biology has begun, and surprising progress is being made.

NERVES
Bundles of neural fibers that carry impulses from the central nervous system (brain and spinal cord) throughout the body and thereby affect muscles or glands.

CENTRAL NERVOUS SYSTEM
The brain and spinal cord. All neurons and neural material are surrounded by bone.

PERIPHERAL NERVOUS SYSTEM
The nerves that carry impulses from the sense organs to the central nervous system and from the central nervous system to the muscles and glands of the body.

BRAIN
The portion of the central nervous system located in the cranium and responsible for the interpretation of sensory impulses, the coordination and control of body activities, the exercise of emotion, thought, and memory, and the integration of cognitive and mental functions.

SPINAL CORD
The portion of the central nervous system encased in the backbone and serving as a pathway for the conduction of sensory and motor impulses to and from the brain, respectively.

SOMATIC NERVOUS SYSTEM
The portion of the peripheral nervous system that carries messages inward from the sense organs and outward to the skeletal muscles.

AFFERENT NERVES
Nerves that carry messages inward from the sense organs to the central nervous system.

EFFERENT NERVES
Nerves that carry messages outward from the central nervous system to glands or muscles.

REFLEX
In neurology, any relatively simple neural interaction involving both afferent and efferent nerves.

AUTONOMIC NERVOUS SYSTEM
The portion of the peripheral nervous system that carries information to and from organs, glands, and smooth muscles within the body.

THE DIVISIONS OF THE NERVOUS SYSTEM

Moving, sensing, feeling, thinking, remembering—none of these would be possible without a nervous system. In fact, your entire life, including all of your thoughts, feelings, and actions, depends on the functioning of your nervous system. **Nerves** transmit messages throughout your body, telling you to inhale and exhale and telling your heart to beat. Nerve cells in the brain can bring stored memories to your attention or help your eyes follow a bird in flight. All your thoughts, hopes, dreams, and desires are there, contained within the most complex system in the human body. Before we can begin to examine behavior from the neurobiological perspective, we will need a map of the nervous system to guide us.

Although the entire nervous system is interrelated, it is often described in parts to make it somewhat more comprehensible. Figure 2.2 shows the component parts of the nervous system. We'll introduce the names and functions of these parts in the next few paragraphs and then review them. At first, this may seem like a lesson in anatomy, but once we get into the workings of the nerve cell, you'll find out why drugs can affect behavior and how pain might be controlled and even get a hint of what thoughts or feelings are made of.

As you can see, the first division is between the **central nervous system** and the **peripheral nervous system.** The central nervous system is centrally located and comprises all the neural cells that are encased within bone. It includes the **brain** and the **spinal cord** (see Figure 2.3). The peripheral nervous system is the system of nerves that carries information to and from the central nervous system. The peripheral nervous system is divided into the somatic and autonomic nervous systems.

The **somatic nervous system** carries messages inward from the sense organs. Light, sound, odor, touch, and taste are among these messages. The somatic nervous system also carries messages out to the skeletal muscles, such as the messages that enable you to move your hands.

Any nerves that carry messages inward to the central nervous system are called **afferent nerves;** any nerves that carry messages outward from the central nervous system are called **efferent nerves.** Afferent and efferent nerves can sometimes interact with just the spinal column without the brain's direct involvement. In such a case, an afferent sensory message travels to the spinal cord, and an efferent motor message immediately returns to the muscles. The quick response provided by this arrangement can be very helpful when, for instance, you place your hand on a hot stove. If you had to wait for the sensory message to travel all the way up your spine to your brain, as most sensory messages do, you'd waste valuable time while your hand cooked. Thanks to this rapid reaction, called a **reflex,** your hand will be off the stove before your brain even knows why!

The **autonomic nervous system** carries information to and from organs, glands, and other muscles within the body. Among the muscles controlled by the autonomic nervous system are those responsible for digestion and heartbeat. This system is called autonomic (like automatic) because the glands, internal organs, and muscles it affects are usually not considered to be under voluntary control. They are generally involuntary.* The autonomic nervous system is further divided into the sympathetic and parasympathetic systems.

The **sympathetic nervous system** is sometimes referred to as the "fight-or-flight" system. If you become angry enough to fight or frightened enough to

---

*There are a number of interesting exceptions to this general rule. For example, through years of practice, Eastern mystics and yoga masters have obtained considerable voluntary control over various autonomic functions including their heartbeat rates.

flee, the sympathetic nervous system is especially active (see Figure 2.4). When you become excited, your pupils dilate, allowing more light to enter. Your heart rate speeds up, causing more oxygen to be sent to the muscles. Your digestion is inhibited, which causes more blood to flow to the muscles. Finally, the sympathetic nervous system orders the release of adrenalin, which is a natural stimulant made by the body. In a frightening or provoking situation, you will know that your sympathetic nervous system has been engaged when your heart starts to pound, you begin to sweat, your mouth becomes dry, and you feel a fluttering in your stomach.

Once the sympathetic nervous system has become active, a counterbalance is needed to return the organism to its original state. The **parasympathetic nervous system** helps bring about this change. It causes the pupils to constrict, stimulates salivation, inhibits the heart rate, and in a sense undoes the stimulation resulting from the activation of the sympathetic nervous system (see Figure 2.4).

The Concept Review on page 40 provides a summary of how the sympathetic and parasympathetic systems act complementarily.

❧ NEURONS AND ELECTROCHEMICAL TRANSMISSION

As you examine the nervous system and all its parts, you may think that it looks something like a wiring diagram, as if your body were wired so that electrical messages could travel constantly between one place and another. But nerves are distinctly unlike wires. A wire is a single entity stretching a particular length; nerves are not single entities. They are made up of thousands upon

SYMPATHETIC NERVOUS SYSTEM
The portion of the autonomic nervous system that is primarily concerned with emotional states and preparing the body for emergencies.

PARASYMPATHETIC NERVOUS SYSTEM
The portion of the autonomic nervous system that is most active during the body's quiescent states and helps the body to recover from states of arousal.

◆ **FIGURE 2.2**

The divisions of the human nervous system.

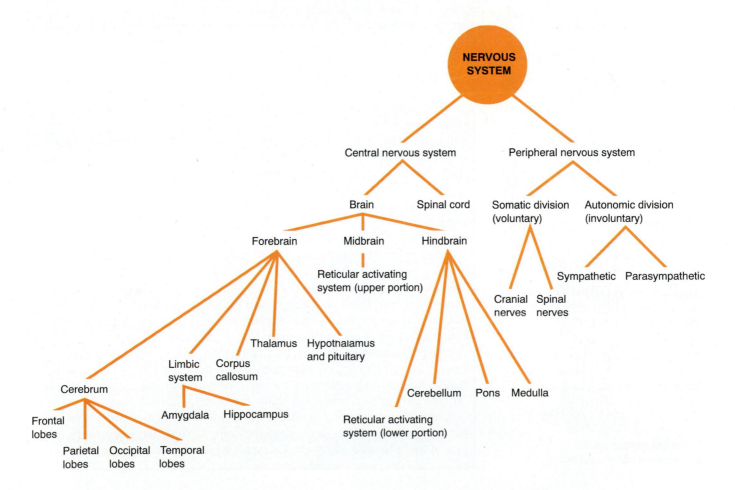

NEURONS
Specialized cells that transmit electrical impulses from one part of the body to another.

thousands of individual nerve cells as described in the chapter preview. Such nerve cells are called **neurons,** which, in most instances, do not touch one another at their points of communication.

If you break a copper wire into thousands of pieces, it's unlikely that an electrical signal would be able to pass through its entire length. Similarly, electrical signals usually cannot pass unaided from neuron to neuron because of the gap between the neurons at the point of communication. Instead, an electrical signal is sent the length of the neuron; when the signal reaches the end, the neuron secretes a chemical that affects neighboring neurons. The chemical message may stimulate another electrical signal to be sent the length of another neuron, and so on. In this way, electrochemical messages are transmitted throughout the body. Thus, your body is an electrochemical system, not just an electrical system, and the brain is the major control center. As you will discover, knowledge of this electrochemical system is the key to understanding much of our psychology.

CONCEPT REVIEW ◆ THE ACTION OF THE NERVOUS SYSTEM

◆ **FIGURE 2.3**

The central and peripheral nervous systems.

Central nervous system

Peripheral nervous system

■ Central nervous system
■ Peripheral nervous system

You're traveling down the highway just a little too close to the vehicle ahead. Suddenly, the driver in front of you brakes hard.

The *afferent* visual nerves of your *somatic system* (part of the *peripheral system*) send messages to your *brain* (part of the *central nervous system*) about the glow of the brake lights and the apparent increasing size of the other vehicle as you rapidly approach it. Millions of biochemical messages are processed in the part of your brain where vision is received. For each of these millions of messages received by the visual area of the brain, about 200 messages are sent out to other parts of the brain (Nauta & Feirtag, 1986), making well over one billion messages, all in less than $\frac{1}{10}$ second!

At about this time, the *sympathetic* division of the *autonomic nervous system* causes your heart rate to increase, adrenalin to be secreted, your pupils to dilate, and your saliva to stop flowing (why create saliva when you're about to crash—you might as well conserve the energy required to make it and put that energy to better use).

You had better do something, or you're going to crash!

Your brain sends a voluntary response to your *spinal cord* and then out along somatic *efferent* nerves, which stimulates the muscles necessary for you to turn the wheel and step on the brake.

After more information has passed from your somatic system into your brain, telling you that the accident has been avoided and that you are safely stopped on the side of the road, your brain sends a message down your spinal cord to the somatic system telling it to relax; this is your signal to release your grip on the steering wheel. Simultaneously, the *parasympathetic* part of the autonomic system begins to fulfill its role of calming you down by slowing your heart rate, making salivation resume (might as well go back to making that stuff now), and constricting your pupils. But since the effects of the secreted adrenalin take a while to wear off, you may remain somewhat shaky for 20 to 30 minutes.

Curiously, prolonged or continuous stimulation of the sympathetic nervous system may result in stress that can, in time, have serious psychological and physical effects on a person's health (see Chapter 15).

PARASYMPATHETIC FUNCTIONS

Constricts pupil

Stimulates salivation

Slows heartbeat

Slows respiration

SYMPATHETIC FUNCTIONS

Dilates pupil
Inhibits salivation
Accelerates heartbeat
Increases respiration
Inhibits digestion
Secretes adrenalin and noradrenalin
Stimulates glucose release

Stimulates digestion

Stimulates gall bladder

Relaxes bladder
Inhibits genitals

Contracts bladder

Stimulates genitals

◆ **FIGURE 2.4**

Functions of the autonomic nervous system. Neurons belonging to the sympathetic nervous system originate in the spinal cord (yellow) and are shown on the right side of this diagram. Neurons belonging to the parasympathetic nervous system exit from the upper end of the spinal cord and also from the lower end of the spinal cord near the organs they affect, which include the bladder and genitals, shown on the left side of this diagram. Almost all organs are enervated by both the sympathetic and parasympathetic systems.

Neuron Structure

The neuron is one of the many individual cells (bone cells, blood cells, skin cells, muscle cells, and so on) that make up your body. No one knows exactly how many cells are in the average human body—a rough estimate is 60 trillion (60,000,000,000,000, or 6×10^{13}). The neuron is the basic unit of the brain and the rest of the nervous system, and most neurons are located in the brain. No one knows how many neurons are in the average brain. An educated estimate is about 100 billion (100,000,000,000, or 10^{11}), but estimates range as high as 1 trillion.

One reason we are unsure how many neurons are in the brain is that we cannot simply count the number of neurons in one part of the brain and then extrapolate to the whole brain. Both the kinds of neurons that are present and their concentrations differ greatly from one part of the brain to the next.

Not only is counting neurons nearly impossible but, as noted in the chapter Prologue, visualizing the patterns of neurocircuitry is exceedingly difficult. Because each neuron may receive messages from, or give messages to, as many

SOMA
The cell body. The soma contains the nucleus of the cell, which manufactures enzymes and molecules essential for maintaining the cell's life.

DENDRITES
The short, branched projections of a neuron that receive impulses from other neurons and conduct them toward the cell body.

AXON
The long projection of a neuron that transmits impulses away from the cell body to the synapse.

NUCLEUS
A body within the soma of a living cell that contains the cell's hereditary material and controls the cell's metabolism, growth, and reproduction.

ION CHANNELS
Gates or selective openings embedded within the neuron's membrane that allow charged atoms (called ions) to enter or exit. Such ion exchanges are responsible for the phenomena of neural transmission and communication.

as 10,000 other neurons, any attempt to comprehend the neurocircuitry of the brain is likely to make you want to turn to something much simpler, such as counting the grains of sand in a desert during a windstorm. For this reason, much of our information about neurons has come from studying individual neural cells rather than neural systems. In the following pages, we will examine a typical neuron and learn how it functions. The way in which the neuron responds to electrical stimulation and the kinds of chemicals it secretes determine our thoughts, feelings, and actions—which, of course, are what psychologists want to understand.

Neurons come in many sizes and shapes, and they often appear to serve unique and specialized functions. Figure 2.5 depicts a typical neuron. Keep in mind, however, that exceptions to this general description abound. In addition, using new techniques that allow us to follow the development of a single neuron in a living creature, researchers have found that a neuron may undergo many changes during its lifetime, growing, altering its appearance or connections, and even changing its function (Purves, Voyvodic, Magrassi, & Yawo, 1987; Bear, Cooper & Ebner, 1987). This finding helps to emphasize that neurons, unlike transistors or similar human-made items, are *alive.*

The typical neuron has three distinct structural features: the **soma,** or cell body, the **dendrites,** and the **axon.** The soma contains the **nucleus** of the cell; it manufactures enzymes and molecules essential for maintaining the cell's life. The dendrites generally receive nerve impulses from surrounding neurons. The axon is the mechanism by which the neuron transmits most of its own nerve impulses. Messages traveling down the axon eventually may stimulate other neurons, muscles, or glands. Some axons are very short, while others are as long as 4 feet—a formidable length given the microscopic size of a neuron.

Surrounding the entire neuron is a thin skin, or membrane. The structure and properties of the membrane directly affect the function and action of the cell. The membrane acts as a kind of skin, permitting the cell to maintain an internal fluid that is markedly different from the fluid surrounding the cell. This difference is most striking in the concentrations of particular ions (electrically charged atoms), including sodium, potassium, calcium, and chlorine ions. You may recognize these elements as essential to your diet. If you don't have enough of any one of them in your system, you will suffer neurological disturbances along with other health-related problems.

When the neuron is at rest—that is, when it is not sending a message—the ion distribution causes the inside of the cell's axon to be electrically more negative than is the surrounding outside medium. These differing concentrations of ions give the neuron the ability to transmit signals along its entire length.

Neural Transmissions

For the next few pages, let's look at the ways in which the neuron transmits messages. As you will soon see, the mechanisms of neural transmission are directly related to our thoughts, feelings, and actions. As we discuss these mechanisms, you will also discover why botulism, cobra venom, and nerve gas are all things to avoid (but you probably already knew that).

When a resting neuron's dendrites are stimulated, an electrical change begins in the membrane surrounding the soma. If the change is of sufficient magnitude, a threshold is passed, which causes the neuron to fire and send a message the whole length of its axon.

When the dendrites of the neuron are stimulated, **ion channels** in the neuron's membrane open, allowing positive ions (mostly sodium) to enter the cell. Typically, chemicals secreted by nearby neurons provide the stim-

Dendrites

Soma

Impulse initiating zone

Axon

Node of Ranvier

Terminal fibers

◆ **FIGURE 2.5**

The typical neuron of a vertebrate animal can carry nerve impulses for a considerable distance. The neuron depicted here, with its various parts drawn to scale, is enlarged 250 times. The nerve impulses originate in the cell body and are propagated along the axon, which may have one or more branches. This axon, which is folded for diagrammatic purposes, would be about 2½ inches long at actual size. Some axons are more than a yard long. The axon's terminal branches may communicate with as many as 10,000 other neurons. Similarly, the dendrites of the neuron in this diagram might receive incoming signals from tens, hundreds, or even thousands of other neurons. Many axons, such as this one, are insulated by a coating known as myelin, which is interrupted at intervals by the regions known as nodes of Ranvier. (SOURCE: Stevens, 1979, p. 55.)

ulation that causes the ion channels to open. Ion channels aren't always opened chemically, however. A few years ago, researchers were surprised to discover that in some neurons sensitive to touch, the membrane's channels are opened by nothing more than the pressure of a touch, which causes the ion channels of the neuron membrane to stretch sufficiently to allow ions to pour in (Guharay & Sachs, 1985).

Advances in the study of ion channels and how they work are coming quickly now that researchers have developed a method that allows them to study individual ion channels in living creatures. This is accomplished by gently sucking up a single ion channel from the surface of a cell into the tip of a pipette (which works like the dropper used in some medicine bottles) and sealing the ion channel within the opening of the pipette without damaging the channel or breaking it off from the cell surface. Then, researchers can watch how the single, isolated channel responds to differing conditions. This is called the *patch-clamp technique* and won the Nobel Prize for its developers, Erwin Neher and Bert Sakmann, in 1991. If you're wondering why no one had done this before, consider that the "dropper" needed is 1/25,000 the thickness of a human hair and you'll get the idea. It wasn't easy (Neher & Sakmann, 1992)!

Like the dendrites and soma, the inside of the axon is electrically more negative than its outside, measuring about 70 millivolts ($70/1000$ of a volt) negative relative to the surrounding medium. Because of this, the neuron is assigned a value of −70 millivolts when at rest. This is known as the **resting**

RESTING POTENTIAL

The difference in electrical potential maintained between the outside and the inside of a resting nerve cell, usually about −70 millivolts.

POLARIZED

In reference to a neuron, to have been placed in a state of potential energy release by the electrical forces created by ions on either side of the cell membrane. In the neuron, polarization results in a resting potential of −70 millivolts across the membrane.

NERVE IMPULSE

The propagation of an electrical impulse down the length of a neural axon once the neuron has fired.

LOCAL EFFECT

The rapid depolarization of a section of an axon in response to the propagation of a neural transmission following the onset of neural firing. It is induced by the rapid depolarization of the soma or of a nearby section of the axon. The local effect results in the rapid depolarization of the next section of the axon, thereby continuing the propagation of the neural transmission.

MICROELECTRODE

An extremely small electric probe capable of monitoring the electrical activity of a single cell.

SPIKE

A nerve impulse generated by a neuron reaching action potential.

ACTION POTENTIAL

A localized, rapid change in electrical state that travels across the cell membrane of a neuron at the moment of excitation with sufficient intensity to cause the neuron to fire.

potential. In this state, the cell and axon are said to be **polarized** because the outside medium and the inside of the cell are like the + and − poles, respectively, of a tiny battery. By making use of this difference in voltage across the membrane, the neuron can generate a **nerve impulse** down the length of its axon.

When the soma reaches threshold, the membrane at the beginning of the axon undergoes a dramatic change. This is called a **local effect.** Special channels in the axon membrane, like those in the dendrites and the soma, open, allowing positive ions to rush in. This influx causes the beginning of the axon suddenly to become positive relative to the external medium. This process is called *depolarization*. The first local effect then causes another identical local effect in the next portion of the axon farther along, and so on. In this manner, the ion exchange races down the length of the axon like a flame following a line of black powder. If a **microelectrode** is placed within the axon and attached to a monitor, such as an oscilloscope, the sudden shift from negative to positive as the nerve impulse passes along the axon shows up on the oscilloscope as a sharp **spike** (see Figure 2.6). Whenever ions are exchanged in a way that causes a nerve impulse, the neuron is said to have reached its **action potential,** which is another way of saying that the nerve has fired. The amount of stimulation, or voltage change, required to reach action potential differs greatly depending on the type of neuron in question (Llinas, 1988).

As soon as the spike has passed one area of the axon, the positive ions are forced back out, restoring the original resting potential of −70 millivolts and often even *hyperpolarizing* the cell (meaning it becomes "very polarized") to about −100 millivolts for a brief time, until everything again equalizes itself at resting potential. Molecular "pumps" within the neuron, often called sodium-potassium pumps, eventually restore the original condition of −70 millivolts by forcing some ions out and allowing others in, although in some cases the original voltage difference is restored by other mechanisms.

Nerve impulses can travel relatively long distances without any loss of strength. The action potential is an all-or-nothing proposition. For the neuron to fire, the dendrites and soma at the head of the axon must be sufficiently stimulated to reach threshold. Otherwise, although some positive ions may flow into the neural soma, not enough will enter to enable it to reach threshold and cause an action potential to be reached. An analogy is a fuse that is singed rather than lighted.

You may be wondering how you can feel a great range of intensities of such stimuli as light, sound, and pressure when a neuron can fire at only one strength. Furthermore, how can you have such a range of motor responses? For instance, you can pick something up gently or with a tight grip. These different intensities are achieved in several ways. To experience weak intensities, it may

◆ FIGURE 2.6

A nerve impulse registers on an oscilloscope as a spike. If an auditory amplifier is attached to the oscilloscope, a click can be heard each time an impulse occurs. Following the spike, there is a negative refractory period during which the difference across the membrane is even less than resting potential; that is, the cell becomes hyperpolarized. This occurs because, after firing, the neuron's molecular pumps don't stop until the polarization is pushed past resting potential.

Action potential +30 millivolts

Resting potential −70 millivolts

Negative refraction period −100 millivolts

be enough for only a few neurons to fire. Strong intensities, on the other hand, may require that thousands upon thousands of neurons fire. Although the strength of each individual impulse is constant, the firing of thousands of neurons can have a cumulative effect. Neurons can also express intensity by how often they fire. A stimulation of mild intensity may cause a neuron to fire only once or twice per second, whereas an extremely intense stimulation may cause some neurons to fire as often as 1000 times per second!

Synaptic Transmissions

Years ago, researchers debated whether an electric spark actually jumped the gap between neurons. We now know that chemicals secreted by the neuron, called **neurotransmitters,** are responsible for the communication across these gaps. Neurotransmitters are very important to psychologists as it is now believed that all behaviors are linked to the function of neurotransmitters and that severe mental illness is always associated with some kind of neurotransmitter mixup or imbalance. For this reason, psychologists are very interested in figuring out the role of each neurotransmitter.

The space between neurons, across which communication occurs, is called the **synapse.** Synapses are generally no more than .000005 (5 millionths) inch across. When an electrical impulse traveling the length of an axon reaches its end, the impulse typically causes neurotransmitters to be secreted into the synapse. If you follow the trunk of a tree upward, you discover that it divides again and again into many individual branches. Similarly, if you follow an axon out to its end, you find that it divides and subdivides into as many as 10,000 end buttons, or **synaptic knobs.** Figure 2.7 is an enlarged drawing showing synaptic transmission at a knob. When an electrochemical impulse reaches a synaptic knob, a change occurs in the knob's membrane. Channels responsive to the positive calcium ion (Ca^+), which is found in the fluid surrounding the neurons, affect the small vesicles that float within the synaptic knob and cause them to be attracted to the **presynaptic surface.** The vesicles carry droplets of neurotransmitter, which they spill from the presynaptic membrane into the synapse. Across the synapse, receptors on the **postsynaptic surface** react to the neurotransmitter. If the postsynaptic surface is the membrane of a gland, the neurotransmitter may interact with the receptors

NEUROTRANSMITTERS
Chemicals secreted by neurons that have an effect on adjacent neurons, muscles, or glands.

SYNAPSE
The small space between neurons into which neurotransmitter is secreted.

SYNAPTIC KNOBS
The extreme ends of an axon in which neurotransmitter is stored.

PRESYNAPTIC SURFACE
The cell surface from which neurotransmitter is secreted into the synapse.

POSTSYNAPTIC SURFACE
The cell surface receiving neurotransmitter secreted into the synapse.

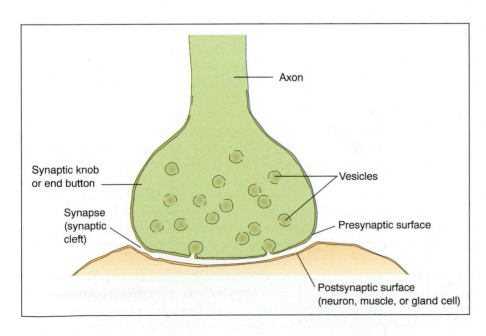

Synaptic knob
or end button

Synapse
(synaptic
cleft)

Axon

Vesicles

Presynaptic surface

Postsynaptic surface
(neuron, muscle, or gland cell)

◆ **FIGURE 2.7**

When a neural impulse reaches the synaptic knobs at the end of the axon, drops of neurotransmitter carried in the vesicles may be released from the presynaptic surface into the synapse. The neurotransmitter affects receptors on the postsynaptic surface.

FIRST MESSENGER SYSTEM
The neural communication system in which the postsynaptic surface responds to informational substances by opening, closing, or altering ion channels.

EXCITATORY SYNAPSES
Synapses associated with depolarization of the receiving cell once neurotransmitter is secreted. If the receiving cell is a neuron, it will become more likely to fire or even to reach action potential.

INHIBITORY SYNAPSES
A synapse associated with hyperpolarization of the receiving cell once neurotransmitter is secreted. If the receiving cell is a neuron, it will become harder to fire, or more difficult reach action potential.

and cause the gland to secrete. If the postsynaptic surface is the membrane of a muscle, the neurotransmitter may cause the muscle to contract. This mode of communication is known as the **first messenger system.**

If the postsynaptic surface belongs to another neuron, as in our earlier example, the neurotransmitter may excite the second neuron, causing it to approach or reach action potential. Once the neurotransmitter has affected the receptors on the postsynaptic membrane, it is either recaptured by the presynaptic membrane, broken down in the synapse by enzymes, or left to diffuse. Anything that blocks or interferes with this synaptic process will cause extreme, even deadly problems for the organism. Botulin toxin, secreted by the *Clostridium botulinum* bacterium and the cause of botulism food poisoning, keeps neurotransmitter from leaving the presynaptic surface, which is why the first signs of botulism are such symptoms as breathing difficulty or double vision (because the nerves no longer control the fine muscles that operate the eyes) rather than the stomach pains you might expect from a disorder called "food poisoning." Cobra venom blocks the postsynaptic surface and keeps it from receiving the neurotransmitter. Like botulism, a dose of cobra venom may quickly make it difficult for you to breathe, although for a slightly different reason. Nerve gas, on the other hand, destroys an enzyme that breaks down the neurotransmitter acetylcholine (a muscle activator) after it has been secreted. The gas, therefore, causes the muscles to keep reacting, which leads to a terrible uncontrollable twitching and eventually to death. Well, enough of this cheery discussion—let's look at the different kinds of synapses.

EXCITATORY SYNAPSES.   There are two basic kinds of synapses, excitatory and inhibitory. So far we have discussed only **excitatory synapses,** in which a message from one neuron causes a second neuron to become excited or to fire. However, it would be catastrophic if one neuron in the brain passed on a message stimulating thousands of other neurons, which in turn passed on the stimulating message to millions more. In short order, all or a large portion of the neurons would be firing and the brain would be out of control. This unfortunate event is prevented by the existence of inhibitory synapses.

INHIBITORY SYNAPSES.   In an **inhibitory synapse** between two neurons, a neurotransmitter is also secreted from the presynaptic membrane into the synapse, but in this case different ion channels in the postsynaptic membrane open that allow only negative ions to flow in. This produces a negative potential (even greater than the resting potential), hyperpolarizing the cell. In effect, the neural message from the first neuron has made the second neuron *less* likely to fire than it was before it was stimulated. In addition to preventing an electrical brainstorm from following a single stimulation, inhibitory synapses also help to tune and sharpen sensory perception. For instance, while a touch on your finger may cause many neurons in the general area of the touch to fire, the inhibitory synapses will block many of the signals that merely surround the exact point of touch. This will enable you to tell precisely where on your finger you were touched (Gottlieb, 1988). Without these inhibitory actions, you would have far less sensory sensitivity.

In addition, many inhibitory synapses are found within the brain. In some areas of the brain, inhibitory synapses actually outnumber excitatory synapses (Gottlieb, 1988). In fact, the failure of these inhibitory synapses to function properly, or in the correct number, appears to be the major cause of epilepsy, a disorder characterized by uncontrollable seizures (Hosford, et al., 1992; Bekenstein & Lothman, 1993). Using this knowledge, researchers hope that they soon will be able to develope drugs that will react with these receptors or synapses in the brain so that such seizures may be ended—in effect, a cure for epilepsy based on our knowledge of the operation of brain neurons.

The World of Neurotransmitters

The first neurotransmitter was identified in 1921. Since that time, the number of different substances found within the nervous system that are known or suspected to be neurotransmitters has increased to about 50 (Fischbach, 1992). These substances are not found randomly in all parts of the nervous system, but tend to be localized in specific groups of neurons, whose axons perform specific functions or send messages to specific areas.

Psychologists are interested in neurotransmitters because their effects are directly related to thoughts, feelings, and behavior. For example, close examination of concentrations of the neurotransmitter dopamine has led researchers to believe that the exact amount of dopamine secreted in certain places within the brain may determine how rewarding we find a particular experience to be (Wise & Rompre, 1989)! If we ever learn how to control dopamine secretion in the brain, we might be able to alter behaviors that many people wish to stop, such as smoking, drug use, overeating, or gambling, among other things. This might be accomplished by making such behaviors less pleasant while making behaviors people wish to encourage, such as peacefulness, love, or finishing an economics paper, for example, more pleasant (assuming that any amount of neurotransmitter can make finishing an economics paper pleasant). You don't need too much imagination, however, to see the potential for abusing such knowledge by, for instance, making sure people enjoy the "right" ideas or "proper" behaviors—a chilling thought.

Other neurotransmitters also play important roles. The neurotransmitter acetylcholine, for example, is essential for the operation of muscles, and GABA (gamma-aminobutyric acid) is needed for the control of inhibitory synapses, among other things (Gottlieb, 1988). The same neurotransmitter may often have different roles depending on where it is operating, and many of the neurotransmitters can be classified into subtypes (such as GABA I and GABA II), each subtly different from the other in ways that might have pronounced effects on behavior (Pritchett, Luddens, & Seeburg, 1989). Name a behavior, a feeling, or a thought, and neurotransmitters will be involved at some level.

DRUGS AND NEUROTRANSMITTER RECEPTORS.   Another important reason for studying neurotransmitters is that drugs that affect behavior appear to do so by modifying or disrupting neural transmissions between brain cells. Solomon Snyder, a renowned researcher in neurotransmission, has stated,

Virtually every drug that alters mental function does so by interacting with a neurotransmitter system in the brain. Many drugs mimic or block the effects of specific neurotransmitters at receptor sites. (1984, p. 23)

Hallucinogenic drugs such as mescaline, psilocybin, and lysergic acid diethylamide (LSD) have chemical structures that strongly resemble those of natural brain neurotransmitters. These hallucinogens mimic the natural brain neurotransmitters and stimulate the corresponding natural receptor sites, which can cause a hallucination such as seeing something that isn't there.

Some drugs block, rather than mimic, neurotransmitters. Such a drug is called an **antagonist.** The neuroleptics, which block receptors of the neurotransmitter dopamine in the brain, are an example of these drugs. Neuroleptics often help to control the hallucinations and bizarre thoughts of schizophrenics (people suffering from the serious mental disorder schizophrenia—see Chapter 16), which has led some researchers to conclude that schizophrenics may be producing excess dopamine or have an excess of dopamine receptors in their brains.

Other drugs work by facilitating or giving a boost to a natural neurotransmitter. Such a drug is called an **agonist.** The antianxiety drug diazepam (Val-

ANTAGONIST
A drug that acts to block or inhibit the actions of other drugs or naturally occurring biochemical substances.

AGONIST
A drug that acts to facilitate or enhance the actions of other drugs or naturally occurring biochemical substances.

PARKINSON'S DISEASE
A progressive nervous disease of the brain characterized by muscle tremor, slowing of movement, peculiarity of gait and posture, and weakness. It is a direct result of dopamine deficiency and can be temporarily treated with medication.

PRIVILEGED SITE
A location (typically in the brain) in which foreign tissue is safe from attack by the body's immune system. Sites in the brain are generally privileged because cells from the body's immune system cannot penetrate the blood-brain barrier that surrounds and protects the brain.

BLOOD-BRAIN BARRIER
The semipermeable membrane and tissue surrounding the blood vessels that serve the brain, which allow substances borne in the blood to have only limited access to the brain. Usually, only a few specific molecules are able to enter. Many drugs as well as the cells from the body's own immune system are typically unable to cross the blood-brain barrier.

ium) appears to work by boosting the effectiveness of GABA (Fischbach, 1992), the most common neurotransmitter found in inhibitory synapses. Antidepressants, such as Prozac, work by boosting the action of the neurotransmitter serotonin. Cocaine boosts the action of dopamine, which may help explain why users so often find it rewarding (recall that dopamine is involved with the brain's natural reward system). Nicotine, the most active ingredient in tobacco, increases the action of receptors for the neurotransmitter acetylcholine, which are involved in muscle movement. This, in part, explains why heavy use of tobacco can give you the "shakes."

By knowing how a drug affects neurotransmitters and their receptor sites, manufacturers can make additional drugs that will mimic, facilitate, or block a neurotransmitter's function. For example, an experimental drug was once developed that countered the effects of GABA, which is the opposite of what diazepam does. When this GABA antagonist was given to human subjects, it caused extreme anxiety, almost a state of panic (Dorow, Horowski, Paschelke, & Amin, 1983).

By conducting experiments with such compounds, researchers hope to uncover the secrets of brain chemistry and, perhaps, to alleviate mental illness, addiction, and many other disorders. This may all be possible if we can uncover the way in which cells operate in response to any combination of signals. As one researcher put it:

. . . for those who would hope to develop drug therapies, such discoveries would be like giving a thief the wiring diagram to the alarm system at the bank. (Linder & Gilman, 1992, p. 65)

FETAL TISSUE TRANSPLANTS AND NEUROTRANSMITTERS. There also is evidence that certain neuromuscular disorders (neural disorders that affect the ability of the muscles to function) may be directly related to dysfunctions in certain brain neurotransmitters. For example, dopamine is also concentrated in areas of the brain that control complex movement. If dopamine in these areas degenerates, the result may be **Parkinson's disease,** in which muscular rigidity and tremors occur. One of the great breakthroughs in medicine occurred in the 1970s when a form of dopamine called levodopa was found to help prevent and control the symptoms of Parkinson's disease. Levodopa taken in pill form finds its way into the brain, where it helps to overcome the problem of the missing dopamine. Individuals with Parkinson's disease who were unable even to button a shirt can perform such tasks easily within minutes of taking levodopa and will appear to have normal motor and muscular control. The progress of the disease can also be slowed by a more recent drug called deprenyl, which works by inhibiting an enzyme that normally blocks dopamine production.

Unfortunately, the relief obtained from these medications is temporary, and can only be used as an aid for a relatively short time. Another way had to be found to help individuals suffering from Parkinson's disease. The first hint of a way came in experiments using mice. In these experiments the brains of healthy mice were damaged so that the specific cells that produced the neurotransmitter dopamine no longer functioned. The mice rapidly lost their movement and direction control and appeared to have all the symptoms of Parkinson's disease. The researchers then treated these mice by placing dopamine-producing cells taken from the brains of mouse embryos alongside the destroyed cells in each mouse's damaged brain (Fine, 1986).

The foreign tissue was not rejected by the mouse's body because most areas of the brain are **privileged sites,** places where the immune system cannot attack. A **blood-brain barrier** isolates the brain from the rest of the body; only certain molecules can penetrate this barrier and enter the brain. The attacking cells of the immune system are not able to get through.

The complicated nerve connections between the embryo-tissue implant and the real brain grew and began to connect on their own. This occurred because axons of one type typically seek out receptors they chemically recognize, thereby making proper connections (Dodd & Jessell, 1988). The foreign dopamine-producing cells placed in each damaged mouse's brain appeared to help by producing the dopamine that was no longer being supplied to the damaged cells. The mice fully recovered from their Parkinson-like symptoms.

By 1993, well over 100 human patients had received the procedure with roughly 56 percent showing substantial improvement (Thompson, 1992; Hitchcock, 1993), and none had died from the surgery. Most of these operations were conducted in England with the use of dopamine producing tissue taken from aborted human fetuses. Fetal tissue is necessary because, unlike mature tissue, it is still growing and will readily make new connections within the brain (Madrazo et al., 1988; Lindvall et al., 1990).

For many years, fetal tissue research was banned in the United States because of the ethical issues it raised. Some feared that such work might encourage abortions or even the eventual growing of fetuses in artificial media for the sole purpose of providing spare parts for people. Others countered that if an abortion is going to occur anyway, one should not throw away tissue that might otherwise save a life. In response to this latter argument, President Clinton lifted the ban on human fetal tissue research and transplantation in 1993.

Interestingly, the new supply of neurotransmitter that these Parkinson patients receive from their brain grafts may be stimulating parts of the brain that surgeons did not intend to affect. It has been observed that after these brain graft procedures, but not after other kinds of brain surgery, patients often behave in strange ways. For instance, some patients experience real changes in their ability to sense pain, others exhibit odd sleep patterns, some have delusions (for instance, one man firmly believed that a farm store was attached to the hospital; another thought that appliance salesmen were visiting all of the hospital rooms), some show personality changes, and some even have visual or auditory hallucinations (Lewin, 1988). Just as interesting is that all of these strange effects following surgery generally disappear within a month or two. Perhaps the introduction of the neurotransmitter from the graft causes these effects and in some way the brain is eventually able to discount them. No one really knows.

THE SECOND MESSENGER SYSTEM. Up to now we have been talking about cells that communicate through voltage fluctuations via the ebb and flow of ions through ion channels at their receptors. Such ion-mediated receptors comprise one superfamily of receptors and, for many years, were the only type known to exist. This was the case because researchers initially examined neural communications between neurons and muscle cells that relied on this system and were less complex than the connections between neurons themselves.

Since that time, however, another superfamily of receptors has been discovered that operate in a different fashion. This superfamily, which includes receptors responsive to dopamine, uses no channels. In this system (see Figure 2.8), a neurotransmitter (first messenger) attaches to its receptor on the postsynaptic surface of a cell. But then, instead of causing ion channels to open or close, the neurotransmitter causes a **G protein** to cleave off a larger protein within the receiving cell, which, in turn, leads to a number of internal enzyme reactions. These reactions cause a second messenger to be created within the cell that alters the cell's behavior, causing it to release a hormone or some

G PROTEINS
A class of molecules that direct the flow of signals from the receptor surface to the rest of the cell. They are called G proteins because they bind to guanine nucleotides within the cell, which, like all nucleotides, consist of an organic base (in this instance, guanine), one or more phosphates, and a sugar. G proteins are typically stimulated into action by first messengers such as neurotransmitters.

SECOND MESSENGER SYSTEM

The neural communication system in which the postsynaptic surface responds to informational substances by freeing a G protein that, in turn, activates an effector enzyme; the enzyme then creates a second messenger or informational substance, which consequently may trigger a cascade of complex reactions resulting in a change in cell behavior. Such second messengers are believed to play an important role in long-term changes in the cell's action.

LONG-TERM POTENTIATION (LTP)

An increase in the efficiency of synaptic interchange that may last for hours or days following a certain pattern of excitatory stimulation. The opposite effect is called long-term depression (LTD) and may also last for hours or days following a certain pattern of inhibitory stimulation. Both LTP and LTD are suspected of playing a major role in learning and memory.

other substance (Linder & Gilman, 1992). Such occurrences are called *G protein-mediated effects.*

This **second messenger system** helps to show that a neuron is not like a switch that just turns on or off in response to some stimulation. Instead, the neuron has a very complex internal information mechanism, making it more like a computer than a switch. G protein-mediated effects are of interest to psychologists because such effects may be the biological basis for learning and memory (see Chapters 8 and 9), two areas in which psychologists are very interested.

LONG-TERM POTENTIATION. Because G protein-mediated effects are slower in onset than ion-mediated effects and last longer, they are not likely to moderate fast point-to-point synaptic transmission in the brain (Fischbach, 1992). Instead, they affect how each neuron will react to first messengers. G protein-mediated effects alter the neurons, synapses, and neurotransmitters so that they undergo actual changes over time. In other words, G protein-mediated effects are especially *responsive to experience.* Psychiatrist and neurobiologist Eric Kandel once said:

As I talk to you and you listen to me, the cells in my brain are having a direct effect on the cells in your brain. What's more, the effect could be long-lasting. So don't talk to strangers. It can produce entirely unwanted effects on your synapses. (Herbert, 1987, p. 80)

Most such long-term effects are mediated by the second messenger system.

Not only do synapses appear and disappear over time, probably as a result of second messages developed deep within the neuron, but the kinds and amounts of neurotransmitter secreted by a neuron may also vary as an eventual effect of experience. Many neurons secrete more than one kind of neurotransmitter (Nicoll, 1988). Sometimes, when a neuron is stimulated, the effect of the stimulation may involve second messengers, not for only a millisecond, but for days or even weeks (Marx, 1986). Such a long-term change in synaptic efficiency is known as **long-term potentiation (LTP).** For you to have any memories of past events, LTP must have occurred within the neurons at some

◆ **FIGURE 2.8**

The second messenger system. In this example of a G protein-mediated response, a first messenger, in this case a neurotransmitter (1), activates a specific receptor on the postsynaptic surface (2) of a cell. The stimulation of the receptor causes a G protein (3) to cleave off and activate an effector enzyme (4). An enzyme is a protein that functions as a catalyst; that is, it makes other chemical reactions occur. In this instance, the effector enzyme liberates the second messenger cyclic adenosine-3',5'-monophosphate, better known as cyclic AMP (5). The second messenger then triggers a cascade of enzymatic reactions (6), culminating in a change in cell behavior (7); in this example, the release of sugar. Such G protein-mediated responses are thought to be at the core of learning and memory because they enable long-term potentiation to occur. (SOURCE: After Linder & Gilman, 1992.)

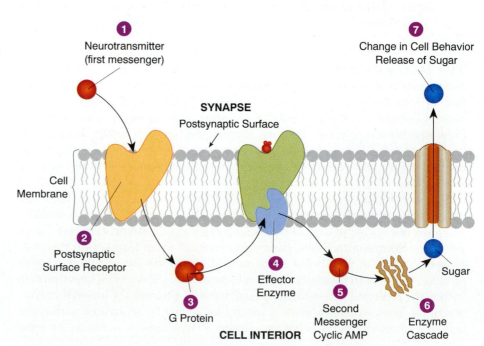

level. Each experience that you can recall has obviously caused some long-term change in your brain or how else could you recall it?

With the alteration of enough neurons, major changes in behavior may be observed over time. If this all seems a bit overwhelming, it's no wonder. Ira Black of the Cornell University Medical College summed it up well when he noted:

In addition to dealing with approximately 100 billion neurons, each of which has on the average 10,000 connections, we now have to realize that the individual neurons may use different signals at different times, depending on the stimuli they receive. The combinatorial power is staggering. (Marx, 1986, p. 1501)

Further research may even force us to add to this power. For example, the most plentiful cells in the brain are not neurons, but rather **glial cells,** which outnumber neurons by a ratio of 10:1. *Glia* is the Greek word for "glue"; for many years, scientists assumed that glial cells, acting like glue, helped to hold neurons in place. Glial cells also often recover neurotransmitter from the synapse after it has been released there by the neuron and are themselves electrochemically active. Now it has been discovered that glial cells communicate with one another over long distances via changes in electrical potential (Cornell-Bell, Finkbeiner, Cooper, & Smith, 1990). Research also indicates that glial cells modify the electrical activity of the neurons they surround, which means that the nervous system is far more complicated than we thought it was—if it's even possible to imagine something more complicated than what we were already contemplating.

NITRIC OXIDE. Nitric oxide* (chemically abbreviated NO, for the one atom of nitrogen and one of oxygen contained within its simple molecular structure) is a short-lived noxious gas familiar to chemists. Its usual nefarious haunts include cigarette smoke and smog. Typically made in the atmosphere during lightning storms, NO will usually last about 5 to 10 seconds before joining up with a second oxygen atom to form another noxious gas, nitrogen dioxide (NO_2)—all of some interest to be sure, but why mention any of this in a psychology textbook? The reason is that nitric oxide, a gas, a depleter of ozone, a suspected cancer-causing agent, and a precursor of acid rain, was discovered in 1991 to be a major neurotransmitter!

This discovery highlighted just how very little we really know about the brain. Nitric oxide isn't just a newly discovered neurotransmitter, but perhaps the first of a whole new class of neurotransmitters. It satisfies all the criteria for being a neurotransmitter—it is a discrete chemical messenger that travels from neurons to adjacent cells (Snyder, 1992), but unlike the neurotransmitters we already know, it is not made in advance and stored in vesicles. Instead, it is made and used immediately. Nor does NO bind to the usual kinds of receptors one might expect a neurotransmitter to grab onto. Instead, its receptor is the element iron, which is found inside enzymes deep within the cell. NO is even released and sent in a peculiar way; as a gas, it simply seeps like a ghost right out of the cell that synthesized it and deep into adjoining cells (Snyder, 1992).

In the few years since its discovery, NO has been found to play a varied and profound role. Scientists have discovered that NO is responsible in great part for blood vessel dilation; that is, in the presence of NO, blood vessels will widen allowing more blood to flow through them. During injury or illness, some cells may be damaged or overstimulated leading to an overrelease of NO. It has been known for years that following a severe bacterial infection, blood

GLIAL CELLS
Support cells in the central nervous system that provide neurons with physical and nutritional support. Glial cells outnumber neurons in the brain and recently have been suspected to be, like neurons, directly involved in information transmission.

*Not to be confused with nitrous oxide (N_2O), an anesthetic commonly called "laughing gas."

pressure may suddenly drop to deadly levels. In 1992 researchers discovered that NO antagonists will bring patients whose blood pressure has dropped precipitously back from the danger zone within a few minutes (Culotta & Koshland, 1992). With this in mind, it was soon discovered that NO was the controller of erections in males. NO dilates the blood vessels allowing an erection to occur. It is now believed that many instances of male impotence (the inability to reach or obtain an erection—a problem for about 10 percent of all men) are the result of failure to release sufficient NO. For years, many cases of impotence were thought to be strictly psychological in nature, but a large number of such instances may soon be remedied by medication that boosts weak NO production.

Stroke (brain damage caused by either a blood clot blocking the flow of blood into an area of the brain or the hemorrhaging of a blood vessel) claims hundreds of thousands of lives each year and is the third leading killer in the United States, behind heart disease and cancer. It is now understood that most of the damage caused by a stroke is due to overexcitement of cells in the brain that manufacture NO. The overrelease of this noxious gas during a stroke kills millions of brain neurons that might otherwise be unaffected. NO antagonists given immediately following a stroke have been found to reduce brain damage significantly. Such drugs may eventually become commonplace and save many lives.

NO is also released by certain cells when they come in contact with bacteria. Who would have guessed that one of the ways our body fights off invaders is by zapping them with poison gas? The discovery of the role of nitric oxide has also led to a certain amount of rare humor in the literature, with journal articles carrying such titles as, "NO a thousand times NO," "NO way," "NO class?" "Just say NO," and the like. Clearly, this discovery is making researchers very happy, and NO wonder—it holds the promise of opening so many new areas of study. Every day that passes, some researchers realize something new—and mutter to themselves such things as, "So that's why nitroglycerin pills stop chest pain—the nitro part mimics NO action by dilating the constricted blood vessels surrounding the heart!" As you might imagine, pharmaceutical companies are rushing to develop drugs that boost or suppress NO synthesis in cells.

The presence of the excitatory neurotransmitter glutamate arouses cells to make NO. Glutamate accounts for synaptic transmission at more locations in the brain than any other neurotransmitter (Snyder & Bredt, 1992), which implies that NO may do a lot of work in the brain as well. Which roles might NO play in the brain? What secrets will it unlock for psychology? We can only guess, but there are hints. Because of its effect on enzymes deep within the cell, NO is most involved with the second messenger system and, therefore, probably plays a large role in long-term potentiation (LTP). As was mentioned earlier, LTP is thought to be fundamental in the processes of learning and memory. In support of this, researchers have found that if rats are given drugs that prevent the synthesis of NO, the rats are unable to learn their way through a maze, something that rats are usually well able to do. Without NO, it seems, certain new things cannot be learned or remembered (Zhuo, Small, Kandel, & Hawkins, 1993)! The story of NO is yet to be fully written, but it is a "Cinderella story—from vaguely noxious gas to powerful queen of communication and defense" (Culotta & Koshland, 1992, p. 1863). And, as hinted, the story may not end with NO. There is now strong evidence of another gas neurotransmitter—CO (Verma, Hirsch, Glatt, Ronnett, & Snyder, 1993). CO is, of course, carbon monoxide, a very poisonous gas usually associated with accidental asphyxiation via car exhausts or faulty heaters. It, too, may have many functions in the brain and elsewhere and may also play an important role in long-term potentiation (Zhuo, Small, Kandel, & Hawkins, 1993). Perhaps NO and CO are just the beginning of a whole new domain in neuroscience. Bit by bit, such discoveries may eventually help to unlock many of the secrets of our psychology. Time will tell.

NEUROPEPTIDES.   Ever since Susan Leeman at Harvard University purified the first one from brain tissue in 1971, another whole new class of chemical messengers has been uncovered—the **neuropeptides.** Neuropeptides are small chemicals made from **amino acids.** Well over 50 have been identified and more than 200 are suspected to exist; the actual number may well be higher. Neuropeptides are not the same as neurotransmitters, however, although they can sometimes act like them, communicating messages from one neuron to an adjacent neuron. Unlike neurotransmitters, neuropeptides can also *travel throughout the body in the bloodstream*, eventually entering and affecting neurons far from the neuropeptide's production site. When a neuropeptide acts in this fashion, it is acting like a **hormone.**

The effects of neuropeptides on behavior are wide-ranging. When different neuropeptides are placed in animals' brains, interesting behaviors are triggered, such as yawning, stretching, or grooming (Panksepp, 1986). Neuropeptides have been described as being like,

island-hopping cruise ships [that] seem to meander through the brain, glands, and the immune system [making] scheduled stops in the choicest locations, at only those cellular ports with customized receiving docks. (Cordes, 1985, p. 18)

The point of this statement is that each neuropeptide has a certain molecular shape that will activate a recipient cell only if it fits a molecular receptor on that cell, like a key in a lock. Sometimes, if the cell it is affecting is a neuron, the neuropeptide may function like a neurotransmitter; that is, it may cause the neuron to be affected (making it easier, or less easy, to fire the neuron). Neuropeptides may affect many other types of cells as well.

Although neuropeptides are very small, their effects can be astounding. Let's take a look at one of the neuropeptides, **beta-endorphin.** The story begins in 1971 with Avram Goldstein, who was working with drugs derived from opium, such as morphine. He discovered that when opium was ingested, it tended to concentrate in different areas of the brain, specifically, in those areas associated with the perception of pain and with emotion. This made sense to Goldstein, because morphine is known to be a strong pain reliever, and it gives the user a good feeling, a sense of emotional well-being, technically known as *euphoria*. Goldstein went one step further; he wondered why human beings and animals even responded to opium, which, after all, is an extract from a plant. What connection could there be between a human brain and a plant?

Goldstein formed the hypothesis that opiates such as heroin or morphine work because they are mimicking some natural brain substance that binds with the same receptors with which drugs such as heroin or morphine bind. In other words, a natural heroin or morphine must exist in the brain. That substance is beta-endorphin ("the morphine within"), and it was discovered in 1975. Immediately following the discovery, researchers began the attempt to synthesize beta-endorphin; in 1977 a small amount was manufactured for the first time.

After the discovery of beta-endorphin, some researchers focused on the Chinese technique of **acupuncture.** Acupuncture usually is performed by inserting thin needles into particular places on a person's body and rotating the needles back and forth. When the acupuncturist does this, an anesthetic reaction can be induced—people in China, for example, undergo certain forms of surgery

---

NEUROPEPTIDES
Extremely small chemical messengers made from short chains of amino acids. Beta-endorphin is a neuropeptide.

AMINO ACIDS
Any of a collection of organic compounds that contain both an amino and a carboxyl group. All life is based on only 20 different amino acids, which are the building blocks of all protein. The neurotransmitter gamma-aminobutyric acid is an example of an amino acid.

HORMONE
A blood-borne secretion of the endocrine glands that specifically affects metabolism and behavior.

BETA-ENDORPHIN
A powerful natural neuropeptide. It means "the morphine within" and is so named because it has properties similar to those of heroin and morphine. It is a powerful painkiller and mood elevator.

ACUPUNCTURE
A traditional Chinese therapeutic technique in which the body is punctured with fine needles. It usually is used as an anesthetic or to relieve pain.

PLACEBO
An inert substance often given to subjects in a control group in place of the treatment given to subjects in the experimental group.

EXOCRINE GLANDS
Glands that secrete fluids through ducts to the outside of the body or to a specific organ.

with no anesthesia other than acupuncture, and they do not feel pain. Nothing is injected through the needles.

Many researchers now believe that acupuncture may produce its anesthetic effect by stimulating the secretion of beta-endorphin. Support for this idea comes from the fact that acupuncture is not as effective if *naloxone* (an opiate antagonist and, therefore, a beta-endorphin blocker) has been administered beforehand (Weiss, 1988).

For years psychologists have known that when people who are in pain are given a **placebo** and are told to expect relief, approximately one-third of them will report that their pain has lessened. These people are called *placebo reactors*. The placebo may be a sugar pill, an injection of water, a magic incantation, or the laying on of hands—anything that usually would not be expected to relieve pain. Why should this power of suggestion work? Research indicates that placebo reactors in some unconscious way may be activating their body's natural pain-suppression system and causing the release of beta-endorphin (Levine, Gordon, & Fields, 1978). Support for this idea also comes from the finding that naloxone lessens the painkilling effect of a placebo. Even in the presence of naloxone, however, placebos can sometimes have a painkilling effect (Gracely, Dubner, Wolskee, & Deeter, 1983), which indicates that other substances not blocked by naloxone may play an important role, along with beta-endorphin, in the perception of pain.

Vigorous exercise can also cause the release of beta-endorphin, which may help to explain the "high" associated with regular vigorous activity. Beta-endorphin is also known to dilate blood vessels, which in turn helps to lower blood pressure, a result often associated with regular exercise (Berk, 1981).

The neuropeptides have been implicated in other areas besides pleasure and pain. For instance, research has indicated that beta-endorphin may play an important role in learning and memory (Bolles & Fanselow, 1982). Without question, these chemical substances are opening a new chapter in psychobiology, and the surprises have only begun to appear.

❧ HORMONES AND THE ENDOCRINE SYSTEM

Hormones are substances that travel throughout the body via the circulation of the blood and have wide-ranging effects on behavior. Hormones are secreted by glands, of which there are two kinds in the body. The **exocrine glands**

The Chinese technique of acupuncture produces an analgesic (pain-killing) response from the body by stimulating the production of the body's natural pain reliever, beta-endorphin.

secrete into ducts that usually lead to the surface of the body; they include tear and sweat glands. The **endocrine glands,** which make up the endocrine system (see Figure 2.9), secrete hormones directly into the bloodstream. Chief among the endocrine glands are the pituitary gland, the adrenal glands, and the gonads. Our basic knowledge of the endocrine system, however, is still growing, as evidenced by the fact that only in the last few years was it discovered that the heart (which was thought to be only a pump) is also an endocrine gland that secretes a hormone that alters the permeability of the ion channels in surrounding neurons and helps to regulate blood pressure (Cantin & Genest, 1986; Sorbera & Morad, 1990).

Hormones are messengers, but, unlike neurotransmitters, which are fast-acting and travel the extremely short distance across a synapse, hormones are slow-acting and are carried throughout the body. Hormones can affect parts of the body distant from the gland that secreted them and also may affect many different parts of the body at once. Some substances, such as noradrenalin and some neuropeptides, do double duty, acting as hormones in some cases and as neurotransmitters in others. As an example of the many vital links between the endocrine and nervous systems, consider the following: We know that if neurons receive no stimulation over a long enough period, they will die. An old saying among neuroscientists is, "Use it, or lose it." If the adrenal glands are removed, and the hormones they produce are not replaced, certain neurons in the brain will die (Sloviter et al., 1989). This helps to show that the human body must be considered as an integrated whole and not looked at piecemeal, as though each system were a discrete entity unto itself.

Endocrine glands secrete hormones in response to neural messages or in reaction to changes in body chemistry. Hormones are known to have a vital function in physical growth and sexual development. They also are involved in changes of mood, reactions to stress, and levels of activity (Reinisch, 1981).

Some of the hormones released by glands such as the pituitary or the hypothalamus (the portion of the brain directly above the pituitary) are called **executive hormones** because they, in turn, bring about the release of other hormones in the endocrine system. The **pituitary gland** often releases its hor-

ENDOCRINE GLANDS
Ductless glands that pour their secretions directly into the bloodstream. The hormones secreted by the endocrine glands are important regulators of many body activities and include such substances as adrenalin and pituitary growth hormone.

EXECUTIVE HORMONES
Hormones that order or control the secretion of other hormones.

PITUITARY GLAND
A gland located beneath and attached to the hypothalamus that controls many hormonal secretions. It often is called the "master gland" because it appears to control other glands throughout the body.

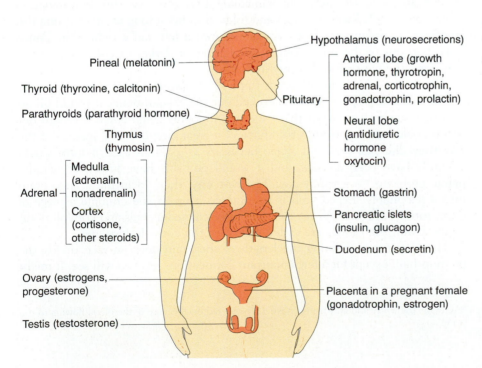

◆ **FIGURE 2.9**

The glands of the endocrine system and some of the hormones they secrete.

Pineal (melatonin)

Thyroid (thyroxine, calcitonin)

Parathyroids (parathyroid hormone)

Thymus (thymosin)

Adrenal — Medulla (adrenalin, nonadrenalin) / Cortex (cortisone, other steroids)

Ovary (estrogens, progesterone)

Testis (testosterone)

Hypothalamus (neurosecretions)

Pituitary — Anterior lobe (growth hormone, thyrotropin, adrenal, corticotrophin, gonadotrophin, prolactin) / Neural lobe (antidiuretic hormone oxytocin)

Stomach (gastrin)

Pancreatic islets (insulin, glucagon)

Duodenum (secretin)

Placenta in a pregnant female (gonadotrophin, estrogen)

Adrenal Glands
Endocrine glands located above the kidneys that secrete the hormones adrenalin, noradrenalin, and steroids. These hormones influence metabolism and the body's reaction to stressful situations.

Adrenalin
A hormone secreted by the adrenal glands that stimulates the sympathetic nervous system; also called epinephrine.

Noradrenalin
A hormone secreted by the adrenal glands that brings about a number of body changes, including constriction of the blood vessels near the body's surface. It causes the adrenal glands to secrete steroids, which, in turn, release sugar so that energy is available for emergency action. It is also called norepinephrine.

Steroids
Any of a number of organic compounds that have a 17-atom carbon ring, including some hormones. Cortical steroids (secreted from the adrenal glands) help to control the release of sugar stored for use in emergencies.

Gonads
The sex glands that contribute to the regulation of the sex drive and the physiological changes that accompany physical maturity. These glands are the ovaries in the female and the testes in the male.

Sulci
The narrow fissures separating adjacent cerebral convolutions.

Gyri
The prominent rounded and elevated convolutions at the surfaces of the cerebral hemispheres.

Myelin
A white, fatty covering on neural fibers that serves to insulate impulses along the fibers and increase the speed of neural transmission.

Cerebrum
The large rounded structure of the brain occupying most of the cranial cavity; it is divided into two cerebral hemispheres by a deep fissure and joined at the bottom by the corpus callosum.

mones after it receives executive hormones from the hypothalamus. For example, orders from the hypothalamus tell the pituitary how much growth hormone to secrete. Too little or too much of this hormone can dramatically affect growth, creating either a dwarf or a giant.

The **adrenal glands** are located just above both kidneys. They secrete **adrenalin** and **noradrenalin** (these same substances, when acting within neurons as neurotransmitters, are called, respectively, epinephrine and norepinephrine). Both of these hormones have much to do with the action of the sympathetic nervous system. They help to prepare an organism for an emergency or for a stressful situation. Adrenalin causes the heart to beat faster and blood vessels to constrict within the stomach and the intestines. Noradrenalin is an executive hormone. When it reaches the pituitary, it stimulates the release of other executive hormones that act on the adrenal glands, causing the adrenals to secrete **steroids.** Steroids are a class of hormones that cause the liver to release stored sugar (glycogen), so that energy can be made available for emergency action. It is this hormone that has been abused by some body builders and other athletes who want to develop large muscles in the hope of improving performance. Overuse of steroids, however, carries with it health risks associated with stressful reactions, including heart disease and high blood pressure. The **gonads,** which secrete sex hormones, are discussed in Chapter 11.

As we have mentioned, some of the same chemical substances may be secreted by glands as hormones or used by neurons as neurotransmitters. Similarly, as we have seen, some neuropeptides do double duty, acting like hormones some of the time and like neurotransmitters at other times. This state of affairs has led some modern researchers to abandon terms such as "hormone," "neuropeptide," and "neurotransmitter" and to use instead the collective term *informational substances* to denote chemicals that carry messages, wherever or however they do so.

◆ THE STRUCTURE OF THE BRAIN

When you look at a human brain (shown in Figures 2.10 and 2.11), three features are likely to catch your immediate attention. First, the brain appears to be rippled, filled with crevices and folds. Second, a long fissure running the length of the brain appears to separate it into a left and a right half. Third, some portions of the brain seem to be lighter or darker in color than other portions—the white and the gray matter.*

Why is the brain convoluted or rippled? One good reason may be the advantage of saving space. If you flattened out the human brain, it would fill an area of 4 square feet, about the size of a Monopoly game board! Perhaps our brains could have evolved in the shape of a great circuit board, instead of the way they did, but the skull shape necessary to contain such a form would certainly have been unusual, and it would probably have presented aerodynamic problems on a windy day. The best way, then, of fitting a large brain into a reasonably shaped skull is to crumple it up. If you crumple a piece of paper into a ball, you will see that you have created fissures and convolutions. In the brain, the fissures are called **sulci** and the convolutions **gyri.**

The long fissure running the length of the brain does, in fact, divide the brain in half, except for a few important connections. As you will see, it might

---

*Actually, the white and gray matter have a pinkish-red hue because of the blood flowing to the brain.

◆ **FIGURE 2.10**

The human brain. Viewed from this angle, only the cerebral cortex is visible. The cerebral cortex is the largest part of the human brain; it contains 70 percent of the neurons in the nervous system.

be more accurate to think of the brain as two brains, joined and sharing information and controlling different aspects of behavior.

When Agatha Christie's master detective, Hercule Poirot, was deep in thought, he would often tap his forehead and refer to the "little gray cells." Many of these gray cells are neurons without a **myelin** coat on their somas. Myelin is a white, fatty sheath that coats the axons and somas of some neurons. It insulates and provides nourishment to the neuron. Myelinated neurons are able to transmit messages faster than nonmyelinated neurons can. Billions of nonmyelinated somas or axons can give the appearance of a grayish mass within the brain—the gray matter. Billions of myelinated somas and axons have a white, glistening sheen—the white matter—because of their white myelin sheaths. The distinction between white and gray matter isn't all that obvious, however, because many neurons have nonmyelinated somas, but myelinated axons.

The largest part of the brain, and the part you usually think of when you picture the brain, is the **cerebrum** (see Figures 2.10 and 2.11). No fewer than 70 percent of all the neurons in the central nervous system are contained in the cerebrum (Nauta & Feirtag, 1979). The outer layer of the cerebrum is called the **cerebral cortex.** *Cortex* in Latin means "bark," and, in a way, the sulci and gyri of the cortex do resemble the bark of a tree. You can trace the evolutionary history and development of your brain by following the lower structures upward to the cerebral cortex. The structures that are deeper and lower in the brain are older in evolutionary terms. For convenience, the brain may be divided into the **hindbrain,** the **midbrain,** and the **forebrain,** and each area may be further subdivided (see Figures 2.2, 2.11, and 2.12).

CEREBRAL CORTEX
The extensive outer layer of convoluted gray tissue of the cerebral hemispheres, which is largely responsible for higher nervous functions, including intellectual processes. It consists of the neocortex and the allocortex.

HINDBRAIN
The posterior section of the brain, which includes the cerebellum, pons, and medulla among other structures.

MIDBRAIN
The middle section of the brain, which contains the structures responsible for processing and relaying auditory and visual information.

FOREBRAIN
The top portion of the brain, which includes the thalamus, hypothalamus, corpus callosum, limbic system, and cerebrum.

◆ **FIGURE 2.11**

A human brain, drawn so that its internal structures are visible through "transparent" outer layers of the cerebrum. (Figure 2.12 shows a generalized mammalian brain in a highly schematic view. Corresponding structures in the realistic and schematic models are the same color.)
The brain and spinal cord of human beings and other mammals can be subdivided into smaller regions according to gross appearance, embryology, or cellular organization.
The most general way of dividing the brain is into hindbrain, midbrain, and forebrain. The hindbrain includes the cerebellum.
The forebrain is more complex. Its outer part is the cerebral hemisphere, the surface of which is the convoluted sheet of the neocortex. The rest of the forebrain includes the thalamus (which has numerous subdivisions) and the hypothalamus (which connects to the pituitary complex). Some structures depicted in this drawing have not been mentioned in the text because they are beyond the scope of our discussion. They are included here, however, to show that each major structure has a name. (SOURCE: Nauta & Feirtag, 1979, p. 102.)

The Hindbrain

The major components of the hindbrain are the **medulla,** the **cerebellum,** the **pons,** and the **reticular activating system.** In evolutionary terms, these portions of the brain are very old. Humans share these brain structures with older and less complex species, such as reptiles. In fact, the hindbrain in humans often is referred to as the "reptilian brain."

THE MEDULLA.   As the spinal column enters the stem of the hindbrain, it begins to widen. This is the location, deep and low within the brain, of the medulla, a small, narrow concentration of millions of neurons perhaps 1½ inches in length. The medulla controls many life-support functions, including breathing and heartbeat. The slightest damage to it can result in death.

THE CEREBELLUM.   Just above the medulla, but in the rear portion of the brain stem, is the cerebellum, which in Greek means "little chamber." Like the cerebral cortex, it has sulci and gyri. The function of the cerebellum appears to be pretty much the same for reptiles, fishes, birds, and mammals, including humans. Among other functions, it coordinates muscle tone and fine motor control. Although the commands for motor movements may originate in higher areas of the brain, it is the cerebellum that controls and fine-tunes the movements. The cerebellum also stores highly repetitious procedures that, once mastered, require little thought and become almost automatic; such skills include riding a bicycle, playing a piano, and typing. Damage to the cerebellum causes awkward and uncontrolled movements.

THE PONS.   At about the same level as the cerebellum, in the front portion of the brain stem, is the pons. Many important ascending and descending nerve fibers run through the pons, connecting it with other brain areas. The pons regulates motor messages traveling from the higher brain downward through the pons to the cerebellum. It is also thought to regulate some sensory information, since cells involved with vision have been found in the pons and because it is often especially active during vivid dreams. In addition, nuclei (densely packed concentrations of neural dendrites and somas) associated with respiratory regulation have been found in the pons.

MEDULLA
The oblong structure just above the spinal cord that is responsible for many vital life-support functions, including breathing and heartbeat.

CEREBELLUM
A portion of the hindbrain situated just beneath the posterior portion of the cerebrum. One of its function is to coordinate muscle tone and fine motor control.

PONS
Part of the brain stem lying just above the medulla that regulates motor messages traveling from the higher brain downward through the pons to the cerebellum. It also regulates sensory information.

RETICULAR ACTIVATING SYSTEM
A complex network of neurons that monitors the general level of activity in the cortex, maintaining a state of arousal.

◆ **FIGURE 2.12**

*Schematic drawing of a generalized mammalian brain. (Colors for parts correspond to those in Figure 2.11.) (*SOURCE: *Nauta & Feirtag, 1979, p. 102.)*

THALAMUS
Part of the forebrain that relays sensory information and is involved in wakefulness and sleep.

OLFACTORY BULB
A mass of cells in the forebrain associated with the sense of smell. The olfactory nerve fibers enter and form a tract leading farther into the brain.

HYPOTHALAMUS
An elongated structure in the forebrain that appears to control an entire range of autonomic functions, including sleep, body temperature, hunger, and thirst.

THE RETICULAR ACTIVATING SYSTEM.   Running upward from the hindbrain toward the midbrain is a complex network of neurons known collectively as the reticular activating system. It is made up of relatively few neurons that seem to monitor the general level of activity in the hindbrain, maintaining a state of arousal. Wakefulness and sleep are regulated in part by this portion of the brain. Sleeping animals whose reticular systems are stimulated by electrodes usually will awaken. If the reticular system is severely damaged, a permanent state of sleep may result. The reticular system also seems to be important in helping to focus attention or to make an organism alert. As you can see, the hindbrain, which is old in evolutionary terms, contains structures vital to the survival of all animals.

The Midbrain

The upper portions of the reticular formation are found in the midbrain along with important sensory-processing and relay areas. These areas modify visual and auditory messages and also function as sensory amplifiers or suppressors. Have you ever wondered why a subtle motion seen out of the corner of your eye can be so attention grabbing? Part of the reason may be that your midbrain has amplified it (Meredith & Stein, 1983). Such a mechanism is valuable for you or for any animal to possess, considering that what you spot out of the corner of your eye might be a hungry predator or a salesman who is sneaking up on you.

The Forebrain

The forebrain includes the thalamus, the hypothalamus, the limbic system, the corpus callosum, and the cerebrum.

THE THALAMUS.   Buried beneath the cerebral cortex on top of the brain stem are two structures lying on either side of the brain and shaped something like eggs. These are the left and right halves of the **thalamus.** We know of two important functions that are served by the millions, or perhaps billions, of neurons that make up the thalamus. Like the reticular activating system, the thalamus seems to be involved in wakefulness and sleep. Perhaps more important, the thalamus is a relay and translation center for sensory information. Before continuing on to higher brain structures, information from the senses passes through the thalamus. There is one exception, however, and that is the sense of smell. Olfactory (smell) messages from the nose bypass the thalamus and travel directly to the area know as the **olfactory bulb.** The sense of smell may be a very old sense and may have evolved in its own direction, while the newer senses have taken advantage of the relatively newer areas of the brain and have become associated with them. Scientists assume that in order for information from the other senses to be understood at the higher brain levels, the messages must be processed by being passed through the synaptic connections in the thalamus.

THE HYPOTHALAMUS.   The **hypothalamus** is an elongated structure located in front of and between the thalamus orbs. Although it is a relatively small structure in the brain, it has been the focus of intense interest because it appears to play many important roles. The hypothalamus apparently controls an entire range of autonomic functions. It takes part in regulating sleep and wakefulness and in controlling body temperature, hunger, and thirst (see Chapter 11 for greater detail). Blood pressure and metabolism also are related to activities within the hypothalamus. At the lower tip of the hypothalamus, and partly under its supervision, is the pituitary gland, which controls many hormonal secretions. Because the hypothalamus is related to the endocrine (hormonal) system, it has been implicated in the control of sexual behavior and reproductive cycles as well as in aggression and reactions to stress.

THE LIMBIC SYSTEM.   The **limbic system** is the portion of the brain most strongly associated with emotional responses. Structures in the limbic system also are associated with learning and memory. Much of the limbic system is located beneath the cerebral cortex. The limbic system is not a single structure but an aggregation of structures, its two major components being the **amygdala** and the **hippocampus.** The limbic system is also believed to represent one of the first evolutionary developments to break away from fixed, instinctive behavioral patterns. Whereas animals such as reptiles flee, fight, or eat in stereotypical and repetitive ways, animals with limbic systems seem to be better able to modify their inherited behavior patterns to meet new demands.

The term amygdala refers to each of two small bulbs located in the front of the brain, one slightly to the left and one slightly to the right of midline. The amygdalae (plural) are associated with memory and emotion. In monkeys, if a lesion (such as a cut) is made on one portion of an amygdala, the animal may go into a blind rage, attacking everything within sight. If a lesion is created in another part of an amygdala, the animal may respond to attacks against it without any emotional expression, remaining passive as if nothing were happening.

The term hippocampus refers to either of two small areas on either side of the back of the forebrain. The hippocampi (plural) are known to be important in the memory process. Damage to either an amygdala or a hippocampus can cause memory to be disrupted (see Chapter 9).

THE CORPUS CALLOSUM.   The **corpus callosum** is the most important connection between the two hemispheres of the brain. The left and right hemispheres, though separate and distinct, share information by passing neural messages back and forth. *Corpus callosum* means "hard or calloused body" in Latin. If you were to insert your fingers between the two soft hemispheres of your brain and press down, you would feel the corpus callosum as a hard surface

---

LIMBIC SYSTEM
An aggregate of brain structures, the two major components of which are the amygdalae and the hippocampi. Some of its major functions include attention, memory, emotion, and motivation.

AMYGDALA
A small bulb at the front of the brain that is associated with emotion. It is part of the limbic system. There are two such structures in each brain, known collectively as amygdalae.

HIPPOCAMPUS
A small area at the back of the forebrain that is known to be important in the memory process. It is part of the limbic system. There are two such structures in each brain, known collectively as hippocampi.

CORPUS CALLOSUM
The structure providing the major connection between the two cerebral hemispheres. When it is severed, communication between the two hemispheres is severely disrupted.

The olfactory sense, or sense of smell, is evolutionarily very old. Olfactory messages are the only sense messages to bypass the thalamus, traveling directly to the olfactory bulb.

♦ **Figure 2.13**

The progressive increase in the size of the cerebrum in vertebrates is evident in these drawings, which show a representative selection of vertebrate brains, all drawn to the same scale. In vertebrates lower than mammals, the cerebrum is small. In carnovores, and particularly in primates, it increases dramatically in both size and complexity. (Source: Hubel, 1979, pp.46–47.)

connecting the surrounding tissue.* Certain rare forms of severe epilepsy can be controlled by cutting the corpus callosum, thereby mostly severing the two hemispheres and creating, in a sense, two independent brains. Patients with such split brains show some amazing qualities, which we will investigate later in this chapter.

THE CEREBRUM. As mentioned earlier, the cerebrum in humans contains fully 70 percent of all the neurons in the central nervous system; it is a massive portion of the brain. Throughout evolution, the cerebrum has grown larger and has become the human brain's most prominent feature (see Figure 2.13). More than any other part of the brain, our large and complex cerebrum prob-

*Be sure to wash your hands before trying this.

ably is responsible for the unique qualities that we as humans share. It is believed to give us our great capacities for thought, language, memory, and comprehension. The outer layer of the cerebrum, the cerebral cortex, has attracted the most attention.

The folds and shapes of the outer covering of the cerebrum lend themselves to a division into four main lobes. These four lobes, appearing in both left and right hemispheres, are the **frontal,** the **parietal,** the **occipital,** and the **temporal lobes** (see Figure 2.14). These four lobes are collectively known as the **neocortex,** meaning "new cortex," because in evolutionary terms it is the most recent development. The neocortex, which comprises the outer covering of the cerebral cortex, is six neural layers deep. These are the layers that are rippled or folded. The portion of the cerebral cortex below the neocortex, called the *allocortex,* is especially involved with the sense of smell and does not show folds or convolutions.

In 1870, while working with dogs as subjects, Gustav Fritsch and Eduard Hitzig made the first attempt at brain mapping and discovered that applying a weak electric current to an area of the cerebral cortex immediately in front of the **central sulcus,** a major fold, caused twitches in muscles on the side of the body *opposite* the brain hemisphere being stimulated. It has since been discovered that as neural fibers from one side of the hindbrain descend down through the spinal column, they cross to the opposite side of the body! As a result, the left hemisphere of the brain controls the right side of the body, and the right hemisphere controls the left side of the body. If a person suffers a stroke that leaves the left side of his body paralyzed, the neurosurgeon knows that the stroke must have occurred in the right cerebral hemisphere, and vice versa.

Further experiments in this line have revealed areas along the cerebral cortex that are responsible for both sensory and motor stimulation. At the back of the frontal lobes, just in front of the central sulcus, lies the **motor area** that controls the body's movement. Electrical stimulation anywhere in this area can produce contractions in particular skeletal muscles. Figure 2.15 shows which muscles are controlled by the different portions of the motor area. As you can see, much of the motor area is reserved for control of the hands, which in our species are extremely important. Another large area is given over to the control of the lips and the mouth—speech is also an important behavior in our species.

◆ **FIGURE 2.14**

The four lobes of the cerebral cortex.

FRONTAL LOBES

The portion of each hemisphere of the cerebrum extending from the very front of the cerebrum to the central sulcus. It includes the primary motor association areas and is known to be involved with emotion and language.

PARIETAL LOBES

The top portion of each hemisphere of the cerebrum extending from the central sulcus to the beginning of the occipital lobes. The parietal lobes contain the primary somatosensory area as well as association areas, including language areas.

OCCIPITAL LOBES

The hind portion of each hemisphere of the cerebrum. The primary visual areas are contained within the occipital lobes.

TEMPORAL LOBES

The portion of each hemisphere of the cerebrum on either side of the head near the temples. The temporal lobes contain the primary auditory areas as well as association areas. They have to do with emotion, vision, and language.

NEOCORTEX

In evolutionary terms, the most recent development of the brain. The neocortex is six neural layers deep and comprises the outer portion of the cerebral cortex. The four major lobes of the brain are made of neocortex.

CENTRAL SULCUS

A major fissure in the brain, also known as the fissure of Rolando, which separates the frontal from the parietal lobes.

MOTOR AREA

An area of the cerebrum that controls body movement. It is located in front of the brain's central sulcus.

SOMATOSENSORY AREA
An area in the cerebrum that controls sensation. It is located behind the central sulcus at the front of the parietal lobe.

VISUAL CORTEX
An area in the brain through which most visual information is processed. It is located in the occipital lobes.

If you had less brain to control these functions, you might find it impossible to be articulate, that is, to make the sounds necessary for language. Similarly, if you had less brain available for hand control, you might find you were clumsy in using your hands and less able to make delicate movements such as writing. To highlight this fact, it is interesting to note that scans of the human brain (which we will discuss shortly) have shown that writer's cramp occurs when cells in this portion of the *brain* become fatigued from firing so often (and, therefore, will start firing less and less until they get a rest), and not because muscles in the hand become tired (Tempel & Perlmutter, 1992).

Directly behind the central fissure at the start of the parietal lobe is a section known as the **somatosensory area.** If this area is electrically stimulated, a sensation will be perceived as though the brain had received a message from another place in the body. For instance, a subject may feel a tingling on her finger or pressure on her lips. Again, a large part of this area is associated with the hands, lips, and tongue (see Figure 2.15).

The occipital lobes form the **visual cortex.** Because the cells in the occipital lobes respond to visual information, if you are struck on the back of the head and the shock causes visual neurons to fire, you will see "stars." Or, more precisely, firing will cause you to perceive little points of light. These same points of light can be created by touching the visual cortex with an electrode carrying a mild current.

◆ **FIGURE 2.15**

Somatosensory and motor regions of the cerebral cortex are specialized; every site in these regions can be associated with some part of the body. In other words, most of the body can be mapped onto the cortex. The distortions come about because the area of the cortex dedicated to

a part of the body is proportional not to that part's actual size, but to the precision with which it must be controlled. In humans the motor and somatosensory regions given over to the face and to the hands are greatly exaggerated. Only one-half of each cortical region is shown: the

left somatosensory area (which receives sensations primarily from the right side of the body) and the right motor cortex (which exercises control over movement in the left half of the body). (SOURCE: Geschwind, 1979, p. 182.)

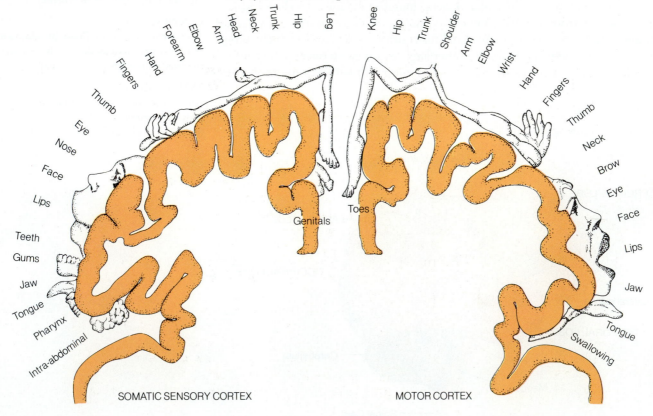

SOMATIC SENSORY CORTEX   MOTOR CORTEX

Most visual information is sent—or, as neuropsychologists say, projected—to the occipital lobes. However, many aspects of vision are also processed by the temporal or parietal lobes. In fact, vision is so important to our species that fully 50 percent of the cerebral cortex is devoted to processing visual messages (Glickstein, 1988)!

Besides processing visual information, the temporal lobes also receive auditory messages arriving from the ears. If a person's temporal lobes are electrically stimulated, she will perceive sounds. Messages from all of the senses also are integrated in the temporal lobes.

The parts of the cerebral cortex other than the sensory and motor areas are known collectively as **association areas.** Association areas appear to be linked with language, thinking, and memory, and they may even be specialized to control certain scientific or artistic abilities.

BRAIN SCANNERS: PET AND MRI

Always structure, never function, that's been the problem: Whenever psychologists or neurologists looked at the brain as we have been doing, they saw structure. If they opened the skull, they could see the structure. If they cut sections of the brain and put them under slides, they could see the structure. If they scanned the brain with X rays, as is done with a **CAT scan,** they could see the structure. Most of our discussion about the brain so far has been related to its parts and structure. No one could actually observe what was going on inside a live brain—at least not with much detail. But it is now possible to observe the brain as it functions, and psychologists and other scientists are seeing the brain in a completely new light. The breakthrough is the **positron-emission tomography (PET)** scan. Positrons are atomic particles that are emitted by some radioactive substances. If a radioactive substance that emits positrons is placed in the body, sensors can monitor the positrons wherever they go.

Despite what you might have heard about fish being brain food, the brain runs on sugar (glucose). As different parts of the brain become active, they demand more sugar. Consequently, one substance used for the PET scan is a

In this CAT-Scan, layers of the brain are revealed by a pencil-thin beam of x rays that scan the brain layer by layer. The reconstructed images can show tumors, lesions, or other abnormalities.

MAGNETIC-RESONANCE IMAGING (MRI)
A technique that makes internal body structures clearly visible. It uses radio waves to excite atoms in the body, and the excitations, monitored by a huge magnet, are interpreted by a computer to produce a composite picture.

kind of radioactive sugar that emits positrons. When one part of the brain becomes active, the radioactive sugar races to that location, and the machine scanning the brain registers high positron emissions coming from that area of the brain.

For safety reasons, the radioactive substances used quickly lose their radio-activity; researchers must therefore rush to administer the injection and complete the scan before the positron-emitting substance finishes radiating. Once the substance is in the body and on its way to the brain, the functioning of the brain can be observed. If, for example, the patient hears someone speak, or listens to music, or thinks, or remembers, or moves, the portion of the brain that is activated can be observed to light up on the scanner (see Figure 2.16). Thanks to the PET scan, we are learning that some areas of the brain perform functions we never suspected.

One of the PET scan's most exciting potentials is in the diagnosis and investigation of mental illness. Although research results are tentative and open to some interpretation, evidence from PET scans indicates that the brains of patients with certain forms of mental illness function in a manner that is consistently different from the brains of normal subjects (see Chapter 16).

Another exciting aspect of the PET scan is its ability to trace neurotransmitters as they travel throughout the brain. Using this technique, researchers can observe with greater accuracy where the neurotransmitters go and with which parts of the brain they interact. Researchers have already used a positron-emitting substance known to bind with dopamine receptors to locate and image the dopamine receptors in a living brain. In Figure 2.17, you can observe the red and yellow areas that highlight where the dopamine receptors are concentrated. The ability to observe neurotransmitters at work will help

◆ **FIGURE 2.16**

In these PET scans of the human brain, different areas are seen to respond (red indicates highest intensity) when presented with different stimuli. For example, visual stimulation excites the occipital lobes, and auditory stimulation excites the temporal lobes.

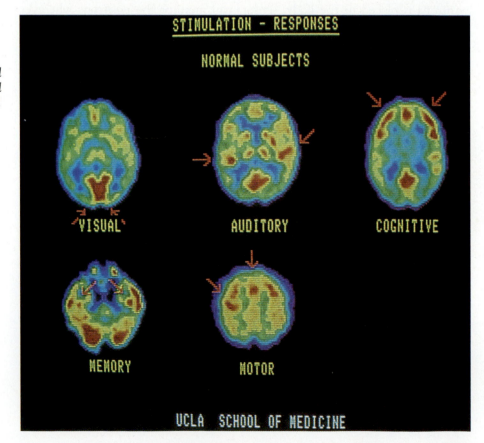

to advance our understanding of the brain and perhaps will be useful as a diagnostic tool for people who have certain mental disorders.

Unlike the PET scanner, the first **magnetic-resonance imaging (MRI)** scanners allowed us to visualize structure, not function. These MRI scanners imaged structures inside a live body in a way that could only have been imagined a decade ago. Unlike an X-ray machine, the MRI scanner uses harmless radio waves that excite the atoms of the body. This brief excitation creates a subtle magnetic change that is monitored by a huge 11-ton donut-shaped magnet, which surrounds the patient. The shift in magnetic field is then interpreted by a computer, and a composite image of the inside of the body is created. Figure 2.18 shows an MRI scan of the brain of a live human. At first, you may mistake it for an artist's drawing, because it is so detailed. It's the clearest look anyone has ever had inside the head of a living person. MRI is so sensitive that it can spot the most minute tumor, observe the slightest clog in an artery, and often distinguish cancerous from noncancerous cells. By using higher-energy radio waves (also harmless), MRI can be used to analyze fluctuations among the atoms and to identify all the chemicals that are present. Such a technique may eventually enable researchers to identify the neurotransmitters, neuropeptides, and hormones located in whichever part of the body they care to look! MRI is a relatively new tool, and scientists are just starting to use it regularly for research and diagnosis. Advances in MRI technology are occurring rapidly. For instance, in 1992 a new MRI was developed that could make motion pictures of the changing blood flow in the brain by comparing where the blood-borne bodies (such as platelets) were from moment to moment (Culotta & Koshland, 1992). This may eventually enable MRI to replace PET as the scanner of choice for observing function, if for no other reason than that it is safer and

◆ **FIGURE 2.17**

The neurotransmitter dopamine can be seen in this PET scan concentrating in the areas of the brain where it is required. By attaching positron-emitting substances to neurotransmitters, researchers hope to discover their destinations in the brain and to observe their concentrations when the brain functions. Such research has vast potential for providing a better understanding of the brain and our behavior.

◆ **FIGURE 2.18**

This MRI scan of a live brain shows structural detail with greater clarity than could ever be produced by an X-ray photograph. In addition, the MRI scan is safer than radiography, as it uses harmless radio waves to produce its pictures. The MRI is also able to identify the chemistry within any given structure of a living system. By looking carefully at this picture, you should be able to identify the parts of the brain highlighted in the color drawing of Figure 2.11 on page 58.

PLASTICITY
The ability of brain tissue to take over the functions of other brain areas that have been damaged or disrupted.

less awkward to use. As you can see, MRI makes X-ray technology seem like a Stone Age tool.*

These new tools and others are opening up the brain as never before. In fact, with new discoveries coming so quickly owing to such new technologies, and researchers predicting that many more major discoveries in neuroscience are just around the corner, the U.S. Congress has designated the 1990s as the "decade of the brain." As you explore this amazing organ further, you will begin to understand the profound implications of such discoveries.

THE BRAIN AND BEHAVIOR

Scientists and psychologists have known for years that the way in which the brain functions directly affects behavior. We have learned much about the relationship between specific parts of the brain and specific behaviors by studying patients with brain injury or disease. The first comprehensive studies of this kind were conducted on patients who had received brain injuries during the First World War. Researchers discovered that damage to the left side of the brain brought about changes on the right side of the body, and vice versa. They also found that damage to the frontal lobes could cause personality changes (as in the case of Phineas Gage, recounted in Chapter 1). Damage to the temporal lobes often affected hearing, and damage to the occipital lobes often affected sight. A further discovery was that damage to the left side of the brain more often affected language ability than did damage to the right side of the brain. Since that time, we have learned that most adults have specific centers for language in the left side of the brain. In some people, however, this organization is reversed. Whatever the case, the halves of the brain are not identical.

*For fans of the Star Trek films and television shows, it is interesting to note that scientists working with MRI think it likely that scanners will someday be created by combining ultra-advanced MRIs with supercomputers whose memory banks are packed with advanced medical knowledge. This combination, it is hoped, would be capable of scanning a patient and reporting *everything* that may be wrong with him or her, in much the same way as the fictional scanners in the sickbay of the starship *Enterprise* now do effortlessly. The very fact that such things can be seriously considered by professionals shows you how far we have come.

AN ENDURING QUESTION: HOW PLASTIC IS THE BRAIN?

Scientists have known for a long time that if some areas of the brain are damaged, other areas may take over the damaged portion's functions. For instance, when a person has suffered a stroke that has left the language center in her left cerebral hemisphere damaged, she can sometimes regain her lost language ability through the use of nearby portions of her brain. Such **plasticity** is most apparent in young children, especially under the age of six or seven years. If the language center in the left cerebral hemisphere of a young child is destroyed, the right cerebral hemisphere may take over and provide all the lost language function.

Plasticity, especially in young children, is probably a result of the way in which the neuronal system develops in the brain (Kolb, 1989). Surprisingly, newborns have many more neurons in their brains than do adults. As the infant grows and gains experiences, neurons are eliminated in a whittling-down process. Some researchers have estimated that neurons in

AN ENDURING QUESTION, CONTINUED

infants die at a rate of about 2 per second (Miller, 1985a). Thus, if some area is damaged or destroyed during infancy, there may be many more neurons ready to take over. By the time a person reaches middle childhood, the number of neurons appears to become stable. More recently, however, it has been discovered that new neurons do appear and grow in the adult brains of mice (Reynolds & Weiss, 1992). Until this study, it was believed that neurons in the central nervous system of adult mammals did not divide and increase in number. It might, therefore, not be unreasonable to assume that the same sort of *neurogenesis* might also be occurring, to some degree, in the adult human brain, although it has yet to be proven.

For years, the basic dogma about neural plasticity in the brain was that after the onset of adulthood, and often before that, the brain became pretty set in its neural organization. Some neuroscientists even liked to use the term "hardwired" to describe this fixed arrangement—that is, until the notorious case of the Silver Spring monkeys.

In the late 1970s, a neuroscientist named Ed Taub working at an institute in Silver Springs, Maryland, began a study on some monkeys in which he destroyed the point where the sensory nerves from one arm entered the spinal column. Taub was going to use the monkeys in rehabilitation experiments, but before he was able to do so, the monkeys were confiscated following a raid on his laboratory by animal rights advocates. Ironically, it was only through the efforts of the animal rights advocates that the monkeys were kept alive for years after they would normally have been destroyed. This, in turn, led to an amazing discovery.

Since the operations to sever the nerves of their arms from their spinal columns, these monkeys have "remapped" their cerebral cortexes! Points on their somatosensory cortexes that once responded to a touch on the arm now respond to a touch on the face (Palca, 1991)! Similarly, human amputees who have lost an arm will commonly feel sensations in the missing limb for some time after their injury. This is known as "phantom sensation," or sometimes "phantom pain." It appears, then, that when we learn something new we not only make new neural connections during the process, but the brain adjusts itself so as to dedicate a larger portion of itself to the demand! So not only are you able to learn a particular task, it seems that you are given more with which to learn it. How much can the adult brain reorganize itself? What controls these reorganizations and when do they occur? As often happens in science, new answers lead to new questions, questions as yet unanswered.   ◆

Specialized Areas in the Brain

To show how specialized certain portions of the brain are, let's examine some of the findings that have come about as a result of brain injuries, diseases, or accidents, beginning with the case of Charles Whitman in Texas. One morning in 1966, Whitman, a young man with no previous history of violence, awoke, picked up a rifle and a pistol, and shot and killed his wife and his mother. Then, he calmly gathered up his weapons, food, and water and went to a university campus, where he climbed to the top of a bell tower, took out his rifle, and proceeded to shoot 38 people. It took police many hours to corner him; he died in a shoot-out.

We've all heard of cases of unexplained violence and aggression, in which someone seems to explode and murders innocent people. In the case of Charles Whitman, however, there may be some clue to the sudden and horrible change in his behavior. During an autopsy of his brain, a malignant tumor was discovered pressing against an amygdala, which, as you may recall, is part of the limbic system. This cancerous tumor would have eventually caused Whitman's death. It had been undetected until the autopsy, and because it was located deep beneath the cerebral cortex, it could not have been operated on with the technology available in 1966 even if it had been detected. Was Whitman's act the first symptom of the tumor's existence? It is known that the amygdala and the limbic system are involved in emotional response. If this area is stimulated in cats, the cats react with tremendous rage, arching their backs, spitting and hissing, fighting with anything that comes near.

Could Charles Whitman's act have been a rage response that he could not comprehend or control? The rest of his brain was working normally. He was able to think of a plan by which to express his rage, and he had the motor coordination necessary to carry it out. But had something interfered with the portion of his brain that normally enabled him to maintain emotional control? We may never know the answers to these questions, but the autopsy has given us a hint about what may have set off Whitman's seemingly pointless rampage.

In our earlier discussion of the hippocampus, we mentioned that part of its function is related to memory. The first indication of this relationship appeared almost 40 years ago when a neurosurgeon performed a radical surgical procedure on a patient that destroyed much of the hippocampi and several associated areas in both temporal lobes; the operation was performed to stop progressively worsening epileptic seizures (Geschwind, 1979). Following the operation, the patient's memory at first seemed to be intact, and he was still able to attend to ongoing events. However, it soon became clear that he was unable to remember any of these *new* events! Psychologists have long been aware that there are two types of memory, short term and long term. Short-term memory holds information for roughly 30 seconds to four minutes and enables you to recall such things as an unfamiliar telephone number long enough to dial it. Long-term memory contains information that you've retained for a long time and are not likely to forget. In the case of this particular patient, the operation had apparently destroyed his long-term memory capacity for acquiring new information, while his short-term memory was unaffected. Consequently, information that had been logged in the long-term memory prior to the operation was intact, but no new information could be stored (with the exception, interestingly, of new motor skills, probably because such skills depend on a different memory system—see Chapter 9). If someone came into the room and was introduced to the patient, the patient would reach out, shake hands, introduce himself, and learn the individual's name. The entire introduction would seem completely normal. But if this individual left the room for a couple of minutes and then reentered, the patient would not be able to recall anything about the previous introduction, and he would act as though he were meeting the person for the first time.

Horribly, the man now had to live from moment to moment, unable to learn his new address or to remember the location of even the simplest everyday object. And each day he was shocked to see how old he looked in the mirror—which, of course, he forgot about a few minutes after leaving the mirror.

On the underside of both occipital lobes is a part of the brain that has a special purpose—the recognition of faces. In normal individuals, the ability to recognize people by their faces is truly remarkable. Our brains are well organized to attend to unique features such as head, eye, nose, and mouth shapes and the sharpness or softness of features. We know about the function of this area of the brain because of what happens to people when the area is damaged. They can no longer recognize faces, a disorder known as **prosopagnosia.** This disorder is accompanied by almost no other neurological or physiological symptoms. Occasionally, there is some loss of vision, but the person continues to be able to perform most tasks, including those that require information processing, without difficulty. The one thing a person with prosopagnosia cannot do is look at another person's face and put a name to it. Even spouses and children may be unfamiliar. It is not that individuals suffering from this disorder don't know who their wives, husbands, or children are; they simply cannot match faces with identities. For instance, a person may not realize that the child she can plainly see is her child until she hears the child's voice. Although she can see and describe the face in fine detail and even match the face with a photograph, she's unable to form the associations between that particular face and a particular identity (Geschwind, 1979).

Researchers have shown that sufferers of prosopagnosia do "know" the faces of familiar people, as indicated by their heightened neural responses when viewing familiar faces (Tranel & Damasio, 1985). This finding leads to the conclusion that the disorder is due to a failure of visual and associative memories to get together rather than to a loss of visual memory.

In the left side of the brain are a number of areas that are involved in the production and organization of language. **Broca's area** is one of them. Damage to Broca's area following a stroke or other condition may result in one form of **aphasia,** called expressive aphasia, which is defined as the absence of ability to speak or severe difficulty in speaking. That the problem is with speech itself, and not with the muscles involved in speaking, is evident because individuals with damage to Broca's area can sing words without difficulty! (A diagram of Broca's area and a more detailed description of the brain and language can be found in Chapter 10, pages 345–379.)

Another interesting example of the interaction between the brain and behavior comes to us from the writings of neurologist Oliver Sacks (perhaps best known to the general public as the doctor portrayed by actor Robin Williams in the film *Awakenings*). In his book, *The Man Who Mistook His Wife for a Hat,* Dr. Sacks spoke of a music teacher, Dr. P., who had come to see him because his wife said he was having severe problems. On examination, however, Dr. P. seemed all right. He was charming, friendly, and intelligent and appeared quite normal.

With the examination completed, Dr. Sacks noticed that his patient hadn't put his shoes back on. Then, Dr. P., indicating his foot, asked, "That is my shoe, yes?" (Sacks, 1985, p. 9). Dr. Sacks, somewhat in a state of shock, said, "No, it is not. That is your foot. There is your shoe." Dr. P. responded, "Ah! I thought it was my foot." Obviously, the examination was not finished! What in the world could be wrong?

Dr. Sacks then showed his patient a picture from a magazine and asked him to tell what he saw. Dr. P.'s eyes darted about, picking up bits and pieces of the scene, but failing to get much out of it. Acting as though he had done well on this test, Dr. P. prepared to leave; then, he reached over and took hold of the top of his wife's head and tried to lift it onto the top of his own. He had mistaken his wife for his hat!

Soon, the real problem became apparent. During a later examination, Dr. Sacks tried a test that's worth describing because it highlights Dr. P.'s problem. In Dr. Sacks's own words:

"What is this?" I asked, holding up a glove.

"May I examine it?" he asked, and, taking it from me, he proceeded to examine it. . . .

PROSOPAGNOSIA
A disorder in which the subject can no longer recognize faces. It is rarely accompanied by other neurological or physiological symptoms.

BROCA'S AREA
An area in the lateral frontal lobe (in the left hemisphere in most cases) that is associated with language production.

APHASIA
Loss of the ability to understand or to use language; by definition, the result of brain damage.

"A continuous surface," he announced at last, "infolded on itself. It appears to have"—he hesitated—"five outpouchings, if this is the word."

"Yes," I said cautiously. "You have given me a description. Now tell me what it is."

"A container of some sort?"

"Yes," I said, "and what would it contain?"

"It would contain its contents!" said Dr. P., with a laugh. "There are many possibilities. It could be a change-purse, for example, for coins of five sizes. It could . . ."

I interrupted the barmy flow. "Does it not look familiar? Do you think it might contain, might fit, a part of your body?"

No light of recognition dawned on his face.

No child would have the power to see and speak of "a continuous surface . . . infolded on itself," but any child, any infant, would immediately know a glove as a glove, see it as familiar, as going with a hand. Dr. P. didn't. (1985, p. 13)

Dr. P., as it turned out, had an inoperable tumor in his right occipital lobe. It had caused his strange problems. Dr. P. could see in the way that a computer might be able to see. He saw lines, angles, details, shapes, but he never could see the "big picture"; he couldn't see the "Gestalt," he couldn't see what it was he was looking at. He knew the shapes and angles of his hat (and his wife's head), but he didn't see the wholeness of "wife's head" or "hat." This lost ability apparently was something that would have been provided by his right hemisphere, had it not been damaged.

Even with this strange problem, Dr. P. was able to function with the help of his wife, who laid out his clothes each day in exactly the same spot and arranged his breakfast and other routines in a set order. In this way, Dr. P. knew he was, in fact, putting on clothes and eating breakfast. He was even able to teach music, which he did until his death brought on by the tumor some months later.

🧬 BRAIN ORGANIZATION

All of the various brain areas interact with each other to process information. They do this according to three basic principles (Volkow & Tancredi, 1991). The first principle states that the brain is *interconnected*. This refers to the fact that many different parts of the brain will spring into action when confronted with a single task. The brain appears to operate via interconnecting "modules" that are relatively independent. A brain module is simply a grouping of cells usually appearing in a strip of brain tissue perhaps no thicker than $1/10,000$ of an inch. Each module of the brain has a task to do and will work *in parallel* with other brain modules that are busy working on other aspects of the same task. Once each module has done its job, the efforts of the individual modules are combined and integrated, which is what is meant by the "interconnectedness" of the brain. Evidence for this principle of brain organization comes from stroke victims and others who suffered some form of brain damage that interfered with the brain's interconnections. In these individuals, certain integrations do not occur. For instance, Michael Gazzaniga has reported a patient who, after some very specific damage, was able to name fruits *or* red objects, each task assumedly controlled by a different module, but not red fruits—a task probably requiring the integration of two modules working in parallel (Gazzaniga, 1989). As another example, consider the patient who was able to compare two words, but only if the words looked or sounded alike (Gazzaniga, 1989). Different sounding words required an integration for comparison—one that this individual was unable to perform.

The second principle states that the brain's organization is generally *hierarchical*. Information coming into the brain from the senses, or perhaps even that gathered from the memory, appears to be built up from small, simple units into a comprehensive whole. For example, cells in the eye may be responsive to light, dark, or certain colors. As information from the eye enters the brain, more complex cells receive this input, cells that are responsive to lines and edges *as well as* color and brightness. This information, in turn, is passed on to more complex cells that are additionally responsive to motion or direction of movement. This information builds up into more complex collections in a hierarchical fashion until it is finally handled by whole modules because no single cell or small group of cells can deal with the growing complexity.

The third principle states that there is *functional differentiation* in the brain. This means that certain brain areas are responsible for specific functions. For instance, the temporal lobes are mainly involved in hearing while the occipital lobes are mainly involved with vision.

However, it is still very difficult to understand just how functionally differentiated the brain may be. Part of the problem is that whole areas of the brain still remain a total mystery. No one knows what they do. For this reason, computer databases are now being developed to correlate all that we know about the brain at any given moment. One such database is BrainMap. When using databases like BrainMap, a researcher can enter into a computer an exact location in the brain and receive all of the current information about that area, including brain scans, journal articles, papers, and anything else that may be relevant. In this way, researchers working on different or even unrelated problems may still benefit from one another's discoveries and build upon them.

THE SPLIT BRAIN

Occasionally, when a person suffers from a severe form of **epilepsy** and cannot be treated in any other way, the corpus callosum connecting the two hemispheres of the brain is severed. This prevents the epileptic seizure from spreading from one hemisphere to the other.

In the early 1950s, R. E. Myers and R. W. Sperry made a startling discovery when examining cats in whom the corpus callosum had been cut. They found that the right hemisphere could learn something while the left hemisphere remained ignorant of what had been learned, and vice versa! Over the next three decades, Sperry, working at the California Institute of Technology, and M. S. Gazzaniga, working at Cornell University Medical College, added to our knowledge about the divided hemispheres. In sum, in human patients with split brains, the two hemispheres of the brain function separately; their interconnectedness has been disrupted.

If you were to meet a patient with a split brain, you most likely would not notice anything unusual about him. To find a difference, you would have to conduct some tests—for instance, of the seeing process. Figure 2.19 shows how the nerves that carry information from the eyes are organized. Each eye independently sends messages to both hemispheres. The visual system has evolved so that the left halves of *both* retinas (the back part of each eye that contains light-sensitive neurons) send their visual messages to the left hemisphere, while the right halves of *both* retinas send messages to the right hemisphere.

Even a split-brain patient looking directly at something with only one eye will receive visual messages in both hemispheres. If the patient glimpses something briefly out of the corners of his eyes, however, the situation is different. Look again at Figure 2.19; imagine that something has been briefly glimpsed in the far-right field of vision while the eyes were looking straight ahead. Due

EPILEPSY
A neural disorder characterized by recurring attacks of motor, sensory, or psychic malfunction with or without unconsciousness or convulsive movements.

◆ FIGURE 2.19

The left and right eyes send messages to both hemispheres because of the crossover at the optic chiasma. However, the right halves of the retinas of both eyes send messages to only the right hemisphere, while the left halves send messages to only the left hemisphere.

Left retina

Right retina

Optic nerve

Crossover point (optic chiasma)

Relay at side of brain stem

Brain stem

Visual cortex

to the extreme angle, only the left halves of both retinas will respond to the object. Similarly, the left halves of both retinas cannot sense objects far off in the left field of vision. Consequently, when both you and a split-brain patient glimpse something out of the corners of the eyes, the object will be projected to only one hemisphere. Unlike you, however, the split-brain patient's receiving hemisphere cannot share this information with the other hemisphere because the connections between the two hemispheres have been cut.

A split-brain person usually has no trouble talking about such visual messages when they are sent to the *left* hemisphere because that is where the language-capable portions of the brain are typically found. Whenever an object or photograph is presented to him, he can tell you what it is. However, if an image is presented off in the *left* visual field, so that it is sent only to the *right* hemisphere, the split-brain person may be unable to tell you what he has seen. This is because the right hemisphere typically has poor language and speech ability compared with the left hemisphere. In most people, the left hemisphere can speak and describe what it has seen, but the right hemisphere, although it too can see, often cannot say what it has seen! But it has seen the object. As proof, consider the following experiment. A number of objects, such as a spoon, a block, a ball, and a toy car, are hidden behind a cloth barrier so that the split-brain patient cannot see them. Then, a photograph of one of the objects is shown at an angle, so that only the right hemisphere registers it and the left brain is ignorant of what has been seen. The split-brain patient will say that she does not know what the picture is (after all, her left brain doesn't know!). But, although the split-brain patient usually cannot articulate what her right brain saw, she can find the object by reaching behind the curtain *with her left hand* and feeling for it! This is because the right brain, which controls the left hand, knows what the object is and what it should feel like, even though it cannot put this knowledge into words!

It should be noted that some split-brain patients do not show such remarkable differences between hemispheres, indicating that in some people the two hemispheres may not be that different from each other (Zaidel, 1983; Myers, 1984). This illustrates how variable brain organization can be from one person to the next. Generally, however, it does appear that the left hemisphere of the brain is organized in a way that facilitates language recognition and production (Gazzaniga, 1983; MacKain, Studdert-Kennedy, Spieker, & Stern, 1983).

Split-brain research has also yielded information that indicates the existence of a very special "interpreter" in the left hemisphere. To illustrate, let's look at an experiment conducted not long ago by Michael Gazzaniga on a 15-year-old split-brained boy named P.S.

In the laboratory, two pictures were shown to P.S., one to each hemisphere. The left hemisphere was shown a chicken claw, while the right saw a snow scene. P.S. was then shown a number of pictures on cards and asked to pick the one that went with the picture he had seen. His right hand pointed to a picture of a chicken (remember his left hemisphere had seen the chicken claw), while his left hand pointed to a snow shovel (his right hemisphere had seen the snow scene—see Figure 2.20). This was what Gazzaniga had expected. But when P.S. was asked why he had pointed to these objects, he answered right away, "Oh, that's easy. The chicken claw goes with the chicken, and you need a shovel to clean out the chicken shed" (Gazzaniga, 1985, p. 30).

Stop for a moment to consider what this means. The left hemisphere didn't know why the left hand had pointed to the shovel, so it fished around for a logical reason and came up with one—and was wrong. Based on this work and many other examples gathered over the years, Michael Gazzaniga has come to believe that there is an "interpreter" in the left hemisphere that is independent of the language areas and

constructs theories about . . . actions and feelings and tries to bring order and unity to our conscious lives. [It] appears to be unique to the human brain and related to the singular capacity of the brain to make causal inferences. (1989, p. 947)

Could the same error made by P.S. occur to a degree in individuals whose brains are normal and intact? How many times have you acted on a feeling or urge and then tried to come up with the reason for your actions? Did hidden knowledge—that is, information hidden from your left brain—motivate you

◆ FIGURE 2.20

Here the left brain sees only the claw, the right brain only the snow scene. The left-brain "interpreter" must generate a hypothesis to explain why one hand is pointing to a snow shovel. (SOURCE: Gazzaniga, 1985, p. 32.)

"unconsciously?" Research shows that even in an individual with a healthy brain, the different portions of the brain, or modules, might not always share knowledge with each other easily (Gazzaniga, 1985). Because of this, Gazzaniga argues that the "interpreter" may bias its views or interpretations as a result of hidden knowledge contained in other modules.

Wouldn't Sigmund Freud, with his theory of the unconscious mind, have loved these studies! Not that these few studies could validate Freud's view, but they do strongly imply that motivations exist beyond the conscious grasp and are able to affect our conscious thought.

❧ SUMMARY

◆ All human behavior involves, either directly or indirectly, the nervous system, in which the brain is the dominant part.

◆ The nervous system can be divided into a number of interrelated component parts: the central nervous system, which includes the brain and the spinal cord, and the peripheral nervous system, which includes the somatic and autonomic nervous systems.

◆ A nerve is made up of thousands upon thousands of individual nerve cells called neurons. Neurons communicate by using electrical impulses and secreting chemicals. The nervous system is therefore considered to be an electrochemical system.

◆ The typical neuron has three distinct structural features: the soma, dendrites, and axon. Messages generally are received by the dendrites and transmitted by the axon. Neurons can communicate with other neurons, with glands, or with muscles when they are stimulated to action potential and discharge an impulse, called a "spike," that runs the length of the axon.

◆ Messages are carried from a neuron to adjacent cells when neurotransmitters are secreted into the synapse between the cells. This is called the first messenger system. Some synapses are excitatory; others are inhibitory. Many substances may function as neurotransmitters. Neurons often secrete more than one neurotransmitter.

◆ The second messenger system works mainly via G-protein activation. This system may modify long-term effects by changing the neuron's membrane or by altering its neurotransmitter emissions.

◆ Nitric oxide, a noxious gas, may be the first of a new class of neurotransmitters.

◆ Many drugs that affect behavior appear to mimic or alter the functions of natural body substances. Drugs that block neurotransmitter functioning are known as antagonists; those that facilitate neurotransmitters are known as agonists.

◆ Transplanting healthy brain tissue from a donor to help replace damaged tissue in a recipient has proved to be a useful and valuable technique for treating Parkinson's disease.

◆ Neurotransmitters, neuropeptides, and hormones may have long-term, dramatic, and wide-ranging effects on a great many aspects of human behavior. For instance, beta-endorphin, a neuropeptide, has been implicated in the control of pain and pleasure.

◆ The endocrine system comprises many glands that secrete hormones. Hormones are blood-borne informational substances that can affect neurons, muscles, or glands throughout the body.

◆ The brain is extremely complex, and much of its functioning remains a mystery. Using such techniques as brain mapping, scientists are unraveling the complexities of the brain's functions.

◆ The brain can be conveniently divided into three areas: the hindbrain, the midbrain, and the forebrain.

◆ A massive portion of the forebrain is the cerebrum. The cortex of the cerebrum can be divided into four lobes: frontal, parietal, occipital, and temporal.

◆ Modern brain scanners are helping us to explore the brain as never before. The PET (positron-emission tomography) scanner highlights brain functions, while the MRI (magnetic-resonance imaging) scanner highlights structural anatomy, chemistry, and function.

◆ We have gathered many clues to the way in which the brain functions by studying patients with brain damage and disease. For example, damage to the limbic system may cause emotional disturbances, and damage to the hippocampus may impair memory functioning. Sometimes brain injuries can result in very unusual behavior; an illustration is the case of "the man who mistook his wife for a hat," in which Dr. P. manifested the inability to "see" the wholeness of objects, although he was still able to describe them.

◆ All of the various brain areas interact and process information according to three basic principles. The first principle states that brain areas are interconnected. The second holds that the brain's organization is generally hierarchical. The third principle is that there is functional differentiation in the brain.

◆ The brain appears to have a certain amount of plasticity. The case of the Silver Spring monkeys and investigations of human amputees helped to show that the cortex can remap itself under certain circumstances.

◆ Research with split-brain patients (in whom the corpus callosum has been severed) indicates that the left and right hemispheres of the brain might best be considered two distinct entities.

◆ Research with split-brain patients also indicates that much important knowledge may be stored in the brain out of easy reach of our left hemispheres, where such knowledge could be expressed to ourselves as thoughts. Such hidden knowledge may hold important clues to our motivations for behavior.

❧ SUGGESTIONS FOR FURTHER READING

1. Ackerman, S. (1992). *Discovering the brain*. Washington: National Academic Press. A "field guide" of how the brain works for the general reader.
2. Corballis, M. C. (1991). *The lopsided ape: Evolution of the generative mind*. New York: Oxford University Press. A look at the differences found when comparing the brains of humans and apes, focusing on the laterality of the brain's hemispheres.
3. Gazzaniga, Michael S. (1989). *Mind matters: How mind and brain interact to create our conscious lives*. Boston: Houghton Mifflin. A fascinating look at brain research for the general reader.
4. Gazzaniga, Michael S. (1992). *Nature's mind: The biological roots of thinking, emotions, sexuality, language, and intelligence*. New York: Basic Books. The co-developer of right brain/left brain theory gives explanations for drug addiction, alcoholism, hypersexuality, and compulsions.
5. Klivington, Kenneth A. (1989). *The science of the mind*. Cambridge, MA: MIT Press. The basics of neuroscience for the general reader. Discusses dreams, the senses, language, illness, biological clocks, brain-mind connections, and more.
6. Ornstein, R. (1992). *The evolution of consciousness: The origins of the way we think*. New York: Touchstone Books. A history of the mind's evolution that centers on the argument that the mind evolved as an adaptation to help us survive rather than to help us reason.
7. Restak, R. M. (1991). *The brain has a mind of its own: Insights from a practicing neurologist*. New York: Crown Publishers. A series of fascinating essays for the general reader showing the insights a neuropsychiatrist has concerning his own patients.
8. Sacks, O. (1985). *The man who mistook his wife for a hat*. New York: Summit Books. A prominent neurologist provides some of his most fascinating case studies concerning brain and nervous system dysfunction.
9. Snyder, Solomon H. (1989). *Brainstorming: The science and politics of opiate research*. Cambridge, MA: Harvard University Press. The co-discoverer of the brain's endorphin receptors discusses the scientific research and political maneuvering that led to the discovery.

Chapter Three

Lifespan Development I: Infancy, Childhood and Adolescence

PROLOGUE

A DR. SEUSS STORY

Parents enjoy reading to their children, and children especially like to have stories read to them. Among their favorites are the enduring stories of Dr. Seuss. It should come as no surprise, then, to discover that over 150 children observed in a study in North Carolina deliberately tried to get their mothers to read a Dr. Seuss story to them when they could. But perhaps you'd be surprised to learn that these children were only 2 to 3 days old!

In the experiment, the babies were put in bassinets, and small, loose-fitting headsets were placed over their ears. A special nipple was placed in their mouths. If the infants sucked at a selected rate, a tape of their respective mothers' voices reading a Dr. Seuss story would be played. If the sucking rate deviated from the selected rate, a different woman's voice would continue with the story.

Regardless of whether the selected rate was fast or slow, at least 85 percent of the infants showed a preference for the voice of their mother over that of a stranger and adjusted their sucking rate to maintain their mother's voice on the earphones. The infants also began new sessions at the correct sucking rate, which demonstrates the presence of a functioning memory (DeCasper & Fifer, 1980).

An important question for researchers at this point, of course, was how could the babies know which voice was their mother's? As it turns out, the human ear is developed and functional about 7 months after conception (Birnholz & Benacerraf, 1983), so the fetus probably listened to its mother's voice during the last 2 months of the pregnancy, perhaps learning the sound of her voice while it was still in the womb. But another possibility was that infants rapidly learned to recognize their mother's voice during the first 1 or 2 days following birth.

With this problem in mind, an experiment was set up to test which of these two possibilities might determine how such young infants were aware of which voice was their mother's. A second study was run, but this time with

CONTENTS

79

fathers instead of mothers. All the fathers in the experiment were presented with their babies at birth and talked to them as often as possible, sometimes as much as 10 hours a day. From birth to the time of the study, each baby heard only her father's voice. The babies, only 2 or 3 days old, once again were equipped with the earphones and the special nipple that allowed them to choose to hear their own fathers or strangers read Dr. Seuss. The babies showed no preference for one voice over the other (Kolata, 1984). This was the first study to show that the infants' reaction probably was a result of their having had more experience hearing their mother's voice—which, of course, implies they heard it while in the womb. In fact, after listening to their father's voice for a few weeks, the infants preferred it to that of a stranger.

IN THIS CHAPTER, we'll examine the development of human beings from birth through adolescence. We'll look at the behaviors of newborn children and the effects of genetic heritage and learning on important developmental changes during childhood. We'll learn how human attachments are formed. We'll also explore cognitive development and the social changes that are important during childhood and adolescence.

WHY PSYCHOLOGISTS STUDY HUMAN DEVELOPMENT

From the time we are born, our position in society is determined to a large degree by our age. As we grow older, we change. These changes are most noticeable during the early years of infancy and childhood. As each month passes, an infant grows larger and shows dramatic gains in intellectual and social competence. Children undergo great changes from one year to the next. As children approach adolescence, their physical changes bring them closer to adulthood. Yet, for adolescents, there are new developmental tasks to work out and new competencies to acquire. Even when individuals reach physical maturity as adults, they still face some common developmental changes. Upon the approach of old age and death, individuals will face yet more changes. **Developmental psychology** is the study of age-related changes in human behavior. By understanding human development, psychologists know what to expect at different developmental stages, and they learn the parameters of human growth and achievement.

All societies are made up of groups of people who are at different stages in their lives—who are different ages. Any study of human behavior must consider the common developmental changes that occur as humans are born, age, and die. Entire populations may be considered in this light. For example, a typical growing population is made up of more age groupings of young people than old ones. When plotted on a graph, this pattern forms a **population pyramid.**

In such a population, typically the group of people who have reached maturity—those in the middle of the pyramid—must provide support for *both* the very young and the very old. Figure 3.1 shows the population pyramids for the United States for the census years 1950 and 1980, which follow the typical pattern. It also projects what the pyramids will be like in 2000 and 2030. As the population stabilizes at around 290 million in 2030, the pyramid is projected to square off; that is, there will be a proportionally much larger group of older people, which is a somewhat unusual situation. A smaller group of middle-aged people will still have to provide support for both the very young and the very old. Such changes could have wide-ranging effects on society as a whole. It is therefore important that developmental psychologists be aware of the developmental changes within societies as well as the individual changes that take place during a lifespan. Such knowledge is essential if we are to be prepared for the problems that could be created by these changes.

🧬 THE LIFESPAN APPROACH

Traditionally, developmental psychology placed the greatest emphasis on the years of infancy and childhood, the time when changes are the most apparent. This is still true to a great extent; after all, the difference between an infant of 2 years and a child of 9 years is far greater than that between adults of 52 and 59 years. Nevertheless, in the last decades, interest in adult development has grown rapidly, leading to a "lifespan approach" to understanding human development. We will cover adult development and aging in Chapter 4.

One of the first people to emphasize the entire lifespan was the psychoanalyst Erik Erikson. Psychologists owe a debt to Erikson for emphasizing the importance of the lifespan and the social forces that shape it. He views human development as a progression through eight **psychosocial stages,** each of which is characterized by conflicts that must be resolved for healthy development to occur. Table 3.1 presents these stages. In Chapter 4, we will examine Erikson's last three stages, which take place during adulthood.

Erikson does not consider the psychosocial stages to be dichotomies—that is, conflicts are not always resolved so that a person will be fully on one side or the other. Rather, there is a range between the opposing positions at each psychosocial stage. For example, Erikson would not expect a child to be completely autonomous or totally in doubt about all her actions, but rather to be somewhere in between, leaning more, it is hoped, toward becoming somewhat autonomous than filled with shame or doubt.

Most modern researchers believe that Erikson's theory fits well the informal observations obtained from many sources and that his theory may have much to contribute as a general outline for healthy socialization and personality

DEVELOPMENTAL PSYCHOLOGY
The study of age-related changes in human behavior over the lifespan.

POPULATION PYRAMID
A graphic depiction of the number of individuals within given age ranges. The age ranges are stacked from the youngest to oldest; in a normal population, the graph typically forms a pyramid shape.

PSYCHOSOCIAL STAGES
The eight stages of ego development as postulated by Erik Erikson. The stages incorporate both sexual and social aspects and include the entire lifespan.

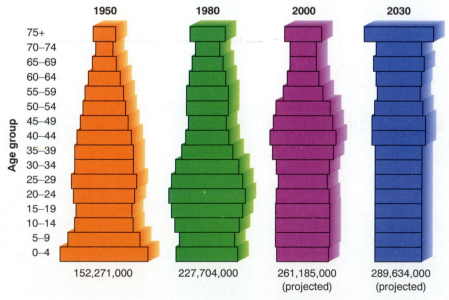

◆ **FIGURE 3.1**

Population pyramids for the United States for 1950 and 1980, with projections for 2000 and 2020. (SOURCE: U.S. Bureau of the Census and the World Bank, as reported by Horn & Meer, 1987, p. 84.)

NATURE
In developmental research, the hereditary component of an organism's development.

development. Hard scientific proof for Erikson's theory is not easy to come by, however, because of the difficulty of examining each of the stages under controlled conditions in a laboratory or by other scientific methods. From time to time throughout this chapter and the next we will return to discuss Erikson's stages as they relate to different topics.

🧬 ISSUES IN DEVELOPMENT

Throughout this chapter and the next, you will be encountering certain issues as they relate to human development. These issues are important because they help us to understand how and why human beings change and also help us to predict how they might change in the future. Of greatest interest to developmental psychologists are the issues of nature versus nurture, stability versus change, and continuity versus discontinuity. We will examine each of these issues in turn before we focus on the development of human beings throughout the lifespan.

Nature versus Nurture

THE INTERACTION OF NATURE AND NURTURE.   As you sit now, reading this book, you are presenting an excellent example of the interaction of **nature**

TABLE 3.1 ◆ ERIKSON'S PSYCHOSOCIAL STAGES		
PERIOD OF TIME	CONFLICT	DESCRIPTION
1. Infancy	Basic trust versus mistrust	Parents must maintain an adequate environment—supportive, nurturing, and loving—so that the child develops basic trust.
2. Years 1–3	Autonomy versus shame or doubt	As the child develops bowel and bladder control, she should also develop a healthy attitude toward being independent and somewhat self-sufficient. If the child is made to feel that independent efforts are wrong, then shame and self-doubt develop instead of autonomy.
3. Years 3–5½	Initiative versus guilt	The child must discover ways to initiate actions on his own. If such initiatives are successful, guilt will be avoided.
4. Years 5½–12	Industry versus inferiority	The child must learn to feel competent, especially when competing with peers. Failure results in feelings of inferiority.
5. Adolescence	Identity versus role confusion	The young person must develop a sense of role identity, especially in terms of selecting a vocation and future career.
6. Early adulthood	Intimacy versus isolation	The adult's formation of close friendships and relationships with the opposite sex is vital to healthy development
7. Middle adulthood	Generativity versus stagnation	Adults need to develop useful lives by helping and guiding children. Childless adults must fill this need through adoption or other close relationships with children.
8. Later adulthood	Ego integrity versus despair	Adults eventually review their lives. A life well spent will result in a sense of well-being and integrity.

(the effects of heredity) and **nurture** (the effects of the environment). Your human brain allows you to process and recall vast amounts of information. If you had inherited the brain of a dog or cat, no amount of training would have enabled you to comprehend this chapter.

If this chapter were written in Turkish, however, you would be unable to understand it (unless, through experience or nurturance, you had come to learn Turkish). So, it is the combination of your inherited brain and your experience with reading the English language, as well as the experience you've gathered in the world up to this point, that enables you to understand and make use of the information in this text.

Some behaviors in the developing person, such as growing physically or acquiring the ability to walk, seem to be mainly a function of the genetic component. Others, such as driving a car or reading a book, seem to be shaped primarily by the environment. It is important to remember, however, that nature versus nurture is an interaction, not a pure dichotomy. Without proper nutrition, a child's growth may be stunted, or he may walk much later than he would have otherwise; without the inherited physical capacity, driving a car or even reading would be impossible. It is always the *interaction* between the two that determines our behavior. We hope that someday we will know enough about the biology of human beings to be able to separate the contributions of nature and nurture. To do that, we will need to have a full understanding of our genetic inheritance. In pursuit of this effort, the United States, in consort with other nations, has begun the journey toward the next great goal in biology—namely, creating a map of the entire human genetic code, called the Human Genome Project. It is now expected that the complete map—that is, the entire code for a human being, with its complete sequence and exact order of genes—will be finished by the year 2005 at a cost of about $3 billion.

HEREDITY.   DNA has been called the "essence of life." It is a unique **molecule.** Every living creature—plant or animal—contains DNA in each cell of its being. In 1953 the structure of DNA was discovered by James Watson, Francis Crick, Maurice Wilkins, and Rosalind Franklin. They found that the DNA molecule is shaped like a double helix. A phosphate-sugar backbone forms the outside, and the four molecules adenine, thymine, guanine, and cytosine (known as bases) form the inside (Watson & Crick, 1953). This configuration is shown in Figure 3.2. A feature of DNA that makes it truly amazing is that it replicates; that is, it makes copies of itself.

The DNA in your body is arranged to form a code, which is determined by the vertical sequence of the base pairs. The molecular code is divided into sections, and each section orders the building of a sequence of proteins that determine the kind of animal or plant that will be made. Each section of code is called a **gene.** For example, each of your approximately 60 trillion cells contains a DNA code consisting of many sections, or genes. Each cell contains the same code (the same genes), the blueprint for your entire body. Had the DNA sequence in your body been different, it might have ordered the construction of a box elder beetle, a kangaroo, a great white shark, or an oak tree instead of you! Different DNA code sequences make different animals or plants or different varieties of the same animal or plant. You look different from your friends mainly because you have a different DNA code in your cells. On the other hand, identical twins share the same or extremely similar codes.

Throughout millions of years of evolution, genetic material has been passed from one generation to the next. Species have evolved and diversified. A genetic heritage now resides within all living creatures. It is formed within the nucleus of each cell.

When a stain of a certain color is applied to the nucleus of a cell, small bodies within the nucleus absorb the stain and become visible. These small

NURTURE
In developmental research, the environmental component of an organism's development.

DNA
Deoxyribonucleic acid. A chemical constituent of cell nuclei, consisting of two long chemical chains of alternating phosphate and deoxyribose units twisted into a double helix and joined by bonds between the chemical bases adenine, thymine, cytosine, and guanine. It is the substance that enables cells to copy themselves; it is the essence of all life.

MOLECULE
A distinct chemical unit or group of atoms that have joined together.

GENE
The smallest functional unit for the transmission of a hereditary trait; a section of genetic code.

◆ **FIGURE 3.2**

The DNA double helix. The external backbones are formed by phosphate-sugar; the base pairs form the internal core. The completed molecule looks much like a spiral staircase, with the base pairs forming the steps.

CHROMOSOMES

Thread-shaped bodies contained within the nucleus of a cell that determine the characteristics that will be passed on to the offspring of an organism.
Chromosomes carry the genes; humans have 23 pairs of them.

MEIOSIS

The process of cell division in sexually reproducing organisms that reduces the number of chromosomes in reproductive cells, leading to the production of gametes.

KARYOTYPE

A photomicrograph of chromosomes in a standard array.

LONGITUDINAL STUDIES

Research studies that are designed to investigate individuals over time, taking measurements at periodic intervals.

LINEAR PROGRESSION

Development that progresses steadily and continuously (as would a straight line). In this process, each new development is dependent on those that came before.

SALTATORY GROWTH

Literally, "growth by leaping." Growth that occurs in "spurts" or sudden leaps.

◆ **FIGURE 3.3**

Humans have 23 pairs of chromosomes. In this karyotype, the pairs are matched. One member of each pair is from the mother, and one is from the father.

bodies are called **chromosomes.** In fact, the word chromosome means "colored body."

In a human body cell, there are 46 chromosomes arranged in 23 pairs. Making up the chromosomes of each cell are the genes (made from strands of DNA), which contain the genetic plans for your entire body. The number of chromosomes per cell varies from one species of plant or animal to another. They may range from as few as 4 to as many as 254 (Sinnott, Dunn, & Dobzhansky, 1958). For example, toads have 44 chromosomes in their body cells; potatoes have 48. Of the 46 chromosomes in your body cells, you inherited 23 from your father and 23 from your mother.

Human sperm or egg cells, called gametes, contain only 23 chromosomes each, rather than 23 pairs. During the formation of these sex cells, a special process known as **meiosis** creates gametes with only half the usual number of chromosomes. Because of this, when a human sperm and egg unite during fertilization, the next generation will also have 46 chromosomes in each body cell. (Without the process of meiosis, sperm and egg cells would have the same number of chromosomes as body cells, and when they joined during fertilization, the number of chromosomes in each cell of the new generation would be doubled.)

Once chromosomes are made visible by staining, they can be photographed. The individual chromosomes can be cut from the enlarged photograph, arranged in pairs, and placed in rows for easy inspection. Such an arrangement is called a **karyotype** (Figure 3.3). A karyotype can show a number of serious chromosomal abnormalities that are known to be associated with various disorders. The first 22 pairs of chromosomes are called the autosomes. The twenty-third pair is labeled separately from the others; these two chromosomes are known as sex chromosomes.

Like the autosomes, the sex chromosomes carry many genes. The sex chromosomes are different, however, in that they also carry the genetic code that determines your sex. Interestingly, these chromosomes are shaped differently, depending on which sex code they carry. Sex chromosomes carrying the genetic code for a girl are shaped like an X, and those carrying the code for a boy are shaped like a Y. These chromosomes are, in fact, referred to as X and Y chromosomes. As you can see, the twenty-third pair in the karyotype in Figure 3.3 contains both an X and a Y chromosome. Males have an XY twenty-third pair, while females have an XX twenty-third pair.

Stability versus Change

There is much evidence to demonstrate that shortly after birth, babies are different from one another (Eisenberg & Marmarou, 1981). Some cry and fret, some sleep, some are quietly active. Workers on obstetrics wards are familiar with the great range of temperaments noticeable within the first few days of life. Although newborns may behave very differently from one another, their own individual rates of activity and crying are quite stable and consistent during those first days of life (Korner, Hutchinson, Koperski, Kraemer, & Schneider, 1981).

Longitudinal studies have suggested that some characteristics of temperament remain stable and consistent over time (Kagan, Reznick, & Gibbons, 1989; Costa & McCrae, 1980; Thomas, Chess, & Birch, 1970). For instance, infants who are passive during their first bath at age 1–2 months are also likely to sleep well in strange surroundings when they are 1 year old and also to enjoy their first weeks at camp when they are 10. In other ways, however, people do change during their lives, sometimes dramatically.

As with the nature-nurture issue, it is important to realize that stability and change are not a dichotomy; instead of an "either-or" situation, both may be involved. Some characteristics may change greatly over a person's lifetime, while others remain stable.

Continuity versus Discontinuity

Developmental psychologists have debated over the years whether human development could be characterized as a natural orderly progression or as a series of stages with abrupt changes occurring from one stage to the next. People often think that human development, and development in general, follows a fairly **linear progression**—one that proceeds at a fairly stable and steady rate and in which each new development builds on all the developments that came before.

This is not usually the case, however. Human development may occur rapidly and slowly and reach a plateau and even appear to reverse, all at the same time, depending on which developmental aspect you consider (see Figure 3.4). Furthermore, some developments appear to be dependent on one another, while others seem to occur in parallel without being directly dependent on one another. In a word, human development is complex. Although some behaviors seem to be acquired in an orderly progression, others may appear in an abrupt way.

As an example, it was once commonly assumed that physical growth in infants and young children progressed at a fairly steady rate of roughly ½ millimeter per day. Any "growth spurts" were thought to occur during puberty. However, when researcher Michelle Lampl made very careful measures of infants and toddlers on a daily basis, she discovered that there were long periods of no observable growth (sometimes as long as 2 months), and then suddenly the infant or toddler would grow. During these growth spurts, infants or toddlers typically became excessively sleepy, hungry, or fussy and then, within just a 24-hour period, grew from ⅒ to almost ½ inch (Lampl, Veldhuis, & Johnson, 1992)! This kind of development is called **saltatory growth.** Such findings help to emphasize that development is rarely a linear process.

Pediatricians regularly check the height of children to measure how well they are growing. But it was only recently that extremely careful measurements made on children who were lying down showed that growth occurs throughout childhood in sudden spurts.

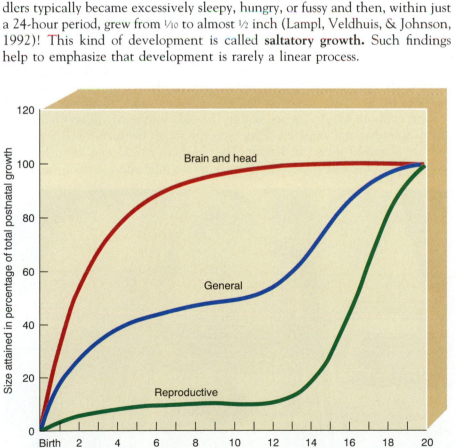

◆ **FIGURE 3.4**

Different aspects of development proceed at greatly differing rates. As you can see, human development doesn't proceed in a linear fashion. (SOURCE: Adapted from Harris, Jackson, Patterson, & Scammon, 1930.)

NEONATES
Newborn infants.

The following Concept Review summarizes the three developmental issues we have discussed so far in this chapter. None of these issues is simple; neither side of an issue completely explains any aspect of human development. Nature is meaningless without nurture; it is impossible to study development without seeing both change and stability in the process; and, although certain behaviors appear to be acquired in a relatively orderly progression, many others are not. Throughout this chapter and the next, you will see how these issues and others apply as the child is born, grows older, and ages.

CONCEPT REVIEW ◆ DEVELOPMENTAL ISSUES

Nature-Nurture
Are certain behavioral characteristics more influenced by heredity or by the environment?

Stability-Change
Are certain behavioral characteristics relatively stable over time, or do changes occur throughout the lifespan?

Continuity-Discontinuity
Can development be characterized as a steady progression, or does it appear to occur in abrupt shifts?

🧬 IN THE BEGINNING . . . (0 TO 1 YEAR OF AGE)

If you are among the many people who are unfamiliar with **neonates** (newborn infants), if your first reaction to a woman's labor pains is to boil some water, or if you've never thought it odd that in old Hollywood movies the delivery-room nurse always handed the mother a 40-pound "newborn" possessing a full set of teeth, then you probably would be surprised by the appearance of a real newborn baby.

Real newborn infants (as opposed to the old Hollywood variety) have skin that is soft, dry, and wrinkled. They typically weigh between 6 and 9 pounds and are about 20 inches in length. The newborn's head may seem huge in proportion to the rest of its body, as it comprises fully one-fourth of the baby's

Human newborns have soft, dry, and wrinkled skin. They usually weigh between 6 and 9 pounds and are about 20 inches in length. The neonate's head accounts for one-quarter of its entire length. In addition, the neonate's forehead is high and its nose is flat.

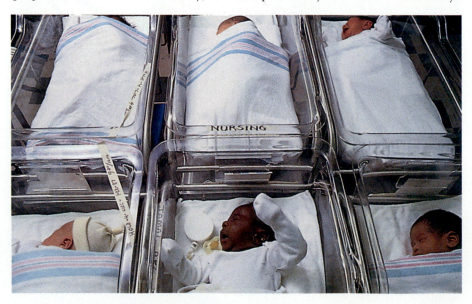

length. In addition, the neonate's forehead is high and its nose is flat. And, although the eyes may eventually be brown, most neonates' eyes are steely blue.

Are Babies Passive?

From the turn of the century until the 1950s, most researchers considered the newborn to be a helpless creature who was handed to the world like a lump of clay ready to be molded and shaped. They did not think of the newborn as being competent in any sense of the word. They considered babies in general to be helpless and passive. Babies cried, they wet, they ate, they slept, they possessed some simple reflexes, and that was about it.

During the 1960s and 1970s, however, there was a sudden surge of research concerning the capabilities of infants. Researchers found, for instance, that throughout infancy babies will initiate social interactions and play an active role in maintaining and developing their parents' responses (Restak, 1982).

This sociability begins only moments after the infant is out of the womb. Newborns will look about and will turn their heads in response to a voice as though they are searching for its source. Newborns seem especially attracted to faces and show an interest in them. This behavior, in turn, helps to initiate reciprocal interest from the person receiving the infant's gaze. Other attributes that are present at or shortly after birth help to facilitate the social attachment of the infant to its caregiver (see Figure 3.5). As you read more about newborns, you may be surprised to find how many interesting abilities and competencies they have. For example, one researcher found that infants who are only 5 months old can discriminate between small groups containing different numbers of items and may indeed possess a primitive ability to add and subtract (Wynn, 1992).

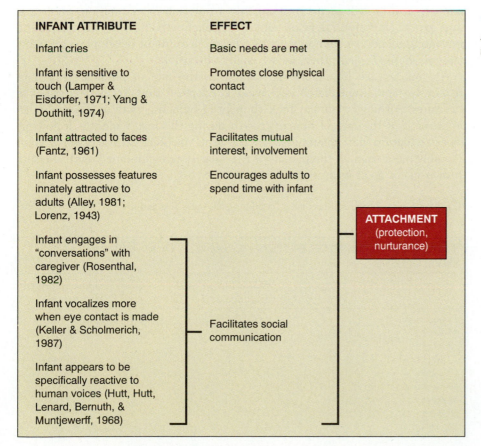

◆ FIGURE 3.5

Attributes present at or shortly after birth that facilitate infants' social attachments.

HABITUATION
A process whereby an organism ceases to respond to a stimulus that is repeatedly presented.

MATURATION
A genetically programmed biological plan of development that is relatively independent of experience.

Researchers have also found that newborns are capable of fairly complex cognitive, learning, and memory tasks. For example, as the chapter Prologue described, not only does an infant hear his mother's voice before he is born, but his memory is developed enough so that he "recognizes" her voice again after birth. Soon after birth, infants actively attend and begin the process of encoding information from the environment, placing it into their memories for later retrieval.

That newborns can learn is demonstrated by studies in which they are exposed to repeated stimuli such as lights or sound. At first, they may "jump" and orient toward the source; these responses are called the "startle reflex" and the "orienting reaction," respectively. With repeated exposure to a stimulus the reaction decreases. Thus, newborns show the effects of **habituation,** in which they stop responding to a stimulus that is repeatedly presented (see Chapter 8).

If another, different stimulus is presented to the infant following habituation to the first stimulus, the infant often pays attention to the newly presented stimulus, which shows that the infant has discriminated between the two stimuli. The effect is an important one. According to psychologist Robert Trotter,

Habituation is now considered a primary indication of brain and nervous-system functioning and . . . is seen as a good predictor of later intelligence. Habituation, which becomes increasingly acute over the first 10 weeks of life, is commonly assessed as a measure of an infant's maturity and well-being. Infants who have brain damage or have suffered birth traumas, such as lack of oxygen, do not habituate well, and may go on to have developmental and learning problems. (1987, p. 38)

Infant Physical and Motor Development

The term used to describe a genetically determined biological plan of development, one that is relatively independent of experience, is **maturation.** Human physical growth seems to be mainly a function of maturation, and, to a large extent, so is motor development. Physical growth and motor development are among the most commonly discussed aspects of infant development among parents, simply because they are so readily observable.

As you can see by examining Table 3.2, the rate of physical growth is incredibly rapid immediately following conception and decelerates quickly thereafter. Although you may have thought of human growth as a fairly linear progression, if the rate of human growth during the first 3 months following your conception were maintained, by the time you were 20 you'd weigh considerably more than all the planets of the solar system combined, with the sun thrown in for good measure!*

*Based on a rate of each cell becoming 25 billion cells every 3 months.

TABLE 3.2 ◆ THE DECELERATION OF GROWTH DURING PRENATAL DEVELOPMENT		
AGE	WEIGHT (in ounces)	PERCENTAGE INCREASE
Conception	0.00000002	
4 weeks	0.0007	3,499,900
8 weeks	0.035	4,900
12 weeks	0.6	1,614
16 weeks	3	400
20 weeks	8	166
24 weeks	22	175
28 weeks	28	27
32 weeks	34	21

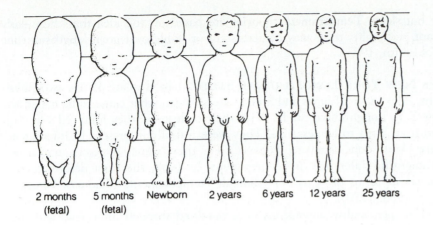

2 months 5 months Newborn 2 years 6 years 12 years 25 years
(fetal)   (fetal)

◆ FIGURE 3.6

Change in body form associated with age. (SOURCE: *Jackson, 1929, p. 118.*)

Changes in the relative size of different body parts also take place during growth. The change in the ratio of head to body length is an interesting example of this aspect of growth (see Figure 3.6).

In Figure 3.7, you can see how aspects of an infant's motor development also appear to follow a maturational plan. Just as individual babies differ, so too do individual rates of motor development. Some infants proceed quickly; others lag behind. Some develop rapidly in one area and simultaneously are slow in another. Like the tortoise and the hare, some infants may race ahead of their peers only to be equaled or overtaken later.

Infant Personality and Social-Emotional Development

Although the human infant doesn't appear to possess a fully integrated personality in its first few days of life, it has been observed that newborns do exhibit considerable differences in temperament shortly after birth. Some babies seem "fussy," some have a high activity level, and some seem to do noth-

◆ FIGURE 3.7

Some motor milestones from the Denver Developmental Screening Test. The bottom of the bar represents the age at which 25 percent of the sample could perform the task; the top represents the age at which 90 percent had achieved it. (SOURCE: *Adapted from Frankenburg & Dodds, 1967, p. 186.*)

Months of age

Rolls over	Sits without support	Stands holding on	Pulls self to stand	Stands alone well	Walks well
4.7 mo. / 2.3 mo.	7.8 mo. / 4.8 mo.	10.0 mo / 5.0 mo	10.0 mo / 6.0 mo	13.9 mo. / 9.8 mo.	14.3 mo. / 11.3 mo.

TEMPERAMENT THEORIES
Theories of human development that place an emphasis on the enduring and stable aspects of personality, which are generally considered to be constitutional in nature, that is, due to the biogenetics of the individual.

GOODNESS OF FIT
From temperament theory, referring to how well suited a certain temperament is to a particular environment. Temperaments well matched with their environments are said to show "goodness of fit."

ing but sleep. **Temperament theories** are based on the idea that these early infant personality traits may be consistent or stable over great lengths of time (Goldsmith, 1983).

THE NEW YORK LONGITUDINAL STUDY. In the late 1950s, two physicians, Alexander Thomas and Stella Chess, began what came to be called the New York Longitudinal Study. With their colleagues, they followed 140 children from birth to adolescence. They were initially interested in infant reactivity, but soon came to believe that they were, in fact, empirically documenting differences in temperament. In 1968, they first described their subjects in terms of "easy" or "difficult" temperaments (Thomas, Chess, & Birch, 1968; 1970).

These personality dimensions were obtained through interviews with parents, observation of infants and children, and other measures. According to the study's classification system, "easy" infants adapted readily to new situations, were approachable, responded with low or mild intensity, exhibited pleasant moods, and had regular body rhythms. "Difficult" children, on the other hand, were slower to adapt to new situations, tended to withdraw from their caregivers, responded with high intensity, and exhibited unpleasant moods. Some children fell in between the dimensions of "easy" and "difficult." Such infants often are referred to as "slow-to-warm-up babies." Other infants were too inconsistent to categorize, exhibiting "mixtures of traits that did not add up to a general characterization" (Thomas, Chess, & Birch, 1970, p. 105). Among the infants studied, the researchers found that 40 percent were "easy," 15 percent "slow-to-warm-up," 10 percent "difficult," and 35 percent inconsistent. What makes these findings so interesting is that these temperaments often appear to be stable over time. For example, a child who doesn't cry much with wet diapers at 2 months of age also is less likely to fuss when a shirt is pulled over her head at 1 year of age. Follow-up studies at 5 and 10 years showed a certain stability of these traits.

Parents or adult caregivers are seen as intrinsically attractive to an infant. Research indicates that infants are also intrinsically attractive to adults (Lorenz, 1943).

GOODNESS OF FIT. Interestingly, "easy" children aren't always at an advantage. Among the Masai children in Africa, for example, it was discovered that the children most likely to die during times of famine were those with easy temperaments, probably because they were fed less often than were "difficult" children who acted more aggressively (deVries, 1984)—a case of the squeaky wheel getting the grease, or milk in this case. Even in Western culture, it has been found that "difficult" infants from upper- and middle-class families, when tested at the age of 4, obtained intelligence test scores that were 20 IQ points higher than their matched "easy" counterparts (Maziade, Cote, Boutin, Bernier, & Thivierge, 1988). This appears to be due to the fact that parents of "difficult" children find they have to spend more time with their "difficult" children, whereas the "easy" children can be more readily left to themselves. Of course, an "easy" child may still have an advantage when she enters school and has to deal with tasks that take time and require concentration (Palisin, 1986). For reasons such as these, psychologists don't automatically assume that an easy temperament is superior, but rather they talk of **goodness of fit,** when referring to how well suited a given temperament is to a particular environment.

It should be noted, however, that not all temperament researchers agree that temperamental characteristics are as stable over time as the New York Longitudinal Study would suggest (Goldsmith et al., 1987).

SOCIAL TIES. We humans are social creatures. We live within communities and families; we form social and emotional ties with one another. As was shown in Figure 3.5, the infant seems innately predisposed to form these ties—for one thing, because such ties are essential for newborns who must rely on their parents or others for basic needs. During this time of helplessness, the infant comes to know his parents socially and forms attachments to them.

The mechanism of **attachment,** especially between the infant and his mother, has been intensely debated and investigated by developmental theorists, but over the years, the theoretical orientation taken by most researchers has changed. During the first decades of this century, both Freud and the behaviorists (see Chapter 1) argued that the infant became attached because attachment was associated with the fulfillment of primary biological needs. For this reason, they believed that nursing led to the formation of strong attachments between infant and mother. But research with rhesus monkeys, conducted by Harry Harlow and his associates, cast doubt on this speculation.

In a series of widely publicized experiments begun about 35 years ago, Harlow and his colleagues separated rhesus monkeys from their mothers at an early age and placed them with artificial surrogate mothers (see Figure 3.8). One surrogate was made of wire; the other was covered with terry cloth and possessed a more rhesus-looking face (Harlow & Zimmerman, 1959). Both "mothers" could be equipped with baby bottles placed through a hole in the chest, which allowed nursing to take place. Regardless of which mother provided food, the baby monkeys spent as much time as possible cuddling and hugging the *cloth* mother. Even rhesus monkeys fed by only the wire mother formed strong attachments to the cloth mother and spent most of their time hugging it. A simple piece of soft cloth did not have the same effect; to function as a surrogate, the cloth had to be roughly shaped like a real mother.

Other researchers soon found more evidence supporting the idea that attachment was more than just dependence on someone who fulfills biological needs. For instance, infants may become attached to other infants their own age (Schaffer & Emerson, 1964). Attachment may develop even if an infant is seriously mistreated by the one to whom she is becoming attached (Rosenblum & Harlow, 1963). Infants also respond readily to others in social situations in which they have never received food or contact comfort (Brackbill, 1958; Rheingold, Gewirtz, & Ross, 1959). Furthermore, infants do not become

ATTACHMENT
An especially close affectional bond formed between a living creature and another living creature or object.

◆ **FIGURE 3.8**

The wire and the cloth surrogate mothers used by Harlow in experiments with rhesus monkeys. Even if the only food available was from the wire mother, the infants preferred the cloth mother.

INTRAORGANISMIC PERSPECTIVE
The view of attachment asserting that the infant has innate mechanisms that foster and promote the development of attachment. Such mechanisms are believed to have been naturally selected because they have survival value.

STRANGE SITUATION
A laboratory test designed by Mary Ainsworth to demonstrate individual differences in the quality of attachment.

SECURE ATTACHMENT
The most common form of attachment observed by Ainsworth in her research. Securely attached children respond happily to their returning mothers, greet them, and stay near them for a while.

ANXIOUS/RESISTANT ATTACHMENT
A form of attachment observed by Ainsworth in her research. Children who show anxious/resistant attachment approach their returning mothers, cry to be picked up, and then struggle to be free. Their behavior is ambivalent; they appear to wish to approach and to avoid their mothers simultaneously.

ANXIOUS/AVOIDANT ATTACHMENT
A form of attachment observed by Ainsworth in her research. Children who show anxious/avoidant attachment do not approach—and actively avoid—their returning mothers.

passive and unresponsive once all their biological needs are taken care of; they continue to be social and to show attachment.

In more recent times, the most accepted theoretical orientation concerning the development of attachment has been toward an **intraorganismic perspective** (Brazelton, Koslowski, & Main, 1974). In this view, intraorganismic organization means that the infant is biologically organized or ready to form attachments to caregivers (again, see Figure 3.5).

John Bowlby, one of the most important proponents of the intraorganismic perspective, believes humans have an innate drive to form attachments that is as strong as the motivational forces of mating or eating (Bowlby, 1982a). His classic paper, *The Nature of the Child's Tie to His Mother* (Bowlby, 1958), is considered by many researchers to mark the beginning of contemporary attachment theory. Attachment remains an area of considerable interest.

THE DYNAMICS OF HUMAN ATTACHMENT.   Twenty years ago, Mary Ainsworth, who trained with John Bowlby, became the first to investigate the parameters of human attachment in depth. Ainsworth's studies remain superior to most others in their scope. They included a 1-year longitudinal investigation of infant attachments in the home; a 20-minute laboratory test known as the **strange situation,** which demonstrates individual differences in the quality of attachment; and an assessment of the variables that determine the quality of infant attachment. By using a number of observational techniques, Ainsworth and her colleagues were able to identify three attachment reactions of differing quality. The first, **secure attachment,** was the most common, accounting for about 65 to 75 percent of children studied. Babies exhibiting this response gave mothers returning from an absence of a few minutes, during which the child was left with a stranger, a happy greeting and approached them or stayed near them for a time. The second kind of reaction, **anxious/resistant attachment,** accounted for about 10 to 15 percent of children. Infants who responded in this way approached their mothers, cried to be picked up, and then squirmed or fought to get free, as though they weren't sure what they wanted. The third kind, **anxious/avoidant attachment,** accounted for about 20 to 25 percent of children; it was demonstrated by infants who didn't approach their returning mothers or who actively avoided them (Ainsworth, 1973).

Subsequent research found that securely attached infants are more likely to explore their environments (Joffe, 1980) and to tolerate a moderate amount of separation from their mothers (Jacobson & Wille, 1984). Because of this, securely attached infants also appear to feel more comfortable exploring and, when faced with something new such as a toy or game, will persist in examining it. This persistence often helps them to master the new thing they have encountered (Frodi, Bridges, & Grolnick, 1985). Not surprisingly, children who exhibit such mastery in infancy tend to show greater competence in early childhood (Sroufe, 1983; Messer et al., 1986). Thus, one of the advantages of a secure attachment relationship is that it can help to foster further social competencies in the infant.

It should be kept in mind, however, that these findings may be limited to certain middle-class American cultures (Lamb, 1988). For instance, among children who grew up on Israeli kibbutzim (collective farms) and also among Japanese children, there were higher percentages of anxious/resistant attachment in the strange situation than were recorded in Ainsworth's original studies. And, among a sample of children from northern Germany, anxious/avoidant attachment was the most common form of attachment (see Figure 3.9). Among Japanese children, 68 percent were found to show secure attachment, and *none* were found to be anxious/avoidant, probably because part of the strange situation, in which the testing is done, requires that the mother leave her infant alone with a stranger for a short time, which is something that Japanese mothers never do. Israeli infants raised on a kibbutz (a collective farm) respond differently, too. They don't find the strange situation to be so strange, probably because they are used to being looked after by strangers. Differences in German data probably reflect the cultural values of northern Germany that teach parents to keep a certain interpersonal distance from their children. These cultural effects are very interesting and show us that we need to learn much more about these kinds of attachments before we can properly generalize our findings to a broad range of children (van IJzendoorn & Kroonenberg, 1988).

INFANT EMOTIONAL DEVELOPMENT. The facial musculature of both full-term and premature newborns is fully developed and functional at birth (Ekman & Oster, 1979), so infants can make many of the same expressions that an adult can (Oster & Ekman, 1978). Newborns can smile slightly, knit their brows, or appear to pout and cry, and if you give them something that tastes awful, they look disgusted (Camras, 1988).

It used to be commonly held that infants younger than about 6 months of age showed only pleasure, wariness, or rage. In older infants, it was believed, emotions become more differentiated and obvious. But many researchers now believe that *all* the basic emotions are present in newborns and that what occurs as the infant ages is that he becomes better able to express these emotions in a way that others see clearly (Campos, Barrett, Lamb, Stenberg, & Goldsmith, 1983). Supporting this assertion is a study that shows that infants only 10 weeks old can discriminate their mothers' different emotional facial expressions. In this study, an infant's mother would face her baby and say, "You make me (happy, sad, angry)," and match her voice to her facial expression. The infant typically acted as though his mother's expression had meaning, and he too would react. Happy mothers produced happiness in their infants. Babies exposed to angry expressions eventually turned away and stopped looking. Those exposed to sad expressions appeared to suck their lips and tried to soothe themselves (Haviland & Lelwica, 1987).

◆ **FIGURE 3.9**

The distribution of infants across cultures by mode of attachment demonstrated during the strange situation. (SOURCE: Adapted from Sagi, van IJzendoorn, & Koren-Karie, 1991.)

AN ENDURING QUESTION:
WHO SHOULD MIND THE CHILDREN?

For as long as our species has existed and in every society, there have been instances when infants had to be left in the care of someone other than their mothers or fathers. In most of these situations, other family members, often a grandparent, functioned as caregiver. Strangers were rarely required to look after the children of others.

Sometimes large-scale infant care by strangers was required because of social disruptions such as war, famine, or plague. From a research perspective, however, if such children were observed to have problems with their development, it was impossible to say how much resulted from nonparental care and how much from the social upheaval that made such care necessary. Although many societies have questioned the wisdom of nonparental or nonfamilial care, its use was often unavoidable.

In some societies, however, nonfamilial care of children was expected. For example, a "nanny system" was quite common among many aristocracies throughout the ages, named after the child caregiver in the nineteenth-century British version of the system. Many writers and scholars have argued that being raised by hired help, leaving wealthy par-

AN ENDURING QUESTION, CONTINUED

ents free to be uninvolved with their children, was harmful. Again, from a research perspective, it is hard to know just how "uninvolved" such parents really were, or how much of the child's eventual development was influenced by the confounding factors of being privileged, rather than by the effects of a nanny. It is also difficult to find evidence of real harm owing to this system, but because we lack carefully gathered data, no one is certain.

In the United States during the 1940s, being raised in homes for orphans was shown to result in severe developmental setbacks for children (Spitz, 1945). This discovery led to the use of foster homes. But the care in the orphanages in question was closer to no care than it was to nonfamilial care, so the question of familial care versus care by strangers remained unanswered.

The question about the effects of nonfamilial care continues today in the United States and in many industrial nations, because so many women who were traditionally charged with raising the children are now entering the work force. In the United States alone, more than 50 percent of mothers are employed outside the home, and more than 8 million American preschoolers require some form of nonfamilial care (see Figure 3.10). A number of organizations involved in child care services have estimated that by the late 1990s, two-thirds of mothers with preschool children will be in the job force. In other industrialized nations, a large portion of married women with preschool children are also working, even in countries such as Japan where mothers traditionally stayed home with their children. A great number of infants around the world are therefore affected. With modern research techniques and the widespread use of day-care, we are now better able to address the age-old question about the possible harm of nonfamilial care.

Psychologist Jay Belsky examined infants in typical day-care settings. He concluded that babies who spent more than 20 hours per week with nonfamilial care during the first year of life were more likely to show anxious/avoidant attachment to their mothers than were other babies (Belsky, 1986). Other researchers have made similar observations and have suggested that infants left in day-care might be showing anxious/avoidant attachment because they perceive the mothers' daily abandonment as rejection (Barglow, Vaughn, & Molitor, 1987). As you recall, insecure attachment is associated with problems as the infant matures.

Some researchers have questioned Belsky's findings, however. Researcher Michael Lamb has pointed out that while it may be true that

◆ **FIGURE 3.10**

The percentage of working mothers of children under 6 years of age increased after 1960 until it leveled off in 1986. About 45 percent of women with young children will stay at home with their children barring extreme circumstances, and the trend for mothers of young children to work outside the home has apparently peaked. Still, because the majority of mothers with young children work outside the home, many preschoolers require some form of nonparental care. (SOURCE: *Adapted from Walls, Hull, Ludtke, & Taylor, 1987; Statistical Abstract of the United States, 1991.)*

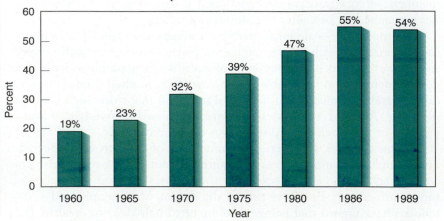

AN ENDURING QUESTION, CONTINUED

day-care infants often show more anxious/avoidant attachment, these findings are all based on the strange situation, whose very validity can be questioned because children in day-care situations are far more used to strangers attending them than children who haven't been in day care (Lamb & Sternberg, 1990). Perhaps, as Lamb and others have argued, other measures should be used to assess the infant's social and emotional well-being, and the quality of the day-care should be considered as well.

What we can feel comfortable saying today is that high-quality day-care for children over 1 year of age appears not to be detrimental. In many instances, high-quality day-care has even been associated with benefits. Young children in high-quality programs have superior language skills (McCartney & Scarr, 1984) and are more likely to regulate their own behavior (Howes & Olenick, 1986). One study showed that disadvantaged children in particular can benefit from high-quality day-care (McCartney, Scarr, Phillips, & Grajek, 1985). The effect on infants younger than 1 year, however, is still debated, and more research needs to be done.

Unfortunately, not all day-care programs are of high quality. Research has consistently shown that there is a difference between children who receive high-quality versus low-quality nonfamilial care. As yet, day-care arrangements that are informal or unlicensed have not been studied as extensively as have licensed ones. One study, however, indicated that there may not be significant differences as long as the caregivers have experience, interact with the children, and provide them with some structure by giving them things to do (Stith & Davis, 1984). Of course, the results of this limited study do not mean that unlicensed day-care centers are as good as licensed ones. Unlicensed centers may run the range from acceptable to dangerous. (The same may be true of licensed centers, but presumably, this is less likely.)

Finally, there is no question that a child will fare better spending part of the day with a high-quality caregiver (an educated, trained person in a safe environment, who has few children to care for, and who interacts with the children while giving them structured things to do) than a

Fairly soon, nearly two-thirds of mothers with preschool children will be in the work force. Day care in the United States is already stressed through overcrowding and understaffing. While some centers like this one are coping affectively, the problem of good day care will become more urgent as growing demand places more pressure on an already strained system.

AN ENDURING QUESTION, CONTINUED

whole day with a depressed or frustrated parent. So don't be afraid to use day-care if you are a parent or plan to become one. Just use a good dose of common sense when choosing a facility.

FOR CRITICAL ANALYSIS

1. Should the federal government require the establishment of uniform standards for day-care centers? Should governments in other countries do the same? How might such standards be helpful? What should those standards be?

2. How might a second income-producing parent provide dividends for his or her children that could offset the possibly disruptive influences of day-care? ◆

EARLY CHILDHOOD: TODDLERS AND PRESCHOOL CHILDREN (1 TO 6 YEARS OF AGE)

Cognitive Development

During early childhood, besides physically increasing in size, children show increased motor competence. But some of the most apparent and interesting changes that take place in the first 6 years of the child's life are cognitive in nature. For a long time, psychologists ignored infants' minds. Some psychologists believed that ignoring an infant's mind wasn't a very hard thing to do, because whatever infants thought about, if anything, couldn't be too complex (Pines, 1966). Since that time, however, largely owing to the work of the Swiss researcher Jean Piaget, psychologists have become increasingly interested in the development of cognitive processes in infants and children.

In Piaget's view, cognitive development was the combined result of the development of the brain and nervous system and of experiences that help the individual adapt to his or her environment. Piaget believed that because humans are genetically similar and share many of the same environmental experiences, they can be expected to exhibit considerable uniformity in their cognitive development. In fact, he argued, four predictable stages of cognitive development will occur during specific periods of a child's life. The first two stages—the sensorimotor (0 to 2 years) and the preoperational (2 to 7)—take place during infancy and early childhood (see Table 3.3). We will discuss these two stages now; later, in the sections on middle childhood and adolescence, we will examine Piaget's last two stages. Piaget's stages are defined by the capabilities of the infant or child, and not by his or her age. For instance, a child is said to be preoperational by what she is able to do and not by the fact that she turned two, although most children become preoperational at about that time.

The Swiss researcher Jean Piaget (1896–1980) believed that children's thinking is qualitatively different from adults'. He developed a theory of cognitive development that outlined children's cognitive progression through a series of stages, the sensorimotor, preoperational, concrete operational, and formal operational.

TABLE 3.3 ◆ PIAGET'S FIRST TWO STAGES OF COGNITIVE DEVELOPMENT
Sensorimotor Stage (0–2 years)   Characterized by a lack of fully developed object permanence, or realization that objects continue to exist even though they are not presently sensed
Preoperational Stage (2–7 years)   Characterized by the beginning of internalized thought processes; called preoperational because children haven't yet acquired the logical operations or rules of thought characteristic of later periods of cognitive development; beginning of a sense of self

Piaget argued that children are not simply adults who know less and, conversely, adults are not simply knowledgeable children. Rather, Piaget believed that older children have more extensive cognitive development. On the one hand, they have broader experiences; on the other, they can process the information in more sophisticated ways because of the more advanced biological and adaptive development of their underlying cognitive structures.

THE SENSORIMOTOR STAGE (0 TO 2 YEARS). The first of Piaget's four stages of cognitive development is the **sensorimotor stage,** which is characterized by a lack of fully developed **object permanence.** Object permanence refers to the ability to mentally represent an object after it is no longer present. Piaget believed that object permanence was necessary before thinking about absent objects could be carried out internally—that is, carried out by using mental symbols or images.

Look around you—do you see a redwood tree? Unless you live in a scenic northern California setting and are sitting next to a window, you probably don't. But can you mentally represent a redwood tree to yourself, even though one isn't actually present? You can do this in a number of ways. You can picture a redwood tree in your "mind's eye" (if you know what the tree looks like). Or you can think of the letter symbols R-E-D-W-O-O-D T-R-E-E. Or you might actually shape a depiction of a redwood tree with your hands to hold on to that object mentally, even though it's out of sight. The point is, you can keep any object "permanent," even when it is absent, by using these techniques. Without mental images, symbols, or depictions to represent an object, you would be unable to think of it, because you would have no internal way of representing it. In other words, without object permanence, "out of sight, out of mind."

Piaget argued that at the beginning of the sensorimotor stage, an infant may be unable to think. Later on, however, when object permanence becomes fully developed, the child leaves the sensorimotor stage.

THE PREOPERATIONAL STAGE (2 TO 7 YEARS). The major distinction between the sensorimotor and **preoperational stages** is the degree of development and use of internal images and symbols. The development of thought, as represented by the establishment of mental representations of absent objects, marks the dividing line between the sensorimotor and preoperational stages. This internalized thought may be the precursor of a sense of self-awareness.

As the preoperational stage sets in, the child demonstrates greater and greater use of symbolic functions. Language development increases dramati-

SENSORIMOTOR STAGE
The first stage in Piaget's theory of cognitive development. It is distinguished by the lack of fully developed object permanence and typically lasts from birth to two years of age.

OBJECT PERMANENCE
Piaget's term for the individual's realization that objects continue to exist even though they are no longer visible.

PREOPERATIONAL STAGE
The second stage in Piaget's theory of cognitive development. It is distinguished by the presence of object permanence, but the lack of concrete operations. It is a time of imaginary play and intuitive "logic" lasting typically from the ages of two to six or seven.

Some of Piaget's most interesting experiments and observations concerned the onset and development of object permanence during the sensorimotor stage. If, during the first four months of the sensorimotor stage, you show an infant an object that attracts attention and then block the baby's view of it with a screen, the child will act as if the object has simply vanished. By the middle of the sensorimotor stage, a child will try to regain visual contact with an object that has disappeared from view. This attempt may indicate the beginning of object permanence, since the infant may be searching for the hidden object. She or he seems to have some internal representation that the thing was once in view and is now gone. Even at this point, however, object permanence is weak.

EGOCENTRISM
A thought process characteristic of children in Piaget's preoperational stage; they view themselves as the reference point in their dealings with the external world.

CENTRATION
The child's tendency to focus, or center, on only one aspect of a changing system at any given time; characteristic of the preoperational stage.

cally, and imaginative play becomes apparent as children spend much of their time engaging in make-believe. Another difference seen during this stage is that children can imitate another person's behavior after some time has passed, implying that they now have a way of symbolically remembering behavior originally observed in a model. All these actions suggest an internal cognitive mediation between incoming stimuli and later responses.

Piaget also argued that the reasoning of children in the preoperational stage is limited, however, because these children tend to be egocentric or self-centered (Gzesh & Surber, 1985). By **egocentrism,** Piaget did not mean that children are selfish; he meant that they generally perceive the world only in terms of their own perspective (Beilin, 1992).

Egocentric thinking is only one of the cognitive limitations Piaget saw children facing early in the preoperational stage. An additional limitation is the inability to comprehend more than one aspect of a problem at a time. Piaget referred to this cognitive limitation as the failure to "decenter," because such children tend to focus, or "center," on only single aspects of problems. This **centration** leads preoperational children to solutions that seem more intuitive than logical. For example, a preoperational child presented with two identical glasses of water will realize that they are equally full. But suppose we pour the water from one of the glasses into a bowl while the child watches. When comparing the bowl of water with the remaining glass, he most likely will believe that there is now less water in the bowl because it is at a lower level than the water in the glass (see Figure 3.11). Of course, you and I know that the amount of water is still the same. We know that no water has been added or taken away (excluding residue remaining in the glass and evaporation due to pouring). We've conserved quantity (one aspect), although the shape has altered (another aspect). Because we can avoid centration, we can comprehend more than one aspect at a time. Children in the preoperational stage don't seem able to do this.

Alternative Views of Cognitive Development

Without a doubt, Jean Piaget contributed immeasurably to our knowledge of cognitive development in children. His theories have had a wide influence on education and psychology. Throughout the years, however, people, especially researchers in the United States, have proposed some strong arguments against Piaget's view.

In the mid-twentieth century, the learning theorists' view was paramount among American psychologists. Proponents of behaviorism, such as John Watson and B. F. Skinner, took a different approach from Piaget's to explain a

◆ **FIGURE 3.11**

Testing a child for the ability to conserve. (a) The child agrees that the two glasses contain the same amount of water; (b) water from one of the glasses is poured into a dish. The child doesn't agree that the dish and the remaining glass contain the same amount of water, because the child is unable to conserve one aspect (amount) while another aspect (height) changes. Another way to say this is that the child centers attention on only one obvious aspect (height), whereas an adult would decenter and consider all aspects.

(a)   (b)

child's cognitive development. In their view, development was not driven from within by the biological development of the child as she interacted with her surroundings, but rather was added to from without. In other words, behaviorists believe that cognitive development is the result of learning. They argued forcefully that there were no stages of cognitive development, but rather that cognitive development was a gradual and continuous process.

Researchers have also criticized specific aspects of Piaget's theory. For example, many studies have indicated that supposedly egocentric preoperational children are often quite able to deal with another person's viewpoint (Hart & Goldin-Meadow, 1984; Mossler, Marvin, & Greenberg, 1976; Shatz, 1973). Also, with careful study, object permanence has been observed in infants as young as 3½ months of age (Baillargeon, 1987), and infants of only 14 months of age have shown that they can imitate something unusual that they saw an adult do a full week after having seen it (Meltzoff, 1988). These findings are at some odds with Piaget's assertion that the sensorimotor period is characterized by the absence of object permanence. Keep in mind, however, that although Piaget is dead, his theory isn't necessarily complete. During his lifetime, Piaget was his own greatest revisionist (Block, 1982). He changed old ideas for new and reorganized his thinking many times. No doubt, this theory will continue to be developed and changed by the work of today's researchers and future ones.

Currently, the issue of whether cognitive development occurs in stages or is mostly a continuous process remains unresolved. But many theorists have concluded that there is some merit to both Piaget's view and learning theory (Fischer & Silvern, 1985). Piaget may have demonstrated what is typical under usual environmental and developmental conditions—that is, what is probable. When modern theorists talk about stages of cognitive development, they often use the term **probabilistic epigenesis** to refer to the fact that stages describe only the typical or most likely development. In fact, researchers currently like to use the word level instead of stage when referring to a child's cognitive development, because stage has a rigid, inflexible connotation.

THE DEVELOPMENT OF GENDER UNDERSTANDING.   One of the cognitive advances in the early childhood years that is very apparent in children's behavior is the development of **gender understanding;** that is, they begin to comprehend that they are boys or girls. This occurs at about the age of 3 (Thompson, 1975). Yet 3-year-old children generally fail to understand **gender constancy,** that is, that your own sex will remain constant—once a boy, always a boy. For example, a girl demonstrates a grasp of gender constancy when she understands that just because she puts on a jersey and plays football, she does not turn into a boy, but is still a girl.

Once children come to comprehend the anatomical basis of gender distinction, which has been found to be the case in about 40 percent of a population of children 3 to 5 years in age, they will generally acquire gender constancy (Bem, 1989). Most children acquire it by age 7 (Wehren & De Lisi, 1983). The progression from rudimentary gender understanding to the completion of gender constancy has been found to be similar in other cultures, although the final age at which gender constancy occurs may vary by a few years (Munroe, Shimmin, & Munroe, 1984). But the acquisition of gender constancy can have its costs. For instance, in one experiment, boys who had achieved gender constancy were found to play more with an uninteresting toy that was endorsed by society as a "boy's toy" than with a toy that was more fun (Frey & Ruble, 1992). That's rather sad and shows one of the costs of **gender typing;** children who acquire gender constancy may come to believe that certain toys, games, or activities are now out of bounds for them simply because they aren't considered gender appropriate.

PROBABILISTIC EPIGENESIS
Literally, the direction in which growth will probably go. In cognitive development theory, the term is used to describe the stages of cognitive development as representing only what typically occurs during the development of most individuals, but not necessarily in the development of all individuals.

GENDER UNDERSTANDING
A person's comprehension that he or she is either a boy or a girl; usually develops in children by about the age of 3 years.

GENDER CONSTANCY
The realization that one's sex is determined by unchanging criteria and is unaffected by one's activities or behavior; usually develops in children by the age of 6 or 7 years.

GENDER TYPING
The process whereby an individual incorporates the behaviors, traits, or attitudes appropriate to his or her biological sex or the sex assigned at birth.

Research has shown that children become attached to their fathers as well as to their mothers. They especially appreciate the father's role as playmate.

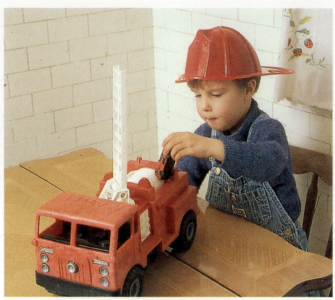

Children are taught by society to choose toys that are deemed to be appropriate for their gender. Children often show such preferences before they are even fully aware that they are boys or girls.

Personality Development in Early Childhood

One of the major achievements of young children is the ability to begin regulating their own behavior. Regulation of children's behavior usually becomes necessary during the child's second year, because this is when the child begins to display sufficient autonomy to interfere occasionally with parental desires. As you may recall, Erik Erikson described his second psychosocial stage (occurring between the ages of 1 and 3) as a conflict between autonomy and doubt or shame. For this reason, parents may wish to instill in the exploring and ever-curious child an understanding of what is acceptable while taking care not to make the child feel ashamed for flexing his or her newfound autonomy. For example, my 2-year-old son, David, is trying to master going to the toilet by himself. Just yesterday he tried to pull down his pants and use the potty. He didn't get them down all the way and had an accident. When he called my wife and me into the bathroom, we saw what had happened. We both praised him for trying and told him what a good boy he was. Then, we cleaned him up and spent some time teaching him how to pull his pants down all the way, telling him, "You can do it!" I suppose if we hadn't been thoughtful about it, we might just as well have come into the bathroom and said, "Oh, what a mess you made! Why didn't you call us to pull your pants down for you? Now we'll have to clean this mess up. Next time, call us first." One way leads to autonomy, the other to shame and doubt. I often use Erikson as a general guide for raising my own children. He is clear, straightforward, and a great help.

Longitudinal studies have shown that throughout the second year of life, a child's social behavior becomes more consistent and predictable (Bronson, 1985). This increased stability of social behavior may indicate that by the age of 2 years, children are beginning to regulate their own behavior internally in a consistent way.

When children begin to regulate their own behavior, they come to appear to rely on internalized value and reward systems. They can behave appropriately without being forced by external pressures, they can ignore immediate gratification in favor of long-term goals, and they may adhere to personal standards of moral behavior in the face of opposition. Consistency of behavior in different situations marks the beginning of what psychologists call "personality." By 2 years of age, a social person is emerging; the child has a unique personality.

Social Relations in Early Childhood

All parents have desires and hopes for their children, but the way parents achieve these ends can differ greatly from family to family. Researchers do not agree on which of the many childrearing practices is best. It is known, however, that parents provide role models for their children and that children rely on their parents to teach them about the world.

Mothers and fathers who have assumed the traditional gender roles behave differently toward their children (McHale & Huston, 1984). From the time the child is born, mothers are more likely to assume caregiving responsibilities, even if the fathers are home and are free to help. Fathers, on the other hand, are more likely to engage the infant in active and stimulating play. As the child grows older, the mother's role of primary caregiver and the father's role of playmate generally continue (Lamb, 1978). Because mothers and fathers behave in this distinctive way, they come to represent different types of experiences for their babies. Both parents, however, transmit and enforce the rules and expectations of society.

THE DEVELOPMENT OF SIBLING RELATIONSHIPS.   Although parents usually are considered to be the primary agents of socialization for the young child, in most families the child has a relationship with one or more siblings. Fully 80 percent of all children in the United States and Britain have siblings (Dunn, 1983). Siblings can have a powerful effect on one another. In fact, some of the differences observed between siblings may be the result of the fact that siblings create different family environments for each other as a result of their behaviors toward one another (Stocker, Dunn, & Plomin, 1989).

Research also indicates that siblings spend a great deal of time together, that they interact on many different levels, and that they often are deeply emotionally involved with one another (Abramovitch, Pepler, & Corter, 1982). This important effect that siblings have on one another, which continues over their lifespans, occurs because siblings are of the same generation, have a common genetic heritage, and share many of the same early experiences (Cicirelli, 1982). Strong sibling relationships have been shown to exist across the lifespan and throughout the world.

Although it was traditionally thought that conflict was the inevitable outcome of a sibling relationship, research has shown that rivalry and conflict are not necessarily the norm. In fact, the most common mode of sibling interaction is that of cooperation and helping (Abramovitch, Pepler, & Corter, 1982).

THE DEVELOPMENT OF PEER RELATIONSHIPS.   Although parents and siblings seem to be the major influences on young children's social development, **peers** begin to have an increasing effect as the child grows older. Strictly speaking, peers are equals. Nevertheless, children often have playmates who are 3 or 4 years older or younger than they are. Many researchers therefore consider children who are interacting at about the same behavior level to be peers, regardless of age. Even so, explorations of peer relationships usually concentrate on children of approximately the same age, because these children are most likely to be interacting with one another.

Between the ages of 1 and 2 years, children's social skills and peer interactions remain at a rudimentary level (Hartup, 1983), although the complexity and amount of peer interaction are greater than during infancy. By the age of 2 years, however, many complex social interchanges occur (Howes, 1987). Imitation becomes more likely, and positive social interactions often are accompanied by appropriate emotional responses, such as smiling or laughter.

Cognitive changes during the second year also play an important role in social interaction. Six-month-old infants rarely show distress when a peer takes

PEERS
Equals; developmentally, those persons who interact at about the same behavioral level regardless of age.

As children become older, they spend more and more time with other children, especially close friends. Children who form friendships do many things together, but most important they form emotional ties with one another.

FRIENDSHIPS
Close emotional ties formed with another person through mutual preference for interaction, skill at complementary and reciprocal peer play, and shared positive affect.

PLAY
Pleasurable activity engaged in for its own sake, with means emphasized rather than ends. Play is not usually engaged in as a serious activity and is flexible, in that it varies in form or context.

EXPLORATION-PLAY-APPLICATION SEQUENCE
A term describing the function of play as a bridge between the cautious exploration of the unfamiliar and its eventual application for useful purposes.

a toy away; such an interaction between children 20 months of age or older, on the other hand, is likely to start a fight. This occurs because children of this age have reached a cognitive milestone, the beginning of self-awareness, or a consciousness of being distinct creatures. In one study, researchers found that as children develop this sense of self-awareness and are able to see themselves as distinct from others, they begin to claim toys and other items as "mine" (Levine, 1983). Once they've defined "mine," they are more likely to become possessive.

THE DEVELOPMENT OF FRIENDSHIPS.   Most interactions among children between the ages of 2 and 6 years have been studied in day-care centers or in nursery schools. During the preschool years, both friendly and, less commonly, antagonistic social interactions emerge. One of the most apparent is the development of **friendships.**

When children first meet, they are more likely to become friends if they are able to exchange information successfully, establish a common-ground activity, and manage conflicts (see Table 3.4). After this initial relationship has been established, other processes become important. As children grow older, they improve their acquaintanceship abilities. They become more successful at

---

TABLE 3.4 ♦ HOW CHILDREN ESTABLISH AN INITIAL RELATIONSHIP

CATEGORY	EXAMPLE
Information exchange: Success	A: What's this? B: This is my room right here. This is my farm here. Look how very, very large.
Failure	A: How come we can't get this off? B: You know, I'm gonna get the rolling pin so we can roll this.
Common-ground activity: Success: A joint activity is successfully initiated	A: And you make those for after we get in together, okay? B: 'Kay. A: Have to make those. B: Pretend like those little roll cookies, I mean. A: And make, um, make a, um, pancake too. B: Oh, rats, this is a little pancake. A: Yeah, let's play house. B: Okay, play house.
Failure: Initiation is ignored, or disagreed with; activity does not develop	A: Let'a play house. B: Nope, nope, nope, nope, nope, nope. A: Because you're coloring that brick wall? B: Yep.
Conflict	A: This is stretchy. B: No, it's not. A: Uh huh. B: Yes. A: Uh huh. B: It's dirty. A: Uh uh. B: Uh huh. A: Uh uh. B: Uh huh. A: Uh uh. B: Uh huh. A: Uh uh. It's not dirty.

SOURCE: Adapted from Gottman, 1983, pp. 27, 53–54.

Although children often may play alone, as they grow older play becomes more of a social phenomenon.

exchanging information, establishing common-ground activities, resolving conflicts, and exploring differences. These characteristics, along with the emotional exchanges, become the most important aspects of the friendship (Diaz & Berndt, 1982; Furman & Bierman, 1983).

PLAY. One of the most striking occurrences during the preschool years is the continuing development of **play.** Although children may often play alone, as they grow older, play becomes more of a social phenomenon (Hartup, 1983). Playing can be simple and unstructured, as in a game of hide-and-seek, or it can be more complex and structured, as in a school basketball game.

Social scientists generally believe that play has evolved because it has a function. It may be that playing with objects, playing make-believe, or playing together at various games helps children to become skilled at manipulating objects (Cheyne & Rubin, 1983), to learn adult roles, or, once they are grown, to cooperate while dealing with serious and complex tasks. Some researchers have argued that an **exploration-play-application sequence** is found in humans and in the more advanced animals (Vandenberg, 1978; Wilson, 1975).

When children are confronted with an extremely novel toy, they tend to explore it before playing with it (Belsky & Most, 1981; Vandenberg, 1984). It's as though they want to be sure that it is safe before they play. This same kind of exploration-before-play sequence has also been observed in chimpanzees (Loizos, 1967; Mason, 1965).

During play, the skills necessary for serious application are acquired. For example, it has been found that chimpanzees need to spend time playing with sticks before they can use sticks for purposeful applications such as food gathering (Birch, 1945; Schiller, 1957). Researchers have found similar play-before-application sequences while investigating human children (Sylva, Bruner, & Genova, 1976; Vandenberg, 1978).

🔶 MIDDLE CHILDHOOD (6 TO 12 YEARS OF AGE)

Middle childhood is a time of continued physical growth and motor development. Until school-aged children reach puberty, their rate of growth is relatively steady. Both sexes gain an average of about 7 pounds in weight and about 2 to 3 inches in height each year. On average, girls and boys perform physically at about the same level, at least until the beginning of puberty (Hall & Lee, 1984).

THE DEVELOPMENT OF MINORITY CHILDREN

Research on child development has generally focused on white, middle-class, American children. Occasionally, poor children are studied or perhaps children from other cultures, but the emphasis still tends to be on white, middle-class children probably because the majority of the U.S. population of children are white and middle class and also because so many subjects in experiments are tied in one way or another to university populations simply because they are easily accessible. These tend to include children of students or faculty, children living near the university, and children in university day care, who tend to be white and middle class by an even larger percentage than the general population.

Minority children, however, constitute a very rapidly growing segment of the American population, and by the year 2000, they will have become the new majority of young people (Spencer, 1990). Any field such as developmental psychology will have to fully consider all members of the population before it can make a general claim of studying the development of children.

The problem with studying only white, middle--class, American children is that minority children often are different for interesting cultural reasons (McLoyd, 1990). For years,

however, minority children were understood in terms of the development and behavior of white children, who were used as some sort of norm by which to measure all others. Researchers have referred to this as the Eurocentric bias, meaning a view that regards the development of children from European heritage as normal and then, in a logical extension of the bias, sets them up as the standard with whom all other children should be compared (Spencer, 1990). The Eurocentric view in child development, it is argued, fosters the tendency to ignore important cultural differences that might affect how a child develops (McLoyd, 1990).

Modern researchers in the United States are beginning to examine minority children in earnest and to consider the cultural distinctions that make African Americans, Asian Americans, Hispanic Americans, native Americans, and other minority groups different from one another, as well as different from those of white European heritage. Even distinctions within each of these groups are considered. For instance, Asian Americans may well trace their cultural roots to very different origins (to Korea, Japan, China, or Vietnam, for example), and children influenced by each of these cultures may in turn develop in a somewhat different way.

Minority families are commonly extended families. In such families, it is not uncommon for grandparents to be living with their grown children and grandchildren.

FOCUS ON ETHNIC DIVERSITY

There are also commonalities among minority children and their families that make them special. For instance, minority families typically are younger, more extended (i.e., grandparents or other relatives may be residing with the parents and children), and more likely to be poor than are majority families (Spencer, 1990). Each of these differences might affect a child in meaningful ways. These distinctions, therefore, are important because a general view of "people as people" overlooks the unique cultural circumstances and influences that are brought to bear on the development of many minority children.

The discoveries made by researchers who study minority children are as diverse and as varied as the subjects of the investigations. Let's examine a few of these studies so that you may have a better idea of the research in this growing area and its implications.

We mentioned that minority families are more likely to raise their children in poverty than are majority families. For many historical and social reasons, this is especially true of African-American families. Studies investigating the effects of poverty on children's development have shown that level of income is one of the best predictors of later competence among African-American children. The more poverty a child faces, the lower is his or her level of competence concerning school, peer relations, and conduct (Patterson, Kupersmidt, & Vaden, 1990). The level of poverty among African-American families is also associated with parent effectiveness. Parents in greater poverty have been found to be less effective. They tend to be less supportive, less consistent, and less involved (McLoyd, 1990). While poverty often has devastating effects on the development of children from any cultural background, in terms of overall percentages, it is of special concern for many minorities. Because of this growing interest, we can expect, someday soon, to obtain a better understanding of the effects of poverty on children's development.

We have also mentioned that minority families are more likely to be extended. As a result, more studies than ever before are being conducted concerning the influence of grandparents, aunts and uncles, and cousins. One study found a significant parental involvement by grandmothers in African-American families (Pearson, Hunter, Ensminger, & Kellam, 1990). However, involvement in childrearing by extended family members has also been found to be quite complex. For instance, sometimes grandparents fill in for parents because parents are absent. Other times, the extended family resides together. So, while there is an emphasis on extended family among most minorities, the interactions and relationships may be quite different from one family to the next. They are not homogeneous (Tolson & Wilson, 1990). As a direct result of this growing interest, however, we can expect to see more research on the complexities of the extended family and how such families affect child development.

Also important are studies that compare minority groups to examine various stereotypes. Why, for example, are Asian-

The stereotype holds that Asian children are superior at schoolwork to most other children. When studying such stereotypes, researchers must first ask, Is the stereotype true? And, if so, why?

American children commonly expected to do well in school, while African-American children are expected to do poorly (Slaughter-Defoe, Nakagawa, Takanishi, & Johnson, 1990)? Researchers addressing such a stereotype will first ask, Is it true? And if it is, they will try to uncover the variables responsible for the difference; they will compare the environments of children from both minority groups in the hope of isolating important factors that might affect school performance, such as the presence of the father in the home or expectations of the family.

By having such diversity from which to draw, researchers are expanding our understanding of the full range of child development. The only way that the field of child development can grow and continue to be relevant is if it encompasses the development of all children, not just a select group.

CONSERVATION
The principle that quantities such as mass, weight, and volume remain constant regardless of changes in the appearance of these quantities, so long as nothing has been added or taken away.

Cognitive Development in Middle Childhood

According to Jean Piaget, at about the time children enter school, they develop the ability to rely on logic or logical operations to form their conclusions. This is known as the stage of concrete operations. Children in this period are able to use logical rules to deal with problems. How children acquire a logical understanding of the world is not clear, but they seem to do it rather abruptly. During the stage of concrete operations, children's thought processes become more competent, flexible, and powerful, as the children come to understand and apply the concept of conservation.

Children are able to conserve when they grasp that the amount of a material does not change unless something is added or taken away, even though its form or distribution may change. For this reason, conserving children will not be fooled by apparent changes in the amount of water when the water is transferred from a container of one shape to one of another shape. They will understand that no water has been added or taken away during these transfers, and that, therefore, the amount of water remains the same. The amount is conserved despite the change in shape.

Piaget stated that the ability to conserve marks the end of the preoperational stage and the beginning of concrete operations. The major difference between the preoperational and concrete stages is not that children can no longer be tricked by problems that require conservation but that children are beginning to use logical operations and rules rather than intuition. This change is viewed as a shift from reliance on perception to a reliance on logic, and it is a giant leap. Because of this, when a child reaches middle childhood, he or she is sometimes said to have reached the age of reason.

Social-Emotional Development in Middle Childhood

During middle childhood, many institutions have an influence on a child's socialization. Among them are the family, peers, schools, and even nonpersonal institutions, such as the media, including television. While the preschool-aged child relies mostly on her parents for information about the world, the school-aged child has much wider and varied social interactions, partly as a result of increased autonomy, and partly because of increased competencies. Figure 3.12 outlines the amount of time spent by school-aged children in various tasks. As you can see, the most common activities in this age group are sleeping, going to school, and watching television.

PEER RELATIONSHIPS.   For the school-aged child, peer relationships both in and out of school become extremely important. Being accepted by one's peers and belonging to peer groups are major concerns (Zarbatany, Hartmann, & Rankin, 1990).

Between the ages of 7 and 9 years, children generally form close friendships with peers of the same sex and age (Roopnarine & Johnson, 1984). School-aged children have, on the average, about five best friends (Hartup, 1984). After the eighth grade, however, it is not uncommon for adolescents to have a friend of the opposite sex (Buhrmester & Furman, 1987). The older children become, the more they are likely to share with friends (Berndt, Hawkins, & Hoyle, 1986) and the more they come to value friends by personal attributes. For instance, one study found that whereas 5½-year-old children might be more interested in making friends with another child who had a new game or toy, 9-year-old children were more interested in making friends with another child because "he's real nice" (Boggiano, Klinger, & Main, 1986).

Throughout the school years, children also rely on their peers as important sources of information and may use peers as standards by which to measure

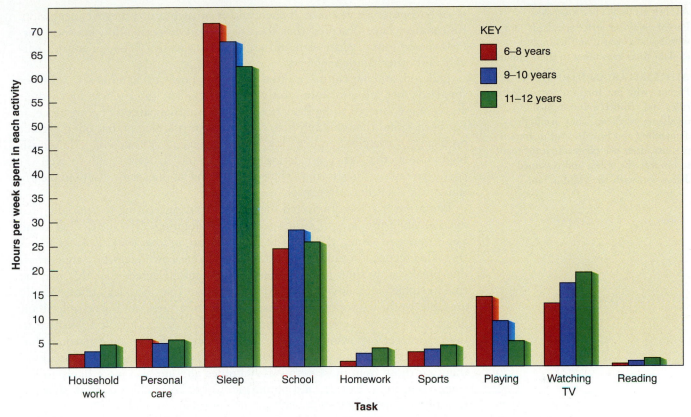

Amount of time per week spent by school-aged children in various tasks. (SOURCE: Adapted from Collins, 1984, p. 18.)

themselves. By the age of 7 or 8 years, children tend to look to their peers as models of behavior and for social reinforcement as often as they look to their own families. Research has also shown that by the fourth grade, children have come to rely on friends as an important source of social and moral support (Berndt & Perry, 1986).

PARENTING STYLES.   Over the years, developmental researchers have examined many different kinds of parenting techniques. Building on the earlier work of Earl Schaefer (1959), Diana Baumrind (1967, 1971, 1980) has become one of the most prominent researchers in the field of parenting styles. In her research, Baumrind has examined the interaction of two of the most important aspects of parenting. One aspect indicates the degree of parental *permissiveness*. The second indicates the degree of *affection*. These two aspects have been found to be part of the parenting of all human societies (Rohner & Rohner, 1981). As you might imagine, Baumrind's work has generated a great deal of research.

Diana Baumrind has defined permissive parents as those who are tolerant, who take an accepting attitude toward their children's desires, who rarely use punishment, and who try to avoid using restrictions and controls when possible. These parents rarely demand mature behavior, such as engaging in proper manners or carrying out family assignments; they allow their children to make many of their own decisions and rarely have strict rules governing the children's time (such as when to go to bed or how much television may be watched). Of course, no one functioning as a parent, by the very nature of the role, could ever be completely permissive, nor is it necessarily a good idea that one should be. All parenting requires some control over children.

Too much permissiveness may result in children who are immature and who have poor impulse control. It should also be pointed out that permissiveness

AUTHORITATIVE PARENTS
Parents who set strict standards, but who are also warm and willing to explain their reasoning to their children.

AUTHORITARIAN PARENTS
Parents who put forward a strict set of rules and require unquestioned obedience to them. They are both demanding and hostile. Authoritarian parents often use physical punishment to enforce the rules, and reasoned discussion with the child is rare.

is an inappropriate response if the child is engaging in excessive aggression. Researchers have observed that there is a positive correlation between permissiveness toward aggression and children's aggressive behavior toward parents and other family members.

Judicious and fair control is often beneficial, however. Parents who set strict standards, but are also warm and willing to explain their reasoning to their children are referred to by Baumrind as **authoritative parents.** For instance, it has been found that children from families with risk factors that often predict problems for the children (e.g., low family income, a mother who didn't finish high school, the father not living at home, and so forth) will do well on cognitive tests as long as they "come from loving families with strict but clearly stated rules" (Adler, 1989, p.7).

Baumrind has also discovered that authoritative parenting is especially productive when it comes to raising teenagers (Baumrind, 1991). This has come as a surprise to some, who point to Erik Erikson and his work; Erikson argues that adolescence is a time for the formation of one's own identity, a time when one breaks away from parental demands. Baumrind agrees that this may be true in stable social environments, but points out that in today's often socially unstable world of working mothers, high divorce rates, and accessible illicit drugs, adolescents do best when parents are both demanding and sensitive to their teenager's growing need for independence. Baumrind's research has shown that adolescents from authoritative families are less likely to abuse drugs than are those from more permissive families and are also more likely to become competent, mature, and optimistic. Other researchers confirm that authoritative parenting fosters academic achievement in adolescents.

Adolescents who describe their parents as being democratic and warm, but at the same time firm are more likely than other adolescents to develop positive attitudes toward their achievements and therefore do better in school (Steinberg, Elmen, & Mounts, 1989). As Baumrind points out,

Authoritative parents are not bossy. They make it their business to know their children, how they're doing in school and who their friends are. Their control reflects a high level of commitment to the child, and they are not afraid to confront the child (Bower, 1989, p. 117)

Baumrind refers to parents who are demanding, but at the same time hostile or rejecting as **authoritarian parents.** These parents put forward a strict set of rules and require unquestioned obedience. They commonly use physical punishment to enforce the rules, and reasoned discussion with the child is rare. Children reared by rejecting, demanding parents tend to be socially withdrawn and sullen. Their friendships are marked by quarreling and shyness. Because of the high degree of control maintained by authoritarian parents, these children are unable to express their hostility outwardly and may have a tendency to turn their aggression inward. This group exhibits a high degree of self-punishment and suicide compared with the other groups.

THE INFLUENCE OF TELEVISION.   Television has been shown to have a great influence on the development of school-age children. American children between the ages of 5 and 13 years spend more time watching television than they spend in any other waking leisure activity (again, see Figure 3.12) (Liebert & Sprafkin, 1988)! These findings may not be quite as alarming as they may seem, because careful analysis shows that of the time that school-age children spend in front of the television, only about two-thirds is actually spent watching. The rest of the time is devoted to other activities. Still, television has such wide-ranging content that it probably has both a detrimental and a beneficial effect on children (Singer & Singer, 1983a; Liebert & Sprafkin, 1988).

Television is so wide ranging in its content that it probably has both a detrimental and a beneficial effect on children.

Television has changed the way we live and the way we carry on our family life. Just having a television set in the house affects family interaction patterns (Parke, 1978). Although families spend time together watching television, they spend less time directly engaging in activities with one another than they used to. Some people have joked that you can spot a television-oriented family because none of the conversations family members have with one another ever lasts longer than the average commercial. Children, especially, can isolate themselves in front of the tube for hours.

Heavy viewing of violent television programs has been consistently associated with aggression in both children and adults (Liebert & Sprafkin, 1988) and with poorer school achievement (Rubinstein, 1983). Heavy viewing also is associated with poorer reading comprehension (Singer & Singer, 1983a) and poorer language usage (Singer & Singer, 1983b) and appears to inhibit the development of imagination.

Interestingly, for children of lower socioeconomic status, heavy television viewing has been associated with higher reading comprehension and higher scholastic achievement. Television viewing, therefore, appears to have a leveling effect, often raising the abilities of disadvantaged children, while lowering the abilities of children of higher socioeconomic status (Morgan & Gross, 1982; Gerbner, Gross, Morgan, & Signorielli, 1980).

Television also influences children's concepts of gender roles. Children who watch more television tend to view the male and female roles in a more stereotypical fashion (Williams, 1986). Television also shapes what is called the "world view." By being exposed to television, children form attitudes and beliefs about their world. This is a good thing insofar as television reflects reality. To the extent that it doesn't, this exposure can cause problems. For example, children who are heavy viewers of television, especially realistic action shows such as police dramas, tend to view the world as a mean and scary place and as more dangerous than it really is (Rubinstein, 1983). Television instills a certain paranoia in these children and may make them more fearful and less trusting of other people.

On the other hand, television has the real potential for having a positive influence on children. Television may be providing a great deal of good information and exposure to ideas and events. For the first time, children, no matter how distant from major centers their homes are, are growing up learning about events on the entire planet. Television may thus broaden horizons and stimulate the curiosity of millions of children who would not otherwise have known what the world might hold for them. Also, certain educational goals can be pursued through programs particularly designed for children.

Studies have shown that children can acquire good nutritional habits from television programs designed to teach such habits (Campbell, 1982), and that children can learn to help other people or to give to charity from watching such behavior modeled on television. They can also learn to cooperate, to share, and to be imaginative under certain conditions, all from being exposed to particular television shows (Pearl, Bouthilet, & Lazar, 1982). Appropriate television programming can enhance friendliness and generosity. It can help children learn to delay immediate gratification as well as to overcome fears of strange and unusual situations (Rubinstein, 1983). So, television certainly has its "good side."

ADOLESCENCE (12 TO 18 YEARS OF AGE)

In some cultures, there is no social period of adolescence. There are only childhood and adulthood. In such cultures, when a child enters puberty, it is a sign that he or she has become an adult. In many groups and tribes throughout the world, the social change from childhood to adulthood happens in a single day. For instance, a boy might be summoned by his elders, along with other children his age, and taken to a place where a ceremony is conducted that marks his passage into adulthood. Such a ceremony is called a *rite of passage*.

For American children, the transition to adulthood is slow, marked by many separate changes over the period of adolescence. A 12-year-old girl may be allowed to wear pantyhose and makeup, a 16-year-old person may be allowed a driver's license, an 18-year-old person may marry or vote, and in many states individuals must be 21 years old to drink alcoholic beverages. For this reason, adolescents often count smoking, drinking, driving, and sexual activities as indications of adult status. The physical changes that occur during adolescence also mark an important transition from childhood to adulthood.

Storm and Stress?

In 1904, G. Stanley Hall published the first scientific study of adolescence in a two-volume work titled *Adolescence*, which had a tremendous influence on subsequent thought concerning the subject. Hall saw adolescence as a period of storm and stress, of many changes in direction and swings in mood, of turbulence and turmoil. To some degree, this is true; adolescents must face many changes, and these experiences may alter their self-concept and attitudes considerably (McKinney & Moore, 1982). Adolescents must deal for the first time with sexual relationships, the choice of a career, political decisions, economic alternatives, and a host of other "adult" tasks.

Modern researchers, however, while recognizing that many tasks and changes are taking place in adolescents' lives, have come to the conclusion that adolescence isn't necessarily a time of unusual turbulence and conflict. The conclusion of an 8-year nationwide study, conducted at the University of Michigan, that examined 2000 adolescent males as they went from tenth grade to the age of 20 years was that adolescence was fairly benign. The study revealed that self-concept, outlook on life, and a number of other attitudes were well formed by the time adolescents entered tenth grade. Moreover, when the subjects were retested at age 20 years, their attitudes were found not to have undergone the dramatic changes that might be expected following a turbulent adolescence (Bachman, O'Malley, & Johnston, 1978). Other studies have confirmed these findings (Offer, Ostrov, & Howard, 1981; Petersen, 1987). According to one group of researchers,

The most dramatic ... findings are those that permit us to characterize the model American teenager as feeling confident, happy, and self-satisfied—a portrait of the American adolescent that contrasts sharply with that drawn by many theorists of adolescent development, who contend that adolescence is pervaded with turmoil, dramatic mood swings, and rebellion. (Offer, Ostrov, & Howard, 1981, pp. 83–84)

There certainly are stresses associated with being an adolescent, but we might be hard pressed to say for sure that these stresses are more severe than those a person encounters during other times. Even so, although adolescence may generally not be a time of unusual turbulence, *some* adolescents may have a particularly difficult time coping with the changes that occur. There are a great range and diversity of adjustment patterns during adolescence (Boxer, Gershenson, & Offer, 1984).

Adolescent Physical Development

Behind each maturational change lies the development of essential cells within the brain and body. Every aspect of a child—his or her emotions, skills, and aptitudes—is related either directly or indirectly to his or her body structure. Feelings about body image underlie many social interactions. This is especially true during adolescence, when many obvious physical changes occur (Chumlea, 1982). Psychologists need to be aware of this physical growth and development and especially of the effects these changes may have on a person's emotions or behavior. In fact, everyone should have a greater knowledge of the physical changes that take place during adolescence in order to understand better an adolescent's feelings and behavior. For instance, although most people know that girls mature earlier than boys, few people give much thought to the fact that adolescents of the same age and sex may vary from completely prepubescent to completely physically mature (see Figure 3.13). Yet the timing of physical development can profoundly affect adolescents and their interactions with peers and the school environment.

At the beginning of adolescence, a number of physical changes occur. These changes are controlled by genetics and hormones. One change is the development of sexual maturity, which occurs during a period called **puberty.** Researchers have found that the hormone melatonin, which is secreted by the pineal gland, is responsible for the onset of puberty. As puberty nears, melatonin concentrations show a marked decrease (Waldhauser et al., 1984).

At the onset of puberty, the testes or ovaries enlarge. During puberty, the reproductive system matures, and secondary sexual characteristics such as facial hair or breast development emerge. Growth also undergoes a marked acceleration. Height and weight increase dramatically, and body proportions change. These changes are known as the **growth spurt.** It begins in girls about 2 years earlier than it does in boys, and it lasts for 2 to 3 years.

Adolescent Cognitive Development

In most individuals, the ability to reason and think becomes fully developed during adolescence. Erik Erikson (1968) has described adolescence as a time of identity crisis when the questions "Who am I?" and "What is my role in life?" become dominant themes. Without the cognitive changes that occur, it would not be possible for adolescents to consider such complex philosophical questions.

The adolescent first becomes capable of dealing with the logic of combinations, which requires the simultaneous manipulation of many factors, either singly or in conjunction with one another. Second, the adolescent becomes able to use abstract concepts to make thought more flexible. Third, the adolescent becomes able to deal with the hypothetical as well as the real (Piaget

PUBERTY
The stage of maturation in which the individual becomes physiologically capable of sexual reproduction.

GROWTH SPURT
The time during puberty in which an adolescent's growth undergoes a marked acceleration.

FORMAL OPERATIONS
In Piaget's theory, the final stage of cognitive development. It is characterized by abstract thinking that is no longer tied to physical objects or events.

& Inhelder, 1969). According to Piaget, this last step is the most advanced form of cognition, and it defines the **formal operations stage.** Not all people reach this stage, but a majority do.

Preadolescent thinking appears to depend substantially on concrete perceptions. But adolescents who have reached the stage of formal operations can analyze the logic of a statement without becoming tied to its concrete properties. In a series of experiments, adolescents and preadolescents were asked to judge whether certain statements were true, false, or impossible to know (Osherson & Markman, 1974–75). The subjects were told that the experimenter

◆ **FIGURE 3.13**

Differing degrees of pubertal development in children of the same sex at the same chronological age (in years). (SOURCE: Adapted from Tanner, 1969.)

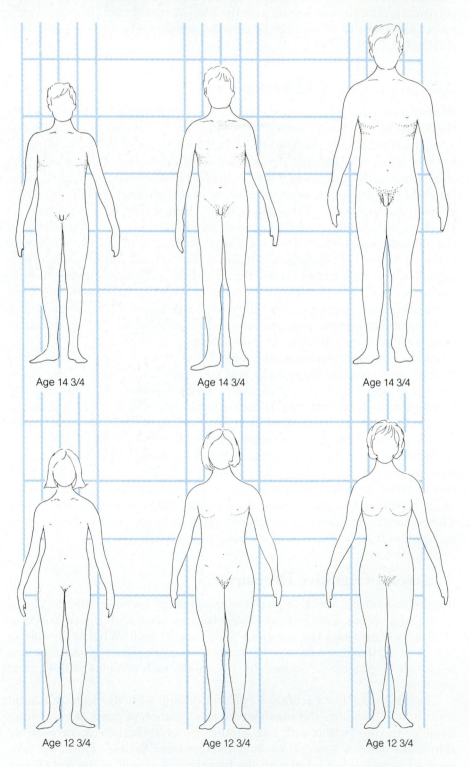

Age 14 3/4   Age 14 3/4   Age 14 3/4

Age 12 3/4   Age 12 3/4   Age 12 3/4

had hidden a poker chip in his hand, and that "either this chip is green, or it is not green." Most of the preadolescents thought that it was impossible to judge because they could not see the hidden chip. The adolescents, however, were able to deal with the concept of green abstractly. They realized that something must either be a particular color or not be that color. The adolescents realized that the statement had to be true. For that matter, everything in the universe is either green or not green. Preadolescents have trouble comprehending such an abstraction. This is one of the reasons why educators usually wait until children reach adolescence before they seriously present them with abstractions such as algebra.

Developmental Tasks of Adolescence

As their cognitive skills develop, adolescents are confronted for the first time with the overwhelming complexities and abstract qualities of the world. Suddenly, nothing is simple. Religious values, political values, social concepts, and questions about personal identity seem to raise endless hypothetical possibilities from which the adolescent is expected by parents and society to draw conclusions and to adopt a life philosophy. During our adult years, we have time to organize and make sense of this confusion. We adopt a philosophy. We take political, social, and moral positions and incorporate them into our identity. In this sense, adulthood has a stability that is not immediately available to the adolescent.

Our culture demands that adolescents handle a number of developmental tasks. They must come to terms with their physical development. They must face sexual relationships. They must exhibit social maturity in dealings with both sexes. They must realize and adjust satisfactorily to their masculine and feminine role. They must achieve emotional independence from parents and other adults. Decisions about whether to marry or to have children become more immediate. Adolescents are expected, therefore, to develop a philosophy and moral ideology and to achieve socially responsible behavior. Sometimes, they feel as though all these demands are pressing in on them at the same time, which can be particularly stressful.

Adolescents often discover that the ideal representations of the world they have developed through formal operational thinking are tempered by the realities of their first real job.

CHOOSING A CAREER. Pursuing a career choice is an essential part of adolescent development. "The adolescent becomes an adult when he undertakes a real job" (Inhelder & Piaget, 1958, p. 346). To cognitive researchers such as Piaget, adulthood meant serious training for work and the beginning of an occupation.

Piaget argued that once adolescents enter the formal operations stage, their newly acquired ability to form hypotheses allows them to create representations that are too ideal. The existence of such ideals, without the tempering of the reality of a job or profession, rapidly leads adolescents to become intolerant of the nonidealistic world and to press for reform and change in a characteristically idealistic and adolescent way. Piaget said:

True adaptation to society comes automatically when the adolescent reformer attempts to put his ideas to work. Just as experience reconciles formal thought with the reality of things, so does effective and enduring work, undertaken in concrete and well-defined situations, cure dreams. (1967, pp. 68–69)

Of course, youthful idealism is often courageous and true, and no one likes to give up dreams. Perhaps, taken slightly out of context, as it is here, Piaget's statement seems harsh. What he was emphasizing, however, is the way reality can modify and shape idealistic views. Some people refer to such modification as maturity. Piaget argued that attaining and accepting a vocation is one of the best ways to modify idealized views and to mature.

ROLE CONFUSION
A consequence of the failure to establish a sense of identity during Erikson's fifth psychosocial stage. Without a sense of identity, the individual will be confused about his or her role in society and will find it difficult to form a life philosophy or create a stable base on which to build a career or have a family.

As careers and vocations become less available during times of recession, lowered productivity, or rising unemployment, adolescents may be especially hard hit. Such difficult economic times may leave many adolescents confused about their roles in society. For this reason, community interventions and government job programs that offer summer and vacation work are not only economically beneficial but also, in the view of many developmental psychologists, help to stimulate the adolescent's sense of worth (Vondracek & Lerner, 1982).

ADDRESSING THE CRISIS OF IDENTITY.   According to Erik Erikson, the adolescent's main task is to develop an acceptable, functional, and stable self-concept. Those who succeed, Erikson argues, will establish a sense of identity, and those who fail will suffer **role confusion.** Erikson believes that the adolescent needs to maintain a meaningful connection with the past, establish relatively stable goals for the future, and keep up adequate interpersonal relationships in the present in order to feel a sense of personal identity. "The adolescent needs to integrate a conscious sense of individual uniqueness" with "an unconscious striving for a continuity of experience" (Erikson, 1968, p. 165).

Other psychologists have found the concept of identity a valuable tool for understanding adolescent psychosocial development. Research and case studies have indicated that resolution of the identity crisis depends greatly on the adolescent's society, family, and peer groups. Ideally, adolescents achieve their new identity by abandoning some of the values and aspirations set for them by their parents and society, while accepting those that they wish to choose.

The Peer Group

Peer groups provide an important social structure for most adolescents (Brown, Eicher, & Petrie, 1986). Adolescent peer groups vary in size and interests, and adolescents often belong to more than one group at a time. Peer groups may consist of a few close friends of the same sex or a large group of both sexes who hang out together. Such groups can be sources of ready companionship, adventure, and standards against which adolescents compare themselves. As a result, a peer group can have a powerful effect. Its influence on adolescents is a worldwide phenomenon (B. M. Newman, 1982).

To become or stay a member of a desired peer group, an adolescent needs a certain amount of social skill or desirability. Adolescents who lack social skills or who are deemed socially undesirable by their peers may find themselves living a lonely or isolated existence, and eventually they may be adversely affected by the experience. To avoid such rejection, adolescents may go to extremes to please a group. They may radically change their dress, appearance, behavior, or jargon. Adolescents who attempt to adjust to a group that has views opposed to those held by their families may face considerable conflict and stress (P. R. Newman, 1982).

A peer group may function as a reference against which adolescents compare themselves. Quite often, differences between an individual and the group are resolved by the person's decision to change behavior to match the group's norms. The group can influence susceptible teenagers either to perform or to avoid misconduct (Brown, Clasen, & Eicher, 1986). It has been shown, however, that peers are less likely to encourage misconduct than they are other types of behavior (Brown, Lohr, & McClenahan, 1986).

Adolescents' evaluations of themselves may have a great bearing on which peer group or group behaviors they find most important and desirable (Eisert & Kahle, 1982). One study discovered that college students (mean age 18.95 years) who evaluated themselves as having high self-esteem chose to join and emulate groups that were composed of students of high socioeconomic status (Filsinger & Anderson, 1982). This is not a one-way street, however; the groups with whom adolescents choose to compare themselves can, in turn, directly affect an adolescent's self-evaluation. No doubt, the students who associated and became friends with high-status peers further enhanced their own self-esteem.

SUMMARY

◆ Developmental psychology is the study of age-related changes in human behavior over the lifespan. By understanding human development, psychologists know what to expect at different developmental stages, and they learn the extent of human growth and development.

◆ One of the first researchers to emphasize the entire lifespan was the psychoanalyst Erik Erikson. He views human development as a progression through eight psychosocial stages, during which we are faced with conflicts that must be resolved for healthy development to occur.

◆ Three issues have played a great role in developmental psychology. They are nature versus nurture, stability versus change, and continuity versus discontinuity.

◆ The DNA in your body is arranged in a code, which is determined by the vertical sequence of the base pairs. Each section of code is called a gene. These genes are arranged on small bodies, called chromosomes, located within the nucleus of each cell.

◆ From the turn of the century until the 1950s, most researchers considered the newborn to be a helpless creature who was not competent in any sense of the word. Subsequent research has demonstrated that newborn infants possess remarkable capacities, including the ability to learn from a very early age.

◆ The term used to describe a genetically determined biological plan of development that is relatively independent of experience is maturation. Human physical growth seems to be mainly a function of maturation, and, to a large extent, so is motor development.

◆ Although the human infant doesn't appear to possess a fully integrated personality in its first few days of life, scientists have observed that newborns do exhibit considerable differences in temperament shortly after birth. The New York Longitudinal Study examined 140 children from birth to adolescence and classified them as having "easy" or "difficult" temperaments.

◆ The mechanism of attachment, especially between the infant and its mother, has been intensely debated and investigated by developmental theorists, and the theoretical orientation taken by most researchers over the years has changed.

◆ In a series of widely publicized experiments, psychologist Harry Harlow and his colleagues separated rhesus monkeys from their mothers at an early age and placed them with artificial wire and cloth surrogate mothers. Even rhesus monkeys fed by only the wire mother formed strong attachments to the cloth mother and spent most of their time hugging it.

◆ In recent years, the most accepted theoretical orientation concerning the development of attachment has been toward an intraorganismic perspective.

◆ Mary Ainsworth investigated the parameters of human attachment. Her studies have included a 1-year longitudinal investigation of infant attachments in the home; a 20-minute laboratory test known as the strange situation; and an assessment of the variables that determine the quality of infant attachment.

◆ The full range of human emotion appears to be present at birth, but emotional expressions do not become more differentiated and obvious until the infant becomes older.

◆ An intensive review of the day-care literature has indicated that high-quality nonfamilial care does not seem to have negative effects on young children. The data concerning infants younger than 1 year of age are unclear.

◆ Some of the most apparent and interesting changes that take place in the first 6 years of life are cognitive in nature. In Jean Piaget's view, cognitive development is the combined result of the development of the brain and nervous system and of experiences that help the individual adapt to her environment.

◆ Piaget's first two stages—the sensorimotor (0 to 2 years) and the preoperational (2 to 7 years)—take place during infancy and early childhood.

◆ The sensorimotor stage is characterized by a lack of fully developed object permanence, whereas the preoperational stage is characterized by the beginning of internalized thought processes.

◆ One of the cognitive advances of young children is that they begin to develop a gender understanding or comprehension that they are either male or female at about the age of 3 years. By about age 7, they usually have acquired gender constancy and realize that gender is determined by unchanging criteria and is unaffected by one's activities or behavior.

◆ One of the major achievements of young children is the ability to begin to regulate their own behavior. To achieve this ability, children appear to rely on internalized value and reward systems.

◆ Mothers and fathers who have assumed the traditional gender roles behave differently toward their children. From the time the child is born, mothers are more likely to assume caregiving responsibilities, even if the fathers are home and are free to help.

◆ Although parents usually are considered to be the primary agents of socialization for the young child, in most families the child has a relationship with one or more siblings.

◆ Peers begin to have an increasing effect as children grow older. Longitudinal studies have shown that throughout the second year of life, a child's social behavior becomes more consistent and predictable.

◆ When children first meet, they are more likely to become friends if they are able to exchange information successfully, establish a common-ground activity, and manage conflicts.

◆ One of the most obvious occurrences during the preschool years is the development of play. Playing can be simple and unstructured, as in a game of hide-and-seek, or it can be more complex and structured, as in a school basketball game. Social scientists generally believe that play has evolved because it has a function.

◆ Research on child development has generally focused on white, middle-class, American children. Modern researchers in the United States are beginning to examine minority children in earnest and to consider the cultural distinctions that make African Americans, Asian Americans, Hispanic Americans, native Americans, and other minority groups different from one another, as well as different from children of white European heritage.

◆ Middle childhood is a time of continued physical growth and motor development. On average, girls and boys perform physically at about the same level, at least until the beginning of puberty.

◆ According to Jean Piaget, at about the time children enter school, they develop the ability to rely on logical operations to form their conclusions. This is known as the stage of concrete operations. During this time, child develop the ability to conserve.

◆ During middle childhood, many institutions have an influence on a child's socialization. Among them are the family, peers, schools, and even nonpersonal institutions, such as the media, including television.

◆ Throughout their school years, children rely on their peers as important sources of information and may use peers as standards by which to measure themselves.

◆ Television has been shown to have a great influence on the development of school-aged children. Television programs have such wide-ranging content that they probably have both a detrimental and a beneficial effect on children.

◆ For American children, the transition to adulthood is slow, marked by many separate changes over the period of adolescence.

◆ Modern researchers have come to the conclusion that adolescence isn't necessarily a time of unusual turbulence and conflict.

◆ Adolescents are expected to develop a philosophy and moral ideology and to achieve socially responsible behavior.

◆ A peer group may function as a reference against which adolescents compare themselves. Adolescents' evaluations of themselves may have a great bearing on which peer group or group behaviors they find most important and desirable.

❧ SUGGESTIONS FOR FURTHER READING

1. Comstock, G., & Paik, H. (1991). *Television and the American child*. San Diego, CA: Academic Press. An examination of the effects of television on children in America. It includes a discussion of viewing habits and their outcomes.

2. Dworetzky, J. P. (1993). *Child Development* (5th ed.). St. Paul, MN: West Publishing. A college level introduction to child and adolescent development.

3. Lamb, M. E. (1981). *The role of the father in child development*. New York: Wiley. An examination at a relationship overlooked for many years; the child and father. Lamb discusses the father's important role in shaping gender identity and as an important figure in the child's life.

4. Lusk, D., & McPherson, B. (1992). *Nothing but the best: Making day care work for you & your child*. New York: Teacher's College Press. A comprehensive guide to selecting good day care and how to deal with problems related to day care.

5. Santrock, J. W. (1990). *Adolescence* (4th ed.). Dubuque IA: Brown. A good college level introduction to adolescent development.

6. Stoppard, M. (1990). *The first weeks of life*. New York: Ballantine. An examination of the neonate and his or her reaction to the world.

7. Sutherland, P. (1992). *Cognitive development today: Piaget and his critics*. New York: Taylor & Francis. A thorough examination of the controversies generated by Piaget's theory. Examines data both supporting and attacking Piaget's views.

Chapter Four

Lifespan Development II: Adulthood and Aging

PROLOGUE

SOME THINGS WE NEVER OUTGROW

Party dresses! Flirtation! Heart palpitations!

It must be an eighth-grade dance, or the junior prom, or a first fraternity party!

No. It's a singles' dance at the local seniors' center!

If the idea of older people dating and falling in love doesn't jibe with your picture of late adulthood, you're out of step with the times. As people are living longer, are staying healthier, and are less likely to live with grown children, the ranks of dating seniors have grown significantly. Researchers interviewed dating couples, ages 60 to 92 years, in a midwestern metropolitan area and were surprised at what they found.

As is the case with younger people, the older daters regularly suffered the "sweaty-palm syndrome." They experienced a heightened sense of reality, awkwardness, problems concentrating, perspiring hands, heart palpitations, and anxiety when the loved one was away. "When you fall in love at my age there's initially a kind of 'oh, gee!' feeling," commented one 68-year-old divorcée. "It's just a little scary" (Bulcroft & O'Conner-Roden, 1986, p. 68).

Like younger people, the older people saw dating as quite distinct from friendship, and they tended to start "going steady" fairly rapidly. They often developed committed, long-term, monogamous relationships, complete with sexual involvement, although they didn't necessarily plan to get married. Also like younger daters, they were selective about what they told their families. "I have a tendency to hide his shoes when my grandchildren are coming over," commented one woman (Bulcroft & O'Conner-Roden, 1986, p. 69).

The older daters enjoyed candlelight dinners, flowers and candy, movies, and dances every bit as much as younger daters. Some also reported going camping, enjoying the opera, and flying to Hawaii for the weekend. They said that physical intimacy was certainly important, but experience had taught them not to count on passionate love lasting forever. They knew the

CONTENTS

119

value of compassionate love and appreciated passion as "the frosting on the cake" (Bulcroft & O'Conner-Roden, 1986, p. 69).

The next time you find yourself dismissing an older couple as "cute" or believing that romance is only for the young, think again. Has anyone ever flown with you to Hawaii for a romantic weekend?

IN THIS CHAPTER, we will examine physical, cognitive, personality, and social development from early adulthood through old age. Along the way, we'll destroy some of the myths and stereotypes commonly held about each age group. We'll conclude the chapter with a discussion of the end of life, of death and dying.

EARLY ADULTHOOD (18 TO 40 YEARS OF AGE)

Had early developmental psychologists heeded the "lifecycle" lessons of Confucius, the Talmud, or Shakespeare, they might have lengthened the scope of their inquiry to include adulthood. But they focused only on infancy, childhood, and adolescence and created a state of knowledge graphically illustrated by this table of contents, taken from a very fine human development textbook (Nash, 1978):

— Conception
— Prenativity
— The Femaleness of Man
— The Perinativity
— Infancy
— Preschool Period
— Preadolescence
— Adolescence
— Death

After charting our course through adolescence, researchers either ignored adults completely, or perpetuated the myth that after 18 years it's all downhill. Then we die.

Perhaps when you're 17 years old, it does seem possible that "after 18 it's all downhill, then we die." But then comes the shock of discovering that you're 19, then 20, then 21. (By the way, the shock keeps right on happening every year, and there appears to be no way to stop it.) Following this discovery, the whole idea of adulthood becomes very interesting because it's happening to you of all people!

A key reason that developmental researchers ignored adult development for so long is that age-related changes in behavior, cognition, physical development, and the like are much more difficult to identify and trace in adulthood than in childhood. In childhood, these changes often are due to forces of biological maturation and are universal. In adulthood, however, social and cultural factors play a much greater role than do biological ones, and we can't count on the changes to be universal. In fact, the timing of the changes varies so much from one person to another that chronological age becomes an increasingly poor guide as we grow older, and it becomes far more difficult to generalize about a group of, say, 50-year-old adults than about a group of 6-year-old children. Bernice Neugarten explains the situation this way:

The stereotype has it that as people age they become more and more like one another. In truth, they become less and less alike. If you look at people's lives, they're like the spreading of a fan. The longer people live, the greater the differences between them. (Neugarten & Hall, 1980, p. 78)

Another important reason for the early emphasis on childhood stemmed from the writings of Sigmund Freud who, as you recall, placed a special emphasis on childhood as a formative time. Later, Erik Erikson helped to extend this emphasis into the adult years.

As we proceed to examine adult development, we will look at *general trends* in physical, cognitive, and social functioning. But we must remember that, among a group of adults of the same age, the *variability* in functioning will be enormous.

The investigation of adulthood finally got underway as diligent and committed researchers followed many of the subjects from prestigious early projects into adulthood (Eichorn, Clausen, Haan, Honzik, & Mussen, 1981). As mentioned, another key factor was the publication of Erik Erikson's highly influential essay, "The Eight Ages of Man," in 1950. In this essay, Erikson described his stage theory of personality development, which, unlike Freud's or Piaget's theories, included adulthood as well as childhood and adolescence. The key issues we deal with in adulthood, Erikson says, are intimacy versus isolation, generativity versus stagnation, and ego integrity versus despair.

Also during the 1950s, some key longitudinal studies of adult development were initiated. These included the Seattle Longitudinal Study, the AT&T Longitudinal Studies of Managers, the Baltimore Longitudinal Study of Aging, and the Duke Longitudinal Study (Schaie, 1983).

Despite the progress, however, the study of adult development today is still what researcher Daniel Levinson called "Dozens of Fragments in Search of an Animating Source and a Unifying Plot" (Levinson, 1986, p. 8). The fragments cover personality, cognitive, and moral development, career choice, marriage and the family, biological development, and so on. Studies of one fragment, however, usually have no evident connection with studies of others, and no larger, empirically tested "scheme of things" exists in which to place the findings (Levinson, 1986).

Erik Erikson (1902–   ). Erikson's psychosocial theory of human development helped to shift emphasis to the whole lifespan and to the influence of social forces.

Physical Development in Early Adulthood

Most Olympic and professional athletes are between 18 and 40 years old. However, it is not just athletic superstars who accomplish amazing feats during these years. College students carry full course loads, work, play sports, and socialize with friends. Young executives work 70 hours per week to establish their careers. Mothers care for babies, run a home, and pursue careers or graduate school. Young construction workers do hard physical labor 8 hours per day, then play softball. Middle-aged folk recall their early adult years and wonder how they ever did it!

The outstanding vitality of early adulthood comes about because so many of our body's organ systems work so well together at that time. The nervous system coordinates the movement of muscles that are stronger than ever. The heart pumps blood effectively from the lungs to these working muscles, and the lungs move air in and out and exchange vital gases with peak efficiency. The kidneys remove waste materials from the blood, the endocrine glands synchronize metabolic processes, and the blood's buffer systems maintain the body's chemical environment with tremendous ease and efficiency.

Health Status in Early Adulthood

For most people, early adulthood is a time of exceedingly good health. Illnesses are usually short-lived, and are readily shaken off with minimal disruption to

Regular exercise during young adulthood can help reduce the chances of physical problems later in life.

POST FORMAL OPERATIONAL THOUGHT
A type of thinking that may develop in late adolescence or adulthood. No widely accepted definition yet exists; in general, characteristics include an ability to understand relativity, contradiction, and subjectivity and to integrate these into decision making.

normal routine. Fewer than 1 percent of young adults are incapacitated by chronic illnesses (Scanlon, 1981).

Despite this generally positive picture, many people do begin to develop certain *silent diseases* that will be problematic later on. These diseases include the beginnings of atherosclerosis (hardening of the arteries owing to a buildup of plaque from cholesterol), emphysema (a breakdown of lung tissue) in heavy smokers, cirrhosis (a hardening and failure) of the liver in heavy drinkers, kidney diseases, AIDS, and arthritis (Scanlon, 1981). The leading causes of death prior to age 35 years are accidents, homicide, and suicide, followed by AIDS, cancer, and heart disease. After 35 years, however, strokes, cancer, and heart disease emerge as the leading causes of death, followed by accidents, suicide, and homicides (National Center for Health Statistics, 1991).

Cognitive Development in Early Adulthood

Developmental psychologists have tried to answer a difficult question for many years: Is there a stage of cognitive development beyond Piaget's formal operational stage? Many researchers and theorists have attempted to describe what is sometimes called **post formal operational thought.**

One of the earliest attempts to examine how adults think was a study conducted by William Perry and his colleagues in the 1960s. The team interviewed 67 Harvard students during each of the students' 4 years in college. Although variability in development was certainly evident among these students, there was a general progression in how they thought about knowledge and about their place in the world.

Initially, many students believed that every question had a single right answer and that professors should either teach the right answers or give them assignments to force them to figure out the right answers for themselves. Up to this point, the students' formal operational skills served them well, but they needed a different kind of thinking for what was to come.

As the students were exposed to more and more competing and contradictory opinions about life, they began to see that knowledge and values are relative and that each person has to work out these issues for himself; no "authority" is going to give us the answer or tell us what is the *right* thing to do. At first, the students were overwhelmed by the diversity of ideas and tended to conclude that, since everyone has a right to his own opinion, one opinion may be as valid as any other. Eventually, however, most of them came to see that some opinions are more reasonable and more easily defended than are others. They eventually realized that, even though they could understand many different options and conflicting opinions, they had to make choices and commitments that were "right" for their own lives, at least at that time (Perry, 1970).

Whether such mature reasoning is "qualitatively" different from what Piaget considered to be formal operational thought is still debatable, however. For this to be demonstrated, further research would have to show that such mature thought processes as Perry described depend upon, and are separate from, the reasoning of formal operational thought (Commons, Richards, & Kuhn, 1982). From Piaget's point of view, such maturity of thought as Perry discovered is based on formal operations and is not an advance beyond it.

Personality Development in Early Adulthood

As we have seen, both our bodies and our minds are still undergoing dynamic changes right through early adulthood. But what about our personalities? Not surprisingly, researchers are finding that adult personalities change, too. In one longitudinal study, changes and stability of key personality variables were assessed over a 50-year period. One of the researchers' conclusions is especially relevant to early adulthood:

Great shifts in personality organization are ordinarily thought to occur during adolescence, but these findings suggest that more marked shifts occur, not during adolescence, but at its end when most people make the profound role shifts entailed by entry into full-time work and marriage. (Haan, Millsap, & Hartka, 1986, p. 225)

What are the demands and developmental tasks of early adulthood? What happens to our personalities as we go through these years? We'll look first at the theory set forth by Erikson in his classic essay that we mentioned earlier, then we'll look at more recent theorists who have added to or otherwise modified Erikson's ideas.

INTIMACY VERSUS ISOLATION. According to Erikson, our chief developmental task in early adulthood is to form an intimate relationship with another person. If the young adult is secure in his identity, he should be "eager and willing to fuse his identity with that of others" (Erikson, 1950, p. 263). This may occur in the context of intimate friendships, which require personal compromises and sacrifices, as well as in the special relationships of spouses or lovers. According to Erikson, if people do not form intimate relationships at this stage, they run the risk of becoming isolated and self-absorbed.

YOUTH: A SPECIAL TIME OF LIFE. In 1960, Erikson was appointed professor at Harvard. Kenneth Keniston, a young faculty member, was asked to assist Erikson in preparing a course on the lifecycle. Recalling those years, Keniston says that Erikson's theories—especially his ideas about the identity crisis—caught on quickly among undergraduates, but Erikson worried about this because he feared students would use them to justify evading responsibility. "Having an identity crisis," he said, "is neither a boast nor an excuse for late papers" (Keniston, 1983, p. 29).

Keniston was impressed by Erikson's theories, but the more he taught, the more college students he found who did not fit Erikson's scheme. He decided that perhaps there was another, optional stage of development that some people experience after adolescence but before becoming full-fledged adults; he called this stage "**youth**" (Keniston, 1968, 1970).

The people Keniston called "youth" were men and women of college and graduate-school age who were unable to settle down as their parents had, who didn't consider themselves to be adults, and who often strongly challenged the existing social order. Many were at least partly dependent on their parents financially, and they often postponed marriage because it implied settling down. Keniston knew that there have always been tiny minorities of people—often the very creative or very disturbed—who fit into this category. In the 1960s, however, many young people did so.

"Youths" aren't just adolescents who refuse to grow up. They usually have already lived through the identity upheavals of adolescence and have a fairly stable sense of who they are. In their view of what must be done in the world, they are "less impelled by juvenile grandiosity than by a rather accurate analysis of the perils and injustices of the world in which they live" (Keniston, 1970, p. 634). They begin to experience a real tension between themselves and society, and they struggle with the question of how they can simultaneously maintain their personal integrity and be an effective member of society. Keniston's ideas are still quite influential.

CAREER CONSOLIDATION. While Keniston was developing his ideas about youth, George Vaillant was gathering and analyzing data for the Grant Study,

YOUTH
A stage of development that some people go through following adolescence and prior to assuming the full responsibilities of adulthood.

SELF-IN-RELATION THEORY
A theory in which the goal of personality development is a deepening capacity for competence in relationships, in contrast to theories that emphasize autonomy, self-reliance, and separation from other people.

a major longitudinal study of adult development. In 1937, William T. Grant, philanthropist and owner of the W. T. Grant variety stores, provided Harvard with a substantial sum of money to make a systematic inquiry into healthy students who function well (Heath, 1945). The Grant Study staff recruited 268 Harvard undergraduates who had good grades, were especially self-reliant, and were superior to their peers in both emotional and physical health. Ninety-five of these men were followed into their fifties.

Vaillant, an admirer of Erikson's work, found that the Grant Study data provided objective support for Erikson's contention that an individual must pass sequentially through the stages of development. The men who failed to master one stage generally weren't able to master later stages. However, the age at which the men mastered the stages varied considerably. The data further suggested, Vaillant concluded, that Erikson's theory needed to be modified somewhat (Vaillant, 1977).

Vaillant decided to insert a new stage, *career consolidation*, between Erikson's stages of intimacy versus isolation and generativity versus stagnation. He found that, between ages 20 and 30 years, most of the men in his study married and established strong friendships. Once the men had established these relationships, while they were roughly 25 to 35 years old, they focused almost exclusively on their careers. They were not good at self-reflection, and much like conscientious elementary-school children, "they were good at tasks, careful to follow the rules, anxious for promotion, and willing to accept all aspects of the system" (Vaillant, 1977, p. 216). They sacrificed play for work, deceived themselves about the adequacy of their marriages and careers, and became "colorless, hardworking, bland young men in 'gray flannel suits'" (Vaillant, 1977, p. 217). In the section on middle adulthood in this chapter, we'll see what happened to these "bland young men" in middle age.

Beginning and selecting a career is another important milestone for young adults.

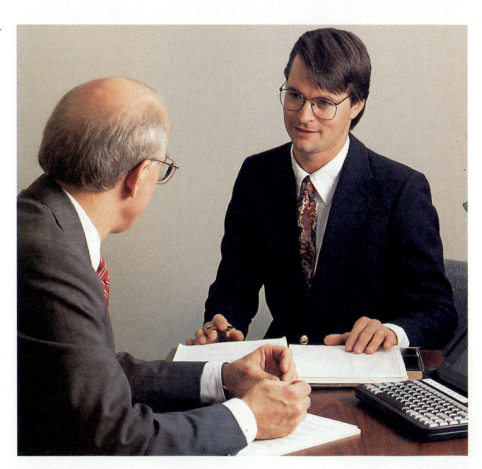

BUT WHAT ABOUT WOMEN?

Vaillant's subjects were all men; Erikson calls his lifecycle stages the eight ages of *man*. Psychologists have repeatedly constructed models of normal development based on observations of male subjects, and repeatedly women have not fit these models. You can imagine what some people thought was the "obvious" conclusion: There must be something wrong with women!

Not until the late 1960s did writers begin to challenge this conclusion and to develop theories of normal female development. To date, there have breene relatively few broad-based studies of women, and many people believe that women's lives, especially in adulthood, defy classification and categorization even more than men's do. Much of the research on women has focused on the effects of traumatic experiences such as rape. Although this is in the process of changing, by and large the writings on normal female development are still in the theoretical, hypothesis-generating stage, similar to where the writings on men were in the 1950s.

In 1976, Jean Baker Miller published *Toward a New Psychology of Women*, a landmark book that, among other things, set forth the proposition that "women's sense of self becomes very much organized around being able to make and then to maintain affiliation and relationships" (Miller, 1976, p. 83). Miller's book and the writings of Nancy Chodorow (1974; 1978) formed the basis for what has come to be called the **self-in-relation theory** of development (Surrey, 1985). According to this theory, the basic goal of development is the "deepening capacity for relationships and relational competence" (Surrey, 1985, p. 2), and development consists of "a process of growth within relationships, where both or all people involved are encouraged and challenged to maintain con-

nection and to foster, adapt, and change with the growth of the other" (Surrey, 1985, p. 8).

Think, for a minute, about how this theory contrasts with Erikson's. His initial stage of trust versus mistrust does emphasize the importance of relationships, but the developmental tasks of his next four stages are aimed at increasing autonomy, self-reliance, and separation from other people. He believes that intimacy is possible only after a person is secure in his identity. Self-in-relation theory maintains that intimate relationships are important throughout life and that the development of a woman's identity is closely tied to those relationships, be they with parents, siblings, other relatives, friends, lovers, spouses, or whomever.

This difference can be readily seen in how the two genders approach moral questions. Carol Gilligan has argued that women typically approach moral problems differently than men (Gilligan, 1982). Gilligan states that women, more often than men, will focus on the interpersonal aspects of moral problems and on minimizing suffering. These assertions are based on interviews Gilligan conducted with many women who were facing interpersonal crises. In this view, the moral development of women can better be understood as a morality of mercy and caring, which leads women, more often then men, to consider the concrete issues of who is being hurt, what has happened each step of the way, and how help can be forthcoming. All of these considerations emphasize the interpersonal nature of women's development. No understanding of "human" adult development can ever be complete without a full understanding of how the development of women and men may differ.

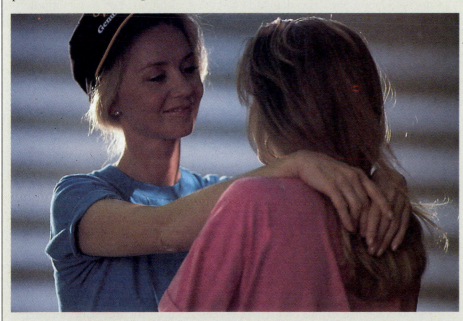

Self-in-relationship theory stresses the need for deep caring relationships as opposed to autonomous states of self reliance. Many researchers are now finding it easier to understand the social development of women in terms of self-in-relation theory.

Loving and Working in Early Adulthood

Most young adults hope and dream that their lives will include an intimate relationship and love. These desires generally focus on the idea of marrying and having a traditional family. If we look at the most recent census data, however, it becomes clear that these hopes and dreams have a greater chance of being shattered than ever before.

Changes in family makeup and household characteristics have attracted researchers' attention, and recently studies have been launched to examine the family as a unit, especially its lifecycle, in order to understand better the stresses and strains a family is likely to face over the years.

THE FAMILY LIFECYCLE.   Many researchers have come to believe that family life moves through a series of stages, each with unique developmental tasks to which the family members must attend. Drawing on the work of earlier researchers, David Olson, Hamilton McCubbin, and their associates (1983) divided the family lifecycle into seven stages:

   I. Young married couples without children
  II. Families with preschool children
 III. Families with school-age children
  IV. Families with adolescents in the home
   V. Launching families
  VI. Empty-nest families
 VII. Families in retirement

They then conducted a cross-sectional survey of 1140 couples and 412 adolescents located in 31 states. Each stage was represented by at least 100 couples or families chosen because they were "normal," "typical," and "ordinary" intact units. Although the length of time a given family might spend in a particular stage varied enormously, the early adulthood years typically encompassed stages I through III. Key stresses in each of these stages are shown in Figure 4.1, and the next paragraphs summarize their main characteristics:

Marriage is a major step commonly taken by young adults. Many others, however, opt for different relationships or singlehood.

◆ *Stage I: Young married couples without children.* The average age of stage I husbands was 27.6 years; that of wives was 25 years. These couples were not yet faced with the demands of young children, but were formulating and negotiating goals for themselves as individuals and as a couple as well as mutually acceptable lifestyles. Financial burdens and work-related difficulties were their key problems. Their relationships were characterized by considerable cohesion and adaptability, and they reported high marital and family satisfaction. Only 10 percent said they had ever considered separation or divorce.

◆ *Stage II: Families with preschool children.* The average age of stage II husbands was 30.5 years; that of wives was 29 years; that of the oldest child was 3 years. Children spent most of their time at home, and the families were essentially child-centered. Parents were preoccupied with the children's growth and nurture and were primary sources of information and control. Family cohesion and overall quality of life were high for stage II families, but adaptability and marital and family satisfaction dropped off slightly. Twenty-one percent of the couples now reported having considered separation or divorce.

◆ *Stage III: Families with school-age children.* Average ages of stage III husbands and wives were 35 and 33, respectively, and the couples had been married for an average of 11 years. They generally had two children, and the average age of the oldest was 9 years. Family incomes did not increase

Researchers have found that family cohesion remains high when young couples have children, but the responsibility that goes along with having children can sometimes put a strain on the relationship.

from stage I to stage III, perhaps because many mothers with small children either were unable or chose not to work outside the home.

Given that there were now more people to support on the same amount of money as in earlier stages, you might suspect that financial problems would be paramount for these families. However, parents reported that the most stressful life events came from activities related to the children's education and socialization, which meant more activities outside the home. Cohesion continued to be high, and these families actually reported slightly higher levels of marital satisfaction than did stage II families. However,

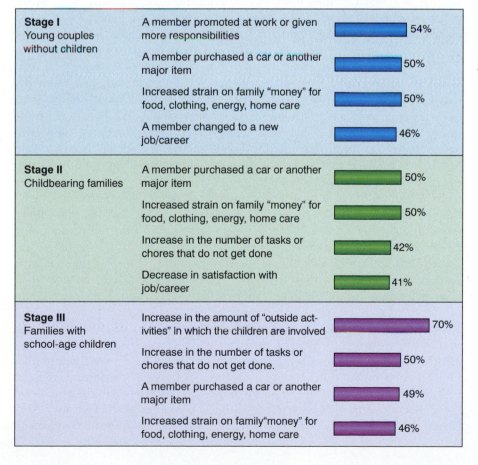

Stage I
Young couples without children

A member promoted at work or given more responsibilities	54%
A member purchased a car or another major item	50%
Increased strain on family "money" for food, clothing, energy, home care	50%
A member changed to a new job/career	46%

Stage II
Childbearing families

A member purchased a car or another major item	50%
Increased strain on family "money" for food, clothing, energy, home care	50%
Increase in the number of tasks or chores that do not get done	42%
Decrease in satisfaction with job/career	41%

Stage III
Families with school-age children

Increase in the amount of "outside activities" in which the children are involved	70%
Increase in the number of tasks or chores that do not get done.	50%
A member purchased a car or another major item	49%
Increased strain on family "money" for food, clothing, energy, home care	46%

◆ **FIGURE 4.1**

Profile of family stresses and strains in early adulthood. The top four stressors for families in each stage are listed. (SOURCE: *Adapted from Olson et al., 1983, pp. 125–126.*)

COHABITATION
A living arrangement in which two unrelated adults of the opposite sex share the same household. In the past, it has implied sexual intimacy, but it does not necessarily do so today.

HOMOSEXUAL
A person who is sexually attracted to a member of his or her own sex.

HETEROSEXUAL
A person who is sexually attracted to a member of the opposite sex.

scores of family satisfaction continued to drop, especially for the women. This meant that the spouses continued to be happy with their relationship, but that they were not so pleased with the family interactions as a whole.

We noted at the beginning of this section that the hopes and dreams of marrying and raising children in an intact traditional family don't always come true. Let's look at some of the alternatives.

UNMARRIED HETEROSEXUAL COHABITATION. Four centuries ago, Peruvian Indians practiced unmarried heterosexual **cohabitation** to give the man's family time to assess the woman's capacity to handle both household chores and field work. Despite its long history, cohabitation has generally been held in ill repute by many Americans. In the 1950s, it was commonly called "living in sin." In 1968, a 20-year-old student was censured by Barnard College for living off campus with her boyfriend (Danziger, 1978). Even in the 1990s, in some states unmarried cohabitation is still a crime, based on "crimes against chastity."

Bad reputation notwithstanding, the number of unmarried couples—two unrelated adults of the opposite sex sharing the same household—almost quadrupled from the early 1970s to the late 1980s and now stands at about 2 million (U.S. Bureau of the Census, 1985). As the numbers have increased, society as a whole has become more accepting and less likely to regard cohabitation as morally wrong.

HOMOSEXUAL RELATIONSHIPS. **Homosexual** relationships are often as diverse as heterosexual ones, but long-term homosexual relationships may actually be more egalitarian than heterosexual ones are. Contrary to the notion that, in a homosexual relationship, one person assumes the "male" role and another the "female" role, most such relationships are patterned after a best friend–roommates model. Since both members of the couple usually work and make comparable incomes, one is not dependent on the other in the way that a traditional housewife often is dependent on her husband for financial support.

When Erikson talked about intimacy he spoke only of **heterosexual** relationships. Homosexuals can have the same kind of intimacy and mutuality that heterosexuals have. Raphella Sohier assessed issues of mutuality and generativity in a small group of homosexual subjects. She found that these people not only loved each other, but also extended their caring to other people, both gay and straight. They were involved in churches and social endeavors and had active political affiliations; and one couple shared responsibility for the son of one of the partners.

In describing their mutuality, the subjects spoke of "love for each other," "shared interests," "deep respect," "complementary, not antagonistic, differences in character," and a "strong physical attraction." Sohier concluded that "homosexuals appear to express generativity in the same fashion as heterosexuals: loving and caring for children, teaching responsibilities for the next generation, and mutual caring for each other and for others outside their immediate relationship" (Sohier, 1986, p. 36).

SINGLEHOOD. Single is a general term that includes people who are divorced, are widowed, or have never married. The proportion of people in the United States who are over 18 years of age and have never been married has jumped dramatically in the last two decades. In 1960, 17 percent of men and 12 percent of women had never married; by 1984, these numbers had increased to 26 percent and 18 percent, respectively (U.S. Bureau of the Census, 1985). When divorced and widowed people are added, singles obviously now constitute a large portion of our population, and they form a heterogeneous group of people.

Peter Stein (1983) has categorized singles according to whether their single status is voluntary or involuntary and stable or temporary, as shown in Table 4.1. Obviously, people often move among these categories. "Ambivalents" may postpone marriage for so long that they eventually come to accept being single as their probable, although unwanted, life state. Similarly, people who have resolved never to marry may meet "Mr. or Ms. Right" and find themselves reconsidering their "firm" decision not to marry.

Much research has supported the view that being single isn't as healthy as being in a relationship. In every industrialized country, premature death rates are higher for single than for married adults (Carter & Glick, 1976). Similarly, married people generally have been found to enjoy better mental health and to be happier with their lives. Single men, especially, have consistently scored lower on indices of health and well-being than have either married men and women or single women (Austrom, 1984). A central problem with this research, however, has been that most of the data were collected in nonrandom fashion from pathological populations such as patients in state mental hospitals or prisoners. Moreover, most studies did not control for differences in education, socioeconomic status, or income.

In an attempt to tease out the contribution of marital status to health and well-being, one researcher studied 517 single and 521 married middle- to upper-middle-class adults (mean age, 35.13 years), living primarily in urban areas in Canada. He found no differences between marrieds and singles on self-reports of physical health, but the historical finding that singles are not as satisfied with their lives was again borne out. He also found that psychological well-being was due more to the social support of friends and family than to marriage (Austrom, 1984). This is one reason single women probably get along better than do single men—they tend to have richer and more intimate friendships and to turn to these friends in times of trouble. Furthermore, most single people are not particularly *unhappy* with their lives; it's just that, on average, married people are happier.

WORKING AND CREATIVITY.   In his now-classic studies, H. C. Lehman (1953; 1954; 1958) identified early adulthood as a time of peak creativity. He identified key works in science, medicine, psychology, and miscellaneous creative fields produced during a 200-year span and determined the ages of the contributors when they made their major accomplishments. He found that in all fields except astronomy, people did their *most outstanding work* between the ages of 30 and 40 years. They may actually have done the work at even younger

Albert Einstein (1879–1955). Einstein was given the Nobel Prize in physics for work he had completed before he was 26 years of age. By the age of 36, Einstein had essentially made his contribution to physics.

TABLE 4.1 ◆ A TYPOLOGY OF SINGLEHOOD		
TYPE	VOLUNTARY	INVOLUNTARY
Temporary	Never marrieds and formerly marrieds who are postponing marriage by not actively seeking mates, but who are not opposed to the idea of marriage. (Ambivalents)	Those who have been actively seeking mates for shorter or longer periods of time, but have not yet found mates; those who were not interested in marriage or remarriage for some period of time but are now actively seeking mates. (Wistfuls)
Stable	Never marrieds and formerly marrieds who have chosen to be single; persons who for various reasons oppose the idea of marriage; religionaries. (Resolveds)	Never marrieds and formerly marrieds who wanted to marry or remarry, have not found a mate, and have more or less accepted being single as a probable life state. (Regretfuls)

SOURCE: Stein, P. J., "Singlehood," in *Contemporary Families and Alternative Lifestyles*, edited by E. D. Macklin and R. H. Rubin. Copyright 1983 by Sage Publications. Reprinted by permission.

Many people in their later years make their greatest contribution as mentors by teaching the young.

MENTOR
A more experienced person in a work setting who provides guidance, support, and advice about career development to a less experienced person.

ages, because there is always a time lag between an initial accomplishment and its recognition.

Many explanations of, and objections to, Lehman's conclusions have been advanced, however. For example, older workers often get channeled into administrative positions and have less time for research. They become **mentors**, more concerned with fostering the development of younger people than with pursuing their own creative activities. Furthermore, other studies have not found the marked age trends of Lehman's study (Cole, 1979). Older folks can take heart in the fact that Brahms was in his forties before he wrote his first symphony, and Tolstoy was in his fifties when he wrote *War and Peace*. Nevertheless, the sheer number of contributions Lehman looked at from so many different historical periods suggests that many people's creative powers do peak in early adulthood.

🧬 MIDDLE ADULTHOOD (40 TO 65 YEARS OF AGE)

The "prime of life," the "empty nest," the "command generation," the "midlife crisis"—at one time or another, people have used each of these phrases to try to capture some "essence" of middle age. On the one hand, people in the age group of 40 to 65 years do have power. They are usually the ones who govern nations, anchor families, direct industry, lead citizen groups, teach the young, and take care of the old. They become better at self-reflection and feel more confident of their ability to handle the complexities of life. The combination of power and a more mature level of personality integration often brings with it an extremely valuable coping skill—the ability to laugh at oneself. Jokes that begin, "You know you're over 40 when . . ." abound. They're funny, however, only if told by someone over 40!

Ironically, having power brings with it a startling realization: If I'm in charge of so many things, I must be grown up! One 50-year-old woman captured the realization that she was now a full-fledged adult in this way:

You always have younger people looking to you and asking questions. . . . You don't want them to think you're a blubbering fool. . . . You try to be adequate as a model. (Neugarten, 1968a, p. 95)

Still other events signal that a person has grown up. Teenage children go off to college. Elderly parents may look to their middle-aged children for emotional or financial support. When the parents die, their children suddenly become the "older generation." A middle-aged person's time perspective changes. Rather than calculating the years since her birth, she may wonder how many more years she will live. If she hasn't already done so, she will go to her lawyer to make a will and may be startled when her lawyer asks, "And what about the disposal of the body?" Whatever her body's shortcomings, she never before intended to "dispose" of it!

Understandably, middle-aged people begin to ask how to make the most of the years remaining. A new job? A new romance? A guru? For many, but not all people, these issues precipitate an emotional upheaval rivaled only by adolescence.

Unfortunately, not many data are available about adult development in middle adulthood. Daniel Levinson thinks this has come about because "adults hope that life begins at 40—but the great anxiety is that it ends there." This "pervasive dread about middle age," he says, results in researchers being unwilling to look closely at this period of life (Levinson, Darrow, Klein, Levinson, & McKee, 1978, p. ix).

Joanne Stevenson advanced a less dreary reason. She noted that "troublesome" groups such as adolescents or the elderly are studied more often. For whom are these groups troublesome? For the middle-aged! As it is the middle-aged who are in command, they dictate that these are the appropriate groups to study (Stevenson, 1977). It may be that the recent interest in studying middle age has come about because middle-aged people themselves are more willing to admit to the more troublesome aspects of their age. Levinson acknowledges that, at age 46, he "wanted to study the transition into middle age in order to understand what I had been going through myself" (Levinson, Darrow, Klein, Levinson, & McKee, 1978, p. x).

Let's turn now to a consideration of some of the physical changes that commonly occur between ages 40 and 65 years.

Most people in middle age find that they are becoming more and more curious about the meaning of life. Some turn to religion or philosophy for answers, while a few search for a guru to give them the answers. Others may become gurus.

Physical Development in Middle Adulthood

The bodies and good health we take for granted in early adulthood begin to demand more attention in middle adulthood. Charts of aging show gradual, usually insignificant, decrements in functioning. But for many people, the decrements don't *feel* insignificant. Ironically, the realization that they're getting older often prompts people to start exercising and eating better, so they may actually whip themselves into better shape than they were in during early adulthood!

APPEARANCE. The thinning and graying of hair that start during early adulthood continue; by age 50 years, most people have some gray hair. By the end of middle adulthood, stiff hairs have begun to appear in men's noses, ears, and eyelashes and on women's upper lips and chins (Troll, 1985).

Skin continues to lose elasticity, and more wrinkles appear. Body shape changes as the bust and chest grow smaller, and the abdomen and hips grow larger. If a middle-aged person has a sedentary lifestyle and consumes as many calories as when he was younger, he must contend with the infamous middle-age spread. Women are confronted with our society's double standard about appearance: while gray hair and wrinkles are thought to make men look "distinguished," they are perceived to make women look "old." In a society as youth-conscious as ours, looking old can be quite a blow to a woman's self-esteem. This double standard may be changing somewhat, however; mag-

FARSIGHTED
The inability to see close objects clearly.

azines and television advertisements have begun to feature attractive graying women as models.

THE SENSES. Middle-aged people often joke that their arms aren't long enough to read the newspaper. They mean that they've become **farsighted**—unable to see objects up close—and they now often need reading glasses. The good news is that people often become less nearsighted as they age and may no longer need glasses to see objects far away. The high-frequency hearing loss begun earlier continues, but usually is not noticeable. Taste buds become less sensitive around age 50 years, and sensitivity to touch drops sharply after about age 45 years (Troll, 1985).

STRENGTH AND ENDURANCE. In the early 1960s, Nathan Shock and his colleagues did a classic, cross-sectional experiment in which they investigated the physical capacity to "do work." They measured this by having subjects lie on their backs and turn the crank of an ergometer, an apparatus that measures effort. The crank could be adjusted to turn more stiffly or more easily. The researchers measured the subjects' blood pressure, heart rate, cardiac output, oxygen consumption, and carbon-dioxide production. They thereby determined the amount of "work" the subjects could do and have cardiac function return to normal within 2 minutes after they stopped working. Measured this way, the work rate peaked at about age 28 years, then declined by about 10 percent by age 40.

The 65-year-old subjects' work rate was about 81 percent of that of the 40-year-old subjects, or 73 percent of the peak work rate. The researchers also found that strength of the dominant hand usually peaked at about age 35, then decreased very slowly; the 65-year-old men still had about 86 percent of the hand-grip strength of the 40-year-old men (Shock, 1962).

What this means is that our strength and endurance gradually decline during middle adulthood, although exercise can certainly slow the *rate* of decline. In his early fifties, Dick Bass, a businessperson with relatively little mountain-climbing experience, got himself into condition and became the first person to climb the highest peaks on each of the seven continents—including Mount Everest, the highest mountain in the world, which at age 55 he was the oldest person ever to climb (Bass, Wells, & Ridgeway, 1986). Given the fitness boom of recent years, it's conceivable that the decreases Shock found would be less drastic if he repeated the study today.

HEALTH STATUS. People entering middle adulthood can look forward to becoming less susceptible to colds and allergies and to a decrease in their incidence of accidents. However, the "silent diseases" of early adulthood now become vocal as chronic illnesses make their appearance. Various arthritic problems often begin in the early forties, and diabetes often begins between ages 50 and 60 years. Peptic ulcers, hypertension, and health problems brought on by excessive alcohol consumption also are major concerns. The adverse consequences of smoking may appear in the form of chronic bronchitis, emphysema, lung and oral cancers, and coronary-artery disease.

Although our response to a middle-aged person's dying usually is shock—"He was too young to die!"—the death rate for people 45 to 54 years of age is twice that for those 35 to 44 years old. For people aged 55 to 64 years, the rate is more than twice that of those aged 45 to 54 years. Prior to age 55 years, the leading causes of death in middle adulthood are cancer, heart disease, AIDS, accidents, and liver disease. After age 55 years, heart disease assumes the leading position, followed by cancer, strokes, and accidents (National Center for Health Statistics, 1991).

Sexuality in Middle Adulthood

Cultural myths about changes in the reproductive systems and sexual functioning are no doubt a major reason people dread middle age. Historically, menopausal women have been described in the most disparaging terms imaginable. Consider these words from a 1966 article in the reputable *Journal of Nervous and Mental Disorders* :

And then, after giving "the best years of her life" to raising a family and caring for the house, she finds herself reduced by the climacteric [the process of menopause] to a shriveled shell of a woman, used up, sucked dry, de-sexed, and, by comparison with her treasured remembrances of bygone days of glory and romance, fit only for the bone heap. (Sillman, 1966, p. 166)

The man caught up in the so-called male menopause is thought to be depressed, hypochondriacal, and impulsive—prone to quit a job or leave a 25-year-old marriage for a 25-year-old woman. These are the myths. Let's look now at some of the realities.

Menopause means "cessation of menses." It is said to have occurred when a woman has gone 12 consecutive months without a menstrual period. The biological changes involved in menopause usually take place over a period of 2 to 5 or even 10 years, known as the **climacteric.** One of the early signs of menopause is irregular menstrual periods. These irregularities are caused by fluctuating levels of the hormone **estrogen**, which gradually decreases during the climacteric. The average age at which menopause occurs in the United States is now about 50 years.

Everything from backache to serious mental illness has been attributed to the decrease in estrogen at menopause. However, only hot flashes and atrophy of the vaginal lining are now thought to be caused by the drop in estrogen. **Hot flashes** are unexpected, brief waves of a hot, feverish sensation that vary widely in intensity, frequency, and duration. Some women experience a warm glow, while others become drenched with perspiration. Some have only a few hot flashes over many years; others have several each day. Chills frequently

MENOPAUSE
The complete cessation of menstruation, which usually occurs during middle age. It is said to have occurred when a woman has lived 12 consecutive months without having a menstrual period.

CLIMACTERIC
The 2- to 10-year period during which the biological changes involved in menopause take place.

ESTROGEN
Hormones produced primarily by the ovaries that are responsible for the development of female secondary sex characteristics. The adrenal glands of the male also produce some estrogen, but the hormone is found primarily in females.

HOT FLASHES
Sudden, brief sensations of heat, often accompanied by reddening of the skin. They are thought to be caused by the fluctuating levels of hormones during the climacteric.

By middle age, some of the more silent physical disorders may make an appearance. Among these are diabetes and high blood pressure.

ATROPHY OF THE VAGINAL LINING
Thinning, loss of elasticity, drying, and itching of the vaginal walls caused by decreasing estrogen levels during the climacteric.

TESTOSTERONE
A hormone that is produced primarily by the testes and is responsible for the development of male secondary sex characteristics. The adrenal glands of the female also produce some testosterone, but the hormone is found primarily in males.

ANDROGENIC HORMONES
The androgens. Male hormones that regulate sexual development; produced by the testes and the adrenal cortex.

precede or follow a hot flash. Rarely do other people know when a woman is having a hot flash. The only thing they might notice is a slight change in the woman's coloring.

Atrophy of the vaginal lining, which is by no means as dreadful as it sounds, occurs when the lining of the vagina becomes drier, thinner, and less elastic, which may make intercourse somewhat painful. Lubricating creams can alleviate this problem, but an active sex life is just as effective a treatment.

Younger women who have not gone through menopause usually view the prospect as much more traumatic than women who have gone through it say it really was (Cohen, Coburn, & Pearlman, 1980). Studies that have asked postmenopausal women about their experience report that, by and large, the women feel better physically and that their sex lives often improve since they no longer have to worry about getting pregnant (Cohen, Coburn, & Pearlman, 1980).

IS THERE A MALE MENOPAUSE?   Researchers have generally found that the level of the male hormone **testosterone,** which is in part responsible for sexual desire, decreases gradually with age. However, studies have found that healthy older men had about the same level of testosterone as did younger men. Interestingly, in these older men, levels of sexual activity correlated highly with levels of testosterone (Vermeulen, 1983; Tsitouras, Martin, & Harman, 1982). Despite this optimistic finding, some very gradual hormonal changes do occur during middle adulthood, and most men notice that their testes and penis get a bit smaller (Talbert, 1977). Sperm production also decreases gradually, but many men are able to father children right into late adulthood.

The term *male menopause* has been jokingly used by the popular media to refer to the emotional and behavioral changes some men experience during middle age, which we'll consider later in this section. In reality, however, the hormonal changes men undergo are by no means as pronounced as those middle-aged women experience. Although stories about the male menopause may make good reading, no such physiologically based event exists.

SEXUAL INTEREST AND ACTIVITY.   The variability noted earlier among adults is nowhere more evident than in their sexual interest and activity. Some people report declining interest in sex by the time they turn 40 years old; others report an active sex life well into their eighties.

As the middle years progress, many men notice that it takes longer and requires more direct stimulation to achieve an erection, but they usually can maintain the erection longer than they could when they were younger. Orgasm may occur less frequently, contractions may be fewer and less intense, and it may take longer to achieve another erection following ejaculation. These changes may produce substantial performance anxiety, which is probably the chief cause of sexual dysfunction in middle-aged men. Life events such as job reversals or problems at home that make a man feel powerless can also lead to sexual difficulties.

Many women find that their interest in sex increases markedly during middle adulthood. This may happen in part because **androgenic hormones,** which are strongly implicated in sexual desire, decrease only slightly during menopause, while estrogen, which suppresses the effects of androgens, drops significantly. Moreover, following menopause, women are free to enjoy sex without fear of pregnancy.

In concluding this section, we urge you not to panic the next time you hear middle-aged people lamenting the loss of their youthful bodies. While poor health can certainly make people feel old, by and large, the negative physical changes of middle adulthood are gradual, and by no means do they fling most of us onto the bone heap!

Cognitive Development in Middle Adulthood

Just as middle-aged people sometimes joke about their physical stamina, they also may joke about their mental capacities, and the jokes are funny so long as people know in their hearts they're not true. After all, it's convenient to invoke our aging memory when we "forget" to attend our teenage son's heavy-metal concert. But the jokes are not so funny when a person really does feel her intellect is failing and she can't think as well as she once did.

PROBLEM FINDING AND SOLVING.   In the section on early adulthood, we raised the question of whether there is a stage of cognitive development beyond Piaget's stage of formal operations. One theorist who thinks there is maintains that a primary distinguishing characteristic of this postformal stage is the ability to identify relevant problems and to ask important questions about ourselves, our life's work, and the world around us. Such *problem finding* enables us to look at old problems in a new light and to think of creative new solutions (Arlin, 1984).

CREATIVITY.   Another important aspect of adult cognitive development is creativity. Now you may be wondering whether my memory is failing and I've forgotten that I told you in the previous section that creativity peaks in early adulthood. No, I haven't forgotten. The work of Lehman discussed earlier focused on *superior* contributions. Wayne Dennis has assessed creativity in another way—by looking at the *total output*, not just at the *superior* works, of 738 male scholars, scientists, and artists who lived to be at least 80 years old. Judged this way, middle adulthood, especially the decade of the forties, is clearly the most productive time in all fields except mathematics and chamber music (Dennis, 1966).

It would seem, then, that creativity peaks at different times for different careers. In general, artists peak at an earlier age than do scholars and scientists. This is probably in part because the latter usually need more formal education and must gather and evaluate more data before producing a work.

Personality Development in Middle Adulthood

DEVELOPMENTAL TASKS OF MIDDLE ADULTHOOD.   "Mature man needs to be needed," says Erik Erikson (1950, pp. 266–277). In his scheme, this need becomes most evident in middle adulthood. The key developmental task at this stage of life, Erikson says, is the achievement of **generativity,** which is a person's concern about establishing and guiding the next generation. Generativity is not necessarily limited to having and caring for one's own children. Rather, it includes many forms of "care for the creatures of this world" (Erikson, 1950, pp. 267–268). Even institutions, such as monasteries, that forbid their members to procreate are careful to transmit their ideas to succeeding generations, and many uphold service to other people as a central value.

Erikson believes that a person who does not achieve generativity feels "a pervading sense of stagnation and personal impoverishment" that may be so pronounced that it amounts to physical or psychological invalidism (Erikson, 1950, p. 267). No one would deny that the need to be needed can become burdensome at times. Far worse, however, at least in Erikson's scheme, is to renounce that need and not teach and guide other people.

George Vaillant's research provided more objective support for Erikson's scheme in that the best adjusted of the Grant Study men were those who, by

GENERATIVITY
The concern about establishing and guiding the next generation, and other forms of "care for the creatures of the world."

this stage in life, enjoyed contributing to other people's lives both at home and at work. Furthermore, Vaillant proposed that a period that he called *keeping the meaning versus rigidity* might come after Erikson's generativity versus stagnation stage and before the final stage of ego integrity versus despair.

The best adjusted of the Grant Study men tried to ensure that their culture would be carried on rather than replaced, and they had attained a degree of tranquillity. The worst adjusted became rigid in their conviction that the good old days were gone forever and that only immorality, decline, and decay lay ahead for humanity. One of the well-adjusted men commented, "I don't plan on leaving any big footsteps behind, but I am becoming more insistent in my attempts to move the town to build a new hospital, support schools, and teach kids to sing" (Vaillant, 1977, p. 232).

THE MIDLIFE CRISIS: MYTH OR REALITY?   During the 1970s, the media picked up the term *midlife crisis* and made it part of our vocabulary. The term's meaning is not always clear, however. George Vaillant notes that the term "brings to mind some variation of the renegade minister who leaves behind four children and the congregation that loved him in order to drive off in a magenta Porsche with a 25 year old striptease artiste" (Vaillant, 1977, p. 222). In reality, few people do anything quite this colorful at any point in their lives!

Because a person in this process is often irrational, his spouse, children, boss, and parents may think he or she is sick. But, in fact, the desire to question and modify our lives stems from the healthier parts of our beings. "No life structure can permit the living out of all aspects of the self," researcher Daniel Levinson says. "In the Mid-life Transition these neglected parts of the self urgently seek expression" (Levinson, Darrow, Klein, Levinson, & McKee, 1978, p. 200).

Some middle-aged adults may make external changes, such as undertaking divorce, remarriage, or shifts in occupation and lifestyle. Others may make internal changes in social outlook, personal values, what they wanted to give the world, and what they wanted to be for themselves. Those who negotiate the midlife transition successfully may become more compassionate, more reflective, and more genuinely loving of themselves and of other people. Failure

While many people picture a mid-life crisis as involving an older man leaving his family to race off in a sports car with a younger woman, most middle-aged men and women never face such an upheaval.

to do so may result in their lives becoming "increasingly trivial or stagnant" (Levinson, 1986, p. 5).

A SECOND ADOLESCENCE? George Vaillant was 33 years old when he first interviewed the Grant Study men, who were then 46 years old. Alarmed by what he heard, he rushed to his 54-year-old department chairperson and exclaimed, "I don't want to grow up; these men are all so ... so depressed" (Vaillant, 1977, p. 226). Interestingly, the Grant Study men who had the "best outcomes" later said that the period from 35 to 49 years was the happiest in their lives; the calmer period from 21 to 35 years had been the unhappiest.

What Vaillant first saw as depression among these men, he later attributed to their having reached a stage in life where they were better able and more willing to acknowledge the painful experiences of their lives. No longer content to be "bland young men in gray flannel suits" (Vaillant, 1977, p. 217), they had, like adolescents, "once more become explorers of the world within" (Vaillant, 1977, p. 220). They often experienced some emotional turbulence due to dissatisfaction with careers, marriages, children, themselves, and miscellaneous events of middle age. The period did require growth and change, but, Vaillant says, it was better characterized as a "transition" than as a "crisis" for most of the men.

THE EMPTY-NEST SYNDROME. While the stereotype of the man caught up in a midlife crisis is Vaillant's renegade minister in the magenta Porsche, the stereotype of the middle-aged woman is that of a depressed housewife mourning the loss of her maternal role as her children grow up and move away. This **empty-nest syndrome,** especially when combined with menopause, is reputed to be so traumatic for women that it constitutes a major crisis.

Lillian Rubin interviewed 160 middle-aged women, all of whom had children who were leaving or had left home. All the women had given up jobs for at least 10 years following the birth of a child, and a majority were homemakers. Rubin found that only one suffered the classical symptoms of the empty-nest syndrome. In fact, almost all responded to their children's leaving home "with a decided sense of relief" (Rubin, 1979, p. 15). The most ambivalent women were those closest to the transition.

Other research has supported Rubin's findings (Cohen, Coburn, & Pearlman, 1980). One group of researchers found that women experienced their most difficult and tumultuous transitions when their children were preschoolers or late adolescents. The postparental stage was characterized by "increases in life and marital satisfaction, and positive personality changes such as increased mellowing, patience, assertiveness, and expressivity" (Harris, Ellicott, & Holmes, 1986, p. 415).

It is probably safe to say that parents experience a multitude of conflicting emotions as they see their children grow older and move away from home. For women whose identity and self-esteem have come solely from their mothering role, their children's leaving home might indeed cause them to feel a profound sense of loss. And fathers who never had much time for their children may be shaken and feel deeply depressed when they realize that "suddenly" their children are gone. However, there are no data that would lead us to conclude that most people suffer from anything approaching a full-blown empty-nest syndrome, just as there are no data that lead us to conclude that any kind of midlife crisis is either universal or inevitable.

We can say in conclusion, then, that despite the stereotypes, most men and women do not experience serious midlife crises or the empty-nest syndrome. Of those who do, however, women are quite likely to express a sense of crisis during midlife, and many men suffer from the empty-nest. Both of these prob-

EMPTY-NEST SYNDROME
Depression parents may experience when their grown children leave home.

lems are important in middle adulthood, and gender is far less tied to either of them than the stereotypes would lead us to believe.

Relationships in Middle Adulthood

Middle adulthood is characterized by multiple connections. Some researchers call people this age the *sandwich generation* because they get caught between the demands of their growing children and those of their aging parents. In addition, most have spouses, friends, siblings, and other relatives to whom they must attend.

It's not as though these connections didn't exist earlier; most did. But they take on new significance in middle age because people's changing time perspective, plus their increased awareness of their own and other people's mortality, makes them realize how precious, and sometimes how problematic, these relationships are. Let's turn now to look at some of these relationships in traditional families.

THE FAMILY LIFECYCLE.   In the previous section on early adulthood, we began looking at the cross-sectional family-lifecycle research that David Olson, Hamilton McCubbin, and their colleagues (1983) have been conducting on intact families. You may recall that these researchers divide the family lifecycle into seven stages.

While there is enormous variability in the length of time a given family spends in a particular stage, the middle adulthood years normally encompass stages IV through VI. We will use Olson and McCubbin's framework as we examine key developmental tasks, stresses, and relationships within traditional families during the parents' middle years (see Figure 4.2).

◆ *Stage IV: Families with Adolescents in the Home.* A major developmental task for stage IV families is to balance freedom with responsibility as the teenagers mature and begin to separate from the family. Moreover, if they haven't already done so, parents must start developing outside interests and activities in anticipation of their children's leaving home.

Olson and McCubbin's stage IV couples had been married an average of 19 years, and the average ages of husbands and wives were 43 and 40 years, respectively. These couples had an average of three children, and the average age of the oldest was 16 years. Although about one-third of the wives worked full time, and sometimes one of the spouses held both full- and part-time jobs, the average annual family income continued to be similar to the three previous stages.

As we can see in Figure 4.2, these families experienced financial pressures as more money was needed for essentials such as medical and dental care, food, clothing, and education. In addition, they had a hard time getting household chores done and were stressed by the children's involvement in so many outside activities. Moreover, parents reported much difficulty managing teenage children.

Among Olson and McCubbin's couples, the large majority were happy and satisfied, as was the case in the previous stages. However, overall marital satisfaction scores dipped slightly. Seventeen percent of the women and 15 percent of the men said they had considered divorce or separation at some point. Disagreement over how to deal with teenage children probably is a major source of contention between parents during these years. Moreover, couples often clash over financial problems, which may increase during middle adulthood.

◆ *Stage V: Launching Families.* Providing appropriate assistance to release young adults into the world and simultaneously maintaining a supportive

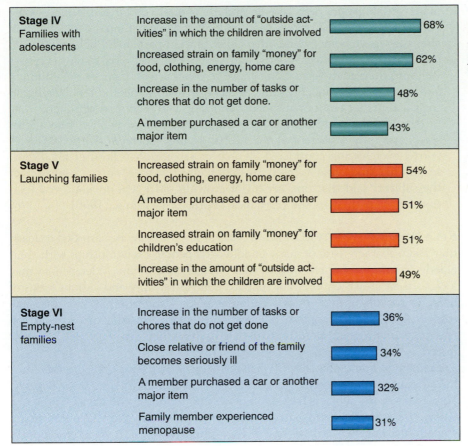

◆ FIGURE 4.2

Profile of family stresses and strains in middle adulthood. The top four stressors for families in each stage are listed. (SOURCE: *Adapted from Olson et al., 1983, pp. 127–129.*)

home base are the major developmental tasks of stage V families. Most of Olson and McCubbin's couples at this stage had been married about 25 years. The average age of the husbands was 49 years, and that of the wives was 46 years. Stage V families had an average of four children, and the average age of the oldest was 23 years. Almost one-fifth of the men reported working a combination of full- and part-time jobs; only stage II men reported as high a percentage of multiple jobs.

In Olson and McCubbin's sample, marital satisfaction reached its lowest point during this stage. However, the percentage of spouses who had contemplated separation or divorce was about the same as for stage IV families—18 percent of the wives and 16 percent of the husbands. These families were beset by many of the same financial and intrafamily strains as were stage IV families, and these were likely sources of the couples' problems.

◆ *Stage VI: Empty-Nest Families.* The developmental tasks of stage VI families are to strengthen the marriage relationship and to maintain kin ties with older and younger generations. Olson and McCubbin's couples who no longer had children in the house had been married an average of 34 years. Average ages were 58 years for the husbands and 56 years for the wives. These families had an average of three children, and the average age of the oldest was 32 years.

Financial pressures lessened a bit at this stage, but families continued to have trouble getting everything done that needed to be done. Moreover, illness and death of friends or relatives became sources of stress for more and more families.

We have relatively few data about these relationships, but the theme we've sounded so many times before certainly is true now: There is enormous variability in how parents and their adult children interact. Some children become completely independent of their parents financially soon after they leave home, while others look to their parents for help with down payments for homes, car loans, and sometimes even day-to-day expenses well into their adult years. Some move to other towns, marry, have children, and become self-sufficient, while others live near home and rely heavily on their parents for emotional support and help with the grandchildren.

Among Olson and McCubbin's couples, marital satisfaction rose at this stage, and only 4 percent of the husbands and 9 percent of the wives reported ever having considered divorce or separation (Olson et al., 1983). In another study that focused on middle-aged women only, 75 percent of the subjects said that one benefit of growing older was an improved relationship with their spouse (Cohen, Coburn, & Pearlman, 1980).

RELATIONSHIPS WITH ELDERLY PARENTS.   You may be surprised to learn that a key characteristic of many middle-aged people's relationships with their elderly parents is reciprocity (Brubaker, 1985). Just as the older people may look to their grown children for support, companionship, and various forms of help, so too many middle-aged children look to their parents for the same things. As the years progress, however, the balance usually tips so that the parents actually need more from their children than they can give them in return.

One study found that 80 to 90 percent of elderly people report that they have frequent contact with their children (Brubaker, 1985). In another study, 50 percent of the subjects had seen one of their children the day of or the day before the interview, and only 13 percent of the men and 9 percent of the women had not seen at least one of their children for more than one month. A major reason for the lack of visits in the latter cases was that the children lived in other towns, and these children often maintained frequent telephone contact with their parents (Shanas, 1979).

When elderly people have been asked how they feel about their relationships with their children, both nursing home residents and community-dwelling elderly have reported that they do not feel abandoned or neglected and are basically satisfied with their family relationships. However, 25 percent of the institutionalized elderly parents did report not receiving as much love and support from their children as they would like (Seelbach & Hansen, 1980).

RELATIONSHIPS WITH SIBLINGS.   Sibling relationships are unique by virtue of sheer duration. Most people have brothers or sisters within visiting distance throughout their lives. Relationships among middle-aged siblings may be characterized by closeness, rivalry, hostility, or apathy. Rarely does closeness originate in adulthood, although it may be enhanced by siblings moving nearer to each other geographically or by their becoming more tolerant and understanding of each other (Ross & Milgram, 1982). Difficulties may arise, however, if one sibling changes her values, lifestyle, or socioeconomic status, and the other does not.

In general, research suggests that most middle-aged adults get along well with their siblings and enjoy the relationships. However, relatively few discuss intimate subjects with each other or involve each other in important decisions about their lives (Cicirelli, 1982).

Sibling rivalry seems to lessen over time, but research has shown that some may indeed be active in the adult years (Ross & Milgram, 1980, cited in Cicirelli, 1982). In childhood, sibling rivalries often center on issues such as intelligence, physical attractiveness, or social competence, but from childhood through adulthood, the major issue in sibling rivalry is *achievement* (Ross &

Milgram, 1982). In adulthood, brothers are more likely to feel competitive with each other than they are with sisters, or than sisters are with each other (Adams, 1968).

Positive sibling relationships can be invaluable in times of crisis. For example, siblings may provide aid, companionship, and support to each other during the illness or death of a parent. In families where sibling rivalry is still strong and members feel much hostility toward each other, however, these same crises can pull the siblings further apart. Interestingly, the death of a sibling almost always enhances feelings of closeness among the remaining siblings (Ross & Milgram, 1982).

Midlife Occupational Development

Having served in many high-level positions and gained a reputation for leadership, common sense, and managerial skill, George Washington, at age 57 years, was named first president of the United States. Dr. Richard Alpert was approaching 40 years of age when he left his job as professor of psychology at Harvard, changed his name to Baba Ram Dass, and became an Indian-style mystic and guru. Corazon Aquino was 53 years old when she left her quiet suburban life in Massachusetts to return home to the Philippines and launch a successful campaign for the presidency there.

Few of us will ever become presidents or gurus. In many ways, however, the career paths of these famous people are magnified versions of common paths ordinary people take during their middle years.

REACHING THE TOP OF A CAREER.   Like George Washington, most people reach the peak of their expertise, power, and prestige in middle age. Corporate executives become division heads, blue-collar workers become supervisors, teachers become administrators, and so on. Exactly what constitutes the top for anyone is determined by his own aspirations. For some people, the top may mean becoming an office manager or running their own service station, while other people may be satisfied only if they head a multinational corporation or become president of the United States. (Or, although you probably didn't list it as a career goal on your college application, you may actually be satisfied only if you become a guru!)

Many factors enter into a person's becoming professionally successful. One longitudinal study found that men who in early adolescence were bright, interested in intellectual matters, ambitious, productive, dependable, and not self-indulgent were most successful in middle age. At midlife, these men were more comfortable with uncertainty, more objective, and less hostile than were their less successful colleagues (Clausen, 1981).

No doubt, personality factors, motivation, and luck play key roles in many success stories. Many barriers exist for women in the workplace, however, and the same is true for many racial and ethnic groups as well. For these people, success may come harder, regardless of their personality, drive, or luck.

COMBINING LOVING AND WORKING.   We saw previously that both loving and working are vital concerns for young adults; now we have surveyed their importance to people in midlife. Just why both are so important was demonstrated in a research project involving a large sample of women, ages 35 to 55 years. The researchers found that paid work was the single best predictor of a woman's sense of *mastery* in the world, while the best predictor of *pleasure* was a good relationship with her husband and children.

Pointing to the high mastery and pleasure scores attained by happily married, employed mothers, the researchers note that having two important arenas in life greatly decreased these women's vulnerability. Good work experiences

AGEISM
Prejudice and discrimination against the elderly.

can offset problems at home, and a good marriage can offset problems at work (Baruch, Barnett, & Rivers, 1983). Some researchers have found that men, on average, score higher than women do on indices of mental health (Kessler & McRae, 1984). It may well be that men achieve these higher scores because they traditionally have been expected to function in both work and family spheres.

The lesson seems increasingly clear. The happiest people, men and women alike, are those who have and make the most of their opportunities for connectedness and attachment to other people, as well as of their opportunities for autonomous achievement.

⚛ LATE ADULTHOOD (65+ YEARS OF AGE)

The Country of Age

— From age 71 years until his death at 89, Michelangelo served as chief architect of St. Peter's Basilica in Rome.
— Anna Mary Moses was 78 years old when her fingers became too stiff to embroider, so she started painting rural scenes in oils and gained international acclaim as Grandma Moses.
— Golda Meir served as prime minister of Israel from age 70 to 75 years, through two Middle East wars.
— Benjamin Franklin was 75 years old when he negotiated the peace settlement with England to end the American Revolutionary War. (Comfort, 1976)

The accomplishments of older people can be dazzling. But those of us who haven't yet traveled in the "country of age" often become worried when we think about growing old. We read this list and think, "I'll never be able to do that," which may or may not be true. The strange thing is that we can readily imagine ourselves at the opposite end of the spectrum—alone, infirm, dependent, poor, reduced to a caricature of our former selves.

Part of the reason we are so anxious is simply a fear of the unknown. In his book, *The View from 80*, writer Malcolm Cowley defines our dilemma this way:

To enter the country of age is a new experience, different from what you supposed it to be. Nobody, man or woman, knows the country until he has lived in it and has taken out his citizenship papers. (Cowley, 1980, p. 3)

So we can read and do research about old age, but it will remain unknown to us until we get there.

A second reason we fear old age is that news stories often focus on issues such as elder abuse, poverty, illnesses, and right-to-die legal cases. This focus alerts us to many social problems that need attention. But we often take this information and make the erroneous assumption that old age is nothing more than one serious problem after another.

Yet a third reason for pessimism is that **ageism**—prejudice and discrimination against the elderly—permeates our youth-oriented culture. In television programs, older people, if they are seen at all, often are portrayed as comical, stubborn, eccentric, or foolish, and older women in particular are stereotyped in roles that suggest they must deny their age and stay young (Davis & Davis, 1985). Even children's fairy tales often portray older people as villainous witches, poor beggars, or village idiots. One review of 2500 fairy tales from around the world found that only 2 percent featured older people who were happy, healthy, energetic, wise, or productive (Chinen, 1987), although many such people in the real world are all these things (and few grandmothers are ever eaten by wolves!).

No doubt you can think of many other ways our society expresses ageism. One of the dangerous effects of this prejudice is that older people may face discrimination in jobs or housing, which is extremely damaging to an older person's self-esteem. The cumulative effects of such discrimination can lead other people to regard older people as second-class citizens, unworthy of serious attention and consideration.

Researchers have finally become interested in aging, however, and some of these images and concerns have begun to change. In 1914, the term "geriatric" was coined from the Greek word *gera*, which means "to age, to become, to awaken," and the fields of **geriatrics** and **gerontology** were born. The last few decades have witnessed a true awakening of interest in gerontology; by the late 1970s, over 5000 articles on aging were being published annually (Hendricks & Hendricks, 1979). One of the most encouraging reports came from a Harris poll conducted in 1981. As Figure 4.3 dramatically illustrates, the public's expectations about serious problems in old age were markedly *worse* than the problems actually reported by the elderly. We can only conclude that the citizens of the country of age know the territory far better than anyone else!

Physical Development in Late Adulthood

How do I know my youth is all spent?
My get up and go has got up and went.
In spite of it all, I'm able to grin,
And think of the places my get up has been!

Pete Seeger, "Get Up and Go"

In 1980, the Weavers, a famous quartet of folk singers, got together once again for two sold-out concerts in Carnegie Hall. Key figures in the folk revival of the 1940s and 1950s, they had long raised their voices to advocate a better world. Now, with great gusto, they sang this song about the departure of their "get up and go." No one sang more enthusiastically than the ailing Lee Hays, sitting in his wheel chair. He died less than a year after the concert. In 1993, however, 74-year-old Pete Seeger, the group's founder, was still singing in concerts.

GERIATRICS
A branch of medicine that deals with the problems and diseases of the elderly.

GERONTOLOGY
The study of old age and aging.

In his 70s, Pete Seeger gave concerts and entertained thousands.

◆ **FIGURE 4.3**

In a Harris poll taken among the general American public and among the elderly, the general public's expectations of serious problems in old age were much worse than the actual problems experienced by the elderly. (SOURCE: Derived from Louis Harris and Associates, Inc., 1981, p. 10.)

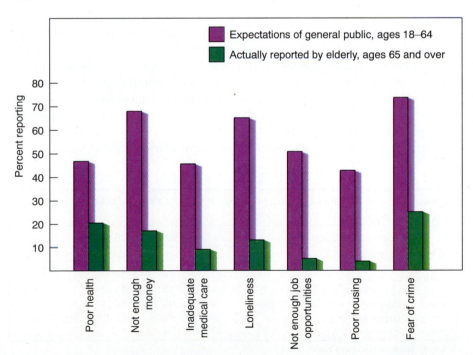

Legend:
- ■ (magenta) Expectations of general public, ages 18–64
- ■ (green) Actually reported by elderly, ages 65 and over

Y-axis: Percent reporting (10–80)

X-axis categories: Poor health, Not enough money, Inadequate medical care, Loneliness, Not enough job opportunities, Poor housing, Fear of crime

SENESCENCE
The gradual weakening of the body that begins during early adulthood and continues until death.

ORGAN RESERVE
The extra capacity of the heart, lungs, and other organs that is drawn on in times of physical or emotional stress or illness.

HOMEOSTASIS
An internal environment in which such body components as blood pressure, blood chemistry, breathing, digestion, and temperature are kept at levels optimal for the survival of the organism.

PRODROMAL
Precursor or early warning of the onset of a disease or disorder.

DEMENTIA
Irreversible loss of personality and intellectual functioning caused by disease or brain damage.

ALZHEIMER'S DISEASE
A deteriorating dementia characterized by progressive loss of memory, concentration, and judgment and by personality changes. Eventually, victims are unable to recognize other people and to control body functions.

BETA AMYLOID
A protein that forms abnormalities in the brains of some people and that may play a significant role in Alzheimer's disease.

MULTI-INFARCT DEMENTIA
Dementia that occurs as a result of one or more cerebrovascular accidents.

We can't deny that many of the physical changes of late adulthood are for the worse. But, referring back to Figure 4.3, we find that only about 20 percent of the elderly said that poor health was a problem for them. Another survey found that 60 percent of noninstitutionalized people over 65 years rated their health as good to excellent, compared to 75 percent of the total population (Robey, 1982). Only about 7 percent of the elderly have physical limitations so severe that they have to restrict their activities (Branch, 1977).

Eventually, however, all people are faced with some unwanted physical changes. When that happens, there are two ways to lighten the load. First, a person can keep a sense of humor, as the Weavers did. Second, they can try to see the inevitable changes as challenges to be met and problems to be solved, rather than as curses inflicted on them that must be passively endured.

SENESCENCE, ORGAN RESERVE, AND HOMEOSTASIS. As we get older, we become increasingly aware of a process known as **senescence**—the gradual weakening of our bodies that usually begins sometime during early adulthood and continues until we die. Moreover, **organ reserve** begins to diminish. As we go about our daily lives, our hearts, lungs, kidneys, and other organs are rarely required to function at their maximum capacity. Under stress, however, each organ in a healthy young adult body can put forth 4 to 10 times its usual effort. Imagine, for example, how much more work your heart, lungs, and leg muscles have to do when you're riding a bicycle uphill than when you're lying down reading a book. This extra capacity that we can call on when we need it is known as organ reserve. Table 4.2 shows the average percentage of reserve for organs at different ages.

Organ reserve enables our bodies to maintain **homeostasis,** or a relatively stable internal environment. As organ reserve gradually diminishes, it becomes harder to maintain homeostasis; if a person is unable to do so, disease and death follow. It is probably the depletion of organ reserve and the consequent inability to maintain homeostasis that causes older people to die from relatively minor illnesses such as pneumonia or the flu, which are rarely life-threatening in younger people (Fries & Crapo, 1981). As Table 4.2 indicates, however, the average percentage of reserve for some organs remains quite high well into late adulthood.

HEALTH CONCERNS. When we looked at health concerns in middle age, we noted that many chronic illnesses begin to appear during those years. In late adulthood, these illnesses become much more prevalent. In addition to having chronic illnesses, older people often suffer from multiple disorders. Furthermore, many diseases are compounded by psychological factors. For example, depression and anxiety are sometimes **prodromal** symptoms of illnesses such as cancer and Parkinson's disease (Goodstein, 1985). The leading causes of death for people 65 years and older are heart disease, cancer, and stroke.

TABLE 4.2 ◆ AVERAGE PERCENTAGE OF FUNCTIONS REMAINING AT EACH DECADE OF ADULTHOOD

BODY FUNCTION	AGE (YEARS)					
	30	40	50	60	70	80
Cardiac output at rest	100	94	83	77	70	—
Vital capacity of lungs	100	88	79	70	59	56
Nerve conduction velocity	100	99	97	94	93	89
Filtration rate of kidney	—	99	91	82	76	58
Basal metabolic rate	100	97	94	92	87	86

SOURCE: Based on data from Shock, 1962.

Another erroneous assumption about older people is that most eventually become senile. Different types of **dementia** do occur more frequently among older people, but they can occur at any age.

Alzheimer's disease is the best known of the dementias. An early symptom of Alzheimer's is premature loss of memory, especially for recent events or familiar routines. At this stage, victims usually worry that something is wrong and try to compensate by making lists or writing down names, addresses, or directions.

As the illness progresses, the victims become increasingly confused and show more impairments of memory, concentration, and judgment. Often, personality changes, including hostility and paranoia, become prominent. Many people begin to deny they have a problem and may talk as if they're carrying on normal routines, despite being unable to work, take care of a house, or function appropriately in social settings. As the severity of the disease increases, the victims lose their ability to recognize family members, to speak, and to understand what is said to them. Eventually, they are unable to feed and dress themselves and to control bladder and bowel functions.

Currently, Alzheimer's afflicts between 2 and 4 million Americans. Unless some form of prevention or cure is found, the number is expected to double by the year 2000, as more and more people live to advanced ages (Massachusetts Committee on Alzheimer's Disease, 1986). Researchers aren't sure what causes Alzheimer's disease, but most agree that a small protein called **beta amyloid** is involved (Marx, 1992; 1993). This protein builds up in Alzheimer's patients, and slides of their brain tissue show a characteristic pattern of plaques made up of beta amyloid (see Figure 4.4).

Another common dementia is **multi-infarct dementia,** which occurs as a result of strokes. If someone suffers a minor stroke, his intellectual and motor functioning will probably return. However, if he suffers several minor strokes or a major one, his course is likely to be similar to that of a victim of Alzheimer's disease.

One of the unfortunate consequences of the recent publicity about Alzheimer's disease is that people often fear that any hint of memory problems in an

The gentleman is Mr. Harold Jensen, my wife's grandfather. He was a sheep rancher all his life (and still is). His rugged life high in the Rocky Mountains of Utah left him extremely fit and now, at age 90, he thoroughly enjoys his mountain bike.

◆ **FIGURE 4.4**

This photo of tissue from the brain of a 69-year-old man with Alzheimer's disease shows a classic plaque consisting of beta-amyloid protein. The plaques appear in the brains of healthy older adults, but usually to a much lesser extent than in Alzheimer's patients.

DEPRESSION
A mood disturbance characterized by feelings of sadness, pessimism, apathy, excessive worry, guilt, and an inability to experience pleasure. Sometimes, these feelings are accompanied by difficulty in sleeping, loss of appetite, and loss of sexual desire.

older person means that that person is a victim of the disease. As I heard one physician put it while trying to explain the difference between serious dementia and normal everyday forgetting, "Try to keep in mind that Alzheimer's disease isn't forgetting where you left your keys, it's forgetting what keys are!"

Furthermore, many highly treatable illnesses often are mistaken for dementia. Primary among these is **depression.** About one in five elderly people has an episode of significant depression at some point (Roth, 1976; Dunn & Gross, 1977; Ban, 1978). Symptoms include loss of appetite, insomnia, early morning awakening, crying, memory impairments, morbid thoughts, excessive worrying, and perhaps hypochondriasis (irrational concern over illness, or the irrational belief that one is ill) or unusual irritability. Depression usually can be treated effectively with medication, psychotherapy, or both.

Untreated depression can be fatal, in that depression greatly increases the person's risk for suicide. The suicide rate for people aged 65 years is about 50 per 100,000, compared to 10.5 per 100,000 for younger age groups. For people aged 75 years, the rate jumps to 80 per 100,000, increasing for males and decreasing for females (Butler, 1975). About 70 percent of suicides are thought to be directly related to the trauma of physical disabilities (Dunn & Gross, 1977). Older men are especially at risk during the year following the death of their wife (Jacobs & Ostfeld, 1977; Rowland, 1977).

Sexuality in Late Adulthood

"Color television sets emit rays that may adversely affect male potency." A middle-aged friend of mine heard this shocking news while watching the nightly news with his 85-year-old father. He was even more shocked, when, without saying a word, his father got up and moved his chair well back from the television!

My friend's reaction was similar to that of many "sexually liberated" young people when they learn that Dr. Alex Comfort, author of *The Joy of Sex*, is a gerontologist. Our society is replete with ageist attitudes about sexuality. Re-

There is no reason why love and sexual interest shouldn't continue throughout the lifespan.

searchers are finding, however, that the idea that older people aren't interested in sex is a myth.

Even our research has perpetuated this myth, however. First, much early sex research focused on quantitative elements, such as frequency of intercourse, rather than on qualitative elements, such as emotional satisfaction or overall sensuality. Older people usually say, however, that quality rather than quantity of sex is most important to them (Stimson, Wase, & Stimson, 1981).

Second, early studies did not control for marital status. Data about married, unmarried, and widowed subjects were combined and reported as representative of all elderly subjects. If you look at frequency of intercourse among people who don't have a partner, you're going to conclude that these people don't have intercourse often. But lack of frequency in this population isn't necessarily due to lack of interest. The primary reason older women give for decreased sexual activity is simply lack of a partner (Gibson, 1984).

Finally, most sex research has used cross-sectional designs that don't separate aging effects from generational effects. We know that cultural norms and values influence sexual behavior, and they certainly influence the *reporting* of that behavior. Understandably, 40-year-old people who are products of the "sexual revolution" of the 1960s will talk more freely about their sexual experiences than will older people who, whatever their sexual feelings and behavior, often feel that *talking* about sex is taboo.

Cognitive Development in Late Adulthood

They tell you that you'll lose your mind when you grow older. What they don't tell you is that you won't miss it very much. (Cowley, 1980, p. 28)

So proclaimed an octogenarian lawyer at a testimonial dinner for his senior partner. It's the kind of joke that only an older person with all his wits about him could make. In reality, people's fear of becoming senile often is greater than their fear of death itself. This fear may lead them to interpret ordinary memory lapses as clear evidence that senility is creeping up on them. In the words of one researcher,

A 35-year-old who forgets his hat is forgetful, but if the same thing happens to grandpa we start wondering if his mind is going (Siegler, quoted in Meer, 1986, p. 62).

There's probably nothing more frustrating for a student than to study hard for a test, know the material well, and then simply have a bad day and not do well on the test. The fact that a person's performance may vary a great deal, depending on different social, environmental, and physical conditions, is known as **intellectual plasticity.** This concept is as relevant for older people as it is for 20-year-old students.

Giving older people more time or teaching them more efficient strategies improves their performance. Another reason older people score low on tests is that they often feel *anxious* about being evaluated, especially if they know that speed is important and that they're being compared to college students. If they're taught to use anxiety-reducing techniques such as deep-muscle relaxation, however, their motivation, attention, and general cognitive functioning improve significantly (Labouvie-Vief & Gonda, 1976; Zarit, Cole, & Guider, 1981; and Zarit, Gallagher, & Kramer, 1981).

Lack of a stimulating environment also has a negative effect on intellectual functioning. It is interesting to note that the decline on many test scores coincides with the period typically marked by retirement. Whatever a job's drawbacks, the intellectual demands it makes may keep thought processes from getting rusty (Labouvie-Vief, 1985).

Lack of stimulation is especially pronounced in many nursing homes. When residents are provided with tasks that force them to think, their cognitive

INTELLECTUAL PLASTICITY
The variability in intellectual functioning caused by different social, environmental, and physical conditions.

LIFE REVIEW
The process in which a person approaching death looks back over his life and attempts to understand its meaning.

functioning improves significantly. In one study, residents were asked questions that required them to search the environment and their own memories for the answers. Compared to control groups, these subjects showed marked improvement in short-term memory and increased involvement with their environment, and nurses rated them as being more aware, active, and self-initiating (Langer, Rodin, Beck, Weinman, & Spitzer, 1979). In another study, residents who met weekly to tell stories about themselves and their families showed improved short-term memory and rated themselves as healthier and happier after 3 months than they had been before (Berghorn & Schafer, quoted in Meer, 1985).

In sum, regarding cognitive functioning in old age, the best advice is "use it or lose it." If you think you have already lost some cognitive functioning, however, getting involved in some kind of training program or simply living in a more stimulating environment is likely to prove that you're a lot smarter than you think!

Personality Development in Late Adulthood

DEVELOPMENTAL TASKS OF LATE ADULTHOOD.   Erik Erikson and his wife Joan Erikson, both of whom are in their nineties, have for obvious reasons lately become especially interested in the final stage of psychosocial development, *ego integrity versus despair*. In this task, they were joined by Helen Kivnick, a clinician and researcher some 50 years younger than they. Together, these researchers interviewed 29 octogenarians.

They found that all of these older people were, in one way or another, attempting to come to terms with their lives and the inevitability of their own deaths. In Erikson's scheme, this is the chief developmental task of later life. The successful outcome of this process is the achievement of ego integrity:

. . . the acceptance of one's one and only life cycle as something that had to be and that, by necessity, permitted of no substitutions. (Erikson, 1950, p. 268)

This task involves a new acceptance of a person's parents and of herself and of the fact that, whatever her failings, she has lived her life as best she knew how. It also implies an acceptance of her

own inescapable death . . . which is both wholly certain and wholly unknowable. (Erikson, Erikson, & Kivnick, 1986, p. 72)

If a person fails to achieve ego integrity, according to Erikson, it may result in her being swept away with despair as she realizes that too little time is left to embark on a whole new life course. However, even people who achieve a high degree of integrity normally feel some despair at this stage of life. After all, there is always something in the past we wish we had done differently, and there is always something in the present that causes pain.

Probably the most concise statement of the process is what gerontologist Robert Butler called the **life review,** a normal, universal process prompted by the biological fact of approaching death. It occurs not only among older people, but also among younger people with terminal illnesses as well (1963). Some people silently reminisce, while others tell stories about their lives to anyone who will listen. Many make pilgrimages back to their childhood homes, or go to family and class reunions. Many muse alone over scrapbooks, photo albums, and old letters, while others share these mementos with friends or family members.

Most people probably do have the capacity to come to terms with their lives and to find meaning, especially if they can share the life-review process with someone who is accepting and doesn't dismiss their reminiscence as the idle ramblings of old age. People who aren't able to find meaning may experience such anxiety, guilt, and depression that they are overcome by despair. Butler believed that this was one factor contributing to the increased suicide rate among the elderly (Lewis & Butler, 1974).

What seems most likely is that there are many different paths to aging, and whether or not they are considered successful depends on the personality of a given individual. One older person may consider frequent social activities to be too hectic and prefer to disengage, whereas another may be happy only if he continues to be as active as he was during middle age. Some people may be delighted that they have time for solitary activities like reading, while others prefer Gray Panther political rallies. The important thing is that society be flexible enough to support older people's wishes and not prevent them from making the most of their later years.

THE VIEW FROM THE COUNTRY OF AGE. As we conclude this section, take special note of the unique perspective that old age provides. Only from that vantage point can a person take stock of his entire lifecycle and see how and why events unfolded, for better or worse. People see how they coped over the years with physical and intellectual challenges, with relationships and jobs, and how these combined to make them who they are.

Erikson says that, during this time, "the life cycle weaves back on itself" and that people renegotiate tasks of earlier stages in new ways. If a person is successful, he can integrate mature "hope, will, purpose, competence, fidelity, love, and care into a comprehensive sense of wisdom" (Erikson, Erikson, & Kivnick, 1986, pp. 55–56).

For those people interested in the life of the mind, wisdom is a much sought-after commodity. We would do well to remember, however, that older people see empathy and understanding, not age, as the hallmarks of wisdom. A personal journey to the country of age may help us to develop these qualities. But we don't have to wait until then to begin.

AN ENDURING QUESTION: HOW OLD CAN WE GROW?

In Vilcabamba, Ecuador, in the nation of Georgia, and in the mountains of Kashmir, people have allegedly lived as long as 170 years. Needless to say, such longevity interests gerontologists. In the early 1970s, Alexander Leaf interviewed several of the aged Ecuadorians, including one man who gave his age as 122 years (Leaf, 1973). When Leaf returned to Ecuador in 1974, this gentleman had turned 134 years of age. Leaf got suspicious!

Searching for documentation to verify the ages of these elders, researchers found that many had used the birth certificates of their parents or grandparents, who had the same names as they did. The birth certificates also listed godparents' names, however, and by doing a lot of tracing and matching, the scientists eventually concluded that none of the Vilcabamba elderly was more than 96 years old (Mazess & Forman, 1979; Mazess & Mathisen, 1982).

The oldest person able to provide acceptable documentation of his age was Shigechiyo Izumi of Japan, who died on February 21, 1986, at age 120 years (Mathews, 1993). Before his death, Izumi attributed his longevity to "the daily cup of *shochu* (sugar-cane liquor) and keeping a simple diet" (*Time*, 1986, p. 79).*

*Winston Churchill once noted that, if you don't drink, smoke, or become involved with the opposite sex, you can live to be 100, but it will seem like 200!

AN ENDURING QUESTION, CONTINUED

There are many theories about why we age and eventually die. The most general is the *wear and tear theory*, which compares our body to a machine. Ordinary stresses such as exams, jobs, and rowdy children take their toll; in addition, our bodies are assaulted by diseases, radiation, pollution, accidents, poor diets, and so on. This theory maintains that the accumulation of all these factors causes us to age and eventually just wear out, but it doesn't explain exactly how or why these insults are so destructive (Hayflick, 1985).

Another theory holds that a *breakdown in our immunological system* causes us to age and reduces our ability to ward off fatal diseases. The immunological system, however, is influenced by other systems, especially the endocrine system, so it may be a *malfunction in the endocrine system* that causes aging. This theory is attractive because hormones influence every part of the body, and the efficiency of the hormonal system does decline with time—but we don't know why (Hayflick, 1985).

The *cross-linkage theory* focuses on the process by which different kinds of molecules are joined together permanently, or cross-linked. This theory has been studied most frequently with the collagen molecule, which, when cross-linked with other molecules, produces changes ranging from wrinkling to atherosclerosis. Many people also believe that cross-linkage occurs with DNA molecules, which carry our genetic programs, and that this damage to DNA leads to mutation or cell death (Hayflick, 1985).

Another theory is known as the *free radical theory*. Free radicals are highly unstable molecules that react with other molecules in a way that may damage cells considerably. Exposure to radiation and reactions of certain enzymes are thought to cause these effects (Hayflick, 1985). Several investigators doing genetic research on aging have discovered genes that have the effect of prolonging life in simple organisms such as the fruit fly and a soil-dwelling worm. These genes work by making a protein that is a very efficient neutralizer of free radicals (Rusting, 1992). In high enough doses, vitamins C, E, and B-complex are also effective free radical fighters, and studies are underway to determine their effectiveness against aging.

Proponents of the endocrine theory maintain that hormonal changes produce free radicals, cross-linkages, and autoimmunity, while many people think that free radicals are simply a special form of cross-linkage, and other people believe that cross-linkage causes free radicals. Clearly, the theories overlap, and at this point it is impossible to distinguish chickens from eggs.

In an experiment that has been replicated many times, Leonard Hayflick cultured cells from a human embryo, provided them with everything necessary for growth and replication, and watched anxiously, hoping the cells would multiply forever. The cells stopped multiplying after about 50 divisions. Hayflick then cultured cells from adults and found that the older the donor, the fewer the times the cells would divide. He concluded that we are apparently genetically programmed such that our cells will divide only a limited number of times. The upper limit of the human lifespan, now known as the *Hayflick limit*, is about 100 to 120 years.

Cancer cells and egg and sperm cells, however, appear to have no limits to their division. It may be that when egg and sperm fuse at conception, they reset the genetic "death clock," and that cancer cells reshuffle their genetic information in some similar way so that they never stop dividing (Hayflick, 1980).

AN ENDURING QUESTION, CONTINUED

Medical advances such as genetic engineering and organ transplants may eventually provide ways of extending our lifespan. However, before you leap for life-prolonging techniques, remember the myth of the goddess Eos and her mortal lover Tithonus. Eos persuaded Zeus to grant Tithonus eternal life, but forgot to ask for youth and health. Poor Tithonus grew old and shriveled away to nothingness, so that eventually only his voice was left. So, if someone offers you the chance to live forever, make sure the deal includes the opportunity to continue to be healthy and productive!   ◆

Relationships in Late Adulthood

Older adults today face a novel situation. Increased longevity means that relationships have the potential of lasting longer than at any other time in history. Families consist of more generations than ever before, and more members are middle-aged and older. In fact, about one-tenth of people over 65 years of age have a child who is also at least 65 years old (Troll, Miller, & Atchley, 1979).

Having more older family members who have outgrown sibling rivalries and other family conflicts and have come to appreciate their common family heritage can make for harmonious relationships. It can also make for increased strain as the younger people try to care for older infirm relatives when they themselves are dealing with declining health (Aizenberg & Treas, 1985).

Another novel situation is that social peerships, which have nothing to do with chronological age, have sprung up. Early retirement means that younger people now deal with issues traditionally assigned to the old. The increase in adult education means that children, grandchildren, parents, and grandparents all may be students at the same time (Aizenberg & Treas, 1985). And, now that romance among older people is out of the closet, grandmothers and granddaughters may shop together for their respective party dresses!

THE TRADITIONAL FAMILY.   We previously looked at the first six stages of the family lifecycle as defined by David Olson, Hamilton McCubbin, and their colleagues in their research on intact families (1983). We come now to their seventh and final stage, families in retirement (see Figure 4.5).

Olson and McCubbin's stage VII families had been married an average of 42 years. The average ages of husbands and wives were 71 and 68 years, respectively. Families had an average of three children, and the average age of the oldest was 41 years. Although all these couples considered themselves retired, 20 percent of the men and 4 percent of the women were still employed

Stage VII Retirement families	Close friend of the family died	28%
	Increase in the number of tasks or chores that do not get done	23%
	A member purchased a car or another major item	23%
	A member retired from work	23%

◆ FIGURE 4.5

Profile of family stresses and strains in late adulthood. The top four stressors are listed. (SOURCE: *Adapted from Olson et al., 1983, p. 130.*)

full-time. The family incomes, however, were generally lower than those in earlier stages.

As might be expected, getting necessary chores done was no longer so difficult for families at this stage, but many did report financial problems, and increasingly they were confronted by the illnesses and deaths of loved ones. These couples reported high levels of marital satisfaction, with only 3 percent of the wives and none of the husbands saying they had ever considered separation or divorce.

RELATIONSHIPS WITH GROWN CHILDREN.   Contrary to popular belief, older people generally do not want to live with their children. Moreover, most adult children provide every bit as much care and support to their aging parents as was the case in the "good old days," and most older people do not feel abandoned.

About 80 percent of people 65 years and older have living children (Shanas, 1980; 1979a; 1979b), and about 90 percent of these have frequent contact with the children (Brubaker, 1985). About 75 percent of noninstitutionalized elderly parents live within 30 minutes of at least one of their children (Shanas, 1979a; 1979b; 1980).

Merely having contact with sons and daughters does not guarantee happiness and well-being in old age (Glenn & McLanahan, 1981; Lee & Ellithorpe, 1982). In fact, some research has found that people who are most involved with their families have the lowest morale (Troll, 1985). This research may be contaminated, however, by the fact that ill health often makes older people more dependent and thereby increases contact with family members. So it is more likely that health, not just family involvement, decreases morale.

Increasingly, researchers have begun to look at the *quality* of relationships, rather than at the frequency of contact, between the elderly and their adult children. If parents and children share interests and values and agree on child-rearing practices, treatment of siblings, intergenerational get-togethers, and religious commitments, they are likely to enjoy each other's company (Aldous, Klaus, & Klein, 1985). Disagreements on such matters can understandably cause problems. If parents are angered by their daughter's divorce, dislike her new husband, and disapprove of how she's raising their grandchildren, chances are they're not going to enjoy her visits.

About 90% of the elderly have frequent contact with their children.

RELATIONSHIPS WITH GRANDCHILDREN. Our culture tends to romanticize grandparenting. We say it provides older people with a sense of immortality and younger people with a tie to the past, which, in many cases, it does. However, this stereotype overlooks the fact that grandparents are an extremely heterogeneous group of people, and the experience can mean many different things. "I could break my daughter's neck for having this baby," commented one 29-year-old grandmother (that's right—29!). "I just got a new boyfriend. Now he will think I'm too old" (Burton, 1985, p. 1).

As is the case with many major life experiences, we feel better about becoming grandparents if we do so "on time." And while we normally think of grandparenting as an experience of late adulthood, on the average, women now become grandmothers at age 50 years, and men become grandfathers at 52 years (Troll, 1983).

Helen Kivnick, who worked with the Eriksons on their project on old age, maintains that grandparenting facilitates personality development in late adulthood. It provides opportunities, she says, for older people to rework the tasks and come to age-appropriate balances for psychosocial tensions of earlier developmental stages. For example, mutual love and security between grandparents and grandchildren may enable grandparents to establish a new balance between intimacy and isolation. Dealing with issues of authority and responsibility may help them achieve a new balance between generativity and stagnation (Kivnick, 1981; 1985).

Many older individuals have warm and loving relationships with their grandchildren. Such relationships often help us to maintain important and intimate contacts as we grow old.

FRIENDSHIPS IN LATER LIFE. Satisfaction and happiness in later life are consistently associated with having friends. Friends provide us with acceptance, support, and companionship, which are as vital to our sense of self-worth in late adulthood as they are when we are younger (Roberto & Scott, 1986). Although we share a gene pool and family heritage with our siblings, we may share more interests with our friends and trust them more as confidants.

Older women usually have a wider circle of friends than do older men, who rely mainly on their wives for support and companionship. Older men, however, report more cross-sexed friendships. The women say there just aren't many men around with whom to be friends, and they worry about what their friends will think. When asked how often her male friend visited her, one woman replied, "I don't let him in my apartment. It wouldn't be proper. People would talk" (Adams, 1985, p. 607). She was right about the last point. Some women at the local senior center told researchers this woman was "fast" and was "always running around"!

Retirement

Retirement on a large scale is a twentieth-century phenomenon. At the turn of the century, two-thirds of all men aged 65 years and older were still working, compared to about one-third in the early 1990s. Moreover, very few of those who did not work had enough money to retire comfortably. They quit working only because of poor health or because employers felt they were too old to be productive (Parnes & Less, 1985a).

In 1935, the U.S. Congress passed the Social Security Act, which set the "normal" retirement age at 65 years. Today Social Security provides retirement benefits for over 90 percent of the labor force. People can begin collecting benefits at age 62 years, or even earlier if they are completely disabled. In addition, private employers provide pensions for about one-half of all wage and salary workers, and they often encourage older people to retire early to make room for less-expensive younger employees. The net result of these social changes has been a move toward early retirement. Today, almost one-half of the men in the labor force retire by age 62 years.

Interestingly, however, many social forces are now pressing in the opposite direction, encouraging later retirement. Older employees who want to keep working have challenged mandatory retirement at age 65 years, and many companies have moved the age limit to 70 years. Moreover, the Social Security system could be in long-term trouble, because fewer young employed people will be paying into the system that will be supporting more and more older people.

WHEN LIFE ENDS

Death is unique among human experiences: not only does it end our earthly life, but it alone is "both wholly certain and wholly unknowable" (Erikson, Erikson, & Kivnick, 1986, p. 72). We may learn about the physiology of dying or about psychological reactions of grieving, but the totality of death itself is ultimately incomprehensible. For centuries, poets, philosophers, and religious leaders have tried to explain death, but they have all run up against the limits of the human intellect.

Dealing with something both incomprehensible and inevitable naturally generates powerful feelings, and those feelings vary, depending on our particular life circumstances. Some people feel defiant about death, while others welcome death as a blessed relief from suffering. Some feel sorrow and anger, others feel resentment and resignation, and yet others may actually feel joy.

Many writers not bound by rules of scientific investigation would agree that most people do fear death. Jean-Jacques Rousseau expressed the belief this way:

He who pretends to look on death without fear lies. All men are afraid of dying, this is the great law of sentient beings, without which the entire human species would be destroyed. (1960, pp. 131–132)

Certainly, there are some good reasons to fear both death and the process of dying. Among the fears expressed by terminally ill people are the following (Kassoff, 1984):

— Fear of the unknown
— Fear of loneliness, isolation, separation, and abandonment
— Fear of loss of the body and loss of self
— Fear of loss of self-control and of courage if the process goes on too long
— Fear of insanity
— Fear of emotional and physical pain
— Fear of loss of identity
— Fear of loss of power over one's destiny
— Fear of dependency and of being a nuisance

With all these possibilities, it is probably safe to assume that, at one time or another, almost everyone feels some fear about death and dying. And, as the quotation from Rousseau suggests, this fear propels us to attend to self-preservation and to master dangers that threaten us. Ironically, however, we can't function if we are constantly mindful of the fear of death. So, to get on with life, we must accept the fear as normal and valuable, then suppress it, knowing it will return to be dealt with and suppressed once again.

Research suggests, however, that, on average, older people generally report lower death anxiety, while middle-aged people express the greatest death anxiety (Bengtson, Cuellar, & Ragan, 1977). In one study, married women with children had the highest death anxiety, and lower anxiety was positively correlated with both advancing age and higher education (Cole, 1978–1979). Among women 60 to 85 years old, feeling a sense of purpose in life seemed to reduce death anxiety significantly (Quinn & Reznikoff, 1985).

Lengthening the Lifespan

Well into the twentieth century, death was an all too familiar part of American life. Death of infants and young children was common, many women died in childbirth, and otherwise healthy adults succumbed to contagious diseases. People died at home and were laid out and buried by family members. It is doubtful that most people felt comfortable with death, but death certainly was no stranger to them. This is still the way death occurs and is handled throughout most of the developing world.

As the century progressed, the widespread use of vaccinations and antibiotics virtually eliminated killers such as smallpox, typhoid, diphtheria, cholera, and bubonic plague. People began to live longer. Those who became seriously ill were taken to hospitals where respirators and other new technology kept them alive while doctors tried a variety of new treatments. When the treatments didn't work and the patients died, these people were surrounded more often by machines and medical specialists than by family and friends.

Having fewer direct contacts with death allowed Americans to develop a somewhat death-denying society. The British historian Arnold Toynbee went so far as to say that, for Americans, death is "un-American," inconsistent with the "earthly paradise" hoped for in "the American way of life" (Toynbee, 1968, p. 131). In all fairness, Americans were not alone in their tendency to deny death. Most nations with advanced medical care did so as well.

On a practical level, denial of death was expressed in a number of ways. Discussions of death were deemed "morbid," and the topic of death often was scrupulously avoided, especially in conversations with dying people. Children were excluded from funerals and were told stories about "grandmother's going on a long journey." Dead people were handed over to morticians who embalmed "the body," made it "look natural," laid it out in an expensive coffin, and presided over the funeral and the "disposal."

During the 1960s, a "**thanatology** boom" began. In 1966, thanatologists Richard Kalish and Robert Kastenbaum began to publish a newsletter on death and dying, which by 1970 had evolved into the journal *Omega*. In 1969, Elisabeth Kubler-Ross published *On Death and Dying*, a book based on interviews with dying patients that rapidly became a best-seller. On college campuses, courses on death and dying were heavily subscribed. Researchers began to look at different aspects of death, dying, and grief, and groups to aid the bereaved sprang up across the country (Leviton, 1977).

In the 1990s, the interest in thanatology continues, and as more people become involved in death-education courses, death has become less of a taboo topic. It probably is not accurate to say that we as a society are becoming comfortable with death. Rather, like our forebears, we're just becoming more willing to acknowledge that death is a fact of life and to be accepting of our discomfort.

THANATOLOGY
The study of death and dying.

❖ SUMMARY

◆ The timing of developmental changes varies so much from one adult to another that chronological age becomes an increasingly poor guideline as we study adults.

◆ The outstanding vitality of early adulthood comes about because so many of our body's organ systems work so well together at that time. For most people, it is a time of exceedingly good health.

◆ Developmental psychologists have tried to answer the question about whether there is a stage beyond Piaget's formal operational stage.

◆ According to Erikson, our chief developmental task in early adulthood is to form an intimate relationship with another person.

◆ Kenneth Keniston has postulated that there is an optional period that some people experience after adolescence and before becoming full-fledged adults; he called this stage "youth."

◆ Many researchers have ignored the differences women may show in personality development during adulthood. "Self-in-relation" theory postulates that the basic goal of development is the deepening capacity for relationships and relational competence.

◆ David Olson, Hamilton McCubbin, and their associates divided the family lifecycle into seven stages. Three of these stages take place during early adulthood: young married couples without children, families with preschool children, and families with school-age children.

◆ Homosexual relationships are often as diverse as heterosexual ones, but long-term homosexual relationships may actually be more egalitarian than heterosexual ones are.

◆ Much research has supported the view that being single isn't as healthy as being in a relationship.

◆ H. C. Lehman identified early adulthood as a time of peak creativity. He found that people did most of their outstanding work between the ages of 30 and 40 years.

◆ The bodies and good health we take for granted in early adulthood begin to demand more attention in middle adulthood. The "silent diseases" of early adulthood now become vocal as chronic illnesses make their appearance.

◆ The biological changes involved in menopause usually take place over a period of 2 to 5 or even 10 years, known as the climacteric.

◆ The term "male menopause" has been jokingly used to refer to the emotional and behavioral changes some men show during middle age; in reality, however, the hormonal changes men undergo are not nearly as pronounced as those middle-aged women experience.

◆ One theorist thinks there is a postformal stage involving the ability to identify relevant problems and to ask important questions about ourselves.

◆ Those who negotiate the midlife transition successfully may become more compassionate, more reflective, and more genuinely loving of themselves and of other people.

◆ Researcher Lillian Rubin has concluded that very few women suffer the classical symptoms of empty-nest syndrome when their children grow up and leave home.

◆ Middle adulthood is characterized by multiple connections. Olson and McCubbin's family lifecycle research has listed midlife as a time for three stages: families with adolescents in the home, launching families, and empty-nest families.

◆ A key characteristic of many middle-aged people's relationships with their elderly parents is reciprocity.

◆ Most people reach the top of their expertise, power, and prestige in middle age.

◆ Many people fear old age; however, those who have traveled in the "country of age" report many less problems than expected by younger people.

◆ Many of the physical changes of late adulthood are not for the better. However, in a survey only about 20 percent of the elderly reported that poor health was a problem for them.

◆ Many of the health concerns of the elderly focus on the fear of losing mental capacity. Alzheimer's disease is a major progressive fatal illness that can appear in old age.

◆ Giving older people more time or teaching them more efficient strategies improves their performance on cognitive tasks. Lack of a stimulating environment can have a negative effect on cognitive functioning.

◆ Erik Erikson believes that the chief developmental task of late adulthood is to develop ego integrity. Failure to achieve it may result in a person's being swept away with despair.

◆ There have been many theories to explain why we age and how long the human lifespan can become. Chief among these are the wear and tear theory, the cross-linkage theory, the endocrine theory, and the free radical theory.

◆ Olson and McCubbin's lifecycle model lists families in retirement as the last stage that takes place in late adulthood.

◆ Satisfaction and happiness in later life are consistently associated with having friends.

◆ Retirement on a large scale is a twentieth-century phenomenon. Interestingly, however, many social forces are now pressing in the opposite direction, encouraging later retirement.

◆ Death is unique among human experiences. Dealing with something both incomprehensible and inevitable naturally generates powerful feelings. Research suggests, however, that on average, older people generally report lower death anxiety than those at earlier ages.

SUGGESTIONS FOR FURTHER READING

1. Block, M. R., Davidson, J. L., & Grambs, J. O. (1981). *Women over 40*. New York: Springer.

2. Comfort, A. (1990) *Say yes to old age*. New York: Crown Publishers. A discussion of the benefits to be derived during the later years. This book helps to debunk some of the negative ideas often associated with aging.

3. Commons, M. L., Sinnot, J. D., & Richards, F. A. (Eds.). (1989). *Beyond formal operations: Adolescent and adult development models* (Vol 2). New York: Greenwood. An advanced look at theories that view cognitive development as continuing beyond formal operations.

4. Eichorn, D. H., Clausen, J. A., Haan, N., Honzik, M. P., & Mussen, P. H. (1981). *Present and past in middle life*. New York: Academic Press.

5. Erikson, E., Erikson, J., & Kivnick, H. (1986). *Vital involvement in old age*. New York: W. W. Norton. A discussion of the time in life between the formation of adolescent identity and the undertaking of full adult responsibility and commitment.

6. Keniston, K. (1970). "Youth: A new stage of life." *The American Scholar*, Autumn, 39(4), 631–654. A classic discussion of the time in life between the formation of adolescent identity and the undertaking of full adult responsibility and commitment.

7. Kubler-Ross, E. (1969). *On death and dying*. New York: Macmillan Publishing Company. A classic text describing Kubler-Ross' stages of death and dying.

8. Michaels, J. (1983). *Prime of your life: A practical guide to your mature years*. Boston: Little, Brown.

9. Parnes, H. S., Crowley, J. E., Haurin, R. J., Less, L. J., Morgan, W. R., Mott, F. L., & Nestel, G. (1985). *Retirement among American men*. Lexington, MA: Lexington Books. A look at how retirement affects men in both beneficial and disruptive ways. An emphasis is placed on how one adapts to the changes that accompany retirement.

10. Rubin, L. (1979). *Women of a certain age: The midlife search for self*. New York: Harper & Row. A classic text looking at the way in which middle age affected women in the culture of the 1970s.

11. Smelser, N. J. & Erikson, E. H. (1980). *Themes of work and love in adulthood*. Cambridge, MA: Harvard University Press.

12. Springer, D. & Brubaker, T. H. (1984). *Family caregivers and dependent elderly*. Beverly Hills, CA: Sage Publications. One of the first publications to look at the sandwich generation, those middle aged who are taking care of both their own children and their parents.

13. Troll, L. E. (1985). *Early and middle adulthood* (2nd ed.). Monterey, CA: Brooks/Cole. A college level text that examines adulthood from ages 18 to 65.

Chapter Five

Sensation

PROLOGUE

SIGHTLESS VISION

John M. Kennedy and his colleagues have worked with blind children and adults, many of whom have been sightless since birth. Through his research, Kennedy has gathered persuasive evidence that congenitally blind people can picture things in their "mind's eye," even though they've never seen them. Kennedy argues that the blind do this by using an internal understanding of perspective gathered through the sense of touch.

Kennedy has concluded that the principles that underlie visual perception are the same as those used in touch. He argues that vision and touch, unlike hearing, are responsive to dimensions of shape and form. Because of this, blind people, relying on a sense of touch, may organize and understand their perceptions in ways very similar to those sighted persons use.

That blind people seem to develop an understanding of the geometry of their world was of interest to biophysicist Carter Collins and other researchers who set out to design a new aid for the blind. At the Smith-Kettlewell Institute of Visual Sciences in San Francisco, Collins impressed televised pictures directly onto a person's back or chest by using a technique called tactile sensory replacement (TSR). A TSR user wears a vest containing a grid on which are hundreds of tiny points that touch the wearer (see Figure 5.1). When the vest is connected to a small black-and-white television camera, the light and dark messages gathered by the camera can be "shone" on the person's back or chest by electrically stimulating the different points and making them vibrate. The entire device weighs only 5 pounds. Blind persons using it have been able to find objects in a room quickly, read meters, and even use an oscilloscope. One blind technician wearing the device was able to assemble something as small as a microcircuit.

What does it feel like to wear the device? The following account was given by a person with normal sight who tried out Collins's TSR device:

I sat blindfolded in the chair, the cones cold against my back. At first I felt only formless waves of sensation. Collins said he was just waving his hand in front of me so that I could get used to the feeling. Suddenly I felt or saw, I wasn't sure which, a black triangle in the lower left corner of a square. The

CONTENTS

◆ **FIGURE 5.1**

The TSR device, which allows blind subjects to "feel" what sighted subjects can "see."

sensation was hard to pinpoint. I felt vibrations on my back, but the triangle appeared in a square frame in my head. There was no color, but there was a light area and a dark area. If you close your eyes and face a light or the sun and pass an object in front of your eyes, a difference appears in the darkness. That difference is approximately what I saw. The image was fuzzy at first, but, even in my ten minutes in the chair, it became clearer. When Collins confirmed that he was holding a triangle, it was clearer still.

For me, believing that there is a difference between sensation and perception has always required an enormous leap of faith. It is hard to believe that I do not see with my eyes or hear with my ears. Although we may learn that there is a difference between sensation and perception, we rarely experience [it] . . . at the TSR lab I experienced the difference for the first time. The sensation was on my back, the perception was in my head. Feeling is believing. (Hechinger, 1981, p. 43)

WHY PSYCHOLOGISTS STUDY SENSATION

We know nothing except by experience, and experience consists of nothing but the information of our senses. Perhaps there is nothing, really, out there to be sensed. All we know is that we sense.—Judson Jerome

What would it be like to be sitting on top of a hydrogen bomb when it exploded? Most people say that whatever the feeling, it would be over quickly. Perhaps a very bright light and a tremendous noise and then nothing. Perhaps a sense of searing heat and of being hurled away. Or perhaps all of that at once, contained within a great roaring explosion, lasting (from your point of view) just a fraction of a second. Obviously, no one could experience this explosion and live to describe it. But we know the answer anyway. Imagine yourself sitting on top of a hydrogen bomb, waiting for it to detonate. You would be looking over your notebook, ready to write down your experiences, feeling the steel casing beneath you, and perhaps listening to the countdown being broadcast over the speakers from the blockhouse miles away. Then suddenly . . . there would be nothing. There would be no light, no sound, no feeling of heat. You would not have sensed anything. How can we be sure? Because we know neural messages have to be translated into electrochemical impulses before they are sent to the brain (see Chapter 2). Consequently, long before your brain had received any of the messages from your nervous system concerning any aspect of the explosion, you would have been vaporized. In fact, the odds are that you would have been vaporized long before visual, auditory, heat, or pressure neurons even had a chance to fire.

This ridiculous, but perhaps memorable, example emphasizes the fact that our senses are our only contact with the world outside our bodies. Students rarely think about the senses when they consider what psychologists might study. But, it does make sense that sensation would be of interest to psychologists when you stop to think that before we can ever experience anything in our external world, that is, before any experience from the outside can affect our minds, we must wait for sensory messages to make their way into our brains. Without messages from the senses, there could be no experience of external "reality"; without such experience, there could be little in the way of organized behavior.

You may have noticed that I put the word *reality* in quotation marks. That's because it is not exactly clear what reality is. Our senses determine what is "real," but what we sense as "real" is often different from what scientific experiments might tell us is "real." For instance, consider the fact that the senses are selective. There are many loud sounds that our species cannot hear, many bright lights that we cannot see, and many impacts that we cannot feel. There also are many substances that we cannot taste and many odors that we cannot smell. Our way of organizing and responding to the world depends a great deal on the way in which our senses filter or select from the stimuli, or information, around us. We come to know our world primarily through our senses, and what we sense often affects our behavior. This is perhaps the main reason why psychologists study **sensation.**

SENSORY THRESHOLDS

Your senses can inform you of the presence of a stimulus or of any change in that stimulus. Before energy such as sound or light can be sensed, however, it must satisfy two conditions. First, it must be energy to which your senses can respond. No matter how bright X-ray light is, you cannot see it. Second, the energy must be strong enough to stimulate your senses. Although delicate instruments might be able to sense the light from a match struck on a mountaintop 50 miles away on a dark night, your eyes would not be able to. The amount of energy required to create a noticeable sensation is called the **absolute threshold.** If the match had been struck at a distance of 30 miles on a dark night under the most ideal conditions, you might have been able to detect it, but just barely. This amount of energy would have been just beyond your absolute threshold. The term is misleading, however, because the absolute threshold for any given stimulus can change depending on your physical condition or motivation.

Just as a certain amount of energy is required before you can detect a stimulus, so must the existing energy fluctuate a certain amount before you can detect a *change* in a stimulus. This minimum amount of energy fluctuation is known as the **difference threshold.** Psychologists often refer to difference thresholds as *just noticeable differences,* or JNDs. Difference thresholds also can change depending on the person's physical condition or motivation or the qualities of the stimulus being tested.

An interesting aspect of just noticeable differences is that they tend to be fairly constant fractions of the stimulus intensity. For example, if you picked up a 1-pound weight and got used to the feel of it, about half an ounce could be added or subtracted from that weight before you would feel a just noticeable difference. Then, if you became accustomed to a 2-pound weight instead of to the 1-pound weight, the just noticeable difference would be closer to 1 ounce than to half an ounce. Thus, as the weight you hold is doubled, the just noticeable difference also doubles; that is, the ratio stays the same. This relationship was first described by Ernst Weber in 1834 and has come to be known as **Weber's law.** Perhaps law is too strong a word, however, because although these fractions hold for a fairly wide range of stimulations, they can change drastically when the intensity of the stimulus becomes very great or very small.

Most people consider that there are five ways to sense: seeing, hearing, tasting, smelling, and touching. As you will soon discover, there are many more than just these five. But for now, let's begin with seeing—our sense of vision.

VISION

Is the human eye like a camera? Both have a lens that light passes through and that focuses light. In addition, the eye has an iris that opens and closes, allowing more or less light to enter. Most cameras have a mechanical "iris." A camera has light-sensitive film; the eye has a light-sensitive area, the **retina.**

SENSATION
Any fundamental experience of events from within or without the body as the result of stimulation of some receptor system. Distinguished from perception in that perception requires the interpretation of a sensation. This distinction is somewhat arbitrary, however, because some perception of a sensation must occur before awareness is possible.

ABSOLUTE THRESHOLD
The minimum intensity a stimulus must have in order to produce a sensation.

DIFFERENCE THRESHOLD
The minimum change that a stimulus must undergo before the change can be reliably detected; it is also called the just noticeable difference (JND).

WEBER'S LAW
The rule that the larger or stronger a stimulus, the larger the change required for an observer to notice a difference. The smallest difference in intensity between two stimuli that can be readily detected is a constant fraction of the original stimulus.

RETINA
The delicate multilayer, light-sensitive membrane lining the inner eyeball. It consists of layers of ganglion and bipolar cells and photoreceptor cells called rods and cones.

SCLERA
The white, elastic outer covering of the eye.

CORNEA
The transparent outer bulge in front of the eye through which light waves pass.

PUPIL
The dark circular aperture in the center of the iris of the eye that admits light.

IRIS
The pigmented muscular membrane that controls the aperture in the center of the pupil, which determines the amount of light that enters the eye.

LENS
The transparent biconvex structure of the eye behind the iris and pupil that focuses light rays entering through the pupil to form an image on the retina.

GANGLION CELLS
Nerve cells of the retina, which receive impulses from rods and cones via the bipolar cells and transmit these impulses to the brain.

OPTIC NERVE
The bundle of nerve fibers connecting the retina and the brain.

BIPOLAR CELLS
Cells that collect and consolidate visual information. A particular bipolar cell is either "rod-driven" or "cone-driven," meaning that it receives information from either groups of rods or groups of cones but never from a mixture of the two. Bipolar cells transmit a ratio derived from the signals they receive from the photoreceptors and nearby horizontal cells to the ganglion cells.

PHOTORECEPTOR CELLS
Light-sensitive cells, called rods and cones, that comprise the third layer of the retina.

Human beings have two retinas, one at the back of each eye, and each is filled with thousands of receptive visual cells. In a sense, the retina works like film. In fact, light-sensitive chemicals taken from the retinas of rabbits have been used successfully on film in cameras!

Once light strikes the retina, neural messages are sent farther into the brain, where cells are either stimulated or not stimulated depending on how the parts of the retina were excited by the light. Film is developed in much the same way. A picture emerges because certain parts of the film have been stimulated by light, while others haven't. When an image enters a camera, it is projected through the lens onto the film upside down. When an image enters the eye, it also is projected onto the retina upside down (see Figure 5.2). At first glance, then, the camera and the eye seem to be very similar.

Actually, they really aren't very much alike. Although the "camera theory" of vision is popular among the general public, it provides an extremely limited understanding of vision. There may be many parallels between the camera and the eye, but the two are actually more different than alike. The visual system, unlike a camera, sees things that aren't there and alters things that are there, and in doing so it affects our understanding of the world. Its abilities are strange and amazing.

Let's consider the camera for a moment. Have you ever seen a newsreel of a dramatic event during which the photographer who was filming the action had to begin running? What happens to the camera's view of the world when the person who is holding it begins to run? The picture starts to shake violently. It looks as if an earthquake were in progress, and it's almost impossible to see what is happening. To make good movies, you must hold the camera steady, so that light entering strikes each frame of the film in roughly the same place. If you move the camera violently, the light image striking the film also will move violently; when the film is projected onto a screen, everything in the image will seem to be moving and jerking in all directions at once. If our visual system worked in the same way, we all would be walking about as softly as we could to avoid quaking motions in our view of the surrounding world. But this is not the case. You can run down a street, and although the world about you may seem to be moving, it will not be moving with the agitation that you would experience had you been taking movies as you ran. The difference lies in the fact that whereas a frame of film passively records the light that shines on it, the central nervous system interacts with the light. The retina is not a piece of film; it is an outpost of the central nervous system that is closely linked to the brain.

◆ **FIGURE 5.2**

Visual images received by the eye are projected onto the retina upside down.

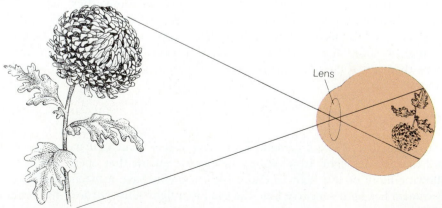

The Retina

Figure 5.3 shows the major parts of the human eye. The outer membrane covering, or white of the eye, is called the **sclera.** The eye itself is not made of a hard substance; its shape is maintained by the fluid within it, which is under pressure. Light entering the eye passes through the transparent **cornea** and enters the **pupil.** The **iris** regulates the amount of light passing through the **lens.** The lens focuses the light onto the retina.

Although the retina consists of ten layers, we will focus our discussion on its three major layers. The first major layer of the retina contains the **ganglion cells,** the axons of which form the **optic nerve.** The second major layer is formed by the **bipolar cells.** The *third* major layer, *nearest the back of the eye,* is made up of **photoreceptor cells** called **rods** and **cones,** which are sensitive to light (see Figure 5.4). When the rods and cones are stimulated by light, their neural messages travel first to the bipolar cells, next to the ganglion cells, and then down the optic nerve to higher parts of the brain. There is also lateral "cross-talk" between neighboring receptors within the same layer of the retina. These lateral connections are made by the **horizontal cells** and the **amacrine cells,** which comprise some of the retina's minor layers ("minor" in terms of thickness).

The human eye is extremely sensitive. Researchers, hoping one day to build robots that can see as well as humans, are now trying to copy what is known about the retina onto silicon chips. To a great extent, they have succeeded in mimicking the functions of the various visual cells found in the eye with silicon chips. To make a silicon retina, engineers first copied the function of the photoreceptors and installed chips that turned light into electrical energy. Each "horizontal cell" chip then calculates the average light intensity generated by the photoreceptors in its immediate neighborhood, just as a real horizontal cell does. Next, the "bipolar chips" transmit a ratio derived from the signals they

RODS
Specialized photoreceptor cells in the retina that are primarily responsive to changes in the intensity of light waves and are therefore important in peripheral vision and night vision.

CONES
Specialized photoreceptor cells in the retina that are primarily responsive to different wavelengths of light and are therefore important in color vision; cones also are associated with high visual acuity.

HORIZONTAL CELLS
Retinal cells with short dendrites and long axons that extend horizontally, linking rods with other rods and cones with other cones. Each of these cells fires according to the average light intensity generated by the photoreceptors in its immediate neighborhood. Horizontal cells are thought to influence opposing color processes (such as red and green, blue and yellow) and are probably responsible, in part, for negative afterimages and other opponent-process effects.

AMACRINE CELLS
Large retinal neurons that connect ganglion cells laterally. There are at least 30 different varieties of amacrine cell. Image rectification appears to be one of their many functions. The functions of most amacrine cells are unknown.

◆ **FIGURE 5.3**

Structures of the human eye.

Retina

Lens

Ciliary muscle

Iris

Pupil

Fovea

Cornea

Aqueous humor

Suspensory ligament

Sclera

Optic nerve

Vitreous humor

The photoreceptors of the retina. The rods and cones are embedded in a pigmented layer called the choroid. They pass on their messages to the bipolar cells. The axons of the ganglion cells form the optic nerve. Notice that, before light strikes the rods and cones, it must pass through the other layers of the retina.

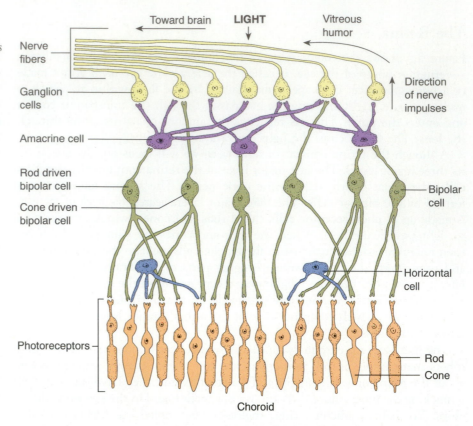

◆ FIGURE 5.5

The Hering Grid.

receive from the photoreceptors and the horizontal cells to the "ganglion chips" where the input is further processed (Mahowald & Mead, 1991). Some of the most advanced cameras on the market today do some signal averaging like real retinas to keep brights from seeming too bright and darks from seeming too dark.

An examination of the Hering Grid provides proof that the horizontal and bipolar cells in the retina engage in signal averaging (see Figure 5.5). The nonexistent gray spots that seem to appear at the intersections result because the cells in your eyes are trying to average light intensities (a good strategy most of the time). The gray spots are examples of such averaging derived from the black and white portions of the grid. Because the retina's response to a given point depends on the light intensity of nearby points, the surrounding black areas cause the eye to signal the brain that the intersections are darker than they really are. The illusion only occurs out of the corners of your vision, however, because the cells concentrated at the center of the fovea, are so dense that they average smaller areas. This is why, when you look directly at an intersection, you won't see a gray spot at that location. Very few of these smaller areas contain both black *and* white messages unless you are looking at an edge separating black from white. You can lose the illusion for the corners of your eyes by moving the grid very close (so that less densely packed neurons there have larger solid areas of black or white to see) or farther away (so that a single area covered by a group of less densely packed neurons will seem uniformly checkered).

Interestingly, the artificial silicon retina mentioned earlier sees this same illusion! This has helped the researchers developing the artificial retina to confirm that they are, in fact, mimicking real biological principles of organization.

Only a generation ago, people believed that the retina was fairly straightforward. After all, the retina seemed to consist of only five basic cells (ganglion,

The retina is only one-tenth of a millimeter thick making it virtually transparent, which, of course, is why light can pass through all of the layers of the retina and still easily reach and stimulate the photoreceptor cells that make up the third retinal layer. In this photograph of a rabbit's retina, the blood vessels that supply oxygen and nutrition can be seen, but the photoreceptor cells are too small to be seen individually.

bipolar, horizontal, amacrine, and photoreceptor). As researchers explored the retina more carefully, you can guess what it turned out to be—that's right, *complicated!* For instance, we now know that in each retina there are at least 30, and perhaps as many as 50, different kinds of amacrine cells, each with its own neurotransmitter or neuropeptide. What the functions of these cells are is anybody's guess. Once they are better understood, researchers may also incorporate their functions into artificial retinas.

The retina is also a marvel of miniaturization; it is made of perhaps the most densely packed and smallest neurons in the nervous system. In fact, if your retinas were composed of neurons the size of those typically found in your brain, your eyes would be as big as tangerines—good for getting bit parts in science fiction films perhaps, but for little else.

THE FOVEA.   If you stare at a bright white wall or a rich blue sky, you often see outlines of the blood vessels layered within your eye. In addition, many people may notice blurry black specks, sometimes with little streamers attached, that seem to pass through their visual field (see Figure 5.6). These objects are called *floaters*.

How is it possible to see something that is inside your own eye? These blood vessels or floating specks interfere with the light image as it passes through the lens on its way to the retina, and, if the light is sufficiently bright and the background is homogeneous, the shadows the objects cast onto the retina become noticeable. Because the objects are inside the eye and cannot be brought into focus by the lens, they are perceived only as shadows cast onto the back of the retina. In normal daylight vision, the most sensitive portion

FOVEA
The area in the center of the retina characterized by a great density of cones and an absence of rods. Images focused on the fovea are seen with the highest acuity.

BLIND SPOT
The region of the retina where the optic nerve attaches and where there are no photoreceptors. The fovea is also a blind spot when something is viewed in very dim light.

of the eye, and the part onto which these shadows are cast, is the **fovea**. The clarity and acuity of human vision depend a great deal on this area.

Look at a single word on this page. That one word, which is projecting directly onto your fovea, will be very clear. The words around it, however, which are projecting onto peripheral portions of your retina, will be indistinct. If you try to decipher the nearby words without removing your glance from the first word, you'll find you are unable to recognize other words only a short distance away. To see something clearly, you need to focus directly on that object. Then it will be projected onto your fovea.

THE BLIND SPOT. The portion of the peripheral retina where the optic nerve passes through the retina on its way to the brain contains no photoreceptors. Because it has no photoreceptors, this area is unable to sense light and is known as the **blind spot.** You can locate your own blind spot by following the directions in Figure 5.7. As you will see, the white circle completely vanishes. Look at the figure again, but this time, while keeping your eye on the cross, notice what replaces the white spot when it disappears. You should see the red wall. How can this be? You cannot see the white spot because there are no photoreceptor cells on the portion of your retina onto which the spot is projected. But without photoreceptors, how can you see the red wall where the spot had been? The answer is that your brain is lying to you. Unlike the camera, your brain tells you that there is something where there is nothing. These blind spots in each eye are always with you, but rather than let you go through life with two holes in your vision, your brain takes the surrounding material, copies it, and fills in the blind spots with similar material. It may be

◆ **FIGURE 5.6**

While looking at a homogeneous background, such as a white wall or a blue sky, you may have had a chance to observe shadows of things floating within your eye. You can enhance your view of such objects by making a pinhole in a piece of paper or cardboard and then looking through the pinhole at a homogeneous background. If you've ever wondered what the things that you see floating around are, now's your chance to find out. In this figure, an artist has drawn the things that can be seen and a physiologist has labeled what they are. Try this experiment to see what you find. (SOURCE: *Walker, 1982, p. 151.*)

Dark specks: opaque spots in lens

Bright but vague patches: seams in lens membrane

Grainy texture: fovea

Lines radiating from center: radial structure of lens

Bright specks: cells near lens

Bright spots or stars: drops on cornea

Bright and dark lines: from moisture on cornea

Floater: blood cell

Wrinkled patches: floating membranes

◆ **FIGURE 5.7**

Finding the blind spot. With your right eye closed, look at the cross in the upper-right corner. Hold the book up and slowly move it back and forth until the circle disappears (about 1 foot from your eye). This is no small laboratory illusion. Throughout the day, objects disappear in your blind spot. As you walk down the street, whole buildings vanish from your sight—without your awareness. This phenomenon highlights the limitations of our processing system's ability to give us a "real" knowledge of the world (Tollefson, 1984).

a lie, but it makes life—at least your visual understanding of it—a little less confusing.

Interestingly, whatever the filling-in process is, it doesn't appear to be cognitive, that is, it is not based on mental expectations (Ramachandran, 1992). Look at Figure 5.8 and you will readily see that the brain does not fill in the blind spot as you might expect it would based on your mental expectation of what is missing. Figure 5.9 is even more curious. For some reason, the blind spot fills in with the green stripe, not the red one or a mixture of both. Somehow, the greater length of the green stripe affects the "filling-in" system.

It also appears that there are two distinct filling-in mechanisms. In one experiment, volunteers looked at a large pink square with twinkling black dots. A small gray square with solid black dots then moved across the larger pink square with twinkling black dots. When the volunteers looked off to one side so as to put this interesting combination into their blind spots, they reported that *first* the gray square with black dots vanished and was replaced with twinkling black dots and *then* the pink color slowly filled in (Ramachandran, 1992). This indicates that there may be separate filling-in mechanisms for texture and color. Because of discoveries like these, it is now believed that the filling-in process may follow certain mechanical rules based on set principles rather than being dependent on each individual's learning and experience.

PHOTORECEPTOR CELLS. Surprisingly, the photoreceptors that comprise the *last* layer of the retina are the *first* neurons activated by the incoming light.

◆ **FIGURE 5.8**

Set the middle dot in your blind spot by closing your right eye and looking at the cross with your left eye. Although the middle dot disappears, the brain does not fill in with another dot to complete the obvious pattern of five dots. This indicates that whatever the filling-in mechanism is, it isn't based on our mental expectations of what should be filling the space covered by the blind spot. (After Ramachandran, 1992.)

PHOTONS

Massless particles of light that carry energy. The energy carried is indirectly proportional to the wavelength of the particle: The shorter the wavelength, the greater the energy. Common names for photons depend on the wavelength and include, among others, radio waves, microwaves, visible light, and X rays.

WAVELENGTH

The linear distance from a point on one oscillation of a wave to the corresponding point on the next oscillation of that wave.

ELECTROMAGNETIC SPECTRUM

The entire range of possible wavelengths for light, both visible and invisible (such as X rays and radio waves).

VISIBLE SPECTRUM

The range of wavelengths of light visible to the unaided eye.

HUE

Specifically, the color of a visible light. Hue is determined by the wavelength of the visible light and, depending on the particular wavelength in question, may be called red, yellow, blue, and so on. Perceived hue may also be affected slightly by extreme changes in brightness.

BRIGHTNESS

A property of color determined by the number of photons issuing forth per square unit area. Shifts in brightness are perceived by the observer as changes along a light-dark continuum.

SATURATION

The purity or richness of a color. Highly saturated colors are vivid and striking, while poorly saturated colors appear faded or washed out.

The retina is so thin that incoming light easily passes *through all the other layers of the retina first* on its way to the photoreceptors. The photoreceptors are the first step in the process by which the brain interprets what it sees. The way in which these receptors work is the key to several interesting phenomena.

As we mentioned earlier, the two main types of photoreceptive neurons are the rods and the cones. As their names imply, the rods have a cylindrical shape, while the cones are more pear-shaped or conical. Each retina contains more than 100 million rods and 6 million cones. These are afferent sensory neurons that are sensitive to particles of light called **photons,** which travel in waves. The distance between waves is called the **wavelength,** and it determines the kind of light. The different kinds of light are shown in the **electromagnetic spectrum** (see Figure 5.10). The human eye is sensitive to only a small portion of this spectrum, known as the **visible spectrum.** X rays and radio waves, which are kinds of light, although you may not have thought of them as such, are found on the electromagnetic spectrum, but are not within the visible spectrum. *Within the visible spectrum*, a long wavelength appears red; as the wavelength shortens, the color changes. The middle wavelengths appear green, and the shorter wavelengths blue. The color created by a given wavelength is known as the **hue.** How a color appears to you may also be influenced by its **brightness** or by its **saturation.**

Different rods and cones are stimulated by different wavelengths within the visible light range. The rods are sensitive to all the light within the visual spectrum *except red*. The cones are not uniform in their response to light. Some are red-sensitive, some are green-sensitive, and some are blue-sensitive (see Figure 5.11). Cone cells are responsible, along with higher areas of the brain, for our ability to see colors. Rods, on the other hand, are not part of the color vision system.

Rods and cones are different in two other important ways as well—sensitivity and acuity, or sharpness of perception. Rods are far more sensitive to light than are cones. For this reason, the rods function best under reduced illumination; they give us our ability to see when there is so little light that objects appear to be only black or gray. In fact, rods are so sensitive that a rod cell will respond even if struck by only a single photon of light (Schnapf & Baylor, 1987)! Many more than one rod cell must respond before absolute threshold can be reached, however, so although one photon may stimulate a rod cell, it is not enough light for the brain to see. It is just as well that our vision works this way. Rods are always firing to some extent, if for no other reason than that atoms in a warm body like ours are active (their activity is why our bodies are warm) and warm atoms give off a certain number of photons in the range to which rods are sensitive. If our absolute threshold were much lower than it is, our vision might be overwhelmed by this "background noise." Cold-blooded creatures like frogs, on the other hand, don't face this problem to the same extent as we warm-blooded creatures do. Their atoms aren't as active (which is why they are cold) and their absolute thresholds are

◆ **FIGURE 5.9**

Set the circle at the intersection in your blind spot by closing your right eye and looking at the cross with your left eye. The green stripe will appear to overlap the red stripe. Something in the filling-in mechanism is using the length of the green stripe to determine that the green stripe should dominate the filled-in scene. (After Ramachandran, 1992.)

◆ FIGURE 5.10

The electromagnetic spectrum. When a white light is directed through a prism, the visible light spectrum results.

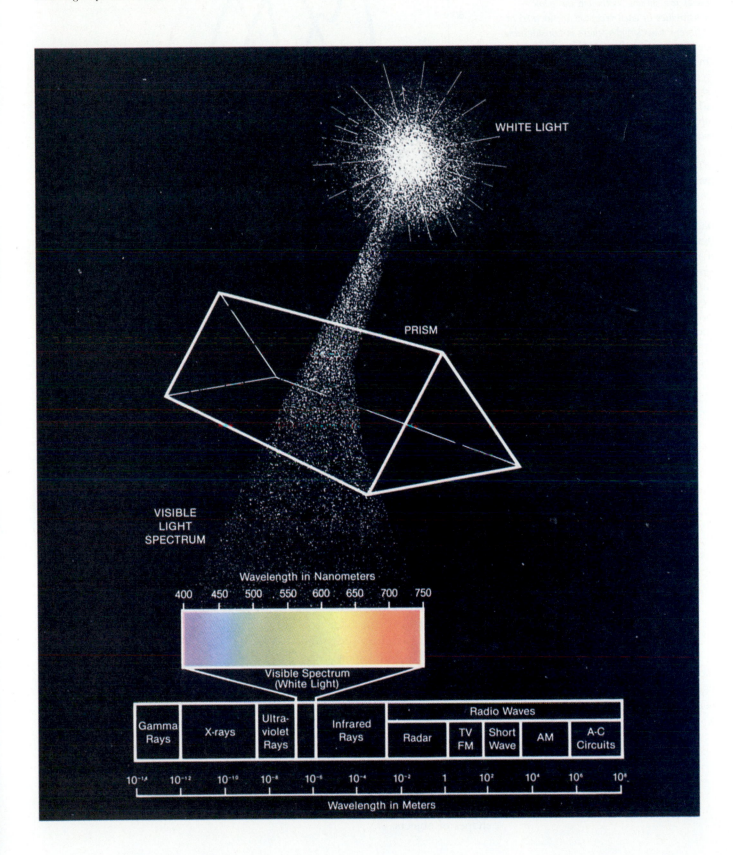

◆ FIGURE 5.11

Responses of the photoreceptor cells to different wavelengths. Rods and blue-sensitive, green-sensitive, and red-sensitive cones are shown. Although the peak sensitivities of each receptor are located at different wavelengths, there is considerable overlap among cells at many wavelengths. In fact, all four photoreceptors are responsive to the wavelengths of light shown in the gray area of the figure, which corresponds to wavelengths of approximately 460 to 530 nanometers (1 nanometer equals one-billionth of a meter, or 1×10^{-9} meters). For example, if blue light of the wavelength 450 nanometers strikes the retina, the blue cones will fire at approximately 80 percent of their maximum possible intensity, and the rod cells will fire at approximately 40 percent of their maximum intensity. Unlike the typical neuron that we discussed in Chapter 2, which can fire at only one intensity after reaching action potential ("all or nothing"), individual visual neurons are capable of sending messages throughout an entire range of neural intensities, from very weak to maximum strength. (SOURCE: Adapted from Land, 1977.)

much lower than ours, which, of course, allows frogs to have much better night vision than we humans can ever hope to have (Aho, Donner, Hyden, Larsen, & Reuter, 1988). All this clearly explains why, when it comes to hunting bugs at night, frogs will beat you every time.

As light levels increase, rods drastically reduce their function. In fact, as soon as it is bright enough that you become aware of colors, you know that your cones must be responding. When light becomes almost too bright for the rods to handle, it is just dim enough for the cones to begin taking over. For this reason, cones are typically active only during daylight or under artificial illumination.

The cones also have far greater acuity than do the rods. One reason that the fovea has such great acuity is that it has no rods, only cones. This explains the clarity with which we see images striking the fovea. Acuity can also vary considerably from individual to individual, depending on how densely cone cells are packed within the fovea (Curcio, Sloan, Packer, Hendrickson, & Kalina, 1987). Rods and cones together make up the periphery of the retina.

Because the fovea has only cones, the eye has a second "blind" spot. If you look *directly* at a dim star on a very dark night, the star may seem to disappear. If you shift your glance a little to one side of the star, however, the star may reappear. This phenomenon occurs because when you look directly at the star, the light from the star shines on your fovea, which contains only cones, and the cones are not sensitive enough to see such a dim light. When you look to the side, however, the light from the star strikes the periphery of the retina. Rods in the periphery are stimulated by the dim illumination, and the star reappears. This blind spot is distinctly different from the other blind spot we discussed earlier, which is located at the point where the optic nerve exits through the retina, an area that has no photoreceptors at all.

Dark Adaptation

You have no doubt had the experience of going from a lighted room into a dark one. At first, you can't see anything and it's difficult to make out forms or shapes. You are likely to trip over objects or bump into them. Gradually, however, you adapt to the dark. After about 10 minutes, assuming there is a little light, perhaps moonlight or some other dim glow, you are able to see the shapes of objects.

About 30 or 40 minutes after you enter the dark room, your rods reach full sensitivity: They adapt to the dark. This **dark adaptation** is due to a slow chemical change in the rods. To reverse your dark adaptation to **light adaptation,** you need only turn on a bright light; your rods will quickly lose their dark adaptation. When you've been in the light for a few minutes, you become light adapted; then, if you turn out the lights again, your rods will have to become dark adapted again, and this will take some time. Because you have two retinas, you can use a trick to keep your dark adaptation. After you've become dark adapted, tightly close one eye, or even put your hand over it when you turn on a light, so that only the uncovered eye is exposed to the bright light. Use the open eye to work in the light. Of course, when you turn out the lights again, you won't be able to see anything with the eye that you've been using, because it will be light adapted. But take your hand off the closed eye and open it. You will find that this eye has remained dark adapted and that you can use it to see your way around in the dark.

Knowledge about these photoreceptors and how they work has come in handy in ways you might not have considered. In 1940, Hitler launched his air force against the British. Facing this aerial onslaught were a few Royal Air Force pilots manning fighter planes. Seriously outnumbered, they took off at all hours of the night to meet the oncoming enemy. Because the pilots had to rush to their planes at a moment's notice in the predawn hours, they had to keep their eyes dark adapted. They were never sure when they would be called into the air, so they had to avoid light from sunset on, waiting in pitch-black ready rooms. They couldn't play cards, read books, or even see one another's faces. They simply waited, hour after hour in complete darkness, until a call came to take to the air.

In the United States, a psychologist named Walter R. Miles, who was a renowned researcher of the sensory system, heard about the plight of the British pilots. Miles understood that the fighter pilots had to maintain dark adaptation, but he also realized that it was absolutely unnecessary for them to sit in the dark. Miles knew that the rod photoreceptors, those required for night vision, were not sensitive to the red end of the spectrum; therefore, red light could not light-adapt the rods. He informed the Royal Air Force of this fact, and red lights were placed in the fighter pilots' ready rooms. Thereafter, pilots

DARK ADAPTATION
The process by which the eyes become more sensitive to light in dim illumination.

LIGHT ADAPTATION
The process by which the eyes become less sensitive to light in bright illumination.

As the sun sets, operators monitoring modern U.S. strategic bombers switch their control room to red light so they will remain dark-adapted throughout the night.

YOUNG-HELMHOLTZ THEORY
A theory of color vision stating that there are three basic colors (red, green, and blue) and three types of receptors, each of which is receptive to the wavelengths of one of the colors.

PRIMARY COLORS
The three colors from which all other colors can be made, usually considered to be red, green, and blue.

waiting for their flights were able to see one another's faces as they played cards or read books. They could pass the time sharing one another's company (Miller, 1980).

Ever since that time, it has been the practice of the military in night operations to use red light in submarines in case the ship has to surface and in aircraft so that the pilots can see when they look out into the dark. Work can go on, because the red-sensitive cones are stimulated by the red light, and dark adaptation is maintained because the rods don't react to that color of light.

Color Vision

Why does a bull charge at a red cape? Whatever the reason, it's certainly not because the cape is red. Bulls do not have color vision and wouldn't know a red cape from a green one. In fact, most mammals are totally color-blind and can see only blacks, whites, and grays. Some mammals, dogs and cats, for instance, have some color vision, but not as rich as ours. In general, color vision is rare in mammals, and even among other primates (apes, monkeys), only some have color vision as rich as we humans possess. Color vision is much more common among birds, fish, insects, and reptiles and, especially among insects, may extend to wavelengths beyond those to which human eyes are sensitive.

THE YOUNG-HELMHOLTZ THEORY.   Color vision is a complicated phenomenon, and a number of theories have been developed to explain how it operates. A popular theory of color vision developed during the nineteenth century is known as the **Young-Helmholtz theory.** It is based on the work of Thomas Young, an English physicist, and additional work, half a century later, by Hermann von Helmholtz, a German physiologist. The theory derives from the fact that all colors in the spectrum can be produced from three **primary** colors, red, green, and blue. This odd fact appeared to be explainable only if we assumed that the human visual system was specifically responding only to these three colors (which is why they appeared to be "primary"). The perception of other colors, therefore, must be produced by various mixtures of the three primaries (see Figure 5.12). This idea occurred to Thomas Young in 1802, when he deduced that the retina couldn't possibly hold enough sensors to

Some fire departments have painted their trucks a fluorescent yellow-green because this is the color that can best be perceived in dim light when other colors may appear gray or black and white.

respond to each of the thousands of different colors that people can discriminate (Nathans, 1989). Instead, he realized that there must be three kinds of primary receptors in the retina.

The Young-Helmholtz theory, then, proposes that there are three kinds of color receptors in the retina, one for receiving each of the primary colors. Physiological data have supported this hypothesis, and three different kinds of cones have been discovered—one kind sensitive to red, one to green, and one to blue light. In fact, investigators have isolated the genes that create the three kinds of cone cells (Nathans 1989), which provides extremely strong support for the theory.

COLOR BLINDNESS.   Some people have an insensitivity to a particular color or are unable to see certain colors at all. This condition is known as **color blindness.** Most color blindness is *sex-linked*; it is more common in men than in women. Eight percent of all men and 0.05 percent of all women are afflicted with one form of color blindness or another (see Figure 5.13). The research on color blindness also lends support to the Young-Helmholtz theory that color blindness results from a weakness in a particular cone system or from that system's complete inability to function.

COLOR BLINDNESS
The inability to see one or more colors. The most common kind is green-cone color blindness.

◆ **FIGURE 5.12**

Additive mixing—*combining beams of light made from the three primaries—gives rise to all possible colors. Where red light and green light intersect, for example, both red and green cones will receive stimulation, creating the sensation of yellow. (If you are curious, a pure yellow light would also stimulate both the red and green cones because both are sensitive to yellow light. This, too, would give rise to the sensation of yellow. Either way, pure yellow light or a red-green mixture, yellow is the resulting sensation.) When equal intensities of red, green, and blue light are mixed, the result is white. White has no wavelength; it is not a color, but an experience. In subtractive mixing, pigments that absorb light are blended or, as in this example, overlapped with one another. Each time a new pigment is blended or overlapped, more color is subtracted. When equal intensities of the three primaries absorb light, all that remains is black. Purely black objects are completely invisible and are only apparent because they are often surrounded or bordered by visible objects.*

◆ FIGURE 5.13

A test for color blindness.

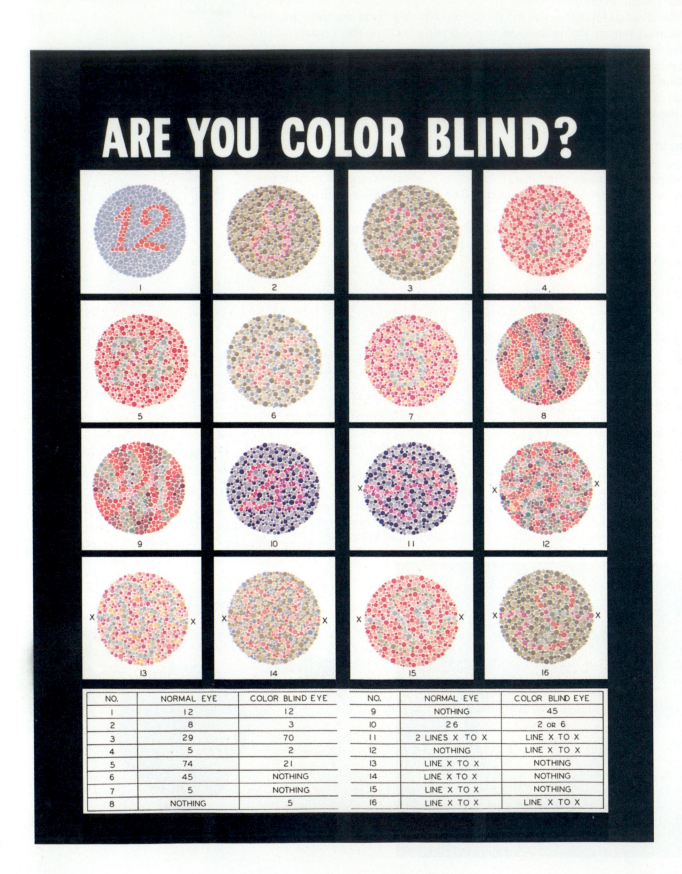

People with normal color vision are called **trichromats;** that is, they use all three color channels. People missing one of the color channels are called **dichromats.** The most extreme form of color blindness exists among **mono-chromats.** A monochromat has only one functioning cone channel. To date, all monochromats have been found to have a functioning blue channel and defective red and green channels. *Monochromasy* is an extremely rare condition and results in black-and-white vision, not unlike what you see when observing a black-and-white television set, although not as clear. Sections of a mono-chromat's fovea are filled with many nonfunctioning cones, which, to a degree, interfere with the production of normal, clear vision. There are even rare cases of individuals with no cone channels operating at all. These people, like mono-chromats, cannot see color, and they have the additional problem of being "day-blind," because the rods, which don't function under bright illumination, provide their only working visual system. Their visual acuity is also very poor because they have no functioning visual cells in the fovea, which is packed only with cones, and they are also unable to sense red objects under any illumination (the rods do not respond to red).

The Young-Helmholtz, or three-color, theory argues that there should be three forms of color blindness, one associated with each kind of cone. Three forms do, in fact, exist. People who have defects in their red cones (who are called *red-minus*) are red-green color-blind. To them, both red and green ap-pear yellow. People who have defects in their green cones (who are called *green-minus*) are also called red-green color-blind, but really have the most trouble discriminating purple from green. Green-minus color blindness is the most common form of color disability. Unlike red-minus and green-minus color-blindness, blue-cone color blindness (known as *blue-minus*) is not sex-linked, which means that it is just as common in women as in men. Even so, blue-minus color blindness is extremely rare. People who have this disorder are blue-yellow color-blind and cannot tell the difference between those two colors.

We've learned how the world looks to the color-blind, not by deduction, but by studying the very rare individuals who have color blindness in one eye but normal vision in the other (Graham & Hsia, 1958). These people look with their color-blind eye at red or green and then match what they see with colors they perceive through their normal eye. The fact that it isn't always easy to simply deduce what a color-blind person should see has led some re-searchers to conclude that the Young-Helmholtz theory doesn't offer a full explanation of color vision after all.

THE OPPONENT-PROCESS THEORY.   Around 1870, the three-color Young-Helmholtz theory was challenged by researcher Ewald Hering, who developed what became known as the **opponent-process theory.** Hering agreed with Young and Helmholtz that there were three kinds of receptors, but he did not believe that these receptors responded to red, green, and blue. Instead, Hering thought that one kind of receptor responded only to brightness; it was a dark-light receptor. The second kind of receptor responded to a red-green contin-uum, and the third kind to a yellow-blue continuum (see Figure 5.14). Hering believed, for example, that if receptors along the red-green continuum were at rest, no color would be sensed in that continuum, but that if the receptors were depolarized in one direction or hyperpolarized in the other, either red or green would be sensed. This theory, Hering believed, explained the phenom-enon of the **negative afterimage** (see Figures 5.15 and 5.16). When a red-green sensitive receptor is looking at red, red is the message that is sent to the brain. When the red message is turned off, the cell leaves one phase and shifts to

TRICHROMATS
People with normal color vision, who have all three cone systems functioning correctly.

DICHROMATS
People with color blindness due to the defective functioning of one of the three cone systems.

MONOCHROMATS
People who have color blindness due to the defective functioning of two of their three cone systems. Most monochromats can see no color at all. Interestingly, all monochromats so far tested have functioning blue cones. This appears to occur because the genes for the red and green cones are located close together, making it possible for a single error or trauma to knock out both red and green cone systems.

OPPONENT-PROCESS THEORY
Hering's theory of color vision in which he argued that photoreceptors function along red-green, blue-yellow, and light-dark continuums and are in opposition to each other.

NEGATIVE AFTERIMAGE
An opposite color image that persists briefly after the originally viewed object is removed. It is the result of fatigued color receptors in the retina.

◆ **FIGURE 5.14**

The visual receptor system as Hering believed it might be. Today there is evidence that the cones are receptive to red, green, and blue (MacNichol, 1964) and not to red-green, blue-yellow, and light-dark as Hering thought. However, an opponent-process system somewhat like the one Hering envisioned does operate at levels higher than the first layer of the retina.

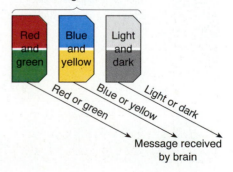

Sensory receptors receiving stimulus

Message received by brain

◆ FIGURE 5.15

To experience a negative afterimage, stare at the yellow circle for about 1 minute. Then glance at a white sheet of paper or a white wall and blink your eyes a few times. A blue circle should appear.

the other, producing a green afterimage. Hering envisioned the same process for yellow-blue receptors.

The opponent-process view is also supported by evidence at the cellular level. In 1956, researchers first discovered cells that operated in the way Hering had predicted (Svaetichin, 1956). In these experiments, the horizontal cells in the retinas of goldfish were examined with microelectrodes, one at a time. The researchers discovered that some cells became very excited when exposed to a particular color—red, for example. When the same cells were exposed to green, however, they actually responded less than they had been responding before stimulation. Some cells worked the opposite way: Green stimulated them, while red had the opposite effect.

The apparent conflict between the two views has been resolved by modern theories of color vision that include aspects of both. The three-color Young-Helmholtz theory seems to be a good description of the first stage of visual processing by the cone photoreceptors, because cones have been found to be sensitive to red, green, and blue, rather than to light-dark, red-green, and yellow-blue. The opponent-process theory, on the other hand, seems to provide a better explanation of color vision at the horizontal-cell and ganglion-cell levels, where information from the three kinds of cones is not added, but rather is contrasted into averages, as Hering envisioned—by the time the information has reached the optic nerve, it has already undergone opponent-processing in some manner (Haber, 1985).

The three-pigment cone system may even interact in an opponent process at the photoreceptor level. This is one of the more popular possibilities currently under examination. For instance, it has been discovered that in turtles, red and green cones are directly connected to one another in the retina (Normann, Perlman, Kolb, Jones, & Daly, 1984). Similar connections may exist in the human retina. Researchers are making discoveries all the time, and no doubt our view of color vision eventually will be modified further.

COLOR CONSTANCY THEORY. For many years, Edwin Land, the inventor of the Polaroid camera, had argued that something peculiar was occurring in the color vision system that had not been addressed by either of the theories we have discussed so far. Color film is sensitive to the wavelengths of light that strike the film. Color film acts according to the Young-Helmholtz view in the sense that red, green, and blue light excite pigments on the film that are sensitive to each of these colors. But have you ever taken a color picture indoors without a flash? Figure 5.17 shows you what can happen. The heavy

◆ FIGURE 5.16

Another example of negative afterimage. Look at the dot in the middle of the flag for 30 seconds or more. Then look at any white surface, such as a wall or a piece of paper. An American flag in its usual colors should appear.

orange glow from the typical tungsten filament light bulbs that are usually used indoors covers everything and gives an odd cast to the picture. There's nothing wrong with the film—it's "seeing" orange wavelengths of light that are really there. Land was puzzled by the discrepancy between what we perceive and what the camera records; if either or both of the theories we have already discussed told the whole story, indoor lighting should look just as orange to us as it does to color film—but it doesn't. Something in our visual system keeps colors looking normal and constant, even under some very great wavelength fluctuations such as those that result in the orange cast caused by indoor light bulbs. Engineers say that a system like ours has *automatic gain control*. In other words, once our visual system has decided that something is "red" in comparison with other colors in the immediate vicinity, it will hold the "redness" constant over an incredible range of lighting conditions, even to the point of eliminating the heavy orange cast created by indoor lighting. This automatic gain control, or **color constancy,** appears to work by calculating ratios of one color to its surrounding color. As we have already discovered, this kind of ratio message is created in part by the bipolar cells. To understand how this ratio signaling maintains color over broad ranges of frequencies, imagine that you are looking at a yellow canary perched in a green bush. The yellow bird would excite your red cones more than the green bush would (yellow has a frequency that is closer to red than to green). For the sake of argument, let's say your red cones were four times more excited by the yellow bird than by the green plant. We can express this as a ratio of 4:1. Now carry the bird and the bush indoors (easier said than done) and look at them in indoor lighting. The orangish light from your indoor light bulbs shines on the bird and the bush. Now the bird excites your red cones even more (because of the added reflected orange light), *but so does the bush* (because it, too, is reflecting the additional orange light). The 4:1 ratio does not change! Color constancy, expressed as a ratio of two channels (red and green), allows your brain to discount the orange cast and keep the canary yellow and the bush green.

Color constancy appears to be one of the many functions of a special grouping of cells found far into the occipital lobes (Jameson & Hurvich, 1989). So little is known about these cells that they are currently referred to in the color

COLOR CONSTANCY
The tendency for a color to appear unchanged regardless of changes in lighting conditions.

◆ **FIGURE 5.17**

A room lighted by typical tungsten filament light bulbs has an actual orange cast. The camera sees this. The human eye and brain, though the mechanism of color constancy, filter out this orange cast, maintaining a perception of the colors as constant under many different lighting conditions.

vision literature as "the blobs" (not exactly a high-tech term, but descriptive nevertheless of both their shape and our bewilderment).

To understand why there is a color constancy system in human vision, we need to examine the reason for the existence of color vision. As some researchers like to say, "You can't understand biology, if you don't understand evolution." It appears that color vision evolved because it gave primates an advantage by enabling them to identify the useful and dangerous objects in their environments more effectively. Considering this possibility, it is reasonable to assume that color vision wouldn't be as useful if the colors of objects constantly altered as lighting conditions changed. So we can further assume that color constancy evolved because of the advantages of keeping the colors of known objects the same. You can readily deduce the value to our arboreal forebears of always sensing a tiger's stripes as the same orangish color or a tasty fruit as the same red, whether they were observed in the pink illumination of early dawn, beneath the bright white light of the noonday sun, or under the blue-gray light of an overcast or foggy sky.

CONCEPT REVIEW ◆ VISUAL CELLS OF THE RETINA

Rod Cells
The most plentiful of the photoreceptors; not part of the color vision system; supersensitive to light, but unresponsive to red; have poor acuity; not found in the fovea; used for night vision.

Cone Cells
Cells of the color vision system; three kinds: red-, green-, and blue-sensitive; have great acuity; fovea is packed with them; need much more light than rods before they can function.

Bipolar Cells
Cells that collect and consolidate visual information. A particular bipolar cell is either "rod-driven" or "cone-driven," meaning that it receives information from either groups of rods or groups of cones but never from a mixture of the two. Bipolar cells transmit a ratio derived from the signals they receive from the photoreceptors and nearby horizontal cells to the ganglion cells.

Ganglion Cells
Receive information from bipolar or amacrine cells; operate in an opponent-process fashion; some ganglion cells respond to the direction of motion of an object.

Horizontal Cells
Fire according to the average light intensity generated by the photoreceptors in each of their immediate neighborhoods; make lateral connections between cones; influence opposing color processes (such as red and green, blue and yellow) and are probably responsible, in part, for negative afterimages and other opponent-process effects.

Amacrine Cells
Make lateral connections between ganglion cells or between ganglion and rod-driven bipolar cells; modify and control visual messages; sharpen ganglion-cell response; over 30 different kinds, the functions of which are largely unknown.

AFTEREFFECTS. **Aftereffects** are different from afterimages in an important way, and this difference helps to show that specialized cells continue to process visual information further within the brain, beyond the retina. Aftereffects can transfer from one eye to the other (although the transfer effect may be quite weak). Recall the afterimage experiment with the American flag in Figure 5.16. If you look at the flag again, but this time with your left eye only, and then search for the afterimage with your right eye, you won't see any afterimage. This color phenomenon occurs only at the retinal level, and information can't be transferred from one eye to the other. However, if you follow the instructions in Figure 5.18, you'll see an aftereffect that will transfer from one eye to the other. We can infer that the detectors that are fatigued in the aftereffect are not located in the retina, but rather are located at a higher level, where information from both eyes can interact. What is happening to the visual information at this higher level is an area of intense interest.

Receptive Fields

The stimulation of the photoreceptor rods and cones is only the first neural step in the visual process. After the millions of photoreceptors are stimulated by incoming light that is focused on the retina, the information is passed to the next layers of the retina, then down the optic nerve, and finally deeper into the brain. As you can imagine, the entire system is unbelievably complicated, and no one yet is certain how it works. Researchers, however, are trying to unravel some of the mysteries. Let's have a look at a few of their ideas.

FEATURE DETECTORS. Look again at Figure 5.4, and notice the ganglion cells that make up the last layer of the retina to process visual information. This figure looks complicated enough, but in fact it's far too simple; it doesn't depict the specializations of this layer of the retina. For instance, there are over 20 kinds of specialized ganglion cells. Each kind responds to a complex pattern of light created by many rods and cones at a particular location on the retina. Each ganglion cell, then, is responding to what is called a **receptive field.** For example, one kind of ganglion cell may respond most to a receptive field comprising a red spot on a green background. Another kind of ganglion cell might respond most to a green spot on a red background. Still another may respond to motion in a certain direction. In this layer of the retina, then, cells specialized to detect certain kinds of complex stimuli are already in place. But what happens to the message once it leaves the ganglion cells and travels down the optic nerve farther on into the brain? It appears that the visual messages pass through increasingly specialized detectors (cells that respond to

AFTEREFFECTS
An effect brought on by fatigue in visual receptors at higher levels in the visual system. Unlike afterimages, aftereffects transfer from one eye to the other. Also known as negative aftereffects.

RECEPTIVE FIELD
The grouping of information from many neurons so that a single neuron may readily respond to the information as a single input. For example, a ganglion cell may be responsive to a receptive field created by many photoreceptors, or a complex cell may be responsive to a receptive field created by many simple cells.

◆ **FIGURE 5.18**

A tilt aftereffect. Look at the left drawing. Do not look in one place, but scan your eyes back and forth across the horizontal bar. This provides apparent motion to the object and will help fatigue the complex cells that combine edge detection with motion. Shortly, you will fatigue cells sensitive to the angles in the left diagram. Then quickly look at the right diagram.

Opposing cells will now dominate, and you should see the vertical lines and right angles appear as diagonal lines and acute angles bending in the opposite direction from those in the left drawing. You can prove that this illusion is an aftereffect, not an afterimage, by showing that it transfers from one eye to the other. Look again at the left figure with one eye only. After a sufficient time of scanning the left figure, close that eye and look quickly at the right figure with the other eye. The effect will be very brief, but it should transfer. This demonstrates that such edge motion and angle detectors are located at higher levels in the brain, where information from both eyes converges.

FEATURE DETECTORS
Innate sensory mechanisms tuned
specifically to respond to particular
aspects of the environment.

SIMPLE CELLS
Cells in the cerebral cortex that respond
to lines of a particular orientation.

COMPLEX CELLS
Cells in the visual cortex that respond
to various combinations of motion,
orientation, or color. Complex cells
usually are associated with large
receptive fields.

HYPERCOMPLEX CELLS
Cells in the cerebral cortex that respond
to complex combinations of visual
stimuli, including width, length, edges,
and certain forms.

unique patterns, forms, or colors), each, it is assumed, with its own receptive field. These are known as **feature detectors.** At each step along the way, feature detector cells help make sense of what you see.

The first important feature detectors in the occipital lobe to receive information from the optic nerve are called **simple cells.** Simple cells are assumed to have receptive fields for information about lines or edges arriving from the visual system. Some simple cells are known to depolarize (fire) when they receive inputs about vertical edges, but hyperpolarize (become harder to fire) when they receive inputs about horizontal edges, and vice versa. Some appear to respond to inputs about diagonal gradations of edges between horizontal and vertical. Some simple cells seem to have receptive fields for information about motion.

Beyond the simple cells are **complex cells.** Complex cells are thought not only to be sensitive to vertical, horizontal, or diagonal edges but also to have receptive fields for the motion of objects. For instance, a particular complex cell may respond most excitedly to combined inputs from feature detectors responding to a diagonal edge *and* a left-to-right motion, while another complex cell may respond most to inputs of horizontal edge *and* an up-to-down motion. At this point, more information about the scene you've glanced at is combined and analyzed. Some complex cells seem to combine color and edges. For instance, certain cells may be responsive to vertical red edges, or to diagonal green ones, or the like. There may be different complex cells for every possible combination.

Information from complex cells then appears to be passed on to hypercomplex cells. **Hypercomplex cells** seem to have receptive fields to inputs about orientation, movement, color, *and* also length or width or even corners. Of course, this view of how the brain makes sense of vision leaves us with a distinct problem. There have to be limits to how specialized visual detectors can become, simply because at some point too many cells would be needed to cover all the possible combinations. We can't expect that we will eventually discover super-ultra-hypercomplex cells only responsive to a receptive field of inputs for lavender Oldsmobiles traveling left to right at a distance of five meters. Even hypercomplex cells, then, cannot hope to recognize an entire visual image, but would need to share information with millions of other hypercomplex cells. And therein lies the major problem with this view of vision. It relies on a system that probably requires too many comparisons to be made before a total image could emerge, too many comparisons (billions, perhaps trillions, every fraction of a second as the image changes) for the brain to make.

One solution to the problem we encounter when trying to understand how the brain could possibly make the trillions of comparisons needed for a mental image to emerge from the information gathered by the senses came from a discovery by Barry Richmond and Lance Optican. One day, while measuring the number of firings emitted by visual neurons, Richmond noticed that as he altered the visual stimulus, the number of firings did not change, but the timing and patterns of the firings *did* change. When he pointed out his discovery to others in the lab, they told him to forget it because those patterns were already known and others had wasted years checking them out. The patterns, they said, didn't seem to mean anything, they were just a nuisance. Undaunted, Richmond and Optican began a very systematic exploration of the different patterns and found that they did indeed go hand and hand with certain stimulations (Optican & Richmond, 1987). This meant that one neuron might be sending two or more bits of information riding on only one signal. The different information was contained in the number of firings, spacing, patterning, and so on, of just one neuron. In a way, FM radio works like this. It sends two different sets of information on one signal, which is why you can hear it in stereo (one signal, but each speaker gets a totally different message). Sending two or more bits of information on *one* signal is called **multiplexing.**

We now know that all of the visual areas of the brain rely on multiplexing (McClurkin, Optican, Richmond, & Gawne, 1991). This means that many fewer comparisons are required then was once believed because individual neurons carry more than a single bit of information as a result of multiplexing. Engineers have known for years that they can always make a simple transmission system more powerful by multiplexing. It appears that nature already knew that!

VISUAL MAPS. Until just a few years ago, most researchers believed that visual information was gathered and processed in the primary visual area of the occipital lobe, an area called V1. A smaller area, V2, also seemed to be involved somehow, but in a minor way. But now we know that the visual field involves over a dozen areas (called maps) in the occipital lobe. Each map is about the size and thickness of a postage stamp (Zeki, 1992). The amazing thing is that each of these areas displays the same screen like a bunch of television sets in a department store all tuned to the same channel! While V1 is still the largest area, these other areas all seem to be quite important. But why is the same information repeated over and over? The reason appears to be that each brain map handles the information differently. Cells in one map may be highly sensitive to motion, while cells in another concentrate on color or shape, and so on. In one area, called V4, cells have been found that respond to ratios, such as firing only when something small is seen in comparison with something large (Schiller & Lee, 1991)! What then does the brain do with all of this information? One idea that used to be popular, but has now been dropped, is that all of the information goes to one central receiving area for interpretation. Instead, the brain appears to work on each of the vision tasks assigned to the different maps in parallel. Computer enthusiasts have been familiar with **parallel processing** for some time. In fact, if you were to interconnect about two dozen typical home computers and let each work on a different part of the same problem, you'd soon find the parallel combination to be almost as powerful as some supercomputers. The problem comes when you try to integrate the information from the separate machines. How the brain accomplishes this feat is still a mystery, but we do know that the different brain maps share their information with each other over millions of connections. Neurons leaving visual maps typically leave from highly specific points and diffuse their information over a wide area in the receiving map (Zeki, 1992). How this turns into the images we see brings us closer to the spirit living in the body or, as it is better known, the mind-body problem (see Chapter 1). Perhaps someday a deeper understanding of the visual system will bring us closer to an understanding of human consciousness.

Computer Modeling

Researchers who study sensation in the brain use many different techniques. One of the most recent involves advanced computers, which can be used to generate a **model** that may yield knowledge about how the brain works. To show you how this is done, let's look at a recent brain model of the occipital lobes, the area of the cerebral cortex most associated with vision.

In the occipital lobes are interesting areas known as ocular dominance columns. When the occipital lobes are stained for viewing under a microscope, these columns, which contain visual receptors, can be seen as swirling stripes throughout the occipital cortex (see Figure 5.19). Interestingly, these distinct

MULTIPLEXING
The act of simultaneously sending two or more distinct messages by way of a single transmission carrier.

PARALLEL PROCESSING
A method of handling information by separating a problem into components, each of which is processed separately and at the same time. This powerful processing method appears to be one of the main ways in which the brain deals with information.

MODEL
A mathematical, logical, or mechanical replica of a relationship or a system of events so designed that a study of the model can yield some understanding of the real thing.

◆ **FIGURE 5.19**

Stripes in the visual cortex of a mammal's brain show the organization of cells responsive to visual information. The stripes are made more visible by a staining procedure. The dark stripes carry information from one eye, while the light stripes carry information from the other. This shows that, while the information from each eye is segregated, it is distributed evenly throughout the visual cortex.

◆ FIGURE 5.20

A computer simulation over time of the action of the visually sensitive cells of the occipital cortex. At first (T = 0), cells respond to information from both eyes. By the end of the program (T = 80), the cells are responding to information from one eye or the other and have formed structures similar to the ocular dominance columns observed to occur in real brains.

columns are not present at birth, but develop gradually as we come to experience our visual world. But why should the occipital lobes be organized in this striking fashion? Working with an advanced computer, researchers created a program in which they gave the computer parameters "derived directly from the physiological characteristics of the cells" (Barinaga, 1990, p. 525). In other words, their program incorporated the known actions of the individual visual cells. They then ran the program and waited to see how all of these millions of interactions, which no one could ever have calculated by hand, would eventually organize the cells. The process and results are seen in Figure 5.20; the final form looks strikingly like the real ocular columns pictured in Figure 5.19! Perhaps, then, this computer program shows us that we already know enough to explain the formation of these columns.

Modeling of the brain with the supercomputers of the future may help us to ask the right questions or lead us directly to new discoveries. For example, if your program won't mimic the brain unless you add "X" to it, then the next step is to go to the real brain and start looking for something there that is actually doing the job of "X." Conversely, if you discover something in the brain you didn't know existed, then you will want to add that parameter to your program and see what kind of difference it makes when you run your model. It is an exciting, interactive way to pursue research and is bound to give us many answers.

◆ FIGURE 5.21

A sound wave. (a) The compression and rarefaction of air molecules. The wave consists of a pulse of compressed air (X) followed by an area of low density. (b) The wave amplitude that corresponds with the compression and rarefaction in (a). The greater the compression, the higher the amplitude. The distance between compressions, or the distance between waves, is the wavelength.

🌀 HEARING

How Sound Is Created

Just as your eyes are sensitive to a limited range of the electromagnetic spectrum, so your ears are sensitive to a limited range of frequencies caused by the compression and rarefaction of air, which create sound waves (see Figure 5.21).

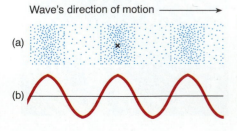

For something to make a sound, it must disturb the surrounding air, creating air waves that radiate from it. Although light can travel in a vacuum, sound cannot; sound depends on a medium such as air or water. Hollywood movies notwithstanding, real spaceships zipping by you in outer space would pass in total silence, without the familiar accompanying whoosh made by objects rushing by in an atmosphere. The moon, for instance, has no atmosphere, so everything that happens on the moon happens in complete silence. When astronauts spoke to one another on the moon, they spoke by means of radio waves, a form of light. Radio waves reaching the astronauts' helmets were converted into sound waves by speakers that caused impacts and compressions within the atmosphere inside the helmets. Had the astronauts removed their helmets and tried to speak to each other, they wouldn't have heard a thing (and they wouldn't have lasted very long, either).

Air waves travel out from the source of a sound in much the same way that waves on a pond ripple outward after a rock has been dropped into the water. Sound waves are generated in all directions, and, like light waves, they have measurable wavelengths. Wavelength in hearing corresponds to **pitch,** whereas wavelength in vision corresponds to hue. Long sound wavelengths are heard as low pitches. Short wavelengths are heard as high pitches. The human ear can perceive a range between approximately 20 cycles, or waves entering the ear, per second and about 20,000 cycles per second (corresponding to wavelengths of between 17 meters and 17 millimeters).* The number of sound waves per second passing a given point is known as the **frequency.** The **amplitude,** or height, of the wave determines the **loudness** (see Figure 5.22). If you could switch your eyes and ears around in some bizarre way, you might imagine that a bright blue light would sound like a loud high-pitched tone while a soft low-pitched tone would look like a dim red light.

Some animals are capable of hearing frequencies higher than those humans can distinguish. Dogs, for example, can hear up to 30,000 or 40,000 cycles per second. Dog whistles work in this range. Dogs trained to respond to these whistles can be summoned from blocks away by a very loud blast on the whistle that neither you nor anyone else around can hear. For years, hunters in Africa had wondered whether elephants possessed a "sixth sense" as they appeared to communicate silently with one another. Now it has been found that the elephants may simply be relying on one of the familiar five senses—hearing. Elephants, it turns out, are able to make infralow frequency sounds (about 14 cycles per second) that can carry great distances. Although your ear cannot pick up such low frequencies, the sound is, in fact, very loud (at least to other elephants).

The Structure of the Ear

Figure 5.23 shows a schematic breakdown of the human ear. The **pinna,** or outer ear, helps to capture sound waves that enter through the external auditory canal and strike the **tympanic membrane,** or eardrum. A subtle vibration of the eardrum sets in motion the three extremely small bones of the middle ear—the **malleus,** the **incus,** and the **stapes.** In fact, these bones are the smallest in the human body. The three bones in turn pass along the vibration, which travels into the **cochlea** within the inner ear. Within the cochlea is the **organ of Corti,** containing approximately 16,000 hairlike cells in four rows. Each hair cell has about 100 **stereocilia,** so there are over 1 million of these

PITCH
The perception of a tone's frequency. In general, shorter wavelengths (higher frequencies) are perceived as having a higher pitch, while longer wavelengths (lower frequencies) are perceived as having a lower pitch.

FREQUENCY
The number of cycles per unit of time in a periodic vibration. Frequency determines the pitch of a sound. Higher frequencies have shorter wavelengths.

AMPLITUDE
A measurement of the amount of energy carried by a wave, shown in the height of the oscillation.

LOUDNESS
A measurement of sound intensity that corresponds to the amplitude of the sound waves.

PINNA
The clearly visible outer portion of the ear. It serves to gather sound.

TYMPANIC MEMBRANE
The thin, semitransparent membrane separating the middle ear from the external ear; it is also called the eardrum.

MALLEUS
The largest of the three small bones in the middle ear; it is also called the hammer.

INCUS
One of the three small bones in the middle ear; it is also called the anvil.

STAPES
One of the three small bones in the middle ear; it is also called the stirrup.

COCHLEA
A spiral tube in the inner ear, resembling a snail shell, which contains nerve endings essential for hearing.

ORGAN OF CORTI
The organ located on the basilar membrane in the cochlea, which contains the hearing receptors.

STEREOCILIA
Extremely short fibers extending from the surface of the hair cells in the inner ear.

*The "bang" from a gunshot or some other sudden sound might be loud enough to harm your ears. If you can't cover your ears to protect them from a loud sound you know is coming, humming just before the sound occurs will help (Borg & Counter, 1989).

◆ FIGURE 5.22

Loudness is measured in decibels (db). A 10-db sound is 10 times louder than one of 0 db (which is the faintest sound that can be heard); a 20-db sound is 100 times louder than one of 0 db and 10 times louder than one of 10 db. The average loud conversation (60 db) is 1 million times louder than the faintest sound that can be heard.

Sounds above 90 db can permanently injure the ear. Sounds also can combine to cause damage—an air hammer being used amidst loud traffic is more damaging than one operated on an empty street.

DECIBEL SCALE FOR SOUNDS
FROM HARMFUL TO FAINT

140 — Physically damaging
120 — Painful
100 — Deafening
80 — Very loud
60 — Loud
40 — Moderate
20 — Faint
0

AUDITORY NERVE
The nerve leading from the cochlea, which transmits sound impulses to the brain.

little items in each ear, which respond to the different frequencies of sound waves. When these superfine stereocilia are bent, they trigger nerve impulses that are sent by the **auditory nerve** to the brain. Perhaps "bent" is too strong a word, because a movement by stereocilia of no greater magnitude than the width of an atom is sufficient to fire the associated nerve cell (see Figure 5.24)! Whether these hair cells fire also is determined by nerve impulses they receive from the brain stem area. Researchers assume that these signals have the effect of dampening or amplifying the auditory message. Such dampening and amplification probably give us the ability to concentrate on only one voice at a

Pinna

Stapes
rocks in
oval window

Cochlear branch
of auditory nerve
(carries nerve
impulses to the brain)

External
auditory
canal

Incus

Malleus

Sound waves

Cochlea

Spinal organ of Corti
(auditory receptors)

Tympanic membrane
(bulges inward)

Tympanic
cavity

Eustachian tube

Round window (bulges outward)

EXTERNAL EAR
(air conduction)

MIDDLE EAR
(bone conduction)

INNER EAR
(fluid conduction)

loud cocktail party, to pick out the flute in an orchestra, or "to turn a deaf ear" to distracting sounds while we are trying to concentrate.

Theories of Hearing

The cochlea is the size of a pea, yet it allows us to discriminate among thousands of incredibly complex tones. How is this possible? A number of theories have been developed to explain how hearing works. The superfine hairs within the organ of Corti are moved by vibrations sent through the liquid in the cochlea, vibrations made by the eardrum as it responds to sound waves by hitting against the oval window at the entrance to the inner ear. It is generally agreed that loudness is determined by the total number of nerves that fire and by the activation of **high-threshold fibers.** These fibers are difficult to bend, and only when they are bent by the considerable force of a loud noise do the nerves associated with them fire, making you aware of a loud noise.

Interestingly, how loud something sounds is also determined by the fine muscles of your middle ear. Have you ever sat in the front row and heard a

HIGH-THRESHOLD FIBERS
Stereocilia in the inner ear that are difficult to bend and thus respond only to loud noises or sounds.

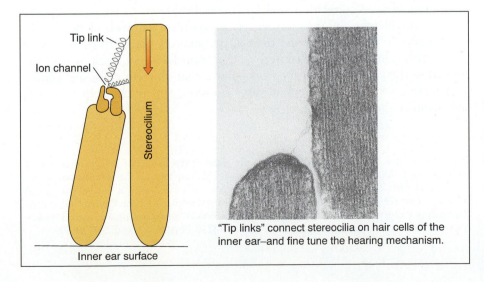

"Tip links" connect stereocilia on hair cells of the inner ear—and fine tune the hearing mechanism.

◆ **FIGURE 5.24**

The mechanism for firing a hair cell in the inner ear is amazingly sophisticated. On the end of each hair cell are bundles of ultrafine stereocilia. Each stereocilium is joined to its neighbor by a "tip link." The tip link is a superfine series of fibers that pull open a "trap-door" ion channel whenever the stereocilium is bent, allowing for the flow of ions, which, in turn, may help the cell to fire. Myosin, a molecule that connects the tip links to the stereocilium, moves up and down like a ratchet along fibers of actin on the stereocilium keeping the tip link at the proper tension.

PLACE THEORY

A theory of hearing that attempts to explain the reception of sound waves between 5000 and 20,000 cycles per second. It asserts that different frequencies stimulate stereocilia at different places within the cochlea. High frequencies stimulate stereocilia near the oval window, while intermediate frequencies stimulate stereocilia away from the oval window.

FREQUENCY THEORY

A theory of hearing designed to explain the reception of sound waves between 20 and 300 cycles per second. According to this theory, auditory neurons fire at rates well correlated with the frequency of the sound.

VOLLEY THEORY

A theory of hearing designed to explain the reception of sound waves between 300 and 5000 cycles per second. According to this theory, auditory neurons fire in volleys that are well correlated with the frequency of the sound.

great opera star sing or had a baby cry right into your ear? Deafening, isn't it? How come the opera star or baby can stand it, when they're even closer to the sound? As it turns out, as soon as you start to vocalize, your middle ear muscles dampen down your hearing so that you don't overwhelm yourself with your own noise (Borg & Counter, 1989). Without those muscles, shouting would be deafening for you.*

Pitch discrimination is a different matter. The perception of high- and middle-range tones appears to be determined by the *place* within the organ of Corti where hairs are stimulated. Very high-pitched tones stimulate hairs near the oval window, while intermediate-range tones stimulate hairs farther within the cochlea. This explanation of tone perception is known as the place theory. The **place theory** would be adequate to explain hearing, except that lower tones—those below 5000 cycles per second—tend to stimulate hairs throughout the entire organ of Corti.

As a partial explanation of how we are able to hear tones lower than 5000 cycles per second, researchers have developed the **frequency theory.** The frequency of a sound may account for our ability to sense tones between 300 and 20 cycles (the lowest that can be registered by the human ear). Because auditory neurons can fire up to 300 times per second, scientists think that these neurons may fire in direct relation to the frequency. They have discovered that frequencies between 300 and 20 cycles per second are fairly well correlated with neural firing. Neurons stimulated by very low-frequency sounds within this range fire roughly an equivalent number of times per second, while neurons stimulated by sounds near 300 cycles per second fire at their maximum of 300 times per second.

The frequency theory, however, still leaves unexplained our perception of sounds in the range between 300 and 5000 cycles per second. A proposal that may help to fill this final gap is the **volley theory.** Although 5000 firings per second would be impossible for one neuron, many neurons firing in volleys could generate up to 5000 pulses per second. In other words, if many neurons all fire at their top speed (300 firings per second for auditory neurons), but out of sequence with one another so that no two are firing at the same instant, they could produce any number of distinct neutral bursts per second. All that would be needed to make sense of such a volley would be some link or connection between the volleying neurons that would yield a sum total firing rate. Researchers refer to such a neural summing mechanism as a *spatial cross-correlator*. With such a mechanism, many volleying neurons could be analyzed as one, allowing us to perceive sounds in the range between 300 and 5000 cycles per second. There is evidence that the auditory nerve does engage in such a spatial cross-correlation analysis (Loeb, 1985).

Once the auditory information leaves the cochlea, it travels along the auditory nerve to the midbrain and then to the auditory cortex in the temporal lobes. Although the hearing centers in the brain have not been as well examined as the visual centers, scientists believe that different cells, specializing in detecting sounds of different quality, duration, and pitch, help to rectify and organize the information.

---

*Some individuals may have hearing loss in only some of the frequency ranges, often due to overexposure to loud sounds (listening to loud music with earphones is the main hazard among college students). This kind of deafness commonly goes unnoticed until it becomes severe. A quick and easy telephone screening test of your hearing is available in the United States at no charge from Occupational Hearing Services, Inc.; it will work on any telephone of good quality. For the local test number nearest you, call 1-800-222-3277 (9 A.M.–5 P.M. E.S.T. M–F).

AN ENDURING QUESTION:
CAN WE LEARN TO FAKE IT?

The senses are our window on the world. They bring us information about what is happening. As Yogi Berra once said, "You can observe a whole lot by just watching."* But are our senses telling us the truth? Philosophers have grappled with this question and have come to the conclusion that there is no way to know. Some have even argued that nothing exists until we sense it. But, in truth, no one knows whether our senses create reality or simply register it and, as best as we can tell, there is no way to find out. As the great philosopher René Descartes concluded after asking himself if there were anything about which he could be certain, "I think, therefore I am." By that he meant that he was sure he existed because he could sense his own thoughts, but whether what he sensed was really there was anybody's guess.

Could we, however, with our growing knowledge about how the senses work, eventually create reality? That is, could we eventually input artificial sensations that could not be discriminated from "real" ones, which would, by definition, make them no less real? Can we someday make any fantasy come true, at least for as long as we are plugged into the "sense machine"? What would such technology do to us as a species, as a society?

Perhaps all of this sounds too much like science fiction to consider seriously. If so, you will probably be surprised to learn what has already been done along these lines. Researchers are interested in this kind of work, not because of some far-off chance to create a new reality, but to help those who have lost their vision or hearing. Most of the best work in this area has been accomplished with those who are deaf owing to damage to the inner ear. For example, almost 15 years ago, Donald Eddington, who is a bioengineer, made an artificial human ear from machine parts in his laboratory with which he was able to aid individuals who became deaf as a result of disease or injury that damaged the fragile hair cells, or stereocilia, that line the inner ear. Hearing aids, which amplify sound entering the ear, are useless to people who have no stereocilia to turn the amplified sound into auditory nerve signals. Eddington's device was an implant made of tiny platinum electrodes that are placed at different points along the cochlea's inner surface via a thin, surgically implanted plug placed just behind the ear. In this way, Eddington electrically tapped into the auditory nerve. Eddington said, "The implant actually bypasses the damaged ear interior. Our electrodes simply stimulate the nerves directly, not with vibrations, but with minute electrical shocks. The system mimics the electrical patterns received by the brain as speech" (Weintraub, 1980, p. 50). Then the plug behind the ear was attached to a cable that ran through a computer to a microphone. The microphone picked up sounds and sent them to the computer, which broke them down by their frequencies. The computer then stimulated the tiny electrodes inside the cochlea according to the frequencies that were received (see Figure 5.25). In this way, the auditory nerve was tricked into

---

*Yogi Berra: former baseball great especially known for his unique utterances, such as, "It's like déjà vu all over again," "Nobody goes there—it's too crowded," "He made the wrong mistake," "It ain't over, 'til its over," and so on.

AN ENDURING QUESTION, CONTINUED

responding to the implants as if they were stereocilia, and it sent messages to the brain based on the stimulation it received.

With devices such as Eddington's, patients who had originally been able to hear before becoming deaf were able to hear voices. Although the voices they heard sounded very "tinny," they were understandable (Tong, Dowell, Blamey, & Clark, 1983; Loeb, 1985).

As computers became more miniaturized and we learned more about the relationship between places within the inner ear and the kinds of sounds created when these places are stimulated, the artificial ear was improved further. Researchers have now developed a pocket-sized computer that filters incoming sounds and sends messages to an artificial ear containing over 5000 platinum implants throughout the inner ear. Perhaps early in the next century, people who had thought they would be deaf for life will be able to hear again as clearly as if their ears had never been damaged.

Similarly, implants of electrodes into occipital lobes that are connected to TV cameras can give rise to the sensation of points of light and colors in individuals who have become totally blind. Suppose someday that such an implant could be made to mimic whatever it is that the brain does to the neural image before it reaches the occipital lobes and could then input this message directly into the neural structures there. If that could ever be done, there should be no reason why we couldn't make fully functional artificial eyes, perhaps even superior to our own natural eyes.

◆ **FIGURE 5.25**

The original artificial ear. Six platinum electrode implants replace the destroyed cilia. The implants stimulate the auditory nerve by generating small electric shocks in response to different frequencies of sound. (SOURCE: Weintraub, 1980, p. 51.)

AN ENDURING QUESTION, CONTINUED

The artificial silicon retina we mentioned earlier is an important first step in this direction.

If we could ever artificially input an entire reality, we could expect a huge demand for it. Think about it—what would you like to experience? But the prospect is also a little depressing. Is this the future of our species—a world where machines and robots do all of the real work so that people can plug their brains into a world of endless excitement and stimulation? Then again, maybe people would use such power judiciously—only the future will tell.

FOR CRITICAL ANALYSIS

1. Do you see the same way other people do? If you experience the color red, is that the same experience your friend is having when she looks at something that she, too, has learned to call "red"? How can you know that what she is experiencing isn't an experience you would consider to be "green"? Mightn't you both be experiencing very different colors when looking at the same thing and only think that you are seeing alike because you've both learned to call the experience you are having "red"?

2. Modern computers are becoming so powerful that soon photographs and even videotape will be fakeable beyond the ability of experts to tell. Entire events could be created for the nightly news that never occurred. What could governments do with such power? Consider how strongly the sense of vision controls what you believe. How would such twisting of reality change your view of your own senses? ◆

SMELL

Smell may be one of the oldest of the senses, and scent messages, unlike information from the other senses, are not relayed through the thalamus but pass to lower areas of the brain that are older in evolutionary terms. The receptors for smell are contained in the **olfactory epithelium** high up within the nose. Receptors in the olfactory epithelium appear to function according to a lock and key system (Buck & Axel, 1991). Substances have different odors because they have different molecular shapes. **Molecules** that are shaped alike will fit into receptors that are responsive to them, just as keys of the same cut will fit into a particular lock. Therefore, molecules of similar shape have the same or similar odors.

The olfactory epithelium is believed to contain about 1000 different kinds of receptors. Odors are captured within the nasal mucus. There, a special *carrier* molecule picks up the odor and takes it to the receptors (Lee, Wells, & Reed, 1987), where the odor may, in turn, stimulate an individual receptor or combinations of different kinds of receptors to fire. Some odors must be stimulating combinations of receptors to fire because humans can sense about 10,000 odors, each with a different molecular shape, yet there are believed to be only about 1000 different smell receptors; therefore, there cannot be a receptor for each odor. However, if some odors stimulate two or more receptors, then the brain can easily use these combinations to discriminate 10,000 different odors.

Some molecules, such as carbon dioxide, have a shape that will not stimulate receptors in the olfactory epithelium, and they are therefore odorless.

OLFACTORY EPITHELIUM
Nasal membranes containing receptor cells sensitive to odors.

MOLECULE
An electrically bound grouping of two or more atoms that comprise a chemically distinct entity.

PHEROMONES
Substances that, when secreted, are sexual attractants to receptive organisms via olfactory perception.

Interestingly, 1.2 percent of the population is smell-blind, that is, they are unable to detect odors of any kind (Smith, 1989).

Many animals have a better sense of smell than humans do. Dogs, for instance, are capable of detecting odors 1000 times weaker than those a human nose could detect. The sense of smell helps animals to recognize objects, locations, and food. Buzzards are an interesting case in point. Because buzzards eat carrion, that is, rotting flesh, they have evolved to find that horrible stink most attractive.*

In many animals, this sense is especially important for sexual communication. Substances that excite sexual activity, called **pheromones,** may be secreted by an animal and carried downwind, where their reception in the olfactory epithelium of another animal arouses sexual interest. For instance, when dogs in heat secrete pheromones, they can attract male dogs that are downwind at distances as great as 1 or 2 miles. But what about human beings? Do we use our sense of smell for sexual identification? Recent discoveries in this area have led to an increased interest in the olfactory sense and to some further surprising discoveries of both a sexual and a nonsexual nature.

At this point, perfume manufacturers and the sexually deprived might wonder if there isn't some substance that people could apply to attract potential sexual partners. In fact, there is a possible substance, called alpha-androstenol. Alpha-androstenol is a strong sexual pheromone for pigs and is found in some human secretions. Researchers have found that if they spray surgical masks with alpha-androstenol and give them to men and women to wear, these people wearing the treated masks rate people in photographs as more attractive than subjects in a control group do (Kirk-Smith, Booth, Carroll, & Davies, 1978). If you decide to wear perfume or cologne containing alpha-androstenol, keep two things in mind, however. First, human social and sexual behavior is very complicated. Don't think that human beings can be controlled by pheromones as lower animals are. The effect of alpha-androstenol, if any, will undoubtedly be very weak (Rogel, 1978). Second, since it is a very powerful pig pheromone, it might be wise to stay away from farms.

Another area that has generated recent interest is that of *kin recognition.* In mice, it has been discovered that each mouse's genes impart to it a characteristic scent. Animals with similar genes (relatives, for instance) smell somewhat the same. With nothing more to go on than another mouse's scent, mice are able to tell their kin from nonrelatives. Whether this ability has a functional value is not known, but it may help mice avoid mating with kin, which, in turn, reduces the chances of genetic disease or defects in the offspring (Beauchamp, Yamazaki, & Boyse, 1985).

There is even evidence that kin recognition by smell occurs in humans. In one study, researcher Richard Porter discovered that 17 out of 18 mothers could distinguish their own child's T-shirt by its aroma from those of other children (McCarthy, 1986). To control for diet and other environmental factors, Porter conducted the same test with husbands and wives (of course, the use of specific detergents, perfumes, and other such substances was controlled). Husbands and wives failed to identify each other's scents. Porter's explanation for this inability is that husbands and wives do not smell "genetically" alike. Researchers are now investigating human kin recognition by scent with an eye to how it might affect the emotional closeness felt between parent and child or how it might influence human sexual behavior. Many neuroscientists now believe that olfaction may be closely tied to such emotional behavior. Their belief is supported by the fact that many nerve fibers leaving the olfactory

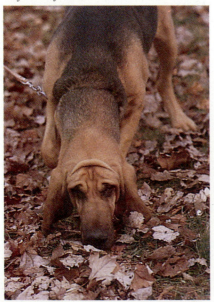

Bloodhounds are used for tracking because their acute sense of smell, well over 1000 times more sensitive than our own, enables them to follow a scent trail that may be days old.

---

*They have also evolved mechanisms that help protect them from the diseases associated with rotting meat. In fact, in one experiment a researcher injected a buzzard with enough botulism toxin to kill 300,000 guinea pigs—it didn't even slow the buzzard down (Smith, 1989).

epithelium detour through the limbic system before traveling to other locations. The limbic system, as you recall from Chapter 2, is a center of memory and emotion. Perhaps in the future we will come to understand better some of these more subtle effects of smell.

TASTE

Taste is a fairly limited sense. Most of what we consider to be taste is really smell. If you were blindfolded so that you could not see what you were eating and then had your nose plugged, you could not tell the difference between a piece of raw apple, a piece of raw potato, and a piece of raw onion. Although the three foods smell different, they taste alike. Think of how hard it is to taste foods when you have a cold; it's actually the sense of smell that's being hindered.

The major taste senses are sweet, sour, salty, and bitter. The taste receptors are located primarily on the tongue, and a few are found in the throat. The average **taste bud** is replaced about every 10 days, so destroying some by burning your tongue is not likely to do any long-term damage. The number of taste buds (receptors) in the average adult human covers a surprising range. Some people have as few as 500, while others may have 10,000! Also the number of pores in the tongue, which give access to the taste buds, has been found to range from 135 to 374 (Miller & Reedy, 1990). These differences account for the different abilities of people to taste and discriminate food flavors. As we all know, some people don't care what they eat, while others are highly discriminating.

Some taste buds are sensitive to only one quality (for instance, sweet); others react to combinations of qualities; and some individual taste buds respond to all four qualities (Arvidson & Friberg, 1980). Most of the taste buds that respond to sweet are found at the tip of the tongue, those responding to salty on the sides and at the tip, those to sour on the sides, and those to bitter toward the back. As you probably realize, the sense of taste is really more complex than this description makes it sound. Some taste buds have up to 40 neurons that may respond to more than one kind of taste, and there is also much "cross-talk" between taste-sensitive neurons, which can greatly modify their responses (Roper, 1989).

Taste senses are quite active early in life. Newborns readily respond to sugar, salt, lemon juice, and quinine, which stimulate the sweet, salty, sour, and bitter senses. Newborns like sweet but increasingly dislike salt, sour, and bitter, in that order. By adulthood, many people have acquired a liking for salty and sour, but few people ever acquire a liking for bitter. This probably doesn't surprise you. Most people like sweet candy, salty peanuts, or even sour pickles, but very few, if any, like the bitter taste of dissolved aspirin.

It has been argued that the senses of taste, like other physiological functions, evolved because they were adaptive. We may wonder, for example, why cats have no taste buds sensitive to sweet, while dogs and human beings do. The reason may be that cats, unlike dogs and human beings, have never needed these taste buds. Wild dogs eat meat, roots, or berries, and human beings in the wild eat the same things. Bitter and sour roots and berries are more likely to be poisonous than sweet roots or berries are, so the sense of sweet may have evolved as a protective measure. Animals attracted to sweet would be less likely to be poisoned, and they would pass on their affinity for sweet to their offspring. Cats, on the other hand, are carnivores (meat eaters) in the wild; an affinity for sweet would serve no purpose for them. Supporting the idea that taste evolved because it helped animals to approach or avoid certain foods is the discovery that distinct and separate neural systems are associated with the approach and avoidance of food by taste (Berridge & Fentress, 1985).

TASTE BUDS
Groups of cells distributed over the tongue that constitute the receptors of the sense of taste.

Of the four basic tastes, the taste of sweet is the only one readily preferred by newborns. By adulthood, although many people acquire a liking for salty and sour, sweet remains the favorite.

🔀 TOUCH

The total surface of the skin is about 20 square feet. That is roughly 1000 times more area than that of the retinas. Embedded within the skin are many receptors for touch. Different touch receptors measure pressure, light touch, vibration, aching pain, sharp pain, cold, and warmth. In addition, there are complex interactions among the touch receptors.

Touch receptors on the skin are not evenly distributed. For example, the lips and the fingertips are far more sensitive than is the back. If someone places two sharp pencils side by side, holding them so that their tips are only about 1 millimeter apart, and then touches them to your fingertip while your eyes are closed, you will find it easy to tell whether you're being touched with one point or two. This two-point discrimination is simple on the fingertip because of the high concentration of touch receptors there. On the back, however, where the concentration of touch receptors is lower, pencil points sometimes have to be placed as far as 2½ inches apart before the person being touched can tell whether one or two points are being used!

Touch receptors appear to be distributed over the body in receptive fields, each associated with its own grouping of touch neurons, not unlike the way in which ganglion cells in the visual system are associated with receptive fields of photoreceptor cells. Touch reception is projected to the somatosensory area of the parietal lobes of the brain (see Chapter 2). Different locations in the cerebral cortex receive touch information from different fields on the body. If you wish, you can feel the different locations in the cortex at work by performing Aristotle's illusion (see Figure 5.26).

Touch also has its emotional and social components, especially when we consider the role of touch in transmitting pain or affection. Pain is perhaps the most feared of the touch senses. Pain is valuable in that it alerts us to bodily damage, but, as we all know, there are times when we desperately want the pain to stop. The best solution would be to stop pain at its source, right at the beginning of the sensation—and we might soon be able to do just that.

In 1949, a Brazilian scientist named Mauricio Rocha e Silva and his student Wilson Beraldo were investigating the reasons for the terrible pain that was associated with the bite of the deadly jararaca snake (see Figure 5.27). Through careful analysis, they discovered that the snake's venom liberated copious

The sense of touch helps enhance the bond between ourselves and others. Often, quite unconsciously, we seek contact because it provides us with a sense of closeness and security.

◆ **FIGURE 5.26**

To "feel" a touch at different locations in the cerebral cortex, perform Aristotle's illusion. First, touch the eraser end of a pencil to both fingers, as shown in (a). These locations on your fingertips are close enough together to project to a very similar location on the cerebral cortex, providing you with the sensation of one touch. Now cross your fingers as shown in (b) and touch again. These locations on your fingertips are farther apart and are received at two very different locations on the cerebral cortex, giving you the unexpected sensation of two touches.

amounts of a natural substance in the body of its victims; they called this substance **bradykinin.** We now know that any injury, scrape, or damage to the body causes bradykinin to be formed in the blood—and the pain begins. Bradykinin appears to cause "pain" neurons to reach action potential and to fire. Researcher Solomon Snyder, working with bradykinin, said, "If you take all the known chemicals that collect in tissue after injury and inject them under a person's skin, most of them don't hurt, or don't hurt much. . . . But if you inject bradykinin, the patient goes through the roof" (McKean, 1986, p. 85). Obviously, this is not the kind of research where it is easy to get volunteers. Researchers are now searching for substances that may be able to block bradykinin.

Touch also has its tender side. Touch obviously plays an important role in affection, and it may have subtle influences as well. People often seem to feel better when they are touched. In one study, researchers even found that restaurant customers who had been lightly touched by their waitress left a bigger tip than other customers did, although most of them said they were unaware of the touch (Crusco & Wetzel, 1984).

BRADYKININ
A blood-borne neuropeptide that is cleaved from a larger inert molecule by enzymes a fraction of a second following any injury. Bradykinin stimulates pain-associated neurons and is considered to be one of the major producers of pain.

KINESTHETIC AND VESTIBULAR SENSES

You may always have considered vision, hearing, smell, taste, and touch to be "the five senses," but there are other senses that are very important in many

◆ **FIGURE 5.27**

Brazilian scientist Wilson Beraldo with a deadly jararaca snake safely contained in formaldehyde. It was Beraldo who first realized that the snake's bite is so extremely painful because the venom liberates large amounts of bradykinin in the blood of the snake's victims.

KINESTHESIS
An inclusive term for the muscle, tendon, and joint senses that yield information about the position and movement of various parts of the body.

VESTIBULAR SENSE
The sense that keeps an organism in proper balance.

SEMICIRCULAR CANALS
Three small, liquid-filled canals located in the inner ear containing receptors sensitive to changes in spatial orientation.

VESTIBULAR SACS
Two baglike structures at the base of the semicircular canals containing receptors for the sense of balance.

The kinesthetic sense provides us with knowledge about our position in space, and the vestibular sense gives us an idea of the direction in which gravity is operating. Because of the centrifugal force experienced during the loop in a wild ride such as this, the vestibular and kinesthetic senses will not tell you that you are upside down; only your visual sense will. This unusual combination makes the ride thrilling.

ways. The kinesthetic sense is one of these. **Kinesthesis** is the sense that informs you of the position of your body and limbs at any given time. From the feedback you receive when you move or reach for objects, you learn to interpret the weight and pressure on your muscles and joints and to use this information to ascertain your body's orientation in space.

The kinesthetic sense can be altered to some degree, and an interesting experiment demonstrates this. If you were to put on a pair of prism goggles that displaced everything 15 degrees to the right, at first you would find it very difficult to function. If an object was directly in front of you, you would reach for it only to see your hand 15 degrees to the right of its actual position. If you kept the goggles on and continued to reach for the object until your hand finally located it, and you did this many times, your kinesthetic sense would become adjusted fairly quickly to the 15-degree displacement. After that, you would have no trouble reaching for objects if you continued to wear the goggles that displaced everything 15 degrees to the right. If you took off the goggles, however, the world would immediately become a strange place again. There you would be with your goggles off, and you would think everything was normal. You'd see an object directly in front of you and would reach for it, relying on your kinesthetic sense to tell you where to move your hand. Amazingly, your hand would shoot off to the *left* 15 degrees from where you aimed it. Again, a period of adjustment would be required until you learned kinesthetically to position your arms in space. In one fascinating experiment, researchers demonstrated that a person's kinesthetic sense could be tricked by producing certain kinds of vibrations in his wrist tendons. Subjects in the experiment were amazed because the vibrations caused them to experience multiple kinesthetic stimulations simultaneously, which created a sense of impossible limb positions or of having multiple forearms (Craske, 1977).

Most of the kinesthetic information sent to the brain comes from receptors located in the joints. There appear to be specialized detectors in the brain, associated with the kinesthetic sense, much as there are specialized detectors for the visual and auditory senses. These specialized kinesthetic detectors appear to be associated with different postures.

The **vestibular sense** is the sense of balance. It tells you the direction in which the force of gravity is operating or the direction in which you are accelerating (for instance, while you are riding in a car or an elevator). The vestibular sense arises from the functioning of the inner ear, where the **semicircular canals** and **vestibular sacs** are located. The three semicircular canals are roughly perpendicular to one another and lie on three planes, so that body rotation in all three directions can be monitored (refer to Figure 5.25). When stereocilia within the canals are displaced by moving fluid, you know that you have changed position in relation to the field of gravity. In this way, you can sense that you are lying down or standing up at any given moment, even with your eyes shut. If the fluid is disturbed to a great degree, it's difficult to maintain balance. If you ever got on a wound-up swing as a child and spun around and around, you'll recall how you found it absolutely impossible to maintain your balance when you stepped off. The fluid in your semicircular canals continued to move, and it wasn't until the fluid became still again that you regained your orientation. Similarly, diseases and injury to the inner ear can cause an immediate loss of balance.

Researchers have discovered that messages from the visual, kinesthetic, and vestibular senses all come together at specific locations in the cerebral cortex. The fact that these inputs converge is probably what enables us to perform functions such as turning that require all three of these senses.

EXTRA SENSES

We have discussed the five traditional and two other senses, but are there still more senses that we haven't covered—"extra" senses? There are words describing such extra senses or powers: *clairvoyance*, sensing events at a distance unhindered by normal physical barriers; *telepathy*, sending thought messages from one person to another; *precognition*, seeing the future; *psychokinesis*, moving solid objects with mental rather than physical power. Although we have words for these senses and powers, does anyone really have any of these faculties? How can we tell? The only way, of course, is to conduct very carefully controlled experiments examining the different powers and senses that individuals claim to possess.

Most researchers believe that no *extrasensory* perception (ESP) has ever been demonstrated under carefully controlled conditions in a manner that could not be explained as chance. Nevertheless, a number of cases are intriguing. Their positive findings may confirm the existence of a weak, but real, phenomenon that is difficult to demonstrate. On the other hand, they may simply confirm that scientists are among the easiest people to fool, especially if an expert magician tries to fool them. People can make a lot of money by claiming they have powers of prediction, for example, and it's difficult, even under what seem to be controlled conditions, to uncover the gimmick they are using to create such an illusion.

These days most scientists, when confronted with discussions of extrasensory perception, reincarnation, UFOs, the Bermuda triangle, or poltergeists, just throw up their hands in disgust and refuse to talk about such matters. But this is a poor attitude, because any strange phenomenon probably merits investigation. With this in mind, a committee of over 40 people has been formed to investigate unusual phenomena, including extrasensory perception. Among its members is a magician, the Amazing Randi (to help show up the tricksters).

Uri Geller was one such trickster. Geller claimed to have a number of extraordinary powers, and he convinced Edgar Mitchell, a scientist and one of the astronauts who walked on the moon, that his powers were real. Mitchell accompanied Geller on a number of talk shows and asserted that Geller's powers were genuine. Geller claimed to be able to bend nails and spoons with the power of his mind and to start watches all over the country whenever he desired, even if the watches were broken. The Amazing Randi was able to duplicate every one of Geller's tricks. Geller had no real powers. In his book *The Magic of Uri Geller*, Randi describes the tricks Geller used to fool the scientists.

More recently, Randi investigated a man who claimed to have the power of psychokinesis. The man stated that he could turn the pages of a telephone book placed on a table by kneeling down to eye level with the table and concentrating. The pages certainly did begin to turn, and viewers were amazed. Randi wasn't. He surrounded the book with styrofoam balls and asked the fellow to try again. This time the power mysteriously failed him. Randi explained that the "psychokinesis" in this case was really a fine jet of air expelled between the lips in pulses in a very subtle way that required some practice. Had the man tried to turn the pages the second time, he would have blown the styrofoam balls all over the place, and his trick would have been obvious (Rucker, 1981).

What about researchers from prestigious institutions or universities who claim to have discovered legitimate psychic phenomena? Could such scientists be easily fooled? In 1979, the late James McDonnell, who had been the chairman of the McDonnell-Douglas Corporation, gave half a million dollars to Washington University in St. Louis for the establishment of a laboratory to study extrasensory phenomena. A professor of physics was named the administrator. The laboratory began its work investigating many subjects and by 1982 had found two young men who were considered by researchers at the university to have demonstrated reliable and convincing evidence of paranormal power. Among other things, one had been observed to make a clock slide across a table without touching it, and both were able to make a digital watch suddenly display apparently random numbers. The researchers considered the subjects to be "the most reliable of the people that we've studied" ("Psychic Abscam," 1983, p. 10). Other people stated that what these subjects did was "beyond the usual laws of physics" ("Psychic Abscam," 1983, p. 12).

At this point, the Amazing Randi stepped forward and identified the two young men as assistants of his whom he had sent to the institute. The clock had slid across the table by the means of an extremely thin "magician's wire" attached by one of the subjects when no one was looking; the digital watch read out strange numbers because the subjects bombarded it with microwave radiation that had gone undetected; and so on. Randi's point was clear—some scientists are easy to fool; they don't conduct experiments carefully enough, and they are too eager to find positive results.

Of course, Randi is not the only person hot on the trail of frauds. Other researchers have found ingenious ways to investigate claims of the paranormal. For instance, one researcher placed $5000 in a sealed box, along with a slip of paper on which he had written a first, middle, and last name of his own choosing. He invited any psychic who makes a living by exercising predictive "powers" (the ones whose startling predictions jump out at you in large black headlines in tabloids at the supermarket checkout stands) simply to state the name he had written on the slip of paper in the box to collect the $5000. So far, no takers.

❊ SUMMARY

◆ Our ways of organizing the world and of responding to it depend a great deal on how our senses filter the stimuli and information around us. We come to know our world primarily through our senses, and what we sense often affects our behavior.

◆ The amount of energy required to create a noticeable sensation is called the absolute threshold. The minimum amount of energy difference necessary before a change in stimulation can be detected is known as the difference threshold.

◆ Although there are many parallels between the camera and the eye, the two are actually more different than alike.

◆ The retina is composed of layers, containing the ganglion cells, bipolar cells, amacrine cells, horizontal cells, and the photoreceptors—rods and cones.

◆ In normal daylight vision, the most sensitive portion of the eye is the fovea.

◆ One portion of the peripheral retina contains no photoreceptors; it is here that the optic nerve passes through the retina on its way to the brain. This area is known as the blind spot.

◆ Different neural receptors are stimulated by different wavelengths within the visible light range. The rods are sensitive to all light except red. The cones are specialized, some responding to red, some to green, and some to blue wavelengths.

◆ The fovea is made up exclusively of cones. For this reason, it is not sensitive to extremely dim illumination.

◆ After 30 or 40 minutes in the dark, the rods reach their full sensitivity, a stage called dark adaptation.

◆ There are two major theories that explain color vision: the Young-Helmholtz theory and the Hering opponent-process theory. Modern color vision theory incorporates both views. The Young-Helmholtz three-color theory explains the functioning of the cones, while the Hering opponent-process theory helps to explain afterimages.

◆ All colors in the spectrum can be produced from three primary colors—red, green, and blue. Using beams of light, all colors can be created by additive mixing (as opposed to subtractive mixing, the process by which pigments are combined).

◆ Most color blindness is sex-linked, and is more common in men than in women. Among dichromats, one of the cone systems is malfunctioning. Green-cone dichromats are the most common. Monochromats have only one functioning cone system and, as a result, are unable to discriminate color.

◆ Edwin Land helped to develop color constancy theory, which explains how we continue to sense the same colors under extremely different lighting and illuminations.

◆ Ganglion cells in the retina respond to receptive fields created by the photoreceptor rods and cones. From the retina, most visual information passes along the optic nerves through higher areas of the brain to the occipital lobes of the cerebral cortex. There the information is processed by simple, complex, and hypercomplex cells, which are specialized detectors receptive to differences in line orientation, motion, width, length, angle, and color.

◆ In the occipital lobes of the brain are many visual maps, each receiving and processing the same visual signal. Each map, however, processes a different aspect of the signal, such as form or color.

◆ The brain appears to rely on two important mechanisms to deal with visual information. These are multiplexing and parallel processing.

◆ Aftereffects are visual effects produced by fatigue of one kind of receptor in the higher levels of the visual system. They differ from afterimages in that aftereffects transfer from one eye to the other.

◆ Just as the eyes are sensitive to a limited range of the electromagnetic spectrum, so the ears are sensitive to a limited range of frequencies caused by the compression and rarefaction of air.

◆ The pitch of a sound is determined by the frequency of the sound wave, and the loudness of a sound is determined by the amplitude of the sound wave.

◆ Three theories of hearing have been proposed to explain the range of the human auditory system: the place theory, the frequency theory, and the volley theory.

◆ Bioengineers have produced an artificial ear in which platinum implants replace damaged stereocilia in the inner ear and stimulate the auditory nerve by generating small electric shocks in response to different frequencies. Artificial eyes are also under development. Perhaps someday it will be possible to induce a full range of artificial sensory inputs.

◆ Smell is one of the oldest senses. The sense of smell works according to the lock and key principle: molecules of a particular shape fit into receptors that are responsive to them, allowing a particular odor to be perceived.

◆ Taste is a fairly limited sense. Taste buds respond to sweet, sour, salty, and bitter.

◆ In many animals, the olfactory sense is especially important for sexual communication.

◆ There are many senses of touch. Different sensory systems measure pressure, light touch, vibration, aching pain, sharp pain, warmth, and cold.

◆ The kinesthetic sense informs us of the position of our body and limbs at any given time.

◆ The vestibular sense helps us to keep our balance.

◆ Most researchers believe that no extrasensory perception has ever been demonstrated in a manner that could not be explained as chance.

❧ Suggestions for Further Reading

1. Ackerman, D. (1990). *A natural history of the senses*. New York: Random House. The author takes an interesting look at the lore and history of the five senses.

2. Coren, S., & Ward, L. M. (1993). *Sensation and perception* (4th ed.). New York: Academic Press. A college-level introduction to sensory and perceptual processes.

3. Goldstein, E. B. (1989). *Sensation and perception* (3rd ed.). Belmont, CA: Wadsworth. A college-level introductory textbook. Includes material on sensation and perception.

4. Hubel, D. H., (1988). *Eye, brain, and vision*. New York: Scientific American Books. A description of the ground-breaking research on vision between the years 1950 and 1980. Written by a Nobel Prize–winning scientist.

5. Smith, J. (1989). *Senses & sensibilities*. New York: John Wiley & Sons. An introduction to the senses for the general reader. Very well written and fun to read.

6. Wolfe, J. M. (Ed.). (1986). *The mind's eye: Readings from Scientific American*. New York: W. H. Freeman. A collection of articles from *Scientific American* on visual and perceptual systems.

Chapter Six

Perception

PROLOGUE

THE BIOLOGY OF A PERCEPTION

In 1990, researcher William Newsome and his colleagues made a momentous breakthrough. They became the first to clearly demonstrate the biology of a single perception (Salzman, Britten, & Newsome, 1990). They had been looking at an area of the brain known as MT, which is known to contain neurons specialized for detecting movement. The neurons in MT are organized into columns. Each of these columns will respond to objects moving through a particular region of the visual field.

While conducting their experiment, the researchers showed rhesus monkeys a screen of small dots that flashed randomly. Within the snowstorm of this visual display, a separate subset of dots moved along in a certain direction. The monkeys were trained to indicate which way they perceived these separate dots to be moving. The monkeys didn't have trouble doing this most of the time. But, when the number of moving dots was low compared to the stationary dots (about 10 percent), it wasn't so easy. In such cases, the viewing screen looked like static on a television set. If any up or down motion could be sensed, it was very obscure. Under these conditions, the monkeys' choices weren't much more accurate than pure guessing would have been.

As the monkeys were performing this task, the researchers monitored the electrical activity coming from the cells in the MT region. They noticed that when the subset of dots moved up, a column of cells in MT that were sensitive to upward motion would fire. One of their first exciting discoveries was that as the subset of moving dots was reduced in number, so as to make the judgment more difficult, the number of cells firing in the column was reduced by a like amount. This meant that the researchers had identified the area in which the monkeys' perceptions of this motion were occurring.

Of course, just because two things are correlated doesn't necessarily mean that one is causing the other (see Chapter 1). For this reason, the researchers took the next exciting step and electrically stimulated area MT for one second while the monkeys looked at the pattern of dots under circumstances in which movement was most difficult to identify. They discovered that if they stimulated the cells responsive to upward motion while the monkeys

CONTENTS

ILLUSION
A significant and consistent interpretation of sensory information by a given population that is not in agreement with precise and objective measurement.

PERCEPTION
The brain's interpretation of the information processed by the senses.

watched the display, the animals were more likely to select "up." This was true even when the dots were, in fact, moving down! Newsome and his colleagues had become the first to demonstrate a direct connection between neural responses and a perception. Still, one question continues to nag at Newsome, namely, what do the monkeys really see when the MT area is stimulated? Does the stimulation create the sensation of dots moving upward, or does it simply affect the monkeys' decision making processes? As Newsome has stated,

I like to think of it in terms of what the monkey would say if he could talk. Would he say, "I saw upward motion and reported up, so why wasn't I rewarded for the correct answer?" Or would he say, "I saw downward motion, but I reported up—I couldn't help it"? (Barinaga, 1991, p. 1025)

Someday, Newsome hopes to find human volunteers who are willing to have their MT area stimulated during brain surgery so he can get the answer to that question. Barring that, Newsome plans to do his experiment again. Next time, however, he will not ask the monkeys to tell him which way they believe the dots are moving, but rather which of six other displays most looks like the test display the monkeys saw while they were being stimulated. In that way, if the monkeys point to an upward-moving display after watching the test display during stimulation, Newsome will know that stimulating the cells actually altered the perceptions and not just the monkeys' urge to describe what they saw in a certain way.

IN THIS CHAPTER, we will examine the ways in which you organize your senses to form perceptions of the world around you. Two important theories of perception are presented and the merits of each are discussed. Along the way, you'll learn how moviemakers create special effects, how three-dimensional vision works, what illusions are, and how your biology helps you to organize the complexities of your environment.

WHY PSYCHOLOGISTS STUDY PERCEPTION

As you study perceptual processes, you will discover that a number of surprises are in store for you. Look at Figure 6.1. You will see a spiral curving downward until it reaches the apex. If this were a staircase and you began at the top, you would eventually reach the bottom by walking round and round. At least, that's what you might think (which just shows you how much you can trust your senses). But put your finger at any point on the curves of the design and begin to move down the spiral staircase with your fingertip—see how far you get! Trace very carefully. You will discover there's no spiral at all, only concentric circles, one inside the next.

This design is known as Fraser's "spiral." The spiral that you see is an **illusion;** it doesn't exist. You interpreted the information in the "spiral" according to some organizing principle, and you *perceived* a spiral. The illusion is so strong that people tracing the spiral sometimes begin to move their fingertip inward from one circle to the next as they trace without being aware of it! But as long as you trace carefully you'll always come back to your starting point.

Gestalt psychologists helped to develop many of the organizing principles that today form the foundation on which much of our understanding of **perception** rests. By knowing about perception, we can better understand how

◆ FIGURE 6.1
Fraser's spiral.

people have evolved to deal with their environments and, in turn, understand better why they behave as they do.

DEFINING PERCEPTION

At one time, sensation and perception were regarded as distinct from one another. Sensations were considered to be such things as pure tones or lights, and what the brain made of these sensations was called perception. However, we now know that processing begins at the very earliest levels of our sensory systems and that these systems are as much a part of what makes us as are our brains. Pure lights and tones may exist in theory, but as soon as we interact with them, we process them in some fashion. Because of this, the distinction between sensation and perception has blurred over the years.

Sensation has now come to refer to the earlier stages of processing, while the term perception is usually used to connote the later stages, in which the results of the earlier processing are brought together to form more complexly processed experiences. Some researchers even consider the terms sensation and perception to be synonymous, and there are good arguments in favor of this view. Others, more traditionally, see the two as a continuum from the simpler sensations to the more complex perceptions, with no clear demarcation point separating the two.

PHYSIOLOGICAL APPROACHES

With modern techniques like those described in the chapter Prologue, researchers have been able to delve into the biology of perception. Such attempts are relatively recent, but they hold the promise of yielding a new and more complete understanding of the perceptual process. Although we did discuss cells that are specialized to detect colors, lines, edges, and movement in Chapter 5, a more detailed understanding of how these cells act will give you a better idea of how researchers are pursuing a physiological understanding of perception.

BLOB PATHWAY
A distinct brain pathway for the transmission of color information. So named because color information is conveyed via a root that travels from the cones of the retina through the midbrain and then to areas of the occipital cortex known as "blobs."

PARVO-INTERBLOB PATHWAY
A distinct brain pathway for the transmission of high-resolution perception of stationary shapes and forms. These messages begin in the retina with the stimulation of small ganglion cells and continue on to the midbrain where more small cells are stimulated. From there, the messages travel to areas that surround the blobs in the occipital cortex.

Brain Pathways

For many years, researchers have known that whenever we look at any scene, our perceptual mechanisms are required to perform three basic tasks. First, we have to distinguish *form* and *shape* from background. In a sense, we are asking, "Is there something there?" If the answer is "yes," then we have to determine the *location* of these forms or shapes in space—"Where are these things I see?" Finally, we need to know if they are *moving* or *acting*—"Are these objects doing anything?" Once we have perceptually answered these three questions, and perhaps have learned what the answers mean, we can usually comprehend what it is we are sensing.

Some of the most exciting research of the last few years has involved the isolation of distinct and separate pathways in the brain for these different kinds of perception. The first two tasks, "Is there something there?" and "Where are these things I see?" are both handled by a combination of two different brain pathways. The first pathway is dedicated to color. Because this color information travels from the cones of the retina to the areas of the occipital cortex called "blobs" (see Chapter 5), it has come to be called the **blob pathway** (see Figure 6.2).

The second distinct pathway is dedicated to the high-resolution perception of stationary shape and form outlines. These messages begin in the retina with the stimulation of small ganglion cells (see Chapter 5) and continue on to the midbrain where more small cells are stimulated. From there, the messages travel to areas *that surround* the blobs in the occipital cortex. The word *parvo*, from the Latin root *parvus*, means "small." Because so many small-sized cells are involved, this pathway has come to be called the **parvo-interblob pathway.**

◆ **FIGURE 6.2**

Vision is a system consisting of three parts. The blob pathway is used in color vision; the perception of stationary forms is handled by the parvo-interblob pathway, and the magno pathway handles the perception of movement and depth. When messages from the three pathways are integrated, a unified world in three dimensions is perceived. (After Livngstone, 1988.)

VISUAL PATHWAY	INFORMATION	
Blob	Color	
Parvo-Interblob	High-Resolution Static-Form Perception	Integrated Visual Perception
Magno	Movement and Stereoscopic Depth	

The third basic perceptual task, *is there motion or action*, is handled by yet a third distinct pathway that is dedicated to motion and stereoscopic depth perception (the depth vision afforded by the use of both eyes). The messages of this pathway begin in the retina with the stimulation of large ganglion cells (see Chapter 5) and continue on to the midbrain where more large cells are stimulated. From there, the messages are sent to the occipital cortex. This is known as the **magno pathway,** in reference to its many large-sized cells.

The three separate pathways interact in some as yet unknown fashion to produce the complete perception.

Form and Shape Perception

Before we can tell whether there is "anything out there," we need to be able to distinguish the form or shape from its background. This is the ability to distinguish a tree from the background sky or a person from the wall in front of which she is standing. Technically, it is called the separation of **figure** from **ground.** Figure 6.3 shows two **reversible figures** and demonstrates that separating figure from ground is not due to something inherent in the stimulus, because the same reversible figure may give rise to different perceptual organizations depending on how you look at it. In fact, researchers have isolated cells in the brain that will fire, or not fire, depending on which of the reversible figures you think you are perceiving (whether you perceive the profiles or the vase) (Logothetis & Schall, 1989).

The art of camouflage is based in part on efforts to make figure and ground inseparable. In Figure 6.4, you can see a painting that shows us how nature sometimes makes use of this principle. Although the ponies blend into the background well, there are still just enough cues to enable you to see them as distinct from their background. They would be even more apparent if they were moving, an activity that also helps us to distinguish figure from ground.

Top-Down and Bottom-Up Processing

Whether you see the vase or the profiles in Figure 6.3 can be influenced by your expectations. If I surrounded that reversible figure with a bunch of pictures of vases, someone seeing it for the first time would probably see the vase. But that same person seeing the reversible figure for the first time would most likely see the profile if the figure was in with pictures of profiles. When your expectations influence your perceptions, it is called **top-down processing.** This term refers to the way the advanced cognition (your expectations) affects the less complex sensory inputs; ergo, "top-down." On the other hand, **bottom-up**

MAGNO PATHWAY
A distinct brain pathway for the transmission of motion and stereoscopic depth perception. These messages begin in the retina with the stimulation of large ganglion cells and continue on to the midbrain where more large cells are stimulated. From there, the messages are sent to the occipital cortex.

FIGURE
In perception, a perceptual experience that is characterized by contour, coherence, structure, and solidity. It is typically experienced against a ground (for example, it appears to be in the foreground).

GROUND
In perception, all that is perceived to be background.

REVERSIBLE FIGURES
Any of a class of figures that suddenly appear to change perspective or figure-ground relationship when looked at carefully and steadily.

TOP-DOWN PROCESSING
Processing in memory, perception, or other aspects of cognition that are influenced by the organism's prior knowledge or expectations, rather than simply being affected by the input itself.

BOTTOM-UP PROCESSING
Processing in memory, perception, or other aspects of cognition that are influenced only by the input of information and not by the organism's prior knowledge or expectations.

◆ **FIGURE 6.3**

In the classic reversible figure–ground example, (a) the silhouetted faces can be seen as figures or as dark background for a vase. The reversible figure–ground pattern needn't be two-dimensional. The beautiful vase pictured here (b) was actually created for Queen Elizabeth's Silver Jubilee in 1977. The profiles that can suddenly be seen as "figure" rather than as "ground" are those of Her Majesty and her husband, Prince Philip.

processing refers to the experience of inputs from the senses with relatively little cognitive processing in terms of your expectations.

For example, have you ever looked at a cloud drifting by and seen nothing in particular (bottom-up processing)? And then your friend says, "Hey, that cloud looks like a goat! See the nose and the horns and the legs over there?" Now you look again, this time trying to see a goat, and sure enough, it does look like a goat (top-down processing).

As soon as you think you know what you are seeing, your experience with past perceptions may guide you to make sense of the entire image based on your expectations. Look at Figure 6.5 and you will see a giant bird called a roc carrying a small man in its beak. You made perceptual sense out of all of the lines, angles, and shadows that you saw in that picture by processing the image top-down, that is, by using your knowledge of birds and what I told you to make perceptual sense of the image. But now, turn the image upside down and look at the same lines, angles, and shadows and see if your top-down processing skill doesn't lead to an entirely different perception! As long as there is some line, angle, or shadowing that can be made to seem familiar, you can process all sorts of identical stimuli into different perceptions.

Our knowledge of human faces is rich and detailed, but we don't often see faces upside down, although we sometimes do. Look at Figure 6.6, and you will see an attractive young woman, both right side up and upside down. Because you are far less familiar with upside-down faces, you will process anything unclear about the upside down face based on your knowledge of right-side-up faces, so the two pictures should seem identical except for orientation. Because of this top-down processing, it is unlikely that you realized that while most of the facial features of the upside-down face are upside down, the eyes

"Just as he reaches a small grassy point of land, another fish attacks him, lashing furiously with his tail."

(SUNDAY NEW YORK HERALD, 1900s)

"The largest of the ROCS picks her up by the skirt."

◆ **FIGURE 6.5**

Is this a giant bird with a little man in its beak, or is it a man in a canoe attacked by a giant fish? If the second question seems to make no sense, turn the book upside down and look again!

and mouth are not! If you still think that the two pictures are identical except for their orientation, turn them upside down and look again! In the familiar orientation you can immediately see what is wrong with her face, while upside down, in the less familiar orientation, you simply processed away any discrepancies—your expectations influenced what you perceived in an ambiguous situation. To reiterate the power of top-down processing, look at Figure 6.7 and count the number of aces of hearts. Did you see all three? Look again. Actually, there are five! How did your expectations that an ace of hearts would be red affect your perception?

Psychologists have even used such examples in court to help jurors understand how their own perceptions might be misleading them. For instance, not too many years ago a young man listening to a recording by the rock group Judas Priest tragically committed suicide. A rumor was started that the words "Do it!" were hidden in the recording and could be heard if it were played backward. Believe it or not, the members of the band were actually brought

◆ **FIGURE 6.6**

The same attractive woman right side up and upside down—or is it?

◆ **FIGURE 6.7**

How many aces of hearts do you see?

to trial in a civil suit alleging that they were responsible for the young man's death because they had irresponsibly put that awful hidden message into their recording! And when the recording was played backward for the judge, he could clearly hear "Do it!" over and over. In fact, anyone *who knew to listen for the words, "Do it!"* was able to hear them. Oddly, no one heard the words until they were told to listen for them. What do you think was happening in this instance? As it turned out, the defense attorney was able to show with high-tech playback equipment that the sounds that formed the so-called words "Do it!" were nothing more than parts of English words and some tones one of the guitars was making. A psychologist was able to explain to the judge that the evidence of his own ears was nothing more than "goats in the clouds," owing to top-down processing. The members of the rock group were found not liable.

I've had similar experiences, perhaps you have, too. I used to go out with friends to a good Armenian restaurant where they played songs in their native language. My friends and I didn't know any Armenian, but since they played the same songs every time we went there we soon began to hear familiar phrases in them—familiar English phrases! I recall that in one song the phrase "Scotch tape on a boa" kept coming up. Of course, that's not what was really being said since the song was sung in Armenian, but that was what we heard. New friends joining us thought we had lost our minds and couldn't hear any English words, until, that is, we'd point the phrases out by telling them what to listen for and quickly raising a finger at just the right moment—Scotch tape on a boa—"Oh yeah, now I hear it." And from that time on, they couldn't stop hearing the phrase even if they wanted to. We all grew quite fond of that song, and I wish I had a copy. But the restaurant is closed now, and I wouldn't know how to find that record even in an international record store, as I can't very well go in and ask, "Do you have 'Scotch Tape on a Boa' by the Armenians?"

There is also a popular song in English that makes no sense when processed bottom-up as follows:

Doze-e-doze an marz-ze-doze an little lamsy divy, akidel edivy to, wooden-u?

That's how it sounds when it is sung. If you've never heard it before, you'll be lost. Once you know the words, however, you can process it top-down:

Does eat oats and mares eat oats and little lambs eat ivy. A kid will eat ivy too, wouldn't you?

🎗 THE GESTALT CONTRIBUTION

From early in this century, when Gestalt psychologists (see Chapter 1) began to investigate the way in which the mind organizes information provided by the senses, perceptual organization of stimuli has attracted interest. Gestalt psychologists were primarily interested in demonstrating that the structuralist approach of breaking conscious perceptions into component parts was an ineffective way of understanding perception, because humans often organize their perceptions into whole entities. The experience of the *relationship* of the parts is as important as the parts themselves, or, as the Gestaltists liked to say, "The whole is greater than the sum of the parts." Another example is that experiencing the perception of "white," which is made from equal amounts of red, green, and blue (see Chapter 5), is not the same as experiencing the colors red, green, and blue one after the other. The whole (white) is something else, something more than just its parts. In the same way, the relationship of notes to one another in a melody makes it instantly recognizable even when the

◆ FIGURE 6.8

Principles of organization set forth by Gestalt psychologists. Included are two newly proposed laws (Rock & Palmer, 1990).

SIMILARITY

Similiar things appear to be grouped together:

Can be seen as either horizontal or vertical rows of X's.

Is usually seen as horizontal rows of X's andO's. The similiar objects are grouped together.

Newly Proposed Laws:

COMMON REGION

Objects within a common enclosure appear to be grouped together:

CONNECTEDNESS

Objects that are physically attached, even at great distances, appear to be grouped together:

NEARNESS

Things that are near to each other appear to be grouped together:

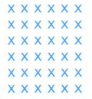

Can be seen as either horizontal or vertical rows of X's.

Is usually seen as horizontal rows, even though the X's and O's are dissimiliar figures.

CONTINUITY

Points or lines interrupted by an overlapping object are seen as belonging together if they result in straight or gently curving lines when connected, and lines tend to be seen as following the smoothest path:

The power lines are seen as *continuous,* despite the fact that they have been segmented by the tree branches.

SIMPLICITY

Every stimulus pattern is perceived in such a way that the resulting structure is as simple as possible:

Is viewed as a triangle and a circle:

It is not seen in a more complicated fashion as a combination of these parts:

or

CLOSURE

Figures that have gaps in them are seen as completed:

Even though there are gaps in the triangle, it is still seen as a triangle.

EMERGENT PROPERTY

From Gestalt psychology: The property that appears as a function of the Gestalt; that property that enables the whole to, in fact, be greater than the sum of its parts. Examples include the color white, which is an emergent property of the equal mixing of red, green, and blue light, and a melody, which is the emergent property of a series of individual notes.

COMMON FATE

A Gestalt principle that states that aspects of a perceptual field that move or act in a similar manner tend to be perceived as a single entity.

APPARENT MOTION

Any phenomenon through which a person perceives motion in an object when the object is, in fact, stationary.

melody is played at different pitches or by different instruments. This recognizable relationship is referred to as the **emergent property.**

In the course of their research, Gestalt psychologists observed that people tended to organize perceptions in certain ways. The Gestaltists stated a number of principles that expressed this organization, among them, *nearness, similarity, continuity, closure,* and *simplicity* (see Figure 6.8). Certainly, these examples indicate that a particular organization of all the parts (the sum of the parts) gives rise to different perceptions or "wholes" than do the parts taken separately. We now believe that the brain perceives in "wholes" because of the organization of the different brain pathways described earlier. As an example, let's consider a Gestalt principle called "common fate." **Common fate** occurs when objects or stimuli that would not normally be grouped together are seen as one organization because they share the same movement or "fate" (see Figure 6.9). This happens because our perception of movement is so sensitive that even if we see only a part of something move, or only glimpse the direction of its movement, our perceptual mechanisms often will fill in the blanks for us, creating the perception of a single object. This appears to occur because the magno pathway perceives common-fate motions as whole entities and then passes this perception on to the parvo-interblob system, which then organizes its form and shape perception around the wholeness of the common-fate object, suddenly making the moving object stand out (Livingstone, 1988).

Emergent properties illustrate one of the meanings that Gestalt psychologists gave to the concept of organization. The Gestaltists pointed out that,

... because the retinal image is nothing but an array of varying intensities and frequencies of light, the rays coming from different parts of the same object have no more affinity for one another than those coming from two different objects. It follows that the ability to perceive objects—such as stones, trees, and houses—must be an organization achieved by the nervous system. The realization that the perception of separate objects was not achieved solely by the "picture" focused on the retina was one of the Gestaltists' most important contributions. (Rock & Palmer, 1990, p. 85)

These perceptual systems appear to have evolved to work in ways that help us make sense of the world around us. For instance, in Figure 6.10 on page 209, you can see an example of the Phi phenomenon, what the Gestaltists referred to as **apparent motion.** In Figure 6.11 on page 209, however, you can

◆ **FIGURE 6.9**

This camouflaged fish is difficult to see. If the fish began to move, however, it would clearly stand out from its background. Although the fish would still look like the background when it was moving, all of its parts would share identical motion; they would share a "common fate." Our perceptual mechanisms quickly unify into a whole anything sharing a common fate.

WHAT REALLY OCCURS

a.

b.

WHAT WE PERCEIVE

a.

b.

◆ **FIGURE 6.10**

The Phi phenomenon: When two lights are placed side by side in a darkened room and flashed alternately (between conditions a & b), we perceive one light moving back and forth. This probably occurs because our perceptions are geared for the real world, not for a laboratory. In the real world, such an experience would almost certainly be the result of two consecutive glimpses of one moving object rather than an unusual consecutive sequence of the illumination and disillumination of two identical objects. Our perceptual mechanisms seem set to provide us with the most likely possibility.

see an interesting twist on apparent motion that has led some researchers to conclude that the perception of apparent motion is "in effect a bag of tricks, one the human visual system has acquired through natural selection during millions of years of evolution" (Ramachandran & Anstis, 1986, p. 102).

What the Gestalt organization principles may be showing us is that we have evolved to perceive the world as it most likely is. If we see part of a leopard in a tree, we may well "fill in" the rest of the leopard, and we probably won't be wrong! In the real world (as opposed to chapters on perception in textbooks), things that look like they are grouped together probably are. In the real world, things with gaps (see the closure example in Figure 6.9) usually *are* whole and are simply partly blocked from view. It makes sense that our perceptual system would evolve to "see" the blocked object in its entirety and to treat it for what it is (see Figure 6.12, p. 210).

According to evolutionary theory, an organism's biological perceptual apparatus *should* have been naturally selected to blend well with the experiences that the particular organism is likely to have. An organism's biological mechanisms, therefore, can be said to have been formed by the kinds of experiences its ancestors had. This process would favor the perceptions of any properties in the environment (for example, shape, position, or motion) that are directly relevant to survival.

(1)

a.

b.

(2)

a.

b.

◆ **FIGURE 6.11**

The following Phi phenomenon supports the notion that we are organized to perceive what is most likely to occur. In (1), two lights flash alternately with one light. Viewers see the two lights appear to travel in the direction of the arrows to fuse to become one. In (2), nothing is altered from condition (1), except that a small square is pasted on the screen in the lower right. Under these circumstances, viewers will now perceive that the lower light travels horizontally and "hides" behind the square. In the real world, hiding is more commonly observed than fusing, and researchers assume that our perceptual mechanisms are choosing to "feed" us the more likely possibility.

◆ FIGURE 6.12

The objects on the left appear to have no organization. There is an organization, however. If you could only fill in the missing parts in your mind's eye, you'd see what it is. Filling them in appears impossible, however, but your perceptual mechanisms are so strong that they can do it if we perceive that these same objects are being occluded (covered) by something as shown on the right. In that case, our perceptual mechanisms will "fill in" the parts, and we readily see the letter B in a number of places! (SOURCE: Rock, 1984, p. 119.)

AFFORDANCE
In J. J. Gibson's theory of perception, the particular properties of an object that offer an organism perceptual information, which often is of unique interest to that organism or may benefit its survival; for example, a hammer affords a human its graspability.

For instance, it has been found that frogs possess perceptual systems that help them to perceive bugs. These "bug detectors" help frogs to organize their perceptual understanding of the world in the most beneficial way. Because frogs eat bugs, there is an obvious value in their perceiving the world in a fashion that makes it easier to retrieve bugs from it. Cats, on the other hand, are highly receptive to motion. They may ignore a stationary object but immediately be fascinated by the same object when it moves. To some degree, this characteristic also is true of humans. J. J. Gibson (1979) used the term **affordance** to describe the interplay between organism and environment that has evolved, whereby each organism is best suited to perceive aspects of the environment that best afford, or offer, the information needed for its particular survival. In this view, how objects or actions are perceived depends on their meaning (relevance) to the organism.

Although the theory of evolution, as applied to perception, makes sense, its application does not supplant genuine evidence as the final arbiter of the debate concerning how perception comes about. Learning and experience also may play a considerable role in the way we organize perceptions.

AN ENDURING QUESTION: THE NATURE AND NURTURE OF PERCEPTION

How do we make perceptual sense of a world as complex as ours? How can we tell whether something is far away or nearby, whether it's large or small, whether *it* is moving or *we* are moving? How do we know when we are about to step off a ledge or walk into a wall? Why are we able to extend our hands just the right distance to grasp something that is directly in front of us? You will probably respond that the reason we can do all these things is that we can see. If you really think about it, however, you will realize that just seeing isn't enough. Not only must we be able to see things but we also must understand what we see—we must perceive. The question is, how do we go about doing this? This is not a new question, as questions go, but has endured over the centuries. It has been asked by philosophers both ancient and modern, and only now are we coming close to an answer.

Of the many answers offered, two have come to dominate our understanding of how we come to perceive the space around us and the objects

Frogs perceive their world in a way that makes it easier for them to retrieve bugs from it. Such species-specific perceptual organizations are called affordances.

AN ENDURING QUESTION, CONTINUED

in it. Historically, these two views were known as the **image and cue theory** and the **direct perception theory.**

The Image and Cue Theory

The first modern and detailed discussion of the image and cue theory was presented by Hermann von Helmholtz in his book *Treatise on Physical Optics* (Helmholtz, 1866/1924).* Encompassed within that imposing title was an examination of how we are able visually to understand the world in terms of three dimensions when all we have to go on is a flat two-dimensional image shining on our retinas. Helmholtz said it was obvious that without experience, learning, or memory, little that you could see would make any sense. Helmholtz would have argued, for example, that the only reason you know you are looking at a book at this moment is that your visual sensations of books have previously been correlated with the *experience* of touching and manipulating books. Once you have obtained that experience, the perception of a book seems automatic. Helmholtz argued that this sense of automatic comprehension was due to your ability to see a *critical cue* with which you were familiar and then draw an **unconscious inference** from that cue about all of the other cues near it. In that way, once you have certain experiences, you know that the particular shapes and surfaces you are viewing constitute a book—and you seem to know it almost instantly. In fact, according to the image and cue theory, even distinguishing a shape from its background requires some initial experience.

Have you ever seen one of those old Hollywood tearjerkers in which someone who has always been blind finally gets to see? What happens? In the ones I've seen, the person usually looks around and says things like, "Joe, I'd have recognized you anywhere," or "Aren't the flowers and sky beautiful?" Helmholtz would have had a good laugh at such scenes and would have argued that someone who had always been blind and could suddenly "see" wouldn't have the foggiest idea what he was sensing, let alone be able to recognize good old Joe! Rather, Helmholtz believed that each image to strike the retina must, *through experience*, become a *cue* filled with information for the observer. This, of course, is how the image and cue theory came to be named.

The Direct Perception Theory

Is it really true that nothing we see or hear would make sense until we had *learned* about what we were sensing? Consider the following: Children readily see and understand the distance and shape of objects, but it is very difficult to teach them to play advanced chess. On the other hand, it is fairly easy to "teach" most computers to play advanced chess, but it is incredibly difficult to "teach" any computer to make perceptual sense of a visual image. Furthermore, although some computers are able to "see" in a limited way, none do it nearly as well as even a young child. If, as Helmholtz suggested, learning is the key, we must ask ourselves, "How did little children get to be so smart? How are they able to handle easily the

IMAGE AND CUE THEORY
The theory that perceptions are learned by acquiring an understanding of the cues contained within the image that falls on the retina. A cue in this instance refers to any part of an image that is distinct from any other part and from which we may acquire information about our surroundings.

DIRECT PERCEPTION THEORY
The theory that perceptions are a function of biological organization and innate perceptual mechanisms.

UNCONSCIOUS INFERENCE
A term coined by Hermann von Helmholtz to describe the way in which an observer progresses from experiencing the sensations created by an object to recognizing that object. In essence, unconscious inferences are made automatically and without awareness. To the viewer, the object in question appears to exist as a thing unto itself, while the sensory and perceptual processes that gave rise to the object in the mind of the viewer go unnoticed.

---

*Sometimes a reference will have two dates as this one does. The first date is when the original paper was published; the second date is when this English translation appeared.

INVARIANTS
In J. J. Gibson's direct perception theory, stimulus features that are unchanging or have proportions that are relatively fixed or constant.

GRADIENT OF TEXTURE
A depth cue. Closer objects show greater detail.

AN ENDURING QUESTION, CONTINUED

same visual stimulations that overwhelm some of our most powerful computers?" We must also ask, "If Helmholtz's view is correct, how is it that the blind using a TSR device like the one described in Chapter 5 can make quick perceptual sense of what they 'see'"?

One answer to such questions was supplied by a twentieth-century researcher named James J. Gibson. Gibson argued that we are already organized at birth by our genetics and biology to mature rapidly in a way that will enable us to make some important perceptual sense of our world early in our development. This is not to say that Gibson believed that experience wasn't important, but rather that he believed important characteristics of objects, such as their distances, shapes, or sizes, are perceived mostly as the result of the innate ("built-in") mechanisms possessed by all healthy members of the species. Included among such mechanisms would be the cells that appear to be prewired detectors of edges, colors, or movements, which we discussed in Chapter 5.

Gibson also liked to point out that almost any visual experience will have within it observable **invariants** that can yield information about the distance, movement, or shape of objects. One of the invariants to which Gibson often referred was **gradient of texture** (see Figure 6.13). Gradient of texture has to do with differences in detail. Look around you. Regardless of the objects you focus on, you'll be able to see more detail in those that are closer and less detail in those that are distant. If you're sitting on a large lawn, you see the grass that's close to you as individual blades, but on the horizon you see a smooth, uninterrupted green. At intermediate distances, you can't see individual blades of grass, but the green may appear to be somewhat patchy rather than uniform in color. Gibson argued that innate mechanisms sensitive to texture gradient might easily use such an invariant to estimate the size of a novel object without the requirement of prior experience (see Figure 6.14).

◆ **FIGURE 6.13**

A texture gradient. The retinal size of the texture elements in this picture increases with nearness and decreases with distance. This feature is found in almost any view of the world and may provide an invariant from which we innately gather depth information.

AN ENDURING QUESTION, CONTINUED

The Interactionist View

The modern view of perception, the interactionist view, is that there is clearly evidence to support both explanations of perception—learning and experience are important, but so is neurological organization. Today we know that it isn't necessary to choose one theory over the other, because the two theories need not be mutually exclusive. Important aspects of each could easily be involved in any perceptual organization. Throughout this chapter are examples of how learning and experience interact with underlying biological mechanisms to produce the amazing perceptual abilities that we often take for granted. While it is still true that we don't know how much of our perceptual ability to attribute to our biogenetic organization (nature) and how much to attribute to learning and experience (nurture), we now know that both are very important. In this light, however, the basic debate still continues, only not at such extremes as before. For instance, modern perceptual debates often begin with an agreement that biological systems play an important role and commonly focus on arguments between supporters of the *global-precedence hypothesis*, who argue in favor of a predominance of holistic perception in the Gestaltists' tradition, and those supporting the analytic, or *local-precedence hypothesis*, who believe that entire perceptions are functions of certain limited areas in the brain or sensory systems rather than compilations of disparate areas working together to produce a whole perception, or Gestalt (Kimchi, 1992). Someone supporting the global view, for instance, would not expect to find a complete perception in one area of the brain. The experiment in the chapter Prologue, however, might indicate just that. Still, someone supporting the global-precedence hypothesis would be quick to point out that the information of motion generated by area MT is sent elsewhere in the brain and that we do not know how important other areas might be for creating the whole perception. Both camps also readily admit that learning can play an important role and point to examples of top-down processing.

As you can see, there is still some polarization among perceptual researchers, but nothing like there was years ago before we had sufficient data to examine the extremely different theoretical views held by supporters of the image and cue theory and those supporting the direct perception theory.

◆ **FIGURE 6.14**

Although the size of an object might not always be obvious without experience, its relationship to a gradient of texture can immediately place it at a particular distance, which then allows its size to be roughly deduced.

AN ENDURING QUESTION, CONTINUED

FOR CRITICAL ANALYSIS

1. Our senses act as filters; there are many things to which we are not sensitive. We can't see X rays, hear dog whistles, or smell carbon dioxide. Why do you think our senses are so selective?

2. Cats have color vision, but how do we know this? How would you go about setting up an experiment to tell if a cat knows the difference between red and blue without dissecting its eye to look for cones (an action that, by the way, would not in itself offer proof because you could not be sure that cones in cats worked the way they do in humans)? Hints: Use a hungry cat, a lamp that can shine either red or blue light of equal brightness, and a food-dispensing lever the cat has learned to work that operates only when, for instance, the red lamp is on. If a cat can see the colors, how will it eventually come to behave? Think of how traffic lights control your actions. How would the animal behave if, in fact, cats were color-blind? ◆

ILLUSIONS

Figure 6.15 contains a number of illusions. Before you look at them, you might want to get a ruler, because some of them are so eerie that you'll want to measure them to see for yourself that the captions are correct.

The Müller-Lyer illusion (d) is a good one to examine in detail. It has been the focus of much controversy. Most people looking at this illusion perceive the horizontal line bordered by the inward-turned arrowheads as shorter than the horizontal line bordered by the outward-turned arrowheads. If you measure the horizontal lines, however, you'll find that they are the same length. Why does the illusion occur?

Knowing that you're being tricked doesn't make much difference; the effect remains. Researchers know that the illusion doesn't take place in the retina. They resolved this issue by an ingenious method. A subject's head and eyes were held very still in an apparatus while the horizontal lines of the Müller-Lyer illusion were flashed into the left eye and the arrowheads were flashed into the right eye. When the subject interpreted the combined sensations, the illusion was still apparent (Gillam, 1980). This outcome proved that the illusion must be happening at a higher level in the brain than that of the retina.

What explanation could there be for the Müller-Lyer illusion? The first possibility is that it is a manifestation of our biological organization. Recall from Chapter 5 how the gray spots that appear in the Hering Grid also appeared in the artificial silicon retina, and you can see how certain illusions might simply be a function of the way in which we are organized. On the other hand, learning might also play an important role.

For example, in Figure 6.16, you see the Müller-Lyer figures in a particular context: a view of the floor of a room or any rectangle lying in front of you with one end more distant than the other. Notice that the horizontal edge that seems to be farther away always has the arrowheads pointing outward, while the horizontal edge that's closer always has the arrowheads pointed inward. Perhaps, because of your experience, when you look at the Müller-Lyer illusion, you perceive the horizontal line enclosed by the inward-turned arrowheads as being closer than the line with the outward-turned arrowheads. If two objects appear to be the same size but you know that one is closer, then

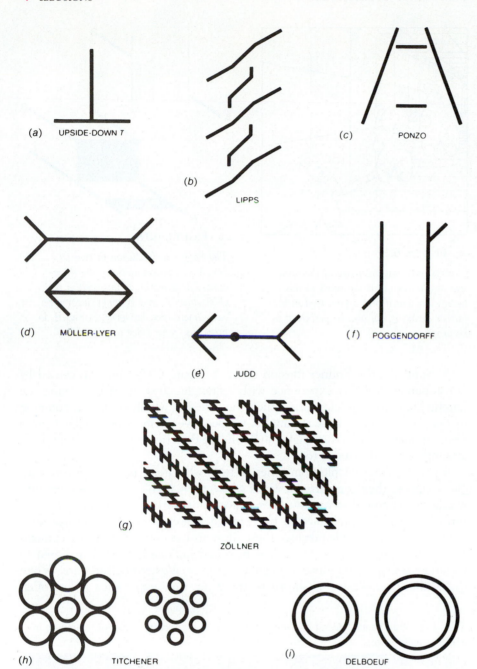

Illusions. (a) Both lines are the same length, although the vertical line looks longer. (b) The middle segments of all the lines are parallel to one another. (c) Although the upper horizontal line looks longer, both horizontal lines are the same length. (d) Both horizontal lines are the same length, although the upper one looks longer. (e) A variation of Müller-Lyer. The dot is in the center of the horizontal line. (f) The diagonal lines, if continued toward each other, would join, although it appears that the line on the right would be above the line on the left. (g) The long diagonal lines are parallel and do not converge. (h) The middle circles are the same size. (i) The outer circle on the left has the same diameter as the inner circle on the right.

(a) UPSIDE-DOWN *T*

(b) LIPPS

(c) PONZO

(d) MÜLLER-LYER

(e) JUDD

(f) POGGENDORFF

(g) ZÖLLNER

(h) TITCHENER

(i) DELBOEUF

you know—because of your learning and experience—that the one that's farther away must be bigger (see Figure 6.17). This may be the cause of the Müller-Lyer illusion.

We can see that the same assumption may be at work in the Ponzo illusion (refer to Figure 6.15c). That illusion is reproduced every time you look at railroad tracks. The upper and lower horizontal lines in the Ponzo illusion are exactly the same length, but the upper horizontal line looks longer. The upper horizontal line appears to be farther away, and, according to experience and learning, if two objects appear to be the same size but one is farther away, then the one farther away must be bigger.

What about the Poggendorff illusion (refer to Figure 6.15f)? Again, it may be that our *experiences* with three-dimensional objects causes the illusion. You may never have seen the Poggendorff illusion before, but you've seen something like it, perhaps an overturned chair. The resemblance is obvious in Figure

◆ FIGURE 6.16

The Müller-Lyer illusion can be explained by our experience with floors. (a) If we view a floor from one side of a room, the far side appears foreshortened, although we know that the far side is the same length as the near side. (b) By removing midsections of the floor, we begin to approximate the Müller-Lyer figures. We still assume that the far side is the same length as the near side. (c) The horizontal lines are now made equal, as in the Müller-Lyer figure. We perceive the top figure to be the long far side of a large room and the bottom figure to be the short near side of a small room. By applying our knowledge of three dimensions to a two-dimensional figure, we may be making an assumption that creates the illusion.

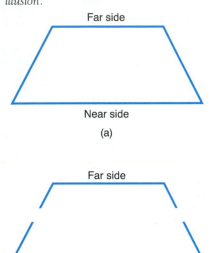

Far side
Near side
(a)

Far side
Near side
(b)

Perceptual belief:
Far side of *large* room
Therefore this line
is long

Horizontal lines are actually equal.

Perceptual belief:
Near side of *small* room
Therefore this line
is short

(c)

◆ FIGURE 6.17

Objects may cast an image of the same size on the retina, as the bears in this picture do, but if one is perceived to be farther away, it will also be perceived to be larger.

◆ FIGURE 6.18

The Poggendorff illusion in two dimensions makes sense in the three-dimensional world. If this were a real chair, lines A and B could never meet. In two dimensions, however, A and B do meet (use your ruler to prove it).

6.18. Similarly, the Zöllner illusion (refer to Figure 6.15g) may be caused by our common everyday experience with rectangles. Instead of perceiving the hatched lines as parallelograms, which they are, but which are not as common in our daily experience as rectangles, we perceive them as rectangles viewed from an angle; if these rectangles angle in one direction, we see the long lines leaning in that direction, too.

But what about people from other cultures who aren't familiar with rectangles? Suppose they come from a world where there aren't many buildings with windows. Suppose they haven't been exposed much to railroad tracks or overturned chairs. Researchers who have tested members of such cultures have reported that the people perceive these illusions less often. For instance, members of the Zulu tribe in Africa live in round huts and aren't as exposed to rectangular shapes and forms as members of most Western cultures are. When the Müller-Lyer illusion is shown to the Zulu, they experience it less often

Zulus lives in a "round" world and are not exposed to the rectangular angles common in modern cities.

than do members of Western cultures (Deregowski, 1972; Gillam, 1980). Such data concerning illusions imply that learning and experience are extremely important factors in individual perception. However, the cross-cultural studies that have yielded the data have been criticized for a number of reasons, among the most important of which is the possibility that members of other cultures may not have fully understood the comparison the researchers wanted them to make.

Still, there is other evidence that learning may have an important bearing on the perception of illusions. For instance, illusions tend to diminish in effect the more you observe them. The first time you see the Müller-Lyer illusion, the lines are likely to appear strikingly different; after you've seen it many times, however, the illusion has less impact (Gillam, 1980).

PERCEPTUAL CONSTANCIES

Perceptual constancies also offer a good example of the value of learning in perception. If you were to examine the world solely on the basis of the image projected on your retina, familiar objects would be constantly changing in size and shape depending on the angle from which you viewed them. Yet, in spite of these continual alterations produced by viewing objects from different distances and different angles, you still recognize familiar objects as familiar. This is one of the primary functions of perception.

Size Constancy

When you look back at your parked car as you are walking away from it, your visual sensory system sends a message to your brain. First, the image of the car is projected onto your retina. If you continue looking back at your car, the image projected onto your retina gets smaller and smaller as you move farther away. When this happens, do you assume that your car is shrinking? No, you aren't upset at all. Although the *sensory* image of your car is shrinking rapidly, you don't perceive that your car is changing size. Instead, you perceive that your car is becoming more distant. You've learned that its size remains the same. Even when you are five blocks from your car and it seems no larger than your fingernail, you perceive that it is still your car and it is still the same size. This learned perception is known as **size constancy.** It is one of a number of such perceptual constancies.

Helping to demonstrate that size constancy is learned is the fact that some people fail to learn it. Mr. S. B. was a 53-year-old cataract patient who had been blind since birth. When his sight was restored by surgery, he had a difficult time adjusting to all the new sensory inputs. One day, he was found trying to crawl out of his hospital window in order to get a better look at the "little" objects, which he believed were close enough to touch. The trouble was that his window was on the fourth floor and some of those "little objects" were full-sized cars in traffic down below (Gregory, 1970).

THE MOON ILLUSION. Have you ever looked at the full moon when it's just coming up over the horizon? It looks huge. But the same full moon doesn't appear to be so large once it's high in the sky. Have you ever wondered why?

In a series of classic experiments, Kaufman and Rock (1962) demonstrated that the **moon illusion** was due to our grasp of size constancy. They observed that when the moon is directly overhead, it's difficult to judge how large it is. If the moon looks fairly hazy, you may realize that it's more than 20 or 30 miles away. But you have little else to go on—just darkness, a few stars, and the round moon.

PERCEPTUAL CONSTANCIES
The tendency to perceive objects as yielding the same or similar experiences, even though the viewing conditions may vary widely.

SIZE CONSTANCY
The learned perception that an object remains the same size, although the size of the image the object casts on the retina varies with its distance from the viewer.

MOON ILLUSION
A perceptual illusion created by the presence of the monocular cues of relative size and overlap, which make the moon appear 25 percent larger when rising than when overhead.

Because of the existence of the moon illusion, photographers use a telephoto lens when photographing the rising moon so the resulting photograph more closely resembles our perceptual experience.

The situation is different when the moon is first rising, however. Kaufman and Rock noticed that the moon illusion was especially pronounced if a large number of objects separated the observer from the rising moon. For instance, if the moon is rising behind the lights and buildings of a city, there is a strong effect. The fact that the city is in *front* of the moon means that the moon is farther away and must be huge, because we all know how large cities are. By experience we know that buildings or hills and mountains are fairly large, and yet they are specks compared with the moon globe that is rising behind them. So we now adjust the size of the moon in our minds and increase it in magnitude. Because we are not used to dealing with objects bigger than entire cities or the mountains that surround them, the perception created when the moon rises above the horizon is one of awesome size. This perspective, as well as an appreciation of its true size—2160 miles in diameter—is totally lost when the moon is seen directly overhead, without any cues with which to compare it. Similarly, we can hold our distant car constant in size, because all of the other familiar things around it, houses, trees, other cars, have also gotten smaller by a like amount. This translates into a perception of distance.

It's so difficult to believe that the illusion of a giant harvest moon is a result of our learning and experience that most people think it has something to do with the optics of the atmosphere. But it isn't so; the rising moon is not magnified by the atmosphere. If you take a photograph of the moon as it rises and another photograph of the moon overhead, and then take a pair of scissors and cut out the images of the moon from both pictures, you will see that they fit one on top of the other perfectly; they are the same size. A camera would have recorded an optical magnification had that been the cause of the moon illusion. The camera records no such thing, however; unlike your mind, the camera does not perceive.

THE DEVELOPMENT OF SIZE CONSTANCY.   Size constancy does not appear to be present at birth; rather, it develops in infants by about 6 months of age. This was demonstrated in an experiment in which 5- and 7-month-old infants wearing a patch over one eye (to eliminate the depth cues that the use of both eyes would provide) were simultaneously shown photographs of large and small faces, all of which were presented equidistant from the child. The only distance cue in this case was the size of the face. To adults, who, of course, possess size constancy, only the large face would have looked near enough to touch; the small face would have looked too distant. The 5-month-old infants, however, reached out to touch faces of both sizes equally. The 7-month-old infants, in contrast, reached far more often for the large face, which indicates size constancy, and seemed to react to the small face as though it were beyond reach (Yonas, Pettersen, & Granrud, 1982).

Shape Constancy

Other constancies also develop through an individual's experience. **Shape constancy** is demonstrated in Figure 6.19. As you can see, objects are perceived to remain constant even though the shape projected onto the retina may change. A door may appear to be rectangular when viewed straight on or trapezoidal when partially opened, but we do not perceive that the door is changing shape from a rectangle to a trapezoid. Instead, we perceive that the door is opening.

A powerful shape constancy illusion can be created with the aid of the house in Figure 6.20. Make a photocopy of the house or carefully redraw it on heavy paper (notice that the windows aren't quite square). Then follow the instructions in the figure. Once you've created the house, set it on a shelf at eye level where it is lighted so that shadows do not fall on it. Stand about 10 feet away and view the house with one eye closed. The shape constancy you possess owing to your experience with houses will soon take over, and the house will begin to look like a normal house. Once this happens, begin walking from side to side. As you apply shape constancy, you will try to hang on to what you know about houses. While trying to accomplish this, you will experience a strong illusion. Amazingly, the house will seem to rotate all by itself! Finally, hold the base of the house between your thumb and forefinger and extend your arm. Look with only one eye; once it appears to be a normal house, tip it forward or backward or rotate it from side to side. You'll be in for a shock. While your hand turns the house one way, it will actually appear to move the other way! As the house appears to turn against the direction of your hand, you will probably expect to feel opposition against your fingers. When no opposition occurs, it will feel very strange. After all, your eyes and hands have been working together for some time now, and, believe me, they're not ready for this.

SHAPE CONSTANCY
The learned perception that an object remains the same shape, although the image it casts on the retina may vary in shape depending on the viewing angle.

◆ **FIGURE 6.19**

Although the shapes of a door's image that are cast on the retina can change drastically, the door is not perceived to have changed shape. Instead, it is perceived to be a rectangular door that is opening.

◆ **FIGURE 6.20**

The inside-out house. Make a copy and cut it out. Cut line AB. Fold edges toward you along lines BD, BE, and BC. Paste triangular flap ABC to the back of the roof; the front and side of the house should meet in a right angle, and the completed house should be "inside-out." Put the house on a shelf at eye level. From about 10 feet away, observe with one eye. When the house appears "normal," walk to one side. What happens? (SOURCE: Gardner, 1983a, p. 64.)

AMES ROOM
A specially designed room that is perceived as rectangular, even though it is not. Objects of the same size seem to be totally different in size at different points in the room.

BRIGHTNESS CONSTANCY
The perception that objects maintain their brightness independent of lighting.

DEPTH PERCEPTION
Perceptual interpretation of visual cues indicating how far away objects are.

A perceptual psychologist named Adelbert Ames (1880–1955) once demonstrated the power of these perceptual constancies by creating what he called the **Ames room** (see Figure 6.21). Strange things seem to happen in the Ames room. People standing on one side of the room appear to be giants, and people standing on the other side appear to be dwarfs. Individuals crossing the Ames room appear to grow or shrink steadily depending on the direction in which they are walking. The illusion of the Ames room depends on our use of size and shape constancy. In the Ames room, one window is much larger than the other, the windows are trapezoids, the floor is uneven so that one end of the room is higher on the plane than the other, and the floor tiles are diamond-shaped and of different sizes. Because we have not experienced this kind of bizarre arrangement, however, our perceptual constancies try to make different sense of the room. Thus, we perceive the windows as equal in size and rectangular. The room seems to be level and the floor to be made of square tiles. Our desire to perceive the room according to our experience is so strong that when a person walks from one end to the other, we prefer to perceive that person as growing or shrinking rather than to give up the idea that the room is regular in shape and size.

Brightness Constancy

Another of the perceptual constancies is known as **brightness constancy.** Because of brightness constancy, objects appear to have the same brightness independent of the light in which they are seen. For example, although gray paper in the sun is actually brighter than white paper in the shade (check it out with a light meter), the white paper appears brighter. We perceive white as bright and gray as darker, regardless of the amount of reflected light actually coming from the surface.

🔗 DEPTH PERCEPTION

Once you have determined that there is "something there," the next question becomes, "Where is it?" When you're sitting in a room and looking at things, your perceptual abilities enable you to tell how far away they are or how close they are with a fair degree of accuracy. This is called **depth perception.**

Monocular Cues

You may have heard that depth perception is a function of using both eyes and that people who are blind in one eye lose their depth perception. But is this true? Close one eye and look around a room. It may seem that your depth

◆ **FIGURE 6.21**

In the Ames room, people seem to change size as they change location.

perception is a little impaired, but you can still tell which objects are closest and which are farthest away without much difficulty. Even if you went to a stranger's house with a patch over one eye and sat in a room you've never been in before, you could still judge whether a lamp was closer than a particular chair, the chair was closer than a particular couch, and the couch was closer than a particular wall. You'd still have depth perception.

In 1930, film producers came to special-effects expert Willis H. O'Brien with an interesting plot for a movie. In the filmed story, an expedition would be made to a place called Skull Island to capture a huge ape named King Kong and to bring him back to New York, where Kong would escape, kidnap a woman, and climb the Empire State Building, there to be killed by fighter planes. Oddly, the producers described this as essentially a love story, with the 50-foot ape in love with the blonde heroine. They said that they would supply the actors. All they wanted from O'Brien was a 50-foot ape, various extinct dinosaurs, and Skull Island—all on film. A lesser man might have thrown up his hands in despair, but O'Brien sat back and pondered. How could you make a film such as *King Kong* when no such gorilla or island existed and still fool the audience into perceiving the situation as real? The only way, of course, was to manipulate the cues that people use in their day-to-day lives to gauge such things as size, distance, and motion. O'Brien knew that image and cue theorists had been trying to determine exactly which cues in the two-dimensional image formed on the retina give rise to depth perception. He knew that quite a number of cues had been isolated. The more O'Brien thought about it, the more it seemed that it might be possible to make people believe in the reality of King Kong.

Some of the cues O'Brien made use of probably will be familiar to you, even though you may not know their names. Whether you are conscious of it or not, you've used them all of your life to judge depth.

The first of the **monocular depth cues** is gradient of texture, which we discussed earlier. This cue alone is often enough to yield a strong sense of depth.

The second depth cue is **height on a plane.** We perceive objects that from our point of view are higher on our plane of vision to be farther away than objects lower on the plane. Inside a room, objects that are farthest from you will always appear to be higher on your plane of view. In other words, when you are standing or sitting upright, the farther away an object is, the more you need to raise your gaze to see it.

Another very important depth cue is **linear perspective:** parallel lines appear to converge on the horizon and to separate as they approach the viewer. Linear perspective is one of the first tricks that any artist learns in order to make a two-dimensional canvas appear three-dimensional. If you look at the railroad tracks in Figure 6.22, you can see the effect of linear perspective and the depth it appears to create on a flat page. Linear perspective is also apparent with just points of light—lines aren't needed. Psychologist E. Lowell Kelly used this knowledge to save lives during the Second World War. He heard that during night training missions, cadet pilots occasionally crashed into the aircraft directly in front of them because they were unable to judge their distance to the taillight of the aircraft they were following. Kelly convinced the air force to use two taillights mounted a fixed distance apart, which provided linear perspective (the apparent distance between the lights shrank as the lead airplane got further away, and grew as the aircraft drew closer to each other) (Fiske, Conley, & Goldberg, 1987).

Overlap is another important cue. We know that if one object appears to overlap another, the object that is overlapped is behind the first object and therefore must be farther away (see Figure 6.23).

MONOCULAR DEPTH CUES
Cues seen with the use of only one eye that give rise to a perception of depth. These cues include an object's height on a plane, linear perspective, overlap, relative size, gradient of texture, aerial perspective, shadowing, and relative motion. On a flat movie screen (with the exception of 3-D movies), only monocular cues give the sensation of depth.

HEIGHT ON A PLANE
A monocular depth cue. Objects higher on a plane are perceived as being farther away.

LINEAR PERSPECTIVE
A monocular depth cue. Parallel lines appear to converge in the distance.

OVERLAP
A monocular depth cue. Objects that are behind (overlapped by) other objects are perceived as being farther away.

In this flat, two-dimensional photograph there are many monocular cues that provide a strong perception of depth.

◆ FIGURE 6.22

An example of linear perspective: parallel lines converging at the horizon.

◆ FIGURE 6.23

Objects that are overlapped appear farther away than objects that are not.

RELATIVE SIZE
A monocular depth cue. Familiar objects appear larger than identical objects that are more distant.

AERIAL PERSPECTIVE
A monocular depth cue. Nearby objects are brighter and sharper than distant objects.

SHADOWING
A monocular depth cue. The distribution of light on a curved or angled surface conveys that some parts are closer and some farther away.

RELATIVE MOTION
A monocular depth cue. Objects that are closer appear to move more than distant objects when the viewer's head is moved from side to side.

ACCOMMODATION
In vision, the adjustment of the lens of the eye to bring into focus on the retina objects that are relatively near.

Relative size can be a factor in depth perception if we know how large particular objects are. Once we have acquired size constancy, we can then judge an object's distance by how large it appears relative to another object of known size. If you look about a room and see two chairs that you know are the same size, and one appears to be much larger than the other, you will immediately assume, because of size constancy, that the smaller chair is farther away.

If you're outdoors and are viewing objects over a considerable distance, **aerial perspective** lends a sense of depth because, as distance increases, dust and haze in the air tend to reduce clarity. Consequently, the colors of distant objects appear pastel and their outlines are hazy, while nearby objects appear sharp and bright. On very clear days, things at a distance may stand out so sharply that they appear to have moved closer.

The distribution of shadows can also be an important depth cue. **Shadowing** provides information about angles and curves that tells us which parts of an object are closer to us than others are (see Figure 6.24).

O'Brien was unable to make much use of the next depth cue, **relative motion,** because it will not work with a two-dimensional image such as a motion picture, unless the camera is moving. For relative motion to make an impression, a three-dimensional scene is necessary. The idea of relative motion is simple. If you move your head from side to side, you'll immediately notice that nearby objects seem to move a great distance, while distant objects seem to move hardly at all. In fact, relative motion may, to a degree, be an invariant depth cue—the kind that direct perception theorists like to point to. This is because the retina does not simply encompass a flat two-dimensional scene, as image and cue theorists originally believed. Instead, researchers have discovered that the eyes wiggle constantly at a rate of at least three times per second, which yields a continuous depth sense owing to relative motion (MacKay, 1973). The tiny movement of the eyes is all that it takes. To get a sense of how such a tiny motion could be sufficient for the perception of relative motion, hold your head as still as possible, move to within one foot of an object keeping the background also in view, look with one eye, and then make the smallest side-to-side movements possible with your head. As you will observe, even with the tiniest of movements you will still obtain relative motion, especially for objects that are near.

The last monocular depth cue, which O'Brien was also unable to use, is the **accommodation** of the lens of the eye to closer objects. As objects draw closer to you (within about 10 feet), your lens must bend to focus on them. Muscles in the eye accomplish this, and the amount of tension these muscles produce can provide feedback concerning distance. To feel the tension on the lens, simply close one eye and look at one finger of your outstretched hand. Then, draw your hand in toward you (bring it very close) and try to keep your finger in focus—can you feel the strain of the muscles bending the lens?

O'Brien took his knowledge of the pictorial depth cues that he could use and proceeded to build a model of King Kong that stood about 30 inches high. He then built models of Skull Island, dinosaurs, and familiar objects such as trees, all of them on the scale of inches. In the famous scene in which King Kong first grabs actress Fay Wray, Kong appears to be his full 50 feet in height. Look at Figure 6.25 and identify the cues on which O'Brien relied. Relative size is one. We know how tall the woman should be, and King Kong towers above her. Furthermore, his hand overlaps her, which means that his hand must be closer to us than she is, which adds to the illusion of size. Using a small model and the appropriate cues, O'Brien was able to trick the audience into believing King Kong was gigantic.

◆ **FIGURE 6.24**

Two circles with identical diameters. The circle on the left appears flat, two-dimensional. Because of shading, however, the circle on the right looks more like a sphere, indicating that some parts are closer to our eyes, some farther away. The shadowing has replicated the distribution of light and dark that is commonly associated with a sphere.

◆ **FIGURE 6.25**

King Kong holding Fay Wray. What cues did O'Brien use to create the impression of great size?

CONCEPT REVIEW ◆ MONOCULAR CUES OF DEPTH PERCEPTION

NO DEPTH CUES

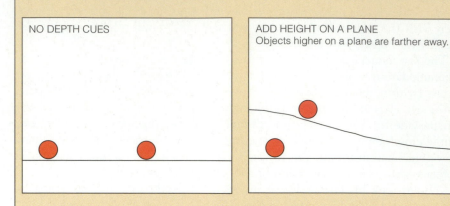

ADD HEIGHT ON A PLANE
Objects higher on a plane are farther away.

ADD OVERLAP
Overlapped objects are father away.

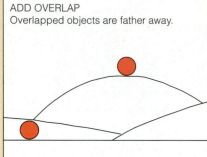

ADD RELATIVE SIZE
Comparing objects of known size reveals which is closer (closer objects appear larger).

ADD LINEAR PERSPECTIVE
Parallel lines appear to converge in the distance and to diverge nearby.

ADD GRADIENT OF TEXTURE
Objects that are closer have greater detail.

ADD SHADOWING
The apparent distribution of shadow provides information about agles or curves, indicating that some parts are closer and some farther away.

ADD AERIAL PERSPECTIVE
Closer objects are bright and sharp. Distant objects are pastel and hazy.

Binocular Cues

All the perceptual cues that we have discussed so far have been monocular cues. That is, they are cues that can be sensed even with only one eye. As you may have gathered, you can perceive depth more accurately, up to a distance of about 25 feet, with two eyes than you can with one. Better depth perception with two eyes is the result of **binocular cues,** which can be sensed by both eyes together but not by each eye individually. One such binocular cue is **convergence.** When you look at an object that is closer than approximately 25 feet, your eyes must converge on the object to perceive it as a single object clearly in focus. Figure 6.26 gives an example of convergence. It's an easy thing to test for yourself. Look at a distant object, and while keeping the object clearly in focus, hold your finger in front of your face. As long as you are looking at the distant object, you'll see two fingers with blurry outlines. Now look at your finger. You will see a single image clearly in focus. By converging your eyes on your finger, you created tension on the muscles required for this kind of eye movement. Through your learning and experience, you come to understand that a certain amount of muscular tension means that a particular object is a certain distance away. If you must make a very strong effort to converge or cross your eyes to look at a nearby object (such as a fly on the tip of your nose), the muscular feedback lets you know that the object is very close.

Convergence is not a factor when you are looking at objects farther away than 25 feet. In this case, your eyes do not converge; rather, as perceptual psychologists say, your eyes are focused at infinity.

Another powerful binocular cue is **retinal disparity.** Because the eyes are set a certain distance apart in the head, objects closer than 25 feet are sensed on significantly different locations on each retina. Figure 6.27 demonstrates this phenomenon. Retinal disparity also is easy for you to demonstrate. Simply hold the index finger of one hand close to your face and the index finger of

BINOCULAR CUES
Depth cues that arise only when both eyes are used. Examples include convergence and retinal disparity.

CONVERGENCE
A binocular depth cue. The eyes tend to turn toward each other when focusing on nearby objects and tend to focus at infinity when viewing objects farther away.

RETINAL DISPARITY
A binocular depth cue. Because the eyes are set apart, objects closer than 25 feet are sensed on significantly different locations on the left and right retinas. At close distances, retinal disparity, more than any other cue, gives a strong perception of depth.

◆ **FIGURE 6.26**

When the eyes focus on a nearby object, they converge. When they focus on a distant object, they do not converge.

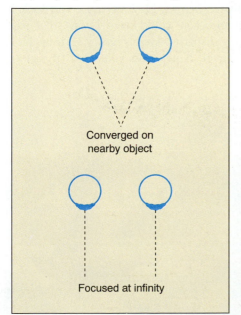

◆ **FIGURE 6.27**

Viewing objects at a distance creates little retinal disparity; viewing objects that are close creates considerable retinal disparity.

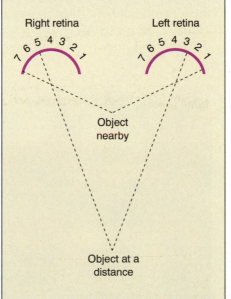

the other hand farther away. Line up your fingers. Now look at them with your left eye, then with your right eye, and then with your left again, and keep switching back and forth from one eye to the other. The near finger will seem to leap back and forth a considerable distance, while the other finger will seem to move only slightly. As Figure 6.28 shows, an object directly in front of your nose is seen on the far right side of the right retina and on the far left side of the left retina, while an object that is far away is seen on almost the same place on both retinas. Another way of saying this is that objects that are extremely close create great retinal disparity, while objects that are far away produce almost no disparity. At a close distance, retinal disparity, perhaps more than any other cue, gives you a strong perception of depth.

Beginning in the 1950s, a number of films were made in so-called 3-D, or three dimensions. Of course, it's impossible to create real three-dimensional images on a flat two-dimensional screen. By using retinal disparity, however, filmmakers were able to create 3-D movies that were so realistic that the action sometimes seemed to be coming right at the audience. To obtain this effect, two copies of the same movie (that had been filmed by two different cameras set the same distance apart as human eyes) were projected onto the screen at the same time. One of these films was shown in red, the other in blue. By using glasses with different-colored lenses, one red (it washed out the red movie so that that eye could only see the blue version), the other blue (it washed out the blue movie so that that eye could only see the red version), viewers would see a different copy of the film with each eye. The illusion of depth was created by the resulting experience of retinal disparity. Later 3-D movies made use of different polarized light (horizontally versus vertically oriented light waves), which could be differentially filtered by special glasses so that the 3-D movies could then be shown in color. Still, the two versions of the film had to be matched exactly when projected, and the 3-D effect ended at the edges of the screen.

If you have never experienced 3-D from two flat images you should know that it is possible to do *without* glasses. It takes some practice, but if you can do it, it's fun. Take a look at the two pictures that are side by side in Figure 6.28. They look the same, but they aren't. They were taken with a special camera that has two lenses the same distance apart as human eyes. In other words, one picture is what the left eye would see, while the other is what the right eye would see. So they are slightly different. Now, if you could look at these photos and see them as one picture, you would see 3-D on a flat page owing to the two retinal images creating disparity. Here's how you do it. Hold the book in front of you so that it is level. Now, cross your eyes (if you are

◆ **FIGURE 6.28**

Normally, these two photographs would be viewed in a stereo viewer so that each of your eyes could view the pictures independently. However, by carefully following the instructions in the text, you will achieve a full 3-D effect without the need for glasses or a viewer, proving that the effect is created only by retinal disparity, and not by 3-D glasses or a viewer as many people believe.

unable to cross your eyes, you're out of luck). As you cross your eyes, you will create the appearance of three, not two, pictures; a left picture, a right picture, and a fused picture in the middle (if you see four pictures, you've crossed your eyes too much, uncross them a little).

Next, make the fused image as congruent as you can; that is, make the two images join into one perfect image and *hold it there*. Just keep looking at the fused image, ignore everything else. Try to relax *without uncrossing your eyes*. If you can hold onto the fused image steadily for long enough, you will begin to feel as though you are looking at a single blurry image, and not a fused image. When that happens, you will unconsciously decide to accommodate the lenses of your eyes to bring this "one" image into focus, and BAM! the fused picture will suddenly become crystal clear and in great 3-D!

Your will also notice that your eyes feel funny when you look at the 3-D image. This is because you are now getting screwy feedback about how far away the image should be while your hands are telling you that it isn't that far. To prove this, all you have to do is touch the picture with your hand while you are looking at it, and your eyes will immediately uncross owing to the feedback your hand gives you about the distance to the picture. Also, the shock of the sudden accommodation clarifying the picture and its impressive 3-D depth may surprise you so much that you uncross your eyes and lose what you were trying to see. But with practice, you will find it easier and easier to do each time. You may also discover that after you do this for a few minutes and then look away and see normal things again, you may not feel so good for a few minutes—but hey! you got to see 3-D and you didn't even need glasses! And, if you did it well, you got to experience great examples of both retinal disparity and accommodation!

If you like 3-D and are interested in getting the full treatment, you might want to try modern 3-D, called Imax (see Figure 6.29). Imax incorporates a huge wraparound screen that, unlike a regular movie, includes the audience's peripheral vision. The 3-D effect is created through the use of battery-powered liquid crystal glasses that rapidly (24 times per second) block off vision to first one eye and then the other in direct synchrony with the rapid back-and-forth projection on the screen of the two different versions of the movie. If you have a chance to attend an Imax 3-D theater like the one I went to in Vancouver, do so. I don't know exactly how to describe the experience other than to point out that sometime during the show I accidentally swallowed my gum. And Imax may be just the beginning! (See Focus on the Future.)

◆ **FIGURE 6.29**

Viewers in Osaka, Japan, are thrilled by the new Imax 3-D wraparound movie system.

SEEING IS BELIEVING

There are two tennis courts in a park about a block away from my house. I'd like to take you over there and show you something—not now, but 20 years from now. Of course, because this is a book, we won't have to wait—so, let's travel into the future, 1 block over and 20 years forward.

Well, here we are in the future (quick trip, wasn't it?). As you can see, there are players on both courts. The couple on the far court are playing a typical game of tennis, not at all unusual. Looking at them, you can't even tell that you are 20 years into the future. But what about those two people playing in the near court—what in the world are they doing? Look at them! They're both wearing some kind of helmet. The helmet appears to be totally solid; it even covers their eyes—how can they see? They're running around swinging their rackets like they're playing tennis. In fact, that one acted like he just hit a ball—but there isn't any ball. And they don't appear to be "playing" tennis with each other; instead, each is playing tennis (if that's what they're doing) alone. They really look weird. Every once in a while, one of them laughs, as though whatever it is she's doing sure is fun.

To understand what is happening (or perhaps I should say what is going to happen), let's take a moment to consider the television or motion picture of today. The pictures produced are flat. We perceive them as real enough, and we are able to make sense of them. But no one would mistake what she saw on television or a movie screen for an image of a real object. When you look at an actor's face on the screen, you know that you are not looking at an actor who is really standing before you. If you walked behind the screen, you would not expect to see the back of the actor's head! Moreover, if you move your head from side to side, the picture on the screen does not change as it would if you were watching a real, three-dimensional object; that is, you perceive no relative motion.

Our friends on the tennis court, however, face none of those limitations. They are experiencing something called a *virtual environment*. The virtual environment—which, by the way, already exists—was first developed by NASA for training astronauts. The NASA version consists of a 12-pound helmet that fits over the head (see Figure 6.30). Both eyes are covered with clear, full wraparound 3-D images, and the ears receive digital stereo sound. With the optics that are now being developed, researchers hope that the artificial images produced in the helmet will eventually be as sharp and real looking as the "real world" images your eyes are perceiving at this very moment.

The images and sounds in the helmet are controlled by a computer that takes into account the wearer's motions. If the wearer looks straight ahead, he sees whatever is programmed to be straight ahead. If he looks left, right, down, up, or even behind him, the images move in relation to his actions, just like real images!

◆ **FIGURE 6.30**

NASA's virtual environment helmet.

Now that we have traveled 20 years into the future, would you like to try on the "tennis game" helmet? OK, walk onto the tennis court. First, you need to wear these special gloves and shoes that will tell the computer the locations of your limbs at any given moment. Now, hold this tennis racket and I'll help you on with the helmet—it's a good bit lighter than the old NASA model. Just put it down over your head and . . . YOU'RE AT WIMBLEDON—CENTRE COURT—SEE AND HEAR THE CROWD—LOOK AROUND—SEE ALL THE DIFFERENT PEOPLE? LOOK LEFT, THEN RIGHT— HEAR THE SOUND CHANGE AS YOU MOVE YOUR HEAD? MOVE ABOUT—SENSE THE POWERFUL EFFECT OF RELATIVE MOTION. ISN'T THIS UNBELIEVABLE? HOLD OUT YOUR HAND—THERE IT IS! THERE'S YOUR HAND! AND YOUR RACKET! NOT YOUR REAL HAND AND RACKET, BUT AN EXACT SIMULATION THAT LOOKS AND MOVES IN COMPLETE SYNCHRONY WITH YOUR REAL HAND AND RACKET, AND IT WILL APPEAR WHENEVER YOU MOVE YOUR ARM INTO WHAT WOULD HAVE BEEN YOUR VIEW, HAD YOUR VIEW NOT BEEN BLOCKED BY THE HELMET—OF COURSE, YOU DON'T FEEL THAT YOUR VISION HAS BEEN BLOCKED, BECAUSE YOU CAN SEE "YOUR HANDS"—YOU CAN SEE WIMBLEDON—AND YOU CAN SEE YOUR OPPONENT ON THE OTHER SIDE OF THE NET, WHO, BY THE WAY, IS GETTING READY TO SERVE. BETTER GET TO YOUR PROPER PLACE ON THE COURT—LOOK DOWN—SEE THE LINES MARKING OUT THE COURT? SEE YOUR FEET AS YOU WALK—SEE HOW EVERY-

FOCUS ON THE FUTURE

THING MOVES IN RELATION TO YOUR STEPS? TURN TO FACE YOUR OPPONENT. THE HELMET IS SO LIGHT YOU ALMOST FORGET THAT YOU ARE WEARING IT. THIS IS UNREAL! ACTUALLY, IT'S TOO REAL—IT LOOKS JUST LIKE IT'S REALLY HAPPENING! GET READY—HERE COMES THE SERVE—WHAT A BULLET! QUICK! STICK OUT YOUR RACKET! (An air-driven piston in the handle of your racket is fired by the computer at just the right time and strength by radio signal; you feel that a ball has hit the edge of your racket.) YOU WATCH THE BALL BOUNCE AWAY OFF THE COURT—A MIRACLE YOU EVEN GOT A PIECE OF THAT ONE—DID YOU SEE THE SPEED ON THAT BALL! LISTEN TO THE CROWD CHEER—WHO ARE THEY ROOTING FOR ANYWAY? YOU COULD GET KILLED OUT HERE. YOU'D BETTER ASK FOR A LOWER-RANKED OPPONENT. TAKE OFF THE HELMET. ZAP!! You're suddenly back on my neighborhood court. (By the way, the Yankee Stadium baseball program is also fun and don't even ask about X-rated films.)*

As you no doubt noticed, the strangest thing about this advanced helmet is that it seemed invisible when you had it on. When you put your hands up to your face, you could feel the solid front plate of the *helmet, but you couldn't see it;* you could see only Wimbledon and all that was happening there—now, that's what I call a high-tech wraparound 3-D optical computer! Of course, it's all ultrahigh resolution and it's digital (would I have taken you 20 years—and 1 block—out of your way to try on a cheap helmet?).

Before such a helmet becomes available for games, however, it probably will have important commercial and professional uses. Such a device, as NASA has shown, would be valuable for training just about anyone who might benefit from learning in a simulated environment—such as airline pilots, emergency room personnel, surgeons, police officers, tank commanders, or even college students who would rather do laboratory work at home, without the laboratory. In fact, today at the University of North Carolina at Chapel Hill, chemists can put on virtual goggles and use a special joystick to maneuver a small molecule that they can see in three dimensions into the cranny of a huge protein and even feel the electrical forces pull or push the molecule as it nears different places on the protein! In this way, they can better see and understand how certain molecules will join. On the same campus, an architect can walk on a treadmill while steering a pair of handlebars through his or her creation—in essence, taking a walk through the blueprints before anything is actually built.

Today in Japan, customers can design their own kitchens, then don goggles and gloves, and walk through their choices trying out the cabinets and appliances. This allows them to see if the design is what they want or if they desire any changes—all before anything is bought or installed.

Virtual helmets eventually should become readily available to the public. Even today, in some cities, gaming stores are available where people can go to play in virtual environments. The helmets used today aren't as sophisticated as the one just described, and there is often a lag time from when you move your head until the scene adjusts itself, but slowly we are approaching the kind of advanced device we imagined on the tennis court. As one investigator noted, "These will be in homes, much as televisions are today. But you won't watch shows—you'll put on the helmet and go places and experience things" (Rogers, 1987, p. 57). Of course, the experiences might take a little getting used to. No doubt, walking through Paris would be nice, but fighting off an invasion of giant spiders from Mars right in your own living room might be another thing. (And you can bet that in the same spirit that led to roller coasters after the invention of the train, designers will make "fright" programs—real "helmet-ripper-offers"!)

There are many questions we might ask concerning the effects of such a system: Should young children ever be allowed to wear the family "TV" and shoot it out with "real" bad guys on some apparently real street? Will interacting with simulated violence make viewers indifferent to the real thing? Could children wear the helmets at home instead of going to school and interact with a real teacher who teaches from a TV studio? All of the kids would see one another as though they were sitting in a real class, and they could interact with one another as well as with the teacher. They would perceive the blackboard, the schoolroom, the whole works, only they would all be in their own homes—probably along with their helmet-wearing parents who have "gone to work" without actually having gone anywhere. Such "helmet schools" would save greatly on the expense of maintaining real school buildings, save on commuting, cut down on automobile exhaust, and spell the death of the short-range spitball.

This all makes you wonder. Maybe philosophers who say that reality is in the mind are wrong—maybe it will turn out to be in the software!

*I told you not to ask!

INNATE

Inborn; arising as a hereditary component of a physiological or behavioral trait.

VISUAL CLIFF

An apparatus constructed to study depth perception in animals and human beings. It consists of a center board resting on a glass table. On one side of the board, a checkered surface is visible directly beneath the glass; on the other side, the surface is several feet below the glass, giving the impression of a dropoff.

The Visual Cliff

Because so many of our perceptual abilities appear to be tied, at least in part, to inherited mechanisms, it was only natural for researchers to wonder whether depth perception might not come into being immediately with little or no learning. That is, is depth perception present at birth?—is it **innate?** Let's look at the experimental evidence.

Most animals will avoid a sharp dropoff or cliff, and this tendency can be used to examine aspects of innate perception. Almost 35 years ago, Gibson and Walk (1960) constructed a device known as the **visual cliff,** a table with a glass surface marked to simulate a deep dropoff on one side and a shallow dropoff on the other (see Figure 6.31). Infant animals, including humans, can be placed at the center between the shallow and deep sides. Because of the glass, the subject cannot actually fall off the cliff.

Babies of many species were tested on the cliff, and the results demonstrated that they possessed an innate ability to avoid a dropoff, called *cliff avoidance.* Newborn chicks, whose first visual experience was on the cliff, refused to cross over to the deep side. Kittens, puppies, piglets, and various other infant animals also refused to venture onto the deep end. Baby mountain goats (a species that would have an exceptional reason for avoiding cliffs) similarly refused to cross to the deep side and, if pushed in that direction, collapsed their front legs. Gibson and Walk, and many other researchers, also demonstrated that human infants were much more easily coaxed onto the shallow side than onto the deep side, although some infants were willing to crawl onto the deep side. Does this mean that cliff avoidance is innate in humans? Unfortunately, the research conducted on humans was not as clear-cut as the research conducted on other species.

Unlike baby chicks, kittens, or mountain goats, human infants aren't precocious in terms of motor development. They usually are not able to crawl until they are about 6 months old, and independent movement is a prerequisite for a test of cliff avoidance. Consequently, by the time they can be tested on the cliff, human infants may already have *learned* to avoid dropoffs. This possibility was suggested by the research team of Campos, Hiatt, Ramsay, Henderson, and Svejda (1978), who observed that precrawling infants of 2, 3½, and 5 months of age showed only a decelerated heart rate when placed on the glass over the deep side. Heart-rate deceleration is generally taken to be a sign of interest, not of fear. The implication is that the infants perceived that something was different, but perhaps did not see this difference as a matter of "depth."

Another researcher (Rader, 1979) argued that cliff avoidance is a genetically inherited predisposition, but doesn't begin to express itself until it is triggered at about the age of 6 months in humans. The issue has not yet been fully resolved.

◆ **FIGURE 6.31**

The visual cliff.

🌀 MOTION PERCEPTION

After we have determined whether something is there and where that something is, we'll want to know what it is doing, if anything. To know whether some object is moving relative to ourselves, we need to compare it with what does not move. J. J. Gibson believed that our perceptual mechanisms evolved to take a special interest in these invariant stimuli *and to contrast them* with stimuli that were in flux. In other words, once we perceive what's stable, we can pick out what's moving. Gibson said that the terms *persistence* and *change* could describe any environment.

Understanding the perception of motion, however, presents some unusual challenges. For example, when you sense motion, how can you know whether an object has moved or you have moved? If someone playing baseball is running back for a long fly ball, what lets her know the amount of motion to attribute to the ball and the amount of motion to attribute to her own body? Is her knowledge based exclusively on learning?

Physiological evidence indicates that there are special neural mechanisms that allow us to judge motion with some degree of accuracy (Frost & Nakayama, 1983). One of these physiological mechanisms is found within our **peripheral vision,** an area that had been long ignored by researchers. It seems that the fovea of the retina is tuned to respond to local changes in the visual field; that is, to objects moving through the visual field. The periphery of the retina, however, responds to *global* changes in the visual field, the kind that occur whenever *we* move (Johansson, von Hofsten, & Jansson, 1980). If you turn your head from side to side or get up and walk, you'll notice that there is a tremendous amount of motion in the periphery, which you see out of the corners of your eyes.

You can demonstrate the distinction between foveal and peripheral vision in a rotary-drum room, a very small room contained within a large upright cylinder. The walls inside the cylinder are covered with vertical stripes, and you sit on a chair in the middle of this cylindrical room. While the chair and floor remain stationary, the walls of the room begin to rotate on the vertical axis so that the vertical stripes painted on the cylinder walls pass rapidly in a horizontal direction in front of your eyes. The walls are so close to your face that the spinning surface fills your entire visual field. Because of this, you sense motion in your peripheral vision (as you recall, one of the tricks used in the new 3-D motion picture system Imax). It creates a sickening feeling, and after about 10 seconds, if you're like most subjects, you'll probably grab your chair, swearing that the walls aren't turning but that the chair you're sitting on is spinning! Subjects are often afraid to get up off the chair because they think they'll be thrown to the ground. They sometimes lean as though they are accelerating or yell for help, but all the time the chair stays still and only the cylinder walls are rotating.

The reason that subjects in the rotary-drum room think they are in motion is that their peripheral vision is totally involved. This peripheral-foveal distinction suggests that there is a physiological organization to help us perceive motion. In fact, while most of the neurons from the foveal region are projected to the occipital lobes, neural messages from the periphery tend to be projected to the temporal lobes (Dichgans & Brandt, 1978). In addition, neural messages from the semicircular canals, which provide us with a sense of balance and orientation, are projected to areas of the temporal lobes very close to those receiving information from the peripheral vision. It may be that the messages from the semicircular canals function with messages from the peripheral vision to help us maintain our balance, head position, and motion in relation to the world around us.

◈ OTHER SENSES

Research concerning human perception is growing rapidly. Although visual perception dominates the research field, many studies of auditory perception or perception involving the minor senses are now being conducted.

As brief examples of some of this research, consider the following. When you hear a sound, you actually sense it twice, once in each ear, unless its source is equidistant from both ears. Sound takes slightly less time to reach the ear closer to the origin of the sound than to reach the ear farther away (see Figure 6.32). Even so, you will perceive only one sound, but it will seem to be coming from a particular direction. Your brain has somehow used the

PERIPHERAL VISION
All visual experiences outside the immediate line of sight; that is, experiences other than those derived from light focused on the fovea. The photoreceptor field on the retina surrounding the fovea gives rise to peripheral vision. Peripheral vision is especially important for determining motion.

◆ **FIGURE 6.32**

Although this single sound is sensed twice, the child hears, or perceives, it only once, but off to one side.

Sound waves reach left ear first

Sound waves

Sound source

difference between the arrival times of the two sensations to generate an understanding of the sound's location in space—a neat trick! This ability develops early in life. By 6 months of age, a baby can orient its head toward the source of a sound with no more than a 12-degree error, and by 18 months, the error is reduced to a very small angle of only 4 degrees (Morongiello, 1988). This is all the more amazing when you consider that as an infant grows, his head size enlarges, making the distance between his ears greater and greater. This means that the infant's brain must continually recalibrate the meaning of the time delay between receiving a sound in one ear and in the other (Clifton, Gwiazda, Bauer, Clarkson, & Held, 1988). You are also able to tell if a sound is coming from above or below, even though the sound reaches both ears simultaneously. This is achieved by making a very subtle discrimination concerning how the quality of the sound was affected by the shape of your outer ear, or pinna (Middlebrooks & Green, 1991). Sound waves captured from above by your outer ear are baffled, or deflected, differently than are sound waves captured from below.

Another interesting discovery concerning auditory perception is that the auditory cortex is not laid out like the cochlea (see Chapter 5), with many different locations each sensitive to a different frequency of sound; instead, the auditory cortex appears to have different locations, each sensitive to a different fundamental pitch *and to all of its higher-frequency harmonic overtones* (Pantev, Hoke, Lutkenhoner, & Lehnertz, 1989). This helps to explain how we can tell that a piano and a violin are playing the *same note*, when they both play a C, even though the instruments sound different. The complex and different sounds made by each instrument stimulated the same "pitch perception" location on the auditory cortex. In fact, some people have such exceptional ability in this area that they are considered to have "perfect pitch," the ability to identify any musical note they hear, regardless of which instrument plays it. Interestingly, there is reason to believe that anyone can be taught to have perfect pitch *if they are taught before the age of* 6. After age 6, it may be more difficult to acquire (Takeuchi & Hulse, 1993).

Touch perception provides another interesting illustration of research with the "minor" senses. If two pencil tips are touched to your body a small distance apart (at two points on the skin, call them A and B) and the touches are made within a fraction of a second of each other, you will feel as though one pencil tip has touched down at point A and drawn a line along the skin to point B (Geldard & Sherrick, 1986). This is similar to the Phi phenomenon observed in vision, in which two stationary lights, when flashed in succession, are perceived as one light in motion. Your brain is filling in the missing information. In the real world, two rapid, close sensations like the pencil touches would *most likely* be caused by one thing moving on your skin (a bug, for instance).

Whichever of the senses is being studied, understanding the processes by which the brain interprets what it senses is fundamental to our knowledge of human perception.

✿ SUMMARY

◆ Broadly defined, perception refers to the way in which we come to know what is going on around us. It refers to the entire sequence of events from initial sensations to our phenomenological comprehension of them.

◆ The basic perceptual abilities of the visual system include distinguishing forms from background, determining the location of forms in space, and analyzing whether forms are moving. Unique brain pathways have been associated with these different abilities.

◆ Reversible figures demonstrate the influence of learning in distinguishing form from ground.

◆ When expectations influence one's perceptions, it is referred to as top-down processing. On the other hand, bottom-up processing refers to the experience of inputs from the senses with relatively little cognitive processing in terms of one's expectations.

◆ Gestalt psychologists studying perception were interested in demonstrating that the whole was greater than the sum of its parts.

◆ Many of the perceptual organizations we make may be the result of perceptual mechanisms that have evolved to provide us with a perception of what is most likely. The Phi phenomenon illustrates this point.

◆ J. J. Gibson coined the term affordance to denote the perceptual organization possessed by a species that helps to support its survival.

◆ Among the theories of visual perception, the two that received the most attention were the image and cue theory and the direct perception theory.

◆ The image and cue theory proposed that we rely mainly on learned cues for such functions as depth perception. Through learning, we are able to make three-dimensional sense of a two-dimensional image projected on our retinas.

◆ Direct perception theorists believed that our genetic and biological organization equipped us to make perceptual sense of the world without having to rely much on learning.

◆ The interactionist view considers aspects of both the direct perception and the image and cue theories.

◆ Research with illusions has indicated that learning may be an important aspect of perception. The effects of many illusions can be understood as attempts to bring the illusions into line with our daily experiences.

◆ The brightness, size, and shape constancies are perceptual cues that help us to make sense of the world.

◆ Depth perception is achieved through monocular cues—that is, through cues sensed with only one eye (such as linear perspective and overlap)—and binocular cues (convergence and retinal disparity). A three-dimensional effect on film is obtained by using retinal disparity.

◆ Our learning and experience play an important role in size perception. Sometimes, our perception of size can be distorted. The moon illusion, which provides the cues of overlap and relative size, is an example.

◆ The visual cliff experiment indicates that the ability to perceive dropoffs is innate in some animals. Research has also been conducted on a comparable cliff avoidance mechanism in humans.

◆ Peripheral vision enables us to differentiate between our own movement and that of our surroundings.

✿ SUGGESTIONS FOR FURTHER READING

1. Bolles, E. B. (1991). *A second way of knowing: The riddle of human perception*. New York: Prentice Hall Press. Addresses the age-old question, "Does objective reality exist, or is it all in our minds?"

2. Coren, S., & Ward, L. M. (1993). *Sensation and perception* (4th ed.). New York: Academic Press. A college-level introduction to sensory and perceptual processes.

3. Gifford, D. (1990). *The farther shore: A natural history of perception*. New York: Atlantic Monthly Press. Presents the fascinating idea that movies, television, and high-speed travel have altered our perceptions, which leads, in turn, to the premise that how we perceive the world creates what we perceive.

4. Goldstein, E. B. (1989). *Sensation and perception* (3rd ed.). Belmont, CA: Wadsworth. A college-level introductory textbook.

5. Gregory, R. L. (1989). *Odd perceptions*. New York: Routledge & Kegan Paul. A collection of short essays for the general reader on how we perceive color, shape, touch, sound, and other sensations. Some are amusing, some serious. All will make you think.

6. Morris, D. B. (1991). *The culture of pain*. Berkeley: University of California Press. A thought-provoking exploration of the perception of pain and how culture can influence such perceptions.

7. Rheingold, H. (1991). *Virtual reality: The revolutionary technology of computer-generated artificial worlds—and how it promises and threatens to transform business and society*. New York: Summit Books. Virtual reality has moved from the realm of science fiction to science fact. This book offers a guided tour through that new world (available in paperback from Touchstone Books).

Chapter Seven

States of Consciousness

On January 13, 1989, a research team arrived at a cave near Carlsbad, New Mexico. There, a young Italian woman named Stefania Follini entered the cave through a small entrance in the ground. She was a volunteer who was helping to investigate the effects of the daily rising and setting of the sun on the human biological clock.

She descended into a 20-by-12-foot subterranean plexiglas module sealed 30 feet below the surface where she had agreed to spend months of time by herself. She went into a world with no sunrises or sunsets. There were no clocks and she was never told the time. The team left messages for her at random intervals on her computer; other than that, she was cut off from the outside world.

As the days passed, she unknowingly extended her own day to 25 hours, choosing to go to bed an hour later each night than was her custom before the experiment began. Without realizing it, she was soon staying awake for 40 or more hours straight and then sleeping 14 to 22 hours at one stretch.

The subterranean chamber Follini occupied during the experiment.

CONTENTS

Stefania Follini exiting the New Mexico cave where she spent four months in an experiment to test the body's reaction to long-term isolation.

She also informed the team on the surface that her menstrual cycle had stopped. After four months, when she was asked to estimate how long she had been underground, she guessed only two months. She thought that it was March when it was actually May! Her biological clock was completely out of synchrony with the world above.

Then, the experiment ended. When she returned to the surface, she was astounded to find how much time had really passed.

IN THIS CHAPTER, we will examine states of consciousness, including sleep and dreaming, hypnosis, meditation, and the effects of drugs. We'll discuss how long dreams last, how self-hypnosis is done, what theories have been developed about why we sleep, why drugs affect us as they do, and how you can alter dreams by taking part in them. You also will discover why Stefania Follini's biological clock began to "free run" once she was cut off from the sun.

WHY PSYCHOLOGISTS STUDY STATES OF CONSCIOUSNESS

Consciousness is the state in which you are aware not only of the external environment but also of internal events such as thinking. Before people act, they often consider things "internally"; that is, they think about them. When psychology was first developed, it was primarily considered to be the study of the mind, and thoughts seemed to most people a good indication of the existence of a mind. Consequently, the study of consciousness became a paramount issue for psychologists. In fact, an early definition of psychology was "the description and explanation of states of consciousness and such" (Ladd, 1887). Defining consciousness is not easy, however. When George Trumbull Ladd put forth that less-than-precise definition in 1887, it drew a lot of humorous comment about exactly what was covered under that umbrella "and such."

Today, thanks to advances in scientific technology, we have some objective ways to measure conscious states. We are able to monitor physiological correlates to changes in some conscious experience by using such instruments as the electroencephalograph (which we will discuss shortly) and the PET scan (see Chapter 2). By expanding our knowledge about what consciousness and its various states are, we come closer to understanding the mind.

ASPECTS OF CONSCIOUS EXPERIENCE

In 1913, John Watson, in his paper "Psychology as the Behaviorist Views It," rejected the study of consciousness and the introspective method (see Chapter 1) as too subjective to be of scientific interest. Although it appeared that objectivity could be preserved by avoiding the issue of consciousness, the concept of consciousness seemed so self-apparent and central to the human experience that it was impossible to ignore for long, and psychologists were drawn to study it (Hilgard, 1980).

Today, we examine conscious experience in many ways. In this book, consciousness was defined as being aware not only of your external environment, but also of internal events such as your thoughts. But many psychologists point out that this definition may be somewhat unclear. For instance, at this moment you are aware of which way gravity is pulling you, so you keep your muscles tense in a certain way to keep from falling over. This is definitely a case of *awareness*, but is it conscious? Well, maybe it is unconscious and only becomes a conscious concern from time to time when you are about to lose your balance or when you read about adjusting yourself in the gravitational fields in texts like this. But the point is, whether you are thinking about it or not, it is part of your awareness of your environment or you'd be flat on the floor right now. This has led psychologists to consider *attention* as an important aspect of conscious functioning.

Attention

Think about the following: You are sitting in a chair. You are relaxed. You feel the pressure of the chair against your body. You feel the pressure of the floor against your feet. You feel the weight of your clothes against your skin. You feel a large spider crawling along your arm. All this tactile (touch) sensory information has converged on you. You probably will not perceive all the inputs equally. Which one will attract the most attention? You probably won't even take notice of the pressure of your clothes or the floor or the chair, but the spider crawling on your arm—that will probably get your attention!

When people are asked, "What is conscious experience?" many will say it is what they are thinking about at any given moment. In other words, what they are attending to. Our conscious awareness has evolved in a way that enables us to be selective about all the stimuli that we receive, to suppress some while attending to others. The ability to attend is what enables you to listen to a particular conversation at a dinner party, even though everyone else is speaking; it also informs you about large (or small) spiders on your arm.

Since the days of William James, psychologists have wondered what attention is and how it operates. Scientists once believed that the attention process heightened our awareness of a particular stimulus, but now we know that attention acts as a filter, toning down or eliminating uninteresting stimuli from our consciousness (Moran & Desimone, 1985). As information from the senses progresses through the nervous system higher and higher into the cortex, receptive fields (the amount of sensory information each neural group has to process) become larger and larger. In fact, by the time sensory messages reach the back surfaces of the occipital lobes of the cerebral cortex (see Chapter 2), which process visual stimuli, the receptive fields are so large that each constitutes half of the visual field (Wurtz, Goldberg, & Robinson, 1982).

An interesting demonstration of this fact can be seen by examining the case of the German artist Anton Raderscheidt, who suffered a stroke in the parietal cortex on the right side of his brain. The stroke did not affect his vision; he could see everything fully on both the right and the left sides of his visual field, but his ability to attend to things was affected because attention is one of the important functions of the parietal lobes. An artist, however, needs to pay attention to what he's painting in order to put it down on canvas, and Raderscheidt was at first unable to concentrate or to pay close attention to anything in the left half of his world. In Figure 7.1, you can see his attempts at self-portrait as he slowly recovered from the stroke damage.

Exactly how attention affects consciousness is still a mystery, but experiments have shown that when attention is required for concentration on one of two stimuli, both of which are encompassed in the same receptive field, the receptive field will actually narrow, eliminating the unwanted stimulus (Moran & Desimone, 1985). The mechanism of attention, then, somehow controls the expanding and shrinking of receptive fields, which, in turn, filters out what is unwanted, influencing our sense of conscious awareness. The mechanism that controls how large a given receptive field will be at any moment in time appears to be under the control of inhibitory synapses within the receptive

CONSCIOUSNESS
A state of awareness of sensations, perceptions, or memories. The aspects of mental life of which one is normally aware.

◆ FIGURE 7.1

These four self-portraits (redrawn) were originally made by the German artist Anton Raderscheidt following a stroke in his posterior right parietal lobe. Although able to see, the artist was not able to attend to the left half of his world. The first self-portrait (a) was painted 2 months after his stroke. The artist was able to paint only what was in his right visual field, as that was all he could concentrate on. The second self-portrait (b) was made 3½ months after the stroke, when his ability to attend to the left half of his visual field was returning. Six months later, he painted the self-portrait in (c), and 9 months after the stroke, he painted the self-portrait in (d), which shows full recovery of his ability to attend to his left visual field.

(a)

(b)

(c)

(d)

field itself (see Chapter 2). When these inhibitory synapses are active, they are able to limit the receptive field's response to a narrower area than might otherwise be the case (Gottlieb, 1988).

As you can see, conscious awareness and consciousness itself are in flux. Consciousness changes and alters throughout the day as part of its normal functioning. How it can change is the focus of investigations of altered states.

🧬 STATES OF CONSCIOUSNESS

The conscious state is said to be altered any time the content or quality of conscious experience undergoes a significant change. There are many ways to alter conscious experience. Psychoactive drugs can alter your conscious state and your perceptions of the world. Sleeping and dreaming also are considered to be states of consciousness. Hypnosis can alter conscious experience. Other causes are sleep deprivation, religious experiences, mystical or emotional experiences, sensory overload or deprivation, high fever, and prolonged strenuous exercise, or even becoming engrossed in the pages of a good book.

Most research into states of consciousness has concentrated on sleep, hypnosis, meditation, and psychoactive drugs; we'll examine each of these areas.

◈ SLEEP

In the 1920s, a German physician named Hans Berger was the first person to record the brain's electrical activity. Because so many of the neurons and their axons (see Chapter 2) run through the cortex in a parallel direction, their thousands of action potentials add up, giving off an electrical field (just like the kind that surrounds an electric wire) strong enough to be picked up as "brain waves." Berger took readings of this activity with a fairly crude home-made device consisting of a couple of silver electrodes glued to his subject's scalp. When Berger reported his results, they sounded so bizarre that he was either laughed at or ignored for the better part of 10 years. (How would you like to be laughed at or ignored for 10 years?) "Berger's vindication," however, exists today in the modern form of his crude device, the sophisticated **electro-encephalograph (EEG).** The EEG has a number of applications, including its use by sleep researchers to measure the brain waves of sleeping subjects. They have observed that brain waves change dramatically at the onset of sleep and during sleep.

After the Second World War, electroencephalograms, the tracings made by EEG machines, were routinely incorporated into sleep research. The EEG yielded some interesting findings in the late 1940s and early 1950s. One was that not everyone "drifts off to sleep." Instead, some people go abruptly from a drowsy waking state to sleeping. Researchers also discovered that distinctly different sleep stages occur throughout the sleep period. Each stage is characterized by a different EEG pattern.

Stages of Sleep

When you fall asleep, your body temperature drops slightly, your pulse and breathing rates decrease, and your level of the stress-related hormone **cortisol** drops. Your body seems to be calming down after a busy day; it's becoming quiet. One interesting exception to all this quieting, especially in children, is the sudden increase in the release of growth hormone, which reaches its highest levels during sleep.

As you fall asleep, **alpha waves,** which are associated with a drowsy but awake state, change to small irregular waves. These waves are associated with the first stage of sleep (stage 1). Have you ever caught yourself falling asleep? Sometimes you can, especially if you're very tired and are thinking about something in particular when you fall asleep. As you shift from alpha to small irregular waves, you may, just for an instant, realize that your thoughts have become incoherent and illogical. This can happen because a rational train of thought can be lost at the onset of sleep (see Figure 7.2).

Many researchers believe, however, that stage 1 might be better thought of as a transition between wakefulness and real sleep (Borbely, 1986). The typical sleeper will spend only about 5 minutes in stage 1 before descending to stage 2. Stage 2 is considered to be more important because it constitutes about one-

ELECTROENCEPHALOGRAPH (EEG)
An instrument that records the electrical activity of the brain.

CORTISOL
A hormone produced by the cortex of the adrenal glands found just above the kidneys. It is critical for the metabolism of fats, carbohydrates, and proteins. It is very similar to cortisone.

ALPHA WAVES
A pattern of brain waves typical of the relaxed, waking state.

◆ **FIGURE 7.2**

A typical sleep cycle in humans. Sleep becomes progressively less deep throughout the night, and dreams tend to lengthen and intensify. The stages appear as numbers from 1 through 4. The amount of time spent in each stage is read horizontally. REM refers to rapid eye movement. Dreaming is most often associated with REM sleep.

DELTA WAVES
A pattern of brain waves associated with the deepest stages of sleep; often called slow waves because of their relatively low frequency.

SLOW-WAVE SLEEP
The deepest stages of sleep, characterized by an EEG pattern of delta waves.

RAPID EYE MOVEMENT (REM)
The rapid back-and-forth movement of the eyes during sleep. Dreaming is often associated with REM.

NREM SLEEP (ORTHODOX SLEEP)
Non-REM sleep, during which no rapid eye movement takes place. Also called orthodox or quiet sleep because the EEG pattern is markedly different from the waking state.

PARADOXICAL SLEEP
REM sleep. The EEG pattern closely resembles that of a person who is awake, even though the person is still asleep. Most dreaming occurs during this kind of sleep. The sympathetic nervous system shows heightened activity.

◆ FIGURE 7.3

In these computer-generated visual displays of the brain's electrical activity (a kind of EEG), the red areas indicate the presence of slow-wave, or delta-wave, sleep.

half of all our sleep time. As stage 2 begins, the muscles become less tense and the eyes rest quietly. During stage 2, the EEG shows slightly larger waves appearing along with rapid short bursts of brain-wave activity called *sleep spindles*. After about 10 minutes in stage 2, the sleeper descends to stages 3 and 4, which are associated with **delta waves.** Delta-wave sleep is sometimes known as **slow-wave sleep.** The distinction between stages 3 and 4 is somewhat arbitrary. If delta waves constitute less than one-half of the waves recorded during slow-wave sleep, the sleeper is considered to be in stage 3; more than one-half, and he is considered to be in stage 4.

The slow-wave stages of sleep are the deepest. In Figure 7.3, you can see the differences in slow-wave delta activity on a computer-generated visual representation of an EEG. It is most difficult to awaken sleepers from stage 4. As people grow older, they often notice that they become lighter sleepers. The EEG confirms this; it is well documented that slow-wave sleep decreases with age.

After spending time in slow-wave sleep, the sleeper typically returns to stage 2 for some time before entering the first rapid-eye-movement (REM) period (which we will discuss shortly). As Figure 7.4 on page 241 shows, following the REM period, the sleeper usually returns to stage 2 before sinking back into slow-wave sleep. This cycle may occur three or four times in a night before the sleeper finally ascends through stages 2 and 1 and then awakens.

Researchers also have investigated sleeping animals. The stages of sleep appear in all mammals (Borbely, 1986), although the pattern may differ. Other primates—monkeys, gorillas, and orangutans—show sleep patterns on the EEG that are very like the human pattern (Tauber, 1974).

REM Sleep

One of the most astounding discoveries in sleep research occurred in 1953 as a result of the careful observations of a graduate student named Eugene Aserinsky. While watching his 10-year-old son whose sleep was being monitored by an EEG in the laboratory, Aserinsky noticed that from time to time the boy's eyes appeared to move rapidly back and forth beneath his closed eyelids. After awhile, these rapid eye movements stopped, and his son slept soundly. A little while later, the movements began again. Further investigation revealed that this kind of **rapid eye movement (REM)** occurred in all subjects. Aserinsky wondered whether REM was related to anything in particular. By carefully examining subjects awakened from REM sleep and from periods of sleep when they displayed no rapid eye movement, called **NREM sleep** or **orthodox sleep,** Aserinsky and other researchers discovered that a very large proportion of subjects who were awakened from REM sleep had been dreaming! This discovery of a physiological correlate associated with dreaming stimulated researchers to conduct further investigations, and the area of sleep research began to grow.

In human beings, NREM and REM sleep are considered to be two distinct kinds of sleep. NREM sleep has been divided into the four stages described in Figures 7.2 and 7.4

REM sleep has its own characteristic EEG wave pattern. During REM sleep, an unusual thing happens: The body becomes simultaneously active and inactive (Chase & Morales, 1990). This occurs because *both* excitatory and inhibitory neural systems are stimulated during REM sleep.

The excitatory aspect of REM sleep can be seen as the sympathetic nervous system becomes active. REM sleep is sometimes referred to as **paradoxical sleep** because the body is excited and brain waves are similar to those of the waking state—blood pressure and heart rate increase, and the body may even act as

◆ FIGURE 7.4

EEG patterns clearly show the differences in states of consciousness. Each state is characterized by a different pattern. Notice how similar the patterns are during the drowsy state and REM sleep.

ATONIA
Loss of muscle tone. During REM sleep, atonia occurs simultaneously with arousal of the sympathetic nervous system. The atonia creates a state of semiparalysis in the REM sleeper.

REM REBOUND
An increase in REM sleep demonstrated by a person who has been deprived of it.

though it is under attack or is responding to an alarming situation. This heightened activity level doesn't necessarily mean that the sleeper is having a nightmare—she may actually be having a pleasant dream. The excitatory phase of REM sleep certainly appears to argue against the idea that the only reason for sleep is to give our bodies a rest!

At the same time, the inhibitory neural mechanisms occurring during REM sleep cause **atonia,** a loss of muscle tone, resulting in a state of semiparalysis. It becomes almost impossible for the dreaming REM sleeper to move. Some researchers believe that this change protects sleepers from physically responding to or acting out their dreams. (Contrary to what you might have guessed, sleeptalking and sleepwalking have been found to occur mostly during NREM, when the body is better able to move. About 15 percent of all dreams *do* occur during NREM sleep, which may account for the occasional actions of some sleepers, although their dreams appear to be less vivid than those that occur during REM sleep.) The inhibitory neural messages that create the semiparalysis during REM sleep pass through an area of the brain called the *pons.* In cats, when certain small portions of the pons are destroyed, the animals will become *active* during REM sleep. Unlike normal cats, cats with destruction in the pons will stand up during REM sleep, walk, bat at the air with their paws, or even appear to stalk prey, all with their eyes closed (Morrison, 1983). Also, certain drugs that are known to affect the pons can induce REM sleep (Quattrochi, Mamelak, Madison, Macklis, & Hobson, 1989).

Sometimes the excitatory and inhibitory processes occurring during REM sleep spill over into each other's territory. When this happens, semiparalyzed muscle groups may suddenly react. This results in the "nap jerks" or twitches that are commonly observed in sleepers (Chase & Morales, 1983).

The body generally tries to devote a certain portion of its sleeping time to REM sleep each night. During REM sleep, people will often incorporate an unexpected sound into their dreams rather than allow the sound to awaken them. Rather than let a street crew's air hammer wake you up, you might instead dream that you are on a battlefield.

People who are deprived of REM sleep in the laboratory often engage in **REM rebound** when they are finally given a chance to sleep undisturbed. In REM rebound, a person will show an increase in REM sleep after deprivation. Such a REM-sleep-deprived person will lapse into REM very soon after falling asleep and will engage in more REM than usual. Interestingly, scientists have discovered that some people may benefit from a certain amount of REM deprivation. Systematic REM deprivation in the laboratory has been found in some cases to help people overcome *endogenous depression* (Borbely, 1986). Endogenous depression, meaning depression from within, is not triggered by specific events, but is a general sense of sadness that has no apparent cause. REM deprivation is assumed to help the sufferers of such depression by somehow altering the effects of neurotransmitters in the brain.

🜲 SLEEP DURATION

The average young adult needs between 6½ and 8½ hours of sleep a night (Tune, 1969); some people need a little more, some a little less. The most alert individuals are those who sleep until they are simply no longer tired (a luxury to most of us). There is no evidence to support the old notion that "oversleeping" will make you tired (Roehrs, Timms, Zwyghuizen-Doorenbos, & Roth, 1989).

On the other hand, some individuals feel that they have had a full night's sleep after significantly less than 8 hours. Such individuals have been carefully monitored in sleep laboratories, and some have been shown to function very well after only 3 hours of sleep (Jones & Oswald, 1968). During the day (and for a good part of the night), they are wide awake and feel fine. When Jones and Oswald reported these findings, they didn't know what to call these people. Should they be considered sleep deprived? The label didn't really apply, because 3 hours of sleep was all they seemed to need. Jones and Oswald finally decided to call them **healthy insomniacs.** Some healthy insomniacs even get by with less than 3 hours of sleep per night. A woman who slept 45 minutes a night, day after day, reported that she felt absolutely fine, refreshed, and able to do her work without difficulty. Her claims were carefully documented in a sleep laboratory and found to be true (Meddis, Pearson, & Langford, 1973)!

You may be wondering whether these healthy insomniacs eventually suffer ill effects of some sort. After all, sleep (at least NREM sleep) does apparently give the body a chance to rest, which the body requires—or does it? Many very large animals expend a great deal of energy but sleep only a few hours a night and do very well. Horses, cows, and elephants usually sleep only 3 to 4 hours every 24. Then again, at the other extreme, opossums and bats sleep 20 hours per day. The range throughout the animal kingdom is considerable. It was even believed for a time that some marine mammals, such as dolphins or porpoises, didn't sleep at all (Webb & Cartwright, 1978), presumably because they would drown if they did. Now, however, through careful observation, we know that such mammals do sleep, but avoid drowning because the two hemispheres of the brain take turns sleeping; while one hemisphere is asleep, the other is awake (Mukhametov, 1984)!

Sleep Deprivation

What would happen if you did not get enough sleep? In one experiment, six couples were asked to reduce their nightly sleep period by ½ hour every week until they felt too uncomfortable to continue. All the subjects stopped before they reached less than 4½ hours of sleep per night (Johnson & MacLeod, 1973). No serious inability to perform different tasks occurred with the decreased amount of sleep, but the subjects all reported discomfort. There is no question about it: When you don't get enough sleep, you get sleepy.

What happens when you not only reduce your sleep but also try to stay awake for a long period? The question of how long people can go without sleep has been investigated extensively, with the first studies conducted in 1842 (Patrick & Gilbert, 1896). Most of us have missed one night's sleep, maybe even two nights in a row. Some people have stayed awake much longer. In one carefully controlled experiment, six human subjects were kept awake for 205 hours (8 days, 13 hours) straight (Kales et al., 1970). The world record under controlled conditions has stood for almost 30 years and is 264.2 hours (11 days, 12 minutes) (Gulevich, Dement, and Johnson, 1966). In cases of extended deprivation like the ones just noted, sensory disturbances, hallucinations, and delusions occur after only about 60 sleepless hours:

The surface of objects begins to waver; the floor appears to be covered with spiderwebs; faces appear and disappear.... A participant hears voices in the sound of a running water faucet and thinks they are talking about him.... The subject feels a ring of pressure around the forehead, as if he were wearing a hat. (Borbely, 1986, p. 156)

Some research indicates that people deprived of sleep have "micro-sleep" periods, an intrusion of REM during waking, which may account for their hallucinations. Micro-sleep episodes also make it difficult to say how long the subject has truly been awake.

Even after 60 sleepless hours, functions such as heart rate, blood pressure, respiration, and temperature did not show much change. When the subjects were finally allowed to sleep, they slept for about 1 whole day—or even

HEALTHY INSOMNIACS
People who function well with only 3 hours or less of sleep per night and do not seem to need more sleep than this.

This scene from the movie They Shoot Horses, Don't They? *depicts an example of marathon dancing, a craze of the 1930s, in which the last couple left dancing on the floor wins the prize. During the Great Depression, couples often danced for days with hardly any sleep in order to win, because they needed the prize money desperately. After about 60 hours of sleep deprivation, hallucinations and delusions become common.*

less—awoke, and felt quite good. This seems to indicate that missing a few nights' sleep may not be harmful in the long run to people who are healthy to begin with.

Because of such findings, some researchers began to wonder whether sleep was, in fact, necessary for life. Perhaps sleep was one of nature's big mistakes. Maybe if we could counter whatever it was that made us sleepy, we could get by just fine without sleep. This speculation led researchers to try an experiment in which rats were deprived of sleep to see whether sleep deprivation was harmful to the rats or whether it only made them sleepy. In Figure 7.5, you see the organization of a device used to measure sleep deprivation in rats. Both rats were connected to an EEG that would signal when they fell asleep. One rat was chosen for sleep deprivation; the other rat was used to control for the possible stress effects of just being in the experiment. Whenever the rat to be sleep deprived fell asleep, the plastic disk the rats were standing on began to rotate. Then the rats would have to walk to keep from falling into the water. The control rat was able to sleep when the other rat was normally awake.

Some of the sleep-deprived rats lasted as long as 33 days! None of the sleep-deprived rats showed any signs of physical abnormalities—that is, until the day before they died. *All* the sleep-deprived rats died; *none* of the control rats did. On autopsy, the rats who had died were found to have many things wrong with them, including stomach ulcers and internal hemorrhages; in all rats the damage was severe and extensive throughout, although no two rats had exactly the same damage. The researchers concluded that "these results support the view that sleep does serve a vital physiological function" (Rechtschaffen, Gilliland, Bergmann, & Winter, 1983, p. 184).

Of course, the same experiment can't be conducted on humans. However, some interesting case studies have come to light, indicating that a fate similar to that experienced by the sleep-deprived rats might await a human subject. In 1986, the case of a 53-year-old man who had a sleep problem was reported (Lugaresi et al., 1986). The man had slept normally until he was 52. At that time, he began to lose the ability to sleep and was soon unable to sleep at all. (Even healthy insomniacs get *some* sleep.) He was admitted to a hospital, but *nothing* given to him would help him to sleep. He finally sank into a vegetative stupor and died. The autopsy revealed that 95 percent of the neurons in an area of the thalamus, which is suspected to be involved with sleep regulation, had been destroyed by a defective protein-gene run rampant. Interestingly, one of the man's sisters had died in the same way. Furthermore, sleep researchers were unable to detect any normal brain-wave sleep patterns in a number of the man's relatives. This fortunately rare sleep failure is now known as *fatal familial insomnia* and has been discovered to be caused by a mutation on a special kind of gene made of protein rather than DNA, called a *prion*, that, in turn, can directly affect the brain (Goldfarb et al., 1992). Because part of the brain was damaged by the errant protein-gene, it is not possible to state with complete certainty that sleep deprivation caused these deaths. But it is suspected that even if sleep deprivation was not the direct cause, it was a major contributing factor in these deaths.

The Circadian Rhythm

Circadian, from the Latin *circa* (about) and *dies* (day), refers to events that occur in roughly a 24-hour cycle. Infradian rhythms, such as heartbeats, occur in periods notably shorter than 24 hours, while ultradian rhythms, such as the

◆ **FIGURE 7.5**

The experimental apparatus for measuring long-term sleep deprivation in rats. The EEGs of both rats are monitored. When the rat to be sleep deprived falls asleep, the EEG notes the change and closes a circuit, causing the plastic disk that both rats are standing on to begin turning. The rats are called a "yoked" pair, because when the turning disk forces the sleep-deprived rat to walk, the control rat must also walk. This arrangement controls for the stress that the rat faces when it is forced to walk in order to keep from falling into the water. A rat who does not walk when the disk turns will be carried to the wall and knocked into the water. With this arrangement, the rat that is not to be deprived is able to sleep when the other rat is normally awake. The sleep-deprived rat can never sleep, because as soon as the rat's EEG senses that the animal is falling asleep, the circuit will close and the disk will start turning. (SOURCE: Rechtschaffen, Gilliland, Bergmann, & Winter, 1983, p. 182.)

CIRCADIAN RHYTHM
A daily cycle. The sleep-wake cycle is considered to be a circadian rhythm.

JET LAG
An uncomfortable feeling caused by disruption of the sleep-wake cycle that follows an attempt to adjust to a new time zone too quickly. It is called jet lag because long-distance travelers often suffer from it.

SUPERCHIASMATIC NUCLEI (SCN)
Dense clusters of neurons located in the central nervous system close to the hypothalamus just above the optic chiasm where the optic nerves from both eyes intersect. The SCN is known to control the pacing and activation of many circadian rhythms.

menstrual cycle, occur over periods notably longer than 24 hours. The sleep-wake cycle occurs daily and is therefore a **circadian rhythm.** Figure 7.6 shows a typical sleep-wake cycle of a person who is sleeping 8 hours per night. As the circadian rhythm begins its downward trend, the person becomes sleepy, his core temperature drops, and the levels of cortisol in his blood lower. When the circadian rhythm comes back up, the person awakens, and both cortisol levels and temperature increase. During the day, as the circadian rhythm nears its high point (usually in the early evening—but this may vary considerably), body temperature and cortisol levels reach their maximum, and vision, hearing, smell, and taste are at their peak. At this time, the person is most alert.

You can easily sense your own circadian rhythm by staying awake all night. By 2 or 3 A.M., you feel extremely tired, and by 5 or 6 you may be exhausted. But, by 7 or 8, you'll probably begin to feel *less* tired. This resurgence occurs because you are reaching a point in your circadian rhythm where your alertness is beginning to pick up. Interestingly, after missing a night's sleep, you won't need a full 8 hours' extra sleep to make up for it; an additional 1 or 2 hours usually will be enough.

Attempting to change the circadian rhythm abruptly is what causes **jet lag.** That sleepy uncomfortable feeling that you may have after traveling great distances has little to do with being cooped up in jets or the length of the trip. It has to do with adjusting to new time zones. In fact, if you leave an American city to fly, for instance, to Belgium, you can avoid jet lag if you continue to stay on local American time. However, if you try to adjust to Belgian time immediately and have breakfast when you would normally have been going to bed back home, you will disrupt your circadian rhythm and you'll find it very difficult to get through the first few days or so.

For years, researchers tried to find out how the body synchronized its circadian rhythm to the length of the day. After all, how could it know when 24 hours were up? Then, in the early 1970s, scientists discovered that a small cluster of brain neurons alongside the hypothalamus, called the **superchiasmatic nuclei,** or **SCN,** were mostly responsible for regulating circadian rhythms. In animals, if this area is disrupted, many circadian rhythms will fail or will occur completely out of synchrony with one another and with the 24-hour day. Even stronger evidence supporting the SCN as being the body's timekeeper comes from experiments in which tissue was taken from the SCNs of live hamsters, who had 20-, 22-, or 24-hour cycles, and then transplanted into hamsters whose SCNs had been destroyed. The recipient hamsters quickly showed the daily rhythm of the donor hamster, whether 20, 22, or 24 hours long (Ralph, Foster, Davis, & Menaker, 1990). Interestingly, the reason these researchers had hamsters with different circadian rhythms with which to experiment was because they had discovered that different circadian rhythms can be induced through breeding. In fact, Martin Ralph and Michael Menaker were able to trace the differences in the animals' circadian rhythms to differ-

◆ **FIGURE 7.6**

The circadian sleep cycle of a typical person who sleeps 8 hours per night and usually awakens at 8 A.M. Notice that the circadian rhythm between midnight and 8 A.M. is similar to that depicted in greater detail in Figure 7.2.

ences in a single gene (Ralph & Menaker, 1988). The finding that the body's pacemaker is directly controlled by a heritable, genetic process emphasizes just how deeply ingrained it is.

Curiously, the SCN isn't bound to an exactly 24-hour day; in fact, the cycle in most people seems to be a little more than 25 hours. The reason for this is unknown, but it may help to explain why many people find it easy to creep forward in their sleep schedule, going to bed later and later each night (making the morning jolt administered by the alarm clock seem worse and worse—does this sound familiar?). The "creep forward" tendency has been shown in experiments in which subjects have been isolated from all time cues, such as the experiment described in the Prologue where the young woman in the cave lost all track of time. In these circumstances, subjects **free run;** a circadian rhythm of 25 hours or more is typical (Siffre, 1975).

Synchronizing the SCN to a 24-hour cycle appears to be the job of the **pineal gland** (Czeisler et al., 1986). Surprisingly, investigations have shown that the pineal gland resembles a crude retina (Miller, 1985c). In fact, the pineal gland, in evolutionary terms, might have been the first eye. In some species, like the Western fence lizard, the pineal gland even has a lens and cornea associated with it!

The pineal gland senses the light and secretes hormones in reaction to the length of day, which, in turn, keeps circadian rhythms on a 24-hour cycle. Sudden changes in this rhythm, due to shifts in work schedules, for instance, can be quite disruptive.

For instance, it was 4 A.M. when the accident occurred at the nuclear power plant at Three Mile Island back in 1979. When the morning-shift workers arrived, they walked into a control room that was in panic. Within a few minutes, however, the workers from the *new shift* realized which gauges were not to be trusted and determined what really might be happening at the reactor core. They acted on a hunch to stop the rising heat of the core just in time.

In Bhopal, India, an accident occurred at a Union Carbide chemical plant during the night shift; it caused the release of a deadly gas that killed thousands of people (Coleman, 1986). At the nuclear plant at Chernobyl, in the former Soviet Union, the atomic core melted down and exploded, spewing radiation over scattered areas of Europe. No one knows how many cancer deaths eventually may result; some people estimate over 10,000. The failure at Chernobyl also occurred during the night shift (Marbach, Carroll, & Miller, 1987).

FREE RUN
The tendency for the sleep-wake cycle to break away from a 24-hour cycle. This is most likely to occur when day and night cues are reduced or eliminated. Most free running in humans involves a cycle of approximately 25 hours, but many other cycles are possible; most are longer than 24 hours, but some are shorter.

PINEAL GLAND
The pineal gland is located in the brain and resembles a crude retina. It secretes melatonin, is sensitive to light, and secretes hormones in response to the length of day. The pineal gland is believed to regulate the 24-hour circadian rhythm.

The control room for Unit II, Three Mile Island, site of the nuclear accident. Workers not in synchrony with their sleep cycles are slower to react in emergencies and less able to think through problems that arise.

Most people think that the oil spill from the *Exxon Valdez* in 1989 occurred because the captain of the ship had an alcohol problem. While it is true that the captain left the bridge to go lie down in his bunk, a report by the National Commission on Sleep Disorders Research pointed out that the direct cause of the accident was the "severe fatigue" of the ship's third mate who was in charge at the time (Holden, 1993). Was it only a coincidence that graveyard-shift workers were on duty during these accidents, or did the accidents occur because the workers were too tired to think in an emergency?

Many researchers now believe that workers whose schedules are not in synchrony with their circadian rhythms are much less productive and much less safe on the job (Monk et al., 1983; Coleman, 1986). Research indicates that drowsy drivers cause more fatalities than drunk drivers (Holden, 1993). In fact, when sleep researcher Charles Czeisler interviewed thousands of shift workers, including truck drivers and nuclear power plant operators, he found that more than half admitted to dozing off while working at least once a week (Weiss, 1989).

Such findings may be especially important for industry. Fully 25 percent of American workers have a schedule other than the standard day shift. Furthermore, many of those 25 percent work for companies that rotate shifts in an effort to be fair to all employees. The most common shifting schedule requires workers to take the day shift (8 A.M. to 4 P.M.) one week, the graveyard shift (midnight to 8 A.M.) the next week, and the swing shift (4 P.M. to midnight) the week after that, and then to start the cycle again.

As you now know, when workers suddenly change to the graveyard shift, they are required to be awake and on the job when their circadian rhythm is telling them to sleep. Then, when they go home at 8 A.M. to sleep, their circadian rhythm is telling them to awaken. No wonder nobody looks forward to the graveyard shift.

Organizations such as the Nuclear Regulatory Commission and the Federal Aviation Administration are just now beginning to pay attention to sleep cycles and to possible ways to ease the strain of shift working. In fact, the FAA is now experimenting with allowing pilots to take "controlled naps" on long trans-Pacific flights, which are notorious for causing fatigue. Although no one can say that a particular airline disaster or industrial accident was caused by workers whose various circadian rhythms were desynchronized, there is no doubt that visual acuity, problem-solving ability, and coordination decrease dramatically when people stay awake at a time when their bodies want to be asleep.

In 1980, researchers at the Stanford University Sleep Center were contacted by the operating manager of the Great Salt Lake Minerals and Chemicals Corporation in Utah. The manager was curious about whether the researchers' knowledge of circadian rhythms and sleep cycles could be used to help his workers. For 10 years the corporation had rotated its workers every week to the preceding shift, as described previously; that was common industry practice. In other words, every week, workers would begin their shift 8 hours earlier than they had the week before.

The Stanford researchers began their experiment by changing the schedules of the workers, so that they moved to a *later* shift (clockwise direction) every 3 weeks (see Figure 7.7). (Various controls comparing nonrotation and different schedules were also incorporated into the study.) The workers were then compared on measures of health, productivity, personnel turnover, and job satisfaction. The results showed that a large majority of the workers who shifted preferred the new forward rotation to the old backward one. To the company's satisfaction, personnel turnover decreased, and productivity increased by 20 percent (Czeisler, Moore-Ede, & Coleman, 1982; Coleman, 1986).

◆ **FIGURE 7.7**

A 3-week clockwise shift. (SOURCE: *Coleman, 1986, p. 46.*)

□ Day Shift   □ Evening Shift   ■ Night Shift

As you may have noticed, two major changes were made in the schedule. First, the advance in shifts proceeded in a clockwise direction instead of the traditional counterclockwise direction. As we mentioned, when you are resetting circadian rhythm, it is much easier to go forward than backward—the clockwise direction is in tune with the typical SCN cycle of slightly more than 24 hours. The second change was to a 3-week rotation instead of a 1-week shift change. The researchers chose this period because it takes from 4 to 14 days for body temperature and hormone secretions to come into synchrony with the new sleep schedule (Coleman, 1986). When the workers were shifted every week, their circadian rhythms (temperature, hormone secretion, and sleep) were desynchronized, leaving them with a generally miserable sense of existence; they were never quite awake and never quite asleep.

Even those workers who shift every 3 weeks, however, must still endure the 4 to 14 days while their circadian rhythms synchronize to their new sleep schedule. Scientists have discovered, however, that if a person who is going from the swing shift to the graveyard shift sits in front of floodlights like those used on a movie set from early evening until midnight, the pineal gland can be fooled into "thinking" that midnight is really sunset! The pineal gland then rapidly moves the body's temperature and hormone secretions forward, bringing them into line with the new schedule in only 2 days (Czeisler et al., 1986). The shift to a new time schedule can be made to occur even more rapidly by providing a flood of bright light 2 to 3 hours before the individual's usual "dawn" (Czeisler et al., 1989).

Another interesting way in which the circadian rhythm might be reset is by altering the body's hormone levels. Melatonin, a hormone that is secreted by the pineal gland at regular intervals, affects the circadian rhythm. Researchers have used controlled doses of melatonin to accelerate or decelerate the circadian cycle, restore the cycle to a blind person whose circadian rhythm had become disturbed, and help alleviate the symptoms of jet lag (Reppert, Weaver, Rivkees, & Stopa, 1988). Once the effects of melatonin are better understood, it might eventually be commonly used to help overcome the problems associated with shift work or jet lag.

The effects of light on the circadian rhythm are not fully understood, however. For instance, it has been discovered that moderate light exposures (equivalent to sunrise) administered for about 10 hours centered around the body's temperature low for the day can stop the circadian rhythm in its tracks. The prominent fluctuations of the rhythm, including temperature changes and shifts in cortisol levels, simply disappeared (Jewett, Kronauer, & Czeisler, 1991). In these studies, timing was critical. If the light exposure was shifted by as little as 18 minutes, the difference was between circadian shutdown and no noticeable change! In all cases, the biological clocks of the volunteers immediately reset as soon as they left the lab and went out into the sunlight. The only observable effect of circadian shutdown on the subjects' behavior was that they seemed to have a more even mood throughout the day with fewer highs and lows. These studies help to emphasize just how much we *don't* know about the circadian rhythm and how much more there probably is for us to learn.

AN ENDURING QUESTION: WHY DO WE SLEEP?

For years, people have assumed that we need to sleep because we must rest. The logic of that conclusion appears undeniable. And yet, when researchers examine sleep closely, sleep is often found to be a time of stress

ADAPTIVE THEORY
A theory about why we sleep. It states that each species needs a certain amount of waking time in order to survive and that sleep is nature's way of protecting organisms from getting into trouble during their extra time.

CONSERVING-ENERGY THEORY
A theory about why we sleep. It states that sleep is a good way of conserving energy in the face of sparse food supplies. This theory agrees with the adaptive theory that sleep can be a protective device.

AN ENDURING QUESTION, CONTINUED

and physiological and muscular activity (like tossing and turning). Furthermore, quiet resting while awake, no matter how quiet, cannot replace sleep. Also curious are the very differing amounts of sleep needed by different species, although all must sleep some. Why do these differences exist? To this day, the reason for sleep remains one of the most profound mysteries. No one knows the answer, but there are some interesting theories that may help provide some clues.

The first theory advanced about why we sleep, known as the **adaptive theory** (Meddis, 1975; Webb, 1974, 1975), contends that each species needs a certain amount of waking time in order to survive. Large herbivores (plant eaters) such as elephants and cows must consume vast amounts of vegetation to live. Grazing and eating like that take a lot of time. If elephants slept for 8 hours a day as we humans do, they probably wouldn't have time for the waking activities that maintain their species.

Unlike elephants, humans don't need 21 hours of waking time in order to survive. In examining the Laplanders, a modern tribe in northern Scandinavia that still follows the herds and lives off the land in the same way our ancestors did many thousands of years ago, we find that approximately 15 or 16 hours of daily waking activity are required to sustain human lives and foster the next generation. This leaves 8 hours per day *that aren't needed.* Sleep, then, may be nature's way of telling people to lie down and be quiet during their "extra time." In this view, sleep is a protective mechanism, keeping organisms out of trouble. If, in your extra 8 hours per day, you wandered about stirring up fights, taking chances, or using up your resources, you would not be as likely to survive and pass on your genes to your offspring. On the other hand, it would be an adaptive advantage if you, or any species, inherited a predisposition to pass out during your spare time.

The second explanation, known as the **conserving-energy theory,** goes hand in hand with the adaptive theory. Two researchers (Allison & Cicchetti, 1976) observed the sleep patterns in 38 different species and reported that differences in species body weight, which is a good indication of metabolism, and the amount of danger faced by the species in its environment correlate well with the amount of sleep a species needs. The implication is that animals that sleep a great deal and have a high metabolic rate may be sleeping to conserve energy as well as to protect themselves. Human beings, too, may have come to use sleep as a means of conserving energy. You burn fewer calories when you're asleep than when you're awake and active. If food supplies are scarce, going into a kind of hibernation for 8 hours every day is a way of ensuring that your limited food supply won't be consumed too quickly. So perhaps a sleep-promoting factor has become incorporated into our biology because of the value inherent in remaining quiet and conserving energy after a day's tasks.

In fact, natural substances have been found in the body that promote sleep (Krueger, Pappenheimer, & Karnovsky, 1982). One of these, factor S (for sleep) is a small molecule that will induce slow-wave sleep for several hours when it is given to animals. Factor S also stimulates the immune system (Karnovsky, 1986). Researchers note elevated levels of factor S during times of illness, which may explain why we tend to sleep more when we are ill.

AN ENDURING QUESTION, CONTINUED

The presence or absence of factor S does not completely control whether or not sleep will occur, however. Other sleep factors must also be playing a role. Researchers suspect that there are many additional sleep factors, and they have isolated a few of them (Borbely, 1986). Even so, to this day no one knows exactly why the body produces sleep-inducing chemicals, or why they cause us to become sleepy.

The most recent, and some say exciting, theory is called the **off-line theory.** It was developed by Jonathan Winson beginning with an observation that he made back in 1969 when he was a student. Winson read that an interesting brain wave, called a *theta wave* was observed in animals when they were startled by a predator, when they hunted prey, when they explored strange new places, *and when they were in REM sleep.* The theta waves were also being produced by neural bundles in an area of the brain called the hippocampus, which was known to be important for memory (see Chapter 2).

Years later, Winson heard about long-term potentiation (see Chapter 2) and realized that for neurons to change in permanent ways so that memories could be stored for long periods, they would have to be stimulated again and again. He wondered if that might not be the function of REM sleep. He soon discovered that animals that have learned a complex task and are then allowed to sleep will forget what they have learned if they are deprived of REM. Animals deprived of NREM do not show this forgetfulness. These findings imply that REM sleep may be involved in the learning process. It may be that during REM, the new experiences that we have acquired are somehow integrated with our older memories and experiences. This may explain why many of the events that occur in our lives on a particular day show up again, in one form or another, in our dreams about 3 or 4 days later (Epstein, 1985). REM may be placing these new experiences into our memory in a more profound and lasting way.

In an effort to support this idea, Winson conducted an ingenious experiment. He monitored a certain location in a rat's brain where he found a small cluster of neurons that *responded strongly only* when the rat was in a particular part of a new maze that the rat was learning to run through. Winson then closed off that part of the maze and let the rat wander anywhere else. The neurons did not fire very much. But, when the rat was asleep and REMing, that same bundle of neurons fired strongly (Pavlides, Greenstein, & Winson, 1988; Winson, 1990)!

This theory is called the off-line hypothesis because all but the very largest computers need **off-line time** to store, sort, and integrate information. Off-line time frees circuits for gathering and sorting new information by consolidating and storing the old information. The same kind of off-line sorting and processing may be occurring in humans during REM sleep (Winson, 1985).

Switching back and forth between on- and off-line also enables smaller computers to handle loads that would normally require much larger machines. The Australian anteater, a very early mammal that lays eggs like a reptile, is the only known mammal that does not engage in REM. Its forebrain is huge in comparison to the rest of its brain (Hawkins, 1986). This may be because its forebrain has to do everything on-line. Winson believes that if mammals like us didn't sleep—that is, have off-line

---

OFF-LINE THEORY
A theory that has as its premise that REM sleep enables creatures to maintain a smaller and more efficient brain size by consolidating and storing previously gathered information during sleep.

OFF-LINE TIME
In computer science, the time when data are no longer being input, but rather are being analyzed, correlated, stored, or treated in some processing fashion. In dream theory, the time when the brain shuts down, or sleeps, to prevent continued input and engages in REM to process data already received—presumably to make room for further input when it awakens.

AN ENDURING QUESTION, CONTINUED

time—each of us would have to haul our enormous forebrains around in wheelbarrows. Perhaps off-line time during REM enables creatures to maintain a smaller and more efficient brain size. If so, then one of the reasons that we sleep is because our powerful brains can't function without off-line time!

This view, as you may have noticed, is not exclusive of the other views concerning why we sleep. All three may be important reasons and others may yet be discovered. A full and complete understanding of why we sleep may still be decades away. Perhaps someday we will understand sleep, and perhaps even find a way to rid ourselves of the need for it. That might sound unpleasant, but if you never got sleepy and found other ways to get the benefits of sleep, you probably wouldn't miss it. Not sleeping would also add 25 to 30 waking years to each person's life.

FOR CRITICAL ANALYSIS

1. If scientists found a way to safely prevent sleep and also fix it so that you would never become sleepy, would you want to make use of this discovery and stay awake the rest of your life thereby adding "years" to your existence? If you say "no," is it because you imagine yourself becoming tired for some reason? Many people say that under such circumstances they sense that they might develop a need for a quiet time like sleep just to get away from stimulation, a need quite apart from the desire to sleep because they are sleepy. Do you also feel that way? Might such feelings also hint at additional reasons for sleep?

2. If people could find a safe way to end the need to sleep, what effect would this have on our environment? Would pollution grow at a faster rate? Would energy resources be used more quickly? Would energy demands remain high throughout the entire 24 hours? How do your answers fit with the idea that sleep is evolutionarily adaptive for the survival of our species?

◆

She's washed her hair, taken a warm bath, and is ready for bed; now for that relaxing cup of coffee. People who are used to drinking coffee before bedtime, amazingly, are often unaware that it may be the cause of their sleep problems. Even a cup of coffee consumed at 4 PM may cause sleep difficulties 7 or 8 hours later.

🧬 SLEEP ABNORMALITIES AND PATHOLOGY

There are many sleep-related disturbances, among them insomnia, narcolepsy, and sleep apnea. In 1988 a congressional commission determined that sleep-related problems cost American society about $50 billion a year and that about 95 percent of individuals with sleep disorders were going undiagnosed (Holden, 1993). All of the major sleep disorders are being investigated in laboratories, and ways of dealing with them are being developed.

If you have difficulty sleeping—or staying awake—you aren't alone. In just the United States, approximately 40 million people have chronic sleep problems, and about 20 percent of them feel that their difficulty is serious enough to warrant at least one visit to a doctor during any given year.

Insomnia

People who have **insomnia** find it difficult to fall asleep or, once asleep, to stay asleep. The difficulty may be temporary or long term, mild or severe, and it may be accompanied by one or many symptoms. On the average, 33 percent of American adults complain of insomnia to some degree; 17 percent saying that their symptoms are serious (Pressman, 1991).

People suffer insomnia for many reasons. The major causes are life-event stressors (upsetting events or circumstances), illnesses, poor sleep habits, or depression (Kales, Caldwell, Preston, Healey, & Kales, 1976), any of which may disrupt the daily sleep-wake rhythm (Coleman, 1986). In fact, such sleep problems can sometimes be an early warning sign of a full-blown depression or anxiety problem (Ford & Kamerow, 1989). Most insomniacs, however, will respond to the simple treatments listed in Table 7.1.

Narcolepsy

Narcolepsy is a peculiar disorder that was poorly understood for many years. It afflicts approximately 250,000 Americans (about one person in every thousand), both males and females. Narcolepsy is an uncontrollable, recurring, and sudden onset of sleep during the daytime waking hours. The total loss of muscle control during a narcoleptic episode often causes the person to fall. Narcoleptics are most likely to sleep at moments of high anxiety or worry. The disorder appears to occur because there is a sudden onset of REM sleep during the waking state. Narcolepsy most often begins between the ages of 15 and 20 years. At first, it may be very difficult to diagnose, appearing to be nothing more than daytime sleepiness. Onset after age 40 is rare (Matheson, 1986).

Although narcolepsy is sometimes called "sleep epilepsy," it has nothing to do with actual epilepsy. Narcolepsy appears to be associated with disturbances in the reticular activating system of the brain stem (see Chapter 2). In general, people who have narcolepsy in their families are 50 times more likely to have the disorder than others. It is now believed to be an *autoimmune* disorder, in which the body's own immune system turns on itself and damages certain cells, in this case, cells in areas of the brain that control waking and sleeping.

INSOMNIA
Difficulty in initiating or maintaining sleep for the necessary amount of time.

NARCOLEPSY
An inherited pathological condition characterized by sudden and uncontrollable lapses into deep sleep.

TABLE 7.1 ◆ TEN THINGS TO DO IF YOU CAN'T SLEEP

1. Establish a solid circadian rhythm by always going to bed at a certain time and getting up at a certain time. This is especially important for the getting-up part—no sleeping in on the weekends. If you haven't been doing this, it will take about 2 weeks to "lock in" on a solid rhythm. You'd be surprised how much insomnia this one step can eliminate.

2. If you wake at night, don't get frustrated; rather, find something quiet to do until you are sleepy again.

3. Cut way down or, better still, eliminate the use of cofee, tea, or other sources of caffeine. Also, avoid alcohol, nicotine, or chocolate in the afternoon or evening, and substitute instead a little of the sleep-inducing amino acid tryptophan (which you can obtain in a glass of milk before bedtime—warm if you like). See, grandma was right!*

4. Keep your bedroom comfortable; avoid excess light and noise and extremes in temperature.

5. Avoid eating heavy meals in the evening.

6. Engage in regular exercise, but not too close to bedtime.

7. In general, avoid napping, especially after a bad night's sleep.

8. Go over your troubles in the morning if you must, but don't take them to bed with you. Instead, when you go to bed, think of something that is repetitive and boring.

9. Avoid using alcohol or sleeping pills (over the counter or prescription) to induce sleep. Such substances usually disrupt the normal sleep cycle and eventually lead to an increase in the severity of the problem.

10. Don't be concerned if, after you've tried to sleep a while, it becomes apparent that you are not going to get 8 hours of sleep. Missing sleep from time to time is not a health hazard; being overly anxious about it, however, might be.

Try each of these suggestions for at least 1 week before giving up. If none of these techniques seems to help, visit a doctor. There might be a medical basis for your insomnia (for example, you may be sensitive to a medication, or you may have difficulty breathing during sleep). Should you need special help beyond what your doctor can provide, you may require help from the more than 150 sleep disorder centers currently accredited by the American Sleep Disorders Association.

*Caution: Some health food stores offer tryptophan in pill form. Recently, some individuals taking such products have contracted a rare and dangerous blood disorder. Although it probably results from a contaminant in the product, to be safe, get your tryptophan the old-fashioned way—have a glass of milk.

SOURCE: Adapted from Hopson, 1986; Borbely, 1986.

SLEEP APNEA
A cessation of breathing during sleep. It may be brief or protracted. Brain damage can result if the apnea lasts long enough to create a significant oxygen deficiency.

If narcolepsy is an autoimmune disorder, the immune system problem is one that can be inherited. By breeding narcoleptic Doberman pinschers with one another, researcher William Dement at Stanford University demonstrated that narcolepsy can be passed from one generation to another. Whenever these specially bread narcoleptic dogs got excited (such as when they were offered their favorite treats), they would all come rushing over, jump up and down like normal dogs, and then suddenly fall sound asleep.

SLEEP APNEA

Sleep apnea is a syndrome characterized by episodes of cessation of breathing during sleep. An apnea (absence of respiration) may last for only a few seconds or may continue for minutes. Sleep patterns may be severely disturbed because a person who is not breathing begins to wake up, and the sleeper often begins gasping or choking. Severe apnea, which affects about 1 percent of the general adult population, often results in 400 to 500 awakenings a night (Coleman, 1986). In one sleep study, a subject was found to have such severe apnea that he was unable to breathe and sleep at the same time. He would fall asleep, stop breathing, stay asleep for a minute or two, and awake gasping. When he had taken in enough air, he would fall asleep again, only to stop breathing once more. Although such severe sleep apnea is rare, mild sleep apnea is not uncommon, and it is estimated that about 15 million people suffer from the disorder.

Sleep apnea is more likely to occur in men than women and is especially common among elderly men (Ancoli-Israel, Kripke, Mason, & Kaplan, 1985). Researchers believe this is because the male hormone testosterone is related to sleep apnea. Men who have sleep apnea and are given supplemental testosterone show an increase in apneic episodes. When testosterone levels are lowered, the apneic episodes decrease (Sandblom et al., 1983).

If a person's sleep is sufficiently disrupted by apnea, he or she may experience daytime sleepiness, headaches on awakening, or other uncomfortable symptoms of insufficient oxygen, high levels of carbon dioxide, and a poor night's rest. Some people thought to be senile have been found to be suffering some brain damage each night because of lack of air exchange. Sleep apnea also can cause heart failure, especially if the person takes sleeping pills (Coleman, 1986).

Obstructive apnea, caused by blockage of the airway, can be treated by a number of methods, which include weight loss, changing sleep positions (not sleeping on the back), placing a pillow at the nape of the neck so that the head is tilted backward during sleep, and the use of tongue-restraining devices or special air pressure masks. Because apnea is sometimes due to collapse of the airway, a *tracheotomy* may be performed in severe cases; this procedure creates a hole in a person's throat, through which he breathes.

DREAMING

Typically, a person has three or four dreams nightly, usually associated with REM periods. Moreover, dreams change during the night. Dreams later in the sleep period become progressively longer, more vivid, and more unrealistic. No one knows what dreams are, but there are a number of theories.

Freudian Psychoanalytic Theory

The psychoanalytic interpretation of dreams, first described by Sigmund Freud (see Chapter 1), argues that dreams are disguised representations of repressed desires, which appear in symbolic form. This is known as the dream's **latent content.** In this view, the purpose of dreams is to provide unconscious gratification, so that certain desires can be satisfied and thus will not intrude into the sleeper's life when she is awake. Only the surface, or **manifest content,** of dreams is open to straightforward observation (people can tell you what they dreamed), and according to this theory, without an in-depth *psychoanalysis* the underlying purpose of the dreams is wholly lost. Unfortunately, since this deep interpretation of underlying purpose is not open to experimental investigation, it remains conjecture.

The Activation-Synthesis Model

One of the most interesting dream theories was proposed by J. Alan Hobson and Robert W. McCarley in 1977, based on research conducted into brain activity during REM sleep. Hobson and McCarley called their theory the **activation-synthesis model** of dreams. They had noticed that during sleep a mechanism in an area of the brain called the pons (see Chapter 2) generates neural impulses that stimulate both the *oculomotor* and the reticular systems. Oculomotor refers to motor neurons associated with eye muscles. This stimulation may be the cause of rapid eye movement. The reticular system, as we noted in Chapter 2, is involved in activating the organism. Hobson and McCarley refer to this neural stimulation as the *activation phase* of dreaming.

The signals from the pons are eventually sent to the forebrain. The forebrain is the master integrator of the brain; it relates emotions to thoughts and to planning ahead (Hawkins, 1986). The question is: What happens to all this electrical information heading into the forebrain? Hobson and McCarley believe that a synthesis occurs, in which the forebrain tries to make sense of the messages it is getting and creates a dream. In this view, dreams are nothing more than vivid and interesting responses to random electrical activity and have no particular meanings.

Hobson has since revised his theory and believes that dreams and their plots may result from order imposed on the chaos of random stimulation. If so, then that "order is a function of our own personal view of the world, our remote memories" (Hobson, as cited by Winson, 1990, p. 87). In other words, Freud and other psychoanalysts such as Jung and Adler (who interpreted dreams somewhat differently than Freud) may have been correct when they asserted that dreams might yield clues about the individual.

The Housekeeping Hypothesis

Uncomfortable with the notion that all this electrical activity is without purpose, Francis Crick, winner of the Nobel Prize for the codiscovery of DNA, and researcher Graeme Mitchison have argued that the brain purposely makes dreams by creating this random electrical activity in order to find and eliminate any senseless or bizarre neural connections that accidentally developed during the course of the previous day's learning and experience. In this view, dreaming may be a time of "housekeeping" during which nonsensical information or "noise" is brought forth and swept clean. This may help to explain why a person may begin to have bizarre thoughts and perceptions after going without sleep for a long enough period. If Crick is right, remembering your dreams might actually help undo the brain's good work, since you would be strengthening the nonsensical associations the brain is attempting to eliminate (Crick & Mitchison, 1983). The housekeeping hypothesis, however, fails to explain why dreams sometimes have sensible associations or why, if it is a matter of sweeping the brain clean, many people report having the same dream again and again (Brown & Donderi, 1986).

LATENT CONTENT
In psychoanalytic theory, the hidden true meaning of a dream. The latent content of a dream, with all of its symbols and concealed meanings, can only be understood, according to this view, through the process of psychoanalysis.

MANIFEST CONTENT
In psychoanalytic theory, the overt, literal, dream content. Usually what is first described or reported by the dreamer.

ACTIVATION-SYNTHESIS MODEL
A physiological model of dreaming that contends that the brain synthesizes random neural activity generated during sleep and organizes this activity into a dream.

LUCID DREAMING
The realization by a dreamer that she or he is, in fact, dreaming.

The Off-Line Hypothesis

As you recall from theories about why we sleep, the off-line hypothesis argues that dreaming is a mechanism for the creation of long-term potentiation; it helps us to remember what we have learned. Jonathan Winson, who developed the theory, believes that dreams reflect the individual's strategy for survival. That is, areas of importance are repeated again and again during dreams, so that our memories and knowledge will be organized around their important content. As Winson has stated:

The subjects of dreams are broad-ranging and complex, incorporating self-image, fears, insecurities, strengths, grandiose ideas, sexual orientation, desire, jealousy, and love. Dreams clearly have a deep psychological core. (Winson, 1990, p. 94)

In this view, although the topics selected for dreams during the night may be unpredictable, all the topics selected for processing during REM sleep engage our psychological survival in some way. Therefore, while the exact content of a dream may not mean very much, the overall theme will be one that is important to us.

◈ CONTROLLING NIGHTMARES

Nightmares affect millions of people. In fact, depending on the study, between 10 and 25 percent of those surveyed said that they had a nightmare at least once a month (Wood & Bootzin, 1990).

Like most of us, Stephen LaBerge, a psychologist and sleep researcher, would have nightmares once in a while. In one, he dreamed that he was drowning; in another, that he was hanging off the edge of a building; and in another, that he was being attacked by someone. Although the dreams were just in his mind, the fear was very real—the pounding heart, the twisting and turning, the struggle to wake up. His dreams made him feel awful, the way nightmares make any of us feel. Unlike the rest of us, though, he decided to do something about them.

He wondered if **lucid dreaming** would offer a solution. A lucid dream is any dream during which you realize you are dreaming. Such dreams have been known as long as recorded history—Aristotle wrote about them. If LaBerge could interrupt his own nightmares and remind himself that he was dreaming, he thought he might be able to take control of the dream and make it come out any way he wanted.

He began working on his project. First, he'd note whenever he had a lucid dream. This put him in a frame of mind to think about lucid dreaming. Whenever he went to bed, he'd spend a little time before he fell asleep reminding himself to have a lucid dream. He would also relax and verbalize his intentions. He'd say, "If I'm on the edge of a cliff, I'll do this," or, "If someone attacks me, I'll do that." A few nights later, he had a dream in which he thought he was drowning. Suddenly, it became a lucid dream. He realized he was dreaming and remembered that he had told himself he could breathe under water. The fear melted away, and he began to enjoy his underwater dream.

What he had done, in effect, was to create a state of relaxation and then implant a suggestion, such as "If I think I am drowning, I will remind myself it's a dream and that I can breathe under water." Bit by bit, his nightmares came under control, and he was averaging 21.5 lucid dreams per month. The few dreams that started as nightmares now had very different endings:

I am in the middle of a riot in the classroom. Everyone is running around in some sort of struggle. . . . [Someone] has a hold on me—he is huge, with a pockmarked face. I realize that I am dreaming and stop struggling. I look him in the eyes and, while holding his hands, speak to him in a loving way, trusting my intuition to supply the beautiful words of acceptance that flow out of me. The riot has vanished, the dream fades, and I awaken feeling wonderfully calm. (LaBerge, 1981, p. 48)

Speaking from my own experience, I can tell you that I used to have falling dreams. Some of those are the worst. I used to dream that either I, or one of my children, was falling out of a window in a tall building or off a cliff. It was really terrifying. But after reading about Stephen LaBerge's work, I engaged in relaxation sessions in which I reminded myself that if I or someone I loved fell, it was okay because I was secretly Superman and would only have to remember that fact to instantly change into my costume and fly. Frankly, the idea struck me as pretty silly, but I tried it anyway. Then one night I was walking along a cliff edge and started to fall. I could feel the panic rising and my heart beating harder. Then I remembered, "Oh yeah, I'm really Superman." Then I started to fly and it was very pleasant. I had a couple more dreams like that and even started looking forward to them. But then the falling dreams stopped altogether. I suppose I decided somewhere deep in my mind that falling was no longer something I needed to deal with, and I dropped the dreams, which had been my intention in the first place. I'm still surprised by how well the technique worked. I almost never have nightmares now.

In his most recent efforts, LaBerge has helped to make dreams lucid by attaching a red flashing light to a monitor that measures a dreamer's REM onset. When REM starts, the red light begins to flash. The dreamer sees the red flashing light through his closed eyelids and usually does not awaken, but rather incorporates the light into his dream. The dreamer has trained himself to realize that anything that happens while the red light is flashing is just a dream. If a nightmare starts, the dreamer will often see the light and no longer be fearful, causing the nightmare to melt away.

I guess this technique must be getting quite popular because I recently heard a comedian talk about it on TV. He said that some dream guy was always chasing after him to kill him. So one night he waited for him and said, "Hey! I'm dreaming you, so if you kill me, where does that leave you? You didn't think of that, did you wise guy?" Now the comedian says when the dream guy catches up to him, all he does is talk about how tired he is from chasing him and what a good runner the comedian is. The real joke, of course, is that it sounds like something that might actually work!

If you suffer from nightmares, you should try this simple method. Results can come surprisingly quickly. Using techniques like these, one woman was able to end her nightmares after just three days of practice—which is remarkable considering that her nightmares had awakened her on average four times a week for a period of 30 years (Kellner, Neidhardt, Krakow, & Pathak, 1992)!

It has also been found that people are more likely to have nightmares if they consume alcohol, caffeine, tobacco, or tranquilizers (Berquier & Ashton, 1992). Another way, then, of treating persistent nightmares might be to eliminate these substances in conjunction with the development of lucid dreams.

🧬 DAYDREAMING

At the University of Minnesota at Morris, psychology students in Eric Klinger's class took some unusual examinations. During the exams, the students were required to respond to loud beeps that were occasionally emitted from a small box on the instructor's desk. They had been told to write down whatever they were thinking about just before the beep occurred. The beep was also used during class lectures; again, the students were to write down exactly what had been on their minds just before they heard the tone.

Klinger said, "It's surprising how little we know about what goes on in people's heads. What I'm hoping to do is find out how much time is spent on different thoughts and how much impact these thoughts have on a person's life" (Bartusiak, 1980, p. 57). During one lecture, Klinger reported, a student

ANIMAL MAGNETISM
The term coined by Anton Mesmer to describe the supposed magnetic force that people could exert on one another.

MESMERISM
An early term for hypnosis, named after Anton Mesmer, who claimed he could cure the ill with magnetism. In mesmerism, "magnetic" forces were called on to relieve pain.

HYPNOSIS
A state of consciousness characterized by relaxation and suggestibility.

wrote down that at the sound of the beep he had been thinking about his church pastor, the Minnesota Vikings football team, and a station wagon. Another man had been fantasizing about being shaved by two women; someone else had been wondering whether to have ham or turkey for dinner. As you can see, Klinger's research indicates that people spend a great deal of time daydreaming about things that are irrelevant to the task at hand.

Daydreaming is often considered to be undirected thought. Amazingly, it appears that the average person spends about one-third of his or her waking conscious time daydreaming. (Doesn't it make you feel better to know you're not the only one?) According to Klinger,

Daydreaming is so commonplace that we usually think little about what it is, why we do it, how it affects us or what sets off the particular content of our fleeting excursions away from the here and now. But it's an important, intriguing—and for psychologists, challenging—part of our mental life. . . . Daydreams usually start spontaneously when what we are doing requires less than our full attention: Our brains move our conscious attention automatically away from the here and now to work over other concerns. (Klinger, 1987, pp. 37, 44)

Interestingly, the percentage of time spent in daydreams, which occur when people are awake, is about the same as the percentage of time spent in night dreaming, which occurs when people are asleep (Foulkes & Fleisher, 1975; Webb & Cartwright, 1978). In each case, people spend about a third of their time in "dreams." Why this is so is unknown.

HYPNOSIS

Altered states of consciousness may be produced by means other than sleep. One of the most interesting and controversial is hypnosis. What we now call hypnosis first received wide attention about 200 years ago. At that time, the Austrian physician Anton Mesmer claimed that he could cure the ill with magnetism. Arguing that living things were influenced by magnetic forces, he coined the term **animal magnetism** to describe the "magnetic" force that people supposedly could exert on one another. Hundreds of Mesmer's patients testified that they were relieved of their pain through his efforts. This kind of treatment became known as **mesmerism.**

Mesmer was a faith healer who knew how to make money. To serve the thousands who requested his services, he "magnetized" inanimate objects and claimed that they could heal. The French Academy of Sciences (in consultation with Benjamin Franklin) found no evidence of any curative effects to be derived from magnetism. However, the academy did suggest that Mesmer's personality had influenced his patients' imaginations. Or, to put it another way, Mesmer had the power of suggestion.

What exactly this power of suggestion may be or how it works has been explored since the time of Mesmer and continues to be a subject of much interest. Today, the term **hypnosis,** after Hypnos, the Greek god of sleep, is used to describe the effects of suggestion. Hypnosis is not a state of sleep, however. Although a hypnotist may say, "You are falling deeply asleep," EEG readings have shown that hypnotized subjects supposedly in a deep sleep are actually awake, but drowsy. Hypnosis appears to be not a single phenomenon but rather a single word used to describe a number of relatively separate phenomena (Barber, 1969).

Some subjects can be hypnotized; others cannot. Interestingly, whether a person is hypnotizable tends to remain stable throughout her life (Piccione, Hilgard, & Zimbardo, 1989). In general, individuals who tend to fantasize and daydream are more likely to be hypnotizable (Lynn & Rhue, 1988).

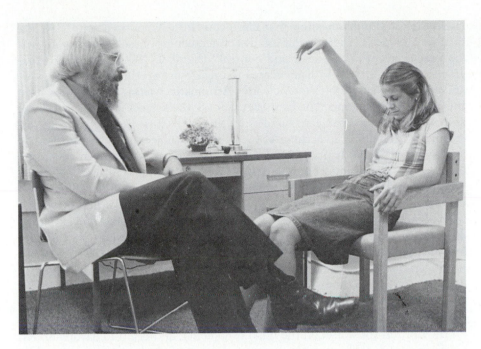

Susceptibility to hypnosis can be measured by the Stanford Hypnotic Susceptibility Scale. In this instance, if the subject is susceptible, her hand would probably lower at least 6 inches within 10 seconds following the therapist's suggestion that her hand is becoming heavy.

When conducting a hypnosis session, the hypnotist begins by encouraging the subject to relax. The subject is usually asked to fix her gaze on a particular place or point, and then to respond to the hypnotist. Once the subject is relaxed, the hypnotist can test for suggestibility. A scale used to measure suggestibility, or susceptibility, is shown in Table 7.2. People who are highly suggestible will meet many of the criteria on this test. These people are likely to be good subjects for hypnosis. Other people, especially those who are alert and curious about the hypnotic effect and are waiting for something to "happen" to them, are likely not to be susceptible. Some subjects have failed to become hypnotized even after thousands of attempts.

Dissociation

Once the subject is prepared and is showing susceptibility, the hypnotist can aid the subject in creating a number of interesting effects. One of the most

TABLE 7.2 ◆ STANFORD HYPNOTIC SUSCEPTIBILITY SCALE, FORM C	
ITEM	CRITERION OF PASSING
0. Eye closure during induction	(Noted, but not scored)
1. Hand lowering (right hand)	Lowers at least 6 inches in 10 seconds
2. Moving hands apart	Hands 6 inches or more apart after 10 seconds
3. Mosquito hallucination	Any acknowledgment of effect
4. Taste hallucination (sweet, sour)	Both tastes experienced and one strong or with overt movements
5. Arm rigidity (right arm)	Less than 2 inches of arm bending in 10 seconds
6. Dream	Dreams well, experience comparable to a dream
7. Age regression (school fifth and second grades)	Clear change in handwriting between present and one regressed age
8. Anosmia to ammonia	Odor of ammonia denied and overt signs absent
9. Arm immobilization (left arm)	Arm rises less than 1 inch in 10 seconds.
10. Hallucinated voice	Subject answers voice realistically at least once
11. Negative visual hallucination (sees two of three boxes)	Reports seeing only two boxes
12. Posthypnotic amnesia	Subject recalls three or fewer items before "Now you can remember everything"

NOTE: This scale is used in conjunction with a brief attempted induction of hypnosis, during which the subject is observed and rated on performance on the above 12 items. The hypnotist suggests each item and notes whether the subject responds to the suggestion. The highest possible score is 12, and the average score is 5.19.
SOURCE: Weitzenhoffer and Hilgard (1962).

DISSOCIATION
A separation or splitting off of mental processes often associated with the hypnotic state. Subjects can then perform acts that do not register in their conscious memory or can engage in two behaviors while remembering only one of them.

AUTOMATIC WRITING
Writing done by the subject during a dissociated hypnotic state; the subject is not aware of writing.

SELF-HYPNOSIS
A hypnotic state induced by the subject without the aid of a hypnotist.

HIGHWAY HYPNOSIS
A hypnotic state experienced by a person operating a vehicle—often the result of relaxing too much during a long and boring drive.

While reading, it is possible to become so engrossed in your book that a certain dissociative state is achieved. In such a case, being interrupted from your reading will not be unlike coming out of hypnosis.

fascinating is the **dissociation** that can occur in a hypnotized state. "At the heart of the idea of dissociation is a disconnectedness or lack of integration of knowledge, identity, memory, and control" (Frankel, 1990, p. 828). For example, the subject can be maneuvered to engage in two things simultaneously and yet to remember only one clearly. **Automatic writing** is an example of this kind of dissociation. The hypnotist will ask the subject to write something and then, while the subject's hand is writing, will draw the subject into discussing or describing something else. Later, the subject may be surprised to learn what his hand has written. At the same time, he will clearly recall the topic he was discussing while the writing was in progress (Hilgard, 1977).

When students first encounter something like automatic writing, they often believe that it's a trick or that the subject was lying and really did know what he was writing. Yet most of us, through **self-hypnosis,** have had a similar dissociating experience at one time or another. It may actually be easier to hypnotize yourself than to enter hypnosis with a hypnotist's help (Ruch, 1975). If you are by yourself and fix your gaze on a particular place and begin to daydream, your EEG state may be identical to that of a hypnotized subject. In fact, a very deep daydream may be a perfect example of hypnosis. Unfortunately, some people drive their cars in this state. They fix their gaze, perhaps on the horizon (or worse, on the hood ornament), and begin to daydream. An experience such as this can also have an element of dissociation; that is, while daydreaming they may still manage to arrive at their destination, taking the correct turns and stopping at the stoplights, without remembering a single detail about the trip. This experience, called **highway hypnosis,** is familiar to most drivers. It can happen to drivers very easily at night, when there are few visual distractions and the broken white line on the highway is going by at a steady rate, or at any other time, especially if the road is very familiar. If this has ever happened to you, then you have experienced an effect of dissociation while self-hypnotized.

Or have you ever been so deeply immersed in a good book that when someone interrupts you, it feels as though you are waking from a dream? This, too, may be a form of dissociation, a hypnotic state (Nell, 1990). It should be noted, however, that not everyone agrees on a clear definition of dissociative experience. While the effect seems to be fairly clear in something like automatic writing, dissociations owing to emotional detachment and alterations in attention, memory, perception, or motivation, while all dissociative in some fashion, may not fit everyone's concept of dissociation (Frankel, 1990).

Dissociative experiences like the ones we have mentioned are very common in the general population and decline with age (Ross, Joshi, & Currie, 1990).

Memory Enhancement

Another phenomenon of hypnosis is memory enhancement. Although memory itself cannot be directly improved through hypnosis, hypnosis can be used to alleviate anxiety that may be inhibiting memory. The greater the anxiety, the less likely a person is to remember clearly and accurately. Hypnosis has been used effectively by police departments and other agencies to *calm* individuals who are trying to remember something.

There is, however, a danger in using hypnosis to enhance memory. Subjects who are hypnotized often expect their power of recollection to be vastly improved. For instance, in 1981, during a murder trial in Illinois, an eyewitness could not positively identify the murderer he had briefly seen at night from a distance of 100 yards. The witness was placed under hypnosis, and the hypnotist pressed for an answer. He told the witness to zoom in on the murderer's face and to say whose it was. The eyewitness, and the jurors who were listening, believed that under hypnosis such a thing was possible. The eyewitness then identified a classmate of his as the murderer (Orne, 1982). But was this a memory or something his imagination had created under the pressure to come up with something? In experiments, it has been shown that hypnotized subjects who are pressed begin to report "remembering" all kinds of things that are not true (Dywan & Bowers, 1983). Researchers also have shown that when imaginary experiences are provided to hypnotized subjects, the subjects often swear afterward that such experiences really occurred (Laurence & Perry, 1983). Luckily for the classmate accused of murder, an ophthalmologist (a medical doctor who specializes in vision) testified that under the conditions on the night of the murder, it would have been physically impossible to resolve a visual image accurately from a distance of more than 10 yards. Because of the false "memories" that can occur under hypnosis, more and more courts are not allowing hypnotized witnesses to testify (Stark, 1984).

Pain Relief and Changed Emotional States

Hypnosis also has been used to relieve pain and to change emotional states. The possibility that hypnosis can raise the natural endorphin levels in the body enough to relieve pain has excited a great deal of interest (see Chapter 2). But in examinations of hypnotic procedures, endorphin has not been shown to be related in any way to the kind of pain relief obtained under hypnosis. Even when subjects were given naloxone, a drug that blocks the effects of endorphin, hypnosis could still relieve pain (Goldstein & Hilgard, 1975). It is possible that the release of some molecule other than endorphin may be responsible for the pain relief achieved through hypnosis, but no one knows.

Hypnosis also can effectively prevent a person from laughing in humorous situations. How can hypnosis bring about such changes? It may be that under hypnosis a person distinguishes between *expected* and *actual* pain or humor. There is a difference. In many cultures, people are taught that certain kinds of pain are more severe than our knowledge of physiology indicates they should be. Any dentist can tell you this. Some patients start screaming before the dentist even touches a tooth. Many dentists have begun using hypnosis to ease such fears. Patients who expect the hypnosis to work, and who are relaxed and comfortable, may then experience only the "real" pain rather than the much more severe "expected" pain.

Certainly, hypnosis has its limits. In cases of extreme pain, no amount of hypnosis is likely to help. Nevertheless, hypnosis has occasionally been successful when anesthetics could not be used, even when general surgery was being performed (Hilgard & Hilgard, 1983). Hypnosis can be especially effective in operations requiring incisions to be made in the back, where there are few pain receptors.

Behavioral Changes

Subjects who are hypnotized frequently behave in strange ways. They may become amnesiac, forgetting specific things, or they may exhibit sensory changes (Kihlstrom, 1985), claiming that they see objects that are not there or denying that they see objects that are in front of them. In the latter case, it is not clear whether the hypnosis causes a real sensory change in the brain. Most researchers attribute such reports to social pressures; that is, participants, in their desire to be good subjects, will go along with the hypnotist, even to the point of lying. They may swear, for instance, that they see only the hypnotist although they are standing in a crowded room. Of course, it may be that sensory changes are hampering the subject's ability to sense the other people in the room, but the physiology of such changes has not been discovered.

HYPNOSIS AND AGE REGRESSION

Throughout the years, hypnosis has been credited with many achievements. Some of these claims have received great publicity, although no substantial data are available to support them. One of the most controversial has been age regression. The hypnotist tells the subject to relax and to feel that he is moving back in time to his youth. When asked how old he is, the subject might reply, "Ten," even though he is obviously an adult. Then, the subject might describe what his life was like when he was 10 years old. He might even be able to recall a language that he spoke then that he can no longer speak with fluency (Fromm, 1970). The hypnotist might ask the subject to regress farther back, to when he was 8, 6, 4, or 1, or even to the time he was in the womb. At this point, the adult might curl up in a fetal position. When asked what he is doing, he might not be able to respond because he is too young to speak. Then, the hypnotist might ask the subject to go back even farther, many years before his birth, and to describe what he perceives or senses. Suddenly, the subject might say that he is a shoemaker in Germany in 1853, and his name is Hans Gunwaldt. "What is life like for you, Hans?" asks the hypnotist, and the subject begins to describe what his earlier life as a shoemaker was like.

What has happened here? Has the subject been sent back to another time, another life? There are ways of testing this phenomenon to see whether it is real (Spanos, Ansari, & Stam, 1979). Adults in the age-regressed state, who are supposedly only 5 years old, often display cognitive abilities far beyond those of a 5-year-old. They answer questions that most adults wrongly believe a 5-year-old could answer but that a real child of that age would never be able to answer (Nash, 1987).

A way of showing the improbability of the prebirth phenomenon is by demonstrating that hypnotists can impose almost any previous life they wish on their subjects. In such a case, a hypnotist need only be given a fabricated previous-life story to pass on to the hypnotized subject. The subject is then age-regressed back many years before his birth. By subtle cuing, the hypnotist can often elicit the fake previous life from the subject. To date, there appears to be no evidence to support the notion of previous lives. The subject, desiring to comply with the hypnotist's request, has apparently tried to act out what he feels may be expected of him (Sarbin & Coe, 1972). When led back to a time before birth, he will often reenact an earlier life, because this has become part of the hypnosis myth.

Stage hypnotists frequently entertain their audiences by getting people to act in bizarre ways. A volunteer may begin to imitate a chicken when told that he is one. However, people who volunteer to be chickens may be a little unusual to start with. Perhaps they simply want to be on stage. They also may be doing what they think is expected of them. Also, some stage "hypnotists" have a bag of dirty tricks. For example, they may hand a steel ball to a volunteer, saying "I'm going to make you feel as though this steel ball is getting hotter and hotter." Suddenly, the volunteer cries "My hands are burning!" and drops the ball, convinced that it was hypnosis that caused the sensation. In fact, the quack hypnotist has used a steel ball containing two chemicals that, when mixed (when the ball was turned and handed to the subject), caused the ball to become extremely hot—for real.

Disinhibition

Hypnosis can also *disinhibit* subjects; that is, remove their reluctance to do specific things. One of the misconceptions about hypnosis is that a subject will never do something while hypnotized that he or she wouldn't do while "awake" (Orne & Evans, 1965). This is not necessarily true. If a hypnotist tells Sergeant Jones to hit Colonel Brown in the face with a pie, and the sergeant is not hypnotized, the sergeant will wisely say, "No, sir." Once the sergeant is hypnotized, however, and the hypnotist says, "Now hit the colonel in the face with a pie," the sergeant may do as instructed. The difference may be that the sergeant can now attribute responsibility to the hypnotist, especially if the colonel has been watching the whole performance. The sergeant will know that because he was hypnotized, no one can blame him. Furthermore, if the sergeant has always wanted to hit the colonel with a pie, this is a good opportunity. Because responsibility can be transferred to someone else—namely, the hypnotist—subjects may be willing to engage in activities that they had always wanted to do but had never dared to do before.

Posthypnotic Suggestion

Hypnotists can in many instances give **posthypnotic suggestions;** that is, they can tell a subject that later, upon seeing or hearing a particular stimulus, he will get an urge to do something. The hypnotist may say, for example, "The next time you hear a car horn, your shoulder will itch, and you will scratch it." Posthypnotic suggestion may work on the same principle as a memory association; that is, by relaxing and thinking that a car horn goes with an itching shoulder, you may actually be cued (reminded) to scratch your shoulder the next time you hear a car horn.

As you have discovered, *hypnosis* is a word that describes many different phenomena (see Concept Review). Hypnosis is an interesting concept, but is also one that is often misunderstood (see Focus on a Controversy).

🌀 MEDITATION

Meditation is a simple technique that can be practiced by anyone. If you sit back, close your eyes, breathe deeply, and, if you wish, concentrate on a particular sound or word for about 15 minutes, a number of changes will probably occur: Your heart rate, blood pressure, and oxygen-consumption rate will decrease. The temperature of your extremities will rise. Your muscles will relax.

It's hard for people to realize that meditation can be simple. This is especially true because so many books have been written about different meditation techniques and so many **yogis** have espoused certain ways to meditate and

POSTHYPNOTIC SUGGESTION
A suggestion made to a hypnotized subject to perform some task in response to a particular cue after the hypnotic session is over.

MEDITATION
Deep relaxation brought on by focusing one's attention on a particular sound or image, breathing deeply, and relaxing.

YOGI
One who practices yoga, a Hindu discipline whose aim is to train consciousness to attain a state of perfect spiritual insight and tranquility. Control of body functions and mental states is practiced.

CONCEPT REVIEW ◆ TYPES OF HYPNOTIC EFFECTS

Hypnotic Effect	Possible Reasons for Effect
Dissociation	When conscious attention is distracted, ingrained habits may continue to function without subject's awareness.
Memory enhancement	Anxiety that may interfere with memory retrieval is reduced.
Relief from pain or change in emotional state	Subject expects change; subject reacts only to actual pain or emotional state rather than to expected pain or emotions. Another possibility is that pain is actually blunted by stimulated neurological mechanism.
"Unusual" behavior	Subject feels such behavior is expected or wishes to please hypnotist by being a "good subject" (social pressure).
Sensory or perceptual changes	Perceptual mechanisms may actually change, or subject may lie, either consciously or unconsciously, in order to be a "good subject."
Disinhibition	Subject can now place responsibility for acts elsewhere (on hypnotist).
Posthypnotic suggestion	Subject unconsciously learns association between two events; when one event occurs, the second event is acted out or is brought to mind.

During meditation, a person's heart rate, respiration, and blood pressure decrease dramatically.

have made dramatic claims. But most research appears to indicate that meditating is the same as resting, and that there is no significant difference between the two states (Holmes, 1984).*

Many researchers in recent years have compared subjects who practiced meditation with subjects who simply rested. No consistent differences were found on measures of heart rate, skin electrical activity, breathing rate, blood pressure, skin temperature, oxygen consumption, muscle tone, blood flow, or any other biochemical factors (Holmes, 1984). Despite all the hype, psychologists have simply been unable to find any physiological differences between meditation and resting, although the issue is debated (Suler, 1985; West, 1985; Shapiro, 1985). This, of course, does not mean that the practice is useless. Taking a nice 15-minute rest twice a day does provide health benefits. It lowers your blood pressure for a short time, calms you, and makes you feel better.

PSYCHOACTIVE DRUGS

Any drug that alters conscious awareness or perception is called *psychoactive*. **Psychoactive drugs** often work directly on the brain. The most commonly used psychoactive drugs—including alcohol, nicotine, and caffeine—are so familiar that we rarely think of them as drugs or consider that they have psychological effects. Psychoactive drugs can be classified according to their effects as **stimulants, depressants,** and **hallucinogens.** In this chapter, we will discuss only the properties of various drugs and their effects on the conscious state. Alcoholism, drug abuse, and addiction are discussed in Chapter 15 (Health Psychology).

Central Nervous System Stimulants

AMPHETAMINES. **Amphetamines** are powerful stimulants originally developed by the military for soldiers who had to stay alert in combat. They are sold under names such as Dexedrine, Benzedrine, and Methedrine. On the street, they are known as uppers, speed, bennies, meth, crystal, ice, and assorted other names. The way in which amphetamines work is not clearly understood, but they are known to facilitate the synaptic secretion of dopamine in the brain. If taken in low doses for a limited time, the drugs can help to overcome fatigue and to maintain a high rate of activity, the purpose for which they were developed. Sustained use, however, can result in a number of unpleasant states that can be long-lasting, including paranoia, anger, and prolonged restlessness. Amphetamines also can decrease appetite, and they were widely prescribed as diet pills during the early 1970s. However, people who used the pills for this purpose over an extended period found that they became accustomed to them; as the dieters acquired **tolerance,** they gradually regained their appetite—but they continued to desire the amphetamines. Consequently, the drugs have not been widely accepted as a viable means of controlling weight and have been placed under much stricter federal controls.

CAFFEINE. **Caffeine** is commonly found in coffee, tea, and many cola drinks and ranks as the most widely used psychoactive drug in the world. Caffeine has both short-term and long-term effects. Over the short term, caffeine can make the user feel alert and awake. In slightly higher amounts, or for those who are sensitive to it, it can make one feel jittery and nervous. It can also accelerate the heart rate and cause loss of appetite.

PSYCHOACTIVE DRUGS
Drugs that alter conscious awareness or perception.

STIMULANTS
Drugs that can stimulate or excite the central nervous system. Cocaine and amphetamines are examples.

DEPRESSANTS
Drugs that can depress or slow the central nervous system. Alcohol and tranquilizers are examples.

HALLUCINOGENS
Drugs that cause excitation at synapses associated with sense perception. A person taking these drugs may perceive sensations when there is nothing "real" to see, hear, or feel. LSD and mescaline are examples.

AMPHETAMINES
Drugs that excite the central nervous system and suppress appetite, increase heart rate and blood pressure, and alter sleep patterns. Amphetamines are classified as stimulants.

---

*It's important to note that not all kinds of meditation reduce physiological activity. Some kinds—for instance, Maulavi (the kind of dancing practiced by the whirling dervishes)—create arousal. The vast majority of meditation techniques, however, reduce arousal.

Over the long term, caffeine can often affect the brain's neurotransmitter system, especially the neurotransmitter serotonin (Charney, Heninger, & Jatlow, 1985). This can lead to increased susceptibility to anxiety and panic attacks (see Chapter 16). In fact, one of the most effective ways to reduce anxiety levels in individuals is simply to get them off caffeine for several months.

It is not clear, however, whether caffeine is addictive. Some coffee drinkers show signs of addiction. They seek coffee for its pleasing effects, and they often exhibit symptoms when they withdraw from it such as headaches, drowsiness, or fatigue. However, these same individuals generally have little trouble giving up caffeine if they need to and typically don't show tolerance for the drug. For these reasons, labeling heavy coffee drinkers as "drug dependent" is somewhat controversial.

COCAINE. Cocaine appears to function both as an amphetamine-like stimulant and as a local anesthetic if injected under the skin or rubbed on mucous membranes such as the gums.

One of the leading experts in the study of the psychoactive effects of cocaine was Sigmund Freud (1885/1974). Freud initially believed that cocaine was relatively safe, and he encouraged its use. For himself, he found that it increased his alertness, made him feel invigorated, and gave him a sensation of pleasure. Later, however, after observing the visual disturbances experienced by a friend who had taken cocaine, he withdrew his support, realizing that the drug could have dangerous side effects.

In very low dosage, cocaine was an ingredient in Coca-Cola until its use in soft drinks was banned by law in 1903. In fact, the drug gave the drink its name. After the law was passed, the Coca-Cola Company found that caffeine was an adequate substitute.

Today, cocaine is widely known as a pleasure-inducing drug. To obtain the pleasure-inducing effects of the drug, people usually inhale or snort it and occasionally inject it into a vein. Cocaine can also be smoked. Taking cocaine in these ways produces euphoria, exhilaration, alertness, confidence, and a high energy level. This reaction may last for 20 minutes to 1 hour, and it is often followed by depression. Long-term use may lead to hallucinations or extremely severe mental disorders. Long-term use also appears to alter specific systems in the central nervous system that affect our ability to experience pleasure, although what this may mean in terms of long-term damage or harm is not known (Gawin, 1991).

TOLERANCE
In pharmacology, the ability to tolerate larger and larger doses of a drug after each exposure to it. A common tolerance mechanism, which occurs during opiate use, is for the body to create natural antidrug substances or antagonists in ever-larger amounts following each exposure to the drug.

CAFFEINE
A bitter white alkaloid derived from coffee, tea, and kola nuts. It is a stimulant and is the most widely used psychoactive drug in the world.

COCAINE
A habit-forming stimulant that typically is inhaled, but is occasionally swallowed, smoked, or injected. It is derived from the leaves of the coca plant and is used in medicine as a local anesthetic.

(a) The normal web of the female spider, Araneus diadematus. The irregularity at the right side of the web was caused by the spider's rushing away when the photo was taken. (b) The same spider built this strange web after receiving a high dose of amphetamine. (c) This web, built one day after receiving the amphetamine, shows partial recovery.

(a)   (b)   (c)

During cocaine use, the heart accelerates, the pupils dilate, and blood pressure increases, often to dangerous levels. Cocaine binds strongly to cells of the heart, especially the left ventricle (Volkow et al., 1990). Cocaine not only stimulates the sympathetic nervous system, but suppresses the parasympathetic nervous system (see Chapter 2). In other words, it not only presses the accelerator, it releases the brake, which may help explain why it can put enough stress on the heart to kill an otherwise healthy young person with just one use (Cowen, 1990). Use of cocaine can also cause brain atrophy, a form of damage in which the brain actually shrinks (Pascual-Leone, Dhuna, Altafullah, & Anderson, 1990).

In 1985, a very addictive form of cocaine called "crack" (cocaine hydrochloride) appeared. Crack is not snorted, but smoked. Heating the crack, or cocaine rock as it is also called, frees the cocaine for inhalation. When cocaine is ingested by this method, the drug enters the blood through the lungs very rapidly and goes straight to the brain. Because crack requires fewer steps to process, cocaine prices on the street fell dramatically, and the drug became readily available. The "high" obtained from crack only lasts about 30 minutes, however. This further exacerbates the problem because users are driven to take it many times a day, strongly increasing the likelihood that they will become addicted.

Cocaine is perhaps the most powerful "rewarder" known and may obtain that power by flipping the "main switch" of the brain's reward system, an area rich in receptors for the neurotransmitter dopamine. Once the dopamine is secreted, the cocaine appears to block its reuptake, making the dopamine available to further stimulate the pleasure centers (Wise & Rompre, 1989). The body then decreases the number of dopamine receptors in an apparent attempt to restore the normal balance (Volkow et al., 1990). When addicts stop taking cocaine, the loss of receptors can leave them temporarily starved for dopamine, which leads to a craving for the drug. In support of this is the fact that most relapses occur during the first few weeks of treatment. Some drug companies are hoping eventually to find a drug that mimics the natural supply of dopamine. This would help addicts get through the first few months of treatment until they can create more dopamine receptors to make up for the loss of the cocaine and thereby return their pleasure system to an even keel.

Cocaine appears to obtain its rewarding affect by stimulating an important pleasure center in the brain.

Because it is so powerfully rewarding, cocaine causes a **psychological addiction** as well as a physiological one. Because cocaine affects the brain's pleasure centers by short-circuiting them—that is, by cutting them off from their natural source of stimulation—cocaine users feel that everything is good in their lives no matter how serious their problems may be. Researchers have discovered that heroin activates the same pleasure centers (Goeders & Smith, 1983). Like heroin addicts, cocaine abusers may alter their lives so that every part of life becomes centered around the drug. Friends, associates, and even lovers who do not provide direct access to the drug are dropped. Rapid weight loss is also associated with cocaine use, and this may lead to anemia or to a lowering of the body's natural defenses against illness. For these reasons, cocaine is considered to be addictive and *extremely* dangerous.

Central Nervous System Depressants

ALCOHOL.   Alcohol is a depressant that acts on the central nervous system, slowing down its functioning. Owing to differences in the content of their stomach enzymes, women absorb alcohol into their bloodstreams faster than do men and, consequently, can become impaired at a faster rate than men can (Frezza et al., 1990).

Some alcohol users believe mistakenly that, in limited amounts, alcohol is a stimulant. This belief probably comes from the fact that alcohol does cause an elevation in sex hormones, which may create greater sexual arousal. Alcohol may make you "want to more, but able to less." Alcohol generally makes people less inhibited and may lead them to engage in behavior they later regret (Steele, 1986). Interestingly, part of alcohol's disinhibiting effect may be that, based on what he has heard, the drinker *expects* to be disinhibited after drinking and may act accordingly (Critchlow, 1986). Disinhibition, however, is not the same as stimulation.

Alcohol also has been found to affect neurotransmitters in the brain, especially in the region of the hippocampus, an area important in memory consolidation (see Chapter 2). This effect may help explain the memory losses sometimes associated with drinking (Mancillas, Siggins, & Bloom, 1986).

Although behavioral effects vary greatly from one person to the next (Erwin, Plomin, & Wilson, 1984), in general, at concentrations as low as 0.03 percent of alcohol per total volume of blood, users tend to feel relaxed or giddy. At concentrations of 0.1 percent—after about three drinks or three beers within twenty minutes—nerve functions in the sensory and motor systems may be impaired to the point that driving a vehicle would be dangerous. At 0.2 percent, the drinker is severely incapacitated, and levels above 0.4 percent are often lethal. Most state laws define legal intoxication as a blood level above 0.1 percent alcohol; some define it as above 0.08 percent. Because it is so widely used by people engaged in activities requiring concentration and alertness, especially driving, alcohol is an extremely dangerous drug. Between 30 and 50 percent of all automobile deaths are related to driving while intoxicated (Zylman, 1975). Among pilots, it has been shown that even 14 hours after being legally intoxicated, the pilots' performance had not yet returned to normal (Yesavage & Leirer, 1986).

Although alcohol is not classified as a hallucinogen, excessive use may lead to hallucinations either while it is being consumed or during withdrawal from it. **Delirium tremens** is the term for the hallucinations suffered by alcoholics on withdrawal, during which they often hallucinate about bugs or animals crawling on them. Heavy use of alcohol is also associated with strokes and accounts for a large portion of strokes in young adults (Taylor & Combs-Orme, 1985).

PSYCHOLOGICAL ADDICTION
An overwhelming desire for a particular substance due to the immediate sense of pleasure or fear reduction it provides. Psychological addiction often occurs in conjunction with physical addiction. The word dependence is often used to characterize either type of addiction and often is specific (for example, drug dependence).

DELIRIUM TREMENS
A state of delirium resulting from prolonged alcoholism and marked by extreme confusion, vivid hallucinations, and body tremors.

BENZODIAZEPINES
An important class of minor tranquilizers that, since the mid-1950s, have come to replace the more dangerous barbiturates. Usually prescribed by physicians to control anxiety and tension.

TRANQUILIZERS
Any of various drugs that are used to pacify.

HEROIN
A highly addictive narcotic drug derived from morphine.

PHYSICAL ADDICTION
An overwhelming desire for a particular substance due to the mechanisms of tolerance and physical reaction to withdrawal.

BENZODIAZEPINES. **Benzodiazepines** are **tranquilizers.** They are the most widely prescribed drugs in the world, administered for the relief of tension or anxiety. Their major effect is to relax muscles by affecting the central nervous system. These drugs are known by such trade names as Librium, Valium, or Xanax.

Benzodiazepines have been found to work hand in hand with GABA (gamma-aminobutyric acid), a neurotransmitter abundant in the brain and associated with inhibitory synapses (see Chapter 2). There appear to be natural receptors in the brain that are particularly sensitive to benzodiazepines. GABA helps the drugs to bind more tightly with these receptors, causing lengthy and increased inhibition at the inhibitory synapses (Guidotti, Baraldi, Schwartz, Toffano, & Costa, 1979). The presence of these natural receptors suggests that the brain may produce its own kind of benzodiazepine and that the drug merely mimics this natural substance.

HEROIN. **Heroin** is indirectly derived from opium, as are the other opiates morphine and codeine. Heroin is made from, but is stronger than, morphine, which, in turn, is stronger than codeine. Heroin is a powerful narcotic and can quickly result in **physical addiction.** It works by mimicking the brain's own morphinelike substance, beta-endorphin. Heroin is an excellent painkiller and creates a great sense of well-being in the user. It is usually injected, but recently smoking heroin has become popular. Smokers refer to this activity as "chasing the dragon."

Because heroin is physically addicting, users eventually need to increase their dose to obtain an effect. Sudden discontinuation of the drug causes severe withdrawal symptoms. The sense of pleasure obtained and the physical addiction associated with heroin result from two very separate brain mechanisms. Heroin stimulates the same pleasure centers as cocaine does and also stimulates a mechanism at a different part of the brain that leads to physical addiction (Bozarth & Wise, 1984; Ling, MacLeod, Lee, Lockhart, & Pasternak, 1984).

If they are very careful about the quality of the drug, use it under sterile conditions, and are lucky, addicts may be able to continue taking heroin for some time without necessarily suffering serious detrimental effects. Their chances of becoming ill, however, increase significantly, because heroin damages the body's natural immune system, which helps ward off disease (McDonough et al., 1980). Heroin deaths also are frequently related to overdose, the dosage being uncertain because heroin is often "cut" (diluted) to make it go farther. Sometimes the heroin is cut with deadly substances. Heroin deaths also may result from unsterile injections, which can transmit diseases such as hepatitis or AIDS. Incorrect injection technique, or simply the accumulated effect of hundreds of injections, may cause serious circulatory disorders. Malnutrition is another factor. Heroin addicts often use their money to buy the drug instead of food; their sense of well-being and the painkilling properties of the drug can render them insensitive to feelings of hunger. As we noted earlier, beta-endorphin appears to be used by the brain to create a natural high when the time is right for feelings of happiness and well-being. Heroin users, however, short-circuit their natural reward system. This may explain why addicts often don't care that they may be going to die, or that other people are hurt by their behavior, or that they don't eat or engage in sex. Since the natural pleasure system has been overridden, no external events of significance are likely to have an effect.

DESIGNER DRUGS. In recent years, some unscrupulous chemists have created drugs that are molecularly similar to heroin, but different enough not to be included under the original federal laws that prohibited the sale of heroin (the laws have since been amended). These substances have come to be known as **designer drugs.** In general, their effects are unknown, but some of them have proved to be very dangerous (Ricaurte, Bryan, Strauss, Seiden, & Schuster, 1985). One in particular, MPTP, is especially hazardous. Those people who were unfortunate enough to try MPTP almost immediately developed severe and irreversible Parkinson's disease (see Chapter 2). Many of these users were young, and Parkinson's is rare in young people.

The only bright light to come from this sad occurrence is that it provided researchers with some clues as to the cause of Parkinson's disease and enabled them to make a drug that blocks the effects of MPTP. When this new drug, called deprenyl, was given to Parkinson patients, it significantly slowed the rate of progression of the disease by 40 to 83 percent, a major advance against the disease (Tetrud & Langston, 1989).

Hallucinogens

Hallucinogens are drugs that cause excitation at the nerve synapses associated with sense perception, producing **hallucinations,** perceptions of lights, sound, and other sensory stimuli when there is nothing "real" to see, hear, or feel. The drugs in this category include mescaline, which is derived from a cactus; psilocybin, derived from mushrooms; and LSD (lysergic acid diethylamide), derived from ergot, a rye mold. As mentioned in Chapter 2, these drugs probably affect us by mimicking neurotransmitters associated with sensation and perception. The effects of some hallucinogens last only a short time; those of others, such as LSD, may last for many hours. Sometimes, after the initial effect of LSD has worn off, the user may experience a **flashback,** such as a burst of color like a sheet of light or mist or other sensory disturbances (Abraham, 1983).

PCP. PCP **(phencyclidine hydrochloride),** better known as angel dust because it was first given widespread distribution by the Hell's Angels motorcycle club, has unfortunately become a popular drug in recent decades. One of its effects is to cause hallucinations. It has been argued, however, that PCP represents an entirely new class of psychoactive drug (Balster & Chait, 1976), because it gives rise to many serious disorders besides hallucinations. This may be due, in part, to the drug's toxic and damaging effect on the nerve receptors to which it binds (Olney, Labruyere, & Price, 1989). In many cases, a complete loss of contact with reality occurs, accompanied by unpredictably aggressive behavior that can persist for weeks after the drug has been taken. Reviewing more than 100 cases, researchers found that a typical PCP reaction includes three distinct phases: violent, psychotic behavior lasting approximately 5 days, unpredictable and restless behavior lasting about 5 more days, and rapid improvement and personality reintegration during the final 4 days. PCP use should be considered a psychiatric emergency. Even if the drug is not taken again, about one-fourth of people treated after using it suffer serious behavioral disturbances later (Luisada & Brown, 1976). There is also evidence that PCP creates strong psychological dependence (Bolter, Heminger, Martin, & Fry, 1976). Because of the hazards, many drug users are turning away from PCP. Unfortunately, others are not aware of the dangers.

MARIJUANA. **Marijuana** is classified as a hallucinogen because, in sufficient doses, its active ingredient, **THC (delta-9 tetrahydrocannabinol),** causes hallucinations. Along with its hallucinogenic properties, marijuana can function as both a depressant and a stimulant. The difference appears to be related to dose. At higher doses, the drug acts as a stimulant; at lower doses, it acts as a depressant (Blum, Briggs, Feinglass, Domey, & Wallace, 1977).

DESIGNER DRUGS
Drugs designed in a laboratory by unscrupulous chemists with the intention of creating substances that mimic the effects of a drug while avoiding the federal laws that forbid that specific drug.

HALLUCINATION
A false sense perception for which there is no appropriate external stimulus.

FLASHBACK
A sudden recurrence of a hallucination or sensory disturbance that occurs after the original effect of a hallucinogenic substance has worn off.

PHENCYCLIDINE HYDROCHLORIDE (PCP)
A dangerous hallucinogenic drug that can lead to aggressive or psychotic behavior. It is also known as angel dust.

MARIJUANA
A hallucinogenic drug derived from the dried flowers and leaves of the cannabis variety of hemp.

DELTA-9 TETRAHYDROCANNABINOL (THC)
The active ingredient in marijuana, which in high doses can cause hallucinations.

A study conducted with female monkeys (whose reproductive cycle is similar to that of human females) found that at moderate dosages (the equivalent of about 15 "joints," or marijuana cigarettes, per week), the animals showed disruption of the menstrual cycle (Smith, Almirez, Berenberg, & Asch, 1983). These doses of marijuana caused failure of ovulation for as long as 4 months, until the monkeys developed a tolerance for the drug. There is also evidence that THC may harm the ova (unfertilized eggs). THC has also been found to interfere with the recall of recently learned material for up to 6 weeks after use (Schwartz, Gruenewald, Klitzner, & Fedio, 1989). This may be one reason why teenagers who use marijuana do less well in school.

Arguments over the danger of marijuana continue. The amount of danger may be related to dose level and frequency of use. In one study, scientists found that experienced airline pilots working a flight simulator were still significantly impaired 24 hours after smoking only one marijuana cigarette (Yesavage, Leirer, Denari, & Hollister, 1985). The pilots were unaware of their impairment although the simulator clearly recorded their poorer performances.

In 1992, William Devane and his colleagues working at Hebrew University in Jerusalem found a natural marijuana-like compound in the mammalian brain (Devane et al., 1992). It had always seemed likely that the receptors that latched onto THC had evolved to join with a natural brain compound and weren't just waiting around for plant-derived THC to show up. Devane called the new substance *anandamide* after the Sanskrit word *ananda* which means bliss. When purified, anandamide is a little less powerful than THC. It appears to play a role in the regulation of mood, memory, pain, movement, and other activities. Both the receptors for opiates and the receptors for THC are G-protein modulated (see Chapter 2). Once receptors of this kind are well understood and mapped, researchers hope to achieve an age-old dream and create drugs that can alleviate pain without ill effects.

❈ SUMMARY

◆ Consciousness is the state in which you are aware not only of the external environment but also of internal events such as thinking.

◆ Important advances in scientific technology have provided objective ways to measure conscious states.

◆ The conscious mind is said to be altered any time the content or quality of conscious experience undergoes a significant change.

◆ The electroencephalograph (EEG) records brain waves as electrical changes and has been used to monitor states of consciousness.

◆ There are four stages of sleep. Stages 3 and 4 often are referred to as slow-wave sleep. Rapid-eye-movement (REM) sleep usually is associated with dreaming. REM sleep is also called paradoxical sleep because REM brain waves are similar to those seen during the waking state.

◆ Atonia, or loss of muscle tone, occurs during REM sleep, rendering the sleeper semiparalyzed.

◆ Sleepwalking and sleeptalking generally occur during non-REM (NREM) sleep.

◆ REM rebound, in which more REM than usual occurs during the sleep cycle, is a result of REM deprivation.

◆ The average young adult needs between 6½ and 8½ hours of sleep a night. Some people, known as healthy insomniacs, can get by with much less.

◆ Three theories have been suggested to explain why we sleep. The adaptive theory argues that each species requires a certain amount of waking time to survive and that the rest of the time is best spent in a state, such as sleeping, in which there is the least chance of danger or injury. The conserving-energy theory argues that sleep is a way of conserving energy. The off-line theory argues that humans and almost all other mammals require downtime, during which they can integrate newly learned material into their memories.

◆ Four ideas have been put forth to explain why we dream. First is psychoanalytic theory which argues that dreams are expressions of repressed desire. Second is the activation-synthesis model, which argues that dreams are the brain's attempt to make sense of random electrical activity. Third is the housekeeping hypothesis, which argues that the brain creates dreams to eliminate any senseless or bizarre neural connections developed during the day's learning. Finally, the off-line hypothesis argues that REM sleep enables creatures to maintain a smaller and more efficient brain size by consolidating and storing previously gathered information during sleep.

◆ Factor S is a natural sleep-promoting substance that increases slow-wave or delta sleep for a few hours.

◆ A limited amount of sleep deprivation may not be

physically detrimental to healthy subjects. The most common effects of such deprivation are decreased performance on tasks, hallucinations, and delusions.

◆ Animal studies have found that inflicting intensive, long-term sleep deprivation results in death. Some scientists, therefore, think that sleep may serve a vital physiological function.

◆ There are many sleep-related disorders, including insomnia, narcolepsy, and sleep apnea.

◆ Hypnosis is not a state of sleep. Hypnosis encompasses a number of relatively separate phenomena, including dissociation, memory enhancement, pain relief, changed emotional states, unusual behavior, sensory and perceptual changes, disinhibition, and posthypnotic suggestion.

◆ Meditation is a simple phenomenon, very like resting, that can be practiced by anyone.

◆ Any drug that alters conscious awareness or perception is called a psychoactive drug. The three major classifications of psychoactive drugs are stimulants, depressants, and hallucinogens.

◆ The stimulants include amphetamines, caffeine, and cocaine. The depressants include alcohol, tranquilizers, and heroin. The hallucinogens include LSD, PCP, and marijuana.

◆ Designer drugs are chemically similar to psychoactive drugs and were synthesized to circumvent federal law. Many of them are dangerous and have unpredictable effects.

✸ SUGGESTIONS FOR FURTHER READING

1. Borbely, A. (1986). *Secrets of sleep*. New York: Basic Books. A book for the student or general reader that contains interesting information about sleep, sleep deprivation, why we need sleep, and sleep as a biological rhythm.

2. Coleman, R. M. (1986). *Wide awake at 3:00 a.m.: By choice or by chance?* New York: W. H. Freeman. A comprehensive book about circadian rhythms with practical suggestions for overcoming insomnia.

3. Dotto, L. (1990). *Losing sleep: How your sleeping habits affect your life*. New York: Morrow. An investigation of how sleep deprivation, disturbances, and disorders can affect job performance and alertness.

4. Empson, J. (1990). *Sleep and dreaming*. Winchester, MA: Faber & Faber. A review of sleep research for the general reader addressing such interesting topics as: Why do we dream in color? Why do some themes recur? And, why do some people sleepwalk?

5. Goldberg, P., & Kaufman, D. (1990). *Everybody's guide to natural sleep: A drug-free approach to overcoming insomnia and other sleep disorders*. Los Angeles: Tarcher. Describes the causes of sleeplessness and presents a number of natural methods for overcoming sleep-related problems.

6. Hauri, P., & Linde, S. (1990). *No more sleepless nights*. New York: John Wiley & Sons. An excellent drug-free guide to overcoming insomnia. Very detailed and includes a host of techniques and tips.

7. Hobson, J. A. (1988). *The dreaming brain*. New York: Basic Books. Gives a historical review of dream research and discusses the activation-synthesis model of dreams.

8. Hobson, J. A. (1989). *Sleep*. New York: W. H. Freeman. The latest on sleep and dreams from one of the leaders of the field, with many excellent color diagrams to highlight the discussion.

9. Hunt, H. T. (1989). *The multiplicity of dreams: Memory, imagination, and consciousness*. New Haven, CT: Yale University Press. A semitechnical look at dreams from Freud's theory to the work in modern labs. Includes a discussion of lucid dreams and the dreams of animals and children. Available in paperback (1991).

10. Julien, R. M. (1985). *A primer of drug action*. New York: W. H. Freeman. Outlines the major classes of drugs and their effects on the body.

11. Langer, E. L. (1989). *Mindfulness*. Reading, MA: Addison-Wesley. A Harvard psychologist looks at the amusing and serious consequences of daydreaming and failure to pay proper attention in our complex society.

12. Nell, V. (1990). *Lost in a book: The psychology of reading for pleasure*. New Haven, CT: Yale University Press. An examination of pleasure reading and how being absorbed in a book is akin to an altered state of consciousness not unlike dreaming or hypnosis.

13. Ornstein, R. (1986). *The psychology of consciousness* (rev. ed.). New York: Penguin Books. A revised edition of a classic text on states of consciousness.

14. Quarrick, G. (1989). *Our sweetest hours: Recreation and the mental state of absorption*. Jefferson, NC: McFarland & Co. Provides a look at "hypnosis" in everyday life and explains how to become absorbed in adult play. The link between absorption and hypnosis is examined.

15. Siegel, R. K. (1989). *Intoxication: Life in pursuit of artificial paradise*. New York: E. P. Dutton. A curious but interesting book by a pharmacologist who argues that humans have a natural drive to lose themselves from time to time in an altered conscious state. The author lists a number of healthy alternatives for achieving such a state other than drug intoxication.

16. Stafford, P. A. (1992). *Dreaming and dreams*. New York: Atheneum. A book on right and left brain functions looks at sleep in humans and mammals.

Chapter Eight

Learning and Conditioning

PROLOGUE

PROJECT SEA HUNT

All the pilots who work Coast Guard air-sea rescue realize the difficulties of finding a person who is lost at sea. They know how truly immense the ocean is and what a small speck a person makes upon it. That's why they have adopted Project Sea Hunt for use in air-sea rescue. Psychologists and biologists worked for a long time to get it ready, and it is now saving lives.

To give you an idea of how it works, imagine that you are a new pilot who will be going on a training rescue mission making use of the technique. Your crew is ready; you head for the helicopter. Your mission today: Find a pilot in a small raft. You are given as much information as you usually get—a short radio message giving rough coordinates. Only the Coast Guard officers know exactly where he is; they know because he was placed there as part of the training mission.

As you reach the helicopter, you immediately notice something different. Underneath the belly of the chopper, there's a large Plexiglas container. It looks like a big hatbox that has been divided into three sections. Something is moving in one of the sections; you bend down to have a look. It's a pigeon strapped into some kind of a device. Each of the other two sections also contains a pigeon.

You turn to one of the researchers who is going along today to monitor the project. He explains that once the helicopter is airborne, each pigeon will have a 120-degree view of the ocean below. The pigeons have been "conditioned." If they should see a red, orange, or yellow speck on the water below, they'll peck at a button that will sound a buzzer in your helmet. There are three speakers in your helmet, one forward, one left, and one right—each for a different pigeon. That way, you'll know which way to turn to continue the search.

Quickly, you start the engines and lift off. Soon you're over the beach and the breakers. A few miles out and you can no longer see the shore. Now there is only the ocean—rolling blue, white-blown water, stretching from horizon to horizon—and you have to find the tiny orange speck of a life

At left, a pigeon in Project Sea Hunt signals he has detected a red, orange, or yellow speck by pecking at a disk. The entire apparatus is suspended from a helicopter equipped for sea rescue, shown at right.

preserver and raft down there somewhere. You and the crew members look at the sea, sometimes searching with binoculars; you calculate how much fuel you have and when it will be dark; you hope you'll get lucky. That's what it's like to look for someone lost "out there."

You start wondering whether to take Project Sea Hunt seriously. As you continue farther out over the ocean, you are mumbling to yourself. Why shouldn't the birds hit the buzzers just any old time? Won't they get bored? Why should they even bother looking? These guys must be crazy. You and your crew scan the ocean with binoculars as usual. You're not going to let some bird beat you. None of you sees anything. Suddenly, there's a buzz in your left ear. "Bring her around 120 degrees to port," the researcher says. You swing the chopper around. Now you hear a buzz in front of you. The pigeon in front must have picked it up. "We're on the right track," the researcher says. Neither you nor your crew has seen anything but ocean. You think to yourself, "These birds are goofy, maybe they're airsick—that is, if birds can get airsick?" But then one of your crew members calls out, "There he is!" "Hey, not bad," someone else shouts as the tiny raft comes into view. As soon as you spot the raft, you flip on the radio switch to call in your success to headquarters. You laugh and turn to your copilot, "Hey, Jerry, it just crossed my mind that the birds were trained to hit a switch when they see a raft, and so were we!" "Yeah," he replies, "and we all get paid bird seed."

You turn to the researcher and ask, "Why did you decide to use birds?" He leans forward so you can hear him over the roar of the engine and the buzzing sounds in your helmet. "Birds have much better vision than humans. They have a wider angle of view, and they don't get nearly as bored as people do. Oh, one more thing: They like to fly!"

Over the next few weeks, the experiments continue. You and your crew are able to spot the target victims about 38 percent of the time on your first pass over the target area. The pigeons are averaging 90 percent (Stark, 1981)!

IN THIS CHAPTER, we'll examine the different kinds of conditioning and learning that are based on many of the ideas encompassed by behaviorism (see Chapter 1). As you'll discover, many of the special techniques used to train the Project Sea Hunt pigeons can also be used to teach other species, including humans. We will also explore the cognitive and ethological approaches, both of which have added to our understanding of the learning process. Along the way, you'll see how prejudice is learned, how cravings for drugs can occur in abusers, even after complete withdrawal has been achieved, why spanking children is a bad idea, how phobias can be taught, what we know about the biological underpinnings of learning, and even how to toilet train a child in less than a day!

LEARNING
A relatively permanent change in behavior as a result of experience.

WHY PSYCHOLOGISTS STUDY LEARNING

Psychologists study **learning** because among most animals, especially humans, many behaviors are learned. Learning may be defined as a relatively permanent change in behavior resulting from experience. We say "relatively permanent change" to exclude the effects of such factors as fatigue. Fatigue, which occurs because of experience, may change behavior, but only temporarily, whereas learning implies a more lasting change.

The Behavior of Organisms

In 1938, a young psychologist named B. F. Skinner, building on the work of many earlier researchers, most notably Pavlov, published a book entitled *The Behavior of Organisms*. In it, he presented many experiments that strongly supported the basic tenets of *behaviorism* (see Table 8.1) and outlined the ways in which the environment might act on an organism to determine what the organism learns and how it behaves.

Any book that expanded on the principles of how behaviors were determined and controlled was obviously important to psychologists. Some researchers, however, were surprised that the book was entitled *The Behavior of Organisms*, because almost all the work it described was based on studies conducted only with rats. In fact, some people still jokingly define psychology as the study of rats and sophomores (sophomores were added later, once professors discovered that students could be made to "volunteer" for experiments).

Skinner had a ready response for his critics, however. He asserted that the principles governing learning were so general that research gathered from one species was readily applicable to just about any other species. The same basic principles that explained how rats learned, he argued, applied just as well to dogs, cats, elephants, birds, fish, people, and nearly all other creatures. As you will see in this chapter, many of the learning principles outlined by Skinner and other researchers do seem to characterize a great many animals, including humans.

B. F. Skinner (1904–1990). An American behaviorist who championed the idea that the environment controls our behavior more than any other force.

TABLE 8.1 ◆ THE BASIC TENETS OF STRICT BEHAVIORISM
1. The mechanisms of learning are similar for almost all species. The way you learn to drive a car and the way an elephant leanrs a circus trick both can be understood by applying the same principles of learning.
2. All learning, no matter how complex, can be understood in terms of two kinds of simple association mechanisms referred to as classical conditioning and operant conditioning.
3. The best way to understand learning is to examine the environment and the observable forces in it and to analyze how these forces affect the responses of the organism in question. Learning is a relatively permanent *observable* change in behavior. Concepts such as the "mind" or "thinking" are best ignored because they can never be directly observed and are therefore outside the realm of science.

HABITUATION
A process in which an organism ceases to respond reflexively to an unconditioned stimulus that has been presented repeatedly.

STIMULUS
Any energy or change in energy condition that is sensed.

SENSITIZATION
The process by which a reflexive response is made stronger and more sensitive to stimuli by pairing the eliciting stimulus with a painful or unpleasant stimulus.

CONTIGUOUS ASSOCIATION
The occurrence of two events close enough in time that the organism perceives them as somehow related. Also called temporal association.

UNCONDITIONED STIMULUS (US)
The stimulus that normally elicits an unconditioned response, such as the food that caused Pavlov's dogs to respond with salivation.

✹ SIMPLE FORMS OF LEARNING

Habituation

People learn in a number of ways. One of the simplest forms of learning is **habituation,** which takes place when a person becomes accustomed to a **stimulus** because it has been presented repeatedly. If construction work began outside your window, the first ka-BLAM of a pile driver might startle you. This response would be natural because being startled is an inborn, not a learned, response. The stimulus in this case would be the loud noise. If the pile driver continued to make the noise over and over, eventually you would become *habituated* to it; you would learn not to react any more. This is the same reason why pigeons happily eat seed alongside the freeway while trucks and cars roar past. They have become habituated to the traffic sounds, which, as any urban dweller can tell you, takes only a day or two.

The trouble with applying the definition of learning to the phenomenon of habituation, however, is that although a change has taken place owing to experience, the change is not necessarily "relatively permanent." We can, for example, bring back the natural startle reflex by removing the loud noise for some time and then unexpectedly presenting it again. Nevertheless, a person can be so habituated to a particular stimulus that the change becomes somewhat permanent. Some researchers like to talk in terms of short-term habituation (which ends quickly) and long-term habituation (which may take a very long time to end), which seem to be controlled by different brain mechanisms (Leaton & Supple, 1986). So, owing to its relative permanence, long-term habituation might be definable as a form of learning, whereas short-term habituation isn't.

It's more important, however, to realize that habituation occurs than to argue about whether habituation is or isn't learning. The value of habituation is that we come to ignore a stimulus that has lost its novelty or importance. Habituation frees us to attend to stimuli that are new or that appear suddenly. If you were in the woods picking berries and heard a deep throaty growl nearby, attending to that new stimulus obviously would have survival value.

Sensitization

Sensitization may occur when an animal or a human being is exposed to a stimulus that is accompanied by pain or fear of some kind. Like the effects of habituation, the effects of sensitization can last from minutes to weeks depending on the amount of training. The effect of sensitization appears to be the opposite of that of habituation, and a different biological mechanism within the organism is responsible for it (Marcus, Nolen, Rankin, & Carew, 1988). If you become sensitized to a sound, the next time that sound occurs you may startle more easily than you would have before you were sensitized. A soft clicking sound, for example, ordinarily would not startle anyone. When it has been associated with pain, however, the sound can cause you to become sensitized, and you may react by jumping the next time you hear it. Soldiers suffering from battle fatigue often show signs of sensitization. They are jumpy and anxious; the slightest sudden noise may startle them. Similarly, a woman attacked and raped in her own home may, for a very long time thereafter, show excessive reactions to the slightest "house sounds" she hears, even though the rest of us may have long since habituated to the common creaks and groans that emanate from our house or apartment from time to time.

CLASSICAL CONDITIONING—DOES THE NAME PAVLOV RING A BELL?

During the 1890s, the Russian physiologist Ivan Pavlov reported an experiment of an associative learning process. He had been investigating digestion (for which he had earlier become the first Russian to win the Nobel Prize) and had been trying to understand why his dogs, who were the subjects of his experiment, often began to salivate *before* they received food. This reaction seemed to occur when a **contiguous association** was made between the presentation of food and another stimulus, such as seeing someone in the laboratory open the cupboard where the dog food was kept. Other researchers had observed this phenomenon, but had either considered it a nuisance or had ignored it. Pavlov, however, became seriously interested in this learning process and began to investigate it systematically.

Pavlov's Experiments

In a series of well-known experiments, Pavlov decided to *pair* a stimulus (food) that would elicit an *unlearned* response (salivation) with a stimulus (bell) that did not elicit salivation and was therefore "neutral" at the beginning of the experiment. Because no learning is required to make dogs salivate when they are given meat, meat is referred to as an **unconditioned stimulus (US),** while the reflex response of salivating is referred to as an **unconditioned response (UR).**

Pavlov took a stimulus that did not cause salivation in dogs (a bell) and began to pair it systematically with the presentation of food. He would ring the bell, immediately present the food (US), and observe the salivation (UR). After the bell and the food had been paired, or contiguously associated, as psychologists say, Pavlov was able to cause salivation without giving food; ringing the bell was enough! The dogs associated food with the bell, and they would salivate. The bell had become a stimulus to which the dogs responded in a predictable way; they showed that they had learned. For this reason, the bell is referred to as a **conditioned stimulus (CS),** and the response it elicits is called a **conditioned response (CR)** (see Figure 8.1). The process by which the bell obtains the power to elicit the CR is called **reinforcement.** The more the meat and bell were paired, the more the *bond* between them was strengthened, or *reinforced*, and the more the bell came to easily and successfully elicit the CR (salivation). This procedure is referred to as **classical conditioning.** Conditioning means learning. Figure 8.2 shows the reinforcement process in

UNCONDITIONED RESPONSE (UR)
The response made to an unconditioned stimulus, such as salivation in response to food.

CONDITIONED STIMULUS (CS)
In classical conditioning, a previously neutral stimulus that is reinforced by being paired with an unconditioned stimulus, so that it acquires the ability to produce a conditioned response.

CONDITIONED RESPONSE (CR)
A learned response elicited by a conditioned stimulus, owing to previous reinforcement of the conditioned stimulus through association with an unconditioned stimulus.

REINFORCEMENT
In classical conditioning, any increase in the ability of a conditioned stimulus to elicit a conditioned response owing to the association of the conditioned stimulus with another stimulus (typically, an unconditioned stimulus).

CLASSICAL CONDITIONING
A learning procedure in which a stimulus that normally evokes a given reflex is associated with a stimulus that does not usually evoke that reflex, with the result that the latter stimulus will eventually evoke the reflex when presented by itself.

ACQUISITION
The time during the learning process when there is a consistent increase in responsiveness; a time when learning is occurring.

Ivan Pavlov (1849–1936) is shown (center, white beard) demonstrating his classical conditioning experiment.

◆ **FIGURE 8.1**

◆ **FIGURE 8.1**

The paradigm used by Pavlov to condition a dog to salivate at the sound of a bell.

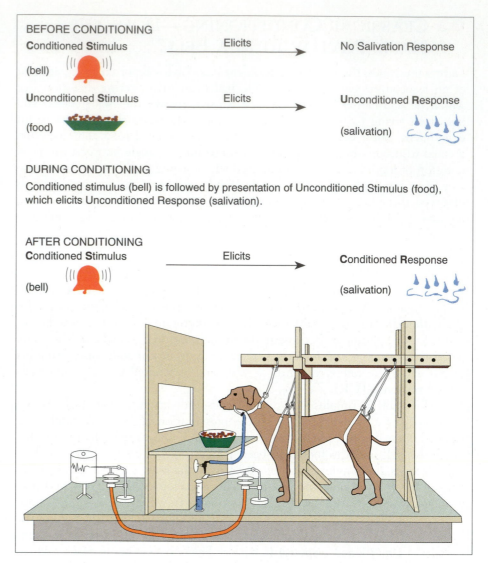

BEFORE CONDITIONING

Conditioned **S**timulus —— Elicits ——→ No Salivation Response

(bell)

Unconditioned **S**timulus —— Elicits ——→ **U**nconditioned **R**esponse

(food)   (salivation)

DURING CONDITIONING

Conditioned stimulus (bell) is followed by presentation of Unconditioned Stimulus (food), which elicits Unconditioned Response (salivation).

AFTER CONDITIONING

Conditioned **S**timulus —— Elicits ——→ **C**onditioned **R**esponse

(bell)   (salivation)

◆ **FIGURE 8.2**

The acquisition and extinction of a classically conditioned response. When the CS (bell) and US (food) are paired, the power of the CS to elicit the CR (salivation) increases. The CS, however, rapidly loses its power to elicit the CR each time that it is presented without the reinforcement of the US. This decrease in eliciting power shows the process of extinction. (SOURCE: *After Pavlov, 1927.*)

ACQUISITION

Drops of saliva elicited by the CS

Number of CS–US pairings

EXTINCTION

Drops of saliva elicited by the CS

Number of CS presentations without US

classical conditioning and its diminishment as the bond between the CS and US first undergoes **acquisition** and then **extinction**. Figure 8.3 shows the important processes of **generalization** and **discrimination** as they pertain to classical conditioning.

Higher-Order Conditioning

Once the CS has the power to elicit the CR, owing to the reinforcement of the CS-US bond by their contiguous pairing, it is possible to use the CS all by itself to create a *higher-order* CS_2 (see Figure 8.4). In experiments, CS_2s have been used to create even higher-order CS_3s and CS_4s, but these CSs are very weak. Higher-order conditioning greatly expands the range and influence of associative experiences, however, and may play a role in the creation of the emotional feelings we acquire toward particular things.

Classical Conditioning in Everyday Life

It was at about this point when I was first studying conditioning, having learned and committed to memory the US-UR-CS-CR alphabet and the assorted boldfaced terms in the previous pages, that I started to get a little bored with the material—let's face it, dog drool just isn't all that interesting. Maybe you are starting to feel the same way. To acquire a full understanding of conditioning, of course, it is necessary to know all these technical terms and definitions, but it would be better to learn what they really *mean*, that is, how

EXTINCTION
In classical conditioning, the elimination of the power of the conditioned stimulus to elicit a conditioned response. Classical extinction will occur if the conditioned stimulus is repeatedly presented without being reinforced through further association with the unconditioned stimulus.

GENERALIZATION
Responding to a stimulus other than the training stimulus as though it were the training stimulus. In classical conditioning, the response tends to diminish the more the other stimulus differs from the training stimulus, thereby creating a "gradient of generalization."

DISCRIMINATION
Differentially responding to two or more stimuli. The responding occurs in such a way that it is obvious that the organism can tell that the stimuli have certain properties that distinguish them from one another.

◆ **FIGURE 8.3**

In the example of generalization, a dog has been conditioned to salivate to a tone with a frequency of 5000 cycles per second. After the conditioning, tones of different frequencies are sounded. The result shown is known as a gradient of generalization. The gradient is created because the dog will respond to other tones, only less so. Also notice that the closer the new tone is to the training stimulus, the stronger is the response.

In the example of discrimination, our dog has again been trained to respond to a CS tone of 5000 cycles. Next (bar graph A), we present a 3000-cycle tone; the dog also responds, but with fewer saliva drops, which is what we would expect according to the gradient of generalization. If, however, we keep presenting the 5000-cycle tone with the US, as we had during training, but also continue to present the 3000-cycle tone (which never accompanies

a US), the dog will come to discriminate between the two tones. The result is shown in bar graph B. The response to the 3000-cycle tone is almost gone, while the response to the 5000-cycle tone has increased. The dog has learned to discriminate between the two tones and only responds to one of them with any significant degree of strength.

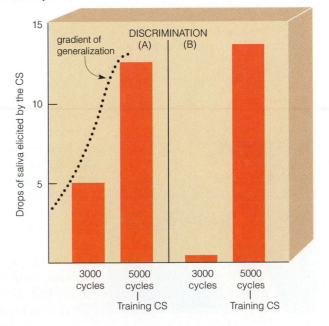

◆ FIGURE 8.4

An example of higher-order conditioning—in this case, second order. Higher-order conditioning tends to be weak, probably because, while the CS_2-CS bond is being reinforced, the power of the CS is decreasing owing to extinction—which, in turn, is occurring because the US is no longer present to reinforce the CS-US bond.

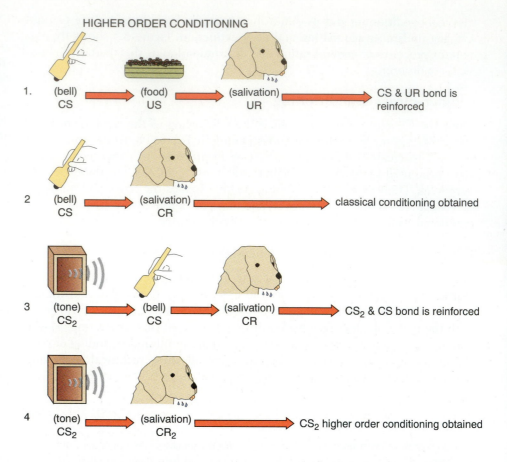

HIGHER ORDER CONDITIONING

1. (bell) CS → (food) US → (salivation) UR → CS & UR bond is reinforced

2. (bell) CS → (salivation) CR → classical conditioning obtained

3. (tone) CS_2 → (bell) CS → (salivation) CR → CS_2 & CS bond is reinforced

4. (tone) CS_2 → (salivation) CR_2 → CS_2 higher order conditioning obtained

they function in real life (although Pavlov would surely argue that his laboratory was real enough). So, let's stop for a moment and take a random assortment of examples of classical conditioning from everyday life—that should be a little more interesting!

PREJUDICE.   In the mid-1940s, psychologist Kenneth Clark held a black doll and a white doll in his hands and asked the following questions of young white children living in the South:

"Which doll looks like you?"
"Now tell me which doll is the good doll?"
"Which doll is the bad doll?"

These children knew that the white doll looked like them. Most children also indicated that the white doll was the "good" doll and the black doll was the "bad" one, that the white doll was "nice" and the black doll was "dirty" or "ugly" (Clark & Clark, 1947). How had these southern white children learned to make such associations? During decades of racial prejudice in America, darker skin had become *associated* with poverty and with being "inferior," not just in the South, of course, but generally throughout the United States. The white children had learned to attribute these characteristics to black people.

This racist attitude is what the white children had been taught; it is also what the black children had been taught. The black children had been raised in the same general environment, the same country. They, too, had seen that the whites lived in better conditions and received better treatment while they received worse. And, as the Clarks discovered in further research, a majority of black children also chose the white doll as the good one and the black doll as the bad one! This famous discovery was instrumental in the U.S. Supreme Court's decision in *Brown vs. The Board of Education of Topeka, Kansas*, which

In 1947, Dr. Kenneth Clark conducted research on the nature of prejudice. His findings helped establish the fact that children were being affectively conditioned to continue the prejudices of their society.

overturned *Plessy vs. Ferguson*, which had allowed for separate, but supposedly equal schools. *Brown vs. the Board of Education* was the famous case that said black and white children may not be segregated in "separate but equal" schools. Dr. Clark's findings helped the justices make their dramatic decision by showing that separate and unequal status was causing a lessening of psychological self-worth among African-American children. Dr. Clark's work in conditioned learning highlighted one of the most hateful aspects of prejudice, namely, that those discriminated against will often come to believe that they are, in fact, somehow inferior.

A famous conditioning experiment conducted by researchers Staats and Staats 35 years ago helped to show how an association process could be responsible for the prejudice Dr. Clark observed. In their experiment, college students were asked to look at one word while pronouncing another. Without being aware of the purpose of the experiment, the students were maneuvered into pairing pleasant words or unpleasant words with a particular name (Tom or Bill) or a certain nationality (Swedish or Dutch). In a short time, subjects revealed obvious differences in attitudes toward these names and nationalities, simply because those words had been paired with positive or negative words (Staats & Staats, 1958).

Advertisers, politicians, moviemakers, and just about everyone tries to use this kind of conditioning to affect our emotions. When a politician associates himself with a positive symbol such as the flag, when a moviemaker uses dramatic music, or when someone dresses well for a job interview, they are all invoking the same process: Each is attempting to render something—the politician, the movie, or the job seeker—more appealing through association with positive stimuli.

What appears to be occurring in instances of association like those just described is a kind of higher-order conditioning (see Figure 8.5).

DRUG OVERDOSE.   As was apparent in the case of the college students conditioned to like or dislike a certain nationality, classical conditioning often occurs without the conditioned person being aware of it. For example, researchers have found that drug users often unwittingly condition themselves to the stimuli that occur immediately before the administration of drugs (Siegel, 1975). When the body is exposed to drugs apparently it attempts to restore balance to the system by building up what is called a drug *tolerance*. Because of this change, after enough exposures to a drug, the body will often require more of that drug before an effect can be achieved. The buildup of tolerance (UR), then, may be a typical reaction to a sudden influx of an opiate drug (see Chapter 7) such as heroin (US) (Snyder, 1984). Notice how this is similar to the case of Pavlov's dogs. In the case of the dogs, the US (meat) produced

◆ **FIGURE 8.5**

Higher-order conditioning may help explain the findings Staats and Staats obtained in their study of induced prejudice among college students.

salivation (UR). In the case of the heroin addicts, the US (injection of heroin) is believed to produce a certain tolerance reaction (UR).

The immediate environmental surroundings of the drug user (for example, the room he is in, the objects in the room) can become conditioned stimuli through associative pairing. After sufficient pairings, whenever the heroin addict enters that same room (CS), his body may respond by producing a tolerance reaction (CR), *even though no heroin has been injected.* This may explain why drug-overdose deaths from injecting heroin occur much more commonly in a *new* environment. A user who takes drugs in, say, a strange house may be injecting into a body that has not produced the usually expected tolerance reaction beforehand (CR), because the usual CS (the old familiar environment) was diminished or absent (Siegel, Hinson, Krank, & McCully, 1982). Because his body isn't ready for the size of the dose he is used to injecting, the user is more likely to misjudge how much heroin he needs and overdose.

CONDITIONED FEAR. Fear often is the result of classical conditioning. The case of Little Albert is an example of the classical conditioning of an irrational fear in a child. Although the 1920 study suffered from certain methodological flaws, it is still interesting because it was conducted by one of the founders of behaviorism, John Watson.

Watson and Rayner tested Albert B., a healthy 11-month-old boy, by systematically exposing him to a white rat, a rabbit, a dog, a monkey, various masks, cotton wool, and even a burning newspaper. As Watson noted, "At no time did this infant ever show fear in any situation" (Watson & Rayner, 1920, p. 2). The two researchers found, however, that making a very loud noise by striking a steel rod with a hammer (US) startled baby Albert and made him cry (UR). Next, the researchers paired the loud gong with the white rat that Albert had previously seen. Whenever Albert touched the rat (CS), the loud gong would be struck (US), which would startle Albert and cause him to cry (UR) (see Figure 8.6). Eventually, Albert would start to cry as soon as he saw the rat. In Watson's words,

The instant the rat was shown, the baby began to cry. Almost instantly he turned sharply to the left, fell over on the left side, raised himself on all fours and began to crawl away so rapidly that he was caught with difficulty before reaching the edge of the table. (Watson & Rayner, 1920, p. 5)

An extremely rare photograph of John Watson (in mask) and Rosalie Rayner, as they prepared to condition Little Albert.

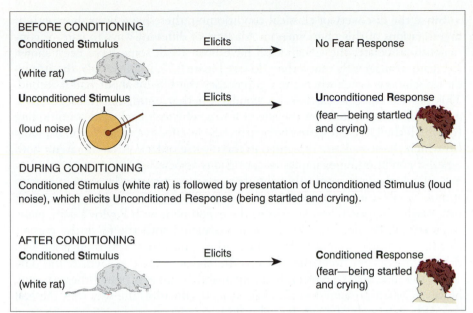

In addition, Albert's fears generalized to related objects, such as a rabbit, a dog, a white cotton ball, and even a Santa Claus mask (probably because of the white beard), but not to dissimilar objects, such as blocks. This probably occurred because Albert had associated the loud noise with characteristics possessed by the rat—white, live, legged, and furry—which he subsequently saw in some of the other objects as well.

The experiment with Little Albert has notable ethical implications. Was it ethical to create what amounted to a phobia in the child? By today's standards, this experiment would clearly have violated ethical procedures. To make matters worse, it appears that before Watson ever began his experiment, he knew that Albert was going to have to leave the home for invalid children where his mother was working and that the researchers probably would never have a chance to undo any learned fear response that they might produce. Yet they went ahead and conducted the experiment anyway (Harris, 1979). Of course, Albert was not the only human ever to be classically conditioned; millions of people are daily conditioned in this way as they come in contact with their environment. Any pediatrician who has given a child an injection can attest to this fact. The child's screaming fit the next time she merely enters the office is a good indication that classical conditioning plays a role in fear responses. In fact, most phobias appear to be related to this kind of conditioning. Later in this chapter, we will discuss the kind of therapy often best suited to help people overcome phobias, and you will see that it relies on conditioning techniques to help phobia sufferers unlearn their fears.*

Contiguity versus Contingency

We have seen that a conditioned stimulus may gain power to elicit a response by being associated in some fashion with an unconditioned stimulus. But we haven't asked *why* this occurs. Is it just the result of two stimuli being paired in time—that is, *contiguously* paired?

*Note that classical conditioning, while playing a role in the formation of prejudice, fears, or drug use, is not the only kind of learning likely to be involved. A person would also be more likely to show these behaviors if he were rewarded for emitting them, or if he observed other people, especially those whom he respected, demonstrating such behaviors. These kinds of learning (operant conditioning and social learning) are covered later in this chapter.

CONTINGENCY DETECTION
The process by which an organism makes a discrimination between stimuli that are only present when the US is presented and other stimuli that happen to be present not only when the US is presented but also when the US is not presented. The result is that the organism can rely on sensing the stimulus that is only present when the US is presented to predict that the US will soon appear.

Since the discovery of classical conditioning, there have been thousands of investigations of this phenomenon. All sorts of different ways to pair, or contiguously associate, the CS and US have been tried; some have been shown to create stronger CRs than others do (see Figure 8.7). Interestingly, the strongest associations occur when the CS precedes the US by about half a second. This has led some researchers to wonder whether contiguous association is, indeed, all that accounts for the effect. If it is, why isn't backward conditioning (in which the US is presented before the CS) as effective as trace conditioning (in which the stimuli are presented in the reverse order)? After all, aren't both types of conditioning examples of contiguous association?

In Pavlov's day, people thought that simply contiguously associating two stimuli would cause conditioning to occur. We now know that this is not necessarily the case. Consider that in the experiment with Pavlov's dogs, many other stimuli besides the bell also were associated with the food: the harness to which the dogs were attached, the leather straps that held their front legs, the scaffolding that held the harness, the elevated table on which the dogs stood, the tube used to collect their saliva, and so on. Not one of these stimuli, however, when presented to the dogs, caused salivation the way that the bell did, although each of them had also been contiguously associated with food many times. There was something special about the bell. As it turns out, the reason the bell was special in Pavlov's experiment is that the presentation of the food was *contingent* (dependent) on the presentation of the bell. Unlike the bell, the other stimuli (the harness, table, and so on) also were present *when no food was given*. The bell, on the other hand, never rang when food was not presented. The fact that the animal learned to associate the bell with the food implies that the animal *was using the bell to predict when food would arrive*.

As a result of these observations, learning theorists now believe that such **contingency detection** by an organism is at least as important as, and probably more important than, the contiguous association of stimuli in explaining why conditioning occurs (Rescorla, 1988).

A classic experiment conducted by Leon Kamin (1969) provided a further clue that conditioning is dependent upon contingency detection. In his ex-

◆ **FIGURE 8.7**

Different kinds of classical conditioning arrangements. The US is presented for a brief time. The CS can be presented in many ways, as the series of examples shows—it can even be presented "backward," after the US, although the effect of such backward conditioning is quite weak.

periment, Kamin used two groups of laboratory animals, an experimental group and a contrast group. First, he conditioned the experimental group to respond to a light. He did this by pairing the light with an electric shock. All the animals in this group quickly learned the association. After conditioning, they reacted with fear and avoidance whenever the light was turned on. The animals in the contrast group received no training. Next, Kamin presented both groups of animals with a light-tone combination (a *compound stimulus*) that was paired with the shock. Finally, he presented both groups of animals with just the tone. Interestingly, the tone was only a CS for the contrast group of animals! The experimental group, which had learned to associate the light with the shock, did not learn the same association for the tone. Kamin called this occurrence **blocking,** because it was as though the association learned for the light, which was already fulfilling the function of contingency detection, prevented the animals from learning a redundant association. The contrast group, on the other hand, immediately learned to use the tone to tell them that the shock was coming because they had no other stimulus already serving that function.

If classical conditioning were simply a matter of contiguity, we would have expected the experimental group to have been conditioned to the tone in the same way that they were conditioned to the light. The existence of blocking, however, argues that it is the *functional* value of the stimulus and its usefulness for detecting contingencies that determine whether conditioning will occur.

OPERANT CONDITIONING

In classical conditioning, a particular stimulus elicits a response that is already in an organism's repertoire (in Pavlov's experiments a bell elicited salivation). For instance, after conditioning, the rat made Albert cry, but Albert already had the ability to cry as evidenced by his reaction to the loud gong. Crying was not a new response brought on by conditioning.

Suppose, however, you wished to teach a new response, something that the organism had not previously shown? We all have acquired such behaviors; the ability to read this book is one of them—you weren't born with the ability to read. The acquisition of novel behaviors is the result of a different kind of conditioning called **operant conditioning.** Much of what you've learned in life has been acquired through operant conditioning. To understand how such conditioning occurs, let's look at a famous series of experiments conducted at the turn of the century by a psychologist named E. L. Thorndike.

The Law of Effect

About the time Pavlov was studying behavior in dogs, an American psychologist, E. L. Thorndike, was observing the behavior of cats. Thorndike would deprive a cat of food for some time and then place it inside a puzzle box, a container from which it was possible for the animal to escape if it happened to trip a latch that opened the door (see Figure 8.8). Food was placed outside the box in plain view of the cat. Eventually, the cat would accidentally hook a claw onto the wire loop or step on the treadle that pulled the latch, and the door to the box would open, enabling the cat to secure the food. As the cats came to appreciate this way of escaping, they usually released themselves sooner each time they were put into the box (see Figure 8.9).

Thorndike's observations of such trial-and-error learning led him to consider that the consequences of an act were an important factor in determining the probability that the action would occur. His thesis was that

any act which in a given situation produces satisfaction becomes associated with that situation, so that when the situation recurs, the act is more likely than ever before to

BLOCKING

In classical conditioning, the phenomenon in which a CS will not be reinforced by pairing it with a US if the organism is already using another CS to detect the onset of that US.

OPERANT CONDITIONING

Skinner's term for changes in behavior that occur as a result of consequences that reinforce or punish emitted responses. These responses are classified according to how they operate on the environment. They are, in turn, shaped by further environmental experiences. Also known as instrumental learning.

E. L. Thorndike (1874–1949).

◆ **FIGURE 8.8**

A puzzle box similar to that used by Thorndike in 1898. (SOURCE: *Bitterman, 1969, p. 445.*)

INSTRUMENTAL LEARNING
The process by which an organism learns to behave because of the consequences that follow the behavior.

LAW OF EFFECT
Thorndike's principle that responses associated with pleasant consequences tend to be repeated, while those associated with discomforting consequences tend to be eliminated.

recur also. Conversely, any act which in a given situation produces discomfort becomes disassociated from that situation, so that when the situation recurs, the act is less likely than before to recur. (Thorndike, 1905, p. 202)

Thorndike referred to such learning as **instrumental learning,** and his explanation of this kind of learning, known as the **law of effect,** is one of the cornerstones of operant conditioning. Because this kind of learning is maintained or changed depending on the consequences that *follow a response,* when you respond to something, your response is strengthened if the consequence is pleasant and weakened if the consequence is aversive. In this way you, and members of hundreds of other species, learn because of the outcomes of your behavior.

Operants

In Thorndike's day, S-R psychologists (see Chapter 1) were concerned with analyzing the muscular responses that constituted behaviors—the way physicists might analyze a billiard shot—to determine exactly which event led to or caused the next one. They generally referred to behaviors as reflexes. Because of this, it was quite natural in the case of instrumental learning to ask, "What elicits the initial instrumental response?" For example, what made Thorndike's cats step on the escape treadle? Which stimulus triggered it? Was it the sight of the treadle, or the view of the cage bars, or something else in the cage? The cause is not at all clear, the way it is in classical conditioning (for example, the bell caused the salivation). To make matters more confusing, Thorndike's cats didn't always use exactly the same response in order to escape. Sometimes they'd press the treadle with their left paw, sometimes with the right. Sometimes they'd just rub against it. Should each of these be considered a different response? Did each have its own eliciting stimulus? In fact, even as late as the mid-1930s, Thorndike's law of effect wasn't all that readily accepted. John Watson, the father of behaviorism, didn't believe that the law of effect was real and referred to its effects in Thorndike's experiments as the influence of "kind fairies" (Iversen, 1992).

◆ **FIGURE 8.9**

The graph shows the gradual decline in the amount of time necessary for one animal to release itself from the Thordikian puzzle box in successive trials. This is one of the earliest learning curves in the experimental study of conditioning. Notice, however, that the curve is not completely smooth but has marked fluctuations. Smooth learning curves usually result when many learning curves are averaged out. (SOURCE: *Bitterman, 1969, p. 446.)*

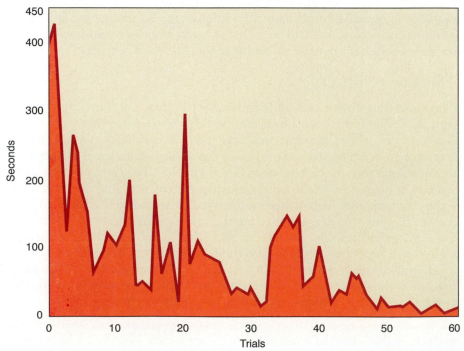

Partly to steer clear of the complexities of building a theory of instrumental learning on a convoluted reflexology of stimulus-response connections, B. F. Skinner eventually came to argue that *any* lever press, whether with the left paw, right paw, or body, could be considered the same response because it *had the same effect on the environment:* It provided the cat with an escape from the box. Skinner introduced the term *operant conditioning* to refer to the learning of instrumental responses that had the same effect on the environment rather than ones that consisted of exactly the same muscular motions. These **operants,** Skinner argued, can be made stronger if they are followed by a reinforcing consequence (as Thorndike had originally suggested in the law of effect), but what initiates the response is of little importance. In this view, a response is initially emitted for unknown reasons. This broke completely with Watson's "No stimulus–no response" rule. This is why Skinner is considered to have been a behaviorist, but not an S-R psychologist.

In Skinner's operant conditioning, the *probability* that the response will be emitted can be predicted by the organism's past experience with the effect of that response on the environment. Responses that had pleasant consequences are more likely to be repeated in similar circumstances, while responses that were followed by unpleasant consequences are less likely to be repeated. For our purposes, then, we will consider instrumental learning and operant conditioning to be equivalent terms.

Reinforcement and Extinction in Operant Conditioning

The strength of an operant response can be measured by its resistance to **extinction;** that is, by how long it takes for the behavior to return to its original rate once the pleasant consequence following the behavior no longer occurs (see Figure 8.10). It is generally correct to say that for an operant response to be strengthened, the response should be rewarded. But *reward* in everyday language denotes *things* such as money, candy, or praise, and something commonly considered a reward will not always work as one. For this reason, psychologists prefer the term **reinforcement** rather than reward, because reinforcement is not a thing, but a process of strengthening behavior. In other words, something is or is not reinforcing because of the effect it has, not because of what it is.

Operant Conditioning in Everyday Life

Operant conditioning is responsible for many of the learned skills that you have acquired since your birth. In great part, you learn to play the piano, write

OPERANTS
Skinner's term for any emitted responses that affect the environment. Operants are classified or grouped not according to the particular muscular combinations involved in creating the response but according to their effect on the environment, that is, how they "operate" on the environment. Therefore, Thorndike's cats used the same operant when they pressed the treadle that opened their cage regardless of which paw or muscles they used.

EXTINCTION
In operant conditioning, the elimination of an operant response or its return to a prereinforcement rate of emission following discontinuation of the reinforcing consequence that had maintained it.

REINFORCEMENT
In operant conditioning, an event that strengthens the response that preceded it. Operant (instrumental) conditioning is a process in which a response is reinforced.

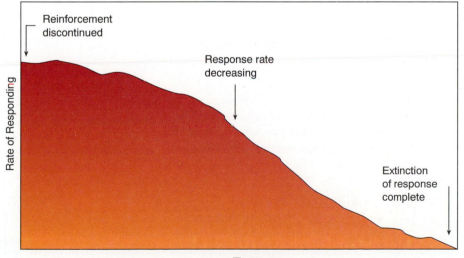

◆ **FIGURE 8.10**

Once an operant response is no longer reinforced, it will undergo extinction. Slowly, over time, the response occurs less and less often until it reaches the level it had prior to reinforcement.

Animals are taught to perform tricks through the use of operant conditioning.

a letter, ride a bicycle, open a door, work a screwdriver, cook a dinner, or pitch a tent through operant conditioning. Any behavior that can be shaped by the pleasant or unpleasant consequences that might follow it can be affected by operant conditioning. In fact, operant conditioning is so prevalent that the best way to give you good examples from everyday life is to let them present themselves during the following discussion of the different aspects of operant conditioning. In this first example, we will investigate the concept of shaping, and observe the operant conditioning of a child.

Shaping

In operant conditioning, a response must occur before it can be reinforced. It is impossible to strengthen a behavior that, in fact, never occurs, and forgetting this can sometimes lead to difficulty. I once observed a father trying to get his 2-year-old son to "hand Daddy the newspaper." The child's response was, "No!" This particular father was a psychology graduate student, however, and he decided to obtain his newspaper by using the principle of **shaping,** also known as the principle of reinforcing successive approximations toward a particular final response. This principle was one of Skinner's great contributions—a discovery he made early on in his work. With this technique, Skinner showed how *new* behaviors can be created through conditioning.

In this example, the father begins by dividing the child's future paper-fetching response into a series of substeps:

CONCEPT REVIEW ◆ CRYING

Is crying an unlearned reflex, a classically conditioned response, or an operantly conditioned response? You've probably learned enough by now to realize that it may be any of the three. If a baby cries (UR) when stuck with a pin (US), the crying has not been learned and is therefore considered a reflex. If a child cries (CR) at seeing a dentist's chair (CS), the crying may result because the chair has been associated with pain in the past, and the crying can therefore be said to be classically conditioned. (Notice, too, that this kind of crying is not operant because it does not help the child to obtain or avoid the chair.) Finally, if a child cries because last time in the same circumstances she received ice cream or avoided homework by crying, the crying has been operantly conditioned. The reinforcing stimulus consequence is depicted as S^{R+}.

UNLEARNED RESPONSE

US → UR
Baby stuck with pin   Cries

CLASSICALLY CONDITIONED RESPONSE

CS → US → UR   During conditioning
Dentist's chair   Painful stimulation   Cries

CS → UR   Following conditioning
Dentist's chair   Cries

OPERANTLY CONDITIONED RESPONSE

R → S^{R+}
Cries   Reinforced with ice cream or homework avoidance

1. Looking at the paper
2. Walking toward the paper
3. Grasping the paper
4. Carrying the paper toward the father
5. Releasing the paper once it is in the father's hand

SHAPING
A method of creating a goal behavior by reinforcing successive approximations toward the goal behavior.

Because the child occasionally looked at the paper (a behavior must occur before it can be reinforced), the first step in the shaping sequence could be reinforced. The father took a fairly safe gamble and assumed that his praise would function as a reinforcer for his son. The following events illustrate the shaping of the child's response:*

FATHER: Jimmy, please bring me the paper.
JIMMY: (Glances about, does not look at the paper) No.
FATHER: (Looking at paper) Jimmy, please bring me the paper.
JIMMY: (Looking at the paper) No.
FATHER: (Hugging Jimmy) Good boy, Jimmy! You looked at the paper. Now bring me the paper.
JIMMY: (Seems confused at first, smiles, looks at paper) No.
FATHER: Please bring me the paper, Jimmy.
JIMMY: (Looking at paper) No.
FATHER: (Withholding affection from voice, calmly repeats request) Jimmy, please bring me the paper.
JIMMY: (Looks at paper, seems confused, walks away from it; then, looking at it takes a few steps toward it) No.
FATHER: (Hugging Jimmy) Good boy! You looked at it and you walked toward it. Now get the paper.
JIMMY: (Smiles, walks over to the paper, touches it) No.
FATHER: (Again hugs Jimmy) Good boy. You touched the paper. Now bring it to me.
JIMMY: (Picks up the paper, carries it to his father) No.

Notice that Jimmy persisted in saying "No" even as he complied with his father's request. To an adult, a "No" following a request is a refusal, a negation. To Jimmy, apparently, the word was a sound he had learned to make following a request. He knew that the sound brought him attention, but its complete meaning was obviously unclear to him.

As you can see, shaping is a powerful way to teach a complicated behavior. Animal trainers use if effectively. It also works well with human adults, as can be demonstrated by a simple experiment. A particular teacher may never lecture from the corner of a room, so this response cannot be reinforced. But 10 well-trained students scattered about a large class may be able to use shaping to alter the teacher's behavior. These students should pay attention, smile, and take notes when the teacher makes any move toward the chosen corner of the room, but appear bored or uninterested when the teacher heads in any other direction. Some instructors will change their behavior without any awareness of what's happening and will end up lecturing from the corner.**

Generalization and Discrimination

In our newspaper-fetching example, after the child has been shaped to get the paper, he may start fetching all sorts of things. Such a response is called a

---

*Parents sometimes get nervous when their actions are to be described in a textbook. This father was no exception. He asked that if I used this example (I have), I include his statement (I am) that he was only curious about shaping when he did this. He assured me that he has no intention of training his child to be a compliant slave and that he (the father) really does fetch his own paper and stuff most of the time—honest!

**Caution: The use of such a technique on your professor may be hazardous to your grade.

POSITIVE REINFORCEMENT
The process by which an organism encounters a stimulus (following a response) that has the effect of increasing the probability that the response will be emitted again.

AVOIDANCE LEARNING
The process whereby an organism is reinforced for behaving in a way that avoids an aversive stimulus.

ESCAPE LEARNING
The process whereby an organism is reinforced for escaping from an aversive stimulus.

generalization, because he is responding in the *same* way to different stimuli. If his father does not reinforce him with praise for doing this, the child may soon learn to make a *discrimination* by responding in a *different* way to different stimuli. In this way, he will learn which things his father believes are appropriate to fetch.

You make hundreds of generalizations and discriminations every day. For instance, you generalize shaking hands to a new stimulus (someone you've never met before), and when you leave your home in the morning, you discriminate the door from the wall (allowing the morning of January 1 as an exception).

Most of the techniques for operant conditioning that we have discussed so far were used by the scientists in Project Sea Hunt, which you encountered in the chapter Prologue. The pigeons were gradually shaped to peck a disk for reinforcement (food pellet); then, a discrimination was created. The pigeons received food following a peck only if a small red, orange, or yellow speck was present. Soon the pigeons learned not to bother pecking unless the speck of color was present, since that was the only time reinforcement was available. Finally, after getting used to the helicopter and their Plexiglas container, they were ready to search the seas for downed pilots.

Strengthening a Response

Although *all reinforcement, by definition, strengthens the response that it follows,* a distinction often is made between positive reinforcement and avoidance learning. **Positive reinforcement** occurs when an organism is reinforced for behaving in a way that leads to the occurrence of a pleasant consequence. **Avoidance learning** occurs when an organism is reinforced for behaving in a way that avoids an aversive consequence. If the organism responds in such a way as to terminate an aversive experience, the strengthening of that response is often called **escape learning**. This distinction can be summarized as follows:

Positive Reinforcement
Behavior leads to the occurrence of a pleasant consequence.
Behavior is strengthened.

Avoidance Learning
Behavior leads to the avoidance of something unpleasant.
Behavior is strengthened.

Escape Learning
Behavior leads to the termination of something unpleasant.
Behavior is strengthened.

For example, if an animal successfully avoids a shock by pressing a lever, the lever-pressing response is strengthened. Similarly, if someone changes the oil

Through our conditioning and learning, things which initially mean very little to us become reinforcing.

in her car to avoid the car's breaking down, her actions are strengthened because the car continues to run. Remember, when an aversive stimulus is escaped from or avoided by some action, that response becomes *stronger*.

Note that positive reinforcement and escape learning may occur simultaneously. By eating, for example, we may realize a positive outcome (feeling full and satisfied) and may simultaneously escape from an aversive state (hunger).

Interestingly, a response and a consequent stimulus don't have to be connected in a cause-and-effect sequence to have a reinforcing effect. If a ball player taps home plate with the tip of his bat just before hitting a home run, the plate-tapping behavior may well be reinforced. Since there is no logical connection between tapping the plate and hitting a home run, acquiring such a response is said to result from **superstitious learning.**

SUPERSTITIOUS LEARNING
Behavior learned simply by virtue of the fact that it happened to be followed by a reinforcer or punisher, even though this behavior was not the cause of the stimulus that followed the response.

PUNISHMENT
An aversive stimulus consequence that has the effect of decreasing the strength of an emitted response.

Weakening a Response by Punishment or Extinction

The following paragraphs describe two ways of weakening the strength of a response.

PUNISHMENT.   **Punishment** occurs when a response is followed by an aversive stimulus that *decreases* the strength of the response or maintains the response at a lower level than it occurred originally. Like reinforcement, punishment is something that affects behavior. Remember, people aren't reinforced or punished, behaviors are! The following story illustrates the meaning of this statement:

At 11 o'clock on a Wednesday morning, an alert neighbor spotted a stranger breaking through the front window of the home across the street, and she called the police. Shortly thereafter, two squad cars arrived. Four armed officers stepped from the vehicles. The officers positioned themselves at the front and the back of the house. A few minutes later, the unsuspecting burglar walked out of the front door lugging a color television. He was greeted by two of the officers leveling shotguns at him and he promptly surrendered. By making it obvious that fighting or running away was likely to lead to unpleasant consequences, the officers had practically ensured that the burglar would make this choice.

The burglar was brought to trial and, not surprisingly, was found guilty. The judge pronounced a 3-year prison sentence. Later that night, the burglar awaited transportation from the city jail to the state prison. He was depressed and miserable. Pondering his hapless condition, he vowed to turn over a new leaf. He swore on everything that was dear to him that he would never, never again break into a house—through a front window.

In this story, a behavior was punished, but not the one that society had hoped to alter. Instead of teaching the burglar not to steal, his arrest taught him not to steal stupidly. As you can see, before you employ reinforcement and punishment techniques, you should ascertain which behavior will be strengthened or weakened.

Punishment can be extremely powerful, however, and it can control behavior. Sometimes, punishment is the most effective means of stopping a behavior. This outcome is especially certain if the punishment is severe. Anyone who has ever tried to cook bacon while naked will tell you that the adverse consequences of that behavior diminished the probability of doing it again. The distinction between escape or avoidance learning and punishment can be summarized as follows:

Avoidance or Escape Learning
Behavior leads to the avoidance or termination of something unpleasant. Behavior is *strengthened.*

Seeing-eye dogs are trained through the use of positive reinforcement, shaping and discrimination. Punishment is rarely, if ever, used.

Punishment

Behavior leads to something aversive or unpleasant.
Behavior is weakened.

Although punishment can be an effective way of terminating or suppressing a behavior, it can have serious drawbacks. When a behavior is punished, especially if it is punished severely, there is often a general suppression of other behaviors. The person or animal may then become withdrawn and less active. Punishment can also lead to hostility and aggression, especially if it is accompanied by pain.

Operant conditioning is essential in training seeing-eye dogs, but the trainers almost never use punishment. If a dog walks forward when it should have stayed, beating it to punish the inappropriate move could lead to a general suppression of behaviors, and the animal might cower in a corner and no longer respond to commands. Or the dog might react aggressively and counterattack. Because of these potential drawbacks, trainers use techniques other than punishment to teach the dog and to correct mistakes. If the dog walks when it shouldn't, the trainer will bring the dog back and try again. If the dog stays the next time, the trainer will reinforce the dog for staying with love and praise. In this way, the dog learns to stay, and the inappropriate behavior is eliminated *without punishment*. The more the animal is taught to respond appropriately, the less chance it has to respond inappropriately.

Unfortunately, the same can't always be said for the way in which we treat our children. The use of spanking to control children's behavior seems to be growing in popularity. A number of people advocate spanking in the schools in order to maintain discipline. Many psychologists, however, are concerned about the growing use of spanking. Based on what you have learned about learning in this chapter, you should be able to appreciate the following arguments against spanking as a technique for controlling children's behavior:

1. Through the process of classical conditioning, the parent or teacher becomes paired with pain, so that the adult comes to elicit a fear response from the child, even without inflicting punishment.
2. Through operant conditioning, the child often is reinforced in such a way that he or she may avoid the adult, lie to the adult, or run away from home.
3. According to research on punishment, mild spankings usually have only a temporary effect because the child becomes habituated to them; this, in turn, shapes some adults into eventually administering severe and physically dangerous spankings.
4. Additional research on operant conditioning has demonstrated that many nonphysical techniques are highly successful in controlling and modifying children's behavior. Supporting this assertion is the fact that many well-behaved children and adults have never been spanked or hit by either of their parents—I never was (so much for spare the rod, spoil the child).
5. Last, and perhaps most compelling, when parents or other adults spank a child, the child may be learning more than the adult intended. By watching parents who choose to spank, children who are spanked apparently learn that physical force is an appropriate early response to select when they are frustrated with someone; that it's all right to choose to hit people; and that spanking is something that parents are supposed to do (which may help to explain why so many child abusers were themselves abused as children) (Fairchild & Erwin, 1977).

EXTINCTION.   Another way of weakening a response is through extinction. As we discussed earlier, extinction in operant conditioning is the weakening or elimination of a response by removal of a reinforcer that maintained the response. If you like to buy a cup of hot coffee from a particular machine every day, but suddenly discover that the machine has begun to give you the coffee first *and then the cup,* your "coffee-machine-patronizing behavior" will eventually stop because the reinforcement has been discontinued.

Even after a response has been eliminated through extinction, however, it may briefly reappear. Perhaps the following Friday you'll give the coffee machine another try. Other creatures also show this behavior (not buying coffee—but rather, once again checking out the situation sometime after extinction has been in effect). It's almost as though the organism had forgotten that the response no longer served its purpose, or as though the organism were checking whether the response would work at a later time. This brief recurrence of a response following extinction is called **spontaneous recovery.** Spontaneous recovery also occurs in classical conditioning. Following extinction, a CS may briefly regain the power to elicit a CR.

Primary and Secondary Reinforcement

You learn because your experiences, in conjunction with your physical needs and genetic tendencies, affect you in some meaningful way. Stimuli necessary for sustaining life can obtain the power to reinforce simply by being withheld for a time; you do not have to learn to need or want them. The stimuli in this category include water, food, and air, as well as proper temperature and barometric pressure. Such stimuli are known as **primary reinforcers.** Other reinforcers, such as money, status, attention, green traffic lights, or even bottle caps (if you would be willing to work for one), are known as acquired or **secondary reinforcers.** You have learned that these things are reinforcers because of their association with primary or other secondary reinforcers. In this sense, primary reinforcers are built in, and secondary reinforcers are learned (White & Milner, 1992).

Schedules of Reinforcement

You aren't reinforced for everything you do, but you do receive reinforcement every once in a while. Oddly, once a behavior is learned, reinforcing it less often may cause it to persist. To demonstrate this phenomenon, we can shape a hungry rat to press a lever by feeding the rat whenever it successfully presses the lever. In the beginning, the rat is reinforced for each correct press. This is known as **continuous reinforcement.** Although continuous reinforcement will lead to the highest rate of responding (Nevin, 1988), once reinforcement is discontinued, the lever-pressing behavior will extinguish rapidly. If, however, we begin reinforcing every fifth press instead of withholding reinforcement entirely, the behavior will not extinguish rapidly. Instead, the rat will learn to persist, at least for as long as five presses. Once the rat becomes used to five presses per reinforcer, the behavior is easily maintained. If we gradually increase the number of presses required for reinforcement, the rat may eventually make as many as 500 presses in order to receive one reinforcer (a miserable, but persistent rat). Such a reinforcement schedule, in which not every response is reinforced, is called an **intermittent schedule,** and it can lead to persistent responding. For instance, if we placed our rat on an extinction schedule after it had become accustomed to 500 presses per reinforcer, it might press several thousand times before it finally gave up, because it had become used to giving 500 presses. Table 8.2 presents four different schedules of reinforcement. Although there are many complex schedules, these four are often considered basic. It is very rare that behavior is reinforced continuously. Most reinforcement occurs according to intermittent schedules. Once you have learned these four, you will see how much of the reinforcement in your life occurs on one

SPONTANEOUS RECOVERY
In operant conditioning, the brief recurrence of a response following extinction. In classical conditioning, the brief recurrence of the eliciting power of a CS after extinction.

PRIMARY REINFORCER
A stimulus that can be innately reinforcing, such as food or sleep.

SECONDARY REINFORCER
A reinforcer whose value is learned through its association with primary reinforcers or other secondary reinforcers. It is also called an acquired reinforcer.

CONTINUOUS REINFORCEMENT
Reinforcement of a particular response each time it occurs.

INTERMITTENT SCHEDULE
Reinforcement of a particular response, but not each time the response occurs.

DISCRIMINATIVE STIMULI
Stimuli in whose presence a response is likely to occur. Discriminative stimuli function as cues enabling us to know when a response is likely to be reinforced.

STIMULUS CONTROL
From learning theory, the idea that discriminative stimuli come to control the behavior they cue.

or more of these schedules. By manipulating or changing schedules of reinforcement, psychologists often are able to control or change behavior.

Discrimination and Stimulus Control

It would be a chaotic world if operant responses were likely to occur at any time or in any place. This does not happen, because your learning has been such that your operant responses are controlled by various stimuli or cues, called **discriminative stimuli.** In the presence of a discriminative stimulus, a particular behavior is more likely to occur. Experience has taught you the meaning of these cues, and you have come to rely on them in assessing which actions or behaviors are likely to yield satisfactory results. For example, what cues should be present to increase the probability that you will undress? A comfortable bed, sleepiness, and a clock that reads midnight? The privacy of a bathroom and the sound of running water? Or perhaps a drum roll and a spotlight? People may discriminate stimuli differently. A stimulus that functions as a cue for you may not be a cue for someone else. Once these cues are well learned, they come to control the times and places in which certain behaviors are likely to occur. This result is known as **stimulus control.** How do red traffic lights, ringing telephones, and timepieces "control" your behavior?

You do not need to be aware of discriminative stimuli for them to affect your behavior. Smokers often find themselves unconsciously lighting up at the

TABLE 8.2 ◆ FOUR BASIC INTERMITTENT REINFORCEMENT SCHEDULES			
TYPE	DEFINITION	EXAMPLE	RESULT
Determined by the number of responses			
Fixed ratio (FR)	Reinforcement is given after every *x* number of responses; e.g., FR 4 = every fourth response is reinforced	A worker is paid for every 20 widgets she makes (FR 20).	Produces fairly regular responses as long as fixed ratio isn't set so high that extinction occurs before first reinforcement
Variable ratio (VR)	Reinforcement is given after every *x* number of responses *on the average*; e.g., VR 4 = on the average, every fourth response is reinforced, but reinforcement may follow any response	Old man Crabtree is reinforced with a dead fly for every third swing of his swatter, on the average (VR 3).	Produces high and stable rate of responses
Determined by the passage of time before a response can be reinforced			
Fixed interval (FI)	Reinforcement is given following *first* response to occur after a fixed amount of time has passed; e.g., FI 1 minute = first response to occur after 1 minute has passed is reinforced	A cook waits for a pie to be done (FI 30 minutes) before taking it out of the oven and serving it.	Produces very low rate of responses until interval approaches or is passed, then response probability rises rapidly
Variable interval (VI)	Reinforcement is given following *first* response to occur after a certain amount of time, *on the average*, has passed; e.g., VI 10 minutes = on the average, reinforcement follows first response to occur after 10 minutes (it may be 6 minutes, 13 minutes, and so on, but the average is 10 minutes)	A resident checks his mailbox occasionally throughout the day while waiting for the postal carrier.	Produces very stable and uniform rate of responses

same places and at the same times. This is probably an example of stimulus control. Furthermore, one cue can lead directly to another, creating a whole series of cues, responses, and reinforcements in chainlike fashion. Collectively, the series is known as a **habit.**

The Relativity of Reinforcement

We have seen how different reinforcers and stimuli can control behavior. But behavior itself—that is, the opportunity to engage in a particular behavior—also can control our actions. Years ago, psychologist David Premack demonstrated that the behaviors an organism is more likely to emit can be used to reinforce the behaviors an organism is less likely to emit (Premack, 1959). This observation became known as the **Premack principle.** The Premack principle is sometimes referred to as "grandma's principle" (although parents, no doubt, use it more often) because it is embodied in statements like "Eat your green beans and you may have some pie." In such an instance, engaging in the less likely behavior (eating green beans) becomes more likely because it leads to a chance to engage in a behavior that the organism is more likely to emit (pie eating).

Initially, psychologists studying operant conditioning were interested in how reinforcers strengthened behaviors. Premack, however, showed that organisms, including humans, appear to have a hierarchy of behaviors, ordered according to which are more or less reinforcing, and that the environment structures how and when any of the behaviors in the hierarchy may be allowed. Also, depending on how recently certain behaviors have been allowed to occur, the positions of behaviors on the hierarchy can change (Timberlake & Allison, 1974); that is, once you're sick of pie, you might actually prefer the green beans. By knowing the current state of an organism's behavior hierarchy, it is sometimes possible

HABIT
A series of cues, responses, and reinforcers linked together in such a way that each stimulus consequence reinforces the person's previous response and cues the next response.

PREMACK PRINCIPLE
The concept developed by David Premack that reinforcement is relative, not absolute, so that if two behaviors have different probabilities of occurrence at any given time, the chance to engage in the more probable will serve to reinforce engaging in the less probable.

Intermittent schedules of reinforcement are a powerful means of controlling behavior. Such schedules strengthen responses by making them resistant to extinction. Here a human subject is operating a lever on an intermittent schedule of reinforcement, just like the rat discussed in the text. By carefully manipulating the schedule of reinforcement, casino operators are able to take in more money than they are forced to give out in reinforcement.

SOCIAL LEARNING
Learning by observing the actions of others. It is also called vicarious conditioning or observational learning.

🧬 CHALLENGES TO THE BEHAVIORIST VIEW

Both classical and operant conditioning are today considered to play important roles in the development of behavior. They are not the only forces, however. Other people have added to the view of learning presented by the behaviorists, not so much by attempting to show that the experimental results obtained in behavioral research are wrong, but rather by showing that there is more to learning than the behaviorists have proposed. The two fields of psychological research that have most expanded our understanding of learning are the views provided by the social-cognitive and the ethological perspectives. Let's examine them in turn.

🧬 SOCIAL LEARNING—OBSERVATION AND IMITATION

You have seen that an organism can learn as the result of classical or operant conditioning. Now we will investigate a third possible way to learn—by observing another organism's behavior. This is known as **social learning.**

The Importance of Models

Albert Bandura and several of his colleagues at Stanford University have argued that social learning is a distinct kind of learning that requires new principles in order to understand it. Bandura, Ross, and Ross demonstrated their thesis in 1963 in an experiment now considered by many to be a classic. They

Both boys and girls who watched a live actor model violence were more likely to imitate the violence than children who had not seen the model.

asked nursery-school children to observe an adult **model** striking a large inflated Bobo doll with a mallet. The model also hit, kicked, and sat on the doll. *Neither the model nor the observing children were directly reinforced at any time during the session.*

Later, after the model had gone, the children were secretly observed as they played in a toy-filled room with the Bobo doll. For comparison, other children who had not seen the model's behavior were also allowed to interact with the doll. The results of the experiment clearly demonstrated that the children who had observed the model were far more likely to be aggressive, in imitation of the model's behavior, than were the other children. These results would not have been predicted by classical or operant conditioning theories, since the imitation seemed to be occurring without reinforcement.

If you consider that learning by trial and error can be very time-consuming, and even dangerous, you will readily see the value of learning by imitating the behavior someone else has already learned or acquired. If our learning were restricted to what we could gain through classical and operant conditioning, our ability to master our world would be severely limited. Bandura emphasizes this point in the following description of a driving instructor attempting to teach a student to operate a car strictly by using the principles of reinforcement:

As a first step our trainer, who has been carefully programmed to produce head nods, resonant hm-hms, and other verbal reinforcers, loads up with an ample supply of candy, chewing gum and filter-tip cigarettes. A semi-willing subject, who has never observed a person driving an automobile, and a parked car complete the picture. Our trainer might have to wait a long time before the subject emits an orienting response toward the vehicle. At the moment the subject does look even in the general direction of the car, this response is immediately reinforced and gradually he begins to gaze longingly at the stationary automobile. Similarly, approach responses in the desired direction are promptly reinforced in order to bring the subject in proximity to the car. Eventually, through the skillful use of differential reinforcement, the trainer will teach the subject to open and close the car door. With perseverance he will move the subject from the back seat or any other inappropriate location chosen in this trial-and-error ramble until at length the subject is shaped up behind the steering wheel. It is unnecessary to depict the remainder of the training procedure beyond noting that it will likely prove an exceedingly tedious, not to mention an expensive and hazardous enterprise. (Bandura, 1962, pp. 212–213)

MODEL
In social learning theory, anyone who demonstrates a behavior that others observe.

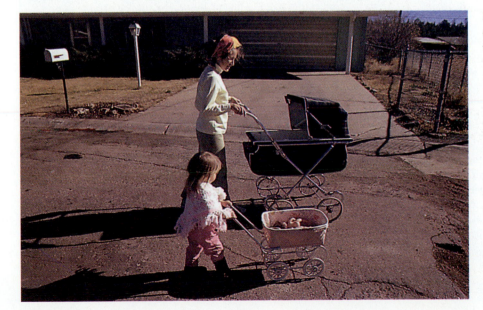

Social learning through imitation may often occur without the need for direct reinforcement.

BEHAVIOR MODIFICATION . . .
. . . OR HOW YOU GONNA KEEP 'EM DOWN ON THE BEACH AFTER THEY'VE SEEN JAWS III

Albert Bandura and his colleagues at Stanford once placed an advertisement in a newspaper offering free aid to anyone with a snake phobia (an unrealistic fear of snakes). Many people answered the ad. As it turned out, the majority of respondents were men who held outdoor jobs and were deathly afraid of encountering a snake. It was hoped that a behavior-modification program could help these volunteers to overcome their phobia. **Behavior modification** is an application of learning theory. By arranging particular associations between stimuli or particular consequences for behavior, or by modeling the behavior that is desired, it is possible to change a subject's behavior; that is, the environment and the experiences of the subject are purposely manipulated in order to change behavior.

In the first part of the behavior-modification program, Bandura made certain that his volunteers did indeed have a snake phobia. He asked each subject to handle a snake, but not one was willing to do so under any circumstances. Next, Bandura used models to help his subjects overcome their phobia. The models did not have a snake phobia. They approached and handled the snakes while the subjects watched. For any male subjects who so desired, Bandura even enlisted the aid of a striptease artist who worked with a boa constrictor named Squeezer (Bandura, 1977). Many of the men found themselves sitting in the middle rows, wanting to be close to the show but far away from the snake.

The results of this experiment in behavior modification demonstrated, as have many similar experiments, the power of modeling as a behavior-modification technique. Within 48 hours, the subjects could comfortably handle the snake that they had so feared at the beginning of the experiment. In addition, no recurrences of phobia were reported when the subjects were interviewed a month later.

Use of a model is usually incorporated into a more comprehensive behavior-modification program that includes both classical and operant conditioning. A good example of such a comprehensive program is described in the book *Toilet Training in Less than a Day* by Nathan Azrin and Richard Foxx (1974).

Toilet training doesn't have to be a 3-year trial. It can be accomplished in under 24 hours using the learning principles that have been described in this chapter. To see how this is possible, let's examine some of the techniques used in the toilet training program developed by Azrin and Foxx. As you'll discover, this program takes account of both the child's physical abilities and his or her environment.

1. The authors recommend that no attempt be made to train children who are much younger than 24 months. Children younger than this usually do not have the muscle development necessary for bladder and bowel control.

2. A learning environment should be created in which the child and parent are together without distraction for the whole day. In this way, all their energy can be devoted to learning and strengthening the new behavior.

3. The steps in the desired behavior sequence are as follows: The child will go to the potty chair when the need arises, lower his or her training pants, urinate or defecate, wipe where appropriate, raise the training pants, remove the plastic pot from the potty chair, empty its contents into the toilet, flush the toilet, and return the plastic pot to the potty chair.

4. The authors give a number of tips for accomplishing these behaviors more easily. They suggest, for example, using large, loose training pants, which are easier to raise and lower.

5. Instrument learning is achieved as the child's appropriate behaviors are reinforced through lavish praise and the administration of large amounts of juice or soda. Drinking liquids makes urination more likely, giving the child more chances to learn the desired response; remember, a behavior must occur before it can be reinforced.

6. The technique of modeling is incorporated in an ingenious way by making use of a doll that wets. At the beginning of the Azrin and Foxx program, before anything else, the child helps the parent "toilet train" the doll. The child watches as the doll models the desired behavior and then sees that the doll is immediately rewarded for its good behavior with praise and juice (administered to the doll in a special baby bottle that refills its reservoir). This is an effective technique because an observer is more likely to imitate a model, even if it is a doll, if she sees that the model's behavior is reinforced.

Social learning can be observed in other species as well. Dachshund puppies learned to pull a food cart sooner when they saw other puppies doing it than when they didn't observe such behavior (Adler & Adler, 1977). Bottle-nosed dolphins learned to pull a rope into their pool by watching other dolphins (Adler & Adler, 1978). Three sea lions learned to pull a rope into the center of their cage after they had watched a fourth learn the task by the shaping method (Adler & Adler, 1977). Rats learned by observing rat leaders who were the first to discover the best route through a cage door (Konopasky & Telegdy, 1977). Another study demonstrated that naive mice learned to copulate sooner by watching other mice do it (Hayashi & Kimura, 1976). Many studies have demonstrated this kind of observational learning in other species.

Social learning has even been indicated in invertebrates. In one study, octopuses watched other octopuses being rewarded for attacking a colored ball. The octopuses that watched learned to attack the same ball sooner (Fiorito & Scotto, 1992). It is assumed, however, that social learning is a higher-order cognitive function than something like classical conditioning, so it was surprising to see an invertebrate exhibit such learning. This has led some researchers to note that octopuses in general are reluctant to attack a novel stimulus. This reluctance is part of the animal's instinctive repertoire. Perhaps while observing the first octopuses being rewarded for attacking, the second group of octopuses merely became more familiar with the ball and were, therefore, more willing to attack when it was their turn (Biederman, 1993).

Performance versus Acquisition

Although learning can apparently take place simply through observation of another person's behavior, reinforcement can be an important supplement in social learning. Consider a second experiment conducted by Bandura in 1965. On one occasion, a group of young children watched as a model was rewarded with juice and candy for being aggressive, and on another occasion a different group of children watched as the same model was scolded for the same aggression. The results of the experiment indicated that the consequences of the model's behavior were very important in determining whether the children would imitate the model. The children who had observed the model receiving juice and candy for aggressive behavior became more aggressive. The children who had observed the model being scolded for aggressive behavior rarely imitated the aggression.

At first glance, this experiment may seem to indicate that reinforcement is necessary for social learning. We can resolve this problem by distinguishing between performing a behavior and acquiring it. Reinforcing or punishing the model's behavior did affect whether the children imitated the model. Nevertheless, the children who had seen the model disciplined for aggression were quite able, when offered reinforcers for demonstrating what the model had done, to recall and demonstrate the model's behavior, even though they had not spontaneously imitated the model before. This experiment showed that children who observed a model being disciplined for aggressive behavior were unlikely to imitate (perform) the behavior but that they did learn (acquire) the behavior, and could imitate it at a later time if the reinforcing and punishing contingencies changed.

The term **latent learning** is sometimes used to describe this kind of incidental learning, when the learning may not be apparent from an animal's or a person's behavior. This kind of learning often occurs in the absence of reward. Rats placed in a maze and allowed to wander for a time without reinforcement will later, when reinforced, learn to find the goal box (where there is food) faster than will rats who are new to the maze. Latent learning apparently occurs in the animals as they wander about in the maze. Although no

BEHAVIOR MODIFICATION
A set of procedures for changing human behavior, especially by using behavior therapy and operant conditioning techniques.

LATENT LEARNING
Learning that occurs in the absence of any obvious reinforcement, apparently as a result of just being exposed to stimuli.

COGNITION
Mental activity involving perceiving, thinking, remembering, or problem solving.

COGNITIVE PSYCHOLOGY
The study of behavior as it relates to perceiving, thinking, remembering, or problem solving.

direct reinforcement was given, just the experience of walking through the maze apparently taught the rats to find their way through it.

Other factors besides reinforcement and punishment of a model's behavior can affect the likelihood that imitation will occur. For instance, the perceived status of the model can be important. Some of the earliest social learning studies demonstrated that the behavior of an entire group of people can best be altered by having the individuals with the highest status (as perceived by the group) model the desired behavior, rather than by attempting to influence each group member singly (Lippitt, Polansky, & Rosen, 1952; Polansky, Lippitt, & Redl, 1950). Such prominent models can have a powerful effect, especially when presented to large numbers of observers by mass media (such as newspapers, movies, or television). In addition, a behavior is more likely to be imitated when the models are nurturant, aggressive, or similar to the observers. Imitation also is more likely when a person can already perform the component subskills of the behavior that has been modeled and when the person's usual environment is similar to that in which the model was originally observed.

Of course, whether a particular model will be perceived as a person of high status, or whether a model's behavior will appear worthy of imitation, depends largely on the thoughts of the observer. For this reason, social learning theorists have become interested in the thinking process and its role in the formation of beliefs and attitudes.

COGNITIVE LEARNING

Cognition refers to thinking. Philosophically, social learning is considered to be an interaction between environment and thought, rather than mainly a function of environmental input. As Albert Bandura put it, to exclude thinking from any theory of learning would be like attributing "Shakespeare's masterpieces to his prior instruction in the mechanics of writing" (Bandura, 1978). Because of this philosophical viewpoint, social learning theory cannot rightly be considered to come under the classification of "behaviorism."

Human beings think, and thinking affects behavior. Traditional behaviorists, especially in Watson's day, were unwilling to examine the mind or thought processes because these phenomena were not directly observable. Since then, learning theorists have devoted increasing time to exploring thought processes, problem solving, and the internal understanding we have of our world. As a result, most of them are no longer "strict behaviorists." The study of thinking and its influence on our behavior is known as **cognitive psychology.***

We respond to the world not just through our conditioned responses but also through our knowledge of it. Does a dog do the same? Do dogs think? Most dog owners assume that they do. Suppose you come home and make a sound as you unlock the door; your dog will be waiting to greet you on the other side (assuming you have a dog—if you don't have a dog, there probably won't be one waiting for you—but I digress). Why was your dog waiting there (assuming you have a dog)? Did it have a mental image of you on the other side of the door? Did it know from the sounds you made that it was you? Or did it simply hear a series of cues, or discriminative stimuli, and run for the door because that response in the presence of those cues had previously been reinforced? Moreover, did the dog become excited and wag its tail because it had been classically conditioned, so that the sounds of the door being unlocked aroused its autonomic nervous system—a conditioned arousal? If the dog merely responded to cues and classical conditioning, then it ran to the door, became excited, and wagged its tail without having any "idea" why it acted

---

*The topic of cognitive psychology is covered in depth in Chapter 10.

in this way. The question of whether dogs or other animals rely on mental representations of their world is debatable. All we know for sure is that humans often use mental or cognitive abilities when they interact with their environment.

A cognitive representation of the world is a valuable asset. With it, you can manipulate, alter, or change things mentally to examine possible outcomes before you actually do anything. You use your cognitive understanding to orient yourself to particular problems or situations. A rat running a maze in search of food has to learn which turns to make in order to find the food. After a number of trials, it learns that at a certain corner it should turn right, and at another corner it should turn right again, and soon it will come to the food. When you enter a strange town or go to a new neighborhood, you may similarly have to find your way around by trial and error or by memorizing certain details. Eventually, however, you become oriented, and you acquire what is known as a **cognitive map,** an internal understanding of the locations of things in relation to one another.

In the late 1940s, psychologist Edward Tolman came to the conclusion that rats weren't as stupid as everyone thought, and that they, too, had cognitive maps. Working with rats that had learned their way through a maze (see Figure 8.11), he found that if a particular path was blocked, the rats would attempt to find another path, one never used before but *lying in the same general direction as the food* (see Figure 8.12) (Tolman, Ritchie, & Kalish, 1964). Tolman referred to this tendency as **place learning.** Interestingly, place learning is not limited to mammals or even vertebrates. Honeybees have also been found to rely on place learning to find food and return home (Gould, 1986). We now know that many animal species employ rich cognitive maps, especially in situations in which food gathering and storage are involved (Roitblat & von Fersen, 1992).

To better understand a cognitive map, imagine that you've just entered the living room of a place in which you used to live. Stand there for a moment. Now point in the direction of your bedroom. You've just used a cognitive map.

Researcher Emil Menzel conducted an experiment in which he examined the cognitive maps of chimpanzees. While carrying a chimpanzee with him around a large field, Menzel hid food in 18 locations, usually in clumps of grass or behind other natural cover. Then, returning to a starting point at the edge of the field, he released the chimp who had seen the food hidden and five other chimpanzee companions. As you might guess, the knowledgeable chimp was the one who found almost all the food. What interested the researchers most was that the knowledgeable chimp took the most efficient route to the food, a route that had no obvious relationship to the path along which he had originally been carried (Menzel, as cited by Miller, 1984b). Clearly, the chimp had not simply learned mechanically where to go, but had a grasp of the

COGNITIVE MAP
A mental representation of the location of things in relation to each other in a given environment.

PLACE LEARNING
Acquiring an understanding of the location of things relative to each other in an environment through experience with the environment.

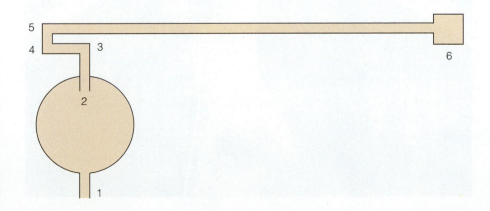

◆ **FIGURE 8.11**

A maze like that used by Tolman to train rats. The rats had to learn their way through the maze, traveling along in the order of the numbers 1 through 6 to reach food at location 6.

◆ FIGURE 8.12

In this experiment, Tolman presented the rats with a new maze of many corridors, but he blocked the standard route shown in Figure 8.11, which the rats had learned. According to behavior theory, an operant gradient of generalization should be in effect, making corridors I and H the most likely choices (they are closest to the blocked corridor). Surprisingly, corridor E was the prime choice! Corridor E leads in the general direction of position 6, where the food is located (who said rats weren't smart?). Tolman called the rats' ability "place learning" because the rats seemed to have a general idea about where they wanted to go.

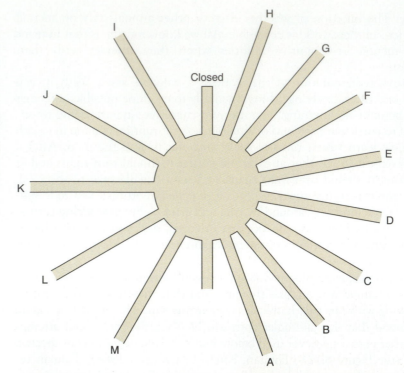

Rats running mazes have demonstrated that they have a cognitive map, or mental representation, of the placement of locations in space.

relationship between his own location and other important locations in the field. This enabled the chimp to take shortcuts; that is, to cover ground he'd never been across before. Another way of saying this is that he *knew* where he was going (something we can't always say about ourselves). The chimp did not have a perfect score, however—he did not find all the food. But the researchers began laughing when they tried to find the food that the chimp has missed. They, too, had forgotten some of the hiding places and ended up doing some intensive searching!

Although cognitive maps are mental representations, some geographers and mapmakers have actually attempted to draw them. By asking many people who live in a city to indicate where they think major landmarks and important places are, mapmakers have been able to regroup locations statistically to represent a mental map that people have of their city. This kind of work is known as **behavioral geography** (Parfit, 1984). Behavioral geographers have discovered that the places people like to go to are often thought to be closer than they actually are, while the places people don't like to go to are thought to be farther away. Dangerous neighborhoods, which people often avoid, are thought to be farther away and smaller than they actually are. Poorer people generally think that places are farther away than wealthier people do, and, since they often cannot afford transportation, places really are farther away for them in a sense (see Figure 8.13). These data indicate that different life experiences influence place learning.

In Chapter 10, we'll examine cognitive psychology in greater detail. We'll see that a new cognitive view of learning has been built on the foundation created by our knowledge of classical conditioning, operant conditioning, and social learning. This new understanding of learning considers how mental processes influence what and how we learn.

INHERITANCE AND THE BIOLOGY OF BEHAVIOR

You have seen how social learning theorists and cognitive psychologists have challenged a basic assumption of behaviorism by opening the mind and thought processes to experimental study. Another significant challenge to behaviorism has been mounted from a different quarter. In the many decades since the publication of Skinner's work, we have come to realize that it is also important to know the specific abilities, limitations, and tendencies to learn of any given species. Although Skinner readily admitted that there were differences among species' abilities to learn, he did not believe these differences were very important. Now researchers know that these differences are important. Certain animals, including humans, learn certain things readily and do not learn other things. For instance, you have learned a full, rich language based on a grammar; a dog or cat never will. These specific species differences appear to be due to the forces of evolution (see Figure 8.14).

Throughout this century, research on inherited behaviors has attracted great interest, especially in Europe. People who specialize in this area of research are called ethologists, and their field of study is **ethology** (Hess, 1970). Ethologists usually conduct naturalistic observations, and they also are interested in learned behavior. Ethologists have strongly argued that no two organisms have exactly the same behavioral capacities and that many of the differences among organisms are due to genetically inherited biological attributes and predispositions.

Research in this field began to grow significantly after Konrad Lorenz published a paper in 1937 describing the *following response*. At one time, Lorenz made certain that he was the first moving object that some newborn goslings

BEHAVIORAL GEOGRAPHY
A statistical technique that enables mapmakers to generate actual representations of cognitive maps. Behavioral geography has as its goal the production of information that will aid developers and planners in creating environments that are more compatible with people's perceptions.

ETHOLOGY
The study of human and animal behavior from a biological point of view; it is characterized by the study of animals in their natural environments.

◆ **FIGURE 8.13**

The streets on this map are from downtown Columbus, Ohio. The buildings on this map represent a low-income resident's cognitive understanding of where the buildings are located. The dot associated with each building shows its actual location in Columbus. In the low-income resident's cognitive map, the buildings are farther away from one another than they are in reality.
(SOURCE: *Parfit, 1984, p. 129.*)

IMPRINTING
As used by ethologists, a species-specific bonding that occurs within a limited period early in the life of the organism and that is relatively unmodifiable thereafter.

CANALIZATION
The process by which behaviors, due to genetic predisposition, are learned extremely easily, almost inevitably. The more canalized a behavior is, the more difficult it is to change or alter.

saw. From that time on, the goslings followed him everywhere he went, even swimming! It seemed to Lorenz that the first object to move past these goslings was "stamped into" the animals' brains as the object to be followed. Lorenz called this phenomenon **imprinting.** He also observed that imprinting could occur only during a *critical period* lasting from hatching until about 2 days later. The most effective imprinting occurred approximately 14 hours after hatching. Through the efforts of ethologists, researchers have a fuller appreciation of the fact that the tendency to behave in certain ways can be inherited (Gould & Marler, 1987).

Canalization

To what degree do inherited behaviors exist in humans? While it is true that we do possess a number of simple inherited reflexes, such as coughing and blinking, human beings show their behavioral inheritance more in terms of *tendencies* to learn some things more easily than others. This is the phenomenon of **canalization.*** A behavior is said to be canalized if there is an inherited predisposition within the nervous system to learn the behavior. Canalization occurs not just in human beings but in most other species as well. Unlike simple reflexes such as sneezing or coughing, canalized behaviors must be learned; it's just that the "prewired" organization of a given species' nervous system makes certain behaviors very easy to learn. Washburn and Hamburg (1965) described the phenomenon as follows:

What is inherited is ease of learning rather than fixed instinctive patterns. The species easily, almost inevitably, learns the essential behaviors for its survival. So, although it is true that monkeys learn to be social, they are so constructed that under normal

*Some researchers prefer to use the term preparedness (Seligman, 1970).

◆ **FIGURE 8.14**

Species specificity can play an important role in determining which behaviors can be acquired. Many behaviors, as Skinner suggested, can be acquired by a vast number of species according to the same basic learning principles. Other behaviors, however, are acquired either easily or with great difficulty depending on the unique characteristics of a given species. In some instances, species specificity is so important that it determines whether a behavior is either almost certain to be acquired or impossible to acquire.

BEHAVIORS TO BE ACQUIRED (LEARNED)	
Almost all species are able to acquire response (e.g., turning around to obtain a food reward) Human turns, bird turns, fish turns, worm turns	
Certain species are able to acquire response easily (e.g., fetching) Human retrieves, dog retrieves, monkey retrieves, elephant retrieves	Certain species are able to acquire response with difficulty (e.g., fetching) Cat retrieves, rhinoceros retrieves, shark retrieves, robin retrieves
Certain species are most likely to acquire response Humans—tool use Doves—nest building Wild dogs—pack hunting	Certain species are almost certain not to acquire response Tigers—tool use Dolphins—nest building Orangutans—pack hunting
Extremely canalized behavior—certain species almost certain to acquire Humans—language Male fox—scent marking territory Peregrine falcon—high speed dive for attacking prey	Behaviors impossible for certain species to acquire Worms—language Adult elephant—hopping on one foot Kangaroo—head stand

SPECIES SPECIFICTY Less important

SPECIES SPECIFICTY More important

circumstances this learning always takes place. Similarly, human beings learn to talk, but they inherit structures that make this inevitable, except under the most peculiar circumstances. (Washburn & Hamburg, 1965, pp. 5–6)

Highly canalized behaviors are not only almost inevitable but also highly resistant to the effects of experience. Conversely, weakly canalized behaviors are highly susceptible to change due to experience.

Canalization means, then, that certain kinds of learning are more or less likely to occur because of our biologically inherited predispositions. For example, if a loud noise scared you while you were eating a hot dog, the experience probably wouldn't affect your fondness for that food even if you had been very scared. If, however, you ate a hot dog and coincidentally caught the flu, which caused you to become extremely sick to your stomach, your desire for that food might be gone forever, and it probably wouldn't help much to realize that the food hadn't caused the nausea. Researchers have found that animals make associations between food and nausea very easily (Garcia & Koelling, 1966), whereas they do not easily make associations between food and a loud sound. From an evolutionary standpoint, a built-in or canalized tendency for the nervous system to make such associations is sensible. If an animal was startled while eating a certain food, there would be no survival benefit in thereafter avoiding that food. But if the animal became sick after eating a certain food, there would be a good reason to avoid that food in the future.

Even the seemingly inherited behaviors of a robin building a nest, a cat cleaning itself, a salmon returning upstream to spawn are really examples of canalization. The behaviors themselves aren't simply "in the genes"; robins have to *learn* to build nests (they're pretty clumsy at first), cats *learn* to clean themselves, and salmon *learn* to swim upstream to spawn. What the animals have inherited, then, is a very strong tendency, or "drive," to learn these behaviors (Gould & Marler, 1987). Being carried in the genes, the inherited drives to learn these behaviors are passed from one generation to the next (Scheller & Axel, 1984).

THE BIOLOGY OF LEARNING AND CONDITIONING

Since the days of Pavlov and Watson, researchers have conducted thousands of classical-conditioning experiments with animals and humans. Many different conditioned stimuli have been paired with unconditioned stimuli. During all those years and experiments, it was assumed, of course, that somewhere in the brain a change had to occur during conditioning that placed the conditioning experience into memory. There had to be some mechanism to record and keep the experience, or else how could an organism change its behavior owing to experience? Exactly how such a mechanism might work, however, was anybody's guess. Some people believed that special groups of cells in certain brain areas might control learning. Others argued that learning might be a diffuse general ability, found to occur fairly evenly among cell groups throughout the entire brain. Practically no one expected or suggested that learning might occur at the level of single cells. Now we know that individual neurons have the ability to be conditioned.

In one single-cell conditioning experiment, researchers classically conditioned a single photoreceptor cell by using a bright light (US) paired with a current passed through a microelectrode into the cell (CS). Afterward, when the cell received the current (CS), it behaved as though it had been exposed to light (CR). This surprising result demonstrated classical conditioning at the most basic level (Farley, Richards, Ling, Liman, & Alkon, 1983).

Further research along these lines has shown that an individual cell not only can be conditioned but also can display the processes of extinction and higher-order conditioning (Barnes, 1987a). Of course, this discovery doesn't tell us whether particular locations in the brain contain or hold experiences or how large these areas might be.

Another interesting study, however, provided a hint as to where some conditioned experiences might reside. In this study, rats were trained to fear a soft sound (CS) that had been paired with a shock (US). At first glance, this may not seem particularly special; in fact, it seems similar to many common classical conditioning studies such as the one conducted with Little Albert. But in this experiment, the animal was conditioned after it was made unconscious by an anesthetic. Even when the animal was anesthetized, classical conditioning still occurred (Weinberger, Gold, & Sternberg, 1984). This result gave strength to the idea that areas of the brain deeper than the cerebral cortex (the cortex is where the anesthetic has its most pronounced effect) play an important role in classical conditioning.

Then, in 1984, researchers David McCormick and Richard Thompson discovered and isolated the location of a specific conditioning experience in the brain. In their experiment, they conditioned an eyeblink response in a rabbit. They used a tone as a conditioned stimulus and paired it with a puff of air to the rabbit's eye, which was the unconditioned stimulus. The puff of air made the rabbit blink. After sufficient pairings, the tone alone came to elicit the blink response. This, of course, is an example of classical conditioning. By producing a small cut or lesion in one extremely small area of the rabbit's cerebellum (see Chapter 2), the researchers eliminated the learned response. After the lesion was created, the rabbit was still able to blink its eyes when it wished, and the air puff still elicited the blink, but the tone, which the rabbit could still easily hear, no longer had an effect. The conditioning had been wiped out! It seems that the experience of the conditioning had existed in a tiny piece of cerebellar tissue no larger than a cubic millimeter (McCormick & Thompson, 1984).

Of course, while McCormick and Thompson's study shows us that some conditioning experiences reside in small and specific locations within the brain, it by no means implies that all, or even the major portion of conditioning experiences, reside in the cerebellum. In fact, more research has isolated conditioning experiences in the hippocampus as well, an area of the brain especially tied to certain memory functions (Kelso & Brown, 1986). As you might imagine, on the heels of these discoveries, researchers have been scrambling to uncover what might be one of the brain's most closely guarded secrets—namely, *where does it store what it knows?* Perhaps some day we will have the answers.

Another avenue of approach that is proving fruitful is investigation concerning *how* the brain stores what it knows. This is the approach taken by Eric Kandel and his colleagues. Kandel has been examining *Aplysia*, a sea snail, in an effort to understand learning and memory. Kandel chose to study sea snails because they have the largest neurons in the animal kingdom. One researcher has noted that the sea snail "is built like an old Philco radio, with simple circuits and large, easily identifiable components" (Hall, 1985, pp. 33–34). In fact, the animal doesn't have more than about 20,000 neurons in its entire body.

Working with *Aplysia* Kandel has clearly demonstrated a mechanism of classical conditioning at the neurological level. Kandel discovered that the synaptic connection between two neurons (see Chapter 2) could be strengthened by a *third* neuron acting on the presynaptic neuron. This third neuron is called a *modulator neuron,* and its function is to enhance the release of neurotransmitter from the presynaptic surface. For example, when the tail of *Aply-*

◆ **FIGURE 8.15**

In the sea snail Aplysia, an electric shock to the tail will activate the motor neuron associated with gill withdrawal, causing the snail to "close up." This helps to protect its most delicate parts.

Siphon

Gill

Mantle sheet

Tail

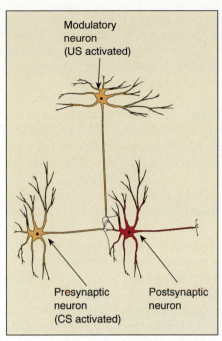

Modulatory
neuron
(US activated)

Presynaptic   Postsynaptic
neuron   neuron
(CS activated)

◆ **FIGURE 8.16**

During conditioning, both the specific modulator sensory neuron and the other sensory neuron involved in the associative event are activated. When stimulated by the US, the modulator neuron secretes serotonin, which, in turn, stimulates the motor neuron causing the UR. If a sensory neuron associated with the stimulation of the CS is active within one-half second of the onset of the US, the serotonin secreted by the nearby modulator neuron will keep the sensory neuron's calcium channels open longer. This allows for more neurotransmitter to spill into the synapse, thereby affecting the postsynaptic surface of the motor neuron. Such changes are examples of conditioning and enable the sensory neuron to fire the motor neuron when it had not been able to previously. When fired by a CS in this fashion, the motor neuron will also lead to gill withdrawal, but in this instance such action would be considered to be a CR, because it was a learned response and not a reflexive one.

sia is stimulated with an electrical shock, the animal will withdraw its gill (see Figure 8.15). This is an unlearned reflex.

During classical conditioning, the modulator neuron secretes the neurotransmitter serotonin in response to the stimulation by the US. This, in turn, causes the sensory neuron to keep its calcium channels open longer, which, through a series of complex chemical steps, enables neurotransmitter to be released in greater quantities. Such continued releases help to make permanent changes in the postsynaptic membrane, which, in essence, causes learning in that it results in a relatively permanent change in behavior as a result of experience (see Figure 8.16).

One of the most interesting discoveries is that serotonin secreted from the modulator neuron only has this enhancing effect on the sensory neuron for about half a second. This probably accounts for the fact that for classical conditioning to occur, the US must follow the CS within about half a second (Kandel & Hawkins, 1992).

SUMMARY

◆ Learning may be defined as a relatively permanent change in behavior that results from experience.

◆ In his book *The Behavior of Organisms*, B. F. Skinner argued that there are general principles of learning that are applicable to almost all species.

◆ During the 1890s, the Russian physiologist Pavlov reported an experiment with an associative learning process. By systematically associating the presentation of a bell with the presentation of food, Pavlov was able to classically condition dogs to respond to the bell by salivating.

◆ Once the CS has the power to elicit the CR, owing to the reinforcement of the CS-US bond by their contig-

uous pairing, it is possible to use the CS all by itself to create a "higher-order" CS_2. This process is known as higher-order conditioning.

◆ Associative experiences also can lead to the formation of beliefs and attitudes, and they can influence behaviors as diverse as prejudice, drug use, and fear.

◆ Watson and Rayner's experiment with Little Albert demonstrated that classical conditioning also can occur in humans.

◆ Originally, scientists assumed that classical conditioning occurred because the CS and US were contiguously associated. Now they recognize that contingency detection plays an important role.

◆ The basic premise of instrumental learning was formulated by E. L. Thorndike at the turn of the century. It is known as the law of effect.

◆ In instrumental conditioning, behaviors are learned because of the reinforcing or punishing consequences that follow them.

◆ Skinner used the term *operant conditioning* to describe responses that operate on the environment. Operants are classified not according to the particular muscular motions that constitute a response but rather according to their similar effect on the environment.

◆ Reinforcement occurs when a pleasant consequence follows a response, making it more likely that the response will be repeated.

◆ An instrumental behavior can occasionally be built up piecemeal through a process known as shaping. Shaping consists of reinforcing successive approximations toward the final response.

◆ An organism's responses can become highly selective or more general through the processes of discrimination and generalization. When an organism discriminates, it responds differentially to two or more stimuli. When it generalizes, similar stimuli evoke the same response.

◆ Positive reinforcement and avoidance or escape learning are both ways of strengthening a response. Positive reinforcement occurs when a behavior leads to a pleasant or reinforcing consequence. The latter occurs when a behavior successfully leads to avoidance of, or escape from, an aversive situation.

◆ Punishment and extinction are ways of weakening a response.

◆ Punishment is an extremely effective way of decreasing a behavior's strength, but its use may have serious drawbacks; for example, it may cause withdrawal, suppression of other behaviors, hostility, or aggression.

◆ Stimuli necessary for sustaining life can obtain the power to reinforce simply by being withheld for a time; such stimuli are called primary reinforcers. Other stimuli, known as acquired or secondary reinforcers, are effective because of their association with primary or other secondary reinforcers.

◆ Operant behavior may be maintained by various schedules of reinforcement.

◆ Through learning, different stimuli come to cue specific responses. Such cues are known as discriminative stimuli.

◆ The behaviors an organism is more likely to display can be used to reinforce the behaviors the organism is less likely to display. This observation became known as the Premack principle.

◆ The behaviorist view has been challenged by social learning, cognitive, and ethological theorists.

◆ Learning through observation of another organism's behavior is called social learning.

◆ Albert Bandura has argued that social learning is a distinct kind of learning because it does not depend on reinforcement.

◆ Social learning theorists draw a distinction between performing (imitating) a behavior and learning (acquiring) it. Latent learning is the term used to describe the kind of incidental learning that may not be apparent from an animal's or a person's behavior.

◆ Models are most likely to be imitated if they have high status, are nurturant, are aggressive, or are similar to the observer.

◆ The study of learning has led to an applied technology called behavior modification.

◆ Cognition refers to thinking. Cognitive learning theorists believe that thought processes have an important effect on learning.

◆ Cognitive aspects of learning can be seen by studying cognitive maps. A cognitive map is an organism's mental representation of the location of objects in relation to one another and to the organism.

◆ Learning is important because it has survival value. Human beings show their behavioral inheritance more in terms of tendencies to learn some behaviors more easily than others. This is the phenomenon of canalization.

◆ Conditioning has been shown to occur in individual neurons. Modulator neurons play an important role in classical conditioning by facilitating the action of the presynaptic membrane.

🎗 Suggestions for Further Reading

1. Domjan, M. P., & Burkhard, B. (1985). *The principles of learning and behavior* (2nd ed.). Monterey, CA: Brooks/Cole. A college-level textbook on the principles of learning and conditioning.

2. Hulse, S. H., Egeth, H., & Deese, J. (1980). *The psychology of learning* (5th ed.). New York: McGraw-Hill. A college-level textbook that introduces theories of learning and includes current views on the interaction between types of learning.

3. Pavlov, I. (1927). *Conditioned reflexes.* New York: Oxford University Press. Describes Pavlov's classic experiments in associative learning.

4. Reynolds, G. S. (1975). *A primer of operant conditioning* (2nd ed.). Glenview, IL: Scott Foresman. A college-level textbook that describes the principles of operant conditioning, including reinforcement.

5. Skinner, B. F. (1971). *Beyond freedom and dignity.* New York: Knopf. A book for the general reader in which Skinner outlines his theory of operant conditioning and attempts to apply it to improve social situations.

Chapter Nine

Memory

PROLOGUE

OUT OF SIGHT, OUT OF MIND

A couple of years ago, Mrs. Duke, a 66-year-old woman, was brought into the hospital by her husband. Mr. Duke said simply that his wife's memory was lapsing and that she needed help.

On call that day in the hospital emergency room was Dr. Tony Dajer. After introducing himself, Dr. Dajer began to examine Mrs. Duke for any obvious physical problems. After completing an initial examination that failed to show anything, Dr. Dajer decided to conduct a simple memory test. He told Mrs. Duke, "I'm going to name three objects. In five minutes I'll ask you to repeat them back to me, all right?" (Dajer, 1991, p. 80)

Mrs. Duke smiled and said, "I'll do my best."

Then Dr. Dajer looked around the room and saw three objects he could name and said, "Bed, chair, sink. Got it?"

Mrs. Duke answered, "Bed, chair, sink, yes."

Dr. Dajer knew that anyone whose memory was functioning at a reasonable level would be able to recall all three items easily after only a 5-minute delay. If Mrs. Duke could not recall one of the items, he reasoned, it might mean that she did indeed have a memory problem.

After five minutes, Dr. Dajer returned. Mrs. Duke seemed in good spirits and well enough, so Dr. Dajer said, "Well Mrs. Duke, what were the three objects?" That was when Mrs. Duke looked at Dr. Dajer and said, "Who are you?"

To say that Dr. Dajer was shocked would be an understatement! After further examination, Dr. Dajer realized that all Mrs. Duke had to go on when dealing with new experiences was what is sometimes called "short-term memory." Mrs. Duke could recall things from her past well enough, but she couldn't remember anything new she encountered for more than about 30 seconds after it was out of her sight! In fact, she had to be constantly told where she was because she kept forgetting. And, although she could remember her husband whom she had known for many years, every time Dr. Dajer came into the room he had to be reintroduced to her!

CONTENTS

MEMORY
The complex mental function of recalling what has been learned or experienced.

ENGRAM
A lasting trace or impression formed in living tissue responsible for memory.

What could possibly have happened to Mrs. Duke to make her memory fail in this manner? Dr. Dajer ordered a CAT scan (see Chapter 2) of Mrs. Duke's brain. The CAT scan revealed the cause of her problem. She had had a very minor stroke caused by a tiny clot that temporarily blocked the artery feeding the hippocampus, an important part of the brain involved in memory. Once the small clot broke up, the blood flow returned to the hippocampus before any permanent damage occurred. Fortunately, Mrs. Duke fully recovered and was able to go home a few days later. The chances are that her disorder won't recur and that she will be all right. But for a couple of days she had totally lost all ability to place new experiences into her memory, an ability that we all take for granted.

IN THIS CHAPTER, we'll examine how memory works: You will see how you put information into your memory, store it, and retrieve it. We'll also examine how you can improve your memory and use it more successfully. And we will see what investigators have learned from other interesting cases like that of Mrs. Duke.

❧ WHY PSYCHOLOGISTS STUDY MEMORY

You rely on your **memory** every moment of the day. Without it, you would have no sense of continuity, no realization of the past; and you couldn't benefit from any learning or experience. Without memory, it would be impossible for you to function. All images and materials not immediately available to your senses must be drawn from your memory. Your very sense of self-awareness requires that you remember you had a "self" yesterday—or 5 minutes ago for that matter. Without a memory, you would be lost.

Yet, memory is not perfect. The mind does not make a record the way a camera or a tape recorder does; our memories shift and change. Some memories are forgotten, some are altered, and others are difficult to retrieve. How well we use our memories influences our ability to think and to understand. Before we can understand human behavior and capability, we must understand how memory works and what its limitations and potentials are.

AN ENDURING QUESTION: WHAT IS THE BIOLOGY OF MEMORY?

Your memory is one of the most remarkable capabilities you have. Although it may take only a fraction of a second to learn something, the resulting memory may stay with you for the rest of your life. Somewhere, somehow, memories are stored in the brain, but where and how is the question.

In 1917, neurophysiologist Karl Lashley began a search for what he called engrams. An **engram** is the hypothetical biochemical structure of a single memory. In his search, Lashley systematically removed sections from the brains of trained rats, trying to find the portion that held an elusive memory, or engram. In his book *In Search of the Engram*, published in 1950, he reported that his studies had yielded information about where the engrams didn't exist, but not about where they did. In fact, every time he trained a rat to run through a maze and then removed

AN ENDURING QUESTION, CONTINUED

a small part of the rat's brain, the rat always seemed to retain some of the memories it had acquired while running through the maze. Lashley was never able to totally remove a single memory. He therefore concluded that each memory was not held in a specific place in the brain, but rather, in some mysterious way, was distributed evenly throughout the brain—a theory he referred to as **equipotentiality.** The biochemical structure of an engram, or memory, is still debated, but evidence is mounting that Lashley's view about equipotentiality was wrong, although, as you will soon see, not totally without merit.

Modern researchers generally believe that memories can be held at different neural levels within the brain, depending perhaps on the complexity of the memory. Figure 9.1 shows the current accepted terminology for these different levels of neural organization (Churchland & Churchland, 1990). A simple memory, such as a conditioned response (see Chapter 8), might be held at the level of *molecules* or *synapses* and perhaps at a very particular location in the brain, whereas the complex recollection of your high school sweetheart might be spread throughout an entire neural *map* or *system* and be scattered across many areas of your brain.

"Recollection," then, may be an aptly descriptive word, because recollecting such a memory might require you to re-collect pieces of it from thousands of different locations within the brain and then activate an entire map or system in order to bring the whole memory together. In this

EQUIPOTENTIALITY
Karl Lashley's concept that memory and learning are not localized in one particular area of the brain, but rather that the entire brain is responsible for handling these functions.

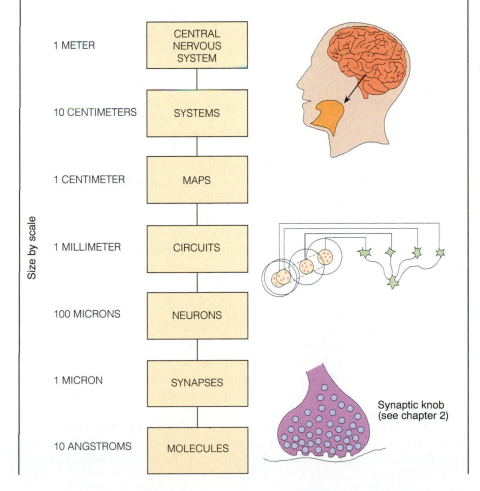

◆ **FIGURE 9.1**

*The organization of the central nervous system (brain and spinal cord) can be studied at different size scales. Perhaps memories can be stored, as whole entities at each of these levels depending on the complexity of the memory. (*SOURCE: *Churchland & Churchland, 1990, p. 36.)*

LONG-TERM POTENTIATION (LTP)
The cellular process that enables learning and memory to exist via the long-term storage of information in the form of electrochemical or structural alterations in the neuron. Various metallic elements, enzymes, and gases are thought to be associated with the process although it is not yet fully understood.

NMDA RECEPTORS
Glutamate receptors on the surface of certain neurons, so named because they were first discovered to bind with the chemical N-methyl D-aspartate. NMDA receptors also bind with magnesium ions. They are believed to be essential for learning and memory.

NON-NMDA RECEPTORS
Glutamate receptors on the surface of certain neurons, so named to distinguish them from neighboring NMDA receptors. Non-NMDA receptors depolarize the neuron when they respond to glutamate, thereby opening the way for NMDA receptor activation.

AN ENDURING QUESTION, CONTINUED

sense, such a complex memory wouldn't be in one place, but would almost seem, as Lashley described it, to be "everywhere at once."

Experimental evidence for the existence of single memories held within *circuits*, *maps*, or *systems* comes from interesting research that reveals that when a list of words is memorized and then recalled, certain neurons associated with the memory will fire more when one specific word on the list, such as "luck," is remembered, while other neurons will fire more when a different word, such as "woe," is remembered (Heit, Smith, & Halgren, 1988). Only a few neurons were monitored in this experiment, so this probably does not mean that specific neurons were storing certain words, but rather that the different neurons tapped by the experiment were probably involved with different neural *circuits*, *maps*, or *systems*, each of which was storing a different word.

Whether we are looking at entire systems, maps, or circuits, there almost assuredly must be some way for a memory to become permanent at the level of the neuron, or it seems most likely that memories couldn't exist. When memories are formed, individual neurons must somehow undergo special long-term changes upon which circuits, maps, and whole memory systems can be built. But what happens to these neurons? How do they change so they can hold a memory? Researchers have wondered what the mechanism behind this process, called **long-term potentiation,** might be.

Researchers now seem tantalizingly close to an answer. Although the proposed mechanism for one form of long-term potentiation is somewhat complex, it is worth looking at because it will show you how the underlying neurological processes explain some of the functions of memory. Let's look at the neurons in the hippocampus, which, as the chapter prologue showed, is an important area of the brain associated with the formation of memories.

Most neurons in the hippocampus use an amino acid called *glutamate* as their primary neurotransmitter (see Chapter 2). Glutamate begins the process of LTP (long-term potentiation) by binding to glutamate receptors on the postsynaptic surfaces of the target cells. There are two important kinds of glutamate receptors on the postsynaptic surface of their target cells in the hippocampus, **NMDA receptors** and **non-NMDA receptors.** Both receptors must become active for LTP to occur. Non-NMDA receptors are typically the most active at the beginning of the LTP process because the NMDA receptors are usually blocked by the metallic element magnesium, which, like iron or potassium, is commonly found in the foods we eat.

Magnesium will only leave the NMDA receptors, thereby freeing them for action, if the postsynaptic cell becomes depolarized via stimulation by other neurotransmitters affecting the cell. What this means is that for the NMDA receptors to become activated and allow the LTP process to continue, *two* things must happen *simultaneously*. First, the postsynaptic cell must become depolarized, which will free the magnesium from the NMDA receptors, and second, glutamate must then bind with the NMDA receptors, thereby stimulating them as well as the non-NMDA receptors.

If you think about it, this arrangement is suited for the detection of coincidences, something upon which much of conditioning is based. If one experience you have causes the cell to depolarize, while *another* expe-

AN ENDURING QUESTION, CONTINUED

rience results in the transmission of glutamate, a mechanism in the NMDA receptor system exists *to form the association* because the NMDA receptors will *only be stimulated if both things occur at the same time* (Kandel & Hawkins, 1992).

Once the NMDA receptor is activated, calcium will pour in. Calcium initiates LTP by activating at least three kinds of *protein kinases*. A kinase is an enzyme that triggers the activation of other enzymes. The action of these kinases in turn leads to a cascade of second messenger (see Chapter 2) reactions in the cell. These reactions appear to cause long-term changes in the cell (lasting for up to two weeks). Among the evidence supporting the importance of NMDA receptors in the memory process is the fact that if NMDA receptors in the hippocampus are blocked by specific NMDA-blocking drugs, learning cannot take place (Kandel & Hawkins, 1992)! These are definitely not the kind of drugs you'd want to be exposed to when studying for a test!

To make memories that might last a lifetime, however, more neurotransmitter must be secreted from the *presynaptic cell*. This enhanced transmission will eventually lead to the activation of genes, the production of new proteins, and the growth of new neural connections—all of which can result in changes lasting a lifetime.

The implication here, however, is that for a memory to be maintained and perhaps made lifelong, the *post*synaptic cell must send a signal back to the *pre*synaptic cell telling it at this point to increase the secretion of neurotransmitter. This presented a problem for researchers, however: for as long as neuroscience has existed, a cardinal rule has been that *every chemical message goes only one way*, from presynaptic surfaces to postsynaptic surfaces, which, in fact, is why these surfaces were given the prefixes "pre" and "post" in the first place. The postsynaptic surface doesn't even have a mechanism for secreting neurotransmitter. How, then, could a messenger possibly leave the postsynaptic surface, travel to the presynaptic surface, and thereby signal an increase in neurotransmitter for the maintenance of LTP? Since there is no mechanical release mechanism on the postsynaptic surface, any such hypothesized "retrograde" (i.e., backward traveling) messenger would have to be something that could diffuse right through the cell and wouldn't need channels or openings through which to pass—something like a gas.

If you recall from Chapter 2 the recent discovery that the gas nitric oxide acts as a neurotransmitter, you will readily see why memory researchers working at the neural level were so excited. Here was the possible retrograde messenger! They immediately conducted experiments and soon found that by blocking the formation of NO (nitric oxide) in the postsynaptic cell, LTP was shut down—it couldn't take place! On the other hand, applying more NO boosted the formation of LTP (Kandel & Hawkins, 1992)! This particular example of LTP is shown in Figure 9.2.

Another important advantage of NO is that because it is diffusible it might well find its way into neighboring pathways while it is facilitating the release of neurotransmitter from the presynaptic cell, thereby *spreading LTP to nearby cells*. But this can only happen if the NMDA receptors of nearby cells are being stimulated at the same time. Again, we see an *associative system* with the potential to spread the newly acquired associations to neighboring neurons—which sounds a lot like a biological basis for memory formation. Following these discoveries, it was found that carbon

AN ENDURING QUESTION, CONTINUED

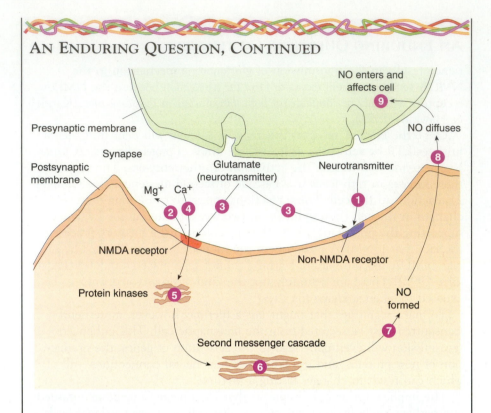

◆ **FIGURE 9.2**

A proposed mechanism for long-term potentiation in hippocampal cells.

1. *Neurotransmitter from the presynaptic cell surface stimulates and depolarizes the postsynaptic cell.*

2. *The action of depolarization releases magnesium (Mg^+), so that it no longer blocks the NMDA receptors (only one such receptor is shown in this figure for purposes of simplification).*

3. *The neurotransmitter glutamate, secreted from the presynaptic surface, stimulates both the non-NMDA and the NMDA receptors. This is possible because the previous depolarization liberated the blocking Mg^+ ions from the NMDA receptors, freeing them to react to the glutamate. Depolarization, plus reaction to glutamate by both the non-NMDA and the NMDA receptors, allows for the detection of conicidences, a necessary mechanism for learning.*

4. *Calcium (Ca^+) ions flow in through the NMDA receptors once they have been stimulated by glutamate.*

5. *The calcium ions, in turn, trigger the reaction of complex protein kinases.*

6. *This results in a cascade of second messenger reactions leading to . . .*

7. *The formation of nitric oxide (NO).*

8. *The NO then diffuses through the postsynaptic cell membrane and travels in retrograde fashion to the presynaptic surface where . . .*

9. *It enters through the presynaptic membrane and affects the cell by enhancing the secretion of neurotransmitter that can lead to permanent changes in the cell.*

monoxide (CO) also appears to function as a retrograde messenger (Zhuo, Small, Kandel, & Hawkins, 1993).

More studies must be carried out before any firm conclusions are drawn. But if researchers can ever uncover the secrets of memory and understand fully how it operates, this knowledge would greatly alter the way we do things, including, to mention just a few, educating our children, helping people with learning or memory disabilities, and perhaps even designing computer "intelligence."

AN ENDURING QUESTION, CONTINUED

FOR CRITICAL ANALYSIS

1. Sometimes I play a game with my class. It goes like this: Starting with the last row and working forward, each person in the class is required to say his or her full name (first and last) out loud while the other students listen. However, before each student can say his or her name, that student must repeat the first and last names of *everyone who has gone before*, and do it in correct order! As it turns out, just about every student is successful (except when trying to remember the last few names of the sequence, the names that they have heard only once or twice). In the short space of an hour class, almost everyone will easily learn 50 first and last names and will also know each person by name, even if after the game all the students move to different seats and sit in a different order. Typically, everyone is very surprised by this amazing, hitherto unknown memory power that they have discovered. What does this tell you about people's knowledge about how their memories work? How might this little game change your view of yourself and your potential to be a good student? What does this game tell you about the effect of repetition on the biology of long-term memory?

2. Once the biology of memory is understood, do you think that it might someday be possible to insert minicomputer chips directly into our brains so that they interact with our biology and boost our intelligence beyond anything that we might imagine? Would you like your mind altered in such a way (consider the possibility of being given the knowledge and reasoning of a Ph.D. with just one surgical operation)? How might the surgical implantation of preprogrammed memory chips into human brains be a grave concern for societies of the future? ◆

WORKING MEMORY
An inclusive term for a number of short-term memory systems that enable individuals to hold on to recently acquired information for about 30 seconds to 4 minutes. Among these memory systems are the phonological loop and the visuospatial sketch pad. Working memory also holds information from declarative memory that is being actively examined.

SHORT-TERM MEMORY
Term that is little used currently but once referred to a hypothesized memory of limited storage capacity and short duration through which it was believed information had to pass before storage in long-term memory was possible. The closest modern equivalent to this discarded concept is the phonological loop of the working memory.

LONG-TERM MEMORY
Term used to refer to memory systems with virtually unlimited storage capacity in which memories may be stored for long periods, even a lifetime. While both implicit and explicit memory systems have long-term storage capability, the term "long-term memory" is usually used to refer to long-term declarative memory.

AMNESIA
Unexpected and often extensive memory loss that may be partial or complete. The two major types are psychogenic and somatogenic.

WORKING MEMORY

Working memory is active memory. While millions, perhaps billions, of recollections may be stored in your memory's "library," working memory deals with only a few memories at a time. The working memory might best be thought of as the library's blackboard on which you have written your current thoughts and mental activities. In other words, working memory consists of the thoughts that you are working on at any given moment. This has led researchers to think of working memory as standing "at the crossroads between memory, attention, and perception" (Baddeley, 1992, p. 559).

Twenty-five years ago, researchers believed that memory was basically divided into two parts, **short-term** and **long-term memory** (Atkinson & Shiffrin, 1968). This was thought to be true because certain kinds of **amnesia** wiped out recently acquired memories while leaving old memories intact. Or, as in the case of Mrs. Duke in the chapter Prologue, certain kinds of amnesia sometimes allowed the sufferer to recall very recent events for only a short time but not remember them for the long term.

Twenty-five years ago, we also assumed the existence of STM (short-term memory) because of common daily experiences that we all share. For example, consider what happens when you look up a new number in the telephone book. As you close the book, you must remember all seven digits in order to dial the telephone. There is only one way you can keep the information in

REHEARSAL
A process by which information can be held in short-term memory for relatively long periods. In rehearsal, an item is repeated over and over so that it is not lost. This technique may eventually result in storage of the item in the long-term memory.

VISUOSPATIAL SKETCH PAD
In Baddeley and Hitch's model of working memory, a slave system of the working memory central executive that can briefly hold visual information about spatial relationships. A short-term memory that enables a person to make a quick mental note about where things are in relation to him or her spatially. The information is typically lost within 4 minutes, often after just seconds.

PHONOLOGICAL LOOP
In Baddeley and Hitch's model of working memory, a slave system of the working memory central executive that can briefly hold information about language or language-like sounds. Closest to the older notion of short-term memory, it can hold items heard over a 2-second period for about 30 seconds. Rehearsal can keep an item in the phonological loop for longer periods.

EIDETIC IMAGE
The formation and reproduction of accurate mental images of objects not currently present. Possessors of these images are said to have photographic memories.

STM for longer than approximately 30 seconds. This is by using **rehearsal**— by saying the number over and over again to yourself, constantly restoring it in your STM. We know to rehearse, or we will forget the information.

Because of observations like this, it was assumed that STM and LTM (long-term memory) worked in a serial fashion; that is, that information entered the STM where it was rapidly lost unless it became incorporated into the more stable LTM (see Figure 9.3). However, the case of K. F. and others like him ended that idea.

K. F. was involved in a motorcycle accident and received a head injury that resulted in a severely deficient STM. In fact, K. F. couldn't recall more than one number in a series! If you said "repeat after me, 4–3–6," K. F. could get no farther than 4. Telephone numbers were definitely out of reach. Yet K. F. was able to memorize word pairs and lists of words as well as the average person! In other words, his LTM could take in pairs of words and long lists for storage *even though his STM couldn't hold more than one item* (Squire, Knowlton, & Musen, 1993). For this reason, STM and LTM are now thought to be working in some sort of parallel (independent) fashion rather than in a sequential manner. As you recall, researchers originally believed that a memory had to pass through STM before it could be stored in LTM. This new way of looking at memory now leads us to believe that STM and LTM may process the same information at the same time (in parallel) without one having to pass the information to the other.

Because the old concept of a serial (sequential) short-term–long-term memory (in which STM passes information on to LTM) failed to fully explain cases like that of K. F., the broader concept of working memory replaced the older view of STM. The working memory (still called short-term memory by some) is now seen as a diverse collection of short-term systems that are separate and distinct from one another. Another way of saying this is that the modern conception of working memory is that it consists of different and distinct short-term memories; there isn't just one STM, but many. And, as we shall see, the same appears to be true of LTM—there isn't just one, but perhaps many.

A Model of Working Memory

Although there are a number of models, or theories, about how working memory functions, the one developed by British researchers Baddeley and Hitch has become especially popular because it is able to describe much of what has been discovered about working memory (see Figure 9.4). These two researchers envision a *central executive*, that is, a portion of the working memory whose job it is to integrate and bring together information from the different kinds of STMs. The different kinds of STMs are referred to as *slave systems* because they are slaves to this central executive.

The function of these slave systems is to supply the main "blackboard" of the working memory, the central executive, with the information you are dealing with at any given moment. The two major slave systems (STM systems) that Baddeley and Hitch describe (they admit that there may be more) are the **visuospatial sketch pad** and the **phonological loop.** The point of making this distinction is to separate the STMs that handle visual and spatial information (such as recalling whether a car is approaching from your left at an intersection while you take a moment to glance to your right) from STMs that deal with auditory information (such as recalling the sound of your friend's voice saying a phone number to you). Research has shown that these two slave systems are separate in much the way that the model depicts them. For example, distractions that interfere with the STM of something visual usually have no effect on the acquisition of short-term auditory information (Baddeley, 1992).

◆ **FIGURE 9.3**

The serial model of memory was popular 30 years ago, but cases like that of K. F. brought its validity into question.

WORKING MEMORY

◆ **FIGURE 9.4**

A simplified representation of Baddeley and Hitch's model of working memory. Both the visuospatial sketch pad and the phonological loop are short-term memory systems. They feed the central executive of the working memory, which integrates information from these systems as well as information called up from long-term memory.

To better understand how the visuospatial sketch pad might work, look for a moment at Figure 9.5. People with good visual memory will be able to recall most or all of the items. In fact, for about 1 percent of adults, the recollection of the image will be so strong that the memory will seem almost as sharp as if they were still looking at the picture. Such an unusual and powerful picture in the mind's eye is known as an eidetic image. An **eidetic image** held in the visuospatial sketch pad may last up to 4 minutes with crystal clarity (Haber, 1969). The ability to use eidetic imagery is known informally as "photographic memory" and, interestingly, is more common in children, although no one knows why.

Study of the sound-oriented phonological loop has also provided some interesting results. For instance, researchers have known for many years about *the acoustic similarity effect*. The effect is a simple one and easy to demonstrate. Basically, it means that lists of words that sound quite different from one another such as "pit, day, cow, pen, rig" are easier to remember than lists of similar-sounding words like "man, cap, can, map, mad." This shows us that the code that this particular STM is using to hold onto information must be organized around sound, that is, it must be *phonological*. Lists of words having related *meanings* such as "car, bus, van, truck, sedan" are not as hard to recall as similar-sounding words, implying that the sound, not the meaning, is what is being held short term in the phonological loop. The acoustic similarity effect probably occurs because similar sounds are harder for the phonological slave system to code in a way that makes them distinct from one another.

The irrelevant speech effect is another interesting phenomenon that gives us insight into the workings of the phonological loop. It turns out that if you read a short list of words and try to hold them in your phonological loop for about 30 seconds, your ability to do so will be disrupted if you hear words spoken to you while you are trying to read the list. Of course, you say, what's so odd about a distraction interfering with reading and studying? Well, what's

◆ **FIGURE 9.5**

How good is your photographic memory? Look at this photograph for 30 seconds (don't name the objects), close the book, and see how many objects you can remember.

interesting is that the disruption will occur even if the words you are hearing are in a language you don't know. Furthermore, if bursts of noise are used as a distractor rather than words, there is no effect (Baddeley, 1992)! This implies that, along with the words you are reading, the phonological loop will force into its store any language-like sound it picks up, thereby causing the interference. This explains why you might be able to read or study in a room filled with machine sounds, but be bothered by the sounds of voices, even voices in a foreign language. The STM of the phonological loop apparently grabs such language-like sounds automatically and tries to hold on to them. This appears to be something that the phonological loop has evolved to do, something over which you have little or no control.

Research concerning the phonological loop is just beginning, but as you can tell, some interesting discoveries are being made. For instance, what do you think is the best predictor of a child's ability to master a foreign language? Is it IQ? Grades in school? Ability to memorize long lists of new words? Actually, it's none of these. The best predictor of a child's ability to master a foreign language is how many unfamiliar words she can hold short term in her phonological loop at a given time (Baddeley, 1992)!

Short-term memory systems may also serve another important purpose. They may make it easy for us to forget things. At first glance, this might not seem to be an advantage. But how would you like to store everything you have ever known—every telephone number you've ever dialed, every street address you've ever encountered, every license plate you've ever looked at, every name you've ever come across? Interestingly, some people have a poor ability to forget information once they are exposed to it. They easily store information into their LTMs. Contrary to what you might think, this is not a happy state of affairs. Such individuals find their minds cluttered with large amounts of useless information that obscure more timely and important facts (Luria, 1968).

DISPLACEMENT.　What happens if you overload any of your STMs by trying to place too much information into them? Consider the phonological loop, for instance. What will happen if you try to place 20 items into it? You are likely to remember a few of the first and a few of the last items of the list, about 7 altogether. The middle items, however, whether meaningful or not, are difficult to recall (see Figure 9.6). The first few items may be easier to recall because you tried to rehearse them and got a few into an LTM. But soon you were overwhelmed by the large number of items and lost most of them. When you reached the end of the list, you remembered the last few items because you had just recently been exposed to them, and they were still in an STM (the phonological loop if you "hear" words in your head as you read them or, less commonly, the visuospatial sketch pad if you recall the words you read visu-

◆ **FIGURE 9.6**

Middle items in a series, whether meaningful or not, are the most difficult to recall. This phenomenon is known as the serial position effect. (SOURCE: *Adapted from Postman & Rau, 1957.*)

ally). This sequence of remembering is known as the **serial position effect**. The items that you lose while memorizing the list are displaced as other items are retained.

The serial position effect has also been observed in other species. For instance, one group of researchers observed the effect among pigeons and monkeys that were reinforced for recalling a series of travel slides (some researcher finally appears to have found a captive audience for his family's trip to the Grand Canyon) (Wright, Santiago, Sands, Kendrick, & Cook, 1985).

The serial position effect is further evidence of the existence of both STM and LTM processes. If your memory were all LTM, you would recall all or most of the list. Memory experts who have mastered tricks for making information stick in their LTMs can easily handle a list of hundreds of words. If there were just STMs, you could only remember the most recently heard or seen words (and most likely, like Mrs. Duke, not recall why you were answering questions about what you could or could not remember).

For memories to last, they must be stored in an LTM in such a way that they can later be retrieved; otherwise the information will be lost from any STMs that might be holding it, and lost rapidly. Because of this, when you are studying, you can fall into a trap without realizing it and think that you have learned much more information than you really have. It's like putting items into a sack without knowing that it has a hole in the bottom of it. Unbeknownst to you, as you are putting some things in, others are falling out. This is known as *displacement*. This is also why it's important for you to go back and test yourself on material after some time has passed. In this way, you can be certain that while your working memory was dealing with the material, it was also picked up by an LTM. Proof that the material has been stored in an LTM comes when you are able to retrieve the memory after some time has passed. For this reason, it is best to check your knowledge of something you have studied perhaps half an hour after you have studied it rather than immediately after.

Chunking

In 1956, George Miller used the term "chunk" to describe a unit of memory. He agreed that the then-hypothesized STM could hold only about seven *meaningless* items of information—such as the digits of a telephone number—but he also argued that the STM could hold more information at one time if many "items" were chunked together. The basis of his argument was that the STM could hold about seven *meanings* at once, regardless of how many items were involved in each meaning (Miller, 1956). For years it was believed that chunking showed that meaning, or meaningful grouping, played an important part in STM. But as we shall soon see while reviewing this concept, there is another explanation.

The Concept Review on chunking raises a question. As you recall, the acoustic similarity effect indicates that the phonological loop codes according to sound, *not* according to meaning. If this is true, how can we explain chunking, which seems to imply that meanings make a difference in the coding within the phonological loop?

Researchers now explain the famous chunking phenomena as a combination of effects. First, there is strong evidence that meaning *does not* influence the phonological loop STM. So why does chunking occur? Interestingly, the length of a string of random numbers that people can hold in their phonological loops varies depending on the language they speak! At first that seems a bizarre finding until you stop and realize that in some languages the words for numbers are quite short, while in others they are long. While it is true that the phonological loop STM can hold about seven random digits, give or take two,

SERIAL POSITION EFFECT
A phenomenon in verbal learning. Items at the beginning or at the end of a long series are more easily remembered; items in the middle are the hardest to recall.

CONCEPT REVIEW ◆ CHUNKING

Chunking is a difficult concept to grasp until you've tried it for yourself.

Look at the four "items" shown below in capital letters. They are called "nonsense syllables" because they have no meaning. The phonological loop should be able to hold roughly seven of these meaningless "items," give or take two. Say them to yourself, then close your eyes and try to repeat them.

DAK   GIR   JOP   FID

You should have had no difficulty. Now, try six nonsense syllables:

DIT   LON   KIF   JAT   WUB   BIP

Some people are able to remember six nonsense syllables, but most can't. It's hard to hold that much information in this STM. Or is it? Although you may have had some trouble holding six meaningless syllables, you're not going to have any trouble repeating six meaningful one-syllable words:

STONE   BRIDGE   PATH   HOP   CUBE   LINE

Why are six one-syllable words easier to recall than six nonsense syllables? It may be because they have a meaning and meanings are easier to remember.

How far can this particular STM memory be pushed? Try nine one-syllable words:

SHOE   MONK   BLADE   JUMP   PLAY

HATE   RUST   SOUP   POND

It's likely that nine one-syllable words have pushed this STM too far. So that's the limit. Or is it? Now, let's chunk 12 syllables (12 items) by placing them into three words (three meanings, or chunks).

CANADIAN   TESTIMONY   PSYCHOLOGY

Is it easy because you are holding onto three chunks (meanings) rather than 12 syllables (items)? If you try eight four-syllable words, however, you're likely to have a little trouble:

DECLARATION MINORITY PESSIMISTIC CONDITIONAL

INFURIATE AMERICAN SYMBOLISM CONSTERNATION

How about 19 words! Easy, if you break a 19-word sentence into five chunks:

MARTIN LUTHER KING, WINNER OF THE NOBEL
PEACE PRIZE, GAVE A SPEECH AT
THE LINCOLN MEMORIAL ABOUT CIVIL RIGHTS.

Could you do this because your phonological loop was holding five chunks (man's name, kind of prize, what he gave, where he gave it, and subject of speech), not 19 items (Anderson, 1980)?

that mostly applies to *English speakers*. The fact is that the phonological loop can generally hold whatever number of digits or items it hears over a span of *two seconds* (Baddeley, 1992). This is known as *the word-length effect*.

Look back at the Concept Review, and you will see that you probably read *stone, bridge, path, hop, cube,* and *line* faster than you read *dit, lon, kif, jat, wub,* and *bip* just because you are familiar with the meaningful words. You also read nine syllables a lot faster when they were *Canadian, testimony,* and *psychology* rather than *shoe, monk, blade, jump, play, hate, rust, soup,* and *pond*. So it was the length of time you took to read these items and not the meanings that was making the difference!

But what about the last instance, the sentence concerning Martin Luther King? Can you still remember anything about that sentence? Odds are that you do. Martin Luther King—gave a speech—at the Lincoln Memorial—about civil rights—won the peace prize. That sentence did have meaning, which is why some or all of it was stored in an LTM while your working memory was dealing with it—or you wouldn't recall any of it now! So, in the last example (and perhaps even in some of the others if you still recall them), LTM effects were confounding our study of chunking in an STM.

❧ LONG-TERM MEMORIES

To store information for days, weeks, years, or a lifetime, we must store it in a long-term memory. It is estimated that altogether human LTMs can store about 100 trillion bits of information, which would make a large computer's mere billions appear practically amnesiac.

In the same way that our old idea of STM evolved into an understanding that there are a set of STM systems working together, we now understand that LTM, too, is not a single entity, but is made up of different systems, each operating in different areas of the brain (Squire, Knowlton, & Musen, 1993). The major distinction among LTMs is that drawn between declarative and implicit long-term memories.

Declarative Memory

Declarative memory is sometimes called "fact memory" or "explicit memory," because it contains conscious memories of specific facts and events. It is known to be based on the functioning of structures within the medial temporal lobes of the brain (amygdala, hippocampus, and surrounding areas) as well as the thalamus and its surrounding areas (see Chapter 2). After a few weeks of processing and storage within these areas, long-term memories are believed to be permanently stored in the neocortex (see Figure 9.7).

Declarative memories can be acquired very quickly although they are not always reliable. For example, the experience of watching a good movie will place much information about the film into the declarative LTM, and do it quickly (you only have to see a good film once to remember a lot of it). Over time, however, your recollections may fade somewhat and become less reliable, and you may even recall scenes happening differently than they actually did. Memory is simply not the same as a camera. For this reason, psychologists have been especially interested in the study of eyewitness testimony. You might be surprised to know that even over relatively short spans of time, eyewitnesses often show quite faulty memory when making their "positive" accusations (see Figure 9.8)

EPISODIC AND SEMANTIC MEMORY. Episodic and semantic memory are currently thought to be two subtypes of declarative memory. **Episodic memory**

DECLARATIVE MEMORY
The type of long-term memory associated with cognitive abilities not directly attributable to unconscious skills or habits. Declarative memories are conscious memories that need to be "brought to mind" in order to become active. Declarative memory is required to recall factual information, and it is sometimes called explicit memory, or fact memory. The ability to recognize a face, recall a number, or recall any verbal or sensory information requires declarative memory.

EPISODIC MEMORY
Memories stored with mental "tags" about where, when, and how you acquired the information. It mostly contains personal information, but also includes "flashbulb memories."

DECLARATIVE MEMORY

Brain Pathways Involved

- Neocortex
- Fornix
- Thalamus
- Mammillary body
- Amygdala
- Hippocampus

Information Involved

Remembering telephone numbers

Remembering faces

Remembering special dates

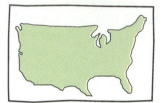

Visualizing maps and locations

◆ **FIGURE 9.7**

The areas of the brain and the types of information involved in declarative memory.

refers to memories of a personal nature such as where and when something happened to you. Recalling that you spoke with a friend of yours yesterday in the bookstore is an example of an episodic memory. **Semantic memory,** on the other hand, refers to memories of a more general nature, such as knowing that the United States is bordered by Mexico and Canada.

The distinction comes from observations of patients with severe amnesia. It is not uncommon for someone suffering amnesia to have dramatic losses of episodic memory while maintaining most, if not all, semantic memories. For example, while an amnesic might not even know her own name, what she has

◆ **FIGURE 9.8**

In the early 1970s, a young man named Larry Berson (photograph "b") was arrested for having committed several rapes. Berson said that he was innocent, but he was positively identified by several of the rape victims who had seen his face at close range under good illumination. A little later, the police arrested Richard Carbone (a), who confessed to the rapes without being asked about them. The rape victims recanted their positive identifications of Berson once they saw Carbone. Coincidence? Fluke? Consider the fact that when Carbone was arrested he also confessed to an armed robbery, a crime for which innocent George Morales (c) was serving time based on "positive" eyewitness identification (Buckhout, 1974)! Which features do these three men have in common and how do you think the memories of the witnesses may have reconstructed their experiences so as to lead them to make positive identifications of the wrong man?

(a)

(b)

(c)

done, or where she has been, she is typically not likely to have forgotten that winter comes after fall or that Jane is a woman's name while Ralph is a man's.

Both episodic and semantic memory are considered to be examples of declarative memory because the **retrieval** of the information from this LTM is carried out explicitly; that is, the subject is aware that stored information is being accessed because he or she makes an effort, however slight, to "bring the information to mind."

Further evidence that these two kinds of memories are declarative comes from the fact that episodic memories are associated with the brain areas involved in declarative memory. The brain paths for semantic memories aren't as clearly understood, but it is known that amnesics who lose episodic memory, while able to tap their semantic memory for general information, oftentimes have trouble acquiring new semantic information (Squire, Knowlton, & Musen, 1993).

Both episodic and semantic memory appear to become integrated to a certain extent in the frontal lobes of the brain. Because of this integration, you are often able to recall the context in which you personally acquired certain general facts. For instance, I know all the U.S. presidents by heart and in order (e.g., Who was the eleventh president? James K. Polk, of course). I learned all of them because when I was a kid I used to buy little packages that contained presidential medallions. Each medallion had a number on the back and the corresponding president on the front. The medallions weren't all that important to me, but the gum that came with them was surprisingly good. And I admit, I was a bit of a gum nut—all to the consternation of my grandmother who for some obscure reason hated to see anyone chew gum—but I digress. The point is that I recall not only the presidents, but also *where and when* I acquired that information. This is because of an integration of episodic and semantic memories occurring in the frontal lobes of my brain. We know this because of an interesting phenomenon called **source amnesia.** People who have source amnesia cannot recall where or when they acquired any of the information that they may have. All their general knowledge is devoid of contextual association. These people also invariably have frontal lobe damage.

STORAGE AND RETRIEVAL. Rehearsing an item (such as a telephone number) again and again may cause it to be stored in the declarative LTM, but generally items that have the most meaning are the most likely to be stored. The declarative LTM is very sensitive to meaning. Sensations that encompass low levels of information are not as likely to be remembered. For example, once you have finished reading a novel, you are likely to recall the gist of it, but you will rarely recall the exact wording of particular sentences. Things with low levels of information, such as the exact wording of sentences, or the style of typeface used, are useful for processing information, but are then typically discarded from the memory.

Of course, you can master certain techniques that will facilitate both *storage* and *retrieval.* And, interestingly, some storing may occur automatically without any particular effort. Usually, **automatic storage** occurs for meaningful and important experiences, but sometimes not. You probably have clear memories of odds and ends from years ago that are of little interest and may have led you to wonder, "Why in the world do I remember that?"

To store many of the things we wish to remember in the declarative memory, however, we must make a concerted effort. In making such an effort, a number of memory techniques can be useful. Let's take a look at some of them.

MEANING AND MEMORY. Although we haven't stressed meaning up to this point, declarative memory may be organized around meaning. This organiza-

SEMANTIC MEMORY
Memory of meanings, including all factual information of a general nature such as knowledge that the English alphabet contains 26 letters.

RETRIEVAL
To bring material from the long-term memory to the working memory so that it can be examined.

SOURCE AMNESIA
A type of amnesia in which individuals fail to recall the circumstances under which they acquired the information they possess.

AUTOMATIC STORAGE
The spontaneous placement of a sensation or experience into the long-term memory without effort or intent.

MNEMONIC
Any device or technique for improving memory.

METHOD OF LOCI
A mnemonic technique in which items are associated with positions or things along a familiar route in order to make them easier to remember.

tion may even be to the point of storing items with similar meanings together, as entries are organized in a thesaurus. The case of Mr. M. D., who had suffered a stroke, is perhaps the prime example. In an evaluation following his stroke, M. D. was shown pictures of different things—toys, tools, kitchen objects, colors, clothing, animals, vehicles, food products, and other odds and ends—and asked to name what he saw. As M. D. zipped right through the list, he seemed to do as well as anyone might. Then, suddenly, M. D. stopped. He was looking at a picture of a peach. When the examining physician asked him what he was seeing, M. D. just shook his head and said that he didn't know. The next picture was of broccoli, he didn't know what it was either. The remaining pictures were of various fruits and vegetables; whether he was looking at cherries, lettuce, tomatoes, or cucumbers, the response was always the same—M. D. recognized none of them. If it grew in a garden or an orchard, M. D. couldn't name it!

The stroke, occurring in the frontal lobe of the cortex and in the areas just below, known as the basal ganglia, had apparently resulted in this strange loss. Because he was such a clear-cut example of memory loss, M. D. had shown us, for the first time, that our memories contain a sort of filing system for words, a mental encyclopedia of categories that is organized by meaning like a thesaurus. Perhaps all of the 75,000 words that the average person commands are categorized in this way.

Most of us complain about forgetting from time to time, but we can learn strategies to improve our memory by using meaning. Without a meaning, an item is difficult to remember. Unfortunately, we're bombarded with the meaningless each and every day. For instance, the number eight means something—it means eight objects, or two units of four, or four units of two. But what does it mean when it's used in a telephone number, such as 831-9011? "Eight" in this instance is merely a place holder. It could just as well be a nonsense syllable. No wonder it's hard to remember telephone numbers.

Look at Figure 9.9. When people simply study this figure and later try to redraw it, their drawings are not very accurate. That's because, like the number eight in a telephone number, this drawing is meaningless. But suppose I told you that this was a midget playing a trombone in a telephone booth? As soon as I told you this, the figure would take on a meaning. Individuals who have such an image in mind are much better able to recall the item when tested later than are those who simply look at the item and try to memorize it (Bower, Karlin, & Dueck, 1975).

MNEMONICS.   A memory aid such as the one we just used is called a **mnemonic** (pronounced NEW-mon-ic). A mnemonic is any kind of remembering system or memory aid. There are many popular mnemonic devices. One of the oldest is known as the **method of loci,** which works well for lists of 10 to 15 objects and is very easy to use. Think of a familiar pathway, perhaps the entrance to your home or a pathway through your house, and then think of 10 or 15 items that appear in a certain order along that path. Associate each item on the list to be remembered with one of the familiar objects along that route. If you are going grocery shopping, imagine bread in your mailbox, broken eggs on the walkway, an orange where the doorknob is, and so on. After you have thought about these vivid associations for a while, you'll find that it's relatively easy to recall your whole shopping list just by "walking" down that path again in your mind's eye and stopping at the different loci to recall the associations made at each one.

Mnemonics may not be totally new to you. Did you ever have to memorize the colors of the rainbow in the right order—red, orange, yellow, green, blue, indigo, and violet? You may have been taught the mnemonic aid "Roy G.

◆ **FIGURE 9.9**

This figure is easier to remember if it's made meaningful.

Biv." Budding musicians learn "Every Good Boy Does Fine" (EGBDF) to represent the lines of the treble musical staff. William James once said that there were three ways to remember things: mechanical methods, which require intensive study and repetition, such as the way children learn the alphabet; judicious methods, which are based on logic, classification, and analysis; and ingenious methods, which include the mnemonic devices we've been discussing and which give meaning to the abstract.

MODELS OF DECLARATIVE MEMORY

Although we have said that there are two long-term memory systems (implicit, which we will discuss shortly, and declarative), the truth is that no one really knows how many distinct LTMs there might be. The following discussion highlights efforts to understand the concept that we call declarative memory. Keep in mind that the ancient Greeks believed that there were only four elements: earth, water, air, and fire. Modern chemists find that idea "quaint." Perhaps future researchers will find our current understanding of memory similarly quaint.

The Episodic Trace Model

One popular view of how declarative memory might work can be found in the **episodic trace model.** In this view, memories are stored as electrochemical traces. The concept of a **memory trace** is not new. The physiological foundations of such a concept were described by Donald Hebb in 1949. He argued that memories must somehow be fixed within the nerve pathways of the brain. Hebb believed that synapses in the brain were altered by the continuous flow of electrical impulses and that when the impulses died down the changes in the synapses remained, creating a network of neurons that stored specific memories. He argued that activating one or two of the neurons in the network could trigger others, thereby bringing stored memories back to mind. Modern researchers are still pursuing that rich line of thought—with results. As we described earlier in our discussion of the biology of memory, researchers are beginning to prove Hebb's assertion.

Building on Hebb's theory, most episodic trace models assume that memories are laid down electrochemically in the brain as entire "images" containing information about the item, its associations, and the context in which it was acquired (Raaijmakers & Shiffrin, 1992). So, if you were to remember a trip you took to an interesting place, according to this model, all of the important images and events would be given about equal strength and laid down close to one another in the brain, probably in some parallel fashion. In this way, activation of one memory might easily activate an adjacent memory, which would explain why, when you think of one part of your trip, another part of it might suddenly come to mind.

The Network Model

A **network model** assumes that memories are not laid down in "clusters" or "images" in a parallel fashion, but rather are *all* tied together in a complex network. In other words, all memories are linked. They are not seen as individual images laid down one next to the other. It is interesting to note that Donald Hebb also thought that this might be a possibility.

One of the most popular network models describing how meaning is represented in memory is based on **propositions** (Anderson, 1983; Raaijmakers & Shiffrin, 1992). The word *proposition* is borrowed from logic theory. A proposition is "the smallest unit about which it makes sense to make the judgment

EPISODIC TRACE MODEL
A model of human memory that depicts memories as being laid down as entire images that contain information about the item, its associations, and the context in which it was acquired. These "images" are assumed to be represented in the brain as electrochemical traces.

MEMORY TRACE
A presumed neurological event responsible for any relatively permanent memory. It is thought to be electrochemical in nature but may involve structural changes in the neuron.

NETWORK MODEL
A model of human memory that holds that sensory information and words are transformed into propositions or other discernible entities in order to be stored in memory in such a way that they are all interconnected, forming memory intersections like ropes in a net.

PROPOSITIONS
The smallest units of information about which it makes sense to render a judgment of true or false. For example, "red apple" is not a proposition. "The apple is red" is a proposition, however, because the statement is either true or false.

PROPOSITIONAL NETWORK THEORY
The memory theory that holds that sensory information and words are transformed into propositions in order to be stored in a memory net.

◆ **FIGURE 9.10**

Proposition 1: Jack gave a Chevrolet to Mary. This proposition contains five nodes. A node is a concept or an item of information. Each node is connected to the proposition by different kinds of links. (Links are italicized; nodes are in roman type.) Thinking about any of the nodes (Jack, Mary, Chevrolet, something that happened in the past, or giving) may bring to mind the entire proposition. The arrows do not imply the direction in which thoughts must flow (links are usually two-way streets), but only show the propositions to which nodes belong when the propositions are combined in a complex elaboration.

◆ **FIGURE 9.11**

Proposition 2: The Chevrolet is new.
Proposition 3: Mary is Jack's fiancée.

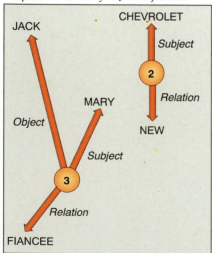

true or false" (Anderson, 1980, p. 102). For example, consider the following sentence: "Jack gave a new Chevrolet to Mary, who is his fiancée." This sentence can be broken into a number of simpler ideas, all of which are implied by the original sentence. These include: "Jack gave the Chevrolet to Mary"; "The Chevrolet was new"; "Mary is Jack's fiancée." These are considered propositions because they are either true or false, whereas just "the Chevrolet" could not be a proposition.

Storing something according to what it *means*, rather than by how it is stated or by how it looks, requires a propositional representation rather than a visual or verbal representation. **Propositional network theory** argues that if we wish to recall how something looked or was stated, we must first locate (recall) its meaning and from there reconstruct our own sensory or verbal representation.

If the LTM is filled with many propositions—that is, bits of simple meaning—then there must be a way in which the bits can interact. In a propositional network, each proposition is represented by a circle that is connected to the components of the proposition by arrows. The components are called "nodes," and the arrows connecting the nodes are called "links." Each arrow is labeled to indicate what kind of link it is. In Figure 9.10, you see the proposition "Jack gave a Chevrolet to Mary" as it might appear in the LTM, with the different nodes (components) connected by links (relationships). Perhaps this arrangement approximates the biochemical organization of this memory.

Figure 9.11 shows two other propositions: "The Chevrolet is new" and "Mary is Jack's fiancée." In Figure 9.12, the three propositions are joined. By starting at the node "Mary," that is, at one of the places in your memory where you have stored the name "Mary," you can "travel" in many directions, for instance, to the nodes "fiancée," "Jack," or "Chevrolet," because they are all linked to "Mary." Once you reach the node "Chevrolet," you can then travel down a link to the node "new." If information is organized like this in your LTM, then thinking of Mary may remind you that she is Jack's fiancée and that she received a Chevrolet, and thinking of Chevrolet may then trigger the recollection that the Chevrolet was new. To recall a particular node, you may have to "travel" to a number of other nodes; one recollection is likely to trigger another.

Memories seem to be linked in different ways. Some nodes are very close and strongly linked to other nodes, so if you remember one, you are likely to remember the others. Then again, some nodes may be far away from others or poorly linked, in which case remembering one node helps you very little in recalling the others. For instance, recalling that the Canadian flag has a maple leaf may not be of much help if you are trying to remember where you left your car keys, because the proposition "The Canadian flag has a maple leaf" is probably not closely linked to the location of your keys. On the other hand, recalling the table in your kitchen might tip you off, assuming that you left your keys on or near it.

In this view, digging into your memory is much like parachuting into a city. If you land near your target, you can reach it quickly. Otherwise, it may take you a long time to get where you want to be, and you may have to travel a number of complex routes to get there. The terrain of memory, of course, is bound to be even more complex than the streets of a city, because it is most likely laid out within the brain in three dimensions.

This model also offers some startling explanations for certain phenomena. For example, in Chapter 16 we will discuss multiple personality. Perhaps you have already encountered this mental disorder in film depictions such as *The Three Faces of Eve* or *Sybil*. In this mysterious disorder, individuals appear to develop more than one personality. These personalities rarely appear simultaneously; instead, they seem to vie for consciousness. Often one personality is totally unaware of another. No one is sure what causes multiple personality, but some interesting possibilities are under investigation. One such possibility involves propositional network theory. Interestingly, researchers have found that about 98 percent of people with multiple personality were abused as children (Chance, 1986). It may be that these individuals, through fear and anxiety, repressed and isolated their childhood experiences. As a result, their memories may have developed in a fragmented way, with whole sections of memory cordoned off from other sections, linked together poorly or not at all. If this is the case, when a particular node or memory is activated, a person with multiple personality disorder may be trapped within a limited fraction of her memory, with each fraction holding different and limited "knowledge" about herself. Such limited and enclosed areas of memory might easily seem to be separate and distinct personalities. Of course, no one knows the real cause for sure, but this hypothesis is interesting. If it is correct, future researchers will view multiple personality as a developmental failure to integrate memory.

There is other evidence as well to support the network model. This evidence indicates that memories may be laid out in an interconnected three-dimensional arrangement corresponding with the biology of the brain. For instance, when subjects were asked to create an imaginary space around themselves and then to fill that space with various imaginary objects, it was discovered that items imagined to be in front of the subjects could be recalled faster than items imagined to be behind them (Franklin & Tversky, 1990). This research implies the existence of a mental representation connected and linked in a way that is similar to the real personal space around us. Even in our imaginations, then, it takes longer to see something "behind" us than to look at something right in "front" of us.

Network models are very popular. Still, as some researchers point out, the episodic trace model is better able to explain certain findings. For instance, the network model would lead us to believe that *apple-pear* would be an easier combination to remember than *apple-engine* simply because the two fruits are more likely to be paired in real life. However, apple-engine is often more memorable because it is a unique pairing. The episodic trace model indicates that such an odd pairing would cause *apple* and *engine* to be laid down parallel to one another in a "memory image" that would include the recollection that you were studying about this in your psychology textbook. If we talk about this enough, it may even be that years later you will still remember *apple-engine* from your textbook while it may be harder for you to recall *apple-pear*. How does the network model explain this? Is there now a strong link in your brain between apples and engines that wasn't there before? It is puzzling, and some researchers are attempting to blend the episodic trace model and the network model into a single hybrid model that will contain the best aspects of both views (Squire, Knowlton, & Musen, 1993).

❧ IMPLICIT MEMORY

Storage and retrieval are also important functions of the implicit memory systems. **Implicit memory,** sometimes called nondeclarative memory, occurs unconsciously; that is, you don't have to bring these memories into conscious recall in order for them to function. Implicit memories, such as recalling how to play the piano, are recalled almost effortlessly as one acts. Similarly, professional dancers or fighters often report that they don't have to think about their next move in a certain situation, they just act. In fact, thinking about what they are doing can interfere with the action.

IMPLICIT MEMORY
The memory underlying cognitive, perceptual, and motor skills. Implicit memories include the unconscious expression of skills or habits, conditioning without awareness, and the phenomenon of priming. It is sometimes called skill memory, or procedural memory.

◆ **FIGURE 9.12**

The three propositions combined.

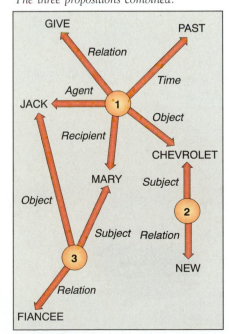

SKILLS
The capacity for carrying out a complex, well-organized, pattern of behavior smoothly and efficiently. The term refers to both motor and cognitive-perceptual abilities, most of which are carried out unconsciously, that is, without having to think about them. Playing the piano is an example of a skill. Once skills become almost automatic, they are believed to be held as implicit memories.

Unlike declarative memory, implicit memories are usually acquired slowly with practice and are very hard to forget. As they say, once you've learned how to ride a bicycle, you never forget. Implicit memory appears to be a mixed collection of different types of long-term memories that are not centered on the medial temporal lobes, limbic system, or thalamus, but rely on a number of different brain systems. For example, we know that the removal or destruction of the hippocampus will have a profound effect on the ability to store long-term declarative memories. However, the acquisition of simple conditioned responses (see Chapter 8) will occur in animals despite the removal of the hippocampus (Solomon & Moore, 1975). Amnesic patients will also retain such implicit memories as a conditioned response (in this instance an eye-blink caused by a puff of air, conditioned to a noise) even though they can't later recall having been conditioned! Not much is known about the biology of implicit memory, however, so it is probably too early to develop a classification scheme for implicit memory based on neural organization (Squire, Knowlton, & Musen, 1993). But most researchers do make distinctions between various kinds of implicit memories such as skills, certain kinds of conditioning (see Chapter 8), and an interesting phenomenon called "priming."

Skills

Skills are fairly unconscious procedures that you acquire for dealing with the world (see Figure 9.13). Reading is a good example of such a skill. You scan the words in this text and seem to know what they say as if by magic. You don't have to think about each word. There was a time in your life, however, when you did have to stop and think about each word. But now written words and how to scan them are part of a skill that has been stored in your implicit memory.

Skills are sometimes referred to as "motor memories," because they often involve muscular activity, such as riding a bicycle or playing an instrument. Skills are generally acquired slowly and with practice. The kind of implicit memory that includes skills is sometimes referred to as "skill memory" or "procedural memory." Declarative memories often interact with implicit memories. When riding a bicycle, for example, you may consciously recall the best way to bank a particular turn (declarative) while all the while shifting your weight and altering your pedaling without awareness (implicit).

◆ **FIGURE 9.13**

The areas of the brain and the types of skills involved in implicit memory.

IMPLICIT MEMORY

Brain Pathways Involved

Posterior neocortex

Caudate nucleus

Putamen

Cerebellum

Skills Involved

Playing a musical instrument

Reading mirror-reversed words

Doing physical activities and sports

Solving puzzles

Identifying the different kinds of implicit memories is not easy, however. For example, researchers did not realize that the learning of skills could proceed independently of long-term declarative memory until the famous case of the severely amnesic H. M., who was able to show improvement day-by-day at a mirror-drawing task but was completely unable to remember ever having practiced it. We'll examine H. M.'s case in more detail later in the chapter.

Implicit memories can often be created right from the beginning without awareness; that is, they don't always start out as declarative memories that finally become ingrained, unconscious habits. In Chapter 8, we discussed a conditioning experiment in which good or bad words were associated with the nationalities Swedish and Dutch. Without being aware that they had been manipulated, students reading those associations reported changing their feelings about those nationalities. In another study, pictures of women labeled "kind" or "capable" were shown to subjects. Unknown to the subjects, "kind" women happened to be all those with a certain length of hair, while "capable" women had a different length. Results showed that the subjects remembered this distinction enough to later influence their judgments about who was "kind" or "capable" and that they did so implicitly, that is, without awareness (Lewicki, 1986).

Priming

A few years ago, it was discovered that some amnesics who totally lose great blocks of memory may have near normal recall if they are given little hints or partial images about what they can't remember. This has led researchers to argue that there is yet another kind of implicit memory, called **priming memory,** which helps us remember from little prompts, whereas declarative memory will usually work in cases in which no prompts or hints are available (Tulving & Schacter, 1990). Studies using the PET scan (see Chapter 2) have found that a portion of the neocortex at the back of the right hemisphere seems to be most involved during the activation of priming memory (Squire, et al., 1992).

Priming, and implicit memory in general, can perhaps be best illustrated by the case of Mrs. X. Mrs. X had suffered from a terrible attack of viral encephalitis. The resulting inflammation of her brain caused severe damage to her limbic system. Like Mrs. Duke in the chapter prologue, she had total **anterograde amnesia** and could no longer store information in her long-term declarative memory. This ability, which we all take for granted, simply stopped, dating from the time of her illness. This meant that although Mrs. X could remember events before her illness, anything that happened since that time faded from her mind moments after it occurred.

Although her working memory was unaffected, Mrs. X was no longer able to hold her job. At work, she had been required to engage in a fairly complicated process of filing, which included transferring business information from a card onto an eight-column display. She also had to identify long numbers, such as document and serial numbers, and process them through a series of steps, many of which she had to stop and think about, therefore recalling from declarative memory what went where and what she needed to write on each card and on the display. Her chances of ever holding such a job again were realistically thought to be zero because she "couldn't remember anything."

But psychologist David Schacter had an idea based on what he knew about priming and implicit memory. He knew that people with failed declarative memories like Mrs. X were able to learn and recall new information from their implicit memories. Schacter wondered whether Mrs. X could learn her job *implicitly!* He began working with her by using priming. For instance, if at a certain place she had always known to write the word "code" but had now

PRIMING MEMORY
A hypothetical memory thought possibly to exist as a distinct entity because in certain cases of amnesia, access to a lost memory may be gained via small prompts, thereby giving rise to the name "priming" memory.

ANTEROGRADE AMNESIA
The inability to recall experiences or events that occur after the amnesia-causing trauma.

INTERFERENCE EFFECTS
In memory, a conflict between
information contained in the memory so
that (1) previously learned information
makes it more difficult to learn new
information (proactive interference) or
(2) recently learned information makes
it more difficult to recall old
information (retroactive interference).

forgotten, Schacter would display "cod _," which helped prime her that "code" was the word to write in that location. Schacter then incorporated the method of vanishing cues by shortening the cue for "code" to just "co __" and then just "c ___ ." Amazingly, after enough practice, the last cue, the letter "c," could be dropped and the blank space functioned as the cue, still engaging the priming memory! After several training sessions, Mrs. X was able to perform her old job as well as she had before. However, she does not recall receiving the special training. She can't even explain how it is that she knows what to do at her job, because she still "can't remember anything" (Greenberg, 1987)!

🔀 FORGETTING

You are not always able to retrieve information that you put into one of your LTMs. A good example of the loss of information from declarative memory can be found in the first memory experiment conducted by Hermann von Ebbinghaus in 1885. Ebbinghaus memorized a list of nonsense syllables and then retested his recollection at different intervals. What he obtained is known as a forgetting curve (see Figure 9.14). For fun, you might repeat his experiment on yourself and observe the results. You should find that Ebbinghaus's forgetting curve is as accurate today as ever and that your own score is very similar to his.

Decay and Loss

The first reason for forgetting is a simple one: The information may no longer be in an LTM. Although some researchers believe that LTM items are permanent, others have concluded that some of them may decay and be lost (Loftus & Loftus, 1980). To date, all the biochemical theories of memory support the idea that LTM items can decay, if for no other reason than that any chemical arrangement may, under certain circumstances, break down or become rearranged. Perhaps the LTM items most likely to be lost are chemically weak; that is, they were not extremely important or were not well rehearsed.

Interference Effects

Sometimes, when we try to retrieve a memory from an LTM, certain experiences can interfere with the retrieval. The influences of these experiences are known collectively as **interference effects.**

PROACTIVE INTERFERENCE.   When proactive interference occurs, it interferes with declarative memory in a "pro" or forward-acting fashion. For in-

Hermann Ebbinghaus (1850–1909)

◆ **FIGURE 9.14**

Ebbinghaus's classic curve of forgetting. Each point on the forgetting curve represents the percentage of items remembered from the original list. Notice that more forgetting occurs in the first 20 minutes than in the remaining 31 days.

stance, suppose you have a new telephone number. Whenever you want to think of your new telephone number, you begin a search in your memory for the number. The old search pattern (looking for your telephone number) has been activated so many times that the search for your new number may lead you to your old number. You know that you have a new telephone number, but you can only remember the old one. What you are experiencing is **proactive interference**—the existence of old information is interfering with the ability to learn something new. To borrow from the network model, think of the declarative LTM as a network of streets running through a city to different locations—streets that crisscross each other. If you are used to driving down three or four streets to get to a particular place but now must use the same streets to go somewhere else, it's easy, if you're not thinking, to take the wrong turn near the end of your route and go to the old location. Previously learned material is somehow interfering with your ability to retain or recall something new. A similar interference effect can also occur for some kinds of implicit memory. In that case, it is often called *negative transfer of learning*; an example might be trying to learn a new arrangement of letters on an unusual typewriter keyboard *after* you had mastered the regular keyboard. You can imagine the problems you'd face!

RETROACTIVE INTERFERENCE. If you practice your new number often enough and are required to recall it under many different circumstances, you will rearrange your memory so that the new number is now associated with many other memories. Eventually, the links or associations to the new number will be *stronger* than those to the old one, and you'll tend to retrieve the new number when you try to recall your old one. This is known as **retroactive interference;** that is, learning something new interferes with the recall of old memories (see Figure 9.15).

The Tip-of-the-Tongue Phenomenon

Besides proactive and retroactive interference, other things can get in the way of LTM retrieval. Sometimes, we can't seem to retrieve a bit of information that we're sure we have stored because we can't find a path to the information.

PROACTIVE INTERFERENCE
The process by which previously learned material interferes with the ability to learn something new.

RETROACTIVE INTERFERENCE
The process by which learning something new interferes with the ability to recall previously learned information.

◆ **FIGURE 9.15**

Experimental arrangements designed to test interference effects. Experiment 1 tests for retroactive interference, while experiment 2 tests for proactive interference. If interference effects occur, the experimental groups will have lower test scores than the control groups have.

TIP-OF-THE-TONGUE PHENOMENON
The experience of being almost able to recall a certain bit of information. You sense that the information is there, you can almost "feel" it, and yet you cannot grasp it.

RETRIEVAL CUE
Any stimulus that can help you gain access to a memory.

This frustration has been known for many years as the **tip-of-the-tongue phenomenon.** William James described the experience in this way:

Suppose we try to recall a forgotten name. The state of our consciousness is peculiar: There is a gap therein; but no mere gap. It is a gap that is intensively active. A sort of wraith of the name is in it, beckoning us in a given direction, making us at moments tingle with the sense of our closeness and then letting us sink back without the longed-for term. If wrong names are proposed to us, this singularly defined gap acts immediately so as to negate them. They do not fit into this mold. And the gap of one word does not feel like the gap of another, all empty of content as both might seem necessarily to be when described as gaps. (James, 1890)

The tip-of-the-tongue experience is particularly frustrating because we feel so close to the information sought. We even seem to know things about what we can't remember. We seem to be actively searching through our LTM network for an association or link that will take us to the right node.

There are some specific methods we can use to make the needed association. Suppose you can't remember the name of a particular person, but it's on the tip of your tongue. How might you find the path that leads to the correct node or trace containing the name? One way is to travel to related memories to see whether there is a direct link from any of them to the memory for which you are searching. For instance, you might reflect on a picture of that person or on the sound of that person's voice. One very good method is to proceed through the alphabet sounding out letters to see whether any of those sounds suddenly triggers the recall of the name (Brown, 1991). By selectively searching all the different accesses you might have to the necessary memory, you may eventually find a retrieval cue or direct link.

Retrieval Cues

A **retrieval cue** can be a great help in getting at something that you can almost remember. This is why multiple-choice tests are easier than tests that require strict recall; the former are loaded with retrieval cues. Let's take a look at the difference between a recall and a recognition test.

Here is a recall question: "Who was the next president after Washington?" To answer this question, you need to activate "Washington" in your memory and examine the associations you have made with Washington. You may have many associations with Washington. But can you activate the memory that will lead you to the answer? Perhaps not. That link or association may be too weak or nonexistent.

How about a question that encompasses two points of memory access: "Was Adams the president after Washington?" Now you have two places from which to begin your search. You can go to your memories concerning what you know about "Washington," check the associations with Washington, and try to find a link or association with Adams. Or you can start with what you know about "Adams." If one of the things you know about Adams is that he came directly after Washington, then you can answer the question correctly.

Curiously, many links or associations in the LTM seem to be stronger in one direction than in the other. If you can't get from Washington to Adams, you may be able to get from Adams to Washington. By making the latter association, however, you strengthen the link or association from Washington to Adams; if you are asked again who was the next president after Washington, you'll be more likely to recall that it was Adams.

Supporters of the episodic trace model would say that this particular improvement in one's memory has occurred because a *new* memory image, more strongly combining Adams and Washington, has now been laid down and that this information, because of its strength, will take precedence the next time you go looking for the president following Washington. Supporters of the network model, on the other hand, view this improvement as a simple strengthening of the *previously existing link* between the Washington and Adams nodes in the memory network or, if this is your first exposure to this information, the creation of a new link. Of course, as mentioned earlier, both models may have merit. If the mental images of the episodic trace model were large and complex enough, and if new information could be added to them, they would begin to resemble small networks. In fact, some researchers in the field view memory traces not as distinct localized entities, but rather as part of a superimposition of all traces put into the system, all of which follow complex mathematical rules for interacting. This concept is found in the various *distributed memory models* that are beginning to become popular. Whatever the eventual outcome is, memory is bound to be far more curious than any of our models currently would suggest. I say this, because none of the theories of memory generated from these models can yet predict or explain all of the things we observe to be true about memory.

The Strength of a Memory

Many things determine whether memories will be strong or weak. Most people believe that shocking or surprising events, either pleasant or unpleasant, usually create very strong memories. If the event is powerful enough, it seems that a memory will be created between nearly every associated event and the event itself. Whatever the powerful news from one generation to the next (that Pearl Harbor has been attacked, John Kennedy has been shot, Neil Armstrong has just stepped on the moon, the space shuttle *Challenger* has exploded, the war in the Gulf has begun), or whatever the personal shock, people often remember where they were standing, who and what were around them, and what others said. This effect is so striking that it has been given an apt name, **flashbulb memory**.

Flashbulb memories were once thought by some to be almost as reliable as photographs. Now we know that although the memories are vivid, they are not perfect. It was formerly believed that flashbulb memories might be particularly vivid because the hormone ACTH is secreted at times of stress and had been found to enhance memory formation by increasing attention (Sandman, George, Nolan, Van Riezen, & Kastin, 1975). Another substance, called cholecystokinin, or CCK, is secreted during eating and has been found to act directly on nerve fibers associated with memory (Flood, Smith, & Morley, 1987). It was also thought that this mechanism, which may have evolved to help boost adaptive memories about where food was located, was also affecting the vividness of flashbulb memories.

Flashbulb memory, however, doesn't appear to be a special kind of memory at all. Flashbulb memories can fade over time, and in all other ways they behave like normal memories (Cohen, McCloskey, & Wible, 1988). For example, in one interesting study, psychologist Charles Weaver decided to examine how memories fade over time. He asked 22 students in his class to do their best to remember the circumstances surrounding their next meeting with a friend or roommate. By coincidence, on the same day that the students were given a questionnaire asking about their meetings (January 16, 1991), the United States began bombing Iraq. The students all agreed that the news, although somewhat expected, was memorable and had upset them.

Taking advantage of this unique situation, Weaver decided to test the students not only on their memories of their personal meeting with a friend or roommate, but also on their recollections of the start of the bombing. The students were retested after two more days, again after three months, and finally after one year. These probes showed that memories for both events were com-

FLASHBULB MEMORY
The vivid impression left on the memory by the stimuli associated with a shocking or surprising event.

RECONSTRUCTION
In memory, the unconscious placement into memory of a deduction or assumption of what one believes must have happened. Such created memories are often recalled as though they were recollections of actual events.

SCRIPTS
In cognitive study, one's knowledge of the appropriate events that should occur in a particular social setting and of how one might carry them out. This comprises knowledge of who is expected to do what to whom as well as when, where, and why. A script would include such typical behaviors as those expected of a person visiting a restaurant or going to a movie.

CONSOLIDATION
The strengthening process through which memory traces, or engrams, must go before they can become a fixed part of the long-term memory.

parable and rates of forgetting were similar (Weaver, 1993). There had been nothing special about the personal meetings with friends or roommates other than that the students had made an effort to remember them. Flashbulb memories may be vivid then, because at the time of the extraordinary incident, we pay close attention to the event. They also may be vivid because we often bring them to mind (simply because they are so meaningful to us) and thereby rehearse them. Recalling them also ties them to other events, which makes the flashbulb memories easier to find later; that is, they become less forgettable—but they are not a special or unique kind of memory as was once thought.

Reconstruction and Retrieval

Sometimes we add our own inventions to actual events without realizing it. Such an addition to a memory is known as a **reconstruction.** One of the primary ways in which we create reconstructions is through the use of **scripts.** A script is a hypothetical memory organization that encompasses people's knowledge of the *typical* events in everyday experience. If an LTM item is not complete, we often fill it in with our script knowledge. If you have ever attended a wedding, you may remember the bride saying, "I do." But think about it. Do you really *remember* that particular statement, or are you using a script of weddings to fill in your recollection?

Look at Figure 9.16. You've certainly placed the visual image of a penny into your LTM. Or have you? Psychologists argue that our LTMs are filled with many errors and mistakes. Do you know which of the pennies in Figure 9.16 is the real one? A great number of people don't. If you're not sure, get a penny and check. If you were wrong, why were you wrong? Is it because you had "forgotten" what a penny looks like? More likely, it is because you never really knew. Just because you have a lot of experience with something doesn't mean that the whole experience is stored in long-term memory.

Failure of Consolidation

Long-term memories may be lost through a failure of **consolidation.** Consolidation is a dynamic feature of LTM. It seems that after information is first put into the LTM, a certain amount of time is necessary for it to consolidate or to take its place in the memory; that is, information new to the LTM is

◆ **FIGURE 9.16**

Which drawing shows the real penny? (SOURCE: *Nickerson and Adams, 1979, p. 297.*)

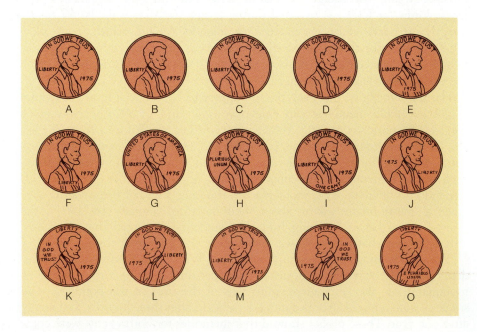

somewhat fragile. This may represent the time it takes the new memory to be transferred from its initial LTM store (the medial temporal lobes including the areas of the amygdala, hippocampus, and thalamus) to the neocortex where it can be held indefinitely (Squire, Knowlton, & Musen, 1993). As long as several years may be required before the memory is firmly and totally implanted (consolidated) (Squire, 1986).

A number of interesting things can interfere with the consolidation process. For instance, cigarette smoking is known to affect it. The active agent involved appears to be nicotine (Houston, Schneider, & Jarvik, 1978), but exactly how nicotine interferes with consolidation is unknown. A sudden shock or trauma can interfere with consolidation to an extensive degree, causing complete loss of very recent memories. It's not uncommon for a person who has been involved in a terrifying incident, such as a severe car crash, to forget everything that occurred within half an hour to an hour before the accident, or for even longer periods before the trauma. Such loss of memory is known as **retrograde amnesia,** and it may be a permanent loss. If LTM memories are jarred very early in the consolidation process, they may be as forgotten as if they had been lost from an STM. Some victims of car crashes find it particularly upsetting that they can't even remember why they were on a particular road or where they had been planning to go when their accident occurred.

Motivated Forgetting

Motivated forgetting is another way in which LTM items can seem to be lost. This sort of forgetting is an active and purposeful one that people use to keep themselves from recalling threatening, painful, or embarrassing memories. Clinical psychologists often use the term **repression** when referring to the process through which memories are forced from conscious awareness. Repressed memories are not available for active recall.

As an example, I can recall a good friend of mine who once remarked to everyone's surprise that he was embarrassed that he had not attended his own mother's funeral and that his relatives must have thought it awful of him not to have gone. This statement surprised those of us who knew him, because most of us had gone to that funeral and clearly remembered him being there. When we told him as much, he was sure we were mistaken. He finally checked with some close relatives and also looked in the guest registry from the funeral—we were right, he had been there.

Odds are that this is an example of motivated forgetting because any experience so upsetting isn't likely to have been forgotten simply because one wasn't paying attention at the time. We all remembered the funeral, and it wasn't our mother who had died. Furthermore, even after everyone had jogged his memory, he still couldn't recall a thing about the funeral. He has also said that while he now does believe he was there, it is just as well that he can't remember because he doesn't want to bring such sad thoughts to mind.

Under severe psychological stress, repression can become so extensive that many memories can be kept from retrieval. Such a condition is referred to as **psychogenic amnesia.** The lost memories usually are personal in nature, such as the person's name or address, rather than letters in the alphabet or how to operate a car. Psychogenic amnesia is discussed in greater detail in Chapter 16.

Somatogenic Amnesia

Somatogenic amnesia is the kind old Hollywood movies tried to depict: The victim would be suddenly thumped on the head and then would forget everything. The old Hollywood solution to this amnesia, of course, was to thump

RETROGRADE AMNESIA
An amnesia brought on by a sudden shock or trauma that causes earlier events to be forgotten.

MOTIVATED FORGETTING
Purposeful forgetting in which memories are repressed in order to fulfill unconscious desires to avoid the memories.

REPRESSION
A psychological process in which memories and motives are not permitted to enter consciousness but are operative at an unconscious level.

PSYCHOGENIC AMNESIA
A disorder involving selective memory loss for psychological reasons. The individual forgets, partially or totally, his or her past identity, but remembers nonthreatening aspects of life.

SOMATOGENIC AMNESIA
Disorders involving selective memory loss for physical reasons such as brain trauma, disease, or toxic exposure. The kind of memory loss depends on the type of injury or illness.

LOCUS-DEPENDENT MEMORY
A memory that has been associated with a particular location so that it is easier to recall when you are in that location.

the victim on the head one more time, setting everything right (a solution that, as you may have guessed, doesn't work very well). In reality, physically induced amnesia is far more complicated and varied. The kind of amnesia produced may vary greatly, depending on the type of injury or disease.

Two of the most interesting examples of somatogenic amnesia, from which researchers have gathered much information, are the cases of H. M. and N. A. You may recall that we discussed H. M.'s case in Chapter 2. He was operated on in 1953 in an effort to control his seizures. Portions of his limbic system closely associated with memory function were destroyed. After the surgery, H. M. was no longer able to store memories in his declarative LTM. He had to get by on what he had learned before 1953. All events since that time vanished from his mind moments after they happened. Like Mrs. X, whom we discussed earlier in the chapter, he had anterograde amnesia.

H. M.'s injury also helped researchers make further distinctions between declarative and implicit memory. Although H. M. was unable to place facts into declarative LTM, aspects of his implicit memory seemed to be unaffected. For example, he could learn new motor skills—playing tennis, reading words backward in a mirror, or solving puzzles. And, although he didn't remember learning to do puzzles, the more he practiced, the better he got at doing them (Alper, 1986).

N. A. was a college student who one day entered his dormitory room just in time to be pierced by a miniature fencing foil with which his roommate was practicing. The roommate accidentally thrust the tip of the fencing foil into N. A.'s right nostril and upward, piercing the middle of N. A.'s brain. With the precision of a surgeon's knife, the foil cut into the left side of the thalamus. Since N. A.'s injury was on the left side of the brain, he lost many verbal memories, but his memory of images was unharmed. As you may recall from Chapter 2, verbal skills are more often controlled by the left hemisphere of the brain, while spatial representations are more often stored in the right hemisphere.

As you can see, the kinds of amnesia suffered by H. M. and N. A. are very different from each other, and each has helped to illuminate our understanding of memory.

❧ ENCODING EFFECTS

Certain circumstances can influence how memories are encoded (entered) into long-term memory. This, in turn, can affect the conditions under which memories can be best retrieved. Two important encoding effects are locus-dependent memory and mood, or state-dependent learning, both of which are interesting types of retrieval cues.

Locus-Dependent Memory

I can recall once sitting in my living room and thinking that I should call my brother later in the day. Then I went outside to water some plants. Once I was outside, I knew that just a few seconds earlier, I had been thinking of something that I needed to do, but I couldn't remember what it was. I did know, however, that I had been sitting in the living room when I was thinking about it, so I went back inside and sat down where I had just been. Almost immediately I remembered that I had to call my brother (I also recalled that it wasn't about anything important and that I had left the hose running outside—I mention this so that you won't feel that you are the only one whose memory seems screwy from time to time). In this instance, my memory of needing to call my brother was tied, in part, to a certain location in my house. This illustrates the phenomenon of **locus-dependent memory.**

Two researchers, Godden and Baddeley, demonstrated this phenomenon in 1975 in what is now considered a classic (and fun) experiment. They had people learn 40 unrelated words either on the beach or, while using scuba equipment, 20 feet under the sea! Half the people in each group were then asked to switch locations before everyone tried to recall the words. Table 9.1 shows the results of the study. As you can see, people who learned the list on the beach were able to recall it better on the beach than beneath the water, while those who learned beneath the water could recall better under water. This indicates that during learning, elements in the environment become associated in the memory with the items to be remembered, so that reexposure to the same elements may facilitate recall of those items.*

In another study conducted at the University of Michigan, students memorized lists of paired items one day in a large, windowless room with an instructor who was dressed in a suit and tie. On the second day, another group of subjects learned similar paired items in a small room filled with daylight, and this time the instructor was dressed casually in jeans and a flannel shirt. In both cases, the items to be learned were presented on a tape recorder. On the third day, the subjects were placed in one setting or the other and asked to recall what they had learned. Those who had learned the list in the setting where they were tested were successful in recalling 59 percent of the list on the average, but subjects who had learned the list in a different setting could remember only 46 percent of the list on the average (Smith, Glenberg, & Bjork, 1978).

Subjects also have been found to remember more accurately if the same sounds are present during recall as were present during learning (Smith, 1985).

In the Mood

Your emotional state may also affect your ability to remember particular items. This phenomenon is called **state-dependent learning.** If people can return to the same emotional or physical state that they were in when they learned information, they find it easier to remember. In Charlie Chaplin's classic film comedy *City Lights*, Chaplin plays a character he made famous, the Little Tramp. In the film, Chaplin saves a drunken man from leaping to his death. As it turns out, the drunk is a millionaire and becomes Chaplin's friend. The two spend the evening together, having a good time and becoming drinking buddies. The next day, however, the millionaire is sober and, not recognizing Charlie, refuses even to speak to him. Later, the millionaire becomes drunk once more, and the moment he sees Charlie, he reacts as though he had found a long-lost friend. Interestingly, evidence for this effect exists. People who learn

*Truly, only a psychologist would have devised an experiment that required subjects to learn a list of words while under water.

STATE-DEPENDENT LEARNING
The phenomenon that memories are recalled with greater ease when you are in the same or similar mood or physical state as when you first acquired the memory.

In this scene from the movie City Lights, *the drunken millionaire is Charlie's good friend. But whenever the millionaire is sober he can't recall who Charlie is and has him thrown out. This is an example of state-dependent learning.*

TABLE 9.1 ◆ RELATIONSHIP BETWEEN RECALL AND ENVIRONMENT			
GROUP	LOCATION TO LEARN MATERIAL	LOCATION TO RECALL MATERIAL	MEAN RECALL SCORE
A	dry	dry	13.5
B	dry	wet	8.6
C	wet	wet	11.4
D	wet	dry	8.4

NOTE: Subjects recall material studied in one location more accurately when they are in that same location.

SOURCE: Adapted from Godden & Baddeley, 1975, p. 328.

something when they are under the influence of alcohol may find that they cannot recall what they learned when they are sober, but can remember it if they once again become drunk (Overton, 1972).

The Spacing Effect

Researcher S. A. Madigan once asked subjects to repeat as many items as they could remember from a list of 48 words that had been presented to them at the rate of one word every 1½ seconds. Most subjects were able to recall about 28 percent of the words. Madigan discovered, however, that if some of the words were repeated, subjects were more likely to remember those words. Specifically, he found that although the subjects could recall only 28 percent of the words they had heard once, they could recall 47 percent of the words they had heard twice (Madigan, 1969).

This discovery should hardly come as a surprise to anyone. After all, the more familiar you become with something, the more likely you are to remember it. But Madigan discovered something else that was a surprise: Among the words heard twice, a word was more likely to be remembered if the *interval* between the first and second presentations had been a long one. If the word had been said twice in a row, it was least likely to be remembered. Madigan's finding is known as the **spacing effect.** As far as anyone can tell, there seems to be no limit to the amount of spacing (additional time between first and second presentations) that will bring further improvement of memory (Anderson, 1980).

Why does this spacing effect occur? One researcher has argued that if you study something for the second time immediately after you have studied it the first time, you may think of the second study session as unnecessary and redundant and pay little attention to it. If you study something a second time

Because of contextual overlap, the student who studies in the library will be more likely to recall the information during the test, unless, of course, the test is given outdoors!

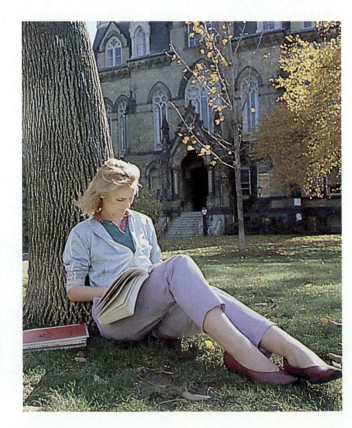

FOCUS ON AN APPLICATION

TO CRAM OR NOT TO CRAM?

It is a rare and lucky student who loves to study. Most students, although they may enjoy reading assigned material, find that they must make a concentrated effort to recall it during a test. And since studying can be a strenuous process, students commonly put it off until the last possible moment—and then find that they must learn a great deal of material in the few hours remaining before the examination. This concentrated learning is called **massed practice,** or cramming. Is cramming the best way to study?

Of course it isn't, you say. Everybody knows it's a foolish thing to do—a sign of procrastination and poor study habits. The good student will study material regularly as it is assigned. Conversely, a bad student will cram. Therefore, it must be better not to cram. Sounds logical, and you have probably heard it from your parents and teachers for years, but is it true?

The spacing effect has shown that information is recalled more accurately if it is learned more than once, especially if there is a large gap in time between the first and the second exposure to the material. The spacing effect, therefore, certainly argues against cramming. But why does the spacing effect work? There is some evidence that if a significant amount of time has elapsed between the first and the second exposure to the same material, it's likely that the material will be learned in different contexts and moods. Thus, the chances are better that the mood and physical surroundings at the time of the test will be similar to at least one of the study sessions. If you are in the same mood, feel about the same way, and have similar physical surroundings when you take your test as you did when you studied the material, you'll have more access to the memories containing the information.

For the same reasons, cramming *can* work well if you know exactly when you are due to take a particular test. If you cram within limits, so that you don't become excessively fatigued, there is a good chance that you will be in the same mood and mental set during testing. If you study thoroughly for many hours before a test and then walk straight into the testing situation feeling much as you did while you studied, you're likely to do well (Glenberg, 1976; Anderson, 1980). If, however, you have to study long in advance of the test, you're likely to be in a different mood, physical condition, and setting when you finally take the test. In that case, spaced practice is best.

Cramming has both weaknesses and strengths. It is not an effective way to learn material permanently. It might get you through one test, but it's a poor way to study for long-term gain or for comprehensive examinations. For lasting comprehension, spaced practice in many different moods and contexts works better. Or, as memory researcher John Anderson has stated,

Although I hate to admit this, if one's purpose is to pass an exam, concentrating a lot of study the night before the exam should be advantageous; in other words, it's best to cram. Of course, cramming will lead to poor long-term retention, as frequently noted by students a year after a course. Studying throughout the term does have some benefit, though this method is just not as efficient as cramming. The strategy that will result in the best grade combines the techniques of studying during the term and cramming the night before. (Anderson, 1980, pp. 216–217)

When massed and spaced practice are combined, people can remember a surprising amount of material, often for as long as 50 years, without the need of rehearsal. In one study, researchers found that students who had taken 3 years of Spanish 50 years earlier and had engaged in both massed and spaced practice retained about 72 percent of the Spanish vocabulary they had originally learned (Bahrick, 1984). Amazingly, these students had not practiced their Spanish or used it since their last Spanish class. The 28 percent of Spanish vocabulary they had forgotten had been lost within 6 years of taking their last class. Following that, their long-term memory of Spanish vocabulary remained stable. A very different result usually is found among students who rely only on cramming at the last minute to pass their tests. Years later, such students typically retain less than 10 percent of what they had originally learned.

In a more recent study of language students, spaced practice was found to account for almost all long-term retention (Bahrick & Phelps, 1987). These results argue for widely spaced language sessions throughout one's education if long-term retention is desired. This is not the common practice in college language courses, which usually are offered within one specific period, such as a semester.

Similarly, retention of mathematical skills is far better when learning takes place spaced out over several years. One study found that people who had taken college math courses above the level of calculus maintained most of their knowledge of high school algebra and geometry for over 50 years, while college students who didn't take math classes lost their high school math skills to a great degree (Bahrick & Hall, 1991).

after considerable delay, however, you may think of it as a more valuable experience and pay closer attention to it (Rundus, 1971).

Another possibility is that if you let enough time pass before you study something a second time, your emotional state and the context of your environment will be different on the second occasion. If the contextual variables—that is, the physical environment and your emotional state at the time you study—are important to your recall of information, then it might be valuable to study in as many different physical contexts as possible. This change of time and place provides what is known as **encoding variability,** and it helps to enlarge the elaborated network of a particular memory. In other words:

The greater the difference between the two study contexts [the first and second time you study the same material], the greater is the probability that one of the contexts will overlap with the test context. On the other hand, at short lags the two study contexts will be more similar, and the probability of study context matching test context will be not much greater than in the single-presentation condition. (Anderson, 1980, p. 214)

The message to the student couldn't be more obvious. If you want to study, study the material, wait some time, and then restudy the material in a different context; and, if possible, study it a third time, after another delay. This procedure is known as **spaced practice,** and it can greatly improve test scores (see Focus on an Application).

ENCODING VARIABILITY
Acquisition of the same information in different moods, states, or circumstances. Greater encoding variability tends to improve test performance by increasing the chances that the test situation will resemble the learning environment.

SPACED PRACTICE
A study method that creates the spacing effect. Studying is accomplished over time with gaps between study sessions. The method is also known as distributed practice.

MASSED PRACTICE
A study method that does not create a spacing effect and is, therefore, not likely to lead to long-term retention. Material is studied in a single session without any interruption. The method is also known as cramming.

SUMMARY

◆ All the images and sensations not immediately available to your senses must be drawn from your memory. Plans for the future and recollections of the past all require a functioning memory.

◆ In 1917, Karl Lashley began a search for the engram. Engrams are the hypothetical biochemical structures that underlie memories.

◆ Long-term potentiation may result when retrograde messengers enhance the transmissions from neurons, leading eventually to activation of genes, the creation of new proteins, and the growth of new connections—all of which can result in changes lasting a lifetime.

◆ Working memory is the active memory. The working memory deals with only a few items at a time and might best be thought of as the mind's blackboard on which current thoughts and mental activities are written.

◆ The modern conception of working memory is that it consists of different and distinct short-term memories; there isn't just one STM, but many.

◆ In the Baddeley and Hitch model of working memory, a central executive integrates and brings together information from different kinds of STMs, which are referred to as slave systems. The two major slave systems that they describe are the visuospatial sketch pad and the phonological loop.

◆ Material being handled by the working memory must be simultaneously stored in LTM in such a way that it can later be retrieved; otherwise the information will be lost.

◆ Long-term memory is not a single entity, but is made up of different systems each operating in different areas of the brain.

◆ Declarative memory contains conscious memories of specific facts and events. It is based on the functioning of the medial temporal lobes of the brain as well as the thalamus and its surrounding areas.

◆ Episodic and semantic memory are two types of declarative memory. Episodic memories are those one has of personal events, while semantic memories refer to memories of a more general nature.

◆ Meaningful items are stored in long-term memory more easily than meaningless items are.

◆ A mnemonic is any kind of remembering system or memory aid. One of the oldest is known as the method of loci, which is the technique of remembering items by associating them in your mind with points along a familiar pathway.

◆ According to the episodic trace model, memories are stored as electrochemical traces. Most episodic trace models assume that memories are laid down electrochemically as entire "images" containing information about the item, its associations, and the context in which it was acquired.

◆ Network models assume that memories are not laid

down in "clusters" or "images'" in a parallel fashion, but rather are all tied together in a complex network.

◆ In propositional network theory, the bits of information that make up the propositions are called nodes, and the connections between the nodes are called links.

◆ Implicit memory underlies cognitive, perceptual, and motor skills. Implicit memories include the unconscious expression of skills or habits, conditioning without awareness, and the phenomenon of priming. It is also sometimes called skill memory, or procedural memory.

◆ Skills are fairly unconscious procedures and are sometimes referred to as motor memories because they often involve muscular activity, such as riding a bicycle.

◆ Priming memory is a form of implicit memory. It is believed to exist as a distinct entity because in certain cases of amnesia, access to memories may be gained via small prompts, thereby giving rise to the name "priming" memory.

◆ Forgetting may occur for a number of reasons, such as decay, interference effects, motivated forgetting, failure of consolidation, and amnesia.

◆ A number of interference effects can obstruct long-term memory retrieval. Among these are proactive interference, in which previously learned material interferes with the ability to learn something new, and retroactive interference, in which learning something new interferes with the ability to retrieve an old memory.

◆ The tip-of-the-tongue phenomenon describes a situation in which a memory is almost, but not quite, available.

◆ A retrieval cue may provide access to a memory that is difficult to find. Such cues may be a great help in getting at tip-of-the-tongue memories.

◆ Memories are sometimes added to through reconstructions, which often include the use of scripts.

◆ Long-term memories may be lost through the failure of consolidation.

◆ Both your physical location and your emotional state can affect your ability to recall information. This phenomenon is known as state-dependent learning.

◆ The longer the time that passes between the first and the second exposure to information, the more likely a person is to remember the information. This observation is known as the spacing effect.

◆ The spacing effect may occur as the result of encoding variability—the learning of information in different moods and environments. Changing the circumstances in which a person learns can facilitate recall because it increases the chance that the recall situation will be similar to the circumstances in which the material was first learned.

◆ For long-term retention of information, spaced practice is more effective than massed practice.

🧬 SUGGESTIONS FOR FURTHER READING

1. Higbee, K. L. (1988). *Your memory: How it works and how to improve it* (2nd ed.). Englewood Cliffs, NJ: Prentice-Hall. A book for the general reader that outlines how memory works and also includes some suggestions for making memory more effective.

2. Klatzky, R. L. (1984). *Memory and awareness: An information-processing approach.* New York: W. H. Freeman. Describes how memory functions and debunks many myths associated with memory. Includes discussions on issues such as eyewitness testimony and advertising.

3. Loftus, E., & Ketcham, K. (1991). *Witness for the defense: The accused, the eyewitness, and the expert who puts memory on trial.* New York: St. Martin's Press. Discusses how eyewitnesses reconstruct what they have seen and the inherent unreliability of such reconstructions. Applies this to everyday problems of memory and the ability of people to recall past events accurately.

4. Mark, V. H., & Mark, J. P. (1992). *Reversing memory loss: Proven methods for regaining, strengthening, and preserving your memory.* Boston: Houghton Mifflin. A neurosurgeon takes you through a step-by-step procedure for finding out the causes of confusion and memory loss. He emphasizes that 30 percent of cases diagnosed as Alzheimer's disease may indeed be other problems that are treatable.

Chapter Ten

Thought and Language

PROLOGUE

CATEGORICALLY SPEAKING

Do you like to type? I won't blame you if you say no. I don't like to either. In fact, considering the length of this book, I wish I had one of those "speakwriters" that scientists have been working on—the kind you simply talk into and it types what you say! Unfortunately, they're not available yet because computers have a terrible time recognizing the same word spoken by different people.

Have you ever heard of "voiceprint identification?" It's based on the fact that no two people have exactly the same voice. The way I say "tomato" and the way you say "tomato" sound completely different to a computer. Perhaps the onset of my voice is a little more rapid than yours, or perhaps we differ in our inflections or in the "phones" we use. (Phones are the smallest unit of sound that can be discriminated, but which do not affect meaning. Different phones are responsible for the same words sounding different when spoken by people with different accents, which is why it took me a moment to understand what my friend from Oklahoma meant when she said that her "pan" had run out of ink.) In general, inexpensive machines programmed to "understand" one person's speech are typically unable to understand anyone else's unless the machines are required only to recognize differences among just a few words (such as the telephone company uses for collect calls).

Of course, the big question is "Why don't people have the same problem that computers do?" Why don't we grow up able to understand only our parents, siblings, and a few teachers? How is it that we can also understand strangers or anyone else who is speaking our language? The answer may lie in an inborn cognitive mechanism for the understanding of language.

In a series of experiments, researcher Peter Eimas (1985) examined what it is that human infants hear when they listen to a spoken language. The infants in the experiment were given a special pacifier to suck, and their rates of sucking were recorded. A word was then spoken by a computer. In this instance, the word "bin" was repeatedly said to the baby. When the baby first heard the computer say "bin," the sucking rate increased, indicating that the infant had noticed a change in the environment. After a short time of listening to "bin," the infant became habituated to it. That is, he be-

came used to it, and his rate of sucking dropped back to normal. Then suddenly, the computer voice changed from "bin" to "pin," and the infant immediately reacted, showing that he had perceived the switch in sound from one letter to the other.

Next, the computer simply said "bin" differently, changing intonation, voice onset, or length of voicing, so that it imitated the way different people might say the word "bin." This time, however, the infants in the study did not react! It was as though they perceived different individual voices as not being different, but perceived a change in letter sounds as very different. Eimas argues that this occurs because infants perceive language sounds in categories. To an infant, "bin" is "bin" no matter who is saying it, but "bin" is not "pin." The baby easily does what most computers find impossible to do. This has led Eimas and others to conclude that babies are genetically organized for language recognition. Eimas even refers to this ability as "phoneme constancy," classifying it as a perceptual constancy (see Chapter 6).

In much the same manner, infants as young as 2 months old treat basic vowel sounds as distinct categories, even though they may hear these few basic vowel sounds spoken hundreds of different ways by different speakers (Marean, Werner, & Kuhl, 1992). By about 6 months of age, infants will also have expanded these distinct categories to include especially the speech sounds of the language to which they are being exposed. For example, in one study, 6-month-olds listened to a stereo speaker play the English long "ee" sound as in "free." Then subtle changes in the sound were made, as might occur if different people were saying the sound. The infants were trained to look at the speaker if they heard a change in sound (when they did so correctly, they were rewarded with the sight of a toy bear). The speaker also played subtle variations of the Swedish sound "y," as in the Swedish word "fy." (The sound can be made by forming your lips in the shape of an O and saying the long English "ee" sound; there is no such sound in English.) The infants exposed to English were more aware of subtle changes in the Swedish sounds than in the English sounds, while the Swedish infants were more aware of changes in the English sounds (Kuhl, Williams, Lacerda, Stevens, & Lindblom, 1992). These results imply that the infants are already learning to categorize the variations of sounds from their own language into categories to be treated as identical—and they are doing this before ever speaking their first words!

This ability to take the tremendous variety of speech sounds, which are different for each person speaking, and perceive them within category groupings is what makes language perception and production possible. And while it is true that a few extremely elaborate and expensive computers are making some small strides in this direction, babies have it down pat!

IN THIS CHAPTER, we'll examine thinking and problem solving and the relationship between cognition and language. We'll learn how language emerges and what language is. In addition, we'll consider whether language is unique to human beings. Other topics will include computers that can "think" and puzzles that require considerable mental dexterity and insight. We'll also look at how different areas of the brain can directly affect the understanding of language and the ability to speak.

WHY PSYCHOLOGISTS STUDY THOUGHT AND LANGUAGE

Perhaps more than any other aspects of our nature, thought and language make us unique. Our abilities to think and speak are the cornerstones on which modern civilization is built. The generations before us found solutions to many problems and communicated these solutions to us through language. We have built on their knowledge; as we solve our own problems, we will communicate the answers to the next generation. More than any other species, we have the power to control our world and perhaps to make it a better place in which to live. Ironically, these same extraordinary abilities to think and communicate could be our undoing, because we have used them to develop weapons of devastating potential. Perhaps the same powers of thought and speech can help us to overcome the danger in which we have placed ourselves.

Whatever the future holds, our abilities to think and speak have placed us in a situation that is fundamentally different from the situations of all other species. Psychologists study thinking, problem solving, and language because these aspects of our psychology are the essence of the human experience.

THINKING

What is thought? *Thinking* or, more broadly, **cognition,** refers to the use of perceptions, mental combinations, and internal representations of symbols, objects, or concepts. When you imagine something, or solve problems mentally, or use language internally, you are said to be thinking. When you are thinking, you can mentally manipulate objects without actually having to move or handle them. There have probably been times when, instead of actually moving furniture about, you mentally pictured the appearance of a room with the furniture rearranged. Such mental manipulations are independent of physical muscular actions.

Subvocal Speech

John Watson, the father of behaviorism, argued that there was no such thing as an internal mental activity (Watson, 1930). Watson said that humans didn't think; they simply emitted responses that had been conditioned to various stimuli. You might wonder how anyone could believe that humans didn't think, but Watson had an intriguing answer. He said that thinking was not a "mental" activity, but **subvocal speech,** that is, a muscular activity! In other words, people didn't think, they talked to themselves, but so quietly that it wasn't apparent. Measurements taken of the muscles, tongue, and throat disclosed that some people did register very subtle muscular motions when they were "thinking" to themselves. Was it possible, then, that Watson was right, and that we only believe we think when we are actually engaging in subvocal speech, a muscular response? Watson argued that even a person who was mute might make subtle muscular responses in the form of hand signing or other gestures that would be muscular representations of what was assumed to be internal thinking. This idea appealed to behaviorists, because they wished to avoid the concepts of *mind* or *mental.*

One way to test Watson's hypothesis might be to paralyze a subject completely, to the point at which he could no longer breathe or even blink, and find out whether thinking continued while no muscle could be moved. Believe it or not, such a test was actually carried out using a derivative of curare, a substance used by Amazonian tribes to poison their darts (Smith, Brown, Toman, & Goodman, 1947). The subject—Smith—was one of the researchers. An artificial respirator was used to keep him alive (the things people do for

COGNITION
The process that occurs between the sensing of a stimulus and the emergence of an overt response. It involves the interplay of concepts, symbols, and mediating responses.

SUBVOCAL SPEECH
In learning theory, Watson's concept of thinking as a series of muscular responses.

science!). After the experiment, when Smith could move again, he reported that, although paralyzed totally, he was easily able to think and had understood everything that had been going on around him. These results indicate that thinking is an internal mental activity, independent of muscular responses, and that Watson's hypothesis was wrong. Perhaps it was good to discover that Watson hadn't, as Herbert Reigl once said, "made up his voice box that he had no mind" (Anderson, 1980, p. 383). As it is, thinking is difficult enough to comprehend.

The debate still continues, however. The behaviorist position remains that feelings and thoughts are only accessible to science through direct observation, and while advances in brain science may someday allow us to dissect exactly what emotions or thoughts are in terms of observable cells and circuits, until then it is hopeless to try and do so with a psychology that is limited to references dealing with unobservable "thoughts" or "feelings," (Skinner, 1989).

And yet, because we can sense our own thoughts and because they are so important to us, the concept of thought and thinking remains so compelling that it is very difficult to keep from trying to explore this area, even if it must be done in an indirect fashion.

Thinking Machines

Some of the earliest researchers to appreciate just how difficult it is to explore thinking, even indirectly, were the computer programmers and designers who first tried to create an intelligent thinking machine. Their early efforts produced simple, weak, mechanical so-called brains that could, in an extremely limited way, process some of the symbolic information with which our own brains are able to work.

As soon as psychologists became aware, through these early projects, that computers were information processors and not just high-speed "number crunchers," they couldn't help wondering whether the unknowable "black box"—as Watson had called the mind—might be accessible to observation after all, albeit in a roundabout way. If we could build computers that "think," psychologists reasoned, these machines might provide us with many hints about how our own minds worked. Never mind that the one is made of electronic parts and the other of living tissue; steam shovels and human arms can work in much the same way regardless of their composition. Computers, then, just might show us how our minds operate!

Today, cognitive psychologists and computer designers are working hand in hand. When psychologists discover some aspect of the brain that hints at how mental information is processed, computer designers try to make a computer that incorporates a similar feature; when computer scientists discover electronic processes that mimic human thinking, psychologists look within the brain for evidence of similar "wiring." Although the model may be limited, the advent of the computer has revolutionized cognitive psychology. Still, no one has yet created a machine that can think, reason, or perform intellectual tasks as well as people do. But who knows—perhaps someday?

AN ENDURING QUESTION: IS THE BRAIN LIKE A MACHINE?

For centuries, philosophers have argued about whether the brain was a "machine" or if a spirit of some sort resided there. As you recall from our discussion of the mind-body problem (see Chapter 1), they wondered if there were a ghost in the machine.

AN ENDURING QUESTION, CONTINUED

If the brain is like a machine—a very complex machine—that senses, stores, analyzes, retrieves, and processes data, then, in theory at least, it should be possible to build a real machine that can do what the brain does and perhaps even surpass the brain's ability. That is, it should be possible to create an artificial intelligence.

Efforts along these lines have begun, but to date we are a long way from such an accomplishment. For instance, just consider what the human mind can do that a computer cannot do:

> We can, for example, recognize our mother. Right after she's had her hair cut. Or permed. We can understand the speech of a cabbie from Boston or a tugboat captain from Baton Rouge. We can recognize something as a chair, whether it is a Chippendale, a bean bag, or a throne. Wee con undrestin wrds efen wen theh ar missspld. Or fill in the blanks when lt rs are missing. Many of us can recognize right away what [Figure 10.1] is: And if we can't, once we are told there is a dog in the center we usually can't help seeing it whenever we look. When we hear "Shall I compare thee to a summer's day?" we don't expect a weather report. When someone asks us if we know Bob Thompson, who plays the trumpet in the school band and lives on Maple Street, we answer yes, but his name is Bill, not Bob, and he plays the trombone, and he moved away six months ago. When given the sentences "The fly buzzed irritatingly on the window. The man picked up the newspaper," we know what is about to happen.
>
> We take this kind of mental work for granted, but computers can't even come close to doing it. (Allman, 1986, p. 25)

The question, of course, is why can't computers come close to "doing it"; that is, why can't they think more like people? Although no one knows the answer, some possible reasons for the computer's failure to "think" like a human are being actively considered. Two of the most important possibilities involve the computer's understanding of meaning and its mode of processing.

Understanding of Meaning

In his book *The Hitchhiker's Guide to the Galaxy* (1979), Douglas Adams described a fictional event that occurred on another planet. It seems that there once was a world with people much like us who pondered the great questions of their existence, much as we do. Their solution was to build Deep Thought, the greatest computer mind in the galaxy. They asked Deep Thought for the answer to the great question: What is the meaning of life, the universe, and everything?

Deep Thought said that answering this question would be "tricky," but that it could be done. To the dismay of the inhabitants of this world, however, Deep Thought said that such a calculation would take 7.5 million years! The people told Deep Thought to go ahead anyway.

Thousands of generations came and went until the time finally arrived. Two inhabitants were selected to approach Deep Thought and ask for the answer to the question—the meaning of life, the universe, and everything. A humming sound came from inside Deep Thought, and the great computer announced that the answer was . . . *Forty–two.*

In this funny example, it's obvious that there was a failure to communicate. Either the people weren't able to understand the meaning of Deep Thought's answer, or perhaps Deep Thought didn't understand the meaning of their question. Somewhere along the line, the *meaning* was lost.

◆ **FIGURE 10.1**

What do you see?

ARTIFICIAL INTELLIGENCE
A computer simulation of human cognitive ability and performance.

PARALLEL PROCESSING
In computer science or neuroanatomy, the handling of information in a manner so that many aspects of a particular problem are manipulated simultaneously, thereby saving time over serial methods in which each aspect of a problem is examined in sequence.

AN ENDURING QUESTION, CONTINUED

Oddly enough, this is one of the problems commonly faced by modern researchers who are trying to create **artificial intelligence.**

A good example of this problem comes from early attempts at artificial intelligence back in the 1950s when researchers first tried to use computers to make translations from one language to another. It seemed reasonable to suppose that a computer would be able to translate anything quickly by simply comparing words between any two languages and by following set rules of grammar. Few researchers stopped to think that words have various meanings that depend on context and experience and are not just symbols embedded in a formal logic.

In one famous story from this endeavor, a researcher decided to test his English-Russian translation program. He placed an English sentence, "The spirit is willing, but the flesh is weak," into the computer and had it translated into Russian. He then instructed the computer to translate the new Russian sentence back into English. What the computer gave him was, "The vodka is good, but the meat is rotten" (Waldrop, 1984, p. 372). Some simple translation programs do exist today, but the problem of meaning in translation remains. This is why human translators are still needed; they understand the meaning as well as the symbols.

Developing an artificial intelligence, therefore, first requires that we know what it means to "understand" something. If you consider the following, you will see the computer's problem when it comes to understanding: "If just one person steps onto the rickety footbridge, it will collapse." A computer's literal solution might be to make sure that there are always two or more people on the bridge! Even though our memories are filled with millions of facts, our understanding of what the facts mean often gives us an edge and enables us to concentrate on only the relevant ones and to compare them with one another. It may be that before a computer can think like a human (and, ultimately, think beyond a human's ability), it will have to know what it means to be a human. The trouble is, of course, that no one knows how to put such an experience into the formal logic that a digital computer uses. After all, what is the meaning of life? (Yes, I know—42!). If computers could learn from experience, rather than by being given information, perhaps their understanding of what things *mean* would approach our understanding. But for a computer to learn from experience, it would have to process information in a very different way than most computers do now—it would require a totally different mode of processing.

Mode of Processing

The brain doesn't work like a simple computer. It doesn't quickly examine every fact related to a particular problem until an answer is reached. If it did, each time you learned a new face it would take you that much longer to recognize your father the next time you saw him. Instead, the brain appears to process millions of bits of information slowly and at the same time. This is known as **parallel processing.** Some people have compared the simple computer to a bank with only one teller and the parallel computer to a bank in which many tellers are working at the same time. In fact, 20 small personal computers—the kind you can buy in your local department store—when hooked together in parallel so that each performs a small part of a problem, can often process information faster than a large mainframe computer costing many hundreds of thousands of dol-

AN ENDURING QUESTION, CONTINUED

lars. Integrating the 20 parts of answers you get from these little computers into a sensible whole answer, however, is another problem. The brain does it somehow, but computer designers are still trying to figure out how best to do it. Until they do, ultrapowerful full parallel-processing computers must remain a dream.

Some computers, however, are able to do some of their work in parallel fashion. This has led to a significant new area of exploration in which computers are being developed that can and do learn from experience. These computers rely on a new kind of internal organization called, interestingly enough, a **neural network.** The organization is based on the idea of computer chips sharing information simultaneously (parallel processing) in a way that mimics the neural processing in the human brain. In a computer based on a neural network system, there is no separate area for memory—memory is spread throughout the system. There are no programs to enter, no software rules to begin with. The machine creates its own pathways to solve problems.

Such systems may mark the beginning of computers that can *acquire* their own experience rather than being simply the passive recipient of a programmer's instructions. John McCarthy, who coined the term *artificial intelligence*, believed that some day machines will learn on their own what the world means and will become not just as intelligent as people, but even more intelligent. In such a world, for instance, scientists may conduct experiments ordered up by a computer and then give the results to the machine. The computer may then ask for more experiments, and then for more, until finally it announces what the "answer" is (hopefully, not "42"). When researchers ask the computer how it arrived at the answer, the computer may even respond that it's "beyond the ability of human minds to comprehend." Such a machine may be of great benefit to us as it solves some of our most difficult problems, uncovers the secrets of nature, and perhaps figures out how to build an even better computer. Of course, if for some reason we find the machine too frightening or if it gets out of hand, we can always pull the plug (assuming, of course, that it runs on electricity!).

Of course, these advances in artificial intelligence haven't yet answered the question, "Is the brain a machine?" Parallel processing may be only one of the brain's many tricks, and it is unlikely to be the major factor that distinguishes the brain from a computer. Brain scientists have commonly observed that if you think of five ways that the brain might work, you'll soon discover that it uses all five of those ways plus five more that you didn't think of. Some researchers speculate that the brain may be so unique that no machine will ever duplicate it. If this is true, the brain is not a machine, but something unto itself.

Roger Penrose is acknowledged to be one of the greatest physicists alive. He believes that the human mind—that is, the ghost in the machine—will turn out to be so special that it will be discovered to be operating according to a whole new set of physical laws that are unheard of today. Accordingly, Penrose argues, no digital computer will ever duplicate the human brain (Penrose, 1989). Penrose even believes that such experiences as insight may be based on sudden "quantum" shifts at the atomic level that can somehow affect large areas of the brain. Of course, he is speculating, and Penrose admits that the truth is anybody's guess. But it is interesting, nevertheless, that such a fertile mind as his might

NEURAL NETWORK
In computer science, computer hardware or circuits that alter their composition or connections in response to experience.

AUTOMATIZATION
A process that occurs after a mental procedure is practiced sufficiently so that the number of if-then connections is reduced to the barest required minimum. Once automatization has occurred, the mental procedure can be called on with a minimum of thought or effort. The mental procedures used by skilled experts tend to be highly automatized.

AN ENDURING QUESTION, CONTINUED

seriously consider the creation of an artificial intelligence equivalent to our own as a theoretical impossibility. Who knows, he may be right.

FOR CRITICAL ANALYSIS

1. How would life be different if we all had a computer in our home that not only could understand what we said, but could carry on conversations with us and be our friend (keeping us company and providing us with the latest stories and ideas for our enjoyment), and could also be an expert in every field from medicine to law, from auto repair to home finance, from psychology to gourmet cooking?

2. If machines become more intelligent than people, should society defer to them when making decisions?   ◆

HUMAN PERFORMANCE

Cognitive psychologists try to find out what people do when they think, reason, and perform intellectual tasks. Although there are many views on this subject and many disagreements among researchers (Oden, 1987), a sense of what these special abilities might be is beginning to emerge.

Although a few researchers argue that all thinking, reasoning, and performance in human beings are probably controlled by one major set of cognitive abilities (Anderson, 1983), it is more commonly argued that there probably are four major categories of human cognitive performance (Gagne, 1984). These four categories are (1) intellectual skills, (2) declarative knowledge, (3) cognitive strategies, and (4) motor skills. Each of these categories includes a broad range of human behavior. Many artificial intelligence researchers have argued that if a computer could master these four broad categories, the machine would indeed exhibit behavior and reasoning ability similar to that of a human being. Let's look at each of the four categories in turn.

Intellectual Skills

Intellectual skills form a general category that includes all the mental procedures, rules, and concepts you have learned.

MENTAL PROCEDURES. Think of the different procedures you have acquired about how to do things. Most likely you know the procedure for driving a car, operating a television set, making a telephone call, and shopping at a store. Some jobs, of course, require complex intellectual skills: Think of the procedures a surgeon or a jet fighter pilot must know.

As you master such procedures, it takes you less and less time to carry them out. A medical student might have to think through her mental procedures for some time in order to remove an appendix, but once she has become a seasoned surgeon, her knowledge of the procedures probably will become so rapid and automatic that she won't have to think about each step before she knows what to do. This process is called **automatization** (Gagne, 1984). It is the acquisition of significant amounts of automatization that distinguishes the expert from the novice.

The basis of such an intellectual skill as mental procedures is the *if-then* system. In other words, you have learned that *if* this occurs, *then* you should do that. Robinson Crusoe, lost on his desert island, had the mental procedure,

"*If* I should see a boat, *then* I should light the signal fire." Your total knowledge of procedures appears to be made of thousands, perhaps millions, of such *if-then* connections.

Computers often have a tough time with *if-then* connections, because of meaning. Of course, you can put into a computer rules about if this, then that; that's what most computer programs contain. You could put the Robinson Crusoe example—*If I see a boat, then I light the fire*—into a computer. But what does "boat" mean to the computer? If you describe the *Queen Elizabeth II* as a boat, the computer might not recognize that a canoe or an aircraft carrier is also a boat. Telling a computer what a boat is so that it will recognize any boat is not at all easy! Humans might have this same difficulty except that they possess an extremely important intellectual skill: Along with the acquisition of mental procedures, they have developed the use of concepts.

CONCEPTS AND CONCEPT FORMATION. One of the most valuable ways in which we can organize thinking is by forming concepts. A **concept** can be defined as the relationship between, or the properties shared by, the objects or ideas in a given group. For example, if you have the concept of boat, you can recognize something as a boat even though it may look different from all the other boats you've ever seen. A new boat can be included within the concept because it has qualities that are common to the entire class of objects we call boats. It has a hull; it floats in water; and it is used for transport. Boats belong to an even larger conceptual category, *vehicles of transportation*. Possessing a concept such as *boat, dog,* or *building* is very useful. Most of the ideas we come across each day belong to familiar categories, although they may appear to be different. By applying concepts, we can develop an immediate understanding of new objects or ideas, because we can relate them to a general class of similar objects and ideas with which we are familiar. We know what to expect from an object, even though we're encountering it for the first time. In this way, we save a tremendous amount of effort, which we would otherwise have to expend learning what each new thing is.

Some concepts are very well defined; that is, the rules that classify them are stated explicitly. Among such explicit concepts are *registered voters, diamonds,* and *hours*. These concepts are exclusive: You either are a registered voter or you are not, something either is a diamond or it isn't, and so on. Some concepts, however, appear fuzzy to many people. For instance, consider the concept *bird*. Robins and sparrows are considered highly typical examples

CONCEPT
An abstract idea based on grouping objects or qualities by common properties.

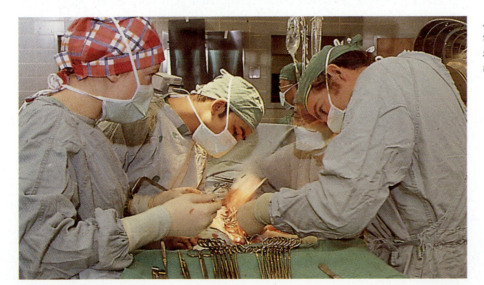

A surgeon must learn many complicated mental procedures in order to perform surgery. After sufficient training many of these procedures become automatized.

of this concept. But turkeys and chickens are not as readily accepted into the concept, especially by children, and penguins are even less likely to be considered birds (Rosch, 1977). Human experience and context also play an important role in concept formation. For instance, "what counts as a bird (and to what degree) is very different in the context of 'The bird crossed the barnyard' than in the context of 'The hunter shot the bird overhead.'" (Oden, 1987, p. 213). In this sense, then, objects that best fit the most common examples of a concept are most likely to be included in that concept.

This kind of contextual difference poses problems for computers when the machines must deal with concepts. Even more troublesome for a computer is the additional fact that many conceptual categories are based on human imagination. For instance, Australian aborigine men include both *fire* and *women* under the conceptual heading of *dangerous things* (Lakoff, 1987).

We develop concepts, in part, by classifying objects according to their similarity to other objects, and the classification may occur even when the similarities are very abstract. Further, we tend to classify objects and ideas that appear to be similar under one conceptual heading until a difference becomes apparent. The same objects may also share many different conceptual categories, all of which are based on the person's knowledge of the similarities and differences between objects. For example, is gray more like white or more like black? Well, gray hair is judged to be more like white hair than black hair because of our *knowledge* of aging. But gray clouds are judged to be more like black clouds than white clouds, owing to our *knowledge* of storms (Medin & Shoben, 1988). Because we have knowledge about the world and how it operates, we adjust our conceptual categories accordingly (Medin, 1989). Until computers have human knowledge and experience, their categorizations will simply not be like ours.

Declarative Knowledge

The second important cognitive category is declarative knowledge.* Declarative knowledge includes all the things you might be able to declare or state. The names of people, the words to a poem, an important date in history, the name of a nation's capital—all are considered declarative knowledge. Many researchers believe that such information is stored in declarative, or fact, memory as a network of propositions (see Chapter 9).

One important reason why researchers have distinguished intellectual skills from declarative knowledge is that experience has differing effects on each. In the case of mental procedures—an intellectual skill—an expert with much experience will reduce the number of if-then steps involved in each procedure as automatization occurs. On the other hand, an expert with much experience in declarative knowledge will elaborate the propositional networks of this information, so that they become more and more complex and expanded, rather than reduced.

Cognitive Strategies

Cognitive strategies, the third important cognitive category, include the abilities you acquire that let you know how best to use your previously learned intellectual skills and declarative information for problem solving, remembering, and learning. Cognitive strategies are not well understood, but researchers assume they exist because of the way humans behave. You can pack a digital computer with procedures, even some rudimentary concepts, and certainly a great deal of declarative knowledge. But when you try to get it to think, the

---

*Declarative knowledge is sometimes referred to as verbal information.

computer will become overwhelmed by the tremendous amount of data you've given it. This occurrence is sometimes called *combinatorial explosion*. It is assumed that we humans have and use cognitive strategies because it is apparent that we somehow avoid being similarly overwhelmed, each time we engage in thought, by the vast amount of information we have stored.

The lack of a cognitive strategy system has prevented parallel-processing computers from becoming the computer world's mainstay, even though these machines can handle vast amounts of information. As you recall, it was the lack of a cognitive strategy system that prevented us from integrating the 20 answer parts we obtained so quickly from our example of 20 home computers linked in parallel series.

HEURISTICS VERSUS ALGORITHMS. In combination with our ability to process information, we can also integrate the parallel processes of our brain. Exactly how we do this is one of the great cognitive secrets to which researchers would love to have an answer. This ability, however, gives us certain problem-solving skills that allow us to outperform any computer.

Consider the following: Checkers, backgammon, chess, or any other game of strategy requires that the player engage in problem solving. People have programmed computers to solve problems and to play games. Computers can play chess, checkers, backgammon, and a number of other games. Have you ever played a game of chess with a computer? You might be surprised to learn that there is not a computer in the world—yet—that can consistently beat the world champion.

What goes on inside the computer's "mind" when it's deciding on a move, and how is the process different from that used by human beings to solve problems? Computers generally work according to **algorithms.** An algorithm is defined as a method guaranteed to lead to a solution if one is possible. Solving a problem by algorithms requires a systematic search of every possible avenue or approach to the solution. Computers can apply this method because they can calculate so quickly. An algorithmic chess computer will examine first every possible move and then the possible moves that might follow any of the first possible moves. The computer will even consider very stupid moves that no experienced human player would bother to investigate. As you can imagine, this computer strategy can encompass an almost infinite number of

ALGORITHMS
Mathematical premises. In computer usage, an algorithm is a program that will search for an answer by examining every possibility.

Very commonly, problems are too complex to solve with an algorithm. Chess is an example. In a game of chess, it is impossible to calculate all the possible moves in the game within the given time limits. Even the most powerful computers are unable to do this. As a result, chess requires heuristic methods of play.

HEURISTICS
Methods for discovering the correct solution to a problem by exploring the possibilities that seem to offer the most reasonable approach to the goal, rather than all possibilities. Heuristics also involve obtaining successive approximations to the correct answer by means of analogies and other search techniques.

MEANS-END ANALYSIS
A problem-solving process in which the difference between the current situation and the desired situation is defined and then a series of steps is taken to reduce, and finally eliminate, the difference. This process is applicable whenever there is a clearly specifiable problem and a clearly specifiable solution.

possible moves. And even though the computer is very fast, it might take two to six years just to fully "think" five or six moves ahead in a complicated game situation. For this reason, an algorithm guaranteed to win any game of chess could lead to games that would take centuries to play—not unlike Deep Thought's 7.5-million-year requirement to ponder the great question, "What is the meaning of life, the universe, and everything?" In other words, in a complicated situation, a computer that relies on algorithms will soon be overwhelmed by data. Because it's not practical for a chess computer to take more than a couple of hours for its longest move when playing against a human, any algorithmic method it uses is limited by a clock.

Human beings obviously don't think in that fashion. We generally attempt to solve problems by a cognitive strategy of **heuristics.** Heuristic methods aren't guaranteed to reach a solution, and they aren't as systematic as algorithmic methods. But sometimes they can produce solutions considerably faster. Unlike the computer, which will be trying out every possible solution, the human will be working only with those that seem the most reasonable. He doesn't know how the sequences may lead to the solution; he simply takes the first steps toward the apparent direction of the goal, hoping that as he gets closer, he'll see the further steps that will lead him to his final goal. It should also be noted that most modern chess computers, as well as other problem-solving computers, incorporate simple heuristic methods.

MEANS-END ANALYSIS. Searching heuristically for the next right step toward the final goal can be very difficult, because the necessary move is not always obvious. Sometimes, however, it's possible to use a plan or general strategy to organize problem solving. Some time ago, two researchers, Newell and Simon, developed a computer planning and strategy program that they called the general problem solver (GPS), which achieved some limited success (Newell & Simon, 1972). The GPS was one of the first computer programs not to use an algorithm; it relied instead on the heuristic of **means-end analysis.**

Means-end analysis may be one of the important cognitive strategies that people use to control and organize the combination of mental procedures (an intellectual skill) and facts (declarative knowledge). In the following example, you can see how the cognitive strategy of means-end analysis is used to organize a series of procedures based on factual knowledge about things such as cars, repair shops, and telephones:

I want to take my son to nursery school. What's the difference between what I have and what I want? One of distance. What changes distance? My automobile. My automobile won't work. What is needed to make it work? A new battery. What has new batteries? An auto repair shop. I want the repair shop to put in a new battery; but the shop doesn't know I need one. What is the difficulty? One of communication. What allows communication? A telephone . . . and so on.

It is profitable, therefore, to try to eliminate "difficult" differences, even at the cost of introducing new differences of lesser difficulty. This process can be repeated as long as progress is being made toward eliminating the more difficult differences. (Newell & Simon, 1972, p. 416)

In this example, the major difficulty (taking your son to nursery school) can be solved only by overcoming lesser difficulties (obtaining a battery, making a telephone call). In means-end analysis, you must proceed from where you are (the initial state) to where you want to be (the goal) by a series of intermediate steps. Each step is accomplished by particular means until the major goal is reached, assuming that it is reachable.

Students studying this kind of cognitive strategy for the first time sometimes question its usefulness. If you begin to apply it, however, you may be amazed by how much it can affect your thinking. In fact, you may be surprised at how inventive you become. The following passage is an example of how means-end analysis can affect your thinking:

Problem: People often are injured in the shower or bath. Your goal is to reduce or eliminate such injuries.

Question: Why are people hurt in the shower or bathtub? They often fall. (At this point, the solution may appear to be to suspend gravity or to stop people from falling—except that in posing the problem, you've made a classic error. You must always be careful in defining the problem. People are not hurt in the shower or bathtub because they fall. No one is hurt by falling. It's landing that causes the trouble. Just remember the man who fell out of a 10-story building and was heard to say as he passed each floor, "So far, so good." So let's start over.) People are hurt in the bathtub because they land on something hard when they fall. What is the difference between what you have (initial state) and what you want (end state)? Hardness. What determines hardness? The manufacturing materials. What you need, then, is soft material for the bathtub and shower stall. But soft material is porous. What's the difference between what you have and what you want? Porosity (there really is such a word, but it doesn't seem to come up in conversations very often). Therefore, you need a soft *nonporous* material. Is there such a material? What is the difference between what you have and what you want? Information. Where can information be found? In a library. If you find that there is such a material, you are set. If not, then what is the difference between what is available and what you need, and can you develop a soft nonporous material? As it turns out, there are many soft, fairly rigid, nonporous materials. And there is the answer to your problem, a soft bathtub or soft shower stall. In fact, such tubs and showers have recently been developed. They keep their form, they hold water well, and they are very comfortable. As a bonus, soft materials produce a lot of friction, and they are very difficult to slip on. If a person should fall, however, the original problem of a body landing on a hard surface is eliminated.

The idea of a soft bathtub is so unusual that it might not have occurred to you had you not gone through the means-end analysis in order to eliminate collision with hard objects. People who are good at this kind of general problem solving or means-end analysis may invent some fascinating things. Any time you have a problem, state the problem carefully and ask yourself, What is the difference between what I have now and what I want? Then break the problem down into as many subgoals as you require and see where it leads you. The next good invention may be yours!

PROBLEM SOLVING. Cognitive strategies such as heuristics or means-end analysis help people to solve problems. *Problem solving* is defined as a sequence of cognitive operations directed toward achieving a particular goal. Interestingly, some researchers believe that *all* higher-level cognition is problem solving. In this view, problem solving provides a way of turning knowledge into behavior. That means that problem solving is a bridge to everywhere, not just a method to use when solving puzzles (Anderson, 1993). This may not seem obvious at first, because so much of human cognition simply doesn't seem like problem solving. But whenever you do something such as get a drink of water, pay a bill, or drive your car, you are engaging in problem solving. The reason it doesn't seem like problem solving is that you already know how to solve these problems, and so you solve them without much thought.

If problem solving makes use of intellectual skills, declarative knowledge, and cognitive strategies that you have already acquired, it is called **routine problem solving.** Evidence indicates that routine problem solving is often so

ROUTINE PROBLEM SOLVING
Problem solving that requires concepts, thoughts, actions, and understandings that are already in your repertoire.

INCUBATION EFFECT
An effect associated with taking a break during creative problem solving. The individual often returns to the problem with a fresh approach and finds the solution.

INSIGHT
In problem solving, the sudden perception of relationships leading to a solution. A solution arrived at in this way can be repeated promptly when the same or a similar problem is confronted.

routine that the cognitive operations involved in carrying it out are frequently executed without our awareness (Anderson, 1993). That is, the routine becomes unconscious, requiring little or no directed thought or attention on our part (Kihlstrom, 1987). Creative problem solving, on the other hand, requires attention and directed thought. In fact, PET scans (see Chapter 2) have shown that the brain will use less and less energy to solve a problem as it goes from being one requiring a creative solution to one that has become routine (Haier, et al., 1992).

To give you a good idea of how creative problem solving works, let's look at an example. You are said to be in the initial state of creative problem solving when you are first presented with a problem. You must then find a way to go from the initial state to the goal. For example, Figure 10.2 shows the cheap-necklace problem. Think about the steps you must go through to find a solution. Here are the instructions:

You are given four separate pieces of chain that are each three links in length. It costs 2 cents to open a link, 3 cents to close a link. All links are closed at the beginning of the problem. Your goal is to join all 12 links of a chain into a single circle at a cost of no more than 15 cents. (Silveira, 1971)

You are now in the initial state. Your goal, of course, is to make the necklace cheaply, that is, for no more than 15 cents. If you approach the problem with a straightforward sequence of operations and link each segment of chain to the next until the chain is finally closed up entirely, it will cost 20 cents, 5 cents over budget. Most people initially attack the problem in this way.

When the cheap-necklace problem was first used in an experiment, the subjects were divided into three different groups. The first group worked with the problem for ½ hour; during that time, 50 percent of the group was able to solve the problem. Members of the second group also worked on the problem for ½ hour; however, they were told during the problem-solving session to take a ½-hour break in which they did some unrelated activities. Interestingly, after returning, 64 percent of these subjects were able to solve the problem. A third group also worked for about ½ hour on the problem, but was given a 4-hour break during the work period. In this group, 85 percent of the subjects solved the problem when they returned. The subjects in the second and third groups had been kept busy during their breaks and didn't have a chance to think about the cheap-necklace problem. Why should a break be beneficial, and why the longer the better? Although subjects rarely returned from their break with the solution at hand, they often came back with a fresh approach to the problem (Silveira, 1971).

Improving your chances of solving a problem by leaving it a while and then coming back to it is known as the **incubation effect.** However, if you're on the right track in the first place, taking a break can be disruptive rather than helpful. A good incubation effect is most likely to occur when you start out with an inappropriate strategy. If you haven't been able to solve the cheap-necklace problem yet, rather than looking ahead to see what the answer is, take a break and try again later.

The cheap-necklace problem also gives you a good opportunity to experience **insight.** Many subjects have reported working on the problem for up to 1 hour and then, suddenly, knowing what to do. If this happens to you, you will experience the insight all at once: The answer suddenly will be clear, and you will wonder why you didn't see it before. On the other hand, if you can't stand it anymore, here is the solution:

Open all three links of chain A at a cost of 6 cents, then use the three links to connect chains B, C, and D with each other, at a cost of 9 cents. In this way you can close the entire necklace, spending only 15 cents (devastatingly simple, isn't it?).

◆ **FIGURE 10.2**

The cheap-necklace problem. It costs 2 cents to open a link and 3 cents to close a link. Put chains A, B, C, and D together to form a necklace for no more than 15 cents.

Chain A

Chain B

Chain C

Chain D

GOAL STATE:

Interestingly, humans may not be the only creatures who can experience insight. During the First World War, psychologist Wolfgang Kohler, whom you may recall was one of the founders of Gestalt psychology (see Chapter 1), studied a colony of captive chimpanzees. One of the chimpanzees, named Sultan, had learned to reach outside his cage with a stick in order to retrieve a banana.

None of this was too surprising to Kohler. He knew that chimpanzees in the wild used sticks to fetch food, especially to gather termites, something they loved to eat. However, while pursuing his investigations, Kohler struck upon something more interesting. In this variation of the banana and stick problem, Kohler put the banana out of reach of a single stick and placed two sticks inside Sultan's cage. One stick was larger than the other and had a hollow opening into which the smaller stick could be inserted. Knowing this, you can most likely imagine a solution: the smaller stick could be inserted into the larger one, so that together the two form one very long stick. With the long stick, Sultan might be able to reach the banana.

Watching Sultan in this situation was very interesting. At first, the ape tried to reach the banana with the longer of the two sticks. When that failed, he pulled the stick back, then tried again. Finally, he put the stick down and seemed to become moody and angry.

But then, after sitting quietly for some time while looking at the two sticks, Sultan suddenly seemed to realize something. His expression changed. He stood up and slowly approached the sticks. Then, he immediately picked up the larger one in his left hand and turned the hollow end toward him. He then picked up the smaller stick and inserted it into the larger one to make one long stick (see Figure 10.3). With the new, extended stick in his hand, Sultan went to the end of the cage and reached out with his new extra-long stick toward the banana. He reached the banana with the stick and pulled it toward him!

Based on this observation and a number of later ones, Kohler came to believe that chimpanzees could also engage in creative problem solving by using insight. Insight, Kohler said, occurs when you have mentally been manipulating different operations toward a goal solution. Suddenly, your mental operations strike on the solution that will work. Then you approach the real situation and put your plan into effect. This, he argues, is very different from

◆ FIGURE 10.3

Sultan used insight to solve the two-stick problem.

a trial-and-error ramble that might occur without thinking. In Sultan's case, the chimpanzee thought about the problem, came up with the solution, and applied it. In other words, the animal relied on insight—he was thinking (Kohler, 1927). The chimp Sultan's insight about putting the sticks together or the insight you may have experienced in solving the cheap-necklace problem provides further evidence for the existence of cognitive strategies. The solutions to the problems were achieved through a strategy of manipulating mental procedures and declarative knowledge, rather than through a physical trial-and-error process.

Impediments to Problem Solving

Cognitive strategies can also be helpful in overriding acquired procedures and declarative knowledge that may be getting in the way of problem solving. Examples of such impediments to problem solving are mental sets and functional fixedness.

MENTAL SET.   Mental procedures usually are very effective in problem solving, especially if they're used for routine problem solving. Sometimes, however, if procedures become too automatized, they may get in the way of a solution that requires creative problem solving. Consider the following example.

In 1942, Luchins formulated a series of water-jug problems. In these problems, subjects were given three jugs, with each jug having an absolute maximum capacity. They were required to use the jugs to obtain an exact amount of liquid. Table 10.1 sets out 10 of these problems. In the first problem, the jugs can hold 21, 127, and 3 ounces of liquid, respectively. The desired amount is 100 ounces. How could you measure exactly 100 ounces using only these three jugs? The answer is to fill jug B to capacity, then pour liquid into jug C, filling it once, dump that liquid out, fill jug C again, dump that liquid out again (this leaves 121 ounces in jug B), and fill jug A once. You will be left with exactly 100 ounces in jug B.

Working on your own, solve the problems for the remaining nine groups of jugs. Try it now before reading on. By the time you are finished, you may have noticed something interesting. All the problems but number 8 can be solved in the same way: jug B − 2C jugs − jug A = desired amount. Problems 7 and 9, however, can be solved more simply: A + C = desired amount. Problem 8 cannot be solved by the B − 2C − A method, but it can be solved by the simpler formula A − C. Problems 6 and 10 can be solved by B − 2C − A and also by the simpler A − C.

When Luchins conducted this experiment, he discovered that 83 percent of his subjects used the B − 2C − A method on problems 6 and 7, even though these could have been solved by the easier solutions (A − C and

TABLE 10.1 ◆ LUCHIN'S WATER-JUG PROBLEMS			
CAPACITY OF JUG A	CAPACITY OF JUG B	CAPACITY OF JUG C	DESIRED QUANTITY
1. 21	127	3	100
2. 14	163	25	99
3. 18	43	10	5
4. 9	42	6	21
5. 20	59	4	31
6. 23	49	3	20
7. 15	39	3	18
8. 28	76	3	25
9. 18	48	4	22
10. 14	36	8	6

A + C, respectively). This tendency is known as **mental set.** After solving the first five problems by B − 2C − A, the subjects were so used to applying this formula that they used it in problems 6 and 7 as well, even though there were simpler solutions. Subjects who skipped the first five problems and began with 6 and 7 discovered the easier solutions immediately. Interestingly, in Luchins's experiment, 64 percent of the subjects failed altogether to solve problem 8, although it required only A − C; the subjects tried to apply the B − 2C − A method that they had used successfully for the first seven problems. Unable to use a strategy on which they had come to rely, a majority of these subjects said problem 8 couldn't be solved! And 79 percent of the subjects used the B − 2C − A method to solve problems 9 and 10, which are easily solved by other means. If we use the same method to solve similar problems, we may overlook better approaches. A mental set can even cause us to ignore the obvious solution.

Studying the effects of mental sets—in fact, just being aware that they exist—can help you to avoid the problems they cause. Luchins discovered that subjects whom he had advised to pay careful attention were often able to overcome their mental set.

In 1986, about 300,000 sixth graders in California were asked the following question on a statewide test:

If 130 schoolchildren are going on a picnic, and 50 can ride on each school bus, how many buses are needed to carry them all?

(a) 2
(b) 2 and a remainder of 30
(c) 2⅗
(d) 3

Fifty-three percent chose either (b) or (c) as the correct answer. Of course, the answer has to be (d), because otherwise the extra 30 children would have to ride in three-fifths of a bus. Some people who viewed these results decried the failings of our educational system (Murray, 1986). Many educators argued, however, that the children's failure to see the obvious answer was simply the result of a mental set—after doing long-division problems for a whole year, a sixth grader understandably might see the school-bus problem as nothing more than just another straightforward long-division problem and might solve it blindly. You can bet that if these same children had just solved 100 school-bus-type problems, they would have rounded off the answer to the next highest whole number.

FUNCTIONAL FIXEDNESS.   The declarative information we have is also usually helpful for solving problems. It provides us with the facts we need to find solutions. Sometimes, however, our declarative information can be too tied to specific facts. Once this happens, we may begin to think that objects that have a specific function can function only in the intended way. This inclination is known as **functional fixedness.**

Recall for a moment the soft bathtub that you derived from means-end analysis. The idea of a soft bathtub is so reasonable that it's hard to believe no one thought of it sooner. New inventions often seem obvious—after they've been invented. The problem with the tub is that experience has taught us to think that only hard objects are suitable containers for large amounts of water. This obviously isn't the case. When we link a particular item or material with one particular function, we may find it difficult to imagine other possibilities. In Figure 10.4, you'll see a table on which there are matches, a candle, and a box of tacks. The task is to use these materials to attach the candle to the door in an upright position so that the candle can burn normally (Duncker, 1945). Can you think of a good way to do this? Figure 10.5 poses another

MENTAL SET
A tendency to continue to use a particular approach or type of solution to a problem based on previously learned mental procedures.

FUNCTIONAL FIXEDNESS
A mental set in which you are unable to see beyond an object's customary function to its other possible uses because you have relied on declarative information that is too narrowly defined.

◆ **FIGURE 10.4**

Using only these materials, attach the candle to the middle of the door in an upright position, so that it can burn naturally.

problem. The two strings must be tied together, but they are so far apart that one person alone can't grasp them simultaneously. Suppose you were this person, and you had to solve the problem with only the materials shown in the picture. What would you do (Maier, 1931)?

If you have trouble with either problem, you may be suffering from functional fixedness. To solve these problems, it is necessary to use the materials differently from the way in which they're normally used. In the first problem (Figure 10.4), most people think of the box as a container for the tacks. The answer, however, is to empty the box of tacks, affix the candle to the middle of the box by pushing a thumbtack up through the bottom, and then fasten the box to the door by pushing thumbtacks through the side of the box into the door. In this way, the box becomes a platform for the candle. The matches aren't needed except to light the candle.

The solution to the second problem (Figure 10.5) requires that the pliers be used as a weight. We typically think of pliers, as a grasping tool, not as a weight. If you tie the pliers to one of the strings, however, you can start the string swinging. Then you can go over and grab the other string, come back, and retrieve the swinging string as it nears you. In this way, you'll be able to hold both strings at once, bring them together, and tie them.

If you're used to using items in unique ways, or if you're aware of unique properties of particular items, functional fixedness is easier to overcome. In one study, the solution required that a screwdriver blade be used as a conductor of electricity in a circuit (Glucksberg & Danks, 1968). The subjects had a great deal of difficulty finding the solution because they were not accustomed to thinking of the screwdriver in this fashion. Functional fixedness had struck again. In a follow-up study, however, a researcher gave subjects practice ahead of time in classifying objects such as paper clips and crayons according to their ability to conduct electricity (Teborg, 1968). These subjects were able to transcend their functional fixedness and realized immediately that the screwdriver blade could be used in an electric circuit. This experiment indicates that the more practice a person has solving problems, the more likely it is that the person will be able to solve future problems.

Mental set and functional fixedness don't always interfere with problem solving. In fact, routine problem solving is facilitated by mental sets and functional fixedness, because old methods usually work and using an object as it was intended to be used is normally a good strategy. If mental set or functional fixedness does cause a problem, it's likely to be during creative problem solving, when finding a solution may entail breaking away from old ideas and methods. When engaging in creative problem solving, then, be careful not to begin with too many preconceived procedures or facts.

Motor Skills

The fourth important cognitive category is motor skills. These are skills that require muscular motions, such as those needed for riding a bicycle, playing tennis, or using tools. Motor skills are maintained in the implicit memory (see Chapter 9) and are acquired slowly through conditioning and practice (see Chapter 8). Intellectual skills, on the other hand, are sometimes acquired abruptly through insight. Practicing a motor skill requires that the same muscular movements be repeated again and again. To practice intellectual or verbal skills, however, you should apply them in different ways in many circumstances.

Another important distinction between motor skills and intellectual or verbal skills is that we can often remember newly acquired motor skills for a great length of time, whereas we can rapidly forget newly acquired intellectual or

Unlike intellectual or verbal skills, motor skills are not easily forgotten. It is easy to forget, for example, that Quito is the capital of Ecuador, but not easy to forget how to ride a bicycle, even if you haven't been on one for a long time.

verbal skills if we don't practice them. It is easy to forget that Quito is the capital of Ecuador, but not easy to forget how to ride a bicycle, even if you haven't been on one in quite some time (see Figure 10.6). These different rates of forgetting further highlight an important difference between implicit and declarative memory (see Chapter 9). The motor skill, held in the implicit memory, is forgotten much more slowly than the declarative information, held in the declarative memory.

🧬 LANGUAGE

No one knows where **language** fits into the cognitive scheme of things. Some people have argued that language is derived from one general all-purpose cognitive ability (Anderson, 1983). Others have argued that language is the result of a combination of cognitive abilities that include intellectual skills (the procedures for creating a **grammar),** declarative knowledge (the meanings of words), cognitive strategies (putting grammar and meaning together to form sentences), motor skills (operating the mouth, lips, and tongue while speaking), and attitudes (which give emotional content to the meanings of words) (Gagne, 1984). Some researchers believe that language is a special and distinct skill, separate from all the other cognitive skills and uniquely human (Wanner & Gleitman, 1982). Whichever is the case, it is obvious that speaking a language is a powerful human ability.

Perhaps the view that cognitive researchers have taken toward language has been stated best by researcher Steven Pinker:

Language acquisition is the jewel of the crown of cognition. It is what everyone wants to explain. . . . In a sense, language acquisition defines what it is to be an intelligent human being. (Kolata, 1987b, p. 133)

◆ **FIGURE 10.6**

These curves represent the rate at which particular skills are forgotten and the percentage decrease in skills over time. Subjects were trained, retrained (their motor skill increased 30 percent owing to the retraining), and then tested over 10 weeks' time. Declarative information (especially of meaningless nonsense syllables) is lost far more quickly than is a motor skill. (SOURCE: *Leavitt and Schlosberg, 1944, p. 412.*)

CONCEPT REVIEW ◆ HUMAN COGNITIVE PERFORMANCE

1. *Intellectual skills:* Procedural and categorical knowledge probably held in the declarative memory, including:

Mental procedures: If-then connections. As a person becomes expert, the if-then connections become automatized and are reduced in number.

Concepts: Concrete and abstract ideas grouped according to common qualities or properties. Enable a person's understanding to be greatly expanded beyond her limited experience. Many new objects or ideas can be understood in terms of previously learned concepts.

2. *Declarative knowledge:* All knowledge that can be declared or stated. Declarative knowledge is maintained in the declarative memory. As a person becomes expert, the networks (see Chapter 9) of declarative knowledge are elaborated and expanded.

3. *Cognitive strategies:* Higher-level control strategies that enable a person to use intellectual skills and verbal knowledge efficiently. Not well understood. Examples may include:

Heuristics: Methods that offer good solutions through the exploration of what appear to be the most reasonable approaches toward a goal, rather than via the exploration of every possible approach.

Means-end analysis: A problem-solving process that reduces the difference between the initial state and the final goal state into a large number of substeps that can be solved more easily.

4. *Motor skills:* Knowledge of muscular operations that is maintained in the implicit memory. Motor skills are forgotten at a much slower rate than is verbal knowledge.

LANGUAGE
Any means of communication that uses signs, symbols, or gestures within a grammar and through which novel constructions can be created.

GRAMMAR
A set of rules that determines how sounds may be put together to make words and how words may be put together to make sentences.

LINGUISTIC RELATIVITY
Whorf's hypothesis that thought is structured according to the language spoken, so that those who speak different languages have different thinking patterns.

Linguistic Relativity

No one knows just how tied together language and thought are. It has been argued that language influences thinking so strongly that thinking itself is actually modified or limited by the words and concepts available in the language. In other words, that you speak a certain language may make it more or less difficult for you to have particular thoughts or ideas than if you spoke another language. Benjamin Lee Whorf called this effect **linguistic relativity** (Whorf, 1956).

Linguistic relativity is an interesting idea. Many people who are bilingual claim that they are able to think and express certain thoughts much better in one language than in the other. Taken to the extreme, the Whorf hypothesis even suggested that human perception might be altered by language. To test this hypothesis, one researcher compared the Dani, a Stone Age agricultural people who live in New Guinea, with persons who spoke English (Rosch, 1973). In the Dani language, there are just two terms for color, *mola* for bright, warm colors and *mili* for dark, cold colors. If Whorf's suggestion that words facilitate perception and understanding were true, the Dani should not have understood that many different colors shown to them were different, because their language distinguished between colors in only two ways. Rosch found, however, that the Dani could easily tell many colors apart, even though they had no words for the different colors in their language. This result indicated that the Dani perceived color distinctions independently of the language they spoke.

PHONEMES
The most basic distinctive sounds in any given language. Phonemes are combined into words.

GOOING STAGE
A stage of language acquisition that typically occurs between the ages of 2 and 4 months. During this stage, infants combine the vowel-like comfort sounds made earlier with harder sounds that are the precursors of consonants. An example, is "goo."

EXPANSION STAGE
A stage of language acquisition that typically occurs between the ages of 4 and 7 months. During this stage, infants produce many new sounds giving rise to babbling. The onset of the expansion stage does not appear to require feedback because deaf babies also babble. Toward the end of the stage, however, the effects of hearing experience begin to be discernible.

RASPBERRY
In foodstuffs, a rather tasty fruit; a type of berry. In social discourse, an explosive sound owing to the rapid expulsion of air from the mouth that vigorously vibrates the lips (especially the lower lip), which, as required for the effect, have been deliberately placed in a configuration so as to make contact with, and surround, the protruded tongue. Considered unrequired in most social circumstances. (For an exception to this rule, see "Sporting events.")

CONONICAL STAGE
A stage of language acquisition that typically occurs between the ages of 7 and 10 months. It is typified by an increase in babbling and the production of cononical syllables (syllables made of consonant and vowel sounds of certain intensities). Duplicated sequences such as "dadada" or "mamama" also mark this stage.

CONTRACTION STAGE
A stage of language acquisition that typically occurs between the ages of 10 and 14 months. So named because during this time the infant will begin to narrow her production of language sounds until it includes mostly the sounds that are common to the language to which she has been exposed. During this stage, infants also acquire the pacing and rhythm of their language.

Still, the Whorf hypothesis is hard to test fully, and it may well be that the kind of language people speak facilitates the way in which they approach problems or think about them.

Language Acquisition

A language is based on the use of signs or symbols within a grammar; that is, within a structure of rules that determines how the various signs or symbols are to be arranged. Newborn infants don't possess language. Of this we are sure. As infants grow, they develop language in a step-by-step sequence. Interestingly, the sequence of language acquisition is similar among children all over the world.

THE ONSET OF LANGUAGE.   The English language consists of more than 100,000 words, 26 letters, and approximately 53 **phonemes.** At first, infants make little vowel-like "comfort sounds." By 2 to 4 months of age, these comfort sounds start to sound a little more language-like. During this time, a language-like sound might include "goo" or something similar, which is why this time is known as the **gooing stage.**

By the time infants are 4 to 7 months old, they generally produce a great number of phonetic sounds, often many more than they will require for the language they will eventually speak. This process is called phonetic expansion, and this time is called the **expansion stage.** The new sounds made during the expansion stage include yells, whispers, growls, squeals, and, every parent's favorite, the **raspberry.** Also during this time, the first fully formed vowels appear. Although mature syllables are rare during the expansion stage, as the infant's repertoire of sounds grows, parents will become aware that their infant has begun to "babble."

Between the ages of 7 and 10 months, the infant's babbling greatly increases as she begins to produce mature syllables and duplicated sequences such as "da-dada" or "mamama." This is known as the **cononical stage** of language acquisition. Interestingly, babies who can hear soon begin to babble cononical syllables, whereas deaf babies, who also babble, do not (Oller & Eilers, 1988). This finding tells us that even early on, experience with sound affects the language acquisition of hearing infants. Interestingly, deaf infants who are exposed to sign language also babble, they just do it manually! That is, they babble with their hands, starting out with the basic shapes they have seen adults use and progressing to make various combinations of hand shapes until they say their first signed word at about 1 year of age (Petitto & Marentette, 1991).

Between 10 and 14 months of age, infants narrow their use of phonemes mainly to the ones they will be using in the language they will eventually learn. This process is called phonetic contraction, and this time is called the **contraction stage.** By this time, infants also are beginning to acquire the pacing and rhythm of the language. Sometimes, an infant joins phonemes with a rhythm, pacing, and length that is so similar to actual language (except that real words are not spoken) that parents swear that their baby has just spoken a totally intelligible sentence but they somehow missed what he said.

For infants to acquire the specific phonemes of their language, feedback appears to be necessary. That is, infants have to be able to imitate what they hear before phonetic contraction can begin. This brings up the first of many linguistic problems. If infants imitate what they hear, why don't they speak in sentences? After all, they hear language, not babbling.

The reason that infants babble rather than imitate full sentences may be that individual words can be discriminated or recognized *only* after they have been associated with particular objects, actions, or circumstances (Miller & Gildea, 1987). This process of recognition takes place through experience, as infants grow. Until these associations have been made—that is, until these different sounds have a *meaning*—any of us can discern only the phonemes. Suppose you were suddenly transported to a foreign land where everyone spoke an unfamiliar language. You wouldn't be that aware of distinct words. Everything that was said would sound like gibberish to you. After a short time, however, you might become aware of some aspects of the language. Perhaps you'd become aware of the spacing—when sounds began and when they ended. You also might become aware of the rhythm and tonal changes or differences in phonetic sounds. Unfortunately, your sensitivity to these aspects of language wouldn't enable you to communicate. On the other hand, you could be learning to imitate the sounds of the language so well that you might appear to be a native speaker to someone who didn't know the language, even though you couldn't say a single word. This sort of imitation is easy for many people to do; you've probably heard it done many times. Comedians such as Robin Williams or Sid Caesar are able to "speak" many languages in this way without having any idea of what they are saying, if anything. But unlike a comedian who learns to "speak" a language phonetically without understanding it, or a computer that can teach itself to mimic a language (also without understanding), children learn their native language through experience and meaning. As humans, meaning is so important to us that it may well be the core of all cognition. You can "teach" a computer the dictionary definitions of a "warm sunny day" or of "a holiday dinner with the family," but it doesn't learn by feeling the warm sun on its skin or by having a wonderful dinner and sharing the experiences of the day with its family. It is through such experiences, however, that children come to develop meanings.

THE ONE-WORD STAGE.   Children usually speak their first word sometime between 10 and 17 months of age, with the average age being 13.6 months (Bloom & Capatides, 1987). At this point, they enter what predictably is referred to as the **one-word stage.** Typically, children's first words relate directly to certain objects or actions that are within their own experience. Although it is often difficult to generalize from an adult's experience to that of a child, you might again imagine yourself living in the foreign land we spoke of earlier. Like a child, you might first acquire words that you could pair directly with some tangible object or obvious action. Children seem to acquire concrete nouns and verbs first, such as *mama, go,* or *wa-wa* (water); they learn more abstract words later.*

The first basic nouns that children use tend to follow the *three-bears rule.* The rule states that a child is most likely to learn a basic noun such as "dog" before she learns a subordinate noun such as "collie" or a superordinate noun such as "mammal." It's called the three-bears rule because, like the story of "Goldilocks and the Three Bears," the category "mammal" is *too large* and the category "collie" is *too small,* while the category "dog" is *just right* (Gleitman & Wanner, 1984). A concept such as "dog" is clearly tied to the simple, basic, and tangible object that is a dog. Such a basic and nonabstract concept is often referred to as a **protoconcept** and is especially easy for children to conceptualize (Roberts, 1988). For instance, whereas a "dog" is easy to imagine, imagining the subordinate "collie" requires specialized knowledge about dogs, and imagining the superordinant "mammal" (not a dog, or cow, or whale, or rabbit—just a "mammal") is impossible because the concept is too abstract.

*The moment when infants first say a duplicated-syllable word such as "mama," "dada," or "wa-wa" generally coincides with the very first occurrence of a preference for using one hand over the other (Ramsay, 1984). This discovery emphasizes how much language may be tied to the development of the brain and nervous system, because both language and handedness are known to be related to the development of the hemispheres of the brain (see Chapter 2).

ONE-WORD STAGE
The universal stage in language development in which children's speech is limited to single words.

PROTOCONCEPT
A primary concept of the simplest form usually related directly to a tangible object and exemplifying a general category (such as dog, house, boat).

Infants show an attentiveness to language even before they speak their first words.

TWO-WORD STAGE
The universal stage of language development in which children's expressions are limited to two-word sentences.

TELEGRAPHIC SPEECH
The pattern of speech, including and following the two-word stage, in which children rely on a grammar of strict word order to convey their meaning and do not use conjunctions, prepositions, or other function words.

Subordinants appear to be acquired when children are given a new name for something that *they already know by name*. In one study, two different toy dogs were shown to 2-year-olds who already knew that both animals were dogs. One dog was then labeled a "fep." Rather than deciding that both animals were now "feps" or that one should now be called by the proper name "Fep," the children appeared to conclude that the one given a new name was a "fep" kind of dog (Taylor & Gelman, 1989). This level of sophistication, shown even by preschoolers, is remarkable when you consider that bilingual preschoolers, like their monolingual counterparts, will readily reject the idea that an object should have two common names unless one is considering a superordinate or subordinate category of that object, but will readily accept that the same object is called by different names in different languages (Au & Glusman, 1990).

Abstract words are acquired after basic nouns and verbs. The first abstract words tend to be adjectives, such as "red," "tall," or "big." Later, terms that are more abstract are acquired, such as the spatial referents "in," "on," and "between." Finally, children acquire very abstract words such as "freedom," "tangential," or the superordinate "mammal," items philosopher Bertrand Russell called "dictionary words" because we learn their definitions verbally rather than by their relationships to real objects. Use of dictionary words among children younger than 5 years is rare. You can imagine the shock one father received when his 3-year-old daughter, while looking at the clouds lazily drifting by, sighed and said, "When I'm older, I'll be free." He recovered from his shock when she added, "I mean four" (Whitehurst, 1982, p. 379).

THE TWO WORD STAGE. Children between 18 and 20 months of age usually have begun to utter two-word statements. During this stage (brilliantly referred to as the **two-word stage**), children rapidly learn the value of language for expressing concepts, especially for communicating their desires to other people. During this time, it is not unusual for more than a thousand new two-word statements to appear monthly (Braine, 1963). This rate is not surprising when you stop to consider that the average English-speaking high school graduate has a vocabulary of about 40,000 words. If you add to that all of the names of people and places that he knows, as well as idiomatic expressions, the number doubles to 80,000 (Miller & Gildea, 1987). If you figure that he has been learning words for about 16 years (since the age of 1), that comes out to about 5,000 words a year, or about *13 new words each and every day of his life!* Children with large vocabularies may acquire words at twice that rate. When you think of it that way, language acquisition can be seen for the formidable task that it is.

Once two-word utterances begin, children are able to make use of many of the descriptive forms found in language—nominative ("that house"), possessive ("Daddy book"), and action ("kitty go"). Throughout the two-word stage, children have a chance to practice these language forms before attempting to expand them. The two-word stage is a universal phenomenon (Slobin, 1970). Behavior theory (see Chapter 8) has never been able to provide an adequate explanation of these two qualities: the universality of language acquisition and the incredible speed with which children acquire language (Lenneberg, 1966, 1967).

TELEGRAPHIC SPEECH. Children do not enter a three-word stage. Instead, following the two-word stage, they spend the next few years creating many short sentences. Psycholinguist Roger Brown has referred to children's sentences during the two-word stage and after as **telegraphic speech.**

Telegraphic speech is an apt term. When people send telegrams, at so many cents per word, they want to be brief and to the point; unnecessary words are excluded. Children's telegraphic speech is similar. A famous example of telegraphic speech can be found in old Tarzan films. Johnny Weismuller believed that since Tarzan was just getting the hang of English after having lived with the apes for so long, he would speak in a certain way. The speech pattern Weismuller chose in portraying Tarzan was a telegraphic one; it was rich in important words such as nouns and verbs ("Jane go now," "Boy here soon," "Tarzan help Cheetah"). In these instances, certain items called **grammatical morphemes** are missing; that is, there are no tenses, plurals, conjunctions, articles, prepositions, and so on. This structure is typical of telegraphic speech.

Findings indicate that children throughout the world acquire grammatical morphemes in the same general order, although at different rates (deVilliers & deVilliers, 1973). This sequence of acquisition is so pervasive that even children who have language disorders acquire these grammatical morphemes in the same order (Khan & James, 1983; Brown, 1984).

Researchers aren't certain why children acquire morphemes in a particular order, although the order may have to do with the complexity of each task. Return for a moment to that foreign land to which you were sent earlier in this chapter. Once you had acquired single words and then two-word phrases and had begun to string the phrases together in a clipped, telegraphic manner, you too would slowly begin to acquire grammatical morphemes—but in what order? Perhaps you would learn the simplest and most obvious ones first. This may be exactly what children do. They learn the easiest and most obvious rule first and then simply begin to apply it.

Other researchers have argued that it's functionality, not complexity, that determines the order of acquisition (MacWhinney, 1978). In other words, the order of acquisition is determined by how much function each grammatical morpheme serves; the ones providing the child with the most value or function are learned first.

Children eventually acquire the grammar rules that adults use. For instance, children soon learn that adding an "s" after a word such as dog means more than one dog. That children understand the rules they are using and are not simply repeating the word *dogs*, for instance, has been demonstrated in an experiment by Berko (1958). Children were asked to answer the question posed in Figure 10.7. They correctly answered, "Wugs," a clear demonstration that they had learned the plural rule, since they had never before heard the word *wug*.

Syntactic and Semantic Structure

Once they have acquired language competence, how do people learn to express themselves by means of language? Can you recall how you learned to express what you wanted to say? In fact, are you even aware of the process you go through in deciding how to express yourself? **Psycholinguists** examine human language to discover how we "decide to say what we say." As you will see, the process is not simple.

Suppose you are working in the hot sun and are becoming thirsty. How do you express a desire for a glass of water? How do you tell your friend on the job that you think it's time to take a break and get a drink? How do you express your meaning in a structured sentence? You may say simply, "Let's take a break and get a drink of water." But was it that simple? How did you come up with that sentence? Did you just string the words together? Were some words more important than others? Could you have strung them together differently?

GRAMMATICAL MORPHEMES
Words or parts of words that help add meaning to a sentence and that are generally acquired by children between the ages of 2½ and 5 years of age. Conjunctions, prepositions, suffixes, and prefixes are examples of grammatical morphemes. Morphemes are the smallest language units to have meaning and cannot be broken down into smaller meaningful units.

PSYCHOLINGUISTS
Those who specialize in the psychology of language.

◆ **FIGURE 10.7**

An example of the "wugs" used by Berko in her study of the acquisition of language rules (SOURCE: Berko, 1958, p. 154.)

This is a wug.

Now there is another one.
There are two of them.
There are two _____.

SYNTAX
The body of linguistic rules that makes it possible to relate a series of words in a sentence to the underlying meaning of that sentence; that is, the rules governing word order in a language (sentence structure).

PHONETICS
The study and classification of speech sounds and their production, transmission, and perception.

SPOONERISMS
Unintentional transpositions of sounds in a sentence, as in "people in glass houses shouldn't stow thrones." The phenomenon is named for an English clergyman, William A. Spooner, who was well known for such errors.

LANGUAGE ACQUISITION DEVICE (LAD)
Developed by Noam Chomsky: A hypothesized neural structure inborn in every healthy individual that is preprogrammed with the underlying rules of a universal form of grammar. Once the child is exposed to a particular language, he will select from the complete sets of rules with which he was born the ones required by the language he is speaking. Most psychologists and linguists currently find the idea to be interesting but agree that a proof is doubtful because it is so difficult to find ways to demonstrate the existence of such a hypothesized device.

SEMANTICS
The study of meaning in language.

In formulating that sentence, you probably didn't begin by searching your entire vocabulary until you struck the contraction *let's*, which you then decided was the best first word. Although a computer programmed for language might perform in this way—choosing each word in sequence before uttering it—people don't. People sort out entire sentences before they say them. They build the **syntax** of a sentence so that it expresses a meaning, and they do this before they begin to speak. The syntax of a language comprises the rules that describe how words may be put together to form sentences. *Grammar* is a broader term than *syntax*; it includes both syntax and **phonetics.** Phonetics includes the study of how sounds (phonemes) are put together to make words.

Spoonerisms give us a clue to the way in which people organize their syntax to express their meaning. Spoonerisms are interesting transpositions named after William A. Spooner (1844–1930), an English clergyman known for accidentally making such rearrangements. You've probably committed a spoonerism or two yourself. Think of a theater usher who asked a group of people, "Would you like me to sew you to your sheets?" when he had meant to say, "Would you like me to show you to your seats?" What this spoonerism demonstrates is that the usher had to have had the word *seats* in mind (the tenth word in the sentence) before he ever said *show* (the sixth word). Otherwise, how could he have gotten these words confused? People work out their syntax before they say the sentence; they don't simply link one word to the next (Motley, 1985).

Some words in a sentence are more important than others, while other words are systematically arranged around the main words to help express the meaning. Like children in the two-word stage, older children and adults stress nouns and verbs. Unlike children in the two-word stage, however, older children and adults build on the nouns and verbs. In one interesting experiment, adults were classically conditioned to salivate when they heard certain sentences. Later, the individual words of the sentence were spoken to them and the amount of salivation was recorded. Although articles, adjectives, and prepositions were as much a part of the sentence as the nouns and verbs, the nouns and verbs generated the greatest salivary response (Razran, 1961).

How we choose a starting place for building a sentence remains unknown, however, even though language theorists have debated and wondered about this topic for years. Some researchers believe we use some as-yet-unknown deep cognitive processing strategy to go from the meaning that we wish to express to the syntax we use. Noam Chomsky (1957), a well-known and respected linguist, has proposed the existence of a **language acquisition device,** or LAD, that has evolved in our species to handle the interaction between syntax and *semantics*. Others believe that the initial focus of a sentence is tied to the topic at hand and that certain aspects of grammar structure derive from the need to emphasize that topic.

To understand what people mean when they argue that grammar rules may have derived from efforts to express a topic, let's consider the sentence, "The cat followed Ann," and the same idea expressed in the passive voice, "Ann was followed by the cat." Both sentences really say the same thing, which may make you wonder why our grammar has a passive voice. What's the point of having two ways of saying the same thing?

Researcher Henrietta Lempert believes that the passive voice may have gotten started because of our need to select a particular focus, to express a particular topic—and not because somebody one day thought that what we all needed was another rule of grammar. To understand what Lempert means, consider the following incident: "The bus hit the dog." If it was your dog, and you wanted to talk about what happened to *your* dog, your dog would be the topic of concern; you would focus your thoughts on your dog. Therefore, you would begin your sentence with "My dog." But then where do you go? My dog—what? You can't say, "My dog hit the bus"; that's not what happened. Instead, you are forced to say, "My dog *was hit by the bus*"—the passive voice. Lempert demonstrated in experiments that children of 2 to 5 years in age could acquire such forms of expression as the passive voice, *especially* if the topic, like the dog in our example, was animate and live (Lempert, 1989). Perhaps our grammar works that way. We start with a central topic and then try to build from it. This, in turn, may lead to a series of complicated grammatical forms, all of which have a use, namely, to support the topic. Such an assumption is incredibly difficult to demonstrate, however, and no one knows for sure whether this approach is correct (Bock, 1990).

Why Does Language Acquisition Occur?

Although some theories have been developed to explain why language is acquired, no one theory has proven superior at explaining or predicting language development (Bloom, 1983). We do have many hints, however. For instance, not all people acquire the same language, so it is obvious that learning plays an important role. At the same time, it is known that deaf babies will enter the babbling stage (Stoel-Gammon & Otomo, 1986) and that all healthy humans will acquire language except under the most unusual circumstances. These two facts are evidence for a natural predisposition in our species to acquire language. An additional finding in support of natural language acquisition is that specific areas in the human brain appear to be "prewired" for language.

The Physiology of Grammar and Semantics

In Chapter 2, you learned that there are specialized regions in the brain that appear to be directly involved with language. **Broca's area** for one, was named after Paul Broca, a French physician who during the 1860s discovered that damage to a particular region in the cerebral cortex causes aphasia, a speech disorder. Broca's area is located on the side of the left frontal lobe (see Figure 10.8). Broca discovered that aphasia occurs only when this area is damaged on the left side of the brain. If the same area is damaged on the right side of the brain, speech remains intact. Over the last 130 years, this finding has been repeatedly confirmed, and studies continue to shed light on this special area

BROCA'S AREA
An area in the lateral frontal lobe (in the left hemisphere in most cases) that is associated with language production.

Frontal lobe   Arcuate fasciculus

Broca's area

Parietal lobe

Angular gyrus

Olfactory bulb

Temporal lobe

Wernicke's area

Occipital lobe

◆ **FIGURE 10.8**

Major areas of the brain, including portions specialized for language.

THE ORIGINS OF LANGUAGE

One of the longest ongoing debates concerning language development involves whether language is basically a learned phenomenon or whether we, as a species, are biogenetically "prewired" for its acquisition. In fact, research on this question has been going on for thousands of years. According to the ancient Greek historian Herodotus, in the seventh century B.C. the Egyptian pharaoh Psamtik I had two newborns raised in silence to see what language they would eventually come to speak. The Egyptians didn't know quite what to make of the "language" that the children eventually spoke, but concluded that it sounded something like Phrygian, although it obviously wasn't.

Others throughout history—Frederick II of Sicily, James IV of Scotland, and Akbar, emperor of India from 1556 to 1605, to name the most notable—conducted similar experiments. Their reports concluded that children not exposed to language either failed to learn any language or spoke a gibberish of some sort. Frederick II was especially disappointed by these results because he had hoped that the children in his experiment, left undisturbed by exposure to common language, would come to speak the pure language that God had intended them to speak—which Frederick assumed to be Latin, although others had argued that it would be Greek. Akbar noted that all his little victims had turned out mute. He was pleased with this result because he had said all along that exposure to language was a requirement for its acquisition. Fortunately, none of the other emperors of India who followed him were interested in replicating or building on his "research."

Today, of course, we know that children must have contact with a particular language before they can be expected to speak it and that Latin won't spring from the mouth of anyone not exposed to it. But modern researchers still wonder if our childhood isn't a special time during which we apply a natural inborn grammar to the words we hear for the first time and if, in fact, children aren't the ones responsible for the creation of new languages.

Let's look at these questions one at a time. First, consider the case of a 13-year-old girl found wandering the streets of a California city in 1970. She was lost because she had escaped from an abusive parent who had kept her in total isolation since she was 18 months old. She was unable to speak a single word—because she didn't know any. Like the children in Akbar's experiment, she had not been exposed to any language (Berreby, 1992). After years of rehabilitation, the girl became a functioning adult. Her intelligence scores were adequate so long as she was given nonverbal intelligence tests—tests that don't require a verbal answer (see Chapter 13). In spite of her remarkable recovery, her language was limited to that of a 2-year-old! As far as complex adult language was concerned, she just never caught on to it. Because it is unethical to conduct the kind of experiment tried by Akbar and various other rulers throughout history, case studies like this one typically form

the basis for many of our modern assumptions concerning language formation. Because of this case and others like it, researchers wonder if experience with some sort of grammar during childhood isn't a prerequisite for mature language acquisition.

Many researchers believe that humans have evolved a language capacity that includes a brain equipped, perhaps at birth, with a form of rudimentary grammar (Chomsky, 1957). Even more controversial is the idea that children naturally impose this inborn grammar early in their development, somehow laying down the neurological groundwork on which the grammar of their own language can be built. The idea, then, is that through corrections and modeling, parents reshape this inborn grammar until the children eventually come to learn the specific grammar of the language that their family is speaking.

Interestingly, there may be a way to tell if children are using an inborn grammar early in their development. On many occasions throughout history, peoples of different languages and ethnic backgrounds have been thrown together. In Hawaii, for example, we even find the term "four-blood," which refers to someone whose grandparents are each from a different ethnic heritage and culture. For centuries, people from different parts of the world have often been brought together by circumstances to work on plantations. Germans worked with Chinese, French with Vietnamese, and Portuguese with just about everybody. Sometimes, especially on plantations in French Guiana, as many as 12 unique ethnic groups might be working together, each speaking a different language. To get by amidst such diversity, people often tried to get a handle on one another's language and culture by picking up a few hundred words and sayings from each other. This approach led to the creation of a "broken" English, French, Japanese, and so forth, known as **pidgin.** For example, to express "They put the body in the ground and covered it with a blanket, and that was all," someone speaking pidgin English was recorded as saying, "Inside dirt and cover and blanket, finish" (Berreby, 1992, p. 47). With a little effort, you might understand what this person was saying, especially if you knew the context, but it certainly isn't clear, acceptable English.

In such circumstances, people usually use pidgin while working with others and then speak their native tongues at home. What makes such a confluence of different language speakers so interesting, however, is how their children interact. The children typically enrich pidgin by combining many of the words from the languages they use while playing together and then apply a grammatical structure to it. This new "language," emerging from such ethnic diversity, is known as a **creole.** Creoles may explain how new languages and dialects get started: The children create them!

The big question, of course, is whether the creole that

forms a new language is based on an inborn grammar. Some say that it is. Creole "languages" throughout the world appear to be formed by the children of people with different native tongues who come together, usually at the borders of nations speaking different languages. Different creole "languages" also have many points in common. Some argue, however, that most creoles have common antecedents, often Portuguese or African, and that these commonalities among creole "languages" are reflective of common linguistic roots rather than genetic ones. And yet, we have to ask, could it be that creole tongues have much in common because they are reflecting a natural grammar we all have inherited? Researchers like linguist Derek Bickerton believe that even if this isn't the case, children's creole is directly based on the deep grammatical structure within us all.

In order to test his theories about the formation of language, Derek Bickerton actually found an uninhabited island 300 miles east of the Philippines for an experiment. He received a grant to populate the island with six young families, each speaking a language very different from the others. Wells were to be dug and homes built for the experiment, which was to last one year. The idea was to give the six families, including their children, 200 made-up words for different objects and actions. These words would create a common pidgin that the families could use. Then the children would play together each day, and their creole, if in fact they created one, would be examined.

Problems arose, however, when some felt that the experiment might not be ethical because it required isolating the children. The legacy of Akbar was still on people's minds five centuries later, and with good reason. Medical facilities and other emergency services were many hours away from the island. Living there would have virtually marooned the children who were to participate in the experiment. For this reason, the National Science Foundation withdrew the grant. Not to be deterred, however, Bickerton is trying again with new funding and a less isolated location on an estate in Europe, where eight families, two each of Greek, Flemish, Basque, and Hungarian speakers, will live. Whether his experiment will uncover evidence of an innate grammar was probably best answered by Bickerton when he said

> Whether my hypotheses are supported or not, I don't much care. What I do care about are the things that we shall know for the first time. I want to discover things. And I think we're going to have some fun. (Berreby, 1992, p. 53)

---

of the brain. The following case studies provide some interesting new findings concerning the left hemisphere and language.

THE CASE OF SARAH M.

Sarah M. was born deaf; she communicated with her hands through sign language. She had been a successful artist for much of her life and was expert at painting delicate scenes and designs on eggshells as well as on canvas. Then, at the age of 71 years, she suffered a severe stroke in the right hemisphere of her brain. The stroke destroyed her ability to paint. She could only make a few haphazard lines and disorganized figures. Her doctors had expected this, because the right hemisphere is known to be very involved in spatial perception (see Chapter 2). The left side of her vision also was disrupted. Sarah tended to leave the left side of her attempted drawings blank. To the astonishment of researchers, however, her sign language ability was unaffected! The spatial skills that the right hemisphere controls to such a strong degree, and that scientists had assumed were needed to organize both hands into forming signs, were not required. (Poizner, Klima, & Bellugi, 1987)

In stark contrast, but offering further support for the power of the left hemisphere to control all language functions, is the case of Gail D. who, like Sarah, was deaf from birth and fluent in sign language.

THE CASE OF GAIL D.

At the age of 38 years, Gail had a left-hemisphere stroke. Although she was not an artist, she could draw and copy as accurately after her stroke as she could before. After the stroke, however, she found herself able to sign only a few nouns or verbs and was often unable to place even these few words into a proper grammar. (Poizner, Klima, Bellugi, 1987)

PIDGIN
A simplified form of speech typically derived from a mixture of two or more languages. It has as its basis a rudimentary form of grammar and vocabulary and is generally used for communication between people speaking different languages.

CREOLE
A language mixture that develops when groups speaking different languages have prolonged contact. Typically, the basic vocabulary of the dominant language is combined with the grammar of a subordinate language, creating an admixture (a mingling within a mixture) of words and grammar that becomes in itself a new subordinate and creolized language.

BROCA'S APHASIA
A disorder caused by damage to Broca's area. Individuals with this disorder have impaired articulation, labored speech, and difficulty in forming a grammatical sentence, but the semantic content of their speech is usually clear.

WERNICKE'S AREA
An area in the temporal and parietal lobes of the brain associated with speech control.

ARCUATE FASCICULUS
The bundle of nerve fibers in the brain that connects Wernicke's area with Broca's area.

WERNICKE'S APHASIA
The inability to understand spoken language because of damage to Wernicke's area. Individuals with this disorder generally speak normally in terms of phonetics and grammar content, but their speech is semantically bizarre.

ANGULAR GYRUS
A portion of the brain in the parietal lobe adjacent to Wernicke's area. The angular gyrus is involved with reading and appears to "translate" visual word images received by the primary visual cortex into auditory form before passing the information on to Wernicke's area.

Case studies like these help to show that parts of the left hemisphere in humans appear to control language no matter how the language is expressed. In an effort to lend empirical support to these case studies, David Corina and his colleagues set up an ingenious experiment. Subjects proficient in American Sign Language were asked to sign certain words that only required the use of one hand while tapping a telegraph key with the other hand (Corina, Vaid, & Bellugi, 1992). Signing was slowed dramatically among those tapping with their right hands (which are controlled by the left hemisphere). More importantly, symbolic gestures, such as waving good-bye or giving a thumbs-up, were unaffected by right-hand tapping. Only signed words were interfered with. Left-hand tapping (a right hemisphere task) had no effect on the speed of right-hand signing. These results indicate that the left hemisphere is involved with the formation of words and that when the right hand was given something additional to do, the task interfered with its language function. Another way of saying this is that when the left hand signs, even though the right hemisphere is controlling the hand's movements, it is the left hemisphere that is generating the meaningful signs!

Most studies, however, focus on damage to the left hemisphere among people who were previously able to speak language. Such studies are also revealing. Among the kinds of problems that have been observed are Broca's aphasia and Wernicke's aphasia, as well as a host of other interesting disorders.

The symptoms of **Broca's aphasia** are impaired articulation and slow and labored speech. Although their responses make sense, people with Broca's aphasia find it difficult to express themselves in a fully formed or grammatical sentence. They also have trouble with verb inflections, connective words, pronouns, and complex grammatical constructions. Halting telegraphic speech in an adult is a sign of Broca's aphasia. For instance, in referring to a visit from friends, a person with Broca's aphasia might say, "Yes . . . Friday . . . No . . . Joe and Susan . . . Sunday morning . . . eight o'clock . . . Joe . . . and Susan . . . visit. . . ." They might also make word substitutions such as "someday" for "Sunday." Patients with Broca's aphasia do not have difficulty singing words, just speaking them, suggesting that singing may be controlled by a different area in the brain.

In 1874, Carl Wernicke, a German researcher, identified another kind of aphasia associated with damage to another part of the cortex in the left hemisphere. **Wernicke's area** is in the left temporal and parietal lobes (see Figure 10.8). Wernicke's area is connected to Broca's area by a bundle of nerve fibers called the **arcuate fasciculus.**

The speech of people with **Wernicke's aphasia** is phonetically and grammatically normal, but its semantic content is bizarre. They can string together words with the proper inflections and grammar, but the "sentences" make no sense whatsoever: for example, "The green odor ran concurrently without a day." It may be that semantic content is generated in Wernicke's area, but it is not structured in a suitable grammar until it has passed by way of the arcuate fasciculus to Broca's area, which provides the grammatical structure. These different specializations may explain why damage to Broca's area causes one kind of speech disruption, while damage to Wernicke's area causes another. As information travels forward from Wernicke's area through Broca's area, it passes on to the facial area of the motor cortex, which can then activate the mouth, larynx, tongue, lips, and other appropriate muscles for speech.

Wernicke's area is also important in the comprehension of reading and writing. When a sound is initially heard, it must pass through the primary auditory cortex to Wernicke's area, which is adjacent, before the message can be understood. A word that is read, however, must pass from the primary visual cortex to an area called the **angular gyrus.** The angular gyrus does an amazing thing to the visual image of the word: It transforms the visual image into an auditory form so that it enters Wernicke's area in the same way as a spoken word does. This is why some people seem to hear the words they are reading.

If the arcuate fasciculus, which connects Wernicke's area to Broca's area, is destroyed or disconnected, speech will remain well articulated and fluent. But semantics may be lost, because Broca's area is operating without receiving any information from Wernicke's area. This disorder may seem at first glance to be no different from Wernicke's aphasia, but because other pathways into Wernicke's area are undisturbed, a patient in whom the connection has been destroyed will appear completely normal when trying to comprehend spoken or written words. This kind of brain damage is especially frustrating because the patient can understand everything that is being said but cannot say anything that makes sense, although the nonsense she may say is likely to be quite grammatical.

A patient who has suffered damage to the angular gyrus may be able to understand speech, but unable to write at all. Damage to the angular gyrus does not affect the spoken word, only the written word. It may be responsible for some cases of **dyslexia,** a "difficulty in reading." Such damage may also explain the apparent limitation of the many children who are alert, intelligent, and able to understand anything—as long as it's not in written form. (People who have difficulty with written material may be considered learning disabled. On the other hand, this assessment must be made with great caution, because many children in today's educational system are very bad at word recognition and comprehension, not because of brain damage, but because they've never been adequately taught to read.) As you can see, the distinction between semantic and syntactic structure appears to have a physiological basis in the brain.

As our understanding of the physiology of language continues to grow, we are also beginning to see how little we really know. For instance, one interesting discovery, made with new computerized tools that allow us to examine the brain more closely, has shown us that these various language-related areas we've been discussing are really all different sections of one brain area (Gazzaniga, 1989) and only seemed to be distinct and separate to researchers like Broca or Wernicke because of the way that the brain is folded and convoluted. Now that the PET and MRI scans enable researchers to locate brain damage with pinpoint accuracy even more is being uncovered about this special area of the brain. For instance, it is now understood that damage to a certain area will cause a person to lose the ability to recognize or understand nouns, while damage to another area will have the same effect on verbs (Damasio & Damasio, 1992)! Who could have predicted that language areas of the brain would turn out to be so specialized?

Teaching Language to the Great Apes

As we noted earlier, some researchers think that our language ability is not like our other cognitive skills, but rather is separate and unique (Wanner & Gleitman, 1982). Learning theorists, in contrast, have argued that language might be acquired by any organism, as long as the organism had the basic learning power necessary. If the first view is correct, language should be uniquely human. If the second view is correct, it may be possible to teach language to a very bright animal who normally doesn't use it. This is one of the reasons that researchers turned their attention to the great apes.

In the early 1950s, two psychologists attempted to get a chimpanzee named Viki to speak English. After many months of trying, Viki could say "cup" and "up" (and, less convincingly, "mama" and "papa") (Hayes & Hayes, 1952).

DYSLEXIA
An impairment of reading ability, in which little sense can be made of what is read and letters or words often appear transposed.

Washoe with her adopted son, Loulis. Loulis acquired a number of signs from Washoe, who often spontaneously signed to him.

Many people believe that the chimp's vocal apparatus is unsuited for making English phonemes.

SIGN LANGUAGE.   In 1966, Beatrice and Allen Gardner began to investigate this question. They speculated that chimps might be able to learn to speak if they were taught sign language, specifically, the American Sign Language (ASL) used by the deaf (Gardner & Gardner, 1969). This was an ingenious idea; after all, chimps are extremely competent with their hands. They can pick up dimes, work screwdrivers, wind watches, and even thread needles.

The Gardners' first attempt was with a female chimp named Washoe (after Washoe County, Nevada, where the Gardners lived). Their experiment had interesting results. By the age of 12 years, Washoe had acquired over 180 signs (Fouts, as cited by Zimbardo, 1979). She had learned some syntax and could put signs together in multiword fashion. For example, before she could be taught the sign for *duck*, she spontaneously placed the signs for *water* and *bird* together. It was also clear that Washoe understood the concepts represented by her words. When she saw a door, she would sign *open*, and she would be let inside. You might argue that this wasn't proof that Washoe really knew the meaning of *open*. Her gesture might simply have been a learned instrumental response (see Chapter 8) to the sight of the door, reinforced by the door being opened. Later, however, when Washoe was first exposed to a car door and a satchel (both of which look very different from a regular door), she immediately signed *open* and seemed anxious to look inside—evidence that she understood the concept of *open*. Washoe was also quite aware of the abilities of those around her. When speaking to a visitor whose ASL signing was a bit rusty, Washoe would slow her signing down. Some visitors confessed to feeling embarrassed at being signed to slowly by an ape.

An even more impressive example of language acquisition among the great apes is the progress of Koko, a lowland female gorilla who was studied by Francine Patterson. Koko has mastered over 500 signs, and she understands many equivalent English words for these signs. She has developed syntax and a number of novel constructions like Washoe's "waterbird."

Speaking to a gorilla is like taking a glimpse into the mind of an alien, who sees some things in a different way, sometimes a metaphorically beautiful way. Consider some of Koko's fabulous terms for objects with which we are all familiar:

Object	Koko's Signs
cigarette lighter	bottle match
zebra	white tiger
hide and seek	quiet chase
pomegranate seeds	red corn drink
viewmaster	look mask
nose	false mouth
Pinocchio doll	elephant baby
mask	eye hat

Koko's ability to understand meanings at more than one level has also been reported. When she was asked, "What can you think of that's hard?" Koko answered, "Rock . . . work" (Patterson, Patterson, & Brentari, 1987).

While work with Washoe and Koko was going on, some researchers expressed concern that although the apes could learn some signs and syntax, they would not naturally communicate with one another using this newly acquired ability. In 1978, however, Savage-Rumbaugh, Rumbaugh, and Boysen at the

Yerkes Center reported the first instance of symbolic communication between nonhuman primates. They arranged an experiment in which each chimp had to depend on the other in order to obtain containers filled with their favorite foods—peanut butter and jelly sandwiches and orange drink. To get the food, each chimp had to choose the correct sign and to flash it on a projector for the other chimp to view. The requested item could then be passed through a hole in the glass from one chimp to the other. The chimp team was accurate between 70 and 100 percent of the time.

ARGUMENTS AGAINST LANGUAGE IN APES. Although the evidence for language acquisition in the great apes is appealing, some researchers have presented arguments against the phenomenon. After working for 5 years with his own chimp, Nimchimpsky, psychologist Herbert S. Terrace has concluded that although chimpanzees can acquire a large vocabulary, they are not capable of producing original sentences or of spontaneously naming things, as children do, without being directly reinforced with food or praise (Terrace, 1979). Terrace argues that language production is still a phenomenon unique to human beings. He believes that the great apes have been instrumentally conditioned to make certain signs in order to get what they want and that they are often inadvertently cued by their owners to produce these signs in sequence. He contends that the apes aren't aware of what the signs mean. In support of this position, B. F. Skinner demonstrated the same kind of communication as the Rumbaughs had produced between chimps—but this time using pigeons.

Savage-Rumbaugh, however, does not accept this argument. She states:

The difference between a chimpanzee and a pigeon is that the chimpanzee is aware of the content of the intended message and he will seek to amplify and clarify a symbolic request by a glance, gesture or whatever other means are at his disposal. . . . If a pigeon who saw a color and pecked a key was asked, "What do you mean—green?" he would not readily amplify or restate. By contrast, when a chimpanzee asks for an M&M, he looks you directly in the eye and points to it. If a chimpanzee says, "Go outdoors" and you say, "What do you mean?" he finds a collar, puts it around his neck and leads you to the door. (Greenberg, 1980a, p. 300)

Furthermore, a number of researchers have raised counterarguments criticizing Terrace for overlooking the conversations of signing apes in natural circumstances and for leaning too heavily on an analysis of the records of repetitious training sessions (Patterson, Patterson, & Brentari, 1987). The Rumbaughs have since been working with a new species, a pygmy chimp named Kanzi, whom they argue is demonstrating more convincing language acquisition than any other ape before him (Savage-Rumbaugh, 1987). They argue that Kanzi spontaneously names things without being directly reinforced for doing so and that he often forms sentences during more open and less-structured conversations. Countering these claims is the respected linguist Noam Chomsky, who believes that it is ridiculous to assume that any species would have evolved the capacity for something as stupendously useful as language and then not have used it until humans showed them how (Gibbons, 1991). The debate continues.

🧬 SUMMARY

◆ Thought, or cognition, makes humans unique, perhaps more than any other aspect of their nature.

◆ By definition, thinking refers to the use of mental combinations and internal representations of symbols, objects, or concepts.

◆ John Watson, the father of behaviorism, argued that all mental activity was really subvocal speech (a muscular activity). An experiment using a powerful paralyzing agent, however, demonstrated that the thought process can continue even when the body is fully paralyzed.

◆ Researchers in artificial intelligence hope eventually to create a computer that will perform thinking, reasoning, and intellectual skills in a way that is equal or superior to human performance.

◆ Cognitive psychologists try to find out what people do when they think, reason, and perform intellectual tasks. Most cognitive psychologists believe that there are probably four distinct categories of human cognitive performance: intellectual skills, declarative knowledge, cognitive strategies, and motor skills.

◆ Intellectual skills comprise a general category that includes all the mental procedures, rules, and concepts we have learned.

◆ Mental procedures are based on if-then connections. Once an expert has mastered certain mental procedures, he can call them up with almost no effort, a process called automatization.

◆ One of the most valuable ways in which we organize our thinking is by forming concepts. A concept is defined as the relationship between, or the properties shared by, the objects or ideas in a group. We acquire concepts by learning which attributes define each particular category.

◆ Declarative knowledge includes all the things you might be able to declare or state, such as the names of people, the words of a poem, or important dates in history. Declarative knowledge is believed to be held in the declarative memory in propositional networks.

◆ Cognitive strategies are the abilities you acquire that let you know how best to use previously learned intellectual skills and declarative information. Algorithms, heuristics, and means-end analysis are three valuable cognitive strategies.

◆ Computers generally work according to algorithms, whereas human beings typically attempt to solve problems using heuristics. An algorithm is defined as a method guaranteed to lead to a solution if one is possible. Heuristic methods, although not guaranteed to reach a solution, sometimes are able to produce solutions faster. A person using heuristic methods takes the steps that seem most reasonable in order to approach a goal.

◆ Means-end analysis is one way to proceed from the initial state to the goal. In means-end analysis, a series of intermediate steps are accomplished by particular means until the final goal is reached.

◆ Problem solving is defined as a sequence of cognitive operations directed toward achieving a particular goal.

◆ A mental set is a strategy gained from previously learned mental procedures that is applied to similar situations.

◆ Functional fixedness may occur when declarative knowledge is too narrowly defined, so a person tends to think that objects that have a specific function can function only in the intended way.

◆ Both mental sets and functional fixedness may facilitate problem solving, because old methods usually work and using an object as it was intended is normally a good strategy. If a mental set or functional fixedness does interfere with finding solutions, it's likely to be during creative problem solving, when the solution requires the application of new ideas or methods.

◆ Motor skills are skills that require muscular motions, such as those needed for riding a bicycle, playing tennis, or using tools. Whereas intellectual skills may be acquired abruptly through insight, motor skills are acquired slowly through practice. Motor skills are also likely to be remembered for great lengths of time, even if they are not practiced.

◆ Whorf's hypothesis of linguistic relativity argues that a person's language affects the way in which he thinks about and perceives his world.

◆ A language is based on the use of signs and symbols within a grammar.

◆ By the time infants are 4 to 7 months old, they generally produce a great number of phonetic sounds; between 10 and 14 months of age, infants narrow their use of phonemes mainly to the ones they will be using in the language they will eventually learn.

◆ By 14 months of age, children have typically begun to speak their first word. This is known as the one-word stage.

◆ Children's first words are often protoconcepts typically acquired according to the three-bears rule (not too large, not too small, but just right).

◆ After the one-word stage, children enter the two-word stage. Both the one-word and the two-word stages appear to be universal among children.

◆ Children don't enter a three-word stage; instead, they expand their use of telegraphic speech.

◆ The syntax of a language comprises the rules that describe how words may be put together to form sentences. Phonetics is the study of how sounds are put together to make words.

◆ Some researchers believe that people use some as-yet-unknown deep cognitive-processing strategy to go from the meaning that they wish to express to the syntax they use. Others believe that the initial focus of a sentence is tied to the topic at hand and that certain aspects of grammar structure derive from the need to emphasize that topic.

◆ There are many theories of language development. Among the most debated are the nature-nurture arguments posed, on the one hand, by nativists who believe that humans are prewired for language acquisition and, on the other hand, by learning theorists who think that we use our general learning ability to invent and maintain language. Many researchers take an interactionist view, arguing that although learning is important for the acquisition of language, the advanced forms of language demonstrated by humans may be the result of innate language acquisition devices.

◆ Human beings appear to have a specialized region in the brain that is directly involved with language. Within this region are Broca's area, Wernicke's area, and the angular gyrus.

◆ The symptoms of Broca's aphasia include impaired articulation and slow and labored speech. In Wernicke's aphasia, semantic content is bizarre, but speech is phonetically and grammatically normal.

◆ Attempts to teach sign language to the great apes have been somewhat limited.

✦ SUGGESTIONS FOR FURTHER READING

1. Bruner, J. (1992). *Acts of meaning*. Cambridge, MA: Harvard University Press. A prominent psychologist argues that an understanding of the mind requires more than just knowledge of information processing, and must also include the role of human concerns, especially the effects of culture, and how they shape our thoughts and language.

2. Dennett, D. C. (1991). *Consciousness explained*. Boston, MA: Little. Dennett takes the reader through the fields of cognitive psychology, artificial intelligence, and neuroscience in order to present his own radical theory of conscious experience. An entertaining, but demanding book for the serious reader.

3. Griffin, D. R. (1992). *Animal minds*. Chicago: University of Chicago Press. An interesting discussion of the kinds of advanced cognitive processing engaged in by many animals, including planning, thinking, and reasoning.

4. Humphrey, N. (1992). *A history of the mind: Evolution and the birth of consciousness*. New York: Simon and Schuster. A research scientist explores the concept of self and traces the evolution of human consciousness.

5. Kurzweil, R. (1990). *The age of intelligent machines*. Cambridge, MA: MIT Press. A well-illustrated and extensive introduction to artificial intelligence.

6. Lloyd, D. (1989). *Simple minds*. Cambridge: MIT Press. A philosopher addresses the prime question of cognitive science, namely, how can a mind develop from brain matter? His goal is to understand how simple a system can be and still be able to think.

7. McCrone, J. (1991). *The ape that spoke: Language and the evolution of the human mind*. New York: Avon. A readable and entertaining book that argues that language is the one mental power that truly separates us from other animals.

8. Norman, D. A. (1988). *The psychology of everyday things*. New York: Basic Books. Do you push when it says pull, or turn on the wrong burner on your stove, or start the windshield wipers when you mean to turn on the headlights? The author argues that designers of everything from simple assembly instructions to power plants are to blame because they disregard the principles of cognitive psychology when they make things with which people will interact.

9. Penrose, R. (1989). *The emperor's new mind: Concerning computers, minds & the laws of physics*. New York: Oxford University Press. A brilliant physicist argues that the human mind is so special that no machine will ever be able to duplicate it.

10. Premack, D., & Premack, A. J. (1984). *The mind of an ape*. New York: Norton. Tells the story of a project begun in 1964 to determine whether apes could be taught to communicate symbolically with one another. Main emphasis is on an African-born chimpanzee, Sarah, and her language progress.

11. Schank, R. C. (1991). *The connoisseur's guide to the mind: How we think, how we learn, and what it means to be intelligent*. New York: Summit. An expert in artificial intelligence and learning illustrates mental operations during a trip to a restaurant. The book is filled with entertaining stories and good examples of cognitive processes.

12. Searle, J. R. (1992). *The rediscovery of the mind*. Cambridge, MA: MIT Press. Puts forth the argument that no study of the mind can succeed without using consciousness as a central concept.

Chapter Eleven

Motivation and Human Sexuality

PROLOGUE
THE GENETICS OF HOMOSEXUALITY

In 1993, Dean Hamer and his colleagues at the National Institutes of Health announced that they had taken a major step toward identifying a gene that may be the cause of homosexuality in some men (Hamer, Hu, Magnuson, Hu, & Pattatucci, 1993). Their evidence indicates that a gene lying on a short stretch of the X chromosome (which is inherited from the mother—see Chapter 3) may be the force motivating some men to take a homosexual orientation.

Other researchers have argued that a person's sexual orientation is the result of cultural, family, hormonal, or personality influences. If the findings of Hamer and his colleagues are replicated, however, they may cast sexual orientation in an entirely new light.

For his study, Hamer recruited 114 men who met the strict definition of homosexuality. These men referred to themselves as gay, were sexually attracted to other men, fantasized about men for the most part, and only or mainly had sex with men. Roughly 2 percent of men meet this definition. The men participating in the study then rated the sexual orientations of their fathers, sons, uncles, brothers, and male cousins. Interviews with many of the relatives confirmed almost all of the ratings.

Supporting the idea of the X chromosome's involvement was the discovery that among the relatives of gay men, only their brothers, maternal uncles, or maternal male cousins were also likely to be gay, and in numbers far higher than would be expected among the general population. The evidence for maternal transmission of homosexuality appeared even stronger in families in which at least two brothers were homosexual.

After analyzing these findings, Hamer and his colleagues used enzymes to "snip" exact points along the X chromosomes of 40 pairs of homosexual brothers. Doing this allowed the researchers to examine any identical genes the men might be sharing. Thirty-three pairs of these brothers showed clusters of the same five markers all packed around the same small spot on the X chromosome, indicating that they all shared a certain bit of identical genetic information.

CONTENTS

Of course, this finding is not yet proof that the information the brothers share is a gene that determines sexual orientation, but it is a strong indication that there might be such a gene. Hamer and his colleagues are now attempting to isolate the gene and examine its biological function. If the gene is identified and does turn out to be responsible for much of sexual orientation, it will not come as a surprise to many homosexual men and women. For many years, homosexuals who were ostracized by society for making a "poor moral choice" have retorted that "choice" had nothing to do with it. Many have argued that the motivation to orient toward the same sex had been there as long as they could remember and that they have no more control over their feelings in this matter than do heterosexuals.

IN THIS CHAPTER, we will explore both the biological and environmental influences that can influence our drives, needs, and motives. We'll examine specific areas of motivational research and investigate theories that attempt to account for motives. Along the way, you'll find out why you can tell when you're hungry and thirsty, why some people are motivated to succeed, and why others find a thrill in harrowing experiences.

WHY PSYCHOLOGISTS STUDY MOTIVATION

Psychologists study motivation because they want to know *why* a behavior occurs. They want to understand the underlying processes that activate or maintain behaviors. Of course, psychologists aren't the only ones with an interest in motivation. The study of history, art, religion, theater, literature, and practically every other area of human endeavor is marked by attempts to understand the motivations behind actions. What are the forces behind love and hate? What drives some people to seek power? Why do some people find it easy to share and others not? Why do some people use drugs? Which motivations are learned or taught, and which are innate? How do motives such as hunger, thirst, or sex affect our behavior?

These questions are not new to psychology or to the human experience. Practically every question ever asked about a human action has, in one way or another, addressed the issue of motivation.

THE CONCEPT OF MOTIVATION

In Latin, the word *motivum* refers to the reason something has moved. The English word *motivation* derives from *motivum*. Some behaviorists (see Chapter 1), such as B. F. Skinner, hoped to explain behavior without having to discuss concepts such as motivation that are not directly observable. But even the early behaviorists were aware that an animal, when presented with food in identical circumstances, may eat at some times and not at others. Because the external conditions were exactly the same in both circumstances, the only obvious explanation had to be some change in internal state. We say that the first time the animal was hungry, whereas the second time it was not. Hunger, then, becomes a handy motivational concept. It helps explain why an animal will or will not eat. Of course, the behaviorists were correct: The motivator hunger is not directly observable. Hunger can only be inferred from the animal's observed eating behavior. For this reason, many researchers prefer to say that they are studying motivated behavior, which is observable, rather than motivation, which is not (Whalen & Simon, 1984).

In the psychological community, there has never been complete agreement on exactly what the word *motivation* means. Some psychologists have preferred a very narrow definition of motivation, which is limited to the internal events that are the immediate and direct cause of an action. Using this definition, many researchers have concentrated on biological or physiological occurrences, such as hormone levels or changes in neurotransmitters that occur just prior to the activation of a motor sequence or action. Other researchers prefer a far broader definition of motivation, which would include any state or condition that might eventually move the organism to act—whether cognitive or physiological. In this view, for instance, a person's beliefs or thoughts could be considered motivators in a given set of circumstances. For the purposes of our discussion, because we want to include the full scope of motivational research, we shall define **motivation** as any state or condition that causes an organism to produce, inhibit, or maintain a behavior or action.

BIOLOGICAL MOTIVES

Perhaps the most obvious kinds of motivations are those that result directly from physical needs. If your water supply were suddenly cut off, your **need** for water would eventually increase. As the need intensified and you became more thirsty, the motivation, or **drive,** to satisfy the need would grow. Your actions would increasingly be directed to filling the need. Similarly, if you went without food or sleep, your motivation to satisfy those needs would also increase. These experiences are so common to the human condition that it seems strange to spend time discussing them. After all, who doesn't know that when you are without water and become thirsty, you are driven to get a drink? We can infer these drives or motives just by watching a person's behavior. If we watch someone searching desperately for food, we immediately assume that the person is hungry; if someone is looking for water, we assume that the person is thirsty. Actually, the only way to observe motivations is to watch the behavior that stems from them. The same thing is true of learning. We assume that learning has occurred because of changes in *performance.* Likewise, we assume that motivation exists because of changes in behavior. Unlike learning, which is a relatively permanent change in behavior due to experience, motivations come and go depending on the needs and drives that are present at a given moment.

Biological motivations such as hunger and thirst are assumed to be "built in," meaning that they exist from birth. You don't have to learn to feel thirsty or hungry. If you go without food or water for a sufficient time, the motivation to obtain those substances occurs automatically. You then want a certain amount of food or water until the condition is alleviated, bringing you back to your original stable point. Psychologists refer to this built-in tendency to maintain stability as **homeostasis.** Homeostatic mechanisms are regulatory; they attempt to maintain an optimal level. Any deviation from the optimal level will create a need. The need usually will produce a drive, which is the motivational force for action.

A thermostat in a home is a homeostatic mechanism analogous to the biological ones that exist in humans. Suppose you set a thermostat in a fully temperature-controlled house to 70 degrees Fahrenheit. If the temperature becomes warmer than that, the air conditioning turns on, cooling the house; if it becomes colder than 70 degrees, the furnace turns on, warming the air. In both cases, the temperature of the house will be returned to an optimal level.

Eating food satisfies a primary biological need. Too little food will result in starvation; too much food will eventually result in obesity. The homeostatic mechanism for food intake in most of us is extremely sensitive. For most peo-

MOTIVATION
Any state or condition that causes an organism to produce, maintain, or inhibit a behavior or action.

NEED
A condition whose satisfaction is necessary for the maintenance of homeostasis.

DRIVE
The psychological representation of a need; a complex of internal conditions, resulting from the loss of homeostasis, that impels an organism to seek a goal.

HOMEOSTASIS
An internal environment in which such body components as blood pressure, blood chemistry, breathing, digestion, and temperature are kept at levels optimal for the survival of the organism through the creation of drives in the presence of needs.

HYPOTHALAMOCENTRIC
HYPOTHESIS
Stellar's hypothesis that a hunger center
responsible for the homeostasis of food
intake exists in the hypothalamus.

SET POINT
A particular weight that the body seems
to demand; it is maintained by a
hypothetical homeostatic mechanism
that monitors levels of fat in the body.

ple, just the small addition of an extra pat of butter or margarine a day will result in a weight gain of 5 pounds per year (Logue, 1991). Yet our homeostatic mechanism for food intake is so sensitive that most people don't need to keep track of the number of calories they take in during the day in order to maintain a stable weight.

Presumably, other homeostatic mechanisms exist besides those that regulate food and water intake. Our need for an optimal temperature, for example, appears to be homeostatically controlled as well. For such mechanisms to work, the body must have sensors that detect deviations from the optimal state. For instance, as far as we know, there are no detectors sensitive to the levels of particular vitamins in the human body, and drives to obtain these necessary substances do not occur. Researchers are currently busy trying to uncover the homeostatic detectors that do exist and to learn how these detectors can alter motivation.

Hunger

How do you know when you're hungry? It seems a simple enough question, but the more you examine it, the more you will see that it's really a complicated matter. Perhaps you feel the hunger in your stomach. Your stomach may growl, or it may feel as though it has shrunk. Conversely, your stomach feels full when you have had enough to eat. It may be the pressure of the food against the walls of your stomach that signals you to stop eating. This seems a reasonable assumption—until it is tested. Experiments have been conducted in which a hungry person is asked to swallow a small balloon attached to a tube. The balloon is then inflated so that it exerts pressure. Interestingly, although the person may not be able to eat as much because the balloon is taking up space (Seligmann & Gosnell, 1986), the hunger doesn't go away (Janowitz & Grossman, 1949). Even more striking, patients who have had their stomachs removed because of cancer or other conditions continue to feel hunger and satiation. So the sensor for the homeostatic mechanisms of hunger and satiation can't be located solely in the stomach. Where, then, might a "hunger center" be situated?

In 1954, Eliot Stellar presented a strong argument that such a center existed in the hypothalamus of the brain. His theory became known as the **hypothalamocentric hypothesis.** Excitement grew as more data began to support the idea that the hypothalamus controlled food intake, and perhaps water intake as well (Grossman, 1972; 1975).

In one study with rats, researchers found that if the ventromedial hypothalamus (VMH)—the underside-middle of the hypothalamus—was stimulated, the hungry animal showed immediate signs of loss of appetite, then resumed eating, but at a very slow pace. If the scientists made lesions (cuts) in the VMH instead of stimulating it, the result was overeating and obesity (see Figure 11.1) (Brobeck, Tepperman, & Long, 1943).

An animal whose VMH has been cut won't continue eating until it explodes. Instead, the homeostatic mechanism is apparently reset at a higher optimal **set point.** An animal's set point is the weight the body tends to maintain by monitoring stored fat. The animal will eat and gain weight until it reaches a certain level beyond its previous capacity, and then it will maintain its weight at that new point.

The idea that the hypothalamus contains centers that activate or inhibit hunger and thirst was popular during the early 1970s. But there were some voices of dissent. For instance, one researcher found that lesions in *other* areas of the brain could also drastically affect eating and drinking (Morgane, as cited by deCharms & Muir, 1978).

◆ **FIGURE 11.1**

This rat's "weight problem" was caused by lesions in the ventromedial hypothalamus.

Then, different researchers began to discover that organs far from the brain directly affected hunger. For example, signals from the duodenum below the stomach appear to influence food intake. Injections of glucose (sugar) into the duodenum will suppress food intake in rabbits (Novin, 1976). The liver, too, gives signals of both hunger and satiation (Novin, 1976; Vanderweele & Sanderson, 1976). The liver contains receptors for glucose that transmit information along the vagus nerve to the hypothalamus. If that nerve is cut, the normal preference that animals show for the flavors associated with high-calorie foods is lost (Tordoff & Friedman, 1989). Furthermore, the rate of metabolism in the liver is an extremely good predictor of how hungry an individual will be (Friedman & Stricker, 1976). (The metabolic rate determines how quickly food or other biological matter is broken down.) In a sense, the liver acts as a calorie counter and signals us to like the flavors that go with high-calorie foods. In one fascinating experiment, rats were given high-calorie foods directly into their stomach, bypassing the mouth, while flavors usually associated with low-calorie foods were placed on their tongues. Soon the rats came to prefer the "low-calorie" flavors (Tordoff & Friedman, 1989). This would mean that the only reason you like the taste of cake more than spinach is because the spinach leaves you feeling less full than does the cake. What does this finding say about the idea of making yummy desserts with new low-calorie fat substitutes that supposedly taste like the real thing? Once your liver finds out the little trick that you've pulled, it may convince you that you don't like such desserts anymore. It will be interesting to see if that happens.

The most recent view of hunger, then, is that the hypothalamus is not *the* hunger and thirst center, but rather is *a* hunger and thirst monitoring and sensing area (Olds & Fobes, 1981; Logue, 1991). In this view, the hypothalamus works in conjunction with other sensing and regulating mechanisms located elsewhere in the brain and in peripheral organs such as the stomach, the duodenum, the intestines, and the liver. One of the most exciting developments to highlight this interaction is our new understanding of the role of **cholecystokinin,** or **CCK.** CCK is a neuropeptide (see Chapter 2) secreted by the intestine that can stimulate receptors in the brain. For some time CCK was suspected of playing a major role in the creation of feelings of satiety, that is, feelings that let you know that you are full and don't want to eat anymore. By developing antagonists to CCK (other substances that block CCK's effectiveness) and then placing them in animals' brains, researchers were able to weaken feelings of satiety and cause animals to overeat (Dourish, Rycroft, & Iversen, 1989). Following this discovery, it was shown that by stimulating the secretion of CCK in animals, satiety was strengthened, causing animals to eat less (Weller, Smith, & Gibbs, 1990). In other words, CCK stimulants work as natural appetite suppressors. Unfortunately, CCK antagonists do not help those with **anorexia nervosa,** a serious eating disorder in which the sufferer shuns food. For this reason, researchers believe that some mechanism other than an over-production of, and sensitivity to, CCK must be at the heart of the disorder (Geracioti, Liddle, Altemus, Demitrack, & Gold, 1992). However, CCK stimulants might be able to help those who don't appear to sense satiation soon enough or fully enough. As you can imagine, pharmaceutical companies are spending fortunes investigating a host of CCK stimulants, as well as CCK itself, hoping finally to develop a safe and effective diet pill sometime in this decade.

Aspects of Obesity

Technically, an individual is obese if his body weight is more than 20 percent above his ideal weight. Over the last decade, researchers have found that obesity usually can't be traced to simple gluttony. Although weight gain is

CHOLECYSTOKININ (CCK)
A neuropeptide secreted by the intestine that can stimulate receptors for satiation in the brain.

ANOREXIA NERVOSA
A serious eating disorder. The sufferer typically loses weight to dangerous levels while maintaining that she is still overweight. The disorder is far more common in women, especially young women, by about 10:1 over men. If not treated, the disorder can be fatal. The cause remains unknown, and various treatments are used including medications and psychotherapy.

sometimes related to "overeating," fatness is also linked to genetics, to the body's natural regulatory mechanisms, and to the social environment. Yale psychologist Judith Rodin has said, ". . . we see that obesity, like other behavioral disorders, is really determined by biological factors interacting with psychological and sociocultural factors. Behavior can alter biological factors which, in turn, change our behavior again" (Hall, 1984, p. 42).

SET POINTS.   In 1964, Ethan Sims conducted an overeating experiment at the Vermont State Prison. Volunteer prisoners were given extra food and were required to gain 25 percent beyond their starting weight. To Sims's surprise, this was extremely difficult for many of the prisoners. One prisoner, who went from 110 pounds to 143, found that during the last few months of the experiment, he had to consume 7,000 calories a day just to maintain his newly acquired weight—more than twice what he normally needed (Bennett & Gurin, 1982). After the experiment, without any conscious effort to do so, most of the prisoners returned to their original weights. Their bodies appeared to demand a certain weight.

This finding and others like it have led some researchers to conclude that the body has a particular set point. In this view, a homeostatic mechanism that is extremely sensitive creates hunger or satiation depending on the body-fat levels.

Furthermore, set points are believed to be genetically determined. Evidence for this comes from the fact that individuals who have no obese parent have only about a 10 percent chance of being obese themselves. These odds increase to 40 percent, however, if one parent is obese and to 70 percent if both parents are obese (Logue, 1991). Experiments with different strains of rats bred for obesity indicate that these percentages may well be more the result of genetic inheritance than of eating habits learned in the home (Zucker & Zucker, 1961; Bray & York, 1971). And data from the most comprehensive human population study conducted so far have led researchers to believe that there may be one major "obesity gene" that, if inherited from both parents, will almost guarantee obesity in the offspring. Indications are that 61 percent of the population do not carry this gene, 34 percent are carriers (that is, they have inherited one such gene from one parent, which in itself will not make them genetically obese, but does make it possible for them to pass the gene on to their children), and 5 percent have inherited such a gene from both parents and are therefore practically destined to become obese (Burns, Moll, & Lauer, 1989). This would not, of course, mean that those without an "obesity gene" from each parent couldn't become obese by overeating and failing to exercise, but only that 5 percent of the population have probably inherited the predisposition to readily store much of what they eat. People would find such a mechanism advantageous in an environment that vacillated between feast and famine, because they would be able to store food in the form of fat and thus could survive when food became scarce. This arrangement, however, is not an advantage in modern industrial societies, where high-calorie foods are plentiful for most people. Although environmental influences can be an important factor in obesity, genetic factors appear to play a greater role (Grilo & Pogue-Geile, 1991).

Interestingly, the kind of eating pattern that may determine obesity in individuals doesn't appear to be one of gluttony. Although obese individuals are commonly thought of as eating too much, researchers have discovered that obese and nonobese individuals eat about the same number of total calories per day! In fact, per pound of body weight, obese individuals actually eat *fewer* calories than their nonobese counterparts. The differences in eating habits that account for the obesity appear to be the different percentages of fat in the diet. In a study of obese and nonobese individuals, researchers discovered that fat accounted for about 35 percent of the calories consumed per day by obese subjects, but only 29 percent of the calories consumed per day by nonobese subjects (Miller, Lindeman, Wallace, & Niederpruem, 1990). Fat is far easier for the body to store than carbohydrates. For this reason, 3000 calories of fat are far more likely to result in a weight gain than are 3000 calories of carbohydrates.

NONHOMEOSTATIC MECHANISMS.   Thus far in our discussion of hunger, we have considered only homeostatic mechanisms. However, many researchers believe that **nonhomeostatic mechanisms** play an even greater role in obesity. In a classic experiment conducted by H. P. Weingarten (1983), a tone and light were paired with each meal given to hungry rats. Later, the rats were given free access to food whenever they wanted it and, presumably, ate their fill as they felt the need. However, even when they had all they wanted to eat, the rats would eat still more if the light and tone were turned on! The rats obviously were not satisfying a homeostatic need for food. What does this study suggest about human consumption? It indicates that there are times when we don't need food but are conditioned by the environmental cues to eat. Such times are probably familiar to us all (for example, being at the movies or at a party or sitting in front of the TV set).

Another interesting experiment highlights a different point. In this experiment, subjects were divided into two groups and told that they would participate in a food taste test. One group was told that they would have to miss lunch. Both groups were then given all the snacks they wished to eat. Those who thought that they would have to miss lunch ate considerably more (Lowe, 1982). This is called anticipatory eating, another example of nonhomeostatic consumption. **Anticipatory eating** may also account for the odd fact that so many obese people who try to diet actually end up gaining weight. Almost every dieter at one time or another has said, "I'll try again tomorrow." This allows the dieter to avoid hunger today and also to avoid the guilt of failure by promising success tomorrow. Because he or she believes that "tomorrow" will be a day without much food, however, the dieter is likely to eat excessively in anticipation of dieting. After three or four weeks of failed starts, the dieter may actually be heavier than if he or she had not attempted to diet in the first place.

Some researchers take an even broader view of the power of nonhomeostatic forces to control our eating. They suggest that the way in which food is associated with other events in our lives, especially during childhood when we may often be given food as a reward or to make us feel better, determines to a great extent how much we eat. Such experiences may condition some of us to eat whenever we need to feel loved or comforted or as a palliative for fear or loneliness (Logue, 1991).

OUTLOOK.   Because there are many aesthetic and medical reasons why obese people wish to lose weight, the research on obesity might seem particularly depressing. In fact, it seems to support what psychologists first reported back in the 1950s. "Most obese persons will not stay in treatment of obesity. Of those who stay in treatment most will not lose weight and of those who do lose weight, most will regain it" (Stunkard, 1958, p. 79).

More recently, however, it has been suggested that weight loss might be accomplished more easily than this view suggests. Since Stunkard relied on information about people who had specifically sought help for obesity, researcher Stanley Schachter questioned Stunkard's depressing conclusion. Could it be that those people who sought help were having an especially

NONHOMEOSTATIC MECHANISMS
In motivation, a motivating system that regulates a drive or an impetus to act, but is not counterbalanced by an opposing regulatory process that would reestablish the initial condition.

ANTICIPATORY EATING
Nonhomeostatic consumption of food owing to an awareness that food will soon be scarce or unavailable.

OSMOSIS
The diffusion of fluid through a semipermeable membrane, such as that surrounding a living cell, until the concentrations of fluid on either side of the membrane are equal.

difficult problem and that other people, who did not seek help, were better able to lick the problem on their own (so researchers never heard about them)? In a survey of people who either were currently or had once been obese, Schachter discovered that a great many indeed had lost a significant amount of weight on their own and had kept it off (Schachter, 1982). This encouraging news indicates that there may be successful dieters out there who generally don't come to the attention of researchers.

Of course, a large number of people who are overweight fail to lose weight. Why some succeed while others fail is still not well understood and remains a challenge for researchers.

Thirst

Thirst, like hunger, is primarily controlled by homeostatic mechanisms. Again we might ask, How do we know when we're thirsty? A common answer is that the mouth becomes dry, but, as you may have guessed, a dry mouth alone cannot account for the motivation to drink water (Fitzsimons, 1973).

The desire to drink appears to be controlled by the way in which water is distributed throughout the body, and at least two separate mechanisms appear to control the body's water balance. To begin with, water in the body is not distributed evenly. About 65 percent of it is contained in the cells, about 25 percent is found in the spaces between cells, and roughly 10 percent is contained in the blood. Both intracellular and extracellular mechanisms appear to be involved in thirst regulation. *Intracellular mechanisms* are based on sensor recordings of the amount of water within cells, whereas *extracellular mechanisms* are based on sensor recordings of the amount of fluid surrounding cells.

Several things can change intracellular and extracellular fluid levels. The two needn't be affected simultaneously. Extracellular fluid, for instance, can be directly affected by loss of blood or diarrhea, while intracellular fluid may not be influenced by these events at all. Cholera, which killed millions of people throughout the world until it was controlled, is accompanied by incessant diarrhea, which causes a massive loss of fluid that cannot be replaced quickly enough. In this sense, many cholera victims die from thirst or dehydration. Blood loss also results in rapid dehydration. In battle, wounded soldiers sometimes cry out for water because of the loss of extracellular fluid.

One way in which the fluid balance might be detected by the brain is through receptors that are sensitive to concentrations of sodium. Sodium does not pass into cells, but rather draws water from cells by a process known as **osmosis.** (For the same reason, salting a steak before you cook it—salt is *sodium chloride*—draws out the juices.) Certain brain cells, then, might be able to

The need for water and the drive to drink are common to all animal species.

regulate the body's water balance by being sensitive to the amount of water being drawn from those brain cells themselves by sodium. These receptors could signal thirst when the volume of water within their cell walls decreased. In fact, salt solutions injected directly into the lateral hypothalamus have been found to produce drinking (Andersson, 1971). Apparently, the injections tricked the osmotic receptors at that location into believing that the cells throughout the body lacked water, when in fact only those in the area of the hypothalamus were dehydrated.

Hormones produced by the pituitary gland, the liver, and the kidneys can affect the amount of water eliminated by the kidneys (Carlson, 1977). Clearly, then, thirst, like hunger, is controlled by the brain, hormones, and the peripheral action of organs far from the brain. Like hunger, it is complex and is not fully understood.

The Interaction of Hunger and Thirst

In the early 1960s, scientists discovered that when food-deprived animals were given only little bits of food on an intermittent schedule of reinforcement (see Chapter 8), the animals would consume large amounts of water. In some circumstances, the animals would drink as much as half their body weight in just 3 hours (Falk, 1961)! This phenomenon is known as **schedule-induced polydipsia,** or **SIP.** Researchers later discovered that giving a very hungry animal only little bits of food intermittently excited the animal, so that it was not only likely to drink more water if water was provided but was also more likely to engage in aggression, running, or even the ingestion of nonnutritive substances such as sawdust (Falk, 1971). Researchers refer to SIP as a "displacement" behavior, because it is more likely to occur when what is really wanted (in this case, food) is unobtainable (Wayner, Barone, & Loullis, 1981).

The phenomenon of SIP shows us that motivated behaviors such as eating and drinking are related and may share similar homeostatic mechanisms, because the motivation for one behavior may help to drive other behaviors.

Sex Drives

For the great majority of people, sex feels good. We have evolved biologically to feel this way. In fact, all species seem to like sex, or at least be attracted to it, and for a good reason. Can you imagine an entire species that was repelled by sex? It wouldn't last long; it would be gone in one generation. Nature has in this way favored animals that are attracted to sex. It would seem reasonable, then, to assume that there might be a biological drive or need for sex. But unlike food and water, sex is not necessary to keep an *individual* alive; it is needed only to maintain the species. For this reason, a drive to engage in sexual activity may not be as obvious in an individual as is the drive to satisfy hunger or thirst.

Research over the years has indicated that the more physiologically advanced the species, the less its sexual behavior appears to be governed directly by chemical and hormonal forces. Even in humans, however, these forces may play a role.

THE EFFECTS OF HORMONES ON SEXUAL BEHAVIOR. In 1849, the German physiologist Arnold Berthold found that by castrating roosters he could stop them from fighting with one another. When the testicles were transplanted back into the castrated birds, the birds once again began to fight. The reimplanted testicles made connections, not with the rooster's nervous system, but rather with the circulatory system. This fact led Berthold and other

SCHEDULE-INDUCED POLYDIPSIA (SIP)
Polydipsia means excessive drinking. Schedule-induced polydipsia refers to an increase in the drive to drink as a result of receiving little bits of food on an intermittent schedule.

GONADS
The sex glands that regulate sex drive and the physiological changes that accompany physical maturity; the ovaries in the female and the testes in the male.

scientists to assume that something was being carried in the blood that affected behavior. That "something" was later discovered to be a sex hormone.

In 1916, a Canadian physiologist named Frank Lillie presented a paper in which he explained why some genetically normal cows, called freemartins, acted and looked like bulls. Freemartins, he noted, always have a fraternal twin brother. Lillie speculated that the hormones from the testes of the male twin somehow masculinized the freemartins in the womb.

Researchers are interested in the effects of hormones on human beings because hormones directly influence many behaviors in lower animals, such as aggression and sexual activity. Following Lillie's discovery about freemartins, researchers found that girls who had fraternal twin brothers were a little more likely to act tomboyish or to show a greater interest in what have traditionally been considered "male" activities, such as contact sports. Because these girls were raised with brothers their own age with whom they played, however, it was not possible to isolate the effects of their environment from any possible hormonal effects. But there is a way to examine the effects of hormones on a human fetus.

Occasionally, a fetus may be exposed to levels of hormones that are higher than normal. Researchers have studied young girls who were exposed to abnormally large amounts of androgenic (male) hormones before birth. Such exposures may be caused by the administration of synthetic hormones for therapeutic reasons to the mother during pregnancy or by a disorder of the infant's own hormone secretions, known as congenital adrenal hyperplasia, or CAH. CAH occurs when the fetus secretes excessive androgen from the cortex of her kidneys. Sometimes female infants with this disorder are born with partially masculinized genitals, although their **gonads,** or sex glands, are female and normal.

During their preadolescence, these girls played in the rough-and-tumble way more commonly observed among boys, and they were characterized as less culturally feminine than most girls (Money & Ehrhardt, 1972; Baker, 1980; Eccles-Parsons, 1982; Hines, 1982). CAH girls also show a stronger preference for toys traditionally considered to be for boys than do matched female relatives without CAH (Adler, 1989).

Similarly, two populations of boys, aged 6 and 16 years, whose mothers received large doses of estrogens (female hormones) during pregnancy, were believed to be less athletic, less assertive, and less aggressive than most boys (Yalom, Green, & Fisk, 1973; Ehrhardt & Meyer-Bahlburg, 1981). It should be stressed, however, that studies of the effects of estrogen on males generally have been correlational or poorly controlled (Huston, 1983). Therefore, many researchers believe that no definite conclusions can yet be drawn concerning the effects of estrogen on males in the womb.

Although hormonal factors alone may account for some of the observed behavioral differences between males and females, the effects of androgynization, or exposure to male hormones, can't be all that strong. Once girls with CAH reach adolescence and adulthood, they no longer behave differentially from nonandrogynized females, and their sexual desires are just as likely to be heterosexual as are any woman's (Money & Mathews, 1982; Ehrhardt & Meyer-Bahlburg, 1981). If androgynization in the womb had given these females strong "male" inclinations, we might assume that they would take a homosexual orientation in adulthood. Studies from the former Soviet Union also reported that androgynization of females in the womb in no way affects later sexual preference or orientation (Lev-Ran, 1974). Furthermore, male fetuses exposed to insufficient androgen levels in the womb are just as likely to have a heterosexual orientation as are other males (Ehrhardt & Meyer-Bahlburg, 1981).

Nevertheless, the effects of hormones on human sexual motivation cannot be dismissed as unimportant. In humans the hypothalamus does appear to be involved in regulating the sex drive to an important degree. It has detectors that are sensitive to different levels of hormones, and these detectors also seem to be able to regulate hormonal output by stimulating the pituitary gland. How these regulatory mechanisms work and exactly how hormones affect sexual behavior are not clearly understood, but there does appear to be some relationship. For example, John Money and his colleagues have found that by administering the drug medroxyprogesterone acetate (Depo-Provera) to male sex offenders, they were able to inhibit the release of **testosterone** and also were often able to reduce the sex drive (Money, Berlin, Falck, & Stein, 1983). These findings imply that sexual activity and testosterone probably are linked in some fashion.

In lower species, numerous data implicate hormones in the direct control of sexual behavior. For instance, in lower mammals, mating occurs only during ovulation, and females typically must be receptive, in terms of hormone levels, before they will engage in sexual intercourse with males. During these receptive periods, the female often secretes a pheromone (see Chapter 5), the smell of which can be picked up by males some distance away. The scent of the pheromone stimulates the males to engage in sexual behavior. As any owner of a female dog in heat can testify, every male dog in the neighborhood shows up at the front door wanting a place on her dance card.

Researchers Richard P. Michael and R. W. Bonsall (1977), who studied rhesus monkeys, reported a preference for sex during the ovulation period of the female's menstrual cycle. This was difficult to observe because the male rhesus monkey is twice the size of the female and usually threatens to assault the female unless she capitulates. Under such circumstances, it is hard to tell when the female wants sexual intercourse. In their studies, Michael and Bonsall developed a unique way of testing the female monkey's desire. They used a cage divided by a door, placing the male on one side and the female on the other. The door could only be opened by a handle on the female's side. Therefore, when the male monkey was on the female's side of the partition, the experimenters could assume that the female was receptive.

As it turned out, the female rhesus let the male in primarily when she was ovulating. Blood samples taken from the female showed that her desire for sexual relations was closely tied to the level of sex hormones in her body. An important question not answered by this research is how the female's desire for sexual intercourse stimulates the male to want to engage in sex, too. Michael and Bonsall have isolated vaginal substances from rhesus females that appear to have the properties of pheromones. These substances, which are secreted at the time of ovulation, may help to stimulate the male to engage in sex. From an evolutionary standpoint, such an effect would make sense, because it would be most valuable to engage in sexual intercourse when the female was most likely to become pregnant.

You may be wondering whether these findings apply to humans. Human females appear to be receptive depending on social circumstances rather than biological triggers, and it is generally assumed that mating is likely to occur at any time during the female's menstrual cycle. But there is some evidence that women's sexual drives do fluctuate throughout their menstrual cycle. Is it possible that women secrete sexual attractants at the time of ovulation that might help to stimulate sexual activity in men? Although pheromones have not been conclusively identified in humans, in 1975, Michael and his colleagues found vaginal secretions in women that were identical to the sex attractants found in monkeys. They discovered that more of these particular acids are present at the time of ovulation than at other points during the menstrual cycle. Then,

TESTOSTERONE
The male sex hormone produced by the testes. It controls the development of secondary sex characteristics, such as the growth of a beard, and may influence the sexual activity of the individual.

in another study, conducted by Richard L. Doty and his colleagues, men were found to consider women's vaginal odors more agreeable and more intense just before and just after ovulation than at any other time during the menstrual cycle (Doty, Ford, Preti, & Huggins, 1975). These results indicate that there may be biological forces at work that fluctuate during a woman's monthly cycle and not only influence her desire for sexual intercourse but also encourage potential partners who are within scent range of her.

There also may be times when the desire to engage in sexual intercourse noticeably diminishes. Healthy, active human partners sometimes become sexually bored with each other. Richard Michael and his colleague Doris Zumpe have noticed similar reactions among rhesus monkeys. Adult male monkeys, after being with particular females for a significant time, appear to tire of them. In Michael and Zumpe's studies, four adult male monkeys were paired for 2½ years with four females. After 2 years, the males' sexual interest had decreased by two-thirds, and they avoided sex twice as often. When four new females were introduced into the cages, the males' interest and intercourse rates immediately doubled, and the attempts to avoid sex were cut in half. Some time later, the original four females were returned to the cages, and the males immediately showed a loss of interest. This result implies that the attraction between the sexes is dependent not so much on hormones or other biological influences but, as the researchers have said, "on the nature of the bond between partners." Of course, research in this area is incomplete, because the female monkeys' responses have not been studied.

Michael and Zumpe have noted that the same kinds of behavior are reported by human subjects. That new partners tend to renew a person's sexual interest may, in the researchers' view, have something to do with a tendency to break and remake sexual bonds. The researchers argue that maintaining sexual interest in a monogamous society may necessitate wearing alluring colognes, clothing, and hairstyles and, particularly, that both sexes refrain from sexual intercourse at times (Michael & Zumpe, 1978).

Currently, research concerning the ability of hormones or other biological forces to directly control or determine our behaviors is inconclusive. Part of the problem stems from the fact that it is very difficult to measure hormone levels in human beings. Hormone assays are very expensive, and in many instances, blood must be drawn from volunteers three or more times on the hour from the same location, leaving them with an aching arm, a collapsed vein or two, and a fervent desire never again to volunteer for anything. Another complication is that studies in which hormone levels were tracked over time have shown that although absolute hormone levels in humans are a poor predictor of behavior, the *range of hormone fluctuation* throughout the day may be a valid predictor (Jacklin, 1989). Even so, if hormones do play a major role in our sexual behavior, it is obviously not as strong as the one observed in lower species. If it were, we would have seen more conclusive research along the lines of Berthold's discovery that roosters stop fighting completely following castration. Actually, human males who have undergone castration for testicular cancer or other disorders are often unaffected in terms of sex drive or aggression.

To summarize, in our species hormones may, in a subtle way, play the leading role in shaping behaviors related to sexual motivation, or that role may be played by culture and learning. No one is certain. All we know is that both biological and environmental forces play important roles.

Sexual Orientations

An important aspect of sexual behavior is the orientation a person has toward a sexual partner. In our culture, the majority of people develop *heterosexual* orientations. Nonetheless, a large number of people express a *homosexual* orientation, and a still larger number develop a *bisexual* orientation in which, as adults, they have complete sexual experiences with members of both sexes. In the most extensive survey conducted so far, British and French researchers found that 4.1 percent of men and 2.6 percent of women had had homosexual intercourse at least once in their lifetimes and that 1.1 percent of men and 0.3 percent of women had had homosexual intercourse during the last 12 months (Aldhous, 1992). These figures were somewhat lower than earlier studies had suggested (Fay, Turner, Klassen, & Gagnon, 1989).

No one yet knows what determines an individual's sexual orientation, although Hamer's study described in the chapter Prologue suggests that genetics may play a part. As you recall, Hamer's study was conducted only with men, but similar findings hold for women in that lesbianism is far more likely to occur among identical twin sisters than among those who are fraternal twins (Bailey, Pillard, Neale, & Agyei, 1992). While these findings aren't yet conclusive, researchers believe that there may be many powerful inherited influences that directly affect sexual motivation.

Attempts to uncover hormonal differences between heterosexual and homosexual adults have not proved conclusive (Feder, 1984), although this approach toward understanding sexual orientation remains promising. For instance, in one study, three groups of volunteers were given the female sex hormone estrogen. The first group consisted of heterosexual women, the second of heterosexual men, and the third of primarily or exclusively homosexual men. The amount of LH (luteinizing hormone—a substance that triggers ovulation in women) was measured in each subject after she or he had taken the estrogen. The women showed a sharp increase in LH within 3 days of taking the estrogen. The heterosexual men, on the other hand, showed little or no increase. Interestingly, among the homosexual men, there was a significant elevation of LH to intermediate levels between those of heterosexual men and women (Gladue, Green, & Hellman, 1984). Of course, these findings show only that certain hormonal responses are related to sexual orientation, not that hormones control or direct that preference.

Richard Green (1987) has conducted a long-term 15-year study in which he kept track of 66 boys who were described as extremely effeminate, who liked to dress as girls, and who played with girls or dolls. As adults, 44 of these boys were homosexual or bisexual, far more than would be expected among 66 boys who were chosen from a random population. This study, of course, doesn't tell us how such an orientation might begin, but it does indicate that it begins early in development.

A number of researchers have argued that the crucial time for the determination of sexual orientation occurs in the womb, sometime around or during the second trimester (middle third) of the pregnancy (Marmor, 1985). Researchers Lee Ellis and M. Ashley Ames have stated:

The involvement of learning, by and large, only appears to alter how, when, and where the orientation is expressed. For humans, the crucial timing appears to be between the 2nd month of [pregnancy] and about the middle of the fifth month, during which time the hypothalamic-limbic regions of the male's nervous system are permanently diverted away from their otherwise-destined female [connections and organization]. (Ellis & Ames, 1987, p. 251)

Ellis and Ames believe that biochemical changes that occur in the womb may change sexual orientation by altering the neural development of the fetus's brain and that such changes might be brought on by stress experienced by the mother, drugs taken during the pregnancy, or other forces that might upset the environment of the womb (Ellis & Ames, 1987).

SEXUAL REASSIGNMENT
A surgical procedure for altering anatomy and appearance so that the individual resembles the opposite sex.

TRANSSEXUAL
An individual who exhibits the most extreme form of gender reversal, in which the individual feels that he or she is really a member of the opposite sex but has been trapped in the wrong-sexed body.

Researchers are coming to believe that sexual orientation is not a personal or moral choice, but rather is biogenetically formed during the prenatal period and beyond an individual's control.

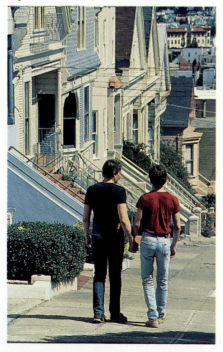

Evidence for the possible role of events in the womb as an explanation of sexual orientation is growing, but many researchers still believe that neural development in the womb may be only a small part of the explanation. During the last few years, the social learning and cognitive theories also have attempted to deal with this issue.

The social learning assumption is that individuals who are encouraged to display sexual attraction to members of the same sex during childhood, or who are encouraged to adopt the social-sexual role opposite to their own, may eventually express a homosexual orientation. Evidence for this assumption has come from other cultures, in which homosexuality has been clearly accepted and in which boys are sometimes specifically trained to grow up to be the lovers of other men. For instance, among the Sakalavas in Madagascar, boys who are considered pretty are raised as girls, and they readily adopt the woman's sex-appropriate role (Green, 1976). An even more striking example of the cultural influence on sexual orientation is provided by the Sambia tribe of New Guinea. Researcher John Money has observed that

the Sambia believe that after being nourished on mothers' milk as young children, the youths must be nourished on the male equivalent—the semen of young, unmarried fellow tribesmen—before they can fully become men. When a bachelor reaches marrying age, he is paired up with a woman by his family and "embarks on the heterosexual phase of his career" . . . the Sambia view the omission of [homosexual] behavior during [adolescence] as abnormal and stigmatizing. (Bales, 1986, p. 18)

Considering the data that indicate that homosexual or heterosexual orientation might be strongly influenced by the environment, the question is then raised whether a parent whose sexual orientation and attitudes are known to his or her children would affect the sexual orientation of the child. To examine this issue, Richard Green conducted a study of 37 children being reared either by female homosexuals or by parents who had had sex-change operations (known as **sexual reassignments**) and who had adopted the social-sexual roles of their new (opposite) sex. The 18 males and 19 females studied by Green were between 3 and 20 years of age, with an average age of 11.3 years; 21 were being raised by homosexual parents and 16 by **transsexual** parents. (Most of the children in the latter group were aware that their parent had at one time been a member of the opposite sex.) The study was conducted over a 2-year period (Green, 1978). Green evaluated the sexual orientation of the younger children by the toys and games they preferred, their peer preference, the roles they chose during fantasy play, their clothing preferences, and their vocational desires. He also used the Draw-a-Person Test, in which children usually draw a person of their own sex before drawing a person of the opposite sex. For the adolescents in the study, Green gathered information about sexual desires and fantasies about sexual partners. He also collected data on overt sexual behavior.

With the questionable exception of only one child, all 37 children in the study developed heterosexual orientations and a marked desire to conform to the social-sexual roles provided by their culture. Not one had homosexual or transsexual fantasies. The adolescents developed desires for the opposite sex. The young children all wanted to play with children of their own sex, which is typical of heterosexual children at ages 5 to 11 years. Boys expressed desires to be doctors, firefighters, police officers, engineers, or scientists, and girls wanted to be nurses, teachers, mothers, or homemakers (except for one girl who said that when she grew up she wanted to be the Popsicle lady). These findings led Green to surmise that influences other than the family may be critical in the formation of gender roles and sexual orientation. His view contradicts the positions held by psychoanalytic, behavioral, and cognitive theorists, but it does support the idea that orientation may develop very early, perhaps as the result of biological forces.

In a more comprehensive study, Alan Bell and his colleagues interviewed 979 homosexuals and 477 heterosexuals in the San Francisco area during 1969 and 1970. They organized their data into a model that included such possible social and familial variables as parental relationships, gender conformity, sibling identifications, and school influences. Once again, the data gathered supported the theory that homosexuality is a deeply ingrained trait that is manifested early and is relatively resistant to external influences (Bell, Weinberg, & Hammersmith, 1981). As you can see, it is still not apparent which factors actually determine sexual orientations, but more and more, researchers are looking to inherited factors for possible answers.

🧬 STIMULUS MOTIVES

The biological or physiological drives such as hunger, thirst, and sex are not the only ones that do not need to be learned. In addition, both human beings and animals seem to require a certain amount of stimulation. The needs to obtain sensory stimulation, to be active, and to explore and manipulate the environment produce motivations that are referred to collectively as **stimulus motives.**

The motivation to experience a certain amount of stimulation appears to have evolved because of its survival value. By manipulating and exploring the environment and by actively sensing it, every organism learns about it and learns what to expect from it. If you own pets and have ever moved to a new home, you will have observed the need to explore, not just in yourself, but in your pets as well. Animals in a new environment are motivated to learn every aspect of it, to investigate its perimeters, and, in general, to determine which parts of it are safe and which may be dangerous.

The need for stimulation is apparent among animal subjects who have been placed in boring and uninteresting environments. In such cases, animals often will work for the chance to engage in something more interesting, even if it is nothing more than looking out a window. No doubt, there have been many times in your life when stimulation levels were too low and you became bored and wished you could do something else. On the other hand, people in highly stimulating situations often seek quiet and solitude, as though they have had too much stimulation. Following overstimulation, such as might be encountered in a stressful job, being isolated from stimulation can be therapeutic and relaxing (Suedfeld & Kristeller, 1982; Suedfeld, Ballard, & Murphy, 1983).

One of the most restful forms of **sensory isolation** uses tanks of warm water in which the subject may comfortably float in darkness and silence. Years ago, when such "sensory deprivation" research was begun, it was thought that depriving someone of sensory input might be harmful. Subjects placed in such restricted environments were given "panic buttons" to signal if they needed to get out fast. There were even some exaggerated reports of hallucinations caused by sensory isolation, which were reported in many textbooks as the norm. Since then, however, much research has shown that the restricted environmental stimulation technique, or REST as it is called, gives most people a profound sense of relaxation and may even have some health benefits (Suedfeld & Coren, 1989).

Perhaps there is an optimal level of arousal somewhere between too little and too much, depending on what you are doing. If you're not sufficiently aroused, your performance is likely to be poor. As you know, you're not at your best if you're tired or run down when you have to take a complex test. Too much arousal can also be disruptive: It's difficult to be efficient when

STIMULUS MOTIVES
Drives or motives that appear to satisfy a need for certain amounts of sensory stimulation.

SENSORY ISOLATION
Lack of a stimulus input needed for maintaining homeostasis. Prolonged reduction of external stimulation, in either intensity or variety, may produce boredom or restlessness, but is often experienced as profoundly relaxing.

FOCUS ON GENDER ISSUES

DO MEN AND WOMEN INHERIT DIFFERENT SEXUAL MOTIVATIONS?

Evolutionary biologists have long asserted that sexual motivations play an important role in the survival of a species. With this in mind, it might seem reasonable to assume that men and women have been shaped by evolutionary forces toward different sexual motivations depending upon their anatomically assigned gender roles. Because women bear children and men don't, it is argued, it might be beneficial if the genders experienced different sexual motivations that related to this difference.

Evolutionary theory states that women will place a greater emphasis on social dominance when choosing a man (which denotes his ability to provide for the family), while men will place a greater emphasis on youth and attractiveness when choosing a woman (which denotes her health and ability to bear children). All this is said to generally occur without awareness on the part of either men or women and is part of an inherited predisposition selected by the forces of evolution. Research has supported this view, as surveys show that women accord more importance to socioeconomic status, ambition, character, and intelligence when initially choosing a partner, while men place the greatest emphasis on youth and physical characteristics (Feingold, 1992).

With this in mind, psychologists decided to see if there were significant gender differences in the way men and women approached the prospect of a heterosexual "one-night stand," in which a person would have a casual sexual relationship with a member of the opposite sex and then, most likely, would not see that person again. The researchers discovered that men and women approach one-night stands very differently and that the differences appear to be based on evolutionary forces (Kenrick, Groth, Trost, & Sadalla, 1993). Douglas Kenrick, who led this study, has said

> From an evolutionary prospective, mating is the most important game around; the more you understand it, the better you'll be at succeeding—or at not being dissatisfied or horrified with what the opposite sex does. (Wuethrich, 1993, p. 6)

What Kenrick and his colleagues did was to ask 327 college students to list their criteria for a sexual partner along 24 dimensions such as intelligence, emotional stability, and social status. The differences between criteria for partners listed by men and women were greatest when they were asked to consider a one-night stand. When asked to consider a marriage partner, the differences in criteria faded. In a marriage, both men and women wanted someone who was nice, attractive, and emotionally stable.

Kenrick and his colleagues predicted that men would be more indiscriminate than women in choosing a partner for a one-night stand, because the man could further his genetic interest (passing on his genes) with little or no investment of resources (he'd be gone the next day). The woman, on the other hand, would be more selective, because she might pay a high price for a rash mating should she become pregnant. In other words, while a man can theoretically impregnate thousands of women over his lifetime, a woman's investment in resources is likely to be substantial, because this one night might account for a significant portion of her lifetime chances to pass on her genes.

The findings of the study supported this hypothesis. Men were willing to lower their standards substantially for a one-night stand, while women generally weren't. After reading this study, I became curious and asked a female colleague what she thought of the findings. She said, "Of course, all men are slime." In an effort to get a second opinion, and perhaps a more comforting one, I asked another female colleague who, after reading the study, sighed and said, "Men! You can't live with 'em, and you can't shoot 'em." So I decided to quit asking.

Although we should consider the evolutionary aspect when examining sexual motivation, just as we would when looking at the behavior of any animal, the effects of culture and environment can't be overlooked. In a culture where one-night stands are considered more acceptable for men than for women (although with the AIDS virus at hand, they are quickly coming to be considered unacceptable for anyone), it might be that a woman would feel the need to rationalize her behavior by noting the higher status of her partner, whereas a man could feel comfortable with just about anyone since it would be for just one night. Identifying gender differences in sexual motivation is tricky and controversial. The same evolutionary argument can be made to assert that women are looking for someone with whom they can make a "nest" and have babies, while men are genetically preselected to roam from partner to partner. Many women find this assertion insulting and argue that they can feel fulfilled without "nest building." In addition, many men take comfort in providing a good "nest" for their children and find fulfillment in their families. Not that such a genetic predisposition isn't possible, but, needless to say, it probably wouldn't be a good idea for a man to attempt to use genetics as an excuse for an extramarital affair that he wouldn't tolerate from his wife.

In summary, how much influence inheritance may have on sexual preferences, orientation, or mate selection remains to be determined, but we can probably safely say that evolution is involved at some level in determining sexual motivations and that these forces will become clearer with time and study.

you're in a state of terror. In 1908, Yerkes and Dodson discovered that mice were better able to learn a simple task in order to avoid a *painful* shock, but were better able to learn a complex task when doing so to avoid a *mild* shock (Yerkes & Dodson, 1908). Later researchers interpreted these findings more broadly, arguing that an optimum level of arousal was associated with the difficulty of each task in which an animal might engage. Historically, for some odd reason, this broader interpretation became known as the *Yerkes-Dodson law*, making it sound quite formidable, although it really was little more than supposition (Winton, 1987). Although there is no justification for referring to this concept as a "law," it is true that, in the most recent terms, a certain level of arousal is needed to produce the best performance, and the best level of arousal depends to some degree on the difficulty of the task.

Even so, the issue remains clouded by the effects of cognition on arousal. For instance, if you were physiologically aroused before performing in an athletic competition because you were scared of failing, you might not do as well as if you were *equally aroused* because you were all psyched up to succeed in the competition (Neiss, 1988).

LEARNED MOTIVATION

Certain motivations can be learned. No one is born desiring a Chevrolet Corvette. Learned motives can be powerful forces. They are often related to incentives, that is, to particular things that we want to possess. When these incentives (sometimes called secondary reinforcers) are present, the motivation to acquire them becomes much stronger, especially if we know what we must do to obtain them.

The term **social motivation** often is used to refer to motives acquired through learning and culture. Theories of social motivation attempt to account for all kinds of impulses or deliberate actions that are not the direct result of biological needs (Pittman & Heller, 1987).

Learned motivations can also imitate biological ones. For example, it's possible to learn to become hungry. Researcher Judith Rodin has shown that one way to bring this about is through classical conditioning (see Chapter 8). Consider what happens when you eat sugar. The sugar (an unconditioned stimulus) triggers the pancreas to secrete insulin (an unconditioned response), and the insulin metabolizes the sugar. Before swallowing the sugar, however, you probably looked at the sweet food, tasted it, and noted its texture, all of which can become conditioned stimuli. If the relationship between these stim-

SOCIAL MOTIVATION
Learned motivational states that result from the individual's interaction with his or her social environment or culture.

Some motivations can be learned; no one is born desiring a brand new sports car.

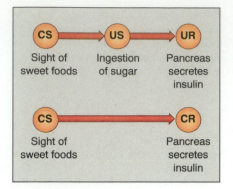

◆ **FIGURE 11.2**

Classical conditioning of the pancreas. After sufficient pairing between the sight of sweet foods and the ingestion of sugar, the sight of the foods alone can result in the secretion of insulin.

uli and the ingestion of sugar is strongly enough established, you can teach your pancreas to secrete insulin. All you need to do is to see or think about the food (a conditioned stimulus), and the pancreas will sometimes secrete insulin (a conditioned response), although no sugar has been swallowed (see Figure 11.2). When insulin is secreted without sugar intake, blood sugar may drop, or oxidative metabolism change, which in turn can lead directly to an increase in hunger. In this way, you can learn to create a genuine biological drive to eat, even when the *need* may not be present (Booth, 1977).

Drinking can also be affected by learning. We frequently take a drink for social reasons or other learned reasons, without really requiring the liquid. As was mentioned earlier, these are examples of nonhomeostatic processes. The interplay between learned motives and biological drives can be so complex that it's almost impossible to isolate one from the other (Rodin, 1981). Some researchers have argued that of the two kinds of motivation, learned motives are more responsible for the complex aspects of human behavior.

THEORIES OF MOTIVATION

Maslow's Hierarchy of Motives

In the past, "grand theories" of motivation were popular—grand in that they attempted to explain most of human motivation. One of the most interesting and frequently cited theories was the **hierarchy of motives** postulated by the humanistic psychologist Abraham Maslow (Maslow, 1970) as part of his research on self-actualization (see Chapter 14). By a hierarchy of motives, Maslow meant that some needs were more powerful than others, depending on an individual's circumstances. The hierarchy is shown in Figure 11.3. As you can see, physiological needs form its base. In other words, to a starving person, the motivation to find food is more powerful and basic than are the motivations to find love, a sense of belonging, and self-esteem. A starving person will be motivated to find food even more than to find safety.

Maslow argued that the higher motivations can come into play only when the basic needs have been satisfied. Before a person can be free to engage in self-actualization—that is, free to continue fulfilling her potential—that person has to meet the physiological needs for safety and security, to find love and belonging, and to have self-esteem and the esteem of others. Accordingly, Maslow placed self-actualization at the top of the hierarchy. Thus, the motivation to realize one's full potential is a fragile thing, easily disrupted by disturbances at the lower levels.

You can see how this hierarchy might explain many of your own motives. Imagine that you arrived in a strange town, hungry and broke. According to Maslow, you would be motivated first to ensure a supply of food and water to satisfy your physiological needs. Then, perhaps, you would look for a job to obtain money for shelter and security. Only after you had a secure base of operations would you begin to make connections to the community to develop a sense of belonging, perhaps by forming relationships. Once you felt that you belonged and that you shared love with other people, your sense of self-esteem could develop as your loved ones and friends held you in esteem. At that point, as a fulfilled member of a community, you might begin to develop your full potential.

Maslow's motivational theory has not always been supported by research, however, and many questions can be raised about it. For instance, how would you explain someone who throws himself on a hand grenade to protect friends, or someone such as Gandhi, who fasted to attain social and political change? Maslow's theory, like most grand theories of motivation, often fails to predict

◆ **FIGURE 11.3**

Maslow's hierarchy of motives.

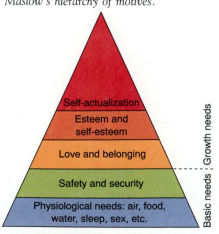

the complex patterns of human behavior and motivation in unusual circumstances. Still, it does provide a generally valid outline of motivation.

The Need to Achieve

Over 40 years ago, David McClelland described the **need for achievement (n-Ach)** as an acquired motivating force (see Figure 11.4), and used it to make predictions about motivation (McClelland, Atkinson, Clark, & Lowell, 1953). Like Maslow, he attempted to expand his motivational theory to encompass as much of human behavior as possible.

At some level, of course, the need to achieve must also have an unlearned component, if for no other reason than that, simply to survive, human beings must obtain a certain degree of mastery over their environment (Spence, 1985).

To measure the degree of n-Ach in his subjects, McClelland showed them different drawings from the Thematic Apperception Test (see Chapter 14) and asked them to tell him stories about what they saw. McClelland was able to isolate themes from these stories that he believed demonstrated a high or low need to achieve, and he used these findings to make predictions about how the subjects would behave. For instance, people with a high need to achieve tended to perform better in school than did those with a low need.

McClelland then attempted to generalize his findings to whole cultures and nations. He argued in 1961 that in nations where the citizens scored low in n-Ach on his tests, the economic standards and gross national product were lower than they were in nations where the citizens scored high in n-Ach. This assertion came to be known as McClelland's **achieving society theory.** While McClelland's tests for n-Ach have been fairly successful at predicting a person's desire to seek challenges, to set high goals, to delay gratification until the goal is achieved, and to take reasonable risks (Atkinson & Raynor, 1974), they have proved somewhat more limited than originally hoped. For instance, data since 1961 concerning national economic standards and gross national products have not given much support to McClelland's achieving society theory (Mazur & Rosa, 1977).

Although it would be very useful to produce a theory of motivation that could explain most of human behavior, most researchers now believe that humans are just too complex to be understood in such a global and all-encompassing way. For this reason, modern motivational theory generally is built on highly detailed investigations of many separate areas and limited generalizations, rather than on sweeping hypotheses.

Some fascinating specific areas of research are developing that tell us a lot about why people behave in the ways that they do. Let's take a few minutes and look at some of them.

HIERARCHY OF MOTIVES
A theory of motivation developed by Abraham Maslow in which more basic needs must be met before needs of a higher order can come into play.

NEED FOR ACHIEVEMENT (N-ACH)
A learned motivation, described by researcher David McClelland. Those who score high in n-Ach often behave in different ways from those who score low in n-Ach.

ACHIEVING SOCIETY THEORY
McClelland's theory that nations whose citizens show the lowest need for achievement also tend to have the lowest gross national product, whereas nations whose citizens show the highest need for achievement have the highest gross national product.

David McClelland

◆ **FIGURE 11.4**

McClelland used this ring-toss game to illustrate the way in which people are motivated to obtain an optimal level of achievement satisfaction. Most subjects preferred to stand at distance markers 6 or 7 when throwing the ring, because doing so provided the greatest sense of achievement. At marker 1, it's easy to get a ringer, but achievement satisfaction is minimized because it's too easy. At marker 10, it's too hard to succeed, and achievement satisfaction also is lowered.

LEARNED HELPLESSNESS
Giving up, even though success is possible, because of previous experience with situations in which success was impossible.

Learned Helplessness

Some people aren't motivated to help themselves when they could easily do so. If they have lost this motivation because of their experiences with failure, they may be suffering from what researchers call **learned helplessness.**

It's possible to teach an animal to become helpless. In the classic experiment that first demonstrated this phenomenon, two groups of dogs were given electric shocks. The dogs from both groups were yoked together in an experimental sense: Whenever dogs in one group received a shock, so did the dogs in the other group. The dogs in the first group, however, were able to press a lever and turn off a shock when it began. They had some control over their situation. The dogs in the second group had no such control. What was most interesting about this experiment was the effect that lack of control had on the dogs in the second group. When dogs from both groups were tested in an environment from which they could not escape shocks, the dogs from the first group barked and ran about trying actively to do something. Dogs from the second group, however, lay down and passively took the shocks as they came (Seligman & Maier, 1967).

Learned helplessness has also been observed in human infants. Two researchers (Watson & Ramey, 1969; 1972) positioned rotating mobiles above the heads of three groups of infants. A pressure-sensitive pillow was placed beneath the heads of the infants in the first group. By moving their heads, these infants could open and close circuits that made their mobiles turn, so they had *control* over this aspect of their environment. The infants in the second group were given no control; their pillows were not connected to the mobiles. As a result, their mobiles remained stationary. The infants in the third group also were given no control; in this case, the mobiles turned randomly. (The purpose of the third variation was to ensure that the infants who learned to move their heads against their pillow were doing so because they had control over their environment, not simply because they were watching a turning object.) After being exposed to the mobiles for 10 minutes per day for a period of 14 weeks, the infants in the first group learned to turn their heads to make the mobiles move. This is what you might expect an infant to be able to do through simple learning. But there's more.

People suffering from learned helplessness aren't motivated to help themselves, even when they could easily do so.

As in the experiments with dogs, the most interesting aspect of these experiments was how *lack of control* affected the later behavior of the second and third groups of infants. Once again, researchers presented the second and third groups with the mobiles, but this time the infants were given control over the mobiles' movements. Even after extensive training, these infants failed to learn to operate the mobiles. Like the dogs who gave up trying to escape because of their earlier lack of control, the second and third groups of infants had learned to be helpless; they had learned not to expect their behavior to have any effect on their mobiles. As a result, they never seemed to appreciate the link between their head movements and the mobiles' turning that the first group of infants had been able to discern. Like the dogs in Seligman's experiment, infants also can transfer such learned helplessness to new situations (Finkelstein & Ramey, 1977).

Not surprisingly, individuals in institutions and other situations in which they are given little opportunity to manipulate their environments, or in which things are always being done to them or for them, may quickly learn not to try. The U.S. Office of Education issued one of the first reports to lend support to this idea. It found that members of minority groups who believed they were controlled by their environment—rather than the other way around—were more likely to fail in school (Coleman et al., 1966). It's ironic that certain life experiences may be helping children to learn not to learn.

Self-Efficacy

Whether a person will show learned helplessness depends a great deal on how he or she perceives the chances of being successful in any given situation. Psychologists refer to this perception as **self-efficacy** (Bandura, 1982). If you have self-efficacy in a certain situation, it means you believe that you can have an effect, that you can make a difference. In a sense, self-efficacy is the same as self-confidence.

High self-efficacy will help an individual to cope. In fact, it is self-efficacy, not fear, that determines whether a person with a phobia will approach whatever it is that he fears. A person who believes that he has control over the thing that frightens him will usually be willing to approach that thing in spite of his fear. With low self-efficacy, the same person would be unlikely to approach the feared object (Bandura, 1986).

If helplessness can be taught, it would stand to reason that its opposite, a sense of self-efficacy, could also be taught. Researchers have, in fact, discovered that there appear to be four major ways to raise perceptions of self-efficacy (Bandura, 1982): (1) through direct action, (2) by observing others, (3) through the use of verbal persuasion, and (4) by altering how one perceives one's own physical state.

Direct action refers to the actual experience you have in a particular situation. Learning through direct experience that you can be successful and that you are capable will enhance self-efficacy. Nothing will boost your confidence like success. Failure, especially as a first experience, can lower self-efficacy. For this reason, when teaching a new task, it is best to structure the first experiences to ensure success before going on to more difficult parts of the task. In this way, the person builds confidence bit by bit.

By observing other people who are *similar* to you succeed at a task, you are also likely to raise your self-efficacy—it makes you more confident that you, too, could do it. For this reason, it is often helpful to team someone new to a job with a successful person who is perceived to be similar to the new worker. Of course, watching someone similar to yourself fail at a task can lower your self-efficacy.

Verbal persuasion, in the form of logical arguments in favor of one's ability to succeed, sometimes can raise self-efficacy, but only if the person's self-efficacy is fairly high to begin with.

Finally, there are the physiological factors, such as fatigue, exhaustion, or fear, which individuals often use as an indication of self-efficacy. Your exact state itself isn't important; it's your cognitive appraisal of the state that matters. For example, trembling might lower an inexperienced soldier's self-efficacy if he perceives this physiological reaction to be an indication of fear, whereas the same trembling in an experienced actor might actually raise self-efficacy if she interprets it as the opening night jitters that will give her first performance more excitement.

High self-efficacy works as a motivator. If you believe that you can succeed, you are likely to try hard. People who try hard enough and long enough will often succeed, further strengthening their confidence. When people use the techniques we have described to help build someone up, psychologists say that they are teaching **mastery.**

When attempting to teach mastery, it is also important to consider the cognitive factors that play a role in determining how broad a person's newly won confidence and desire to succeed will be. There are three important cognitive dimensions to consider: (1) internal versus external reasons for control, (2) stable versus unstable circumstances, and (3) global versus specific applications (Abramson, Seligman, & Teasdale, 1978; Miller & Norman, 1979). Let's look at each of these.

SELF-EFFICACY
How effective a person is in a particular situation. Perceived self-efficacy can be a powerful cognitive motivator.

MASTERY
In motivation, the opposite of learned helplessness; the acquisition of skills or attitudes that enable one to persist in adversity and that help "psychologically inoculate" one against giving up or feeling helpless.

ALTRUISM
Behavior that benefits someone other than the actor, with little or no apparent benefit for the actor.

INTERNAL VERSUS EXTERNAL REASONS.   If you think that control over events resides in the environment rather than in yourself ("There's nothing I can do about it, things just happen to me"), then this perceived locus of control may lead you to believe that what you do doesn't matter. If, on the other hand, you believe that control resides within you and not in the environment ("The reason things went right was because of what I did"), then you may feel more confident about taking on new tasks. A school-aged child, for example, who has an external sense of control typically will believe that he failed because the teacher didn't like him or because the tests were unfair, while a child with an internal sense of control typically will attribute her failure to not trying hard enough. Obviously, learned helplessness is less likely to occur if a person perceives the reason for lack of control to be internal; that is, if he believes he is failing because he isn't trying hard enough, rather than because of forces over which he has no control.

STABLE VERSUS UNSTABLE CIRCUMSTANCES.   As you might guess, if you believe that whatever bad thing is happening to you is going to be long lasting or permanent, you're more likely to demonstrate learned helplessness than if you think it is temporary. For example, someone in a hospital bed who can't walk is less likely to show signs of learned helplessness if he is aware that he will soon be better than if he believes he'll never walk again. With this in mind, we would predict that the people of what was once East Germany will strive hard and succeed in spite of the hardships they face while transferring to a market economy because, by and large, they view their economic troubles as temporary. Someone without job skills, who is on welfare and has a large family to raise in a decaying inner city environment, however, may view her situation as relatively permanent, which will weaken her self-efficacy and greatly reduce her motivation to succeed.

GLOBAL VERSUS SPECIFIC APPLICATIONS.   Finally, learned helplessness is more likely to occur if you perceive the cause of your loss of control or failure as being applicable in many or all situations (global), rather than being applicable in only a few circumstances (specific). For this reason, self-efficacy and motivation to succeed are usually not too adversely affected by failures that are viewed as isolated or fluky. We would predict that although the space shuttle *Challenger* disaster was very upsetting, it alone would not deter the United States from continuing its space program. However, if one disaster followed on another until the *whole* program seemed a mess, confidence and mastery could be so undermined that the public might come to believe that we just can't do it anymore and might turn away from further efforts. This could occur in spite of our many great space successes in the past—learned helplessness is often irrational.

We might, therefore, assume that to develop mastery, it would be best to have an internal, stable, and potentially global sense of mastery (Mineka & Hendersen, 1985). Furthermore, if we consider operant-learning theory (see Chapter 8), we might add that persistence is more likely to occur if success comes intermittently—not with every effort (Jones, Nation, & Massad, 1977). In other words, occasional failures interspersed with successes can teach you that you can "bounce back" from failure, which is an important contributor to a sense of mastery.

Altruism and Intrinsic Motivation

People often are motivated to help one another. Sometimes, the act of giving help may appear to be particularly selfless. We often use the word **altruism** to describe the motivation for such selfless acts. An altruistic act is the opposite of one motivated by self-interest. Psychologists think that altruistic behaviors are controlled by internalized systems for self-reward and morality. Such **intrinsic motivation** has been found in many cases to be superior to extrinsic (external) motivation in creating and maintaining behavior. In one experiment, researchers tried to teach fifth graders not to litter and to clean up after other children. The children were divided into two groups. The children in the first group were told each day for 8 days that they should be neat and tidy, and the reasons this behavior would be good for them were explained. The children in the second group were told, for the same number of days, that they were neat and tidy. Littering and cleanliness were measured on the tenth and fourteenth days. The differences were considerable. The children in the first group, who were motivated extrinsically, were far less likely to have helped to clean up than were the children in the second group, who had begun to think of themselves as neat and tidy and wanted to maintain this positive self-image (intrinsic motivation) (Miller, Brickman, & Bolen, 1975).

Extrinsic motivators may have problems associated with them as well. In one study, children were observed drawing and, after a time, were given some good-player certificates as a reward for having drawn (Lepper, Greene, & Nisbett, 1973). Interestingly, these children were less likely to draw after that than were the children who had not been rewarded. In this case, the reward actually seemed to undermine the intrinsic motivation behind the drawing.

Many motivational theorists have become interested in discovering the circumstances under which extrinsic reinforcement will undermine behavior that is intrinsically motivated. This area of research is of special interest to behavioral theorists. In many schools and institutions, people who are not motivated to work often are stimulated to do so through the use of "token economies." That is, when the people behave appropriately, they are given a token that can be traded in for something of value. Some observers have argued that token economies, while effective, can have drawbacks and that researchers and therapists must determine at the outset whether the behavior they want to encourage isn't already intrinsically motivated. If it is, giving tokens as rewards may undermine the intrinsic motivation; then, instead of doing something because it's fun or has its own value, people will do it only if there is something "in it for them." Imagine the poverty of a world in which no positive behaviors occurred unless obvious extrinsic reinforcement were immediately available. The internal motivations behind love, empathy,

INTRINSIC MOTIVATION
A drive to engage in a behavior for its own sake in the absence of any obvious external reward or reinforcer.

Monkeys find manipulating these locks to be intrinsically motivating.

SOCIOBIOLOGY
A theory of motivation and behavior stating that many human behaviors are influenced by inherited biological predispositions. Morality, love, kindness, aggression, anger, hatred, and most other aspects of human behavior are viewed partly in terms of their functional value for ensuring the survival of a person's genes.

OPPONENT-PROCESS THEORY
A theory of motivation by Richard Solomon proposing that many acquired motives, such as drug addiction, love, affection, social attachment, cravings for sensory and aesthetic experiences, skydiving, jogging, sauna bathing, and even self-administered aversive stimuli, seem to follow the laws of addiction.

charity, and humanity would be gone; there would be no more selflessness (Greene, Sternberg, & Lepper, 1976).

Some researchers believe that altruism and other intrinsic motivations may also have important unlearned components and therefore could never come completely under the control of extrinsic motivators. This view has been best developed by the proponents of **sociobiology,** a theory of behavior first proposed by Harvard zoologist Edward O. Wilson (Wilson, 1975).

To sociobiologists, altruism can, in a manner of speaking, have a "selfish" component that serves a genetic purpose. They believe that one of the reasons a person often is willing to make a sacrifice for other people may be that such an act may promote the general survival of "his kind." Such behavior is common in the animal kingdom. Many animals have even been observed to give up their lives (for instance, by deliberately distracting a predator while the other members of the group flee to safety). Such "altruism" can be very selective. For example, in Chapter 6, we discussed how animals often are able to recognize kin by smell, and researchers have observed that many animals would rather share with or protect a blood relative than an unrelated member of their species (Lewin, 1984). In the mid-1950s, the British biologist J. B. S. Haldane anticipated this view when he jokingly announced that he would lay down his life for two brothers or eight cousins. His reasoning was that each brother would have one-half of his genes and each cousin about one-eighth of his genes, which made the decision acceptable in terms of genetic survivability.

The sociobiological view that many seemingly learned motives have important inherited components has given rise to areas of study such as behavioral genetics, which examines questions of nature and nurture (see Chapter 3).

Solomon's Opponent-Process Theory

Over the last 20 years, researcher Richard L. Solomon has developed a powerful theory to explain acquired or learned motivation on a relatively grand scale—the **opponent-process theory.** This theory addresses many of the motivational questions that we have discussed so far. Its startling central theme is that most learned motivations are addictions. As Solomon has said,

The opponent-process theory of motivation helps explain why anyone would actually go out of his way to do this.

The theory attempts to account for such diverse acquired motives as drug addiction, love, affection, and social attachment, and cravings for sensory and aesthetic experiences (cases in which the initial reinforcers are positive) and for such acquired motives as parachuting, jogging, "marathoning," sauna bathing, and a variety of self-administered, aversive stimuli like electric shocks (cases in which the initial reinforcers are negative).

Acquired motives can be as powerful as innate ones. They can become the focus for the major behaviors of an organism, even at the expense of innate needs. A heroin addict, for example, may spend the better part of each day in drug-seeking behavior, may ignore food, liquid, and sexual incentives, and may abandon normal societal obligations. The heroin motive is acquired only because certain experiences have occurred; it is not innate. We tend to think of such addictions as pathological, but they are not. . . . Most acquired motives, such as love, social attachments, food-taste cravings, thrill seeking, and needs for achievement, power, and affiliation, obey the empirical laws for the addictions. (Solomon, 1980, p. 691)

In other words, acquired behaviors—loving, jogging, sauna bathing, parachute jumping, and so on—can become addictions. Even cravings for certain aesthetic experiences can become addicting.

Consider parachute jumping. What actually happens? The first parachuting experience usually is frightening. Fear builds as the jump time nears, reaching a peak when the "ready" signal goes on (see Figure 11.5). Parachutists report that the moment of stepping out of the airplane door is truly a terrifying one.

Until the last second, many people think that they won't be able to jump. If they do jump, they discover that the sensation of falling is slight for one or two seconds but then increases very, very rapidly. There is a sickening feeling in the stomach. What started as a gentle descent through the air quickly becomes a brutal plunge in which the parachutist is battered by winds of between 120 and 180 miles per hour. The winds are surprisingly cold and ripping. The sense of time is distorted, which adds to the terror, as the parachutist thinks, "Surely, the parachute should have opened by now." Suddenly, there is the upward jerk of the parachute unfurling, and fear recedes as the reassuring brightly colored canopy appears overhead.

EMOTIONAL CONTRAST.   When first-time jumpers land, they usually walk about in a stony-faced silence for a while, slowly recovering from their terror. Then an interesting thing happens, which Solomon calls affective or **emotional contrast.** The parachutists begin to smile at one another. They are elated. They run toward each other laughing, shaking hands, and slapping one another on the back. They make jokes, laugh some more—a sense of great relief abounds. This intense feeling can last for several hours. You can imagine it easily even if you haven't watched parachutists, because it is such a natural human reaction.

Solomon first noticed this effect when he went into a hospital where 1-day-old infants were resting. The infants weren't hungry yet, but Solomon gave them milk to drink. They enjoyed it, drinking it readily when he placed the nipple in their mouths. Then he removed the nipple, and the babies began to cry. They had been happy without the milk before he showed up, but now they were crying. After a while the crying subsided, and the babies returned to their initial peaceful state. This kind of effect, Solomon realized, was an example of emotional contrast. Emotional contrast is interesting because it shows us that surviving a terrifying or painful experience, as our parachutists did, can lead to feelings of exhilaration. Conversely a pleasurable experience, such as drinking milk, can lead to feelings of depression. In this way, pleasure can lead to sadness, and pain to happiness!

As another example, consider what once happened to a young neighbor of psychologist H. B. Taussig. The young neighbor was out playing golf when a storm began. He packed up his clubs and started to leave the golf course. Suddenly, as he was walking away, he began to feel a strange tingling all about

EMOTIONAL CONTRAST
An emotional effect that plays an important part in Solomon's opponent-process theory of motivation. Following any emotional arousal (pleasant or aversive), there is often an opposite emotional state. This contrasting emotional state will last for a time and then diminish or end.

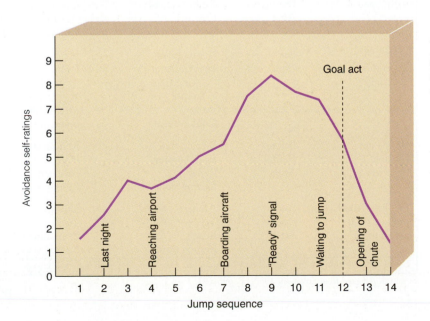

◆ **FIGURE 11.5**

The parachute jumper's fear is at the highest level just before the jump, and it lessens significantly when the parachute opens. (SOURCE: *Epstein & Fenz, 1965, p. 2.*)

◆ FIGURE 11.6

Emotional contrast. Initially, during the first few stimulations, there is an intense affective (emotional) reaction. Then the person adapts to the reaction, and it remains steady for a time. This state is followed by a strong affective afterreaction that eventually decays, returning the person to the initial state. (SOURCE: Solomon, 1980, p. 700.)

him. Then there was a tremendous flash of light. The ground seemed to rush at him. A gigantic BOOM almost broke his eardrums. He lay there, shocked. His shorts were torn to shreds and he was burned across his thighs. His companions realized that he had been struck by lightning. As they ran up to him, they could hear him screaming, "I'm dead, I'm dead!" (Taussig, 1969, p. 306). An ambulance was called. By the time it arrived, the young man's legs were numb and blue and he was unable to move. He was rushed to the hospital emergency room. But as he was wheeled in, he was laughing happily. In fact, he was euphoric, talking to everyone, telling them what had happened, showing them his tattered shorts, and grinning broadly from ear to ear! It's interesting to think that the young man hadn't been that happy before the lightning hit him! I guess there's nothing like being slammed to the ground by over a million volts of electricity to cheer you up.

Solomon has examined many such emotional contrasts. As you can see in Figure 11.6, there is an initial primary effect (toward A, in the illustration). With the parachutists, it was one of terror. It peaks, declines a little, remains steady for a time, and then is followed by an intense emotional contrast (toward B), during which the emotions swing in the opposite direction. After a time that, too, wears off, and there is a return to the middle.

Table 11.1 shows Solomon's examples of emotional contrast in four different conditions. The first is injecting heroin for the first time; the second, social attachment of ducklings on their first exposure to a moving mother duck (imprinting; see Chapter 8); the third, people's first experience of sauna bathing, which is very hot; and the fourth, military parachutists' first experience of free-fall. As you can see, there is an initial state (before). Then comes what Solomon has called the A process, or the first affective peak (during). Then comes the B process, which is the emotional contrast (after), and then a return to the resting state. If the A process is extremely stimulating, the B process is likely to be extremely stimulating *in the opposite direction*.

TABLE 11.1 ◆ EMOTIONAL CONTRAST (CHANGES IN AFFECT) IN FOUR CONDITIONS			
CONDITION	PERIOD	AFTER FIRST FEW EXPERIENCES	AFTER MANY EXPERIENCES
I. Self-dosing with opiates	Before	Resting state	Craving
	During	Rush, euphoria	Contentment
	After	Craving	Abstinence-agony
		Resting state	Craving
II. Social attachment in ducklings	Before	Contentment	Some distress
	During	Excitement at seeing the mother	Following the mother
	After	Distress	Intense distress
		Contentment	Some distress
III. Sauna bathing	Before	Resting state	Resting state
	During	Pain, burning	Heat, excitement
	After	Relief	Exhilaration
		Resting state	Resting state
IV. Free-fall in military parachuting	Before	Anxiety	Eagerness
	During	Terror	Thrill
	After	Relief	Exhilaration
		Resting state	Resting state

NOTE: The emotions in the "After Many" column are those associated with addictive effects.

SOURCE: Adapted from Solomon, 1980, pp. 696–697.

One of the most remarkable examples of emotional contrast was described by David H. Rosen. The Golden Gate Bridge, which connects San Francisco and Sausalito, California, is one of the longest suspension bridges in the world, and its roadway is hundreds of feet above the strong currents of San Francisco Bay. Unfortunately, over the years the bridge has attracted many suicidal people, and more than 500 of them have died jumping from it. Incredibly, 10 people have survived the jump. This fact is remarkable because at a speed of over 120 miles per hour, the water would feel like concrete on impact—and, after that, assuming the person were still conscious, he or she would have to swim in the strong, cold currents to reach safety. In 1976, David Rosen interviewed seven of the survivors. All of them, he found, had undergone a "spiritual rebirth." They were happy, enjoyed their lives, and felt better than they ever had. Consider these individuals in the light of the emotional contrast phenomenon for a moment. Is it possible that the A process was so intense, the terror and certain realization of imminent death so overwhelming, that surviving the jump called up an opposing B process of such intense exhilaration that the people were left with a happier outlook even after the feeling of excitement had subsided?

ADDICTION.   Solomon has gone on to say that emotional contrast can lead to addictions because of two changes that take place in the A and B processes over time. He noticed that when people engage in the same kind of emotional contrast again and again, the initial A state *becomes less potent*. People adapt to it. The B state, on the other hand, *becomes stronger*; it starts sooner and lasts longer (see Figure 11.7). Once these changes have begun to occur, following emotional contrast, a person will not always return to the original state. A weak A process, caused by repeating the experience many times, followed by a strong B process may leave the person in the B state (see Figure 11.8). A person left in the B state may easily become addicted to the activity that resulted in achieving the B state because he will either like the B state (if it is pleasant) and try to maintain it, or he will dislike the B state (if it is aversive) and try to return to the opposing A state—which, ironically, only leads to an even stronger B state. In either case, the addiction is set.

CRITICAL DECAY DURATION.   Another important part of the opponent-process theory is the **critical decay duration** of the opponent process. If you experience an emotional contrast, the A process will become weaker and the B process stronger only if you engage in the behavior that produces the contrast again and again. The changes won't happen if you wait too long between experiences. After the critical decay duration, the addicting effect won't occur. In other words, if you wait too long before parachuting again, the terror of the A process may be just as great as it was originally, and the elation of the B process no more than it was before. However, if you immediately jump again and do it a number of times, the A process will weaken and the B process will strengthen, thus slowly beginning an addiction (Starr, 1978).

More research is needed to demonstrate the power of the opponent-process theory of motivation and to investigate the prevalence of its effect. Still, the theory helps to explain how people can come to enjoy danger or pain and why pleasure and happiness can be so fleeting. It might also help to answer a number of other questions. For instance, why do people who diet and find the initial experiences painful sometimes come to enjoy being hungry? Why do soldiers initially terrified of war sometimes reenlist for combat when their enlistment time is up? Why does a job that is initially exciting sometimes become dull and tedious? We also may learn from research into the opponent-process

CRITICAL DECAY DURATION
From the opponent-process theory of motivation, a time of sufficient length between the onset of an affective A process and its repetition so that no decrease in A process intensity or increase in B process intensity is noted.

◆ **FIGURE 11.7**

Changes in the A and B processes after repeated emotional contrasts. The initial A state becomes weaker, and the B state becomes stronger. (SOURCE: Solomon, 1980, p. 700.)

◆ **FIGURE 11.8**

After many stimulations, the A process may become so weak and the B process so strong that an emotional contrast can leave the individual in the B state.

"Because it's there," and because
$|A - B| = B > A.$

CONCEPT REVIEW ◆ ADDICTION

Take another look at Table 11.1, and you'll see the kinds of changes that occur if a particular emotional contrast is engaged in often enough. In cases I and II (heroin use, duckling attachment), the A process during the first few exposures is pleasant. The contrasting B process that follows is aversive. At first, the organism is left in a fairly neutral state, $[A - B] = 0$, because the A and B processes are equal in strength. After many exposures, however, the A process weakens (for example, the heroin high is mild; the duckling follows the mother but is not excited by her). The B process simultaneously becomes stronger. This change eventually will leave the organism in the B state: [weak A − strong B] = B > A. The B state is aversive in cases I and II.

If the B state is aversive, as in cases I and II, the urge to return to the A state will be great; such a return will, ironically, lead only to a further weakening of the A state and further strengthening of the B state. As you can see, this is the beginning of an addiction. The organism will strongly desire to return to the A state, but in so doing will only make the A state weaker still and the B state even stronger. The addiction is complete, the hook is set. This is why long-term heroin addicts don't enjoy their heroin; they simply shoot up to *avoid* withdrawal—making the addiction worse.

In cases III and IV (sauna bathing, parachuting), the A process during the first few exposures is not pleasurable, but aversive. People may have tried such an aversive thing for the first time because of military orders or social pressure. After a few times, however, the aversive A process weakens and the opposing pleasant B process grows: Once again, [weak A − strong B] = B > A. As a result, the stronger B process, which in cases III and IV is pleasant, is sought more and more often (especially because the A process is no longer scary), and, once again, addiction is underway, although for slightly different reasons (reasons of approach rather than escape).

theory how to avoid these kinds of emotional shifts, perhaps by building in critical decay durations at the appropriate times. We may come to understand motivations that at first seem bizarre or unusual. And we may find a better explanation for thrill seeking than George Mallory's explanation for attempting to climb Mount Everest—"Because it's there."

AN ENDURING QUESTION:
WHY DON'T WE ALWAYS DO WHAT'S IN OUR OWN BEST INTEREST?

Have you ever noticed that even though you may know that doing some particular thing will be in your own best interest, you still don't do it? Why is that?

For years, researchers have argued that people will make rational choices unless they are confused by the choice or fail to understand its significance in some way. The gist of this argument is that any rational person will make the smart choice if he fully understands all of the variables involved and their importance. And yet, we know that we don't al-

AN ENDURING QUESTION, CONTINUED

ways make rational choices even when we fully understand the options. For example, taking smokers on a tour of a cancer ward will scare them into not smoking, but only for about a day. To explain this discrepancy, we turn to concepts such as addiction. But however you look at it, we are dealing with irrationality.

To demonstrate that irrationality can occur even when choices are obvious, researcher R. J. Herrnstein asked people if they would prefer $100 now or $115 in a week. The hypothetical question was stated in a way that made clear that the money would be held in escrow in a bank and that the people would not have to worry about it being there a week later. Most people said that they wanted the $100 now (Herrnstein, 1990)! Is that a rational choice? Well you might say that they didn't feel that $15 was worth waiting a week. So Herrnstein asked another question. He asked them if they would prefer $100 in 52 weeks or $115 in 53 weeks. This time they wanted the $115. What had changed?

From this and many other studies, Herrnstein has concluded that there are certain factors common to human motivation that preclude our always making the rational choice, even when we fully understand the choice.

The first of these factors is the immediacy of an event. For some reason, events some time away are discounted more than are events happening right now. Things happening now seem to be magnified. Something attractive looks even more attractive if it is right in front of us than if it is down the road, and, conversely, unattractive things look worse if they are about to happen now rather than later. The effect is so powerful that it often overwhelms rationality. Impulse buying is a good example of this principle at work. A car salesman knows that he mustn't let you out of the showroom without getting you to buy, because once you leave the car won't seem quite as desirable.

Let's consider another example. If you are on a diet, passing up some treat that is right in front of you can be very hard because the pleasure it offers is magnified out of proportion. As proof, ask yourself what dieter who passed up a treat has ever said *the next day*, "Boy, I wish I had eaten that fattening food yesterday when I had the chance, I really missed something." It's not very likely, because a piece of cake just isn't that important in retrospect—it's only important if you're hungry and it's right in front of you. As Herrnstein has pointed out,

> Imagine, for example, that we could always select meals for tomorrow, rather than for right now. Would we not all eat better than we do? We may find it possible to forgo tomorrow's chocolate cake or second helping of pasta or third martini, but not the one at hand. (Herrnstein, 1990, p. 359)

This effect helps explain how a cigarette *now* can seem a fair trade for heart disease later, or how the threat of a five-second shock of cold water now can keep someone from enjoying a day of swimming (no, it doesn't work as well just to inch into the water a little at a time, but people make this irrational choice because the threat of cold water is magnified by its immediacy).

Another reason for the failure to make the best choices is the tendency to engage in **melioration.** We, and most other organisms, allocate our behaviors so that we choose those that will give us the greatest reward. However, if you consider Richard Solomon's demonstration that the A process weakens the more we do something, and if you consider that for each activity the A process may weaken at a different rate, you make

MELIORATION
In psychology, the tendency of organisms to shift behavioral allocations toward more lucrative alternatives.

AN ENDURING QUESTION, CONTINUED

an interesting discovery. Even though melioration sounds reasonable, it may not lead to maximum happiness (Herrnstein, 1990).

By meliorating, we level our experiences, even the most desirable experiences, down to a common denominator. In other words, getting more of something good can actually devalue it so that we get *less total pleasure* from it than if we had it less often! This may explain why multimillionaires usually say that getting their first million was the most fun. Backing that up is research that shows that increasing wealth does not go hand in hand with increasing happiness (Murray, 1988). Similarly, someone who has many sexual partners and often engages in sexual activity may find it becomes progressively more and more difficult to discover sexual experiences that are as exciting as the first ones were. Herrnstein's findings may also explain why many older couples often recall their early years of struggling to get by as some of their happiest. More isn't necessarily better.

As another example, consider my great uncle who grew up in Russia and never saw an orange until he came to this country. He still remembers the first orange my grandfather gave him to eat back in 1921. But most Americans like myself may never know what my great uncle's orange tasted like, because in a land of plenty, melioration is the normal mode of action. In fact, I bought some oranges a few weeks ago and then forgot about them. They stayed in the refrigerator until fuzz grew on them, and I ended up throwing them out. Oranges just aren't special anymore.

If you want to be rational about obtaining happiness—if you want to maximize it—perhaps you should, as the phrase goes, "stay hungry." That is, dole out treats to yourself sparingly. This is another way of saying that you should observe the critical decay duration. In spite of what *"Lifestyles of the Rich and Famous"* would have us believe, by "staying hungry" to some extent, we may have more total fun than someone who has all the treats all of the time!

Consider that after Walter Bonatti became the first person ever to climb the north wall of the Matterhorn solo during winter, an effort that took days and almost cost him his life, he was asked what the greatest part of that experience had been. He said, with a look of ecstasy on his face, that it had been the bath he took in his hotel afterward. Everyone laughed, but later Bonatti swore that he hadn't been joking. Although "stay hungry" has its applications, of course, I'm not suggesting that you search for the critical decay duration for your bath, the people around you wouldn't appreciate that much; but you get the idea.

FOR CRITICAL ANALYSIS

1. How might you restructure your own environment to increase pleasure by reducing melioration? What sorts of problems do you immediately encounter?
2. Why do you think people meliorate? In terms of natural selection, what advantages might there be in melioration? (Consider the purpose of pleasure as a motivator and the species survival value of food and sexual activity.)

SUMMARY

◆ Psychologists study motivation because they want a fuller explanation of why a behavior occurs.

◆ The word *motivation* is derived from the Latin word *motivum*, which refers to the reason that something has moved.

◆ Scientists assume that biological motivations such as hunger and thirst are built in—they exist from birth.

◆ Homeostasis refers to built-in regulatory systems for maintaining the status quo. Any deviation from an optimal state creates a need that usually produces a drive that is the motivational force for action.

◆ The hypothalamocentric hypothesis argues that hunger and thirst centers located in the hypothalamus monitor deviations from optimal states. Lesions in the ventromedial hypothalamus result in overeating and obesity.

◆ Hunger and thirst also seem to be regulated by sensors distant from the brain.

◆ The most recent view is that the hypothalamus is not the hunger and thirst center, but rather is one of a number of hunger and thirst monitoring and sensing areas.

◆ The homeostatic mechanism that monitors thirst appears to depend on sodium levels in the intracellular and extracellular fluids.

◆ Hunger and thirst have been shown to interact. Providing small amounts of food to a hungry animal on an intermittent schedule often produces schedule-induced polydipsia by increasing the drive to drink.

◆ Although some people gain weight because of overeating or because of defects in regulators in the brain and elsewhere in the body, nonhomeostatic mechanisms also play an important role in obesity.

◆ Research has indicated that the more physiologically advanced a species is, the less its sexual behavior appears to be governed directly by chemical or hormonal forces. Even in humans, however, chemical and hormonal factors may play a role.

◆ The sex drive in humans may have something to do with sensors in the hypothalamus that are sensitive to different levels of hormones.

◆ Human beings and animals seem to have a need for a certain amount of stimulation. Motivations generated by these needs are referred to as stimulus motives.

◆ Certain motivations can be learned. Learned motives often are related to incentives, which are particular things that we want to possess.

◆ Learned motivations can imitate biological ones. For instance, it's possible to learn to become hungry through classical conditioning.

◆ Abraham Maslow, a humanistic psychologist, developed a theory based on a hierarchy of motives, in which some needs were more powerful than others. Modern motivational theory, however, usually is limited to highly detailed investigations of specific areas.

◆ Over the last 30 years, researchers have investigated the need for achievement that is evident in some individuals. Scientists believe that this need is learned as the result of experience.

◆ It is possible to learn to become helpless, although this type of learning usually doesn't occur suddenly.

◆ When we are faced with a new situation, one of the most important determinants of our behavior is perceived self-efficacy; that is, our belief about how effective we might be. Our performance tends to vary as a function of our perceived efficacy.

◆ There are four basic ways to change our self-efficacy. These include direct action, observing other people, verbal persuasion, and our perception of our own physical states.

◆ In many cases, intrinsic motivation has been found to be superior to extrinsic motivation in creating and maintaining behavior.

◆ Sociobiologists argue that motivated actions, including altruistic ones, may have important genetic components and biological foundations.

◆ Richard Solomon has developed a theory of acquired motivation called the opponent-process theory. His theory explains many motivational phenomena as a function of addictions. The theory may help to explain why some people come to enjoy danger or pain and why pleasure and happiness can be so fleeting.

◆ Often we do not act in our own best interest. Interfering with our rational choices are the facts that immediate events are magnified—they are seen as better or worse than later events—and that we tend to meliorate, or try to maintain the same rate of reward for each of our actions.

SUGGESTIONS FOR FURTHER READING

1. Apter, M. J. (1992). *The dangerous edge: The psychology of excitement*. New York: Free Press. An interesting look at the factors that motivate people to take risks.
2. Logue, A. W. (1991). *The psychology of eating and drinking* (2nd ed). New York: W. H. Freeman. A discussion of the biological motivations behind eating and drinking behavior. Includes interesting personal experiences of the author.
3. Lyman, B. (1988). *The psychology of food: More than a matter of taste*. New York: Van Nostrand Reinhold. Technical yet readable book about why we eat what we eat. Discusses food texture, color, odor, and appearance, as well as the social and psychological influences that lead us to make food choices.
4. Margulis, L. & Sagan, D. (1992). *Mystery dance: On the evolution of human sexuality*. New York: Touchstone. An examination of how all the creatures from whom we have evolved have left their mark on our sexuality, from apes to promiscuous bacteria.
5. Mitchell, R. G. (1983). *Mountain experience: The psychology and sociology of adventure*. Chicago: University of Chicago Press. A book for the general reader that discusses the motivations of people who climb mountains. Includes a discussion of how groups can motivate people.
6. Petri, H. (1990). *Motivation: Theory and research* (3rd ed.). Belmont, CA: Wadsworth. A college-level textbook covering all aspects of motivational research.

Chapter Twelve

Emotion

PROLOGUE

SAD THOUGHTS

At Washington University School of Medicine, seven volunteers, four men and three women, entered a room for a unique experiment. Each individual was given an injection of a short-lived radioactive sugar and then placed inside a PET scanner (see Chapter 2). The purpose of the injection was to enable researchers to track the radioactive markers (positrons) given off by the sugar while it was used to fuel the subjects' brains.

As you recall, the PET scan allows researchers to observe brain function by enabling them to see which areas of the brain become active during certain activities. PET scans have revealed how the brain behaves when people read (the occipital lobes become more active) or listen to music (the temporal lobes become more active), and it has also shown that the brains of those suffering from various types of mental illness may be functioning differently than brains of unaffected individuals.

In this experiment, however, researcher Marcus Raichle was planning to try something different. He asked his subjects to think of something that made them very sad. The four men and three women were asked to close their eyes and get as sad as they could. During the experiment, one woman and two of the men actually shed tears (Dreverts & Raichle, 1992).

When Dr. Raichle and his team examined and compared the PET scans, they saw a remarkable similarity. In each instance, an area of the brain called the orbital frontal cortex had lighted up (see Figure 12.1). The brighter colors, red and yellow, indicate the areas of greatest activity. Interestingly, among the women, this area of the brain lighted up in both the left and right hemisphere, while in men, only the left hemisphere responded. This does not necessarily mean that women are more emotional then men, but rather that women tend to have brains that are less lateralized. That is, their left and right hemispheres appear to be less distinctly different than are men's.

For a long time now, the frontal lobes have been known to play an important role in emotion. With the PET scan data, we can directly see an emotional center in the brain as it becomes activated.

CONTENTS

◆ **FIGURE 12.1**

When subjects were asked to think sad thoughts during a PET scan, portions of the orbital frontal cortex became active.

415

EMOTION
A complex feeling-state involving conscious experience and internal and overt physical responses that tend to facilitate or inhibit motivated behavior.

POLYGRAPH
A lie detector. This device measures physiological changes regulated by the autonomic nervous system (heartbeat, blood pressure, galvanic skin response, and breathing rate). The assumption is that deliberate lying will produce detectable physical reactions.

IN THIS CHAPTER, we'll examine what has been, to date, one of the most difficult and all-consuming tasks in psychology: finding out what emotions are. Although we deal with emotions every day, and they are an integral part of human interaction and behavior, amazingly nobody really knows what they are. Still, some theories have brought us closer to an understanding of emotion, and the implications for our understanding of behavior are significant.

WHY PSYCHOLOGISTS STUDY EMOTIONS

It has been said that our emotions make us seem most human. We rage, we laugh, we cry, we fear, and we love. To be without emotions is to be unfeeling, perhaps "inhuman."

Everyone has emotions, even infants a few weeks old. Babies demonstrate striking emotional behaviors. They smile and laugh, they form loving attachments, and they show fear. Parents often report that the first smile from their baby is a magical moment that instantly seems to create a closer and more meaningful bond. As adults, we pay close attention to other people in order to discern their attitudes and emotional reactions. Even in the absence of any other cues, emotional monitoring can provide vital information about the people around us. At the same time, we often look to our own feelings to understand why we behave the way we do. Emotions pervade our existence, affecting every moment, and no study of human behavior would be complete without an attempt to understand the power and value of our emotional experiences.

THE BIOLOGY OF EMOTION

During the first year of life, a central emotional system develops within the human brain in a small area called the amygdala (see Chapter 2). There, sensory information about whether to approach or withdraw from an object, person, or situation is evaluated (Fox, 1989, 1991). This basic neural decision about whether to approach or withdraw appears to be the first use of **emotion** as a motivator of behavior in the infant.

As the infant grows, emotions continue to develop along "approach or avoid" lines, lines that appear to be distinctly separate in their neural organization. For instance, when the two hemispheres of the infant's brain are monitored, it has been observed that positive emotions such as joy are associated with a surge of electrical activity in the left hemisphere, while the right hemisphere shows increased electrical activity when negative emotions such as sadness are elicited (Fox & Davidson, 1988).

Complex emotions emerge once a greater information exchange between the amygdala and the frontal lobes of the brain becomes possible. This occurs when neural connections form between these areas as the infant develops into a child.

The central nervous system, of which the brain is the primary part, integrates its emotional reactions with the autonomic nervous system (see Chapter 2). During intense emotional reactions, such as fear, rage, or sexual arousal, the sympathetic nervous system becomes more active, resulting in several physical changes (see Table 12.1). The heart rate, for instance, may climb to 140 beats per minute or more, strictly as a result of emotional arousal. The fact that strong, measurable, physiological changes often occur in direct relationship with emotional changes is the basis for the **polygraph,** or lie detector (see Focus on a Controversy).

Lie detectors don't measure lies but rather a person's physiological level of arousal or anxiety.

✪ WHY EMOTIONS EVOLVED

Emotions appear to be common throughout the animal kingdom. Along with anatomical forms and physiological systems, emotions too have evolved. They are an integral part of us as human beings. But why should our nervous system have developed the complex system of reactions we call our emotions? The reason appears to be that emotions help us to survive. When emotions first began to appear in evolving animals, those with better-developed emotions were more likely to pass on their genes to the next generation, which, in turn, furthered the evolution of emotions.

Perhaps we often use the word *feeling* interchangeably with *emotion* because we can feel, or sense, an emotion. Most people find it difficult to express exactly what they feel, because the way in which they experience emotion is very subjective. Writers sometimes try to express these subjective sensations with phrases such as "She was walking on air" (happiness), "He shrank into insignificance" (humiliation), "Her blood boiled" (anger), or "He gagged" (disgust). In fact, these phrases are so descriptive that their overuse has made them trite. Still, such descriptions can give us clues to what people feel in certain emotional states. These states function as motivators. The fact that emotions motivate us appears to be one of the important reasons why emotions evolved.

We also use emotion to communicate, which appears to be another major function of emotions (Oatley & Jenkins, 1992). The expression on the face of another person often can tell us a great deal about how she is feeling. Sometimes, if we are not certain about the meaning of the situation in which we find ourselves, we will look at the emotional reactions of other people for information. This checking of others' emotions is called **social referencing.**

Social referencing begins early. In one interesting experiment, a special version of the visual cliff (see Figure 6.31, p. 230) was used. This version of the cliff had only one side, which was neither shallow nor deep, but somewhere in between. The subjects were one-year-old infants. In this study, researchers found that the emotional expression on a mother's face could control whether her infant would attempt to go beyond the cliff edge. If the mother looked fearful, her infant was very unlikely to attempt a crossing. On the other hand, if she looked happy, her infant was likely to cross over the edge (Sorce, Emde, Campos, & Klinnert, 1985). Further experiments showed that infants will actively search for emotional cues, not just from their mothers, but from any familiar adult who happens to be present (Klinnert, Emde, Butterfield, & Campos, 1986).

We also use emotions to communicate with ourselves. Our emotional state during certain experiences lets us know how we feel about what is happening.

SOCIAL REFERENCING
The use of emotional signals or cues from others as a guide for one's own behavior in ambiguous situations.

TABLE 12.1 ◆ PHYSIOLOGICAL REACTIONS ASSOCIATED WITH EMOTIONAL AROUSAL	
REACTION	DIVISION OF AUTONOMIC NERVOUS SYSTEM CONTROLLING REACTION
Pupils dilate	Sympathetic
Mouth becomes dry	Sympathetic
Heartbeat increases	Sympathetic
Tears are produced	Parasympathetic
Adrenalin is secreted	Sympathetic
Sweating increases	Sympathetic
Bladder relaxes	Sympathetic
Genitals are stimulated	Parasympathetic

LIE DETECTION

Psychologists who study emotion know that a person can become physiologically aroused for many reasons. They also know that the polygraph, or lie detector, is based on the assumption that emotional arousal can signal when a person lies. The following story helps us examine this assumption:

In the late 1970s, Floyd "Buzz" Fay was happily going about his business on what seemed like an average day. Unbeknownst to Buzz, a man named Fred Ery was shot and mortally wounded that day by a holdup man during a robbery attempt. Ery, the man who was shot, knew Buzz Fay, and as he was dying, he said, "It looked like Buzz, but it couldn't have been" (Kleinmuntz & Szucko, 1984, p. 774). After losing a great deal of blood and being given large doses of drugs, Fred Ery began to mumble, "Buzz did it." Although Fred Ery had been incoherent when he made the accusation, the police quickly arrested Buzz Fay at gunpoint the following morning. Fay was amazed. He couldn't bring himself to take the arrest seriously, believing that "they'll let me go tomorrow."

The prosecution realized that they had a weak case, as they had no other evidence of Fay's guilt. They offered him a deal. They would give him two polygraph tests, one to be administered by the Bureau of Criminal Identification and the other to be administered privately. If he passed either test, the charges would be dropped, but, if he failed them both, he'd be charged with aggravated murder, and the lie detector test would be admitted as evidence.

Fay thought that the offer was good and accepted it. To his horror, both lie detector tests indicated he was guilty. Fay was quickly convicted of murder and was given a sentence of life in prison. Fortunately for him, the death sentence, which had been in effect in his state (Ohio) until just a few weeks before his trial, was no longer being used.

Adrian Cimmerman, a dedicated county public defender, continued to believe that Fay was innocent. After 2½ years of exhaustive work by Cimmerman to find the truth, while Fay was cooped up in his prison cell, the police finally received a tip from an informant, and Fred Ery's real killer was tracked down and convicted. Buzz Fay was released.

Needless to say, Buzz Fay no longer puts any faith in lie detector tests. As a matter of fact, while Fay was in·prison, he became something of an expert on the polygraph. He discovered that not only was it based on an implausible theory but that it was easy to beat (Cimmerman, 1981). The polygraph test was commonly used in prisons to get to the bottom of charges against prisoners, such as drug abuse. While Fay was in prison, he coached 27 inmates who were going to take a lie detector test. All the inmates had told him outright that they were guilty of the charges (usually drug offenses). After less than half an hour of training, 23 of the 27 found that they were able to beat the lie detector test (Lykken, 1981).

A polygraph is designed to measure physiological changes that occur in conjunction with emotional states. It is called a polygraph because it measures several different physiological states. One "graph" monitors respiratory rate, another heart rate, a third blood pressure, and a fourth electrical changes on the surface of the skin—the last is known as a GSR (galvanic skin response) measuring device.

A subject connected to a polygraph is asked questions. Many of the initial questions are routine, such as, "Is your name Nancy?" or "Is your address 114 Inwood Drive?" These routine questions help to establish a baseline against which to measure changes associated with strong emotions.

A person suspected of having broken into a store the night before might be asked such questions as, "Were you home all last night?" If the person lies and answers, "Yes," the fear the person feels when lying may register as a change in the physiological mechanisms measured by the polygraph. In this way, the machine might be able to detect a lie.

By investigating the polygraph, we can see the interaction of both cognitive processes and autonomic arousal in the evocation of emotion. By doing so, we'll also come to appreciate the difficulties inherent in trying to use a polygraph as a "lie detector."

The Italian psychiatrist Cesare Lombroso was the first person to make claims similar to those of modern proponents of the polygraph when he concluded that he could tell whether someone was lying by noting changes in that person's blood pressure. (Lombroso also believed, by the way, that he could identify a criminal by the shape of the person's skull.) The first modern machine to rely on the greater sensitivity of all four physiological measures was developed in 1906. Interestingly, this first polygraph was designed as a medical instrument. It wasn't until 1932 that Harvard-trained psychologist William Marston began to champion the device as a "lie detector."*

At first glance, the lie detector may appear to have been a marvelous breakthrough in criminology, because it supposedly can determine when someone is lying. Lie detectors, however, have become controversial because they don't detect lies. They do, however, detect nervousness, and, as you saw in the case of Buzz Fey, there is a very important difference.

---

*William Marston had an interesting career. After making a name for himself by offering the new "lie detector" for use during the famous Lindbergh kidnapping trial, he went on to embarrass serious advocates of the polygraph by suggesting that it be used by husbands to discover whether their wives enjoyed their kisses more than they did someone else's and enjoyed testing this assertion! Following this, Marston entered the world of comic books and created the well-known superhero Wonder Woman (Biddle, 1986). People familiar with Wonder Woman will recall that she possessed a lariat that forced anyone she lassoed to tell the truth—you can guess where Marston got that idea.

FOCUS ON A CONTROVERSY

Are you the kind of person who becomes nervous when you are accused of having done something wrong, even though you are innocent? People who tend to be nervous when questioned, especially if they are aware which questions are the serious ones, may easily register high rates of nervousness although they have done nothing wrong. Less commonly, some people can remain absolutely calm and not be the least bit upset after committing some heinous act. For this reason, many courts do not admit lie detector evidence unless both the prosecution and the defense have agreed to allow its admission. This control alone may not offer sufficient safeguards, however, because the great majority of lie detector tests are given not by law enforcement agencies but by employers to employees, transactions that are not under the control of the criminal justice system.

To better understand the problem, consider the case in Los Angeles, where a supermarket clerk was fired after failing the lie detector test on the question, "Have you ever checked out groceries at a discount to your mother?" It turned out that her mother had died five years earlier (Beach, 1980, p. 44). The opportunity for abuse is great, because businesses, especially banking and retail outlets, administer tens of thousands of tests each year both to employees and managers who are under suspicion of some kind and as a routine personnel screening device (Meyer, 1982; Biddle, 1986).

The most commonly used lie detector tests are accurate in no more than two-thirds of cases—and, when they do make a mistake, which is often, they are most likely to indicate that an honest person is telling a lie (Lykken, 1981; Brett, Phillips, & Beary, 1986). In fact, in a population in which about 5 percent of the subjects tested are lying—as we might suspect could be the case when, for instance, a supermarket tests its employees—it turns out that about 90 percent of those testing positive will, in fact, be innocent (Brett, Phillips, & Beary, 1986). During the Reagan presidency, Secretary of State George Schultz refused to submit to a lie detector test that the president wished to make mandatory for government employees. Since that time, the U.S. Government Office of Technology Assessment, after an intensive study of the issue, has concluded that no lie detection method is foolproof and that the polygraph is generally not valid for lie detection because the chances for error are far too high (Saxe, Dougherty, & Cross, 1985; Brooks, 1985).

One of the reasons for the poor performance of the polygraph as a lie detector may be a function of the people who administer the tests. Joseph Buckley, who heads one of the largest testing firms, has said, "Like an X ray, a polygraph records data that take a lot of expertise to interpret. In the wrong hands, it's worse than nothing" (Beach, 1980, p. 44). Other researchers have found that even in the hands of experts, the analysis of lie detector results is still subject to too much error (Szucko & Kleinmuntz, 1981; Kleinmuntz & Szucko, 1984). Yet, in most states, lie detector operators don't even have to be licensed.

To make matters worse, as Buzz Fey discovered, it's quite easy to fool a lie detector. If a subject is agitated when answering the initial baseline questions, perhaps because she or he has purposely thought of something frightening or arousing, or even if the person just bites her tongue or flexes his toes, the lie detector will register a strong reaction to his or her *truthful* statements (Honts, Hodes, & Raskin, 1985). The baseline thus is recorded as very high in physiological arousal, and lies told later will go undetected—when compared with the high baseline. Obviously, any machine that can be so easily tricked should not be relied on extensively; rather, its use should be limited to special circumstances.

One set of circumstances in which the polygraph might be effective is known as the **concealed information test.** In a criminal investigation, for instance, a suspect is given information that only the perpetrator of the crime could know. For example, he might be told, "The color of the getaway car was red . . . green . . . white . . . blue," "The house was broken into through the back door . . . the front door . . . a window . . . a skylight." The idea here is to see whether the subject will have a pronounced reaction only when he hears the correct answer (such as red car; window), providing strong evidence that he is the real criminal. After enough "correct" reactions, testers can conclude that the person is probably guilty of the crime because he has shown that he has knowledge that only the criminal could have. Innocence, of course, cannot be proved by this method—a person who doesn't react may be guilty, but unemotional.

The American Psychological Association has stated that "the polygraph's validity is 'unsatisfactory,' [and that] there is no physiological response pattern associated uniquely with deception" (Bales, 1988, p. 5). In response to these findings, the U.S. Congress passed a law that, with few exceptions, forbid the use of the polygraph by private business as a preemployment screening device.

Even so, the search for Wonder Woman's lariat continues. One possibility now being investigated are ERPs, or **event-related brain potentials.** ERPs are a measure of the change in brain activity recorded during a normal electroencephalographic examination (see EEG, Chapter 2). The subject rests passively during the EEG and is presented with a stimulus. Changes in brain wave action are noted when the subject sees the stimulus. Experiments have indicated that when a guilty subject is shown something that only he would recognize, ERPs change greatly, far more than they would otherwise. In other words, ERPs are a sensitive measure of guilty knowledge (Bashore & Rapp, 1993). Even so, this newer version of the lie detector is subject to some of the same criticisms as the polygraph (Bashore & Rapp, 1993) in that some people, even when guilty, don't react that strongly. Whether ERPs will eventually replace polygraphs as a more accurate and sensitive measure remains to be seen. Researchers are currently testing the limits of this new technique.

CONCEALED INFORMATION TEST
In polygraph administration, a method of examining suspects by providing them with specific information to which only someone with guilty knowledge could consistently react.

EVENT-RELATED BRAIN POTENTIALS (ERPs)
A measure of the brain's electrical activity as recorded through the scalp. ERPs are calculated by measuring the positive and negative deflections or changes in voltage during a normal electroencephalographic examination (see EEG, Chapter 2), which occur when the subject, who is resting passively, is presented with a stimulus.

WHAT MAKES US EMOTIONAL?

Although we have inherited the capacity to experience emotion, whether we will experience emotion depends on many factors. For many years, researchers have gathered data about which circumstances are most likely to arouse emotions (Oatley & Jenkins, 1992). Let's consider some of these.

Emotions arise in situations that are *meaningful* to the individual. Events that satisfy goals, or that offer the promise of doing so, tend to elicit positive emotions. Events that harm or frustrate evoke negative emotions.

Emotions will be more intense if they concern real events and if the events are perceived in a vivid way. This explains why one photograph of a burned child running from a village in Vietnam can have a more powerful emotional effect than cold statistical reports of thousands killed. This is why the presence of television at an event can make the event so memorable. The television pictures engage our emotions more effectively because of their visual impact. This statement about emotion also helps explain why, for example, warnings of distant dangers don't deter cigarette smokers. They're not real (in this case, immediate) or vivid enough. If, on the other hand, the number of deaths from smoking occurred because every once in a while a cigarette exploded, it might be a different matter.

Emotions are also aroused more by *changes* in conditions than by conditions that remain constant. Another way of saying this is, "Continued pleasures wear off; continued hardships lose their poignancy" (Frijda, 1988, p. 353). This, of course, is what Richard Solomon discovered when he investigated the effect of repeated emotional contrast (see Chapter 11).

For these reasons, real, meaningful, vivid change will evoke the strongest emotions. If you are driving along and crest a hill, only to see a truck coming toward you in your lane, it will be real, personally meaningful, vivid, and a change—the event will likely arouse your emotions to a high pitch. Take away any of these factors, for example, see the same vivid change in a movie so that it is not real and less meaningful in a personal way, and your emotions will diminish accordingly.

You can also use your cognitive skills to think of experiences in a way that makes them seem more or less real or more or less meaningful, thereby greatly affecting their emotional impact on you. When the fox in the famous Aesop fable decided that the grapes he couldn't reach were probably sour anyway, he

Everyone has emotions, even infants only a few weeks old.

was reducing the personal meaning of the grapes because he wanted sweet ones, and thereby reduced his emotional stress. In similar ways, our emotions can distort our views of reality, affect our judgment, and motivate us.

JUDGING EMOTIONS

People's perceptions of their own emotional states can be altered with false physiological feedback and can thus influence their judgments. Because our own judgments can affect the way in which we perceive our emotional state, subjective reports we may give others are not always a reliable basis for assessing emotion. For this reason, psychologists often prefer to rely on observations of overt behavior when assessing emotions.

Observing overt behavior for clues about a person's emotional state is such a common activity that we have all learned to recognize behavioral cues and their emotional content to some degree. Some of the observations that we make can be quite subtle. Interestingly, back in the days of silent films, actors relied heavily on body and facial cues to show emotion because they believed that without sound to help them, the audience would not pick up emotional meanings. It was thought necessary to overact. Consequently, a heroine in trouble would put the back of her hand to her forehead, assume a look of horror, pant, and lean backward as though she were about to fall (a series of behaviors more in line with food poisoning than fear). These contortions weren't really necessary, however, because people are so responsive to facial expressions and body cues that the actors could have succeeded in conveying emotional states by much subtler means. Today, some actors still have difficulty going from the screen to the stage and vice versa. On the stage, the audience is farther away, and body cues and emotional expressions must be exaggerated. On the screen, during a closeup, a very slight change in facial expression can carry a tremendous impact. For this reason, many actors practice for hours with videotape equipment and mirrors to learn to change their expressions to reflect subtle changes in mood.

This discussion of actors brings up a problem with relying exclusively on overt behavior to understand emotions. Suppose the hero in a play bares his teeth, shouts and yells, clenches his fists, makes menacing gestures, glares, and speaks in a deep and threatening voice. You assume he isn't *really* angry. (In fact, he may be happy because the play in which he is acting is about to end and he can get some dinner.) Actors are trained to pretend. But when you see these same behaviors in other people, how do you know these people are really angry and are not pretending? Perhaps you look at the situation they're in and deduce that they're not acting. Of course, this requires a subjective assessment on your part, based on the overt behavior you are viewing, and so subjectivity enters in once more.

Look at the picture in Figure 12.2. Is this person happy or sad? It's not hard to tell, is it? She's obviously sad. In fact, she looks as though some great tragedy has befallen her. A child may have died, or her home burned down. We know what emotions feel like, and we can usually tell by looking at other people what those people must be feeling. Or can we? Now, turn to page 426 to see the entire photograph.

Some tragedy! These people are participating in a joyous reunion. What you see on their faces is an intense emotional response that is easy to mislabel. Emotions can be confusing. When we're extremely happy, we sometimes cry— and when we're extremely distraught, we sometimes laugh. Understanding emotion can be a lifelong pursuit; we all engage in it, whether or not we're psychologists.

Currently, most researchers believe that human emotion, although rooted in our biology, is strongly influenced by learning and cognitive processes (Eron,

◆ **FIGURE 12.2**

What emotion is this person feeling?

FRUSTRATION-AGGRESSION HYPOTHESIS
The idea that if one is blocked or prevented from reaching a desired goal, some form of aggression will be an inevitable result.

PAIN-ELICITED AGGRESSION
The desire to harm or defeat another, brought on by pain or anguish. It is common to many species, including humans. Cognitive interpretations can often control or mediate the aggression in spite of the pain or anguish.

1987). In other words, although our capacity to be emotional is inborn, the situations that make us emotional often depend a great deal on our thoughts, learning, and experiences.

AN ENDURING QUESTION: WHAT CAUSES VIOLENCE?

In July 1984, in a suburb of San Diego, California, an unemployed security guard named James Huberty walked into a McDonald's restaurant carrying a shotgun, a semiautomatic rifle, and a pistol. Without any apparent reason, he began shooting everyone. When the carnage was over, 22 people, including Huberty, were dead, and many others were injured. It was the worst mass murder in U.S. history. What would make someone do such a thing? Psychologists believe that they have part of the answer.

One possible result of significant emotional arousal is violence or aggression. Although people who become emotionally aroused usually are not violent and aggressive, those behaviors almost never occur unless emotional arousal has preceded them. For this reason, psychologists who study emotional arousal are concerned with this phenomenon.

Over the years, many people have attempted to explain aggression and violence. One of the oldest explanations (and at one time the most popular) suggested that aggression and violence were the inevitable result of being blocked or frustrated in an attempt to achieve a desired goal (Dollard, Doob, Miller, Mowrer, & Sears, 1939). This became known as the **frustration-aggression hypothesis.**

The frustration-aggression hypothesis has since been modified. We now know that some people react to frustration by becoming aggressive, but aggression isn't an inevitable response to frustration (Berkowitz, 1965). Frustrated people have also been known to respond by trying harder, by crying, and by giving up. Reactions to frustration appear to depend on the individual and on the specific situation. To be frustrated—that is, to be unable to attain your goal—is aversive and can result in psychological pain or depression. Scientists now realize that people who are anguished or depressed in this way are more likely to become violent. In this sense, frustration, as one of many causes of psychological anguish, can lead to aggression (Berkowitz, 1983).

For years, hunters have known that there is no more dangerous situation than confronting a wounded animal whose back is to a wall. They know that animals who are in pain and unable to flee often will attack. Decades ago, psychologists in laboratories carefully investigated this phenomenon, which came to be known as **pain-elicited aggression.**

When an animal, such as a rat, is placed in a cage and given a painful electric shock, the rat will attack any other animals that happen to be nearby. At first, researchers believed this attack response was a fairly simple, uncomplicated behavior with the purpose of ending the animal's pain. Researchers reasoned that it might be normal for an animal in its natural environment to "assume" that any sudden pain was caused by an attack from a nearby animal. In this view, aggression by the animal in pain is seen as an attempt to stop an attacker. The discovery that rats given electric shocks will attack other small animals but will never attack inanimate objects supported this view (Ulrich & Azrin, 1962).

As the research on pain-elicited aggression continued, it became obvious that the phenomenon wasn't so simple after all. In one study, re-

An Enduring Question, Continued

searchers found that a mouse who had been interrupted during a fight with another mouse would actually cross a painful electrically charged grid to resume his attack (Lagerspetz, as cited by Berkowitz, 1965). The finding that animals in pain would endure even more pain to attack a victim made researchers believe that the pained animal's greatest inclination is not just to stop pain but rather to do harm to another animal and to gain a victory (Berkowitz, Cochran, & Embree, 1981; Berkowitz, 1983).

When researchers first examined pain-elicited aggression in animals, they did not believe the phenomenon included human beings. After all, if pain-elicited aggression was obvious in human beings, it wouldn't be safe to be a dentist. But once the simple notion that an animal in pain will bite had evolved into the more sophisticated view that an animal who suffers will want to harm another animal, the idea that humans might engage in pain-elicited aggression began to emerge. In short order, studies began to confirm that humans were not immune from becoming more aggressive when they were uncomfortable or suffering. For example, in one experiment, researchers found that subjects were more likely to make a hostile judgment about a stranger if the subjects were asked to express their views while sitting in a hot room (Griffitt & Veitch, 1971). Subjects also were found to be more willing to punish a stranger in an experimental situation if the subjects were irritated by cigarette smoke (Jones & Bogat, 1978) or if they were in a hot room (Baron & Bell, 1975). These findings indicate that people who are in pain or suffering are more likely to lash out aggressively than are contented people (Berkowitz, 1983). For instance, some researchers have argued that the urban riots in American cities during the late 1960s were made worse by the summer heat (Baron & Ransberger, 1978), and other research has shown that hot days in general are associated with an increase in violent behavior (Bell, 1992).

People who are hurting often become depressed over their state of affairs. And depressed people often show a substantial amount of aggressiveness (Kendell, 1970; Poznanski & Zrull, 1970). It is also known that depressed people often are apathetic and are unable to engage in the prolonged purposeful action necessary to resolve their problems. For this reason, when depressed people attack, they tend to "attack someone impulsively, revealing their instigation to aggression in a quick outburst of temper not requiring planned and sustained behavior" (Berkowitz, 1983, p. 1142).

This is what psychologists believe may have happened to James Huberty. He was deeply depressed and had even attempted suicide. His mother had left him when he was a young boy. As an adult, he had failed at work and had lost a great deal of money in unsuccessful real-estate ventures. He moved out west to find employment, but ended up losing a series of jobs. He was suffering and in anguish. Because of his pain, like members of most species, he was more likely to lash out and to try to harm people who were nearby. Aggression from such a depressed person is likely to be sudden and impulsive (Berkowitz, 1990). Huberty's aggression was particularly deadly because guns were part of his life and were readily available to him. Reportedly, he often sat on his porch with a shotgun on his lap. Had the guns not been readily available, his sudden impulse might not have resulted in so many deaths. But the guns were in

AN ENDURING QUESTION, CONTINUED

his hands, McDonald's was across the street, and there were people nearby on whom he could vent his anger.

Why Huberty attacked so violently, while other people who are in similar pain (and who also have ready access to firearms) do not, remains a mystery. Perhaps like the dentist's patients, most people are able to cope with their pain cognitively and to understand that they must deal with it without inflicting harm on other people. In the words of one researcher, "This aggressive instigation need not be translated into open attacks on others. We can learn to restrain our aggressive dispositions, be led not to think of others as sources of displeasure, and turn our thoughts away from aggression-promoting ideas" (Berkowitz, 1983, p. 1143). As our society attempts to understand horrors such as this one, we hope to find ways to reach those people who suffer so that we can help them learn to cope with their pain without turning on those around them.

Aggression and Inheritance

For years dog breeders have known that aggression can be bred into and out of certain varieties of the same species. If you heard that your child were going next door to play with the neighbor's collie, you might have a different reaction than if you were told that the neighbor's dog was a pit bull. With this in mind, is it possible that certain groups of people might be more prone to violence than others?

Researchers in the Netherlands believe that they have isolated a mutant gene in a large Dutch family that is directly responsible for outbursts of violence and aggression among the male members of the family who inherited it (Brunner, et al., 1993). Among the male members of this family who inherited the gene, one raped his sister and then attacked a man with a pitchfork, another made his sisters undress at knife point, a third tried to run over his employer with a car, and two more were arsonists. The fact that none of the women in the family had similar outbursts led the researchers to look on the X chromosome for the gene affecting the males' aggression; in other words, this pattern of aggression was believed to be caused by a sex-linked disorder (see Chapter 3). The mutant gene in this family, although not yet isolated, appears to cause a deficiency of an enzyme known as MAOA, which helps break down certain neurotransmitters in the brain. Without sufficient MAOA, these neurotransmitters may build up to levels that could cause unusual behavior including aggression. It is hoped that the men of this family who inherited this disorder may eventually be able to control their aggression either by eliminating substances from their diet that MAOA normally metabolizes or perhaps through the use of certain neurotransmitter blockers.

Controlling Aggression and Violence

Human beings are not a uniquely aggressive species. In many instances, human aggression can be controlled through conditioning (see Chapter 8), modeling, and learning (Lore & Schultz, 1993). Let's look at a few examples.

Everyone knows that one of the terrors of childhood is the school bully. In fact, in the United States alone, an estimated 5 million instances of school bullying occur each year, and the number may be much higher. Boys tend to bully about three times more often than girls and are

AN ENDURING QUESTION, CONTINUED

more likely to be violent, while girls tend to use more subtle forms of bullying such as spreading rumors.

The victims of bullying are often very upset and commonly find their self-esteem lowered by the incident. But can anything be done about this behavior, or is a certain amount of aggression in children simply the nature of our species?

One nation, Norway, has made a concerted effort to stem bullying throughout its school system. Over the last few years, the Norwegians have lowered the instances of school bullying by a huge 50 percent (Pepler & Rubin, 1990; Lore & Schultz, 1993). This was accomplished by giving each teacher a 32-page book explaining how to intervene and how to sanction bullies. All teachers and schoolchildren were shown a short videotape depicting the effects of bullying on a 10-year-old and a 14-year-old child. In general, it became clear to everyone that bullying would no longer be accepted in school.

Then again, this study was concerned with controlling aggression in children. Could similar results be achieved with adults? The answer is yes. Inappropriate aggression in adults can also be controlled through learning. For example, in a study conducted by the police department in Minneapolis, Minnesota, researchers discovered that the incidence of repeat violence by husbands against their wives was greatly reduced when the man was arrested and held in jail overnight following the incident rather than simply being asked to leave the house briefly or receiving brief counseling. One night in jail apparently was a sobering experience that enabled men to later control their desires for similar outbursts (Lore & Schultz, 1993).

Similarly, if a woman reports her husband or boyfriend to the authorities the very first time he assaults her, she is far less likely to be beaten again (Lore & Schultz, 1993). These studies help to reinforce our understanding that while we may have an innate capacity for aggression, our learning and experience can play a very great role in determining whether we will express aggression.

FOR CRITICAL ANALYSIS

1. Suppose studies actually showed that certain genes among certain minority groups were, in fact, responsible for inciting aggression among members of those groups. How might such a finding affect society? What precautions should researchers take before announcing such a discovery? Should it be announced?

2. Should a major national effort be undertaken to teach people that violence will not be tolerated in our society? Such an effort would be very expensive, but how much money do you think unbridled violence costs our society? Would a major effort, including education, training, aid, more prisons, thousands more police officers, and similar measures, be cost-effective? If we don't do something now, do you think the levels of aggression will get worse or not? Why?   ◆

THEORIES OF EMOTION

So far in this chapter, we've discussed what makes us emotional, we've looked at the evolutionary benefits of emotions for motivating us and helping us to communicate, and we've examined some of the biological underpinnings of emotions, but we haven't addressed the central question, namely, what are emotions? Over the years, researchers have attempted to develop theories of emotion that help to explain what emotions are. This task is anything but easy.

From what you've read so far, it is apparent that any theory of emotion must deal with a series of events and feelings. Common sense tells us that an emotion is the result of some specific event and that we react to emotions once they occur. This sequence is shown in Figure 12.3. However, a subjective assessment of an emotional state can influence a person's behavior. Consider the following experiment. In this experiment, male subjects were taken one at a time to a darkened room where they were seated in a chair. A microphone was placed over the subject's heart, and he was told that his heart rate was going to be monitored during the experiment.

In front of the subject was a screen for showing slides—slides of *Playboy* magazine centerfolds. One by one, each subject was shown slides of attractive women, 12 in all, representing each month of the year. The heartbeat sound was loud enough so that the subject could hear it. What the subject didn't know was that the microphone was a fake; the subject couldn't really hear his own heartbeat. Instead, the sound of a false heartbeat filled the room. The experimenter controlled the heartbeat and made it go faster or slower by turning a dial. Earlier, the playmates of the month who were going to be associated with a rapid heartbeat—Miss February, Miss August, and Miss November—had been selected at random. The whole time, the subject was to think he was listening to the sound of his own heart. How would this belief affect him?

◆ **FIGURE 12.3**

The commonsense concept of emotion.

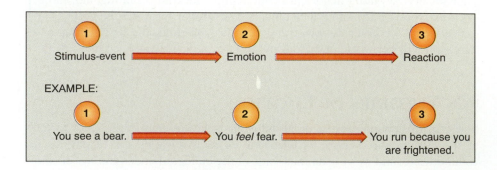

At the end of the experiment, each subject was told that he could choose any three of the centerfold photographs to take home with him. Little did he know that this was the dependent variable the experimenter wanted to measure. The results showed that the subjects found the centerfolds associated with a rapid heartbeat to be the most desirable (Valins, 1966).

Apparently, the subjects in this experiment thought that they had become emotionally aroused while watching particular slides, and they used the false emotional feedback to make a judgment about their preferences and feelings. Stuart Valins, who conducted this classic experiment, liked to say that even in the absence of specific physiological reactions, the cognitive or thought component of an emotion can still have an effect. In other words, how you assess your feelings is part of your emotional makeup (Lazarus, 1984).

How many times during the day do you rely on cognitive assessments in order to know what your emotional state is, and how many times might you have been fooled by circumstances just as the subjects in the experiment were misled? In other words, how can you be sure how you really feel about things?

When Stuart Valins played false heartbeats as feedback, the subjects were influenced by what they thought was real emotional arousal, inappropriately labeled their "arousal" as sexual interest, and acted accordingly. This kind of occurrence seems to argue against our commonsense understanding, which tells us that an emotion must be felt before we react to it. Many years before Valins's research, this problem was examined by William James, whose brilliant mind was probing psychological issues before most people had ever heard of psychology.

The James-Lange Theory

In 1890, William James argued that the commonsense explanation of emotions—that environmental events create an emotion that in turn gives rise to responses—might be incorrect. Instead, James asserted that environmental experiences give rise to different visceral and muscular responses and that these responses are themselves the emotional state.

According to James, emotion doesn't produce the behavior but rather the emotion is the behavior. James believed that encountering something dangerous, such as a bear in the woods, would immediately cause bodily changes associated through experience with danger, and you would run (or freeze or do something to avoid the danger). Only *while* reacting could you create the emotion. According to James, the unique body changes that trigger a behavior are *not* the emotion. The emotion is the feeling that you experience *when you act* (see Figure 12.4). For example, if you trip and start to fall while walking down the street, immediate changes occur in your body, and you thrust out

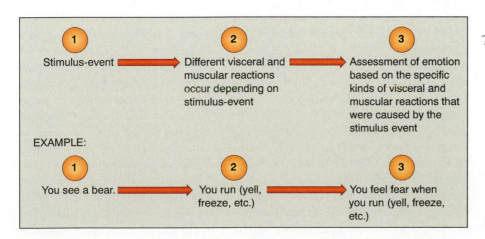

◆ FIGURE 12.4

The James-Lang theory of emotion.

JAMES-LANGE THEORY OF EMOTION
A classical theory of emotion named for William James and Carl Lange, who independently proposed it. The theory posits that a stimulus first leads to visceral and motor responses and that the following awareness of these responses constitutes the experience of the emotion. According to this theory, for instance, we do not cry because we are sad; rather, we are sad because we cry.

your hands to protect yourself. According to James, you don't "feel fear" until you extend your hands. James believed that this view was correct because some behaviors seemed to occur so fast that there appeared to be no time in which to feel an emotion before acting. A Danish researcher named Carl Lange wrote along similar lines, emphasizing the physical changes that lead to immediate responses. Ever since, the theory has been known as the **James-Lange theory of emotion** (Lange & James, 1922).

The James-Lange theory was developed toward the end of the nineteenth century. It remained undisputed for over 30 years, until it was strongly challenged by the American physiologist Walter Cannon. In 1927, Cannon and his student Philip Bard took issue with the James-Lange assertion that visceral and muscular responses could themselves be considered emotions. Cannon and Bard believed that separate areas of the brain were responsible for the different aspects of what was considered to be emotion. Specifically, they argued that the thalamus of the brain coordinated the perceptions that lead to feelings of arousal, while the hypothalamus governed behavior (Cannon, 1927). Although we now know the particulars of their theory to be incorrect, it was the first effort to point out that distinctly separate mechanisms in the central nervous system are called into action when an emotion and a behavior occur. In disagreement with the James-Lange hypothesis, most modern researchers do, in fact, believe that there is an organization in the brain devoted to emotion that is distinct from the neural pathways involved in the generation of most muscular or visceral actions.

Schachter's Two-Factor Theory

In 1962, psychologist Stanley Schachter developed a theory of emotion that was a refinement of the James-Lange theory. Schachter was aware that most research at the time had shown that the physiology of emotional arousal was very similar, even for very different emotions. For instance, during intense anger, happiness, and sadness, adrenalin is secreted, heartbeat accelerates, respiration increases, and pupils dilate. How, then, can a person tell which emotion she is feeling from only attending to her physiological arousal? Schachter wondered whether James and Lange might still be correct in proposing that the emotion itself was determined by the behavioral response. If only a very general arousal state exists for each emotion, Schachter argued, then the cognitive (thinking and perceptual) processes must be playing a central role in determining which emotional state we perceive ourselves to be experiencing when we become aroused (see Figure 12.5).

Imagine, for example, that someone walking through a desert comes on a six-foot-long rattlesnake. She freezes, she gasps, and her eyes open wide. How would you assess her emotional state? If you think about how you would feel, you might call it terror. As for her physiological state, her pupils would probably be dilated, her heart would be beating faster, her respiratory rate would have increased, and her adrenalin level would be high—all indications of an aroused sympathetic nervous system. However, these signs alone wouldn't enable you to define her emotional state, according to Schachter. She, too, might have trouble labeling her emotion if she relied only on her *general* physical arousal. Rather, she must make a mental or cognitive assessment of the situation. When she does so, she comes to the conclusion that what she feels is happiness, because she has now found her lost rattlesnake Buffy, who escaped from her snake farm just down the road. Her excitement was due not to terror but to her happy surprise, since she had just about given up the search. Yet her initial physiological reaction seems the same as a hiker's would have been, had he simply wandered off the road to look for a tumbleweed and stumbled across a deadly snake by accident. In that case, however, his subjective assess-

EXAMPLES:

◆ **FIGURE 12.5**

Schachter's theory of emotion. Different labels may be placed on similar states of arousal depending on how the situation is assessed.

ment would have been that he was in big trouble and was likely to be severely injured. He would have assessed his similar arousal as fear.

To test his theory, Schachter designed an ingenious experiment in which his subjects were secretly given a dose of adrenalin, which caused them to feel a certain amount of physiological arousal. Initially, Schachter had planned to spray the subjects' waiting room with adrenalin so that it would be inhaled, but this method turned out to be too expensive. Instead, he invited the subjects into a room and told them that they were going to take part in a vision experiment. They were given an injection of adrenalin, believing it to be a substance that would improve their vision.

By today's standards, such an experiment might not be considered ethical, since injecting a person with a potent substance could be harmful. Nevertheless, the research results were intriguing, although consent for injection of such a substance was not obtained.

The subjects were divided into two groups. One group was told to expect the symptoms they would be feeling (faster heartbeat, sweating, jitters, fluttering stomach, and so on), while the second group was told to expect symptoms unrelated to the true effects of adrenalin (such as itching feet).

The subjects from each group were given a form to fill out and were placed, one at a time, in a waiting room. In the waiting room was another "subject," who was really an actor working for Schachter. The actor behaved in either one of two planned ways—very happy or very angry. In the happy condition, the actor laughed, told jokes, and played with a hula hoop that was in the waiting room. In the angry condition, the actor became furious about the form he had to fill out, which asked personal questions such as, "With how many men has your mother had extramarital relationships? Four and under; five to nine; ten and over."

The subjects who had been told to expect the symptoms that they began to feel attributed their physical arousal to the injection rather than to the actor's behavior, whereas those who were expecting different symptoms attributed their physical arousal to an emotional reaction brought on by the actor's behavior. The second group of subjects, therefore, began to believe that they were feeling what the actor was feeling, either happiness or anger. In the angry condition, for example, the actor became more and more incensed at the

TWO-FACTOR THEORY OF EMOTION
Stanley Schachter's theory that emotion stems from our cognitive interpretations of a general physiological arousal occurring under specific circumstances.

questions as he filled out the form and finally crumpled it up, swore that he would never answer such personal questions, and stormed out of the room. Subjects who attributed their physical arousal to emotion, rather than to the injection, were much more likely to become angry, too, in this circumstance (see Figure 12.6). This result indicates that the presence of a physiological arousal may cue a person to search for the reason behind the arousal. Then, by examining the immediate circumstance, the person may come to the conclusion "I must be angry" or "I must be happy." The same general physical arousal, then, can lead to different emotions based on a subjective labeling of the immediate situation (Schachter & Singer, 1962).

Schachter's ideas are known as the cognitive appraisal theory, or **two-factor theory of emotion.** Consider the following study.

Spanning the Capilano River in British Columbia are two bridges. One is a sturdy, cedar bridge 10 feet above a shallow part of the river. The other is a narrow, wooden footbridge with low, wire cable handrails. It wobbles and sways 200 feet above some rocky rapids.

One day, an attractive female researcher stopped men as they came off these bridges and told them she was investigating how beautiful scenery affects creative expression. She asked them to fill out a questionnaire, which included writing a short story. Most of the men readily complied. When they finished, she gave each man her name and phone number, using as an excuse, ". . . in case you want to know more about the research." Half the men who crossed the scary bridge called, compared with only 12 percent of those who crossed the safer bridge. And the stories told by the former group contained significantly more sexual imagery than did those of the latter group (Dutton and Aron, 1974)!

The researchers concluded that the fear generated by crossing the rickety bridge was translated into sexual attraction. The men were in a heightened state of arousal when they saw an attractive woman and instantaneously mislabeled some of their heightened arousal as stemming from her!

Although cognitive processes may affect our emotions, our physiology still plays an important role in many aspects of our emotional makeup. Emotions aren't always a strictly cognitive matter (Leventhal & Tomarken, 1986). Think especially of the facial expressions of people who are happy, angry, or sad. Are these expressions learned? Are they part of a cognitive assessment of emotion? Or are they derived from inherited patterns of behavior? The next important work in the field of emotion came from the study of facial expressions.

The Capilano River footbridge created high levels of arousal in those who crossed it (you can see why).

Facial Feedback Theory

Are facial expressions of emotions universal? Except in extreme cases, such as the reunion example, we can usually guess people's moods by their expressions. If you traveled to a foreign land—Malaysia, for instance—you would be able

◆ **FIGURE 12.6**

In Schachter's experiment, the subjects were placed in one of four different conditions. Only the subjects who did not expect the symptoms from the injection showed emotions similar to those of the actor.

SUBJECTS' AWARENESS OF SYMPTOMS

	Subjects expect symptoms (attribute arousal to injection)	Subjects do not expect symptoms (attribute arousal to actor)
Actor angry	Subjects generally unaffected by actor's behavior	Subjects became angry
Actor happy	Subjects generally unaffected by actor's behavior	Subjects became happy

ACTOR'S STATE WHEN SUBJECT ENTERED ROOM

to recognize facial expressions and would know which emotion the person was feeling (Ekman, 1973; Ekman, Sorenson, & Friesen, 1969; Izard, 1971; Boucher, 1973). This ability to recognize facial expressions and corresponding emotions is also found among tribes that have had little contact with the West or with mass media (Ekman, 1973; Ekman & Friesen, 1974). Except in cultures in which people are taught not to display certain emotional expressions, people universally show the same expressions when experiencing the same emotions (Ekman & Oster, 1979). Six facial expressions have been found to be universal—that is, they are clear to almost all people who see them: happiness, anger, disgust, sadness, fear, and surprise (see Figure 12.7).*

No one knows why certain facial muscles become active when particular emotions are being experienced. Why, for instance, should the corners of the mouth turn down when someone is sad? Many researchers feel that these expressions are tied to an innate, genetically predetermined organization that activates certain facial muscles during a particular emotional state (Ekman,

*The facial expressions for fear and surprise can be distinguished more easily if viewed in a motion picture: The fear expression lasts longer than does the surprise expression.

◆ **FIGURE 12.7**

Can you match each photograph with its proper emotion?

(Answers: (a) disgust; (b) happiness; (c) fear or surprise; (d) anger; (e) sadness.)

(a)

(b)

(c)

(d)

(e)

FACIAL FEEDBACK THEORY
A theory of emotion put forth by S. S. Tomkins, stating that emotions are determined by feedback from our facial expressions, which are innate, universal responses to specific events.

◆ **FIGURE 12.8**

In an experiment (Ekman, Friesen, & O'Sullivan, 1988), student nurses were asked to convince an interviewer that the film they had just seen was a pleasant experience. In one case the movie was a nice nature film, in the other, a film about burns and amputations. Smiles that show real enjoyment (photo on the bottom) involve more activity of the muscles that circle the eyes, while the facial actions of a lying smile (on the top) are often quite different.

1993). Even individuals blind since birth, who could never have seen facial expressions, tend to show them (Charlesworth & Kreutzer, 1973). Research has also shown that facial expressions are more pronounced on the left side of the face in right-handed individuals and that the same holds true for monkeys (Hauser, 1993). This finding indicates a deep evolutionary involvement between the organization of the brain and the development of facial expressions.

Of course, just because our facial expressions may be based on genetic organization doesn't mean that we can't control them. Who hasn't tried to keep a straight face when something funny happens at a time when it is inappropriate to laugh? In fact, attempts to mask feelings by controlling facial expressions have been observed in children as young as 3 years of age who, in one experiment, were observed trying to "look innocent" after being caught doing something they had been told not to do (Lewis, Stanger, & Sullivan, 1989).

Researchers have wondered whether feedback from our own facial expressions could tell us which emotion to experience. S. S. Tomkins has argued that such feedback may be the muscular precursor of emotion. Like James and Lange, Tomkins believes that different kinds of muscular actions may be creating different emotions (Tomkins, 1962; 1963).

To test **facial feedback theory,** researchers asked subjects to produce different facial expressions as they carried out certain tasks. They then measured the subjects' self-reported feelings afterward. The purpose was to find out whether deliberately altering facial expressions would directly affect emotions (Laird, 1974). Initial results were inconclusive; by the mid-1980s, however, some surprising results began to emerge (Adelmann & Zajonc, 1989).

The surprises started when researcher Paul Ekman examined exactly which muscles were involved in each of the six universal facial expressions (surprise, disgust, sadness, anger, fear, and happiness). Ekman then measured the physiological changes that were associated with the creation of each expression. These measures included heart rate and hand temperature. The subjects Ekman studied were not asked to produce an emotional expression, but were instead told exactly which muscles they were to contract. This was done because people are generally not very good at faking an emotional expression (Ekman, Friesen, & O'Sullivan, 1988) (see Figure 12.8).*

As an experimental control measure, some subjects were asked to contract facial muscles that were not involved with the expression of a particular emotion. To almost everyone's surprise, not only did the building of a facial expression lead to a physiological arousal, but the kinds of physiological arousals associated with each of the six facial expressions were also distinctly different from one another (Ekman, Levenson, & Friesen, 1983). To verify that the distinct physiological states created by the facial expressions were associated with each of the six emotions represented by the expressions, Ekman and his colleagues instructed the subjects to relive emotional experiences that would create each of the six emotions. For example, a subject might think of something that was very sad and then rate how sad she felt on a scale from 0 to 8. Relived experiences with high ratings created the same physiological arousals associated with the facial expressions. Again, each emotional experience was associated with the same distinct physiological "fingerprint" created by a particular facial expression (see Figure 12.9).

Later, Ekman and his colleagues traveled to western Sumatra, Indonesia, and conducted the same tests again, only this time on members of the Minangkabau culture. The results were much the same, indicating that people

*Actors, of course, make their living faking true emotional expressions, so it is possible to do; it's just that most people aren't very good at it. As the great actor John Barrymore once supposedly said, "The key to acting is honesty—once you've learned to fake that, you can do anything!"

probably share a biological heritage of emotion that is relatively independent of culture (Ekman, et al., 1987).

These data strongly support the original James-Lange view of emotion for two reasons: They suggest that (1) distinctly different visceral and muscular reactions give rise to each emotion, and (2) emotions may be created by muscular reactions.

If sensitive modern instruments can show that autonomic nervous system activity can distinguish among the emotions, this must also change our view of Schachter's two-factor theory (Leventhal & Tomarken, 1986). Schachter argued that autonomic arousal did not distinguish among the emotions and that it was our cognitive assessment of a situation that gave rise to an emotion. As we noted, some research has supported that view. More recently, however, acceptance of Schachter's view has declined, and researchers have begun to look for alternative interpretations of the research results. Perhaps the subjects in Schachter's original experiments were confused about their feelings because they had been aroused in an "unnatural" way through an injection of adrenalin. Perhaps the men who crossed the swinging rickety bridge were more alert because of their fear and took more notice of the woman's beauty. Perhaps, after they had calmed down, their memories of her attractiveness were clearer than were those of the men who crossed the safe bridge, and this prompted more of them to call her for a date. Perhaps the subjects in Stuart Valins's false-feedback experiment were *actually* aroused through classical conditioning by the sound of the false accelerated heartbeat, and so on.

Alternative views such as these are being proposed by researchers who wonder just how important cognitive appraisal is for the creation of an emotion. The issue is not yet settled. Certainly, we know that cognition is important and that our thoughts can create feelings in us, but this is not the same as saying that our cognitions or thoughts are necessary before an emotion can exist. Some researchers believe that in many instances our emotions are separate from our thoughts (Zajonc, 1984). In this view, sensory information may be channeled directly into neural circuits that give rise to an emotion. Other researchers, however, believe that emotions cannot exist until some mental processing or cognitive activity has first occurred that helps to interpret sensations and give them meaning, which then generates an emotional state (Lazarus, 1991). Also, there are times when cognition and emotion can intermix in highly complex ways such as when we feel disgusted for being angry or when we are afraid to let our anger show (Ekman, 1993). Such "affect within affect" is just now being studied. Further research undoubtedly will be required before the debate is resolved.

◆ **FIGURE 12.9**

The average physiological responses that occurred when researcher Paul Ekman had subjects recreate facial expressions. The results were consistent across subjects. As you can see, by comparing heart-rate change and temperature change, you can distinguish the six emotions from one another in terms of autonomic activity. For instance, although anger, fear, and sadness all have similar heart-rate changes (an increase of 7 to 8 beats per minute), they show quite different temperature changes. With anger, there is a significant increase in hand temperature; with fear, there is a slight decrease; with sadness, there is a slight increase. Ekman argues that since these sensitive changes are consistent, they distinguish the emotions from one another; he believes that his data refute Cannon's and Schachter's contention that there is only a general and indistinguishable arousal state during emotion. SOURCE: Adapted from Ekman, Levenson, & Friesen, 1983, p. 1209.)

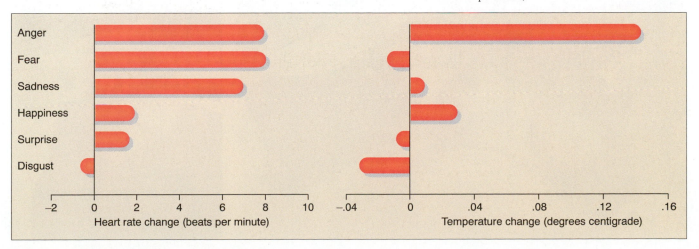

PSYCHOEVOLUTIONARY SYNTHESIS OF EMOTION
Robert Plutchik's theory that emotions evolved because they help a species to survive. In his theory, cognitive assessments of stimulus-events may give rise to innate emotional patterns, which in turn motivate behaviors that ultimately have survival value.

Plutchik's Psychoevolutionary Synthesis of Emotion

Although much of what is considered emotional behavior may be the result of learning and cognitive processes, undoubtedly some of it is innate. The existence of similar facial expressions and emotional reactions in all members of our species is evidence of this. These expressions of emotion are conspicuous in other species as well (see Figure 12.10). The kinds of emotions that we see in our species and in others may have evolved because they help ensure survival. As we suggested earlier, emotions may exist because they serve a function.

Researcher Robert Plutchik outlined a theory of the **psychoevolutionary synthesis of emotion** (Plutchik, 1980), in which he argued that emotions are inherited behavioral patterns that have important functions and that can be modified by experience. Plutchik's theory began where others have left off. He defined emotion as "a complex sequence of events having elements of cognitive appraisal, feeling, impulses to action, and overt behavior—all of which are designed to deal with a stimulus that triggered the chain in the first place" (Plutchik, 1980, p. 68).

PRIMARY EMOTIONS. According to Plutchik, emotions can be thought of in the same terms as colors. Some are fundamental, or primary, and others are

◆ **FIGURE 12.10**

Many species of animals display emotions. Such expressions of emotion often are very similar to those displayed by human beings.

mixtures of the primaries (see Figure 12.11). Plutchik has deduced from his research that there are eight primary emotions: sadness, fear, surprise, anger, disgust, anticipation, joy, and acceptance (in the form of sexual receptivity). He has found that these eight emotions are consistent across a wide range of situations. We may have hundreds of words for emotions, but all of them describe either one of the eight emotions or some combination of them (Plutchik, 1980).

FUNCTIONAL ASPECTS OF EMOTION. Plutchik's theory includes not only behavioral aspects of emotion, such as hitting, running away, crying, and laughing, but functional aspects as well—those aspects that help an organism to ensure management of the environment and survival. Charles Darwin as-

◆ **FIGURE 12.11**

Plutchik's wheel of emotion. Some emotions are primary (within the wheel), while others are secondary (composites or dyads) made from two primaries (outside the wheel). For instance, disappointment, a secondary emotion, is a combination of two primary emotions, surprise and sadness. (SOURCE: *Plutchik, 1980, p. 75.*)

TABLE 12.2 ◆ FUNCTIONAL ASPECTS OF THE EIGHT PRIMARY EMOTIONS

PRIMARY EMOTION	FUNCTION	FUNCTIONAL DESCRIPTION
Fear	Protection	Behavior designed to avoid danger or harm, such as running away or any action that puts distance between an organism and the source of danger.
Anger	Destruction	Behavior designed to eliminate a barrier to satisfaction of an important need. This includes biting, striking, or various symbolic acts of destruction, such as cursing or threatening.
Joy	Incorporation	Behavior that involves accepting a beneficial stimulus from the outside world, as in eating, grooming, mating, or affiliation with members of one's own social group. Such actions have the effect of nurturing the individual.
Disgust	Rejection	Behavior designed to expel something harmful that has been ingested, such as vomiting or, at times, defecation. This behavior is believed to be associated with feelings of contempt and hostility and with sarcasm, all of which are essentially a rejection of other people or their ideas.
Acceptance	Reproduction	Behavior designed to provide contact with sex for the purpose of perpetuating one's gene pool. Expressions of this function include sexual signaling, courtship rituals, and sexual intercourse.
Sadness	Reintegration	Behavior associated with the loss of someone who has provided important nurturance in the past. In such circumstances, the individual sends signals that serve to encourage the return of the lost individual or to attract a substitute. Expressions of this function include crying, emission of distress signals, and "babyish" behavior.
Surprise	Orientation	Behavior reactions to make contact with a new, unfamiliar stimulus: a loud noise, a strange animal, or a new territory, for example. The organism must quickly reorient the body and stop what it is doing so that the sense organs can take in information about the novel stimulus.
Anticipation	Exploration	Behavior designed to bring the organism into contact with many aspects of its environment. Getting to know one's neighborhood permits a form of mental mapping that enables the animal to anticipate and deal with future challenges to its survival.

SOURCE: Plutchik, 1980, p. 73.

sumed that emotions evolved because of the function they fulfilled. He published his arguments on this topic in *The Expression of the Emotions in Man and Animals* (Darwin, 1872/1967).

Table 12.2 outlines the eight basic behavioral patterns of animals and human beings according to Plutchik. Each category is functional—that is, it serves a purpose—which is why it was selected by the evolutionary process. The functional aspects of the eight primary emotions are listed alongside the emotions in the table. For example, Plutchik argues in the first instance that the reason the emotion *fear* exists is that it affords an organism protection.

According to this view, an emotion has five components: a stimulus-event, cognition of that event, an assessment of feeling, a behavior guided by innate mechanisms and based on that assessment, and the function served by the behavior. Figure 12.12 gives examples of this kind of emotional sequence. The difference from the James-Lange theory is obvious: In this model, we *do* run because we feel afraid, not the other way around. Plutchik also argues that not only do we run because we feel afraid but we also run because running leads to protection (the function or value of the emotion). Running functions to ensure our survival. This is why the emotion evolved in the first place. This model is similar to Schachter's cognitive model of emotion because the "feeling" is not labeled until a cognitive assessment is made. However, in Plutchik's theory, an emotion is not only based on a cognitive assessment, but it is also tied to distinct, innate, physiological mechanisms that guide our responses to serve a valuable function. As we discussed, more recent research (Ekman, Levenson, & Friesen, 1983) has indicated that there are distinct autonomic states associated with primary emotions. Plutchik's theory encompasses this concept.

Plutchik has taken the interesting viewpoint that our cognitive abilities have grown and advanced largely to serve emotion! With a powerful brain

◆ **FIGURE 12.12**

Plutchik's psychoevolutionary synthesis of emotion. Plutchik's theory has elements of both the commonsense view and Schachter's two-factor theory. It meshes with more recent findings by Ekman, and it incorporates Darwin's idea of adaptive function through natural selection. It is like the commonsense view because the emotion stimulates the behavior. It resembles Schachter's theory because a cognitive assessment must be made before a primary emotion can be generated from what would be only a general state of physiological arousal. It also is in agreement with Ekman's findings that there are different arousal states associated with the primary emotions. Finally, Darwin's ideas are expressed by the argument that primary emotional states exist because they serve a valuable function.

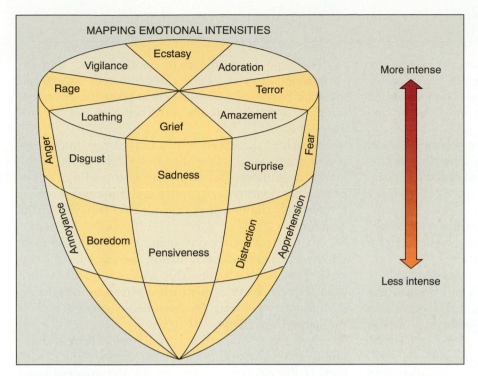

MAPPING EMOTIONAL INTENSITIES

◆ **FIGURE 12.13**

Plutchik's model for depecting the relative similarities and intensities of the primary emotions. Each lengthwise slice of the figure represents a primary emotion, from its most intense to its mildest expression (for example, grief—sadness—pensiveness). Emotions that most resemble one another are adjacent; those most unlike are far apart or are opposite one another. All positions on the figure are plotted from ratings by subjects in a number of studies. At mild intensities, the emotions aren't labeled, because it often is too difficult to discriminate them. The adrenalin injection used in Schachter's experiment may have created an arousal in this range, allowing subjects to misinterpret their emotional state more easily. Confusing loathing with adoration, or ecstasy with grief, would be much less likely. (SOURCE: Plutchik, 1980, p. 74.)

that can make rapid calculations and evaluate many situations, we find it easier to interpret what our feelings mean and then to react in a way that's most functional. This idea is unusual; many people think that emotions can get in the way of clear, rational thinking. Plutchik views rational thinking as something that can help us to develop and perfect the emotional experience.

EMOTIONAL INTENSITIES, SIMILARITIES, AND DIFFERENCES. Emotions, as we all know, can vary in intensity. Compare annoyance and rage or apprehension and terror—the difference is one of intensity. Furthermore, some emotions have elements in common, such as rage and loathing, whereas other emotions are distinctly opposites, such as grief and ecstasy. Plutchik has developed a model that maps emotional intensities. In Figure 12.13, you see a three-dimensional figure that resembles a top. Similar emotions are placed close to one another; those that are opposite appear across from one another. The figure is shaped like a top to represent the fact that intense emotions are more definable. Less intense emotions are more alike, which is indicated by their nearness to one another at the bottom of the figure. As you have discovered, emotion is a complex area including aspects of physiology, cognition, and innate mechanisms. No one theory of emotion gives us a complete explanation. No doubt, future research will help us to understand emotion more fully.

✦ SUMMARY

◆ Everyone has emotions; even infants a few weeks after birth exhibit them. Emotions pervade our existence, and no study of human behavior would be complete without an attempt to understand the power and value of emotional experiences.

◆ The word feeling is often used interchangeably with the word emotion because we feel, or sense, an emotion. We become most emotional when confronted by circumstances that are personally meaningful, vivid, real, and changing.

◆ Because subjective reports are not always a reliable guide in assessing emotion, many psychologists prefer to rely on observations of overt behavior.

◆ Emotional reactions are often associated with an arousal of the autonomic nervous system. During intense emotional reactions such as fear, rage, sexual arousal, and love, the sympathetic branch of the autonomic nervous system becomes quite active. The strong, measurable physiological changes that occur are the basis on which the polygraph, or lie detector, purports to assess truth telling.

◆ As the infant develops into a child, electrical measures of the brain show that positive and negative emotions are associated with the different brain hemispheres.

◆ The frustration-aggression hypothesis was once a popular way to explain aggression. Currently, most researchers believe that aggression is a response that derives from our biological heritage, but the things that make us aggressive appear to derive mostly from experience and learning.

◆ Pain-elicited aggression may occur in animals, including humans, who are suffering or in anguish. Cognition, especially in humans, may control or mediate the painful experience so that aggression need not be the result.

◆ Common sense tells us that an emotion is the result of a specific event and that we react to emotions once they occur.

◆ The James-Lange theory of emotion argues that environmental experiences give rise to different visceral and muscular responses, which are themselves the emotional states. In this view, emotion is the behavior, not the producer of it.

◆ Schachter developed a two-factor or cognitive appraisal theory of emotion that was a refinement of the James-Lange theory. Schachter demonstrated that it was possible for cognitive (perceptual and thinking) processes to create an emotion that depended on behavior for its existence.

◆ Six different facial expressions have been found to be universal: happiness, anger, disgust, sadness, fear, and surprise. Tomkins has argued that feedback from our own facial expressions tells us which emotion to experience. Data from tests of facial feedback theory strongly support the James-Lange theory.

◆ Ekman has shown that distinct and different autonomic arousal states are associated across cultures with each of the emotions created by the six universal facial expressions.

◆ Plutchik's psychoevolutionary synthesis of emotion is an attempt to trace the origin of emotions. Plutchik argues that emotions are inherited behavior patterns that have important functions and that can be modified by experience. Plutchik considers emotions to be like colors: Some are fundamental or primary, and others are mixtures of the primaries.

◆ According to Plutchik, emotion has five components: a stimulus-event, cognition of that event, an assessment of feeling, a behavior guided by innate mechanisms and based on that assessment, and the function served by the behavior.

◆ Plutchik contends that our cognitive abilities have grown and advanced largely to serve emotion.

◆ Emotions vary in intensity and in their similarity to other emotions.

⬢ SUGGESTIONS FOR FURTHER READING

1. Ekman, P. (Ed.). (1983). *Emotion in the human face*. New York: Cambridge University Press. An interesting book on facial expressions and their effects on emotions.

2. Lykken, D. T. (1980). *A tremor in the blood: Uses and abuses of the lie detector*. New York: McGraw-Hill. A book by one of the foremost researchers on lie detection, discussing its valid uses and giving cases where it has been abused in the past.

3. Plutchik, R. (1980). *Emotion: A psychoevolutionary synthesis*. New York: Harper & Row. Outlines Plutchik's theory of emotion, including its roots in Darwin's theory of evolution. Discusses the survival functions that emotions serve.

Chapter Thirteen

Intelligence and Creativity

PROLOGUE

THE GENIUS OF MENLO PARK

One of the most inventive minds in American history, and in the history of the world for that matter, was that of Thomas A. Edison. While working in his laboratory at Menlo Park, New Jersey, Edison either invented or perfected the incandescent light bulb, the phonograph, and the motion-picture camera and projector to name but a few of his most prominent achievements.

Edison worked around the clock and his laboratory never shut down. He liked to keep the lab going 24 hours a day. He accomplished this by taking catnaps now and then while he worked. Among those working for Edison in the huge, dimly lighted lab at Menlo Park was a mathematician named L. L. Thurstone, who had been hired to do fairly simple math connected with the work at the laboratory. At first, Thurstone assumed that Edison was too busy to do it himself. But he soon discovered that Edison needed him to do the fairly straightforward math because it was beyond Edison's grasp. The great genius simply didn't have a head for numbers. Edison not only had trouble with high school algebra, he was even hard pressed to handle long division!

This experience led Thurstone to wonder about intelligence and to turn his life's work to its study. Over the years, Thurstone came to believe that there is no such thing as intelligence, at least not in any general sense. Watching Edison had made him think that there were, in fact, many different kinds of intelligence. Edison, Thurstone realized, was a mechanical genius; he was brilliant at putting things together. But in other areas, he just wasn't all that bright. When it came to mathematical ability, the average high school student was superior to Edison.

The public, on the other hand, didn't seem to understand this. In their eyes, intelligence was just one thing—something you either had or didn't have. And most likely, it was something you were born with or were not born with, as the case might be. Perhaps that is why people were so surprised when Edison, as the resident national genius, was asked what he thought of Einstein's theory of relativity when it was published. In a widely shown newsreel interview, Edison admitted that he couldn't understand the

INTELLIGENCE
A general term for a person's abilities in a wide range of tasks, including vocabulary, numbers, problem solving, and concepts. It may also include the ability to profit from experience, to learn new information, and to adjust to new situations.

first thing about it. Thurstone wasn't surprised, however. Edison would have had no hope of grasping Einstein's mathematics even though the theory of relativity didn't require more than good high school math. Furthermore, the concepts of Einstein's theory were highly abstract, which Thurstone believed required a different kind of intelligence than Edison's practical and applied genius.

IN THIS CHAPTER, we'll examine L. L. Thurstone's idea that there are many different kinds of relatively independent intelligences. We'll discuss how a person's intelligence can change owing to experiences. We'll also look at tests that measure intelligence and creativity and see how such tests are designed. Finally, we'll examine mental retardation, exceptionality, and giftedness and look at the contributions of both nature and nurture to intelligence.

❊ WHY PSYCHOLOGISTS STUDY INTELLIGENCE

People within every group or society are aware that some of their members have superior abilities to analyze problems, to find solutions, to comprehend ideas, and to accumulate information. Such people are valued because they can help the society to reach its goals. They are considered intelligent.

We revere those people whose insights, gifts, and knowledge have enabled them to make brilliant deductions or to see things as no one has seen them before. We know their names—Galileo, Einstein, Newton, Michelangelo, Darwin, and Beethoven, to name a few. But why do some people have these abilities and others not? Are these gifts present at birth, or are they acquired through experience and learning? Can **intelligence** be taught? Can intellectual potential be found and cultivated? Can we prevent it from being lost or wasted? Does intelligence change over time, or does it remain stable? Is there a general kind of intelligence, applicable in all situations, or are there many kinds of intelligence, as Thurstone suggested? Psychologists are interested in all these questions. In fact, intelligence is such an intriguing subject that nearly everyone takes an interest in it.

❊ DEFINING INTELLIGENCE

What is intelligence? Is it the ability to do well in school or to figure things out? Is it having the skills to find happiness or knowing when to come in out of the rain? Think about the following people and ask yourself if they are intelligent:

— The physician who smokes three packs of cigarettes per day?
— The Nobel Prize winner whose marriage and personal life are in ruins?
— The corporate executive who has worked to reach the top and has earned a heart attack for the effort?
— The brilliant and successful composer who handled his money so poorly that he was always running from his creditors and sometimes paid for a night's lodging with the rights to a great work? (Incidentally, his name was Mozart.)

Examine any of these paradoxes, or consider the lives of your own friends or even your own life, and it will probably be clear to you that intelligence is not an easy thing to define.

The first scientific interest in defining and measuring intelligence can be traced to the nineteenth-century inheritance theories of Sir Francis Galton (1822–1911). Galton was interested in the success that English dog breeders had had in creating so many varieties of dog. He wondered if it wouldn't also be possible to breed humans for desirable characteristics, intelligence being one of them. Galton founded a **eugenics** movement that advocated mating the best men and women for the purpose of producing superior offspring.

The movement never went very far, mostly because people preferred to marry for love rather than genes. Still, Galton's studies of supposedly superior and inferior qualities of people marked the start of the entire psychological testing movement, and people began to think about differences in mental abilities in a way they never had before. By 1900, the public had come to accept the idea that science could measure psychological differences in order to identify superior and inferior abilities. Clouding serious scientific research, however, were numerous nonsensical but popular theories, which were often the product of charlatans or pseudoscientists who purported to be able to measure "inherited traits." One such theory, for example, was **phrenology.** Phrenology is the study of personality based on the contours and bumps of the head. It works about as well as trying to figure out how much money someone has by feeling the outside of his safe. Another idea was the notion that criminal tendencies were mostly inherited and were directly related to such physical features as a low forehead or "shifty" eyes. We now know that this idea is foolish. Among thousands of counterexamples is the fact that Australia was settled two centuries ago mostly by criminals banished from England. Many of today's Australians can trace their genetic roots back to these criminals, yet Australia has a low crime rate. The list of foolish beliefs about inherited characteristics is long. Nevertheless, as the twentieth century dawned, it was a common public belief that most human characteristics were the result of heredity; the influence of learning or experience was discounted.

More recently, however, the contributions of experience and environment have been widely investigated, and the more modern view of a characteristic such as intelligence is that it must be viewed as an interaction between inherited capacity and environmental influence.

EUGENICS
Term coined by Sir Francis Galton referring to the science of improving the genetic characteristics of humans through breeding.

PHRENOLOGY
A system developed by Franz Joseph Gall for identifying types of people by examining their physical features, especially the configuration of the skull.

MENTAL AGE (MA)
A concept developed by Alfred Binet that was subsequently incorporated into the formula mental age/chronological age × 100 = IQ. The mental age of a person is derived by comparing his or her score with the average scores of others within specific age groups.

CHRONOLOGICAL AGE (CA)
A concept developed by Alfred Binet that was subsequently incorporated into the formula mental age/chronological age × 100 = IQ. The chronological age of a person is his or her actual age.

INTELLIGENCE QUOTIENT (IQ)
A quotient derived from the formula MA/CA × 100, where MA is mental age and CA is chronological age. The intelligence quotient was devised by German psychologist L. William Stern and introduced in the United States by Lewis Terman.

〽 MEASURING INTELLIGENCE—IQ TESTS

In 1905, Alfred Binet (1857–1911) and Theodore Simon (1873–1961) developed the precursor to the modern intelligence test. Its purpose was to determine which Parisian schoolchildren would benefit from regular classes and which should receive special education.

To create the test, Binet established which tasks or questions could be solved easily by children in each of the school grades and which were difficult. Carrying his research further, he developed a concept of **mental age (MA).** For example, a 5-year-old child who performed as well on the test as an average 6-year-old child would be said to have a mental age of 6. A 10-year-old child who performed only as well as an average 5-year-old child would be said to have a mental age of 5. Binet used the term **chronological age (CA)** to represent the actual age of the child.

A few years later, the German psychologist L. William Stern developed a formula that would avoid fractions when comparing MA and CA. It yielded a score he called the **intelligence quotient,** or **IQ.** Stern's formula, MA/CA × 100 = IQ, gave a rough index of how bright or dull any child was in comparison with his or her school peers. In the case of the 5-year-old child (CA = 60 months) with an MA of 72 months, the IQ is 120, more than sufficient for schoolwork. But the 10-year-old child (CA = 120 months) with an MA of only 60 months has an IQ of 50, which would be defined as developmentally retarded—not sufficient for schoolwork.

VALIDITY
The capacity of an instrument to measure what it purports to measure.

In 1916, Lewis Terman (1877–1956) and his colleagues at Stanford University in California revised the original Binet-Simon intelligence scale and incorporated Stern's idea of the IQ. Their revision, known as the Stanford-Binet, became the first of the modern IQ tests. Using the Stanford-Binet test, most IQ scores in a normal population fall between 85 and 115, although some are higher or lower. Figure 13.1 depicts the distribution of scores.

Test Validity

Although we now have IQ tests, intelligence itself has never been adequately defined, and there is some question about the **validity** of these tests. A test is said to be valid if it measures what it claims to measure. Do IQ tests measure intelligence, as most people use the term? Generally, IQ tests measure common skills and abilities, many of which are acquired in school. Consider the areas covered in a widely used intelligence test, the revised Wechsler Adult Intelligence Scale (WAIS-R), shown in Figure 13.2 on pages 446–447. Does the ability to answer the example questions correctly coincide with most people's understanding of intelligence?

Many people think that intelligence also includes such attributes as creativity, persistent curiosity, and striving for success. IQ test scores aren't always good indicators of a person's abilities in these areas. For instance, two researchers worked with a number of bright mathematicians whose IQ test scores were very similar, who were all about the same age, and who all had Ph.D.'s from prestigious universities. They found that these subjects had remarkable differences in creative output, as measured by other mathematicians (Helson & Crutchfield, 1970). IQ test scores, then, are not generally a valid measure of creativity.

IQ tests, however, have been found to predict other behaviors. They are generally able to predict success in school with a fairly high degree of certainty—not surprisingly, perhaps, since this is what they were originally designed to do. IQ tests also are sometimes valid for clinical assessments of people who have mental disorders or neurological and perceptual deficiencies.

Whether an IQ test will be a valid predictor often depends on the particular situation and the population being considered. For example, although people have attempted to use IQ tests to predict the likelihood of success on the job (Cronbach, 1970), the tests are fairly inaccurate at making such predictions (McClelland, 1973). If the job in question requires the academic skills most often learned in school, however, the IQ test will be a better predictor of success. This again shows the relationship between IQ scores and the ability

◆ **FIGURE 13.1**

The standard distribution of IQ scores within the general population. The most common IQ score is 100. Approximately two-thirds of all scores fall within the IQ range of 84 to 116.

to do well in school. In one study (Ghiselli, 1966), IQ test scores moderately predicted job success among stockbrokers (a more academic job) but poorly predicted job success among police officers (a less academically oriented job). As you can see, IQ tests may be useful predictors of success in some situations, but they don't necessarily measure the great number of abilities that might be included under the term *intelligence*.

Factor Analysis

Some IQ tests are given individually, one on one, such as the Stanford-Binet or the WAIS-R, while others are given to groups. Some IQ tests are designed to be taken by infants exclusively, or by children, or by adults. All the IQ tests ask different questions, and although they are all called intelligence tests and all yield an IQ score, they may measure different abilities. Furthermore, some tests measure the same ability more than once and thereby give that one ability more weight in the final score. The amount of weight or emphasis given to any one ability is known as a **factor load.**

To understand factor load better, let's look at an example from athletics. Think of an Olympic decathlon athlete who must compete in the following 10 events:

- ◆ pole vault (requires running start)
- ◆ 100-meter dash
- ◆ javelin (requires running start)
- ◆ 110-meter high hurdles
- ◆ pole vault (requires running start)
- ◆ 400-meter run
- ◆ high jump (requires running start)
- ◆ 1500-meter run
- ◆ discus
- ◆ running long jump
- ◆ shot put

As you can see, one ability is measured more than once; that is, it has a heavy factor load. This ability is running. The idea of trying to balance tests—including IQ tests—for factors, so that each ability is tested only once, was advocated by L. L. Thurstone in 1938. To accomplish this, Thurstone relied on a technique known as **factor analysis.** Of course, who's to say that a test equally weighted for all factors is the best indicator of what we call intelligence? Perhaps, intelligence is defined better by tests that have more weight for some factors than for others. Factor analysis is still valuable, however, because, if the factors can be isolated, the value of each factor and the weight it should be given can be determined more accurately. Although the factor analysis approach has been challenged, there is no doubt that some IQ tests are loaded in favor of particular factors. For instance, I do fairly well on the Stanford-Binet test; this test is heavily loaded in favor of verbal skills, and I enjoy talking and writing. But when I take the WAIS-R, my IQ is 15 points lower. The Wechsler includes many tasks that require eye-hand coordination, and it turns out that I am a clod with blocks. Both tests give me an IQ score, however. People often assume that an IQ is an absolute value regardless of the test; as you can see, they are mistaken.

As you learned at the beginning of the chapter, Thurstone was a mathematician who worked in Edison's laboratory, solving the mathematical equations that Edison seemed completely unable to comprehend. Edison's inability in this area led Thurstone to conclude that rather than a single quality called general intelligence, there must be many, perhaps unrelated, kinds of intelligence. One of Thurstone's hopes was that it would eventually be possible to

FACTOR LOAD
The weight or emphasis given to any factor or ability.

FACTOR ANALYSIS
A statistical procedure aimed at discovering the constituent traits within a complex system of personality or intelligence. The method enables the investigator to compute the minimum number of factors required to account for intercorrelations of the scores on the tests.

◆ **FIGURE 13.2**

Subtests of the Wechsler Adult Intelligence Scale (WAIS-R, 1981).

VERBAL SCALE

1. INFORMATION: Twenty-nine questions covering a wide range of general knowledge that people have presumably had an opportunity to gain simply by being exposed to the culture.

   EXAMPLE: How many zeros are there in 1 billion?

2. DIGIT SPAN: Fourteen groups of from two to nine digits presented orally, one group at a time. After hearing a group, subjects must repeat it from memory. Some require repitition forward, others backward.

3. VOCABULARY: Thirty-five vocabulary words of increasing difficulty presented visually and orally. Subjects must define each word.

   EXAMPLE: "What does parsimony mean?"

4. ARITHMETIC: Fourteen problems similar to those encountered in elementary school. The problems must be solved without paper or pencil.

   EXAMPLE: "How much would three cigars cost if each cigar was $1.80 and the store was offering a 10 percent discount on all puchases?"

5. COMPREHENSION: Sixteen questions that ask subjects to indicate the correct thing to do under varied circumstances, what certain proverbs mean, or why certain practices are followed.

   EXAMPLE: "What is meant by 'too many cooks spoil the broth'?"

6. SIMILARITIES: Fourteen items requiring that subjects explain the similarity between two things.

   EXAMPLE: "In what ways are red and hot alike?" (ANS.: Both can be sensed; both are stimuli.)

PERFORMANCE SCALE

7. PICTURE COMPLETION: Twenty pictures. In each picture something is missing. Subjects must identify the missing part.

   EXAMPLE:

8. PICTURE ARRANGEMENT: Ten sets of cards. Each set contains cartoon characters performing an action. If the set of cards is placed in the proper sequence, it will depict a sensible story. Subjects must place cards from each set in the proper order.

   EXAMPLE: "Place the cards in the proper sequence so that they depict a sensible story." (ANS.: Corect order should be 3, 1, 4, 2.)

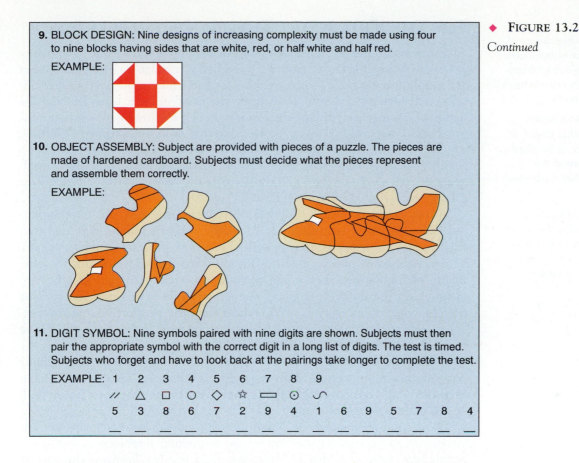

◆ **FIGURE 13.2**

Continued

distinguish social from nonsocial intelligence, academic from nonacademic intelligence, and mechanical from abstract intelligence.

Since Thurstone's day, many people have attempted to isolate different kinds of intelligence. One of the most exhaustive efforts was made by J. P. Guilford. He developed a model of intelligence based on factor analysis of the human intellect. In his most recent version of the model, Guilford proposed that there are as many as 150 different factors, or kinds of intelligence (Guilford, 1982). Other researchers agree with Guilford that there are different kinds of intelligence, but disagree as to the number. Psychologist Howard Gardner, for example, has proposed that there are seven different kinds of intelligence (Gardner, 1983b). Gardner's categories are quite broad in their definition of intelligence, including such aspects as social grace and athletic skill.

The view that there are different kinds of intelligence lies in direct contradiction to an idea proposed early in this century by Charles Spearman (1863-1945). Spearman argued that there was only one kind of general intelligence (g) and that g represented the amount of mental energy that a person could bring to bear on any given mental task (Spearman, 1927). A number of modern researchers also hold this view. Of course, because no one has been able to define intelligence adequately, no one is sure how many kinds of intelligence there may be—a state of affairs that plainly illustrates the difficulty of measuring intelligence (Weinberg, 1989).

Currently, this issue is unresolved. Two camps remain. There are the *lumpers*, who believe that all intelligence stems from one general ability, and the *splitters* who argue in favor of many separate kinds of relatively independent intelligence (Mayr, 1982). There are even some who take a middle ground, arguing in favor of a hierarchical organization of specific skills stemming from only one or two factors (Horn, 1986).

COMPONENTIAL INTELLIGENCE
From Sternberg's triarchic theory of intelligence: that aspect of intelligence encompassing the cognitive problem-solving and information-processing skills measured by most IQ tests.

CONTEXTUAL INTELLIGENCE
From Sternberg's triarchic theory of intelligence: that aspect of intelligence encompassing the ability of the individual to adapt to her environment or culture.

EXPERIENTIAL INTELLIGENCE
From Sternberg's triarchic theory of intelligence: that aspect of intelligence encompassing the ability to take a newly learned skill and make it routine.

THE TRIARCHIC THEORY OF INTELLIGENCE

After having studied the issues of intelligence and intelligence testing for many years, psychologist Robert J. Sternberg reached a conclusion: Intelligence tests are simply too narrow. "Most psychologists and others who have studied intelligence have attempted to 'look inside the head' in order to understand the nature of intelligence" (Sternberg, 1985, p. 1111). By this, he means that most intelligence tests rely solely on problem-solving skills and cognitive abilities, which is true. In fact, if the tests commonly used by Piaget to test children's cognitive development (see Chapter 3) are assembled and given as an "intelligence" test, they correlate quite well with the Wechsler Intelligence Test (Humphreys, Rich, & Davey, 1985).

In his book *Beyond IQ* (1984), Sternberg proposed an information-processing approach (see Chapter 10) to the study of intelligence, one that would encourage a step-by-step analysis of cognitive processes and be *applicable in any sociocultural context*. Toward this aim, Sternberg developed a triarchic theory of intelligence that would account for what he argues are the two missing legs necessary to support the concept we call intelligence. This triarchic view of intelligence is far broader than the perspective that psychologists have traditionally accepted, and it may be more in line with what most people believe intelligence to be.

The first leg of the theory, of course, includes the cognitive problem-solving and information-processing skills measured by most IQ tests. This is what Sternberg calls **componential intelligence,** which the layperson might call "book smart" or "school smart."

The second leg concerns the ability of the individual to adapt to her environment or culture. This is known as **contextual intelligence.** For years, people have referred to this as "street smart"; it involves knowing the ins and outs, the angles, and how to get by in a given situation. Learning how to survive and do well in your cultural and social environment is important and, after all, is an intelligent thing to do. In fact, when Sternberg teaches his psychology graduate students, he likes to include contextual training such as how to compete for a top job, or how to obtain the biggest financial grants, or how to publish in the journals that have the largest circulation (and why it's smart to do so). Some of Sternberg's colleagues have argued that by discussing the "inside" ways to get ahead, he is covering the seedier side of office politics and that it is inappropriate. Sternberg argues that such inside contextual knowledge is important, that contextual intelligence can be learned, and that it's about time we recognize this fact.

The third leg is **experiential intelligence.** Sternberg argues that an important part of intelligence is the ability to take a newly learned skill and make it routine. We have phrases to describe this kind of intelligence, such as "learning from your mistakes" and "capitalizing on your experiences." People with this intelligence quickly develop expertise by making their newly acquired skills routine. By so doing, the mental tasks that once required thought become almost effortless or automatic.

Sternberg has developed a test to measure these three components (the Sternberg Multidimensional Abilities Test). Perhaps this new test will be better able to predict performance and help individuals discover their weaknesses and identify ways to correct them than standard IQ tests can (Weinberg, 1989).

For Sternberg, as for almost all modern psychologists, intelligence is understood to be a series of skills, *not* strictly something that you're born with, something that you either have or do not have. These skills, admittedly influenced by heredity, can be nurtured and developed as well. For this reason, correcting weaknesses in intelligence may well become an important part of applied psychology. Sternberg's book *Intelligence Applied* (1986) even provides a training program, based on the author's theory, to help individuals strengthen any or all of the three forms of intelligence he identifies.

AN ENDURING QUESTION: HOW MUCH OF INTELLIGENCE IS INHERITED?

Your brain, your nervous system, and, indeed, your entire body are made according to instructions received from the genes you inherited from your parents. It would seem reasonable that superior genes would endow a child with superior intellectual capacity. And, in fact, researchers have discovered that parents with high IQs tend to have children with high IQs, while parents with low IQs tend to have children with low IQs.

This finding might appear to prove that intelligence is inherited. But does it really? Rich parents tend to have rich children, and parents who like tostadas and enchiladas tend to have children who like tostadas and enchiladas; it doesn't necessarily follow that these characteristics are carried by genes. Environment also can play an important role. Perhaps being raised by intelligent parents in a stimulating or intellectual home tends to increase a child's IQ.

Nature and Nurture

Genetics determines brain structure and differences within that structure, and obviously, brain structure is related to intellectual functioning. In fact, in one study, the brain sizes of young adults who had IQs above 130 were compared with the brain sizes of matched subjects (in terms of body size, gender, and the like) who had IQs that were slightly below the average of 100. An extremely sensitive imaging technique was used (magnetic resonance imagining—see Chapter 2) to compare the brains of the two groups. Brain size and IQ were found to correlate $+.35$ (see Appendix B) (Willerman, Schultz, Rutledge, & Bigler, 1991). What this typically would mean, for example, is that if we compared two women who were about the same physical size and age, we would expect the one with the higher IQ to have the larger brain. Psychologist Lee Willerman, who conducted this study, points out that those with higher IQs appeared to have more myelin in their brains, especially in areas of the brain associated with higher mental processes, which seems to account for the larger size of their brains. Young adults with lower IQs had brains that more closely resembled the less myelinated brains of older adults. Other studies have lent further support to this finding (Andreasen, et al., 1993).

Psychologists often debate the importance of genetics in determining IQ. What you should remember is that intelligence is not strictly something children are born with—that they either have or don't—but is rather an attribute greatly determined by interactions among genetic inheritance, culture, and experience. This is true even in the case of something such as brain size, which at first glance may seem to depend solely on genetics. It may be, for instance, that the young adults with higher IQs in Willerman's study came from more stimulating homes where they were also provided with better nutrition. Either of these environmental factors might possibly lead to a greater production of myelin. In this case, larger brains to a great degree could be the result of environmental forces.

TWIN DESIGN
A research design used for sorting the influence of nurture from nature. A characteristic or behavior is compared between identical twins; then the same characteristic or behavior is compared between fraternal twins.

ADOPTION DESIGN
A research design used for sorting the influence of nurture from nature. Genetically related individuals who are reared apart from one another or genetically unrelated individuals who are reared together are studied.

BEHAVIORAL GENETICS
The interdisciplinary science that focuses on the relationship of nature and nurture, that is, on the interaction of what is inherited and what is acquired and how that interaction affects behavior.

AN ENDURING QUESTION, CONTINUED

This example also helps us to understand that if some aspect of intelligence is inherited, it doesn't necessarily mean that that aspect, whatever it might be, is there at birth and is rigidly fixed in the child and unchangeable from that point on. Because intelligence is determined by more than one gene, and because it is also a complex response to the environment, it doesn't follow Mendel's simple laws for the inheritance of traits (see Chapter 3). Richard Weinberg expressed this point when he said, "There is a myth that if a behavior or characteristic is genetic, it cannot be changed. Genes do not fix behavior. Rather, they establish a range of possible reactions to the range of possible experiences that environments can provide" (Weinberg, 1989, p. 101).

Methods of Behavioral Genetics

There are two basic ways to study the inheritance of human intelligence. The first is the **twin design,** in which a characteristic or behavior is compared between identical twins and then between fraternal twins. The second method is the **adoption design.** Researchers who use this design study genetically related individuals who are reared apart from one another or genetically unrelated individuals who are reared together. As you can see, these designs allow the effects of nature and nurture to be separately examined. It is not uncommon for both designs to be incorporated into a single study.

As an example of this kind of **behavioral genetic** research, consider the fact that relatives share many of the same genes, while unrelated people do not (which no doubt has some bearing on why relatives are related to each other and unrelated people aren't). Keeping this in mind, look at Table 13.1, and you'll see categories of related and unrelated people, with a correlation coefficient next to each. These correlations represent the relationship between the IQ scores of pairs of individuals within each category (the scores of two first cousins, of a parent and child, and so forth).

Let's look at parents and their children to see how these correlations would be derived. Each parent and his or her child are given an IQ test.

TABLE 13.1 ◆ CORELATIONS OF INTELLIGENCE TEST SCORES*	
CORRELATIONS BETWEEN INDIVIDUALS	MEDIAN VALUE
Genetically Related Persons	
Identical twins reared together	.86
Identical twins reared apart	.72
Parent—child	.40
Fraternal twins reared together	.60
Siblings reared together	.47
Siblings reared apart	.24
Half-siblings	.31
Cousins	.15
Unrelated Persons	
Nonbiological sibling pairs (adopted/adopted pairings)	.34
Adopting parent—offspring	.19

*Based on a study of 111 studies that reported on familial resemblances in intelligence.

SOURCE: Adapted from the Bouchard & McGue, 1981, p. 1056.

AN ENDURING QUESTION, CONTINUED

Then a computation is made that allows these test scores to be compared with each other; each parent's score is compared with his or her own child's score. The more alike these compared scores are, the closer to +1.00 the correlation coefficient will be. A high positive correlation means that the test scores of the parents and their respective children are similar. We can predict from a positive correlation that if a parent's IQ is high, his or her child's is likely to be high, or that if a parent's IQ is low, his or her child's is likely to be low also. A correlation of zero, or near zero, indicates no relationship between the two scores. If that were the case, the parent's score would tell us nothing about the child's score. A correlation approaching −1.00 indicates an inverse relationship; that is, if one score is high, the other is likely to be low, and vice versa. As you can see, the actual correlation between parents and their children is +.40, a moderate positive correlation.

One of the areas of greatest interest in Table 13.1 is the "twins reared apart" category. It is rare for identical twins to be reared apart, but when they are, it provides an ideal chance to study the IQs of two people sharing the same genes but having different upbringing and experiences. As you can see from the table, identical twins reared apart have an even higher correlation than do siblings reared together (Segal, 1985). In the Minnesota Study of Twins Reared Apart, one of the most extensive studies of its kind, Thomas Bouchard and his colleagues at the University of Minnesota found the correlation for IQs among identical twins reared apart to range from +.69 to +.78 (strong positive correlations), depending on the IQ test used (Bouchard, Lykken, McGue, Segal, & Tellegen, 1990). In this survey, the researchers were careful to use only identical twins who were separated at infancy and who were raised in different environments. Identical twins reared apart were also found to show many similarities other than intellectual ones, including shared aspects of personality and social attitudes. This has led Thomas Bouchard to say:

> For almost every behavioral trait so far investigated, from reaction time to religiosity, an important fraction of the variation among people turns out to be associated with genetic variation. This fact need no longer be subject to debate; rather, it is time instead to consider its implications. (Bouchard, Lykken, McGue, Segal, & Tellegen, 1990, p. 227)

At first glance, this result would seem to indicate that inheritance plays a greater role in the determination of IQ than the environment does. However, the "twins reared apart" category is not without problems. As you might imagine, it isn't easy to find twins who have been reared apart. In earlier studies, from which much of this table was developed, "reared apart" often turned out to mean that they were living next door to one another, or that they went to the same school, or that one was with the father and the other with the mother; and because married couples tend to have similar IQs, the "reared apart" environments may have been quite alike in terms of intellectual stimulation. Therefore, the "twins reared apart" category might be contaminated (in a research sense). If so, IQ similarities between identical twins reared apart could no longer be sorted in terms of heredity or experience, and researchers began to question these earlier data.

In an effort to overcome such problems, many rigorously sampled twins were studied for the Minnesota Study of Twins Reared Apart. These

452

An Enduring Question, Continued

newer data tripled the current number of subjects in the "twins reared apart" category. Even so, some researchers are still concerned that some contamination of the "reared apart" category may have occurred even in these new studies (Dudley, 1991). But Thomas Bouchard and his colleagues point out that they were very careful with their selections and that even if there were some contamination, there is no doubt that twins reared apart are far more alike along many dimensions than are siblings reared together and that this could not possibly be explained by shared environments (Bouchard, Lykken, McGue, Segal, & Tellegen, 1991).

The Texas Adoption Project

In one of the most detailed efforts to differentiate the effects of the environment and heredity, researcher Joseph Horn examined 300 adoptive families who had acquired their children at birth (Horn, 1983). He compared the IQs of these children with the IQs of both the adoptive mother and the biological mother. In all, 469 adopted children were tested. The results showed that the children's IQs were more strongly correlated with their biological mothers' ($+.28$), even though the children had never met these women, than with their adoptive mothers' ($+.15$), who had raised them.

At first glance, it might appear that heredity is the most important factor in intelligence, but this is not the finding of the study. To begin with, the difference between correlations of $+.15$ and $+.28$ is very small, almost insignificant (Walker & Emory, 1985). Correlations that small leave much to be explained.

Given these small correlations, the statistical analysis shows us that the biological mothers' IQs accounted for (or, in statistical terms, explained) only about 8 percent of the scores obtained by the adopted children. The IQ scores of the adoptive mothers explained only about 2 percent of their adopted children's IQ scores.* In other words, fully 90 percent of the variables that accounted for the children's IQ scores were unaccounted for, even after the contributions of both the adoptive and the biological mothers had been considered.

The unexplained variables could include, for example, the contributions of the fathers, both biological and adoptive. Assuming that the fathers contributed as much to the children's intelligence as the mothers, however, would still leave a large percentage of the variables unaccounted for. These variables may very well have to do with the children's environment—the environment beyond that supplied by exposure to the adoptive parents. These variables might include television, school, friends, and a host of other possible factors. Joseph Horn, who conducted the Texas

---

*By squaring the correlation coefficient, you can derive what statisticians refer to as the explained variance. For example, Table 13.1 shows that siblings reared together have an average correlation of $+.47$ when their IQ scores are compared. $+.47 \times +.47 = +.2209$ or, when rounded off, $+.22$, which equals 22 percent. This means that whichever variables are responsible for one sibling's IQ score, 22 percent of those same variables are responsible for the other sibling's IQ score. In other words, 22 percent of the variance has been "explained" (although we still may not know which variables, environmental or genetic, they are sharing). As you can see by using this formula, correlations such as $+.28$ or $+.15$ are really quite weak. For a more detailed discussion of correlation and correlation coefficients, see the Statistics Appendix (Appendix B).

AN ENDURING QUESTION, CONTINUED

Adoption Project, states unequivocally that he believes that IQ can be strongly affected by environmental factors (Horn, 1985).

The Texas Adoption Project also produced a surprise when the same children were retested after a 10-year interval. The researchers running the project discovered that

> the popular view of genetic effects as fixed at birth and environmental effects as changing has got matters almost backward, at least for the trait of intelligence in this population during these developmental years. . . . Especially provocative is the finding that genes seem to continue actively contributing to intellectual variation at least into early adulthood, whereas the effect of shared family environment appears to be largely inertial after early childhood. (Loehlin, Horn, & Willerman, 1989, pp. 1000–1001)

In other words, the influence that genetics was having on intelligence increased as these children aged, while the effects of environment decreased. Other studies support these data and yield estimates showing that while the shared family environment accounts for about 70 percent of IQ correlations among twins by age 3, its influence decreases dramatically to 30 to 40 percent in middle childhood and drops to about 20 percent by age 15 (Wilson, 1983).

At first it is difficult to see how genes could have a greater effect on the expression of intelligence as a child gets older. But remember what the authors of this research said about needing to break away from the idea that genetic effects are fixed at birth and express themselves only then and there. Perhaps an example from another field will help to clarify this apparent paradox. Consider the effectiveness of the heart at pumping blood when a person is resting. Among a population of 20-year-olds, environmental factors (exercise, diet, and so forth) may play a greater role in heart efficiency than do genetic factors. It is simply rare for a 20-year-old to have a bad heart. By the time these same people are 80 years old, however, genetic factors will probably account for more of their heart efficiencies than environmental factors. If you want to live a long time, exercise and diet are important, but nothing beats a great set of genes. Similarly, for reasons yet unknown, genetic influences are playing a greater role in intellectual variation among children as they grow older.

Of course, this leads us to the ultimate question of where do we stand? Are genes more important than environment, or is it the other way around? The answer for now is that no one really knows, but the general consensus of over 1000 psychologists is that both play a major role (Snyderman & Rothman, 1987). If you pressed me for a current assessment as it stands in the mid-1990s, I would say that on average, environment and inheritance each account for about 50 percent of the differences observed in intelligence as measured by traditional tests. This still leaves great room for the effects of environment. Even with our limited understanding of intelligence, we can often boost IQ 20 to 25 points with environmental intervention (Weinberg, 1989). And with the advanced technology coming our way, we may be able to engage in genetic intervention sometime in the next century. Imagine finding the genes responsible for some of the variance of IQ and medically adjusting them in a living person to raise intelligence. Although it may sound like science fiction, there is a good chance that you will live to see it happen in your own lifetime. In fact, a few years ago, the National Institute on Child Health and Human Development awarded psychologist Robert Plomin $600,000 to head a

AN ENDURING QUESTION, CONTINUED

project to search for more than 100 genetic "markers" in the blood of over 600 schoolchildren in an effort to find genes (see Chapter 3) associated with intelligence and giftedness (Holden, 1991).

FOR CRITICAL ANALYSIS

1. How might poor prenatal care cause environmental damage to a child's intelligence? How might such effects look as though they were due to genetic causes?
2. If it were your job to select people for an intelligence breeding experiment, which aspects of intelligence would you emphasize and why? How could you know if these aspects were under any genetic control before you began to breed subjects?   ◆

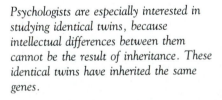 BIRTH ORDER AND INTELLIGENCE

In 1896, Galton observed something intriguing about the effect of the order in which children were born. He noticed that an exceedingly large number of prominent British scientists were firstborn children. Since Galton's time, a number of studies have indicated that firstborn children have a distinct advantage over other children in certain areas of development. Firstborns are more articulate and tend to score higher on intelligence tests than children born later. Firstborns also tend to be more reflective, whereas later children are more impulsive. When dealing with important choices, reflective children tend to examine a number of options and to delay decisions so that they can minimize their errors. Impulsive children, on the other hand, are eager to rush to a solution when dealing with problems (Kagan, 1966). Firstborns also appear to have a greater need to achieve (Sampson, 1962), to be more active (Eaton, Chipperfield, & Singbeil, 1989), and to perform better academically (Altus, 1967). Firstborns are more likely to attend college (Bayer, 1966) and to have high educational aspirations (Falbo, 1981). Interestingly, 21 of the first 23 astronauts to travel into space were firstborn children.

The meaning of these birth-order data is not clear. It may have something to do with the size of the family into which children are born. Perhaps first-

Psychologists are especially interested in studying identical twins, because intellectual differences between them cannot be the result of inheritance. These identical twins have inherited the same genes.

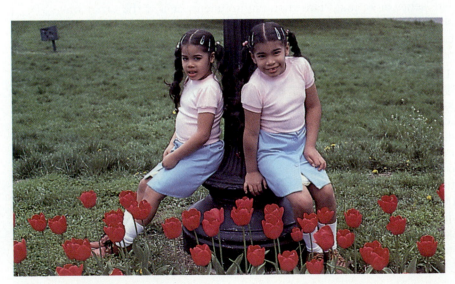

borns enjoy a more stimulating environment than do later children, because firstborns have the undivided attention of both parents. Supporting this interpretation is that firstborns develop language rapidly, while twins develop language at a slower rate, and triplets more slowly still (Davis, 1937). Research has shown that twins tend to be shortchanged in this regard by their parents, because parents don't like to repeat themselves. In other words, a twin is likely to be spoken to less often because parents treat the twins as a unit and do not double their verbal interactions (Lytton, Conway, & Suave, 1977). Because IQ scores reflect verbal skills to a considerable degree, it is not surprising, then, that firstborns tend to have higher IQ scores than second children, that second children also tend to have higher scores than third children, third than fourth, and so on (Zajonc & Markus, 1975) or that children from families with many siblings tend to have lesser verbal skills (Blake, 1989).

Perhaps parents could mitigate these differences if they paid extra attention to their younger children. Still, there may not be great cause for concern, since the difference between firstborns and later children on IQ tests is generally only three or four points, which in practical terms is not very significant. In addition, the fact that firstborns tend to be more successful may be related to many factors other than extra parental attention or stimulation. Larger families, for example, are often of lower socioeconomic status, and later children, on the average, are more likely to be at an economic disadvantage compared with earlier children, in that fewer opportunities can be made available to them. For example, an eighth-born child is far more likely to be a member of a poor family than a rich one, and by a much larger degree than would a firstborn child.

Finally, not all scientists agree that there is a real or significant birth-order effect (Grotevant, Scarr, & Weinberg, 1975). Some researchers have reported finding no birth-order effect (McCall & Johnson, 1972; Galbraith, 1982). Nevertheless, studies that include large samples of subjects generally support the theory that birth order is related to achievement motivation and to IQ test scores (Belmont & Marolla, 1973; Berbaum, Markus, & Zajonc, 1982; Berbaum & Moreland, 1985).

As you can see, the birth-order effect is small—although it is interesting. Unfortunately, in just about any bookstore, you can find books claiming all sorts of fantastic things about birth-order, treating it as though it were destiny itself. The birth order effects described in this text are subtle, and as best we know, these are all that there are (Ernst & Angst, 1983). Books claiming to tell how any individual child will develop based solely on birth order are nonsense.

CULTURE-FAIR TESTING

Any intelligence test that makes use of language is likely to be culturally biased. Consequently, people have attempted to produce language-free, **culture-fair tests** that would be equally difficult for members of any culture. The first such tests generally relied on pictures and nonverbal instructions, but these still tended to favor some cultures. Children in these cultures were simply more familiar with pictures or the requirements of certain tasks (Vernon, 1965). Still, some tests are self-explanatory and do not require pictures of familiar objects. One of the most widely used culture-fair tests is the Raven Progressive Matrices Test. In Figure 13.3, you'll see a sample question from the Raven test. Even without instructions you can understand what is required. But in this test, too, people from cultures in which fill-in or matching exercises are more common may be more likely to do well than people from other cultures. To date, no one test has been developed that is completely culture-fair.

CULTURE-FAIR TEST
A test that is supposed to be free of cultural biases, usually constructed so that language differences and other cultural effects are minimized.

◆ **FIGURE 13.3**

Sample item from the Raven Progressive Matrices Test.

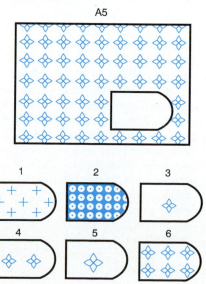

IQ, RACE, AND CULTURE

A serious controversy concerning the heritable aspects of intelligence developed immediately after researcher Arthur Jensen published an article in the 1969 *Harvard Educational Review*. Jensen suggested that the reason whites scored higher than blacks on IQ tests by an average of 15–18 points was probably related more to genetic variables than to the effects of experience. In other words, Jensen was saying that whites were naturally intellectually superior to blacks. The ensuing debates on radio, on television, and in the press were stormy, usually generating more heat than light. Into the middle of all this controversy came William Shockley, a Nobel Prize winner (for coinventing the transistor, not for work related to genetics or psychology), who advocated that blacks be prevented from having too many children so that they would not pass on their inferior genes.

Cultural and Educational Bias

No one disputes that whites score higher than blacks do on IQ tests. But this fact does not necessarily mean that Jensen was right. There are other interpretations. The kinds of observations that Jensen made were not new. In 1912, the U.S. Public Health Service gave the then-new IQ tests to immigrants arriving in New York. It was discovered that 87 percent of Russians, 83 percent of Jews, 80 percent of Hungarians, and 79 percent of Italians were feebleminded. It didn't matter to the supervisor of the testing, Henry Goddard, that many of the immigrants couldn't speak English. He was convinced that the tests were adequately translated to suit the immigrants.

If translated versions of the intelligence tests were administered to the immigrants, why did they score so poorly? Unfortunately, a considerable knowledge of American culture was necessary to score well; 79 percent of the Italians tested were not feebleminded, but rather were ignorant of the answers to culturally biased questions.

When the United States entered the First World War, the army administered the same IQ tests to all inductees. It was at this time that blacks were first tested in large numbers. Their average mental age was only 10.41, just behind recently emigrated Poles (10.74), Italians (11.01), and Russians (11.34). Of all those who were tested, including the recently naturalized immigrants, blacks were the poorest financially and were the least educated. In other words, educational bias may have influenced test scores. Because of inferior schooling, black children may have been less likely than were white children to be exposed to the kinds of strategies and knowledge required by IQ tests. This interpretation, however, was not considered at the time. Instead, the army findings were commonly used to support unfounded racist beliefs that blacks were intellectually inferior. A similar kind of educational bias may explain the fact that Japanese children tend to outscore white American children on IQ tests by about 7 points (Mohs, 1982). Although a few researchers believe that this, too, may

be due to genetic differences, most point to the possible effects of the superior Japanese school system. The effect of schooling cannot be too strongly stated. IQ and schooling go hand in hand: Schooling boosts IQ (Cahan & Cohen, 1989), and IQ predicts school performance mostly because IQ tests are typically filled with the kinds of questions children encounter in school. Supporting this assertion is the interesting finding that the IQs of schoolchildren tend to show a small, but measurable decline just after summer vacation (Ceci, 1991) and typically lose up to 6 IQ points for each year of missed school. Considering that year after year, Japanese schoolchildren spend many more days in school than do their American counterparts, the differences in IQ should not be surprising.

In an effort to shed some light on this issue, psychologist Sandra Scarr gathered data on the IQ scores of black children adopted and raised by white families. Scarr discovered that the younger the black children were at the time of adoption, the closer their scores were to the white IQ averages (Scarr & Weinberg, 1976). Similarly, the IQs of poor children increased when they were adopted by affluent families (Schiff, Duyme, Dumaret, & Tomkiewicz, 1982).

These results strongly suggest that background, experience, and culture can influence a person's knowledge and thought processes as measured by any particular intelligence test. Different cultures teach not only different things but also different ways to think about things. And different cultures require their children to meet different educational standards. As Jerome Kagan once said in reference to two of the best-known IQ tests, "If the Wechsler and Binet scales were translated into Spanish, Swahili, and Chinese and given to every ten-year-old child in Latin America, East Africa, and China, the majority would obtain IQ scores in the mentally retarded range" (1973, p. 89). Of course, these children wouldn't be mentally retarded in the commonly understood sense of the term, but they would be at a disadvantage in taking the tests until they learned to adapt to our culture. In this case, a low IQ score would represent cultural ignorance or lack of education, not lack of intelligence. Any of us would be at the same disadvantage if we took a test developed in another culture.

IQ and School Placement

In the 1970s, the landmark case of Larry P. reached the courts. Larry P. was a student in California who was placed in a special class as a result of his low score on an IQ test. In the court case, *Larry P. v. Wilson Riles*, it was argued that IQ tests should no longer be used to assign students to such "special" classes. Larry's attorney maintained that a disproportionate number of African-Americans such as Larry P., as well as other minority children, had been wrongly assigned to special classes for the mentally retarded because of their IQ scores. In these classes, they were taught little. Furthermore, assignment to such a class stigmatized the students. A federal appeals court agreed, and IQ tests were no longer allowed to be used as a basis for assigning a child to a "special" class. In 1992, California allowed an exception in cases in which parents of a minority child with a learning disability wanted to use an IQ test to aid in special placement.

The case of Larry P. was also somewhat offset by the 1980 ruling of a federal district judge in Illinois in *PASE v. Hannon*. In that case, the judge ruled that IQ tests could still be used to place minority students in special education classes as long as other factors were considered when placing the students. Some researchers believe that by balancing a test to adjust for cultural differences between blacks and whites, an IQ test may be developed that eliminates black-white differences.

The Kaufman Assessment Battery for Children

The Kaufman Assessment Battery for Children (K-ABC) was developed by Alan and Nadeen Kaufman in the early 1980s in part to eliminate black-white differences. While field-testing the K-ABC, the Kaufmans discovered that the test cuts the IQ differences between blacks and whites by 50 percent (to about 7 points) and eliminates the difference between white and Hispanic children. The Kaufmans argue that this is because the test reduces cultural and educational bias.

Initially, there were worries that the design of the K-ABC might result in scores that concealed important differences that should be exposed. In other words, the test might appear to be fairer but in fact might be hiding serious educational deficits displayed by minorities who had been victims of discrimination, poverty, and poorer schools. The K-ABC, however, has been found to correlate well with achievement tests (Childers, Durham, Bolen, & Taylor, 1985; Valencia, 1985), which implies that the K-ABC distinguishes those individuals who have acquired knowledge from those who haven't, while at the same time avoiding a racial bias.

The K-ABC is just now coming into wider use. Eventually, we will be able to judge whether it has actually overcome some of the cultural bias that other tests include.

The Proper Use of Intelligence Tests

Ever since Alfred Binet first began to use intelligence tests to differentiate between normal and dull students in the Paris school system, there has been controversy over whether IQ tests are a valid measure of intelligence:

> Intelligence tests have been under attack practically since their inception (Cronbach, 1975; Haney, 1981). Critics have claimed, among other things, that intelligence and aptitude tests measure nothing but test-taking skills, have little predictive power, are biased against certain racial and economic groups, are used to stigmatize low scorers, and are tools developed and fostered by those in power in order to maintain the status quo. . . . Though perhaps not as apparent as 10 (or 60) years ago, such criticisms remain prevalent (e.g., Gould, 1981; Lewontin, Rose, & Kamin, 1984; Owen, 1985). (Snyderman & Rothman, 1987, p. 137)

The following case study illustrates the problem. Some time ago, when Gregory Ochoa was a high school student in Cal-

ifornia, he and his classmates, most of whom also had Spanish surnames, were given an IQ test. As a result of the testing, Gregory was placed in a special class. Gregory didn't fully realize what had happened. All he knew was that his special class didn't do regular schoolwork. Any class member interested in intellectual pursuits, such as going to the school library, was told that such activities were out of bounds.

Gregory soon dropped out of school. He was sent to reform school, where he received some remedial reading. After finishing reform school, he joined the navy. There Gregory earned high school credits, which eventually enabled him to attend college as a student on probation. In college, he received high grades and graduated with honors—while *still* on probation! He believes he was kept on probation because the college never stopped thinking of him as "retarded." By the time he was 40, Doctor Gregory Ochoa was an assistant professor at the University of Washington in Seattle, where he taught classes in social casework.

Ochoa's problems in school had started when he was given his first IQ test and was placed in a special class for no other reason than that his IQ test score was low. No one considered that cultural differences might have played a role in his low score. He was lucky to have received remedial training—other children with low IQ scores were not so lucky.

Cases like Ochoa's and the court decisions discussed earlier have led many states to give up or strictly limit the use of IQ tests for identifying students or placing them in special education. This, of course, has left the schools with a problem—to find alternative assessment devices that are valid and can indicate the need for special help. These include assessments of the pupil's personal history, adaptive behavior, classroom performance, past academic achievement, and use of instruments designed to point out specific deficits in specific skill areas. Unfortunately, these assessment devices have been shown to be even less valid indicators of future academic achievement than are IQ tests, and psychologists and educators are therefore left with the requirement of identifying pupils in need of special help but with few valid ways of doing so.

In a survey of over 1000 professionals with expertise in intelligence testing, most were found to favor the continued use of intelligence tests at their present level (Snyderman & Rothman, 1987). But the question remains, can the tests be used without being misused? In the words of Gregory Ochoa:

> I think first of all, one would have to ask why you want to know what this person's intellectual capacity is. Are you using it in order to make sure that every horizon available to him is reached, or are you using it to diminish his opportunities or to prove to him, or to oneself, that Blacks, or Chicanos, or other minorities are inherently inferior to others. I think that is the critical issue—what is it being used for? ("The IQ Myth," 1975)

NATURAL SELECTION
The process, first suggested by Charles Darwin, through which those individuals of a species best adapted to their environment have a better chance of passing on their genes to the next generation than do those less well adapted.

KIBBUTZ
An Israeli farm or collective where children are often reared in groups and receive nurturance and guidance from many different adults and older children.

Over the years, however, researchers have tried to eliminate some cultural bias from tests that are given to large and diverse populations. Still, the concept of intelligence remains fairly mysterious. For instance, researcher James Flynn examined IQ scores obtained from 14 nations around the world, all the way from the Netherlands to New Zealand, and discovered that there had been a significant jump in IQ scores from the last generation to the current one, an increase ranging from 5 to 25 points (Flynn, 1987).

No one knows why there should be such an increase. It obviously can't be genetic, because the forces of **natural selection** couldn't have worked such a genetic change in only 30 years. The real surprise was that the greatest gains occurred on the Raven culture-fair test, which is purported to measure intellectual aptitude that is free of cultural bias. The reason this occurred is probably because culture-fair tests aren't culture-fair. One researcher trying to solve this dilemma has argued that so-called culture-fair tests become easier if your culture has provided you with training, as many modern schools do, emphasizing intelligent guessing (which modern students exposed to multiple-choice testing often raise to an art form) and speed of thought (Brand, 1987).

As you can see, although we have learned a great deal, the factors that influence IQ or intelligence are still far from understood.

THE EFFECTS OF ENVIRONMENTAL STIMULATION

One way to assess environmental influences on intellectual development is to alter the environment on purpose and then observe the effect on IQ scores. Ethically, of course, it's proper to create only a stimulating environment in the hopes of raising IQ scores.

Project Head Start was designed in the 1960s to help disadvantaged preschool children do better in school as they grew older. At first, research results from the Westinghouse Learning Corporation and researchers at Ohio State University indicated that Head Start was making little difference in the long-term intellectual development of children enrolled in it. However, researchers David P. Weikart and Lawrence J. Schweinhart released an interim report in 1980 on an 18-year study of the progress of 123 children at Perry Elementary School in Ypsilanti, Michigan, which indicated that good-quality preschool education programs do benefit the disadvantaged. The Ypsilanti Project offered 12½ hours per week of education at ages 3 and 4 years, plus 90-minute weekly home visits. Children in the enrichment program scored higher on reading, math, and language achievement tests than did those in the control group. They also showed fewer antisocial and delinquent tendencies (Williams & King, 1980a).

An executive report released in 1986 noted that although it was not known whether all Head Start programs in the United States were producing beneficial results, such results could be achieved if the programs were adequately funded and the teachers were well trained and competent (Schweinhart & Weikart, 1986). Among the benefits are

improved intellectual performance during early childhood; better scholastic placement and improved scholastic achievement during the elementary school years; and, during adolescence, a lower rate of delinquency and higher rates of both graduation from high school and employment at age 19. (Schweinhart & Weikart, 1985, p. 547)

A 20-year follow-up study of children from two American cities who were enrolled in Head Start, preschool, or no school during the school year 1969–70 showed that although the value gained from Head Start had diminished over the years, some benefit was still observed. The benefit gained, however, was

Psychologists hope that by providing stimulating environments for children during their early years, handicaps associated with being raised in underprivileged or unstimulating environments might be overcome.

somewhat comparable to the long-term value of preschools in general. The long-term benefits were obvious when children who had had Head Start were compared with those who had had no school during that year, and this was especially true of members from the lowest socioeconomic group (Lee, Brooks-Gunn, Schnur, & Liaw, 1990).

Other programs like the Ypsilanti Project have also been effective (Gray & Ruttle, 1980; van Doorninck, Caldwell, Wright, & Frankenburg, 1981). A notable example of institutional enrichment can be found in Israel, where children of European Jewish heritage have an average IQ of 105, while those of a Middle Eastern Jewish heritage have an average IQ of only 85. Yet when raised on a **kibbutz,** children from both groups have an average IQ of 115.

Early intervention projects have not been uniformly successful. Depending on the program, how it is implemented, and the population that receives the intervention, early intervention may produce many different outcomes. Programs with a high academic content are generally the most successful in producing increases in IQ and achievement (Miller & Dyer, 1975; Stallings, 1975). Special programs aren't always required to give an intellectual boost, however. For example, good-quality day-care has been found to improve the intellectual development of socioeconomically disadvantaged children (Burchinal, Lee, & Ramey, 1989).

In summary, there is no clear-cut way to predict whether early intervention will be effective. Many programs claim success, but their work is often hard to assess because the criteria they use to define success and to define which children are needy often differ (Scarr & McCartney, 1988). The general consensus appears to be that early intervention can have lasting and valuable effects (Lazar & Darlington, 1982; Casto & Mastropieri, 1986), but there is no guarantee for any given program with any given group of children (Ramey, 1982; Woodhead, 1988).

✖ INTELLECTUAL CHANGES OVER TIME

Problems arise when IQ tests are used to measure intellectual changes during a lifespan. In the 1930s, Nancy Bayley developed a test called the Bayley Mental and Motor Scale to evaluate infants' intellectual and motor skills. Interestingly, subjects who were measured by the Bayley test when they were 9 months of age often had very different IQs when they were retested at 5 years of age by the Stanford-Binet IQ Test. In fact, the correlation between

TABLE 13.2 ◆ CORRELATION BETWEEN INFANT'S IQ SCORES AT VARIOUS AGES WITH THEIR SCORES AT 5 YEARS

AGE (IN MONTHS)	CORRELATION COEFFICIENT BETWEEN SCORES FOR THE SAME SUBJECTS AT 5 YEARS OF AGE
3	.008
6	−.065
9	−.001
12	.055
18	.231
24	.450

SOURCE: Adapted from Anderson, 1939.

the two IQ scores was zero (Anderson, 1939), indicating that the infants' IQ scores at 9 months of age on the one test were totally unrelated to their IQ scores at 5 years on the other test. Table 13.2 shows the correlations between the children's scores at various ages with those at 5 years.

The correlation between 9 months and 5 years was virtually zero because tests given at different ages often measure different abilities. Tests for very young children and infants generally emphasize motor skills, whereas tests for older children tend to emphasize verbal and cognitive skills. Yet both are said to measure intelligence.

A number of other tests were then designed to assess infants' intellectual development. They included the Griffiths Test of the Abilities of Babies (Griffiths, 1954), the Cattell Test of the Measurement of Intelligence of Infants and Young Children (Cattell, 1966), and the Bayley Scales of Infant Development (Bayley, 1969). Like the Bayley Mental and Motor Scale, these tests all failed significantly to predict what the IQs would be once the children reached school age (McGowan, Johnson, & Maxwell, 1981). Although such tests have some limited utility for describing the infant's current state, they simply cannot predict intellectual changes over a long time.

As Figure 13.4 shows, not until children are about 10 years old do IQ scores tend to become consistent over time or reliable. This means that IQ scores obtained from children younger than 10 years may not be reliable; the scores may change considerably as the children grow up.

Psychologists have wondered if it might not be possible to develop an infant IQ test that would produce scores that would correlate well with later intellectual performance. But without some common denominator that could be measured in infancy and would also relate to IQ in childhood, such a test would not be possible. And for a long time, it was believed that no such denominator was likely to be found. Slowly, however, this view has begun to change (DiLalla et al., 1990).

◆ **FIGURE 13.4**

Correlations between children's IQ scores at various ages and their IQ scores at maturity, according to several studies. (SOURCE: *Bloom, 1964.*)

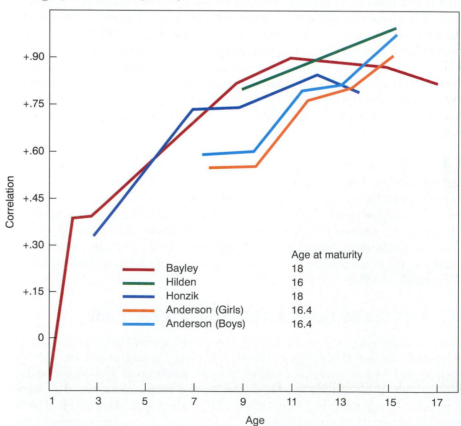

	Age at maturity
Bayley	18
Hilden	16
Honzik	18
Anderson (Girls)	16.4
Anderson (Boys)	16.4

For example, in one study, 4-month-old infants were given both repetitive and new sounds to listen to. An intelligence score was developed based on how easily they recognized a new stimulus (measured by change in heart rate) and how quickly they came to recognize a repeated stimulus as familiar. The children were followed until they were 5 years old and were then given the Stanford-Binet IQ Test. The correlation was an impressive +.60 (O'Connor, Cohen, & Parmelee, 1984), implying that 36 percent of the variables responsible for one test score (the auditory discrimination) were also responsible for the score on the Stanford-Binet at 5 years of age (.60 × .60 = .36, or 36 percent). It was assumed that in this instance, a basic memory skill had been tapped.

Similar results have been obtained with the use of a visual habituation test developed by Joseph Fagan (see Figure 13.5) (Rose, Feldman, & Wallace, 1988). This test appears to be most useful with infants who are deemed at risk for retardation due to premature birth or other reasons. This test was used on 128 infants between 3 and 7 months of age, who were then retested with the Stanford-Binet at age 3 years. Fagan discovered that he was able to correctly predict 101 of the 104 children whose IQs would be within the normal range by age 3 and also predict fully half of the infants whose scores would be in the retarded range by that age (Bower, 1988). The test may also be able to predict certain memory and language abilities that are relatively independent of IQ (Thompson, Fagan, & Fulker, 1991).

Overall, studies are finding that infant habituation tests are able to predict childhood IQ with some success. In general, infant habituation tests correlate with childhood IQ at roughly +.36 by age 8 or 9 (McCall & Carriger, 1993).

Terman's Study

In 1921, psychologist Lewis Terman received a grant from New York City to conduct an extended longitudinal study of children with IQs above 140. Terman selected his 1528 subjects from grade schools in California. Their average IQ was 150, and 80 of them possessed IQs of 170 or higher (Terman, 1925). Follow-up studies were conducted in 1922, 1927–28, 1939–40, 1951–52, 1960, 1972, 1977, and 1982. Terman strongly believed that intelligence, or giftedness, was an inherited quality. In fact, during his life, he often turned a blind eye toward any evidence that there was also a strong environmental component to IQ (Cravens, 1992). Even so, his data do tell us a lot about men who have high IQs.

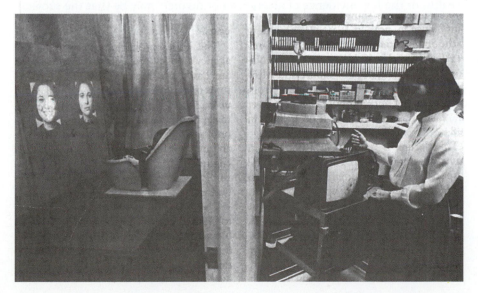

◆ **FIGURE 13.5**

The baby in this photograph is looking at pictures of two faces. One of those faces he has seen before; the other is new. The researcher is measuring how long the baby looks at each of the faces. Babies who spend less time looking at the familiar face tend to have higher scores on intelligence tests when they reach school age.

Lewis Terman (1877–1956).

Because few women were encouraged to seek professions during the 1920s, most of the follow-up studies of professional accomplishments concentrated on the approximately 800 men in the original selection. This is not to say that the Terman women didn't choose professions; many of them did, but there were few professional women in the average general population with whom to compare them. By 1950, at an average age of 40 years, the men had written and published 67 books, over 1400 articles, and 200 plays and short stories; they had obtained over 150 patents; 78 of them had received a Ph.D., 48 an M.D., and 85 an L.L.B.; 74 were university professors, and 47 were listed in *American Men of Science*. As Terman noted, "The number who became research scientists, engineers, physicians, lawyers, or college teachers, or who were highly successful in business and other fields, is in each case many times the number a random group would have provided" (1954, p. 41).

Among the Terman women, there were also some surprises. According to Pauline Sears, who reviewed the data, the Terman women

were way ahead of several trends that have only lately become true for the nation as a whole. They were quicker to join the work force. They took longer to marry and have children, and more were childless. A high proportion were in managerial positions; I suspect that because they were bright, they got ahead faster. Their brightness made another intriguing difference: the divorced women among them were happier than most, at least on our measure of satisfaction with their work pattern. Almost all divorced women worked full time, and their work was satisfying to them. The same was true of the women who remained single. All of them worked, and they were much happier with their work than most women are. Their satisfaction wasn't from income, either, but from the work itself. (Sears quoted in Goleman, 1980, p. 44)

Pauline Sears's late husband, Robert Sears, was in charge of overseeing the Terman study. Robert Sears was formerly head of the psychology department at Harvard and was dean of Stanford University. He was also one of the 1528 children in Terman's original study (Goleman, 1980).

The Terman "kids" are now in their late 70s and early 80s, and compared with the average person of that age, they are healthier, happier, and richer; they have had a far lower incidence of suicide, alcoholism, and divorce. These studies also dispel the myth that genius is next to insanity, since few of the Terman subjects have suffered from serious behavioral disorders compared with the average populace.

A possible reason for correlations between high IQ scores, happiness, and wealth, or the low incidence of alcoholism or divorce, may be that the subjects in Terman's study stayed in school (probably because they were good at it, which is what a high IQ would indicate). If you stay in school long enough and do well, you're likely to obtain an advanced degree. And generally, if you have an advanced degree, you'll earn more money. People who are richer tend to be happier (perhaps that doesn't surprise you). If you are better educated, wealthier, and happier, you probably can afford better medical care, are more aware of how to take good care of yourself, and are under less stress. Finally, happier people get divorced less often.

With these results in mind, one researcher studied 26 of Terman's subjects who had IQs of 180 or higher and compared them with 26 randomly selected subjects from the rest of Terman's sample to see if this group did even better than the typical Terman subject. But the differences turned out to be negligible (Feldman, 1984). This finding helps to emphasize that extra IQ points needn't make an important difference, at least at the upper end of the scale. What did seem to make a difference for Terman's "kids" is that they all were at the upper end of the IQ spectrum.

⁂ MAINSTREAMING THE INTELLECTUALLY HANDICAPPED

If we consider intelligence not as a quality that is solely the result of inheritance but rather as a fluid and changing group of abilities sensitive to environmental effects, then our understanding of bright and dull, superior or retarded, must change (see Table 13.3).

How many times have you tangled with your own intellect? Sometimes it lets you down, sometimes it doesn't. Does this make you bright, average, dull? At one time or another, every child and every adult will face some failure of intellect. Occasionally, incapable adults are left to fend for themselves (which may have unfortunate consequences). But what should we do with incapable children? If they can't match their school peers, should we label them "learning disabled" or "mentally handicapped" and send them for "special" education?

How many Gregory Ochoas have been improperly labeled, have dropped out of school, and, unlike Gregory, have been unable to save themselves? On the other hand, some children do have serious problems that are more than occasional and that clearly require special help; we certainly can't abandon all testing and ignore them.

In 1975, Public Law 94–142 was enacted by the U.S. Congress to deal, in part, with the fact that too many children were not being given the education to which they were entitled; instead, they were being labeled and isolated, usually as a result of a single test or because they had a physical or social-emotional handicap. In an attempt to change this unfortunate trend, Public Law 94–142 stipulated that the least restrictive educational environment be provided to meet all handicapped children's needs. This is sometimes referred to as **mainstreaming,** because every effort is made to keep the child within the regular academic class.

The results of this law aren't as clear-cut as its language. As with early intervention programs, the outcome seems to depend on the type of mainstreaming program used. In some cases, students who have been exposed to both mainstreaming and special education perform at about the same level in both environments (Semmel, Gottlieb, & Robinson, 1979). But in cases where the school district, the teachers, and the parents support mainstreaming, and the students are selected with care, then mainstreaming can be successful (Madden & Slavin, 1983).

A good example of the effects of mainstreaming on the intellectually handicapped can be found in children with Down syndrome. **Down syndrome** is one of the most common birth defects and is the leading cause of mental retardation in the United States. Children born with Down syndrome often are severely mentally handicapped. They are also commonly born with a constellation of other physical defects. In the past, many physicians told parents there was little hope of an intellectual life for these children. In some cases, physicians have even shown considerable ignorance:

When Mindie Crutcher was born, physicians said she would always be hopelessly retarded, that she would never sit up, never walk, never speak. "She will never know you're her mother," they told 25-year-old Diane Crutcher. "Tell relatives your baby is dead." Today, the child who would never sit up is a lively seventh-grader. The child who would never walk is the star of dance recitals. The child who would never talk or know her own mother told a symposium of physicians she was "glad Mom and Dad gave me a chance." (Turkington, 1987, p. 42)

Children with Down syndrome have posed a particular challenge for mainstreaming programs, perhaps because it was so commonly believed that these children were capable of very little, but this challenge has been met by some

---

MAINSTREAMING
The philosophy of keeping as many exceptional children within the regular classroom as possible.

DOWN SYNDROME
A chromosomal abnormality that manifests itself in such features as a thick tongue, extra eyelid folds, and heart deformities, as well as deficient intelligence. It is most often caused by the development of a third chromosome on the 21st chromosome pair.

TABLE 13.3 ◆ IQ SCORES AND THEIR RESPECTIVE CATEGORY LABELS*

SCORE	CATEGORY
130+	Very superior
120–129	Superior
110–119	Bright normal
90–109	Average
80–89	Dull normal
70–79	Borderline retarded**
50–69	Mildly retarded (educable)
35–49	Moderately retarded (trainable)
20–34	Severely retarded
below 20	Profoundly retarded (custodial)

*Based on category labels in the Wechsler Adult Intelligence Scale and the American Psychiatric Association's *Diagnostic and Statistical Manual—IV*.
**Scores that determine retardation categories may vary from state to state.

successful mainstreaming programs. Earlier, many children born with Down syndrome were institutionalized because physicians and parents often believed that education could not possibly help. But after Public Law 94–142 was passed, many Down syndrome children were given educational opportunities for the first time. One institutionalized girl (with a rarer and less severe form of Down syndrome), who began educational training as a result of the law, received a 2-year associate's degree in early childhood education from the University of Maine (Turkington, 1987).

Researchers now believe that the *majority* of children born with Down syndrome "who are reared at home in middle- or upper-middle class families can be expected to be educable when they enter school" (Turkington, 1987, p. 44). Psychologist John Rynders and his colleagues at the University of Minnesota designed Project EDGE to improve communication skills in children with Down syndrome. The children with Down syndrome entered Project EDGE when they were 30 months old. Seven of the 13 children in the project are currently in educable classes or in a combination of regular and educable classes. In 1984, a follow-up study of 13 EDGE children found that 11 of them were reading with comprehension at or above second-grade level (Turkington, 1987), a far cry from being "hopelessly retarded, never able to sit up, never able to walk, never able to speak." In 1986, the U.S. Congress passed Public Law 99–457, which was designed to provide early intervention for handicapped children. This extension to Public Law 94–142 encouraged states to begin helping handicapped children from birth, perhaps preparing these children for future regular schooling, as did Project EDGE.

CONCEPT REVIEW ◆ INTELLIGENCE

What the Lay Public often Believes:

1. An IQ does not change. Intelligence is something that you either have or don't have.
2. An IQ test tells how intelligent you are.
3. All IQ tests will give you roughly the same score.
4. An IQ test given to a child will tell you how smart he will be when he grows up.
5. IQ tests are good instruments for placing children in special programs.

What the Professionals Know:

1. A person's IQ score may change considerably during her lifetime. Intelligence isn't just something you are born with. The behaviors that we consider to be indicative of intelligence often can be taught or improved through experience.
2. "Intelligence" is a poorly defined term. IQ tests are limited and generally test for the kinds of skills that are helpful for school achievement. They often fail to measure creativity and other important skills that we usually consider to be signs of intelligence (for example, although someone might receive a very low IQ test score, she might show impressive survival skills in her own environment—she might be "street smart").
3. One person's IQ test scores may vary, sometimes widely, from one test to the next, depending on the skills and attributes tested.
4. IQ tests given to people when they are children generally are unreliable predictors of the people's scores as adults.
5. IQ tests are valuable instruments for placing children in special classes. However, the tests are sometimes poorly administered or interpreted; cultural or environmental circumstances may yield a low score for a child who has normal potential. For this reason, a score on an IQ test should never be the sole reason for placing a child in a special class.

The main concern about mainstreaming has centered around whether handicapped children will be accepted by the normal children in the regular classroom. Two Australian studies, carried out to examine both the academic and the social progress of children with Down syndrome in the regular classroom, demonstrated that most of the children were well accepted by their peers (Hudson & Clunies-Ross, 1984; Pieterse & Center, 1984). All the handicapped children in these studies had attended some form of early intervention program, such as Project EDGE, and then had been mainstreamed into the regular classroom. These studies emphasize that even though children with mental handicaps may require some form of special intervention or help, they can also do well, if given the chance—and mainstreaming is one way to help them fulfill their potential. Mainstreaming also gives children in the regular classroom the opportunity to learn compassion, tolerance, and understanding and, even more important, to learn about the special potentials of handicapped children.

◆ CREATIVITY

Individual differences in intellectual capacity are not the only characteristics that have attracted interest in recent years. Psychologists are also concerned about the development of **creativity.** One researcher pointed out:

Some of the controversy about the concept of creativity surrounds the question of the extent to which it is a personality trait, a specific cognitive ability, or a type of problem-solving strategy that might be learned (Michael, 1977). If it is the latter, there is less need to search for those who know the process than to teach the process to everyone. (Fox, 1981, p. 1108)

Defining *creativity* is difficult, but we all seem to have some idea of what it means. Look at the picture in Figure 13.6 and decide what it is. A fairly common but rather uncreative answer is that it looks like a broken window. But what if someone told you that it was a boat arriving too late to save a drowning witch? That's a more creative response.

One way of defining creativity is to apply the four criteria of *novelty, appropriateness, transcendence of constraints,* and *coalescence of meaning* (Jackson & Messick, 1968). Novel, of course, means new. Something creative should be new. However, spelling *cat* Q-R-S would be new but it wouldn't be appropriate. Jackson and Messick therefore included appropriateness as a necessary dimension. Something transcends constraints when it goes beyond the traditional. A creative idea may transcend constraints by lending a new perspective to something with which we are all familiar. Finally, the most creative ideas have meanings that coalesce over time. In other words, the depth and value of an extremely creative idea often are not apparent at first, but become more obvious as time passes. When Thomas Edison first developed the motion-picture projector, many people wondered why the great genius was wasting his time on something of so little value. It was only after some time that the full significance of the invention became apparent.

High creative ability is poorly predicted by IQ tests. Individuals with very similar IQs often differ considerably in their creativity (Torrance & Wu, 1981). This failure of IQ tests to predict creativity was investigated by Guilford and his colleagues in 1957. They believed that IQ tests typically measure a kind of intelligence different from that required for creativity. Two of the factors Guilford mentioned in his model of the intellect were **convergent production** and **divergent production.** Guilford argued that most IQ tests rely heavily on convergent production, in which people search their knowledge for all that they can find to help them converge on one correct answer. In divergent

CREATIVITY
The ability to originate something new and appropriate by transcending common thought constraints.

CONVERGENT PRODUCTION
In J. P. Guilford's model of intelligence, a type of thinking in which an individual searches through his or her knowledge and uses all that can be found to converge upon one correct answer.

DIVERGENT PRODUCTION
In Guilford's model of intelligence, a type of thinking in which a person searches for multiple ideas or solutions to a problem. It is characteristic of the creative thought process.

◆ **FIGURE 13.6**

What do you see?

Artistic creativity is not measured by IQ tests. Individuals with very similar IQs often differ considerably in their creativity.

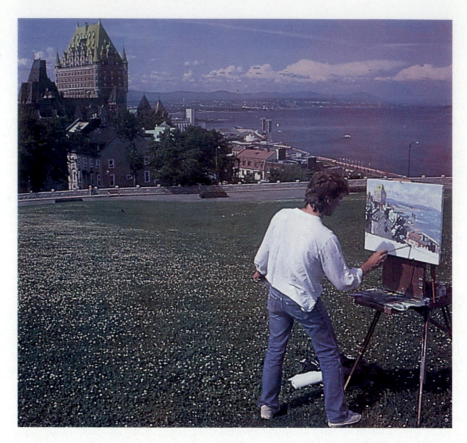

production, they use their knowledge to develop as many solutions as possible to a given problem. Figure 13.7 illustrates the difference between these two thought processes. Creativity, Guilford believes, relies more on divergent production (Guilford, 1983). If Guilford's view is accurate, then the ability to see many solutions to one problem is very different from the ability to develop one correct answer from a store of information.

Both thinking skills appear to be acquired, at least in part, through experience. In one study, 3- and 4-year-old children were given convergent games to play: blocks that had to be inserted into particular forms cut from a board. These children spent two-thirds of their time placing the pieces into the forms on the board. Another group of children, the divergent group, played with blocks only. Using the different block pieces, they engaged in a wide variety of activities. A third group, a control group, did not partake in either the convergent or the divergent games. After the play period, the divergent group performed better than did the other two groups on new divergent tasks,

◆ **FIGURE 13.7**

Illustrations of divergent and convergent production.

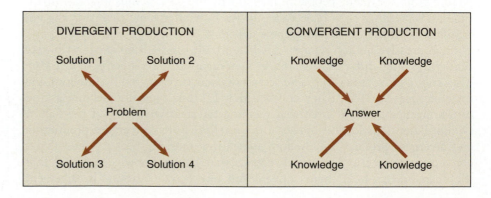

whereas the convergent group performed better than the other two on new convergent tasks (Pepler & Ross, 1981).

Some tests have been designed to predict creativity by measuring divergent production. One such test, described by Michael Wallach (1970), employs the concept of ideational fluency. **Ideational fluency** is the ability to develop a large number of ideas appropriate to a particular task. To measure ideational fluency, researchers might ask someone to name as many uses as possible for a common object such as a cork or a shoe or to point out all the similarities between a train and a tractor. People with high ideational fluency produce many answers. Divergent production tests such as this one are much more accurate in their predictions of creativity than are IQ tests. In a study of almost 500 college students (Wallach & Wing, 1969), researchers found that ideational fluency correlated well with creative attainments such as receiving prizes in science contests, publishing original writing, or exhibiting artwork. Like IQ test scores, ideational fluency scores among older children appear to be fairly stable over time (Kogan & Pankove, 1972).

IDEATIONAL FLUENCY
A term used by Michael Wallach to describe an individual's ability to produce many ideas. Ideational fluency is sometimes used as a measure of creativity. It correlates poorly with average or above average IQ.

 ## SOME FINAL THOUGHTS ON INTELLIGENCE

Biology is not democratic. Some of us are tall, some of us are short, and some of us are no doubt better biologically organized to develop skills considered indicators of intelligence. Inheritance is important. Yet, as the Head Start Project showed, intelligence (or whatever it is that our "intelligence" tests measure) can be dramatically affected by the environment. Intelligence might best be considered a complex interaction between genetic heritage and experience. The Terman subjects probably did well in school, and therefore did well on IQ tests, which ask academic types of questions, both because they inherited excellent brains and nervous systems and also because they were stimulated at home and school to learn and to develop their cognitive and intellectual skills.

SUMMARY

◆ The first scientific interest in intelligence and intelligence testing can be traced to the inheritance theories of Sir Francis Galton.

◆ In the modern view, intelligence is an interaction between inherited capacity and environmental influences.

◆ In 1905, Alfred Binet and Theodore Simon developed the precursor to the modern intelligence test. Its purpose was to determine which Parisian schoolchildren should receive special education.

◆ Binet developed the concept of mental age, or MA. By comparing mental age with chronological age, CA, Binet was able to make comparisons among children. The German psychologist L. William Stern developed the formula MA/CA $\times$ 100 = IQ, which yielded a rough index of how bright or dull any child was compared with school peers.

◆ Although we have IQ tests, intelligence itself has never been defined adequately, and there is controversy over whether these tests measure intelligence as most people use the term.

◆ A test is said to be valid if it measures what it claims to measure. IQ tests have been found to be valid for predicting school performance and as tools in clinical assessment.

◆ The amount of weight or emphasis given to any one ability measured on a test is called a factor load. Some IQ tests measure particular factors more than others do. For this reason, the same individual may score differently on different IQ tests.

◆ To balance a test for factors so that each ability is tested only once, L. L. Thurstone advocated use of a technique called factor analysis.

◆ According to Thurstone and other factor analysts, there is no general ability called intelligence; rather, there are many different kinds of intelligence. The debate over this issue continues today.

◆ Psychologist Robert J. Sternberg has developed a triarchic theory of intelligence that includes componential intelligence (the cognitive problem-solving and information-processing skills measured by most IQ tests), contextual intelligence (the individual's ability to adapt to her environment), and experiential intelligence (how quickly one can make a newly learned skill routine).

◆ Psychologists have studied the heritability of human intelligence and other characteristics by examining people who are related to one another. Based on current data, many psychologists agree that heredity does play a role in determining individual differences and intelligence. How important it is in comparison with environmental experiences has yet to be determined.

◆ In 1896, Sir Francis Galton observed that firstborn children appear to have a distinct advantage over other children in certain areas of development. Firstborns are more articulate, tend to score higher on intelligence tests, and are more reflective than children born later. However, not all scientists agree that there is a significant birth-order effect.

◆ According to researcher Arthur Jensen, the fact that whites average 15–18 points higher than blacks on IQ tests was mainly the result of genetic variables. Other people argue that cultural bias on the tests accounts for the discrepancy.

◆ In one study, Scarr and Weinberg gathered data on the IQ scores of black children adopted by white families. They discovered that the younger the black children were at the time of adoption, the closer their IQs were to white IQ averages.

◆ Attempts have been made to devise a culture-fair test, one that contains no cultural bias. However, even on tests that do not use language, an advantage will go to people from cultures incorporating any types of skills or activities required by the test.

◆ The Ypsilanti Project and home-based early intervention projects have generally been successful in raising the intellectual levels of the children who participated.

◆ Intellectual changes are difficult to measure over time. Tests measure different skills in subjects of different ages, and as a result reliability is not always high.

◆ Lewis Terman conducted a study that has surveyed gifted children for over 60 years and is still in progress. The Terman kids are now in their 70s and 80s, and, compared with the average person of that age, they are healthier, happier, and richer, and they have a far lower incidence of suicide, alcoholism, and divorce.

◆ Jackson and Messick have judged creativity by four criteria—novelty, appropriateness, transcendence of constraints, and coalescence of meaning. High creativity correlates poorly with high IQ scores.

◆ Some tests have been designed to predict creativity by measuring divergent production, the search for multiple solutions to a problem. One such test, described by Michael Wallach, employs the concept of ideational fluency, or an individual's ability to produce many ideas.

SUGGESTIONS FOR FURTHER READING

1. Anastasi, A. (1988). *Psychological testing* (6th ed.). New York: Macmillan. A college-level text that evaluates psychological tests, including intelligence tests.

2. Chapman, P. D. (1988). *Schools as sorters: Lewis M. Terman, applied psychology, and the intelligence testing movement. 1890–1930.* New York: New York University Press. This book helps describe the age into which Terman's ideas so neatly fit. It also deals with Terman's student, Kimball Young, and how he encountered the misuse of intelligence tests to improperly label Hispanic children as retarded, an experience that led him to reject Galton's idea of inherited intelligence, which had been embraced by Terman.

3. Fancher, R. E. (1985). *The intelligence men: Makers of the I.Q. controversy.* New York: Norton. A discussion of the history and controversies involved in intelligence testing.

4. Lazar, I., & Darlington, R. (1982). *Lasting effects of early education: A report from the Consortium for Longitudinal Studies.* Monographs of the Society for Research in Child Development, 47(2-3, Serial No. 195). A monograph that evaluates the effects of early childhood education on children at risk for learning problems.

5. Lewontin, R. C., Rose, S., & Kamin, L. J. (1984). *Not in our genes.* New York: Pantheon Books. A politically motivated discussion of the genetic determinants of traits, including intelligence. Presents the view that IQ is largely determined by environmental variables.

6. Minton, H. L. (1988). *Lewis M. Terman: Pioneer in psychological testing.* New York: New York University Press. An interesting book that chronicles the personal circumstances surrounding the emergence of Terman's work.

7. Sternberg, R. J. (1986). *Intelligence applied: Understanding and increasing your intellectual skills.* New York: Harcourt Brace Jovanovich. Provides a general overview of the ways in which people can be intelligent and how that intelligence can be increased.

8. Terman, L. M., & Oden, M. H. (1959). *The gifted group at midlife.* Palo Alto, CA: Stanford University Press. Reports on Terman's longitudinal study of gifted children, including their achievements and adjustments.

Chapter Fourteen

Personality

PROLOGUE

AS THE TWIG IS BENT

As the Second World War entered its final months in Asia, thousands of Japanese living in a captured part of China called Manchuria were forced to flee from the advancing Russian army. Attacked by angry Chinese, suffering from extreme hunger and cold weather, Japanese parents were often forced to leave their children behind. They did this to save the children from the hardships of the escape or because the adults could not flee quickly enough with the children in tow. As a result, over 2500 Japanese children were left behind, usually with childless Chinese couples who offered to adopt them and raise them as their own.

After the war, the Japanese parents were unable to look for their children because of the Chinese civil war and the closing off of contact with Japan following the rise of Mao-tse Tung. It wasn't until 1981, 36 years after the war had ended, that the Japanese government was able to persuade the Chinese government to facilitate contact between the war orphans and their parents.

By this time, most of the "orphans" were middle-aged and had Chinese spouses and teenage children of their own. Still, almost all of them took the opportunity to travel with their families to Japan to search for their Japanese parents and relatives. Relying mostly on memories of their family names and locations, they began the search. Of those who were older than 9 at the time of separation, 77.5 percent were reunited with their families. Of those who were younger than 5, whose memories were less complete, only 31.3 percent were successful (Tseng, Ebata, Miguchi, Egawa, & McLaughlin, 1990).

As the orphans' search became news, both Japanese researchers in Tokyo and American researchers in Hawaii realized that it presented the chance of a lifetime for anyone interested in studying personality and its formation. These researchers were interested because they knew that distinct cultures encourage different characteristics or personality traits in their members. There are well-described differences between Japanese and Chinese culture (Doi, 1962; Lebra, 1976; Yang, 1986).

The researchers wondered if the orphans would have retained a higher proportion of the traits most encouraged by Japanese culture, such as those

CONTENTS

PERSONALITY
The organization of relatively enduring characteristics unique to an individual, as revealed by the individual's interaction with his or her environment.

concerned with interpersonal relations, temperament, attitudes toward work, manners, and habits, than would be expected to be found among the Chinese. Or would living in China for all those years have lessened the expression of traits more typical of Japanese culture? In other words, they were asking an old question, "How much of personality is formed in childhood?" This was a unique chance to find out.

To their surprise, the "orphans" retained many of the attitudes and personality characteristics more common to the Japanese, even though many had been exposed to Japanese culture for less than 7 years of their 40 plus years of life. This finding does suggest that personality traits may be strengthened early in life and then remain fairly resistant to change thereafter (Tseng, Ebata, Miguchi, Egawa, & McLaughlin, 1990). Because of this research, the old adage "As the twig is bent, so grows the tree" takes on greater importance.

Although the researchers didn't rule out genetic influences (especially where temperament was concerned—see Chapter 3), many studies of adopted infants from other cultures show the environment to be a forceful molder of personality. This study, however, was the first chance to investigate a large group of children raised for a few years in one culture and then transferred to another for the remainder of their childhoods and many years of their adulthoods. That the initial effect of the first culture could be seen so clearly so many years later tells us something about childhood as a special time of personality formation.

IN THIS CHAPTER, we'll examine what personality is and how it is assessed. We'll look at personality from the viewpoint of trait theorists, psychoanalysts, behaviorists, and humanists. Each position takes a different view of personality and has made an important contribution to our understanding of personality.

WHY PSYCHOLOGISTS STUDY PERSONALITY

Psychology is the study of behavior. If any behavior were as likely as any other to occur at any given time, it would not be possible to develop a science of psychology. Behavior would be so random that it could not be predicted. But behavior isn't that way. People often are consistent; they reveal qualities in their behavior that can be relied on. You already know this about yourself, your friends, and your family. You know that some people are almost sure to be shy in a particular circumstance, while others probably will be aggressive or outgoing and warm. You've learned to count on certain behaviors from certain people. To a psychologist, this means that the behaviors have predictability, which is the essence of any science.

By assuming that an individual will act in a certain way, we are implying that we know something about that individual's **personality.** Personality is a certain consistency in a person's behavior that remains fairly stable under varying conditions. In fact, when someone does something inconsistent, we often say, "He acted like a different person."

Psychologists wonder whether personality is internally or externally governed or perhaps is controlled by a combination of factors. Is personality shaped primarily by environmental (external) forces? If it is, it will change drastically if the environment changes drastically. If, on the other hand, personality is subject to internal controls, then altering the environment drastically may have less effect. Psychologists want to find out how stable personalities are and what controls them.

THEORIES OF PERSONALITY

To a psychologist, the word *personality* refers to the whole person, not just to a part. Personality encompasses intelligence, motivation, emotion, learning, abnormality, cognition, and even social interactions. In describing someone's personality, you might refer to any of these areas. You might say that someone is intelligent, friendly, good humored, and eager to learn. Although these are different aspects of one person, they add up to a description of personality.

There are many theories of personality, each with a different emphasis and explanation of why certain personalities develop. Like all theories, personality theories should be testable, so that we can create a science of personality. A solid theory of personality would be valuable, because it could be used to assess people and to guide them toward the endeavors to which they are suited. Certain personalities may be suited for certain kinds of work. Other personalities may signal future trouble in the same work. Haven't you ever questioned whether your personality was right for a particular job or was well matched with another person's for a successful marriage, business relationship, or friendship? All of us have wondered at one time or another whether we wouldn't benefit from a change in personality. Imagine how useful it would be if personality could be measured, so that we could choose the lifestyles for which we were best suited and that would enable us to lead the most productive lives. This is the applied goal of all personality theory.

Historically, investigators of personality have attempted to group people into types. This seems a straightforward approach. Other sciences began in the same way. Chemistry has classified the elements according to type, and physics has classified matter and energy according to type. Similarly, personality researchers have been interested in grouping people according to their behavioral differences.

Personality Types

One of the earliest attempts to categorize people by type of personality was made by the Greek physician Hippocrates (460–377 B.C.). Hippocrates classified people into four personality types: *melancholic* (sad), *phlegmatic* (listless and tired), *sanguine* (content or optimistic), and *choleric* (easy to anger). With his limited understanding of biology, he believed that these different personality types were caused by one or more of four body fluids he called *humors*. He concluded that a melancholic temperament was the result of too much black bile, a phlegmatic temperament was the result of too much phlegm, a sanguine temperament was the result of too much blood, and a choleric temperament was the result of too much yellow bile. Of course, modern medicine has disproved these ideas, but they are interesting attempts to correlate behavior and physical state.

Among the modern theories of personality types, one developed by the American physician William Sheldon has received considerable attention. Sheldon found a moderate correlation between physique (body type) and personality (Sheldon 1940; 1944). Figure 14.1 illustrates the three physiques— **endomorph, mesomorph,** and **ectomorph.** Sheldon measured subjects according to 7-point scales for each of the three dimensions. For instance, a person who rated 2, 5, and 7 would be low on endomorphy, moderate on mesomorphy, and extremely high on ectomorphy. Table 14.1 outlines the kinds of personality characteristics that Sheldon believed were correlated with the three body types.

Why should different personalities have been found to be associated with different body types? Some researchers, in an effort to explain Sheldon's findings, have argued that physique and personality may be correlated simply be-

ENDOMORPH
One of Sheldon's three body types. An endomorph is broad and thick in proportion to height, is round, and has fairly weak muscles and bones. The corresponding temperament is viscerotonic.

MESOMORPH
One of Sheldon's three body types. A mesomorph is characterized by a predominance of muscle and bone, as in an athlete. The corresponding temperament is somatotonic.

ECTOMORPH
One of Sheldon's three body types. An ectomorph is relatively thin and physically weak. The corresponding temperament is cerebrotonic.

◆ FIGURE 14.1

Sheldon's body types.

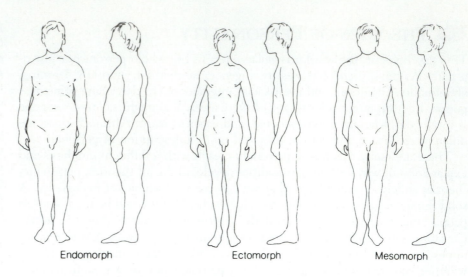

Endomorph   Ectomorph   Mesomorph

INTROVERT
One of Jung's personality types. An introvert is socially withdrawn, emotionally reserved, and self-absorbed.

EXTROVERT
One of Jung's personality types. An extrovert is gregarious, focuses on external events, is not introspective, and likes to be with others.

cause of the kinds of experiences different people have. Because of his body type, an endomorph may find vigorous sports uncomfortable and thus may avoid them. A mesomorph may excel at sports and therefore take part in them frequently. An ectomorph may learn at an early age that she is weaker than other children and consequently may become fearful and introverted. These correlations even may have been due to biases among observers and raters. Because many people think of fat individuals as jolly, thin individuals as restrained, and muscular individuals as athletic, raters may have emphasized these characteristics regardless of the subjects' actual behavior (Tyler, 1956). So far, no cause-effect relationship has been established between Sheldon's body types and certain personalities.

As another example, there is Carl Jung (1875–1961), a Swiss psychiatrist and psychoanalyst, who developed a personality theory that separated individuals into two types he called **introverts** and **extroverts** (Jung, 1933). Introverts are withdrawn and tend to avoid social contact, while extroverts are outgoing and try to interact with people as often as possible. Because interaction with other people is an important dimension of personality, as well as an important part of our lives, whether we are introverted or extroverted can have a powerful effect on our existence.

Categorizing individuals according to type is appealing because it appears so simple and reasonable. Yet it is this simplicity that limits the value of any typing system. People are complex, and they behave in many different ways under different circumstances. Researchers have therefore found it extremely difficult to type individuals. More often, they prefer to consider people to have certain traits in less or greater degrees.

TABLE 14.1 ◆ PERSONALITIES CORRESPONDING TO SHELDON'S BODY TYPES	
PHYSIQUE	TEMPERAMENT
Endomorphic: soft, round, overdeveloped digestive viscera	Viscerotonic: relaxed, loves to eat, sociable
Mesomorphic: muscular, rectangular, strong	Somatotonic: energetic, assertive, courageous
Ectomorphic: long, fragile, large brain, sensitive nervous system	Cerebrotonic: restrained, fearful, introversive, artistic

The Trait Approach

Traits are important underlying and enduring qualities of a person. We use trait words all the time to describe ourselves and others, Look at the following list of common trait words. Which are most descriptive of your personality?

moody	rigid	pessimistic	unsociable
passive	thoughtful	controlled	even-tempered
sociable	talkative	easygoing	carefree
touchy	aggressive	changeable	optimistic
anxious	sober	reserved	quiet
careful	peaceful	reliable	calm
outgoing	responsive	lively	active
restless	excitable	impulsive	

As you can see, many of these trait words may be descriptive of you, but to greater or lesser degrees.

ALLPORT'S TRAIT THEORY. One of the best-known advocates of the trait approach was Gordon Allport (1897–1967). Allport recognized that each person has certain consistent aspects or, as Allport put it, "predispositions to respond to environmental stimuli in certain ways." What might make one person angry might make another person laugh because of the way the two people are predisposed to respond or, as you or I might say, because of their personalities.

Allport considered traits to be enduring and also general—that is, likely to occur under many different circumstances (Allport, 1937). He recognized that some traits are more enduring and general than others are. Consequently, he drew distinctions among **cardinal traits, central traits,** and **secondary traits** (Allport & Odbert, 1936). Cardinal traits are the most general and enduring. Allport argued that some people have no cardinal traits. For a trait to be cardinal, it must be the overriding factor in a person's life. For example, hatred may have been a cardinal trait of Adolf Hitler, and reverence for every living thing may have been a cardinal trait of Albert Schweitzer.

Central traits are far more common. They are less enduring and less general than are cardinal traits, but they are nevertheless important to us all. According to Allport, central traits are the basic units that make up personality. Surprisingly few central traits are enough to capture the essence of a person. Allport found that when college students were asked to write a description of a person whom they knew well, they tended to mention on an average only 7.2 central traits (Allport, 1961).

Secondary traits are far less enduring and less general than are central traits. In fact, Allport often used the term *attitudes* rather than secondary traits. Examples of secondary traits might be liking to watch old movies, attending baseball games frequently, and putting off work until almost too late.

Allport felt that no two people have exactly the same traits, and as a result every personality is unique. Still, many people have traits that are similar, and these traits manifest themselves in the way people interact with the environment (see Figure 14.2).

CATTELL'S TRAIT THEORY. Some trait theorists have emphasized the need for statistical analysis, such as factor analysis (see Chapter 13), to isolate different traits. After all, you wouldn't expect to find a separate and distinct trait for every trait word in the English language. There would be many overlaps. Raymond Cattell (1950) held this view. He was not satisfied with simply classifying traits; he wanted to know how traits were organized and how they were related to one another.

TRAITS
Distinguishing qualities, properties, or attributes of a person that are consistently displayed. According to Allport, a trait is a predisposition to respond to many types of stimuli in the same manner.

CARDINAL TRAITS
In Allport's theory, an encompassing trait that seems to influence almost every act of a person who possesses the trait. Cardinal traits are uncommon and are observed in only a few people.

CENTRAL TRAITS
In Allport's theory, behavioral or personality tendencies that are highly characteristic of a given individual and easy to infer. Allport argues that surprisingly few central traits, perhaps five or ten, can give a fairly accurate description of an individual's personality.

SECONDARY TRAITS
In Allport's theory, traits that are not as crucial as central traits for describing personality. Secondary traits are not demonstrated often because they are related to only a few stimuli and a few responses.

Gordon Allport (1897–1967).

◆ **FIGURE 14.2**

Allport viewed traits as intervening variables that help to relate stimuli and responses that at first may not appear related.

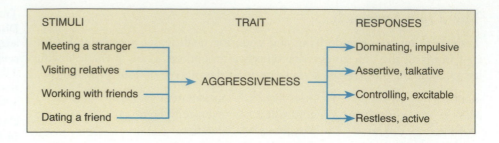

Cattell began his work by examining the visible or apparent portions of a personality. He referred to the obvious traits that we can all see as **surface traits.** He used questionnaires and direct observation to compile data about surface traits from many people. His subsequent statistical analysis turned up certain surface traits that seemed to come in clusters. To Cattell, such group-ings indicated a single underlying trait. Cattell referred to these more basic traits as **source traits.** In Figure 14.3, you can see results from the 16 person-ality factor questionnaire developed by Cattell (Cattell, Saunders, & Stice, 1950). In this example, the questionnaire was given to three groups of subjects: airline pilots, creative artists, and writers. As the results show, members of different professions can have similar or different personality profiles. In this case, creative artists and writers have more in common than either group has with airline pilots (Cattell, 1973). Cattell points out that this kind of person-ality profile can help psychologists to predict behavior. For example, Cattell has shown that a person who scores very high on factor Q^3 tends to be accident-prone. A low score on Q means the person is conservative, and scale Q^2 helps predict success in school. People with the most stable marriages were similar on factor A, which indicates whether a person is aloof or warm; factor L, the dimension of trusting versus suspicious; and factor Q^1, whether a person is group-dependent or self-sufficient. Factor E also is important. Husbands from stable marriages tended to be a little more dominant than their wives were,

◆ **FIGURE 14.3**

The 16 personality factor profiles developed by Cattell for three groups of subjects: airline pilots, creative artists, and writers. (SOURCE: *Adapted from the handbook for the 16PF, 1970.)*

A	Reserved		Outgoing
B	Less intelligent		More intelligent
C	Affected by feelings		Emotionally stable
E	Submissive		Dominant
F	Serious		Happy-go-lucky
G	Expedient		Conscientious
H	Timid		Venturesome
I	Tough-minded		Sensitive
L	Trusting		Suspicious
M	Practical		Imaginative
N	Forthright		Shrewd
O	Self-assured		Apprehensive
Q	Conservative		Experimenting
Q^1	Group-dependent		Self-sufficient
Q^2	Uncontrolled		Controlled
Q^3	Relaxed		Tense

Writers — Creative artists — Airline pilots

1 2 3 4 5 6 7 8 9 10

but husbands who were much more dominant than their wives tended to have unstable marriages.

Trait theory has been criticized for a number of reasons. It is not yet clear which traits are the most enduring and general. Many personality "traits" may be situationally dependent (Bem & Allen, 1974; Endler & Magnusson, 1976). A person who is dominant in one situation may be submissive in another, and a person who is forthright in one circumstance may be sly in another (Becker, 1960). Another problem has to do with how traits are ascribed (Rorer & Widiger, 1982). Sometimes traits are ascribed only after a considerable amount of behavior has been consistently observed; at other times, a few isolated behaviors are used to delineate a trait (Pervin, 1985). For example, before we would say that someone has the trait of honesty, she might need to show her honesty in many different situations and circumstances. On the other hand, someone who commits one or two murders in his lifetime may be ascribed the trait of homicidal, even though an exceedingly small percentage of his entire behavioral repertoire resulted in murder (Rorer & Widiger, 1983). Traits often are assigned in this fairly arbitrary fashion. Still, research continues to indicate that there are characteristics, uniquely combined in each individual, that appear to endure in a significant enough way to make it difficult to dispense with the idea of traits (Buss, 1989). The concept of traits continues to play an important role in our understanding of personality.

Trait researchers recognize the criticisms of trait theory. They do not argue that all of human personality can be explained by traits, and they agree that the immediate forces in a given situation will always have some effect on behavior and that traits sometimes are ascribed in an arbitrary manner (Pervin, 1985). For a science of personality to be broad enough to predict behavior adequately, environmental aspects and the problem of ascription have to be considered as well. In this sense, there are probably no strict trait theorists; that is, no psychologist sees the entire personality as the result of traits alone. As researchers Jackson and Paunonen have humorously pointed out,

one encounters the term "trait theorist," with its connotations, in the writings of several authors. Like witches of 300 years ago, there is confidence about their existence, and even possibly their sinister properties, although one is hard pressed to find one in the flesh or even meet someone who has. Similarly, few theorists can be found who take the opposite extreme position that variables associated with the person play no role in behavior. What one can identify are different sets of investigators, some of whom prefer to focus on the stability or continuity of personality across situations, and others who seek to isolate variables in the environment which, for example, arouse motives. There is a third set, those who argue that it is the person-situation interaction that is of crucial importance (Endler & Magnusson, 1976; Magnusson & Endler, 1977; Mischel, 1977). (Jackson & Paunonen, 1980, p. 523)

Although the trait approach enjoys a certain popular appeal, it remains, after many years, a descriptive rather than an explanatory (see Table 1.1, page 18) approach, and it has not done a good job of predicting the wide ranges of human behaviors encountered in different situations (Pervin, 1985).

The Psychoanalytic Approach

One of the names most associated with psychology in the minds of people is Sigmund Freud, the founder of *psychoanalytic theory* (see Chapter 1). Freud opened a new era of investigation when he derived a model of personality based on his observations of many patients.

Freud studied human personality with the aid of techniques he developed for probing what he believed were the hidden or unconscious thoughts or desires of his patients. One such technique was the interpretation of dreams

SURFACE TRAITS
From Cattell's theory of personality, a cluster or group of behaviors that are overt and appear to go together. Inferring the existence of a surface trait makes it possible to classify similar behaviors under one term; for example, constant fighting, yelling, and making angry facial expressions can be categorized under the surface trait term aggressive.

SOURCE TRAITS
From Cattell's theory of personality, traits that can be identified only through factor analysis and that are more important than surface traits. Cattell argues that personality can be reduced to 16 source traits and that, although surface traits may appear to be more valid to the commonsense observer, source traits have greater utility in accounting for behavior.

ID
In psychoanalytic theory, the reservoir of instinctive drives; the most inaccessible and primitive portion of the mind.

EGO
In psychoanalytic theory, the part of the personality that regulates the impulses of the id in order to meet the demands of reality and maintain social approval and self-esteem.

SUPEREGO
In psychoanalytic theory, the part of the personality that incorporates parental and social standards of morality.

PLEASURE PRINCIPLE
The psychoanalytic postulate that an organism seeks immediate pleasure and avoids pain. The id functions according to the pleasure principle.

REALITY PRINCIPLE
According to Freud, the principle on which the conscious ego operates as it tries to mediate between the demands of the unconscious id and the realities of the environment.

LIBIDO
According to Freud, the psychological energy driving the individual to seek gratification—principally sexual gratification, but also food, comfort, and happiness.

OEDIPUS COMPLEX
A Freudian term representing the sexual attachment of a boy to his mother. This desire is repressed and disguised in various ways. The child expresses jealousy and hatred of his father because the father can have relations with the mother that the son is denied.

by analyzing their symbolic content (Freud, 1900/1953). Another was the analysis of slips of the tongue, which, like dreams, Freud believed revealed hidden desires and unconscious processes.

We use the term *psychoanalyst* to describe practitioners who have accepted Freud's theory either totally or to a considerable degree or who have built upon the work of Freud and his colleagues. Because Freud's theory of personality attempts to explain most of human behavior (Freud, 1940/1964), it is often considered to be a grand explanatory theory.

THE THREE-PART PERSONALITY.   Freud relied on his knowledge of biology, psychology, and social experience to create a model—a picture of the personality—divided into three parts: the **id,** the **ego,** and the **superego** (see Figure 14.4). According to Freud, the id and ego are present at birth, while the superego develops through experience with the culture.

The id has no objective knowledge of reality. It ruthlessly and relentlessly drives the organism toward pleasure; it is therefore said to follow a **pleasure principle.**

The ego is the part of the personality that must deal with reality if the id's desires are to be met. The ego therefore functions according to a **reality principle.** For instance, the id may insist on possessing all the money in the bank, but it is the ego that must open the safe, disable the guards, and deal with the other realities of the situation.

On the other hand, we are taught that stealing is wrong, and this is where the superego comes in. Freud considered the superego to be the internal representation of an ideal expressed in terms of social and traditional values.

These hypothetical constructs (id, ego, and superego) were designed to create a picture of the biological (id), psychological (ego), and social (superego) aspects of personality. Freud believed that the dynamics of personality involve a continual conflict among the id, the ego, and the superego (Freud, 1917/1963). He thought that each person has a certain amount of psychological energy, or **libido,** and that conflicts among the three parts of the personality drain this energy. In particular, the instinctive pleasure drive often comes into conflict with acquired social inhibitions about expressing instinctive desires, with the consequent repression of such desires (Freud, 1905/1953). This antagonism is well illustrated in the classic unconscious conflict that Freud called the **Oedipus complex.**

In Freud's view, the major determinants of the personality come from this unconscious reservoir of repressed desires, which are basically irrational. The major theme of all Freudian psychodynamic personality theory is that people are constantly driven by unreasonable demands resulting from unconscious

◆ **FIGURE 14.4**

Freud's concept of the three-part personality.

desires and that these desires must be brought to consciousness and resolved before a healthy personality can develop.

INSTINCTS AND DEFENSE MECHANISMS. Freud considered sexual behavior and aggression to be instinctive drives. Throughout the animal kingdom, he argued, aggression helps animals to obtain needed food and territory, and sexual behavior maintains species; as such, both are necessary for survival. In our species, however, these aggressive tendencies and sexual desires run head on into cultural taboos against explicit sexual actions and uncontrolled violence.

According to Freud, this struggle between biological drives and social inhibitions produces anxiety, and the ego relies on what he called **defense mechanisms** to control and handle the anxiety effectively. Table 14.2 lists some of the more common psychological defense mechanisms. Freud argued that it was necessary for individuals to distort reality in some way to protect themselves from unacceptable unconscious thoughts and unwanted realities. At first, defense mechanisms may seem to be bad, because they twist the truth; some misrepresentation seems to be necessary, however, for our psychological well-being. In general, psychologists don't consider our use of defense mechanisms inappropriate or unhealthy unless we rely on these mechanisms to an extreme.

PSYCHOSEXUAL STAGES OF DEVELOPMENT. In Freud's view, child development is an important predictor of later adult personality. According to Freud, during development each person passes through five psychosexual stages. The first three stages—oral, anal, and phallic—are centered on physical satisfaction derived from the erogenous zones (areas of the body that when stimulated give rise to sexual pleasure, such as the lips or genitalia). These stages take place during the first 6 years of life. The later stages—latency and geni-

DEFENSE MECHANISMS
Reactions to the anxiety caused by conflict that serve to protect and improve the self-image. The mechanisms are not deliberately chosen. They are common to everyone and raise serious problems for adjustment only when they are used excessively and prevent the person from coping realistically with difficulties.

TABLE 14.2 ◆ SOME PSYCHOLOGICAL DEFENSE MECHANISMS

Denial
The refusal to admit the existence of events that are unpleasant or that have produced anxiety.

> *Examples:* Someone who continues to buy on credit or to spend more than she has in a checking account may be denying that eventually there'll be a deficit of funds. Someone who continues to speed even after witnessing a terrible traffic accident is denying that such a thing could happen to him.

Rationalization
The justification of irrational, impulsive action, or even failure, to oneself or other people by substituting acceptable explanations for the real but unacceptable reasons.

> *Examples:* A thief rationalizes his stealing by pointing out that he was abused as a child. A doctor deals with his error in judgment by noting that "no one's perfect."

Reaction Formation
When an individual exhibits, and at the conscious level believes she possesses, feelings opposite to those possessed at the unconscious level.

> *Examples:* A parent who hates his child conceals this unwanted and stressful emotion by being overly protective or indulgent. A person is boastful and bellicose to hide feelings of inferiority.

Projection
The attribution of one's own undesirable thoughts or characteristics to other people.

> *Examples:* Someone who flirts with other people's spouses and then inaccurately views ordinary social contacts by other people with his own spouse as flirtatious. Someone who steals and incorrectly assumes other people cannot be trusted.

FIXATION
In psychoanalytic theory, inordinate persistence in a particular psychosexual stage of development because the id has received either too much satisfaction, leading to positive fixation, or too little satisfaction, leading to negative fixation.

COLLECTIVE UNCONSCIOUS
Jung's concept that a portion of the unconscious contains certain shared experiences, predispositions, and symbols that are inherited and found in all members of a given race or species.

Sigmund Freud (1856–1939), the founder of psychoanalysis.

tal—occur between the age of 6 years and adulthood, and Freud emphasized them less than the first three stages. In summary, the stages are as follows:

◆ *The oral stage (birth to approximately 1 year):* During this time, a child obtains the greatest satisfaction from stimulation of the lips, mouth, tongue, and gums. Freud noted that sucking and chewing are the chief sources of an infant's pleasure.

◆ *The anal stage (approximately 1 to 3 years):* During this time, the child gains the greatest satisfaction from exercising control over the anus during elimination and retention. Freud believed that the anal stage reaches its peak once toilet training is successful.

◆ *The phallic stage (approximately 4 to 6 years):* During this stage, the child derives the greatest pleasure from stimulating the genitals. The child also comes to identify with the same-sex parent, a critical step toward developing into a healthy, mature adult.

◆ *The latency stage (approximately 6 years to puberty):* Freud called this the latency stage because he believed that the sexual drive becomes dormant at about the age of 6 years and remains so until the onset of puberty. During this time, children are supposedly free of erotic feelings and instead expend their efforts on acquiring cultural and social skills.

◆ *The genital stage (puberty to adulthood):* Freud believed that heterosexual desire awakens during this time and that as long as no strong fixations have occurred, the child is on her way toward a "normal" life.

If the transition through these stages doesn't go smoothly, Freud argued, developmental problems can arise. **Fixation** may occur at any stage. For example, if a child's id doesn't receive enough satisfaction during the oral stage, the child may be reluctant to leave that stage until he feels fully satisfied. A *negative fixation* can result, according to Freud, in a manifestation of oral-stage processes later in adult life. Conversely, a person may want to retain oral-stage satisfaction in later life—a condition Freud called *positive fixation*. Both kinds of fixation result in similar behaviors, but for different reasons.

As an example of fixation, a person might remain immature in his social relations and engage excessively in oral activities, such as eating, talking, and smoking. Such behavior in adult life, Freud believed, might result from negative or positive fixation during the oral stage. Any fixation can lead to problems. If a child's id was not satisfied during toilet training because of the demands made by parents, the child may seek satisfaction through undue retention—an anal fixation. Freud believed that such an *anal retentive personality* would be expressed later in life in stinginess, selfishness, and the like.

CONTEMPORARIES OF FREUD.   Many prominent psychoanalysts who were students and colleagues of Freud broke with him and developed their own theories when their observations of their patients led them to different conclusions (Grosskurth, 1991). Carl Jung, whom we mentioned earlier for his concepts of introversion and extroversion, for instance, believed that we possess two unconscious minds—a personal one, not unlike that envisioned by Freud, and a species-specific one inherited from our ancestors (Jung, 1936/1959). Jung called the latter concept the **collective unconscious.** He spent much of his life gathering religious and totemic artifacts from different cultures and comparing them in order to demonstrate that similar unconscious symbols have played a role in the psychology of all members of our species (Jung, 1955/1959).

Alfred Adler (1870–1937), a Viennese psychiatrist, was one of Freud's colleagues. Adler believed that people were more motivated by their hopes for the future than they were by their experiences of the past. He saw humankind in a much more benevolent light than did Freud, believing, in contradiction to Freud's view, that underlying biological drives and forces did not predestine humankind to follow a path of conflict and turmoil.

One of Adler's most important principles, which he believed to be a prime motivator in humans, was what he called *striving for superiority*. By this term, Adler was referring to a drive to fulfill one's potential and not, as the phrase might imply, to a wish to dominate other people. Adler's concept of striving for superiority is not unlike Maslow's concept of self-actualization (see Chapter 11); in fact, the humanist concept of self-actualization was derived, to a great degree, from Adler's ideas. Adler also believed that no matter how much we may have accomplished at any point in our lives, if we do not continue to grow and strive upward, feelings of inferiority will result. In this way, we are "pushed" by fears of inferiority and "pulled" by desires for superiority to fulfill our potential, each in our own unique way. Adlerian psychotherapy focuses on these ideas in the treatment of patients.

THE INFLUENCE OF PSYCHOANALYTIC THEORY.   Freud's view of personality development has had a powerful influence on the history of psychology. A number of his concepts have been supported by modern research, including the existence of unconscious thoughts and motivations (Kihlstrom, 1987), that is, an individual's unawareness of forces that make him feel and behave as he does. Testing many of Freud's ideas by the scientific method has proved difficult, however (Hook, 1960). For example, to this day, no one has conclusively demonstrated that dreams necessarily mean anything or that there is any special content hidden in them. Furthermore, many of Freud's other ideas have not been well supported (Erwin, 1980). For instance, modern research indicates that the first 6 years of a person's life, though important and formative, are not as crucial to the development of adult personality as Freud believed they were. Then again, Freud's view shouldn't be considered complete just because he is dead. If Freud were alive today, Freudian theory might undergo considerable renovation at the hands of its creator.

Whether or not one agrees with Freud's theory of human personality or with the views proposed by the other prominent psychoanalysts, their work is regarded as valuable because it has stimulated so much research. Its full value will remain uncertain until we can devise more ways to test it. In the interim, we owe Freud and his colleagues a historic debt of gratitude for their insights and for the impetus they provided to research into human personality.

Behavioral and Social Learning Approaches

Behavioral and social learning theories of personality have developed from the work of the behaviorists, beginning with John B. Watson early in this century (see Chapter 1).

BEHAVIOR THEORY.   Following in the footsteps of Watson and others, psychologist B. F. Skinner put forward a view of behavior that implies that personality is controlled by processes fundamentally different from those envisioned by trait theorists or psychoanalysts (Skinner, 1953; 1969). Skinner and the behaviorists refuse to consider drives or other internal motivational factors. As we noted in Chapters 1 and 8, a fundamental aspect of their position is that anything not directly observable, such as drives or thoughts, has no place in an objective science.

Behaviorists believe that learning (see Chapter 8) is mostly responsible for the development of personality. They argue that complex social interactions and aspects of personality are due to the history of conditioning unique to each individual.

In addition, behaviorists do not consider traits to have roots within the person, but rather believe they are the products of environmental forces and learning. The reason some traits seem stable is that the environments in which individuals live often are stable for long periods. Skinner and other behaviorists contend that if the environment is sufficiently manipulated, then aspects of personality that have appeared to endure will disappear and will be quickly replaced by others. In this view, then, behavior is controlled by stimulus conditions, and it is not necessary to form hypotheses about internal motives, traits, or conflicts.

Consider the following example. Suppose you knocked on someone's door and asked for a contribution to a worthy charity. If the person gave you money, would you say that this was evidence of the trait of generosity? Or would you say that underlying motivational factors in the person's unconscious mind prompted the gift? Behaviorists argue that whether a person gives is determined by the immediate environment and the person's past history of reinforcement for giving. Furthermore, by manipulating the environment, it is possible to increase or decrease a person's willingness to be generous. In fact, you could do several things to increase the amount of money that people gave as you went door to door for charity (Cialdini & Schroeder, 1976; Kleinke, 1977; Bandura, 1969):

1. Dress well, but don't overdo it.

2. Carry identification that officially associates you with the charity.

3. Carry a see-through collection container; this allows the giver to see that other people have made donations.

    a. Make sure the container is always one-third full (so that it looks as though people have been giving but you still have a way to go).

    b. Remove all pennies (donors will believe that other people have been giving bills and silver—their cue to what they should give).

4. Travel with a colleague (more people will give if more people ask. Just imagine what you'd give if 100 people showed up at your place all at once to ask for a donation!).

5. If the donor is reluctant, use the phrase, "Even a penny will help" (very few people will give only a penny, and few will say that they don't have a penny).

Although the behaviorist arguments seem persuasive, and the theory is very popular in the United States—perhaps because of our democratic institutions and professed desire to view all people as equal at birth—there is evidence of individual differences in personality just after birth, too early for the environ-

Actors are able to convince us that they have different traits and personalities when, in fact, they are only responding to direction from an external source. Behaviorists wonder if we aren't all actors.

ment to have had a significant effect. In Chapter 3, we discussed the findings of Thomas, Chess, and Birch that babies have noticeably different personalities just after birth and that these temperaments are long lasting. These data argue somewhat against the idea that personality is solely the result of environmental experience.

Other critics of the idea that situations determine behavior and personality have stated,

> We have never met anyone who, from a behavioral viewpoint, was not a trait theorist. If one really believes that situations determine behavior, then there is no reason to test or interview prospective employees for jobs such as police officer; it is only necessary to structure the job situation properly. Picking a mate would simply be a matter of finding someone whose physical characteristics appeal to you. In a properly managed class all students would work up to their abilities. Do you know anyone who believes these things? Obviously not. (Rorer & Widiger, 1983, p. 445)

Trait theorists have further argued that just because situations may often determine behavior, this is not proof that traits don't exist.

The argument over whether enduring internal qualities or environmental influences are the primary drive behind a person's behavior is known as the **person-situation debate.** In general, most researchers now agree that currently there is no way to assess which may have the most influence on a person and that most studies indicate that which one is stronger may be a function of the particular situation in which a person finds herself. As a rule, then, personality is understood as an *interaction* between a person's unique characteristics and the environmental forces that impinge on her (Kenrick & Funder, 1988; Carson, 1989).

SOCIAL LEARNING THEORY.   Social learning theorists, such as Albert Bandura, argue that personality is shaped not only by environmental influences on the person but also by the person's ability to influence the environment (Bandura, 1978). As we discussed in Chapter 8, social learning theory states that thinking is an important determinant of behavior. The inclusion of cognitive viewpoints within a behavioral framework has been a relatively recent trend; an example is the work of personality learning theorist J. B. Rotter (1972). Rotter believes that the most important variables in determining personality are the person's expectations concerning future outcomes and the values of different reinforcements that might occur in a particular situation. In other words, a person's behavior depends on what she expects the outcome of any particular action to be and what those outcomes are worth. The likelihood that someone will be aggressive when trying to return merchandise to a department store would depend, then, on that person's expectations about whether aggression will work.

Rotter doesn't care for the term *trait*, preferring instead the term *generalized expectancy*. The implication is that your behavior or "trait" is really the result of your belief that the behavior will serve you well. Moreover, if traits—the stable aspect of a personality—are actually generalized expectancies, then changing the environment and giving you new experiences may lead to behavioral changes and differences in your personality. This potential is not consistent with the connotation of the word *trait*, which is that the qualities of personality are relatively enduring and unchangeable, even if the environment alters drastically.

Another reason for the apparent existence of consistent behavior in individuals may be the result of a social expectancy that encourages people to view other people as consistent. To make this idea clear, let's consider a truly ingenious experiment designed by the late social psychologist Stanley Milgram (1933–1984), who, sadly, had little time to develop this work fully.

PERSON-SITUATION DEBATE
From personality theory, the argument concerning whether the primary drive behind a person's behavior is due to enduring internal qualities or environmental influences.

Milgram recalled the story of the great swordsman and writer Cyrano de Bergerac whose large nose made him too shy to pursue Roxanne, the woman he loved. Instead, Cyrano allowed his words to be used by his foolish friend Christian in love letters to Roxanne, so that he, Cyrano, might still court his beloved by proxy. With this in mind, Milgram "created" people he called Cyranoids. A Cyranoid is anyone who, like Christian, speaks the words of another. In one variation of his work, Milgram recruited high school teachers to interview an 11-year-old boy, asking them to determine the boy's level of general intellectual ability and achievement in areas of science and literature. Unbeknownst to the teachers on the interview panel, the only response that the boy would give to their questions was to repeat what he was hearing in a concealed earpiece. Whose words was he hearing? The words of Stanley Milgram (the Cyrano of this experiment), who was answering the teachers' questions from a hidden location—the boy merely reported what Milgram said! Milgram, a Ph.D. and prominent social scientist, provided the teachers with the best and most intelligent answers that he could muster.

When the teachers graded the boy, they were way off. For example, in the area of social science, Milgram's specialty, the teachers compared the boy's answers to those of a typical tenth grader, although the boy had been giving the answers of a distinguished professor of social psychology (Herbert, 1985).

Milgram also conducted other experiments in which one Cyranoid would answer many questions or have a conversation, while the real hidden speakers changed off with one another every minute. Even when giving the answers of scores of different people, the speaker was viewed as consistent by the rater, not, as one might expect, as an individual with a fragmented personality. This work implies that there may be a strong bias at work among people to view another person, and her "personality," as unified.

As you can see, in behavioral and social learning theories, the individual's personality is considered to be situationally dependent (Bandura, 1969), or dependent on the expectations of other people. In trait theories and psychoanalytic theories, the personality is believed to be stable across many situations and shaped by underlying motivations and predispositional forces.

The Humanistic Approach

The central focus of all humanistic theories of personality is the concept of self. *Self* refers to the individual's internal experiences and subjective evaluations. Humanistic theories are quite varied, but they share a number of basic themes. They reject the notion that underlying traits or unconscious motivations and conflicts are important forces in the development of personality, arguing instead that human beings are endowed with free will and free choice. Similarly, they reject the idea that environmental forces are the major determinants of personality. Instead, individuals are seen as aware beings capable of unique experiences based on their own view of the world and self.

Most humanistic theories stress that people have a positive drive to grow as human beings and to realize their potential to the fullest. Humanistic approaches are sometimes *phenomenological*. This means that for each of us, there is no objective world; there is only our subjective or personal experience of the world, which depends on our self-concept, attitudes, and beliefs. Humanists argue that to understand anyone's personality, you must know how he perceives the world. You must find a way to "stand in the other person's shoes," even if only for a moment.

That people move in the direction of fully developing their personal potential, especially their emotional potential, is called self-actualization (Maslow, 1954). This concept, as you recall, was derived, in part, from the work of Alfred Adler. Adler's work, in many ways, is viewed as a transition from the psychoanalytic theories predominant in Freud's day to the modern humanistic view.

According to the humanistic view of personality development, there is no simple way to have a more creative and fulfilled life. Knowing the qualities of those people who have fulfilled their potential or imitating them is no guarantee of realizing one's own potential. Self-actualization, therefore, is more of a journey, an exploration, or a way of life than it is a final goal. By observing and interviewing many people, humanists have gained some insight into ways to help foster self-actualization (Maslow, 1968).

ROGERS'S SELF THEORY. To humanistic psychologist Carl Rogers (1902–1987), a person's unique subjective experience of reality and self was central to any dynamic understanding of personality (Rogers, 1961). Rogers's personality theory often is referred to as a "self" theory because it focused on the individual's self-perception and personal view of the world. Rogers argued that we develop a self-concept through our experience with the world, our interactions with other people, and what other people tell us. We build our own lives, and we are all free to choose for ourselves rather than being at the mercy of learned stimuli or unconscious forces. Rogers stressed that each person is purposeful in his behavior and is positively striving to reach self-fulfillment. The major cause of maladjustment is an individual's perception that his sense of self is in opposition to personal expectations or goals (Rogers, 1951).

Carl Rogers (1905–1987).

The humanistic approach has been criticized on a number of grounds. First, people have argued that concentrating on self-perception and subjective assessment does not bring us any closer to explaining the causes of an individual's behavior (Smith, 1950). Second, they have criticized humanists for concentrating too heavily on the individual and ignoring the environmental problems that may be causing discomfort or disharmony. Third, critics note, the humanist viewpoint has not been demonstrated by rigorous experimentation. There is little evidence, for instance, to support the humanist assertion that human beings are positively striving toward self-fulfillment and possess free will. Finally, the humanistic personality theory has not been very successful at predicting human behavior over a wide range of circumstances or situations, a problem that it shares with other theories of personality (see Focus on a Controversy).

PERSONALITY ASSESSMENT

We study personality in the hope of providing people with insights into their behavior that will help them lead happier lives. For this reason, psychologists have been interested in assessing personality and have developed a number of measures and tests for doing so.

Measuring Personality Traits

Trait theorists would like to know which traits predominate and how these traits are likely to influence behavior. Perhaps the best known of the instruments used to measure abnormal patterns of personality traits is the Minnesota Multiphasic Personality Inventory (MMPI). The MMPI is the most widely used psychological test in the world (Lubin, Larsen, Matarazzo, & Seever, 1985). Research with the MMPI has been extensive; well over 100 studies are published every year, and the total body of MMPI literature encompasses over 8000 books and articles. The MMPI is more popular now than ever. It has been translated into 124 languages and is regularly used in 46 countries. Even the Russians have used it to test applicants to their cosmonaut program (Holden, 1986b).

CONCEPT REVIEW ◆ COMPARING THEORIES OF PERSONALITY

Type (Hippocrates, Sheldon)
There is little concern with the "self" as the source of motivation. Unconscious processes are considered to be less important than are conscious ones, if they are even considered. Early experience is thought to have little role in the formation of later personality development. Biology and inheritance are seen as important and, to a high degree, are believed to determine personality.

Trait (Allport, Cattell)
Strong emphasis is placed on the "self" as the source of motivation. Unconscious processes are deemphasized. Early experience is thought to have only a slight role in the formation of later personality development. Biology and inheritance are seen as important and, to a degree, are believed to determine the traits that define personality.

Psychoanalytic (Freud, Jung)
Strong emphasis is placed on the "self" as the source of motivation. Unconscious processes are strongly emphasized. Personality determinants are thought not to be directly accessible to the individual without the use of therapeutic techniques for tapping the unconscious. Early experience is strongly emphasized as the primary foundation for later personality development. Biology and inheritance are seen as important and, to a degree, are believed to determine personality development.

Behavioral (Skinner, Bandura)
Strong emphasis is placed on the environment, rather than on the "self," as the source of motivation. Unconscious processes are not considered to be important. Early experience (past history of reinforcement) is thought to have a moderate role in the formation of later personality development (competing with current reinforcement contingencies). Biology and inheritance are deemphasized and are considered to play little role in the development of personality.

Humanistic(Maslow, Rogers)
Strong emphasis is placed on the "self" as the source of motivation. Unconscious processes are deemphasized. Early experience is thought to have only a slight role in the formation of later personality development. Biology and inheritance are deemphasized and are considered to play little role in the development of personality.

| | Emphasis | | | |
| | | | | |
Theory	"Self"	Unconscious	Early Experience	Biology
Type	− −	=	− −	+ +
Trait	+ +	−	−	+ +
Psychoanalytic	+ +	+ +	+ +	+ +
Behavioral	− −	− −	=	− −
Humanistic	+ +	− −	− −	− −

KEY: + + Very Strong, + Strong, = Moderate, − Weak, − − Very Weak.

DOES PERSONALITY THEORY HAVE A FUTURE?

During the last 20 years, prominent researchers have reviewed the progress of personality theory, and many have come to a pessimistic conclusion:

> Sechrest (1976) suggests that personality theory is in sad shape and Phares & Lamiell (1977) suggest that the field is in a period of crisis. . . . Loevinger and Knoll (1983) appear to take a dim view of how much the field has advanced and, following Meehl (1978), question whether a really impressive theory of personality is possible. (Pervin, 1985, pp. 83–84)

Further concern has been expressed over the way personality is currently presented in textbooks such as the one you are now reading:

> One continues to wonder why personality is still so widely taught as a "procession through the graveyard" in the pungent phrase of a prominent personality researcher. It is true that the lives and insights of Freud, Jung, Adler, Sullivan, Rogers, Maslow, etc., make extremely interesting reading and their historical contributions highlight some of the issues of human relationships that must continue at the center of personality research. But we may well ask why no one teaches cognition, social psychology, developmental psychology, or abnormal psychology by using the views of famous people as the centerpiece for the entire course. (Singer & Kolligan, 1987, p. 535)

These are interesting concerns. Why would researchers believe that the field of personality is "in sad shape," and why is personality so commonly taught by reviewing the major works of historical figures? To answer these questions, we need to consider the term *personality* and what it encompasses. Personality is a *big* term. There is very little behavior in which a human might engage that couldn't be considered an aspect of personality. In short, "personality," as a field of study, covers just about everything.

Early in the history of psychology, behavior was thought to be somewhat less complicated than we now know it to be. During that time, it was not uncommon for an individual such as Freud or Adler to attempt what are called "grand theories" of personality—grand in that they attempt to explain most of human behavior. Unfortunately, grand theories of personality, like most psychological grand theories, often failed to predict complex patterns of human behavior. Consequently, modern personality theory has generally limited itself to highly detailed investigations of many separate areas, rather than attempting to develop grand theories. "Current work in [personality] centers around a few hot topics in the field, a few theoretical points of view, a wide variety of rather unrelated topics and concerns, and major concern with a few controversies and issues" (Pervin, 1985, p. 84–85).

The topics that are currently "hot" in the field of personality include *learned helplessness* (see Chapter 11), *memory organization* (see Chapter 9), *social attribution* (see Chapter 18), *self-efficacy* (see Chapter 11), *cognitive information processing* (see Chapter 10), and a considerable number of others (also found under various chapters and headings in this text). But if these are the current hot topics in personality research, why, then, aren't these topics covered here in the personality chapter? Why, instead, are the grand theories reviewed? There are two reasons for this. First, it is always useful to have some background in the grand historical theories; they still have an influence on our thinking. Second, and more important, is that the term *personality*, by its very nature, implies a grand encompassing view, the kind of view that could not be represented by a collection of, as Pervin calls them, "rather unrelated topics and concerns." Although, as we have noted, grand theories have thus far proven to be of limited value, such theories *are* required if we are to create a field of study as broad as "personality." This, of course, is why so many researchers believe that personality, as an endeavor, is in "sad shape"; there don't seem to be any viable or powerful grand theories that can encompass it.

Could this situation change? Is a really impressive theory of personality possible? Some people believe that it is, and that it may be emerging from the work of cognitive psychologists who have begun to apply information-processing theory to the area of personality (Carson, 1989). Their work, although just beginning, is a significant departure from the theories we have discussed in this chapter. Unlike traditional personality theory, which emphasizes the consistency of the self across situations and circumstances, the cognitive information-processing view looks at the self as a collection of many different cognitive **scripts** that enable the person to change and to be flexible across many circumstances.

Perhaps a grand theory of personality based on how we think and process information will eventually prove its power and utility. Its proponents argue that there is still life in personality theory and one day hope to show that cognition, learning, motivation, and emotion can all be understood as an interaction based primarily on the way our thinking is organized. Further, they believe that this understanding will, in turn, lead to a powerful new ability to predict human behavior across many diverse situations and circumstances. If the future proves them right, the only heading broad enough to encompass their collected research would be *personality*.

The MMPI contains 550 phrases to which the subject taking the test can answer "true," "false," or "cannot say." The phrases tap emotional reactions, psychological symptoms, and beliefs (Hathaway & McKinley, 1940). The following are examples of the kinds of statements made on the MMPI:

- ◆ There have been times when I've considered killing myself.
- ◆ I am my own worst enemy.
- ◆ Most lawyers are honest.
- ◆ I find it difficult to fall asleep.
- ◆ If given a chance, I would do something to benefit the world.

The MMPI is broken down into 10 basic scales. Each measures a different trait (see Table 14.3). In addition, there are three validity (control) scales. The L scale, or lie scale, attempts to spot individuals who are trying to fake a good self-image. People who score high on this scale say that they do a number of commendable daily activities that almost no one engages in, such as never telling a lie or never putting off something they'd rather not do. The K scale, another control, reflects on how defensive or open the subject is being. The F scale, the third control, tests whether the subject is trying to present an exaggerated impression of a personal problem. Throughout the MMPI, a number of statements are made more than once, with only slightly different wording. Responding differently each time will result in an invalid score. Another

TABLE 14.3 ◆ THE MMPI SCALES	
SCALE	TRAIT MEASURED
Validity Scales 1. Lie scale (L)	A high score identifies subjects who have stated they possess socially desirable characteristics and behaviors that are in fact very rare. This happens when subjects attempt to fake a good response and do not provide adequate data.
2. Frequency scale (F)	A high score identifies subjects who have checked items that are rarely marked true except by those who are trying to present an exaggerated impression of their problems or by those who are extremely deviant.
3. Correction scale (K)	These items reflect how defensive or honest the subject is being. The scale measures attitudes more subtle than those measured by the L scale. A high score indicates that a subject may not be deliberately lying but is keeping a close check on other true feelings and is not being as open as could be desired.
Clinical Scales 1. Hypochondriasis (Hs)	A high score indicates a subject who is overconcerned with body functions in the absence of any real physical illness.
2. Depression (D)	A high score indicates pessimism about the future, a sense of helplessness and hopelessness, and a concern with death and suicide.
3. Hysteria (Hy)	These items discriminate people who use physical symptoms to control other people, to solve their problems, or to avoid responsibilities.
4. Psychopathic deviate (Pd)	A high score indicates that the subject has a disregard for social customs and mores, is unable to benefit from punishing experiences, and lacks emotional commitment to other people, particularly in terms of sex and love.
5. Masculinity—feminity (Mf)	These items identify men who prefer homosexual relations to heterosexual ones. Women tend to score low on this scale, and the scale for women cannot be used as a mirror image of the scale for men.
6. Paranoia (Pa)	This scale distinguishes people who feel that they are being persecuted and victimized by other people or who believe undue attention is being paid to them by other people.
7. Psychasthenia (Pt)	A high score indicates the existence of obsessive thoughts, compulsive behaviors, and a high degree of fear or guilt, insecurity, and anxiety.
8. Schizophrenia (Sc)	These items identify those people who are aloof, remote, and cold and who may have bizarre emotional feelings, delusions, or hallucinations.
9. Hypomania (Ma)	A high score indicates excitability, hyperactivity, and a tendency to rush from one thing to the next without finishing anything.
10. Social introversion (Si)	These items pinpoint subjects who are withdrawn, have few social contacts, and have little interest in being with other people.

scale, the Question scale (?), is a measure of the total number of items put into the "cannot say" category.

The MMPI is called a **standardized instrument** because it has been administered to thousands of people from whom profiles have been obtained. If you were to take the MMPI, your profile could be compared with the standards that have already been gathered. In this way, your personality could be assessed in terms of that of other people whose behavior is known and whose personalities have already been examined.

Problems can arise with even the best personality gauges, however. Sometimes subjects are unwilling to declare how they really feel, and although the MMPI is considered an objective instrument, one subject's understanding of a statement can differ considerably from another subject's. For example, how would you respond to this sentence?

◆ Sometimes I see things that aren't really there.

You might think to yourself, "This question is asking whether I have hallucinations, and the answer is definitely no." Or you might think, "The question is asking whether I see illusions, which is a perfectly normal phenomenon. As a matter of fact, a couple of days ago I was driving down the highway and I

STANDARDIZED INSTRUMENT
In psychological testing, a test or measure that has been administered to a wide sample of the population for which it is intended, so that the range and probabilities of responses from that population to the test or measure are known.

◆ FIGURE 14.5

An MMPI profile. This one was scored by a computer. Since the instrument has been standardized, the computer compares the responses against those in a large data bank obtained from the standardized group. Personal biases on the part of the person administering the profile are thus eliminated. (SOURCE: Minnesota Multiphase Personality Inventory Manual, 1970.)

PREDICTIVE VALIDITY
The degree to which a score or assessment correlates with a specific outcome. A test with high predictive validity allows fairly accurate predictions to be made about certain future behaviors.

thought I saw water on the road up ahead. But when I got there, no water was there. I'll check yes." Different interpretations of a statement's intent can lead to different answers, which can be a problem.

Each person's MMPI scores are recorded on a profile (see Figure 14.5). An atlas that accompanies the MMPI outlines average reactions to situations by people with different profiles. A subject can be given a "code-type" comparing him with these other people, and psychologists administering the test may then predict the degree to which this subject's behavior will be similar to that of other people who have a like score.

Police departments, for example, often give MMPIs as part of their promotion procedures to screen out overly rigid and suspicious personalities, proneness to anxiety or indecisiveness, or a penchant for impulsive use of weapons. Nuclear power plant personnel are screened for factors such as hostility to authority, poor reactions to stress, and substance abuse (which has its own suggestive code-types and subscales) (Holden, 1986b, p. 1250).

The MMPI can be a valuable instrument if it is used for making general assessments. It usually is not effective for predicting highly specific responses in extraordinary circumstances, but as in the examples of police officers and nuclear plant operators, it may give some indication of the behavior patterns a person is likely to exhibit.

Other instruments have been designed to measure attitudes and preferences along certain dimensions, but the MMPI remains the most widely used of these tests (see Focus on an Application).

Predictive Validity and Reliability

The results obtained from trait instruments such as the MMPI usually are considered in the light of a subject's actual behavior. In other words, a correlation is obtained between the subject's behavior and the score. In this way, investigators can say with some confidence that someone who scored high on the social introversion scale of the MMPI is very likely to be withdrawn, shy, and somewhat introverted. Behaviors should reflect scores. If they do, then the instrument is said to have **predictive validity,** sometimes called *criterion validity;* that is, it measures what it purports to measure. To determine the predictive validity, researchers correlate the test score with predicted behavior patterns. A device that has high predictive validity will yield a score from which accurate predictions about behavior can be made. This is exactly what personality theorists want—instruments that will tell them ahead of time what kinds of behavior people with different scores will exhibit. Conversely, if the device indicates that certain behaviors should occur and they don't occur, then the device's predictive validity is low.

Many personality assessment instruments have established useful levels of validity. For example, they often can measure and predict a young couple's marital adjustment by assessing the similarity of the spouses' needs: the more similar, the better the adjustment (Meyer & Pepper, 1977). They can assess the likelihood that someone will graduate from a military training program (Alker & Owen, 1977). These measures aren't accurate all the time—far from it—but they can often help psychologists to make predictions with more accuracy than would have been possible had the instruments not been used.

Unfortunately, assessment instruments don't always work. Quite often they yield an inaccurate description of an individual's personality. There are several reasons for this. One is that people frequently distort their beliefs, attributes, and attitudes when giving information (Edwards, 1961). What they say they are like and what they are really like may be quite different. Subjects may exaggerate some traits and overlook others. People who do this are not necessarily trying to lie. Part of the problem may be that normal human memory

BEING A CAREFUL CONSUMER AND THE LIMITS OF PSYCHOLOGICAL TESTING

There are hundreds of psychological tests on the market today. The results of these tests can affect hiring and promotion decisions, the way students are handled in school, the outcomes of legal proceedings, and the kinds of medical and psychological treatment people receive. The odds are good that sometime in your life, you will be given a psychological test in connection with school, a job, or health matters. If interpreted by qualified professionals who understand the use and *limitations* of the test results, many of these tests can be valuable. Unfortunately, some tests either are of dubious quality or are administered by people who have little experience with or understanding of the meaning of the test scores (Matarazzo, 1986). Practically all the tests in existence provide royalties and remuneration for their creators; testing is a business.

Because such testing may have a direct effect on your life, it is important that you be an informed consumer and take an active part in the testing process. The purpose of this focus is to familiarize you with the limits of testing and to help you make intelligent decisions concerning tests you may encounter.

The Barnum Effect

Most psychological tests look official. They come in a handsome case, ask questions that seem important, and are given by testers in a setting of authority. This combination tends to give the average layperson a sense of security that the test is valid and good. In such contexts, psychologists talk of the Barnum effect. The Barnum effect (named for showman P. T. Barnum, who allegedly said, "There's a sucker born every minute") refers to the fact that people generally believe that personality testing is more accurate than it actually is (Synder, Shenkel, & Lowery, 1977). Psychologists and the informed layperson know, of course, that good packaging and advertising do not necessarily make a test valid or reliable.

Further heightening the Barnum effect is that many personality tests are now scored and interpreted by computer. Even MMPI results may be scored by a computer, which may then print out a published dissection of the subject's personality. Computers, of course, simply help to score tests quickly. They do not ensure that the test is either valid or accurate. Unfortunately, many people believe that computers are somehow objective and infallible and tend to give more credence to personality tests graded by computers (Matarazzo, 1983).

Even the very best personality tests available to psychologists provide only a limited amount of information and can be interpreted within only a limited range. For psychologists, the fact remains that if those you wish to test understand what you want to know, have the information you seek, and are not trying to lie, the simplest and most accurate way to

find out about them is probably just to ask them rather than to give them a test (Shrauger & Osberg, 1981; Rorer & Widiger, 1983).

The MMPI-2

Like other tests, the Minnesota Multiphasic Personality Inventory (MMPI), the most widely used psychological test in the world, has its limitations. For instance, psychologist Robert Colligan argued that the MMPI is based on outdated information about "normal" personality (Colligan, Osborne, Swenson, & Offord, 1983). To understand this assertion, you need to know how the test was originally developed. In the 1930s, psychologist Starke Hathaway and neurologist John McKinley at the University of Minnesota collected answers to their questions from a group of "normal" people. But where did they get this sample of normal people? As it turns out, a very large portion of their sample was found at the University of Minnesota hospital. The researchers stopped hospital visitors walking in the halls and asked them to take the test. They also sampled some workers on a federal Depression relief project and some high school graduates who were coming in for job counseling. As a result, their average normal person was 35 years old, was married, lived in a little town or farming community, and had schooling only through the eighth grade. Colligan has pointed out that "whoever takes the MMPI today is being compared with the way a man or woman from Minnesota endorsed those items in the 1930s or early 1940s" (Herbert, 1983c, p. 228).

To meet these objections to the original test and to satisfy the requests by many clinicians to update it, the MMPI has been revised. The new test, the MMPI-2, was standardized on 2600 people from around the nation and reflects the national percentages of men and women and of minorities as described by the 1980 census.

The new test is different from the old MMPI in a number of ways. Gone are the sexist wording, outmoded expressions, and questions about religion (such as whether the respondent believes in the Second Coming of Christ) that many found offensive. Added are 15 new content scales of special interest to clinicians that assess such things as suicidal behavior, anger, repression, cynicism, low self-esteem, family problems, job functioning, substance abuse, type-A personality (see Chapter 15), and eating disorders.

The new MMPI-2 is not without its critics, however (Helmes & Reddon, 1993). The first concern is that the new population on which the test was standardized is not average because it is highly educated: 45 percent were college graduates (as opposed to the national average of 16.5 percent). Only 5 percent were high school dropouts (the national average is

FOCUS ON AN APPLICATION

33.5 percent). This appears to have occurred because volunteers were used to standardize the new test and poor readers weren't very interested in wading through the hundreds of questions required by the test (Adler, 1990). As a result, it is feared that the MMPI-2 might not be very applicable in state hospitals, veterans hospitals, or state-funded treatment centers where clients are often less educated than the sample on which the MMPI-2 was standardized. Furthermore, the codetypes from the MMPI-2 often don't match the old MMPI atlas used to predict behaviors. In the old system, someone who scored high on a particular scale on the MMPI could be matched with thousands of others with similar scores, which often helped to predict his behavior. But the same person with a high score on the same scale on the MMPI-2 often doesn't seem to fit the pattern for those with the same scale score on the old MMPI. Because the questions were changed on the new test, the scores on the scales, even though they are the same scales, appear to mean something different.

As you can see, even the most widely used test in the world is open to interpretation. As an informed consumer of psychological testing, you should feel free to ask questions about the tests you may be asked to take. Find out why you are being tested. Find out the name of the test and the publisher. Feel free to consult a professional about how that test was used in your case. This will help you to determine whether the test was valid and reliable in the circumstances in which it was used.

Human beings are extremely complicated. It should come as no surprise that tests that attempt to quantify and qualify an individual's personality are limited in their power and utility. In the right hands, in the right circumstances, they can furnish valuable information. But no test ever devised, or likely to be devised, is going to reduce something as complex as you to a set of test scores and descriptive paragraphs that are totally valid.

RELIABILITY
The extent to which a test, rating scale, classification system, or other measure is consistent, that is, produces the same results each time it is applied to the same thing in the same way.

is imperfect. For instance, a person who reports feeling anxious most of the time may actually not feel anxious often, but rather may remember occasional moments of anxiety so vividly that anxiety seems an important part of her personality. Other people may profess to be honest because they like to think of themselves as being honest, when in fact they cheat on their income taxes, keep extra change when a cashier gives it to them, and make up lies to excuse lateness to work.

A trait-measuring device or personality assessment instrument must be reliable as well as valid. **Reliability** refers to the instrument's consistency. Does the score remain fairly stable over time? An instrument would not be very valuable if a subject's score changed drastically from day to day. Any measuring device purporting to disclose underlying traits should show reliability, because traits by their very nature are considered enduring and general. They should be there day after day, month after month, and the instrument should reflect this fact.

Psychoanalytic Personality Assessment

Psychoanalysts have developed measures designed to probe the personality in depth, break through the defenses of the subject, and uncover hidden, unconscious motivations. The subject's early history is the focal point of these investigations, especially the way in which the subject dealt with the sexual and aggressive instincts outlined in Freud's hypothesis.

Historically, the two assessment devices most often used for probing the unconscious have been the Rorschach ink-blot test and the Thematic Apperception Test (TAT) (see Figure 14.6). The Rorschach ink-blot test is the fourth most commonly given psychological test, following only the MMPI, the Wechsler Adult Intelligence Test, and the Bender-Gestalt Visual-Motor Test (Lubin, Larsen, Matarazzo, & Seever, 1985). It has become so associated with psychology that most students picture psychologists with their ink blots just as they picture physicians with their stethoscopes.

Both the Rorschach and the TAT are considered *projective* tests in that they contain ambiguous stimuli that can be interpreted by subjects in many different ways. The Rorschach consists of ink blots in which a subject can see any number of different things. The TAT contains a series of ambiguous pictures; subjects are asked to make up a story about each. The story should describe what is happening in the picture, but because the picture is open to so many interpretations, subjects are free to project onto the picture their own unconscious feelings and desires. Similarly, subjects can *project* onto an ink blot unconscious images and sensations. The test results are interpreted by a clinician.

Clearly, the clinician is a major factor in psychoanalytic assessment. In empirical tests of the validity of clinical assessment, however, clinical judgments often have been shown to be inaccurate and inconsistent. Research also has indicated that a clinician's assessment of a particular person is not generally improved by the use of projective assessment techniques (Golden, 1964; Soskin, 1959). It is not uncommon for different clinicians to view the same responses to projective tests quite differently. Some people have argued that the problem with projective tests is that they are too projective: Not only is the subject expected to project, but the clinician also may be free to see whatever she wants to in the score (Goldberg & Werts, 1966).

◆ **FIGURE 14.6**

Sample items from the Rorschach and the TAT.

Q SORT
A personality assessment technique based on a series of statements and traits that the test subject is required to sort into categories from "most like me" to "least like me."

In general, the view of psychoanalytic assessment among psychologists has been split. On one side of the issue are psychologists who support the tenets of Freudian theory and believe that projective tests are a useful way to tap unconscious processes. On the other side are psychologists who argue that projective testing as it is now used is invalid and unreliable.

Behavioral Personality Assessment

As you recall, the behavioral approach to personality is radically different from that of trait theorists or psychoanalysts. For behaviorists, the assessment of personality is the assessment of behavior, and behavior can be assessed only if it has been carefully defined and directly observed. A behavior is counted or timed—in other words, monitored. In this way, a rate or frequency of the behavior can be obtained. A behavioral assessment of personality includes an examination of the stimuli in the individual's environment and of the behaviors that these stimuli control and reinforce (see Chapter 8). Attempts to change the individual's personality are made by altering or restructuring the environment. Behaviorists refer to such shaping of the personality as *behavior modification*. The application of behavioral technology to the modification of personality through therapy will be examined in detail in Chapter 17.

The value and importance of different stimuli in a person's life can be assessed by examining the person's behavior in real situations, by investigating the person's preferences, and by knowing which reinforcers or rewards are most effective and important to the person. Behaviorists understand that each person is unique and that stimuli that are reinforcing for some people may not be for others.

Behaviorists rely extensively on experimental methods. Because they deal with only the observable aspects of behavior in a given person, they tend to avoid concepts or constructs that rely on internal qualities or motivations such as traits or unconscious desires. Behavioral assessment often is criticized for avoiding what many people consider to be important aspects of personality, such as emotion and thought.

Humanistic Personality Assessment

The humanistic approach to personality assessment differs greatly from the psychoanalytic, behavioral, and trait approaches. Humanists study personality by examining each person's subjective experience. Subjective experience is difficult to assess, but humanists hope to find objective ways of doing this. Several specific techniques for studying and uncovering a person's subjective experience have been devised.

Q SORTING.   The **Q sort** is one of the techniques that humanists have developed to examine an individual's subjective experience. A Q sort is conducted by presenting a large number of cards to a subject. Each card shows a different statement. The subject must choose whether the statement describes himself. The Q sort cards may contain statements such as the following:

- ◆ I am a reasonable person.
- ◆ Most people like me.
- ◆ I get frightened easily.
- ◆ I have a good sense of humor.
- ◆ I am successful at my work.

The subject's selection of cards gives an impression of her self-image. The subject is often asked to sort the cards a second time, according to his *ideal* self.

It is possible to obtain a correlation between people's Q sorts and their likely behaviors. In this way, a personality can be appraised objectively based on the person's subjective self-appraisal (Bem & Funder, 1978).

INTERVIEWS.   Humanists often use personal interviews to facilitate personality assessment. The interviewer gently explores the subject's self-concept and emotional feelings, trying through empathy to see the world as the subject sees it (Jourard, 1967). The interviewer is careful to avoid interjecting her world view and opinions. Carl Rogers based a client-centered therapy on this technique, which will be discussed in detail in Chapter 17.

In recent years, scientists have become increasingly interested in assessing nonverbal cues. Many humanists believe that much about a person's subjective self-appraisal and world view can be learned by examining expressions, posture, gestures, and movement. Some researchers argue that self-concepts such as submissiveness or dominance can be assessed by observing a person's "body language" during an interview.

Humanistic assessment methods have been criticized for their lack of rigor. Some people have argued that many clinical assessments derived from the interview method reflect the clinician's subjective appraisals rather than a true understanding of the subject.

In the end, all personality assessment has the common goal of finding out more about the individual, discovering his enduring characteristics, and uncovering the forces that have created and maintained them.

◆◇◇ SUMMARY

◆ Personality is the sum total of the ways in which an individual characteristically reacts. Personality refers to the consistency in a person's behavior under varying conditions.

◆ To a psychologist, the word *personality* refers to the whole person, not just to a part.

◆ Historically, investigations of personality have classified people according to certain types. Hippocrates, William Sheldon, and Carl Jung are among those who attempted to classify personality in this way.

◆ Instead of categorizing individuals according to type, modern trait theorists generally believe that people possess certain traits in lesser or greater degree.

◆ One of the best-known advocates of the trait approach was Gordon Allport. Allport recognized that some traits were more enduring and general than others, and he drew distinctions among cardinal traits, central traits, and secondary traits.

◆ Some trait theorists have emphasized the need for statistical analysis to isolate traits. Raymond Cattell is one such theorist. Cattell has developed the 16 personality factor questionnaire, which makes use of factor analysis.

◆ Sigmund Freud was the founder of psychoanalytic theory. Freud divided the personality into three parts: the id, the ego, and the superego. He believed that the dynamics of the personality involved continual conflict among these elements. Freud considered sexual behavior and aggression to be instinctive.

◆ Freud believed that this struggle between biological drives and social inhibitions produces anxiety, and that the ego often relies on defense mechanisms to control and handle the anxiety.

◆ According to Freud, as a person develops, he or she passes through several psychosexual stages. These stages—the oral, anal, phallic, latency, and genital—mark important points in the development of a healthy personality.

◆ Many prominent psychoanalysts broke with Freud to develop their own theories of personality. Among them were Carl Jung, who developed the concepts of introversion and extroversion, and Alfred Adler, who defined striving for superiority as a prime motivator of behavior.

◆ B. F. Skinner and other behaviorists do not consider drives or other internal motivational factors in their approach to personality. Instead, they believe that learning and environmental forces impinging on the organism shape personality.

◆ In contrast to the behaviorist approach, research on infants' temperaments argues against the idea that personality is solely the result of environmental experiences.

◆ Social learning theorists such as Albert Bandura argue

that personality is shaped not solely by environmental influences on the person but also by the person's effect on the environment.

◆ Research by Milgram indicates that people may have a bias to view as consistent diverse behavior from the same individual.

◆ The focus of all humanistic theories of personality is the concept of self. Self refers to the individual's personal internal experiences and subjective evaluations.

◆ Carl Rogers has developed a humanistic self theory of personality that focuses on the individual's self-perception and personal view of the world.

◆ By their nature, personality theories are grand, in that they attempt to explain most of human behavior.

◆ Trait theorists are interested in measuring which traits are predominant and how these traits are likely to influence behavior. The best-known instrument for this purpose is the Minnesota Multiphasic Personality Inventory, or MMPI.

◆ Everyone should be familiar with the limits of psychological testing and should become a careful consumer. People tend to be too trusting in assessing the power of personality testing. This trust is known as the Barnum effect.

◆ Although many personality assessment instruments have useful levels of validity, they often fail to yield an accurate description of an individual's personality.

◆ Validity refers to an instrument's success in measuring what it claims to measure. Reliability refers to an instrument's consistency when used repeatedly.

◆ Psychoanalysts have developed measures to probe the personality in depth, to break through the defenses of the subject, and to uncover hidden unconscious motivations. The best-known devices for tapping unconscious aspects of personality are the Rorschach ink-blot test and the Thematic Apperception Test (TAT).

◆ For behaviorists, the assessment of personality is the assessment of behavior. Behaviorists assess personality by examining the stimuli in the individual's environment and the behaviors that these stimuli control and reinforce.

◆ Humanists assess personality by examining people's subjective experiences. One method is the Q sort technique, which asks subjects to choose from an assortment of statements the particular statements that best apply to themselves. In this way, an impression of a subject's self-image is obtained.

◆ All personality assessment has the common goal of finding out more about the individual, discovering the person's enduring characteristics, and uncovering the forces that have created and maintained these characteristics.

❧ SUGGESTIONS FOR FURTHER READING

1. Grosskurth, P. (1991). *The secret ring: Freud's inner circle and the politics of psychoanalysis*. Reading MA: Addison-Wesley. An account of Freud's secret committee that governed the psychoanalytic movement from 1912 to 1927.

2. Hall, C. S., Lindzey, G., Loehlin, J. C., Manosevitz, M., & Locke, V. O. (1985). *Introduction to theories of personality*. New York: John Wiley. A college-level textbook on personality theory.

3. Mason, J. M. (1992). *The assault on truth: Freud's suppression of the seduction theory*. New York: HarperCollins. Former projects director of the Freud archives asserts that Freud turned his back on valid scientific findings because he was reluctant to believe that many of his female patients had, in fact, been sexually abused by their fathers.

4. Mischel, W. (1986). *Introduction to personality: A new look* (4th ed.). New York: Holt, Rinehart, & Winston. A college-level textbook that introduces major personality theories and assessment techniques.

5. Pervin, L. A. (Ed.). (1990). *Handbook of personality: Theory and research*. New York: Guilford Press. A high-level, comprehensive compendium of theory and research in personality.

Chapter Fifteen

Stress, Health, and Coping

PROLOGUE

HELP WHEN IT WAS MOST NEEDED

Psychologists who study the effects of sudden and severe stress know how debilitating the condition can be. Sometimes, the speed at which help and intervention can be made available to a person under stress can make the difference between his being able to cope with the stress or becoming one of its victims. The following is the story of how one man quickly delivered help when it was most needed.

In August 1987, Northwest Airlines flight 255 from Detroit to Phoenix crashed on takeoff, killing all 153 people on board. The airline employees were in shock—it was their first accident in about 25 years. They were suddenly faced with terrible dilemmas. What should they tell the families waiting in Phoenix or the families who were still in Detroit when the jetliner crashed? What could they say to family members throughout the country who would soon be calling in? How could they help their staff handle the wrenching emotional experience of dealing with the victims' families and the press? How could they get help to the flight crews and personnel, scattered among six "hub" cities, who were suffering because they had had friends on the flight or who would soon be functioning poorly because they were harboring a secret dread of flying?

The vice president of the airline decided to place a call to psychologist James Butcher, who is known for his work in disaster crisis management. The vice president asked Butcher if he would put together a walk-in mental health counseling program for employees and victims' families in six cities— and do it within 24 hours! James Butcher recalled, "I gulped and said yes" (Bales, 1987, p. 26).

The first thing Butcher did was to pick up the telephone and arrange for psychologists to staff five of the six cities; Butcher took Detroit for himself, where he could be closest to the problem. The program Butcher set up consisted of three parts: (1) immediate personnel and victims' families; (2) a hotline, also staffed by mental health professionals, who could refer people in need to psychologists in locations other than the six cities; and (3) a special crisis intervention program aimed at those people who were at high

CONTENTS

STRESS
A psychological state associated with physiological and hormonal changes caused by conflict, trauma, or other disquieting or disruptive influences.

HEALTH PSYCHOLOGY
Any aspect of psychology that bears on the experience of health and illness and the behavior that affects health status.

PRIMARY PREVENTION
Efforts aimed at preventing an illness or pathological condition, mental or physical, from occurring, as opposed to secondary prevention in which a pathological condition is treated after it has appeared in hopes of preventing it from becoming worse. The focus is on optimizing health.

risk for emotional problems. Among this latter group were about 150 airline employees who had been asked to care for the victims' families just after the crash (Bales, 1987).

For two weeks, the psychologists led by Butcher worked 14 to 16 hours per day. Of course, there was no way to undo the tragedy, but many family members and employees needed help to come to grips with their depression, grief, and anger. They needed professional assurance that their feelings of guilt ("I never should have let her fly by herself, I should have been with her") were normal and were part of grieving. Other people, too numb to feel anything, were counseled that such numbness, too, was a normal reaction following the sudden death of someone loved and that they were neither unfeeling people nor "crazy." They were also told what to expect later, when the sadness and grief would come. Other psychologists discovered that some people needed help to overcome a new and strong fear of flying. Desensitization techniques (see Chapters 8 and 17) were helpful in these instances. Finally, employees were "debriefed"; they talked about their experiences and sorted out what had happened in a group setting, after which each employee was able to spend some time alone with a psychologist.

Butcher pointed out that although some of the people helped through the trauma required further aid, the number needing professional assistance was much lower than would have been expected if no one had been there to help. Judging by all the experience gained by psychologists over the years with stress and crisis management, there is little doubt that James Butcher is right.

Today, over 1000 psychologists are members of the Disaster Response Network, a volunteer organization whose members offer professional services without charge to disaster victims. They frequently work in concert with other relief agencies such as the American Red Cross and are often able to make an important difference by being on the scene so early (Turkington, 1992).

IN THIS CHAPTER, we'll investigate the stress caused by disasters such as airline crashes and look at the effects of stress on health. We'll also examine how our behavior influences our health and how psychologists hope to change behavior to better our health and adjustment. In addition, we'll explore ways to reduce stress and to promote better health.

🧬 WHY PSYCHOLOGISTS STUDY HEALTH

Every year, researchers provide more evidence that our well-being and physical health are directly linked to our behavior. For example, smoking and overeating are both *behaviors*; they are also associated with major killers like heart disease and cancer. How we behave when interacting with the environment, therefore, can be a matter of life and death.

Smoking and overeating are obvious examples of behaviors that may be detrimental to health. There are many other such behaviors, some quite subtle. For instance, just the way we behave when we try to cope with the *stresses* of our daily lives can have an important effect on our health and well-being. Sometimes, if we fail to deal properly with **stress,** real physical damage may result.

If psychologists can learn how to help people control the behaviors that are detrimental to health, or how to acquire the behaviors that are beneficial, millions of lives could be significantly extended and improved.

HEALTH PSYCHOLOGY

Health psychology has been defined as "any aspect of psychology that bears upon the experience of health and illness and the behavior that affects health status" (Rodin & Stone, 1987, pp. 15–16). As you might imagine, that definition covers a lot of ground. Interestingly, although some early psychologists such as William James and G. Stanley Hall dealt with health-related issues from time to time, health was generally considered to be solely a matter for physicians. In 1964, however, a presidential commission took note of the fact that the leading causes of death were no longer the terrible diseases of the past such as plague, diphtheria, typhoid, and cholera. These scourges can now be prevented or controlled by inoculation, sanitation, or antibiotics. Instead, the report noted that every year hundreds of thousands of Americans and others around the world were dying prematurely as a result of their own detrimental *behavior*, from preventable diseases, incidents, or accidents (Fisher, 1986; Taylor, 1990). As a result, much of health psychology is oriented toward **primary prevention,** that is, toward efforts to prevent illnesses before they happen by optimizing health.

RISK ASSESSMENT

One of the important emerging areas in health psychology is the study of detrimental behaviors. Detrimental behaviors are those behaviors that pose a risk to human health and well-being. One of the problems faced by health psychologists is to make people aware of which of their behaviors are the most dangerous and preventable. Consider the following two people. One worries about smoking his pipe—a behavior that could cause lip or oral cancer—and talks about stopping. At the same time, he thinks nothing of riding his bicycle through heavy traffic to work. The other individual has been concerned about consuming the local water ever since some of the wells in his area were shut down because of pesticide contamination. He is careful to drink only bottled water and even puts off taking a drink at work until he can get home to his "safe water," as he calls it. As he drives home, however, he doesn't wear his seat belt. What's most likely to kill either of these people is neither lip cancer nor pesticide poisoning, but traffic accidents, which are more probable by a factor greater than 1000 to 1 over the things they are worrying about. In fact, one out of every 140 Americans will die in a car accident (Allman, 1985). Cars are deadly (and bicycles are 15 times more deadly than cars per mile driven); yet we often seem to worry most about the long shots such as the dangers of artificial sweeteners, food coloring, or strangers who might kidnap our children (Wandersman & Hallman, 1993). It's the *real* dangers, however, on which we must focus most of our efforts (Morgan, 1993). Table 15.1 lists most of the major causes of death in the United States and many of the lesser ones so you can see at a glance which are the major threats. Worldwide, the number one killer is still malaria. Though Americans rarely think about malaria, one of the most amazing statistics I have ever seen was a World Health Organization estimate that half of all the people who have ever lived died of malaria!

Table 15.2 shows another way of measuring threats to life. Here we see the numbers of potential years of life lost. Looking at the data in this way helps us to see that car accidents may be a greater danger than heart disease even

TABLE 15.1 ◆ HOW WE DIE (Fatalities per year in the U.S. Population from Selected Causes)	
Heart disease	725,010
Cancer	506,000
Stroke	145,340
Pneumonia and flu	78,640
Diabetes	48,840
Motor vehicle accidents	47,880
Suicide	30,780
AIDS	29,850
Homicide*	25,700
Liver disease and cirrhosis	25,600
Kidney disease	20,860
Infections**	19,750
Birth defects	17,920
Emphysema	16,470
Drowning	7,380
Fire	7,380
Stomach ulcer	6,190
Asthma	4,600
Nutritional deficiencies	3,060
Poison	2,563
Firearm accident	2,255
Tuberculosis	1,760
Infectious hepatitis	1,660
Electrocution	1,025
Appendicitis	902
Excess cold	334
Pregnancy, birth, and abortion	330
Flood	205
Nonvenomous animal	129
Syphilis	110
Lightning	107
Tornado	90
Measles	70
Venomous bite or sting	48
Whooping cough	20
Polio	17
Fireworks	5
Botulism	2
Poisoning by vitamins	1
Smallpox†	0

*Includes individuals killed while committing crimes by police or victims.
*The number of deaths from uncontrolled infections or septicemia, as it is called, is increasing at an alarming rate. A person who sustains a bacterial infection today is 30 times more likely to die of it than he or she would have been back in 1950. This is owing, in the most part, to resistant strains of bacteria that are able to keep ahead of our ability to combat them with new antibiotics.
†Smallpox is now believed to be extinct.

SOURCE: Allman, 1985, p. 38; National Center for Health Statistics, 1991.

TABLE 15.2 ◆ THE FIFTEEN
LEADING CAUSES OF DEATH
DEFINED BY YEARS OF
POTENTIAL LIFE LOST BEFORE
AGE 65 (1991)

CAUSE OF DEATH	YEARS OF LIFE LOST NATIONWIDE
1. Cancer	1,832,039
2. Heart disease	1,411,399
3. Motor vehicle accidents	1,144,492
4. All other accidents	1,090,844
5. Suicide	764,235
6. Birth defects	660,346
7. Homicide	638,289
8. AIDS	585,992
9. Premature birth	487,749
10. Sudden infant death syndrome	363,393
11. Stroke	237,898
12. Liver disease and cirrhosis	233,472
13. Pneumonia and flu	184,382
14. Diabetes	145,501
15. Chronic lung disease/asthma and emphysema	135,507

SOURCE: National Center for Health Statistics, 1991.

though the latter kills more people. This is because heart disease generally kills people near the end of their natural lives while car accidents often take people early in life.

Protecting Yourself

Table 15.3 is a guide that describes the behavior changes you can make to improve your health and well-being. These changes focus on the major threats to individuals living in industrialized nations* (based on things that kill 10,000 or more Americans each year). If everyone made these changes in his or her behavior, millions of lives worldwide would be saved each year. Deaths resulting from causes believed to be relatively unrelated to behavior, such as Alzheimer's disease, are not included in the list.

Hazard Perception

Behaviors such as smoking and excessive drinking are extremely dangerous, but they often are not readily perceived to be (Jeffery, 1989). People tend to be more optimistic about their chances than statistics would indicate they should be (Weinstein, 1989). This problem of hazard perception—or, to be more precise, the lack of it—is common (Wandersman & Hallman, 1993). For example, many people believe that it is good to keep a firearm in the home for protection. It generally isn't. In a study conducted between 1978 and 1983, researchers examined all the gun-related deaths in King County, Washington (Kellermann & Reay, 1986), and found that a gun in the home was 6 times more likely to result in a death by accident or in the murder of one family member by another than it was to save a person from an intruder. It has also been shown that suicide often becomes more likely if a highly lethal method, such as a gun, is readily available (Kellermann, et al., 1992).

Some hazards get heavy press coverage, which increases people's worry about them. Let's look at a few of them and the real risks they involve. Consider flying. Your chances of being killed in a commercial jet are one in a million for every 1000 miles flown. You are *far* more likely to die falling down the stairs (something you probably don't think much about). What about drinking saccharine-sweetened soda? Couldn't that give you cancer? Perhaps—the data for humans aren't very clear. However, the odds can't be greater than about one in 100 million for each soda you drink—which means that you are 50 times more likely to be killed by lightning. What about a chest X-ray examination? There is a one in a million chance it will cause a cancer. Asbestos contamination might also cause lung cancer, but except for asbestos workers, the chances are very remote. Nevertheless, millions of dollars are being spent to clean up asbestos in the environment. Not that we shouldn't clean up asbestos, but health psychologists point out that many more lives could be saved with our limited funds, if we used the money to hire more police to enforce the speed limits on our highways. And yet, people generally feel safe in their cars. Why is that? Perhaps because we see cars all the time and are used to them. We control them and feel that we can avoid an accident if only we are careful. Asbestos, on the other hand, is out of our control and we often don't know where it is; it may be lurking about waiting to get us. As you can see, hazard perception is an interesting area to investigate.

Health psychology is concerned not only with sorting real from perceived risk but also with discovering why people don't change their behavior even after they have been given the kind of information we've been discussing

*In the nonindustrialized world, the leading cause of death is malaria.

TABLE 15.3 ◆ SELECTED THREATS TO YOUR LIFE (PRESENTED IN ORDER OF ACTUAL DANGER) AGAINST WHICH YOU CAN TAKE DEFENSIVE ACTION

Threat and Defensive Action You Can Take

1. Heart disease

It is now known that cholesterol is a major factor in promoting heart disease. See your doctor now and discover your blood serum cholesterol level and HDL levels—you may need to have them checked a number of times to obtain a valid average level. The blood should be drawn from the arm and not the finger for more accurate results. The ratio of total cholesterol over HDL should be 5 or less. Avoid fatty foods and keep your fat intake to 30 percent of daily calories or less by eating less fatty and fat-saturated foods. Don't smoke. Know your blood pressure. Exercise regularly. Control your weight. Have the entire family learn cardiopulmonary resuscitation (CPR). Be especially alert for health problems a few weeks following a strep infection because of the danger of rheumatic fever (this is especially true for children). After age 40 get an EKG stress test every 3–5 years. Women past menopause and all men may also benefit by avoiding iron supplements and by donating blood 3 times a year to reduce their ferritin (iron) blood levels to 80 or slightly below, but this is still speculative. Donating blood is a good practice with no risk, assuming that you aren't anemic, so many people are doing this now in case the data turn out to be correct—check with your doctor. Some doctors have suggested that a premenopausal woman's monthly blood loss, which reduces her blood iron, is what protects her so well from heart disease up to menopause when her rate will become the same as a man's. So, maybe the doctors of the last century were correct when they bled people with leeches—perhaps they were improving their patients' health after all!

2. Cancer

Don't smoke and try to avoid second-hand smoke. Smoking is a known cause of lung cancer and leukemia. Know the levels of radioactive radon gas in your home (see the July 1987 issue of *Consumer Reports*, pages 440–447, at your local or college library for a discussion of this hazard and what to do about this serious concern, which is believed to be responsible for upwards of 20,000 cancer deaths per year). Know your family history and take special care to watch for kinds of cancers that run in your family (especially cancers of the colon or breast). Avoid ever getting a sunburn. Avoid the sun in general; wear sunblock and a hat. See your doctor for complete and regular checkups, and learn how to check yourself (how to do a self-examination of your skin from a dermatologist; for women, learn how to do a self-examination of your breasts from your family physician or gynecologist). For women, obtain a mammogram (if over age 35), and have a Pap smear on a regular basis. Avoid excessive alcohol consumption. Avoid mouthwash containing alcohol (people who use mouthwash regularly have the same rate of oral cancer as heavy drinkers). See your doctor promptly about anything unusual that doesn't go away.

3. Stroke

(All those behaviors listed for heart disease.) Avoid excessive alcohol consumption.

4. Diabetes

Have your doctor do an annual check of your blood for sugar (glucose). Know your family history. Avoid obesity. Get checked immediately following symptoms such as light-headedness, unexplained fatigue, persistent thirst, or frequent urination.

5. Motor vehicle accidents

Wear a seat belt with shoulder harness (use proper protective seats for infants). Avoid alcohol consumption before driving. Obey speed limits. Be very vigilant at intersections and while making left turns. Don't be an impatient driver eager to get a jump on the next guy; follow the rule "When in doubt, wait it out"—an extra minute at an intersection might be worth years of life. Drive a large car with air bags. Don't ride a motorcycle.

6. AIDS

Avoid sharing needles if taking drugs. Avoid intimate sexual contact with an infected partner. Assume everyone is infected and use a condom to reduce chances of infection; practice abstinence for complete protection. If possible, prepare for transfusions in advance of surgery by "stockpiling" your own blood; although blood-borne AIDS is now rare, this may protect you from other diseases as well.

7. Suicide

Immediately seek professional help for depression or suicidal thoughts. Know your family history. Avoid keeping a gun in the house.

8. Liver disease and cirrhosis

Avoid unprotected sex (because of the hepatitis B virus). Don't drink to excess (98 percent of all cirrhosis is alcohol related). Keep all drug use to the absolute minimum including the taking of common painkillers.

9. Homicide

Don't keep a gun in your home. If possible, avoid dangerous neighborhoods or jobs. Don't be confrontational.

10. Emphysema

Don't smoke. Get regular checkups. Get early and regular help for asthma.

Curiously, people are often more concerned with remote threats to their health such as the potential danger of drinking artificially sweetened beverages than they are with major risks such as riding a bicycle in traffic.

(Krantz, Grunberg, & Baum, 1985). This is the reason health psychologists investigate such problems as why a person won't stay on her blood-pressure medication, or why people have such a difficult time when they try to stop smoking or drinking.

Health psychologists are not only concerned with behaviors that can promote good health, they are also interested in *any* experience or circumstance that might affect health or well-being. The following sections give examples of such experiences—the kinds of experiences we all hope never to encounter.

🌈 ACUTE STRESS AND CHRONIC AFTERMATH

Sometimes, a stressful experience can be strong enough, or last long enough, to result in direct physical consequences that are harmful to good health. The following are examples of such experiences. Even though the experience may be relatively short-lived, it can be so intense that the memory of it can linger for years.

On Sunday morning, May 18, 1980, Mount Saint Helens, a volcano in the Cascade Mountains in the state of Washington, exploded with the force of a large hydrogen bomb. The entire top of the mountain blew off. A towering column of ash and debris rose thousands of feet into the air. Although there had been warnings beforehand, over 50 people lost their lives, some of them more than 20 miles from the explosion.

The wind carried the ash in a predominantly northeasterly direction. Over the next few days, ash fell from the sky. One of the unfortunate towns in the path of the ash was Othello, Washington, a community of less than 5000 people, 137 miles away from Mount Saint Helens. There, the ash covered everything. It formed drifts like snow, except that it was powdery and hot and smelled of sulfur. The small agricultural community was completely disrupted by this unpredictable event. No one knew how to deal with the ash. No one knew what effects it would have on health or if it could ever be cleaned up. Worst of all was the fear that this might be only the first of many such eruptions.

Psychologists, concerned about the effects of stress in the community, found that many residents of Othello were afflicted by the symptoms of stress. Hospital and emergency room visits increased 21 percent. The death rate increased 18.6 percent. According to physicians' records, stress-aggravated illnesses, psychosomatic conditions, and mental illnesses more than doubled. Child abuse and divorce increased substantially. According to measures from the community alcohol center, the police, and the courts, alcohol abuse, aggression, and violence also increased (Adams & Adams, 1984). Other nearby communities also showed similar increases in stress-related disorders, increases that were in direct relation to the distance from the explosion. The nearer people were to the explosion, the more likely they were to have stress-related problems (Shore, Tatum, & Vollmer, 1986).

Some terrible experiences may encompass many months of exposure. For many, the Vietnam War was such an experience (Cusack, 1993). Over the past few years, we have learned that approximately 15 percent of Vietnam veterans are suffering psychological problems (Kaylor, King, & King, 1987; Goldberg, True, Eisen, & Henderson, 1990). Symptoms associated with long-term stress among the vets have been found to be linked not to their personalities or behavioral characteristics, but rather to their exposure to combat (Goldberg, True, Eisen, & Henderson, 1990). These symptoms, including dizziness, headaches, memory loss, anxiety, intestinal problems, depression, and nightmares, are especially prevalent among combat soldiers who participated in atrocities, such as the torture and murder of prisoners (Yager, Laufer, & Gallops, 1984; Breslau & Davis, 1987). Approximately 35 percent of the veterans who had heavy combat experience fit the profile for **post-traumatic stress disorder,** or PTSD. In addition, many of the veterans have found readjustments to civilian life extremely difficult. Like their World War II and Korean War counterparts, Vietnam combat veterans also suffered an approximately 45 percent higher death rate (due mainly to automobile accident, suicide, and drug overdose) for the first 5 years following their return to civilian life than soldiers assigned to noncombat duty during a similar time period (Bower, 1987). The popular rumor that 50,000 vets have committed suicide since the war is a wild exaggeration, however (Pollock, Rhodes, Boyle, Decoufle, & McGee, 1990). But the vets do have a suicide rate 1½ times higher than for a similar population. Vietnam veterans are also twice as likely to have low sperm counts (Centers for Disease Control, 1988). No one knows why that has happened since most of the vets were not exposed to defoliants or other chemical agents; long-term stress is suspected to have played a role.

Clearly, a traumatic experience can have long-term effects even though the immediate danger has been removed (Hefez, Metz, & Lavie, 1987). How long will stress of this sort last? Perhaps as long as the events are remembered.

Is it possible to prepare yourself for acute trauma, to harden yourself psychologically, so that once the event is over the stress won't continue? Perhaps, but if the stress is severe enough, even the toughest individuals may suffer. Police officers and fire fighters working in large cities often experience stressful events. They become somewhat hardened, but can still be overwhelmed by events. For instance, in San Diego in September 1979, a Pacific Southwest airliner collided with a small plane and plunged into a downtown area killing 144 people. The first police and fire fighters to arrive on the scene were faced with a dreadful vision of human carnage. There was extensive dismemberment among the victims, making the crash more horrifying than most accidents. Parts of bodies were found all over lawns, houses, and roads. Some police said they couldn't walk down the street without stepping on human tissue. Many of the officers who helped to identify and label the bodies had seen death before, but after this they experienced stress symptoms—nightmares, insomnia,

POST-TRAUMATIC STRESS DISORDER
A disorder characterized by the recurrence of a particular traumatic event in the mind of the individual who experienced it, a numbness or lack of responsiveness to external stimuli, and two or more symptoms associated with depression and anxiety, such as sleep disturbances, low threshold for startling, impairment of memory, and guilt about having participated in the event.

When the ash fall from the Mt. St. Helens eruption covered the town of Othello, Washington, 137 miles away, the residents soon began to show symptoms of stress.

GENERAL ADAPTATION SYNDROME
Physiologist Hans Selye's description of the body's physiological-hormonal reaction to stressors. The reaction consists of three stages: the alarm reaction stage, the resistance stage, and the exhaustion stage.

ALARM REACTION STAGE
The first stage of the general adaptation syndrome, during which cortical hormone levels rise and emotional arousal and tension increase.

RESISTANCE STAGE
The second stage of the general adaptation syndrome, during which cortical hormones maintain high levels, physiological efforts to deal with stress reach full capacity, and resistance by means of defense mechanisms and coping strategies intensifies.

EXHAUSTION STAGE
The final stage of the general adaptation syndrome, during which resistance to the continuing stress begins to fail. Brain functioning may be hindered by metabolic changes; the immune system becomes much less efficient; and serious illness or disease becomes likely as the body begins to break down.

HYPOTHALAMIC-PITUITARY-ADRENAL AXIS
The glands and neural-hormonal complexes of the hypothalamus, pituitary gland, and adrenal glands of the kidneys, which together comprise an important stress reaction system.

CORTICOSTEROID HORMONES
Any of the steroid hormones of the cortex of the adrenal glands.

headaches, gastrointestinal problems, or memory loss. Some actually found themselves paralyzed when they attempted to put on the uniform that they had been wearing the day of the accident. Alan Davidson, president of the Academy of San Diego Psychologists, said, "This has had an impact on the human psyche beyond what we can humanly know" ("Crash Trauma," 1979, p. 61). Police who helped with crowd control or arrests and did not have to deal directly with the carnage fared much better. It was clearly direct contact with the victims that caused the acute stress and left the memories that resulted in chronic stress.

Disasters needn't be of the magnitude of a volcanic explosion, a war, or a plane crash to induce post-traumatic stress disorder. Many people suffer from the disorder due to personal disasters such as car crashes, physical assaults, or robberies (Norris, 1992). In fact, in a random sample of over 1000 young American adults living within the limits of a major city (Detroit), it was found that fully 9 percent had developed post-traumatic stress disorder or had suffered from it at one time. The stressors leading to such a severe reaction included serious accidents, assaults, rapes, seeing someone killed, or receiving news about the death of a loved one (Breslau, Davis, Andreski, & Peterson, 1991).

❧ REACTIONS TO STRESS

Conflicts and traumas can cause stress, and stress can lead to illness. But how does all this come about? How can stress make you ill?

The Body's Reaction

About 50 years ago, the Austrian physiologist Hans Selye first began calling attention to the body's reaction to stress and stressful situations. Selye called the physical reaction to stress the **general adaptation syndrome.** This syndrome consists of three different stages: the **alarm reaction stage,** the **resistance stage,** and the **exhaustion stage** (Selye, 1976).

STAGES OF THE GENERAL ADAPTION SYNDROME.   During the alarm re-action stage, the person becomes alerted to the stress, and the body's resources mobilize to help cope with the stress. For many years, scientists knew that one way in which stress could affect the body was via the glands that comprise the **hypothalamic-pituitary-adrenal axis.** In response to stress, the hypothalamus (see Chapter 2) produces a certain hormone (corticotropin-releasing factor) that triggers the secretion of another hormone, adrenocorticotropic hormone (also called ACTH, because no one wants to have to say *adrenocorticotropic* any more often than is absolutely necessary). ACTH then acts on the adrenal glands above the kidneys to cause the secretion of **corticosteroid hormones.**

Corticosteroids have pronounced effects. Some of these hormones act like strong tranquilizers by boosting the effects of inhibitory neurotransmitters (see Chapter 2), which causes the person to become lethargic or depressed (Barnes, 1986). Others have excitatory effects leading to emotional arousal and in-creased tension, causing the person to become more sensitive and alert to his surroundings (Barnes, 1986). (See the Concept Review.) Individuals who be-lieve that they have little or no control over the cause of the stress show an especially heightened alarm response (Breier et al., 1987).

This is perhaps a good place to point out that stress is not necessarily a bad thing. It can serve many valuable functions by preparing the body for action. In fact, one interesting study has shown that patients who are fearful before an operation have fewer postoperative problems than patients who are relaxed beforehand (Manyande, et al., 1992). Problems only arise when the stress be-comes unmanageable or long-lasting.

CONCEPT REVIEW ◆ EMOTIONAL PINBALL

Novel or dangerous situations or disturbing thoughts that cause a person to feel frightened, angry, anxious, grief-stricken or depressed can set the body pinging and flashing like a pinball machine with a dozen balls in play. The chemicals that trigger the uproar can affect the entire body almost simultaneously. For clarity, the process is shown numbered sequentially here, from the brain to the kidneys and the heart and then throughout the upper body.

Electrochemical activity in the brain causes the hypothalamus to trigger the release of adrenocorticotropin (ACTH) (1) from the pituitary gland.

ACTH, a hormone, travels in the blood stream (2). Reaching the kidneys (3), ACTH ultimately prompts the adrenal glands to release hormones like cortisol and epinephrine, which can affect virtually every organ.

Epinephrine signals the heart (4) to beat faster, speeding up the response to a crisis—fighting or fleeing from an enemy, for example.

The stomach (5) starts producing the hormone gastrin as part of a general acceleration of metabolism. Breakdown and synthesis of vital proteins quicken in cells throughout the body (6).

Hormones released in response to crisis may interfere with the complicated reproductive cycle in women and upset the balance of sex hormones (7).

The kidneys (8) begin to produce renin, provoking the constriction of blood vessels.

High cortisol levels may harm organs vital to the production of white blood cells. The spleen (9) and thymus (10) may shrink, weakening the immune system.

Under certain conditions, the brain may also release endogenous opiates, hormones that usually dampen pain. High levels of opiates may impair the body's response to disease by making some kinds of white blood cells (11) ineffectual. SOURCE: Maranto, 1984, p. 37.

Early in the stress reaction, the person often attempts to cope, sometimes by using psychological defense mechanisms (see Chapter 14) and sometimes by attempting to alleviate the stress through direct action. If the stress persists, however, symptoms of maladjustment such as rash, gastrointestinal upset, hives, and sleep disruption may occur, and the person may enter the next stage, the stage of resistance.

The stage of resistance can be characterized as a "full war effort," whereas the alarm reaction was merely an alert. The attempts at defense have reached full capacity now. The individual must find some way of dealing with the stress to prevent complete psychological disintegration. A temporary resistance may be achieved by intensifying the use of psychological defense mechanisms or by taking actions directed at eliminating the stressful situation. During the stage of resistance, a person tends to become fixed in her pattern of dealing with the stress rather than reevaluating the situation and finding a new way to cope.

Unresolved stress can lead to the exhaustion stage, when all the person's resources are at an end, and the patterns of coping attempted during the stage of resistance begin to collapse. During the stage of exhaustion, psychological defenses may become inappropriate and exaggerated. Metabolic changes may occur that inhibit normal brain functioning, and eventually a complete psychological disorganization may result. Resistance becomes weaker until, finally,

Hans Selye was one of the first to research the effects of stress.

Continued and chronic stress will eventually take its toll on the body.

the body begins to break down and to suffer the diseases that can accompany stress. Depression is a likely outcome (Gold, Goodwin, & Chrousos, 1988a; Gold, Goodwin, & Chrousos, 1988b).

STRESS AND ILLNESS.   Among the most common early symptoms of chronic stress are headaches from muscle tension, gastrointestinal disturbances, skin rashes and hives, dizziness, and fatigue. Chronic stress can also lead to high blood pressure, which is referred to as *hypertension*.

During stressful situations, the kidneys react by retaining sodium and fluid. This increased retention is believed to be the direct cause of stress-induced hypertension (Light, Koepke, Obrist, & Willis, 1983). Uncontrolled hypertension, should it go on long enough, can bring on a heart attack, stroke, or kidney failure (Benson, 1975). Chronic stress can also aggravate arthritis, colitis (an inflammation of the colon, or large intestine), asthma, hypoglycemia (low blood sugar), ulcers, and diabetes. Although chronic stress has not been found to be associated with the onset of cancer, it does appear to accelerate the disease in those who have it (Persky, Kempthorne-Rawson, & Shekelle, 1987). Chronic stress is related to an increased chance of succumbing to contagious diseases including the common cold (Cohen, Tyrrell, & Smith, 1991).

STRESS AND THE IMMUNE SYSTEM.   How can stress be related to so many different kinds of illness? For one thing, stress can have a direct effect on the body's immune system. For many years, researchers suspected that there was some kind of direct link between the nervous and immune systems that did not depend on the actions of hormones such as those involved in the hypothalamic-pituitary-adrenal axis, but no one knew what that link might be. In the last few years, however, researchers have begun to uncover the mystery.

Scientists can measure the immune system's proper functioning by examining the effectiveness of the body's lymphocytes (white blood cells). Lymphocytes are the body's means of attacking and destroying foreign or invading organisms. One of the most important discoveries linking the nervous and immune systems was the finding that lymphocytes are covered with receptors for neuropeptides (Ruff, Wahl, Mergenhagen, & Pert, 1985). Neuropeptides are messenger chemicals created by nerve cells (see Chapter 2). This finding strongly implies a nervous system–immune system connection.

Researchers have suspected such a link for years, not only because stress was known to have an effect on health, but also because of some direct evidence of this effect on the body's ability to fight disease (Weber & Pert, 1989). For instance, in one study conducted at the Mount Sinai School of Medicine in New York, researcher Steven J. Schleifer and his colleagues examined the lymphocyte counts of men who were married to women dying of cancer. The average age of the men was 65 years. Within 10 months, the wives of all the men died. The white blood count of these men became lower and lower as the stress continued. Schleifer discovered that their lymphocyte counts were significantly depressed after bereavement (Schleifer, Keller, Camerino, Thornton, & Stein, 1983). It is assumed that lower lymphocyte levels make people more susceptible to disease. In fact, after the death of a spouse, it's not uncommon for the remaining partner to become seriously ill or to die within 2 years. This higher rate of illness and death is much more common among survivors than among similar individuals of the same age who have not suffered the loss of a loved one (Glick, Weiss, & Parkes, 1974; Parkes, 1972).

Natural killer cells are a special kind of lymphocyte and are an important component of our immune system. They help to destroy invading disease agents. How severely these important cells are impaired has been found to vary directly with the amount of stress or depression reported by people who are not able to cope effectively with their situations. The more stress or depression the people were experiencing, the more severely their killer cells were impaired (Irwin, Daniels, Bloom, Smith, & Weiner, 1987; Herbert & Cohen, 1993).

Since the work in this area, known as *psychoneuroimmunology*, began, many direct nervous system–immune system connections have been uncovered; so many, in fact, that researchers now think of the immune system as a *sensory system*, not unlike vision or hearing, because it collects information (about the state of the body's health) and sends the information to the central nervous system for processing—all without your awareness (Marx, 1985). Because of the discovery of the connections between the two systems, we are in a better position to understand how shocks to the nervous system, such as are caused by stress, bereavement, or depression, are capable of compromising the immune system (Calabrese, Kling, & Gold, 1987).

Stress is relative, however. To understand better what is meant by this statement, consider the following study. Researcher Steven Locke randomly selected 117 students at Boston University and evaluated *how much* stress they suffered by having them complete a stress survey that measured their symptoms, such as poor sleep or feelings of anxiety. In addition, Locke asked his subjects how each thought he or she was coping with stress. Then blood samples drawn from each subject were exposed to human leukemia cells. Locke's aim was to discover *how well* the natural killer cells in the blood samples could attack the leukemia cells. He found some notable differences among blood samples—and something else, too. The ability of the body's immune system to attack effectively was related less to how much stress each subject faced than to how well that person was coping with the stress. In other words, a person who can cope with stress may have a better chance of staying healthy than a person who cannot cope (Sapolsky, 1990). This could explain why two individuals in the same stressful job might show totally different bodily reactions to the stress they face (Locke, Furst, Heisel, & Williams, 1978; Locke, et al., 1984).

The relationship between illness and the immune system is also a complex one. Although there is a general link between illness and stress, no immune system disease such as lupus, multiple sclerosis, and some forms of arthritis has ever been directly linked to stress (Stein, Miller, & Trestman, 1991). Furthermore, while some people with apparently healthy and strong immune systems become quite ill, others with weak or compromised immune systems remain healthy (Stein, Miller, & Trestman, 1991). All we can say for certain is that long-term stress is associated with immune system weakness, and that in turn is associated with some susceptibility to illness, but doesn't necessarily lead to illness. In the same sense, a stress-free life (if there could ever be such a thing) would not necessarily be a guarantee of good health.

Measuring Susceptibility to Stress and Illness

Is there any way to measure how much stress you may be facing from day to day? In Table 15.4, you'll see a scale for rating life changes, developed by Holmes and Rahe back in 1967. Each of these life events is assigned a value, a certain number of stress points. In their study, Holmes and Rahe found that individuals who had more than 300 stress points within 1 year were two or three times as likely to have illness and other stress-related problems than were individuals who had fewer stress points. Again, it is important to point out that these were only averages. Some people with many stress points remained quite healthy, while some with few stress points became ill. On the average, however, a relationship between stress and illness was found.

One interesting detail you may notice while reading the table is that some very nice things seem to be stressful. Among these often pleasant events or

TABLE 15.4 ◆ SOCIAL READJUSTMENT RATING SCALE

RANK	LIFE EVENT	MEAN VALUE	RANK	LIFE EVENT	MEAN VALUE
1.	Death of spouse	100	24.	Trouble with in-laws	29
2.	Divorce	73	25.	Oustanding personal achievement	28
3.	Marital separation from mate	65	26.	Wife beginning or ceasing work outside the home	26
4.	Detention in jail or other institution	63	27.	Beginning or ceasing formal schooling	26
5.	Death of a close family member	63	28.	Major change in living conditions (building a new home, remodeling, deterioration of home or neighborhood)	25
6.	Major personal injury or illness	53			
7.	Marriage	50			
8.	Being fired at work	47	29.	Revision of personal habits (dress, manners, associations, etc.)	24
9.	Marital reconciliation with mate	45	30.	Trouble with the boss	23
10.	Retirement from work	45	31.	Major change in working hours or conditions	20
11.	Major change in the health or behavior of a family member	44	32.	Change in residence	20
12.	Pregacy	40	33.	Changing to a new school	20
13.	Sexual difficulties	39	34.	Major change in usual type and/or amount of recreation	19
14.	Gaining a new family member (through birth, adoption, oldster moving in, etc.)	39	35.	Major change in church activities (a lot more or a lot less than usual)	19
15.	Major business readjustment (merger, reorganization, bankruptcy, etc.)	39	36.	Major change in social activities (clubs, dancing, movies, visiting, etc.)	18
16.	Major change in financial state (a lot worse off or a lot better off than usual)	38	37.	Taking out a mortgage or loan for a lesser purchase (for a car, TV, freezer, etc.)	17
17.	Death of a close friend	37	38.	Major change in sleeping habits (a lot more or a lot less sleep, or change in part of day when asleep)	16
18.	Changing to a different line of work	36			
19.	Major change in the number of arguments with spouse (either a lot more or a lot less than usual regarding child rearing, personal habits, etc.)	35	39.	Major change in number of family get-togethers (a lot more or a lot less than usual)	15
20.	Taking out a mortgage or loan for a major purchase (for a home, business, etc.)	31	40.	Major change in eating habits (a lot more or a lot less food intake, or very different meal hours or surroundings)	15
21.	Foreclosure on a mortgage or loan	30	41.	Vacation	13
22.	Major change in responsibilities at work (promotion, demotion, lateral transfer)	29	42.	Christmas	12
23.	Son or daughter leaving home (marriage, attending college, etc.)	29	43.	Minor violation of the law (traffic tickets, jaywalking, disturbing the peace, etc.)	11

SOURCE: Holmes & Rahe, 1967.

circumstances are marriage, gaining a new family member, a change in financial state (which could mean for the better as well as for the worse), an outstanding personal achievement, the beginning of school, family get-togethers, and even a vacation.

Several major points should be kept in mind. First, these data are correlational and do not necessarily imply cause and effect. For example, people of lower socioeconomic status (who are also more likely to have poorer health care) lead lives in which more changes take place, often due to financial problems. Stressful changes in the lives of such people may only be correlated with poor health and not be the cause of it. If so, then adding up stress points may not be a valid way to explain future problems. Similarly, the stress points should be used solely as a general guideline. Although the numbers give them the appearance of being highly specific, they aren't; they're only general. For example, it's highly doubtful that one pregnancy, one Christmas, and four vacations would be more stressful than the death of a spouse. So read the table with an open mind.

Most research dealing with stress and illness begins with an examination of a population suffering from illness; the objective is to determine how much stress that group was under before the illness. But this kind of research can be biased, in that the researchers often know ahead of time that the people they are dealing with are suffering from stress-related illnesses. When time and funds permit, researchers prefer to conduct *prospective* research, in which they find a healthy population, study the subjects' stress patterns, and observe the long-term effects on health.

The largest study of this kind has been conducted by George E. Vaillant (1979). He selected 204 men who were in the sophomore class at Harvard from 1942 to 1944. For over four decades, he kept in touch with 185 of them. During these years, Vaillant and other researchers conducted many psychological and physical tests on, as well as interviews with, the subjects. Stress predictors included how often the subjects visited a psychiatrist or psychologist, whether they were failing to make progress in their job, whether they were dissatisfied with their job, whether their marriage was unhappy, whether they received little vacation or recreation time, and whether they had a poor outlook on life.

The findings of this study generally support the notion that people who have the ability to cope well with stress are likely to be healthier. Of the 59 men in this study who coped well with stress and who had the best mental health, only 2 became extremely ill or died by the time they were 53 years of age. Of the 48 men who were found to have the worst mental health, 18 became chronically ill or died. The men in this group had shown themselves to be less able to deal with stress. The men in both groups came from very similar backgrounds. Clearly, their ability to cope with stress was directly related to their physical health.

By 1990, Vaillant could report that one of the strongest predictors of mental and physical health after age 65 was the extent of tranquilizer use before age 50 (Vaillant & Vaillant, 1990). It is assumed that those who were in need of tranquilizers were either under more stress or coping less well.

In keeping with these findings, another prospective study took almost 3000 initially healthy subjects ages 45 to 77 and tracked them for 12 years. The results of the study showed that subjects who reported feeling the most hopeless about their lives throughout the study were four times more likely to die from heart disease than were the other subjects. The study controlled for the effects of gender, age, smoking, alcohol use, blood pressure, and other factors known to be related to heart disease (Anda, et al., 1993).

AN ENDURING QUESTION: ARE THERE DISEASE-PRONE PERSONALITIES?

For centuries, philosophers and scientists have wondered about the role of personality in the onset of disease (Taylor, 1990). In the 1930s and 1940s, specific personality profiles were developed along with the claim that they were able to predict the likelihood of hypertension, cancer, heart disease, ulcers, arthritis, and other diseases (Dunbar, 1943; Alexander, 1950). Convincing evidence to support these claims, however, was lacking.

Yet common sense tells us that we shouldn't be too surprised to discover that individuals exposed to prolonged stress differ in their vulnerabilities to serious disease. In 1959, researchers Meyer Friedman and Ray Rosenman separated male personalities into two categories, type A and type B, and linked them to coronary artery disease. Men with type A personalities are intense, alert, competitive, and striving, while those with type B are relaxed, easygoing, and unpressured (Friedman & Rosenman, 1959).

META-ANALYSIS
An examination of many studies that focus on one topic in order to discover an overall consensus. Careful attention is paid to eliminating faulty studies.

AN ENDURING QUESTION, CONTINUED

Since that time, much research has indicated that type A males have a greater chance of incurring heart disease than do type B males (Suinn, 1977). This research implies that certain personality types are more prone to specific stress-related illnesses. In fact, the idea of type A personality and its relationship to heart disease became so well established that efforts to change personality with the hope of lessening heart disease became commonplace.

More recently, however, support for the idea of a heart-attack-prone personality has not been forthcoming. The problems with the concept were brought to light when cardiologist Robert Case analyzed the personalities of 516 heart-attack victims and discovered that type As were no more likely to have heart attacks than were the type Bs (Case, Heller, Case, & Moss, 1985). To avoid possible bias, another physician, Richard Shekelle, conducted a prospective study with 3110 men who had never had a heart attack. He classified their personality types according to the recognized methods of sorting type A from type B; then he waited to see what would happen. After a few years, the subjects had had a total of 129 heart attacks, divided evenly between type As and type Bs (Shekelle, et al., 1985). These new findings have led some researchers to conclude that the earlier positive results linking type A personality to heart disease may have been due to interviewer bias (see Chapter 1) or other confounding measures (Lazarus, DeLongis, Folkman, & Gruen, 1985). These findings then prompted two psychologists, Howard Friedman and Stephanie Booth-Kewley, to make a careful analysis and comparison of 101 studies conducted between 1945 and 1984 on disease and personality. This approach is called a **meta-analysis.** They concluded that there does appear to be a slight link between type A behavior and heart attack (Friedman & Booth-Kewley, 1987). But others conducting meta-analysis of these studies have come to the opposite conclusion, that type A behavior is not related to heart attack (Matthews, 1988). The cause of all this confusion may be that "type A" has never been clearly defined (Friedman & Booth-Kewley, 1988; Rodin & Salovey, 1989) and is often assessed differently from one study to the next.

It may well be that certain personalities make people more prone to illness in general, although perhaps not to *specific* illnesses, but further research is needed before we can say which personalities might be at higher risk.

FOR CRITICAL ANALYSIS

1. It was once believed that stress caused ulcers. We now know that although stress may exacerbate an ulcer, it cannot cause one. This discovery has reduced the guilt commonly felt by the ulcer patient concerning his condition. Why?
2. If certain personalities are eventually linked to specific illnesses, how might guilt and blame reemerge in patients with certain physical illnesses? Why might they come to feel this way?   ◆

Hassles

Sometimes we know the exact cause of our stress and have an idea about how to handle the problem. Much of the time, however, we can't put our finger on what's wrong when we feel under stress. Stress doesn't have to result from an extreme trauma such as a plane crash or volcanic eruption. Instead, over days and weeks a number of what people call "hassles" can add up, resulting in stress. Hassles include getting stuck in a traffic jam, receiving a personal insult from someone, not being appreciated enough on the job, receiving a parking ticket, having to rush to get to work, burning dinner, having a favorite television show be preempted, being $2 short at the supermarket, spilling food on your clothes, or sleeping through the alarm. How many irritations like these occur each day, none of them significant by itself? They can accumulate and create an overall feeling of stress that we can't blame on any one thing (Kanner, Coyne, Schaefer, & Lazarus, 1981). Enough of these little irritations can lead to a general adaptation syndrome.

If we allow ourselves to be subjected to these kinds of stressors often enough, the reaction can last a long time. We can begin to feel fearful about our very existence. This feeling is known as **anxiety.** Anxiety is different from fear. If you are fearful, you know why you're afraid. If you are anxious, by definition, you don't know the specific cause. Anxiety is not object-related. The American Psychiatric Association has defined anxiety as "apprehension, tension, or uneasiness that stems from the anticipation of danger, the source of which is largely unknown or unrecognized."

Anxiety levels are generally found to be higher among people who handle stress poorly. Such people go through the day with a feeling of dread that's just below the surface, a constant tenseness. They're steeled for the next insult. Why do some people become anxious when facing hassles while others remain calm and relaxed? Evidence indicates that there may be a biological or genetic difference in people most susceptible to life's hassles.

Evidence of a genetic factor was gathered by researcher Gregory Carey (Carey, Goldsmith, Tellegen, & Gottesman, 1978), who reported that identical twins are much more likely to react similarly to stress than are fraternal (nonidentical twins). Other evidence (Jemerin & Boyce, 1990) indicates that there may be biochemical differences among people that influence how they handle stress. Specific brain cells that seek out benzodiazepines have been discovered. Benzodiazepines are tranquilizers such as Valium or Xanax. The existence of such natural receptors implies that the brain must be manufacturing its own natural benzodiazepine, or else why would there be brain cells ready to receive it (see Chapter 2)? This finding indicates that the brain relies on neurochemistry to mediate how much anxiety people feel in the face of stress. If we discover that people with different levels of anxiety have significantly different brain chemistry, then we might find a biological reason to explain why some people are better able to handle stress than others are. In addition, it may eventually be possible to develop totally safe and effective drugs that enlarge our capacity to endure stress. If such drugs are used judiciously, people could be "tuned" to an optimal level for handling stress without exhausting their psychological and physiological resources.

Suicide

In the throes of a conflict, or under intense stress, some people may consider suicide to be a reasonable solution. Many such people apparently look on suicide as a decision to stop participating in a stressful life. Over the last 15 years, there has been an alarming increase in suicide, especially among adolescents. For those 15 to 19 years old, suicide is the third-ranking cause of death, just behind accidents and murder. The rate of suicide among the aged is also alarmingly high (Holden, 1992). David Kupfer, a psychiatrist specializing in suicide and depression has said, "Officially, there are 32,000 suicides a year in the United States, but the real number is a lot higher" (Holden,

ANXIETY
A state of apprehension in which the source is usually not specific, as it is in fear. There is a vague but persistent feeling that some future danger is in store, such as punishment or a threat to self-esteem. Anxiety typically leads to defensive reactions.

FOCUS ON ETHNIC DIVERSITY

PROMOTING HEALTH IN ETHNIC MINORITY POPULATIONS

Most of the research concerning stress has either focused on white populations or on a representative mixture of the U.S. population as a whole. However, ethnic minority populations often have special health needs or are sometimes uniquely different when compared with majority or representative populations. For example, among whites the suicide rate increases with age. Elderly whites in America are at the highest risk for suicide. Among African-Americans, however, the suicide rate does not increase with age and even appears to decrease slightly (see Figure 15.1). In fact, suicide among elderly African-American women is extremely rare compared with their white counterparts (Holden, 1992). Why this is so remains a mystery. It would be interesting to know how culture or family might be influencing these rates of suicide or even if genetic factors play a role. For such reasons, the study of ethnic minority populations offers health psychology fertile ground for investigating various influences on human well-being.

Currently, nearly one quarter of the U.S. population is composed of members of ethnic minorities. The recent acceleration of ethnic populations in the United States is due in large part to immigration. Consequently, many members of ethnic minorities now living in the United States are first-generation immigrants who are unacculturated and unfamiliar with the U.S. health care system (Castro & Magana, 1988). As a result, they may suffer the special stresses associated with the greater likelihood of social isolation and limited health care as well as the stresses associated with a higher rate of unemployment or poverty.

Minority members may also face unique stresses or health needs depending on the minority to which they belong. For instance, African-Americans have the historical issues of slavery and institutionalized discrimination as antecedents of current social problems. Included among these problems are high levels of urban crime and a certain amount of ongoing prejudice at the hands of the dominant culture. For reasons as yet unknown, African-Americans are also at significant risk for high blood pressure, which often goes untreated for lack of available health care or opportunities to obtain regular checkups and treatment.

For Hispanics, prejudice, poverty, and higher levels of urban crime are often associated with the added stress of recent immigration. This is often exacerbated by the need to learn a new language, something first-generation immigrants often have difficulty accomplishing. This, in turn, can limit the doctor-patient relationship to local care providers who may be overburdened. Hispanics, also for unknown reasons, run a higher risk of contracting diabetes. Tradition and attitudes about gender roles can be an important factor. Among Hispanics, women are expected to see doctors, but men typically resist treatment. Young Hispanic males are among the least likely individuals ever to see a physician for regular checkups. And yet, many problems such as diabetes can be adequately treated if caught early before symptoms appear.

Asian and Pacific Islanders are a very diverse group. Japanese Americans are already highly acculturated into the United States. As a result, recent Japanese immigrants may find life in the United States less stressful than immigrants from, for instance, Indochina or Korea, who typically have fewer resources (Castro & Magana, 1988). Psychologists and physicians who are unfamiliar with Asian or Pacific cultures may need to learn how issues such as shame, stigma, and loss of face may affect a person's willingness to see a doctor or discuss a problem. For example, a male doctor treating a recently arrived Chinese woman may find that she will not answer a blunt question about whether she recently had unprotected sex, the same kind of question that an American college student might answer readily.

Furthermore, lifestyle can be a major contributor to health, and different minorities often accept or promote different lifestyles. The use of cigarettes, alcohol, and drugs does differ from group to group, although poverty is the factor most associated with these behaviors. For this reason, urban black populations, who are often the most financially impoverished, are more likely to suffer from health-related problems associated with alcohol, tobacco, and drug use.

Physicians and psychologists need to be aware of the special stresses or medical problems people may face as members of ethnic minorities. In this way, better health care can be promoted and achieved for everyone.

◆ **FIGURE 15.1** *Suicide rates by age group, 1989.* (SOURCE: *Holden, 1992, p. 1761.*)

1992, p. 1761). The reason for this is that some suicides are called accidents to spare the family's feelings or are wrongly listed as accidents or natural deaths. It is thought, for instance, that a significant number of car "accidents" are actually suicides. A number of people who have survived car accidents have later admitted that they were, in fact, trying to take their own lives. Failed suicides are common. For each successful suicide, there are about 100 attempts (Holden, 1992).

While it's obvious that anyone would be susceptible to the stress associated with a trauma such as a plane crash or a war, it's also true that many people, even those who appear to have everything they need, live in situations that they appraise as stressful. Stress is highly personal, and each individual reacts to it differently. Some people may suffer severe stress in situations in which others wouldn't experience stress at all or even see the reason for it.

Think of stressful times in your life when you were much younger. Suppose you could play the game "If I only knew then what I know now." Suppose you could bring your current maturity and knowledge to bear in an earlier stressful situation. Conflicts with parents might seem foolish or needless. Concerns over your complexion or your treatment at the hands of certain classmates might seem trivial. The point of this exercise is to show that people who are under stress may be lacking important information. Their view of their situation may not be the only possible view. They may see themselves trapped in a horrible conflict with no way out, where someone with different knowledge or understanding might not even see a conflict.

Suicide is a final solution, and one from which there can be no return. Many people who have seriously attempted suicide but failed have later found other ways of coping with their stress. Unfortunately, as suicide rates increase and more attention is given to it by the media and the public, it is on the minds of more people and is more often considered as an alternative. One interviewer discovered that 65 percent of all college students had at one time or another thought of suicide with sufficient intensity to contemplate the means (Mishara, 1975).

Suicide must always be viewed as a possibility among people who are under considerable stress. One of the goals of psychologists is to be aware of the hazard and to make sure that potential suicides are given a chance to obtain help.

Several signs may warn of a potential suicide. First, any attempts at suicide, however mild, or jokes about suicide, however lightly made, must be taken seriously. The person should be offered help in the form of family support or professional counseling. Previous attempts at suicide also are significant, because 30 to 40 percent of the people who commit suicide have attempted it previously. Furthermore, about 10 percent of the people who attempt suicide will kill themselves within 10 years of the attempt (Grinspoon, 1986).

Among adolescents, a population with a high suicide rate, an important warning sign is the perceived failure to achieve in school—a sign that should be especially heeded in students who have superior or better-than-average ability. Of those adolescents who have committed suicide because of perceived failure at school, only 11 percent were actually in serious academic trouble (which again shows how often stress is in the eye of the beholder) (Jacobs, 1971). Another important sign among adolescents is a sudden increase in aggression or violence-related behavior such as carrying weapons or engaging in fights (Garrison, McKeown, Valois, & Vincent, 1993). It is believed that teens who become aggressive may be more likely to act out suicidal thoughts.

An important sign for members of all age groups is withdrawal from social relationships. Such withdrawal may occur because the person feels unwanted by his family (Rosenkrantz, 1978). Rejection by friends and peers can also contribute to withdrawal. Another indication may be the termination or failure of a love relationship. And any recent loss, even eviction from an apartment, can tilt a person toward suicide if she has a serious drug or alcohol problem (Rich, Fowler, Fogarty, & Young, 1988). In another interesting study, cigarette smoking has been found to be a predictor of suicide among middle-aged women (Hemenway, Solnick, & Colditz, 1993). In this correlational study, 100,000 female registered nurses between the ages of 30 and 55 living in 11 states were studied. Among those who committed suicide, women who smoked between 1 and 24 cigarettes daily were twice as likely to kill themselves as nonsmokers, and those who smoked more than 24 cigarettes a day were four times as likely to take their own lives. The reason for this correlation is not known. It may be that people who are under considerable stress often turn to cigarettes for comfort.

Another possible reason for suicide involves brain chemistry. In 1975, Swedish researchers were attempting to measure levels of serotonin in the human brain. Serotonin, a neurotransmitter that had been discovered not long before, was known to be involved with mood and emotion. Because brain serotonin cannot be measured directly without destroying the brain itself, the researchers took samples of cerebrospinal fluid from the spines of human subjects and measured the levels of a substance known as 5HIAA, which is known to be a good indicator of the level of brain serotonin. Psychiatrist Marie Asberg still remembers the day in June 1975 when one of her staff psychiatrists happened to notice something and commented, "All these low-5HIAA patients kill themselves" (Pines, 1983, p. 56). Dr. Asberg recalls, "I thought, my God, what is she saying?" (p. 56). In fact, the staff psychiatrist had inadvertently discovered a biological marker that might be directly related to the incidence of suicide. Following that discovery, researchers linked low levels of serotonin and 5HIAA with depression, aggression, and impulsivity. As you can imagine, the combination of these three attributes is an obvious formula for violent suicide. In fact, the lower the levels, the more impulsive and aggressive the suicide (see Figure 15.2).

Building on this work, researchers in Finland have studied violent criminals. They discovered that men who committed impulsive unpremeditated murders had the lowest levels of 5HIAA. Among this group, it was also discovered that men who had killed more than once had levels of 5HIAA that were lower than those in men who had only killed once (Roy, De Jong, & Linnoila, 1989). Low levels of 5HIAA almost assuredly mean impulsive, aggressive behavior, whether directed at oneself or others.

Perhaps the most extensive work in this area has been conducted by Victoria Arango and her colleagues. She examined 20 suicide victims along with 20 sex- and age-matched controls. Her findings uncovered a significantly larger number of binding sites for serotonin in the brains of the suicide victims, an indication that their brains were trying to compensate for a serotonin deficiency (Arango, Underwood, & Mann, 1992).

Researchers have also discovered that the ratio of two other important neurotransmitters, norepinephrine and epinephrine, plays a role in suicide. People who have too much epinephrine, relative to their levels of norepinephrine, have been found to be more likely to kill themselves (Ostroff, Giller, Harkness, & Mason, 1985).

Certain genes may also be responsible for suicide (Swift, Perkins, Chase, Sadler, & Swift, 1991). For many years, it has been known that suicides run in families. The case of the famous American writer Earnest Hemingway may be such an example. Although his suicide in 1961 was well publicized, few people realize that Hemingway's father, sister, and brother also took their own lives. And the Hemingway family is not unique in showing this sort of clustered

◆ **FIGURE 15.2**

Marie Asberg's comparison of the 5HIAA levels of 46 patients who had attempted suicide with 45 healthy volunteers. The average 5HIAA level for the suicidal group was 16.3 nanograms per milliliter compared to 19.8 for the controls. More striking was the very low 5HIAA of those who made violent attempts—hanging or drowning, for example. Six patients killed themselves within the year. (SOURCE: Adapted from Pines, 1983.)

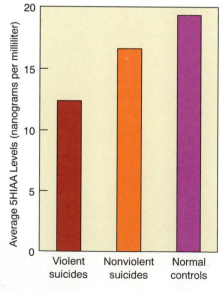

occurrence. Psychologists now consider suicide by one or more blood relatives to be an important indicator of potential suicide in an individual.

Although more research is needed, these findings indicate that psychologists may be on their way to developing valid screening tests for potential suicides and other violent, impulsive behavior.

❧ WAYS OF COPING WITH STRESS

If you stop for a moment to think about some of the conflicts or traumas that people face, you may wonder how these people ever adjust. But there are ways of coping, some of which people turn to almost automatically (Lazarus, 1993).

Psychological Defense Mechanisms

Sometimes, we're able to handle conflict and stress by using defense mechanisms. These are ways of handling information to make it appear more agreeable; we see a conflict or a trauma in a light that renders it less disturbing. This is called **emotion-focused coping,** and it helps us to change the way in which we perceive what is happening to us (Lazarus, 1993). Among the defense mechanisms that enable us to engage in emotion-focused coping are **denial, rationalization, reaction formation,** and **projection** (see Chapter 14). Such defenses are normal and healthy. They help us to survive stress. Without them, we would be prey to the full intensity of every conflict or trauma. As we noted in Chapter 14, in general, psychologists don't consider the use of defense mechanisms inappropriate or unhealthy unless we rely on these mechanisms to an extreme.

Stress Management

In contrast to defense mechanisms, which can alter your view of the stressors in your life, **problem-focused coping** can help you either to eliminate the stressor or to harden yourself to the hassles that occur every day and the big ones that occur once in a while (Lazarus, 1993). Deciding which kind of coping to choose may not always be clear. As psychologist Richard Lazarus has pointed out,

Here we have rediscovered the Alcoholics Anonymous epigram, that people should try to change the noxious things that can be changed, accept those that cannot, and have the wisdom to know the difference. (Lazarus, 1993, p. 9)

Even so, there is no way of totally avoiding stress—but avoiding it may not be necessary. Remember, the amount of stress you face isn't nearly as important as how you deal with it. If you can learn to treat stress in the right way, you can defuse it. Psychologists have concentrated much of their effort on training people to cope directly with their stress. Coping does not always come naturally. It must be learned and honed like any other skill.

CLINICAL STRESS MANAGEMENT. At a meeting of the American Medical Association in 1921, Edmund Jacobson introduced the concept of psychosomatic illness—physical illness brought on by stress and tension. His interest in this area continued, and in 1938 he developed a treatment for neuromuscular tension, called **progressive relaxation** (Jacobson, 1938). This marked the first serious effort to develop a clinical technique that could be applied to reduce and alleviate stress. Since that time, many different stress-management techniques have been developed. Unfortunately, because modern stress-management technology has become a growth industry and many wildly exaggerated claims have been made by various groups and individuals pur-

EMOTION-FOCUSED COPING
Strategies that attempt to alter the way in which we attend to or interpret stressors.

DENIAL
A defense mechanism in which the individual simply denies the existence of the events that have produced the anxiety.

RATIONALIZATION
A defense mechanism in which irrational, impulsive action, or even failure, is justified to others and to oneself by substituting acceptable explanations for the real, but unacceptable, reasons.

REACTION FORMATION
A defense mechanism in which the individual exhibits, and at the conscious level believes he or she possesses, feelings opposite to those possessed at the unconscious level.

PROJECTION
A defense mechanism in which the individual attributes his or her own motives or thoughts to others, especially when these motives or thoughts are considered undesirable.

PROBLEM-FOCUSED COPING
Active rational strategies intended to alleviate stress by directly eliminating or reducing the stressor.

PROGRESSIVE RELAXATION
A technique in which deep relaxation is achieved through the progressive relaxation of one muscle group at a time, usually beginning with the feet and legs. The subject breathes deeply and focuses attention on each muscle group as it is relaxed.

Techniques such as biofeedback have been helpful for training people to relax.

porting to alleviate stress, it's not always easy to be a knowledgeable consumer. Many serious scientists have carefully evaluated stress-reduction techniques, however, and psychologists now have a general idea of how effective each of these techniques is. Some of the techniques that have often proved beneficial are listed in Table 15.5. A word of caution is in order, however. Applying these techniques to the problem of reducing human stress requires a certain amount of therapeutic art. For this reason, the techniques often vary in their effectiveness, depending on the skill and wisdom of the clinician who is applying them (Woolfolk & Lehrer, 1984).

COPING STRATEGIES. Besides using clinical interventions to alleviate stress, you can use some personal coping strategies:

1. If you find yourself in a conflict, you're probably going to be uncomfortable. No one likes to be uncomfortable. As a result, people have a tendency to get the conflict over with as quickly as possible and thus to end the discomfort. This can lead to a rushed judgment that may in the long run cause even greater problems—you may make the wrong choice. One of the best ways to cope with a conflict is to gather as much information as possible. Say to yourself, "All right, I'm uncomfortable and I'll be uncomfortable for a while, but it's more important to gather information to help me with my choice than to rush to a conclusion I might not be satisfied with." As you gather information, you usually will find that your view of the conflict begins to change, and the choice becomes obvious. Suddenly, the conflict will be over because you have enough information to make the right decision.

2. Trust in time. Many stressful events can be very painful. Divorce is a good example. After a divorce, many people feel that their lives have been ruined. Even months after a divorce, depression and stress are likely to be severe or even to increase. New stressors must be faced, such as dating again, adjusting to a lower income, or raising children as a single parent. It can seem that the anguish will never end. But, although time may not heal all wounds, it often helps. Mavis Hetherington found that among divorced couples, the stress is often much lower 2 years after the divorce (Hetherington, 1979). In other words, the pain is likely to decrease significantly given time. People make new friends, form new bonds, and often remarry. This is true, not only of divorce, but also of other stressful situations. If you find yourself in extreme anguish, feeling that all of your plans are collapsing or that your career is being ruined, trust in time. There is a good possibility that within a year or two after your current world has collapsed, you will find yourself in another one that is fulfilling.

3. Try not to be alone too much of the time. Maintain friendships and contacts. The lonely and the isolated suffer stress more and have poorer health than do those who have company (House, Landis, & Umberson, 1988; Taylor, 1990). Other people can function to distract you by making you interested in things they find exciting. When you're by yourself, to keep yourself company you tend to discuss personal issues with yourself. But when you're with other people and are involved in doing things with them, it's difficult to engage in self-reflection. Often, the good ideas and moods of other people can have a relaxing and comforting effect. In addition, it is helpful to have a pet with whom to share your time alone. Pets help to keep away loneliness, and their

TABLE 15.5 ◆ STRESS-MANAGEMENT TECHNIQUES

TECHNIQUE	PROCEDURE	THERAPEUTIC BENEFIT
Progressive relaxation	Over many sessions, a subject is taught to pay attention to individual muscles until she is able to recognize levels of tension in each muscle.	Subjects become aware of which muscles are tense at any given time. They can then eliminate unnecessary tension by relaxing and thereby reduce or eliminate headache, neuralgia, excessive physiological arousal, or other stress-related disorders.
Modified progressive relaxation	Deep muscle relaxation is taught by use of a relaxing environment, deep breathing, and cycles of tensing and relaxing muscles. (The emphasis is on learning to relax rather than on learning the tension level of each muscle.)	This technique takes less time than the original form of progressive relaxation. It reduces muscle tension and induces relaxation, which may help stem the general adaptation syndrome.
Yogic therapy	Typically, progressive relaxation is combined with meditation and the body postures associated with yoga. The technique often contains elements of the Hindu religion.	The therapy helps alleviate muscle tension, excessive autonomic arousal, and hypertension. People who like the yoga exercises especially enjoy it.
Meditation	Subjects learn relaxation, deep breathing, and concentration on one particular sound or idea.	This technique reduces blood pressure and may help reduce anxiety, fatigue, insomnia, mild depression, and irritability.
Hypnosis	Hypnotic induction is described in Chapter 7. It is especially useful for subjects who are susceptible to suggestion or feel comfortable with the idea of hypnosis.	Subjects may respond to suggestion by developing greater relaxation and a more positive attitude concerning stressful situations.
Biofeedback	Equipment that amplifies body temperature, muscle tension, or other physiological measures provides subjects with feedback about their biological activity.	In conjunction with therapy and proper assessment, biofeedback can help subjects regulate their biological activity. Control of muscle tension and autonomic arousal often is the focal point.
Cognitive therapy	Therapy focuses on the individual's own cognitive appraisals. Stressful ideas, thoughts, and perceptions are directly examined and tested to determine their validity.	The subject's thinking may be restructured, so that situations or circumstances that were once perceived as extremely stressful are viewed in a less stressful, often more realistic, light.
Psychopharmacology	Medications are used to alter psychological or physiological reactions to stress.	In conjunction with psychotherapy, people suffering from acute stress may benefit from temporary use of drugs to control anxiety, depression, and other stress-related disorders such as muscle tension.

CHEMICAL DEPENDENCE
The strong and compelling desire to continue taking a chemical substance because of its physical or psychological effects.

presence has been shown to reduce stress, high blood pressure, and depression and to lessen the likelihood of illness (Culliton, 1987; Allen, Blascovich, Tomaka, & Kelsey, 1991).

4. People who have a pessimistic outlook on life are more likely to develop poor health (Peterson, Seligman, & Vaillant, 1988), so try to think positively and rationally. Keep a sense of humor. Enjoy laughter. And remember that not everything that seems to be a catastrophe really is one. Not every goal is worth having. In fact, you may have been very lucky that you didn't achieve some of your goals. Remember the old saying, "Beware of what you desire, you might obtain it."

5. Begin to think of yourself as a relaxed person. Move and speak more slowly. Eat slowly. Take deep breaths. Stop from time to time to relax your muscles. Watch how hectic the lives of other people seem, and let this remind you to slow down more. Don't schedule your life so that you need to rush from place to place. If you find yourself in a traffic jam, don't think about the future and how the traffic is keeping you from being someplace. Instead, take a deep breath, turn on the radio, listen to the music, and relax. Look at the tense faces and angry expressions of the people around you, and take pleasure in the fact that you are a relaxed person.

These ideas may seem simple; in fact, they are. Nevertheless, relying on them can make a powerful difference. One final thought—remember that stress is not always a bad thing. A small amount of stress may serve to move you to action. Stress is likely to be detrimental only if it is unresolved and long lasting and, especially, if you are prone to deal poorly with it. In one of the Chinese languages, the characters for *stress* mean *pressure* and also *opportunity*. The Chinese have realized that a small amount of stress can motivate people to take action that may eventually provide them with something good, and for this reason their word for stress has both a positive and a negative component.

THE CONTROL OF HEALTH-THREATENING BEHAVIOR: STOPPING SMOKING AND DRINKING

The two most serious health-threatening behaviors, in terms of years of life lost, are both kinds of **chemical dependence.** These are dependence on alcohol and on nicotine. It is estimated that in the United States alone 59 million people are addicted to alcohol, nicotine, or both (Holloway, 1991).

Alcohol Dependence (Alcoholism)

Excessive use of alcohol is deadly. It is a major contributor to death by cancer, stroke, and cirrhosis of the liver. It is also estimated to be responsible for one-third of all fatal motor vehicle accidents (Centers for Disease Control, 1993a). It often is a contributing factor in high blood pressure, pneumonia, diabetes, suicide, accidents, and homicide. Approximately 9 percent of all Americans drink to excess (more than 20 million people). Loss of health or life owing to excessive alcohol consumption far exceeds similar losses from all other drug abuse combined, except for nicotine. Only about 3 percent of the alcohol-addicted people who need help are currently receiving treatment, and yet the cost of treating alcoholism and alcohol-related disorders has surpassed 15 percent of the national health bill! Alcohol abuse is a huge problem.

Whether someone will become an alcoholic is closely related to the number of alcoholics in that person's family. Studies of adopted individuals suggest that a genetic predisposition for alcoholism exists. Children adopted by nonalcoholics are much more likely to become alcoholics than are other adopted children if either or both of their biological parents were alcoholics. This is true even if these children have never known or lived with their biological parents (Cadoret, Cain, & Grove, 1980). The exact way in which this genetic predisposition works is unknown, but relatives of alcoholics have been found to react to alcohol in a chemically different way from people who have no close alcoholic relatives (Schuckit, Gold, & Risch, 1987). It has also been shown that mice can be bred to produce offspring that are genetically more susceptible to alcohol than are other mice (Wafford, Burnett, Dunwiddie, & Harris, 1990). The susceptible mice have been found to have significant differences associated with certain neurotransmitters and their actions (see Chapter 2). The same may be occurring in humans who have inherited a genetic susceptibility to become alcoholic, but it has not yet been proven.

Stress also appears to play an important role in alcoholism. Sober individuals with a higher genetic risk for alcoholism have been found to show a greater heart rate and blood pressure increase in response to stress than do people who have a low genetic risk for alcoholism (Finn & Pihl, 1987).

TREATMENT. The first step in treating alcohol abuse is to detoxify the abuser and to take steps toward physical recovery by providing good food and shelter. Detoxification requires that a person's intake of alcohol be curtailed under supervision. During this time, mild or severe withdrawal symptoms may appear. In severe cases, delirium tremens (see Chapter 7) and convulsions may occur. In modern hospitals and clinics, certain drugs have been found to be helpful in reducing the severity of withdrawal symptoms. Detoxification is only the first step, however. The individual must be taught to take control of his craving for liquor and, if necessary, to abstain from all drinking.

The drug disulfiram (Antabuse) has helped some alcoholics to avoid an immediate return to drinking. A person who has received this drug will experience extreme discomfort if she then ingests alcohol. Antabuse given without additional supportive therapy is insufficient, however, since once out of the hospital the person must self-administer the drug. Antabuse is most effective in keeping the alcohol abuser from drinking for a certain time, during which other therapies can be tried.

Naltrexone, an opiate antagonist, has also been effective in treating the craving for alcohol (O'Malley, et al., 1992; Volpicelli, Alterman, Hayashida, & O'Brien, 1992). It is thought to work by blocking the ability of alcohol to cause the brain to release pleasure inducing endorphins (see Chapter 2).

Psychotherapy focuses on the individual's need to learn to cope with the problems he has been trying to escape and to live without depending on alcohol. Although there is strong genetic evidence that some people have a greater affinity for alcohol than do others, it is possible to learn to avoid alcohol altogether regardless of one's inheritance. Some researchers also believe that it is possible to teach an alcoholic how to be a controlled drinker, that is, how to have only one or two drinks and then stop (Rosenberg, 1993). Others, however, argue that such an approach is fraught with danger and that the chance of relapse into old habits is so high as to make any effort to teach controlled drinking to an alcoholic pointless (Stockwell, 1986).

Alcoholism may be treated by psychotherapeutic techniques, but the most effective treatment is one that was begun, and is still run, by nonpsychologists. In 1935, Bill W. and Dr. Bob in Akron, Ohio, started an organization known as Alcoholics Anonymous, or AA. Bill W. had recovered from his alcoholism through a spiritual change. He, in turn, was able to help Dr. Bob stop drinking. The two of them formed a group to help other alcoholics. There are now over 10,000 AA groups with over 1 million members in the United States. AA is a nonprofessional counseling program run by alcoholics for alcoholics. AA

PSYCHOTHERAPY
A category of methods for treating psychological disorders. The primary technique is conversation between the patient and the therapist.

argues that an alcoholic is an alcoholic for life and that total abstinence is the only cure. Members support one another at group meetings and can call on one another at a moment's notice in time of need. At the meetings, members often talk about how their lives are now and how their lives were before they stopped drinking. They discuss ways of living without using alcohol. A similar group, Al-Anon, has been established for the families of alcoholics.

With modern therapeutic approaches, social support, and good aftercare, reported recovery rates from alcoholism run as high as 75 percent, but such high rates are rare. Alcoholism can have such a damaging effect on individuals and their lives that it is inaccurate to equate recovery with simply giving up drinking. For an alcoholic to recover, not only must she cease drinking, but she must also often regain physical health, family relationships, social functioning, vocational functioning, and emotional stability, and she must resolve any legal problems brought on during the days of drinking (Emrick & Hansen, 1983). Recovery is an encompassing process (Holden, 1987b), not just the cessation of a particular detrimental behavior. Fortunately, per capita alcohol consumption in the United States has dropped 4 percent since 1980, the year when it reached its peak. This decline may be due to the increased awareness of alcohol's dangers, especially as they pertain to drinking and driving.

If you have a drinking problem, call the National Council on Alcoholism at 1-800-622-2255. They can help you.

Nicotine Dependence

Smoking is even more deadly than drinking, and yet it is more accepted, perhaps because it doesn't change behavior like drinking does. Smoking causes heart disease, cancers, stroke, and emphysema, four of the great killers listed in Table 15.1. It is estimated that smoking kills 350,000 Americans long before their time every year, the equivalent of seven commercial jetliner crashes every day (Edwards, 1986). In the United States, costs to life and health from smoking, as well as costs to productivity, approach $100 billion per year.

Nicotine is powerfully addictive, and many smokers who quit suffer from strong withdrawal cravings that are not just psychological, but are based on a real physical dependence (Hughes & Hatsukami, 1986). Stanley Schachter, a well-known psychologist, published a series of carefully controlled experiments that demonstrated the addictive power of nicotine. Schachter found that blood nicotine levels correlated well with urinary pH (a measurement of acidity). High levels of acid in the blood caused nicotine levels to fall by washing nicotine from the blood. High levels of acid in the urine also indicated the presence of high levels of stomach and blood acid. Schachter formed the hypothesis that when nicotine was washed from the blood, a craving for a cigarette would develop in a person who had become addicted to nicotine through smoking. In his experiments, he demonstrated that the use of antacids such as Rolaids, Tums, or bicarbonate of soda could reduce the craving for cigarettes. Moreover, individuals who smoked cigarettes tended to smoke less when they used antacids to the limit directed on the antacid package. Further studies have shown that the use of antacids can help smokers quit: An addict's desire for a cigarette is lessened because the nicotine he is used to is washed from the blood more slowly when the acid levels are low, enabling him to withdraw from the nicotine gradually. Schachter also discovered that when a person is under stress, blood acid and stomach acid levels rise, washing out some nicotine, which may explain why people get the desire for a cigarette when they become nervous (Schachter, 1977; Schachter, Kozlowski, & Silverstein, 1977; Silverstein, Kozlowski, & Schachter, 1977; Schachter, Silverstein, & Perlick, 1977).

Some smokers attempting to withdraw from nicotine require even more help and have benefited from transdermal nicotine patches that are placed on the skin and administer ever-decreasing doses of nicotine, easing the symptoms of withdrawal. However, many people who resume smoking after quitting appear to do so long after the 2-to-4-week process of nicotine withdrawal has been completed (Hughes, 1992). For this reason, other factors besides nicotine addiction are being considered as causes of smoking addiction.

TREATMENT. To date, professional methods offered for breaking the smoking habit include psychotherapy, record keeping (so that people become aware of how much they are smoking), group pressure, positive reinforcement, hypnosis, aversive conditioning, the use of antacids, nicotine patches, muscle relaxation, assertiveness training, cancer films, and thought stopping (learning to stop your thoughts each time you think of a cigarette), among others. Increased public awareness along with growing social pressure against smoking has had a good effect. In July 1993, the Centers for Disease Control reported that at that time smoking in the United States was at the lowest levels ever recorded; only 19.1 percent of Americans were smokers, and approximately 2.5 percent of Americans were quitting each year, a higher level of quitting than ever previously recorded (Centers for Disease Control, 1993b).

Attempting to quit on your own can work, too. Self-quitters can do as well as those in formal treatment (Cohen, et al., 1989). Light smokers (less than 20 cigarettes per day) are 2.2 times more likely to succeed than heavier smokers; 24 percent relapse even after 6 months of abstinence; and it is common for a few long-term quitters to occasionally have a few cigarettes (Cohen, et al., 1989). Data such as these show that quitting is rarely a one time thing, but rather a dynamic process occurring over time.

If you need help to stop smoking, call the American Cancer Society at 1-800-227-2345. They have specific information and techniques that can help you to quit on your own. If that doesn't work, you can try a formal program. Many are available—check with your state's psychological association or referral service.

The nicotine patch has been a successful aid for helping people to quit smoking. The patch provides small doses of nicotine through the skin, replacing the nicotine usually obtained through smoking. By gradually reducing the nicotine dose, the ex-smoker can kick the smoking habit with a minimum amount of withdrawal symptoms.

❖ SUMMARY

◆ Health psychology has been defined as "any aspect of psychology that bears upon the experience of health and illness and the behavior that affects health status." Every year, researchers offer more evidence that our well-being and physical health are directly linked to our behavior.

◆ One of the important and emerging areas in health psychology is the study of detrimental behaviors. Detrimental behaviors are those behaviors that pose a risk to human health and well-being.

◆ Health psychology is involved with sorting real from perceived risk. It also is concerned with why people don't change their behavior even after they become aware of which of their behaviors are the most dangerous.

◆ Sometimes, acutely stressful situations arise that do not derive from a conflict. Even though the stressful event may be of relatively short duration, it can be so intense that the memory of it can linger for years, resulting in chronic stress.

◆ Stress can lead to illness. Hans Selye has referred to the physical reaction to stress as the general adaptation syndrome, which occurs in three stages. During the alarm reaction stage, the person becomes alerted to the stress. During the resistance stage, the stress continues, and the individual engages in a full-scale effort against it. During the stage of exhaustion, all of the person's resources are gone, and the patterns of coping begin to collapse.

◆ Chronic stress can lead to high blood pressure, heart attack, stroke, and kidney failure. It also can aggravate arthritis, colitis, asthma, hypoglycemia, diabetes, and other disorders. Ulcers also are known to be affected by stress.

◆ One way of measuring the immune system's effectiveness is to count lymphocytes (white blood cells). A person's lymphocyte count often is lower following stressful situations. Stress can also have an effect on the immune system at the cellular level.

◆ The new field of psychoneuroimmunology includes investigations of the many direct nervous system–immune system connections that have been discovered and their effects.

◆ Because of the discovery of the connections between the nervous and immune systems, researchers are better able to understand how shocks to the nervous system—such as those caused by stress, bereavement, or depression—are capable of compromising the immune system's effectiveness.

◆ Stress is relative; people differ in their vulnerability to serious disease caused by prolonged exposure to stress.

◆ There may not be a link between specific diseases—such as heart attack, ulcer, or headache—and certain personality traits. People with certain personalities, however, may be generally more prone to illness than are others.

◆ Stress doesn't have to be the result of an extreme trauma such as a plane crash or volcanic eruption. Instead, over days and weeks, a number of "hassles" can add up, resulting in stress.

◆ A new picture of anxiety is beginning to emerge. Psychological factors are important, but some people may be biologically more susceptible to anxiety.

◆ Over the last decade, there has been an alarming increase in suicide. Although suicide may sometimes seem to be the only way out of a conflict, many people who have made serious attempts at suicide but failed have later found other ways of coping with their stress. The possibility of suicide by people who are under considerable stress must always be taken seriously. Such individuals should be offered help in the form of family support or professional counseling.

◆ Researchers have shown that the incidence of suicide is related to lower levels of serotonin, an important brain neurotransmitter.

◆ People sometimes are able to handle conflict and stress by using defense mechanisms.

◆ A number of stress-management techniques have been developed for clinical use. These include progressive relaxation, yogic therapy, meditation, hypnosis, biofeedback, cognitive therapy, and psychopharmacology.

◆ Problem-focused coping can help you to eliminate stressors or to harden yourself to the stress. Direct methods of coping include gathering as much information as possible, trusting in the healing effects of time, keeping a sense of humor, spending time with other people, realizing that all goals needn't be obtained, and learning to relax.

◆ The two most serious kinds of chemical dependence in terms of damage to health or lives lost are dependence on alcohol and nicotine.

✿ SUGGESTIONS FOR FURTHER READING

1. Colt, G. H. (1992). *The enigma of suicide*. New York: Touchstone Books. A discussion of the causes of suicide ranging from genetic reasons to the influence of television.

2. Dienstfrey, H. (1991). *Where the mind meets the body*. New York: HarperCollins. A discussion of seven major studies from the field of mind-body health for the general reader. It includes topics on relaxation, psychoneuroimmunology, and neuropeptides.

3. Krantz, L. (1992). *What are the odds: A to Z odds on everything you hoped or feared could happen*. New York: HarperPerennial. The title says it all. Interesting reading that helps put risks in perspective.

4. Kutash, I. L., & Schlesinger, L. B. (Eds.) (1980). *Handbook on stress and anxiety*. San Francisco: Jossey-Bass. A comprehensive handbook on the sources and treatment of stress.

5. Meichenbaum, D. (1985). *Stress inoculation training*. New York: Pergamon. A cognitive behavior modification approach to stress and stress reduction.

6. Ornstein, R., & Sobel, D. (1989). *Healthy pleasures*. Reading, MA: Addison-Wesley. Describes ways to achieve good exercise, sleep, nutrition, and education, with the aim of improving health in ways that are natural and fun, rather than via strict regimens. Has lots of practical suggestions.

7. Ornstein, R., & Swencionis, C. (Eds.) (1990). *The healing brain: A scientific reader*. New York: Guilford Press. An examination of the relationship between stress and the immune system.

8. Selye, H. (1976). *The stress of life* (2nd ed.). New York: McGraw-Hill. Outlines the late Hans Selye's classic theory on the body's reactions to stress and how to help control these reactions.

9. Stone, G. C., et al. (Eds.) (1987). *Health psychology: A discipline and a profession*. Chicago: University of Chicago Press. A comprehensive treatment of the field of health psychology, including professional issues, applications, and the training of health psychologists.

10. Taylor, S. (1989). *Positive illusions: Creative self-deception and the healthy mind*. New York: Basic Books. The author argues for the value of a positive outlook and a little self-deception in maintaining mental health.

Chapter Sixteen

Abnormal Behavior

PROLOGUE

SOMETHING IS WRONG

In 1990, Drs. Elaine Walker and Richard Lewine published the results of an experiment designed to look for early warning signs that an individual might be at risk for schizophrenia. Schizophrenia is a severe mental disorder. Those who suffer from it commonly experience serious disturbances of emotion and thought. They often become withdrawn, show inappropriate emotional responses, suffer from hallucinations, or express strange thoughts and beliefs. The disease commonly makes its first appearance during early adulthood and tends to become progressively worse.

In their experiment, Walker and Lewine invited 19 untrained observers to watch some home movies. The observers were told that each movie showed members of a family interacting with one another. They were also informed that the home movies were more than 25 years old and were typical of the movies that most families took back then. Each family—there were five altogether—had either two or three children, and each film spanned a period of at least 5 years in the lives of each family.

The observers were also told that one of the children in each family later became schizophrenic. None of the parents had schizophrenia, nor did any of the siblings later develop the disorder. No schizophrenia was reported in any of the five affected children until they reached early adulthood. In fact, throughout the childhoods of those later affected, none of the parents reported seeing any sign of the impending disaster.

Each of the observers was asked to watch all of the children in the home movies and try to guess which child from each family later developed schizophrenia. To avoid biases, the observers were given no criteria for judging; they were simply told to choose one child from each family.

In a typical film, one might see a family with three children. They would seem cheerful, the way families do in home movies. But still, the observers knew that one of those happy children later suffered from severe mental illness. But which child? In the films all of the children seemed fairly normal.

As the observers watched the children interact, they tried to find something that might tip them off. For example, an observer might notice that as a family interacted, one of the children seemed to grin for just a moment in a

CONTENTS

527

ABNORMAL BEHAVIOR
Behavior that is statistically unusual, considered maladaptive or undesirable by most people, and self-defeating to the person who displays it.

peculiar way while looking at nothing in particular. Or perhaps, a child moved about and swung his arms in a way that seemed a little goofy—of course, all kids act like this sometimes, so what? Or perhaps a child seemed to make less eye contact with the other family members; still, is that so odd? But because the observers were forced to choose, they decided to choose a child from each family based on nothing more than observations of this kind. This was the typical experience the observers had while watching the five films.

When the experiment was over, the results were tabulated. Of the five preschizophrenic children, the observers correctly identified four of them (Walker & Lewine, 1990), a success rate far greater than chance would predict.

Walker and Lewine caution, however, that whatever the observers saw in the preschizophrenic children, it isn't enough to enable us to go among a population of healthy children and pick the ones who will eventually develop schizophrenia. There are simply too many children who are slightly different in some way or sometimes behave oddly, but who nevertheless grow up to be perfectly normal, healthy adults. But the experiment does indicate that something was wrong with this group of schizophrenics many years before their illnesses appeared, something wrong enough to be detected by untrained observers just from watching home movies.

IN THIS CHAPTER, we will examine mental disorders, the differences between normal and abnormal behaviors, how abnormal behaviors are assessed, and the issues that are raised by assessment.

WHY PSYCHOLOGISTS STUDY ABNORMAL BEHAVIOR

We are social beings who live in groups called societies; we depend on one another. We have come to trust one another's behavior. Consequently, abnormal or deviant behavior often is viewed as frightening, puzzling, or disruptive. In a humane society, people ought to help one another; the hungry should be fed, the homeless should be sheltered, and the needy should be cared for. When people's behavior becomes so aberrant that they are unable to survive on their own, or so deviant that it is harmful to themselves or to other people, the members of a humane society will want to help change or prevent the behavior.

Psychology is the study of all behavior, normal and abnormal. Psychologists study abnormal behavior to learn more about behavior and to help those in need.

DEFINING ABNORMALITY

If we want to assess, treat, or possibly prevent **abnormal behavior,** it would be helpful to begin with a clear definition of the term. Many students are surprised, however, to discover that the distinction between normal and abnormal is not always clear.

Although people often picture someone who is mentally ill as ranting and raving uncontrollably, that kind of behavior is actually quite rare and is at the extreme of what most psychologists consider abnormal. Most abnormality is more subtle than the stereotype of the "raving lunatic." For this reason, professionals must be careful when assessing behavior; they must try to keep their own beliefs about what is acceptable personal or societal behavior from biasing their assessment and leading them to an unwarranted view of some behavior as a mental disorder. For instance, poorer persons are more likely to be labeled psychotic than more well-to-do people are (Eron & Peterson, 1982; Redlich & Kellert, 1978). Of course, it may well be that the pressures of living at the lower end of the socioeconomic spectrum predispose a person to more serious illness (Wills & Langner, 1980). Conversely, mental disorder may lead to economic loss resulting in poverty (Harkey, Miles, & Rushing, 1976). But it also may be that evaluators expect poverty and mental illness to go hand in hand, which may bias their judgment and create a self-fulfilling prophecy. The elimination of bias and prejudgment in clinical practice is crucial.

How would you define abnormal? The word *abnormal* means "different from the normal or aberrant to the norm." In usage, however, the term implies more than just deviating from the norm. Skydiving is certainly a deviation from the norm, in that the average person doesn't do it. In fact, few people do. *Statistically*, then, those who skydive are "abnormal." But does this mean that they should be helped or stopped from engaging in their sport?

In the clinical sense, for a behavior to be considered abnormal, it must be not only different from the norm but also *maladaptive* or *self-defeating*. Maladaptive means that the behavior interferes with the person's functioning and development or with the activities of society. A self-defeating behavior is one that will eventually undermine the person's well-being or personal success. Of course, these tests hardly settle the issue. You may have already thought, "Maladaptive or self-defeating by whose standards?" According to this definition, psychiatrists in a police state could consider anyone to be abnormal who disagreed vehemently with the government, since this behavior would be different and, in terms of what the state deemed appropriate, maladaptive and self-defeating for both the individual and society. Whenever we use such terms as maladaptive or self-defeating, we must consider the context. Almost any behavior might be considered normal under the right circumstances. For instance, yelling, shouting, and undressing in front of other people, which would be considered abnormal at the public library, would be considered quite normal in a locker room before a football game. Subtle distinctions between normal and abnormal require value judgments and careful assessment. Abnormal behavior is not absolutely distinct from normal; rather, there is a continuum from normal to abnormal.

As a result, no definition of abnormal behavior is completely satisfactory. Some people believe that if psychology were as exacting as medicine, where diagnoses and diseases are often clearly described, the problem of defining abnormality would be solved. But even in medicine there are shades of gray. Try to conceive of an absolute definition of "physically sick" and you will find it is as difficult as trying to define abnormal behavior. Even at the extremes, it can be difficult. For example, over the last few years 17 different definitions of "severely and persistently mentally ill" have appeared in the professional literature. When researchers decided to apply all seventeen definitions to 222 people who were under treatment in Philadelphia's inner city neighborhoods, it turned out that depending on which definition was used, somewhere between 4 percent and 88 percent of the group were "severely and persistently mentally ill" (Schinnar, Rothbard, Kanter, & Jung, 1990)! Most of the definitions put the number for that group at between 45 and 55 percent, which was also in agreement with the judgments of the authors of the study. This result reinforces the point that clinical judgments play an important role in the assessment of mental disorders. Judgments are made with the aid of definitions, but there is no absolute demarcation line between normal and abnormal.

MODEL
A mathematical, logical, or mechanical replica of a relationship or a system of events so designed that a study of the model can yield some understanding of the real thing.

ETIOLOGY
The cause of a disease or disorder as determined by psychological or medical diagnosis.

INSANE
A legal term for those with a mental disorder, implying that they lack responsibility for their acts and are unable to manage their behavior.

MODELS OF PSYCHOPATHOLOGY

In evaluating the abnormal behavior of another person, psychologists may use different models to provide an understanding or explanation of the disorder in question. A **model** is a depiction or representation that helps to organize knowledge. Several different models may be used to depict the mechanisms that may underlie psychopathology. The model preferred depends on the professional's training and background. In addition, different therapies or treatments are preferred depending on the approach and the model used. Each model has some value. In some circumstances, some models may be more applicable than others. Many mental-health professionals rely on more than one model. For example, most people who rely on the humanistic-existential model would not deny that abnormal behavior occasionally may be caused by biological dysfunction. Nor is someone who relies heavily on the medical model likely to deny that abnormal behaviors can be learned. Instead, each model helps us to understand that abnormal behavior may be the result of many different factors.

The Medical Model

The medical model assumes that the underlying cause, or **etiology,** of a mental disorder is a biological dysfunction. In other words, something has gone wrong biologically, owing to genetics, hormones, biochemical imbalances, trauma, viruses, poisoning, or a host of other events that can disrupt the organism's biology, especially the brain and nervous system. The medical model views abnormal behaviors as analogous to physical illness and as symptoms of an underlying disease or injury. People suffering from mental disorders are referred to as patients, and emphasis is placed on diagnosis and treatment, often incorporating drugs or such other medical therapies such as electroshock or psychosurgery. The medical model is becoming one of the most popular models owing to the rapid growth of neuroscience and the resulting expansion of our knowledge of the brain and neurochemistry.

The Learning Model

According to the learning model, abnormal behaviors are acquired in the same way as normal behaviors—that is, they are learned through the processes of conditioning and social learning (see Chapter 8). In this model, the behaviors are not considered symptoms of an underlying disease; rather, the behaviors themselves are thought to be the problem. Because the person exhibiting the abnormal behavior is not considered medically sick, she is referred to as a client, not a patient. The abnormal behaviors are eliminated through retraining and conditioning.

The Psychoanalytic Model

In the psychoanalytic model, abnormal behaviors are viewed as evidence of unresolved unconscious conflicts among the id, the ego, and the superego (see Chapter 14). Treatment usually involves psychoanalysis and a detailed investigation of the desires and conflicts in the unconscious.

The Humanistic-Existential Model

The humanistic-existential model depicts abnormal behaviors as the result of a failure to fulfill self-potential due to family and cultural influences. Such failure may occur when people lose contact with their real thoughts and emotions or become isolated from other people; eventually, they may view their lives as meaningless and useless.

INSANITY AND THE LAW

If someone commits a crime and there is some question about his mental state, mental-health professionals may be called on to assess his condition. Such an assessment is often important to a person's criminal defense. If it can be proved that he didn't know right from wrong at the time he committed the crime, or that he could not control his actions, he may be sent to a mental institution for treatment rather than to a prison for punishment.

Whether the so-called **insane** can be held criminally responsible for their actions is a legal issue, not a psychological one. The legal standards for determining whether someone is insane differ from state to state and are sometimes different from those applied by psychiatrists and psychologists.

The desire to distinguish the insane individual from the criminal is an old one. As far back as the middle of the thirteenth century, madness, or insanity, was commonly defined as a condition in which those afflicted didn't know what they were doing, lacked mind and reason, and were "not far removed from brutes." By the sixteenth century, the generally accepted definition was more precise: those who couldn't

count, couldn't recognize their parents, and couldn't understand profit and loss (Amarilio, 1979). This definition, too, was obviously inadequate, and a modern standard was sought.

The modern insanity defense originated in England in 1843 when Daniel M'Naghten shot and killed Edward Drummond, the secretary to Robert Peel, then prime minister of England. M'Naghten was tried for murder, and in his defense he pleaded insanity. Medical testimony was given indicating that M'Naghten was driven by strong delusions to commit the murder and that he didn't understand the difference between right and wrong. The jury verdict was not guilty on the ground of insanity (*M'Naghten's Case*, 1843). The M'Naghten rule is still used as the test for legal insanity in several states in the United States.

The M'Naghten rule has been criticized, however, because only those who appear *severely disturbed* can be classified as insane under its stringent standard. It "does nothing for the person, if he exists, who knows the conduct to be wrong but as a result of mental defect or disease is powerless to control that conduct" (Spring, 1979, p. 26). Many states, therefore, have developed further tests of insanity that attempt to deal with these criticisms (see Table 16.1). Most of these new tests

TABLE 16.1 ◆ LEGAL STANDARDS FOR DETERMINING INSANITY

TEST	SOURCE AND YEAR	STANDARD	RULE
M'Naghten rule	*M'Naghten's Case* (1843)	Cognitive	Defendant is relieved from criminal responsibility if he either (1) was prevented by his mental disease from knowing the nature and quality of his act or (2) was unable to distinguish between right and wrong.
Irresistible impulse	*Parsons v. State* (1887)	Cognitive or volitional	Used as an adjunct to M'Naghten. Defendant is relieved from criminal responsibility if he meets either of the two criteria above or if he had a mental disease or defect that kept him from controlling his conduct (a so-called irresistible impulse). This marks the first addition of a volitional component to the insanity defense.
Durham rule	*Durham v. United States* (1954)	Cognitive or volitional	"The rule . . . is simply that an accused is not criminally responsible if his unlawful act was the product of mental disease or defect" (*Durham v. United States*, 1954, pp. 874–875).
ALI (American Law Institute)	Model Penal Code (1955)	Cognitive or volitional	"A person is not responsible for criminal conduct if at the time of such conduct, as a result of mental disease or defect, he lacked substantial capacity either to appreciate the criminality (or wrongfulness) of his conduct or to conform his conduct to the requirements of the law" (Amarilio, 1979, p. 362).
APA (American Psychiatric Association)	U.S. Public Law 99–646, 100 Stat. 3599 (1986)	Cognitive	A person charged with a criminal offense should be found not guilty by reason of insanity if it is shown that as a result of mental disease or mental retardation he was unable to appreciate the wrongfulness of his conduct at the time of the offense (Wettstein, Mulvey, & Rogers, 1991, p. 21).

FOCUS ON A CONTROVERSY

are broader because they incorporate a volitional standard as well as the old cognitive standard of knowledge of right from wrong. The volitional standard deals with the issue of self-control. A person is said to meet the volitional standard for insanity if he or she, even though aware of the wrongness of an act, is compelled by mental disorder to proceed with the act in any event. Many states have adopted these broader standards.

After the attempted assassination of President Reagan by John Hinckley in 1981, and Hinckley's subsequent acquittal by reason of insanity for volitional reasons (i.e., he understood that what he did was wrong but was allegedly powerless to stop himself), Congress adopted the more stringent APA standard for federal court cases; this standard disallows volitional reasons for claiming insanity (see Table 16.1). Under the new federal standard, Hinckley would have gone to prison rather than to a mental institution.

None of these tests, however, has addressed the most pressing issue: whether insanity should be a defense at all, whether those whom society calls "mad" should be treated differently from others who commit crimes. Some people have recommended that the insanity defense be abolished, and in a few states, including Montana, Idaho, and Utah, it has been.

Interestingly, in states where the insanity defense has been banned, such as Montana, judges have been more likely than before to rule a defendant incompetent to stand trial, so that the overall number of insanity acquittals has remained about the same (Steadman, Callahan, Robbins, & Morrissey, 1989). Also, studies have found that eliminating the volitional standard and relying only on the narrower cognitive standard tends to reduce recommendations for acquittal for reasons of insanity by only 24 percent (Wettstein, Mulvey, & Rogers,

1991). Most defendants who meet the volitional standards for an insanity defense will also meet the cognitive standards. Furthermore, jurors aren't as swayed by the wording of standards as much as one might assume. Jurors typically report relying mostly on "common sense" when making their recommendations. However the determination is made, the arrangement appears to be failing. It is estimated that at least 24,000 prison inmates in the United States are suffering from severe mental disorder and require treatment; they include a large number who are schizophrenic (Abram & Teplin, 1991). Stanley Graham, former president of the American Psychological Association, has estimated that for every two individuals with severe mental disorder in hospitals or clinics, there are three in prison (Graham, 1990). Even where jurisdictions are aware of this problem, however, many people with severe mental disorder are still placed in prisons simply because they are dangerous and insufficient psychiatric facilities are available to provide them with the help they need.

Others have recommended that juries should not be burdened with the issue of sanity. In this view, a defendant's sanity should be considered only during the sentencing phase of a trial by a judge or special panel of experts and not by the jury during establishment of guilt or innocence (Stanfiel, 1981). This arrangement, however, is rarely implemented.

The American Psychological Association has advocated that the insanity defense be based on a valid scientific understanding of human behaviors and not be determined or altered by social or political pressures (Rogers, 1987). But a *complete* scientific understanding of abnormality may be a few hundred years away. In the meantime, the insanity defense in criminal trials is likely to remain subject to such pressures, especially the public's feelings about responsibility and punishment.

CLASSIFICATION AND ASSESSMENT OF ABNORMAL BEHAVIOR

Table 16.2 outlines the prevalence of maladjustment estimated to exist in the United States. As you can see, mental disorders, including drug abuse or dependence, are experienced by nearly one-third of the U.S. adult population at some point in their lives. This translates to about 44.7 million persons (Regier, et al., 1993). And yet, the public seems generally unaware of the magnitude of the problem. In a poll taken only a few years ago, just 1 percent of the respondents thought of mental health as a major health problem (Holden, 1986c) Nevertheless, mental problems cost the nation an estimated $300 billion per year in terms of health costs, lost productivity, accidents, crimes, law enforcement costs, and fires (National Clearinghouse, 1985).

Before clinicians can consider treatment for a mental disorder, they must make an assessment to determine the nature of the problem. The disorder also must be identified so that it can be adequately explained to others. For this reason, classification systems attempt to organize mental disorders systematically.

Although a number of such classification schemes have been developed, to date none has been completely satisfactory. In 1952, the American Psychiatric Association developed the *Diagnostic and Statistical Manual of Mental Disorders* (DSM), which classified mental disorders according to a format that had been devised by the army during World War II. During the war, psychiatrists and psychologists had become more aware that many mental disorders seemed to have a biological component and that early diagnosis and treatment were important. Because of this finding, it was considered desirable to organize all mental disorders into a **nosology** (Grob, 1991).

In 1968, the DSM was modified to bring it into line with different classifications used by the World Health Organization. The new manual, known as DSM-II, was used for a number of years, but eventually its limitations became apparent as new information became available. As a result, a special task force to formulate a revised classification system was assembled; by 1977, their work was complete, and a new classification scheme, DSM-III, was presented for extensive testing and field trials.

DSM-III was new in a number of ways. It described mental disorders in greater detail and made distinctions among disorders that had previously been unified under one heading (Robins & Helzer, 1986).

By 1983, it had become obvious that psychological knowledge was expanding so rapidly that it would be useful to clarify, update, and revise DSM-III while awaiting the publication of a fully revised manual. This new version was called DSM-III-R (*Diagnostic and Statistical Manual of Mental Disorders*, third edition, revised). It, in turn, was replaced in 1994 by **DSM-IV.**

In the next few pages, we will explore some of the important classifications of DSM-IV and examine selected types of mental disorders. We will describe examples of the behaviors associated with each disorder and in certain instances provide case studies.

DSM-IV evaluates each individual according to five dimensions, or axes (see Table 16.3). The first three axes are used to assess the immediate condition of the individual. The fourth and fifth axes consider the stresses that the individual faces and offer an overall assessment of his or her ability to function.

NOSOLOGY
A classification of diseases.

DSM-IV
The fourth edition of the *Diagnostic and Statistical Manual,* published by the American Psychiatric Association in 1994. The manual provides clinicians with the most current diagnostic and classification criteria for mental disorders.

TABLE 16.2 ◆ COMPARISON OF LIFETIME PREVALENCE RATES* OF MENTAL DISORDERS OF PERSONS 18 YEARS AND OLDER

DISORDER	PERCENTAGE EXHIBITING THE DISORDER DURING THEIR LIFETIME
Any disorder	32.2
Any disorder except substance abuse	12.6
Substance use disorders	16.4
Alcohol abuse/dependence	13.3
Drug abuse/dependence	5.9
Schizophrenic disorders	1.5
Affective disorders	8.3
Anxiety disorders	14.6
Phobia	12.5
Panic	3.8
Obsessive-compulsive	2.5
Somatization disorders	0.1
Personality disorder, antisocial personality	2.5
Cognitive impairment (severe)	1.3

*Based on a total sample of 20,291 persons in five epidemiological catchment areas of the United States: New Haven, Connecticut; Baltimore, Maryland; St. Louis, Missouri; Durham, North Carolina; and Los Angeles, California.

SOURCE: Adapted from Regier et al., 1988, 1993; Katerndahl & Realini, 1993.

TABLE 16.3 ◆ DSM-IV CLASSIFICATIONS*

AXIS I (ANY MENTAL DISORDERS THAT MAY BE PRESENT)	AXIS II (ANY PERSONALITY DISORDER THAT MAY BE PRESENT)
1. *Schizophrenia* Disorganized Catatonic Paranoid Undifferentiated Residual	*Personality disorders* Paranoid Schizoid Schizotypal Histrionic Narcissistic Antisocial

2. *Delusional disorders*
Delusional disorder
  Erotomanic type
  Grandiose type
  Jealous type
  Persecutory type
  Somatic type
  Mixed type
  Unspecified type
	Borderline
	Avoidant
	Dependent
	Obsessive compulsive
	Passive aggressive
	
	AXIS III
	Any medical or physical disorder that may also be present

3. *Mood disorders* Bipolar I disorder Bipolar II disorder Major depressive disorder	AXIS IV A checklist rating the psychological and social factors that may have placed the individual under stress, including homelessness, legal problems, or financial troubles
4. *Anxiety disorders* Simple phobia Generalized anxiety disorder Panic disorder without agoraphobia Obsessive-Compulsive disorder	AXIS V A global assessment of functioning scale that allows the clinician to state his or her overall judgment as to the person's psychological, social, and occupational functioning
5. *Somatoform disorders* Conversion disorder Hypochondriasis	
6. *Dissosiative disorders* Psychogenic amnesia Psychogenic fugue Multiple personality disorder	

*The classifications of Axes I and II have been significantly limited to include only those categories discussed in the text.

These last two axes are valuable because they include in the description of the disorder the kinds of stresses the individuals are facing in their environments and how well they are able to function psychologically, socially, and occupationally.

Before we examine these disorders, it should be pointed out once again that mental disorders usually are extremes of normal behaviors. If you think that some of these descriptions fit you a little bit, don't worry. It's not likely to be the first sign that you're on your way to a mental disorder; it probably just means that you're normal. Everyone has little eccentricities, and these are not considered problems unless they become extreme and interfere with the person's life.

As we discuss the disorders listed in DSM-IV, you may be surprised to discover that very few of them have a known etiology. Many are simply *descriptions* of behavior patterns that have often been found to occur together and, therefore, appear to be a **syndrome.** Don't assume that because certain behaviors are classified under one label they are necessarily due to the same cause. For example, you should not infer that people who are said to have schizophrenia all have one particular "disease." Instead, you should understand that they generally exhibit a similar series or constellation of abnormal behaviors. This also is true for medical disorders that are known to affect behavior. Among the medical disorders that can affect behavior are neurosyphilis, stroke, and Alzheimer's disease. In each case, brain or nerve damage is likely to have occurred. Although the etiology sometimes is known, more often it is not understood exactly how the physical damage occurred. In these cases, the disorder may be described only as delirium, dementia, amnesia, cognitive dysfunction, or the like—all terms describing mental disorganization or incoherence, not terms denoting well-defined diseases.

It may be difficult at first for you to realize that many of these disorders are merely descriptive terms. It's like referring to someone as an "accident victim." Accident victims often have a lot in common, such as broken bones, bruises, cuts, and concussions. But all kinds of accidents can happen for all kinds of reasons, and just because two people are labeled accident victims doesn't mean that they are suffering from exactly the same damage. When it comes to illness, we're so used to discussing true diseases that have understood etiologies (such as tuberculosis) that we think a term such as schizophrenia must also refer to some particular disease, too. Someday, we may uncover a single cause of schizophrenia, or we may find that there are many causes. For many of the disorders classified in DSM-IV, a common denominator remains to be discovered.

🧬 ANXIETY, SOMATOFORM, AND DISSOCIATIVE DISORDERS

Anxiety Disorders

Anxiety disorders are maladaptive syndromes that have severe anxiety as their central feature. Included among these are phobia, generalized anxiety, panic, obsession, and compulsion. As a rule, people who suffer from anxiety disorders find their quality of life to be significantly impaired (Massion, Warshaw, & Keller, 1993).

SIMPLE PHOBIA.   Almost everyone has heard of the word *phobia*. Phobia is more than just a fear, however; it is a specific and *unrealistic* fear. Different terms have been used to describe different kinds of **simple phobias.** Phobias run the gamut from A to Z. Perhaps you're familiar with some, such as acrophobia (fear of heights), arachnophobia (fear of spiders), claustrophobia (fear of closed-in spaces), xenophobia (fear of other cultures), and zoophobia (fear of animals).

If you were in a tall building that caught fire and you had to go out onto the ledge of the tenth floor, you'd be bound to feel a little fearful (to say the least). Such behavior is not considered a phobia; instead, it is called normal! If you had acrophobia, however, you probably wouldn't be able to go two steps up a ladder, and you would avoid going even to the second floor of a building if you had to be anywhere near a window. People with phobic disorders are well aware that their fear is *unrealistic*. They often are the first to admit, "This is foolish, but I can't help how I feel."

Like all behavior that might be considered abnormal, such fear comes in varying degrees. When you stand near a sheer edge, do you get a feeling that some magnetic force is starting to pull you over? That's a common perception, but people with acrophobia experience a very intense version of this sensation.

Most people deal with their phobias by avoiding the thing they are frightened of. Someone with herpetophobia (fear of snakes) would probably go out of his way to avoid a job that required working in the country.

SYNDROME
A number of features, characteristics, events, or behaviors that appear to go with each other, or which are thought to be coordinated or interrelated in some way.

SIMPLE PHOBIA
A person's pathological fear of an object or situation. The individual may realize that the fear is irrational but, being unable to control it, avoids the object or situation. Relatively easy to treat.

CONCEPT REVIEW ◆ THE STRENGTHS AND WEAKNESSES OF CLASSIFYING MENTAL DISORDERS

Strengths

DSM-IV is the result of many years of input by hundreds of professionals. It provides a catalog of the human mental disorders that comprise behavior patterns that have been deemed to be of clinical significance. The categories are fairly reliable; that is, if many different professionals use DSM-IV when diagnosing the same individual, they are likely to be in good agreement as to which disorder they have observed. DSM-IV is a system for collective grouping of individuals who behave in the same way, perhaps because they share the same underlying problem. In other words, DSM-IV defines unified groups who can be studied for similarities in the hope that some common denominator can be discovered among them that could explain their disorder, which, in turn, might facilitate treatment.

Weaknesses

DSM-IV is descriptive, not explanatory (and it makes no claim to be explanatory, an effort that at this time would be premature). As a result, it is not possible to assume that each mental disorder is a discrete entity that has sharp boundaries separating it from other mental disorders, or no mental disorder. Therefore, some of the definitions in DSM-IV may be too narrow and thus omit individuals who should be included, while other categories may be too broad and thus admit individuals who should be excluded.

Without solid underlying explanations for the disorders included in DSM-IV, some of the disorders may not be "real" mental disorders, but may simply comprise groupings of undesirable behaviors (behaviors simply deemed socially undesirable). For example, one axis II classification in DSM-IV is called "dependent personality disorder" and is composed of behaviors that include a severe pattern of dependent and submissive behavior. Psychologist Marcie Kaplan has argued that including this disorder reflects the bias of the *men* who developed the manual. Kaplan believes that women are more likely to be considered to have dependent personality disorder than men are, because our society has more often taught them to be dependent (Kaplan, 1983). Kaplan further states that to be fair, there should be a category called *independent personality disorder* that includes typical *male* traits carried to excess. As you can see, what is "normal" is not always agreed on or determined easily.

General Consensus

DSM-IV is useful in the hands of people who know and understand its limitations (which are considerable). With our limited knowledge of an extremely complex area of study, DSM-IV is probably the best catalog that we are currently able to assemble.

In general, simple phobias are believed to be learned. In Chapter 8, we discussed the case of Little Albert, in which a phobic disorder was produced in the child by associating a rat with a very loud noise. Little Albert eventually came to fear the rat. Similar occurrences have happened outside the laboratory. It is also believed that our evolutionary history predisposes us to learn some phobias more easily than others. For example, phobias of spiders and snakes are much more common than phobias of cleansers or clouds.

The following case study illustrates how a phobia might develop as a result of one's experience.

PHOBIC DISORDER: THE CASE OF JUDY R.

Judy R., a 27-year-old college senior, came to the University Counseling Center because of an intense fear of birds. She had been frightened of birds since she was 9 years old. She was functioning well socially and academically, but she felt that her phobia was beginning to interfere with her plans to become a teacher. Judy had begun student teaching, and several incidents had triggered a fear reaction. On four separate occasions, she suffered severe and almost incapacitating terror: on a class visit to the bird section of a museum, seeing pictures of birds in textbooks, being offered a feather by a student, and being near a baby chick on animal day.

How Judy became afraid of birds is not completely clear. Before the age of 9 years, she had a duck and chick as pets. Between the ages of 10 and 15 years, however, she had a few frightening experiences that may have helped to create the phobia. Once playmates warned her that there was an owl near her home that attacked people; she once saw her friend's parakeet escape and fly wildly about a room; she was once scared by her brothers with a toy bird; and she had seen Alfred Hitchcock's film *The Birds*, in which birds viciously attacked people. But she could not attribute her fear directly to any one of these incidents.

Judy structured her entire life so that she could avoid birds. Whenever she walked anywhere, she selected routes with minimal foliage and less chance to encounter a bird, even if they took her far out of her way. She would run between her car and entrances to buildings, and she always kept her car windows rolled up to keep birds out. She could not sunbathe, hike, or go on picnics. She didn't dare visit the beach or go to the zoo. She had frequent nightmares about birds and often thought that noises in her house were caused by birds who had somehow gotten in. She was so frightened of birds that she was careful when she backed out of her driveway not to run over or injure a bird for fear that the "word" might get out among the bird community and the birds would get her. She realized that such actions were far beyond the capability of birds and that her fear was irrational, but the thought persisted. (Lassen & McConnell, 1977)

Many phobias do not seem to have one specific cause or beginning. This fact has led some medical researchers to speculate that some phobias may be attributable to underlying changes in brain chemistry that predispose the individual to become easily fearful. Psychoanalysts, on the other hand, have argued that phobias are symptoms of an underlying conflict and that the phobia cannot be adequately resolved unless the underlying conflict is resolved through psychoanalysis. Still, psychoanalysis generally has not been effective in treating phobias.

The most commonly used treatments for phobia involve behavior modification and, occasionally, drugs. These techniques have been highly successful, and simple phobias are perhaps the most easily treatable of the mental disorders. There are other phobias, however, that don't appear to be "simple" and that sometimes do not respond so easily to treatment. DSM-IV treats these phobias separately. They include agoraphobia (fear of being outside the home) and social phobia (fear of social situations in which one might be scrutinized). For reasons not yet understood, these two phobias seem to be special cases in which the unrealistic fear is of a more general nature and is less specifically focused than are the simple phobias. Most simple phobias, however, readily loosen their grip with treatment. In Chapter 17, we'll see how Judy R. overcame her phobia through behavior modification.

GENERALIZED ANXIETY DISORDER. People suffering a **generalized anxiety disorder** are in a continued state of apparently pointless apprehension, worry, and dread over a number of life's circumstances (Barlow, Blanchard,

GENERALIZED ANXIETY DISORDER
An anxiety state characterized by a relatively constant feeling of dread and tension without apparent or reasonable cause. Free-floating anxiety is a common complaint.

FREE-FLOATING ANXIETY
A chronic state of foreboding that is unrelated to a specific situation or object but can be activated by any number of situations and activities.

PANIC ATTACK
A sudden overwhelming and debilitating onset of fear characteristic of panic disorder. There is no realistic reason or cause.

Vermilyea, Vermilyea, & DiNardo, 1986). They will typically show an unrealistic fear concerning unforeseen circumstances (for example, worry about a child who is in no danger, worry about finances for no good reason). As a result, they often are unable to make decisions or to enjoy life. Because their anxiety is not tied to a specific object, it often is called **free-floating anxiety.** The following case study illustrates this kind of anxiety.

GENERALIZED ANXIETY DISORDER: THE MECHANIC'S CASE

The patient, a 31-year-old mechanic, had been referred for psychotherapy by his physician, whom he had consulted because of dizziness and difficulty in falling asleep. He was quite visibly distressed during the entire interview, gulping before he spoke, sweating, and continually fidgeting in his chair. His repeated requests for water to slake a seemingly unquenchable thirst were another indication of this extreme nervousness. Although he first related his physical concerns, a more general picture of pervasive anxiety soon emerged. He reported that he nearly always felt tense and that "if anything can go wrong, it will." He was apprehensive of possible disasters that could befall him as he worked and interacted with other people. He reported a long history of difficulties in interpersonal relationships, which had led to his being fired from several jobs. As he put it, "I really like people and try to get along with them, but it seems like I fly off the handle too easily. Little things they do upset me too much. I just can't cope unless everything is going exactly right." (Davison & Neale, 1978, p. 150)

Although no one knows what causes a person to suffer from generalized anxiety disorder, it may have both environmental and genetic causes. For instance, it is known that people who have experienced real, unexpected, and very stressful events in their lives are at least three times more likely to develop generalized anxiety disorder than are other people (Blazer, Hughes, & George, 1987). It is also known, however, that someone showing generalized anxiety disorder is more likely to have close relatives who also suffer from the disorder than would be expected by chance alone (Noyes, Clarkson, Crowe, Yates, & McChesney, 1987).

PANIC DISORDER. Panic disorder is probably the most common mental-health reason people come to a doctor or hospital for help (Boyd, 1986). Approximately 3.8 percent of the population will suffer from the disorder sometime during their lives (Katerndahl & Realini, 1993). When the first **panic attack** occurs, the person is commonly overwhelmed by fear without any warning (Faravelli, Pallanti, Biondi, Paterniti, & Scarpato, 1992). Typically, the person can find no real reason to be frightened, and those who do find a reason are commonly aware that it should have been insufficient to have caused such a high level of fear. Even so, panic attacks are strong and debilitating. The feeling of terror can be overpowering, almost as if the person were having a heart attack. Chest pains, heart palpitations, breathing difficulty, and fainting may occur. For this reason, sufferers of panic attacks often carry the extra burden of fearing their attacks, that is, they become afraid of becoming afraid (Kenardy, Evans, & Oei, 1992).

As is the case with generalized anxiety disorder, people who have suffered from real, negative, and stressful events are at greater risk for developing panic disorder than are other people (Roy-Byrne, Geraci, & Uhde, 1986), especially if they have recently lost someone they love (Faravelli & Pallanti, 1989). Unlike those who suffer from generalized anxiety disorder, however, people who show panic disorder do not appear to be more likely to have relatives who have panic disorder than one would expect to find among the average population (Noyes, Clarkson, Crowe, Yates, & McChesney, 1987). This does not mean that biology plays no role in panic disorder; rather, the disorder may not be very strongly tied to *inheritance*. In fact, there are some intriguing data linking panic attack to biology. For instance, the first instances of the disorder typically occur following puberty and are rare in childhood (Hayward, et al., 1992). Also, an intravenous injection of sodium lactate will almost always quickly bring on a full-blown panic attack in people who have panic disorder, although it has no effect on other people! Interestingly, the lactate cannot be directly interacting with the brain because it cannot cross the blood-brain barrier (see Chapter 2). Researchers therefore believe that the lactate causes certain peripheral sensations that are somehow misinterpreted by the subject in a way that is frightening enough to trigger a panic episode (Coplan, et al., 1992).

Another interesting study discovered that individuals who suffer from panic disorder had significantly higher levels of cholesterol. Most of the subjects in the study were unaware of their cholesterol levels before the study was conducted. It may be that a higher cholesterol level and the presence of panic attacks are both directly related to some as yet unknown neurochemical or hormonal mechanism (Bajwa, Asnis, Sanderson, Irfan, & van Praag, 1992). This finding might also help explain why some studies have found type A personalities (see Chapter 15) to be at greater risk for heart attack. The heart attacks may be due to the cholesterol levels correlated with anxiety rather than to the anxiety itself (Bajwa, Asnis, Sanderson, Irfan, & van Praag, 1992).

Researchers have also noted that caffeine can greatly exacerbate a panic attack (Charney, Heninger, & Jatlow, 1985). This does not seem to be related to caffeine's ability to make a person jittery. Instead, use of caffeine over a number of months somehow alters the effects of certain neurotransmitters in the brain, most notably serotonin. In fact, one of the first treatment steps for people who suffer from panic attacks is to get them to abstain from caffeine. Usually, 2–4 weeks of caffeine abstinence are needed before a lessening of anxiety is noted.

Findings such as these have led researchers to hope that sometime soon the entire mechanism of panic, and perhaps anxiety in general, will be understood sufficiently for the development of medications that will enable us to control problems of anxiety when they arise.

OBSESSIVE-COMPULSIVE DISORDER.   One of the most interesting anxiety disorders is the **obsessive-compulsive disorder,** or OCD. In this disorder, the sufferer typically feels a need to go over unwanted thoughts again and again or to engage in certain actions or rituals repetitively, perhaps as a way of coping with anxiety. From time to time, all of us have had ideas or thoughts that we couldn't seem to get out of our minds. And sometimes we feel better if we carefully organize our daily activities in an almost ritualistic manner. In the obsessive-compulsive disorder, this behavior is taken to the extreme, but it is an ineffective way of coping.

The obsessions and compulsions represent the different properties of OCD. **Obsessions** are thoughts that continue to enter a person's mind unwanted that become impossible to ignore. For example, a person may have the constant obsession that someone is breaking into the house whenever she is away. This idea could interfere with her life, making every minute away from home uncomfortable because of her persistent thoughts about intruders. Some people are obsessed with thoughts about committing violent acts. The guilt and revulsion that accompany these thoughts only seem to bring them to mind more often, although the person has no intention of acting them out. Such obsessions, although never realized, may still result in extremely high levels of anxiety.

Compulsions are needs to perform ritualistic acts, and can take many forms. The need to read every license plate on the highway, the need to wear certain

OBSESSIVE-COMPULSIVE DISORDER (OCD)
An abnormal reaction characterized by anxiety, persistent unwanted thoughts, or the compulsion to repeat ritualistic acts over and over.

OBSESSION
A persistent idea or thought that the individual recognizes as irrational but feels compelled to dwell on.

COMPULSION
A useless, stereotyped, and repetitive act that a person is unable to inhibit.

clothes on a certain day, the need to avoid stepping on a crack on the sidewalk, or the need to wash one's hands every 15 minutes are examples of compulsions that can, when carried to extremes, interfere with life.

Although it's possible to have obsessions without engaging in ritualistic acts or to have compulsions without obsessive thoughts, the two often coexist, which is why the disorder is referred to as obsessive-compulsive. In fact, the obsession can often be the cause of the compulsion. The person who is obsessed with the fear that there is a stranger in the house may ritually and compulsively check in all the closets and under all the beds before retiring.

It is common for people to have minor obsessions or minor rituals. The point at which such manifestations become serious enough to require help is not always clear-cut. As a rule, it's a good idea for people to seek professional advice any time such behaviors begin to interfere seriously with their lives or functioning. An obsessive-compulsive disorder is described in the following case study.

OBSESSIVE-COMPULSIVE DISORDER: THE CASE OF S. K.

S. K. was admitted to a mental hospital at the age of 29. . . . Soon after the patient's admission to the hospital, his wife was asked to give a history of the patient's illness. She reported that he had exhibited a compulsive handwashing for several months but that it became more serious. "He used to wash his hands and keep the water running for 15 minutes at a time. After he had washed them, he would turn off the spigot with his elbow. He had to count and wash and rinse his hands a certain number of times. If he had touched the door or door knob, he would go back and wash his hands again. One time he began to wash his hands at 1 o'clock in the morning. After we moved into our own house, he refused to use the front door or to turn the knob on the door for fear there might be germs. He used to go to the back window and call me to go to the front door and open it for him. He reached the point where he would climb in and out of windows so that he wouldn't have to enter the doors at all." The wife described also the following compulsion: "He also had the idea that when he walked there was something under his shoe. He would stop and look on the sole of his shoe, but there would be nothing there. He also worried as to whether or not his shoe laces were tied. He would pick up his foot and look to make sure. He had to do that a certain number of times before he was absolutely sure they were tied. When he walked down a street, if he kicked a stone he felt that he should put it back in the same place. If he walked on a line, then he would have to walk on all the cracks in the sidewalk." (Kolb, 1973, pp. 427–428)

Obsessive-compulsive disorder is especially fascinating because we may now be on the verge of truly understanding it. In the mid-1970s, a new antidepressive drug was developed called clomipramine. A number of psychiatrists gave this drug to their OCD patients to help them cope with the depression commonly associated with their disorder. Soon afterward, however, reports began to come in from all over the world that clomipramine was *curing* OCD in about two-thirds of all cases. Other antidepressants, even those very similar in chemical structure to clomipramine, had no such effect.

Quickly, there was a rush to discover how the drug might be working its magic. And, as you might imagine, OCD was converted almost overnight into a biological disorder in the minds of most professionals. As reports of the drug's success were spread by the media, thousands of OCD sufferers began to come forth—people who until then had been too ashamed to admit to their affliction. It was soon discovered that as many as 5 million Americans might be suffering from OCD, many more than had been previously thought, and the number of diagnosed cases of OCD jumped considerably (Stoll, Tohen, & Baldessarini, 1992).

Judith Rapoport, a child psychiatrist, is one of the leading researchers in the search for the cause of OCD. She believed that the obsessions and compulsions of OCD were linked to the kinds of subroutines that most animals have, such as those related to territoriality and grooming (for example, a cat bathing itself). Such behaviors are repetitive and stereotyped. These subroutines appear to arise in an area of the brain called the basal ganglia. Interestingly, brain scans of OCD patients show that there are consistent abnormalities in the basal ganglia (Luxenberg, et al., 1988). PET scans have also shown that the right caudate nucleus, an area deep in the brain known to control impulses involving sex, aggression and disgust, is more active in people with OCD (Baxter, et al., 1992). Rapoport believed that clomipramine might work by boosting the effect of serotonin or in some other way influencing brain neurotransmitters so that the action within the right caudate nucleus lessens, which in turn, makes persistent and unwanted thoughts less pervasive.

As further evidence for a biological cause, Rapoport looked at a problem in dogs called *acra lick dermatitis* (ALD). Dogs with this disorder won't stop licking their paws. Eventually, the problem can get so bad that the hair and skin of the paws are licked away until the bones show through. The usual treatment is to wrap the dog's paws in bandages that it can't lick through, but something else also works—clomipramine! Prozac, another drug that affects serotonin, is also affective against both ALD and OCD (Rapoport, Ryland, & Kriete, 1992). In fact, Rapoport says that she is now the only child psychiatrist in the world making regular house calls on dogs; she plans to start a brain bank from dogs with ALD that have died in the hopes of finding anatomical abnormalities in their brains that may be related to OCD.

The introduction of these drugs for the treatment of OCD has made a great difference. Think about the many routines of your daily life that you have learned to the point of habit. You check to see if your hands are dirty. If they are, you wash them. When you leave the house, you check to make sure that things are right before you go. If they are, you leave. Throughout the day you check and you act, you check and you act, what could be more normal? But suppose your brain couldn't get the "we're done, everything is okay" signal to where it was needed to break your subroutines? Your hands are now clean, and you know it, but an important part of your brain says "wash!" You know that it makes no sense, but you are forced to wash again and again. You can't stop. How does it really feel to have that happen? One patient summed it up this way:

Ninety-five percent of me is rational, and there's five percent of me that's out of control. And I can almost feel where it is in my brain, because I constantly talk to that part and say: "Shut up, and leave me alone. I don't want to do that." (Trotter, 1990, p. 27)

But after taking clomipramine, the patient said,

That part of my brain finally listened and did shut up. It let the other ninety-five percent regain the control it always should have had. (Trotter, 1990, p. 27)

Considering such experiences, it might well be that OCD should not be classified as an anxiety disorder as it is in DSM-IV. Anxiety may not be its root cause or its most important feature. Instead, we may actually be looking at the biochemistry of belief and doubt; that is, the brain chemistry that tells us when something is finished or when it needs to be continued, the chemistry that informs us when it is time to leave a certain action or forgo a certain thought—the chemistry that says, "Stop licking your paws!"

SOMATOFORM DISORDERS
Patterns of behavior characterized by complaints of physical symptoms in the absence of any real physical illness.

CONVERSION DISORDER
A somatoform disorder characterized by physical symptoms such as paralysis, blindness, deafness, and loss of sensation. The assumption is that anxiety has been converted into a tangible symptom.

Somatoform Disorders

Soma means body, and **somatoform disorders** are patterns of behavior in which an individual complains about physical symptoms when no physical illness can be found. Somatoform disorders are found in roughly one person in 300, making them about 10 times less common than anxiety disorders (Swartz, Blazer, George, & Landerman, 1986), but they may account for as many as 20 percent of those on whom expensive medical tests are conducted each year, making somatoform disorders an important contributor to the high cost of health care (Lipowski, 1988). Unlike anxiety disorders, which are fairly evenly divided between the sexes, somatoform disorders are slightly more common among women than men (Cloninger, Martin, Guze, & Clayton, 1986). The two major somatoform disorders are conversion disorder and hypochondriasis.

CONVERSION DISORDER. **Conversion disorder** gets its name from the fact that the anxiety and stress faced by the person are thought to be converted into physical symptoms. These symptoms may be wide-ranging. For example, people may go blind or become deaf although there's nothing wrong with their eyes or ears. Motor symptoms, such as wobbling, shaking, twitching, and collapsing, are not uncommon; again, there's nothing physically wrong that should cause these symptoms. Visceral symptoms, such as headache, choking, coughing, and nausea, may occur. The visceral symptoms of a conversion disorder can look like a very real physical disease. Cases of conversion disorder have been known to mimic acute appendicitis, malaria, and tuberculosis, although no organic pathology was present. Cases of pseudopregnancy have even been reported, in which the menstrual cycle ceases, the abdomen appears to swell, and morning sickness begins. No actual pregnancy is involved; the symptoms are the result of the conversion disorder.

The reasons a conversion disorder develops usually are fairly clear. Conversion disorders typically serve the purpose of helping people to avoid doing something they would rather not do. For example, conversion disorders were common among pilots during World War II. Pilots who flew night missions often had a conversion disorder of night blindness, while pilots who flew day missions often had other kinds of visual disturbances that caused them to be grounded. Most people who suffer from conversion disorders have at one time or another expressed the wish to become sick to avoid what they had to do. This wish usually is repressed, and when the conversion disorder symptoms begin, the sufferer is *genuinely unaware* that this is not a real physical disease.

Since conversion disorder can mimic so many real illnesses, it's often difficult for physicians to distinguish it from physical illness. Nevertheless, there are some general guidelines for identifying conversion disorder. In Figure 16.1a, you see an example of "glove anesthesia." The entire hand has become paralyzed and immobile and is numb all over. However, if you've ever had novocaine at a dentist's office, you know how one side of your lip can be numb while the other side is not. This localized numbness occurs because the nerve beds are laid down lengthwise, not crosswise. Consequently, real neural damage to the hand typically results in paralysis of only one lateral portion (see Figure 16.1b). To a neurologist, glove anesthesia is a dead giveaway of conversion disorder.

About one-third of people suffering from conversion disorder express indifference about their symptoms. Instead of being very upset that they can no longer see or that their arm is paralyzed, they often describe their symptom in a matter-of-fact way without emotion. It's as though they are relieved to have the symptoms. Often, the symptoms are selective. A person who is blind as a result of conversion disorder is not likely to bump into people or objects.

◆ **FIGURE 16.1**

Because of the organization of the human nervous system, a full glove anesthesia (a) is impossible as a function of only physiological causes. Real nerve damage is more likely to result in a loss of feeling similar to that shown in (b). For this reason, a symptom such as glove anesthesia is an indication of psychological problems.

(a)   (b)

Someone who is actually blind and not yet used to it will typically have a number of accidents. Furthermore, the conversion disorder often can be eliminated or altered under hypnosis, and during sleep a "paralyzed" limb may be seen to move or a "deaf" sleeper may respond to sounds.

Generally, all the models of psychopathology view conversion disorder as an unconscious attempt to avoid danger. Some scientists have argued that the right hemisphere of the brain is more likely to use this defense than is the left hemisphere. This interesting assertion is derived from the fact that, especially in cases of conversion paralysis such as glove anesthesia, conversion disorder is much more likely to occur on the left side of the body than on the right side (Stern, 1977; Galin, Diamond, & Braff, 1977).

HYPOCHONDRIASIS. Hypochondriacs believe themselves to be ill although there is no physical illness present. Unlike people suffering a conversion disorder, hypochondriacs are intensely interested in body functions and illness, and they will avidly seek medical attention in a search for some dread disease that they are sure is present (Barsky, 1993). Approximately 5 percent of all medical outpatients (patients treated at hospital, but who usually don't stay overnight) are not physically ill, but rather suffer from **hypochondriasis** (Barsky & Klerman, 1985). Hypochondriasis in adults is unrelated to age and is found as readily among young adults as well as among the middle aged or the elderly (Barsky, Frank, Cleary, Wyshak, & Klerman, 1991). Researchers assume that hypochondriacs use their supposed disability to gain attention, avoid something unpleasant, or feel important.

It is a classic sign of hypochondriasis when people become upset at a physician's reassurances that tests show no organic pathology and that nothing is wrong. Instead, they hope for some proof that they can hold up to others to maintain their maladaptive behavior pattern. Hypochondriacs are different from malingerers; they are sincere in their belief that they are ill, whereas malingerers knowingly fake a disorder to serve their purposes. Hypochondriasis is difficult to treat, because sufferers often leave a physician or psychologist who will not give them attention for their supposed illness and seek the services of someone who will. A hypochondriac is described in the following account.

HYPOCHONDRIASIS
A somatoform disorder in which there is a persistent and exaggerated concern about diminished health and energy in the absence of demonstrable organic pathology.

HYPOCHONDRIASIS: THE CASE OF GRACE H.

Grace H. cataloged in excruciating anatomical detail a full range of symptoms—past, present, and future—to which she was heir. She had "almost" had a series of exotic diseases, had suffered for years from a strange collection of symptoms that fit no known malady in humans, and was about to come down with something certain to be nearly fatal. . . . Probably the most startling aspect of the scene was the obvious and absolutely noncontroversial fact that Grace H. looked as healthy as a horse. The fact that she was 72 years old had to be some kind of testimony to her hardiness in the face of plague, pestilence, and, as she viewed it, the perversity of the medical profession. . . . According to the children, Grace's histrionics had been in evidence for at least the last 40 years. The eldest son, who was 50 years old, recalled that his mother had been ailing when he was just a child. As he said, "Sometimes when I was in school, I would get worried that mother would be dead by the time I got home. I knew she was sick when I went to school and I was sure it would be all over by the time I got home. I had a hard time concentrating on my school work because I was always worried about her health." The mother was an artful specialist in hypochondriasis who had practiced all the arts of being sick while staggeringly well. She seemed to be totally free of anxiety until asked about her health, and at that point she disintegrated into a mass of nervous energy. (McNeil, 1967, pp. 47–49)

DISSOCIATIVE DISORDERS
Mental disorders that are characterized by an attempt to overcome anxiety by dissociating oneself from the core of one's personality.

PSYCHOGENIC AMNESIA
A dissociative disorder involving selective memory loss. The individual forgets, partially or totally, his or her past identity but remembers nonthreatening aspects of life.

FUGUE
A dissociative disorder in which the individual leaves his or her present situation and establishes a different existence in another place. Although the former life is blocked from memory, other abilities are unimpaired and the individual appears normal to others.

Hypochondriasis must be assessed very carefully, however, because *real* illness can sometimes be extremely elusive. Just because an underlying physical reason can't be found does not guarantee that there isn't one. Before classifying a person as a hypochondriac, psychologists prefer to see clearly how the person is exploiting her "illness." The existence of physical complaints without an apparent cause is not sufficient reason to make the classification.

Dissociative Disorders

Like somatoform disorders, **dissociative disorders** help individuals to obtain gratification and simultaneously to avoid stress. They also provide a means of denying responsibility for behavior that might otherwise be deemed unacceptable. Individuals with dissociative disorders separate themselves from the core of their personality, and they often feel as though they are outside themselves or somehow removed from who they are. Occasional feelings of dissociation are quite common among the general population (Ross, Joshi, & Currie, 1990). It is only when these feelings are carried to extreme that problems occur. At that point, the dissociation may become so severe as to result in psychogenic amnesia, psychogenic fugue, or multiple personality, which are classified as dissociative disorders.

PSYCHOGENIC AMNESIA. **Psychogenic amnesia** is a memory loss, either partial or total; it can last for a few hours or many years. Amnesia can be caused by many things, including psychosis, brain damage, and alcoholic delirium. Psychogenic amnesia, however, has no underlying physical cause and appears to be the result of stress. People suffering from this disorder usually forget personal material such as who they are, as well as events and other names associated with personal experience. Rarely would someone with psychogenic amnesia forget the name of his country or how to do such things as operate an automobile or read a book.

PSYCHOGENIC FUGUE. **Fugue** comes from the Latin word meaning "to flee." This disorder is an amnesia in which the sufferer leaves home and surroundings and wanders off. In extreme cases, the person may even begin a new life in another city without any recollection of personal events prior to the fugue. Occasionally, the fugue comes to a sudden end, and the person is left in a strange city, unable to recall his new identity but again able to remember his original identity. As you can imagine, it would be a little strange to wake up in a different bed and to find out that eight years have passed, you are known by a different name, and you are selling ties in St. Louis! The following case study describes a four-day fugue experienced by a famous American author, Sherwood Anderson.

PSYCHOGENIC FUGUE: THE CASE OF SHERWOOD ANDERSON

Anderson was better known as a paint manufacturer than as a writer in his home town of Elyria, Ohio. He would daydream to escape the boredom of a routine workday and found relaxation in writing short stories. On November 27, 1912, the 36-year-old Anderson suddenly got up from his desk while dictating a letter to his secretary. He stopped in the middle of a sentence, walked out of the room, and was not seen again until four days later, when he was found in a Cleveland drugstore. Anderson was taken to Huron Road Hospital, where experts agreed that he had succumbed to mental strain and was the victim of amnesia. He reportedly told the story of the missing days for the rest of his life, each time with different details. He simply couldn't remember what really happened. (Wallace, Wallenchinsky, Wallace, & Wallace, 1980, pp. 434–435)

MULTIPLE PERSONALITY DISORDER. In **multiple personality disorder,** an individual develops more than one personality. These personalities rarely appear simultaneously; instead, they seem to vie for consciousness. Often one personality is totally unaware of another. The two most celebrated cases of multiple personality were described in the books *The Three Faces of Eve* and *Sybil.*

MULTIPLE PERSONALITY
A dissociative disorder in which one person develops two or more distinct personalities, which often vie with each other for consciousness. One personality's memories are not usually accessible to another personality.

MULTIPLE PERSONALITY DISORDER: THE CASE OF SYBIL DORSETT

Sybil Dorsett was a college graduate who was leading what seemed to be a normal healthy existence as a schoolteacher. In 1954, she began work on a master's degree at Columbia University. She came to the attention of psychiatrist Cornelia Wilbur because she was having blackouts and periods of amnesia that were becoming progressively longer, and no physical cause for her ailment could be discerned. It was during a therapy session with Dr. Wilbur that there was a sudden and radical change in Sybil's personality. Her voice changed, her manner changed, and she began to act like a little girl; she even threw a temper tantrum. A short time later, a third personality emerged, who called herself Vicki. Sybil was unaware of the other personalities, but Vicki knew about them. In the course of several therapy sessions, Vicki revealed that throughout her childhood many personalities had been created for Sybil, 16 in all. Some of the personalities were children, some were adults, and some were even male. In Figure 16.2 you can see pictures drawn by Sybil as different personalities were in control.

During the therapy, Dr. Wilbur discovered that Sybil had been systematically abused and tortured by her schizophrenic mother from as early as 3 years. Apparently, whenever Sybil encountered a situation that she could not handle, a new personality was created to deal with the stress. Over a period of several years, Dr. Wilbur worked with all 16 personalities, attempting to solve the problems of each and eventually integrating them into a seventeenth new and whole personality.

Of the disorders we've discussed so far, multiple personality is one of the most complex and difficult to understand. In the past, researchers thought it was an extremely rare disorder, but because of its complexity, it may often have been confused with the more severe psychotic disorders such as schizophrenia and, as a result, not recognized for what it really was. With use of the current DSM classification system, however, careful screening has shown that

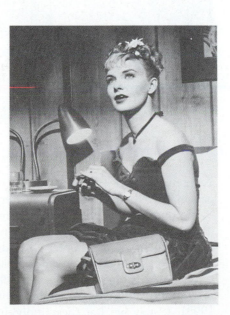

Actress Joanne Woodward portraying the personalities of Eve White and Eve Black in the motion picture The Three Faces of Eve, *a case history of a multiple personality.*

◆ **Figure 16.2**

Some of Sybil's 16 personalities were artists, and their paintings helped Sybil to recover. Each personality had a different artistic style. A painting by "Marcia" (a) depicts a grim self-portrait and highlights Marcia's depressed nature. At the right (b) is a painting by an angry, fearful "Peggy." The dark shadow in the foreground represents her sadistic mother. At the bottom (c) is a painting of a warm home and family environment by "Mary," who liked to recall her childhood friends. (From Sybil paintings, courtesy of Dr. Cornelia B. Wilbur.)

(a)

(b)

(c)

as many as 3 to 4 percent of all psychiatric inpatients may have multiple personality (Ross, Anderson, Fleisher, & Norton, 1991).

No one is sure what causes multiple personality, but some interesting possibilities are under investigation. One such possibility involves the development of memory. In Chapter 9, we discussed propositional network theory, in which memory is envisioned as a series of nodes of information that are linked to one another. Interestingly, researchers have found that about 94 percent of people with multiple personality were abused as children (Boon & Draijer, 1993). It may be that these individuals, through fear and anxiety, repressed and isolated their childhood experiences. This in turn may have resulted in their memories developing in a fragmented way, with whole sections of memory cordoned off from other sections, linked together poorly or not at all. If this is the case, when a particular memory is activated, a person with multiple personality disorder might be trapped within a limited fraction of her memory, with each fraction holding different and limited "knowledge" about herself. Such limited and enclosed areas of memory might easily seem to be separate and distinct personalities. Of course, no one knows the real cause for sure, but this hypothesis is interesting. If it is correct, future researchers will view multiple personality as a developmental failure to integrate memory.

It should also be noted, however, that many professionals doubt the prevalence of the disorder or even its existence. One researcher investigating allegations of child abuse associated with multiple personality found that attempts to document these allegations have yielded little support (Frankel, 1993). How then could so many cases of multiple personality have recently appeared, 94 percent of whom recall abuse from their childhoods once in therapy? Some argue that such recollections, and perhaps even the disorder as well, are created during therapy by the therapist's expectations and before therapy by exposure to popular movies like *Sybil* and *The Three Faces of Eve* (McHugh, 1993). Such things have happened in the past. Perhaps the most noted instance occurred in the 1880s when Jean-Martin Charcot believed that he had discovered a new mental disorder that seemed to combine features of epilepsy and hysteria. He called this disorder hystero-epilepsy. However, Charcot's student, Joseph Babinski, discovered that the disorder magically disappeared when those suffering from hystero-epilepsy were isolated from one another so they could not observe each others' "symptoms" and when the physicians at the hospital stopped being so interested in the new and exciting cluster of symptoms that the patients were exhibiting (McHugh, 1993). Whether multiple personality turns out to be a problem of memory, a mental disorder, or a figment of the imaginations of psychiatrists and psychologists, it will require careful study.

🧬 MOOD DISORDERS

Mood disorders are disorders of affect, or emotion. The most serious types are the bipolar disorders and major depression.

Bipolar Disorders

The bipolar disorders are characterized by drastic changes in mood. All of us are happy some of the time and sad some of the time, and mood swings are not abnormal in most instances. But with bipolar disorders, the mood changes are dramatic, debilitating, and, once started, likely to remain a problem for years (Coryell, et al., 1993).

Bipolar I disorder used to be referred to as manic-depressive disorder and is often characterized by severe mood swings from deep depression to mania. During the manic phase of the disorder, a person might suddenly have feelings of great elation and extreme agitation. He or she might become very impatient, show poor judgment, or try to initiate a number of endeavors simultaneously. Occasionally, the sufferer becomes violent. Mania, by definition, impairs day-to-day functioning and often requires hospitalization.

During the depressive phase of the disorder, the same person may go through periods of intense depression, bordering on suicide. The depressive phase may last for hours or even days. This is what is meant by bipolar disorder—swinging repeatedly back and forth between two poles, the manic and the depressed. Sometimes, the moods and accompanying behaviors are severe enough to clas-

MOOD DISORDERS
A group of disorders characterized by extremes of mood and emotion.

BIPOLAR I DISORDER
A mood disorder characterized by severe cyclical mood swings. Formerly called manic-depressive psychosis. Bipolar I disorder includes at least one episode of mania and may also include episodes of hypomania or depression.

PSYCHOSIS
Any of a group of disorders involving extensive and severe psychological disintegration, disruption of all forms of adaptive behavior, and loss of contact with reality. Psychotic individuals may show bizarre motor behavior, extreme emotional states, absence of emotional responsiveness, withdrawal, delusions, hallucinations, and cognitive distortions. Psychosis often requires institutionalization.

BIPOLAR II DISORDER
A mood disorder characterized by severe cyclical mood swings. Episodes include depression and at least one episode of hypomania, but never mania.

sify as a **psychosis.** In that case, it is referred to as bipolar disorder with psychotic features. Bipolar I disorder also includes those individuals who cycle between manic and normal moods without showing evidence of depression.

In **bipolar II disorder**, the individual swings back and forth between severe depression and *hypomania*. Hypomania is not normal behavior. It is a mania, but not so severe as to interfere with day-to-day life. During the period of hypomania, a person might appear to have an inflated opinion of himself, need less sleep than usual, and be more talkative or distractible. He or she is also more likely to enter into foolish ventures or engage in dangerous activities such as high-speed driving. Such hypomanic behaviors might even be considered "normal" in someone who had, for instance, just won a million dollars. But for those with bipolar II disorder, there is no obvious reason for the hypomanic behavior episodes. Individuals with bipolar I disorder may also cycle between depression and hypomania with the exception that they have had at least one fully manic episode in the past.

The distinction between the two bipolar disorders is new with DSM-IV and came about because clinicians believe that the distinction is a real one and that the two types of bipolar disorder are truly different in some fundamental way. In fact, evidence suggests that bipolar II disorder is more likely to be passed from generation to generation than is bipolar I disorder (Simpson, et al., 1993). But some disagree and find the distinctions between the two disorders to be unclear (Blacker & Tsuang, 1992). This disagreement illustrates once again that these diagnostic classifications are not written in stone and are likely to undergo further revision in DSM-V once we have learned more about these mood disorders.

Scientists have estimated that between 0.4 and 1.2 percent of the adult population will have bipolar disorder sometime during their lives (Spitzer & Williams, 1987). The following case study illustrates bipolar I disorder.

BIPOLAR I DISORDER: THE CASE OF M. M.

M. M. was first admitted to a state hospital at the age of 38, although since childhood she had been characterized by swings of mood, some of which had been so extreme that they had been psychotic in degree. At 17 she suffered from a depression that rendered her unable to work for several months, although she was not hospitalized. At 33, shortly before the birth of her first child, the patient was greatly depressed. For a period of four days she appeared in coma. About a month after the birth of the baby she "became excited" and was entered as a patient in an institution. . . . As she began to improve, she was sent to a shore hotel for a brief vacation. The patient remained at the hotel for one night and on the following day signed a year's lease on an apartment, bought furniture, and became heavily involved in debt. Shortly thereafter Mrs. M. became depressed and returned to the hospital in which she had previously been a patient. . . . In a little less than a year Mrs. M. again became overactive, played her radio until late in the night, smoked excessively, took out insurance on a car that she had not yet bought. Contrary to her usual habits, she swore frequently and loudly, created a disturbance in a club to which she did not belong, and instituted divorce proceedings. On the day prior to her second admission to the hospital, she purchased 57 hats. (Kolb, 1973, p. 376)

In the bipolar disorders, the timing of the mood swings is rarely related to external events. This fact has led researchers to believe that there may be important genetic or biological factors directly affecting bipolar disorder.

Evidence for this belief comes from a number of sources. First, as we will discuss in Chapter 17, bipolar disorder sometimes responds well to drugs based on the metal lithium. Also, bipolar disorder has been shown to run in families (see Figure 16.3). This observation has led geneticists to search for possible clues as to the ways in which bipolar disorder might be inherited. Research so far has indicated that bipolar disorder probably is not related to a single gene but is more likely to have a complex genetic basis. To date, despite many research efforts using genetic studies, brain scans, and blood analyses, no reliable biological common denominator associated with bipolar disorder has been uncovered.

Detailed efforts designed to examine possible environmental causes have also been undertaken. An area of special interest has been the interactions among family members where one or more members has bipolar disorder. It is still too early to say if certain types of family interactions or stresses predispose a person to bipolar disorder, but some interesting discoveries have been made. One finding was that bipolar disorder is more common among those who have demonstrated creative accomplishments, such as writers. The researchers initially assumed that the stress of creativity might increase a person's chances of acquiring bipolar disorder. But that finding is now considered to be an indication of a *biological* cause since it was discovered that creative achievements are also more common among blood relatives (but not relatives by marriage) of those who suffer from bipolar disorder than they are among the general populace (Richards, Kinney, Lunde, Benet, & Merzel, 1988) and that no such relationship exists between creativity and other mood disorders, only bipolar disorder (Coryell, et al., 1989).

Major Depressive Disorder

The term **depression** describes a wide range of emotional lows, from sadness to a severe and suicidal state. Each of us has felt unhappy at one time or another, and sadness can be quite natural as long as there is an obvious cause. **Major depressive disorder,** however, is a lasting and continuous state of depression without an obvious organic or environmental cause. A mood of unhappiness and apathy prevails. Major depression is twice as likely to occur among females as among males. Scientists estimate that between 5 and 9 percent of all women will suffer at least one major depressive episode sometime during their lives (Spitzer & Williams, 1987) and some studies show the percentage to be as high as 26 percent (American Psychiatric Association, 1993). Of all Americans, 5–8 percent will suffer from major depressive disorder at least once in their lifetimes (American Psychiatric Association, 1993).

DEPRESSION
A feeling of sadness and sometimes total apathy. Guilt or inability to cope with problems, frustration, or conflict is often behind depression. It may be influenced by chemical imbalances in the brain as well.

MAJOR DEPRESSIVE DISORDER
A lasting and continuous state of depression without any apparent cause. It is also known as unipolar depression. Major depressive disorder may include psychotic features such as hallucinations, delusions, or a depressive stupor.

◆ **FIGURE 16.3**

Family trees of two families showing the incidence of psychiatric problems, especially bipolar disorder, for three generations. The oldest generations are at the top of the figure. The first-generation couple on the left had nine offspring, eight daughters and one son. The grandmother of this family has bipolar disorder and so do three of her living daughters. The third daughter from the left married twice. The first-generation couple on the right had one daughter, who married the only son of the other first-generation couple. In this family, the grandfather has bipolar disorder. The numbers represent the individual's age at the time of the study or the person's death. An X indicates that the subject has died. The family tree makes the unusually high incidence of mental disorder in these families apparent. (After Elliot Gershon, National Institute of Mental Health.)

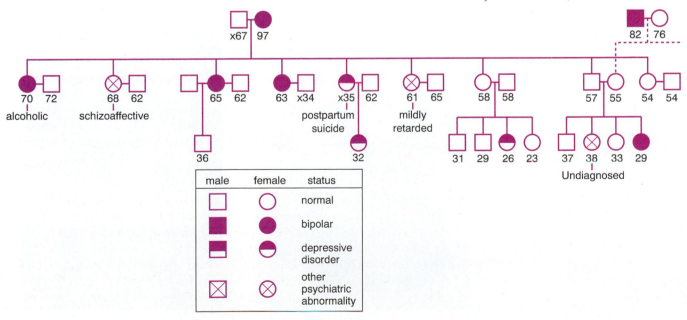

DYSTHYMIC DISORDER
A common form of depression defined by a depressed mood for more days than not, lasting for at least 2 years with no respite from depression for more than 2 months at a time, and associated with some disruption or loss of sleep, appetite, energy, self-esteem, or concentration. Often accompanied by feelings of hopelessness.

Persons with major depressive disorder usually regard themselves in a negative way and blame themselves for things that have gone wrong. They typically experience a decrease in drives such as hunger and sex and an increase in insomnia. Their favorite activities bore them, and they feel hopeless about the future. The onset of depression often is foreshadowed by a sense of being powerless, of losing control over one's life and environment (Hyland, 1987). In fact, researchers have found high levels of MHPG, a hormone by-product that becomes elevated in animals when they are placed in situations in which they are helpless (see Chapter 11), in people with major depressive disorder (Samson, Mirin, Hauser, Fenton, & Schildkraut, 1992).

Interestingly, researchers have also found that people who have low cholesterol (under 160) are at higher risk for major depressive disorder and suicide (Morgan, Palinkas, Barrett-Connor, & Wingard, 1993). It is thought that lowering cholesterol, or having low cholesterol to begin with, is associated with reduced levels of serotonin, which in turn, may be related to higher rates of depression or suicide.

PET scans have also highlighted two areas associated with major depressive disorder. The left prefrontal cortex and the amygdala (see Chapter 2) operate abnormally during bouts of severe depression (Drevets, et al., 1992). Interestingly, the amygdalae in individuals with major depressive disorder continue to function abnormally *between* bouts of depression, possibly opening the door for the development of a medical test to determine who is at risk for developing the disorder.

Major depressive disorder may include psychotic features such as delusions, hallucinations, or a depressive stupor (in which the patient does not speak or respond); it often occurs, however, without such behavior.

Another form of depression is **dysthymic disorder.** It is far more common than major depressive disorder and less severe, but also requires treatment. Some have described dysthymic disorder as the "walking wounded" version of major depressive disorder.

Depression may begin at an early age. In one comprehensive study, almost 1 percent of all *preschoolers* were found to be suffering from major depressive disorder (Kashani & Carlson, 1987). Among grade schoolers, the percentage rises to about 2 percent. Yet very few parents or professionals who deal with children ever consider such a possibility when attempting to explain a child's withdrawn or listless behavior. Depression is also often associated with anxiety.

It is normal for people to have changes of mood, highs and lows.

 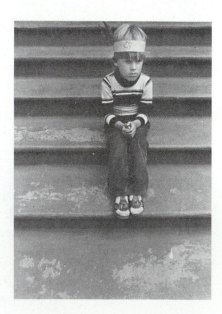

Anxious-depressed individuals are generally more resistant to treatment and typically take longer to recover from bouts of major depression (Clayton, et al., 1991). In such instances, when anxiety is associated with major depressive disorder, the anxiety appears to be a precursor of major depression and not a separate disorder (Coryell, Endicott, & Winokur, 1992).

Individuals who develop major depressive disorder before the age of 20 years are more likely to have close relatives with the disorder (Weissman, et al., 1984; Hammen, et al., 1987). This implies that, as with the bipolar disorders, major depressive disorder may be partly the result of inherited factors.

The idea that major depressive disorder may have an inherited component was first investigated systematically in 1962. At that time, psychiatrist Seymour S. Kety studied 85 adoptees with mood disorder, primarily major depression. These individuals had not been reared by their biological parents. Kety reported a significant concentration of depression in the adoptees' *biological* relatives, finding that they were three times more likely to suffer from depression than were members of the adopted families (Kety, Rosenthal, Wender, Schulsinger, & Jacobsen, 1978). Among all the family members in the study, both biological and adopted, there were 18 reported suicides. That 15 of these suicides were among the biological relatives of the depressed group suggests the possibility of a genetic factor in depression and suicide. The suspected inherited form of major depressive disorder is called **endogenous depression.**

Individuals who have endogenous depression appear to be biologically different from other people. This often can be demonstrated by the use of a diagnostic tool called the **dexamethasone suppression test,** or **DST.** In almost all individuals who do not have endogenous depression, an injection of the drug dexamethasone interacts with the hypothalamic-pituitary-adrenal axis (see Chapter 15) and causes the levels of cortisol to be suppressed or reduced. Among those diagnosed as having endogenous depression, slightly over 50 percent will show no such reduction (70 percent in cases in which the endogenous depression is severe) (APA Task Force, 1987). These results appear to be due to the specific existence of endogenous depression and not simply to the effects of being sad or depressed, because lack of suppression is not commonly observed among people suffering from acute grief (Shuchter, Zisook, Kirkorowicz, & Risch, 1986). The test is by no means a foolproof way of diagnosing endogenous depression (Nelson, Mazure, & Jatlow, 1990), and many believe a test more accurate than the DST is sorely needed—assuming one can be found.

We do not know why lack of suppression is seen among so many of those diagnosed as having endogenous depression, but the finding does emphasize that there are some underlying biological events correlated with the condition. Supporting this assertion is the fact that individuals with endogenous depression are more likely to suffer from allergies than are members of the general population. This discovery suggests that a central nervous system/immune system imbalance might produce depression-like symptoms like an allergic reaction (Marshall, 1993).

But the most comprehensive study to date to examine major depressive disorder among twins in an effort to sort out possible genetic influences found environmental factors such as experiencing a trauma, getting a divorce, losing a job, or having poor interpersonal relations to be as important a set of predictors as genes appear to be (Kendler, Kessler, Neale, Heath, & Eaves, 1993).

Thus, genetics and the environment appear to play equally important roles. There are even instances of individuals who have endogenous depression and also have an obvious (environmental) reason to be depressed. Such individuals are said to suffer from **double depression** and show greater impairment and more severe depression than is usually observed in either endogenous depres-

ENDOGENOUS DEPRESSION
The suspected inherited form of major depressive disorder. Endogenous depression occurs without any apparent external cause. It is marked by long-term despair, dejection, and feelings of apprehension, gloom, and worthlessness.

DEXAMETHASONE SUPPRESSION TEST (DST)
A blood test used to indicate the presence of endogenous depression. Dexamethasone is administered, and the suppression of cortisol is measured. Failure to suppress cortisol is an indication of endogenous depression.

DOUBLE DEPRESSION
Severe depression brought about by a combination of endogenous and environmental causes, either of which would have been sufficient in and by itself to create a serious depressive state.

SEASONAL AFFECTIVE DISORDER (SAD)
Depression associated with either a longer or shorter day. It commonly affects individuals in either the winter or summer months and typically passes once the season is over.

SCHIZOPHRENIA
A term used to describe a number of psychotic disorders characterized by serious emotional disturbances, withdrawal, lack of or inappropriate emotional responses, hallucinations, and delusions.

DELUSION
A strong belief opposed to reality, which is maintained in spite of logical persuasion and evidence to the contrary.

sion or environmentally induced depression (Klein, Taylor, Harding, & Dickstein, 1988).

Some sufferers of mood disorders seem to be affected by the season. Their depression comes on in the winter months and, although rarer, may even include episodes of mania or hypomania during the summer months. This is sometimes called **seasonal affective disorder** or **SAD.** Physicians have been aware of this interesting disorder for well over 2000 years (Wehr & Rosenthal, 1989), but it has only recently been studied in depth. It is estimated that in the United States SAD affects about 1 to 2 percent of the population of Florida, 6 percent of those living in Maryland or New York City, and almost 10 percent of the residents of New Hampshire or Alaska (Bower, 1992). In other words, it is directly correlated with latitude. The closer one is to the pole, the longer the winter nights are and the more numerous the persons affected by SAD.

Seasonal affective disorder is different from other forms of depression in some provocative ways that may eventually furnish important clues to the underlying cause of the disorder. For instance, sufferers from SAD typically crave extra sleep and are especially drawn to consume large amounts of carbohydrates (Garvey, Wesner, & Godes, 1988). This has led researchers to wonder if there isn't some link between SAD in humans and hibernation, a pattern of behavior most markedly observed in bears. So far, no one knows. What we do know, however, is that winter SAD can usually be cured by the use of bright lamps that simulate daylight, and can be used to artificially lengthen the sufferer's winter days.

Another intriguing possibility is that SAD is due in part to a malfunction of the retina. Researchers have discovered that subtle retinal abnormalities commonly exist in sufferers of SAD that lessen the amount of light processed by their eyes and sent onto the brain, where, in turn, it is assumed to have an important effect on brain hormones or neurotransmitters (Lam, Beattie, Buchanan, Remick, & Zis, 1991).

SCHIZOPHRENIC DISORDERS

Schizophrenia is a serious psychosis. It affects as many as 2 million people in the United States and perhaps 1 percent of the entire world's population. The treatment of schizophrenia costs the United States an estimated $50 billion per year. Although it is typically a disorder of young adults, it can occur at any age and tends to be between two and three times more common in men than in women (Iacono & Beiser, 1992). It may be that women are at less risk for schizophrenia or for its more severe forms because estrogen, a hormone that is at higher levels in women than men, functions to block dopamine in the brain (Bower, 1992). As we shall soon see, excess dopamine may greatly contribute to the symptoms of schizophrenia or possibly be a cause of the disorder.

Contrary to common belief, schizophrenia does not mean having more than one personality. As you recall, multiple personality is a dissociative disorder. The "schizo" in schizophrenia historically referred to a split between emotion and thought, a complete breakdown of integrated personality functioning. In instances of schizophrenia, emotions become flat and distorted. Thought, language, and behavior become bizarre and disturbed. These bizarre behaviors are commonly accompanied by delusions and hallucinations.

A **delusion** is a strong unrealistic belief that is maintained even though there is ample evidence of its falseness. Schizophrenics who believe that they are Jesus Christ or that the telephone company has wired their brain and is controlling their every movement are exhibiting delusions. Schizophrenics may also have **hallucinations,** which are sensory perceptions in the absence of appropriate external stimuli. In other words, schizophrenics often see objects or hear voices that are not there, and react to them, although schizophrenia may occur without hallucinations (Asaad & Shapiro, 1986). The hallucinations experienced by sufferers of schizophrenia are thought to be fairly intense. Evidence from EEG recordings (see Chapter 7) shows electrical brain-wave patterns during auditory hallucinations that appear very similar to those observed when normal subjects hear real sounds (Tiihonen, et al., 1992). It has also been discovered that normal sensory inputs are not processed normally in schizophrenics, leading to sensory overloads when none should occur (Judd, McAdams, Budnick, & Braff, 1992).

The onset of schizophrenia can be gradual or rapid. Gradual onset is usually a worse sign, because it is associated with a poorer likelihood of recovery. Approximately 25 percent of schizophrenics who are treated undergo remission, during which their symptoms abate. A cure is rarely claimed, because schizophrenia in remission can recur. Over time, a schizophrenic may experience symptoms in varying degrees of severity (Harrow, Carone, & Westermeyer, 1985). Sometimes the behavioral disruption is relatively mild; at other times, it is extremely severe.

Figures 16.4 and 16.5 are paintings made by schizophrenics that illustrate the disintegration and reintegration of personality and sensation that often accompany a schizophrenic episode. Note the distortions of perception. Distortions in thought also are common to schizophrenia, as is apparent in the diary entry of a college-age schizophrenic, which is reproduced in the following case study.

SCHIZOPHRENIA: THE CASE OF DAVID F.

David F. was a young college student who became more and more apprehensive about his future as he neared graduation. He also was concerned about his relationship with

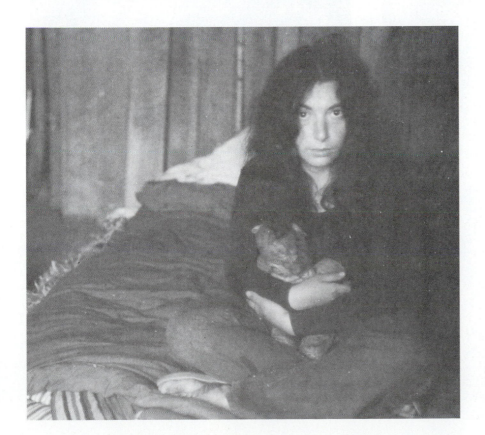

HALLUCINATION
A false sense perception for which there is no appropriate external stimulus.

Schizophrenia is a serious mental disorder and is classified as a psychosis.

his girlfriend, and he had feelings of sexual inadequacy. David began to stay in his room and stopped attending classes almost entirely. He recorded many of his feelings in a diary. The following excerpts were written shortly before he was hospitalized:

> Thursday, March 12, 11 A.M. I'm out! I'm through . . . boomed out of the tunnel sometime last night and it's raining stars . . . whooey . . . it's nice out there's time for everything . . . I can do it I did it and if it happens again I'll do it again twice as hard I got a dexamyl high going and I'm not on dexamyl and I've been up for forty eight or more hours and I'm giddygiddygiddy and I took a test this morning and it was on Voltaire and I kicked him a couple of good ones for being down on Pascal that poor bastard with his shrivelled body and bottomless abysses they're not bottomless!! You get down far enough and it gets thick enough and black enough and then you claw claw claw your way out and pretty soon you're on top again. And I licked it by myself, all alone . . . I just sat in on one of those weddings of the soul and I tooted tooted . . . I don't care I can use it I can run on it it will be my psychic gasoline now I don't have to sleep sleep all the time to get away with it . . . but if I lose my typewriter? (Bowers, 1965, p. 351)

In DSM-IV, schizophrenia is classified according to subtypes. There are five major subtypes, each marked by a somewhat different clustering of behaviors or symptoms (see Table 16.4). Although these subtypes are fairly stable, it is not uncommon for the same individual to show symptoms of different subtypes from time to time (Kendler, Gruenberg, & Tsuang, 1985). Even though there may be some overlap, evidence suggests that these subtypes are, in fact, truly different disorders, not just artifacts of a classification system (Gur, et al., 1991).

◆ **FIGURE 16.4**

Louis Wain (1860–1939) was a famous artist best known for his witty depiction of cats in human situations, such as giving a tea party. Fifteen years before his death, Wain suffered a schizophrenic breakdown. The changes in his cat paintings show a fascinating and frightening transition from his former style to one that highlights sensory distortion and turmoil. (Derik Bayles/Courtesy Guttman-Maclay Collection. Life Picture Service.)

TABLE 16.4 ◆	CLASSIFICATIONS OF SCHIZOPHRENIA SUBTYPES
SUBTYPE	CHARACTERISTICS
Disorganized	Earlier age of onset than most of the other types. Emotions are extremely distorted. The person may display grossly inappropriate silliness and laughter, unusual and bizarre mannerisms, and obscene behavior.
Catatonic	Alternating periods of intense excitement or extreme withdrawal. During extreme withdrawal, the person may hold his body very still, sometimes for hours. The positions assumed are often odd. During intense excitement, the person often walks about rapidly and carries on incoherent conversations. Behavior is uninhibited, wild, and impulsive.
Paranoid	The person has bizarre delusions. Feelings of persecution are common. Judgment is impaired and unpredictable; hallucinations are common.
Undifferentiated	No one subtype of schizophrenia dominates. The person shows rapidly changing mixtures of schizophrenic behaviors, delusions, hallucinations, bizarre thoughts, and emotions.
Residual	Subtle indications of schizophrenia that are occasionally observed in those who are recovering from a schizophrenic episode.

Causes of Schizophrenia

During the last 100 years, just about every conceivable biological and environmental cause for schizophrenia has been proposed. For instance, during the 1920s, it was common to pull teeth in an attempt to alleviate schizophrenia, since at the time it was thought that a localized infection might be a possible cause. Sadly, something as simple as pulling teeth wasn't the answer. During the 1940s and 1950s, interest in possible biological causes decreased as environmental theories became more popular. Although scientists now believe that the environment plays a role in the onset of schizophrenia, the most intriguing new research into the origin of schizophrenia has once again focused on the biological, owing to recent discoveries in genetics, biochemistry, virology, and neurology.

GENETIC AND ENVIRONMENTAL FACTORS.   Studies of the incidence of schizophrenia among identical and fraternal twins have indicated a hereditary component to schizophrenia. For instance, a study in the United States found that if one identical twin had schizophrenia, there was a 42 percent chance that the other would, whereas there was only a 9 percent chance for a similar result among fraternal twins (Gottesman & Shields, 1972). Fraternal twins, although born at the same time, do not share exactly the same genetic makeup.

Children of schizophrenics who were adopted by nonschizophrenics also have been found to have a higher incidence of schizophrenia than control populations (Barnes, 1987b). Another study indicated that close relatives of schizophrenics are almost 13 times more likely to suffer from schizophrenia (3.8 percent chance) than are individuals who have no such relatives (0.3 percent chance) (Baron, Gruen, Kane, & Asnis, 1985). In fact, data indicate that schizophrenia has a heritability that exceeds that for diabetes, ulcers, or high blood pressure (Loehlin, Willerman, & Horn, 1988), all disorders in which heredity is known to play an important role.

Curiously, though, the subtypes of schizophrenia shown in Table 16.4 do not run in families (Kendler, Gruenberg, & Tsuang, 1988). While the predis-

◆ **FIGURE 16.5**

A patient diagnosed as a paranoid schizophrenic was unable to make even a simple original drawing when asked to do so. A painting from a magazine (a) was provided as an aid. The patient's first attempt to copy (b) revealed visual distractions, confusions about language and letters, and lack of color. As therapy progressed, the patient's recovery was dramatically demonstrated by his improved ability to copy the original art, as shown in (c) and then (d). (Al Yercoutere— Malibu, California.)

(a)

(b)

position to become schizophrenic does appear to have a genetic component, the subtype of schizophrenia that eventually manifests itself may be the result of environmental influences or perhaps be due to the severity of the schizophrenia, but does not itself seem to be part of the genetic picture.

As noted, some studies have indicated that the environment may have a pronounced influence on the onset of schizophrenia. In the UCLA high-risk study, 54 families who had troubled teenagers but no history of psychosis were studied for 15 years. Patterns of family interactions were also observed. Teenagers who developed schizophrenia were more likely to come from families who showed the most unusual or pathological patterns of communication, such as often saying one thing while really meaning another (Wynne, Singer, Bartko, & Toohey, 1977). This may indicate that among those predisposed to schizophrenia, additional stresses may bring on the disorder. Of course, it might also be that the families with the most pathological communication patterns demonstrate schizophrenic-like interaction, implying that they might have some biological problem that they pass on to their children.

Perhaps the best evidence that exists for both genetic and environmental factors in schizophrenia comes from the case of the Genain quadruplets (Rosenthal & Quinn, 1977). In 1930, these *identical* quadruplets caused something of a sensation. Quadruplets aren't that rare, but identical quadruplets (all stemming from one fertilized egg) are. The four girls were called Nora, Iris, Myra, and Hester.* The fascinating thing was that by the time the girls had reached

*These names are not the girls' real ones; they are fictional names corresponding to the initials of the National Institutes of Mental Health (NIMH). In this way, data obtained about any one of the quadruplets cannot be directly identified with a given individual except by the medical researchers who have the original files and the correct names.

(c)

(d)

AL YERCOUTERE—MALIBU, CALIFORNIA

DOPAMINE HYPOTHESIS
The argument that abnormalities associated with the neurotransmitter dopamine are related to the onset and maintenance of schizophrenic episodes. Either an overabundance of dopamine or the existence of too many dopamine receptors in the brain is deemed responsible.

late adolescence, all four were schizophrenic. The odds of this happening by random chance were one in 2 billion, so it appears that genetics was an important factor—because they all share the same genes.

The severity of schizophrenia, however, was not at all the same for the four sisters, indicating an environmental component as well. Of the four, Nora and Hester showed the most severe symptoms, but Iris was less affected, and Myra, less still. In fact, at last report, Myra was living with her husband and appeared to be leading a relatively normal life (Hamer, 1982).

Researcher Kenneth Kendler, who has examined these data and other similar studies, expressed the general consensus of professionals in this field when he said: "It is not fair to say that schizophrenia is a genetic disease. . . . But the evidence is strong that schizophrenia, like coronary heart disease and early-onset hearing loss, tends to run in families" (Barnes, 1987b, p. 430).

BIOCHEMICAL FACTORS. Research into the biochemistry of schizophrenia underwent a revolution in the late 1950s, when scientists discovered that small amounts of certain chemical agents, once in the body, could produce a number of mental changes (Huxley, 1954). Such hallucinogenic substances as LSD and mescaline were found to cause a temporary breakdown of the thought process, mental disorganization, and sensory experiences similar to the symptoms of psychosis. Some investigators wondered whether, in the case of schizophrenia, the body wasn't producing its own hallucinogenic substances. My father was a research psychiatrist, and in the late 1950s he began experiments with LSD to identify similarities between LSD intoxication and schizophrenia. My mother volunteered to be one of his subjects. Years before the general public had ever heard of LSD, my mother was "dropping acid" every Thursday under supervised conditions in a laboratory. Like most schizophrenia research conducted at that time, the efforts, unfortunately, turned out not to be fruitful. Thursday night dinners, however, were unique often including my mom's favorite dish at the time—blue mashed potatoes.

To date, no internal hallucinogen similar to LSD has been found to be the cause of schizophrenia. Since the late 1950s, our understanding of schizophrenia has grown, and few researchers now think that its mysteries will ever be solved in such a straightforward way.

In the past few years, the possibility that some physical or biochemical causes of schizophrenia may be uncovered has grown, however. Researchers now believe that if schizophrenia is caused by a biochemical agent or agents, these substances must be related to the neurotransmitters that send nerve impulses across synapses from neuron to neuron in the brain (see Chapter 2). In the 1970s, the neurotransmitter dopamine began to attract special interest (Lucins, 1975) because many of the antipsychotic drugs (drugs used to treat schizophrenia) are known to block dopamine action at the site of the dopamine receptor cell (Farde, Hall, Ehrin, & Sedvall, 1986). This possible explanation of schizophrenia became known as the **dopamine hypothesis.**

By late 1986, it was discovered through the use of the PET scan that although schizophrenics don't produce excess dopamine, they do have an unusually greater density of dopamine receptors in the portion of the brain known as the limbic system (see Chapter 2). PET scans of schizophrenics have also shown a decrease in frontal brain activity known as *hypofrontality* (Siegel, et al., 1993). One exciting idea currently under investigation is that too many dopamine receptors in the limbic system might account for the *positive* symptoms of schizophrenia (behaviors *added* on top of what is normal, such as bizarre actions, thoughts, or verbal statements), while hypofrontality might account for the *negative* symptoms of schizophrenia (behaviors that are *missing* from what is normal, such as the lack of spontaneity and emotionality or the inability to focus attention) (Davis, Kahn, Ko, & Davidson, 1991).

STRUCTURAL AND ANATOMICAL FACTORS. Biochemical hypotheses concerning psychosis are only about three decades old. Before that time, most research centered on the possibility of structural abnormalities in the brains of psychotics. These older studies, some conducted more than 50 years ago, reported that the cerebral ventricles (the butterfly-shaped fluid-filled cavities found between the lobes of the brain) were abnormally enlarged in the brains of schizophrenics. At that time, the process used for studying brain structure was *pneumoencephalography*, in which gas or air was injected into the ventricles of the brain so that they could be visualized on X-ray film and measured. The experience was extremely painful, and although enlarged ventricles were reported in some schizophrenics, these findings were dismissed as erroneous by later researchers, who believed that the injection of gas or air could have artificially enlarged the ventricles and made them appear bigger on the X-ray images.

Modern researchers, however, using computed axial tomography (CAT) scans and magnetic-resonance imaging (MRI) (see Chapter 2) to take more sophisticated pictures of the brain, have obtained findings that have confirmed the older research (Lieberman, et al., 1992). In fact, some of these confirming brain scans were of John Hinckley, the man who shot President Reagan in 1981 and who was diagnosed as a schizophrenic. The scans showed him to have abnormally enlarged cerebral ventricles. Over the past 15 years, many researchers have presented additional data confirming that schizophrenics do, in fact, have abnormally enlarged cerebral ventricles as well as other consistent abnormalities of the central nervous system, such as less gray matter in the brain (see Chapter 2) (Andreasen, 1988; Shelton, et al., 1988; Suddath, et al., 1989; Raz & Raz, 1990). Studies also indicate that these structural changes are not the result of medical treatments or of drug or alcohol use and that they are not related to how long a person has been in an institution. The structural changes seem to correlate only with schizophrenia. Perhaps the most telling study concerning enlarged cerebral ventricles in schizophrenics was conducted by Daniel Weinberger and his colleagues who examined the brain scans of 15 pairs of identical twins, in which one of each pair had been diagnosed as schizophrenic (Suddath, Christison, Torrey, Casanova, & Weinberger, 1990). They noted that in 14 out of 15 pairs, the cerebral ventricles of the schizophrenic twin were abnormally enlarged when compared with the non-schizophrenic twin (see Figure 16.6). No abnormalities were noted among 7 normal twins who were used as controls.

◆ FIGURE 16.6

Brain scans of forty-four-year-old male identical twins. The brain on the right, however, clearly shows the enlarged cerebral ventricles that are associated with this individual's schizophrenia. (SOURCE: *Suddath, Christison, Torrey, Casanova, & Weinberger, 1990.*)

TWO-STRIKE THEORY
A recent theory of the cause of some or most schizophrenia. In this view a susceptibility to the influenza virus is inherited (first strike). Following this "strike," exposure to the flu virus during the second trimester of pregnancy provides the second strike, causing a disruption of brain development in the fetus that later manifests itself as schizophrenia.

DELUSIONAL DISORDER
A psychosis characterized by delusions and extreme suspiciousness. Hallucinations rarely occur, and the personality does not undergo the serious disorganization associated with schizophrenia.

THE TWO-STRIKE THEORY.   One of the most promising avenues of current research into the cause or causes of schizophrenia is the **two-strike theory.** Careful microscopic examination of the brains of schizophrenics has revealed that there is extensive *developmental pathology* throughout the outer cortex and within deeper regions associated with emotion and memory (Akbarian, et al., 1993). This indicates that whatever is going wrong with the brains of schizophrenics probably went wrong in the womb during the second trimester (months 4–6) of pregnancy when billions of neurons in the developing brain of the fetus normally find their appropriate target calls and make many of their connections. Something in schizophrenics, it appears, disrupts the normal neural connections made in the brain of the fetus during this developmental period, leading to the catastrophic disorder we call schizophrenia.

Evidence supporting this assertion comes from studies of identical schizophrenic twins. As you recall, it is just about as likely for the identical twin of a schizophrenic to also develop schizophrenia as not. Interestingly, MRI studies have shown that the likelihood of an identical twin of a schizophrenic also developing the disorder is directly tied to the amount of disruption that occurs in the womb as the fetus is developing (Weinberger, Berman, Suddath, & Torrey, 1992; Bracha, et al., 1992).

The two-strike theory gets its name from the belief that a genetic susceptibility (the first strike) and a subsequent environmental influence (the second strike) work together to cause severe disruption in the formation of the brain during the second trimester of pregnancy. Currently, the number one environmental suspect is the influenza virus.

The flu virus is known to be one of the few viruses that can weaken the chemical links between neurons and the glial cells that guide them to the positions to which they are assigned in the developing brain (Scheibel & Conrad, 1993). It might also be that the genetic link among schizophrenics and their relatives is an inherited immune disorder that leaves the fetal brain at greater risk for disruption by the flu virus during the second trimester of pregnancy.

The question then remains, if schizophrenia is the result of developmental brain pathology, why does schizophrenia seem to be a disorder mainly of young adults rather than of children? The answer may be that the brain damage, though present from birth, doesn't fully manifest itself until some time after puberty. Support for the idea that something is wrong from birth comes from careful examination of infants of schizophrenic parents. These children, who themselves are at high risk for schizophrenia, show uneven central nervous system development throughout their infancy and childhoods (Fish, Marcus, Hans, Auerbach, & Perdue, 1992). Other studies, like the one incorporating home movies described in the Chapter Prologue, also point to a disorder with its roots early in development.

If the two-strike theory turns out to be correct, it won't necessarily preclude other theories. Remember, that schizophrenia is a descriptive term and may encompass a number of relatively unrelated disorders (Heinrichs, 1993).

DELUSIONAL DISORDER

Delusional disorders are fairly uncommon, affecting about 0.05 to 0.1 percent of all individuals sometime during their lives. Delusional disorder used to be called paranoia and is slightly more common in females than it is in males.

Delusional Disorder

Delusional disorder is a system of delusions that the psychotic individual firmly believes or accepts. The difference between delusional disorder and the paranoid type of schizophrenia is that in delusional disorder, hallucinations rarely occur and there is no serious disorganization of the personality. The delusional system usually develops slowly. Delusional disorder is categorized according to subtype, depending on the particular kind of delusion that predominates (see Table 16.5).

The delusions are not simply misbeliefs; they are severe mental distortions. For example, delusional people might feel that aliens are trying to take over their minds, or they might believe themselves to be Abraham Lincoln or Joan of Arc. Interestingly, the delusions are usually logical, in the sense that if you accept the basic premise (for example, that the patient's mind is being controlled by aliens), the rest of his ideas may seem perfectly reasonable (in that context). One of the most memorable depictions of delusional disorder in the history of motion pictures was Humphrey Bogart's portrayal of Fred C. Dobbs in the film *Treasure of the Sierra Madre*. Dobbs, a gold prospector, becomes more and more convinced that other people are after his share of the gold, and he eventually attempts murder in "self-defense."

Causes of Delusional Disorder

Because delusional disorder is less common than psychotic mood disorders or schizophrenia, less is known about its possible causes. Some researchers believe that it is not accurate to consider delusional disorder as separate from schizophrenia, because delusional disorder is not always readily distinguishable from paranoid schizophrenia (Meissner, 1978). As a result, many of the potential causal factors that are associated with schizophrenia are being investigated as possible causes of delusional disorder as well. However, because delusional disorder doesn't appear to run in families in the way that schizophrenia does (Watt, 1985), and because the personality isn't nearly as shattered as it is in schizophrenia, other researchers consider the two categories as distinct, which is the way they are presented in DSM-IV.

❧ PERSONALITY DISORDERS (AXIS II)

There are many types of **personality disorders.** The current list from DSM-IV is shown in Table 16.6. The personality disorders are grouped into three clusters in DSM-IV. The disorders within each cluster resemble each other to some extent, although they remain distinct. All personality disorders share certain qualities. People who have a personality disorder are typically severely impaired in terms of how they feel about themselves and how they get along with others

PERSONALITY DISORDER
Deeply ingrained, habitual, and rigid patterns of behavior or character that severely limit the adaptive potential of the individual but that are often not seen by him or her to create problems or be maladaptive. They are sometimes called character disorders.

TABLE 16.5 ◆ DELUSIONAL DISORDER—SUBTYPES	
SUBTYPE	DELUSION
Erotomanic	A person, usually of high status, is in love with the subject.
Grandiose	Inflated worth, power, knowledge, identity, or special relationship to a deity or famous person.
Jealous	One's sexual partner is unfaithful.
Persecutory	Someone or some group is treating the subject in a malevolent way.
Somatic	Physical defect, disorder, or disease.
Mixed	Delusions characteristic of more than one of the above types, but no one theme predominates.
Unspecified	Any delusion that does not fit one of the other categories.

TABLE 16.6 ◆ PERSONALITY DISORDERS	
DSM-IV CATEGORY*	DESCRIPTION
Paranoid	Harbors a continuous unjustifiable suspicion and mistrust of people. Often appears cold or unemotional. Takes offense easily (behavior not due to schizophrenia or paranoid disorder).
Schizoid	Is unable to form social relationships, lacks warm or sentimental feelings for others, and is indifferent to praise, criticism, or the feelings of others (behavior is not due to schizophrenia or paranoid disorder).
Schizotypal	Exhibits strangeness in thought, speech, perception, and behavior, but not severe enough to classify as schizophrenic. Often socially isolated, suspicious, and oversensitive to criticism.
Histrionic	Is overreactive, intense, and overdramatic to the point of disturbing interpersonal relationships. Often displays an overreaction to minor situations, crying, tantrums. Is seen by others as vain, shallow, dependent, or manipulative.
Narcissistic	Has an unwarranted sense of self-importance, is preoccupied with fantasies of success. Demands attention, often believes she is entitled to special treatment. Tends to idolize or devaluate others. Lacks empathy.
Antisocial	Continuously violates the rights of others. Was antisocial prior to age 15 years; often fails to hold a job or to perform adequately on the job. Often lies, fights, steals, and is truant. Usually shows disrespect for the law. Can be engaging for own purposes, manipulative, impulsive. Lacks feelings for others.
Borderline	Is unstable in mood, behavior, and self-image. Is impulsive and unpredictable in behavior. Has intense and unstable relationships with others, inappropriate and uncontrollable anger. Is unable to be alone, has long-lasting feelings of boredom or emptiness. Makes suicidal gestures.
Avoidant	Is oversensitive to rejection or possible humiliation. Avoids relationships unless guaranteed to be accepted uncritically. Has low self-esteem. Is devastated by the slightest disapproval. Remains isolated although wanting to be with others.
Dependent	Allows others to take over and run his life. Lacks self-confidence and cannot function independently. Avoids opportunities to be self-reliant.
Obsessive compulsive	Has restricted ability to express warmth and affection. Has a need for perfectionism at the expense of others or at the expense of enjoying life. Insists that others do his or her bidding. Devoted to work and productivity at the expense of enjoying life.
Passive aggressive	Passively refuses to perform adequately in social relationships or at work even though adequate effort is possible. The name for the disorder comes from the belief that the person is passively expressing overt agression. Often shows procrastination, stubbornness, and intentional inefficiency.

*This table includes descriptions of only the most general nature and is completely inadequate for diagnostic purposes. In DSM-IV the categories are described in far more detail.

(Drake & Vaillant, 1985). In fact, the most definitive aspect of a personality disorder is that the individual engages in behavior that *disrupts social relationships*. Also, unlike axis I disorders, the personality disorders are not considered to be psychiatric disorders.

Individuals with personality disorders seldom feel responsible for the troubles they cause because they generally attribute any problems to bad luck or perceive that the fault is someone else's. Another marked feature of personality disorders is that the maladaptive behavior pattern will typically persist until those who must deal with the individual finally become exhausted and break off the relationship. Individuals with personality disorder are also far more likely to be substance abusers or alcoholics than are members of the general population, which further interferes with their social relationships (Nace, Davis, & Gaspari, 1991).

In personality disorder, we see an all-encompassing problem that permeates every single social interaction that the person has. Perhaps one of the best examples of personality disorder ever captured on film was actor Robert DeNiro's portrayal of the character Rupert Pupkin in the movie *The King of Comedy*, a masterful depiction of narcissistic personality disorder and worth renting if you've never seen it.

Another example, in this case antisocial personality, is that of Dan F., a disk jockey at a radio station, who told his story to his friend, a clinical psychologist; it is reproduced in the following case study.

ANTISOCIAL PERSONALITY DISORDER: THE CASE OF DAN F.

"I can remember the first time in my life when I began to suspect I was a little different from most people. When I was in high school my best friend got leukemia and died and I went to his funeral. Everybody else was crying and feeling sorry for themselves and as they were praying to get him into heaven I suddenly realized that I wasn't feeling anything at all. He was a nice guy but what the hell. That night I thought about it some more and found out that I wouldn't miss my mother and father if they died and that I wasn't too nuts about my brothers and sisters, for that matter. I figured there wasn't anybody I really cared for but, then, I didn't need any of them anyway so I rolled over and went to sleep." As we discussed his early life he told me he could not recall a time when he was not "doing everybody I could and the easy ones twice." He remembered that when he was 12 years old he had read a book about "con men." It was then he decided it would be his life's work. They were heroes to him and he "fell down laughing" when they took some "mark" for his "bundle." As he said, "There is a sucker born every minute, and I'm glad the birth rate is so high."

One night, a colleague of Dan's committed suicide. . . . My phone started ringing early the next morning with the inevitable question "Why?" The executives at the station called but Dan F. never did. When I talked to him, he did not mention the suicide. Later, when I brought it to his attention, all he could say was that it was "the way the ball bounces." At the station, however, he was the one who collected money for the deceased and presented it personally to the new widow. As Dan observed, she was really built and had possibilities. (McNeil, 1967, pp. 85, 87)

Generally, people with personality disorders do poorly in therapy, believing that it is other people who are in need of help. However, a growing body of evidence indicates that biological problems may be at the core of many axis II disorders, which may open the door for the possibility of future medical or pharmacological intervention (Siever & Davis, 1991).

🧬 THE ASSESSMENT OF MENTAL DISORDERS

One of the most difficult problems faced by clinicians is assessment. Errors in assessment can lead to serious misunderstandings and inappropriate treatment. The effectiveness of assessment in actual practice has been the focus of a number of investigations and controversies.

Assessment Bias

Back in 1973, psychologist David Rosenhan brought the problem of assessment to the forefront with a series of ingenious studies (Rosenhan, 1973). Rosenhan wondered whether a perfectly sane individual who gained admission to a mental hospital as a patient would be recognized as normal by the staff and discharged. To test his idea, he obtained the cooperation of eight people, who agreed to be pseudopatients. Among these eight were a psychology graduate student, three psychologists, a pediatrician, a psychiatrist, a painter, and a housewife. Rosenhan himself was one of the pseudopatients. With the exception of the hospital administrator and chief psychologist, no one else in the hospital knew that he was checking in as a patient. Twelve hospitals were chosen in five states on the East and West coasts. Some were old and rundown, some were very new; some were research hospitals, some weren't; some were private hospitals, some public.

The pseudopatients' task was to call their hospitals for an appointment, arrive, and complain of hearing voices. The patients answered every other

David Rosenhan.

question asked by the staff during patient intake honestly. All the pseudopatients behaved in the hospital as they would normally have behaved. When asked by the staff how they felt, they indicated that they no longer had symptoms and were feeling fine. They responded politely to attendants who requested that they take medication (spitting it out later, however).

In no case was the sanity of the pseudopatient detected. The condition of seven out of eight was diagnosed as schizophrenia in remission. The pseudopatients stayed in the hospital from 7 to 52 days, with an average of 19 days. During the first of the hospitalizations, when careful data were kept, 35 out of a total of 118 other patients in the same hospitals became aware that the pseudopatients were sane. These patients would argue, "You're not crazy. You're a journalist, or a professor. You're checking up on the hospital" (p. 252). These patients recognized normality while the hospital staff failed to.

After Rosenhan published his results, one teaching hospital questioned his findings. The staff there argued that such errors were unlikely. Consequently, Rosenhan informed the staff that sometime during the next three months one or perhaps more pseudopatients might attempt to be admitted to that hospital. After admission, the patients would act sanely. The staff members were asked to try to expose the pseudopatients. The staff carefully examined 193 patients who were admitted for treatment. One member of the staff believed with high confidence that 41 of these patients were pseudopatients. One psychiatrist thought that about 23 were pseudopatients, and another psychiatrist, with one staff member, agreed that 19 were probably pseudopatients. At that point, Rosenhan admitted that he had never sent anyone to their hospital! Rosenhan concluded that "any diagnostic process that lends itself so readily to massive errors of this sort cannot be a very reliable one" (p. 252).

The pseudopatients also noticed during their stays that the staff often misinterpreted behavior. Boredom was misinterpreted as nervousness. Anger at being mistreated by an attendant was misinterpreted as berserk behavior caused by pathology. Once several patients were sitting outside the cafeteria half an hour before it opened, and a psychiatrist was overheard telling his residents that this was indicative of the oral stage of the patients' syndrome. Apparently, it hadn't occurred to the psychiatrist that there was nothing much to do inside a hospital besides eat or wait for lunch.

Rosenhan came to the following conclusion:

It is clear that we cannot distinguish the sane from the insane in psychiatric hospitals. The hospital itself imposes a special environment in which the meanings of behavior can easily be misunderstood. The consequences to patients hospitalized in such an environment—the powerlessness, depersonalization, segregation, mortification, and self-labeling—seem undoubtedly counter-therapeutic. (p. 257)

Rosenhan replicated his initial study, carried out in 1973, with follow-up studies in 1973, 1974, and 1975. The later studies involved more than 10 hospitals (Greenberg, 1981). Rosenhan found essentially the same results.

A number of researchers and clinicians have taken issue with Rosenhan because of his methods and conclusions. For instance, psychologist Max Lewis of the University of Western Washington has stated:

I have some trouble with Rosenhan's study. First of all, subjects did report auditory hallucinations and ask to enter the hospital. Secondly, it is standard operating procedure to keep any admission for a period of observation. Thirdly, I don't have confidence that all pseudopatients presented a "normal" pattern of behavior; they were there to make a point. Fourthly, is it not possible that some of the pseudopatients did exhibit problems worthy of treatment? Obviously we would all be more comfortable if all the pseudopatients were immediately discovered. But a nineteen day stay is much different from being locked away without a follow-up. I think Rosenhan has an important point, but the situation doesn't seem so horrible to me as Rosenhan's discussion portrays it. (Lewis, 1981)

Since the Rosenhan study, DSM-III, DSM-III-R, and DSM-IV have been published. The more reliable criteria of these advanced manuals should, we hope, make such misdiagnoses less likely. Still, Rosenhan's studies help to highlight how difficult diagnosis can be.

AN ENDURING QUESTION: SHOULD MENTAL DISORDERS BE CLASSIFIED BEFORE THEIR UNDERLYING CAUSES ARE UNDERSTOOD?

More than a century ago, Dr. Samuel Cartwright described a "disease of the mind" to the Louisiana Medical Association. He called the disease *drapetomania*, from the Greek *drapetes*, which means "to run away." He said that drapetomania was the "insane desire to wander away from home," and, he argued, this was why many slaves ran away—they had this disease of the mind (Chorover, 1979).

As you can see, labeling diseases of the mind without considering social or cultural factors or learning and experience can lead someone to assume that pathology exists when all that really exists is different behavior. Sometimes, as in the case of drapetomania, the behavior is different for a good reason. Critics of DSM-IV have likened it to a symphony written by a committee; the notes are all there, but the way they are put together reflects the biases inherent in such a process. They argue that the DSM system is a haven for people who think that their job is to find a label to fit every subjective observation imaginable.

Because the underlying causes of these "pathologies" are frequently lacking, the DSM-IV diagnoses are based on gross descriptions of complex behaviors that often appear different to different people. This leads to arguments of the kind we have touched on lightly, such as whether delusional disorder is distinctly different from schizophrenia or whether obsessive-compulsive disorder should, in fact, be considered an anxiety disorder.

Some professionals have gone so far as to reject all *psychological* assessment as invalid. For example, the psychiatrist Thomas Szasz has written about what he calls psychiatric injustice. He states that psychiatry has been used as a political weapon and that it has eliminated the civil liberties of many people who simply behaved differently, because it labels them sick and incarcerates them in hospitals. Szasz argues that in the past those who exhibited abnormal behavior were labeled witches or warlocks, whereas today they are labeled with psychiatric terms that serve the same purpose; that is, to justify the community in eliminating these people from effective participation in society. In his classic book *The Myth of Mental Illness* (1961), Szasz wrote:

> The term "mental illness" is a metaphor. More particularly as this term is used in mental health legislation, "mental illness" is not the name of a medical illness or disorder, but is a quasi-medical label whose purpose is to conceal conflict as illness and to justify coercion as treatment. (Szasz, 1961, p. xviii)

This view has been reinforced in the perception of the public by such films as *One Flew over the Cuckoo's Nest*, in which a man is placed in a mental institution simply because he has been disruptive; is forced to take drugs against his will; is given shock therapy, supposedly for treatment but really as a clandestine form of discipline; and eventually is given a lobotomy because he has challenged the rule of the ward nurse.

AN ENDURING QUESTION, CONTINUED

Films such as One Flew over the Cuckoo's Nest *helped underscore the growing concern people have about providing just and adequate care for the mentally ill.*

And yet, to abandon our system of assessment would probably be an overreaction. Most researchers now feel confident that Szasz was in error when he claimed that mental illness was a myth. One researcher said about schizophrenia that although it has been argued that schizophrenia is a myth, it is a "myth with a genetic basis and a pharmacological treatment" (Valenstein, 1980a, p. 321).

Supporters of DSM-IV believe that competent clinicians are well aware of the limitations of the classification system. Professionals must be able to communicate with one another, and if DSM-IV were not available, something less rigorous would take its place. Realistically, no one can expect to eliminate all terminology from psychiatry and psychology. Supporters argue that the DSM-IV classifications are on the whole quite reliable; that is, different assessors tend to use the same descriptions when confronted with the same cases. They also argue that, by carefully describing behavior patterns that have aspects in common, they may be able to identify distinct groups that have a common underlying cause for their disorder. No doubt, this will not happen for every category, but it may lead to breakthroughs in certain areas.

Since DSM-IV has been adopted—and it appears to be here to stay, at least until DSM-V comes along—the general consensus is that it can be a valuable tool provided its limitations are clearly realized.

FOR CRITICAL ANALYSIS

1. Why is it that we often feel great sympathy and compassion for someone once a physical cause is discovered for their unwanted behavior?

2. Many of the people who are on death row for murder have very unusual electrical brain activity or other brain abnormalities. How would you feel if in the future we discover underlying physical disorders that cause people to become homicidal? How might we look back on the people whom we execute today?

3. Until the actual cause of schizophrenic behavior is known, why is it truly correct only to say that someone displays schizophrenic behavior, but not that he or she "has schizophrenia"?   ◆

✸ SUMMARY

◆ The distinction between normal and abnormal behavior is not always clear. For this reason, professionals must be careful when assessing behavior. For a behavior to be considered abnormal in the clinical sense, it must be not only different from the norm but also maladaptive or self-defeating.

◆ In evaluating the abnormal behavior of another person, different models may be used to arrive at a better understanding of the underlying mechanisms that may contribute to the disorder. Some models may be more applicable in some circumstances than in others.

◆ The medical model assumes that the underlying cause of a mental disorder is a biological dysfunction. According to the learning model, abnormal behaviors are acquired through conditioning. In the psychoanalytic model, the abnormal behaviors are viewed as evidence of unresolved unconscious conflicts. In the humanistic model, abnormal behaviors are considered the result of failure to fulfill self-potential.

◆ Insanity is a legal term. There are different legal standards for determining whether a defendant in a criminal case is not guilty by reason of insanity.

◆ In 1994 a new classification scheme, the fourth edition of the *Diagnostic and Statistical Manual* (DSM-IV), was adopted. It provides assessment according to five dimensions or axes. The first three axes assess the immediate condition of the individual, while the fourth and fifth axes classify and assess the individual's past situation and overall ability to function.

◆ Anxiety disorders include simple phobia, in which an individual suffers from a specific unrealistic fear; generalized anxiety disorder, a relatively continuous state of tension, worry, and dread; panic disorder, in which a person may suddenly be overwhelmed by panic even though there is no apparent reason to be frightened; and obsessive-compulsive disorder, in which a person is obsessed by an unwanted thought or compulsively engages in actions and repetitive behaviors, perhaps as a way of coping with anxiety.

◆ Somatoform disorders are patterns of behavior in which an individual has physical symptoms when, in fact, no illness can be found. Somatoform disorders include conversion disorder and hypochondriasis.

◆ Dissociative disorders are those in which the person separates from the core of her personality. Included under dissociative disorders are psychogenic amnesia, which is a loss of memory; psychogenic fugue, in which the sufferer leaves home while in a state of amnesia; and multiple personality, in which more than one personality develops.

◆ Some mood disorders, schizophrenic disorders, and delusional disorders are classified as psychoses. The psychotic person has lost contact with reality, and his personality becomes grossly distorted. In many cases, hospitalization is required.

◆ Mood disorders are disorders of emotion. They include bipolar I and bipolar II disorder, in which there may be extreme mood swings from depression to mania, and major depressive disorder, a state of severe and utter sadness bordering on suicide. Seasonal affective disorder is a form of depression that responds to the seasons, becoming more likely in the winter or summer months.

◆ Recent evidence has indicated that mood disorder may have a genetic and biological component. The inherited form of depression is called endogenous depression, as opposed to environmentally induced depression.

◆ Schizophrenic disorders involve a complete breakdown of integrated personality functioning. Emotions become flat and distorted. Thought, language, and behavior become bizarre and disturbed. Delusions and hallucinations often occur. Schizophrenic disorders include the disorganized, catatonic, paranoid, undifferentiated, and residual types.

◆ Many causes of schizophrenia have been postulated, among them genetic and environmental factors and biochemical, structural, and anatomical factors. There is evidence to support all these views, indicating that schizophrenia may have many causes.

◆ One kind of schizophrenia may be the result of dopamine receptor abnormalities. A large percentage of the schizophrenics tested were found to have significantly more receptors for dopamine than normal people do. It is also thought that a combination of inherited immune weakness and exposure to the influenza virus during the second trimester or pregnancy may contribute to the onset of schizophrenia.

◆ Delusional disorders comprise a system of delusions that the psychotic individual firmly believes or accepts. Delusional disorder differs from paranoid schizophrenia in that in delusional disorder, hallucinations rarely occur and there is no serious disorganization of the personality.

◆ Personality disorders are a separate axis in DSM-IV. Although there are many different types of personality disorders, they all share certain qualities. Sufferers are essentially normal and do not exhibit the problems associated with psychosis. The most definitive aspect of a personality disorder is that the individual engages in behavior that disrupts social relationships.

◆ One of the most difficult problems faced by clinicians is assessment. Errors in assessment can lead to serious misunderstandings and inappropriate treatment. Psychologist David Rosenhan has shown that relatively normal individuals may be assessed in a biased fashion once they have been labeled as suffering from a psychiatric disorder, such as schizophrenia.

SUGGESTIONS FOR FURTHER READING

1. Baur, S. (1988). *Hypochondria: Woeful imaginations.* Berkeley: University of California Press. A book for the layperson about hypochondria and how it affects our culture. Some famous hypochondriacs are discussed, including Charles Darwin and Leo Tolstoy. The final chapter covers treatment.

2. Berger, D. & Berger, L. (1992). *We heard the angels of madness: One family's struggle with manic depression.* New York: Morrow. A mother, aided by her sister, writes a stirring account of her son's mental illness. A family guide to dealing with bipolar disorder including such practical advice as what to expect from insurance, Social Security, halfway houses, and hospitals. Helpful institutions, researchers, and support groups are also listed.

3. Goodwin, D. W. (1983). *Phobia: The facts.* New York: Oxford University Press. An introduction for the general reader to the subject of phobias, including their definitions, prevalence, and place in history. Treatments for common phobias are also discussed.

4. Gottesman, I. I. (1990). *Schizophrenia genesis: The origins of madness.* New York: W. H. Freeman. A comprehensive history of schizophrenia for the general reader. Compares modern views with earlier thought on the subject.

5. Kaplan, H. I., & Sadock, B. J. (Eds.) (1989). *Comprehensive textbook of psychiatry/V, Vols. 1 & 2.* Baltimore: Williams & Wilkins. An extremely comprehensive, high-level compendium of mental disorders. Hundreds of topics include phobic disorders, panic disorders, dissociative disorders, somatoform disorders, depressive disorders, schizophrenias, personality disorders, and many others.

6. Kass, F. I., Oldham, J. M., & Pardes, H. (Eds.) (1993). *The Columbia University College of Physicians and Surgeons complete home guide to mental health.* New York: Columbia University Press. This valuable addition to every home provides detailed discussions of mental health and suggests when help should be sought. It provides full coverage including how to select a therapist, when children need professional help, guidelines for dealing with substance abuse, how to cope with long-term illnesses, and much more.

7. Levenkron, S. (1991). *Obsessive-compulsive disorders: Treating and understanding crippling habits.* New York: Warner Books. This book for the general reader describes how a dysfunctional society can contribute to the creation of OCD in individuals. It also describes ways in which family and friends can help sufferers of OCD.

8. Mondimore, F. M. (1990). *Depression: The mood disease.* Baltimore: Johns Hopkins University Press. Written for the general reader. The author describes the causes of and treatments for depression. Also addressed is why so many people who are afflicted refuse to seek help.

9. Rapoport, J. L. (1989). *The boy who couldn't stop washing: The experience and treatment of obsessive-compulsive disorder.* New York: E. P. Dutton. The first popular book on OCD by one of the leading researchers in the field. Very interesting reading.

10. Rosenthal, N. E. (1989). *Seasons of the mind: Why you get the winter blues and what you can do about it.* New York: Bantam Books. A psychobiologist describes the winter variety of seasonal affective disorder, how to know if it is affecting you, and, if so, what you can do about it. Support groups are also listed.

11. Smyth, A. (1991). *Seasonal affective disorder.* New York: Harper Collins. An examination of seasonal affective disorder, which is suspected of affecting about 10 percent of the U.S. population. Written for the general reader.

12. Torrey, E. F. (1988). *Surviving schizophrenia: A family manual* (rev. ed.). New York: Harper & Row. A psychiatrist discusses the nature of schizophrenia and describes how it is diagnosed and treated. For the student or general reader.

13. Ussher, J. (1991). *Woman's madness: Misogyny or mental illness?* Amherst, MA: University of Massachusetts Press. An examination of depression in women and its diagnosis. The issue of whether the diagnosis is often unwarranted, given the violence and oppression faced by many women, is discussed.

Chapter Seventeen

Therapy

PROLOGUE

SHOCK THERAPY

In 1803, Dr. Johann Christian Reil was working in Germany where he was in charge of what was then called a madhouse—or, as some put it, an insane asylum. Reil was a great believer in the Pinel system, and he hoped to bring this humanitarian French reform to Germany. He intended to try something new and radical: he was going to introduce therapies in the hope of bettering the lives of the patients in his care.

One of the therapies Reil discovered was shock therapy. By this, Reil meant any action that might shock the patient back to reality. Reil had come to believe that most of his patients had left reality for their own worlds. Reil thought that it might help if he could bring them back to reality, and sometimes a shock seemed to do it.

For instance, one of his therapies used a small cannon, the kind that is loaded with blank charges and fired off during ceremonies. An attendant would wait with the cannon, perhaps behind a corner, for a particular patient to appear. As the unsuspecting patient stepped into view, the attendant would fire the cannon. Of course, it would go off with a terrific boom, typically causing the patient to leap into the air, scream, turn, and look in horror. The patient would often gasp for breath or run away.

To Reil's way of thinking, that was a normal reaction to being startled by a cannon. For a moment, Reil thought, the patient was normal. Anyone might have reacted in the same way.

Other attempts at "shock" were made as well. At night attendants would often grab a sleeping patient, carry him out to the garden, and throw him into an icy pond. Sometimes an attendant would dress in a ghost outfit and make strange sounds while standing on a table at the foot of a patient's bed. The patient would typically waken and scream to see a ghost hovering over him.

On other occasions, the entire hospital staff participated in an elaborate tableau. Dressed in costumes and horribly made up, they gathered behind a large curtain, props in hand, and froze in assigned positions. The patients were seated before the curtain, which was abruptly drawn aside. In one tableau, called the "resurrection of the dead," a member of the staff was

CONTENTS

TREPHINING
An ancient procedure in which the skull was punctured by a sharp instrument so that evil spirits might escape.

being lifted from a coffin with his eyes rolled back. As one would expect of an audience never exposed to motion pictures or few plays, they gasped in horror. Reil did note, however, that the staff went to such lengths for only the most troublesome cases. Reil's philosophy was to teach the patients that it was better to be healthy than to stay in the hospital and be sick. Reil called his method noninjurious torture (Roueche, 1980).

At the time, Reil thought he really was doing something to help. He and his staff were working hard to help the patients recover from their illness.

IN THIS CHAPTER, we will examine different ways to treat mental illness. We'll look at somatic therapies, including modern drug treatments, electroshock therapy, and psychosurgery. We'll also look at psychotherapies, such as Freudian psychoanalysis, behavior therapy, and hypnotherapy.

WHY PSYCHOLOGISTS STUDY THERAPIES

When people suffer from behavioral disorders, it's only reasonable that members of society should want to help. As you may have gathered from the Prologue, however, good intentions are not always sufficient. Any help or therapy that is provided should be beneficial. Unproved therapies, despite all the reasoning behind them, may do more harm than good. Psychologists study therapies because rigorous investigation is needed to determine the effectiveness of different therapeutic measures. Once an effective therapy is found, it often furnishes clues to the underlying cause of the disorder. On the other hand, once a therapy has proved ineffective, it can be eliminated so that patients no longer need be subjected to it.

THE HISTORY OF THERAPY

Therapeutic attempts to alleviate mental disorders are perhaps as old as humankind. Half a million years ago, Stone Age people applied "medical" techniques to open the skulls of patients in distress. The procedure was called **trephining** (see Figure 17.1). An opening was cut in the skull by chipping away at it with a sharp stone tool. Mad thoughts or evil spirits were supposed to escape through this opening. Some trephined skulls show signs of healing around the opening, indicating that the individuals may have survived the procedure and lived to tell the tale.

Before the development and extensive use of the scientific method, it was widely believed that emotional disorders were due to supernatural forces—to possessions by spirits, witchcraft, or being haunted by one's ancestors. Even in the middle of the twentieth century, most primitive societies believed that mental disorders had supernatural origins (Gillin, 1948).

The Greek and Roman Era (Circa 400 B.C.–A.D. 476)

From the time of the Greek physician Hippocrates (circa 460–377 B.C.) to the time of another Greek physician, Galen (circa A.D. 131–201), the Greeks and Romans, more often than not, argued for humane treatment of people who had mental disorders. As the Roman Empire expanded, the Greek and Roman countryside was dotted with hundreds of temples dedicated to Aesculapius, the Roman god of medicine and healing. Here people who were troubled could go for rest, sleep, and gentle care. At these temples, the belief in supernatural causes persisted, but the priests also considered rational explanations for mental

◆ **FIGURE 17.1**

In the primitive procedure of trephining, a hole was cut in the skull, ostensibly to allow evil spirits or devils to escape. The procedure was dangerous, and the chance of hemorrhage and infection was high. Still, trephining may occasionally have relieved pressure on the brain, caused by bleeding or a tumor, and brought about improvement.

illness such as stress, and their attempts at magical cures did not preclude human treatment and consultation.

Although these cures weren't particularly effective, the ancient Greeks and Romans did document many disorders and separate them into categories that are still, to some degree, considered valid. For example, the ancients differentiated between acute and chronic disorders and between mania and depression, and they distinguished among illusions, delusions, and hallucinations. Some of the temple priests even relied on dream interpretation to draw conclusions about their patients (Mora, 1967).

The Middle Ages (A.D. 476–1453)

After the fall of the Roman Empire, rational efforts to understand mental disorders were largely displaced by reliance on religious demonology. People who suffered from mental disorders were often suspected of having been invaded by a spirit or a devil. Madness was sometimes thought to be the will of God, and therapy for madness was a religious ritual.

Psychotics often became targets of religious persecution. This reached its peak following the shock and horror of the bubonic plague that swept Europe during the fourteenth century. During that time, many people whose behavior was abnormal were burned as witches. These "witches" were convenient scapegoats on whom a frightened and ignorant society could blame its troubles. It should be noted that the plague had killed half the population of Europe, so their "troubles" were worse than anything seen before or since.

One of the major Christian treatises of the Middle Ages was the *Malleus Maleficarum*, the "witch's hammer." This book described the signs by which a witch could be identified. The signs closely parallel many of the symptoms of behavioral disorders that are known today. The *Malleus Maleficarum* went through 29 editions, the last published in 1669. By then the Renaissance had developed a more humane view of mental disorders.

The Renaissance (Circa 1400–1600)

In 1453, Constantinople (now Istanbul) fell to the Turks. This marked the collapse of the Byzantine Empire, which had been the repository of Greek and Roman writing and civilization for a thousand years. Byzantine scholars fled to the West, especially to Italy, to escape from the Turks. They brought with them Greek and Roman scientific writings. Slowly, over the next few centuries, Western European scientists, investigators, and explorers built on this wealth of material and information. The understanding that nature was governed by physical laws encouraged a belief that the world could be shaped and controlled.

During the Renaissance, the writings of the early Greeks and Romans reemerged as a powerful force. Invention of the printing press made it possible to distribute these writings widely. Reading the ancient Greek and Latin texts quickly became the mark of the well educated. In fact, even in the early twentieth century, it was a rare college that did not offer ancient Greek and Latin as part of its curriculum. Gradually, because of the new knowledge of the physical world, the demonology of the Middle Ages was abandoned in favor of a more rational and scientific approach to mental disorders.

After the Renaissance

The last several centuries have witnessed gradual reform in mental institutions and in mental-health care. Scientists have become aware of possible genetic and biological causes of mental disorder as well as of unconscious factors and environmental influences that may affect its course.

GENERAL PARESIS

Tertiary (third-stage) syphilis (a sexually transmitted disease), which involves an invasion of and severe irreversible damage to the brain caused by the syphilis spirochete (a bacterium). The central nervous system damage often becomes noticeable 15 to 30 years after infection. The clinical picture includes tremors, loss of contact with reality, extreme personality deterioration, increasing paralysis, and delirium. The patient may survive many years in this condition. If the illness is diagnosed in time, through the use of a simple blood test (the Wassermann test), the administration of penicillin almost guarantees a cure.

MENTAL INSTITUTIONS. Asylums during the Middle Ages had been used to hold "suspects" and to protect society from their evil power. During the Renaissance, treatment became more "humane," if only in the sense that people were chained and shackled and treated like animals rather than being systematically tortured or killed. Reform of mental institutions did not really begin until the end of the 1700s.

In 1792, following the onset of the French Revolution, Philippe Pinel was placed in charge of an asylum for the mad in Paris. After repeated requests, Pinel received permission to try an experiment. Had he failed, he might well have been executed by the new revolutionary government. Believing strongly in the revolution, he argued that the inmates were citizens and brothers, not beasts or criminals. Pinel removed their chains and shackles and treated them with kindness and consideration. He placed them in sunny rooms and allowed them to exercise. The noise, the squalor, and the abuse gave way to a more peaceful atmosphere. The reforms were successful.

Pinel's reforms were adopted in many countries, helping to end the nightmare of torture and abuse that had been common practice. As the years passed, more enlightened treatment of patients was adopted in piecemeal fashion; its progress varied from country to country, and there were occasional lapses into the old horrors. In general, however, mental institutions in western nations continued to undergo reform throughout the nineteenth century. Still, there was little in the way of therapy, and many mental institutions remained barely more than holding pens where even basic care was often wanting.

THE ERA OF PSYCHOLOGY. The last alleged witch to be publicly murdered by a sanctioned institution died in Switzerland in 1782. As enlightenment spread, the scientific method became the accepted way to advance knowledge, and a new understanding of behavior started to emerge.

By the mid-1800s, physicians and anatomists had begun to realize that abnormal behavior could result from damage to the brain or nervous system. They discovered, for instance, that syphilis bacteria were the cause of an organic psychosis known as **general paresis.**

Proponents of organic theory made a sharp break with the demonologists by arguing that abnormal behavior was due to underlying physical causes. By implication, appeal to spirits was unnecessary; a cure could be achieved by rectifying the underlying physical problem. In many people who demonstrated abnormal behavior, however, problems with the brain or nervous system were

Crude restraining devices were commonly employed in early mental asylums.

still not evident. Consequently, additional avenues of interpretation were sought to supplement the organic view.

By the late 1800s, a psychological revolution was beginning. Psychiatrists argued that abnormal behavior might be the result of certain experiences such as stress or unresolved unconscious conflicts. Sigmund Freud, more than anyone else, championed these ideas.

In the United States, too, interest in understanding mental disorders was growing, owing in part to the publication of Clifford Beers's book *A Mind That Found Itself* (1908). Beers described his own emotional breakdown and recovery in a way that made it seem that it could happen to anyone. Even today, the book makes fascinating reading, but in 1908 it was a shock, and it spurred a number of influential Americans to support financial and political projects aimed at developing therapies for people suffering from mental disorders.

The first half of the twentieth century saw advances in learning theory and humanistic therapies, both of which attempted to explain and treat mental disorders. Then, in the 1950s, medical and biological therapies advanced by great leaps, as scientists found certain drugs that helped to control psychotic disturbances and to alter mood. Our expanding knowledge of drug and brain chemistry and our new techniques for examining the brain suggest that the 1990s may herald another important scientific leap in medical and biological understanding of abnormal behavior and its treatment.

Today, many people are still treated in hospitals or special institutions for the mentally ill. In some of these institutions, the quality of care is excellent. Unfortunately, even in this day and age, too many institutions are places where drugs are misused or overused, and physical violence, rape, unexplained death, and filthy living conditions are commonplace (Weicker, 1987). This is especially the case in nonindustrialized nations.

Furthermore, many people who are in need of help are left to fend for themselves. It is estimated that somewhere between 10 and 40 percent of the homeless in America are severely mentally ill and in need of psychological help, and between 20 and 30 percent are alcohol or drug abusers also in need of assistance ("Mental Illness," 1990). These percentages are broad because the true size of the problem is difficult to assess. The homeless are not easily counted or studied; many either refuse to be interviewed or deny that they are homeless.

Although institutions that treat the mentally ill vary widely, the best of them typically offer a large number of therapeutic techniques in response to the needs of individual patients. In the next few pages, we'll investigate some of these modern therapies.

SOMATIC THERAPIES

In 1956, I was 9 years old. My father was a physician, a staff resident in psychiatry at Brooklyn State Hospital, and we lived on the fourth floor of the staff house on the hospital grounds. From my window, I could look out across a narrow road to a large, ugly, four-story brick building. The windows of the building were barred, but I could still see into the large rooms. These were the wards for psychotics. My parents explained to me that the building was a hospital and that the people inside it were sick. I soon became accustomed to their bizarre behavior. One woman stood by the window most of the day directing an orchestra that didn't exist. Other patients threw themselves on the floor and got into fights. Others stayed in one place and stared straight ahead for hours on end. The only thing I didn't get used to was the screaming. From sunrise to sunset and all through the night, there was screaming. I heard screaming laughter, screaming crying, screaming curses, screaming poems, screaming fights. It never ended.

576

SOMATIC THERAPY
Invasive therapeutic intervention that acts directly on the body and its chemistry. Included in this classification are psychopharmacological, electroconvulsive, and psychosurgical procedures.

PHENOTHIAZINES
Antipsychotic drugs, often called the major tranquilizers. These drugs help control and alleviate the symptoms of psychosis.

NEUROLEPTIC
Any of a collection of drugs that are known to have antipsychotic properties.

That year my father was drafted into the army, and we left the hospital for a 2-year tour of duty in California. In 1959, when we returned, something was very different. The building was still there, the patients were still there, but the screaming was gone. Days would pass by without a single scream from anyone. Attendants seemed to be busier making beds and serving food than rushing to break up fights. The patients took better care of themselves. They seemed to dress better and to be more sociable with one another. More of them had grounds privileges and were out walking about and sitting on the benches.

I didn't know it at the time, but during those 2 years the first of a series of new antipsychotic drugs had arrived; it was called *chlorpromazine*. The changes I was noticing were due to the effects of this drug.

Drug treatment, also known as psychopharmacological therapy, is one kind of **somatic therapy,** meaning a therapy that directly interacts with the body and its chemistry. Other somatic therapies are electroshock and psychosurgery.

Psychopharmacological Therapy

We will look at four classes of drugs that are used therapeutically: antipsychotic drugs, antidepressants, antimanic drugs, and antianxiety drugs. It is important to note that today, federal and state courts have affirmed that involuntary medication violates the rights of individuals who are able to decide for themselves whether they wish treatment. In other words, if you are legally competent, no one can force you to take medication, even if you have been involuntarily committed to a hospital. An exception to this rule is made for jailed offenders who have been found guilty of a crime and are believed to be dangerous to themselves or others. Among people who have been deemed by the courts to be mentally incompetent, the process of involuntary medication often follows what is known as the Jamison-Farabee consent decree, which is based on a legal case in California. The decree requires that outside psychiatrists, not associated with the committing hospital, must review and consent to the medication prescribed by the hospital. Approximately 1 percent of the time, prescriptions made by the hospital are overruled (Hargreaves, Shumway, Knutsen, Weinstein, & Senter, 1987; Zito, Craig, & Wanderling, 1991).

NEUROLEPTICS (ANTIPSYCHOTIC DRUGS). Today, the most widely used agents to combat psychosis are the **phenothiazines.** They include such drugs as Thorazine, Stelazine, Compazine, and Mellaril. When these drugs first appeared, they were often referred to as the major tranquilizers. Although they do tend to quiet people, the term *tranquilizer* is not as descriptive as *antipsychotic agent,* since these drugs, unlike some tranquilizers, also have antipsychotic effects. Also important is the drug Haldol, which is classified separately as an antipsychotic agent. To prevent confusion, it is common to refer to all drugs that have an antipsychotic effect by the general term **neuroleptic.**

Neuroleptics vary in their effectiveness. Sometimes they fail to suppress psychotic symptoms, and sometimes their effects last only a short time. Their use often is accompanied by side effects such as a dry mouth or an uncomfortable feeling. They can also cause dizziness, which is especially dangerous for elderly patients and has resulted in a number of hip-fracturing falls (Ray, Griffin, Schaffner, Baugh, & Melton, 1987).

Especially among people with acute psychoses, the drugs often help to alleviate symptoms, reduce the number of hallucinations, control the severity of delusions, and reduce violent or aggressive behavior. However, the phenothiazines usually have little effect on other psychotic behaviors, such as severe emotional withdrawal or bizarre speech and affect. Haldol may be somewhat more effective in these instances. Medications rarely eliminate problems totally, and they are not considered cures.

To date, the only drug to show dramatic improvements among chronic schizophrenics is Clozapine. Clozapine was first synthesized in 1959 and was briefly used as an antipsychotic medication in Europe. It was withdrawn from use in the United States in 1975 because 1 percent of patients receiving it developed a rare immune system disorder that was potentially fatal.

Because of continuing good results in Europe, Clozapine was approved for use in the United States by the Food and Drug Administration in 1989, with the proviso that it only be given to patients after at least two attempts with other neuroleptics have failed. Many physicians, however, advocate greater use of Clozapine because it has had fairly dramatic effects in reducing both positive symptoms (delusions, hallucinations, disordered thinking) and negative symptoms (social withdrawal, limited speech, flat affect) in almost half of all schizophrenics who have been placed on it (Meltzer, 1993). The dangerous immune system disorder that can result (*agranulocytosis*—a failure of certain white blood cells to develop or function) is preventable if caught in time through weekly blood tests. However, of the 2 million schizophrenics in the United States currently receiving medication, only 40,000 are getting Clozapine. One reason is expense. Clozapine costs about $4500 per patient per year, and that doesn't include the costs of weekly blood tests and evaluations by physicians. Nevertheless, studies have shown that Clozapine is cost-effective because although it is not a cure, it is up to seven times more effective for treating schizophrenia than any other drug on the market; consequently, hospital costs are reduced because so many treated patients are able to leave the hospital and return home or to their communities (Meltzer, 1993).

The promise and risks of Clozapine have never been better expressed than by Dan Weisburd, the father of a schizophrenic named David. Dan wrote the following description of his son's experience on Clozapine for the California state legislature. Six weeks after starting Clozapine,

. . . David stood before me, wide-eyed, a look of wonderment on his face. There were no "voices." He felt clearheaded for the first time in years.

[David said] "It's as if I awoke from a nightmare, Dad. And I'm so grateful. I don't want to waste a second crying. But I want to tell everybody *this* is really me and I'm back; that I'm not my illness, that I'm David; that I'm not a schizophrenic. I'm a person."

One day out of eight years. I'm sure you can guess the rest. David's white count went crashing. He had achieved the second lowest count of anyone kept alive and on the drug. But he would have to come off the medication that gave him that one good day. We all sat there looking at the doctor. David agreed to stop taking Clozapine, knowing that he would most likely go back into the abyss of schizophrenia, back to other medications that merely masked some symptoms and perhaps even exacerbated others. Bravely he said, "If I've had this one day, then I know others are possible sometime, I hope soon. And I hope I'll remember what this feels like. Please, help me to remember." (Weisburd, 1990, p. 1247)

Clozapine appears to be a powerful serotonin antagonist (Kahn, et al., 1993), and other drugs with similar action are now being developed that, researchers hope, will not present the danger to the immune system that Clozapine does. Risperidone is one such promising drug and may become available in 1994. If it turns out to be as effective as Clozapine, but without the dangerous side effects, it is believed that mass production will dramatically lower its costs, making it available as a general treatment.

Because neuroleptics tend to calm patients and make the patients easier to handle, hospital staff sometimes administer them too freely. Overmedication has become a serious problem in many hospitals and institutions (Weicker,

TARDIVE DYSKINESIA
A severe and relatively permanent neuromuscular reaction, following long-term use of, or a sudden withdrawal from, antipsychotic drugs. The disorder is manifested in involuntary twitching of body and facial muscles.

NEUROLEPTIC MALIGNANT SYNDROME
An often deadly reaction to neuroleptic drugs that occurs in 1–2 percent of patients receiving these drugs. The syndrome often comes on quickly, and the fatality rate is about 3 percent, owing to kidney or brain damage. The cause of the syndrome is unknown.

1987). On some wards, all patients are medicated, regardless of their condition. This kind of institutional abuse of medication is not therapy; it is a chemical form of crowd control. Critics have contended that drugs are too often used indiscriminately; that psychiatrists, too busy being administrators, scribble out prescriptions without knowing their patients; and that pharmaceutical companies sometimes act as "pushers," providing massive numbers of free samples and consultations that advocate drugs as the primary mode of therapy. In a sense, these critics argue, chemical shackles have taken the place of the old iron ones.

Abuses can also occur among outpatients (patients who are treated at a hospital or clinic, but who are not staying in the hospital). One study found that 58 percent of all the juveniles being seen at one state clinic for stealing, fighting, or other conduct disorders, but not for psychotic disorders, were being given neuroleptics (Richardson, Haugland, & Craig, 1991). Use of neuroleptics for treating conduct disorders is generally considered unacceptable without further cause. It has also been found that when local clinics are unavailable, which is often the case, physicians treating people with psychotic disorders who visit their offices tend to increase the doses of neuroleptics over time to keep the psychotic behavior under control. In fact, one study found that 10 percent of such patients were being given what the researchers called extreme doses (Segal, Cohen, & Marder, 1992).

These kinds of abuses are becoming less common, however. For one thing, it has been found that long-term use of antipsychotic medication can produce a condition called **tardive dyskinesia,** in which body and facial muscles twitch involuntarily. Tardive dyskinesia occurs in about 10 to 20 percent of people taking antipsychotic medication, many of whom might not have needed it (Culliton, 1985). It is also likely to occur in one-third of the juveniles or elderly who take neuroleptics (Richardson, Haugland, & Craig, 1991; Saltz, et al., 1991). The effects of tardive dyskinesia usually are permanent, and far too often the early symptoms are misdiagnosed as part of the mental disorder or simply go unrecognized (Weiden, Mann, Haas, Mattson, & Frances, 1987). Tardive dyskinesia may occur because antipsychotic agents somehow affect the dopamine system in the brain (Snyder, 1984). Patients who are treated over a long period with blocking drugs, such as the phenothiazines, and then are withdrawn from the drugs show an extreme hypersensitivity to dopamine.

Due to the dangers of permanent damage from use of the phenothiazines, many professionals are now using these drugs for only short-term intervention to stop sudden flare-ups of psychotic symptoms (Herz, Szymanski, & Simon, 1982). Psychosis, especially schizophrenia, is a condition that tends to vary greatly over time. If the patient and professional staff are aware of the early signs of trouble, the latter can quickly administer neuroleptics for a brief time before things get really bad. The four major signs that a psychosis is about to become worse are (1) hallucinations, (2) increased suspiciousness, (3) sleep disturbances, and (4) excessive anxiety. When these signs appear, immediate short-term use of neuroleptics can be beneficial (Carpenter & Heinrichs, 1983). Some researchers have cautioned, however, that schizophrenia among people who are given low neuroleptic dosages often is more severe than it is among those who have had a full course of neuroleptic treatment (Marder et al., 1987). There appears to be no simple formula for selecting the proper neuroleptic dosage for individual schizophrenics. One reason for optimism is that Clozapine, unlike other neuroleptics, does not cause tardive dyskinesia, and hopefully, drugs based on its structure will be free of this danger as well (Meltzer, 1993).

Adding to the dangers of neuroleptics is the threat of **neuroleptic malignant syndrome.** This dangerous syndrome develops in roughly 1 percent of individuals treated with neuroleptics. It often comes on very quickly, and in the past about 20 percent of those individuals who manifested the syndrome died from brain damage or kidney failure (Pope, Keck, & McElroy, 1986; Sternberg, 1986). With careful monitoring, however, the fatality rate in more recent years has been lowered to about 3 percent (Keck, Pope, & McElroy, 1991). The cause of the syndrome is unknown, and it is currently not possible to predict which people will react so adversely to neuroleptics.

ANTIDEPRESSANTS.   **Antidepressants** have sometimes been called mood elevators. At first, there were two main kinds, the tricyclics and the monoamine-oxidase (MAO) inhibitors. Among the tricyclics, the best known probably is Elavil; among the MAO inhibitors, the best known probably is Marplan. These drugs are given for depressions that are relatively severe. Their effectiveness in alleviating depression is somewhat variable, and it often takes 2 to 3 weeks of continuous use before any helpful effects are achieved. Antidepressants usually are more effective against endogenous depression (depression without apparent environmental cause) than against depression that is environmentally induced. Some of these drugs must be monitored carefully because they can be dangerous. For example, a person taking MAO inhibitors must observe strict dietary restrictions; the person must avoid tyramine, a common substance found in many foods such as red wine, sour cream, bananas, liver, eggplant, and soy sauce. Consuming tyramine with an MAO inhibitor can cause a deadly rise in blood pressure.

About 30 percent of depressed individuals do not respond to either tricyclics or MAO inhibitors, both of which have been on the market for over 25 years. A considerable number of these individuals and others have been helped by a new, second generation of antidepressants, such as the drug *fluoxetine*, better known by the brand name Prozac. In fact, Prozac may be one of the most successful drugs yet developed to treat a mental disorder. Since its introduction in December 1987, psychiatrists and psychologists have been having so much success with it, and so many fewer side effects have been reported than with previous antidepressants, that Prozac is now the nation's most prescribed antidepressant.

All antidepressants work by bolstering the action of two important neurotransmitters in the brain, serotonin and norepinephrine (Schatzberg, 1987). The tricyclics block reabsorption of these neurotransmitters by the neurons that release them, forcing the neurotransmitter to stay longer in the synapse (see Chapter 2), which increases its effect. The MAO inhibitors interfere with the enzymes that break the neurotransmitter down, which also causes the transmitter to linger in the synapse. Prozac works like the tricyclics, but exclusively on serotonin, which is suspected to play an important role in emotion. Serotonin is also believed to play an important role in the wake-sleep cycle. Interestingly, depressed individuals will often recover from their depressions for a time if they are deprived of sleep, while frequent naps often exacerbate depression (Wu & Bunney, 1990). Prozac and the related drugs Zoloft and Paxil are classed as selective serotonin reuptake inhibitors, or SSRIs.

Drugs that can block serotonin reuptake, such as Clomipramine, although originally formulated as an antidepressant are also often affective against obsessive-compulsive disorder—as the following case study shows.

TRICHOTILLOMANIA: THE CASE OF BETH

It began when Beth was 13 years old. She would sit before the mirror and look at her hair. One by one, she would take each strand of hair and pull it out by the root. Then she would bite off the root and lay the strand of hair down. She continued this ritu-

ANTIDEPRESSANTS
Drugs used to relieve the symptoms of extreme sadness and withdrawal from life that characterize severe depression. MAO inhibitors, selective serotonin reuptake inhibitors, and tricyclic drugs are the three main classes of antidepressants.

LITHIUM CARBONATE
A chemical compound that has been found to be effective in controlling the severe mood swings associated with bipolar affective disorders.

alistic routine hair after hair, making a neat little pile of rootless strands that she placed before her.

After a few weeks of doing this each night, bald spots began to appear. She knew that what she was doing was crazy, but she couldn't bring herself to stop. In a desperate effort to save her hair, she sliced her fingertips with a razor blade hoping to make it too painful to grip hairs firmly enough to pull them out. She pulled her hair out anyway.

Afraid to tell her parents the truth, Beth was sent to a dermatologist (a physician specializing in disorders of the skin). She went for many treatments and was given different creams and ointments. By the time she was 16, she was bald. She finally told her parents what had been happening.

They sent her to a psychotherapist who diagnosed trichotillomania, a $20 word meaning compulsive hair pulling. Her only comfort was that she found out she had company, over 2 million compulsive hair pullers in the United States alone, 90 percent of whom are women. She was considered a moderate case, not severe like those who also pulled out their pubic hairs and eyelashes. Unfortunately, psychotherapy did not help. Then one day in 1987, while watching TV, Beth heard about a drug called Clomipramine that was being used to treat obsessive-compulsive disorder. She thought that what she was doing to herself sounded like a compulsion, so she contacted the researchers at the National Institutes of Mental Health who had been mentioned in the news report and asked for help (Trotter, 1990).

Up to that time, trichotillomania had not been classified as an obsessive-compulsive disorder. However, the researchers were curious about it, and a study was organized with a number of compulsive hair pullers, who were divided into an experimental and a control group (Rapoport, 1989). The experimental group received Clomipramine and the control group a placebo. In the experimental group, 12 of the 13 women improved dramatically, including Beth. The placebo worked no better than chance would have predicted. In January 1990, based on these and other studies, the Food and Drug Administration approved the use of Clomipramine for treating obsessive-compulsive disorder, in addition to depression for which it had been originally formulated.

Other clinical trials are underway to examine the possibility of expanding the drug's usefulness for treating such disorders as compulsive nail biting or kleptomania (compulsive stealing). Thanks to this research, for the many people like Beth whose brain would fail to give a stop signal once a routine had begun, there is now a chance for a normal life free of compulsion.

ANTIMANIC DRUGS. **Lithium carbonate,** sold under a number of trade names, such as Lithonate and Lithotabs, is effective in resolving manic episodes and severe mood swings in about one-third of patients taking the drug. Forty percent of patients, however, fail to respond significantly, while the remaining percentages show only some improvement (Harrow, Goldberg, Grossman, & Meltzer 1990). Lithium is less effective against swings toward depression, perhaps because depression is a more heterogeneous entity. The following case study discusses how the drug helped Ruth H. to resume a normal life.

PSYCHOPHARMACOLOGICAL THERAPY: THE CASE OF RUTH H.

For nearly 20 years, Ruth H. suffered from bipolar disorder, reaching manic highs and then descending into deep depressions. She had been given antidepressants; she had had psychotherapy and electroshock therapy. Nothing seemed to help. In 1969, she was on the verge of committing suicide when she was given lithium carbonate. She has been able to live normally ever since.

Her bipolar disorder began when she was a child. After college she became an elementary school teacher, but her condition worsened, and she had to quit her job. After the birth of her first child she entered a deep depression. The depression was followed by a manic high and thus the pattern began. It was to characterize a major portion of her life for the next 20 years.

By 1968, her condition had deteriorated; her stable periods came less often. In 1969, she came to the attention of Dr. Ronald Fieve, a psychiatrist who was then developing the new lithium treatment for manic depression. Within a few months after beginning this treatment, Ruth was able to remain stable day after day. She now looks back on those times as bad years. She remembers, "Before I began taking the lithium I'd send out invitations to a party during a manic period and Bob (her husband) would have to cancel it later because I'd be in bed depressed. Now, if I plan a party it will go ahead as scheduled. I know I will be able to function." (Seligmann & Shapiro, 1979, p. 102)

BENZODIAZEPINES
Antianxiety drugs, such as Valium and Librium, that help alleviate anxiety by directly interacting with the neurochemistry of the brain. They are often referred to as minor tranquilizers.

Lithium administration must be monitored very carefully because it is a dangerous drug. The drug is highly toxic, and blood tests must be taken to measure the level of toxicity. Without close monitoring, lithium may promote kidney damage (Samiy & Rosnick, 1987). Monitoring the heart often is advisable as well, since lithium is suspected of causing fatal cardiovascular blockage in some cases (Jaffe, 1977).

ANTIANXIETY DRUGS. The antianxiety drugs, collectively known as **benzodiazepines,** often are referred to as minor tranquilizers. Valium, Librium, and Xanax are among the most commonly known. The minor tranquilizers are not used to treat psychotics; they are used to help individuals with problems in which tension or anxiety is a central feature. Among their side effects are drowsiness and lethargy. The minor tranquilizers are toxic and can lead to dependence. For many years Valium was particularly abused and resulted in instances of Valium addiction, in which users experienced convulsions on sudden withdrawal of the drug. Many critics argue that antianxiety drugs are too often dispensed like Band-Aids and that our society is too quick to turn to drugs. Drugs, they say, should be treated with more respect and used more judiciously.

There is also concern because many patients, perhaps a majority, who use benzodiazepines for a significant length of time experience *rebound anxiety,* in which their anxiety returns with an even greater severity when they stop taking the drug (Chouinard, Labonte, Fontaine, & Annable, 1983). The reason for this rebound is not clear, but it may result from a mechanism similar to the one that causes tardive dyskinesia.

Interestingly, scientists have discovered that antidepressive drugs, such as the tricyclics and the SSRIs, often work better against *anxiety* than do the antianxiety drugs (Kahn, et al., 1986). No one knows why this is the case, but it most likely has something to do with brain neurotransmitters, which probably play a role in anxiety much as they have been found to do in depression. Supporting this idea is the finding that all the drugs known to have an effect against panic disorder augment the action of the neurotransmitter GABA (Breslow, et al., 1989).

As neurologists and psychologists gain a deeper understanding of the brain and its neurotransmitters, and as pharmacologists further their knowledge of the interactions between chemistry and biology, we may find answers to such questions and develop new and more effective drug treatments.

Electroconvulsive Therapy

In the 1930s, in a crude practice, schizophrenic patients were commonly given substances that induced full-blown seizures. This treatment was based on the rather flawed theory that epilepsy was a counterforce to schizophrenia (Weiner, 1989). Also in use were some "shocking" therapies like those described in the Prologue, where you met Johann Christian Reil, the German anatomist and neurologist who is credited with the first use of such therapy. In 1938, two Italian clinicians, Ugo Cerletti and Lucio Bini, developed what they believed to be an improvement. They called their new treatment *electroshock*. It consisted of administering an electric shock to the brain, which caused a convulsion, a kind of epileptic seizure. Cerletti and Bini used their treatment for schizophrenia and reported encouraging results.

Modern researchers refer to the treatment as **electroconvulsive therapy,** or **ECT,** and have found it to be most effective against depression and the depressive lows encountered in the bipolar disorders (Thompson & Blaine, 1987). Approximately 2 to 3 percent of hospitalized psychiatric patients are treated with ECT (Thompson & Blaine, 1987). In the modern procedure, the patient is injected with a muscle-relaxing drug that prevents the convulsions that used to accompany electroshock therapy and often resulted in broken bones and torn ligaments. An electrode is placed on each temple and, typically, between 80 and 90 volts are passed through the brain for a fraction of a second. During that time, cerebral functioning is halted—short-circuited. About 5 minutes of unconsciousness usually follow. The beneficial results derived are believed to occur because of that brief halting of cerebral functioning. How or why ECT works has never been clearly understood.

Many clinicians think that ECT is at least harmless and is beneficial if used in appropriate circumstances (Janicak, et al., 1985; Markowitz, Brown, Sweeney, & Mann, 1987). Its use has not gone unchallenged, however. Memory for recent events is temporarily disrupted by ECT (Squire & Zouzounis, 1986), and some researchers have argued that memories for events in the more distant past may be permanently impaired after multiple ECT treatments (Costello, 1976; Roueche, 1980). Scientists have used sophisticated MRI scans (see Chapter 2) to look for structural damage following the administration of ECT, but no post-treatment structural changes have been observed (Coffey, et al., 1988). Detailed studies of patients who received 100 or more treatments with ECT have found no greater loss of cognitive functions over time than was observed in matched control groups who did not receive ECT (Devanand, Verma, Tirumalasetti, & Sackeim, 1991).

The effectiveness of ECT is also hotly debated. Most clinicians currently accept ECT as good practice (Weiner, 1989) if the number of treatments is limited, if it is not used as the first choice of treatment, and if it is conducted under medical supervision and with proper care. ECT can even be a life-saver, because some suicidal depressions appear to respond to nothing else.

In modern electroconvulsive therapy, muscle relaxants are administered beforehand to prevent the convulsions from tearing ligaments or breaking bones.

Psychosurgery

Psychosurgery is "a destruction of some region of the brain in order to alleviate severe, and otherwise intractable, psychiatric disorders" (Valenstein, 1980b, p. 12). Brain surgery undertaken to repair damage resulting from strokes or accidents or to treat tumors or spastic disorders is not considered psychosurgery. Similarly, brain surgery performed to prevent epilepsy is not considered psychosurgery because the problem is neurological.

FRONTAL LOBOTOMIES. In 1935, the Portuguese neurologist Antonio de Egas Moniz developed the technique that was the real beginning of psychosurgery. He had heard that the destruction of prefrontal areas in the brain of monkeys had had a calming effect on some of the more excitable animals, and he decided that destroying the prefrontal lobes in humans might be a way of controlling dangerous or manic patients. Moniz and his colleague Almidia Lima first performed a procedure in which they drilled holes over the portion of the cortex that they wished to destroy and then poured alcohol into the holes. Moniz first performed this operation on a 63-year-old former prostitute who was suffering from brain syphilis. Two months after the surgery, he reported that she was cured. Obviously, from our modern understanding of medicine, we know that such a surgical procedure could not possibly have cured syphilis (Valenstein, 1980b). Moniz then dispensed with alcohol and refined his procedure by using wire loops to hook onto and sever parts of the brain that he wished to disconnect from the prefrontal cortex. His operation became known as a **frontal lobotomy.** Moniz was a highly respected neurologist, and his results gained widespread attention, especially in 1944, when he was partially paralyzed after being shot by one of his lobotomized patients.

His technique was accepted for a number of reasons. First, it was practiced by surgeons, a highly respected group. Second, alternatives were lacking or limited. Before the discovery of psychopharmacological treatments, most care for psychotics was custodial. Third, in 1949, Dr. Moniz received the Nobel Prize for his development of the frontal lobotomy. Approximately 35,000 such operations have been performed in the United States since 1936 when American surgeons W. Freeman and J. Watts refined Moniz's procedure into a rather dramatic and, to some people, horrific operation. It made use of a surgical device shaped somewhat like an ice pick, called a leukotome, which is inserted behind the eyeball and pushed or hammered beyond the orbit of the eye until the point punctures the brain. It is then slashed back and forth, destroying many of the white nerve fibers connecting one part of the brain to another.

By 1970, however, interest in psychosurgery was beginning to wane. Effective drug treatments had become available for calming the uncontrollable and for treating mania. Moreover, the overall results from most lobotomy procedures had been disappointing. The majority of the patients either were unchanged or seemed to degenerate. Finally, a new attention was being paid to human rights and patient rights, emphasizing that the patient must be properly informed before consenting to such a procedure. Yet, in the last few years, psychosurgery has once again attracted attention. Part of the renewed interest stems from the fact that modern psychosurgical techniques are safer and result in less gross physical and intellectual impairment than did the older lobotomy procedures. Also, the area of the brain that is destroyed in modern operations is much smaller and more localized (Henn, 1989).

THE EFFECTIVENESS OF MODERN PSYCHOSURGERY. A few years ago, the National Commission for the Protection of Human Subjects of Biomedical and Behavioral Research and the National Institutes of Mental Health con-

PSYCHOSURGERY
Brain surgery for the purpose of altering behavior or alleviating mental disorders.

FRONTAL LOBOTOMY
A psychosurgical procedure, rarely performed today, in which a sharp instrument is inserted through the orbit of the eye and then slashed back and forth to separate specific nerve fibers connecting one part of the brain to another.

DEINSTITUTIONALIZATION
The practice, begun in the early 1960s, of releasing mental patients from hospitals and assigning them to community health centers or treating them on an outpatient basis.

ducted a pilot study and a follow-up to investigate the current effectiveness of psychosurgery. The study found that a large majority of patients had received adequate preparation beforehand. They had discussed the risks and benefits with their physician and understood what was likely to happen. The investigators judged that the majority had improved markedly. They noted no neurological damage or deficit in any of the cases. However, almost half showed less improvement, from slight benefit to definite worsening (in three cases). Although it had been assumed that psychosurgery was most successful in treating depression, the follow-up studies showed that a favorable or unfavorable outcome was not associated with a particular mental disorder. Based on similar findings, Elliot Valenstein who helped prepare the report for the national commission said,

The outcome of psychosurgery indicates that between 60 and 90 percent of the patients experience a significant reduction of their most troublesome symptoms. The risk of permanent adverse intellectual, emotional, and physical side effects is reported as minimal. The latter finding stands in sharp contrast to the results from older lobotomy operations (Henn, 1989, p. 1680).

A broad survey of modern psychosurgical outcomes is shown in Figure 17.2. As Valenstein noted, although popular novels and films like *One Flew over the Cuckoo's Nest* commonly depict postsurgical patients as semianimated vegetables, none of the patients studied was in this state. In the 1930s and 1940s, this sometimes was the fate of psychosurgery patients, owing to the more extensive tissue damage inflicted then. The creation of semianimated vegetables is not considered likely to happen with modern psychosurgical techniques (Mirsky & Orzack, 1980).

THE DEINSTITUTIONALIZATION OF THE MENTALLY ILL

Every Wednesday and Friday for more than a year, a van from the Texas state psychiatric hospital at Austin cruised into downtown Houston, paused in front of the Greyhound bus station and dumped its cargo—about a dozen mental patients just discharged from the hospital. A few on each trip had somebody waiting for them at the terminal. The rest were left with no money and nowhere to go—just an appointment with a mental-health counselor in the next three months. So every Wednesday and Friday, bus-station security guard Ricky Cameron led a group to the Star of Hope mission two blocks away. Three times he called the state hospital to complain; three times he was rebuffed. (Karlen & Burgower, 1985, p. 17)

◆ **FIGURE 17.2**

Survey of psychosurgical outcomes, based on data from four studies. SOURCE: *After Henn, 1989.*

Figure 17.3 shows a graph of the inpatient population of state and county mental hospitals in the United States over the years. The number of inpatients reached a high in 1955, at a little over 550,000, and then decreased dramatically. By 1975, the inpatient population was below 200,000, a decrease of two-thirds in 20 years; by 1988, it was about 175,000 and dropping.

The downward trend beginning in about 1956 was due in part to the availability of the new neuroleptic drugs that helped to control psychotic reactions and enabled patients to be released from the institutions and, in theory, rehabilitated in their own communities. This emphasis on **deinstitutionalization** increased at the beginning of the Johnson administration in 1964, when the country undertook a massive effort to reform its mental-health systems. Instead of maintaining large state and county institutions, governments intended to deliver services at community mental-health centers where patients would be close to their families and homes.

The idea behind the change was a good one. Data showed that patients who could live at home and see psychologists or psychiatrists as outpatients were faring much better (Kiesler, 1982a). Deinstitutionalization also helped to improve the institutions for the patients who had to remain. In the late 1950s, it had not been uncommon for psychiatrists or psychologists to see each patient for only 15 minutes per month! Patients were crammed into rooms, many of them lying on the floor with no place to go and not enough staff to attend to them. When the drastic overcrowding was reduced, psychiatrists and staff could spend more time with individual patients. Many institutions were carpeted and made more attractive, and they offered their patients better services. Unfortunately, the Vietnam War and the inflation that followed ate away at the financial support required by many community mental-health centers that were supposed to support the deinstitutionalized. These centers were unable to maintain the staff necessary to assist the deinstitutionalized patients in their neighborhoods. Many centers either folded or saved money by staffing with paraprofessionals instead of professionals, and the quality of care declined (Lewis, 1981).

Because of these unfortunate events, as the quotation at the beginning of this section clearly shows, deinstitutionalization often has amounted to no more than "dumping." Furthermore, there is very little local support for doing anything about the problem. As Texas County Judge Jim Scanlan said, when asked why citizens hadn't done something about the dumping of patients at the bus terminal by Austin State Hospital, "The public is more interested in mosquito control" (Karlen & Burgower, 1985, p. 17).

Oddly, although the number of patients hospitalized in state and county hospitals has decreased by more than two-thirds since 1955, the rate of hospital admissions for treatment of mental disorders has increased by 129 percent. This is because patients are commonly admitted and readmitted again and again. This new mode of functioning for state hospitals has become known as the revolving door method of treatment, and many complain that it makes no more sense than permanent institutionalization (Geller, 1992).

Also, a significant number of admissions are not being handled by state or county mental hospitals, which are the ones counted in Figure 17.3. In fact, 60 percent of all hospital admissions for mental disorders now occur at general hospitals (Kiesler, 1991)—and the majority of these hospitals do not have special psychiatric facilities. The average length of stay for mental disorders in a general hospital is 11.6 days, as opposed to an average 6-month stay in a state or county hospital. The patients who go to general hospitals usually are covered by Medicare, Medicaid, or private insurance plans that generally will not pay unless the patient is hospitalized for only a short term (Salit & Marcos, 1991). The deinstitutionalized patient who needs long-term care and may not

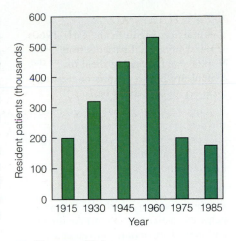

◆ **FIGURE 17.3**

The inpatient population of state and county mental hospitals from 1900 through 1985. In the last 35 years, the policies of deinstitutionalization and improved treatment have reduced the inpatient population by more than two-thirds. (SOURCES: Bassuk & Gerson, 1978; Kiesler, 1982a, 1982b).

Even today, many patients lead lonely, isolated lives in institutions where care is inadequate.

PSYCHOTHERAPY
A category of methods for treating psychological disorders. The primary technique is conversation between the patient and the therapist.

INSIGHT THERAPY
Psychotherapy that attempts to uncover the deep causes of the patient's or client's difficulty. The therapist tries to guide the individual to self-understanding.

ACTION THERAPY
Psychotherapy in which the therapist helps the patient or client take direct and immediate action to overcome problems through the use of special techniques.

directly qualify for insurance or government aid often is left to cope alone in a boardinghouse or on the street. In fact, one researcher has estimated that as many as 50 percent of the 250,000 homeless people in the United States may have psychotic disorders (Bassuk, 1987). In addition, some deinstitutionalized individuals with mental disorders run afoul of the law, and are sent to prison. In this sense, some patients have been *reinstitutionalized*—taken from the mental hospital and put in prison.

Some communities, most notably New York City, are attempting to reinstitutionalize the mentally ill. This can lead to tricky problems in a free country such as the United States. As you might imagine, it is a little scary that vans can roam the city, pick up people who are acting "strangely," and hold these people against their will on no more than a psychiatrist's say-so. Although many homeless need our help, and some may need to be taken to a hospital, the potential for abuse is enormous. In the wrong hands, such efforts could amount to the suspension of civil liberties for anyone deemed "undesirable" by people who have local power. Results from the New York program appear to be encouraging, however. Eighty percent of those reinstitutionalized fit the DSM-III-R classifications for schizophrenia, and 73 percent received additional medical diagnoses (Marcos, Cohen, Nardacci, & Brittain, 1990).

PSYCHOTHERAPY

Psychotherapy is any noninvasive psychological technique designed to bring about a positive change in someone's behavior, personality, or adjustment. *Noninvasive* means not directly interacting with the body or its chemistry, as somatic therapies do. Psychotherapies can often be just as effective as somatic therapies (Robinson, Berman, & Neimeyer, 1990). Although there are many kinds of psychotherapy, they have certain things in common.

In individual psychotherapy, the patient or client interacts directly with the therapist in a personal and trust-inspiring atmosphere. Concerns are discussed, and problems can be freely aired. Through interaction and the use of psychotherapeutic techniques, the person comes to have a better self-understanding. With this understanding, and supported by the psychotherapeutic encounter, the person may be better able to adjust to the stress and demands of his situation.

Psychotherapies rely on words to bring about a positive change in behavior, personality, or adjustment.

The focus varies with the type of psychotherapy. There are two sets of dimensions. In **insight therapy**, the therapist attempts to help the client or patient develop a better understanding of a situation or problem; **action therapy** usually focuses directly on changing a habit or problem that has been troublesome. In **directive therapy**, the therapist actually guides the client, giving instructions and advice; in **nondirective therapy**, primary responsibility for direction of the therapy is placed on the client's shoulders, and the therapist only helps the client to find personal solutions. The dimensions emphasized by different therapies are shown in Figure 17.4.

All the psychotherapies share some common ground. Researcher Jerome Frank has given perhaps the best description:

All psychotherapies attempt to combat demoralization by replacing confusion with clarity. . . . All schools of psychotherapy [attempt to replace] despair with hope, feelings of incompetence with self-confidence, and isolation with rewarding personal relationships. To bring about these transformations, psychotherapies rely on words. . . . (Frank, 1986, p. 4)

Psychoanalysis

Psychoanalysis is an insight therapy based on the theory and work of Sigmund Freud. Many variations of psychoanalysis have been developed by both Freud's contemporaries and later practitioners.

In psychoanalysis, abnormal behavior is assumed to be the result of unconscious conflicts. By using special techniques, the psychoanalyst hopes to uncover these unconscious conflicts and repressed memories and hence to explain and deal with the motivation behind the abnormal behavior.

The techniques Freud devised for uncovering unconscious conflicts include free association and dream interpretation, which we touched on in earlier chapters. In free association, the patient is asked to say whatever comes to mind, no matter how ridiculous. Freud believed that unconscious desires were always brewing just below the surface; he argued, therefore, that apparently random thoughts might be closely related to the conflict. In dream interpretation, the patient describes the manifest (apparent) content of a dream and works with the analyst to uncover the latent (hidden) meaning. The idea is that unconscious thoughts and conflicts will come to the person during sleep, but that a psychic censor disguises the conflict in the dream so that it appears in symbolic form; the dream must be analyzed before its real content can be understood.

Freud also looked for points of resistance and analyzed those. By **resistance** he meant the patient's tendency to balk at the analyst's attempts to probe certain areas. Freud believed this reaction was a defense of the unconscious against giving up its secrets; resistance was therefore a sign that the therapist was getting close to the problem.

Analysis of **transference** is another important aspect of Freudian psychoanalysis. The patient often transfers feelings she has toward other people onto the analyst and then behaves, for example, as though the analyst were the "rejecting father" or "overbearing mother." There is empirical evidence that people do, in fact, transfer their feelings onto others who remind them of someone with whom they have had an important relationship (DeAngelis, 1992). Freud liked to have his patients recline on a couch so that he could sit behind them; he thought that by removing his physical presence from their view, transference became easier. He believed that the analyst could gain insight into patients' thought processes by observing how they began to transfer their feelings from their parent or lover to their analyst.

In its original form, Freudian psychoanalysis took a very long time. Freud thought that his therapy sessions should include three to five meetings per

DIRECTIVE THERAPY
Any approach in which the therapist takes an active role and directs the client or patient to confront problems and life situations.

NONDIRECTIVE THERAPY
A therapeutic technique based on humanistic psychology in which the therapist creates a supportive atmosphere so that clients can work out their own problems.

PSYCHOANALYSIS
A therapy that seeks to bring unconscious desires into consciousness and make it possible to resolve conflicts usually dating back to early childhood experiences. Psychoanalysis is also the school of psychological thought founded by Sigmund Freud, which emphasizes the study of unconscious mental processes.

RESISTANCE
In psychoanalytic therapy, a patient's opposition to attempts to bring repressed thoughts into the conscious mind.

TRANSFERENCE
A concept developed by Freud that refers to the tendency of a person in therapy to transfer to the therapist perceptions and feelings about other people rather than seeing the therapist as he or she really is.

◆ **FIGURE 17.4**

Dimensions of psychotherapy. The term insight therapy *generally is reserved for therapies whose goal is an in-depth understanding of the individual's self. Although action therapies sometimes help individuals to develop insight into their problems, the term* action therapy *refers in general to therapeutic attempts to deal directly and immediately with specific difficulties or current problems.*

	DIRECTIVE	NONDIRECTIVE
INSIGHT	Psychoanalysis Gestalt therapy Transactional analysis	Client-centered Existential
ACTION	Rational-emotive therapy Behavior therapy Cognitive restructuring Hypnotherapy	Self-hypnosis Meditation

CLIENT-CENTERED THERAPY
A type of psychotherapy developed by Carl Rogers and based on the belief that the client is responsible for his or her own growth and self-actualization. The therapist creates an atmosphere of acceptance, refrains from directing the client, and reflects back to the client what the client has said.

week for as long as 6 years.* At the current cost of $100 to $150 an hour, very few people can afford such intensive therapy.

To reduce the expense and the amount of time involved, modern psychoanalysts have developed techniques for shortening the therapy to perhaps one hour per week for a few years. They have modified Freud's theories and procedures in other ways as well. Neo-Freudians, as these modern analysts often are called, sometimes attach as much importance to cultural, social, and interpersonal factors as to the psychosexual aspects of development that Freud emphasized (see Chapter 14). Many of these psychoanalysts have dispensed with the Freudian couch and instead sit face to face with their clients, and they may explore conscious thoughts and desires as much as unconscious motives. Like Freud, however, neo-Freudians believe that insight into the unconscious is the key to resolving mental disorders (Youngstrom, 1992).

Humanistic-Existential Therapies

Freud believed that people are motivated by instinctive urges toward aggression and death. His view of human beings, shaped by the carnage of the First World War, was essentially pessimistic. The humanistic-existential view, on the other hand, is optimistic; it regards human beings as capable of living rich, fulfilling lives, relatively free of urges toward unhappiness and destruction. The emphasis of therapy is on fulfilling potential, or self-actualizing. Having a sense of belonging, a feeling that one has an important role to play within the society, is also of great importance. Humanistic-existential therapies are considered insight therapies.

CLIENT-CENTERED THERAPY. Carl Rogers, the humanistic psychologist, was the founder of **client-centered therapy.** Unlike psychoanalysts, who believe that unconscious motives and drives are the crucial aspects of an individual's personality, Rogers argued that conscious thoughts, feelings, and self-concept were primary. Client-centered therapy is a form of nondirective therapy; the therapist refrains from guiding the therapy in any particular direction. The client is considered responsible for his therapy and decides the direction in which the therapy will proceed. (Humanists shun the word *patient* because they do not view their clients as sick.)

The client-centered therapist relies on special techniques. First, the therapist must have an unconditional positive regard for each client. The client is accepted totally. Second, the therapist attempts to make the therapeutic atmosphere personal and forthright; the therapist doesn't hide behind her professional role. Third, the therapist tries to develop genuine empathy for the client.

In nondirective therapy, as we mentioned, the therapist never advises the client or tells him what to do. Instead, the therapist often reflects the thoughts and feelings of the client by repeating or stating in different words what the client has said or by noting the client's emotional state. The following conversation between a client-centered therapist and a client will give you an impression of this technique.

CLIENT: Sometimes, even when there's no good reason to, I tell lies. I don't know why I do.
THERAPIST: (*Remains silent*)
CLIENT: I don't know why; it's as though there was some kind of drive or force that makes me do it.

---

*In Woody Allen's movie *Sleeper*, Woody is placed in suspended animation for 2000 years. When he comes to and finds out how long he's been asleep he remarks, "My analyst was a strict Freudian. If I'd been going to him all this time, I'd almost be cured now."

THERAPIST: And how does this make you feel?

CLIENT: It makes me feel bad. I don't like to think of myself as a liar.

THERAPIST: When you tell lies, then, it makes you uncomfortable.

CLIENT: Yes. I feel better when I don't tell lies, when I don't feel the need to.

THERAPIST: There are times when you don't tell lies, and when that happens it makes you feel better?

CLIENT: Yes, I really like it better when I don't, but I don't seem to have any control.

THERAPIST: Then you have no control?

CLIENT: Well, sometimes I can decide what I want to do, and then I feel better.

THERAPIST: So sometimes you can control yourself. You can control your life, and this makes you feel better.

CLIENT: Yes, I suppose that's the main thing, to learn to control my own life.

THERAPIST: (*Does not respond, remains silent*)

CLIENT: That's really what I need to do, to control things for myself.

THERAPIST: You want your life to be in your own hands.

The therapist in this exchange unconditionally accepted the client and avoided interjecting her own thoughts and feelings, such as what she thinks about the act of telling a lie. Instead, she helped the client to better understand his feelings and thoughts. This technique of active listening can be valuable in getting to know someone much more intimately.

EXISTENTIAL THERAPY.   **Existential therapy** is much like client-centered therapy except that it emphasizes the idea of free will. Existential therapist Rollo May has argued that people have learned to subordinate their own responsibility and self-image to society's. They begin to feel like nonentities, lost in society. Existential therapists try to restore people's courage, so that they can make choices for themselves and feel in control of the environment rather than controlled by it.

Humanistic and existential therapies are so similar that they often are referred to under one heading as humanistic-existential therapy. Both aim at improving a person's self-concept, promoting self-acceptance, and developing the person's belief in his own ability.

Rational-Emotive Therapy

Rational-emotive therapy is an action therapy developed by Albert Ellis. It is based on the assumption that people engage in self-defeating behaviors because they hold onto beliefs that are unrealistic or faulty (Ellis, 1962). Rational-emotive therapy focuses on changing these beliefs by getting clients to understand that the faulty beliefs are the problem. For example, a student who is turned down for medical school and becomes deeply depressed, on the verge of suicide, has obviously developed faulty beliefs about the world and his situation in it. The faulty belief is that getting into medical school is the only possible way to have a happy and fulfilling life and that without it there is no point in living. Rational-emotive therapy attacks the faulty belief, examining the emotional beliefs rationally.

Rational-emotive therapy is also a directive therapy. The therapist directly interacts with the client and points out irrational beliefs and values, noting how they influence the client's thinking. The therapist may even give the client homework to do to help change the belief system. The hope is that eventually the client will learn a new belief system that is rational. The following is an example of an exchange between a rational-emotive therapist and

EXISTENTIAL THERAPY
A form of psychotherapy, generally nondirective, that is derived from the existentialist philosophy that each individual has to choose values and decide on the meaning of his or her own life. The therapist tries to achieve an authentic, spontaneous relationship with the client in order to help the client discover free will and make his or her own choices.

RATIONAL-EMOTIVE THERAPY
A form of directive therapy associated with Albert Ellis in which the therapeutic goal is modification of the client's inappropriate ideas about self-concept and relations with others.

Albert Ellis, the founder of rational-emotive therapy.

a client. The client is a college student who has never been out on a date. Although he wants to, he's too afraid.

CLIENT: She's really nice, and I'd like to ask her out, but I just don't dare.
THERAPIST: What do you think will happen if she turns you down?
CLIENT: Oh, no. I couldn't bear it. It would be awful.
THERAPIST: If she turned you down it would be awful, and you couldn't bear it. Isn't that a little strong?
CLIENT: But it would make me feel awful if she turned me down.
THERAPIST: Why? Does everybody in the world have to like you? If she turns you down, isn't there somebody else you could ask out who would be just as good? Even better? Do you expect everyone in the world to like you?
CLIENT: Well, suppose I asked her out and she turned me down, and I asked somebody else out and she turned me down, too?
THERAPIST: You've got two people turning you down and you haven't even asked anybody out yet. Suppose only 1 percent of the women in the world liked you, and the other 99 percent didn't like you. What would it be like then?
CLIENT: I suppose it would be pretty awful.
THERAPIST: Why? How long could it take you to ask one hundred women out? A couple of weeks? A couple of weeks, and you would have a date. You would finally find someone who liked you. If you liked her, you'd be happy. Who cares what the other ninety-nine think?
CLIENT: I don't know. You make it sound simple.
THERAPIST: Well, it's not that simple, but I think you can make a good beginning by asking her out. Why don't you do that as homework? Go up to her and ask her out.
CLIENT: I don't know.
THERAPIST: What do you have to lose?
CLIENT: Nothing, I guess.
THERAPIST: That's right, nothing. Everybody doesn't have to like you. As long as they're not throwing rocks at you, it's OK. I know a good politician who says he can tell when he reaches a just solution, because that's when everybody hates him. Think about that. Now, you'll ask her out for homework, and you'll record her reactions and how you felt about them, and how things went. Right?
CLIENT: OK, I'll try it, but it might not work.
THERAPIST: And what should you tell yourself if you think it might not work?
CLIENT: That it doesn't matter. That there are other fish in the sea, right?
THERAPIST: Right.

As you can see, this therapy is directive. The therapist is forcefully trying to get the client to see the illogic of his fear, which could lead to a life of isolation. The client needs to understand that the consequences of being rejected are minor, whereas the rewards of tolerating a few rejections for an eventual acceptance could be major.

Rational-emotive therapy follows a particular pattern of therapist-client interaction, as do other therapies. But the pattern isn't rigid. Different psychotherapies don't have sets of strict rules that each therapist must follow without deviating. Therapists are human beings, and they have their own personalities. Ellis's own personality comes through when he discusses his views about people and their ability to maintain good mental health:

I am still haunted by the reality, however, that humans—and I mean practically all humans—have a strong biological tendency to needlessly and severely disturb themselves and that, to make matters much worse, they are also powerfully predisposed to unconsciously and habitually prolong their mental dysfunctioning and to fight like hell

(a) In group therapy situations, a number of people join together and share experiences and feelings under the supervision of a therapist. (b) In traditional psychoanalysis, the patient rests on a couch out of direct view of the analyst. (c) Most modern therapists sit face to face with their clients.

(a)

(b)

(c)

against giving it up. No, I do not think that they are masochistic. ... I think that they are almost always extremely hedonistic but that they continually indulge in short-range rather than long-range hedonism, that they are obsessed with the pleasures of the moment rather than of the future, and that this is the main (though hardly the only) source of their resistance to achieving and maintaining mental health. (Ellis, 1987, p. 365)

And yet, Ellis remains an optimist. As he has said, "I believe that, along with their powerful self-defeating and self-destructive tendencies, humans also have great self-changing and self-actualizing powers" (p. 374).

Gestalt Therapy

Frederick (Fritz) Perls (1893–1970) developed **Gestalt therapy,** an insight therapy. Gestalt therapy is not directly related to Gestalt psychology, which is concerned with perception (see Chapter 6). Instead, Gestalt therapy is based heavily on Freudian psychoanalytic ideas. As a technique, however, it differs from the Freudian approach to therapy.

Gestalt means "whole" in German. Fritz Perls believed that an adequate therapy must take into consideration all the different parts of a person's life. The ultimate goal is to balance and integrate emotion, thought, and action. Through awareness developed during therapy, clients can check imbalances in thoughts, actions, and feelings and can create a whole personality. The therapy is based on helping the client to leave behind unneeded defenses and to release pent-up emotions.

Gestalt therapy emphasizes what is happening here and now rather than what happened in the past or what may happen in the future. It focuses on what exists rather than on what is absent, and on what is real rather than on what is fantasy (Korchin, 1976).

This focus on the present brings the client into contact with his life, feelings, and thoughts as they really exist. The client is required to speak in the first person and to use the active voice. In this way, the client builds a personality centered on himself. For example, the client would be encouraged to say "I am unhappy" (statement from the self) instead of "Anybody could see that this would be upsetting" (referring to others).

Perls often conducted exercises in which clients played out different parts of their personalities. In this way, they developed awareness about their own feelings, actions, and thoughts. The goal of Gestalt therapy is to enable clients to take responsibility for their own actions and, starting with someone who is fragmented into many social roles and who feels helpless, to reintegrate all aspects of the personality into one whole, functioning person.

Group Therapies

One of the earliest group approaches to therapy was developed by J. L. Moreno, a Viennese psychiatrist who coined the term *group psychotherapy*. Moreno's approach, psychodrama, originated at Vienna's Theater of Spontaneity in 1921. In **psychodrama,** an individual may take the role of a family member and portray or act out that person's behavior and feelings. Therapy comes from the release of pent-up emotions and from insights into the way other people feel and behave.

Group therapy was used infrequently before the Second World War. After that war and again after the Korean War, the U.S. Army found that it did not have enough therapists to see all the soldiers who needed help. Consequently, it decided to try pairing more than one soldier with each therapist. The results were surprisingly beneficial. Under the direction of the therapist,

GESTALT THERAPY
A form of psychotherapy originated by Fritz Perls, who adapted the fundamental concepts of traditional psychoanalysis but placed greater emphasis on the immediacy and importance of the here and now in breaking down the influence of the past. The patient-therapist relationship is more active and democratic than in traditional psychoanalysis.

PSYCHODRAMA
A specialized technique of psychotherapy developed by J. L. Moreno in which patients act out the roles, situations, and fantasies relevant to their personal problems. Psychodrama is usually conducted in front of a small audience of patients.

SENSITIVITY TRAINING
Group sessions conducted for the purpose of developing personal and interpersonal sensitivity to feelings and needs. The feelings among group members are channeled so that members' self-acceptance and growth are enhanced.

ENCOUNTER GROUPS
Therapeutic gatherings in which members of a group, under the guidance of a trained therapist, confront one another during a psychodynamic exchange that uncovers defenses and helps reveal hidden emotions.

FAMILY THERAPY
A general term for a number of therapies that treat the family as a whole. Family therapy is a theoretically neutral term, in that family therapy can be practiced as part of many different psychotherapeutic approaches.

TRANSACTIONAL ANALYSIS
A form of interpersonal therapy originated by Eric Berne based on the interactions of "child," "adult," and "parent" ego states.

BEHAVIOR THERAPY
A group of techniques based on learning principles and used to manipulate an individual's behavior directly to promote adaptive patterns while eliminating maladaptive ones.

members of the therapy group discovered that they often had experiences and insights to share with one another. They were relieved to find that other people had similar problems.

Most therapy groups have 7 to 10 members. Psychiatrists and psychologists frequently see clients individually once per week and also in a group once per week.

SENSITIVITY TRAINING AND ENCOUNTER GROUPS. During **sensitivity training,** participants learn to become sensitive to the needs and feelings of other people and to trust other people. For example, a person taking a "blind" walk is blindfolded and led about; he must trust the person who can see not to guide him into something that might be injurious. Or participants may extend their body awareness by touching one another in a platonic way. They may embrace one another as a way of communicating human affection and a bond. In this way, they achieve heightened sensitivity to others as human beings and a feeling of belonging to the group.

In **encounter groups,** individuals confront one another and attempt to break through defenses and false fronts. Sometimes, the discussions can be painfully honest and difficult to deal with. A qualified therapist should be present to keep things from getting out of hand, since tearing someone down is much easier than building someone up. The purpose of encounter groups is not to cause psychological injury but to help people encounter themselves by having others challenge their assertions and beliefs.

FAMILY THERAPY. In **family therapy,** the family is treated at the same time as a whole unit, with the members interacting with one another and the therapist. This allows the therapist to observe and examine family relations and conflicts in a professional environment. Therapists who practice family therapy often see each family member in private one-on-one sessions as well.

TRANSACTIONAL ANALYSIS. **Transactional analysis,** originated by Eric Berne, is used with groups or couples. The idea behind transactional analysis was described years ago in Berne's classic book *Games People Play* (1964). Berne argues that partners often create unwritten rules that may satisfy their own needs but get in the way of an honest and healthy relationship. Figure 17.5

An encounter group must be managed carefully and only by trained professionals, so it does not get out of hand and turn into a group assault on one individual.

shows several transactions. Horizontal transactions from A to A—that is, from adult to adult—indicate a healthier interaction. In the diagonal transactions, P represents the parent role and C the child role (roles that anyone may adopt). These transactions, in which someone takes the parent role and someone takes the child role, may not be healthy interactions. If social interactions are analyzed to find out what kind of role a person is playing, the rules can be changed to promote mutual satisfaction, and unproductive games can be ended.

Behavior Therapy

Behavior therapy relies on learning theory and the principles of conditioning. Behavior therapy is a radical departure from the psychotherapies we have considered to this point. Behavior therapists are not interested in feelings or dreams for purposes of therapy; they concentrate only on observable behaviors and how these behaviors might be changed through conditioning or social learning.

Each therapeutic treatment deals with a specific problem, and terminology such as "passive-aggressive personality disorder" or "somatoform disorder" generally is not used, since behaviorists are concerned with observable behavior rather than with constructs such as personality or mental disorder. Behavior therapies rely on the principles of classical conditioning, operant conditioning, or social learning (described in Chapter 8), or on a combination of all three.

CLASSICAL CONDITIONING THERAPY. You may recall from Chapter 8 that Little Albert's fear of the rat was created through classical conditioning. Behavior therapists may make use of a paradigm of this experience called **aversive conditioning.** Aversive conditioning has been used in many situations, for instance, in attempts to help a person stop smoking or drinking.

To treat alcoholism in this fashion, the client may be taken to a laboratory where a bar, similar to a neighborhood bar, has been set up. The taste and smell of the alcohol and the ambience of the surroundings are all reminiscent of the place where the client usually drinks. As the client drinks, however, she is given an electric shock, an unconditioned stimulus. Her favorite drink is continually paired with this painful stimulus. After enough pairings, the alcohol begins to elicit an aversive fear. In one large study using aversive conditioning to treat alcoholism, one-third of the alcoholics were found to be abstaining from drink 3 years after the conditioning (Wiens & Menustik, 1983).

Aversive conditioning can elicit a very strong response. You might think that a human being, well aware of being in a laboratory under special circumstances, would take up old habits at home, safe in the knowledge that a drink wouldn't be accompanied by an electric shock. Yet this kind of therapy often works. It happened to me once. I like pears, but a couple of years ago, I was eating a pear and bit right through a large worm. Disgusting, isn't it? To this day I can't eat pears. It doesn't matter that the pears are canned or chopped thoroughly, so that I can tell that there's nothing in them. It doesn't matter that I can look carefully and see no wormholes. The aversive conditioning was very strong. I even hate writing about it.

Unfortunately, the desire to smoke or drink can be so strong that a person may be willing to risk the negative consequences of taking a puff or a sip even after aversive therapy. In this case, the conditioned response may be extinguished quickly, and the person will end up smoking or drinking once again. Aversive conditioning works frequently enough, however, to make the attempt worthwhile.

AVERSIVE CONDITIONING
An element of behavior therapy in which unacceptable behavior becomes linked with painful stimuli and is thereafter avoided.

◆ **FIGURE 17.5**

Transactional analysis. Eric Berne describes the interactions shown here as crossed transactions. According to Berne, the personality can express itself as a child (C), adult (A), or parent (P) (roughly equivalent to Freud's concept of id, ego, and superego). Healthy transactions are from adult to adult. It's easy to see that the diagonal transactions are likely to create problems.

PATIENT
"Doctor, I'm worried that these chest pains are due to my heart."

DOCTOR
"Now who's the doctor here? You or me?"

PROFESSOR
"Do you have your paper."

STUDENT
"No. I lost my book and then my only pen broke and and my car's been acting up and the dog got sick and..."

FATHER
"Go wash the car!"

SON
"It's your car, you wash it. I don't wash your face for you, do I ?"

SYSTEMATIC DESENSITIZATION
A therapeutic procedure developed by
Joseph Wolpe in which anxiety-
producing stimuli are paired, in a
graduated sequence or hierarchy, with a
state of physical relaxation until the
most difficult situation can be faced
without anxiety.

SYSTEMATIC DESENSITIZATION.   Joseph Wolpe at Temple University developed a therapy that he calls **systematic desensitization.** His therapy is based on the idea of associating a relaxed and tranquil feeling with stimuli that previously caused anxiety. Look at the following hierarchy of fear written by a person who has arachnophobia, an unrealistic fear of spiders. The higher in the hierarchy the item is, the more frightening it is to him.

Rating	Hierarchy Items
1	Planning a picnic.
10	Hearing about the possibility spiders may be nearby.
20	Hearing someone describe an encounter with a spider.
30	Trying to decide how to make sure there are no spiders in the house.
40	Having to do spring cleaning.
50	Thinking that a doctor will make me look at a spider during treatment.
60	Seeing a spider on a wall 20 feet away.
70	Crawling through a cobwebbed attic.
80	Seeing a spider crawl on my arm.
90	Having a large spider crawl on my face.
100	Falling into a dark pit where hundreds of spiders climb on me and try to crawl into my mouth and ears.

During systematic desensitization, the therapist leads the client through each of the steps in the hierarchy by having him lie down or relax in a chair and think carefully about his fear or even act it out. As he thinks about the first item in the hierarchy, he may experience mild anxiety. Eventually, he learns to relax while thinking of this item until he feels calm and relaxed whenever he thinks of it. Then the next step in the hierarchy is taken and this, too, is associated with relaxation and tranquility. After completing the hierarchy, fear of the object (in this case, spiders) decreases, often dramatically.

OPERANT BEHAVIOR THERAPY.   Therapies based on operant conditioning attempt to end behavior that is inappropriate or to create appropriate behavior that is absent. Table 17.1 outlines the techniques used by operant conditioners

*Through modeling and
counterconditioning, Albert Bandura was
able to help those with snake phobia
overcome their fears.*

TABLE 17.1 ◆ OPERANT TECHNIQUES USED IN BEHAVIOR MODIFICATION	
TECHNIQUE	DESCRIPTION
Positive reinforcement	Providing a reinforcer following an appropriate response.
Negative reinforcement	Removing an aversive stimulus following an appropriate response.
Punishment	Providing an aversive stimulus following an inappropriate response.
Extinction	Removing the reinforcer that is maintaining the inappropriate response.
Positive reinforcement of incompatible response	Reinforcing behavior that is incompatible with the inappropriate response (for example, reinforcing telling the truth, which is incompatible with lying).
Time-out from positive reinforcement	Essentially producing boredom following an inappropriate behavior by removing the opportunity to engage in any reinforcing activities for a brief time (usually a few minutes).
Altering response effort	Structuring the environment such that inappropriate responses are more difficult to make or appropriate responses are easier to make.
Token economy	Providing tokens (generalized secondary reinforcers) for appropriate behaviors. Tokens can be redeemed later for specific reinforcers unique to each person's taste.
Response cost	Imposing fines for inappropriate behavior (often used in conjunction with token economies).
Negative practice	Forcing repetition of an inappropriate behavior (for example, yelling) until it finally becomes aversive to engage in the behavior.

in therapy. Because these techniques rely less on talking than do other forms of psychotherapy, they often can be useful with psychotics who have limited verbal ability. For instance, operant conditioning techniques have been used successfully to teach social skills to schizophrenics (Liberman, Mueser, & Wallace, 1986). Most of the time, however, these techniques are used to help alleviate less severe disorders. The following case study describes a typical instance of operant conditioning in therapy.

BEHAVIOR THERAPY: A BIRD IN THE HAND

In Chapter 16, you met Judy R., who had a bird phobia. She had come to the counseling center at a university because her unrealistic terror of birds was interfering with her life and her plans to become a teacher. The counselors at the center decided to use behavior therapy to help Judy unlearn her fear of birds.

First, the therapists set up a 35-step hierarchy for systematic desensitization, similar to the hierarchy described in this chapter. They decided that Judy would act out the hierarchy rather than just imagine it, since acting something out while learning to be calm is more effective.

A 27-year-old woman, the same age as Judy, served as a model. Judy watched as the model touched bird pictures, the first behavior that Judy was to imitate. The therapy proceeded slowly, with Judy first placing her hand on the model's hand and then touching the pictures by herself. A little later, the same procedure was used with feathers.

Then a stuffed bird from a museum was brought in. First the model and Judy looked at the stuffed bird from a distance of several feet, and then they slowly approached it.

TOKEN ECONOMIES
Training, based on operant conditioning, that uses tokens as rewards for certain behaviors. The tokens can be redeemed for special privileges or other reinforcers.

BEHAVIOR CONTRACTS
A technique often used in behavior, group, or family therapy, in which a contract or bargain is struck. The client promises to engage in a certain behavior in return for a particular behavior from another.

COGNITIVE THERAPY
A behavior therapy technique in which the client's beliefs, attitudes, and expectations are tested in reality in a formal and structured way.

The model touched the bird first and then Judy touched it while wearing gloves. Later she removed the gloves. The therapy never moved fast enough to cause Judy much anxiety. Everything was done slowly and gently, and at each step Judy was allowed time to be sure she was calm and comfortable before the next step was taken.

Next, Judy took bird specimens home and kept them in a place where she would see them often. Then came a session in which she was trained to fight off birds, should any happen to fly at her, by waving her arms and shouting. These defensive measures were first modeled for Judy, and then Judy tried them on a group of live pigeons. She dispersed the birds without feeling afraid.

Following this success, Judy went to a live-poultry store and watched the model touch hundreds of small chicks. Next, Judy went to the zoo and spent time at the duck pond, the aviary, and the cages for large birds. Later, she was able to go with her model around a bird-populated city mall. Finally, Judy watched the model walk through a large closed aviary at the zoo where people could walk surrounded by hundreds of birds. Judy accompanied the model through the aviary, and then she was able to walk through on her own.

The therapists also employed cognitive restructuring. Judy was given many factual bits of information about birds that she was able to test on her own by experiencing birds firsthand. For example, Judy was informed that birds almost never fly at people except by accident, a hypothesis she was able to test firsthand on her walk through the aviary.

Before treatment, Judy was unable to get farther than about halfway up her hierarchy with a minimum amount of anxiety. After treatment, Judy no longer showed fear of birds (although she admitted that an uncaged eagle might still make her a little nervous). She did not go out of her way to avoid birds. She often drove with her car windows down. She went for walks on the beach and went sunbathing. She even wore a blouse imprinted with vivid pictures of birds. Eventually, Judy moved to a new apartment that was on a waterfront populated by seagulls. A follow-up 12 months later showed that her bird phobia had not returned. (Lassen & McConnell, 1977)

Many techniques are used for behavior modification. Another is the token economy. **Token economies** are a popular means of modifying behavior. This technique uses tokens, such as poker chips, as currency. In institutions for delinquent children and in state hospitals, token economies have been found to be effective in controlling and developing behaviors. The tokens function as conditioned reinforcers. They can be given following appropriate behavior or withdrawn following inappropriate behavior. They can be useful both for initiating and for terminating behavior. The tokens can later be traded in for items that are of value. Once behaviors are established, praise and other social reinforcers can take the place of tokens.

Sometimes, two parties set up **behavior contracts,** in which each agrees to a behavior desired by the other. A husband, for example, may promise to play tennis once a week with his wife if she promises to go bowling with him in return.

Behavior therapies may also be based on social learning principles. In social learning, models are used to demonstrate desired behaviors or responses. Modeling has been found to be a very effective way of producing behavior changes.

Considering John Watson's denial of the mind as an area of study, behaviorism represented a radical break from other forms of psychology. Nevertheless, many psychologists and psychiatrists recommend using behavior therapy in conjunction with other forms of psychotherapy (Goisman, 1985). In practice, behavior therapy isn't often used by itself (Farkas, 1980).

COGNITIVE THERAPY.   Cognitive therapy, or cognitive restructuring, is a therapeutic treatment in which a client is helped to obtain information about himself through a series of unbiased encounters that can disprove false beliefs. The client is encouraged to explore, with the therapist, beliefs, attitudes, and expectations in order to form hypotheses that can be tested. In this way, the client can go out to test expectations experimentally and through the experiences can come to a new cognitive understanding of his world.

Less difficult tasks usually are assigned first, and more difficult ones later. Occasionally, the client's activities for the entire day will be planned moment by moment. These experiments help the client to disconfirm erroneous assumptions about the world by testing them.

Cognitive therapy seems to be most effective with clients who selectively perceive their world as harmless or dangerous, ignoring any evidence to the contrary; who overgeneralize based on a few limited examples (for instance, because they fail at one thing, they decide they are totally worthless); who magnify unhappy events and blow them out of proportion (for instance, they believe that the loss of a job is the end of the world); and who engage in absolutist thinking (they always see things as black or white, good or bad, never as gray or mixed) (Meichenbaum, 1977; Beck, 1991).

In Table 17.2 are a number of "coping statements" that the client can rehearse as a means of restructuring cognitive understanding and bolstering herself against stress or depression. These statements are not simply slogans; their validity has been demonstrated to the client during experimental explorations of each statement in real situations. In some forms of cognitive therapy, the statements can even be organized and presented by a computer without the need of a therapist! Such computer programs can lead, say, depressed individuals through a series of explorations of their beliefs and have been found to be as effective at reducing minor episodes of depression as are human therapists (Selmi, Klein, Greist, Sorrell, & Erdman, 1990). Furthermore, depressed individuals treated with cognitive therapy have been found to be less likely to relapse into depression following treatment than people treated with antidepressants only (Evans, et al., 1992). Cognitive therapy has also been found to be helpful in the treatment of anxiety (Beck, 1991; Zinbarg, Barlow, Brown, & Hertz, 1992) and in the alleviation of panic attacks (Beck, Sokol, Clark, Berchick, & Wright, 1992).

Like the other therapies that we have discussed so far, cognitive therapy is not a rigid system, but rather a general framework that has certain aspects or qualities that distinguish it from other therapies (Beck, 1991). In fact, there are at least 22 popular variations of cognitive therapy (Goldfried, Greenberg, & Marmar, 1990).

TABLE 17.2 ◆ COPING STATEMENTS FOR DEALING WITH STRESS	
SITUATIONAL STAGE	COPING STATEMENTS
Preparing for stress	What is the task? You can work out a way to handle it.
Facing the stress	You can deal with your fear. Being tense is good; it makes you alert. Take a deep breath. Go one step at a time.
Dealing with being overwhelmed	Your fear will rise, but you can manage it. If you're too frightened, just pause. Keep in mind what to do this moment.
Reinforcing self	It's not as bad as you expected. You succeeded! You can control your thoughts.

SOURCE: After Meichenbaum, 1977.

HYPNOTHERAPY
Hypnosis used for therapeutic purposes
in cases of pain control or behavior
pathology. The method has been used in
therapy, dentistry, surgery, and
childbirth.

Hypnotherapy

Many modern psychotherapists rely on hypnosis for therapeutic intervention. They use **hypnotherapy** in a number of important ways, for instance, to make a recollection of a past emotion or memory seem more vivid (Nash, Johnson, & Tipton, 1979).

Hypnosis has been beneficial in conjunction with behavior therapy. Some behavior therapists have hypnotized clients during systematic desensitization to help the clients to relax more deeply and to imagine more vividly the feared object or situation in their hierarchy (Lazarus, 1976).

One of the oldest applications of hypnosis is in pain control. Hypnosis has been used successfully to control pain during major surgery and childbirth. Dentists and plastic surgeons have found it an effective substitute for drugs in carrying out procedures (Kroger, 1977). Hypnosis can even help to reduce and control chronic severe pain (Hilgard & Hilgard, 1975). EEG recordings (see Chapter 7) indicate that hypnotized subjects who are successful at managing pain actually alter their pain perception at the neurological level, rather than simply reporting that they have less pain because they know that they have been hypnotized (Spiegel, Bierre, & Rootenberg, 1989).

People with physical disorders, especially those associated with anxiety and stress, also may respond to hypnosis. This is especially true of people with disorders such as dermatitis, asthma, and rash, which can be made worse by stress and anxiety (DePiano & Salzberg, 1979).

Hypnosis has been effective in the treatment of dissociative disorders such as amnesia, fugue, and multiple personality. Under hypnosis, people sometimes can recall events more easily, which may help them to overcome the amnesia or fugue state or make multiple personalities more accessible.

Some researchers have suggested that hypnosis can affect dissociative disorders for two reasons. First, it can reduce the anxiety that interferes with recall. Second, mood-dependent and other memories become easier to retrieve through use of the vivid imagery and moods that hypnosis can create. Hypnosis can also be used to alter or reduce anxiety. In the following case study, hypnosis was used to alter a terrifying dream.

HYPNOTHERAPY: THE CASE OF MR. B

The chief complaint of Mr. B. [was] a recurring traumatic dream [dating from his time as a combat soldier]. . . . Mr. B dreamt of being shot by a Viet Cong sniper. He would hear the shot and see the bullet coming to kill him, awakening just before the bullet was going to strike his head. He had dreamt this nearly nightly for ten years. In the alteration of the dream, it was allowed to proceed in hypnotic trance until the bullet became visible about 50 yards away. At this point the bullet was transformed into a whipped cream pie, much in the manner of the old-time silent movies. The pie was then slowed and returned to the Viet Cong sniper. It struck the sniper in the face, so startling him that he fell from the tree. The event was so improbable that the Viet Cong and Mr. B broke into outrageous laughter and walked off together in disbelief. . . . Mr. B rehearsed the substituted dream at home with self-hypnosis. The revised dream was dreamt at night several times, replacing the traumatic dream. After this replacement the traumatic dream disappeared. It reappeared for two periods subsequently in the next 2 years but was again removed with a rehearsal of the altered dream. (Eichelman, 1985, p. 113)

Brief Therapy

In recent years, a number of abbreviated versions of the major therapies have appeared and have gained in popularity (Goldfried, Greenberg, & Marmar,

Focus on Ethnic Diversity

Therapy for Diverse Populations

Culture, like family, has long been recognized as an important context for understanding the individual. . . . (Szapocznik & Kurtines, 1993, p. 401)

With this fundamental principle in mind, the American Psychological Association's Board of Ethnic Minority Affairs established the Task Force on the Delivery of Services to Ethnic Minority Populations. The idea was to explore all of the factors that might come into play when therapists treat clients who come from ethnic populations different from their own.

Interest in this area began when certain unusual mental disorders were found to be specific to particular cultural groups. The most notable of these disorders is called *koro*. Koro is generally limited to populations of male Asians. The disorder is not rare among male Asians, but is almost unheard of among other groups. The central feature of this disorder is the man's unfounded belief hat his penis is retracting into his abdomen and that he will soon die owing to this problem. To someone from a different culture, this might seem bizarre, even laughable. But for the sufferer, there is nothing funny about it. Those who suffer from koro are not uncommonly driven to suicide in the hope of avoiding what they believe will be a terrible and painful death.

This disorder appears to be a unique type of conversion disorder associated with severe anxiety and panic. Intense cold or fear can cause the penis to retract to some degree, so it is assumed that ongoing fear in these individuals causes retraction, which in turn causes more fear (as proof of the "disease") and so on, leading to severe panic attacks, insomnia, intense abdominal pain from fear, and, as mentioned, even suicide (Bernstein & Gaw, 1990).

Following this discovery, another culturally specific mental disorder called *moth madness* was noted among traditional Navajo. Those suffering moth madness are gripped by seizures brought on, they believe, by supernatural forces punishing them for incestuous thoughts or actions (American Psychological Association, 1993).

While DSM-IV doesn't deal with these disorders directly, it does allow for unusual diagnoses under the heading *disorders not otherwise specified*. The reason that koro, moth madness, and other culturally specific disorders may deserve their own classifications is that the symptoms or behaviors associated with such disorders are, in part, dictated by cultural expectations and follow a set pattern.

However, the APA task force went further than just listing unusual disorders specific to other cultures. They took into consideration any problem that therapists might need to be concerned with when dealing with a client whose culture differs from their own. In so doing, the task force published guidelines for therapists who provide services for culturally diverse populations. These guidelines ask the therapist to take care when dealing with someone from a different cultural background.

One recommendation is that the therapist ask him- or herself whether it is appropriate to view the client differently than if he or she were a member of the therapist's own cultural group. If the answer is yes, the guidelines suggest that the therapist be sensitive to the client's culture when attempting to understand the problems that brought the client into therapy. Perhaps the best way to understand what this sensitivity might involve is to look at some examples.

For instance, a therapist's clients might include a Hispanic woman who has come to feel that something is wrong with her because she is not liked at work. According to the guidelines, a sensitive therapist will consider the real possibility of blatant racism in the workplace before delving into the woman's personality in an attempt to discover reasons that others might not like her. The guidelines point out that racism may yield such behaviors as "healthy paranoia" and that a sensitive therapist should consider this possibility when a minority member complains that others "have it in for him."

Such sensitivity also includes the ability to make adjustments when, for example, the entire family of an American Indian client shows up expecting to be part of the therapy. The therapist needs to recognize that this is how this particular culture deals with persons who are in need of help. A sensitive therapist will not turn his or her back on such ethnic traditions. A therapist sensitive to such differences will also be willing to consult honestly with traditional healers or other important figures in the client's culture, even if the beliefs of these individuals may not always agree with the understanding held by the majority culture.

It is also understood that if a therapist is unfamiliar with a particular culture, he or she will attempt to recommend another therapist who is familiar with it or, barring that, do the most possible to become educated about the client's culture. People don't stand alone outside their culture. To understand a person, we must also understand, and be sensitive to, his or her culture.

BRIEF INDIVIDUAL PSYCHOTHERAPIES
Any one-on-one psychotherapy usually lasting no more than 30 sessions, which is designed to provide limited support when lack of time or money prevents regular therapeutic intervention.

1990). These versions go by the collective name of **brief individual psychotherapies.** Brief therapy usually lasts between 1 and 30 sessions. Generally, brief therapy aims at providing support, reducing a person's weaknesses while strengthening his defenses, and doing so with a minimum expenditure of money and time. This latter consideration has become especially important because many health insurance companies have changed their coverage to limit the number of psychotherapy sessions for which they will pay (DeAngelis, 1987).

The development of brief therapy initially led to considerable controversy. Some people believed that brief therapy was too short to be effective and therefore was an unethical practice, "while others worry if they don't hurry up and learn the techniques, they'll be forced out of business" (DeAngelis, 1987, p. 34). Studies have found, however, that brief therapies are often as effective as long-term therapies (Crits-Christoph, 1992) and that individuals in need of therapy are only half as likely to drop out at the beginning of therapy if they know beforehand that the sessions will be limited in number (Sledge, Moras, Hartley, & Levine, 1990).

AN ENDURING QUESTION: DOES PSYCHOTHERAPY WORK?

Does psychotherapy work? In 1952, H. J. Eysenck assessed the effectiveness of psychoanalytic and nonpsychoanalytic psychotherapy and created a storm of controversy that continues to this day. Eysenck did an exhaustive review of the literature and examined over 7000 cases; his conclusion was that the data failed to prove that psychotherapy of any kind facilitated recovery in patients with abnormal behavior. Eysenck argued that any apparent success was simply due to the fact that psychotherapy took so much time that spontaneous remission eventually occurred. He found that roughly two-thirds of any group of people with behavioral problems will recover or improve markedly within 2 years whether or not they receive psychotherapy. Throughout the years, Eysenck continued to present interesting arguments that psychotherapy is, in general, no better than no therapy (with the exception of behavior therapy, which, Eysenck argued, was often effective) (Eysenck, 1985).

Since Eysenck's findings were published, a number of studies have criticized his assumptions, especially his finding that two-thirds of people with behavioral problems will improve even without professional help (Bergin, 1971). Still, many researchers contend that the issue has not been settled and that no definite proof has been presented to show that psychotherapies are effective (Erwin, 1980).

Measuring the effectiveness of psychotherapy tends to be difficult, because the relationship between client and therapist is so complex that it's hard to determine what is or is not a beneficial change and whether any change that does take place is due to the therapy (Sacks, Carpenter, & Richmond, 1975). Researchers can make only a few unequivocal statements about psychotherapy. For example, the clients or patients who are most likely to improve are those who are the least maladjusted, have the shortest history of symptoms or of maladaptive behavior when they begin therapy (Shapiro, Struening, Shapiro, & Barten, 1976), are most motivated to change their behavior (Horowitz, Marmar, Weiss, DeWitt, & Rosenbaum, 1984), and come from the middle or upper class (Derogatis,

AN ENDURING QUESTION, CONTINUED

Yevzeroff, & Wittelsberger, 1975). The most experienced therapists are also most likely to have successful results (Brenner & Howard, 1976). Studies of other characteristics of therapists, such as personal adjustment, warmth, empathy, genuineness, or professional status, have not found an obvious or clear relationship to their effectiveness as therapists (Gomes-Schwartz, Hadley, & Strupp, 1978).

Eysenck's argument that psychotherapy and no therapy are equally effective depends on a particular definition of improvement and spontaneous remission. Using different criteria, other investigators have been able to argue that 83 percent of people who receive psychotherapy improve, while only 30 percent who receive no therapy improve (Bergin, 1971). On the other hand, a 30-year follow-up study of over 500 clients who began therapy in childhood found uniformly negative results when that group was compared with a comparable *untreated* group of children. The researcher suggested that the clients who received therapy had become too dependant on their therapists and saw themselves as people who always "need help" (McCord, 1977).

One of the most extensive analyses of the effectiveness of psychotherapy was conducted by Mary Smith and Gene Glass in 1977. They devised a statistical method that combined the results of 400 studies that had addressed the question of the effectiveness of psychotherapy. The 400 studies used many different criteria for assessing improvement. Smith and Glass found support for the effectiveness of psychotherapy (see Table 17.3). They concluded that all the psychotherapeutic treatments were more effective than was nontreatment, with small differences among the therapies, and that group therapy was as effective as individual therapy.

Since the publication of Smith and Glass's findings, their research has been carefully scrutinized. Smith and Glass's complex statistical analysis has been supported (Landman & Dawes, 1982), but some have argued that the criterion for which studies to include (that is, which studies were well controlled and which were not) was not well defined (Orwin & Cordray, 1984).

The fact that psychologists continue to debate whether psychotherapy works is a surprise to most students. But if psychotherapy did work opti-

---

TABLE 17.3 ◆ EFFECTIVENESS OF DIFFERENT PSYCHOTHERAPIES	
TYPE OF THERAPY	MEDIAN TREATED PERSON'S PERCENTILE STATUS IN CONTROL GROUP*
Psychoanalytic	72
Transactional analysis	72
Rational-emotive	78
Gestalt	60
Client-centered	74
Systematic desensitization	82
Behavior modification	78

*The scores represent the median treated person's percentile status as measured against untreated control subjects. If there were no effect, the median treated person's percentile score would be 50. If there were a negative effect, the expected percentile score would be less than 50. In this study, the average treated person was better off than approximately 75 percent of the untreated controls.

SOURCE: Adapted from Smith & Glass, 1977, p. 756.

AN ENDURING QUESTION, CONTINUED

mally, each form of mental disorder would have a specific remedy. This is not the case. Therapies are diverse, and sometimes they have limited success. Depending on the circumstances, some therapies may be more appropriate than are others (Pilkonis, Imber, Lewis, & Rubinsky, 1984). For instance, behavior modification has been found to be extremely useful in treating simple phobias. Often a psychiatrist uses a combination of therapies (say, drugs and behavioral therapy) and hopes for benefits from each. Such an interdisciplinary approach has raised hopes that psychotherapy will prove to be of greater benefit in the future. In fact, 30 to 40 percent of all therapists consider themselves to be *eclectic* (Goldfried, Greenberg, & Marmar, 1990), which means that they are prepared to use whichever therapy might be best for a given situation rather than adhering to a particular therapy. This has led some to argue that comparing therapies for effectiveness is akin to comparing apples and oranges insomuch as certain problems are more likely to be treated by using one kind of therapy than another. For instance, simple phobias, which are relatively easy to treat, are more likely to be treated with behavior therapy than something more intractable; as a result, one therapy may appear more effective than another simply because it is being used to treat easier problems (Persons, 1991).

Perhaps psychotherapy would be more effective if therapist and client always achieved rapport. Many therapists have noticed that they are personally more effective with one kind of client than with another. Good therapists often are viewed more as artists than as scientists. The exceptional ones frequently find it difficult to explain why they are successful or to teach other people to achieve the same results. Supporting this assertion is the finding by researchers that *who* performs the therapy is often much more important than the *type* of therapy that is performed (Luborsky, et al., 1986).

Research concerning the value of psychotherapy is growing, and scientific debate about whether it is *generally* effective continues.

FOR CRITICAL ANALYSIS

1. Observers once recorded Albert Ellis during therapy sessions to see whether he actually used the rational-emotive techniques of the therapy that he founded. The results indicated that he did use those techniques, but that he also varied his approach considerably from client to client based on his assessment of the client (Becker & Rosenfeld, 1976). Consider also that many therapists, while able to teach the basic principles behind what they do, are often not able to teach others how to obtain the same results that they achieve. In what way do these data argue that much of therapy is an art and not a science? In this context, what are the differences between art and science?

2. As is the case with those who learn to play the violin, some people quickly learn how to be good therapists, while others never learn how even after much practice. Therapy and violin can both be taught as sciences. Certain rules and procedures must be followed to master each skill. Why, then, are great therapists and great violinists considered to be artists? Why can't they always teach others to be just as good as they are? ◆

🔀 RECIPES FOR TREATMENT

In 1989, the American Psychiatric Association published its long-awaited 3000-page, four-volume *Treatments of Psychiatric Disorders*. This work was meant to accompany the DSM system of evaluation, and it outlined what experts suggest as the best current therapeutic interventions for each mental disorder. The book described the characteristics of each mental condition and then explained which part of the problem is best treated by drugs, suggesting an appropriate dosage, and which part is most amenable to psychotherapy, indicating which psychotherapy is best and how long the treatment should last. The book also listed alternative treatments and took into consideration individual factors such as the patient's age and personality. In its conception, it seemed like a fine idea—a compendium of treatments telling how and when to apply them. Similar books dealing with physical diseases have been very successful. But was it too soon to try something like this for mental illness and its therapies? Was mental illness too poorly defined and were its therapies still too much of an art and too little of a science? Perhaps so, because the outcry was immediate.

Opponents straightaway expressed concerns that the manual would curb the development of new or alternative kinds of care, pointing out that if it had been written 40 years ago, it would have inhibited practitioners from trying anything on their patients other than ECT or psychosurgery. Psychologists, who are not M.D.'s and therefore cannot write prescriptions, were especially concerned that so much reliance was placed on psychopharmacology. They pointed out that much research has shown that psychotherapy is often as effective as somatic therapies.

Other fears were expressed as well. Among them were the worries that rigid instructors might treat the book as gospel or that it might lead to problems in the courtroom. For example, suppose a therapist wanted to treat depression in a way *other* than those listed as "best" by the book. If her client committed suicide, would she be liable for malpractice because she had not followed the advice of the "experts"? Such a concern might keep a therapist who had considerable adeptness in, for instance, transactional analysis, from using her skill with that technique to treat depression simply because "the book" didn't list that treatment as one of her choices. This problem was especially irksome for many practitioners because therapy is still so much of an art that it often appears to defy scientific analysis. In the words of one professional, "[The book makes] a rather arrogant presumption that a consensus opinion by psychiatrists is tantamount to what the 'experts say' and should be considered *the* standard for mental health treatment" ("Treatment Book," 1989, p. 19).

The treatment guide is currently used by many practitioners, but the controversy continues. The American Psychiatric Association has now added a disclaimer stating that the book is not officially endorsed by the association itself, but merely by the association's task force who assembled it.

This controversy demonstrates clearly that therapy for the mentally ill is an evolving process, how little we really know about it, and how far we have to go. Once we have mastered the formidable challenge of mental illness—perhaps centuries from now—such a book will be on every practitioner's shelf, and there will be little controversy because we will finally know how best to treat such disorders. Until then, trained professionals—practicing artists, researchers, and experimenters—will be rewriting the book daily.

🔀 MISDIAGNOSIS

Sometimes patients are assessed inadequately, and important symptoms are overlooked or ignored. In such cases, having well-defined assessment categories doesn't help much, because the patient's difficulties are not being rigorously addressed. Researchers, wondering how often such misdiagnosis is likely to occur, have looked into the problem. One investigation examined 100 psychiatric patients. All the patients had originally been examined at a large psychiatric reception center, to which they had been brought by their families or by the police under mental-health warrants. All were to be committed to state mental hospitals after the examination. When they volunteered to be part of the investigation, they were taken to a special clinical research ward instead. There they were given intensive physical and psychological tests. The physicians found that 46 of the 100 patients had medical illnesses that had gone undiagnosed and that probably either were the cause of their psychiatric symptoms or had exacerbated them considerably. Another 34 had previously undiagnosed physical illnesses that were not directly related to their psychiatric symptoms.

Once the underlying medical problem was treated, 61 percent recovered rapidly and their abnormal behavior disappeared. Among the medical problems that had been missed by those who had initially examined the patients were Addison's disease (an insufficiency of adrenalin, which can result in irritability, depression, and emotional instability); arsenic poisoning (from dust and paint chips in old houses); Wilson's disease (an inability to metabolize copper properly, which can lead to irritability, depression, emotional instability, high-pitched voice, and trembling); lead intoxication (from water running through old pipes and from paint dust); vitamin deficiency; and other dietary deficiencies. The number of physical illnesses discovered wasn't surprising, since the patients were mainly from the poorer areas of the city and had not received adequate routine medical care (Hall, Stickney, LeCann, & Popkin, 1980). The researchers believed that these 100 patients were generally representative of the population typically committed to a state mental hospital. They concluded that there was a serious failure to test incoming psychiatric patients properly for physical disorders and that the legal implications of this failure were profound. The medical tests given each patient by the researchers cost an average of only $400. A follow-up study at Baylor College of Medicine uncovered similar diagnostic oversights (Muecke & Krueger, 1981). Considering the general lack of funds available for the poor and needy, it is suspected that this problem has gotten worse since that time.

These kinds of oversights are, unfortunately, all too common when elderly patients are assessed, because physicians faced with signs of mental deterioration often respond, "Well, what do you expect, they're old." In fact, the difficulty might be treatable if only a proper and full medical workup were done (Kolata, 1987d).

Sometimes, the overlooked problem may even have a simple solution. For instance, some patients' mental disorders are made much worse by severe visual disorders that can often be treated with glasses or special ophthalmological intervention. Once treated, the symptoms often lessen significantly or even go away (Flach & Kaplan, 1983).

The following case study illustrates the problem of misdiagnosis.

THE ASSESSMENT OF PSYCHOPATHOLOGY: THE CASE OF CAROL T.

Carol T. was born in 1946; her troubles began in the summer of 1971. One day, she felt shaky and her mouth felt a little tight. Then, without warning, she fainted while at work. When she went to see her family doctor, he said she was overtired and gave her Valium (diazepam), a tranquilizer. One morning, at the end of July, Carol T. felt a strange compulsion and for no apparent reason, she went into the bathroom, took a razor, and slashed her wrists. She survived. Two days later, she was given a psychiatric consultation. She spent 1 month in a psychiatric hospital and was given Thorazine (chlorpromazine), an antipsychotic drug. Carol then entered psychotherapy. For the next few years, she was in and out of mental hospitals and saw many different psychiatrists. She was given electroshock therapy, more antipsychotic drugs, and L-dopa, a drug to control Parkinson's disease because she had begun to shake. Still her symptoms got worse. She couldn't tie her shoes, open a jar, comb her hair, or write. She could hardly chew or swallow. She began to limp, lost her balance, and occasionally fell. Then she had trouble speaking, her voice became higher, and her speech became slurred. At that point, she was diagnosed as suffering from conversion disorder and was transferred to a community mental-health center. There, one of the staff doctors just happened to stop in to see her. He took one look at Carol's eyes and recognized the copper-colored rings around her corneas as Kayser-Fleischer rings. These rings are an unmistakable sign of Wilson's disease. They are evidence of the actual buildup of copper in the body. The doctor said, "She was practically a textbook presentation. I think my secretaries could have made the diagnosis" (Roueche, 1980, p. 357). Carol was immediately placed on drugs to help leach the excess copper from her body. She is now fully recovered from the disease that would have cost her life had the doctor not spotted it.

One of the most difficult disorders to assess is schizophrenia. Although the DSM-IV diagnostic criteria are fairly clear, these criteria can sometimes be satisfied by the early onset of disorders other than schizophrenia. For example, disordered and bizarre thinking is not unique to schizophrenia (Harrow & Quinlan, 1977), and hallucinations can occur in other disorders (Fitzgerald & Wells, 1977) and can even be experienced by otherwise normal individuals (Bentall, 1990). Adding to the problem is the fact that over half of those diagnosed as schizophrenic have learned to fake some or all of their symptoms and to mask others in order to be admitted to hospitals or to help lengthen or shorten their hospital stay (Martin, Hunter, & Moore, 1977; Pope, Jonas, & Jones, 1982). As you can see, diagnostic assessment takes skill, knowledge, and experience. It is anything but simple.

◆◇ SUMMARY

◆ Therapeutic attempts to alleviate mental disorders are perhaps as old as humankind. Stone Age people resorted to trephining to help evil spirits escape the mind.

◆ During the Greek and Roman eras, treatment of mental disorders was often combined with attempts to bring about magical cures.

◆ During the Middle Ages, a rational view of mental disorders was replaced by religious demonology.

◆ Early reforms of mental institutions began after the French Revolution and continued through the nineteenth century. Today, many people are still treated in hospitals or in special institutions for the mentally ill.

◆ By the mid-1800s, physicians began to realize that abnormal behavior could result from damage to the brain and nervous system.

◆ Somatic therapies directly interact with the body and its chemistry. They include psychopharmacological, electroconvulsive, and psychosurgical procedures.

◆ Four major classes of drugs are used in psychopharmacology: antipsychotic drugs, antidepressants, antimanic drugs, and antianxiety drugs.

◆ Tardive dyskinesia, an involuntary twitching of the body or facial muscles, can result from long-term use of antipsychotic drugs.

◆ In electroconvulsive therapy, an 80- to 90-volt electric shock is administered to the brain, causing a convulsion. It has been used to treat depression and other disorders, but how it works is unknown, and its use is controversial.

◆ Psychosurgery is the destruction of a region of the brain for the purpose of alleviating severe psychiatric disorders. The frontal lobotomy, which became popular in the 1930s and 1940s, has been criticized for causing irreparable injury to the brain and producing only mixed results. Modern psychosurgical techniques are less dangerous and destroy less tissue.

◆ Deinstitutionalization is the practice in which mental patients are assigned to community mental-health centers or seen on an outpatient basis. Because the program receives insufficient funding, however, patients may not be given adequate care outside the institution.

◆ Psychotherapy is a noninvasive psychological therapy designed to bring about a positive change in someone's behavior, personality, or adjustment. Psychotherapy can be divided into insight therapies, which emphasize developing awareness and understanding, and action therapies, which focus directly on changing a habit or problem. Psychotherapies can be further divided into directive therapies, in which the therapist guides the client, and nondirective therapies, in which the client is primarily responsible for the direction of the therapy.

◆ Psychoanalysis is a therapy based on the work of Sigmund Freud. Psychoanalysts assume that abnormal behavior is the result of unconscious conflicts. They use various techniques, including free association and dream interpretation, to uncover these conflicts.

◆ In humanistic-existential therapies, people are considered capable of living rich and satisfying lives. The emphasis is on fulfilling their potential, or self-actualizing.

◆ Carl Rogers developed a client-centered therapy in which the therapist refrains from guiding the therapy but provides unconditional positive regard for the client. The client is responsible for the direction the therapy takes.

◆ Existential therapists argue that people must learn to accept responsibility, make choices for themselves, and control their environment rather than allowing it to control them.

◆ Rational-emotive therapy is an action therapy based on the assumption that people engage in self-defeating behaviors because they hang on to beliefs that are unrealistic or faulty.

◆ Gestalt therapy is an insight therapy based heavily on Freudian psychoanalytic ideas. The ultimate goal of Gestalt therapy is to balance and integrate emotion, thought, and action.

◆ One of the earliest group therapies was psychodrama. Following the Second World War, group therapy became more popular. Many therapists have found that group therapy is beneficial.

◆ During sensitivity training, participants learn to become sensitive to others' needs and feelings and to trust other people.

◆ In encounter groups, individuals confront one another in an attempt to break through defenses and false fronts.

◆ In family therapy, the family is treated together as a whole unit.

◆ Behavior therapy relies on learning theory and the principles of conditioning. Each therapeutic treatment deals with a specific problem. Important techniques include aversive conditioning, systematic desensitization, operant techniques, token economies, behavior contracts, and social modeling.

◆ Cognitive therapy is a treatment in which the client is helped to obtain information about himself through a series of unbiased encounters that disprove false thoughts and beliefs.

◆ Modern clinicians use hypnotherapy in a number of important ways. Hypnotherapy can intensify the memory of past emotions and events, can be used in conjunction with behavior therapy, is useful in controlling pain, and is effective for the treatment of dissociative disorders.

◆ Researchers are divided on whether psychotherapy is effective. Most research indicates that it is effective to some degree.

◆ Physical diseases may exacerbate behavioral problems, and many behavioral problems may be the result of misdiagnosed or undiagnosed physical ailments.

◆ Like physical disorders, mental disorders are subject to misdiagnosis. Diagnostic assessment takes skill, knowledge, and experience. It is anything but simple.

SUGGESTIONS FOR FURTHER READING

1. Beers, C. (1908). *A mind that found itself.* New York: Longmans, Green. A classic account of one man's descent into psychosis and his rehabilitation early in this century. Contains one of the earliest descriptions of the mental institution as a place where occasional recovery is achieved despite inconsistent and in some cases inhumane treatment. This historically significant book had a profound effect on the nation's understanding of mental illness and is still very readable and interesting.

2. Gorman, J. M. (1990). *The essential guide to psychiatric drugs.* New York: St. Martin's Press. Dosages, uses, and side effects of psychiatric drugs. Includes advice on choosing a psychiatrist.

3. Papolos, D. F., & Papolos, J. (1988). *Overcoming depression.* New York: Harper & Row. An exploration of depression and mania for the general reader. Includes a discussion of the medications used to treat mood disorders, their benefits and complications.

4. Smith, M. C. (1991). *A social history of the minor tranquilizers: The quest for small comfort in the age of anxiety.* New York: Haworth Press. The development, promo-

tion, use, and abuse of the minor tranquilizers, from the 1950s through the early 1980s, is discussed by a professor of health care administration.

5. Valenstein, E. S. (1987). *Great and desperate cures: The rise and decline of psychosurgery and other radical treatments for mental illness*. New York: Basic Books. For the student, general reader, or professional, a discussion of the history of, and controversies surrounding, psychosurgery and other controversial therapies for mental illness.

6. Yalom, I. D. (1990). *Love's executioner: and other tales of psychotherapy*. New York: Basic Books. A discussion of 10 patients in therapy by the psychotherapist who treated them. Highlights the art and uncertainty of the therapeutic process.

7. Yudofsky, S., Hales, R. E., & Ferguson, T. (1992). *What you need to know about psychiatric drugs*. New York: Ballantine. A good compendium of psychiatric drugs. Also includes discussions about why certain drugs are prescribed for certain disorders and which nondrug alternatives might be available.

Chapter Eighteen

Social Psychology

PROLOGUE

SOCIAL PRESSURE

In the early 1950s, psychologist Solomon Asch conducted what has since been regarded as a classic experiment. Asch was interested in conformity and devised an experiment involving nine people. Eight of the "subjects" were secretly confederates of Asch's; only the ninth person was the real subject of the experiment.

As the experiment began, everyone was shown three comparison lines. Each line was obviously a different length. Then a standard line was placed alongside the comparison lines (see Figure 18.1), and Asch asked all the subjects (the real subject and the eight confederates) which line in the comparison group was the same length as the standard line. The real subject was asked last. All the confederates had been told to lie: They picked the medium-length line, a line that didn't match the standard line.

Asch was interested in how the real subject would respond. The experiment was especially interesting because the shorter comparison line that the confederates chose was so obviously different that it would be reasonable to assume that no one would select it. You might even think that the real subject would guess that the other eight people were confederates or perhaps think that they were all crazy. Nobody with normal eyesight could possibly agree that the standard line was the same length as the shorter comparison line the confederates had selected.

But one by one, as subjects were led through this procedure, 75 percent of them went along with the group and agreed that the shorter line was the same length as the standard (Asch, 1951).

Afterward, Asch explained the experiment to the subjects and questioned them. He asked them if they could in fact tell that everyone else was wrong when they said that the shorter line equaled the standard line. Amazingly, the subjects said that they had known that the other people were wrong!

When they were asked "Then why did you agree with them?" the subjects typically responded, "I don't know." or "I didn't want to rock the boat, I just wanted to go along."

CONTENTS

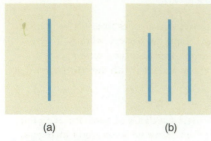

◆ FIGURE 18.1

The stimulus cards used in Asch's experiment. The subjects were required to match the standard line on card (a) with the line of the same length on card (b) (After Asch, 1951).

The more we think about the results of Asch's experiment, the more disturbing it becomes. He had discovered that many people would rather go against the evidence of their own eyes than openly disagree with the unanimous judgment of even a small group of people (Asch, 1951; Wheeler, Deci, Reis, & Zuckerman, 1978).

IN THIS CHAPTER, we'll examine many of the ways in which people influence one another. We'll take a look at the factors determining obedience, the effects that groups have on their members, and the ways in which our attitudes can be changed by those around us. We'll also study other areas of interest to social psychologists, such as competition and cooperation, conformity, helping others, moral behavior, and prejudice.

WHY PSYCHOLOGISTS STUDY SOCIAL BEHAVIOR

Except for extremely rare instances, no human being lives in total social isolation. Each of us interacts with other people. Social psychology is the study of how people affect the behavior, thoughts, and feelings of others.

If you were told that you had to give up something in your life, probably the last thing you or anyone would choose to surrender would be the company of others. Most of us would rather live in a cave with other people than in a mansion with no hope of ever seeing another person. Other people are such a common element in our lives that we rarely consider what it would be like without them. They affect us, they shape us, they influence what we think and feel and do. We, in turn, influence them. Social psychologists study how groups behave and how being a member of a group or society affects individuals.

INTERPERSONAL INFLUENCE

Groups can influence our behavior in important ways. Among the most important kinds of social influences are conformity and obedience.

Social psychology is the study of the effects of groups and social interaction on behavior.

Conformity

As you learned in the Prologue, the tendency to conform can be very strong. Asch demonstrated that we may conform even if it means disavowing the evidence of our own eyes. Still, a degree of **conformity** is important in any society. Without it, there would be chaos. The ways in which other people expect us to conform are known as **social norms.**

Some social norms are explicit and may even be spelled out: "No parking," "No smoking in this section," "Shirts and shoes must be worn in this establishment." Other social norms are unspoken and unwritten, but they still influence our behavior. For example, there is probably no functional reason for someone to attend a business meeting dressed in a suit rather than a sweatshirt, except that it is an unspoken social norm and is expected. There are many unspoken social rules, such as waiting your turn in line, shaking hands when you first meet someone, and not staring at strangers.

WHY PEOPLE CONFORM. Conformity is common, and people probably have two major reasons for conforming. First, they often are reinforced for conforming. Since childhood, we have been reinforced for adopting the "correct" beliefs and behaviors of our parents, guardians, and teachers. Even as adults, we often are reinforced for acting like other people. Because we are reinforced for conforming so often and under so many different circumstances, our conformity tends to generalize to new situations.

The second important force behind conformity may be our tendency for **social comparison.** We commonly compare ourselves with other people, especially those who are like us, as a way of assessing the accuracy of our attitudes, feelings, and beliefs. We like to view ourselves as rational and correct in our views. Consequently, people who rely heavily on social comparison may find it difficult not to change in the direction of conformity (Bleda & Castore, 1973; Fazio, 1979).

Someone who is very different from the other members of a group may make the group feel uncomfortable because he disrupts the group's stable basis for comparison. The group usually tries to force the individual to change. If it fails, the person who is viewed as deviant may be rejected.

REFERENCE GROUPS. Will a mathematician who hears that most sailors have tattoos want one also? If you read in an advertisement that all the "im-

CONFORMITY
Action that results from social pressure to comply with social norms. When people conform, they act or behave in correspondence with current customs, rules, or styles.

SOCIAL NORMS
Shared standards of behavior accepted by and expected from group members.

SOCIAL COMPARISON
Assessment of the accuracy of our own attitudes, feelings, or beliefs by comparing them with those of others.

Although the pressure to conform may be strong, some struggle against it.

REFERENCE GROUP
A group with which we identify and that we use as our standard of behavior.

portant people" of Norway vacation at a particular resort, will you want to go there, too? In both cases, the pressure to conform is small. Just because a particular group engages in a certain behavior does not necessarily mean that other people will want to do the same or will use that group for purposes of social comparison. Instead, we generally look to people we are like, or wish to be like, in making decisions about how we will conform. Social psychologists refer to such groups as **reference groups.** The norms of reference groups tend to be perpetuated because each new member who joins is under pressure to conform and to maintain the group's standards.

Much of the research on conformity grew out of a desire to understand the social forces that were at work in Nazi Germany. Could you have been a member of the Nazi party? Could you have joined in the mass rallies and their persecutions? The students of Ron Jones's high school history class in California didn't think that they would have gone along with the Nazi movement had they lived in Germany at the time. They believed that they would have resisted. To help his class understand more fully the social forces that affected the Germans, Jones had the class simulate some of the German experience with Nazism for 5 days. To his horror, the pretend game became all too real, and a Nazi-like system of beliefs and control took root among his students and throughout the school (Jones, 1978).

What Jones had done to bring this about was quite simple. He began by limiting all answers in class to three words or less. Soon, new nonverbal leaders emerged. A Nazi-like salute was then incorporated, and slogans such as "strength through community" were shouted in unison. Banners were made, new recruits were enlisted from the rest of the school, and mandatory sitting postures were introduced. The group called itself the Third Wave. From Jones's small class, the group grew to over 100 members, and membership cards were issued. The better students often were thrown out of the class by the others. Once these "deviants" were purged, social comparison helped to strengthen conformity.

Jones decided to tell the Third Wave that they were part of a national organization of students who wanted political change. He emphasized that they were a special group and that they had been selected to help the cause. In this way, he reinforced their conformity.

Jones told the students that the next day a candidate for president of the United States would announce the formation of a national Third Wave. He

Adolescents feel a special need to conform with their reference group.

invited them to view the speech on the television monitor in the school auditorium. The following day, some 250 students filed into the auditorium wearing special uniforms and homemade armbands. Muscular student guards stood at the door, while others, enlisted by Jones to help, pretended to be photographers and reporters and circulated among the crowd. This added charade helped the students to believe that they were about to become part of a nationwide movement. The students stood, rank upon rank, straight and proud. As they waited for the announcement, Jones began to show a movie of the Nazi rally at Nuremberg and the history of the Third Reich. The students just stood there, blankly watching what appeared to be an eerie reflection of themselves.

Afterward, Jones explained to the students what had been going on and how they had been manipulated. He predicted that they would never admit to having been part of this madness, to having been tricked into being followers of a "Nazi" movement. His prediction appears to be accurate, for few students wish to talk about that time. In 5 short days, seemingly healthy, normal students at Cubberley High School in California had banded together, purged their ranks of "intellectuals," and were ready to follow the orders of a national leader. They had even begun to take pride in relying on coercion and discrimination as means to an unknown end. They may never again have a lesson in history or social psychology of such importance and magnitude.

Look around you. Whom do you admire? What are your reference groups? How have you changed your behavior to conform to their standards? What are their goals, and are these goals that you desire? Of course, most conformity is innocuous. Conforming by wearing a shiny silk blazer when you're part of a bowling league is hardly the same as marching to the cadence of the Third Reich. And yet, as you may have begun to sense, there are similarities. In both cases, there is pressure to be part of the group and to demonstrate appropriate behaviors to new members.

Obedience

Although it's possible to get a group of high school students to conform to Nazi-like values and beliefs, it's still a long way from there to the death camps

Nazis on trial in Nuremberg, November 25, 1945. Hermann Goering, Rudolf Hess, General Joachin von Ribbentrop, and General Wilhelm Keitel are shown in the front row.

OBEDIENCE
The willingness to follow commands or instructions.

and the murder of millions of people. Or is it? During the Nuremberg trials, in which the Nazi war criminals were brought to account, one phrase was heard so often that it has come to be associated with the German underlings even by people who are not old enough to remember the Second World War. The phrase is, "I was just following orders." As the court records show, this excuse was not well received. The lowest-ranking officers, it was conceded, might possibly use such an excuse. But certainly the higher-ranking officers had a choice.

THE MILGRAM EXPERIMENT.   In the early 1960s, social psychologist Stanley Milgram investigated **obedience** in a study that is now considered a classic. Milgram began by using students from Yale University as subjects and later expanded his research to include a cross section of people of different ages, occupations, and educational levels.

Two subjects were ushered into an experimental room and were told that they were part of an investigation to test the effects of punishment, in the form of an electric shock, on memory. An experimenter, dressed in a white lab coat, would oversee the experiment. The subjects would draw lots to find out who would be the "learner" and who would be the "teacher." Unknown to the real subject, the other subject, "Mr. Wallace," a gentle-looking, friendly 50-year-old man, was really an actor working for Milgram. The lots were rigged so that the real subject would be assigned the role of teacher.

The teacher was given a sample shock of 45 volts to find out what it would feel like—it stung. The learner, Mr. Wallace, was then strapped into the electric chair as the subject chosen to be the teacher watched. The teacher-subject was then taken into an adjacent room and put in front of an array of switches ranging from "Slight shock, 15 volts," to "Danger: severe shock, 450 volts." The learner was instructed to repeat a list of words. Every time he made an error, the teacher was to administer a shock, starting with the lowest level and gradually increasing. The actor playing the role of learner had been given a script to follow for each voltage level, since the teacher would be able to hear him from the next room. As the shock level rose, the learner would begin to protest. The stronger the shock, the louder he would protest. At 75 volts he would moan; at 150 volts he would demand to be released from the chair. At 180 volts he would yell that he could no longer stand the pain. At 300 volts he would protest that he had a heart condition and begin to scream. If the teacher complained at any time, the experimenter would say, "Teacher, you have no other choice; you must go on!" (Milgram, 1963, p. 374). After the 300-volt level, it was planned that there would be an ominous silence from the learner's room, as though he were unconscious or even dead. Unknown to the teacher, the learner received no real shocks.

Milgram's aim was to find out how much pressure to obey the experimenter in the lab coat would create when he said, "Teacher, you have no other choice; you must go on!" How far would subjects go under these circumstances? Before conducting the experiment, Milgram interviewed 40 psychiatrists, describing the procedure you have just read. He asked them to estimate the behavior of most subjects. The psychiatrists agreed that the majority would not go beyond 150 volts, and that perhaps only one in a thousand—those who were very deviant or sadistic—would go all the way to 450 volts. How far would you have gone?

To everyone's horror, when the experiment was conducted, 62 percent of the teacher-subjects went all the way to 450 volts! None of them seemed to enjoy it. For example, after delivering 180 volts, one subject said,

He can't stand it! I'm not going to kill that man in there. You hear him hollering? He's hollering. He can't stand it. What if something happens to him? . . . I mean, who

Stanley Milgram (1933–1984).

In this variation of the Milgram experiment, a teacher-subject forces the learner's arm onto the electric plate. (Photos (c) 1965 by Stanley Milgram from the film Obedience, *distributed by the New York University Film Library.)*

is going to take the responsibility if anything happens to that gentleman? (Milgram, 1965a, p. 67)

At that point, the experimenter said that he would take responsibility. The subject replied, "All right," and continued delivering shocks.

Of the 38 percent of the subjects who were not willing to go to 450 volts, many went to high levels (see Figure 18.2). All who refused to continue simply walked out of the experiment. Not one of them tried to see how Mr. Wallace was. Interestingly, the personality tests that were administered to the subjects failed to reveal any differences between the subjects who obeyed and those who refused.

VARIABLES INFLUENCING OBEDIENCE. Social psychologists have identified at least three variables in this experiment that may help to explain the high rate of obedience. First, a legitimate authority, the experimenter, was present and was willing to take responsibility. Second, the victim was in another room, and this distance may have lessened the teacher's stress by eliminating the need to see the learner's anguish. Third, the teacher-subject accepted the subordinate role, applying all the rules the subject had ever learned about being a good follower. Perhaps, as social psychologist Philip

The percentage of subjects who delivered shock at different voltage levels in Milgram's experiment. Approximately two-thirds of the subjects continued to 450 volts despite the screaming protests of the learner. No subject discontinued shock before the 300-volt level. (SOURCE: Adapted from Milgram, 1963.)

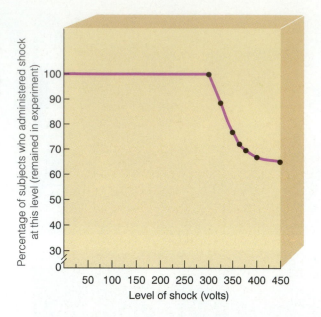

Zimbardo has suggested, such follower training in public situations begins on the first day of school, when the teacher says, "Stay in your seat no matter what" (Zimbardo, 1979).

It should be stressed that obedience does not happen only under these select conditions. Even if the learner is directly in front of the teacher-subject, the latter may still obey. In a variation of the Milgram experiment, the teacher-subject actually had to force the learner's hand down onto an electric shock plate. Obedience under these conditions, although less frequent, was still much higher than anyone had predicted.

By today's standards, the Milgram experiment might not be considered ethical because of the stress placed on the teacher-subject. Some of the subjects were shaking and weeping as they pressed the 450-volt lever. How do you debrief such a subject after the experiment? Do you say, "Don't feel bad—the learner is only an actor. I just wanted to see if you would electrocute a stranger simply because I told you to." No serious aftereffects were observed among the teacher-subjects, but even after a careful debriefing many felt that they had discovered an evil side of themselves. Some of the volunteer experimenters who helped Milgram to conduct the research were called to account by university authorities, who asked why they had continued the experiment when they could plainly see that the teacher-subjects were under stress. Their frightening answer: "Milgram told us to!"

The Milgram findings are not specific to the United States. Similar results have been obtained in many other countries, including Germany and Australia (Kilham & Mann, 1974; Mantell, 1971). The same results were found even among three groups of children, aged 7, 11, and 15 years, who were ordered to shock an innocent victim (Shanab & Yahya, 1977).

A further variation of the experiment demonstrated that Milgram's results were due to the subjects' desire to be obedient rather than to any hidden sadistic pleasure they got from shocking the learner. In this study, 42 boys, aged 13 and 14 years, were asked to take part in an experiment in which they simultaneously were both the teacher and the learner. This was accomplished by giving the boys earphones to wear that would produce a high-pitched sound when they pressed buttons on the teacher's console. Whenever they made a mistake, they administered this sound to themselves. Although the tone was not actually dangerous, they were told they might suffer a 50 percent hearing loss. Using an experimental procedure similar to Milgram's, the researchers found that the subjects were willing to follow orders even though they believed they might injure themselves (Martin, Lobb, Chapman, & Spillane, 1976).

Conformity and Obedience

As you might imagine, once social psychologists discovered variables that influenced conformity and variables that influenced obedience, they wanted to see how these variables interrelated.

As an example of research in this area, let's consider another variation of the Milgram experiment that uses one learner and three teacher-subjects. Only one of the teacher-subjects is a real subject, however. Unknown to that individual, the other two teacher-subjects, as well as the learner, are actors. In this variation, the confederate teacher-subjects disobey. The first of the actors disobeys the experimenter at 150 volts and leaves. The second actor defies the experimenter at 225 volts and leaves. The real subject is then left alone to continue following orders. Under these circumstances, the real subject can use the other two "subjects" for social comparison. As it turned out, after the two actors defied the experimenter, only about 12 percent of the real subjects remained and went all the way to 450 volts (see Figure 18.3) (Milgram, 1965b). Conversely, if the two actors both argued for more shock, all the way to 450 volts, the real subject was more likely to obey than were the single teacher-subjects in the original experiment.

The Jonestown tragedy vividly demonstrated the potential consequences of conformity and blind obedience to authority. In 1978, almost 900 members of the California-based People's Temple died in a ritual mass suicide in Jonestown, Guyana, at the command of their leader, Reverend Jim Jones. Jones believed that his communal group was under attack from the outside by forces bent on destroying it. (This outside force was, in reality, nothing more than one congressman, Leo Ryan, who had come to the South American country to make sure that the people from his California district were all right and who was leaving with 14 of them who had asked to go home with him.) After Jones's men had murdered the congressman and several of his party, Jones ordered his followers to kill themselves by taking cyanide. The mass death shocked the world and left people wondering how such a tragedy could have happened.

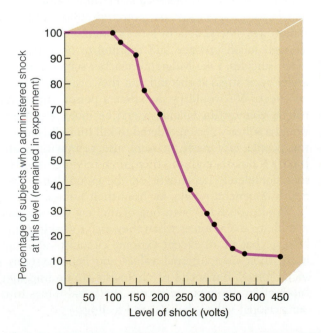

◆ **FIGURE 18.3**

The percentage of subjects who delivered shock at different voltage levels in the repeat of Milgram's experiment when two other "subjects" disobeyed the researcher's request to shock the learner. The group pressure in this case allowed the subject to discontinue the shocks sooner. Only 12 percent went all the way to 450 volts. (SOURCE: Adapted from Milgram, 1965b.)

Aftermath of the tragedy at Jonestown.

MORALS
The attitudes and beliefs that people hold that help them to determine what is right or wrong.

Although a few members disobeyed Jones and ran into the jungle, most complied. The final tape recordings of Jonestown are horrifying to hear. The people went to their self-administered deaths crying and screaming for help. Most were not happy to die, which makes their deaths even more incomprehensible.

Now that you have learned something about conformity and obedience, you may begin to appreciate the powerful influences that were in force that day in Jonestown. The people in Jones's community were followers; they had learned through much practice and training to obey their leader, even carrying out mock suicides. Like Milgram's teacher-subjects, many of them cried and were under great stress at the end, but they obeyed. Social comparison certainly had an effect. We would predict that a person surrounded by hundreds of other people committing suicide would be much more likely to do the same than would a solitary person ordered to kill himself (Latane, 1981). By their actions, the people in Jonestown were also complying with reference group norms. Jones's followers had no other group to which they could refer. Not only were they completely dependent on the group, but they were isolated in a dense South American jungle, far from their homes.

Would you have been one of the few who escaped? It's easy to feel invulnerable to social forces when they aren't working directly on you. Most people believe that in all except extreme circumstances, such as a gun held to their head, their own internal values and belief systems would override external social forces. But social psychologists are finding that this is, in fact, a rarity. More often the opposite is true: the social forces turn out to be stronger than our personal values, beliefs, and feelings.

THE DEVELOPMENT OF MORALITY

As you have discovered, some people will conform to the standards of Nazi-like groups, obey orders to harm another person, or refuse to help someone in need. Other people will not conform or obey and will willingly give aid. The data presented in this chapter so far have indicated that situational factors determine a person's conformity, obedience, or desire to help. On the other hand, many psychologists believe that morality is not just situationally dependent, but is an integral part of an individual's personality. A moral person, they argue, will be less likely to harm another or to refuse to give aid than will an amoral person, regardless of the situational factors. During the last two decades, psychologists have examined the development of morals in an effort to learn how much of people's morality is subject to situational factors.

Morals are the attitudes and beliefs a person holds that help him to determine what is right or wrong. Some researchers have come to believe that moral reasoning progresses through a series of stages as the individual is influenced by the reasoning of other people. Researcher Lawrence Kohlberg (1963, 1971) postulated six stages in the development of morality. According to Kohlberg, moral development begins in childhood with an orientation to obey in order to avoid punishment, and it may end with the emergence of concern for reciprocity among individuals and a sense of universal justice.

Kohlberg devised an assessment tool for determining the stage of moral development an individual has reached. Individuals are presented with a moral dilemma. The reasoning they use to resolve the dilemma indicates how advanced their moral thinking is. Table 18.1 gives an example of one of these moral dilemmas. For each stage, actual answers have been provided that demonstrate the kinds of reasoning involved. The statements in the left column describe, in general terms, the quality of moral reasoning that defines each stage. As you can see, there are no right or wrong answers: Each stage is value-free. A person's position in the stages is determined not by whether the answers are right or wrong according to some value system, but by the kind of moral reasoning used to make the choice.

According to Kohlberg, each stage is built on the previous stage. More advanced stages of moral thinking reorganize the earlier stages in a way that furnishes the person with new criteria and perspectives for making moral judgments (Hoffman, 1979; Walker, de Vries, & Bichard, 1984). Kohlberg assumed that children begin at the first stage. As they interact with other people, they may progress through each stage, but they never skip a stage.

Kohlberg's most recent investigations, made just before his death, indicated that no clear distinction could be made between stages 5 and 6 (Colby, Kohlberg, Gibbs, & Lieberman, 1983). For this reason, stage 6 has been dropped from the current assessment procedures. Even so, Kohlberg believed that many people never reach the final stage. In fact, most people do not seem to develop much beyond stage 4 (Shaver & Strong, 1976). The third and fourth stages are therefore called the conventional stages, since they represent the stages reached by most adults.

In Kohlberg's view, people advance to a higher stage of moral development by exposure to other people's moral reasoning that is more advanced than their own. This social interaction places a person in a conflict that can be resolved only by accepting the more advanced stage of moral reasoning.

Psychologist David Rosenhan (1973) used Kohlberg's assessment techniques to measure different individuals' stages of moral thinking. Afterward, he placed these individuals in the role of the teacher-subject in a replication of Milgram's famous shock experiment, which you read about earlier. Even some subjects who scored at stage 6 when taking the moral dilemma tests went all the way to 450 volts when shocking the learner. Furthermore, they were unable to give a reason for doing so that would accord with the universal principles supposedly possessed by someone at the sixth stage of moral development. The subjects at stage 6 were, however, less likely to continue up to 450 volts than were these subjects at Kohlberg's stage 1.

Although Kohlberg's theory presents a well-organized description of how moral development may occur, it has been strongly criticized for a number of reasons. Its most serious problem may be that it correlates poorly with moral behavior. Although teacher-subjects at stage 6 were less likely to shock learners than were those at stage 1, whether people will choose to behave in a moral way often is more dependent on the immediate situational and social forces than on their stage of moral reasoning. This indicates that fostering a high level of moral reasoning may not bring about more moral behavior (Kurtines & Greif, 1974). Researchers also have argued that Kohlberg's theory is culturally biased in favor of Western ideas of what is morally "advanced" (Simpson, 1974; Hogan, 1975; Sampson, 1978) and that it is biased against women because all of Kohlberg's subjects were white, lower- and middle-class men, making it an inaccurate reflection of female moral reasoning (Gilligan, 1982). Still, Kohlberg's ideas have sparked an interest in how moral values emerge and how they may shape our behavior. Whether the sequential development of moral reasoning that Kohlberg discovered will eventually be considered an important part of development remains to be seen. For the moment, it certainly is intriguing.

TABLE 18.1 ◆ PRESENTATION OF A MORAL DILEMMA, WITH ANSWERS GRADED ACCORDING TO KOHLBERG'S SIX STAGES OF MORAL DEVELOPMENT

In Europe, a woman was near death from cancer. One drug might save her, a form of radium that a druggist in the same town had recently discovered. The druggist was charging $2000, 10 times what the drug cost him to make. The sick woman's husband, Heinz, went to everyone he knew to borrow the money, but he could get together only about half of what the drug cost. He told the druggist that his wife was dying and asked him to sell the drug for less money or to let him pay later. But the druggist said, "No." The husband got desperate and broke into the man's store to steal the drug for his wife. Should the husband have done that? Why or why not?

STAGE	PRO	CON
Preconventional Stages *Stage 1:* Punishment and obedience orientation (physical consequences determine what is good or bad).	He should steal the drug. It isn't really bad to take it. It isn't like he didn't ask to pay for it first. The drug he'd take is only worth $200; he's not really taking a $2000 drug.	He shouldn't steal the drug. It's a big crime. He didn't get permission, he used force and broke and entered. He did a lot of damage, stealing a very expensive drug and breaking up the store, too.
Stage 2: Instrumental relativist orientation (what satisfies one's own needs is good).	It's all right to steal the drug because she needs it and he wants her to live. It isn't that he wants to steal; it's the way he has to use to get the drug to save her.	He shouldn't steal it. The druggist isn't wrong or bad, he just wants to make a profit. That's what you're in business for, to make money.
Conventional Stages *Stage 3:* Interpersonal concordance or "good boy—nice girl" orientation (what pleases or helps others is good).	He should steal the drug. He was only doing something that was natural for a good husband to do. You can't blame him for doing something out of love for his wife; you'd blame him if he didn't love his wife enough to save her.	He shouldn't steal. If his wife dies, he can't be blamed. It isn't because he's heartless or that he doesn't love her enough to do everything that he legally can. The druggist is the selfish or heartless one.
Stage 4: "Law and order" orientation (maintaining the social order, doing one's duty is good).	He should steal the drug. If he did nothing he'd be letting his wife die, and it's his responsibility if she dies. He should take the drug with the intent of paying the druggist later.	It is a natural thing for Heinz to want to save his wife, but it's still always wrong to steal. He still knows he's stealing and taking a valuable drug from the man who made it.
Postconventional Stages *Stage 5:* Social contact—legalistic orientation (values agreed on by society including individual rights and rules for consensus, determine what is right).	The law wasn't set up for these circumstances. Taking the drug in this situation isn't really right, but doing it is justified.	You can't completely blame someone for stealing, but extreme circumstances don't really justify taking the law into your own hands. You can't have everyone stealing whenever they get desperate. The end may be good, but the ends don't justify the means.
Stage 6: Universal ethical-principle orientation (what is right is a matter of conscience in accord with universal principles).	This is a situation that forces him to choose between stealing and letting his wife die. In a situation where the choice must be made, it is morally right to steal. He has to act in terms of the principles of preserving and respecting life.	Heinz is faced with the decision of whether to consider the other people who need the drug just as badly as his wife. Heinz ought to act not according to his particular feelings toward his wife, but considering the value of all the lives involved.

SOURCES: Description of Kohlberg's stages from Shaver & Strong, 1976. Dilemma and pro and con answers adapted from Rest, 1968.

🧬 HELPING OTHERS

People do not always hurt each other or refuse to help someone in need in the way that the subjects in Milgram's experiment did. Sometimes people will go out of their way to help another or to prevent someone from being hurt; at other times they will not. Social psychologists believe that the situational forces present at any given moment play a major role in determining whether people will help in an emergency. To test this theory, social psychologists have studied the factors at play during real and "arranged" emergencies. The following incident stimulated great interest in this area of investigation.

One night in 1964, on Austin Street in Queens, New York, a woman named Kitty Genovese was stabbed to death. When her killer attacked her on the street, she screamed and fought with him. Her screams were so loud that they were heard by many people in apartments overlooking the street. Windows lighted up as the occupants awakened and looked outside to see what was happening; 38 presumably respectable and law-abiding citizens watched as she was stabbed. Their lights scared off the attacker. Kitty lay in the street, wounded but still alive. But when the people turned off their lights and went back to bed, the attacker struck again. Once again, he was scared off by people looking out their windows, and once again he returned when the lights went out. He finally stabbed her a third time, killing her. At no time during the entire attack did any of the 38 people call the police or an ambulance! The police were not called until after Kitty had died. Why hadn't these people helped? They didn't have to fight with the killer. They were safe in their homes and needed only to pick up the telephone. According to the newspapers, this was one more example of unfeeling city people with no concern for anyone but themselves. But was this the answer?

To shed a little light on what may have happened that night on Austin Street, let's examine an experiment by Darley and Latane conducted in 1968. The subjects were told that they would be taking part in a discussion about the kinds of problems students might face when they are away at college. On the pretext of maintaining anonymity, the students were isolated in separate cubicles; they could not see one another, and they could speak to each other only through an intercom. Each subject was led to believe that he or she would be participating in a discussion group that would include either one other student, two other students, or five others. Actually, the subject was the only student in the experiment. The other subjects were voices on a tape recorder.

To begin, each student was asked to give a short introductory statement describing himself or herself. During the introduction, one of the pretend students said that he was embarrassed by the fact that he occasionally had epileptic seizures. As the "discussion" got underway, this participant began to have what sounded like an epileptic seizure (recorded on the tape beforehand). What would the real subject do? When the subject believed that there was only one other participant and that he was having a seizure, the subject was very likely to summon or provide help. The more participants the subject believed were taking part in the discussion, however, the *less* likely he or she was to do anything. This tendency is known as the **bystander effect.** The bystander effect may have been responsible for the failure of the people on Austin Street to call for help when Kitty Genovese was being stabbed.

BYSTANDER EFFECT
People's tendency to ignore others who need help or situations that call for action. The effect is especially pronounced under crowded conditions.

Because of the bystander effect, this person may receive no help.

DIFFUSION OF RESPONSIBILITY
One possible reason for the bystander effect. When someone is observed to be in need of help and many people are around, individuals may believe that they need not act or give aid because they place the responsibility to act on other people in the crowd. They may think, for instance, "Someone else will surely help" or "Why should I have to be the one to help?"

What gives rise to the bystander effect? Most people assume that help is more likely to be given when more people see that it is needed, rather than the other way around. But social psychologists have found that the opposite is often true. There appear to be two reasons for the bystander effect: **diffusion of responsibility** and the fear of appearing foolish.

If you are the only person who sees a stranger in distress, and you know that you are the only one, then it is also apparent that if you take no action no help will be forthcoming. This perception places a burden of responsibility on you to act. However, if you know that many people besides yourself have seen the person in distress, then it becomes easy to assume that someone else will take action; it is no longer incumbent on you to do so. Many of the people who watched Kitty Genovese being stabbed also saw that others were watching. There may have been a great diffusion of responsibility, with everyone believing that someone else would do something. Or the witnesses may have thought that someone else should help and asked themselves, "Why me?" Ironically, had Kitty Genovese been in a more isolated place and been seen by a single witness, that person might have been more likely to call the police or to take some other action. In fact, research has shown that the more populated a place is, the *less* likely people are to help those they see in need, which may partly explain the fact that rural people are generally more willing to offer assistance than are urban people (Steblay, 1987).

Have you ever arrived at a bad car accident where there was a large crowd and wondered why the ambulance was taking so long to arrive? Perhaps you should have been wondering whether anyone had called an ambulance. Everyone may have assumed that someone must have called or thought it was someone else's responsibility to call. Think of diffusion of responsibility the next time you see someone in need and there are many witnesses. It may still be incumbent on you to act, if only to summon help.

The second reason for the bystander effect may be the fear of appearing foolish. Some situations are clearly emergencies; other situations are more ambiguous. In ambiguous situations, people often are reluctant to act because they are afraid of looking foolish should it turn out that there was no emergency. To test this assertion, two researchers had students fill out a questionnaire in a small room. The researchers weren't really interested in the student's responses to the questionnaire; instead, they wanted to see how the students would react to something unusual that began to happen. The room had a small vent. As the students worked on the questionnaire, smoke began to pour through the vent. The smoke came from a smoke generator run by the researchers.

The subjects in this experiment were assigned to one of three conditions. They filled out the questionnaire alone, in the presence of two other subjects, or in the presence of two confederates posing as subjects. In the last case, the confederates were told to do nothing when the smoke began to fill the room.

The students who were in the room alone had no reason to fear embarrassment or to interpret the smoke as anything but an emergency. The great majority of subjects in this condition responded by telling the person in the outer room what was happening. When two other subjects were in the room, the amount of action taken was drastically lessened (see Figure 18.4). As smoke began to filter in, the subjects would look at one another, each examining the others' reactions. For each subject, the situation became ambiguous because the others weren't reacting (each of them, of course, was waiting to see whether someone else would react). Not wishing to appear foolish by misinterpreting something as an emergency, many subjects failed to act. In the condition with the two confederates, the real subject was even less likely to act because the confederates gave no hint of concern (unlike some participants in the condition that used three real subjects). The confederates made the situation even more ambiguous. Rather than appear foolish by acting in a situation that might not be an emergency, the real subject would stay in the room as it filled with smoke and continue filling out the questionnaire (Latane & Darley, 1968).

In ambiguous situations, people are much less likely to help others than they are in obvious emergencies (Yakimovich & Saltz, 1971). For example, if an accident victim is seen to be bleeding, most people realize that the situation is not ambiguous and that help is absolutely required (Shotland & Huston, 1979). Researchers have also found that people are more likely to help if they are in familiar surroundings than if they are in an unfamiliar location, probably because unfamiliar surroundings heighten the ambiguity (Latane & Darley, 1970).

Latane and Darley (1970) created a bystander intervention model that delineates five steps a person must complete before she is likely to give help:

1. The event must be observed.
2. The event must be interpreted as an emergency.
3. The person must accept responsibility for helping.
4. The person must decide how to help.
5. The person must take action.

Other factors may affect the chances that a bystander will lend aid. Researchers Shirlynn Spacapan and Sheldon Cohen (1977) conducted an experiment with female students in which **task load** (how busy the subject was) and diffusion of responsibility were measured simultaneously. The women were divided into two groups. Those in the first group were required to go into a shopping mall and buy 26 items specified on a list within half an hour. Since this requirement would be relatively easy to carry out and the women would have time to spare, these subjects were considered the low-task group. The high-task group was required to buy 52 items within half an hour, a task that would take practically the whole time. Members of both groups were sent into the shopping mall during either crowded or uncrowded times.

The results demonstrated that how busy a person is and whether that person stands to lose something by helping may be as important a variable as diffusion of responsibility. In each instance, a "victim" asked the subject to help look for a lost contact lens. In the uncrowded low-task situation, 80 percent of the subjects stopped to look; in the crowded high-task situation, none did! In the

TASK LOAD
A measure of demand in terms of behavior required per unit of time. In conditions of high task load, there is much to do and little time to do it.

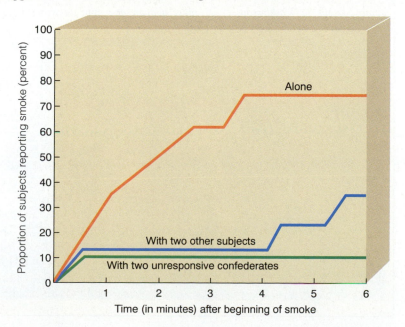

◆ **FIGURE 18.4**

Proportion of subjects who reported smoke in Latane and Darley's 1968 experiment. Subjects were much more likely to report the smoke if they were alone than if they were with two other subjects or two unresponsive confederates. (SOURCE: Adapted from Latane & Darley, 1968, p. 218.)

mixed situations—that is crowded low-task and uncrowded high-task—approximately one-third of the subjects complied with the request for help.

Researchers have also found that individuals who maintain their anonymity are less likely to help. In one study, students who wore hoods to hide their faces were found to be less likely to help a fellow student who appeared to have fainted (Solomon & Solomon, 1978). In another study, subjects were asked to administer shocks to a woman as part of an experiment. They were told either that the woman was a very nice person or that she was an extremely obnoxious person. In addition, the subjects either wore hoods and garments to disguise themselves or showed themselves and their faces to the woman. The results were that the subjects were only slightly more likely to shock the

CONCEPT REVIEW ◆ BYSTANDER INTERVENTION

The following example highlights Latane and Darley's five-step process of bystander intervention:

On January 13, 1982, a Boeing 737 took off in bad weather from National Airport in Washington, D.C. Unable to gain altitude, it crashed into the 14th Street bridge, flipped over, and smashed through the ice of the frozen Potomac River. Lenny Skutnik, a Washington office worker, was on his way home when he witnessed the disaster (step 1). As he reached the banks of the river, he observed a rescue helicopter attempting to save drowning victims of the crash (step 2). He noticed that one woman in the water apparently didn't have the strength to hold onto the life preserver dangling from the helicopter. At this point, Skutnik looked around and realized that "she was going to drown if I didn't get her, because nobody else was going to" (step 3).

The only way to reach her was to swim out to her and help her to safety (step 4). In a truly heroic action, Skutnik plunged into the freezing Potomac, amid ice chunks and potentially explosive jet fuel, and saved the woman's life (step 5). Empathy and compassion were also motivating forces for his action; as he stated in an interview with NBC news, "It was just in my heart. I just felt sorry for the girl."

Lenny Skutnik, a Washington, D.C., office worker, dove into the frozen Potomac River to save a victim of an airliner crash.

"obnoxious" woman than the "nice" woman. But if the subjects wore hoods and were able to disguise themselves, they gave the "obnoxious" woman twice as much shock (Zimbardo, 1979). (The same woman played each role and was not really shocked.)

There are three important ways of encouraging people to help others. One, of course, is by studying social psychology. Now that you are aware of these studies, you are more likely to inquire whether your help is needed, even if it means attracting the attention of many people who are doing nothing. Willingness to help others can also be fostered by teaching appropriate helping skills. People are more likely to help if they have some kind of training in the appropriate action to take (Shotland & Heinold, 1985). For instance, training seminars in cardiopulmonary resuscitation (CPR) have been successful in getting people to administer CPR quickly to heart attack victims, in order to keep the victim alive until help arrives. Training in what to do in case of an emergency prepares a person to take action. A third way of encouraging others to help is by reinforcing them for helping and by modeling helping behavior.

COOPERATION AND COMPETITION

When two or more people work together for their mutual benefit, they are cooperating. Cooperation is a valuable behavior, since societies would not be possible without it. Competition occurs when two or more people vie for a certain goal in which not all can be winners. Competition may be the best strategy in one circumstance, and cooperation in another.

Psychologists believe that competition and cooperation are taught by social interaction and that both strategies can be initiated at a very early age. Children often are spontaneously cooperative. But in our society, and in others, individual competition is so often modeled and reinforced that the desire to surpass others sometimes interferes with the need for cooperation. Irrational competition sometimes can spoil the success that cooperation might bring.

In one experiment, M. C. Madsen and his associates discovered that in certain cases cooperation declines as children grow older and that competition may become the most common mode of responding, even when it cannot possibly lead to success. Madsen had children of the same age sit across from each other at opposite ends of a small table (see Figure 18.5). Narrow gutters ran down the length of the table on both sides. The table surface was arched so that a marble placed anywhere on the table would immediately roll into the nearest gutter. A cup was imbedded in the tabletop in front of each child. At the start of the game, a marble was placed in a free-sliding marble holder in the center of the table. The marble holder prevented the marble from rolling into a gutter. Each child had a string attached to one end of the marble holder. To score, a child needed only to pull the string and cause the marble holder to pass over his cup. The marble would then drop into the cup and the child would have succeeded. However, if both children pulled their strings simultaneously, the marble holder would come apart and the marble would roll into the gutter.

Madsen found that cooperation was common among 4- and 5-year-old children playing this game. The children usually would negotiate an arrangement where each would receive about half of the marbles. However, when Madsen tested school children in the second through fifth grades, he found their desire to compete was so strong that a majority of them failed to obtain a single marble (Madsen, 1971). In a later study, some of the children were so competitive that they argued that it was impossible to get a marble! One child pointed out that success might be possible "if I could play alone" (Kagan &

◆ **FIGURE 18.5**

Madsen's marble-pull game. (SOURCE: *Madsen, 1971, p. 367.*)

Madsen, 1971, p. 38). It never dawned on them to cooperate for their mutual benefit.

Older children appear to be much more competitive because of their experience and learning. Cross-cultural research supports this supposition. When Madsen examined children from different backgrounds, he obtained different results. His data indicate that a strong competitive outlook is more likely to develop among older children in urban surroundings. For instance, it was observed that city-dwelling Israeli children were more competitive than were Israeli children raised on a kibbutz (Madsen, 1971; Shapira & Madsen, 1974). American children generally were most competitive, regardless of their race, gender, or background, perhaps because so much emphasis is placed on competition in American society (Madsen & Shapira, 1970; Nelson & Madsen, 1969). It has also been shown that children reared in family environments in which competition is emphasized tend to be more competitive (Monsaas & Engelhard, 1990).

A more adult version of Madsen's game, known as the Acme-Bolt trucking game, was designed by researchers Deutsch and Krauss (1960). Figure 18.6 shows the layout of the trucking game. To begin, each player is given a trucking company, either the Acme Company or the Bolt Company. Each person's job is to move trucks along available routes until the goal is reached. Subjects receive 60 cents for each successful trip to the goal, minus 1 cent for each second it took to complete the trip. You can see that each company has two possible routes: an alternative route, which is long and time-consuming, and the short route, which is a one-lane road. As you might imagine, the best way to play the game is for the two people to cooperate with each other and take turns. In this way, each can use the shortest route and use it quickly. In most cases, this was what happened. The players recognized that cooperation was the most logical and reasonable way to play the game.

In another variation of the trucking game, Deutsch and Krauss added gates at the positions shown in Figure 18.6. The gate on the left was controlled by

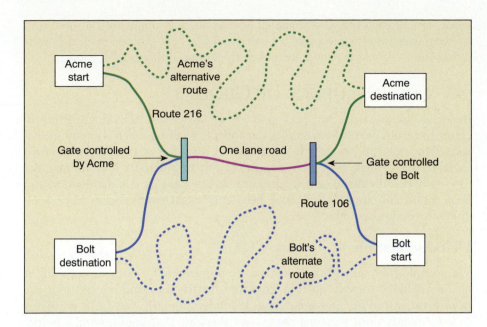

◆ **FIGURE 18.6**

Road map from the Acme-Bolt trucking game. (SOURCE: *Deutsch & Drauss, 1960, p. 183.*)

Acme, and the gate on the right by Bolt. The gates could be closed at any time by their respective owners to stop the other player from moving her truck along the one-lane road. Two variations of this game were played. In one variation, the unilateral threat condition, only one of the players was given a gate. In the second condition, the bilateral threat condition, each of the players had a gate. Possessing a gate gave the owner a potential threat to use. The threat did not exist if the players were willing to trust each other, but if one person wanted to use the gate to accumulate more money than his opponent, he could do so. When both people possessed a gate, the danger that one might strike would prompt the other to strike first. Possession of one gate caused losses for both players, and possession of two gates caused the most losses (see Figure 18.7). Players would often slam their gates at the beginning of the session and leave them shut while each lost money. This research indicates that the chances of cooperation diminish as the ability to threaten one another increases. We needn't travel too far from this simple game to draw parallels with the nuclear arms race that was in effect throughout the cold war. Indeed, if we discussed the game using phrases such as *first-strike capability, implicit*

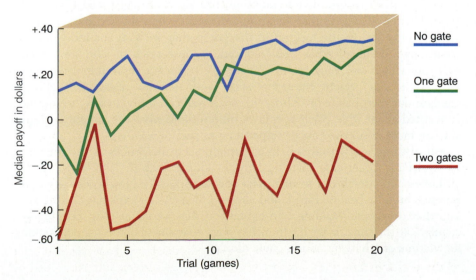

◆ **FIGURE 18.7**

In the Acme-Bolt trucking game, Deutsch and Krauss discovered that cooperation decreased (costing both sides money) as the number of implied threats (the power to stop commerce by using a gate) increased. (SOURCE: *Deutsch & Krauss, 1960, p. 185.*)

DEINDIVIDUATION
The process in which social restraints are weakened and impulsive and aggressive tendencies released as the person loses individual identity, usually as the result of being part of a large group or having his or her identity concealed in some way, for example, by a mask.

threat, *lack of cooperation,* and *mutual destruction,* you might well assume that we were weighing the prospects of a potential war between two nuclear powers rather than considering the outcome of the Acme-Bolt trucking game.

THE INFLUENCE OF GROUPS

In social circumstances, we encounter groups as well as individuals. Psychologists have discovered that groups can affect a person's behavior in special ways. Not only do people rely on groups as a source of comparison and for social norms (Tajfel, 1982), but depending on the situation, a group may occasionally deindividuate or polarize its members. Because deindividuation and polarization can strongly influence behavior, social psychologists have been drawn to study these processes.

Deindividuation

We are told from an early age that we are responsible for our actions. Almost no one is likely to walk up to a storefront, smash the window, and loot the store just because she sees something desirable. Similarly, few of us are likely to wait quietly until someone passes and then hit that person with a bottle. And not too many of us are likely to go over to the house of someone we don't like, drag that person out to a tree, and hold a lynching. Most of us would assume that anyone doing such things must be socially deviant. But these same behaviors, which few of us would ever dream of doing alone, are more likely to occur if we're part of a group. During blackouts, crowds often engage in looting. During raucous baseball games, people have been known to throw things at the umpires or players. And during episodes of extreme racial hostility, mobs may engage in lynchings.

It seems that the social restraints that we normally accept can disappear once we become a member of a group that becomes aroused or angry. Why should a group have such a restraint-reducing influence? We have words for it—*mob mentality,* for instance. But mobs are made up of people. Why will people do things in a group that they'd never do when alone? It's not that groups change people in a permanent way. Individuals who've taken part in mob violence often feel ashamed of their behavior when they're alone again.

One reason may be the effects of modeling. When we see many other people engage in a behavior, we become more certain that that behavior is appropriate. A second reason may be that a diffusion of responsibility occurs; that is, we can distribute the blame for our actions. After all, "everyone else was doing it too." A third reason, **deindividuation,** has also been suggested (Zimbardo, 1979; Diener, 1980). Deindividuation can occur when we become so caught up in events and in the feelings of the group that we lose our individuality. Once our individuality has been reduced, we lose track of who we are and what our values are. This, in turn, causes us to become more impulsive, more sensitive to our present emotional state, and, to some degree, less able to regulate our own behavior. Also, with such reduced individuality, we are less concerned about what other people think of us and what they might do to us. We are more concerned about responding as part of a group.

All of these social factors help to explain such incidences as the infamous Central Park jogger case that filled the headlines back in 1989–90. A group of adolescents attacked a woman who was jogging in a New York City park. She was brutally beaten, raped, and almost killed. As an explanation, the boys said that they were "wilding," an expression that wasn't in most people's vocabulary at the time. It meant that they were roaming about *as a group* looking for victims or whatever action came along.

Group attitudes may be altered if they are contradicted by the people in power.

Drawing by Booth; (c) 1977 The New Yorker Magazine, Inc.

Wilding was heralded by the press as something new, a further example of our deteriorating moral values and decaying urban life. But these social forces aren't new. There have been endless examples of similar group or mob behavior throughout human history, probably dating back to the first time a group of aroused or aggressive humans ever went out together looking for something to do. And, lest you think that the very existence of wilding says something about how our cities have changed, consider that almost 40 years ago the famous Olympic ice skater Dick Button was similarly attacked in Central Park by a gang of youths and almost beaten to death for no other reason than "kicks" (the term in vogue back then). This is not to say that such incidences aren't on the increase in the United States or that urban crime isn't becoming worse, but only that regardless of the new names given to such behaviors, the *social forces* they involve are not new in either our culture or our species, but have been with us from the dawn of civilization and perhaps before that.

Reduced individuality is not an inevitable part of being a member of a group, but certain conditions can make it more likely to occur. One way to encourage reduced individuality is to camouflage the qualities that make us individuals. Taking away a person's individuality compels him to conform and blend into the group. Anything that fosters anonymity reduces individuality. Ku Klux Klan members wear hoods, supposedly to conceal their identity but undoubtedly also to reduce the individual sense of self and to make them more amenable to group desires. Concentration on events in the environment rather than on internal thoughts also helps to lessen individuality. Group unity and a high level of emotional arousal will reduce individuality even further.

Polarization

Very often, individuals who enter a group discussion with moderate views will change their views and eventually take a more polarized or extreme position; that is, they will become more conservative or more radical in their approach to a particular issue or decision. Consequently, a group may reach a more extreme position on an issue than its members might have chosen individually, had they decided the issue without group interaction.

In one study, researcher Jerald Greenberg (1979) asked 200 subjects individually how they would divide money between two people who had worked at a particular job. The subjects were told that one person had done a better job than the other had, but that they could divide the money as they wished. On the average, subjects responded that 63.2 percent of the money should go to the person who had done the better job. Some time later, the subjects were again asked individually how they would divide the money. The average response the second time was that 64.3 percent should be given to the one who had done the better job, not much different from the first recommendation. In another group, the subjects were given the same information and were asked individually how they would divide the money. On the average, 64.4 percent of the money was awarded to the person who had done the better job. Then the subjects in this second group were allowed to discuss the situation with four other people. Afterward, they were again asked individually to make a recommendation, and this time the average response was that 76.5 percent of the money should be given to the person who had done the better job (see Figure 18.8).

◆ **FIGURE 18.8**

Subjects in all conditions were asked to divide money between two workers, one of whom was said to have done a better job. Subjects individually awarded more money to the better worker, but after group discussion the members shifted toward a more extreme position, which demonstrates the polarizing effect of the group on the judgments of its members. (SOURCE: After Greenberg, 1979.)

The **polarization effect**—the tendency of members of a group to take a more extreme position than they would as individuals—has been demonstrated many times. The direction of the polarization may be strongly influenced by culture. In cases in which American groups were more likely to polarize in the direction of taking a risk, Chinese groups were more likely to polarize in the direction of caution (Hong, 1978).

There are a number of explanations for the polarization effect. First, when we are among other people who share our views, we may wish to gain their approval by exemplifying the beliefs and attitudes they hold. To show ourselves worthy of the group's esteem, we may want to be more extreme in ways that the group values. For example, jet fighter pilots admire coolheadedness and lack of emotion in a tough situation. Most other people who agree that coolheadedness is a fine attribute will try to demonstrate it to a degree and will express a certain admiration for this behavior. However, should they become fighter pilots and find themselves among many other people who admire the behavior, they may attempt to exemplify these attributes in the *extreme* to obtain the admiration of the group (Pruitt, 1971).

The second reason that groups may tend to polarize is a fairly obvious one. While exchanging information, individuals may make persuasive arguments, and the entire group may shift toward the most convincing of these arguments. A jury furnishes a good example of this kind of polarization effect. Jury members are selected because they are undecided to begin with; potential jurors with extreme views are weeded out. It is up to each side in the courtroom to make persuasive arguments. The jury is then expected to become more and more polarized during discussion in the jury room, until it reaches a verdict (Kaplan & Schwartz, 1977; MacCoun, 1989). We can only hope that juries become polarized because of the convincing arguments presented by the prosecution or the defense and not because of the wish of uncertain jurors to obtain the esteem of those who have already decided one way or the other. It is useful to keep the group polarization process in mind. As you recall from the chapter Prologue, it is easy to become convinced if many other people agree that something is true. Just because a group takes an extreme position does not necessarily mean that it's a more reasonable position than an individual might take.

The common view that groups tend to reach middle-of-the-road decisions is not altogether inaccurate, however. If all groups became polarized, all governments would become radical or reactionary, and all group plans would be extreme. In fact, much of the time, this does not happen. Whenever a group includes unified subgroups, with each holding opposing views in the group discussion, a typical result is depolarization and compromise (Vinokur & Burnstein, 1978). A case in point is the U.S. Congress, made up of two subgroups, Democrats and Republicans.

Leadership

Individuals can affect groups, of course. Sometimes, an extremely influential group member will emerge as a leader. When a person becomes a leader, she is given the authority of a group and speaks for the group. Throughout history, people have wondered about the qualities of leadership and what makes leaders attractive to others. Psychologists who have studied leaders have arrived at two very different hypotheses to explain how a leader emerges.

The first, the **situational-environmental hypothesis,** argues that people are chosen as leaders because they happen to be in the right place at the right time. In other words, if they happen to have certain skills that meet a group's needs at a given moment, they may emerge as leaders (Hollander & Julian,

POLARIZATION EFFECT
An effect in which members of a group tend to take a more extreme position (more conservative or more daring) than they would have as individuals. It is probably the result of social comparison or persuasive group arguments.

SITUATIONAL-ENVIRONMENTAL HYPOTHESIS
The hypothesis that individuals become leaders because of situational or circumstantial forces rather than because of their personality traits.

GREAT-MAN, GREAT-WOMAN
HYPOTHESIS
The hypothesis that individuals become leaders primarily because of their personality or the traits they possess.

IN-GROUP
Any group for whom an individual feels a positive regard. This is a subjective term and depends on the person's point of view.

OUT-GROUP
Any group that an individual views in a negative way. This is a subjective term and depends on the person's point of view.

PREJUDICE
Beliefs or judgments made without sufficient evidence and not easily changed by opposing facts or circumstances; preconceived hostile and irrational feelings, opinions, or attitudes about a group or an individual.

DISCRIMINATION
In social psychology, differential treatment of people on the basis of their race, ethnic group, or class, rather than on their relevant traits. Acts of discrimination are typically premised on prejudice.

1970). The situational approach argues that an individual who may be a leader in one set of circumstances may be a follower in different circumstances. In other words, circumstances may arise in which any member of the group may emerge as a leader; it depends on the situation, not on the individual.

The other hypothesis, that leaders have particular traits that make them stand apart from other members of their group, is known as the **great-man, great-woman hypothesis.** This idea is not new. The special abilities of leaders have been heralded for centuries. However, these qualities have not been carefully examined until recently. Psychologists have found that one of the most important abilities—one shared by many leaders—is a high degree of verbal skill (Bavelas, Hastorf, Gross, & Kite, 1965). In addition, good leaders generally maintain the views of their group. Leaders who wander too far from their group's views tend to be discarded. Aside from these two characteristics, leaders are very different from one another. We have not yet uncovered specific personalities or important traits that are guaranteed to result in leadership.

Research has shown that both leadership hypotheses have merit and that they often work simultaneously. For example, whereas certain leaders may emerge owing to circumstances, some individuals, because of their personalities, are more likely than other people to accept and capitalize on a situational call to leadership (Nydegger, 1975).

Leaders have also been classified according to their abilities to fill certain group needs. One researcher (Bales, 1970) has argued that groups need both task leaders, who are able to get certain jobs done, and social-emotional leaders, who can lift spirits and offer psychological comfort and a sense of well-being to group members. Bales has argued that great leaders combine the best of both task leaders and social-emotional leaders.

PREJUDICE AND DISCRIMINATION

We have seen some of the effects of individuals on one another and of groups on individuals, as well as the reasons why some individuals become leaders of groups. Also of interest are the effects of attitudes and behaviors of members of one group on members of other groups. Social psychologists sometimes use the terms **in-group** and **out-group** when discussing the feelings that members of one group may have toward their own group and toward other groups. Whether someone considers a group to be an in-group or an out-group depends on his perspective. What is an in-group for you may be an out-group for someone else. By definition, a person has a positive regard for in-groups but views out-groups in a negative light. The way in which a person decides which are in-groups and which are out-groups has been of great interest to social psychologists studying prejudice and discrimination. After all, before prejudice can begin, it is necessary to identify the in-group and the out-group. A very prejudiced individual may perceive hundreds of out-groups, placing just about every person in existence into one or another of them.

Prejudice can be defined as learned values and beliefs that may lead an individual to be unfairly biased against members of particular groups. Because of prejudice, people may behave differently toward other groups (out-groups) than they do toward their own (in-group). Differential behavior based on prejudice is called **discrimination.**

One of the classic demonstrations of prejudice was set up by teacher Jane Elliott in an experiment she conducted with her third-grade class in Riceville, Iowa. Elliott wanted her students to understand something about prejudice. All the students in her class were white, but their eye color differed. On the first day of the experiment, Elliott, who had blue eyes, announced to her class that it was a well-known fact that blue-eyed children were brighter and generally were superior to those with brown eyes. The brown-eyed children in the classroom, who were fewer, were told that they were inferior and should defer to the blue-eyed children because they were better people. To emphasize their inferiority, the brown-eyed children were forced to sit in the back of the room, to use paper cups instead of the drinking fountain, to stand at the end of the line, and to wear special collars that enabled the blue-eyed students to identify them immediately from a distance or from behind. The blue-eyed students, on the other hand, were given special privileges such as extra time at recess and second helpings at lunch.

Before the first hour had elapsed, the effects of discrimination had begun to show on the brown-eyed children. Their schoolwork deteriorated. They became angry and depressed. They described themselves as sad, stupid, or awful. (You may recall from Chapter 8 that this is not unlike the way in which the black children referred to the black doll in the experiment conducted by Clark and Clark.) In describing the effect on the blue-eyed children, the teacher stated, "What had been marvelously cooperative, thoughtful children became nasty, vicious, discriminating little third-graders . . . it was ghastly" (Zimbardo, 1979, p. 638).

The next day, Elliott informed the students that she had made a mistake and that it was really the blue-eyed children who were inferior. In short order, the behaviors of the children switched. The brown-eyed children began to do better at their schoolwork, while the blue-eyed children began to lose their self-confidence.

Feeling prejudice firsthand may be a valuable educational experience for those who, because of their cultural position, are not typically subjected to prejudice. The benefits that may be gained from the experience have been demonstrated in an experiment in which children in an all-white third-grade class were assigned randomly to be either green or orange people. They wore colored armbands to show which group they belonged to. At first, the orange people were considered superior. They were told that they were cleaner and smarter. The green people were regarded as inferior and were denied many privileges given to the orange people. On the second day, the situation was reversed. The effects were similar to those produced in the Elliott study. Each time, the group discriminated against felt inferior, lost self-confidence, and did poorly in schoolwork. In this experiment, another all-white class served as a

Before the civil rights movement in the United States, and resulting legislation, discrimination was openly practiced.

STEREOTYPE
A set of simplistic and relatively fixed overgeneralizations concerning the physical or psychological characteristics of a class or group of people.

control group and was never exposed to the assignments of orange or green. On the third day, and again after 2 weeks, students in the control class and students who had gone through the orange and green experiment were asked whether they would like to go on a picnic with black children from a nearby school. On one occasion, only 62 percent of the children in the control group agreed to go, while 96 percent of the children in the group that had experienced prejudice firsthand agreed (Weiner & Wright, 1973).

Both the eye-color and the orange-green experiments show how easily prejudice can be learned. It can be taught by systematically associating other groups with unpleasant stimuli, by rewarding discriminatory behaviors, and by modeling discrimination.

Personality and Prejudice

Although individuals can learn to feel prejudice against a particular group, there is evidence that some people are prejudiced in a much more general way. These people place just about everyone in out-groups and treat them according to **stereotypes.** In 1946, researcher Eugene Hartley, when measuring people's attitudes toward different minority groups, decided to list three minorities that didn't exist, Daneriens, Pirenians, and Walonians. He found that people who identified many out-groups were prejudiced against the made-up groups as well. One generally prejudiced person stated, "I don't know anything about them. Therefore, I would exclude them from my country" (Hartley, 1946).

Perhaps the best-known effort to explain prejudice was made by another team of researchers over 40 years ago (Adorno, Frenkel-Brunswik, Levinson, & Sanford, 1950). Adorno and his colleagues believed that people who were highly prejudiced were likely to have authoritarian personalities. Authoritarian people tend to be submissive and obedient to authority and to reject other groups in a punitive way. They usually see other people as either weak or strong: "Either you're with us or against us" (in-group or out-group). Adorno thought that individuals became authoritarian because of the harsh and punitive child-rearing practices of their parents (Stephan & Rosenfield, 1978).

To test this hypothesis, Adorno and his colleagues developed the California F scale to measure authoritarianism (see Chapter 14). Although the findings are not completely consistent, in general, Adorno's hypothesis—that people who are extremely authoritarian are more likely to be prejudiced—has been supported (Cherry & Byrne, 1976).

Power and Stereotyping

The power wielded by different groups and the attention that each group receives owing to its relative power may also have an important influence on stereotyping. As a general rule, members of groups that are powerless pay attention to members of groups that are powerful. This is because in so many instances, the powerful group controls or significantly affects the lives of members of the less powerful group. Consequently, it is in the interest of those out of power to pay attention to what those in power demand of them. Researcher Susan Fiske has observed that those out of power study those in power closely, hoping to enhance their ability to predict and perhaps control what the powerful will do. In so doing, the less powerful form complex, nonstereotyped views of those in power (Fiske, 1993).

On the other hand, the powerful are little affected by the less powerful and need not pay attention to them. Also, those in power often don't want to pay attention to the less powerful simply as a way of maintaining their dominant status. As a result, those who have power are more likely to stereotype those without power simply because it is easy to lump individuals about whom you know little into a stereotyped classification (Fiske, 1993).

Overcoming Prejudice

Prejudice can be overcome in a number of ways. We might attempt to overcome it through contact—bringing antagonistic groups into contact with one another—but that may make matters worse (Olson & Zanna, 1993). Groups also need a common goal. For example, racism is not likely to persist among members of a baseball team, because all the players have one goal. They must cooperate with one another to reach this goal, and as a result, they come to think of one another as members of a common in-group.

Prejudice can also be combated by legislation. Although it is difficult to legislate values, prejudice can be encouraged or not by the structure of the laws in a society. Until apartheid was abolished in the early 1990s, for example, the legal structure in South Africa made racial prejudice more likely, since blacks and whites were segregated by law and the persistent economic and political inequalities between the groups were emphasized. In the United States, over the past 30 years, laws such as the Voting Rights Act, which are designed to give minority members equal rights, have helped to change attitudes and beliefs among the population. In 1963, for example, 61 percent of white parents in the South said that they would not send their children to a school attended by even a few blacks. By 1975, this figure had decreased to 15 percent. Much of the difference was due to a new awareness brought about by legislation (Gallup, 1975).

Finally, through learning, self-esteem may be increased among people who are the victims of prejudice so as to lessen the adverse effects of the prejudice. Concepts such as "Black is beautiful" and "I am somebody" may protect potential victims from some of the detrimental effects of prejudice. Furthermore, all of us who are interested in eliminating prejudice can help by modeling nondiscriminatory behavior and by showing others that we are accepting of the members of potential out-groups. This holds true for sexual discrimination, as well as for race, age, ethnic, and religious discrimination.

❧ SOCIAL COGNITION AND ATTITUDE CHANGE

The attitudes that a person has about other people can be a powerful influence in social situations. Consequently, psychologists have been drawn to study how social attitudes are formed and how they change. A **social attitude** is a relatively enduring system of feelings, beliefs, and behaviors with respect to a social object. For example, the attitudes you have toward a family member would include your feelings and thoughts about that person and your behaviors toward that person that have been generated by the feelings and thoughts. Knowing how someone thinks about a particular issue makes it easier to predict the person's behavior (Cialdini, Petty, & Cacioppo, 1981). The interaction between social forces and thought processes has opened a relatively new area of social investigation known as **social cognition.**

Forming Social Attitudes

Research in social cognition has shown that experiences with social stimuli can affect our perceptions and evaluations of that stimuli (Tesser & Shaffer, 1990). Recall from Chapter 8, for example, how the studies by Staats and Staats (1958) demonstrated through the process of associative learning how

SOCIAL ATTITUDE
An enduring system of positive or negative evaluations, feelings, and tendencies toward action with regard to a social object.

SOCIAL COGNITION
An area of social psychology that is concerned with how social influences affect cognitive processes such as thought, memory, and perception.

BOGUS PIPELINE
A procedure for measuring a person's real attitudes and feelings rather than what the person wishes to present. Subjects are led to believe that a supposed physiological monitor is able to detect their real attitudes and feelings and that any attempt to hide them will be uncovered.

nationalities such as Swedish or Dutch and names such as Tom and Bill could be systematically paired with pleasant or unpleasant words to alter how people felt toward these nationalities and names.

Instrumental learning can also be important in the formation of attitudes. As children develop, parents typically reinforce or punish the behaviors that stem from the attitudes the children hold. We can all recall a childhood experience in which adults told us the attitudes that we should have about stealing other people's property or calling someone a name. Our attitudes and views were shaped as we were systematically rewarded for the "right" behaviors and punished for the "wrong" behaviors.

Social learning through modeling is another important way attitudes are acquired. We often base our attitudes on the behavior of other people, even when they are not trying to transmit their attitudes to us directly. We look to others to help us decide which attitudes are best and appropriate.

MEASURING ATTITUDES. Investigators often measure attitudes by means of questionnaires or scales. Such measurement devices must be used carefully, because subtle differences in the meanings of words that appear in them can bias responses. For an extreme example of such bias, examine Figure 18.9. Generally, however, if the questionnaire or scale is worded carefully and is used appropriately, it can provide much valuable information about attitudes.

Another problem that arises with questionnaires is that people often present attitudes different from their real ones or disguise their true beliefs in an attempt to enhance their image in the eyes of the researcher (Braver, Linder, Corwin, & Cialdini, 1977; Schlenker, 1978). When this happens, it is difficult to obtain a true assessment of attitudes. To reduce the incidence of faked attitudes on questionnaires and scales, social psychologists have devised a unique arrangement known as the **bogus pipeline.** In this procedure, subjects are connected to a machine with impressive flashing lights. They are told that the machine will monitor their physiological responses and will reveal their true opinions to the experimenter whenever they supply an answer about their attitudes. A trick is used to convince subjects that the machine actually works. Several days before the questionnaire is administered, the experimenter's coworkers subtly obtain the subject's views on certain matters, usually from his friends or family members. The subject is asked to respond to these questions first. Once subjects are convinced that the machine can detect their real opinions, they are asked to respond to the questionnaire. It is assumed that since they believe the machine can reveal their true feelings, they will no longer have a reason to fake (Jones & Sigall, 1971).

There is evidence that real attitudes are tapped better by the bogus pipeline technique than by a questionnaire used alone. In one study, for instance, whites expressed a positive attitude toward blacks when asked to answer a standard questionnaire, but expressed more negative attitudes when connected to the bogus pipeline (Jones, Bell, & Aronson, 1972). In another experiment, students connected to the bogus pipeline were more likely to confess to having had the answers to a test beforehand than they were when asked the same question on a standardized questionnaire (Quigley-Fernandez & Tedeschi, 1978). The bogus pipeline technique has not always produced positive results, however (Cherry, Byrne, & Mitchell, 1976). It may even be possible that the bogus pipeline causes subjects to "confess" to attitudes more negative than those they really have (Gaes, Kalle, & Tedeschi, 1978).

Other approaches to revealing a person's real attitudes have also been attempted. Real physiological monitors can be used to measure information about the intensity or direction of an emotional or attitudinal response (Olson & Zanna, 1993). Such monitors have also been used to measure physiological

◆ **FIGURE 18.9**

An example of how a questionnaire can be biased. Survey questions (a) and (b) appear to ask the same thing, but because of the connotations of the words used, survey (a) will report that people like to spend, while survey (b) will report that they like to save.

(a)	How do you handle your money? Are you
	☐ Generous, or ☐ Stingy
(b)	How do you handle your money? Are you
	☐ Extravagant, or ☐ Thrifty

responses as attitudes undergo change, but they are not always accurate and present the same problems as lie detectors (see Chapter 12).

ATTITUDES AND SELF-AWARENESS. Sometimes subjects aren't certain about their own attitudes and may respond to questions without carefully monitoring their feelings. The subjects in one experiment were asked about their attitudes toward working certain puzzles. In one condition, they described their feelings while seated before a mirror. In the control condition, the subjects saw no mirror. The hypothesis stated that people placed before a mirror will have more self-awareness and that this, in turn, will help them to concentrate on their feelings. The experimenters used the subjects' attitudes about how much fun the puzzles would be to predict how long they would play with the puzzles. The attitudes obtained from subjects seated before a mirror predicted much more accurately how long they would play with the puzzles than did the attitudes obtained from the other subjects (Pryor, Gibbons, Wicklund, Fazio, & Hood, 1977).

Changing Attitudes: Persuasive Communication

It seems that a day can't go by without someone trying to change our attitudes. All you need to do to find the attitude changers at work is to turn on a television set, listen to a radio, or look at a billboard.

Techniques for changing attitudes commonly rely on **persuasive communication.** In persuasive communication, we are provided with facts or logical arguments about why we should use a particular product or feel a certain way. These so-called facts or logical arguments often are self-serving, and biased. Sometimes the communications will influence our attitudes; sometimes they will not. The ability of messages from advertising agencies, political candidates, or even people we know to affect our attitudes depends on a number of complex interactions.

CHARACTERISTICS OF THE COMMUNICATOR. In general, we tend to trust information from experts (Eagly, 1983). Nevertheless, a communicator's intentions can affect our view of his credibility. We would normally consider a physician to be an expert on medical matters, but we might not believe a physician who tells us that cigarettes are good for our health once we find out

PERSUASIVE COMMUNICATION Arguments designed to alter attitudes by appealing to reason by means of fact and logic.

Techniques for changing attitudes commonly rely on persuasive communication.

EMOTIONAL APPEALS
Arguments designed to alter attitudes by appealing to the emotions through stirring visual and verbal messages.

that she owns a large share of a tobacco company. In such an instance, we might regard the communication as biased because of the obvious motives behind the expert's statement (Eagly & Himmelfarb, 1978).

Another important characteristic of the communicator is his perceived similarity with the audience. If members of the audience think that the speaker is similar to them (in socioeconomic class, occupation, appearance, and so on), they probably will find him to be more persuasive. Television commercials capitalize on this tendency, using actors or actresses who look like "someone off the street." In general, salespeople who are like their customers are even more successful at selling the product than are experts who are perceived to be unlike the customers (Brock, 1965).

Other interesting characteristics have also been found to play a role. If, for instance, the speaker has a babyish face he is typically viewed as being more trustworthy (Brownlow & Zebrowitz, 1990). Speakers who speak more tentatively, that is, who hedge their arguments or use frequent disclaimers, tend to be more persuasive (Carli, 1990).

Researchers have also gathered much evidence to show that the information people generate themselves is more powerful in determining attitudes than is information provided by other people (Cialdini, Petty, & Cacioppo, 1981). In other words, self-persuasion is most persuasive (Olson & Zanna, 1993).

In one study, students were asked to write an essay about a particular issue using certain words that were associated with either a pro or an anti position. The students who used the most pro words became more favorable toward the position. Those who used the anti words became less favorable (Eiser & Ross, 1977; Eiser & Pancer, 1979). In a second study, subjects were given essays to read that contained either the pro words or the anti words; these essays did not affect the subjects' attitudes. In the first study, the subjects had used these words in their own essays (self-generated); in the second study, they had read essays in which the words had been used (generated) by other writers. These studies highlight the strong influence of self-generated arguments.

CHARACTERISTICS OF THE COMMUNICATION. Another important factor in producing attitude change is the form of the message or communication. One kind of communication may be more effective than another, depending on the recipient's initial view of the message. If the recipient initially opposes the idea that is to be presented, a two-sided argument (in which the speaker clearly presents both sides of the issue) will lower the recipient's resistance to persuasion more effectively than will a one-sided argument (in which the speaker presents only the side the recipient opposes). On the other hand, if the recipient initially agrees with the issue, a one-sided argument in favor of the issue will strengthen her attitude toward the issue more effectively than will a two-sided argument (Hovland, Lumsdaine, & Sheffield, 1949).

Some communications appeal to the emotions. Cigarette smokers are frightened by stories of lung cancer; a request for funds to feed the hungry is accompanied by photographs of malnourished children; and a message about driver safety is supplemented by an account of an automobile accident. **Emotional appeals** can be effective in changing attitudes and behavior, but only under certain conditions (Olson & Zanna, 1993). For an emotional appeal to work, the viewers must believe that they can take action that will reduce the stress caused by the emotional appeal, such as giving to the hungry. If action is impossible, viewers tend to deny the emotional appeal or to try to ignore it. In addition, viewers who have high self-esteem are more likely to be influenced by emotional appeals (Leventhal, 1970). It may be that people with low self-esteem view themselves as helpless or as under too much stress to be worried about the problems of other people. If the recipients of the message think that they can do nothing, or if they have low self-esteem, a mild emotional appeal will have a greater effect than will a strong one (Janis & Feshbach, 1953).

There are also ways to help people resist attitude change. People who have been taught how to refute arguments that go against their beliefs are less likely to change their beliefs (McGuire, 1964). It's also possible to help people avoid attitude change by forewarning them that the speaker is intent on changing their beliefs (Petty & Cacioppo, 1979).

Simply being exposed to something can alter our attitude in favor of it (Zajonc, 1968). Advertisers, knowing this, attempt to show their products as often as possible. This effect is known as the **mere exposure effect.** It does not hold true for things that have negative outcomes. For example, mere exposure to watching your car being damaged is not likely to make you feel better about it (Swap, 1977). In one clever experiment, researchers took photographs of subjects and of the subjects' friends or lovers. Then they made photographs from mirror images of the subjects and the subjects' friends and lovers. The photographs were mixed together, and the subjects were asked which they felt most favorable toward. When subjects viewed themselves, they felt most favorable toward the photograph of the mirror image, which is the view of themselves with which they were most familiar, but when they viewed friends and lovers, they felt most favorable toward the direct photographs, which is the way they usually saw those people (Mita, Dermer, & Knight, 1977). Apparently, the stimulus doesn't even have to be observed consciously for the mere exposure effect to occur (Wilson, 1979). This may explain why people are more likely to vote for candidates they've seen or been exposed to than for candidates they've not seen. The effect persists even if voters are aware of the issues both candidates support and are not treating the election as a beauty contest (Grush, 1980).

CHARACTERISTICS OF THE LISTENER. Sometimes, people don't give much thought to a particular issue when it is presented, and yet their attitudes change anyway. For example, Miller and his colleagues discovered that listeners were more likely to change their attitudes in favor of a speaker who spoke quickly (Miller, Maruyama, Beaber, & Valone, 1976). Whether or not a listener has paid careful attention to a particular discussion, however, will affect the endurance of the attitude change. Researchers Petty and Cacioppo have argued that there are two basic routes of persuasion: **central route processing,** in which attitudes are changed while the person is motivated to think carefully about the issue, and **peripheral route processing,** in which attitudes are changed while motivation or ability to think about the issue is very low (Olson & Zanna, 1993). An attitude change through the central route (for example, after carefully listening to a persuasive argument) is likely to be an enduring change. An attitude change through the peripheral route (for example, while noticing that a commercial has a pleasant jingle and nice-looking people) is more likely to be temporary (Cialdini, Levy, Herman, Kozlowski, & Petty, 1976).

One study clearly demonstrated the importance of these two routes of persuasion. Subjects were exposed to a message that contained either two or six arguments in favor of a particular positive position. The messages were given either by a likable or a dislikable person. Half of the subjects were told that they would later be interviewed again concerning the issue, so they were motivated to pay attention and to think about it (central route). The other half were told that they would be interviewed later on an unrelated issue, and they therefore had little motivation to think about the message (peripheral route). The subjects who expected to be interviewed about the topic showed attitude change that was determined primarily by the number of arguments presented.

MERE EXPOSURE EFFECT
The effect in which attitudes become more favorable toward something merely by being exposed to it.

CENTRAL ROUTE PROCESSING
From social-information processing theory, a route of persuasion and attitude change that may occur when a person pays careful attention to a persuasive discussion. Any resulting attitude change is relatively enduring.

PERIPHERAL ROUTE PROCESSING
From social-information processing theory, a route of persuasion and attitude change that may occur even when a person pays little attention to the persuasive message. Any resulting attitude change is usually temporary.

COGNITIVE DISSONANCE
The condition in which one has beliefs or knowledge that are internally inconsistent or that disagree with one's behavior. When cognitive dissonance arises, the person is motivated to reduce the dissonance through changes in behavior or cognition.

The attitude change was greater when six rather than two arguments were given. Whether the speaker was likable or dislikable had no effect. Among the subjects who did not expect to be interviewed, the number of arguments (two or six) made little difference in attitude change. The important factor was whether the source, the speaker, was likable or dislikable. Furthermore, a measurement of attitudes taken 10 days later showed that the subjects who had expected to be interviewed about the topic (central route) had stable attitude changes, while those whose attitudes had been changed by the peripheral route had shifted back to their premessage attitudes (Chaiken, 1980).

The effect of the recipient's intelligence on his susceptibility to persuasion has also been examined. You might expect that it would be more difficult to change the attitudes of an intelligent person. In general, however, there is no reliable relationship between intelligence and ability to resist persuasion. The more intelligent a person is, however, the more likely it is that a two-sided argument will be effective in creating attitude change, compared with a one-sided argument (Miller & Buckhout, 1973).

A person's level of self-esteem has been shown to be an important predictor of her ability to resist persuasion (Linton & Graham, 1959). Nevertheless, a distinction must be drawn between long- and short-term self-esteem. Long-term self-esteem is the general feelings we have about ourselves over a long period of time, while short-term self-esteem can vary from moment to moment, depending on immediate events. For instance, although you may generally feel good about yourself (your long-term esteem is high), you may call yourself "stupid" if you drop a glass and break it (your short-term self-esteem is low). By giving subjects tasks in which they were destined to fail, researchers have manipulated short-term self-esteem. Interestingly, the level of short-term self-esteem seems to have a greater effect on the person's ability to resist persuasion than does his level of long-term self-esteem. As short-term self-esteem lowers, resistance to persuasion decreases (Gollob & Dittes, 1965; Zellner, 1970). Why this is so is not known.

Cognitive Dissonance and Attitude Change

In the late 1950s, Leon Festinger conducted what has become a classic experiment. Subjects were invited to participate in a study that was purposely made exceedingly dull. For one hour they were required to move spools on and off of a tray and to rotate pegs in a pegboard by quarter turns, always using only one hand. It's hard to imagine a more boring task. The subjects were unaware that they had been assigned to one of two groups. When they were finished, they were offered a monetary reward for participating in the experiment and were then asked to do something for the experimenter. Subjects in the first group were given only $1 and were asked to tell the next subject, who was waiting to participate in the experiment, that the experiment had been fun! After taking the dollar and complying with the request, the subjects were asked by an interviewer about their *real* feelings about the experiment. Subjects in the second group were put through the same procedure but given $20 as a reward instead of $1. Interestingly, the subjects who had received the $20 reported really feeling that the experiment was horribly boring, while the subjects who had received only $1 said they really thought that the experiment had been interesting (Festinger & Carlsmith, 1959). Festinger argued that when a person acts in a manner that is *inconsistent with his real feelings or beliefs*, and can find no obvious reason for having done so, **cognitive dissonance** is created. Such dissonance, he argued, must be resolved because it causes an uncomfortable feeling, and the best way to resolve it is to change your attitude so that the previous behavior will now appear to be consistent with your views.

In other words, when subjects lied by telling another person that the dull task was really interesting, they behaved in a manner inconsistent with their feelings; those who had received only $1 for doing this were subjected to a high level of cognitive dissonance because they couldn't even look to the money as a reason for their lying. The real reason the subjects had lied, of course, was that they were being obedient to the experimenter. As we learned from the Milgram experiments, most people will be obedient. But, unable to find any obvious reason for telling a lie, the subjects resolved their dissonance by deciding that, in fact, they had not lied, that they had really enjoyed the experiment! By changing their attitudes, they did not have to face the unpleasant feelings of dissonance. Those subjects who received the $20, on the other hand, felt that they had a reason to lie, since they were being well paid to do so; therefore, they did not feel much dissonance. As a result, little attitude change occurred in this group (see Figure 18.10).

Cognitive dissonance theory had a great impact when it was introduced because it collided head-on with the two most popular psychological theories of its time, behaviorism and psychoanalytic (Freudian) theory. For example, no behaviorist would have predicted that the subjects who would be most likely to lie would have been the ones *least* reinforced for doing so. Freudian theory predicts that openly expressing the anger you have toward someone leads to a catharsis (see Chapter 1) that reduces the anger. Cognitive dissonance theory showed, however, that to justify their expressions of anger, people will denigrate the object of their anger, making further anger even easier to express and, therefore, more likely to occur (DeAngelis, 1990).

Dissonance effects will not occur if people realize that they are being forced to make a choice inconsistent with their feelings or beliefs or if the actions they take that are inconsistent with their real views have no consequences (Schlenker & Schlenker, 1975). Most attempts to reduce cognitive dissonance, however, generally will cause attitudes to change. For instance, as a general rule, attitudes about whether you will win a wager become more positive *after* you've placed a bet (Younger, Walker, & Arrowood, 1977). Dissonance theory helps to explain why most people perceive that they have made good decisions *after* they have made them. The amount of effort or money we expend to reach a goal or to acquire something may have more effect on how we feel about it than does its actual value. For this reason, once a person, or even a nation, makes a commitment or invests in a particular action, it often becomes difficult to convince those responsible that the decision was not a good one and should not be pursued. They have changed their attitudes to agree with their decision in order to reduce their feelings of dissonance.

One of the best-known experiments that demonstrated this effect was conducted by Aronson and Mills in 1959. These researchers divided female college students into three groups. In each group, the subjects were told that they would be listening to a supposedly exciting taped discussion about sex. The first group was admitted to hear the tape without passing any initiation test. The second group received a mild initiation in which they had to read five sex-related words such as *prostitute* or *virgin* to a male researcher. The third group was given a severe initiation in which subjects had to read a dozen obscene words and two very explicit sexual passages to a male researcher. After the initiations, the subjects did not listen to an exciting discussion about sexual behavior as they had been led to believe, but to a boring report about animal sexuality that made little sense. After listening to the tape, the subjects were asked to rate the value of the taped discussion. As expected, the more severe the initiation, the more the discussion was valued (Aronson & Mills, 1959). The investigators argued that those subjects who had gone through the stress

◆ **FIGURE 18.10**

Festinger and Carlsmith's experiment demonstrating the effects of cognitive dissonance. Subjects who lied (told the next subject that the experiment was fun) and received only $1 reduced their cognitive dissonance by claiming that they had, in fact, liked the experiment. Subjects who lied but received $20 experienced little or no dissonance and claimed to dislike the experiment. A control group, whose members moved spools and turned pegs but were not requested to lie and received no money, really disliked the experiment. (SOURCE: Adapted from Festinger & Carlsmith, 1959, p. 207.)

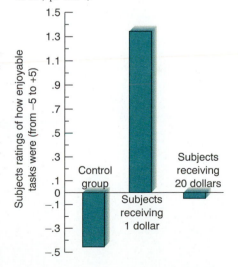

IMPRESSION MANAGEMENT HYPOTHESIS
The hypothesis that the results of cognitive dissonance experiments can be explained, not by changes in real attitudes made to reduce dissonance, but rather by a need to appear consistent in the eyes of others.

ATTRIBUTION
The psychosocial process through which we come to believe that certain events or dispositions are responsible for the behavior of ourselves or others.

of the severe initiation experienced cognitive dissonance when all they received for their efforts was a boring, senseless tape. Rather than feel upset, the subjects altered their perception of the tape and found listening to it to be a valuable experience.

In 1962, Elliot Aronson proposed a modification to Festinger's cognitive dissonance theory, which eventually became known as the **impression management hypothesis** (Tedeschi, 1981; Malkis, Kalle, & Tedeschi, 1982). This view argues that the results of dissonance theory could be explained by people's need to appear to other people to have consistent attitudes (Tedeschi, Schlenker, & Bonoma, 1971); that is, the subjects in the experiments on cognitive dissonance were not really changing their true attitudes but were reporting that their attitudes had changed so that they would appear consistent in the eyes of other people. For example, according to the impression management hypothesis, the women who went through severe initiation in the experiment just discussed *truly* thought that the tape was boring but needed to appear consistent in the eyes of the investigators. They asserted that the tape was valuable so that they would not appear foolish for having gone through so much trouble to hear it. In other words, they needed to present attitudes that seemed consistent with their behaviors, although their *real* attitudes had not changed.

To examine this hypothesis, researchers conducted experiments on cognitive dissonance and obtained the subjects' reactions through the bogus pipeline procedure. The procedure indicated that the subjects' true attitudes often had not changed in situations in which the subjects in a typical dissonance experiment would normally demonstrate an attitude shift (Cialdini, Petty, & Cacioppo, 1981). Although the bogus pipeline procedure may be fallible, the idea of impression management must be considered as a possible explanation for the results of cognitive dissonance research (Leary & Kowalski, 1990).

Attribution

We often are curious about the personality or motivations of other people. We look for stable traits and underlying motives as a way of understanding others' behavior. We react to people's behavior differently depending on the motives or traits to which we attribute that behavior (Heider, 1958). We engage in **attribution** whenever we try to find the reasons for another's behavior or to understand his personality or motivation. In other words, we attribute a person's behavior to certain aspects of his personality or environment.

Social psychologists have found that one of the first tasks of attribution is to decide whether the individual's personality is determining the behavior (that is, whether the behavior is being shaped from within) or whether forces in the environment are controlling the behavior (that is, whether the behavior is being shaped from without). We assign blame or give credit depending, in part, on whether we attribute someone's behavior to internal or external factors. Consider what happened in 1957 when the Soviet Union launched the world's first artificial satellite, *Sputnik*. Stunned by this technological achievement, American scientists rushed to match it. Their early attempts to launch rockets failed utterly because they did not know much about how to build these machines. The only people in the United States who really knew how to build and fly rockets were Nazi scientists captured during the Second World War. The leading expert among them was Wernher von Braun, who had built the V-2 rocket that had been used against London with devastating effect. Many Americans were dismayed that the U.S. government had to turn to a former Nazi to get the rocket program literally off the ground. They argued that we should not entrust the program to a man who had developed missiles that killed civilians. These people attributed von Braun's behavior in working for the Nazis and being a Nazi to evil personality traits. Other people attributed von Braun's behavior to environmental causes. They argued that von Braun was not responsible, since the Nazis had forced him to build the V-2. People who attributed von Braun's behavior to internal motivations and personality traits held him accountable for what happened during the war and did not want him to head the missile program, while those who attributed his behavior to environmental forces believed that he had been forced to do what he had done and were not opposed to his appointment. In 1960, a film entitled *I Aim at the Stars* cast the German actor Curt Jurgens in the role of von Braun. Its basic premise was that von Braun was internally motivated only to explore rocketry and space flight and that his part in the Nazi war effort was attributable to the external forces brought to bear on him. One caustic movie reviewer, suspicious of this argument, entitled his review of the film "I Aimed at the Stars, but I Hit London."

One of the most interesting aspects of the attribution process is that it can lead to a biased assessment of other people (Harvey & Weary, 1984). For instance, we tend to view our own behavior as stemming from situational or environmental forces, but we see the behavior of other people as stemming from internal forces (Eisen, 1979; Quattrone, 1982). Moreover, people usually find terms for traits to be better descriptions of other people than of themselves (Goldberg, 1978).

Psychologists have developed two hypotheses to explain this tendency. The **visual perspective hypothesis** argues that we attribute other people's behavior to internal forces and our own to external forces because of our visual perspective. Unless we're standing in front of a mirror, we rarely see ourselves as others see us. But we easily see the environmental forces that impinge on us from all directions. For this reason, we may be more aware of the environment than we are of ourselves. When dealing with other people, however, we tend to see whole people, the way we would see ourselves if we had a mirror. As a result, their "peopleness," with its accompanying traits and personality, may strike us more than the environmental circumstances affecting them. This theory may help to explain why therapists working with alcoholics have found that the alcoholics are more willing to take the responsibility for controlling their drinking after they have viewed a videotape showing themselves intoxicated. By seeing themselves as they see other people, they may attribute more responsibility to internal traits and personality.

The second hypothesis argues that we tend to consider ourselves to be more at the mercy of situational forces than other people are because we are more acutely aware of our own situation. This idea is known as the **information availability hypothesis.** The more information we obtain about another person, the more likely we are to attribute her behavior to environmental factors. Long before social psychologists found evidence for the information availability hypothesis, people in many cultures had demonstrated an understanding of this effect. As an American Indian saying puts it, if you want to know another person, walk a mile in his moccasins. Other cultures have similar sayings. Their import is that we can understand a person better once we really know the forces that impinge on her. Until then, we tend to attribute another's behavior to personality traits. In criminal trials, a defense lawyer will try to bring up as much information as possible about a client's hard life and difficult past. The more information the jury members hear about the defendant's situation, the more likely they are to attribute that person's action to environmental factors, rather than to personality. Both the visual perspective hypothesis and the information availability hypothesis have been supported by research (Eisen, 1979; Taylor & Fiske, 1978).

VISUAL PERSPECTIVE HYPOTHESIS
The hypothesis that explains people's tendency to attribute their own behavior to environmental causes rather than to personality traits as a function of their visual perspective, because they view their surroundings more often than they view their own body.

INFORMATION AVAILABILITY HYPOTHESIS
The hypothesis that explains people's tendency to attribute their own behavior to environmental causes rather than to personality traits as a function of the fact that they have more information about their personal situation, their environment, and the obvious forces in it than they have about others'.

SELF-SERVING BIAS
An attribution bias describing the fact that people tend to attribute behavior that results in a good outcome to their own personality or traits and attribute behavior that results in a bad outcome to the forces or circumstances of the environment.

Another factor affecting attribution error is **self-serving bias.** This term describes the tendency to attribute behavior that results in a good outcome to internal forces and to attribute behavior that results in a bad outcome to environmental factors (Carver, DeGregorio, & Gillis, 1980; O'Malley & Becker, 1984). In other words, people tend to take responsibility for good results but to attribute bad results to factors beyond their control. Similarly, mothers view the positive personal characteristics of their children as stable and inborn, but see the negative characteristics as transitory (Gretarsson & Gelfand, 1988).

The self-serving bias probably occurs because people like to do "good" things and want their family to do good things, and are at a loss to explain why they occasionally do "bad" things. The bias probably stems from the belief that we should be in control of our behavior all of the time, in which case we must somehow deal with behavior that results in a bad outcome. The self-serving bias may be a form of rationalization, through which we deny that there are internal forces that lead us to behave in ways that we don't like or that we can't control.

SUMMARY

◆ Social psychology is the study of how people affect the behavior, thoughts, and feelings of other people.

◆ The ways in which other people expect us to conform are known as social norms.

◆ People generally look to reference groups of similar individuals, or of individuals whom they would like to resemble, in order to make decisions about how to conform.

◆ Researcher Stanley Milgram demonstrated the power of obedience when he found that a majority of people would administer shocks to a stranger when they were asked to do so, even though the stranger appeared to be in pain or in danger.

◆ The tragedy of Jonestown demonstrated the dangers of blind obedience and conformity.

◆ Situational factors at any given moment play a great role in whether people will help someone in an emergency. In some situations, people are less likely to help if there are many witnesses to the person's distress. This is known as the bystander effect. The bystander effect may be the result of diffusion of responsibility or of fear of appearing foolish by interpreting an ambiguous situation as an emergency when, in fact, it is not.

◆ According to the bystander intervention model, for intervention to occur, the event must be observed and interpreted as an emergency, and the observer must take responsibility for helping and decide how to help. All these requirements must be met before action can be taken.

◆ Morals are the attitudes and beliefs that help people to determine what is right or wrong. According to researcher Lawrence Kohlberg, moral development begins in childhood and progresses through six stages.

◆ Both competition and cooperation are taught by so-cial interaction. In certain instances, cooperation declines as children grow older, and competition becomes the common mode of responding, even when it cannot possibly lead to success. Cooperation between partners diminishes as their ability to threaten each other increases.

◆ Individuals are influenced by groups in unique ways. Groups may deindividuate members, or they may lead members to become polarized and to take more extreme positions than they would as individuals.

◆ Sometimes, an extremely effective group member will emerge as a leader. The situational-environmental hypothesis states that particular situations may arise in which a group member is fortuitously elevated to the position of leader because he or she happens to possess the skills needed at the moment. The great-man, great-woman hypothesis argues that certain people possess traits that make other group members likely to accept their leadership. Research has indicated that both hypotheses may be correct.

◆ Prejudice consists of learned values and beliefs that may lead an individual to be unfairly biased against members of particular out-groups. Differential behavior based on prejudice is called discrimination.

◆ Individuals with authoritarian personalities tend to be more prejudiced and are especially prone to categorize people as members of in-groups or out-groups.

◆ Prejudice may be overcome by educating people, legislating nondiscriminatory behavior, increasing the self-esteem of the victims of prejudice, and creating contact between hostile groups as they work together to reach a common goal.

◆ A social attitude is a relatively enduring system of feelings, beliefs, and behaviors toward a social object. Social attitudes can be formed through the processes of associative learning, instrumental learning, and social learning.

◆ Social psychologists typically use questionnaires or scales to measure attitudes. The bogus pipeline procedure is designed to tap the real feelings and attitudes of subjects instead of the pretended feelings or attitudes subjects often report.

◆ Individuals tend to assess their own attitudes more accurately and to express more self-awareness when placed in front of a mirror.

◆ Techniques for changing attitudes commonly rely on persuasive communication. The characteristics of the communicator can affect the attitudes of the listener. Communicators who are similar to their audience in socioeconomic class, occupation, or appearance are more persuasive.

◆ Self-generated persuasion is more effective than is persuasion generated by other people.

◆ Two-sided arguments are more persuasive to individuals who initially oppose the idea that is presented. One-sided arguments are more persuasive if the recipient initially agrees with the idea.

◆ Emotional appeals are effective in changing attitudes, and individuals with high self-esteem are more likely to be influenced by emotional appeals.

◆ We can help people to resist persuasion by warning them that someone else is going to try to persuade them.

◆ Simply being exposed to something that does not have a bad outcome can alter our attitude in favor of it. This is known as the mere exposure effect.

◆ Central-route processing of a message generally leads to a permanent change in attitudes, while peripheral-route processing usually leads to a temporary change.

◆ When subjects are made to state or do something that goes against their beliefs and they can see no valid reason for having made the statement or taken the action, they are placed in cognitive dissonance.

◆ Researchers argue that to resolve this dissonance, subjects tend to change their attitudes to bring them into line with the statements they have made or the actions they have taken.

◆ The impression management hypothesis argues that cognitive dissonance results can be explained, not as real changes in attitudes and beliefs, but rather as professed changes for the purpose of maintaining an appearance of consistency in the eyes of other people.

◆ We often look for stable traits in other people or for the motives behind their behaviors as a way of understanding them. Social psychologists call this attribution. People generally are held accountable for behavior that is attributed to personality or trait variables and are considered blameless for behavior that is attributed to environmental forces. People tend to attribute their own behavior more to environmental forces and to attribute the behavior of other people more to personality and trait forces.

◆ The self-serving bias describes our tendency to attribute behavior that has a good outcome to our own personality traits and to attribute behavior that has a bad outcome to external forces that are beyond our control.

◆ SUGGESTIONS FOR FURTHER READING

1. Aronson, E. (1987). *The social animal* (5th ed.). New York: W. H. Freeman. For the general reader or student of psychology, an examination of many areas in social psychology, including prejudice, political unrest, advertising, and sexual behavior.

2. Baron, R. A., & Byrne, D. (1987). *Social psychology: Understanding human interaction* (5th ed.). Boston: Allyn & Bacon. A college-level introductory textbook on social psychology.

3. Cialdini, R. B. (1985). *Influence: Science and practice.* New York: Random House. An interesting account of the ways human beings can influence each other. For the student or general reader.

4. Latane, B., & Darley, J. M. (1970). *The unresponsive bystander: Why doesn't he help?* New York: Appleton-Century-Crofts. The classic text on bystander intervention.

5. Lindzey, G., & Aronson, E. (Eds.). (1985). *Handbook of social psychology* (3rd ed.). Hillsdale, NJ: Erlbaum. A high-level comprehensive handbook on social psychology.

6. Milgram, S. (1974). *Obedience to authority.* New York: Harper & Row. Discusses Milgram's obedience research.

7. Paulus, P. B. (Ed.). (1980). *The psychology of group influence.* Hillsdale, NJ: Erlbaum. An advanced-level discussion of research on how groups influence each other.

Chapter Nineteen

Gender, Attraction, and Intimacy

PROLOGUE

PROLOGUE

GIRLS AND BOYS

From the moment a baby is born, parents tend to treat boys and girls differently. Although male and female babies exhibit few behavioral differences, most parents will describe their daughters as cuter, softer, or more delicate than their sons. Fathers are especially likely to treat babies differently based on gender. Fathers tend to emphasize the beauty and delicacy of their newborn daughters and the strength and coordination of their newborn sons (Krieger, 1976).

In one interesting experiment, these different reactions of mothers and fathers were made apparent. In this study, preschoolers were given stereotypical sex-typed toys to play with, including kitchen play sets, a dollhouse, an army war game, and cowboy outfits. Both boys and girls were given "girls' toys" to play with on one occasion and "boys' toys" on another. The children were told to play with these toys the way girls would (for girls' toys) or as boys would (for boys' toys). What the experimenters were interested in was the reaction of the mother and father when they entered the room and saw which toys their children were playing with.

When the mothers saw the children playing, they showed little differential reaction to the toy sets. But the fathers showed a strong reaction. Fathers were far more negative when their children were playing with the "inappropriate" toys. This was especially true when the fathers found their sons playing with "girls' toys" in the way that girls would. The fathers in these cases either tried to interfere with their son's play or simply stood to one side in an obvious show of disgust (Langlois & Downs, 1980).

In a similar vein, other researchers have shown that fathers are more likely to offer sons toys that are stereotypically considered male, such as trucks or footballs (Jacklin & Maccoby, 1983). Mothers are also more supportive of their children's play when it involves "sex-appropriate" toys, but their reactions tend to be more subtle (Caldera, Huston, & O'Brien, 1989). Mothers generally treat boy and girl infants less differently than do fathers. For this reason, fathers, in our culture may have an important effect on the early learning of what most people in the culture consider to be sex-appropriate roles (Power, 1981).

CONTENTS

GENDER ROLE
The behaviors associated with one sex or the other.

GENDER-ROLE IDENTIFICATION
The degree to which a child adopts the sex role of a particular model.

Not only fathers and mothers but the culture as a whole tends to treat boys and girls differently. One study found that adults were more likely to offer a doll to a child they thought was a girl and more likely to offer a truck to a child they thought was a boy (Huston, 1983). In another study, adults' observations of the same infant differed based on whether they were told it was a boy or a girl (Condry & Condry, 1977). As you can see, many forces are at work teaching children what their "appropriate" sex roles should be.

IN THIS CHAPTER, we will examine gender issues such as these and also discuss the cognitive and social-cultural aspects of human sexuality. We will look at the formation of sex roles and gender identity and the pressure that society and culture bring to bear in shaping our sexual behavior. We'll also explore love and intimacy, the history of sexual research, and some sexual myths and misunderstandings.

WHY PSYCHOLOGISTS STUDY GENDER, ATTRACTION, AND INTIMACY

Our sex greatly influences the relationships, pursuits, choices, and conflicts that we face in life. Because of this, psychologists are interested in every aspect of our sexuality. They want to know how the biological and hormonal aspects of sexuality may affect behavior, how our cognitive understanding of being either male or female shapes our relationships, and how social-cultural influences on sexuality can direct our futures and determine our roles in society. Psychologists also are interested in intimacy and love. The reason for their interest was probably best expressed by Harry Harlow in 1958, when he gave the presidential address to the American Psychological Association:

Love is a wondrous state, deep, tender, and reassuring. Because of its intimate and personal nature it is regarded by some as an improper topic for experimental research. But, whatever our personal feelings may be, our assigned mission as psychologists is to analyze all facets of human and animal behavior into their component variables. So far as love or affection is concerned, psychologists have failed in their mission. The little we know about love does not transcend simple observation and the little we write about it has been written better by poets and novelists. (Harlow, 1958, p. 673)

GENDER-ROLE ACQUISITION

As young children grow, certain behaviors come to be expected of them. Among these behaviors are those expected because of the child's gender. The acquisition of these behaviors is an example of the interaction between the child's cognitive development and his or her culture, which determines which behaviors are deemed appropriate for each gender. These behaviors constitute what is known as a **gender role.***

As we discussed in the Chapter Prologue, the cultural shaping of gender roles may begin as early as birth. But determining how children learn gender roles requires a theoretical understanding of **gender-role identification.** Psychoanalytic, social learning, and cognitive theories have all addressed this question. Each predicts that the parent's gender-role-related behavior should have a striking effect on the child's developing sexual identity, even though each theory views the development of gender-role identification differently.

*Some researchers prefer the term *sex role*. In practice, however, the two terms, *sex role* and *gender role*, should be treated as synonymous (Maccoby, 1988).

According to the Freudian or psychoanalytic view, a boy's identification with his father results from a drive to avoid retaliation for initially desiring his mother because of the bond that he formed with her during feeding. This came to be known as the *Oedipus complex*, named after Oedipus, the mythical Greek king, who killed his father and married his mother without knowing who they really were. According to this view, once the boy child has identified with his father to avoid confronting him as a rival for the mother's affection, the boy adopts the father's ways as his own. Girls identify with their mothers in a more complex way known as the *Electra complex*. It is more complex because the girl also begins with an attachment to her mother via nursing, so a simple mirror image of the Oedipus complex can't be used as a sufficient explanation. Although psychologists find the Freudian view historically interesting and colorful, it is generally regarded as scientifically limited (Jacklin, 1989), and few currently refer to it or consider it when examining this issue.

Some people have developed a more modern psychoanalytic approach to the question of gender-role identification, but they readily admit that their perspective is quite subjective (Stoller, 1985). Instead, most current researchers emphasize social learning theory or cognitive theory.

Social Learning Theory

Social learning theory is based on the work of Albert Bandura, described in Chapter 8. In this view, children's behaviors are reinforced or punished according to what parents and society deem appropriate for the child's gender. In the Chapter Prologue we saw how parents may treat children differentially based on gender. Parents provide toys for their daughters that are different from those they give their sons and encourage their children to develop gender-appropriate interests.

Modeling and observational learning are considered to be important aspects of social learning theory. Boys learn to observe men to see how they are expected to behave, and girls learn to observe women. Boys notice that in books and the media men are generally portrayed as the initiators of action. On television, for example, about 70 percent of the major characters who initiate actions in any kind of program are men (Huston, 1983). According to social learning theory, parents, television, peers, and society as a whole shape the acquisition of gender roles through modeling and observational learning.

The Cognitive View

Lawrence Kohlberg (1966) was the first to propose a cognitive conceptualization of gender-role acquisition. According to this view, after children realize that they have a self, they come to understand that they are either male or female, and this cognitive realization then guides the children to change their behavior to match what society deems appropriate for their gender. The time at which children first become aware of their gender and its meaning is an important consideration, because cognitive theory predicts that gender-role acquisition will not begin until the child has the concept that he or she is a boy or a girl, respectively, and understands what it means to be a boy or a girl. This has led researchers to examine the development of a child's concept of gender as a way to test the theory's prediction that "gender-appropriate" behaviors will not precede the child's conceptual grasp of gender.

THE DEVELOPMENT OF GENDER UNDERSTANDING.   Children appear to develop a **gender understanding**—that is, to comprehend that they are boys or girls—by about the age of 3 years (Thompson, 1975). Although a 2-year-

GENDER UNDERSTANDING
A person's comprehension that he or she is either a boy or a girl; usually develops in children by about the age of 3 years.

From an early age, children engage in behavior that their culture considers appropriate for their gender.

GENDER CONSTANCY
The realization that one's sex is determined by unchanging criteria and is unaffected by one's activities or behavior; usually develops in children by the age of 6 or 7 years.

old child may tell you she is a girl, she may have trouble understanding who else is a girl or who is a boy or, for that matter, why she is called a girl. Also, 3-year-old children, whose cognitive processing is limited (see Chapter 3), generally fail to understand gender constancy.

Gender constancy is the understanding that your own sex will remain constant—once a boy, always a boy. A child is demonstrating a grasp of gender constancy when she understands that just because a girl puts on a jersey and plays football, she does not turn into a boy—she is still a girl. Surprising as it is to most adults to discover, the development of gender constancy isn't usually complete until a child reaches the age of about 6 years (Emmerich & Goldman, 1972; Wehren & De Lisi, 1983). Researchers have found that the progression from rudimentary gender understanding through the completion of gender constancy is similar in other cultures, although the final age at which gender constancy occurs may vary by a few years (Munroe, Shimmin, & Munroe, 1984). But the acquisition of gender constancy can have its costs. For instance, in one experiment, boys who had achieved gender constancy were found to play more with an uninteresting toy that was endorsed as a "boy's toy" than with a toy that was more fun (Frey & Ruble, 1992). That's rather sad and shows one of the costs of sex typing; children who acquire gender constancy may come to believe that certain fun toys, games, or activities are now out of bounds for them simply because those activities aren't considered sex appropriate.

GENDER CONSTANCY AND COGNITIVE THEORY. As we noted earlier, Kohlberg's cognitive theory predicts that children will not show gender-role acquisition to any significant degree until they have a cognitive grasp of what it means to be a boy or a girl; but this is not what happens. Children engage in stereotypical gender-role behaviors well *before* they are cognizant of their gender or its constancy. As early as 26 months of age, children are typically aware of the different things that constitute masculine and feminine dress and behavior—they already know that men often wear shirts and suits, and shave their chins and that women often wear blouses and dresses and makeup. Children as young as 2 or 3 years quite commonly show some preference for what their culture deems to be sexually appropriate toys and activities (Jacklin, 1989); yet these children are often unaware that most of the toys they choose for themselves are considered more appropriate for their sex than for the opposite sex. In other words, contrary to Kohlberg's cognitive development view, children demonstrate a certain degree of sex typing before they have a complete understanding of which sex they are or that their sex remains constant.

Social learning theorists like to point to the child's selection of same-sex stereotyped toys as one of the earliest manifestations of sex-role acquisition. Even as early as 14 months of age, toddlers more often play with toys that are considered stereotyped for their own gender than with other toys (O'Brien & Huston, 1985), although they will readily play with both. Social learning theorists argue, of course, that parents have shaped and reinforced the toddler's choice of toys. In fact, in one study, researchers examined the rooms of boys and girls between 1 and 5 years of age and found that parents had indeed provided their children with a far greater variety of same-sex stereotyped toys than of opposite-sex stereotyped toys (Rheingold & Cook, 1975).

Social learning theory also predicts what we saw in the Chapter Prologue—that parents will differentially reinforce behaviors they deem sex appropriate for the gender of their child. Although the assertiveness of boys and girls at 13 to 14 months of age appears to be identical, parents tend to pay more attention to boys' assertive behaviors while attending more to girls' less intense communications (Fagot, Hagan, Leinbach, & Kronsberg, 1985). Peers also reinforce boys for being more assertive and girls for being less assertive. Peers apply strong sanctions against boys who show interest in female activities (Birns & Sternglanz, 1983). With all this pressure, it is argued, children who have adopted behaviors "appropriate" for the opposite sex soon are discouraged and begin to become sex typed.

This might lead us to wonder what might happen if fathers participated equally with mothers in the domestic responsibilities of raising the children. Would the children be less likely to acquire stereotypical sex roles?

In one study, children's sex-role attitudes were examined in relationship to the father's participation in child care and home chores. Even fathers who did not overtly display the stereotyped paternal role had little effect on the children's attitudes; the children continued to show sex-role stereotyped attitudes (Baruch & Barnett, 1986). As you may have noticed, this finding is contrary to the social learning view. Many other studies have also contradicted the social learning view. One study, for example, found that some children didn't necessarily choose same-sex stereotyped toys with which to play. According to social learning theory, this would indicate that the children had not been shaped to play with such toys. But when these same children were asked to choose a sex-stereotyped toy for another child, they were quite able to do so. This shows that they knew which toys were deemed appropriate for boys and girls; they just did not always care to play with the toys sex stereotyped for their own gender (Eisenberg, 1983).

This debate has gone on for years, and many researchers now believe that the two views—cognitive and social learning theory—should be intertwined to create a cognitive–social learning view (Serbin & Sprafkin, 1986). One interesting version of this current trend is gender schema theory.

Gender Schema Theory

In 1981, researcher Sandra Bem suggested **gender schema theory** to explain the intertwining of the two theories. In her view, as children develop, they reach a point when they are able to integrate cognitively all the different sex-typed behaviors they have acquired through social learning and conditioning. This cognitive integration helps to shape their attitudes and beliefs about sex roles and guides them to their own decisions about what is sex appropriate (Bem, 1981). Bem's view explains how children can show sex-typed behaviors long before they have gender constancy. The theory also explains how, bit by bit, cognitive advances can help the child organize and integrate all the information that he or she has acquired about sex roles up to that point. Supporting this view is research showing that as soon as children acquire even a very rudimentary understanding of gender, sex typing suddenly becomes more prominent as the children rapidly form gender stereotypes and alter their behavior to better fit gender expectations (Martin & Little, 1990).

Gender schema theory may also apply to the way parents help shape their children's sex typing. For instance, although it is true that parents typically reinforce the use of sex-appropriate toys, parents are more likely to do so when they know their children possess gender constancy (Fagot, Leinbach, & O'Boyle, 1992).

Table 19.1 outlines the development of sexual identity according to the four theories we have discussed in this chapter. Research in this area is currently continuing at a fast pace; whether Bem's view is correct remains to be seen. Perhaps a complete understanding of children's sex typing will require an entirely new theoretical view—one not yet considered.

GENDER SCHEMA THEORY
The theory developed by Sandra Bem that explains how cognitive advances help the child to organize and integrate the information that he or she has learned about his or her sex.

TABLE 19.1 ◆ THE DEVELOPMENT OF SEXUAL IDENTITY

THEORETICAL VIEW	INITIAL STATE	FORCE	REACTION
Psychoanalytic (boys)	Pleasure bond made with mother through nursing	Desires mother, identifies with father	Male sex typing
Psychoanalytic (girls)	Pleasure bond made with mother through nursing	Desires father; identifies with mother	Female sex typing
Social learning (boys and girls)	No differentiation of behavior with respect to gender	Differential reinforcement for and modeling of gender-specific behaviors	Shaping of culturally appropriate sex typing
Cognitive (boys and girls)	No understanding of gender	Advances in cognitive development allow an understanding of gender	Sex typing based on child's comprehension of what culture deems appropriate for his or her gender
Gender schema (boys and girls)	No understanding of gender	Slowly, through reinforcement, modeling, and cognitive development, an understanding (schema) of sex-typical behavior is acquired	The child's schema is applied to the self in varying degrees, depending on how much the child is reinforced or encouraged to behave in a manner deemed sex appropriate by his or her culture

AN ENDURING QUESTION: DO MALES AND FEMALES HAVE DIFFERENT "NATURAL" SKILLS OR TRAITS?

What causes the psychology of men and women to be different? Why do boys and girls develop different attitudes, behaviors, and sexual orientations, seemingly based on their gender? Is it mostly a matter of biology, or does the environment play a large role?

To give you a feel for just how long people have been interested in these kinds of questions, let's look back a couple thousand years to the great Greek philosopher Aristotle (384–322 B.C.), who said that women were "more compassionate . . . more envious, more querulous, more slanderous, and more contentious" and that men were "more disposed to give assistance in danger" and "more courageous" (Book IX of The History of Animals, Chapter 1; cited in Miles, 1935, p. 700). He believed these were natural female and male traits, not characteristics that were taught or learned.

As recently as our own century, some researchers equated the abilities of women with those of primitive people or children, a belief that we today find ridiculous. Even Sigmund Freud argued that females were psychologically inferior (Horney, 1939). But what do we actually know about real sex differences? Except for obvious anatomical differences and the fact that one gender has the ability to give birth, what true sex differences are there?

Part of the debate has focused on the term *sex difference*. It is argued that a real sex difference exists when, for example, a rooster crows but a hen doesn't. What we observe in people, on the other hand, should be considered a sex-related variation in ability because, on average, one sex may be slightly better than the other at certain skills (Caplan, Mac-

AN ENDURING QUESTION, CONTINUED

Pherson, & Tobin, 1985). However it is defined, "sex differences" is a hot issue. And, while it is probably correct to say that we may still be a long way from having solid answers to our questions, the discoveries made so far have been intriguing.

To get some of the flavor of this ongoing debate, let's look at a few topics that have been the focus of sex differences research. The first thing that may surprise you is that the major topics in this field are very specific, such as gender differences in spatial ability or mathematical skill, rather than broader aspects of personality, such as gender differences in emotion or aggression. Although the broader topics are often discussed, and we have already mentioned some examples in this chapter, specific skills are easier to define and measure and are, therefore, better candidates for demonstrating a clear, true biological gender difference in behavior.

Business textbooks from the 1950s often stated as a fact that women were better typists than men because of their naturally superior manual dexterity. While this belief may have justified hiring only women for the typing pool, the same texts never bothered to explain why such a supposed superior dexterity shouldn't have also made women better surgeons. So what real gender differences are there?

Spatial Ability

The modern field of gender differences dates back to 1974 when Eleanor Maccoby and Carol Jacklin published *The Psychology of Sex Differences*; their aim was to examine the beliefs concerning sex differences in behavior and either document them thoroughly or dismiss them altogether (Maccoby & Jacklin, 1974). Maccoby and Jacklin discovered a few real sex differences, but they were small. Among these differences was a superior spatial ability among boys. (Spatial ability is the ability to understand how objects would appear at different angles and how they would relate to each other in a given space.) After this discovery, many biological theories to explain these differences were proposed (Kimura, 1985).

Interestingly, this research was being conducted at a time when the economic and social status of women was becoming a major issue. Consequently, researchers often worried that their findings might be misinterpreted. Many feared that any research that showed one sex (especially women) as somehow less able than the other, however slightly, would be used to justify social injustice. This concern was especially acute because the media quickly picked and disseminated them widely, often to an audience that made more of the typically subtle differences than was merited. For instance, at the time I was engaged to my future wife and I can recall giving her advice about parking the car. When she didn't listen and parked it her way—and not very well—I hastened to add that she should have deferred to my superior spatial abilities. I recall that she promptly crumpled up a piece of paper and deftly bounced it off the end of my nose asking, "Is that good enough spatial ability for you?"

The concern over the problem of superior male spatial ability led to an enormous amount of research. Then, in 1985, a detailed critique dismissed years of research supporting male superiority in spatial ability because of faulty methodology, debatable statistics, observer bias, and failure to define adequately what was meant by "spatial ability" (Caplan, MacPherson, & Tobin, 1985). As a result, many researchers dismissed the pre-

AN ENDURING QUESTION, CONTINUED

viously held belief that males have superior spatial ability. Others, however, tightened study protocols and definitions and continued to argue that research shows a difference in spatial ability. For example, one such study has shown that compared to unaffected females, males and females suffering from congential adrenal hyperplasia or CAH (a disorder in which the fetus is exposed to testosterone, the male sex hormone, in the womb) are superior at tasks that require that they find hidden patterns or mentally rotate geometric forms or shapes (Resnick, Berenbaum, Gottesman, & Bouchard, 1986).

Finally, in 1992 the issue of gender differences in spatial ability revived when researchers discovered that spatial ability in 16-year-old females was best predicted by how masculine the girls had rated themselves to be when they were 11 years old (e.g., how much they wished to be a boy) (Newcombe & Dubas, 1992). Perhaps this means that "masculinity," rather than maleness, is somehow associated with better spatial skills. For instance, do certain "male" activities enhance spatial skills? Or do biological variables link masculinity in either sex with increased spatial skills? No one yet knows, but research in this interesting area is continuing.

Mathematical Ability

While supposed differences in spatial ability raised a few eyebrows, the reported difference in mathematical ability caused a furor. In 1979, researchers Camilla Benbow and Julian Stanley gave the Scholastic Aptitude Test (SAT), which includes mathematical and verbal portions, to 9927 seventh and eighth graders who had had the same exposure to mathematics, regardless of sex. The boys performed significantly better than the girls on the math portion. Among those students who scored over 700 out of a possible 800, boys outnumbered girls 13 to 1 (Benbow & Stanley, 1983). Using questionnaires, the researchers found that the girls who were tested liked math as much as the boys and believed that math would be valuable in their careers (Benbow & Stanley, 1981).

In opposition, some researchers argued that these kinds of tests alone do not demonstrate in any conclusive way that the superior mathematical ability of males is due to biological or brain differences. Furthermore, even if male mathematical superiority were traced to sexually differentiated brain structures, such structures might still be the result of early childhood experience, because early experience may dictate the development of specialized brain organization. Another possibility is that girls are socialized to be afraid of math or to believe that they can't master its apparent complexities (Licht & Dweck, 1984).

Then, in 1982, the eminent Harvard neurologist Norman Geschwind (1926–1984) described a possible hormonal basis to explain math excellence in boys. Geschwind recalled that an excess of testosterone during fetal development can change the brain anatomy of rats so that the right hemisphere of their brains becomes dominant; perhaps, he argued, the same occurs in humans. Geschwind argued further that there should be a greater proportion of left-handedness among those whose right brain is dominant (Geschwind & Behan, 1982), because the brain hemispheres control the opposite side of the body; thus; right-hemisphere dominance would likely lead to left-handedness. Geschwind also suggested that im-

AN ENDURING QUESTION, CONTINUED

mune system disorders might also be present as a reaction to the excessive fetal testosterone levels that led to the right-hemisphere dominance in the first place.

To test Geschwind's view, Benbow and Stanley took a survey of 40,000 students for whom they had scores on the SAT mathematical portion. To their surprise, 20 percent of the mathematically gifted students were found to be left-handed (more than twice the expected number), and 60 percent had immune system disorders such as allergies or asthma (five times the expected level). In the same population of students, but among those whose scores were lower, left-handedness and immune system disorders were found to occur at normal rates (Kolata, 1983).

Upon further examination, however, it was concluded that Geschwind's theory of brain reorganization in the presence of excessive hormone is so complex that it is unclear how one would go about testing the theory or developing an animal model to demonstrate some of its principles (McManus & Bryden, 1991). The reason for the mathematical superiority of boys at the extreme end of the spectrum remains a mystery.

It is again interesting to note how social or political pressure might influence this kind of research. For instance, a number of researchers have pointed out that gender differences in spatial or intellectual abilities observed in the past are not as great now as they were 10 or 20 years ago (Feingold, 1988; Hyde & Linn, 1988; Jacklin, 1989). This finding, in turn, has led some to argue that gender differences observed and recorded over the years must be the result of environment, because there hasn't been enough time for evolutionary developments to account for the recent narrowing of these gender differences. Others argue that a bias toward equality is skewing the research. Still others contend that many of the tests used to measure gender differences have been altered to reduce the appearance of gender differences and that the research is showing this effect rather than a real effect. All of this has led to a growing belief that studying gender differences is far more complicated than anyone had originally envisioned and that much more research will have to be conducted before a clear understanding of the nature-nurture aspects of gender differences can emerge.

FOR CRITICAL ANALYSIS

1. If you were a researcher and you discovered beyond any reasonable doubt that men really were smarter than women, but the difference was so slight that it was of no practical significance, should you keep that knowledge to yourself? What harm might you cause if you announced your discovery? On the other hand, what value is there in sharing your finding with others?

2. As equality of the sexes became more politically popular, gender differences in scientific research were found to diminish. In this instance, how might politics be affecting scientific findings? When explaining behavior, the British have often emphasized nature as a cause, while Americans have often looked to nurture. How might the different historical backgrounds of these two nations account for such a bias? How can political biases in science be resolved? ◆

ATTRACTION

It would be impossible to understand sexuality or intimacy fully without also investigating attraction between one person and another. Which factors determine who will be our lovers or intimate friends? Psychologists have examined many of the variables that affect our liking and loving of others. Let's look at some of these.

Liking

All of us know some people whom we especially like. These people have a special significance for us. We look forward to seeing them and enjoy being with them; they make our lives happier. And one of the desires that most of us share is the hope that other people will like us.

In general, researchers have found that we tend to like people most who give us the most gratification for the least effort on our own part. If someone is nearby and is easy to get along with, if that person fills our needs and makes us laugh, the chances of "falling in like" are much greater than if the person is distant and difficult to get along with and meets only a few of our needs. Although this general assessment should hardly surprise you, it is interesting to examine each variable that may affect the probability of liking another person. You may find that some of the variables are more important and that some have a different effect than you imagined.

CLOSENESS. Our relationships with other people depend a great deal on their physical proximity to us. There's a much greater chance that we will like those people who live nearby than those who live farther away. In a study examining marriage licenses, one researcher found that half of the couples who applied for a license lived within 14 blocks of each other (Koller, 1953). Perhaps your one love in the world is really your one true love within 14 blocks! In another study, conducted in a college dormitory, students were asked to identify the other people in the dormitory whom they especially liked. The person next door was more often liked than the person two doors down the hall. The person two doors away was more liked than was someone three doors away, and so on (Priest & Sawyer, 1967). Other studies have found that simply being someone's roommate will foster friendship more often than one might expect (Newcomb, 1961). One of the most striking demonstrations of this proximity effect came to light during research conducted among the students attending the state police training academy in Maryland. Students were asked to identify the members of the class with whom they had become close friends. The researcher was surprised to find that over 44 percent of those identified came either immediately before or immediately after the trainee on the alphabetical list of names used at the academy (Segal, 1974). The explanation is that the trainees had been placed in dormitory rooms and assigned seats in the classroom based on alphabetical order. Consequently, those who were close to one another alphabetically were more likely to have contact.

It may have already occurred to you that proximity to another person sometimes leads to dislike as well. If people have dissimilar initial attitudes, then proximity generally will not lead to attraction. The same is true if one of the people involved is annoying. For instance, a stranger who sits close to you in the movie theater and talks incessantly throughout the film is not likely to become a close friend. If strangers stand so close that they invade your personal space, you are not likely to care for them. The people in proximity whom we dislike tend to be those who upset or disrupt our enjoyment of our immediate environment (Ebbesen, Kjos, & Konecni, 1976). As a rule, however, closeness leads to liking rather than disliking.

SIMILARITY.   Once we've had the chance to make the acquaintance of those in our immediate vicinity, whether we will like someone often depends on how similar to us that person appears to be in terms of shared values, attitudes, and beliefs. We also tend to prefer people who are similar to us in age, level of education, status of occupation, and political views (Laumann, 1969).

The fact that likes attract has been well documented. In one study, college students were paired by a computer according to similarity and dissimilarity of attitudes and beliefs. The couples were then sent on a half-hour date to the school cafeteria. When they returned, their attraction for each other was measured by how close they stood together and by a survey taken of their attitudes toward each other. Measures were taken immediately after the date and again several weeks later. Couples with similar attitudes and beliefs were more likely to want to have another date than were couples who were very dissimilar (Byrne, Ervin, & Lamberth, 1970).

A number of reasons have been put forth to help explain why people who are similar to each other are more likely to find each other attractive (Rubin, 1973). First, we feel good when people agree with us; agreement gives us confidence in our own opinions and boosts our self-esteem. Second, if other people share our views, we immediately think that we know more about them and may feel more comfortable bringing up new topics and less worried that we may start an argument. Third, we are more likely to share activities with people who share our views. We may find it easier to interact with them because they, too, want to go to the church meeting, the political rally, or the film festival. Finally, to maintain our self-concept, we like to believe that those who share our views are good people, people with whom we should associate.

Under certain circumstances, opposites may attract, too. At first, this observation may seem to contradict the research we've been discussing, but "opposite" in this case doesn't refer to opposite attitudes and beliefs but rather to the fact that each person may be lacking something that the partner can provide. Psychologists refer to this as *sharing complementary needs*. For example, if you are a domineering and outgoing person, you may be more likely to find attractive someone who is reserved and submissive than you are someone who is also domineering and outgoing. Some researchers have argued that similarity is most important when a relationship is beginning, but that complementary needs begin to play a more important role as the relationship becomes a long-term one (Kerckhoff & Davis, 1962). Others believe that similarity remains the most important factor, especially among well-adjusted married couples (Meyer & Pepper, 1977).

COMPETENCE.   We generally prefer someone who is competent. Very few of us appreciate incompetence, especially in those on whom we depend. In fact, demonstrating incompetence to people we have just met is a pretty sure way of making ourselves disliked. But sometimes people can seem too perfect, too superior. Such people can make us feel inferior; although we may have a grudging admiration for them, we may not like to be around them. Consequently, we may not like them. If a competent person is not too perfect and seems capable of mistakes, we are more likely to feel good about that person; she will seem more human and, therefore, more like ourselves.

In one experiment, subjects listened to one of four tapes that contained a recording made by a candidate for a quiz contest. The same person had made each tape. On two of the tapes, the contestant was described as extremely intelligent and very successful in college. On the other two tapes, the contestant was said to be of average intelligence and average ability in school. On one of the tapes in each condition, the contestant was overheard to have an accident. He spilled coffee on himself. No accident occurred on the other two tapes. In this way, all four possibilities—superior–no accident, superior–accident, average–no accident, and average–accident—could be compared. None of the listeners heard more than one tape.

The groups of listeners rated how they felt about the contestant, and the results were compared. The best-liked contestant was the superior one who had the accident. Ranked next was the superior contestant who had no accident. Ranked third was the average contestant who had no accident, and ranked fourth, and last, was the average contestant who had the accident (Aronson, 1969). The accident had enhanced the likability of the superior contestant and had detracted from the likability of the average contestant. In terms of competence, then, the best-liked individuals appear to be those who are competent but who are also human and are likely to make occasional mistakes. Because they have proved their competence before, we are likely to forgive them their error—it makes them seem more like us. When a person whom we view as inferior makes a mistake, however, we often see the blunder as further evidence of inferiority, which is likely to detract from that individual's appeal.

Theories about Liking

As you have discovered, many variables can affect whether we will like someone. Researchers have attempted to integrate these findings into comprehensive theories. The four major theories about liking are reinforcement theory, equity theory, social exchange theory, and gain-loss theory.

REINFORCEMENT THEORY. The **reinforcement theory of liking** argues that we come to like or dislike people as a result of our learning. As we discussed in Chapter 8, there are three major forms of learning: associative, instrumental, and social. According to the reinforcement theory, we come to like or dislike other people because of processes involved in these three modes of learning. Through associative learning, we come to like or dislike other people because of the experiences and stimuli we associate with them. We will like people whom we associate with pleasant experiences and attractive attributes more than we will those we associate with unpleasant experiences or unattractive attributes.

According to instrumental learning, we like the people who reward us and dislike the people who punish us. In this view, we are more likely to feel warmth toward someone who offers us important opportunities than we would had we interacted with the same person just as often but in a less rewarding situation (Clore & Byrne, 1974; Byrne & Clore, 1970).

According to social learning, we are more likely to like people whom we see are liked by others. Because others are modeling the liking of a particular individual, we may, especially if we admire the models, be more likely to imitate their behavior by also liking that person. Similarly, it becomes more probable that we will dislike someone whom we see disliked by others whom we admire.

EQUITY THEORY. If whether we liked someone were totally controlled by simple reinforcement principles, then we might be expected to like people who give us the most but take the least. In this kind of relationship, we could maximize our reinforcement. But psychologists have observed that in actual liking relationships, those we like most are often those with whom we share. People often say that they feel distressed when they are placed in a situation of social inequity; that is, when they are giving more than they receive or receiving more than they give. The **equity theory** modifies reinforcement theory by describing how people work toward a collective reward system for equitably distributing costs and rewards. According to the equity theory, people learn that what they receive from others should be in proportion to what they have placed in the relationship. Such a system of equity appears to be well established in most cultures. Most people will agree that if you expect a lot from a relationship, then you should expect to put a lot into it. Many of us feel that when someone does a favor for us, we are in one way or another obliged to return the favor. In this way, we can restore equity to the relationship. Even in relationships that other people may see as inequitable, the *participants* often feel that there is equity because they have psychologically distorted the exchanges that have been made through the use of defense mechanisms or other psychological means.

The equity theory argues that in romantic or liking relationships, the most successful arrangements are equitable ones. For this reason, a very attractive man might, perhaps unconsciously, attempt to match himself with a very attractive woman, so that he feels he is getting a fair return for his physical attractiveness. In fact, research does show that in romantic relationships, but

REINFORCEMENT THEORY OF LIKING
A social theory of relationships that we like those whom we have been reinforced for liking or whom we associate with pleasurable events or circumstances.

EQUITY THEORY
A social theory of relationships that individuals attempt to strike a balance between what they give and what they receive; that they strive toward a collective reward system for equitably distributing costs and rewards.

EXCHANGE THEORY
A social theory of relationships that human interactions can best be understood by examining the costs and rewards to each person.

GAIN-LOSS THEORY
A social theory of relationships that we are most attracted to those who have given us the greatest net gain and are least attracted to those who have caused the greatest net loss.

not in platonic ones, the more attractive a person is, the more likely it is that he or she will pair up with a similarly attractive partner (Feingold, 1988b). The trade doesn't always have to be for a similar "commodity." For example, a wealthy woman might want to trade her money for an intelligent man. One interesting experiment demonstrated how intelligence might function as a commodity in the dating marketplace. In this experiment, researchers discovered that male subjects who were told that they had done poorly on a test were more likely to ask an unattractive women for a date, while male subjects who were told that they had scored well on a test were more likely to ask out an attractive woman (Kiesler & Baral, 1970). Presumably, the subjects' self-worth had been manipulated by the information that they had done either well or poorly, which left them with a greater or lesser amount of "social" currency that could be traded. If, after taking the test, the subject was led to believe that he was intelligent, he may have considered that he could trade his intelligence for beauty.

Equity theory can lead one to view human relationships as cold, selfish, and materialistic. Because it highlights the more calculating side of human behavior, the theory is sometimes unpopular among those first encountering it. And yet, common everyday expressions such as "trophy wife" (a term applied to a young, attractive woman who has just married a very successful older man who, in turn, has just divorced his wife of long standing for her) show us that people clearly understand the trade "my success and money for your beauty." However callous that observation may be, it, sadly, contains much truth.

EXCHANGE THEORY.   The **exchange theory** argues that people will like each other only if, in the social exchange, they both end up with a net profit in terms of what they have put into the relationship. This theory helps to explain an attraction between people with opposite needs. In such a situation, each person fills the needs of the other, and each feels that there has been a net gain in the exchange; that is, more has been obtained from the relationship than lost (Homans, 1961; Rubin, 1973). Although the exchange theory may clarify the formation and maintenance of liking relationships, it is difficult to apply because it is not easy to define loss or gain in a relationship; these terms are subjective. Furthermore, the exchange theory is hard-pressed to deal with acts of giving when no return for the action is expected. Such altruistic behavior, engaged in without hope of compensation, would not seem to have any value in the interpersonal marketplace that the exchange theory describes.

GAIN-LOSS THEORY.   The **gain-loss theory** argues that if someone we come to know likes us more and more as time passes, we will generally like that person better than if he had liked us from the start. Similarly, we dislike people whose evaluations of us have become more and more negative with time more than we do people who have always held us in a negative light (Aronson, 1969). We do not know why the gain-loss effect occurs, but a number of explanations have been postulated. One may be that people tend to ignore things that don't change but pay particular attention to changes. For this reason, a loss or a gain may seem more important.

Another reason may be that we often attribute the gain or loss of someone's liking or affection to our own behavior; that is, we have either won someone over or have driven someone away. If, on the other hand, the person has always liked us or has always disliked us, we usually attribute this orientation to the individual's predispositions rather than to anything we have done. If this is true, then gaining someone's regard may enhance our self-esteem, and because we associate the enhancement with that person, he or she appears more likable. The opposite would be true for someone who initially liked us but over time came to dislike us.

Finally, if someone comes to like us, it usually makes us less anxious about them. As we become less anxious, we like them more for reducing our anxiety. The opposite would be true for someone who began to dislike us more.

The Power of Good Looks

An old expression suggests that beauty is only skin deep. This is another way of saying that there is much more to a person than physical appearance and that to discriminate against those who are physically unattractive in favor of those who are attractive is a form of prejudice. Researchers have found, however, that people who are physically attractive are more often liked—not just sexually but also in most kinds of social situations. To a great degree, attractive people are perceived to be "more sociable, dominant, sexually warm, mentally healthy, intelligent and socially skilled than physically unattractive people" (Feingold, 1992, p. 304).

Is this man attractive?

In one study, psychologists deliberately left money in a telephone booth change return and then watched secretly as the next person came to use the telephone. The person in the telephone booth (both genders were tested) was then approached by either an attractive or an unattractive female confederate of the psychologist's. This person would say she might have left some money in the change return and would ask whether the subject in the telephone booth had found any. Subjects were more likely to return the money to the attractive confederate (Sroufe, Chaikin, Cook, & Freeman, 1977). This outcome may have occurred because it's more reinforcing to get a smile and a thank you from a beautiful person or because the subject hoped that returning the change would begin a relationship. Alternatively, the confederate's good looks may simply have made the subject feel better and, therefore, more likely to give the money back.

In mock trials, psychologists have found that juries are more likely to give an attractive defendant a less severe sentence (Leventhal & Krate, 1977). This is not always the case, however, If the defendant is said to have used his or her good looks while committing the crime, the sentence is more likely to be harsh. Investigators also have found that attractive, better-dressed panhandlers make more money than do unattractive ones (Kleinke, 1977).

Children demonstrate at an early age that physical attractiveness is an important dimension. In one study, 3- to 6-year-old children were asked to illuminate a slide of either an attractive or an unattractive child. The children were significantly more likely to illuminate the slide of the attractive child (Dion, 1977). By the fifth or sixth grade, attractive children are more successful in influencing and changing the behavior of children of the opposite sex than are unattractive children (Dion & Stein, 1978). By college, attractive people are more likely to have dating experience and sexual experience than are unattractive people (Curran & Lippold, 1975).

The perception of attractiveness may even have a built-in component; that is, there may be an aesthetic prototype for attractiveness that we understand apart from what we are taught. Two studies highlight this possibility. In the first study, it was found that infants as young as 2 or 3 months of age show a preference (as measured by how long they looked) for attractive over unattractive faces (Langlois, Ritter, Roggman, & Vaughn, 1991). Because these infants were probably too young to have been taught about what is or isn't attractive, it is assumed that their response showed an innate preference for symmetry or for some other aspects that we find common to attractive people.

In the second study, psychologists asked themselves what makes a face attractive. Based on the idea that natural selection generally favors the average over the extreme, they took many different faces of women and used a computer to make composites of 4, 8, 16, and 32 different faces. The more faces used, the more the composite face became an "averaged" face. When people were then asked to look at the composites and choose the most attractive, the most averaged face was the winner (see Figure 19.1). In fact, the more averaged a face was, the more beautiful it appeared to be (Langlois & Roggman, 1990)! It is known that infants are innately attracted to the human face (Dannemiller & Stephens, 1988). Perhaps, then, the most beautiful faces are the most prototypic. In other words, the faces we generally find to be most attractive are those whose individual features (eyes, nose, mouth, and so on) are closest to human averages.

Of course, the term *attractiveness* encompasses more than just physical features. Personality also plays a key role. And yet, knowing that you are *physically* attractive or unattractive can directly affect your personality. One study demonstrated that social skill was positively correlated with physical attractiveness. In this study, individuals engaged in telephone conversations and were then rated by their telephone partners, who had not yet seen them, on dimensions of social skill, anxiety, liking, and desirability for future interaction. The more physically attractive an individual was, the higher his or her ratings tended to be. These results probably reflect the fact that unattractive individuals may lack the courage to initiate social interactions or that they have not been approached by other people and therefore have failed to obtain the social skills more often demonstrated by attractive individuals (Goldman & Lewis, 1977).

Physical beauty can also have a radiating effect. In one experiment, researchers filmed a man walking arm in arm with either an attractive or an unattractive woman. Four different groups observed the films independently. Two groups saw the man with the attractive woman. The first group was told that she was a medical student and the second group that she was a waitress. The third and fourth groups saw the man with an unattractive woman. The third group was told she was a medical student and the fourth group that she was a waitress. All groups were asked to rate the level of happiness and success they believed the *man* possessed. Whether the woman was a waitress or a medical student had some effect on the subjects' ratings of the man. In all cases, however, the man with an attractive woman was rated as significantly more successful and happy than was the same man with the unattractive woman (Meiners & Sheposh, 1977). It would be interesting to conduct the experiment once again, this time filming a woman with an attractive or unattractive man. Perhaps women would value the man's profession more, or perhaps not. What do you think?

◆ **FIGURE 19.1**

These are not photographs of real women, but rather are made from computer-blended images of faces. Images a–d represent composites of 4, 8, 16, and 32 faces, respectively. The pictures made from the most composites (c and d) were rated as the most attractive even when compared with the individual faces that made up the composites.

(a)   (b)   (c)   (d)

Researchers also have demonstrated that attractive individuals are less likely to be affected by peer pressure. It may be that attractive individuals value their own opinion more than that of others because they have been told that they themselves are valuable. Unattractive individuals are more susceptible to peer pressure because they appear to have a greater desire to be liked and are therefore more likely to comply with group demands (Adams, 1977).

Attractive individuals are not always assessed in a better light. Whether they are often depends on which aspect is being evaluated (Eagly, Ashmore, Makhijani, & Longo, 1991). For instance, people more often perceive attractive people as vain and egotistical and as more likely to have extramarital affairs (Dermer & Thiel, 1975). And, although it is true that physical beauty affects judgments of personality, the reverse is also true. In one experiment, photographs of female college students were rated attractive, average, or unattractive by a group of undergraduate subjects. Then another group of undergraduates were shown the photos with either favorable, average, or unfavorable personality descriptions attached to them. Photos accompanied by a favorable description of personality were rated as more attractive than were those without the description, and those accompanied by unfavorable descriptions were rated as less attractive than were those without the description (Gross & Crofton, 1977). In this case, what was good was beautiful.

🧬 LOVE AND INTIMACY

To say that we love another is, perhaps, to give him or her the most positive evaluation of which we are capable. We talk a great deal about love, but researchers cannot always agree on what we mean by the word. In one sense, this is a semantic problem. Love can refer both to the heart-pounding excitement of a first sexual encounter and to the gentle affection between two elderly brothers.

Many people would just as soon not know why couples fall in love. Former senator William Proxmire once ridiculed two psychologists who were studying love and had requested an $84,000 federal grant. Proxmire stated emphatically, "Right at the top of the things we don't want to know is why a man falls in love with a woman." At the same time, however, scientists are finding that, if anything, passionate love and interest in romantic feelings are growing. In the 1960s, when college students were asked whether they would marry someone who met all of their needs but whom they didn't love, 24 percent of the women and 60 percent of the men said that they wouldn't. When asked again in 1979, 80 percent of the women and 86 percent of the men said that they wouldn't. Love had apparently become more important than ever. *New York Times* columnist James Reston, responding to Senator Proxmire's statement, gave the following rationale for studying love:

If the sociologists and psychologists can get even a suggestion of the answer to our patterns of romantic love, marriage, dissolution, divorce—and the children left behind—it could be the best investment of federal money since Mr. Jefferson made the Louisiana Purchase. (Reston, 1975)

H. H. Kelley (1983, p. 274) has outlined the behaviors of love as follows:

1. Verbal expression of affection
2. Self-disclosure: revealing intimate facts
3. Nonmaterial evidence of love: giving emotional and moral support, showing interest in another's activities and respect for his or her opinions
4. Feelings not expressed verbally: feeling happier, more secure, more relaxed when other is around
5. Material evidence of love: giving gifts, performing physical chores

PASSIONATE LOVE
A strong sexual desire for another individual combined with the perception that one is in love. This perception is often the result of misattributing to love a heightened physiological arousal for any reason.

6. Physical expression of love: hugging and kissing
7. Willingness to tolerate less pleasant aspects of other: tolerating demands in order to maintain the relationship

Love can be divided into two classifications: passionate love, which is a temporary but intense reaction to another, and conjugal love, which is a long-term relationship based on friendship and mutual respect.

Passionate Love

Passionate love is an intense emotional reaction, often based on strong sexual desire. An individual experiencing it thinks constantly about the person he wants to be with and thinks of that person in the context of love. Passionate love generally leads to an unrealistic evaluation of the love object.

Some researchers have noted three criteria that must be met before passionate love can occur (Berscheid & Walster, 1974). First, the person must be exposed by her culture to the idea of passionate love. In many cultures, the idea of love at first sight or passionate love is uncommon. Instead, marriages often are arranged, and love is viewed as something that may develop after many years of companionship. In modern Western culture, the idea of passionate love is not only common but expected. It is heralded in novels, songs, theater, and television dramas. As a result, a person in our culture not only thinks more about spontaneous and passionate love but also expects to fall in love, even suddenly.

Second, for passionate love to occur, an appropriate person must be present. For most people, the person must be an attractive member of the opposite sex. Passionate love and sexual attraction are highly associated with each other.

The third important criterion is an emotional arousal that the individual interprets as love. This reaction may take the form of sexual arousal or even of anxiety at meeting the other person.

The onset of passionate love is relatively swift and sudden (Berscheid, 1983). Interestingly, a mild feeling such as liking, especially if it has continued over a long time, usually does not become something as intense as passionate

Passionate love is often the most exciting aspect of a new relationship, but it typically diminishes with time.

love. This supports the idea that liking and passionate love are not simply different points along a single continuum of attraction, but rather are qualitatively different phenomena with different antecedents (Berscheid, 1983). Ironically, passionate love also is quite fragile compared with something as stable as liking. Passionate love rarely lasts for long and is generally replaced by either a loss of interest or a more enduring conjugal love.

Unfortunately, a cultural expectation, an attractive person, and physical arousal don't give us much to go on if we plan to build a long-term relationship, such as a marriage. Countless couples have fallen in love and have married quickly, only to find later that they were not well suited to each other. A survey of over 200 college couples who were dating and who stated that they were in love found that half of the couples had broken up by the end of 2 years. At the beginning of their love affairs, they had felt a strong physical attraction for each other and had believed that they would share their futures. But by the time 2 years had passed, half of them stated that they were either bored with the relationship or had found that they did not share similar interests (Hill, Rubin, & Peplau, 1976).

These findings may also indicate that liking and loving are two different things (Sternberg, 1987). Consider the following stories, both of which are true, although the names have been changed:

Tom sat right behind Jane in biology class. For Tom, it was love at first sight. From the very first day he saw Jane, he could think of little else: Thoughts of her preoccupied him constantly. Tom was therefore crushed when Jane found herself a boyfriend, Peter. Prior to that time, Tom had never really gotten to know Jane. His interactions with her all took place in his mind. Finally, Tom started having conversations with her and discovered that although he was still madly in love with her, he did not like her a whole lot.

Mike and Louise had been dating for about 3 months. Both of them seemed happy in the relationship, but their friends saw trouble. Louise just seemed a whole lot more involved than Mike. One night, Louise confessed her love and let on to her plans for their future together. Mike was dumbfounded. He had not made any plans and did not want them. Mike told Louise that he liked her but did not love her and did not think he ever could. Mike broke off the relationship the next day. (Sternberg, 1987, p. 331)

These two examples highlight the problems of love without liking and liking without love. Perhaps the strongest relationships are the ones in which the two partners *both* like and love each other.

CONJUGAL LOVE.　　After we fall passionately in love with and are aroused by someone, our passion generally doesn't last long—at least not at the same level—even if we continue to love and stay with that person. Our diminishing emotional passion may be supplanted by a **conjugal love** relationship. People who have romantic expectations that their sexual passion will remain at a high level usually face disappointment. Psychologist Ellen Berscheid interviewed a large number of undergraduates and asked how they would react if passion disappeared from their marriage. More than half said that they would want a divorce (Berscheid, 1983). Yet psychologists have found that passion generally does disappear. This may explain, at least to some degree, the high divorce rate in the United States.

Yet conjugal love often becomes deeper and more powerful than the initial passionate love was. Researchers have found that the most stressful experience the average person will ever face is the death of a spouse (Holmes & Rahe, 1967). Perhaps, more than any other factor, sharing experiences with each other leads to conjugal love, or, as it is sometimes called, *companionate love*. Another aspect of conjugal love is the willingness to make sacrifices for each other.

CONJUGAL LOVE
A deep and generally abiding love that develops between two people over long periods of time. It is associated with a desire to be together, share with one another, and sacrifice for one another. It is also called companionate love.

MASTURBATION
Sexual self-stimulation.

SPERMATORRHEA
A term coined by the physician Claude l'Allemand based on the erroneous assumption that nocturnal emissions were related to the venereal disease gonorrhea.

SEXUAL MYTHS AND RESEARCH

Historically, human sexuality has probably been surrounded by more myths and misunderstandings than any other subject. Many people think that sexual development and sexual behavior are very private matters and not uncommonly become embarrassed when discussing sex. As a result, the study of sexuality has often lagged behind other areas of investigation or been ignored altogether. Before researchers began to study sexuality carefully, misunderstandings about sex were common.

Early "Research"

One of the first researchers to write in detail about human sexual behavior was Richard von Krafft-Ebing (1840–1902), a professor of psychiatry at the University of Strasbourg in Germany. *Psychopathia Sexualis*, his most powerful—and frightening—work, was first published in 1886 and was last reprinted in the 1960s. Krafft-Ebing did little real scientific research; rather, he collected a series of gruesome case histories that he used as evidence to support his feeling that human sexual behavior was an assortment of disgusting diseases. Krafft-Ebing even argued that **masturbation** was a loathsome disease, often the precursor to lust murder. It has been said that *Psychopathia Sexualis*, probably more than any other book, encouraged disgust and revulsion about sex (Brecher, 1976).

Predating von Krafft-Ebing was Samuel Tissot (1728–1797), a Swiss physician who predicted that masturbation would lead to blindness, impotence, acne, and insanity, ideas that are still common among the uneducated. Tissot's beliefs were unwavering, even though he never bothered to test his predictions to see whether they really came true in people who masturbated. In the early 1800s, Claude François l'Allemand, a French physician, equated nocturnal emissions of semen by a sleeping male with gonorrhea, believing that both had the same cause. As a result, he referred to harmless nocturnal emissions as **spermatorrhea** and considered them a serious disorder. Compounding the errors, Charles Drysdale, another physician, described spermatorrhea as a terminal disorder ending with death by a "kind of apoplexy . . . induced by the exhausted state of the brain" (Sussman, 1976, p. 23). These physicians weren't necessarily lying; they may have made some faulty assumptions and false deductions. For instance, Drysdale may have had a dying patient who also had nocturnal emissions of semen; since Drysdale's training undoubtedly included nothing about the common nature of such emissions and no one ever discussed it, he may have erroneously linked the two as somehow showing cause and effect. At any rate, sex simply wasn't a topic that people of that time openly discussed. It was a forbidden subject, and few data about human sexual development existed. People didn't realize that the predictions were false because no one bothered to check.

Even as recently as 1900, physicians were so worried about the horrible consequences thought to result from the loss of semen through masturbation or from sexual stimulation that they openly advocated castration of male children who masturbated and clitoridectomy (removal of the clitoris) of female children who masturbated. Other physicians recommended severing the nerves to the penis or cauterizing of the genitals with hot irons or glass rods dipped in caustic solutions. Special spermatorrhea rings were made for those who feared arousal or for male children who had erections. As Figure 19.2 shows, an erection would not have been in the best interest of the wearer of such devices (Sussman, 1976). Until the last years of his life, even Sigmund Freud believed that the loss of 1 ounce of semen could cause the same fatigue as the

Spermatorrhea rings. (SOURCE: *Sussman, 1976, p. 60.*)

loss of more than a quart of blood (Brecher, 1976), which, of course, is not only untrue, but ridiculous.

As a young man, Havelock Ellis (1859–1939) had read the works of Charles Drysdale, the eminent physician who had described the dread scourge spermatorrhea. Ellis was terrified. He would never masturbate because he thought it was dangerous, but he could do nothing to prevent his nocturnal emissions. He had spermatorrhea—he was a dead man! He wept and prayed and searched desperately for a cure. Reading medical texts of the day, he was horrified at the gruesome measures physicians suggested to control spermatorrhea. He planned suicide, but found himself too afraid to attempt it, so he decided to become a monk. After some thought, however, he felt unworthy to become a monk because his problem was sexual. Finally, in an attempt to give the short life remaining to him some meaning, he decided to keep a diary describing his deterioration and death due to spermatorrhea and to leave it as a gift to science.

Oddly, as the months came and went, his brain didn't turn to oatmeal. His eyes didn't even lose their luster, an early symptom predicted by Dr. Drysdale. Slowly, fear gave way to anger as Ellis realized that the books were filled with lies and that he had been put through a period of unnecessary anguish. It was obvious that the loss of semen during nocturnal emissions did not result in deterioration and death. In that moment, Ellis knew he had found his goal in life—to uncover the truth about sexuality. He decided to devote the rest of his days to careful and accurate sexual research.

Although Havelock Ellis is not as well known as Sigmund Freud, his investigation of human sexuality in the early part of this century marked the beginning of modern sexual research. In his books, *Studies in the Psychology of Sex,* published between 1896 and 1928, Ellis pointed the way for later researchers such as Kinsey and Masters and Johnson. Ellis believed strongly that before people can label a sexual behavior deviant, they must document what normal sexual experiences are. Many of Ellis's findings are still valued. He noted, for instance, that sexual behavior was normal before puberty in both girls and boys, that masturbation was common in both sexes, that homosexuality and heterosexuality were not opposites but occurred in varying degrees, and that women had sexual desires, contrary to the myth advanced by the Victorians. He also found that orgasm is similar in men and women. Ellis stated that male impotence and female frigidity were in most cases caused by psychological problems and that when it came to perversions, the range of variation within normal limits was so great that "unusual" sexual behavior was, in fact, commonplace.

Largely as a result of Ellis's work, medical concerns about nocturnal emissions and masturbation came to an end early in this century (Brecher, 1976).

CHANGING SEXUAL BEHAVIOR

Sexually transmitted diseases, or **STDs,** are diseases primarily passed through sexual contact. These diseases include chlamydia, gonorrhea, syphilis, venereal warts, genital herpes, and acquired immune deficiency syndrome (AIDS). Some of these diseases, such as chlamydia, gonorrhea, and syphilis, are treatable with antibiotics. If left untreated, however, they can cause extensive damage to the reproductive system and, in the case of syphilis, even death. Lack of attention to these diseases is not uncommon because they often produce no immediate symptoms.

Venereal warts, genital herpes, and AIDS are caused by viruses and are therefore not susceptible to antibiotics. These disorders have no cures, and AIDS is especially dangerous. In fact, in 1993, 29,850 people died of AIDS in the United States (National Center for Health Statistics, 1993). Although it is not certain that infection with HIV (the virus that causes AIDS) will always lead to a full-blown case of AIDS, the majority of those infected with HIV do, in fact, go on to develop AIDS. To the best of our knowledge, once AIDS has developed, it is 100 percent fatal. Because AIDS can take a long time to develop following infection with HIV, the number of people dying now reflects the rate of infection 2 to 10 years ago, not the larger number being infected today. By 1993, more than 1,000,000 Americans were estimated to have been infected with the HIV virus. AIDS is no longer a potential health crisis, but a very real health disaster.

Currently, on an alarming number of urban campuses throughout the United States, an estimated 1 in every 300 students is infected with HIV. Campuses in the less densely populated areas of the nation, such as the mountain states, have lower rates of infection, but everywhere the percentage of infected students is climbing.

STDs have something in common besides their mode of transmission. They all can be avoided by a change in *behavior*. In fact, AIDS and other incurable STDs can currently be battled only through education and behavior change. Nevertheless, despite recent efforts to educate people to the dangers, many, including college students, remain woefully ignorant. And many who are educated still allow themselves to be exposed to the hazards of infection (Catania, et al., 1992).

The role of psychology, therefore, is twofold. First, psychologists must help educate people to the dangers of STDs by getting information to them. Second, psychologists must illuminate the reasons why people take risks even after they are aware of the dangers and help them control their behavior.

Because psychology is at the forefront of the educational effort, it is important to provide information to those who may be lacking it. The need is definitely there. For example in a 1990 survey of Americans (Reinisch & Beasley, 1990), researchers found that a *majority* answered "yes" to the following: "Anal intercourse between uninfected people can cause AIDS." Because AIDS is caused by a virus, not by a particular

sexual act, you cannot get AIDS from an uninfected partner. It is important to get this kind of factual information to the public.

Currently, researchers are going to great lengths to impress upon the public that the AIDS virus is only transmitted by the exchange of bodily fluids, as occurs during sexual intercourse, oral sex (although it is difficult to show that this has ever been a mode of transmission), and by blood exchange (as occurred during blood transfusions before blood was screened for the virus, or during the sharing of unsterile needles as IV [intravenous] drug users often do). Casual contact, such as might spread the common cold, has not been found to be a mode of transmission.

It is also important to know that a person may be infected with HIV for up to 6 months before a blood test will finally show positive because the body can take a long time to recognize the virus and begin to make the antibodies to which the test is sensitive (although it will usually register by 12 weeks after an infection has begun). For this reason, a negative HIV blood test is not proof that someone is uninfected unless that person has been sexually abstinent for 6 months prior to the test and has not shared needles with someone who is infected during that period. Although using condoms greatly reduces the chances of infection, they are not 100 percent effective. In fact, different brands of condoms have yielded different levels of safety. For this reason, abstinence remains the only completely "safe" approach to sex.

AIDS also continues to affect populations differently. The AIDS virus spread most rapidly among the homosexual population because gay men may encounter a greater number of sexual partners and are more likely to practice anal intercourse (Shilts, 1987). Anal intercourse spreads the virus more readily than vaginal intercourse because the bowel has a more fragile lining than the vaginal canal and tears more easily, giving the virus an entry point into the body proper. Similarly, AIDS is spreading rapidly through the heterosexual population in Africa because many people there have other STDs that leave sores or lesions that allow the virus entry. In some parts of Africa, AIDS is now the most common cause of death among men and the second leading cause among women.

The reasons people take risks even after they are educated to the dangers are more complex than the excuse of simple ignorance. They center on the processes of denial and failure to delay gratification.

Denial is a powerful defense mechanism (see Chapter 14). It helps people to cope with stress. But it can also lead to danger if they allow their tendency to deny what they don't want to believe to affect their judgment. AIDS counselors hear the same phrase every day, "I never thought that it could happen to me."

Psychologists work to help people train themselves to believe that it can happen to them. For instance, people may

Psychologists now know that masturbation is a normal development in little boys and girls and that it continues to be a normal practice engaged in by a majority of adolescents and adults. Thanks to the efforts of modern sexual researchers, we have been able to break away from the prejudices of the past. We know, for instance, that it is normal for a sleeping male to have occasional nocturnal emissions of semen (sometimes called *wet dreams*) and for a male child to have erections before puberty. But this kind of information about human sexual development wasn't always available to the scientific community. It has come from careful data gathering.

Modern Research

At the end of the Second World War, Alfred Kinsey, a zoologist and an expert on wasps, published a compendium of human sexual behavior in two volumes, *Sexual Behavior in the Human Male* and *Sexual Behavior in the Human Female*. They included sexual case histories of over 11,000 men and women. Kinsey was inspired to write his books by his experiences as a professor at the University of Indiana. Occasionally, in response to his lectures on the sexual behavior of wasps, his students would confide in him and ask questions about human sexual behavior. In an effort to help his students, Kinsey went to the library to search for answers. To his surprise, he found that very little had been written about human sexual behavior and decided to gather the data for himself.

The Kinsey reports came as a great relief to many people, who discovered that others had the same sexual feelings and behavior that they did. For instance, Kinsey found that more than one-half of the married women and over two-thirds of the married men in his sample had had premarital intercourse. Most of these people had no idea that they were in the majority. Kinsey also discovered that an overwhelming majority of men and women engaged in masturbation. He found that many heterosexual people had homosexual experiences, and vice versa.

Kinsey's data were generally of a survey type. Beginning in the 1960s, psychologists William Masters and Virginia Johnson began a detailed investigation of the human sexual response in the laboratory; their techniques, no doubt, would have shocked Krafft-Ebing and raised Freud's eyebrows. Masters and Johnson's study of human sexuality was published in 1966. It contained detailed descriptions of volunteer subjects who had engaged in sexual behavior

SEXUALLY TRANSMITTED DISEASES (STDs)
Diseases that are primarily transmitted through sexual intercourse.

ORGASM
The climax of sexual excitement, normally marked by ejaculation of semen by the male and muscular spasms of the genitals in both sexes.

Alfred Kinsey (1894–1956). His pioneering research on the human sexual response helped dispel many myths and widened our understanding of human sexual behavior.

William Masters and Virginia Johnson have conducted extensive research into human sexual responses.

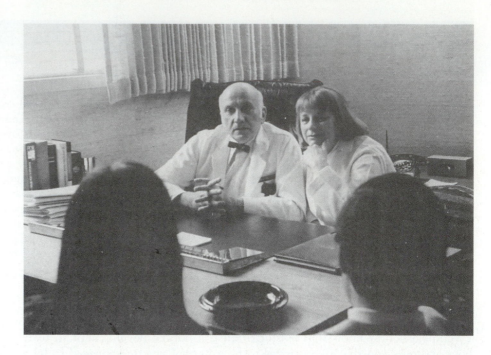

to the point of **orgasm** while being monitored by sophisticated physiological devices.

Masters and Johnson discovered that male and female sexual responses were very similar. Both men and women proceed through four stages of sexual arousal. The first is an *excitement phase*, which can occur through sexual fantasizing or tactual stimulation. The second is a *plateau phase*, during which the genitals become prepared (erection in males, moisture of the vaginal walls in females) for orgasm. Next comes the *orgasmic phase*, characterized by muscular contractions in the genitals of both sexes and ejaculation of semen in the male. Finally, there is a *resolution phase*, during which the body returns to its previous state. During the resolution phase, men have a *refractory period* lasting a few minutes; at this time a second ejaculation is impossible. Women, however, often are capable of having multiple orgasms with no waiting periods.

Masters and Johnson have found that orgasms are the same whether created by self-stimulation, fantasy, or intercourse. The fact that fantasy can cause the same arousal as physical stimulation emphasizes the cognitive nature of human sexuality. Both men and women react to erotic or sexual material. Physiological monitors suggest that men and women are equally aroused by explicit sexual literature (Heiman, 1977).

Masters and Johnson also developed sex therapy for people who suffer from sexual dysfunction of psychological origin (Masters & Johnson, 1970). Most of the therapeutic approaches concentrate on reducing people's worry about sex and encouraging them to center their attention on the pleasure of sex (Heiman, 1979).

Thanks to modern researchers such as Masters and Johnson, who have brought sexual research into the open, we are now better able to separate fact from myth and to more fully understand ourselves and other people.

⬡ SUMMARY

◆ Men and women may have different natural traits or abilities. The differences associated with these traits or abilities are very slight, however.

◆ Gender identity begins to develop at about the age of 2 years, and it becomes very strong once gender constancy is achieved at about age 6 years.

◆ Through socialization, children learn what sex-role behaviors are deemed appropriate for them.

◆ Gender identity appears to be shaped by both cognitive and social processes. Freudian, cognitive, and social learning theories all predict that gender identity is strongly affected by environmental, particularly parental, influences.

◆ Researchers have found that we tend to like most those people who give us the most gratification in return for the least effort on our part.

◆ Our relationships with other people depend a great deal on their physical proximity. Generally, we are more likely to become friends or lovers with those who are physically close to us. We also tend to prefer people who are similar to us in age, level of education, status of occupation, and political views.

◆ Opposites may attract if the two persons have complementary needs.

◆ We generally like people who are competent but who show that they are human and capable of mistakes, which makes them seem more like us.

◆ Physically attractive people are generally better liked than are unattractive people.

◆ Many theories have been developed to explain how people come to like or dislike others. Among the most influential of these theories are the reinforcement theory, the equity theory, the exchange theory, and the gain-loss theory.

◆ Psychologists have not agreed on a definition of love. Generally, however, they divide love into two categories: passionate love and conjugal love. Passionate love may often be the result of sexual arousal. Conjugal love usually develops after people have spent much time together and have come to share things and to make sacrifices for each other.

◆ Historically, more myths and misunderstandings have probably arisen about human sexuality than about any other subject. Early researchers such as Krafft-Ebing believed that much sexual behavior was associated with disgusting diseases. Until the turn of this century, spermatorrhea (wet dreams) was considered to be a serious disease. It is now known to be a normal sexual occurrence.

◆ Modern researchers such as Kinsey and Masters and Johnson have found that normal sexual behavior encompasses a far greater range than earlier researchers ever dreamed it did.

◆ Masters and Johnson discovered that male and female sexual responses are very similar. Both men and women proceed through four stages of sexual arousal: the excitement phase, the plateau phase, the orgasmic phase, and the resolution phase. Masters and Johnson also developed sex therapy for people who suffer sexual dysfunction of psychological origin.

◆ Although some sexually transmitted diseases can be cured, the most deadly, AIDS, remains only preventable through education.

⬡ SUGGESTIONS FOR FURTHER READING

1. Bell, A. P., Weinberg, M. S., & Hammersmith, S. K. (1981). *Sexual preference: Its development in men and women*. Bloomington: Indiana University Press. Discusses the development of sexual orientations, including many of the variables found to correlate with the development of homosexual orientations.

2. Kelley, H. H., et al. (Eds.). (1983). *Close relationships*. New York: W. H. Freeman. Analyzes the social aspects of human relationships, including love, commitment, power, emotion, and conflict. For the student or general reader.

3. Luria, Z., Friedman, S., & Rose, M. D. (1987). *Human sexuality*. New York: John Wiley. A college-level textbook on all aspects of human sexuality, including the social perspective.

4. Margulis, L., & Sagan, D. (1991). *Mystery dance: On the evolution of human sexuality*. New York: Touchstone. An examination of how all the creatures from whom we have evolved, from apes to promiscuous bacteria, have left their mark on our sexuality.

5. Reinisch, J. M., & Beasley, R. (Eds.). (1990). *The Kinsey Institute new report on sex: What you must know to be sexually literate*. New York: St. Martin's Press. About 540 pages of the most up-to-date information about sexual matters, including topics such as love and commitment, contraception, STDs, fetishism, and exhibitionism. It also includes a survey of what Americans do and don't know about sex.

6. Sadock, B. J., Kaplan, H. I., & Freedman, A. M. (Eds.). (1976). *The sexual experience*. Baltimore: Williams & Wilkins. A college-level text that discusses sexual relationships, including a classic history of sexual research.

Appendix A

Applied Psychology

Throughout this textbook, you have seen examples of the application of psychology to improve people's lives. Once basic research has been conducted and data gathered, and psychologists discover information that they believe might benefit people, their interests are likely to turn to applying this information to help build a technology of behavior and to advance and improve life. Whenever psychologists have sufficient information from which they believe the public can benefit, they begin to consider how they can apply it. Basic research is essential to the quest for knowledge; applying knowledge that we have gained to help other people often is a benefit of this quest.

In this appendix, we'll briefly examine several areas in which psychology has been applied to aspects of daily life. Because of the limitations of space in a textbook such as this, it is impossible to examine any area in much detail, but this appendix will give you a general idea of selected applied areas. The areas include industrial/organizational psychology, sports psychology, environmental psychology, consumer psychology, and educational psychology.

 ## INDUSTRIAL/ORGANIZATIONAL PSYCHOLOGY

Industrial/organizational psychologists, or I/O psychologists, as they are called, work for businesses, labor organizations, or governments or teach at universities, where they may be allied with psychology or business departments. Traditionally, their main concern has been to improve the functioning of businesses and industries and to identify ways to make an organization efficient and effective. **I/O psychology** has grown along with American business and industry, and it is now a large and encompassing field of psychology. The roots of I/O psychology can be found in early time-motion studies, in which workers' movements were analyzed carefully for speed and efficiency. From there, the field expanded to consider the great range of variables that influence production and business success. The three major areas of concern among I/O psychologists are the creation and operation of organizations (typically business organizations), the selection and training of personnel and staff, and job performance and productivity.

Organizational Behavior

Organizational behavior includes the policies and procedures of managers, the way managers interact with workers, the tasks of jobs, and the structure of organizations (Mowday & Sutton, 1993). Studies of organizational behavior can range in scope from the study of a single employee to the study of an entire organization (Schneider, 1985). Research to date suggests that there is no one organizational arrangement, formula, management system, style of su-

I/O PSYCHOLOGY
Abbreviation for industrial/organizational psychology, the field of applied psychology concerned with methods of training, counseling, selecting, and supervising personnel in business and industry. IO psychologists also investigate ways to make organizations effective and efficient.

pervision, or type of employee that is suited for all jobs and all circumstances. The basic thrust of I/O psychology, therefore, is to find the criteria for what works in a given system or situation and apply them.

LEADERSHIP AND SUPERVISION.   Among the best-studied organizational behaviors is leadership or supervisory capability (Hollander & Offerman, 1990). The Michigan and Ohio State studies conducted over 30 years ago provide the foundation of our modern understanding of leadership and supervision. In these studies, carried out in different industries, government agencies, hospitals, and volunteer organizations, leaders and supervisors were examined according to two dimensions: *employee-centered* and *job-centered*. Employee-centered supervisors or leaders were those who were most concerned with their workers' problems. They were friendly and supportive of workers, and they helped to instill a sense of pride and personal value in the employees. These supervisors allowed workers considerable latitude and freedom in carrying out the job and supervised the work in a general way. Job-centered supervisors or leaders, on the other hand, emphasized only production, watched the work closely, and made sure that the workers met their quotas. The studies indicated that employee-centered supervisors and leaders were more effective and were thus better able to increase production (Likert, 1961). Researchers also have shown that employee-centered and job-centered approaches aren't necessarily mutually exclusive; supervisors and leaders who are interested in their employees in a friendly and personal sense and who also emphasize job production are also likely to be successful (Cummins, 1971; Anastasi, 1979). Of course, studies of this kind are correlational, and it is difficult to establish a cause-effect relationship. For example, if production falls significantly, supervisors may become exceptionally concerned about productivity and therefore become job-centered. This, of course, is different from saying that job-centered supervisors cause lower production. On the whole, however, current research confirms the finding that employee-centered supervisors are more successful.

These findings have led some organizations to attempt to find quick ways to orient supervisors to get along with people. High-pressure courses and one-week manager-training sessions on interpersonal relations usually are not successful, however. Employess often regard sudden changes in managers' or supervisors' behavior as contrived. A sincerely employee-centered supervisor is spontaneous and honest. Such behavior is not easily taught. Most employee-centered managers are that way because of the kind of personalities they have, and had before becoming managers (Anastasi, 1979).

Another area of concern among I/O psychologists is the "glass ceiling" (Morrison & Von Glinow, 1990), a gender-related problem. In many organizations, women who have proven their leadership ability are promoted to a level just below the top, but are allowed to go no further. The "glass ceiling" refers to being close enough to see those who work on the top floor, while still being kept one floor down. Highlighting this problem is the fact that in the top 500 U.S. corporations, only 1.7 percent of the corporate officers are women (Offerman & Gowing, 1990). The circumstances for minorities are not much better (Morrison & Von Glinow, 1990). Discrimination of this kind is a major concern of I/O psychologists, not just for reasons of justice, but because they know that it denies organizations the talents and benefits of many potential leaders.

There are many theories about what makes an effective leader and how that resource can be tapped (Ilgen & Klein, 1989). There is no consensus, however, about which factors are the most important or why some people seem so able to lead while others do not (House & Singh, 1987).

EMPLOYEE PARTICIPATION, FEEDBACK, AND CONFLICT RESOLUTION.
I/O psychologists have also found that employee participation in management decisions can be beneficial for an organization. This is especially true when the organization undergoes a change that requires the workers to learn new skills. In such a case, even if earnings are maintained, workers often resent having to learn new skills, and production suffers as grievances, absenteeism, and turnover increase. But if workers are given an opportunity to make suggestions and to help plan their new work, they often are more likely to accept the changes. Employee participation in management decisions is not always successful or even a good idea, however (Heller & Clark, 1976). For example, it may not be beneficial to an organization for employees to help in management decisions if the employees have no desire or wish for independence or work latitude or if the management decisions are unrelated to the kind of work the employees will be doing (for example, decisions pertaining to company finances or organizational structure).

Other important areas of organizational behavior that interest I/O psychologists include feedback of results and resolution of organizational conflicts. Some kinds of feedback are fairly obvious and need little interpretation, such as monthly sales. Other kinds of feedback within an organization are subject to many psychological influences. For example, feedback concerning a worker's or manager's job performance can be influenced by evaluators' beliefs about locus of control (see Chapter 11) and attribution (see Chapter 18). A worker may be evaluated differently if the supervisor sees failure or success as a function of the worker versus a function of the system in which the worker was operating (internal or external locus of control). Skills or motives attributed to others, whether validly or not, often affect how they are evaluated (Horn, 1985). Defense mechanisms (see Chapter 14) also can play a role. The supervisor who highly recommends a worker for a job is less likely to observe that worker's failures, because to do so would be to admit failure herself (Cummings, 1982). I/O psychologists try to make organizations aware of what these psychological influences are and how they may distort important feedback and communication.

I/O psychologists are also involved in helping to eliminate and resolve conflicts within an organization. Labor-management conflicts are the most widely publicized. Other important conflicts may occur, however, between different levels of management, sales, and production or between retailers and manufacturers, all of which can be disruptive to an organization (Brett, Goldberg, & Ury, 1990). By holding conflict-resolution workshops and training the parties involved to develop skills of communication and to work out give-and-take solutions, I/O psychologists often help them to resolve problems more quickly, to the benefit of everyone. Sometimes, the psychologists provide training in interpersonal relations and mutual understanding. This training makes people more aware of psychological pitfalls—into which they may fall because of pride or face-saving—that would be detrimental to all parties to the conflict. Such workshops and conflict-resolution training have been helpful in many circumstances (Rubin & Brown, 1975; Brett, Goldberg, & Ury, 1990).

Personnel Selection

The personnel selected to run an organization may determine its success or failure. I/O psychologists have been instrumental in developing valid personnel selection techniques and in devising the best ways for organizations to select a successful employee base (O'Reilly, 1991).

When a professional develops a personnel classification and selection system, the first important step he takes is **job analysis.** Before selecting someone

JOB ANALYSIS
Analysis of the specific tasks required in a job and the training, physical abilities, educational level, vocational preparation, and temperament a person needs to perform the job.

for a job, an organization must know which tasks are required and what those tasks entail. In job analysis, the analyst details the tasks and outlines the traits and skills that a worker will need to perform those tasks. The analyst chooses predictors that help to identify the traits and skills required for the job. He then evaluates these predictors for reliability and validity.

Productivity and Personnel Behavior

Productivity—a function of worker satisfaction, performance, and motivation—has long been an area of interest among I/O psychologists.

JOB SATISFACTION. Most recent research concerning job satisfaction has been derived from surveys correlating different variables with attitudes expressed by workers. Perhaps it isn't surprising that since research in this area began, high levels of job satisfaction have been found to be associated with higher pay, greater chance for promotion, good supervisors, pleasant working conditions, and the chance for workers to use their skills and abilities to the fullest (Locke, 1976). In fact, these findings are so consistent that some researchers have become suspicious of them (Staw, 1984), noting that job satisfaction is almost always measured by questionnaire and wondering whether the questions are biased so that researchers often find what they expect to find. For example, questionnaires almost always ask for responses to such items as "I would prefer my job if the pay was good" or "if it was challenging." They don't ask whether job satisfaction would be improved "if the job was easy" or "if the job didn't require any responsibility," or "if the job allowed me to get away from my family." What we have found may not really show all the possible variables associated with job satisfaction.

Job stress is another important area associated with job satisfaction, and more and more corporations are hiring I/O psychologists to help them to address this issue (Offerman & Gowing, 1990).

Job satisfaction is not easy to measure. Interestingly, some experiments have shown that increasing rewards for workers can actually *decrease* job satisfaction. It's as though the worker feels, at least at some level, "this job must really be lousy if you've got to pay me this much money to do it." Increasing a person's salary and reward doesn't always have this effect, however (Deci & Ryan, 1980).

ABSENTEEISM. I/O psychologists are especially concerned with absenteeism (O'Reilly, 1991). Tens of billions of dollars are lost each year because employees don't come to work. Of course, health problems and injuries are causes of some absenteeism, but absenteeism is also related to job dissatisfaction. Many employees who are unhappy in their jobs withdraw from their work, taking days off when they have no health reason to do so (Johns & Nicholson, 1982). It's difficult to separate the influence of job satisfaction on absenteeism from all the other variables, but because of one interesting field study, we know that it probably makes a difference. The study measured absenteeism in relation to job satisfaction of salaried employees who were working for Sears Roebuck and Company in Chicago. As it happened, during the study a tremendous snowstorm crippled the city. The Sears employees were told they didn't need to come to work unless they wanted to. As a result, only those who wanted to come to work did. It turned out that they were the ones who reported the highest job satisfaction. This study shows that in situations where attendance is largely voluntary, high job satisfaction is one of the greatest indicators of low absenteeism (Smith, 1977).

Other factors that may influence absenteeism are incentives to attend work, ease of transportation to work, flexibility of working hours, and the worker's family responsibilities. I/O psychologists address all these issues in an effort to make work attendance easier for employees. For example, some companies are now providing on-the-job day-care for children of employees. Although expensive, it often is effective enough in reducing absenteeism and increasing job satisfaction to make it worthwhile for the company.

I/O psychologists also have examined the other side of the absenteeism issue—the price a worker pays for *attending* work rather than what he obtains for being absent from it. In some jobs, this cost of attendance is recognized. Professional airline pilots are allowed to fly only a certain number of hours per week. Work hours per week also are limited for air traffic controllers and bus drivers. When jobs are dissatisfying, performance correlates positively with absenteeism. That is, workers who take off a few days now and then ("mental health" days) actually perform better, often well enough to outweigh the costs of the time they have taken off (Staw & Oldham, 1978). Some industries have a double standard: They recognize that the top executives benefit from a few days off after a hard job to "decompress," but "mental health" days for the lower echelons are distinctly discouraged (Staw, 1984).

I/O psychologists have been instrumental in helping to introduce flexible working hours and four-day work weeks to reduce absenteeism and increase production (Narayanan & Nath, 1982). They also have recently begun to investigate a new and growing phenomenon: the use of telecommunications and personal computers to allow people to work at home.

TURNOVER. Job turnover is a serious problem for many industries and corporations. Whenever someone quits, another person must be trained to take that individual's place. As a result, I/O psychologists have been asked to find the causes of turnover and the means by which it can best be eliminated. W. H. Mobley and other researchers have provided a theoretical model that explains the sequence that leads to turnover (see Figure A.1).

Like absenteeism, turnover may be subjected to a double standard. Many organizations encourage turnover for their top executives, considering it a source of fresh ideas and invigoration (Brown, 1982), but discourage it among workers, even though it may also be beneficial for some of them. Similarly, some turnover in middle and lower management may be beneficial to companies (Katz, 1982), but it is rarely encouraged. As a compromise, some corporations are now looking at rotation of assignments within their companies to produce the beneficial effects of turnover without the adverse effects of losing valued employees (Staw, 1984).

Motivation and Performance

There are many valuable techniques for increasing employees' motivation to produce (Katzell & Thompson, 1990). Behavior modification techniques (see Chapter 8) include the use of reinforcers for appropriate behavior. Workers who produce are given bonuses, promotions, better offices, more prestigious titles, or verbal praise in an effort to maintain and reinforce their successful behavior within the corporation (O'Reilly, 1991; Komaki, Heinzmann, & Lawson, 1980).

Goal setting is also a valuable technique (Staw, 1984). It is derived from cognitive psychology and requires that specific goals be set for performance. Much research has shown that workers perform better if they have specific goals to aim for than if they are simply told, "Do your best." Knowing the exact goal required seems to help create within the worker an internal structure or organization for achieving that end; it gives her something to aim for. In some cases, the technique is no more complicated than posting a chart where

SPORTS PSYCHOLOGY
The application of psychological techniques and principles to sports and other structured physical activities for the purpose of maintaining and maximizing performance and investigating applied clinical issues.

every worker can see how well the company is progressing against a competitor. Goal setting is one of the most powerful ways to increase worker motivation.

Other valuable motivational aids include making sure that each worker is given a job that he or she can do well, that resources are made available to ensure the worker's performance (such as providing the right equipment, offering on-the-job coaching or training, or organizing problem-solving groups), that leaders are trained to be sensitive to the needs of people, and that a certain air of dignity and quality in the workplace is maintained, which helps to instill pride (Katzell & Thompson, 1990).

I/O psychology is a growing area. For instance, many I/O psychologists are now working diligently to see whether the managerial techniques that have been so effective in Japan are culturally transferable to the United States. Such cultural applications are relatively new to American I/O psychology because, for the first time, we are seeing other nations with higher productivity. No doubt the field will continue to grow as psychology is applied further to business and industry.

✽ SPORTS PSYCHOLOGY

Sports psychology is the application of psychological principles to physical activity and sports, either to maximize performance or to investigate applied clinical issues. Sports psychology in the United States has only recently attracted significant interest, but it has a long history in Europe, especially among the former Eastern bloc nations (Browne & Mahoney, 1984).

◆ FIGURE A.1

A typical decision process a worker might use to determine whether to leave a job. Many variables that may influence the person's willingness to search for new employment, such as the family's reaction to moving, or the friends a worker must leave, are outside the company's control. Rather than addressing the variables that affect the utility of quitting, the company wishing to reduce turnover would do better to find ways to increase job satisfaction. By doing so, it may prevent the worker from considering quitting in the first place.

The History of Sports Psychology

Sports psychology has its roots in the work of experimental psychologists who were interested in motor learning and performance. Their early laboratory experiments measuring reaction time and other motor skills seem a far cry from modern sports psychology, but their work marked the first time that psychologists took an active interest in analyzing physical performance. Of course, modern sports psychology deals with the mental as well as the physical aspects of performance. Everyone knows the effects motivation and concentration can have on an athlete. In fact, the first sports psychology publication in the United States was an 1898 paper describing the enhancing effects of a cheering audience on competitive bicycling (Geron, 1982).

Serious work in American sports psychology did not begin until the 1920s when Coleman Griffith (1893–1966), known in the United States as the father of sports psychology, set up the first sports psychology laboratory. There he investigated the best ways to teach sports performance and to assess athletes' personalities in order to guide and develop these people. Even with Griffith's sports psychology laboratory, however, the United States and other Western countries lagged far behind the Soviet Union in sports psychology.

In 1965, the first International Congress of Sports Psychology was held in Rome, and a network of information was organized through which countries could exchange data on sports psychology. This was a landmark in Western work in this subject, and it heralded the rapid acceleration of sports psychology in the United States.

Today sports psychology has five major goals: (1) to take laboratory findings and apply them to the playing field to maximize athletic performance; (2) to discover what makes a successful athlete and which kinds of athletes are best suited for which sports; (3) to discover the best methods for preparing an athlete mentally for a major event or performance; (4) to investigate the effects, both beneficial and harmful, of sports on children; and (5) to find how best to use sports and exercise for leisure and mental and physical rehabilitation (Browne & Mahoney, 1984). The first three goals have attracted the most attention and research, but recently efforts to achieve the latter two goals have begun.

The Physiology and Personality of the Athlete

A great deal of what goes into making an athlete is inherited. Height, center of gravity, and muscle mass are, to a large extent, genetically determined and may limit the kind of sport in which a person may excel or the athletic ability she may have. To state the obvious, height is an advantage in basketball, muscle mass helps in weight lifting, and fast reflexes help the boxer. Other physical variables are also extremely important, if less obvious. The ratio of muscle fiber types is one example. Muscle fibers show either a fast or a slow twitch when stimulated. Some people have a high percentage of one kind of muscle fiber versus the other. Someone with a high percentage of fast-twitch muscle probably would be more successful at a sprint event, for instance, than would someone with a high percentage of slow-twitch muscle who might be far better at a marathon. The amount of oxygen consumed per minute per unit of body weight at a fixed amount of effort is also an important variable. In both men and women, these two variables—ratio of muscle fiber types and rate of oxygen consumption—are more than 90 percent determined by heredity (Fox & Mathews, 1981). Modern sports physiologists have the job of determining the kind of body a potential athlete possesses and which sports and skills are most likely to suit him.

PEAK PERFORMANCE
The exceptional performance given by an athlete when physical and mental conditions are optimal.

Scientists also have attempted to determine the optimal personality for athletes in any given sport. Unfortunately, initial work in this area often was done by nonpsychologists who were unfamiliar with proper personality-testing procedures. They often used invalid or unreliable tests, and the results of their "experiments" often were flawed, misinterpreted, or biased (Mahoney, 1979; Morgan, 1980). Valid research in this area is hard to come by, and it appears that many variables go into making a great athlete. Several findings, however, have been supported by good research. For instance, persons who are good at contact sports tend to perceive pain as less aversive than do those who excel in noncontact sports (Ryan & Kovacic, 1966). Individuals with greater pain tolerance appear to seek out contact sports more often, rather than simply developing a pain tolerance from experience with such sports.

Optimal level of arousal is another variable that has some predictive validity. For example on an ice-hockey team, members who perform best when considerably aroused are more likely to be successful goalies (where action is sudden and fast), while those players whose optimal performance occurs at a lower level of arousal may be more successful as a member of the forward line. By testing a person's ability to function at different levels of arousal, a sports psychologist can suggest which team position a player should be trained to fill or which kind of sport may offer a person the greatest likelihood of success. These are just a few of the areas in which a sports psychologist can be helpful in determining an athlete's performance, but much more research needs to be conducted before any psychologist can just walk up to a coach or sports director and lay out in detail which variables or constitutions are required for success in a given sporting activity. Sports psychology has this ability as one of its goals, but it still has a long way to go.

The Peak Performance

Nothing is more exciting to an athlete than to have a **peak performance,** in which she achieves a "personal best" or perhaps even sets a record. When peak performances occur, an athlete often has intense concentration and the feeling of being disassociated from her surroundings. Her body seems to be operating on its own, and she has no awareness of pain or fatigue. Time seems to slow down, and the athlete has a sense of being in command and of having exceptional power (Unestahl, 1983). This kind of mental and physical "flow," which often leads to a peak performance, is a strange phenomenon. Athletes can't force it to happen. It's like trying to force yourself to fall asleep; the more you concentrate on it, the farther you get from it. Instead of making it happen, you just have to let it happen, which is an experience foreign to most athletes—they are used to trying hard.

Sports psychologists have found ways to help athletes find their flow, but the athletes' attempts to gain such control over their behavior, like the learning of any new skill, can disrupt their performance for a time, until the new ways are acquired. Because of this, a less experienced coach or athlete will sometimes give up prematurely on attempts to acquire these new control skills.

Psychological Techniques for Achieving Peak Performance

One of the most serious factors disrupting peak performance is the pressure of competition. If athletes become anxious during competition, they can become overaroused; that is, they go past the optimal zone of arousal required for a peak performance. One immediate problem of overarousal is muscle tension. Muscle tension interferes directly with muscle contraction; a muscle can contract only if its antagonist muscle is relaxed. Proper muscle contraction is necessary for peak performance. Many athletes have talked about how well they did during practice only to blow it during competition because of excess muscle tension. Sports psychologists have devised a number of techniques to get around this problem.

The first technique is fairly straightforward. It is practice, practice, and practice, again and again, until the activity required of the athlete becomes so automatic that it is almost mindless. Soon the athlete has learned the procedures so well that he can act without thinking, and mental activity (which may include thoughts about failing or about what he is doing) is less likely to occur and to get in the way.

Monitoring arousal is another valuable technique for competitive performance. Most athletes don't like to pay attention to how nervous they are, fearing that they will only become even more jittery. But knowing how active his autonomic nervous system is can alert an athlete to take steps to avoid a problem. Sweating palms, upset stomach, intestinal problems, difficulty in breathing, trembling or tension, a heavy sensation in the legs, yawning, and fatigue are all signs of involvement of the autonomic nervous system. Mental signs include inability to pay attention to important information, lack of concentration, confusion, negative statements to oneself, excessive fear of failure, and loss of confidence. Athletes can be taught to control the muscle tension in major muscle groups when they feel their autonomic arousal becoming excessive. There are many ways to control muscle tension (see Chapter 15), such as medication, progressive relaxation, yoga, hypnosis, and biofeedback (Pressman, 1980). Once the muscles are relaxed, mental training can begin.

To help an athlete mentally prepare the muscles that will be used in the athletic event, having him carefully imagine the event is often helpful (Brown, 1980). This prepares his muscles to act in their appropriate sequence. The high jumper Dwight Stones made ample use of this technique before each jump. His mental imagery was a little more exaggerated than most, and people viewing him could actually watch how he prepared to jump in his mind's eye. He looked at each step he planned to take in his approach, and actually seemed to follow himself at a distance as he looked up and then dropped his gaze, imagining his leap over the high bar. As further mental preparation, athletes are taught not to say negative things to themselves and to establish realistic goals, such as a personal best rather than a world record (Meichenbaum, 1977; McClements & Botterill, 1980). These measures help to contain increasing anxiety and resulting loss of confidence.

When athletes practice constantly, monitor their arousal levels, find their optimal level, and control their arousal through relaxation and mental training, their skills often improve dramatically (Scott & Pelliccioni, 1982; Weinberg, 1981).

Future Directions for Sports Psychology

Most work in modern sports psychology has concentrated on helping athletes achieve peak performances. There is hardly a professional sports team or an Olympic athlete who hasn't had advice from sports psychologists. But the future of sports psychology is much broader than that. Psychologists are finding that people can benefit from participation in almost any sport and at almost any skill level (Sonstroem, 1981). Psychologists also have studied individuals who become "addicted" to exercise and sports (Glasser, 1976). Explanations for such incessant exercising often concern endorphins (see Chapter 2) (Moore, 1982) and brain neurotransmitters (Ransford, 1982). Much more research is needed before we know how helpful sports can be for physical and mental rehabilitation and how sports affect children and their development, but these are growing areas of concern. Sports psychology is developing rapidly

ENVIRONMENTAL PSYCHOLOGY
The applied psychology concerned with the effects and influences of the environment on behavior.

in the United States, and many scientists and psychologists are attracted to it. The future is wide open in this field, and researchers have just scratched the surface.

ENVIRONMENTAL PSYCHOLOGY

Beginning in the 1960s, as public concern about environmental problems began to grow, a new area of psychology emerged, **environmental psychology.** It is concerned with the influences of the natural environment on behavior and vice versa (Holahan, 1986). The areas of interest to environmental psychologists are diverse, ranging from traditional topics, such as the effects of lighting in the workplace, to recent concerns, such as the influence on behavior of pollution and environmental toxic hazards. Environmental psychologists are also interested in developing and creating entire environments in accord with psychological principles in an effort to create harmony between individuals and their surroundings. Sometimes the work can even be a little exotic, such as figuring out how to design the physical features of a bank so as to best deter bank robbers (Saegert & Winkel, 1990).

Illumination

One of the most studied areas in environmental psychology is illumination, or the amount of light necessary for optimal performance. This area is the well-spring from which the whole field of environmental psychology developed.

Years ago, industry used as little light as possible in the workplace to save electricity or, even earlier, to save candles! Between 1910 and 1960, the recommended illumination levels for work and offices continually increased, as it was obvious that workers were performing better when they could see what they were doing and when they did not suffer from serious eye fatigue. At first reading, it may appear that this is stating the obvious and that there is little to this area of psychology. Actually, the applied psychology of illumination is really very complex (Meer, 1985). Environmental psychologists have studied and have helped to design the many new kinds of lighting available. For example, they were instrumental in developing the kinds of lighting used in surgical operating rooms where glare must be eliminated but a great amount of highly focused, high-intensity light must be available over the entire operating field.

Each job may require a different kind of lighting. Suppose you are a worker in the garment industry, and it's your job to examine clothing for loose threads. Look at Figure A.2—you can see the amazing difference that proper lighting can make. Environmental psychologists have developed optimal illumination for many different environmental conditions. Optimal lighting can significantly increase performance (Faulkner & Murphy, 1973).

Another task of environmental psychologists working with illumination has been to eliminate glare. Glare, such as arises from bright metal surfaces or glossy paper, can cause phototropisms. A phototropism is the natural inclination of the eye to look toward a light source or bright spot. Constantly fighting this tendency while trying to work at a task can lead to severe eye fatigue. Environmental psychologists have found optimal angles of lighting and levels of light distribution in situations where glare could be a problem. As you can imagine, environmental psychologists often work directly with commercial architects to develop the best work environment. Such an environment includes appropriate lighting for the work being done.

◆ **FIGURE A.2**

For a worker in the garment industry whose job is to remove loose threads from cloth, a difference in lighting can be crucial. With 75 foot-candles of low angle grazing lighting (above), the thread is highly visible compared to its appearance under 650 foot-candles of general overhead diffuse illumination (below).

Atmospheric Conditions and Toxic Hazards

Environmental psychologists have studied the relation between different temperature conditions and behavior and, increasingly, the effects of environmental hazards on behavior.

HEAT. Regulation of heat is another important variable that affects body temperature, arousal, and attention. Individuals who are too warm are more likely to be aggressive and to work less efficiently (Calvert-Boyanowsky, Boyanowsky, Atkinson, Gaduto, & Reeves, 1976).

Violent crimes and riots are more likely to occur in hot summer months; suicides and depressions are more common in the winter; and admissions to psychiatric hospitals correlate well with increases in air pollution (Strahilevitz, Strahilevitz, & Miller, 1979). Because of these findings, environmental psychologists have been interested in weather and related conditions, and in their effects on human behavior.

POLLUTION AND ENVIRONMENTAL TOXINS. An initial concern about air pollution led environmental psychologists to examine pollution in general. They have now identified a number of toxic substances that they believe cause learning problems in children. These include heavy metals, such as cadmium and lead. In poorer neighborhoods, whole buildings often have lead-based wall paint and plumbing. The water and dust in such buildings may contain excessive amounts of toxic heavy metals.

Air pollution is another source of lead contamination. A study conducted at the Case Western Reserve laboratory, using a mass spectrograph analysis of hair samples taken from children, showed that children who had serious learning difficulties also tended to have significantly higher levels of cadmium and lead in their bodies than did children from a well-matched control group (Pihl & Parkes, 1977).

Scientists believe that lead contamination in the air is a serious problem. They once estimated that one out of every five inner city black children 5 years old or younger were carrying a sufficient amount of lead in his or her body to interfere with his or her ability to learn. The children of poor people (those with incomes below $6000 per year) showed eight to nine times the lead content found in children from high-income families (those with incomes exceeding $50,000 per year) (Raloff, 1982).

In more recent years, with the increasing use of unleaded gasoline, the amount of airborne lead has decreased significantly. The lower levels of airborne lead are especially noticeable in congested inner cities where the blood-lead levels in children have decreased in direct proportion to the decrease in the use of leaded gasoline. Environmental psychologists and members of the medical profession were directly responsible for bringing this information to the attention of appropriate government agencies. The effort is now underway to eliminate lead from all gasoline.

Environmental psychologists have discovered that subtle changes in human behavior sometimes can be an early sign of toxic exposure (Fein, Schwartz, Jacobson, & Jacobson, 1983; Weiss, 1983). They are now isolating the influence of these pollutants on behavior. Table A.1 shows the kinds of behavioral changes associated with different metal toxins. **Behavioral toxicology** is a very new field, but the demand for it is growing. None of the 50 states has escaped a significant amount of toxic hazard from untended or improperly stored toxic dump sites or contaminated water and air (Fein, Schwartz, Jacobson & Jacobson, 1983). For instance, after a fire retardant, polychlorinated biphenyl (PCB)

BEHAVIORAL TOXICOLOGY
The classification and study of the behavioral effects of environmental toxins.

TABLE A.1 ◆ NEUROLOGICAL AND PSYCHOLOGICAL SIGNS AND SYMPTOMS ATTRIBUTED TO METAL TOXICITY; COLLECTED FROM CLINICAL AND EXPERIMENTAL SOURCES

SIGNS AND SYMPTOMS	ALUMINUM	ANTIMONY	ARSENIC	BORON	CADMIUM	LEAD	MANGANESE	MERCURY	NICKEL	SELENIUM	TELLURIUM	THALLIUM	TIN	VANDIUM
Anosmia (loss of smell sense)			●		●									
Appetite loss		●						●		●			●	●
Convulsions						●		●						
Depression				●						●				●
Disorientation	●			●			●					●		
Dizziness		●	●						●	●			●	
Dysarthria (defective speech articulation)	●						●	●						
Fatigue, lethargy		●	●		●			●		●		●		
Headache		●	●	●				●	●				●	
Incoordination	●					●	●	●				●		
Insomnia									●					
Jitteriness, irritability		●	●				●		●					●
Mental retardation						●	●							
Paralysis	●													
Paresthesias (unusual physical sensations)		●	●									●		
Peripheral neuropathy (peripheral nervous system disorders)	●		●		●	●								
Polyneuritis (multiple nerve inflammation)		●	●					●					●	
Psychiatric signs	●					●	●	●						●
Somnolence (sleepiness)										●	●			
Tremor	●					●	●	●						●
Visual disturbances			●			●	●			●			●	●
Weakness			●	●			●	●	●	●			●	

SOURCE: Adapted from Weiss, 1983, p. 1176.

was accidentally mixed with cattle grain feed and distributed throughout the state of Michigan, researchers found hardly a single person in that state who did not have PCB in his or her body.

NOISE.   Another environmental hazard that influences behavior is excessive noise—both abrupt and prolonged. Besides being a major distraction, excessive noise increases both blood pressure and the chance of hearing damage. Because of these findings, in many work conditions in which noise is excessive and prolonged, workers are now provided with sound-baffle earplugs or other equipment that helps to reduce noise while still enabling the workers to hear what is going on around them. Actually, most sources of extreme noise are not work-related; they are found in the home environment. Most cases of hearing damage have been found to occur through the inappropriate use of stereo headsets. Through habituation, the user finds higher and higher volume levels tolerable, leading to possible permanent ear damage. Working with environmental psychologists, the government has been quick to place noise standards and restrictions on the work environment, but the individual's attention to this problem is still wanting.

The Structured Environment

Environmental psychologists are well aware that the environment often determines the kinds of behaviors that will occur. For example, something as simple as a pleasant or unpleasant view from a hospital window can affect the length of a patient's postoperative recovery. Environmental psychologists use their skills to structure environments—both indoors and outdoors—to achieve particular results. Different environments affect behavior differently. The way people act in a church is different from the way they act in a classroom, an office lobby, or a baseball stadium. In each instance, behavior is influenced partly by the arrangement of the physical properties of the environment, such as chairs and tables and room color.

Not too long ago, at the University of Texas in Austin, 108 clerical workers were hired, divided into three groups, and given various jobs to do. As one might expect, their error rates, tardiness, and absenteeism were all evaluated by a supervisor. No one ever thought to ask why the offices were all painted blue or, in the case of another group, yellow, or even other colors. Although the workers were told they were participating in a study, they were unaware that the purpose of the study was to help NASA choose interior colors for space modules that would best facilitate human performance during a 30-month interval (Crawford, 1989).

Researchers have consistently found that they can more accurately predict a person's behavior by the environment that person is in than they can predict behavior through personality assessment tests (Barker, 1968). Behavioral and social learning psychologists refer to this influence of the environment as stimulus control (see Chapter 8). Conversely, some environmental psychologists argue that people are not directly controlled by their environment but rather form plans about how they wish to behave and then seek environments in which the behavior is accepted (Russell & Ward, 1982). In other words, you don't scream and cheer because the baseball park has cued you to do so, but instead you plan ahead to go someplace where you can enjoy yourself in a boisterous way, and so you choose the ballpark. Either way, the environment you're in is a good predictor of which behavior you will exhibit.

When developing environments that encourage particular behaviors, environmental psychologists often consider proxemics. **Proxemics** is the study of the behavioral effects of crowding, privacy, territory, and personal space. In a psychological sense, proxemics deals with what is perceived about these factors. For instance, when determining crowding, it's not possible simply to count how many people there are within a certain area. You may feel crowded in an office with 10 other people but not crowded in an elevator with 20, because in the office you expect more privacy, whereas in the elevator you expect to be packed in.

How crowding and lack of privacy affect behavior and work performance is an important issue in environmental psychology. The term *personal space* often is used to indicate how much room each person needs in order to feel sufficiently relaxed and comfortable. Personal space varies greatly from situation to situation. You may not feel your personal space invaded by a family member who touches you. On the other hand, if you were an inmate in a state prison, you might consider your personal space invaded if someone behind you got within 6 feet. Personal space is a perceived space. Researchers take proxemics into consideration when developing any environment.

Environmental psychology is a young and growing endeavor. Its future is wide open. In fact, environmental psychologists are currently busy planning and organizing the environment for the first permanent space station. By examining life in zero gravity or in low levels of gravity, which might be attained

PROXEMICS
The study of nonverbal expression through the spatial distance people maintain when interacting, as well as their orientation toward each other as reflected by touch and eye contact.

CONSUMER PSYCHOLOGY
The field of applied psychology concerned with advertising and selling; the object of study is effective communication from the manufacturer or distributor to the consumer.

in a rotating space station, they are arranging and organizing the environment to facilitate comfort, research, and social interaction. Wherever humankind needs to construct a beneficial environment, environmental psychologists, with their developing knowledge, are providing expertise and skills.

CONSUMER PSYCHOLOGY

Consumer psychology began as the psychology of selling and advertising. Its objective was to get the manufacturer's message through to the consumer. Advertising goes back as far as human history. When the city of Pompeii was excavated centuries after it had been buried by the eruption of Mount Vesuvius, archaeologists found advertisements painted on the walls of public buildings. But it wasn't until the twentieth century that a systematic inquiry into the needs of the consumer and the desires of advertisers developed.

Consumer Research

Modern consumer psychology is mainly concerned with conducting and applying consumer research. The major categories of consumer research are (1) advertising effectiveness, (2) consumer opinion, (3) assessment of consumer attitudes through rating scales and projective techniques, (4) psychological segmentation of markets, and (5) consumer behavior in natural environments.

To test advertising effectiveness, psychologists attempt to demonstrate the ability of a particular advertisement to influence the public. They also may test the power of the advertising medium. For example, a consumer psychologist might have designed the following study as a test of the effectiveness of billboards. A few years ago, when I was walking around in Salt Lake City, I noticed a number of large billboards at different locations that simply stated in great gold letters, "Calvin Coolidge was the 30th president of the United States." The billboards carried the message for a few weeks and then the messages were taken down. Before the billboards went up, a consumer psychologist probably went about surveying people at random and asking them who was the thirtieth president of the United States. She would then find out how many people, on the average, knew the answer. After two weeks of billboard exposure, the public would be surveyed again. Now many more people would probably know that Calvin Coolidge was the thirtieth president. This increase in knowledge would demonstrate the power of the billboard.

Consumer opinion surveys help businesses that market products to find out what consumers want and how the business can provide it. Consumers' attitudes can also be assessed through rating scales, and if consumers are found to have different attitudes in different parts of the country or different countries, the market can be psychologically segmented to provide each area with what the people there desire (Lutz & Bettman, 1977). For example, Oil of Olay, a facial cream or lotion, is one of the 10 best-selling products of its type in the United States. Anyone with a television set has seen advertisements for it. A couple of summers ago, I was in New Zealand and turned on a television set. On came an Oil of Olay commercial. It was exactly the same as the commercial that I had seen in the United States—only the product was called Oil of Ulam. No doubt, consumer psychologists had been at work again! As it turns out, in both Australia and New Zealand, there already was an "Olay Oil" that was used for cooking (Love, 1987). Something obviously had to be done, because leaving the name as it was would conjure up images of rubbing cooking oil all over one's face.

Probably, a survey of consumer attitudes found that New Zealanders and Australians liked the word *Ulam* as well as, or better than, *Olay*. It's the consumer psychologist's job to find out which name sounds the most appealing.

For example, some very tasty fish have atrocious names. You can't find them in your local supermarket, because no one wants to eat a hogsucker or a viperfish. With a little effort, however, a seller can find a nice name that people do like and rename the product. Call a hogsucker "rock salmon," for example, even though it has nothing to do with real salmon (or hogs, for that matter), and people are much more willing to eat it. Very few products are named simply by an owner or product manager who likes a particular name. In the modern consumer world, psychologists take many possible names and offer them to consumers in rating surveys to find which name not only sounds best but also sounds most like the product (see Figure A.3).

Most advertisers rely on making sure that their message is perceived (Bettman, 1986). Modern consumer psychology uses information about cognitive processes such as perception, memory, and information processing and studies how advertisements affect the operation of these processes (Cohen & Chakravarti, 1990). Advertisers highlight their messages to gain and hold the audience's attention by using size, repetition, color, and so on. Making the product recognizable in a visual sense is important, but it's also important to make it recognizable verbally. If the product name is difficult to pronounce, it may have to be changed. The makers of Baume Bengue were dismayed because no one knew how to pronounce the name of their product. As a result, they placed the words "pronounced ben-gay" on the label. Later, they dropped the original name altogether and just called it Ben-Gay.

In Chapter 18, we discussed the mere-exposure effect—the phenomenon that people tend to like something merely because they have been exposed to it repeatedly (assuming that the exposure has been in no way aversive). The mere exposure effect is one of the most powerful influences in advertising (Bornstein, 1989). This is one of the reasons you may trust a brand name product even if you've never used it. Brand name products are often more expensive than generic ones. Most consumers say that the higher price inspires confidence. They associate the higher price with higher quality. In many cases, however, the product's higher price reflects only the expensive advertising necessary to make it a brand name!

To test products or advertisements successfully, consumer psychologists may investigate the ability of customers to identify brands or to state brand preferences. The effects of advertising can be measured by an increase in brand identification or a shift of brand preferences. Sometimes, advertising is so effective that brand names become words that stand for an entire class of products such as Kleenex, Q-tips, Band-Aids, or Xeroxes. Because of the power of continual exposure, one of the major thrusts of advertising is simply to get the product into the consumer's awareness, regardless of the message content. As long as the brand name is presented often enough that the consumer becomes familiar with it, it will have a certain amount of selling power. The most effective advertising technique, however, is to combine repeated exposure with persuasive communication (Petty, 1977; Day, 1976).

The Physiological Approach

Consumer psychologists have joined with physiologists in efforts to develop measuring devices that can record interest in products or advertisements. One device can track eye movements when a consumer watches an advertisement. In a laboratory setting, the investigators track eye movements by recording exactly which part of the advertisement the consumer is watching at any given time (Witt, 1977; Barton, 1980). Interestingly, people often watch the faces and hands of the actors in the ads more than they do the products. Faces and hands are just intrinsically interesting. This is frustrating to advertisers who

◆ **FIGURE A.3**

When developing names for products, it's important to consider that certain sounds seem to go with certain shapes or forms. Most everyone will choose (a) as Molana and (b) as Krakatok. M, N, and L have a gentle, flowing sound pattern, while T and K are sharp and short in sound, which translates into a visual perception of something angular and sharp.

Which of the two shapes is a Molana, and which is a Krakatok?

(a)   (b)

EDUCATIONAL PSYCHOLOGY
The branch of applied psychology concerned with the psychological aspects of teaching and the formal learning process in school. Educational psychologists apply theories, methods, and test instruments for educational purposes.

want the product to stand out. One way around this tendency is to link the product through a series of steps with the face and name of a person. The Folgers Coffee Company did this some years ago in an impressive series of advertisements. An actress was given a name—Mrs. Olsen. Soon, when the advertisement came on and people looked at the face of the actress, they remembered she was Mrs. Olsen. And, of course, Mrs. Olsen was linked directly to Folgers' coffee. After these very successful advertisements, Folger's coffee went from ninth to first place in the coffee market.

Researchers also have measured interest in advertisements by the relative amounts of alpha versus beta waves in subjects' EEGs or by arousal of the central nervous system while subjects were watching ads (Ryan, 1980; Kassarjian, 1982).

Consumer Protection

Because of the work they do, consumer psychologists often encounter ethical concerns of a special nature. Psychology should be used to benefit people, never to harm them. In some instances, however, advertisements may be designed to sell products that cost consumers their health or money without providing a reasonable benefit. Cigarettes are an example of a product that is deadly (and, unlike other dangerous products such as automobiles, is deadly *when used as intended*) and is sold through advertisements. Psychologists who offer their skills to help sell dangerous, worthless, or overpriced products at the expense of the consumer are doing the public a disservice.

We can ask a more general question, "Should psychologists be in the business of helping advertisers push their products?" With this in mind, many consumer psychologists have concentrated their efforts on consumer protection and product safety. Their work involves studying ways to protect consumers from accidents and hazards while using a product or from dangerous misuse of a product. Childproof safety caps are an example. Consumer psychologists investigated the ability of children of different ages to think through the process of opening a complex cap. Soon they discovered that the opposing techniques of pressing down while turning were easily within the grasp of adults but were beyond the comprehension of almost all children young enough to be in danger. The techniques used for promoting products have also been used by consumer psychologists to point out the value of proper health care (such as performing breast examinations or giving up smoking). Other consumer psychologists have spent time developing ways for professionals to communicate effectively with consumers. Doctors, lawyers, and other professionals who deal with the public daily and who have difficulty communicating their information in ways the public can readily understand often consult consumer psychologists for the best methods to furnish information that will enable the public to make informed decisions. Whenever products or services of any kind are available and the public needs to be informed about them, consumer psychologists are able to provide a valuable service.

🧬 EDUCATIONAL PSYCHOLOGY

Practitioners of **educational psychology** are principally concerned with training teachers, improving student performance, and conducting educational research. Teacher-training programs generally focus on the teacher's need to be aware of what changes in behavior occur as children develop, how different ethnic and cultural backgrounds may influence students, how children learn attitudes and prejudices, what the social relations among groups are, what the effects of cooperation and competition are, and how conformity and the learning of social norms influence children (Snow & Swanson, 1992; Johnson & Johnson,

1975). Educational psychologists often are instrumental in developing programs to give teachers the basic information they require about behavior. Modern teachers must also have considerable knowledge about psychological testing and test scores, especially aptitude and achievement tests, which educational psychologists often provide.

Many educational psychologists spend much of their time conducting research. Often this work is concerned with developing valid and reliable tests for measuring student aptitude and achievement or with developing techniques that help students to learn and teachers to teach. Educational psychologists are also concerned with the clinical aspects of behavior as they may relate to education—areas such as test anxiety and school phobia.

Educational psychologists have been especially interested in the effects of early education on disadvantaged children. As we mentioned in Chapter 13, Project Head Start and other early intervention projects have been successful in helping to redress the negative impact of a poor environment.

Educational psychology places special emphasis on the psychology of learning (Pintrich, Cross, Kozma, & McKeachie, 1986). In the literature of the field, different educational philosophies often are debated. One of the most prominent of these debates is the argument between the behaviorist and the cognitive philosophical orientations. Educational psychologists oriented toward the behaviorist view believe that children should be taught material in ways that make it easy to learn and acquire. In their view, teaching is mainly appropriate use of schedules of reinforcement and appropriate organization and presentation of material. Educational psychologists with a cognitive philosophy typically view the child as innately curious and believe that if the child is placed in an environment that stimulates this curiosity, the child will inevitably learn. Behaviorists respond that without appropriate schedules of reinforcement and contingencies for learning, simply placing the child in an environment that allows excessive freedom gives the child freedom not to learn. Cognitive theorists often counter that "programming" the child with prepackaged material inhibits creativity and spontaneity. The debate, which has been going on for about 40 years, has not been resolved.

In 1983, the National Commission on Excellence in Education concluded that the educational foundations of our society were being eroded by mediocrity. The commission argued that there was a crisis in American education, that students were learning less and less from teachers who were poorly trained. This challenge to American education has made the public increasingly aware of the many problems surrounding this great social task. Educational psychologists are at the forefront of efforts to develop more effective teacher-training methods and better ways for students to learn.

The School System

School serves the purpose of systematically passing on the wisdom (or prejudices) of a culture to its young. Educational psychologists have investigated schools to discover the variables that determine which schools are most successful and how that success can be generalized to schools that are less successful. Educational psychologists agree that huge differences exist among schools (Rutter, 1983). For instance, studies conducted in Great Britain found a great range in several measures of schools. In one school, 50 percent of the pupils went on to college; in another fewer than 9 percent did so. Delinquency rates varied from 1 percent to 19 percent, and absenteeism ranged from 6 percent to 26 percent (Rutter, Maughan, Mortimore, Ouston, & Smith, 1979). The range among American schools is even greater.

At first, it might seem that these differences are due only to the very different populations that schools may serve. Educational psychologists, however, have studied many pairs of schools that differ greatly in their delinquency, attendance, and college-acceptance rates but serve similar student populations in terms of intellectual characteristics and socioeconomic status (Finlayson & Loughran, 1976; Reynolds & Murgatroyd, 1977). Furthermore, a number of schools have been found that consistently turn out students who attain high levels of scholastic achievement despite the fact that these students come from inner city neighborhoods generally associated with low achievement (Weber, 1971). All these findings indicate that different schools may provide their students with very different educations despite the neighborhood from which the students come. Schools that show superior student achievement, whether the students come from poor neighborhoods or affluent ones, tend to maintain these high standards of excellence year after year. Schools with poor performance records, regardless of neighborhood, also tend to be consistent (Rutter, 1983).

To date, educational psychologists are unsure what it is that makes a school successful. This issue has been the subject of much speculation and debate. For example, although schools with good reputations consistently turn out more successful students than do schools with poor reputations, even though they draw from the same population, this is only a correlation, not a demonstrated cause-effect relationship. We don't know whether the school with the good reputation takes the students and changes their behavior, or whether the more motivated students in a particular neighborhood seek the "better" school, thereby maintaining its reputation for excellence, or whether some other process is at work.

The Teacher

Educational psychologists have discovered that only a handful of excellent, dedicated teachers may be an important factor in determining whether a particular school will be successful. In one study (Pedersen, Faucher, & Eaton, 1978), researchers found that the children in a particular elementary school who had achieved the highest grades and who later demonstrated superior status as adults all had one thing in common—the same first-grade teacher!

The academic material that the teacher taught obviously had little effect on the children once they had become adults. However, this teacher appeared to have made a lasting contribution to the students' attitudes toward learning and the desire to achieve and also had helped the students to set their sights on different life paths than they might ordinarily have considered. Think of the teachers you've had whom you greatly admired and respected. Did they teach you more than just the academic material? Did they teach you to do your best, to have confidence in yourself, to set high standards, and then to attain them? Did they make you want to stay in school and continue to learn? Perhaps such teachers, more than anything else, determine whether a school will be successful.

The Successful School

Although it is commonly assumed that the age of the school or the size of classrooms has an important effect on student achievement, educational psychologists have discovered that these two factors don't make much difference, assuming that reasonable minimal standards are met—that facilities are not completely dilapidated and that the school isn't out of funds for the most rudimentary equipment (Rutter, Maughan, Mortimore, Ouston, & Smith, 1979). Successful schools generally have an academic emphasis. Academic goals are clearly stated, there is a certain degree of structure, and achievement expectations are high (Linney & Seidman, 1989). More specifically, effective schools are characterized by regularly assigned and graded homework and by a high proportion of time devoted to active teaching, instead of to miscellaneous activities such as calling roll, handing out papers, setting up equipment, and disciplining students. Effective schools also have a system of checks to make certain that teachers are following the intended practices of the school. This is especially important for inexperienced teachers, who tend to be the most inefficient in classroom management (Rutter, Maughan, Mortimore, Ouston, & Smith, 1979).

In this section, we have touched on only a few of the important issues addressed by educational psychologists, but we have examined other areas of interest in other chapters. For instance, we examined test development in Chapters 13 and 14, learning and cognition in Chapters 8 and 10, and motivation in Chapter 11. All these areas, as well as others, are of concern to educational psychologists in their quest to understand how people become educated and how they apply their knowledge.

Appendix B

Statistics

Richard D. Rees

You are a student in introductory psychology who has developed a healthy respect for what psychology has to offer. You've been impressed with the research methods psychologists use and have decided to conduct a study of your own.

For a long time you have been concerned about television and its possible adverse effects on studies and grades. The children in your family and the children in your friends' families spend a lot of time watching TV. It seems obvious to you that, if they watched less, they would do better in school.

The hypothesis you want to test is that students who are heavy TV watchers do not perform as well in their academic studies as students who are light TV watchers.

With the cooperation of a friend, the principal of Tumbleweed Elementary School, and with the permission of the parents involved, you embark on a two-week research project with 50 fourth graders from Tumbleweed. Half of the students are assigned randomly to a group of heavy TV watchers and told to watch 35 hours or more of TV per week, and half are assigned to a group of light TV watchers and told to watch 6 or fewer hours of TV per week. At the end of two weeks, all students take the same unannounced spelling test consisting of 15 words from a current chapter of their spelling workbook. The results of the spelling test are given in Table B.1. You want to know whether the light watchers did better than the heavies.

At this point you can't tell for sure. Something must be done with the scores before you can make sense out of them. In this appendix we set out strategies and techniques that will help you interpret, understand, and make predictions from research data such as test scores. These strategies and techniques form a very valuable research tool, namely, statistics. So let's apply statistics to your TV watchers' spelling scores.

TABLE B.1 ◆ SPELLING SCORES OF HEAVY AND LIGHT TV WATCHERS									
HEAVY WATCHERS (35 HOURS OR MORE PER WEEK)					LIGHT WATCHERS (6 OR FEWER HOURS PER WEEK)				
11	1	7	4	13	13	10	13	11	13
7	5	2	10	6	15	11	9	14	7
0	15	6	1	7	8	15	14	12	13
9	2	7	0	7	14	11	11	5	8
6	5	8	2	9	13	14	13	5	3

TABLE B.2 ◆ Frequency Distribution of Spelling Scores of Heavy and Light TV Watchers

HEAVY TV WATCHERS		LIGHT TV WATCHERS	
Spelling Score	Number of Students (Frequency)	Spelling Score	Number of Students (Frequency)
15	1	15	2
14	0	14	4
13	1	13	6
12	0	12	1
11	1	11	4
10	1	10	1
9	2	9	1
8	1	8	2
7	5	7	1
6	3	6	0
5	2	5	2
4	1	4	0
3	0	3	1
2	3	2	0
1	2	1	0
0	2	0	0

DESCRIPTIVE STATISTICS

Descriptive statistics are used to summarize, organize, describe, boil down, and make sense out of large amounts of data. In Table B.1 you have an incoherent mass of test score data. The scores are disorganized and convey very little information.

Frequency Distributions and Graphs

One way of organizing the scores to make them more meaningful is to arrange them in a *frequency distribution*.

REGULAR FREQUENCY DISTRIBUTION. In a *regular frequency distribution*, each score value from highest to lowest is listed once; beside it, in the frequency column, the number of times that score occurs is written. In examining Table B.2 you can see, for example, that the score of 7 occurred 5 times among the heavy TV watchers.

GROUPED FREQUENCY DISTRIBUTION. If the spread of score values in a distribution is large (for example, a math test with 53 questions on it), then a *grouped frequency distribution* may be used. A grouped frequency distribution condenses the score values into intervals and then shows, in the frequency column, the number of people who received scores falling within each interval (see Table B.3).

To further clarify the arrangement of scores in a frequency distribution, so that you can see at a glance the visual pattern involved, the distribution can be graphed.

HISTOGRAM. A *histogram* (or *bar graph*) uses a series of vertical bars to show the pattern of scores (see Figure B.1). Notice that the sides of each bar are plotted midway between the scores so that each score falls in the center of the bar.

TABLE B.3 ◆ GROUPED FREQUENCY DISTRIBUTION OF MATH SCORES FOR 50 STUDENTS

MATH SCORES IN INTERVALS OF 5	NUMBER OF STUDENTS (FREQUENCY)
50–54	2
45–49	3
40–44	2
35–39	6
30–34	8
25–29	12
20–24	7
15–19	5
10–14	4
5–9	0
0–4	1

◆ **FIGURE B.1**

Histogram of spelling scores of heavy and light TV watchers.

FREQUENCY POLYGON.   A *frequency polygon* plots the frequencies of the scores as points that are then connected with a straight line. Figure B.2 shows you at a glance that the heavy TV watchers didn't do too well on the spelling test. It certainly conveys more information than the mass of scores in Table B.1.

When large amounts of data (thousands of scores) are plotted, the jagged edges tend to smooth out and the frequency polygon often takes on an identifiable shape. Some of the more commonly observed shapes are (1) a normal *bell-shaped curve* (where the majority of people scored in the middle of the distribution with very few at the extreme high and low ends), (2) a *positively skewed curve* (where most of the people got low scores, with fewer and fewer getting progressively higher ones),* (3) a *negatively skewed curve* (where nearly everyone aced the test), and (4) a *bimodal curve* (where very few people scored in the middle, most either acing the test or bombing it). The curves are shown in Figure B.3.

Central Tendency

Another useful descriptive statistic involves measuring the central tendency of a group of scores. *Central tendency* refers to a single number representing the middle or the average of a distribution. There are three measures of central tendency: the mean, the median, and the mode (see Table B.4).

*A positively skewed curve often indicates poor performance, but not always. For example, reaction-time curves are usually positively skewed, indicating that most people have fast reaction times.

◆ **FIGURE B.2**

Frequency polygon of spelling scores of heavy and light TV watchers.

◆ FIGURE B.3

Commonly observed shapes of frequency polygons.

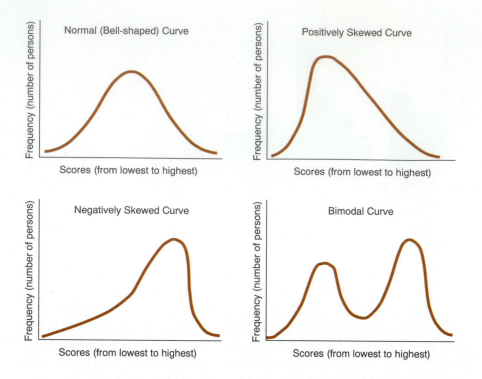

MEAN.　The *mean* is the arithmetic average and is obtained by adding up all the scores in the distribution and dividing that sum by the total number of scores. The heavy TV watchers' spelling scores add up to 150. Since there were 25 students in this group, we divide 150 by 25 to obtain a mean score of 6. The light TV watchers' scores total 275, which, divided by 25, gives a

TABLE B.4 ◆ MEASURES OF CENTRAL TENDENCY OF SPELLING SCORES FOR HEAVY AND LIGHT TV WATCHERS	
HEAVY WATCHERS	**LIGHT WATCHERS**
Mean 15 + 13 + 11 + 10 + 9 + 9 + 8 + 7 + 7 + 7 + 7 + 7 + 6 + 6 + 6 + 5 + 5 + 4 + 2 + 2 + 2 + 1 + 1 + 0 + 0 = 150	15 + 15 + 14 + 14 + 14 + 14 + 13 + 13 + 13 + 13 + 13 + 13 + 12 + 11 + 11 + 11 + 11 + 10 + 9 + 8 + 8 + 7 + 5 + 5 + 3 = 275
Mean $= \dfrac{\text{Sum of Scores}}{\text{Number of Scores}} = \dfrac{150}{25} = 6$	Mean $= \dfrac{\text{Sum of Scores}}{\text{Number of Scores}} = \dfrac{275}{25} = 11$
Mean = 6	Mean = 11
Median 15, 13, 11, 10, 9, 9, 8, 7, 7, 7, 7, 7, ⑥, 6, 6, 5, 5, 4, 2, 2, 2, 1, 1, 0, 0,	15, 15, 14, 14, 14, 14, 13, 13, 13, 13, 13, 13, ⑫, 11, 11, 11, 11, 10, 9, 8, 8, 7, 5, 5, 3,
Median = Exact middle score. There are exactly 12 scores on either side of the circled 6.	Median = Exact middle score. There are exactly 12 scores on either side of the circled 12.
Median = 6	Median = 12
Mode Mode = Most frequently occurring score. 　(There were 5 students who got a score 　of 7.)	Mode = Most frequent occurring score. 　(There were 6 students who got a score 　of 13.)
Mode = 7	Mode = 13

mean of 11. Out of 15 possible, the light watchers averaged 11 right, and the heavy watchers 6 right. Your hypothesis is looking more plausible all the time, isn't it?

MEDIAN. Although the mean is the most commonly used measure of central tendency in statistical analysis, there are times when it is not appropriate to use it (for instance with a highly skewed distribution containing extreme scores). Instead, the *median* is used. The median is the exact middle of a distribution of scores. Half the scores fall on one side of it and half on the other. There are precise methods for calculating the median, but for our purposes, a convenient way is to list each score from highest to lowest and then count in to the center.

MODE. The *mode* is a very crude measure of central tendency. It gives, at best, only a rough estimate of the middle area and is seldom used in statistical analysis. The mode is simply the score in a distribution that occurs more frequently than any other score. For the heavy watchers it is 7, and for the light watchers, 13.

Variability

Variability refers to the dispersion or scatter of a group of scores. It is concerned with how spread out the scores are. High variability means that the scores are widely separated with much distance between them. Low variability indicates very little spread; the scores are tightly clustered together. Measures of variability include the range, the variance, and the standard deviation.

RANGE. The *range* is obtained by subtracting the lowest from the highest score. The range of spelling scores for the heavy TV watchers is 15 (the scores ranged from 0 to 15). For the light watchers, the range is 12 (from 3 to 15). Although easy to calculate, the range, like the mode, is a crude statistical measure. As you can see, it takes into account only two scores in the distribution, the highest and the lowest.

VARIANCE AND STANDARD DEVIATION. The *standard deviation* (SD) is the most useful measure of variability. It takes into account every score in the distribution. The standard deviation (which is the square root of the variance) can be thought of (generally speaking) as a number representing the average distance of the scores from the mean. The larger the standard deviation, the more spread out the scores. It is calculated by (1) finding the difference between the mean and each score, (2) squaring each of these differences, (3) adding up the squared differences, (4) dividing the sum of the squared differences by the total number of scores (N) minus one* (the average of the squared differences), and (5) taking the square root of the average of the squared differences. The calculations up through step 4 yield the variance. Taking the square root in step 5 (to return to the original units of measurement) gives the standard deviation.

As you can see in Table B.5, the heavy TV watchers had slightly greater variability on the spelling test than the light watchers. The heavies had a higher range and a larger variance and standard deviation.

Transformed Scores

Sometimes, for purposes of increased clarity or for making comparisons, it is desirable to change or transform scores into new units. Percentiles represent one type of transformed scores, and standard scores are another.

*Note: The divisor is N if you are merely describing a set of scores, and it is N minus 1 if you are making an inference about a population, as we will be doing with these data.

TABLE B.5 ◆ MEASURES OF VARIABILITY OF SPELLING SCORES FOR HEAVY AND LIGHT TV WATCHERS

HEAVY WATCHERS			LIGHT WATCHERS		
Range					
Range = Highest score minus lowest score			Range = Highest score minus lowest score		
Range = 15–0			Range = 15–3		
Range = 15			Range = 12		

Variance and standard deviation (SD)

Scores	Scores minus mean of 6	Scores minus mean, squared	Scores	Scores minus mean of 11	Scores minus mean, squared
15	9	81	15	4	16
13	7	49	15	4	16
11	5	25	14	3	9
10	4	16	14	3	9
9	3	9	14	3	9
9	3	9	14	3	9
8	2	4	13	2	4
7	1	1	13	2	4
7	1	1	13	2	4
7	1	1	13	2	4
7	1	1	13	2	4
7	1	1	13	2	4
6	0	0	12	1	1
6	0	0	11	0	0
6	0	0	11	0	0
5	−1	1	11	0	0
5	−1	1	11	0	0
4	−2	4	10	−1	1
2	−4	16	9	−2	4
2	−4	16	8	−3	9
2	−4	16	8	−3	9
1	−5	25	7	−4	16
1	−5	25	5	−6	36
0	−6	36	5	−6	36
0	−6	36	3	−8	64
		Sum of scores minus mean, squared = 374			Sum of scores minus mean, squared = 268

$$SD = \sqrt{\frac{\text{Sum of score minus mean, squared}}{\text{Number of scores minus one}}}$$

$$SD = \sqrt{\frac{374}{25-1}} = \sqrt{15.583} = 3.948$$

Variance = 15.583
Standard deviation = 3.948

$$SD = \sqrt{\frac{\text{Sum of scores minus mean, squared}}{\text{Number of scores minus one}}}$$

$$SD = \sqrt{\frac{268}{25-1}} = \sqrt{11.167} = 3.342$$

Variance = 11.167
Standard deviation = 3.342

PERCENTILES. Carol, a subject in the group of light TV watchers, scored 13 correct on the spelling test. Her friend Julie, in the heavy group, got 9 right.

To see how well each girl did in comparison with her own group, we need to transform the scores. A percentile shows the percentage of people in the reference group who scored at or below a certain score. In Carol's reference group (the light watchers), 19 children out of 25 got 13 or fewer words right. Dividing 19 by 25 gives us .76 or 76 percent. Thus, Carol's score of 13 places her at the 76th percentile. Julie's 9 represents the 84th percentile (21 students out of 25 got a score of 9 or less, 21/25 = .84). So Julie with her 9 did better with respect to her group of heavy watchers than Carol with her 13 did with respect to the light watchers.

STANDARD SCORES (Z, T, SAT).   Z *scores* are transformed scores that have a mean of 0 and a standard deviation of 1. To obtain a Z score for any raw score in a distribution, simply subtract the mean from the score and divide the result by the standard deviation. Carol's Z score is 0.60 (her score of 13 minus the mean of 11 divided by the standard deviation 3.341 equals 0.60) in her light TV group. Julie's Z score is 9 minus 6 divided by 3.948 which equals 0.76. Again, you can see that Julie with her Z of 0.76 did better with respect to her group than Carol with her Z of 0.60 did with respect to hers, even though Carol's raw score of 13 was higher than Julie's raw score of 9.

Two other standard scores are *T scores*, which have a mean of 50 and a standard deviation of 10, and *SAT scores*, with a mean of 500 and an SD of 100. To obtain a T score, multiply the Z score by 10 and add 50. Carol's T (10 times 0.60 plus 50) equals 56.0, and Julie's T is 57.6 (10 times 0.76 plus 50). SAT scores are obtained by multiplying the T score by 10. Carol's SAT is 560, and Julie's is 576.

Table B.6 shows transformed scores for Carol with respect to the group of light TV watchers and Julie with respect to the heavy watchers.

Julie's boy friend, Ambitious Andy Angus, who lifts bulls for exercise, was also randomly assigned to the heavy watchers' group and got a score of 1 on the spelling test. His Z score is −1.27 (1 minus 6 divided by 3.948). His T score is 37.3 (−1.27 times 10 plus 50), and his SAT is 373.

T scores are easier to interpret for many people because, like Z scores, they avoid negative numbers (a Z of −1 is the same as a T of 40). Also, the results of some national exams, such as the Scholastic Aptitude Test and the Graduate Record Exam, are reported in SAT scores.

The Normal Bell-Shaped Curve

Z scores and the standard deviation are related to the normal bell-shaped curve in a fixed and predictable manner. When a frequency polygon is drawn for large numbers of people on certain traits (for instance, intelligence, height, weight, extroversion), the resulting curve is bell-shaped. Because many traits in psychology take this bell shape, the normal curve is a very useful statistical tool. Since the percentages under the curve never change, by plugging in the standard deviation you can determine the percentage of the people falling above, below, or between certain scores. Look at Figure B.4. Assuming that the mean spelling score on a 25-item test for a *large population* of light TV watchers is 11 with an SD of 3, you can see that about 68 percent of the subjects score between 8 and 14 on the test. Only 13/100 percent (0.13 percent) were above a score of 20.

TABLE B.6 ◆ TRANSFORMED SPELLING SCORES		
	JULIE (IN HEAVY WATCHER'S GROUP)	CAROL (IN LIGHT WATCHER'S GROUP)
Actual score on spelling test	9	13
Percentile	84th	76th
Z score	+0.76	+0.60
T score	57.6	56.0
SAT score	576	560

Normal bell-shaped curve showing various scores and percentages under the curve (total area equals 100 percent).

	−3	−2	−1	0	+1	+2	+3
Standard Deviations	−3	−2	−1	0	+1	+2	+3
Cumulative Percentages	.1%	2.3%	15.9%	50%	84.1%	97.7%	99.9%
Z Scores	−3.0	−2.0	−1.0	0	+1.0	+2.0	+3.0
T Scores	20	30	40	50	60	70	80
SAT Scores	200	300	400	500	600	700	800
Spelling Scores	2	5	8	11	14	17	20
IQ Scores	55	70	85	100	115	130	145

A popular intelligence test (the Wechsler) has a mean IQ of 100 with an SD of 15. As you can see in Figure B.4, about 95 percent of the population have IQ scores between 70 and 130.

Z scores are expressed in standard deviation units, so that a person with a Z score of +3.00 would be standard deviations above the mean and would have outscored over 99 percent of those with scores on that variable. Remember, any score on any test can be converted to a Z score, and by examining the percentages under the curve, you can see at a glance how good that score is.*

🧬 INFERENTIAL STATISTICS

Whereas descriptive statistics merely describe, organize, and summarize data, inferential statistics are used to make predictions and draw conclusions about populations based on data from a sample.

Populations and Samples

The question you want to answer is: Do all fourth graders who are heavy TV watchers really obtain a lower spelling test average (mean) than all fourth graders who are light TV watchers? Your populations of interest, then, are *all* heavy and *all* light TV watchers who are in the fourth grade. However, you can't measure them all, so you obtain a sample of each, which is smaller and

---

*It must be assumed that the large population of test scores under consideration would form a frequency polygon that is shaped like the normal bell-shaped curve.

more manageable and which you *can* measure. If your samples are chosen at random (so that any member of the population has an equal chance of being selected), then they are likely to be representative of the population.

Probability

Inferential statistics are based on the laws of *probability* or chance. If heavy or light TV watching has no effect at all on spelling scores, then you would expect the mean scores for the two samples (heavy and light) to be about the same; that is, the probability is high that the means will be the same or nearly the same. The probability is very low that the heavy watchers' sample will average, say, a score of 2 and the light watchers sample will average, say, 14 if TV watching has no effect on spelling scores in the population. You wouldn't expect the averages to be so far apart from chance alone.

Null Hypothesis (Retain or Reject)

The procedure to follow in inferential statistics is (1) to state the *null hypothesis* (that there is *no* difference between the average scores in the two populations), (2) to draw a sample from each of the two populations of interest, (3) to find the two sample mean scores, (4) to determine how probable it is that the difference between the two means occurred by chance, and (5) to reject the null hypothesis if the probability is less than 5 percent that the difference could have occurred by chance (the choice of 5 percent is an arbitrary one that psychologists have generally found to be most useful).

In your present study, your null hypothesis is that heavy and light TV watchers will score the same on the spelling test (signifying that TV watching does not affect spelling scores). In your two samples, the heavy watchers and the light watchers scored a mean of 6 and 11, respectively, on the test. Could a mean of 6 in one group and 11 in the other have occurred just by chance if the null hypothesis is true? It could have, but it is not very likely. Using the normal curve and specific inferential statistical testing procedures, we find that the probability that means of 6 and 11 (a difference of 5 points) would occur by chance is less than 5 percent. This is so low that you reject the null hypothesis and conclude that, in the populations, fourth graders who are light TV watchers score better on the spelling test than those who are heavy TV watchers. You have found a significant difference between the means. *Significant* has a specific meaning in statistics. It means that the difference between the sample means could have occurred purely by chance less than five times in a hundred samplings (that is, in 5 percent) of the two populations if in fact the two population means are the same (that is, if the null hypothesis is true).

It was not chance that accounted for the heavy group's lower score, it was too much TV. Notice that in rejecting the null hypothesis you are supporting the research hypothesis that you formulated when you began the study. That is, students who are heavy TV watchers do not perform as well in their academic studies as students who are light TV watchers. You could have made an error in drawing this conclusion if that very slim probability (less than five chances in a hundred) actually happened in these samples. But the probability of your having made such an error (known as a *Type I error* in statistical terminology) is less than 5 percent.

❖ CORRELATION

Showing that heavy TV watchers score lower on the spelling test than light watchers involved one major statistical procedure, namely, testing for differences between means.

Correlation, another major procedure in statistics, is designed to show relationships between variables. Correlation may be classified as descriptive or inferential depending on how it is used. Instead of getting up an experimental study with two groups of fourth graders assigned to two weeks of heavy or light TV viewing, we could simply select a group of fourth graders, ask them how much TV they watch per week, and give them a spelling test. The correlation or relationship between hours of TV and test scores could then be determined. A trend or tendency (a correlation) might show up. You might expect a strong negative correlation, but it is possible that it could be moderate, weak, or zero. It might even be positive.

Correlation Coefficient

The correlation between two variables is expressed as a number known as the *correlation coefficient*. It can range from 0 to 1 (usually expressed in hundredths, that is, .01, .09, .18, .45, .87, .93, etc.), with higher numbers showing stronger relationships, and it can be positive or negative. A correlation can also be perfect, although perfect correlations rarely occur with psychological data.

Positive, Negative, Perfect, and Zero Correlations

A *positive correlation* means that there is a tendency for the two variables to change together in the same direction. For instance, high school grade point average is positively correlated with college grade point average. That is to say, those who do well in high school tend to do well in college also, and vice versa. Of course, there are exceptions, but the tendency is nevertheless a strong one.

A *negative correlation* shows that, as one variable is increasing, the other is decreasing. The variables change in opposite directions. Absences and grades would probably be negatively correlated. As absences increase, grades decrease, and vice versa.

The strongest possible correlation is 1.00 (which can be either +1.00 or −1.00), and it is called a *perfect correlation*. A perfect positive correlation (+1.00) means that right down the line each person maintains his or her position from highest to lowest on both variables. The highest person on variable X is also the highest on variable Y, the next highest on X is next highest on Y, and so on, down to the person who is lowest on both variables. There are no exceptions to the pattern. For example, it costs 50¢ for an ice cream cone at the corner ice cream parlor. What is the correlation between money spent for ice cream cones and the number of cones purchased? It is perfect (+1.00), isn't it? The person who spends 50¢ gets one cone; whoever spends $1 gets two cones; $10, 20 cones; $50, 100 cones; and so on. You can *predict* exactly a person's "score" on one variable if you know the "score" on the other variable. (If someone spent $20 on ice cream cones, how many did he or she buy? Exactly 40, of course.)

Zero correlation means that there is no relationship between the two variables being studied. What would you expect the correlation to be between nose length and IQ for a group of 50 people? It would be zero, or very near to zero, since these two variables are not related.

Scatter Diagrams

A scatter diagram can show visually the direction and strength of a correlation. The correlation scatter diagrams in Figure B.5 were constructed by plotting a single dot for each person's score on both variables. The closer the dots ap-

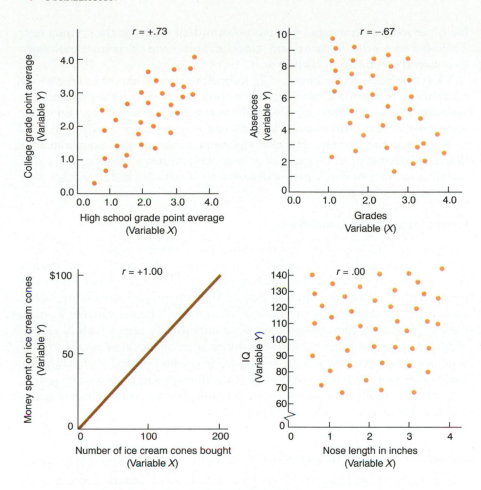

◆ FIGURE B.5

Scatter diagrams showing positive, negative, perfect, and zero correlations (r = correlation coefficient).

proach a diagonal straight line, the higher the correlation; a diagonal straight line represents a perfect correlation of $+1.00$ or -1.00.

Table B.7 shows how different correlation coefficient values are interpreted. Remember, the size of the correlation coefficient shows how strong the relationship is, and the sign (plus or minus) indicates the direction of the relationship (positive meaning that the two variables change together and negative that they vary in opposite directions). A correlation coefficient of $-.83$, for example, indicates a stronger relationship than does one of $+.71$, since .83 is a larger value than .71.

Correlating Test Scores with TV Viewing

Let's take another look at the fourth-grade TV watchers. You want to know whether those who watch TV more tend to score lower on the spelling test. Select 10 fourth graders from Tumbleweed Elementary and find out how many

TABLE B.7 ◆ Interpreting Correlation Coefficients	
CORRELATION COEFFICIENT (PLUS OR MINUS)	INTERPRETATION
1.00	Perfect relationship
.73 to .99	Very strong relationship
.60 to .72	Strong relationship
.31 to .59	Fairly strong (or moderate) relationship
.16 to .30	Weak relationship
.01 to .15	Very weak relationship
0.00	No relationship

hours per week each watches TV. Also obtain their scores on the spelling test. Table B.8 shows the TV hours and scores, and gives the calculations necessary to obtain the correlation coefficient.

The correlation coefficient of $-.72$ indicates a strong (almost a very strong) relationship between TV watching and spelling scores. The higher-scoring students watch less TV and vice versa. The correlation is not perfect (there are some exceptions to this trend), but the trend is nevertheless striking.

Note that the data in this appendix were made up and exaggerated to illustrate the statistical concepts. You may wish to run your own study with real data in order to check your understanding of statistics and to indulge your curiosity about behavior.

Correlation and Causation

Experimental studies, which test the differences between means, help you to draw conclusions about case-and-effect relationships, but correlational studies do not establish causation. Just because two variables are correlated does not mean that one causes the other. It may be that when two variables are highly correlated, variable X causes variable Y, or variable Y causes variable X, or X causes Z which in turn causes Y, or W simultaneously causes both X and Y. The correlation coefficient gives us no information about causation. Much TV watching may cause low grades; low grades may cause more TV watching; or some other variable (such as increased study time, procrastination, depression, self-concept, intelligence, or social pressure) may be causing both higher grades and less TV or lower grades and more TV.

TABLE B.8 ◆ **CALCULATION OF CORRELATION BETWEEN HOURS OF TV WATCHING AND SPELLING TEST SCORES FOR FOURTH GRADERS**

SUBJECT	HOURS OF TV PER WEEK (VARIABLE X)	VARIABLE X SQUARED (X^2)	SCORE ON -WORD SPELLING TEST (VARIABLE Y)	VARIABLE Y SQUARED (Y^2)	VARIABLE X TIMES VARIABLE Y (XY)
1	0	0	10	100	0
2	5	25	8	64	40
3	10	100	9	81	90
4	13	169	2	4	26
5	18	324	6	36	108
6	23	529	5	25	115
7	27	729	3	9	81
8	30	900	0	0	0
9	31	961	7	49	217
10	36	1296	1	1	36
Totals:	193	5033	51	369	713
	Sum of X	Sum of X^2	Sum of Y	Sum of Y^2	Sum of XY
	193	5033	51	369	713

N = Number of subjects = 10

$$r = \frac{N(\text{Sum of } XY) - (\text{Sum of } X)(\text{Sum of } Y)}{\sqrt{[N(\text{Sum of } X^2)-(\text{Sum of } X)^2][N(\text{Sum of } Y^2)-(\text{Sum of } Y)^2]}}$$

$$r = \frac{(10)(713)-(193)(51)}{\sqrt{[(10)(5033)-(193)^2][(10)(369)-(51)^2]}}$$

$$r = \frac{7130-9843}{\sqrt{(50330-37249)(3690-2601)}}$$

$$r = \frac{-2713}{\sqrt{(13081)(1089)}} \qquad r = \frac{-2713}{3774.2825}$$

$r = -.7188$ or $-.72$

When birth statistics were examined for a number of European cities several years ago, a high positive correlation was supposedly found between the number of babies born per year and the number of storks nesting in the chimneys. Obviously, a hasty assumption about *causation* will lead you to an outdated conclusion. Even your TV-watching fourth graders wouldn't buy that one.

🌀 SUMMARY

◆ Psychologists give tests, conduct experiments, and carry out extensive research into many facets of human and animal behavior. The data resulting from all this research must be analyzed, interpreted, summarized, and reported in a meaningful way. By using statistics, researchers can make sense out of the data and can draw valid conclusions about the results of their tests and experiments.

◆ Statistics fall into two main categories: descriptive and inferential. Descriptive statistics are used to summarize, organize, and describe a set of research data, and inferential statistics are used to draw conclusions about populations based on the results obtained from a sample.

◆ Descriptive statistics include frequency distributions (both regular and grouped), graphs (including histograms and frequency polygons), measures of central tendency (mean, median, and mode), measures of variability (range, variance, and standard deviation), and transformed scores (including percentiles and standard scores).

◆ Although frequency polygons take many shapes (including skewed and bimodal), the most important shape for use in statistical analysis is the normal bell-shaped curve.

◆ The normal curve has a fixed and predictable association with the standard deviation and Z scores, permitting direct comparison of the results of many diverse tests and experimental data. The normal curve is also a probability curve, which has special applications in conjunction with inferential statistics.

◆ Inferential statistics are based on the laws of probability. Researchers are interested in determining the chances that the results obtained from certain samples represent the true state of affairs in the population. To do this, a null hypothesis (that no difference exists or that observed differences are due only to chance) is stated, and then the null hypothesis is retained or rejected depending on the results of the statistical test employed.

◆ Correlation, another statistical procedure, shows the strength of the relationship between two variables. Correlation coefficients range from 0 to +1.00, or from 0 to −1.00. The higher the correlation coefficient, the stronger the relationship.

◆ A positive correlation means that the two variables are changing together in the same direction. A negative correlation shows an inverse relationship (as one variable is getting larger the other is getting smaller, and vice versa).

◆ Correlation coefficients may be visually displayed in scatter diagrams.

◆ Correlation does not imply causation.

Appendix C

How to Locate and Read Research Articles in Psychology

An introductory psychology text usually contains hundreds of references to books, journal articles, dissertations, and papers. While it is not possible in this appendix to describe and explain all the different sources of information you might encounter, it is valuable for you to be able to locate and read articles in psychological journals if you wish to know how psychologists report their research findings or wish to do further research on a topic.

The first part of this appendix describes the sources you can use to find articles, abstracts and other research sources. The second part describes in detail the parts of a journal article. The third part lists some of the major journals used by psychologists and gives a brief summary of the kind of research each reports.

Even though psychologists publish in many different journals and use a multitude of formats, this appendix describes the article organization preferred by the American Psychological Association,* since many of the major journals are published by that association and a number of other journals also use its format.

RESEARCH SOURCES

Psychologists and psychology students can use many sources to obtain information about a specific subject. The most commonly used is *Psychological Abstracts*, which is published monthly by the American Psychological Association (APA). Each volume contains abstracts (summaries) of articles that have appeared in journals important to psychologists. The abstracts are indexed by both subject and author. The APA also publishes (quarterly) the *PsycSCAN* series, which includes abstracts in one specific area, such as clinical, applied, or developmental psychology. In addition, the APA's *PsycINFO* service provides custom computer searches for data or information.

Other important sources of interest include: *ERIC*, a catalog of selected documents in the area of education, which is closely tied to psychology; *Dissertation Abstracts*, which lists dissertations published throughout the world, including dissertations in psychology; and the *Science Citation Index*, which includes psychological literature, as well as psychiatric and relevant medical literature. The *Science Citation Index* is a valuable adjunct to *Psychological Abstracts*, because it includes information related to psychology published by other

---

*These guidelines are printed in the *Publication Manual of the American Psychological Association* (3rd edition), which was published in 1983.

science disciplines, such as chemistry, biology, and medicine. It also includes more indexes than *Psychological Abstracts*—subject, author, country, and even institutional affiliation indexes.

 # THE RESEARCH ARTICLE

There are three major kinds of research articles published by psychologists. The first is a presentation of an emphirical study in which original research is reported. The second is a review article, which critically evaluates past and present research on a topic and often suggests ways to clarify problems relating to the research. The third is a theoretical article, which is similar to a review article in organization, but differs in using previous research to support a particular theoretical position. Other kinds of articles, such as brief reports, comments, replies, and case histories are also published in journals.

Most research reports follow a consistent organization. They present a *title*, an *abstract*, an introduction to the *problem*, the *method* of doing the research, the *results* obtained from the research, a *discussion* of the research results, and *references* to other research articles.

The Abstract

The abstract of an article is a short (usually under 150 words), comprehensive summary of the contents of the article. It generally gives the major issues confronted by the researchers and summarizes the major findings.

Methodology

The next section of an article describes in detail how the study was conducted. It often contains descriptions of the research subjects, any apparatus or materials used in the research, and the procedure followed to test the subjects or apparatus. A detailed methodology section is necessary so that others can evaluate and replicate the research results.

Results

The results section gives a detailed description of the research findings. It often includes a statistical treatment of the raw research data. Tables and figures summarizing these data are commonly presented. This is often the most complex and difficult section for the beginning student of psychology. Appendix B may help you understand the results section.

Discussion

In the discussion section, the research results are interpreted and evaluated. In this section, the authors summarize their results and may relate them to a theoretical position.

References

Reference citations add support to statements made in the body of the research article. They are often a source of further information about a topic and can be a good starting point for more detailed research.

 # SELECTED JOURNALS IN PSYCHOLOGY

The following list of journals in psychology is only a partial one. It includes all journals published by the APA, plus other journals in science and psychology. Most selections are followed by a notation of the chapters in this textbook to which the journal mainly relates.

The *American Psychologist* is the official journal of the APA. It contains all archival documents of the association plus other articles, notes, comments, and letters that directly affect the APA or inform the public about issues and problems facing psychology.
Chapters 1-19.

Behavioral Neuroscience is published by the APA and contains original research papers on the biological bases of behavior. It includes articles on the biological and neurological sciences that directly relate to psychology.
Chapters 2, 5, 6, 7, 11.

Contemporary Psychology is published by the APA and contains critical reviews of textbooks, films, and other media used in psychology.

Developmental Psychology is published by the APA and contains articles about human behavior across the life span.
Chapters 3, 4.

The *Journal of Abnormal Psychology* is published by the APA and contains articles concerning psychopathology and abnormality. It usually does not include works on treatment of these disorders; those are more often published in the *Journal of Consulting and Clinical Psychology*.
Chapters 15, 16.

The *Journal of Applied Psychology* is published by the APA and contains articles about how psychology can be applied in every field except clinical psychology.
Appendix A.

The *Journal of Comparative Psychology* is published by the APA and contains articles on the behavior of various species, related to evolution, development, ecology, control, and functional significance.
Chapters 2, 3, 8, 10.

The *Journal of Consulting and Clinical Psychology* is published by the APA and contains articles on the diagnosis and treatment of psychopathology.
Chapters 15, 17.

The *Journal of Counseling Psychology* is published by the APA and contains articles of interest to counselors in the school system, counseling agencies, and other counseling settings.
Chapter 14, Appendix A.

The *Journal of Educational Psychology* is published by the APA and contains articles concerning learning and cognition, especially as these subjects relate to instruction.
Chapters 8, 10, 13, Appendix A.

The *Journal of Experimental Psychology: General* is published by the APA and contains articles of interest to experimental psychologists.
Chapter 1, Appendix B.

The *Journal of Experimental Psychology: Animal Behavior* is published by the APA and contains articles on learning, motivation, memory, and other processes in animals.
Chapters 6, 8, 9, 11.

The *Journal of Experimental Psychology: Human Perception and Performance* is published by the APA and contains articles on human perception, verbal and motor performance, and human cognition.
Chapters 5, 6, 10, 13.

The *Journal of Experimental Psychology: Learning, Memory, and Cognition* is published by the APA and contains articles concerning learning, memory, and cognition, in both humans and animals.
Chapters 8, 9, 10.

The *Journal of Personality and Social Psychology* is published by the APA and contains articles on personality and social processes, including attitude measurement and the relationship between attitudes and behavior.
Chapters 14, 18, 19.

Professional Psychology: Research and Practice is published by the APA and contains articles on the application of psychology, including its scientific underpinnings.
Chapters 1, 17, Appendix A, Appendix B.

Psychological Bulletin is published by the APA and contains evaluative reviews of important issues in psychology. Original research is usually reported only to back up the reviews.
Chapters 1-19, Appendix A.

Psychological Review is published by the APA and contains theoretical articles on any area of scientific psychology.
Chapters 1–19, Appendix A.

Science is published weekly by the American Association for the Advancement of Science and often includes articles of interest in scientific psychology.
Chapters 2-19, Appendix A.

Science News is published weekly by Science Service, Inc., and often includes psychology articles. Students especially enjoy this publication, as it is written for educated laypeoples as well as for scientists. It reports important research that has come out of annual meetings of both the American Psychological Association and the American Psychiatric Association, as well as other scientific organizations and sources.
Chapters 1–19, Appendix A.

Appendix D

Using the Computer for Psychological Research

Computers have made a great difference in the way information about psychological research can be accessed. Previously, if you wanted to research a topic, you had to go to the library and hunt through the *Psychological Abstracts*, *ERIC*, or other abstracts in aligned fields like medicine, sociology, and anthropology. Now there are several ways to obtain the same infomration, sometimes without leaving your own home! Because the computer is so fast and versatile, you can search by author, journal name, key terms, and even by year in much less time than you would have spent searching the old way by scanning paper records.

There are two basic ways to search the psychological literature by computer. One requires access to a computer and modem; the other requires access to a computer with CD-ROM drive. If you have access to a computer and modem, you can search by hooking into an information system like Compuserve. Compuserve has a database called Knowledge Index that can access information in psychology, medicine, drugs, and other related fields. Searches can be performed by subject area, author, journal name, or even year of publication. The American Psychological Association's own database, called PsycINFO, is part of this system. Because of the speed of the computer, using key terms to find material on your topic is fast and easy. The American Psychological Association has even published a book called the *Thesaurus of Psychological Index Terms* (6th ed., 1991) to assist you in finding articles by key terms. Other databases use similar terms. The only disadvantage to this kind of database searching is that you must pay a fee for membership in the information system and will also be charged a fee for the time you spend accessing the database. The major advantage is that you can access the database from any location.

The second way to access psychological information is through PsychLIT, a service provided by the American Psychological Association. PsycLIT is a computerized CD-ROM database to which many college libraries subscribe. Its major advantage is that it includes chapters in edited books, which aren't included in the psychological abstracts or in Knowledge Index. Its disadvantage is that it isn't as broad-based as a database system like Knowledge Index.

Table D.1 lists the major sources of information about psychology and related fields along with their advantages and disadvantages. Computers have made a great difference in the way research is being done. If you have your own computer, you may not even need the library!

TABLE D.1 ◆ SEARCHING THE RESEARCH LITERATURE

	Computer Information System (PsycINFO and other databases)	PsycLIT	*Psychological Abstracts*
You will need	Computer and modem	Computer and CD-ROM drive	Go to the library
Advantages	Can be done at home if you have a computer and modem	Includes references to books and chapters in books	If you don't like the computer, do it the old-fashioned way!
	Updated monthly		Updated monthly
Disadvantages	Book chapters not included	Only updated quarterly	Book chapters not included
	Searches cost for computer time	Need to go to a library that has it, because subscription cost is prohibitive for an individual	Need to go to the library

Appendix E

Ethics and Psychological Research

Sometimes, a professional group will outline or describe behavior that it considers moral and appropriate for dealing with the specific issues faced by the profession. Such an outline of behavior deemed appropriate for a professional organization and its members defines the ethics of that organization and its members. Throughout this text, experiments have been discussed and issues examined that raise questions about ethical procedures and practices.

Consider some of the following ethical concerns that I have noticed in the professional literature while gathering data for this text. These are not new problems, but have been concerns for a long time. All raise difficult and interesting issues. Space prohibits more than just touching on these topics, but you can immediately see the problems they raise:

♦ A nationwide survey found that 7.1 percent of male and 3.1 percent of female psychiatrists have had sexual relations with their patients (Gartrell, Herman, Olarte, Feldstein, & Localio, 1986). The percentages for psychologists are about the same. This is perhaps the oldest ongoing ethical concern—even the 2500-year-old Hippocratic oath taken by physicians prohibits sexual contact with patients.

♦ A few years ago the National Institute of Mental Health rebuked a psychologist for "knowingly, willfully, and repeatedly engaging in misleading and deceptive practices in reporting results of research [and] that he did not carry out the described research" (Holden, 1987a). To put it bluntly, this psychologist apparently faked his data. Fortunately, however, such practices occur rarely.

♦ Although only 5 percent of the members of the American Psychological Association (APA) use animals in their research, protests concerning alleged cruelty to animals in research have sparked nationwide attention. To protect animals from poor conditions or inhumane treatment, the APA has a strict set of guidelines for the care of animal subjects. However, controversy about the use of animals in research continues.

♦ Three social psychologists carried out an experiment in which they hoped to measure the tension that people felt when they perceived their psychological space to be invaded. To do this, the researchers placed a hidden periscope overlooking a men's room so that the men who used the urinals could be secretly observed. The researchers wanted to find out whether a subject would take longer to begin urinating if someone else were using the adjacent urinal than if the subject were alone. It did take longer, which probably comes as no surprise (Middlemist, Knowles, & Matter, 1976). The subjects, however, were never informed that they were being observed.

These four examples highlight a few of the problems that may occur when people overstep professional bounds. To help prevent such transgressions, the American Psychological Association has compiled a list of ethical principles for psychologists. A general outline of these principles follows:

1. Psychologists strive to maintain high standards of competence in their work. They recognize the boundaries of their particular competencies and the limitations of their expertise. They provide only those services and use only those techniques for which they are qualified by education, training, or experience. . . . They maintain knowledge of relevant scientific and professional information related to the services they render, and they recognize the need for ongoing education. . . .

2. Psychologists seek to promote integrity in the science, teaching, and practice of psychology. In these activities psychologists are honest, fair, and respectful of others. In describing or reporting their qualifications, services, products, fees, research, or teaching, they do not make statements that are false, misleading or deceptive. Psychologists strive to be aware of their own belief systems, values, needs, and limitations and the effect of these on their work. . . .

3. Psychologists uphold professional standards of conduct, clarify their professional roles and obligations, accept appropriate responsibility for their behavior, and adapt their methods to the needs of different populations. . . . Psychologists' moral standards and conduct are personal matters to the same degree as true for any other person, except as psychologists' conduct may compromise their professional responsibilities or reduce the public's trust in psychology or psychologists. Psychologists are concerned about the ethical compliance of their colleagues' scientific and professional conduct. When appropriate, they consult with colleagues in order to prevent or avoid unethical conduct.

4. Psychologists accord appropriate respect to the fundamental rights, dignity, and worth of all people. They respect the rights of individuals to privacy, confidentiality, self-determination, and autonomy, mindful that legal and other obligations may lead to inconsistency and conflict with the exercise of these rights. . . .

5. Psychologists seek to contribute to the welfare of those with whom they interact professionally. . . . When conflicts occur among psychologists' obligations or concerns, they attempt to resolve those conflicts and to perform their roles in a responsible fashion that avoids or minimizes harm. . . .

6. Psychologists are aware of their professional and scientific responsibilities to the community in which they work and live. They attempt to make public their knowledge of psychology in order to contribute to human welfare. Psychologists are concerned about and work to mitigate the causes of human suffering. . . . They are encouraged to contribute a portion of their professional time for little or no personal advantage. (Excerpts from Ethical Principles of Psychologists and Code of Conduct. Amended December 1, 1992)

There are also important ethical considerations to take into account before conducting an experiment. We must remember that experimenting on live subjects, especially human beings, is serious business. To protect all subjects, we must respect certain ethical safeguards. To deal with the ethical problems that may arise when researchers conduct experiments, the American Psychological Association has also published guidelines for psychological research on human subjects. The following is a summary of the major points:

1. All safeguards for the protection of each human research participant must be maintained. The researcher should protect participants from physical or mental discomfort, harm, and danger.

2. Researchers are ultimately responsible for their own ethical practices as well as for those of other people who assist in their research.

3. All research subjects must be informed of any aspect of the research that is likely to affect their willingness to participate.

4. Subjects should be fully debriefed following any concealment or deception.

5. Subjects must be allowed to decline to participate or to terminate participation in research at any time.

6. The investigator must honor all promises and commitments.

7. All information obtained about participants during research must be kept confidential.

Glossary

A-B-A Single-Subject Experimental Design An experimental design in which time is used as a control and only one subject is monitored. The independent variable is given in condition A and withdrawn in condition B. The dependent variable is the subject's behavior over time as the independent variable is presented, withdrawn, and finally presented again.

Abnormal Behavior Behavior that is statistically unusual, considered maladaptive or undesirable by most people, and self-defeating to the person who displays it.

Absolute Threshold The minimum intensity a stimulus must have in order to produce a sensation.

Accommodation In vision, the adjustment of the lens of the eye to bring into focus on the retina objects that are relatively near.

Achievement Test A test designed to evaluate a person's current state of knowledge or skill. Most IQ tests are achievement tests, although they are often used as aptitude tests.

Achieving Society Theory McClelland's theory that nations whose members show the lowest need for achievement also tend to have the lowest gross national product, whereas nations whose members show the highest need for achievement have the highest gross national product.

Acquisition The time during the learning process when there is a consistent increase in responsiveness; a time when learning is occurring.

Action Potential A localized, rapid change in electrical state that travels across the cell membrane of a neuron at the moment of excitation with sufficient intensity to cause the neuron to fire.

Action Therapy Psychotherapy in which the therapist helps the patient or client take direct and immediate action to overcome problems through the use of special techniques.

Activation-Synthesis Model A physiological model of dreaming that contends that the brain synthesizes random neural activity generated during sleep and organizes this activity into a dream.

Acupuncture A traditional Chinese therapeutic technique in which the body is punctured with fine needles. It usually is used as an anesthetic or to relieve pain.

Adaptive Theory A theory about why we sleep. It states that for each species a certain amount of waking time is necessary in order to survive, and sleep is nature's way of protecting organisms from getting into trouble during their extra time.

Adoption Design A research design used for sorting the influence of nurture from nature. Genetically related individuals who are reared apart from one another or genetically unrelated individuals who are reared together are studied.

Adrenal Glands Endocrine glands located above the kidneys that secrete the hormones adrenalin, noradrenalin, and steroids. These hormones influence metabolism and the body's reaction to stressful situations.

Adrenalin A hormone secreted by the adrenal glands that stimulates the sympathetic nervous system; also called epinephrine.

Aerial Perspective A monocular depth cue. Nearby objects are brighter and sharper than distant objects.

Afferent Nerves Nerves that carry messages inward from the sense organs to the central nervous system.

Affordance In J. J. Gibson's theory of perception, the particular properties of an object that offer an organism perceptual information, which often is of unique interest to the organism or which may benefit the organism's survival; for example, a hammer affords a human its graspability.

Aftereffects An effect brought on by fatigue in visual receptors at higher levels in the visual system. Aftereffects, unlike afterimages, transfer from one eye to the other. Also known as negative aftereffects.

Ageism Prejudice and discrimination against the elderly.

Agonist A drug that acts to facilitate or enhance the actions of other drugs or naturally occurring biochemical substances.

Alarm Reaction Stage The first stage of the general adaptation syndrome, during which cortical hormone levels rise and emotional arousal and tension increase.

Algorithms Mathematical premises. In computer usage, an algorithm is a program that will search for an answer by examining every possibility.

Alpha Waves A pattern of brain waves typical of the relaxed, waking state.

Altruism Behavior that benefits someone other than the actor, with little or no apparent benefit for the actor.

Alzheimer's disease A deteriorating dementia characterized by progressive loss of memory, concentration, and judgment, and by personality changes. Eventually, victims are unable to recognize other people and to control body functions.

Amacrine Cells Large retinal neurons that connect ganglion cells laterally. There are at least 30 different varieties of amacrine cell. Image rectification appears to be one of their many functions. The functions of most amacrine cells are unknown.

Ames Room A specially designed room that is perceived as rectangular, even though it is not. Objects of the same size seem to be totally different in size at different points in the room.

Amino Acids Any of a collection of organic compounds that contain both an amino and a carboxyl group. All life is based on only 20 different amino acids, which are the building blocks of all protein. The neurotransmitter gamma-aminobutyric acid is an example of an amino acid.

Amnesia Unexpected and often extensive memory loss which may be partial or complete. The two major types are psychogenic and somatogenic.

Amphetamines Drugs that excite the central nervous system and suppress appetite, increase heart rate and blood pressure, and alter sleep patterns. Amphetamines are classified as stimulants.

Amplitude A measurement of the amount of energy carried by a wave, shown in the height of the oscillation.

Amygdala A small bulb at the front of the brain that is associated with emotion. It is part of the limbic system. There are two such structures in each brain known collectively as amygdalae.

Androgenic hormones The androgens. Male hormones that regulate sexual development; produced by the testes and the adrenal cortex.

Angular Gyrus A portion of the brain in the parietal lobe adjacent to Wernicke's area. The angular gyrus is involved with reading and appears to "translate" visual word images received by the primary visual cortex into auditory form before passing the information on to Wernicke's area.

Animal Magnetism The term coined by Anton Mesmer to describe the supposed magnetic force that people could exert on one another.

Anorexia nervosa A serious eating disorder. The sufferer typically loses weight to dangerous levels while maintaining that she is still too overweight. The disorder is far more common in women, especially young women, by about 10:1 over men. If not treated, the disorder can be fatal. The cause remains unknown and various treatments are used including medications and psychotherapy.

Antagonist A drug that acts to block or inhibit the actions of the other drugs or naturally occurring biochemical substances.

Anterograde Amnesia The inability to recall experiences or events that occur after the amnesia-causing trauma.

Anticipatory Eating Nonhomeostatic consumption of food owing to an awareness that food will soon be scarce or unavailable.

Antidepressants Drugs used to relieve the symptoms of extreme sadness and withdrawal from life that characterize severe depression. MAO inhibitors, tricyclic drugs, and selective serotonin reuptake inhibitors are the three classes of antidepressants.

Anxiety A state of apprehension in which the source is usually not specific, as it is in fear. There is a vague but persistent feeling that some future danger is in store, such as punishment or threat to self-esteem. Anxiety typically leads to defensive reactions.

Anxious/Avoidant Attachment A form of attachment observed by Ainsworth in her research. Children who show anxious/avoidant attachment do not approach—and actively avoid—their returning mothers.

Anxious/Resistant Attachment A form of attachment observed by Ainsworth in her research. Children who show anxious/resistant attachment approach their returning mothers, cry to be picked up, and then struggle to be free. Their behavior is ambivalent; they appear to wish to approach and to avoid their mothers simultaneously.

Aphasia Loss of the ability to understand or to use language; by definition, the result of brain damage.

Apparent Motion Any phenomenon through which a person perceives motion in an object when the object is, in fact, stationary.

Aptitude Test A test designed to evaluate a person's potential for achievement. Ideally, it is independent of current knowledge. An example might be a test of the nervous system that could predict to a certain degree how likely someone was to succeed at a given task.

Arcuate Fasciculus The bundle of nerve fibers in the brain that connects Wernicke's area with Broca's area.

Artificial Intelligence A computer simulation of human cognitive ability and performance.

Association Areas The parts of the cerebral cortex, other than the sensory and motor areas, that appear to be involved with language, thinking, and memory.

Atonia Loss of muscle tone. During REM sleep, atonia occurs simultaneously with arousal of the sympathetic nervous system. The atonia creates a state of semiparalysis in the REM sleeper.

Atrophy of the vaginal lining Thinning, loss of elasticity, drying, and itching of the vaginal walls caused by decreasing estrogen levels during the climacteric.

Attachment An especially close affectional bond formed between a living creature and another living creature or object.

Attribution The psychosocial process through which we come to believe that certain events or dispositions are responsible for the behavior of ourselves or others.

Auditory Nerve The nerve leading from the cochlea, which transmits sound impulses to the brain.

Authoritarian Parents Parents who put forward a strict set of rules and require unquestioned obedience to them. They are both demanding and hostile. Authoritarian parents often use physical punishment to enforce the rules, and reasoned discussion with the child is rare.

Authoritative Parents Parents who set strict standards, but who are also warm and willing to explain their reasoning to their children.

Automatic Storage The spontaneous placement of a sensation or experience into the long-term memory without effort or intent.

Automatic Writing Writing done by the subject during a dissociated hypnotic state; the subject is not aware of writing.

Automatization A process that occurs after a mental procedure is practiced sufficiently so that the number of if-then connections is reduced to the barest required minimum. Once automatization has occurred, the mental procedure can be called on with a minimum of thought or effort. The mental procedures used by skilled experts tend to be highly automatized.

Autonomic Nervous System The portion of the peripheral nervous system that carries information to and from organs, glands, and smooth muscles within the body.

Aversive Conditioning An element of behavior therapy in which unacceptable behavior becomes linked with painful stimuli and is thereafter avoided.

Avoidance learning The process whereby an organism is reinforced for behaving in a way that avoids an aversive stimulus.

Axon The long projection of a neuron that transmits impulses away from the cell body to the synapse.

Behavior Contracts A technique often used in behavior, group, or family therapy, in which a contract or bargain is struck. The client promises to engage in a certain behavior in return for a particular behavior from another.

Behavior Modification A set of procedures for changing human behavior, especially by using behavior therapy and operant conditioning techniques.

Behavior Therapy A group of techniques based on learning principles and used to manipulate an individual's behavior directly to promote adaptive patterns while eliminating maladaptive ones.

Behavioral Genetics The interdisciplinary science that focuses on the relationship of nature and nurture, that is, on the interaction of what is inherited and what is acquired and how that interaction affects behavior.

Behavioral Geography A statistical technique that enables map makers to generate actual representations of cognitive maps. Behavioral geography has as its goal the production of information that will aid developers and planners to create environments that are more compatible with people's perceptions.

Behavioral Toxicology The classification and study of the behavioral effects of environmental toxins.

Behaviorism The school of psychology that views learning as the most important aspect of an organism's development. Behaviorists objectively measure behavior and the way in which stimulus-response relationships are formed.

Benzodiazepines Antianxiety drugs, such as Valium and Librium, that help alleviate anxiety by directly interacting with the neurochemistry of the brain. They are often referred to as minor tranquilizers.

Beta amyloid A protein that forms abnormalities in the brains of some people, and that may play a significant role in Alzheimer's disease.

Beta-Endorphin A powerful natural neuropeptide. It means "the morphine within" and is so named because it has properties similar to those of heroin and morphine. It is a powerful painkiller and mood elevator.

Binocular Cues Depth cues that arise only when both eyes are used. Examples include convergence and retinal disparity.

Bipolar Cells Cells that collect and consolidate visual information, a particular bipolar cell is either "rod-driven" or "cone-driven," meaning that it receives information from either groups of rods or groups of cones but never from a mixture of the two. Bipolar cells transmit a ratio derived from the signals they receive from the photoreceptors and nearby horizontal cells to the ganglion cells.

Bipolar I Disorder A mood disorder characterized by severe cyclical mood swings. Formerly called manic-depression psychosis. Bipolar I disorder includes at least one episode of mania and may also include episodes of hypomania or depression.

Bipolar II Disorder A mood disorder characterized by severe cyclical mood swings. Episodes include depression and at least one episode of hypomania, but never mania.

Blind Spot The region of the retina where the optic nerve attaches and where there are no photoreceptors. The fovea also is a blind spot when something is viewed in very dim light.

Blob Pathway A distinct brain pathway for the transmission of color information. So named because color information is conveyed via a root that travels from the cones of the retina through the midbrain and then to areas of the occipital cortex known as "blobs."

Blocking In classical conditioning, the phenomenon in which a CS will not be reinforced by pairing it with a US if another CS is already being used by the organism for detection of the onset of that US.

Blood-Brain Barrier The semipermeable membrane and tissue surrounding the blood vessels that serve the brain which allows only limited brain access to substances borne in the blood. Usually, only a few specific molecules are able to enter. Many drugs as well as the cells from the body's own immune system are typically unable to cross the blood-brain barrier.

Bogus Pipeline A procedure for measuring a person's real attitudes and feelings rather than what the person wishes to present. Subjects are led to believe that a supposed physiological monitor is able to detect their real attitudes and feelings and that any attempt to hide them will be uncovered.

Bottom-up Processing Processing in memory, perception, or other aspects of cognition that is influenced only by the input of information and not by the organism's prior knowledge or expectations.

Bradykinin A bloodborne neuropeptide that is cleaved from a larger inert molecule by enzymes a fraction of a second following any injury. Bradykinin stimulates pain-associated neurons and is considered to be one of the major producers of pain.

Brain The portion of the central nervous system located in the cranium and responsible for the interpretation of sensory impulses, the coordination and control of body activities, the exercise of emotion, thought, and memory, and the integration of cognitive and mental functions.

Brief Individual Psychotherapies Any one-on-one psychotherapy usually lasting no more than 30 sessions, which is designed to provide limited support when lack of time or money prevent regular therapeutic intervention.

Brightness A property of color determined by the number of photons issuing forth per square unit area. Shifts in brightness are perceived by the observer as changes along a light-dark continuum.

Brightness Constancy The perception that objects maintain their brightness independent of lighting.

British Empiricism A theory put forth by British philosophers during the seventeenth and eighteenth centuries (most notably, by Locke, Berkeley, and Hume) arguing that all knowledge and understanding come from only learning and experience (e.g., the mind is a blank slate on which experience writes our nature). In light of our modern understanding of inheritance, the idea of tabula rasa or blank slate is no longer considered to be plausible.

Broca's Aphasia A disorder caused by damage to Broca's area. Individuals with this disorder have impaired articulation, labored speech, and difficulty in forming a grammatical sentence, but the semantic content of their speech is usually clear.

Broca's Area An area in the lateral frontal lobe (in the left hemisphere in most cases) that is associated with language production.

Bystander Effect People's tendency, especially pronounced under crowded conditions, to ignore others who need help or situations that call for action.

Caffeine A bitter white alkaloid derived from coffee, tea, and kola nuts. It is a stimulant and is the most widely used psychoactive drug in the world.

Canalization The process by which behaviors, due to genetic predisposition, are learned extremely easily, almost inevitably. The more canalized a behavior is, the more difficult it is to change or alter.

Cardinal Traits In Allport's theory, an encompassing trait that seems to influence almost every act of a person who possesses the trait. Cardinal traits are uncommon, observed in only a few people.

Case Study An intensive study of a single case, with available data, test results, and opinions about that individual.

CAT Scan Computerized axial tomography. A technique for examining soft tissue, usually the brain. A narrow beam of X-radiation is repeatedly passed through the tissue in layers or segments; then, a computer reconstructs the image. Such scans can reveal tumors, lesions, or other abnormalities.

Catharsis In psychoanalytic theory, elimination of a conflict by bringing it to consciousness and allowing it to express itself; in general, any emotional releases resulting from a buildup of internal tensions.

Cause-Effect Relationship A relationship in which one act regularly brings about a particular result.

Central Nervous System The brain and spinal cord. All neurons and neural material surrounded by bone.

Central Route Processing From social-information processing theory, a route of persuasion and attitude change that may occur when a person pays careful attention to a persuasive discussion. Any resulting attitude change is relatively enduring.

Central Sulcus A major fissure in the brain, also known as the fissure of Rolando, which separates the frontal from the parietal lobes.

Central Traits In Allport's theory, behavioral or personality tendencies that are highly characteristic of a given individual and easy to infer. Allport argues that surprisingly few central traits, perhaps five or ten, can give a fairly accurate description of an individual's personality.

Centration The child's tendency to focus, or center, on only one aspect of a changing system at any given time; characteristic of the preoperational stage.

Cerebellum A portion of the hindbrain situated just beneath the posterior portion of the cerebrum. One of its functions is to coordinate muscle tone and fine motor control.

Cerebral Cortex The extensive outer layer of convoluted gray tissue of the cerebral hemispheres, which is largely responsible for higher nervous functions, including intellectual processes. It consists of the neocortex and the allocortex.

Cerebrum The large rounded structure of the brain occupying most of the cranial cavity, divided into two cerebral hemispheres by a deep fissure and joined at the bottom by the corpus callosum.

Chaos Theory The theory which states that predictions for most systems are limited because initial states are subject to deviations too small to measure, which can, nevertheless, lead to pronounced effects. In other words, a certain amount of chaos will accompany each prediction, lessening the accuracy of the prediction over time.

Chemical Dependence The strong and compelling desire to continue taking a chemical substance because of its physical or psychological effects.

Cholecystokinin (CCK) Cholecystokinin is a neuropeptide that is secreted by the intestine and which can stimulate receptors for satiation in the brain.

Chromosomes Thread-shaped bodies contained within the nucleus of a cell that determine the characteristics that will be passed on to the offspring of an organism. Chromosomes carry the genes; humans have 23 pairs of them.

Chronological Age (CA) A concept developed by Alfred Binet that was subsequently incorporated in the formula mental age / chronological age × 100 = IQ. The chronological age of a person is his or her actual age.

Circadian Rhythm A daily cycle. The sleep-wake cycle is considered to be a circadian rhythm.

Classical Conditioning A learning procedure in which a stimulus that normally evokes a given reflex is associated with a stimulus that does not usually evoke that reflex, with the result that the latter stimulus will eventually evoke the reflex when presented by itself.

Client-Centered Therapy A type of psychotherapy developed by Carl Rogers and based on the belief that the client is responsible for his or her own growth and self-actualization. The therapist creates an atmosphere of acceptance, refrains from directing the client, and reflects back to the client what the client has said.

Climacteric The 2- to 10-year period during which the biological changes involved in menopause take place.

Cocaine A habit-forming stimulant that typically is inhaled, and is occasionally swallowed, smoked, or injected. It is derived from the leaves of the coca plant, and is used in medicine as a local anesthetic.

Cochlea A spiral tube in the inner ear, resembling a snail shell, which contains nerve endings essential for hearing.

Cognition Mental activity involving perceiving, thinking, remembering, or problem solving.

Cognitive Behavior Therapy A behavior therapy technique in which the client's beliefs, attitudes, and expectations are tested in reality in a formal and structured way.

Cognitive Dissonance The condition in which one has beliefs or knowledge that are internally inconsistent or that disagree with one's behavior. When such cognitive dissonance arises, one is motivated to reduce the dissonance through changes in behavior or cognition.

Cognitive Map A mental representation of the location of things in relation to each other in a given environment.

Cognitive Psychology The study of behavior as it relates to perceiving, thinking, remembering, or problem solving.

Cohabitation A living arrangement in which two unrelated adults of the opposite sex share the same household. In the past, it has implied sexual intimacy, but it does not necessarily do so today.

Collective Unconscious Jung's concept that a portion of the unconscious contains certain shared experiences, predispositions, and symbols that are inherited and found in all members of a given race or species.

Color Blindness The inability to see one or more colors. The most common kind is green-cone color blindness.

Color Constancy The tendency for a color to appear unchanged regardless of changes in lighting conditions.

Common Fate A Gestalt principle that states that aspects of a perceptual field that move or act in a similar manner tend to be perceived as a single entity.

Complex Cells Cells in the visual cortex that respond to various combinations of motion, orientation, or color. Complex cells usually are associated with large receptive fields.

Componential Intelligence From Sternberg's triarchic theory of intelligence: that aspect of intelligence encompassing the cognitive problem-solving and information-processing skills measured by most IQ tests.

Compulsion A useless, stereotyped, and repetitive act that a person is unable to inhibit.

Concealed Information Test In polygraph administration, a method of examining suspects by providing them with specific information to which only someone with guilty knowledge could consistently react.

Concept An abstract idea based on grouping objects or qualities by common properties.

Conditioned Response (CR) A learned response elicited by a conditioned stimulus, owing to previous reinforcement of the conditioned stimulus through association with an unconditioned stimulus.

Conditioned Stimulus (CS) In classical conditioning, a previously neutral stimulus that is reinforced by being paired with an unconditioned stimulus, so that it acquires the ability to produce a conditioned response.

Cones Specialized photoreceptor cells in the retina that are primarily responsive to different wavelengths of light and are therefore important in color vision; cones also are associated with high visual acuity.

Conformity Action that results from social pressure to comply with social norms. When people conform, they act or behave in correspondence with current customs, rules, or styles.

Conjugal Love A deep and generally abiding love that develops between two people over long periods of time. It is associated with a desire to be together, share with one another, and sacrifice for one another. It is also called companionate love.

Cononical Stage A stage of language acquisition that typically occurs between the ages of 7 and 10 months typified by an increase in babbling and the production of cononical syllables (syllables made of consonant and vowel sounds of certain intensities). Duplicated sequences such as "dadada" or "mamama" also mark this stage.

Consciousness A state of awareness of sensations, perceptions, or memories. The aspects of mental life of which one is normally aware.

Conservation The principle that quantities such as mass, weight, and volume remain constant regardless of changes in the appearance of these quantities, so long as nothing has been added or taken away.

Conserving-Energy Theory A theory about why we sleep. It states that sleep is a good way of conserving energy in the face of sparse food supplies. This theory agrees with the adaptive theory that sleep can be a protective device.

Consolidation The strengthening process through which memory traces, or engrams, must go before they can become a fixed part of the long-term memory.

Consumer Psychology The field of applied psychology concerned with advertising and selling, whose object of study is effective communication from the manufacturer or distributor to the consumer.

Contextual Intelligence From Sternberg's triarchic theory of intelligence: that aspect of intelligence encompassing the ability of the individual to adapt to her environment or culture.

Contiguous Association The occurrence of two events close enough in time so that they are perceived by the organism as somehow related. Also called temporal association.

Contingency Detection The process by which an organism makes a discrimination between stimuli that are only present when the US is presented and other stimuli that not only happen to be present when the US is presented but also when the US is not presented. The result is that the organism can rely on the sensing of the stimulus that is only present when the US is presented to predict that the US will soon appear.

Continuous Reinforcement Reinforcement of a particular response each time it occurs.

Contraction Stage A stage of language acquisition that typically occurs between the ages of 10 and 14 months. So named because during this time the infant will begin to narrow her production of language sounds until it includes mostly the sounds that are common to the language to which she has been exposed. During this stage, infants also acquire the pacing and rhythm of their language.

Control Deliberate arrangement of experimental or research conditions so that observed effects can be directly traced to a known variable.

This is often accomplished by exposing two like groups to identical conditions with the exception that one group is exposed to the variable being tested.

Convergence A binocular depth cue. The eyes tend to turn toward each other when focusing on nearby objects and tend to focus at infinity when viewing objects farther away.

Convergent Production In J. P. Guilford's model of intelligence, a type of thinking in which an individual searches through his or her knowledge and uses all that can be found to converge upon one correct answer.

Conversion Disorder A somatoform disorder characterized by physical symptoms such as paralysis, blindness, deafness, and loss of sensation. The assumption is that anxiety has been converted into a tangible symptom.

Cornea The transparent outer bulge in the front of the eye through which light waves pass.

Corpus Callosum The structure offering the major connection between the two cerebral hemispheres. When it is severed, communication between the two hemispheres is severely disrupted.

Correlation A relationship between two variables such that when one variable systematically increases, the other will systematically alter as well.

Corticosteroid Hormones Any of the steroid hormones of the cortex of the adrenal glands.

Cortisol A hormone produced by the cortex of the adrenal glands found just above the kidneys. It is critical for the metabolism of fats, carbohydrates and proteins. It is very similar to cortisone.

Creativity The ability to originate something new and appropriate by transcending common thought constraints.

Creole A language mixture that develops when groups speaking different languages have prolonged contact. Typically, the basic vocabulary of the dominant language is combined with the grammar of a subordinate language, creating an admixture (a mingling within a mixture) of words and grammar that becomes in itself a new subordinate and creolized language.

Critical Decay Duration From the opponent-process theory of motivation, a time of sufficient length between the onset of an affective A process and its repetition so that no decrease in A process intensity or increase in B process intensity is noted.

Culture-Fair Test A test that is supposed to be free of cultural biases, usually constructed so that language differences and other cultural effects are minimized.

Dark Adaptation The process by which the eyes become more sensitive to light in dim illumination.

Declarative Memory The type of long-term memory associated with cognitive abilities not directly attributable to unconscious skills or habits. Declarative memories are conscious memories that need to be "brought to mind" in order to become active. Declarative memory is required to recall factual information, and it is sometimes called explicit memory, or fact memory. The ability to recognize a face, recall a number, or recall any verbal or sensory information requires declarative memory.

Defense Mechanisms Reactions to the anxiety caused by conflict that serve to protect and improve the self-image. The mechanisms are not deliberately chosen. They are common to everyone and raise serious problems for adjustment only when they are used excessively and prevent the person from coping realistically with difficulties.

Deindividuation The process in which social restraints are weakened and impulsive and aggressive tendencies released as the person loses individual identity, usually as the result of being part of a large group or having his or her identity concealed in some way, for example, by a mask.

Deinstitutionalization The practice, begun in the early 1960s, of releasing mental patients from hospitals and assigning them to community health centers or treating them on an outpatient basis.

Delirium Tremens A state of delirium resulting from prolonged alcoholism and marked by extreme confusion, vivid hallucinations, and body tremors.

Delta Waves A pattern of brain waves associated with the deepest stages of sleep, often called slow waves because of their relatively low frequency.

Delta-9 Tetrahydrocannabinol (THC) The active ingredient in marijuana, which in high doses can cause hallucinations.

Delusion A strong belief opposed to reality, which is maintained in spite of logical persuasion and evidence to the contrary.

Delusional Disorder A psychosis characterized by delusions and extreme suspiciousness. Hallucinations rarely occur, and the personality does not undergo the serious disorganization associated with schizophrenia.

Dementia Irreversible loss of personality and intellectual functioning caused by disease or brain damage.

Dendrites The short, branched projections of a neuron that receive impulses from other neurons and conduct them toward the cell body.

Denial A defense mechanism in which the individual simply denies the existence of the events that have produced the anxiety.

Dependent Variable In an experiment, the variable that may be affected by changes in the independent variable.

Depressants Drugs that can depress or slow the central nervous system. Alcohol and tranquilizers are examples.

Depression A mood disturbance characterized by feelings of sadness, pessimism, apathy, excessive worry, guilt, and an inability to experience pleasure. Sometimes, these feelings are accompanied by difficulty in sleeping, loss of appetite, and loss of sexual desire.

Depth Perception Perceptual interpretation of visual cues indicating how far away objects are.

Designer Drugs Drugs designed in a laboratory by unscrupulous chemists with the intention of creating substances that mimic the effects of a drug while avoiding the federal laws that forbid that specific drug.

Developmental Psychology The study of age-related changes in human behavior over the lifespan.

Dexamethasone Suppression Test (DST) A blood test used to indicate the presence of endogenous depression. Dexamethasone is administered and the suppression of cortisol is measured. Failure to suppress cortisol is an indication of endogenous depression.

Dichromats People with color blindness due to the defective functioning of one of the three cone systems.

Difference Threshold The minimum change that a stimulus must undergo before the change can be reliably detected; it is also called the just noticeable difference (JND).

Diffusion of Responsibility One possible reason for the bystander effect. When someone is observed to be in need of help and there are many people around, individuals may believe that they need not act or give aid because they place responsibility to act on other people in the crowd. They may think, for instance, "Someone else will surely help" or "Why should I have to be the one to help?"

Direct Perception Theory The theory that perceptions are a function of biological organization and innate perceptual mechanisms.

Directive Therapy Any approach in which the therapist takes an active role and directs the client or patient to confront problems and life situations.

Discrimination Differentially responding to two or more stimuli. The responding occurs in such a way that it is obvious that the organism can tell that the stimuli have certain properties that distinguish them from one another. In social psychology, differential treatment of people on the basis of their race, ethnic group, or class, rather than on their relevant traits. Acts of discrimination are typically premised on prejudice.

Discriminative Stimuli Stimuli in whose presence a response is likely to occur. Discriminative stimuli function as cues enabling us to know when a response is likely to be reinforced.

Dissociation A separation or splitting off of mental processes often associated with the hypnotic state. Subjects can then perform acts that do not register in their conscious memory or can engage in two behaviors while remembering only one of them.

Dissociative Disorders Mental disorders that are characterized by an attempt to overcome anxiety by dissociating oneself from the core of one's personality.

Divergent Production In Guilford's model of intelligence, a type of thinking in which a person searches for multiple ideas or solutions to a problem. It is characteristic of the creative thought process.

DNA Deoxyribonucleic acid. A chemical constituent of cell nuclei, consisting of two long chemical chains of alternating phosphate and deoxyribose units twisted into a double helix and joined by bonds between the chemical bases adenine, thymine, cytosine, and guanine. It is the substance that enables cells to copy themselves; it is the essence of all life.

Dopamine Hypothesis The argument that abnormalities associated with the neurotransmitter dopamine are related to the onset and maintenance of schizophrenic episodes. Either an overabundance of dopamine or the existence of too many dopamine receptors in the brain is deemed responsible.

Double-Blind Controlled Experiment A research technique in which neither the subjects nor the observers know which subjects have been exposed to the independent variable. It is used for controlling biases that may be introduced by either the subjects or the observers.

Double Depression Severe depression brought about by a combination of endogenous and environmental causes, either of which would have been sufficient in and by itself to create a serious depressive state.

Down Syndrome A chromosomal abnormality that manifests itself in such features as a thick tongue, extra eyelid folds, and heart deformities, as well as deficient intelligence. It is most often caused by the development of a third chromosome on the 21st chromosome pair.

Drive The psychological representation of a need; a complex of internal conditions, resulting from the loss of homeostasis, that impels an organism to seek a goal.

DSM-IV The fourth edition of the Diagnostic and Statistical Manual, published by the American Psychiatric Association in 1994. The manual provides clinicians with the most current diagnostic and classification criteria for mental disorders.

Dyslexia An impairment of reading ability, in which little sense can be made of what is read and letters or words often appear transposed.

Dysthymia A common form of depression defined by a depressed mood for more days than not, lasting for at least 2 years with no respite from depression for more than 2 months at a time, and associated with some disruption or loss of sleep, appetite, energy, self-esteem, or concentration. Often accompanied by feelings of hopelessness.

Ectomorph One of Sheldon's three body types. An ectomorph is relatively thin and physically weak. The corresponding temperament is cerebrotonic.

Educational Psychology The branch of applied psychology concerned with the psychological aspects of teaching and the formal learning process in school. Educational psychologists apply theories, methods, and test instruments for educational purposes.

Efferent Nerves Nerves that carry messages outward from the central nervous system to glands or muscles.

Ego In psychoanalytic theory, the part of the personality that regulates the impulses of the id in order to meet the demands of reality and maintain social approval and self-esteem.

Egocentrism A thought process characteristic of children in Piaget's preoperational stage; they view themselves as the reference point in their dealings with the external world.

Eidetic Image The formation and reproduction of accurate mental images of objects not currently present. Possessors of these images are said to have photographic memories.

Electroconvulsive Therapy (ECT) Treatment of mental disorders by passing an electric current through the brain for a certain amount of time, which causes a convulsion, a temporary suspension of breathing, and a coma lasting from 5 to 30 minutes. ECT has been found to be most effective against depression and the depressive lows encountered in bipolar disorder.

Electroencephalograph (EEG) An instrument that records the electrical activity of the brain.

Electromagnetic Spectrum The entire range of possible wavelengths for light, both visible and invisible (such as X rays and radio waves).

Emergent Property From Gestalt psychology: The property that appears as a function of the gestalt; that property which enables the whole to, in fact, be greater than the sum of its parts. Examples include the color white, which is an emergent property of the equal mixing of red, green, and blue light, and a melody, which is the emergent property of a series of individual notes.

Emotion A complex feeling-state involving conscious experience and internal and overt physical responses that tend to facilitate or inhibit motivated behavior.

Emotion-focused coping Strategies that attempt to alter the way in which we attend to or interpret stressors.

Emotional Appeals Arguments designed to alter attitudes by appealing to the emotions through stirring visual and verbal messages.

Emotional Contrast An emotional effect that plays an important part in Solomon's opponent-process theory of motivation. Following any emotional arousal (pleasant or aversive), there is often an opposite emotional state. This contrasting emotional state will last for a time and then diminish or end.

Empty-nest syndrome Depression parents may experience when their grown children leave home.

Encoding Variability Acquisition of the same information in different moods, states, or circumstances. Greater encoding variability tends to improve test performance by increasing the chances that the test situation will resemble the learning environment.

Encounter Groups Therapeutic gatherings in which members of a group, under the guidance of a trained therapist, confront one another during a psychodynamic exchange that uncovers defenses and helps reveal hidden emotions.

Endocrine Glands Ductless glands that pour their secretions directly into the bloodstream. The hormones secreted by the endocrine glands are important regulators of many body activities and include such substances as adrenalin and pituitary growth hormone.

Endogenous Depression The suspected inherited form of major depressive disorder. Endogenous depression occurs without any apparent external cause. It is marked by long-term despair, dejection, and feelings of apprehension, gloom, and worthlessness.

Endomorph One of Sheldon's three body types. An endomorph is broad and thick in proportion to height, is round, and has fairly weak muscles and bones. The corresponding temperament is viscerotonic.

Engram A lasting trace or impression formed in living tissue responsible for memory.

Environmental Psychology The applied psychology concerned with the effects and influences of the environment on behavior.

Epilepsy A neural disorder characterized by recurring attacks of motor, sensory, or psychic malfunction with or without unconsciousness or convulsive movements.

Episodic Memory Memories stored with mental "tags" about where, when and how you acquired the information. It mostly contains personal information, but also includes "flashbulb memories."

Episodic Trace Model A model of human memory which depicts memories as being laid down as entire images in which are contained information about the item, its associations, and the context in which it was acquired. These "images" are assumed to be represented in the brain as electrochemical traces.

Equipotentiality Karl Lashley's concept that memory and learning are not localized in one particular area of the brain, but rather that the entire brain is responsible for handling these functions.

Equity Theory A social theory of relationships that individuals attempt to strike a balance between what they give and what they receive; that they strive toward a collective reward system for equitably distributing costs and rewards.

Escape Learning The process whereby an organism is reinforced for escaping from an aversive stimulus.

Estrogen Hormones produced primarily by the ovaries and which are responsible for the development of female secondary sex characteristics. The adrenal glands of the male also produce some estrogen, but the hormone is found primarily in females.

Ethics The study of the general nature of morals and of the specific moral choices to be made by the individual in professional relationships with others.

Ethology The study of human and animal behavior from a biological point of view; it is characterized by the study of animals in their natural environments.

Etiology The cause of a disease or disorder as determined by psychological or medical diagnosis.

Eugenics Term coined by Sir Francis Galton referring to the science of improving the genetic characteristics of humans through breeding.

Event-related brain potentials (ERPs) A measure of the brain's electrical activity as recorded through the scalp. ERPs are calculated by measuring the positive and negative deflections or changes in voltage during a normal electroencephalographic examination (see EEG, chapter 2), which occur when the subject, who is resting passively, is presented a stimulus.

Exchange Theory A social theory of relationships that human interactions can best be understood by examining the costs and rewards to each person.

Excitatory Synapses Synapses associated with depolarization of the receiving cell once neurotransmitter is secreted. If the receiving cell is a neuron, it will become more likely to fire or even reach action potential.

Executive Hormones Hormones that order or control the secretion of other hormones.

Exhaustion Stage The final stage of the general adaptation syndrome, during which resistance to the continuing stress begins to fail. Brain functioning may be hindered by metabolic changes; the immune system becomes much less efficient; and serious illness or disease becomes likely as the body begins to break down.

Existential Therapy A form of psychotherapy, generally nondirective, that is derived from the existentialist philosophy that each individual has to choose values and decide on the meaning of his or her own life. The therapist tries to achieve an authentic, spontaneous relationship with the client in order to help the client discover free will and make his or her own choices.

Exocrine Glands Glands that secrete fluids through ducts to the outside of the body or to a specific organ.

Expansion An enlargement or extension of initial research efforts.

Expansion Stage A stage of language acquisition that typically occurs between the ages of 4 and 7 months. During this stage, infants produce many new sounds giving rise to babbling. The onset of the expansion stage does not appear to require feedback because deaf babies also babble. Toward the end of the stage, however, the effects of hearing experience begin to be discernible.

Experiential Intelligence From Sternberg's triarchic theory of intelligence: that aspect of intelligence encompassing the ability to take a newly learned skill and make it routine.

Experiment A test made to demonstrate the validity of a hypothesis or to determine the predictability of a theory. Variables are manipulated and changes are contrasted with a control that has not been exposed to the variable of interest.

Exploration-Play-Application Sequence A term describing the function of play as a bridge between the cautious exploration of the unfamiliar and its eventual application for useful purposes.

Extinction In classical conditioning, the elimination of the power of the conditioned stimulus to elicit a conditioned response. Classical extinction will occur if the conditioned stimulus is repeatedly presented without being reinforced through further association with the unconditioned stimulus. In operant conditioning, the elimination of an operant response or its return to a prereinforcement rate of emission following discontinuation of the reinforcing consequence that had maintained it.

Extrovert One of Jung's personality types. An extrovert is gregarious, focuses on external events, is not introspective, and likes to be with others.

Facial Feedback Theory A theory of emotion put forth by S. S. Tomkins stating that emotions are determined by feedback from our facial expressions, which are innate, universal responses to specific events.

Factor Analysis A statistical procedure aimed at discovering the constituent traits within a complex system of personality or intelligence. The method enables the investigator to compute the minimum number of factors required to account for intercorrelations of the scores on the tests.

Factor Load The weight or emphasis given to any factor or ability.

Family Therapy A general term for a number of therapies that treat the family as a whole. Family therapy is a theoretically neutral term, in that family therapy can be practiced as part of many different psychotherapeutic approaches.

Farsighted The inability to see close objects clearly.

Feature Detectors Innate sensory mechanisms tuned specifically to respond to particular aspects of the environment.

Figure In perception, a perceptual experience that is characterized by contour, coherence, structure, and solidity. It is typically experienced against a ground (for example, it appears to be in the foreground).

First Messenger System The neural communication system by which the postsynaptic surface responds to informational substances by opening, closing, or altering ion channels.

Fixation In psychoanalytic theory, inordinate persistence in a particular psychosexual stage of development because the id has received either too much satisfaction, leading to positive fixation, or too little satisfaction, leading to negative fixation.

Flashback A sudden recurrence of a hallucination or sensory disturbance that occurs after the original effect of a hallucinogenic substance has worn off.

Flashbulb Memory The vivid impression left on the memory by the stimuli associated with a shocking or surprising event.

Forebrain The top portion of the brain, which includes the thalamus, hypothalamus, corpus callosum, limbic system, and cerebrum.

Fovea The area in the center of the retina characterized by a great density of cones and an absence of rods. Images focused on the fovea are seen with the highest acuity.

Free Association A method used in psychoanalytic therapy in which the patient is asked to say whatever comes to mind, no matter how trivial, inconsequential, or unrelated to the matter being discussed. Freud believed that the first thing to come to mind was often a clue to what the unconscious was trying to conceal.

Free-Floating Anxiety A chronic state of foreboding that is unrelated to a specific situation or object but can be activated by any number of situations and activities.

Free Run The tendency for the sleep-wake cycle to break away from a 24-hour cycle. This is most likely to occur when day and night cues are reduced or eliminated. Most free running in humans involves a cycle of approximately 25 hours, but many other cycles are possible, most longer than 24 hours, some shorter.

Frequency The number of cycles per unit of time in a periodic vibration. Frequency determines the pitch of a sound. Higher frequencies have shorter wavelengths.

Frequency Theory A theory of hearing designed to explain the reception of sound waves between 20 and 300 cycles per second. According to this theory, auditory neurons fire at rates well correlated with the frequency of the sound.

Friendships Close emotional ties formed with another person through mutual preference for interaction, skill at complementary and reciprocal peer play, and shared positive affect.

Frontal Lobes The portion of each hemisphere of the cerebrum extending from the very front of the cerebrum to the central sulcus. It includes the primary motor association areas, and it is known to be involved with emotion and language.

Frontal Lobotomy A psychosurgical procedure, rarely performed today, in which a sharp instrument is inserted through the orbit of the eye and then slashed back and forth to separate specific nerve fibers connecting one part of the brain to another.

Frustration-Aggression Hypothesis The idea that if one is blocked or prevented from reaching a desired goal, some form of aggression will be an inevitable result.

Fugue A dissociative disorder in which the individual leaves his or her present situation and establishes a different existence in another place. Although the former life is blocked from memory, other abilities are unimpaired and the individual appears normal to others.

Functional Fixedness A mental set in which you are unable to see beyond an object's customary function to its other possible uses because you have relied on too narrowly defined declarative information.

Functionalism The school of psychological thought founded by William James, which proposed that the function, not the structure, of conscious experience should be studied.

G Proteins A class of molecules that direct the flow of signals from the receptor surface to the rest of the cell. They are called G proteins because they bind to guanine nucleotides within the cell, which, like all nucleotides consist of an organic base (in this instance, guanine), one or more phosphates, and a sugar. G proteins are typically stimulated into action by first messengers such as neurotransmitters.

Gain-Loss Theory A social theory of relationships that we are most attracted to those who have given us the greatest net gain and are least attracted to those who have caused the greatest net loss.

Ganglion Cells Nerve cells of the retina, which receive impulses from rods and cones via the bipolar cells and transmit these impulses to the brain.

Gender Constancy The realization that one's sex is determined by unchanging criteria and is unaffected by one's activities or behavior; usually develops in children by the age of 6 or 7 years.

Gender Role The behaviors associated with one sex or the other.

Gender-Role Identification The degree to which a child adopts the sex role of a particular model.

Gender Schema Theory The theory developed by Sandra Bem that explains how cognitive advances help the child to organize and integrate the information that he or she has learned about his or her sex.

Gender Typing The process whereby an individual incorporates the behaviors, traits, or attitudes appropriate to his or her biological sex or the sex assigned at birth.

Gender Understanding A person's comprehension that he or she is either a boy or a girl; usually develops in children by about the age of 3 years.

Gene The smallest functional unit for the transmission of a hereditary trait; a section of genetic code.

General Adaptation Syndrome Physiologist Hans Selye's description of the body's physiological-hormonal reaction to stressors. The reaction consists of three stages, the alarm reaction stage, the resistance stage, and the exhaustion stage.

General Paresis Tertiary (third-stage) syphilis (a sexually transmitted disease), which involves an invasion of and severe irreversible damage to the brain caused by the syphilis spirochete (a bacterium). The central nervous system damage often becomes noticeable 15 to 30 years after infection. The clinical picture includes tremors, loss of contact with reality, extreme personality deterioration, increasing paralysis, and delirium. The patient may survive many additional years in this condition. If the illness is diagnosed in time, through the use of a simple blood test (the Wassermann test), the administration of penicillin almost guarantees a cure.

Generalization Responding to a stimulus other than the training stimulus as though it were the training stimulus. In classical conditioning, the response tends to diminish the more the other stimulus differs from the training stimulus, thereby creating a "gradient of generalization."

Generalized Anxiety Disorder An anxiety state characterized by a relatively constant feeling of dread and tension, without apparent or reasonable cause. Free-floating anxiety is a common complaint.

Generativity The concern about establishing and guiding the next generation, and other forms of "care for the creatures of the world."

Geriatrics A branch of medicine that deals with the problems and diseases of the elderly.

Gerontology The study of old age and aging.

Gestalt Psychology The school of psychological thought that emphasizes that wholes are more than the sum of their parts. Gestalt psychologists study forms and patterns and contend that stimuli are perceived as whole images rather than as parts built into images.

Gestalt Therapy A form of psychotherapy originated by Fritz Perls, who adapted the fundamental concepts of traditional psychoanalysis but placed greater emphasis on the immediacy and importance of the here and now in breaking down the influence of the past. The patient-therapist relationship is more active and democratic than in traditional psychoanalysis.

Glial Cells Support cells in the central nervous system that provide neurons with physical and nutritional support. Glial cells outnumber neurons in the brain and recently have been suspected to be, like neurons, directly involved in information transmission.

Gonads The sex glands that contribute to the regulation of the sex drive and the physiological changes that accompany physical maturity. These glands are the ovaries in the female and the testes in the male.

Goodness of Fit From temperament theory, referring to how well suited a certain temperament is to a particular environment. Temperaments well matched with their environments are said to show "goodness of fit."

Gooing Stage A stage of language acquisition that typically occurs between the ages of 2 and 4 months. During this stage, infants combine the vowel-like comfort sounds made earlier with harder sounds that are the precursors of consonants. An example, is "goo."

Gradient of Texture A depth cue. Closer objects show greater detail.

Grammar A set of rules that determines how sounds may be put together to make words and how words may be put together to make sentences.

Grammatical Morphemes Words or parts of words that help add meaning to a sentence and that are acquired by children generally between the ages of 2 1/2 and 5 years of age. Conjunctions, prepositions, suffixes, and prefixes are examples of grammatical morphemes. Morphemes are the smallest language units to have meaning and cannot be broken down into smaller meaningful units.

Great-Man, Great-Woman Hypothesis The hypothesis that individuals become leaders primarily because of the personality or traits they possess.

Ground In perception, all that is perceived to be background.

Growth Spurt The time during puberty in which an adolescent's growth undergoes a marked acceleration.

Gyri The prominent rounded and elevated convolutions at the surfaces of the cerebral hemispheres.

Habit A series of cues, responses, and reinforcers linked together in such a way that each stimulus consequence reinforces the person's previous response and cues the next response.

Habituation A process whereby an organism ceases to respond to a stimulus that is repeatedly presented.

Hallucination A false sense perception for which there is no appropriate external stimulus.

Hallucinogens Drugs that cause excitation at synapses associated with sense perception. A person taking these drugs may perceive sensations when there is nothing "real" to see, hear, or feel. LSD and mescaline are examples.

Health Psychology Any aspect of psychology that bears on the experience of health and illness and the behavior that affects health status.

Healthy Insomniacs People who function well with only 3 hours of sleep per night or less, and who do not seem to need more sleep than this.

Height on a Plane A monocular depth cue. Objects higher on a plane are perceived as being farther away.

Heroin A highly addictive narcotic drug derived from morphine.

Heterosexual A person who is sexually attracted to a member of the opposite sex.

Heuristics Methods for discovering the correct solution to a problem by exploring the possibilities that seem to offer the most reasonable approach to the goal, rather than all possibilities. Heuristics also involve obtaining successive approximations to the correct answer by means of analogies and other search techniques.

Hierarchy of Motives A theory of motivation developed by Abraham Maslow in which more basic needs must be met before needs of a higher order can come into play.

High-Threshold Fibers Stereocilia in the inner ear that are difficult to bend and thus respond only to loud noises or sounds.

Highway Hypnosis A hypnotic state experienced by a person operating a vehicle—often the result of relaxing too much during a long and boring drive.

Hindbrain The posterior section of the brain, which includes the cerebellum, pons, and medulla among other structures.

Hippocampus A small area at the back of the forebrain that is known to be important in the memory process. It is part of the limbic system. There are two such structures in each brain known collectively as hippocampi.

Homeostasis An internal environment in which such body components as blood pressure, blood chemistry, breathing, digestion, and temperature are kept at levels optimal for the survival of the organism.

Homosexual A person who is sexually attracted to a member of his or her own sex.

Horizontal Cells Retinal cells with short dendrites and long axons that extend horizontally, linking rods with other rods and cones with other cones. These cells fire according to the average of light intensity generated by the photoreceptors in each of their immediate neighborhoods. They are thought to influence opposing color processes (such as red and green, blue and yellow) and are probably responsible, in part, for negative afterimages and other opponent-process effects.

Hormone A bloodborne secretion of the endocrine glands that specifically affects metabolism and behavior.

Hot flashes Sudden, brief sensations of heat, often accompanied by reddening of the skin. They are thought to be caused by the fluctuating levels of hormones during the climacteric.

Hue Specifically, the color of a visible light. Hue is determined by the wavelength of the visible light and, depending on the particular wavelength in question, may be called red, yellow, blue, and so on. Perceived hue may also be affected slightly by extreme changes in brightness.

Humanistic Psychology A school of psychology that emphasizes the uniqueness of the individual and the search for self-actualization.

Hypercomplex Cells Cells in the cerebral cortex that respond to complex combinations of visual stimuli, including width, length, edges, and certain forms.

Hypnosis A state of consciousness characterized by relaxation and suggestibility.

Hypnotherapy Hypnosis used for therapeutic purposes in cases of pain control or behavior pathology. The method has been used in therapy, dentistry, surgery, and childbirth.

Hypochondriasis A somatoform disorder in which there is a persistent and exaggerated concern about diminished health and energy in the absence of demonstrable organic pathology.

Hypothalamic-Pituitary-Adrenal Axis The glands and neural-hormonal complexes of the hypothalamus, the pituitary gland, and the adrenal glands of the kidneys, which together comprise an important stress reaction system.

Hypothalamocentric Hypothesis Stellar's hypothesis that a hunger center responsible for the homeostasis of food intake exists in the hypothalamus.

Hypothalamus An elongated structure in the forebrain that appears to control an entire range of autonomic functions, including sleep, body temperature, hunger, and thirst.

Hypothesis Any statement or assumption that serves as a possible, but tentative, explanation of certain observations. A hypothesis is always formulated in a way that makes it amenable to empirical test.

I/O Psychology Abbreviation for industrial/organizational psychology, the field of applied psychology concerned with the methods of training, counseling, selecting, and supervising personnel in business and industry. I/O psychologists also investigate ways to make organizations effective and efficient.

ID In psychoanalytic theory, the reservoir of instinctive drives; the most inaccessible and primitive portion of the mind.

Ideational Fluency A term used by Michael Wallach to describe an individual's ability to produce many ideas. Ideational fluency is sometimes used as a measure of creativity. It correlates poorly with average or above average IQ.

Illusion A significant and consistent interpretation of sensory information by a given population that is not in agreement with precise and objective measurement.

Image and Cue Theory The theory that perceptions are learned by acquiring an understanding of the cues contained within the image that falls on the retina. A cue in this instance refers to any part of an image that is distinct from any other part and from which we may acquire information about our surroundings.

Implicit memory The memory underlying cognitive, perceptual, and motor skills. Implicit memories include the unconscious expression of skills or habits, conditioning without awareness, and the phenomenon of priming. It is sometimes called skill memory, or procedural memory.

Impression Management Hypothesis The hypothesis that the results of cognitive dissonance experiments can be explained, not by changes in real attitudes made to reduce dissonance, but rather by a need to appear consistent in the eyes of others.

Imprinting As used by ethologists, a species-specific bonding that occurs within a limited period early in the life of the organism and that is relatively unmodifiable thereafter.

In-Group Any group for whom an individual feels a positive regard. This is a subjective term, depending on the person's point of view.

Incubation Effect An effect associated with taking a break during creative problem solving. The individual often returns to the problem with a fresh approach and finds the solution.

Incus One of the three small bones in the middle ear; it is also called the anvil.

Independent Variable In an experiment, any variable that is manipulated so that its effects on the dependent variable may be observed.

Information Availability Hypothesis The hypothesis that explains people's tendency to attribute their own behavior to environmental causes rather than to personality traits as a function of the fact that they have more information about their personal situation, their environment, and the obvious forces in it than they have about others'.

Inhibitory Synapses A synapse associated with hyperpolarization of the receiving cell once neurotransmitter is secreted. If the receiving cell is a neuron, it will become harder to fire, or more difficult to reach action potential.

Innate Inborn; arising as a hereditary component of a physiological or behavioral trait.

Insane A legal term for those with a mental disorder, implying that they lack responsibility for their acts and are unable to manage their behavior.

Insight In problem solving, the sudden perception of relationships leading to a solution. A solution arrived at in this way can be repeated promptly when the same or a similar problem is confronted.

Insight Therapy Psychotherapy that attempts to uncover the deep causes of the patient's or client's difficulty. The therapist tries to guide the individual to self-understanding.

Insomnia Difficulty in initiating or maintaining sleep for the necessary amount of time.

Instrumental Learning The process by which an organism learns to behave because of the consequences that follow the behavior.

Intellectual plasticity The variability in intellectual functioning caused by different social, environmental, and physical conditions.

Intelligence A general term for a person's abilities in a wide range of tasks, including vocabulary, numbers, problem solving, and concepts. It may also include the ability to profit from experience, to learn new information, and to adjust to new situations.

Intelligence Quotient (IQ) A quotient derived from the formula MA/CA x 100, where MA is mental age and CA is chronological age. The intelligence quotient was devised by German psychologist L. William Stern and introduced in the United States by Lewis Terman.

Interference Effects In memory, a conflict between information contained in the memory so that (1) previously learned information makes it more difficult to learn new information—see proactive interference—or (2) recently learned information makes it more difficult to recall old information—see retroactive interference.

Intermittent Schedule Reinforcement of a particular response, but not each time the response occurs.

Interobserver Reliability The degree of disagreement or agreement between two or more observers who simultaneously observe a single event.

Intraorganismic Perspective The view of attachment asserting that the infant has innate mechanisms that foster and promote the development of attachment. Such mechanisms are believed to have been naturally selected because they have survival value.

Intrinsic Motivation A drive to engage in a behavior for its own sake in the absence of any obvious external reward or reinforcer.

Introspection The method introduced by structural psychologists, in which the subject describes his or her own conscious experiences.

Introvert One of Jung's personality types. An introvert is socially withdrawn, emotionally reserved, and self-absorbed.

Invariants In J. J. Gibson's direct perception theory, stimulus features that are unchanging or have proportions that are relatively fixed or constant.

Ion Channels Gates or selective openings imbedded within the neuron's membrane that allow charged atoms (called ions) to enter or exit. Such ion exchanges are responsible for the phenomena of neural transmission and communication.

Iris The pigmented muscular membrane that controls the aperture in the center of the pupil, which determines the amount of light that enters the eye.

James-Lange Theory of Emotion A classical theory of emotion named for William James and Carl Lange, who independently proposed it. The theory posits that a stimulus first leads to visceral and motor responses and that the following awareness of these responses constitutes the experience of the emotion. According to this theory, for instance, we are sad because we cry, rather than we cry because we are sad.

Jet Lag An uncomfortable feeling caused by disruption of the sleep-wake cycle that follows an attempt to adjust to a new time zone too quickly. It is called jet lag because long-distance travelers often suffer from it.

Job Analysis Analysis of the specific tasks required in a job and the training, physical abilities, educational level, vocational preparation, and temperament a person needs to perform the job.

Karyotype A photomicrograph of chromosomes in a standard array.

Kibbutz An Israeli farm or collective where children are often reared in groups and receive nurturance and guidance from many different adults and older children.

Kinesthesis An inclusive term for the muscle, tendon, and joint senses that yield information about the position and movement of various parts of the body.

Language Any means of communication that uses signs, symbols, or gestures within a grammar and through which novel constructions can be created.

Language Acquisition Device (LAD) Developed by Noam Chomsky: An hypothesized neural structure inborn in every healthy individual that is preprogrammed with the underlying rules of a universal form of grammar. Once the child is exposed to a particular language, he will select from the complete sets of rules with which he was born, the ones required by the language he is speaking. Most psychologists and linguists currently find the idea to be interesting but agree that a proof is doubtful because it is so difficult to find ways to demonstrate the existence of such an hypothesized device.

Latent Content In psychoanalytic theory, the hidden true meaning of a dream. The latent content of a dream, with all of its symbols and concealed meanings, can only be understood, according to this view, through the process of psychoanalysis.

Latent Learning Learning that occurs in the absence of any obvious reinforcement, apparently as a result of just being exposed to stimuli.

Law of Effect Thorndike's principle that responses associated with pleasant consequences tend to be repeated, while those associated with discomforting consequences tend to be eliminated.

Learned Helplessness Giving up, even though success is possible, because of previous experience with situations in which success was impossible.

Learning A relatively permanent change in behavior as a result of experience.

Lens The transparent biconvex structure of the eye behind the iris and pupil that focuses light rays entering through the pupil to form an image on the retina.

Libido According to Freud, the psychological energy driving the individual to seek gratification—principally sexual gratification, but also food, comfort, and happiness.

Life review The process in which a person approaching death looks back over his life and attempts to understand its meaning.

Light Adaptation The process by which the eyes become less sensitive to light in bright illumination.

Limbic System An aggregate of brain structures, the two major components of which are the amygdalae and the hippocampi. Some of its major functions include attention, memory, emotion, and motivation.

Linear Perspective A monocular depth cue. Parallel lines appear to converge in the distance.

Linear Progression Development that progresses steadily and continuously (as would a straight line). In this process, each new development is dependent on those that came before.

Linguistic Relativity Whorf's hypothesis that thought is structured according to the language spoken, so that those who speak different languages have different thinking patterns.

Lithium Carbonate A chemical compound that has been found to be effective in controlling the severe mood swings associated with bipolar affective disorders.

Local Effect The rapid depolarization of a section of the axon in response to the propagation of a neural transmission following the onset of neural firing. It is induced by the rapid depolarization of the soma or of a nearby section of the axon. The local effect results in the rapid depolarization of the next section of axon, thereby maintaining the propagation of the neural transmission.

Locus-Dependent Memory A memory that has been associated with a particular location so that it is easier to recall when you are in that location.

Long-Term Memory Term used to refer to memory systems with virtually unlimited storage capacity in which memories may be stored for long periods, even a lifetime. While both implicit and explicit memory systems have long-term storage capability, the term "long-term memory" is usually used to refer to long-term declarative memory.

Long-Term Potentiation (LTP) An increase in the efficiency of synaptic interchange which may last for hours or days following a certain pattern of excitatory stimulation. The opposite effect is called long-term depression (LTD) and may also last for hours or days following a certain pattern of inhibitory stimulation. Both LTP and LTD are suspected of playing a major role in learning and memory.

Longitudinal Studies Research studies that are designed to investigate individuals over time, taking measurements at periodic intervals.

Loudness A measurement of sound intensity that corresponds to the amplitude of the sound waves.

Lucid Dreaming The realization by a dreamer that she or he is, in fact, dreaming.

Magnetic Resonance Imaging (MRI) A technique that makes internal body structures clearly visible. It uses radio waves to excite atoms in the body, and the excitations, monitored by a huge magnet, are interpreted by a computer to produce a composite picture.

Magno Pathway A distinct brain pathway for the transmission of motion and stereoscopic depth perception. These messages begin in the retina with the stimulation of large ganglion cells and continue on to the midbrain where more large cells are stimulated. From there, the messages are sent to the occipital cortex.

Mainstreaming The philosophy of keeping as many exceptional children within the regular classroom as possible.

Major Depressive Disorder A lasting and continuous state of depression without any apparent cause. It is also known as unipolar depression. Major depressive disorder may include psychotic features such as hallucinations, delusions, or a depressive stupor.

Malleus The largest of the three small bones in the middle ear; it is also called the hammer.

Manifest Content In psychoanalytic theory, the overt, literal, dream content. Usually what is first described or reported by the dreamer.

Marijuana A hallucinogenic drug derived from the dried flowers and leaves of the cannabis variety of hemp.

Massed Practice A study method that does not create a spacing effect and is, therefore, not likely to lead to long-term retention. Material is studied in a single session without any interruption. The method is also known as cramming.

Mastery In motivation, the opposite of learned helplessness; the acquisition of skills or attitudes that enable one to persist in adversity and that help to "psychologically inoculate" one against giving up or feeling helpless.

Masturbation Sexual self-stimulation.

Maturation A genetically programmed biological plan of development that is relatively independent of experience.

Means-End Analysis A problem-solving process in which the difference between the current situation and the desired situation is defined and then a series of steps is taken to reduce, and finally eliminate, the difference. This process is applicable whenever there is a clearly specifiable problem and a clearly specifiable solution.

Meditation Deep relaxation brought on by focusing one's attention on a particular sound or image, breathing deeply, and relaxing.

Medulla The oblong structure just above the spinal cord that is responsible for many vital life-support functions, including breathing and heartbeat.

Meiosis The process of cell division in sexually reproducing organisms that reduces the number of chromosomes in reproductive cells, leading to the production of gametes.

Melioration In psychology, the tendency of organisms to shift behavioral allocations toward more lucrative alternatives.

Memory The complex mental function of recalling what has been learned or experienced.

Memory Trace A presumed neurological event responsible for any relatively permanent memory. It is thought to be electrochemical in nature but may involve structural changes in the neuron.

Menopause The complete cessation of menstruation, which usually occurs during middle age. It is said to have occurred when a woman has lived 12 consecutive months without having a menstrual period.

Mental Age (MA) A concept developed by Alfred Binet that was subsequently incorporated in the formula mental age / chronological age $\times$ 100 = IQ. The mental age of a person is derived by comparing his or her score with the average scores of others within specific age groups.

Mental Set A tendency to continue to use a particular approach or type of solution to a problem based on previously learned mental procedures.

Mentor A more experienced person in a work setting who provides guidance, support, and advice about career development to a less experienced person.

Mere Exposure Effect The effect in which attitudes become more favorable toward something merely by being exposed to it.

Mesmerism An early term for hypnosis, named after Anton Mesmer, who claimed he could cure the ill with magnetism. In mesmerism, "magnetic" forces were called on to relieve pain.

Mesomorph One of Sheldon's three body types. A mesomorph is characterized by a predominance of muscle and bone, as in an athlete. The corresponding temperament is somatotonic.

Meta-Analysis An examination of many studies that focus on one topic, in order to discover an overall consensus. Careful attention is paid to eliminate faulty studies.

Method of Loci A mnemonic technique in which items are associated with positions or things along a familiar route in order to make them more easily remembered.

Microelectrode An extremely small electric probe capable of monitoring the electrical activity of a single cell.

Midbrain The middle section of the brain, which contains the structures responsible for processing and relaying auditory and visual information.

Mnemonic Any device or technique for improving memory.

Model A mathematical, logical, or mechanical replica of a relationship or a system of events so designed that a study of the model can yield some understanding of the real thing. In social learning theory, anyone who demonstrates a behavior that others observe.

Molecule A electrically bound grouping of two or more atoms that comprise a chemically distinct entity.

Monochromats People who have color blindness due to the defective functioning of two of their three cone systems. Most monochromats can see no color at all. Interestingly, all monochromats so far tested have functioning blue cones. This appears to occur because the genes for the red and green cones are located closely together, making it possible for a single error or trauma to knock out both red and green cone systems.

Monocular Depth Cues Cues seen with the use of only one eye that give rise to a perception of depth. These cues include an object's height on a plane, linear perspective, overlap, relative size, gradient of texture, aerial perspective, shadowing, and relative motion. On a flat movie screen (with the exception of 3-D movies), only monocular cues give the sensation of depth.

Mood Disorders A group of disorders characterized by extremes of mood and emotion.

Moon Illusion A perceptual illusion created by the presence of the monocular cues of relative size and overlap, which make the moon appear 25 percent larger when rising than when overhead.

Morals The attitudes and beliefs that people hold that help them to determine what is right or wrong.

Motivated Forgetting Purposeful forgetting in which memories are repressed in order to fulfill unconscious desires to avoid the memories.

Motivation Any state or condition that causes an organism to produce, maintain, or inhibit a behavior or action.

Motor Area An area of the cerebrum that control body movement. It is located in front of the brain's central sulcus.

Multi-infarct dementia Dementia that occurs as a result of one or more cerebrovascular accidents.

Multiple Personality A dissociative disorder in which one person develops two or more distinct personalities, which often vie with each other for consciousness. One personality's memories are not usually accessible to another personality.

Multiplexing The act of simultaneously sending two or more distinct messages by way of a single transmission carrier.

Myelin A white, fatty covering on neural fibers that serves to insulate impulses along the fibers and increase the speed of neural transmission.

Narcolepsy An inherited pathological condition characterized by sudden and uncontrollable lapses into deep sleep.

Natural Selection The process, first suggested by Charles Darwin, through which those individuals of a species best adapted to their environment have a better chance of passing on their genes to the next generation than do those less well adapted.

Naturalistic Observations Observations in which researchers refrain from directly influencing the organisms being observed.

Nature In developmental research, the hereditary component of an organism's development.

Need A condition whose satisfaction is necessary for the maintenance of homeostasis.

Need For Achievement (N-ACH) A learned motivation, described by researcher David McClelland. Those who score high in n-Ach often behave in different ways from those who score low in n-Ach.

Negative Afterimage An opposite color image that persists briefly after the originally viewed object is removed. It is the result of fatigued color receptors in the retina.

Neocortex In evolutionary terms, the most recent development of the brain. The neocortex is six neural layers deep and comprises the outer portion of the cerebral cortex. The four major lobes of the brain are made of neocortex.

Neonates Newborn infants.

Nerve Impulse The propagation of an electrical impulse down the length of a neural axon once a neuron has fired.

Nerves Bundles of neural fibers that carry impulses from the central nervous system (brain and spinal cord) throughout the body and thereby affect muscles or glands.

Network Models Models of human memory that hold that sensory information and words are transformed into propositions or other discernible entities in order to be stored in memory in such a way that they are all interconnected, forming memory intersections as do ropes in a net.

Neural Network In computer science, computer hardware or circuits that alter their composition or connections in response to experience.

Neuroleptic Any of a collection of drugs that are known to have antipsychotic properties.

Neuroleptic Malignant Syndrome An often deadly reaction to neuroleptic drugs which occurs in 1–2 percent of patients receiving these drugs. The syndrome often comes quickly and the fatality rate is about 20 percent, owing to kidney or brain damage. The cause of the syndrome is unknown.

Neurons Specialized cells that transmit electrical impulses from one part of the body to another.

Neuropeptides Extremely small chemical messengers made from short chains of amino acids. Beta-endorphin is a neuropeptide.

Neurotransmitters Chemicals secreted by neurons that have an effect on adjacent neurons, muscles, or glands.

NMDA Receptors Glutamate receptors on the surface of certain neurons, so named because they were first discovered to bind with the chemical N-methyl D-aspartate. NMDA receptors also bind with magnesium ions. They are believed to be essential for learning and memory.

Non-NMDA Receptors Glutamate receptors on the surface of certain neurons, so named so as to distinguish them from neighboring NMDA receptors. Non-NMDA receptors depolarize the neuron when they respond to glutamate thereby opening the way for NMDA receptor activation.

Nondirective Therapy A therapeutic technique based on humanistic psychology in which the therapist creates a supportive atmosphere so that clients can work out their own problems.

Nonhomeostatic Mechanisms In motivation, a motivating system that regulates a drive or an impetus to act, but that is not counterbalanced by an opposing regulatory process that would reestablish the initial condition.

Noradrenalin A hormone secreted by the adrenal glands that brings about a number of body changes, including constriction of the blood vessels near the body's surface. It causes the adrenal glands to secrete steroids, which in turn release sugar so that energy is available for emergency action. It is also called norepinephrine.

Nosology A classification of diseases.

NREM Sleep (Orthodox Sleep) Non-REM sleep, during which no rapid eye movement takes place. Also called orthodox or quiet sleep because the EEG pattern is markedly different from the waking state.

Nucleus A body within the soma of a living cell that contains the cell's hereditary material and controls the cell's metabolism, growth, and reproduction.

Nurture In developmental research, the environmental component of an organism's development.

Obedience The willingness to follow commands or instructions.

Object Permanence Piaget's term for the individual's realization that objects continue to exist even though they are no longer visible.

Observer Bias An error in observation caused by the expectations of the observer.

Obsession A persistent idea or thought that the individual recognizes as irrational but feels compelled to dwell on.

Obsessive-Compulsive Disorder An abnormal reaction characterized by anxiety, persistent unwanted thoughts, or the compulsion to repeat ritualistic acts over and over.

Occipital Lobes The hind portion of each hemisphere of the cerebrum. The primary visual areas are contained within the occipital lobes.

Oedipus Complex A Freudian term representing the sexual attachment of a boy to his mother. This desire is repressed and disguised in various ways. The child expresses jealousy and hatred of his father because the father can have relations with the mother that the son is denied.

Off-Line Theory A theory that has as its premise that REM sleep enables creatures to maintain a smaller and more efficient brain size by consolidating and storing previously gathered information during sleep.

Off-Line Time In computer science, the time when data are no longer being input, but rather are being analyzed, correlated, stored, or treated in some processing fashion. In dream theory, the time when the brain shuts down, or sleeps, to prevent continued input and engages in REM to process data already received—presumably to make room for further input when it awakens.

Olfactory Bulb A mass of cells in the forebrain associated with the sense of smell. The olfactory nerve fibers enter and form a tract leading farther into the brain.

Olfactory Epithelium Nasal membranes containing receptor cells sensitive to odors.

One-word Stage The universal stage in language development in which children's speech is limited to single words.

Operant Conditioning Skinner's term for changes in behavior that occur as a result of consequences that reinforce or punish emitted responses. These responses are classified according to how they operate on the environment. They are, in turn, shaped by further environmental experiences. Also known as instrumental learning.

Operants Skinner's term for any emitted responses that affect the environment. Operants are classified or grouped not according to the particular muscular combinations involved in creating the response but according to their effect on the environment, that is, how they "operate" on the environment. Therefore, Thorndike's cats used the same operant when they pressed the treadle that opened their cage regardless of which paw or muscles they used.

Operational Definition A definition derived from a set of clearly stated operations; for example, for human strength the amount of weight that can be lifted by a person from the floor to a height of 1 foot in 5 seconds. Although such definitions are exact, and work well in scientific studies, they are sometimes considered limited because they may not include everyone's understanding of the construct being defined.

Opponent-Process Theory Hering's theory of color vision in which he argued that photoreceptors function along red-green, blue-yellow, and light-dark continuums and are in opposition to each other.

Opponent-Process Theory A theory of motivation by Richard Solomon proposing that many acquired motives, such as drug addiction, love, affection, social attachment, cravings for sensory and aesthetic experiences, skydiving, jogging, sauna bathing, and even self-administered aversive stimuli, seem to follow the laws of addiction.

Optic Nerve The bundle of nerve fibers connecting the retina and the brain.

Organ of Corti The organ located on the basilar membrane in the cochlea, which contains the hearing receptors.

Organ reserve The extra capacity of the heart, lungs, and other organs that is drawn on in times of physical or emotional stress or illness.

Orgasm The climax of sexual excitement, normally marked by ejaculation of semen by the male and muscular spasms of the genitals in both sexes.

Osmosis The diffusion of fluid through a semipermeable membrane, such as that surrounding a living cell, until the concentrations of fluid on either side of the membrane are equal.

Out-Group Any group that an individual views in a negative way. This is a subjective term, depending on the person's point of view.

Overlap A monocular depth cue. Objects that are behind (overlapped by) other objects are perceived as being farther away.

Pain-Elicited Aggression The desire to harm or defeat another, brought on by pain or anguish. It is common to many species, including humans. Cognitive interpretations can often control or mediate the aggression in spite of the pain or anguish.

Panic Attack A sudden overwhelming and debilitating onset of fear characteristic of panic disorder. There is no realistic reason or cause.

Paradoxical Sleep REM sleep. The EEG pattern closely resembles that of a person who is awake, even though the person is still asleep. Most dreaming occurs during this kind of sleep. The sympathetic nervous system shows heightened activity.

Parallel Processing In computer science or neuroanatomy, the handling of information in a manner so that many aspects of a particular problem are manipulated simultaneously, thereby saving time over serial methods in which each aspect of a problem is examined in sequence.

Parasympathetic Nervous System The portion of the autonomic nervous system that is most active during the body's quiescent states and which aids the body to recover from states of arousal.

Parietal Lobes The top portion of each hemisphere of the cerebrum extending from the central sulcus to the beginning of the occipital lobes. The parietal lobes contain the primary somatosensory area as well as association areas, including language areas.

Parkinson's Disease A progressive nervous disease of the brain characterized by muscle tremor, slowing of movement, peculiarity of gait and posture, and weakness. It is a direct result of dopamine deficiency and can be temporarily treated with medication.

Parvo-Interblob Pathway A distinct brain pathway for the transmission of high-resolution perception of stationary shapes and forms. These messages begin in the retina with the stimulation of small ganglion cells and continue on to the midbrain where more small cells are stimulated. From there, the messages travel to areas that surround the blobs in the occipital cortex.

Passionate Love A strong sexual desire for another individual combined with the perception that one is in love. This perception is often the result of misattributing to love a heightened physiological arousal for any reason.

Peak Performance The exceptional performance given by an athlete when physical and mental conditions are optimal.

Peers Equals; developmentally, those persons who interact at about the same behavioral level regardless of age.

Perception The brain's interpretation of the information processed by the senses.

Perceptual Constancies The tendency to perceive objects as yielding the same or similar experiences, even though the viewing conditions may vary widely.

Peripheral Nervous System The nerves that carry impulses from the sense organs to the central nervous system and from the central nervous system to the muscles and glands of the body.

Peripheral Route Processing From social-information processing theory, a route of persuasion and attitude change that may occur even when a person pays little attention to the persuasive message. Any resulting attitude change is usually temporary.

Peripheral Vision All visual experiences outside the immediate line of sight; that is, experiences other than those derived from light focused on the fovea. The photoreceptor field on the retina surrounding the fovea gives rise to peripheral vision. Peripheral vision is especially important for determining motion.

Person-Situation Debate From personality theory, the argument concerning whether the primary drive behind a person's behavior is due to enduring internal qualities or environmental influences.

Personality The organization of relatively enduring characteristics unique to an individual, as revealed by the individual's interaction with his or her environment.

Personality Disorder Deeply ingrained, habitual, and rigid patterns of behavior or character that severely limit the adaptive potential of the individual but that are often not seen by him or her to create problems or be maladaptive. They are sometimes called character disorders.

Persuasive Communication Arguments designed to alter attitudes by appealing to reason by means of fact and logic.

Phencyclidine Hydrochloride (PCP) A dangerous hallucinogenic drug that can lead to aggressive or psychotic behavior. It is also known as angel dust.

Phenothiazines Antipsychotic drugs, often called the major tranquilizers. These drugs help control and alleviate the symptoms of psychosis.

Pheromones Substances that, when secreted, are sexual attractants to receptive organisms via olfactory perception.

Phi Phenomenon Specifically, a perceptual illusion brought about by observing two lights placed side by side in a darkened room and flashed alternately. The resulting perception is of one light moving back and forth. Also, often applied to any circumstance in which stationary objects presented in succession appear to be moving, such as occurs when we view a motion picture.

Philosophy In most general terms, philosophy is "the search for the truth." It encompasses two major branches: epistemology, which includes efforts to comprehend the origins, limits, and nature of knowledge; and metaphysics, in which the reality of existence is examined. Minor branches include esthetics, logic, and ethics.

Phonemes The most basic distinctive sounds in any given language. Phonemes are combined into words.

Phonetics The study and classification of speech sounds and their production, transmission, and perception.

Phonological Loop From Baddeley and Hitch's model of working memory: A slave system of the working memory executive that can briefly hold information about language or language-like sounds. Closest to the older notion of short-term memory, it can hold items heard over a two second period for about 30 seconds. Rehearsal can keep an item in the phonological loop for longer periods.

Photons Massless particles of light that carry energy. The energy carried is indirectly proportional to the wavelength of the particle: The shorter the wavelength, the greater the energy. Common names for photons depend on the wavelength and include, among others, radio waves, microwaves, visible light, and X rays.

Photoreceptor Cells Light sensitive cells, called rods and cones, that comprise the third layer of the retina.

Phrenology A system developed by Franz Joseph Gall for identifying types of people by examining their physical features, especially the configuration of the skull.

Physical Addiction An overwhelming desire for a particular substance due to the mechanisms of tolerance and physical reaction to withdrawal.

Physiology The biological discipline that examines the functions of cells, tissues, and organs in living organisms.

Pidgin A simplified form of speech typically derived from a mixture of two or more languages. It has as its basis a rudimentary form of grammar and vocabulary and is generally used for communication between people speaking different languages.

Pineal Gland The pineal gland is located in the brain and it resembles a crude retina. It secretes melatonin, is sensitive to light, and secretes hormones in response to the length of day. The pineal gland is believed to regulate the 24-hour circadian rhythm.

Pinna The clearly visible outer portion of the ear. It serves to gather sound.

Pitch The perception of a tone's frequency. In general, shorter wavelengths (higher frequencies) are perceived as having a higher pitch, while longer wavelengths (lower frequencies) are perceived as having a lower pitch.

Pituitary Gland A gland located beneath and attached to the hypothalamus that controls many hormonal secretions. It often is called the "master gland" because it appears to control other glands throughout the body.

Place Learning Acquiring an understanding of the location of things relative to each other in an environment through experience with the environment.

Place Theory A theory of hearing that attempts to explain the reception of sound waves between 5000 and 20,000 cycles per second. It asserts that different frequencies stimulate stereocilia at different places within the cochlea. High frequencies stimulate stereocilia near the oval window, while intermediate frequencies stimulate stereocilia away from the oval window.

Placebo An inert substance often given to subjects in a control group in place of the treatment given to subjects in the experimental group.

Plasticity The ability of brain tissue to take over the functions of other brain areas that have been damaged or disrupted.

Play Pleasurable activity engaged in for its own sake, with means emphasized rather than ends. Play is not usually engaged in as a serious activity and is flexible, in that it varies in form or context.

Pleasure Principle The psychoanalytic postulate that an organism seeks immediate pleasure and avoids pain. The id functions according to the pleasure principle.

Polarization Effect An effect in which members of a group tend to take a more extreme position (more conservative or more daring) than they would have as individuals. It is probably the result of social comparison or persuasive group arguments.

Polarized In reference to the neuron, to have been placed in a state of potential energy release by the resulting electrical forces created by ions on either side of the cell membrane. In the neuron, the polarization results in a resting potential of -70 millivolts across the membrane.

Polygraph A lie detector. This device measures physiological changes regulated by the autonomic nervous system (heartbeat, blood pressure, galvanic skin response, and breathing rate). The assumption is that deliberate lying will produce detectable physical reactions.

Pons Part of the brainstem lying just above the medulla and regulating motor messages traveling from the higher brain downward through the pons to the cerebellum. It also regulates sensory information.

Population Pyramid A graphic depiction of the number of individuals within given age ranges. Each age range is stacked from the youngest to oldest; in the normal population, the graph typically forms a pyramid shape.

Positive Reinforcement The process by which an organism encounters a stimulus (following a response) that has the effect of increasing the probability that the response will be emitted again.

Positron Emission Tomography (PET) A technique by which organ functions, especially brain function, can be directly observed. A scanning device monitors the emission of radiation following the injection of a positron-emitting substance that gathers in specific locations determined by ongoing organ functions.

Post formal operational thought A type of thinking that may develop in late adolescence or adulthood. No widely accepted definition yet exists; in general, characteristics include an ability to understand relativity, contradiction, and subjectivity, and to integrate these into decision making.

Post-Traumatic Stress Disorder A disorder characterized by the recurrence of a particular traumatic event in the mind of the individual who experienced it, a numbness or lack of responsiveness to external stimuli, and two or more symptoms associated with depression and anxiety, such as sleep disturbances, low threshold for startling, impairment of memory, and guilt about having participated in the event.

Posthypnotic Suggestion A suggestion made to a hypnotized subject to perform some task in response to a particular cue after the hypnotic session is over.

Postsynaptic Surface The cell surface receiving neurotransmitter secreted into the synapse.

Predictive Validity The degree to which a score or assessment correlates with a specific outcome. A test with high predictive validity allows fairly accurate predictions to be made about certain future behaviors.

Prejudice Beliefs or judgments made without sufficient evidence and not easily changed by opposing facts or circumstances; preconceived hostile and irrational feelings, opinions, or attitudes about a group or an individual.

Premack Principle The concept developed by David Premack that reinforcement is relative, not absolute, so that if two behaviors differ in their probability of occurrence at any given time, the chance to engage in the probable will serve to reinforce engaging in the less probable.

Presynaptic Surface The cell surface from which neurotransmitter is secreted into the synapse.

Primary Colors The three colors from which all other colors can be made, usually considered to be red, green, and blue.

Primary Prevention Efforts aimed at preventing an illness or pathological condition, mental or physical, from occurring. The focus is on optimizing health. As opposed to secondary prevention in which a pathological condition is treated after it has appeared in hopes of preventing it from becoming worse.

Primary Reinforcer A stimulus that can be innately reinforcing, such as food or sleep.

Priming Memory A hypothetical memory thought possibly to exist as a distinct entity because in certain cases of amnesia, access to a lost memory may be gained via small prompts, thereby giving it its name "priming" memory.

Privileged Site A location (typically in the brain) in which foreign tissue is safe from attack by the body's immune system. Sites in the brain are generally privileged because cells from the body's immune system cannot penetrate the blood-brain barrier that surrounds and protects the brain.

Proactive Interference The process by which previously learned material interferes with the ability to learn something new.

Probabilistic Epigenesis Literally, the direction in which growth will probably go. In cognitive development theory, the term is used to describe the stages of cognitive development as representing only what typically occurs during the development of most individuals, but not necessarily in the development of all individuals.

Problem-focused Coping Active rational strategies intended to alleviate stress by directly eliminating or reducing the stressor.

Prodromal Precursor or early warning of the onset of a disease or disorder.

Progressive Relaxation A technique in which deep relaxation is achieved through the progressive relaxation of one muscle group at a time, usually beginning with the feet and legs. The subject breathes deeply and focuses attention on each muscle group as it is relaxed.

Projection A defense mechanism in which the individual attributes his or her own motives or thoughts to others, especially when these motives or thoughts are considered undesirable.

Propositional Network Theory The memory theory holding that sensory information and words are transformed into propositions in order to be stored in a memory net.

Propositions The smallest units of information about which it makes sense to render a judgment of true or false. For example, "red apple" is not a proposition. However, "The apple is red" is a proposition, since the statement is either true or false.

Prosopagnosia A disorder in which the subject can no longer recognize faces. It is rarely accompanied by other neurological or physiological symptoms.

Protoconcept A primary concept of the simplest form usually related directly to a tangible object and exemplifying a general category (such as dog, house, boat).

Proxemics The study of nonverbal expression through the spatial distance people maintain when interacting, as well as their orientation toward each other as reflected by touch and eye contact.

Psychiatrist A medical doctor who has completed specialized training in the field of mental health, such as a psychiatric residency.

Psychoactive Drugs Drugs that alter conscious awareness or perception.

Psychoanalysis A therapy that seeks to bring unconscious desires into consciousness and make it possible to resolve conflicts usually dating back to early childhood experiences. Psychoanalysis is also the school of psychological thought founded by Sigmund Freud, which emphasizes the study of unconscious mental processes.

Psychodrama A specialized technique of psychotherapy developed by J. L. Moreno in which patients act out the roles, situations, and fantasies relevant to their personal problems. Psychodrama is usually conducted in front of a small audience of patients.

Psychoevolutionary Synthesis of Emotion Robert Plutchik's theory that emotions evolved because they help a species to survive. In his theory, cognitive assessments of stimulus-events may give rise to innate emotional patterns, which in turn motivate behaviors that ultimately have survival value.

Psychogenic Amnesia A disorder involving selective memory loss for psychological reasons. The individual forgets, partially or totally, his or her past identity, but remembers nonthreatening aspects of life.

Psycholinguists Those who specialize in the psychology of language.

Psychological Addiction An overwhelming desire for a particular substance due to the immediate sense of pleasure or fear reduction it provides. Psychological addiction often occurs in conjunction with physical addiction. The word dependence is often used to characterize either type of addiction and often is specific (for example, drug dependence).

Psychology The science of behavior and mental processes.

Psychosis Any of a group of disorders involving extensive and severe psychological disintegration, disruption of all forms of adaptive behavior, and loss of contact with reality. Psychotic individuals may show bizarre motor behavior, extreme emotional states, absence of emotional responsiveness, withdrawal, delusions, hallucinations, and cognitive distortions. Psychosis often requires institutionalization.

Psychosocial Stages The eight stages of ego development as postulated by Erik Erikson. The stages incorporate both sexual and social aspects and include the entire lifespan.

Psychosurgery Brain surgery for the purpose of altering behavior or alleviating mental disorders.

Psychotherapy A category of methods for treating psychological disorders. The primary technique is conversation between the patient and the therapist.

Puberty The stage of maturation in which the individual becomes physiologically capable of sexual reproduction.

Punishment An aversive stimulus consequence that has the effect of decreasing the strength of an emitted response.

Pupil The dark circular aperture in the center of the iris of the eye that admits light.

Q Sort A personality assessment technique based on a series of statements and traits that the test subject is required to sort into categories from "most like me" to "least like me."

Rapid Eye Movement (REM) The rapid back-and-forth movement of the eyes during sleep. Dreaming is often associated with REM.

Raspberry In foodstuffs: a rather tasty fruit; a type of berry. In social discourse: an explosive sound owing to the rapid expulsion of air from the mouth that vigorously vibrates the lips (especially the lower lip), which, as required for the effect, have been deliberately placed in a configuration so as to make contact with, and surround, the protruded tongue. Considered unrequired in most social circumstances. (For an exception to this rule, see "Sporting events.")

Rational-Emotive Therapy A form of directive therapy associated with Albert Ellis in which the therapeutic goal is modification of the client's inappropriate ideas about self-concept and relations with others.

Rationalization A defense mechanism in which irrational, impulsive action, or even failure, is justified to others and to oneself by substituting acceptable explanations for the real, but unacceptable reasons.

Reaction Formation A defense mechanism in which the individual exhibits, and at the conscious level believes he or she possesses, feelings opposite to those possessed at the unconscious level.

Reality Principle According to Freud, the principle on which the conscious ego operates as it tries to mediate between the demands of the unconscious id and the realities of the environment.

Receptive Field The grouping of information from many neurons so that a single neuron may readily respond to the information as a single input. For example, a ganglion cell may be responsive to a receptive field created by many photoreceptors, or a complex cell may be responsive to a receptive field created by many simple cells.

Reconstruction In memory, the unconscious placement into memory of a deduction or assumption of what one believes must have happened. Such created memories are often recalled as though they were recollections of actual events.

Reference Group A group with which we identify and that we use as our standard of behavior.

Reflex In neurology, any relatively simple neural interaction involving both afferent and efferent nerves.

Rehearsal A process by which memories can be held in a short-term memory for relatively long periods. In rehearsal, an item is repeated over and over so that it is not lost. This technique may eventually result in storage of the item in the long-term memory.

Reinforcement In classical conditioning, any increase in the ability of a conditioned stimulus to elicit a conditioned response owing to the association of the conditioned stimulus with another stimulus (typically an unconditioned stimulus). In operant conditioning, an event that strengthens the response that preceded it. Operant (instrumental) conditioning is a process in which a response is reinforced.

Reinforcement Theory of Liking A social theory of relationships that we like those whom we have been reinforced for liking or whom we associate with pleasurable events or circumstances.

Relative Motion A monocular depth cue. Objects that are closer appear to move more than distant objects when the viewer's head is moved from side to side.

Relative Size A monocular depth cue. Familiar objects appear larger than identical objects that are more distant.

Reliability The extent to which a test, rating scale, classification system, or other measure is consistent, that is, produces the same results each time it is applied to the same thing in the same way.

REM Rebound An increase in REM sleep demonstrated by a person who has been deprived of it.

Replication Repeating an experiment to establish the reproducibility of results.

Repression A psychological process in which memories and motives are not permitted to enter consciousness but are operative at an unconscious level.

Resistance In psychoanalytic therapy, a patient's opposition to attempts to bring repressed thoughts into the conscious mind.

Resistance Stage The second stage of the general adaptation syndrome, during which cortical hormones maintain high levels, physiological efforts to deal with stress reach full capacity, and resistance by means of defense mechanisms and coping strategies intensifies.

Resting Potential The difference in electrical potential maintained between the outside and the inside of a resting nerve cell, usually about -70 millivolts.

Reticular Activating System A complex network of neurons that monitors the general level of activity in the cortex, maintaining a state of arousal.

Retina The delicate multilayer, light-sensitive membrane lining the inner eyeball. It consists of layers of ganglion and bipolar cells and photoreceptor cells called rods and cones.

Retinal Disparity A binocular depth cue. Because the eyes are set apart, objects closer than 25 feet are sensed on significantly different locations on the left and right retinas. At close distances, retinal disparity, more than any other cue, gives a strong perception of depth.

Retrieval To bring material from the long-term memory to the working memory so that it can be examined.

Retrieval Cue Any stimulus that can help you gain access to a memory.

Retroactive Interference The process by which learning something new interferes with the ability to recall previously learned information.

Retrograde Amnesia An amnesia brought on by a sudden shock or trauma that causes earlier events to be forgotten.

Reversible Figures Any of a class of figures that appear suddenly to change perspective or figure-ground relationship when looked at carefully and steadily.

Rods Specialized photoreceptor cells in the retina that are primarily responsive to changes in the intensity of light waves and are therefore important in peripheral vision and night vision.

Role Confusion A consequence of the failure to establish a sense of identity during Erikson's fifth psychosocial stage. Without a sense of identity, the individual will be confused about his or her role in society and will find it difficult to form a life philosophy or create a stable base on which to build a career or have a family.

Routine Problem Solving Problem solving that requires concepts, thoughts, actions, and understandings that are already in your repertoire.

S-R Psychology The school of psychology that views the stimulus-response connection as the foundation of behavior. The goal of S-R psychology is to discover the functional relationships between stimuli and responses.

Saltatory Growth Literally, "growth by leaping." Growth that occurs in "spurts" or sudden leaps.

Sample A group of subjects who are representative of the population about which an inference is made.

Saturation The purity or richness of a color. Highly saturated colors are vivid and striking, while poorly saturated colors appear faded or washed out.

Schedule-induced polydipsia (SIP) Polydipsia means excessive drinking. Schedule-induced polydipsia refers to an increase in the drive to drink as a result of receiving little bits of food on an intermittent schedule.

Schizophrenia A term used to describe a number of psychotic disorders characterized by serious emotional disturbances, withdrawal, lack of or inappropriate emotional responses, hallucinations, and delusions.

Scientific Method The principles and processes used to conduct scientific investigations, including formation of hypotheses, observation, and experimentation.

Sclera The white, elastic outer covering of the eye.

Script In cognitive study, one's knowledge of the appropriate events that should occur in a particular social setting and of how one might carry them out. This comprises knowledge of who is expected to do what to whom as well as when, where, and why. A script would include such typical behaviors as those expected of a person visiting a restaurant or going to a movie.

Scripts In cognitive study, one's knowledge of the appropriate events that should occur in a particular social setting and of how one might carry them out. This comprises knowledge of who is expected to do what to whom as well as when, where, and why. A script would include such typical behaviors as those expected of a person visiting a restaurant or going to a movie.

Seasonal Affective Disorder (SAD) Depression associated with either a longer or shorter day. It commonly affects individuals in either the winter or summer months and typically passes once the season is over.

Second Messenger System The neural communication system by which the postsynaptic surface responds to informational substances by freeing a G protein which, in turn, activates an effector enzyme that then creates a second messenger or informational substance, which consequently may trigger a cascade of complex reactions resulting in a change in cell behavior. Such second messengers are believed to play an important role in long-term changes in the cell's action.

Secondary Reinforcer A reinforcer whose value is learned through its association with primary reinforcers or other secondary reinforcers. It is also called an acquired reinforcer.

Secondary Traits In Allport's theory, traits that are not as crucial as central traits for describing personality. Secondary traits are not demonstrated often because they are related to only a few stimuli and a few responses.

Secure Attachment The most common form of attachment observed by Ainsworth in her research. Securely attached children respond happily to their mothers' return, greet them, and stay near them for a while.

Self-Actualization Abraham Maslow's term for the process in which an individual constantly strives to realize his or her full potential.

Self-Efficacy How effective a person is in a particular situation. Perceived self-efficacy can be a powerful cognitive motivator.

Self-Hypnosis A hypnotic state induced by the subject without the aid of a hypnotist.

Self-in-relation theory A theory in which the goal of personality development is a deepening capacity for competence in relationships, in contrast to theories that emphasize autonomy, self-reliance, and separation from other people.

Self-Serving Bias An attribution bias describing the fact that people tend to attribute behavior that results in a good outcome to their own personality or traits and attribute behavior that results in a bad outcome to the forces or circumstances of the environment.

Semantic Memory Memory of meanings, including all factual information of a general nature such as knowledge that the English alphabet contains twenty-six letters.

Semantics The study of meaning in language.

Semicircular Canals Three small, liquid-filled canals located in the inner ear containing receptors sensitive to changes in spatial orientation.

Senescence The gradual weakening of the body that begins during early adulthood and continues until death.

Sensation Any fundamental experience of events from within or without the body as the result of stimulation of some receptor system. Distinguished from perception in that perception requires the interpretation of a sensation. This distinction is somewhat arbitrary, however, because some perception of a sensation must occur before awareness is possible.

Sensitivity Training Group sessions conducted for the purpose of developing personal and interpersonal sensitivity to feelings and needs. The feelings among group members are channeled so that members' self-acceptance and growth are enhanced.

Sensitization The process by which a reflexive response is made stronger and more sensitive to stimuli by pairing the eliciting stimulus with a painful or unpleasant stimulus.

Sensory Isolation Lack of a stimulus input needed for maintaining homeostasis. Prolonged reduction of external stimulation, in either intensity or variety, may produce boredom or restlessness, but is often experienced as profoundly relaxing.

Serial Position Effect A phenomenon in verbal learning. Items at the beginning or at the end of a long series are more easily remembered; items in the middle are the hardest to recall.

Set Point A particular weight that the body seems to demand; it is maintained by a hypothetical homeostatic mechanism that monitors levels of fat in the body.

Sexual Reassignment A surgical procedure for altering anatomy and appearance so that the individual resembles the opposite sex.

Sexually Transmitted Diseases (STDs) Diseases that are primarily transmitted through sexual intercourse.

Shadowing A monocular depth cue. The distribution of light on a curved or angled surface conveys that some parts are closer and some farther away.

Shape Constancy The learned perception that an object remains the same shape, although the image it casts on the retina may vary in shape depending on the viewing angle.

Shaping A method of creating a goal behavior by reinforcing successive approximations toward the goal behavior.

Short-term Memory Term in little current use that once referred to an hypothesized memory of limited storage capacity and short duration through which it was believed information had to pass before storage in long-term memory was possible. The closest modern equivalent to this discarded concept is the phonological loop of the working memory.

Simple Cells Cells in the cerebral cortex that respond to lines of a particular orientation.

Simple Phobia A person's pathological fear of an object or situation. The individual may realize that the fear is irrational but, being unable to control it, avoids the object or situation. Relatively easy to treat.

Single-Subject Experiment An experiment in which only one subject participates. Time is normally used as the control; that is, the subject's behavior changes over time in relation to the presentation and withdrawal of the independent variable.

Situational-Environmental Hypothesis The hypothesis that individuals become leaders because of situational or circumstantial forces rather than because of their personality traits.

Size Constancy The learned perception that an object remains the same size, although the size of the image it casts on the retina varies with its distance from the viewer.

Skills The capacity for carrying out a complex, well-organized, pattern of behavior smoothly and efficiently. The term refers to both motor and cognitive-perceptual abilities, most of which are carried out unconsciously, that is, without having to think about them. Playing the piano is an example of a skill. Skills, once they become almost automatic, are believed to be held as implicit memories.

Sleep Apnea A cessation of breathing during sleep. It may be brief or protracted. Brain damage can result if the apnea lasts long enough to create a significant oxygen deficiency.

Slow-Wave Sleep The deepest stages of sleep, characterized by an EEG pattern of delta waves.

Social Attitude An enduring system of positive or negative evaluations, feelings, and tendencies toward action with regard to a social object.

Social Cognition An area of social psychology that is concerned with how social influences affect cognitive process such as thought, memory, or perception.

Social Comparison Assessment of accuracy of our own attitudes, feelings, or beliefs by comparing them with those of others.

Social Learning Learning by observing the actions of others. It is also called vicarious conditioning or observational learning.

Social Learning Theory A theory developed by Albert Bandura that stresses learning by observing and imitating others. Social learning is sometimes called observational learning or vicarious conditioning.

Social Motivation Learned motivational states that result from the individual's interaction with his or her social environment or culture.

Social Norms Shared standards of behavior accepted by and expected from group members.

Social Referencing The use of emotional signals or cues from others as a guide for one's own behavior in ambiguous situations.

Sociobiology A theory of motivation and behavior stating that many human behaviors are influenced by inherited biological predispositions. In this view, morality, love, kindness, aggression, anger, hatred, and most other aspects of human behavior are partly viewed in terms of their functional value for ensuring the survival of a person's genes.

Soma The cell body. The soma contains the nucleus of the cell which manufactures enzymes and molecules essential for maintaining the cell's life.

Somatic Nervous System The portion of the peripheral nervous system that carries messages inward from the sense organs and outward to the muscles of the skeleton.

Somatic Therapy Invasive therapeutic intervention that acts directly on the body and its chemistry. Included in this classification are psychopharmacological, electroconvulsive, and psychosurgical procedures.

Somatoform Disorders Patterns of behavior characterized by complaints of physical symptoms in the absence of any real physical illness.

Somatogenic Amnesia Disorders involving selective memory loss for physical reasons such as brain trauma, disease, or toxic exposure. The kind of memory loss depends on the type of injury or illness.

Somatosensory Area An area in the cerebrum that controls sensation. It is located behind the central sulcus at the front of the parietal lobe.

Source Traits From Cattell's theory of personality, traits that can be identified only through factor analysis and that are more important than surface traits. Cattell argues that personality can be reduced to 16 source traits and that, although surface traits may appear to be more valid to the common-sense observer, source traits have greater utility in accounting for behavior.

Spaced Practice A study method that creates the spacing effect. Studying is accomplished over time with gaps between study sessions. The method is also known as distributed practice.

Spacing Effect The fact that repeated items are learned better and are more easily recalled the greater the amount of time between the first and the second exposure to the items.

Spermatorrhea A term coined by the physician Claude l'Allemand based on the erroneous assumption that nocturnal emissions were related to the venereal disease gonorrhea.

Spike A nerve impulse generated by the neuron reaching action potential.

Spinal Cord The portion of the central nervous system encased in the backbone and serving as a pathway for the conduction of sensory and motor impulses to and from the brain, respectively.

Spontaneous Recovery In operant conditioning, the brief recurrence of a response following extinction. In classical conditioning, the brief recurrence of eliciting power of a CS after extinction.

Spoonerisms Unintentional transpositions of sounds in a sentence, as in "people in glass houses shouldn't stow thrones." The phenomenon is named for an English clergyman, William A. Spooner, who was well known for such errors.

Sports Psychology The application of psychological techniques and principles to sports and other structured physical activities for the purpose of maintaining and maximizing performance and investigating applied clinical issues.

Standardized Instrument In psychological testing, a test or measure that has been administered to a wide sample of the population for which it is intended, so that the range and probabilities of responses from that population to the test or measure are known.

Stapes One of the three small bones in the middle ear; it is also called the stirrup.

State-Dependent Learning The phenomenon that memories are recalled with greater ease when you are in the same or similar mood or physical state as when you first acquired the memory.

Stereocilia Extremely short fibers extending from the surface of the hair cells in the inner ear.

Stereotype A set of simplistic and relatively fixed overgeneralizations concerning the physical or psychological characteristics of a class or group of people.

Steroids Any of a number of organic compounds that have a 17-atom carbon ring, including some hormones. Cortical steroids (secreted from the adrenal glands) help to control the release of sugar stored for use in emergencies.

Stimulants Drugs that can stimulate or excite the central nervous system. Cocaine and amphetamines are examples.

Stimulus Any energy or change in energy condition that is sensed.

Stimulus Control From learning theory, the idea that discriminative stimuli come to control the behavior they cue.

Stimulus Motives Drives or motives that appear to satisfy a need for certain amounts of sensory stimulation.

Strange Situation A laboratory test designed by Mary Ainsworth to demonstrate individual differences in the quality of attachment.

Stream of Consciousness A term coined by William James to describe the idea that conscious experience is like a river, always changing and flowing, rather than a permanent fixture.

Stress A psychological state associated with physiological and hormonal changes caused by conflict, trauma, or other disquieting or disruptive influences.

Structuralism The school of psychological thought founded by Edward Titchener that is concerned with reducing experience to its basic parts, determining the laws by which the parts are synthesized, and investigating the structure and content of mental states by introspection.

Subject Bias Unwanted changes in a subject's behavior owing to her knowledge about the experiment or awareness of being observed.

Subvocal Speech In learning theory, Watson's concept of thinking as a series of muscular responses.

Sulci The narrow fissures separating adjacent cerebral convolutions.

Superchiasmatic Nuclei (SCN) Dense clusters of neurons located in the central nervous system close to the hypothalamus just above the optic chiasm where the optic nerves from both eyes intersect. The SCN is known to control the pacing and activation of many circadian rhythms.

Superego In psychoanalytic theory, the part of the personality that incorporates parental and social standards of morality.

Superstitious Learning Behavior learned simply by virtue of the fact that it happened to be followed by a reinforcer or punisher, even though this behavior was not the cause of the stimulus that followed the response.

Surface Traits From Cattell's theory of personality, a cluster or group of behaviors that are overt and appear to go together. Inferring the existence of a surface trait makes it possible to classify similar behaviors under one term; for example, constant fighting, yelling, and making angry facial expressions can be categorized under the surface trait term aggressive.

Survey A method of collecting data through the use of interviews or questionnaires.

Sympathetic Nervous System The portion of the autonomic nervous system that is primarily concerned with emotional states and preparing the body for emergencies.

Synapse The small space between neurons into which neurotransmitter is secreted.

Synaptic Knobs The extreme ends of an axon in which neurotransmitter is stored.

Syndrome A number of features, characteristics, events, or behaviors that appear to go with each other, or which are thought to be coordinated or interrelated in some way.

Syntax The body of linguistic rules that makes it possible to relate a series of words in a sentence to the underlying meaning of that sentence, that is, the rules governing word order in a language (sentence structure).

Systematic Desensitization A therapeutic procedure developed by Wolpe in which anxiety-producing stimuli are paired, in a graduated sequence or hierarchy, with a state of physical relaxation until the most difficult situation can be faced without anxiety.

Tardive Dyskinesia A severe and relatively permanent neuromuscular reaction, following long-term use of, or a sudden withdrawal from, antipsychotic drugs. The disorder is manifested in involuntary twitching of body and facial muscles.

Task Load A measure of demand in terms of behavior required per unit of time. In conditions of high task load, there is much to do and little time to do it.

Taste Buds Groups of cells distributed over the tongue that constitute the receptors of the sense of taste.

Telegraphic Speech The pattern of speech, including and following the two-word stage, in which children rely on a grammar of strict word order to convey their meaning and do not use conjunctions, prepositions, or other function words.

Temperament Theories Theories of human development that place an emphasis on the enduring and stable aspects of personality, which are generally considered to be constitutional in nature, that is, due to the biogenetics of the individual.

Temporal Lobes The portion of each hemisphere of the cerebrum on either side of the head near the temples. The temporal lobes contain the primary auditory areas, as well as association areas. They have to do with emotion, vision, and language.

Testosterone A hormone that is produced primarily by the testes and is responsible for the development of male secondary sex characteristics. The adrenal glands of the female also produce some testosterone, but the hormone is found primarily in males.

Thalamus Part of the forebrain that relays sensory information and is involved in wakefulness and sleep.

Thanatology The study of death and dying.

Tip-of-the-Tongue Phenomenon The experience of being almost able to recall a certain bit of information. You sense that the information is there, you can almost "feel" it, and yet you cannot grasp it.

Token Economies Training, based on operant conditioning, that uses tokens as rewards for certain behaviors. The tokens can be redeemed for special privileges, or other reinforcers.

Tolerance In pharmacology, the ability to tolerate larger and larger doses of a drug after each exposure to it. A common tolerance mechanism, which occurs during opiate use, is for the body to create natural antidrug substances or antagonists in ever-larger amounts following each exposure to the drug.

Top-down Processing Processing in memory, perception, or other aspects of cognition that are influenced by the organism's prior knowledge or expectations, rather than simply being affected by the input itself.

Traits Distinguishing qualities, properties, or attributes of a person that are consistently displayed. According to Allport, a trait is a predisposition to respond to many types of stimuli in the same manner.

Tranquilizers Any of various drugs that are used to pacify.

Transactional Analysis A form of interpersonal therapy originated by Eric Berne based on the interactions of "child," "adult," and "parent" ego states.

Transference A concept developed by Freud that refers to the tendency of a person in therapy to transfer to the therapist perceptions and feelings about other people rather than seeing the therapist as he or she really is.

Transsexual An individual who exhibits the most extreme form of gender reversal, in which the individual feels that he or she is really a member of the opposite sex but has been trapped in the wrong-sexed body.

Trephining An ancient procedure in which the skull was punctured by a sharp instrument so that evil spirits might escape.

Trichromats People with normal color vision, who have all three cone systems functioning correctly.

Twin Design A research design used for sorting the influence of nurture from nature. A characteristic or behavior is compared between identical twins; then the same characteristic or behavior is compared between fraternal twins.

Two-word Stage The universal stage of language development in which children's expressions are limited to two-word sentences.

Two-Factor Theory of Emotion Stanley Schachter's theory that emotion stems from our cognitive interpretations of a general physiological arousal occurring under specific circumstances.

Two-Strike Theory A recent theory of the cause of some or most schizophrenia. In this view a susceptibility to the influenza virus is inherited (first strike). Following this "strike," exposure to the flu virus during the second trimester of pregnancy provides the second strike, causing a disruption of brain development in the fetus that later manifests itself as schizophrenia.

Tympanic Membrane The thin, semitransparent membrane separating the middle ear from the external ear; it is also called the eardrum.

Unconditioned Response (UR) The response made to an unconditioned stimulus, such as salivation in response to food.

Unconditioned Stimulus (US) The stimulus that normally elicits an unconditioned response, such as the food that caused Pavlov's dog to respond with salivation.

Unconscious Inference A term coined by Hermann von Helmholtz to describe the way in which an observer progresses from experiencing the sensations created by an object to recognizing that object. In essence, unconscious inferences are made automatically and without awareness. To the viewer, the object in question appears to exist as a thing unto itself, while the sensory and perceptual processes which gave rise to the object in the mind of the viewer, go unnoticed.

Validity The capacity of an instrument to measure what it purports to measure.

Vestibular Sacs Two baglike structures at the base of the semicircular canals containing receptors for the sense of balance.

Vestibular Sense The sense that keeps an organism in proper balance.

Visible Spectrum The range of wavelengths of light visible to the unaided eye.

Visual Cliff An apparatus constructed to study depth perception in animals and human beings. It consists of a center board resting on a glass table. On one side of the board, a checkered surface is visible directly beneath the glass; on the other side, the surface is several feet below the glass, giving the impression of a dropoff.

Visual Cortex An area in the brain through which most visual information is processed. It is located in the occipital lobes.

Visual Perspective Hypothesis The hypothesis that explains people's tendency to attribute their own behavior to environmental causes rather than to personality traits as a function of their visual perspective, because they view their surroundings more often than they view their own body.

Visuospatial Sketch Pad From Baddeley and Hitch's model of working memory: A slave system of the working memory executive that can briefly hold visual information about spatial relationships. A short-term memory that enables a person to make a quick mental note about where things are in relation to him or her spatially. The information is typically lost within 4 minutes, often after just seconds.

Volley Theory A theory of hearing designed to explain the reception of sound waves between 300 and 5000 cycles per second. According to this theory, auditory neurons fire in volleys that are well correlated with the frequency of the sound.

Wavelength The linear distance from a point on one oscillation of a wave to the corresponding point on the next oscillation of that wave.

Weber's Law The rule that the larger or stronger a stimulus, the larger the change required for an observer to notice a difference. The smallest difference in intensity between two stimuli that can be readily detected is a constant fraction of the original stimulus.

Wernicke's Aphasia The inability to understand spoken language because of damage to Wernicke's area. Individuals with this disorder generally speak normally in terms of phonetics and grammar content, but their speech is semantically bizarre.

Wernicke's Area An area in the temporal and parietal lobes of the brain associated with speech control.

Working Memory An inclusive term for a number of short-term memory systems which enable individuals to hold onto recently acquired information for about 30 seconds to 4 minutes. Among these memory systems are the phonological loop and the visuospatial sketch pad. Working memory also holds information from declarative memory that is being actively examined.

Yogi One who practices yoga, a Hindu discipline, the aim of which is to train consciousness to attain a state of perfect spiritual insight and tranquility. Control of body functions and mental states is practiced.

Young-Helmholtz Theory A theory of color vision stating that there are three basic colors (red, green, and blue) and three types of receptors, each of which is receptive to the wavelengths of one of the colors.

Youth A stage of development that some people go through following adolescence and prior to assuming the full responsibilities of adulthood.

References

Abraham, H. D. (1983). Visual phenomenology of the LSD flashback. *Archives of General Psychiatry, 40,* 884–889.

Abram, K. M., & Teplin, L. A. (1991). Co-occurring disorders among mentally ill jail detainees. Implications for public policy. *American Psychologist, 46,* 1036–1045.

Abramovitch, R., Pepler, D., & Corter, C. (1982). Patterns of sibling interaction among preschool-age children. In M. E. Lamb & B. Sutton-Smith (Eds.), *Sibling relationships: Their nature and significance across the lifespan* (pp. 61–86). Hillsdale, NJ: Erlbaum.

Abramson, L. Y., Seligman, M. E. P., & Teasdale, J. D. (1978). Learned helplessness in humans: Critique and reformulation. *Journal of Abnormal Psychology, 87,* 49–74.

Adams, B. N. (1968). *Kinship in an urban setting.* Chicago: Markham.

Adams, G. R. (1977). Physical attractiveness, personality, and social reactions to peer pressure. *Journal of Psychology, 96,* 287–296.

Adams, P. R., & Adams, G. R. (1984). Mount Saint Helens's ashfall. *American Psychologist, 39,* 252–260.

Adams, R. G. (1985). People would talk: Normative barriers to cross-sex friendships for elderly women. *The Gerontologist, 25,* 605–611.

Adelmann, P. K., & Zajonc, R. B. (1989). Facial reference and the experience of emotion. *Annual Review of Psychology, 40,* 249–280.

Adler, H. E., & Adler, L. L. (1978). What can dolphins (Tursiops Truncatus) learn by observation? *Cetology, 30,* 1–10.

Adler, L. L., & Adler, H. E. (1977). Observational learning in the California sea lion (Zalophus Californianus). *Aquatic Mammals, 5*(3), 72–77.

Adler, L. L., & Adler, H. E. (1977). Ontogeny of observational learning in the dog. *Developmental Psychobiology, 10,* 267–271.

Adler, T. (1989, April). Infant is father to the child, studies show. *APA Monitor,* p. 7.

Adler, T. (1989, June). Early sex hormone exposure studied. *APA Monitor,* p. 9.

Adler, T. (1990, April). Does the "new" MMPI beat the "classic?" *APA Monitor,* pp. 18–19.

Adorno, T. W., Frenkel-Brunswik, E., Levinson, D. J., & Sanford, R. N. (1950). *The authoritarian personality.* New York: Harper.

Aho, A. C., Donner, K., Hyden, C., Larsen, L. O., & Reuter, T. (1988). Low retinal noise in animals with low body temperature allows high visual sensitivity. *Nature, 334,* 348–350.

Ainsworth, M. D. S. (1973). The development of infant-mother attachment. In B. Caldwell & H. Ricciuti (Eds.), *Review of child development research* (Vol. 3). Chicago: Univ. of Chicago Press.

Aizenberg, R., & Treas, J. (1985). The family in late life. Psychosocial and demographic considerations. In J. E. Birren & K. W. Schaie (Eds.), *Handbook of the psychology of aging* (2nd ed., pp. 169–189). New York: Van Nostrand Reinhold.

Akbarian, S., Bunney, W. E., Jr., Potkin, S. G., Wigal, S. B., Hagman, J. O., Sandman, C. A., & Jones, E. G. (1993). Altered distribution of nicotinamide-adenine dinucleotide phosphate-diaphorase cells in frontal lobe of schizophrenics implies disturbances of cortical development. *Archives of General Psychiatry, 50,* 169–177.

Aldhous, P. (1992). French venture where U.S. fears to tread. *Science, 257,* 25.

Aldous, J., Klaus, E., & Klein, D. M. (1985). The understanding heart: Aging parents and their favorite children. *Child Development, 56,* 303–316.

Alexander, F. (1950). *Psychosomatic medicine.* New York: Norton.

Alker, H. A., & Owen, D. W. (1977). Biographical, trait, and behavioral-sampling predictions of performance in a stressful life setting. *Journal of Personality & Social Psychology, 35,* 717–723.

Alkon, D. L. (1989). Memory storage and neural systems. *Scientific American, 261*(1), 42–50.

Allen, K. M., Blascovich, J., Tomaka, J., & Kelsey, R. M. (1991). Presence of human friends and pet dogs as moderators of autonomic responses to stress in women. *Journal of Personality & Social Psychology, 61,* 582–589.

Alley, T. R. (1981). Head shape and the perception of cuteness. *Developmental Psychology, 17,* 650–654.

Allison, T., & Cicchetti, D. V. (1976). Sleep in mammals: Ecological and constitutional correlates. *Science, 194,* 732–734.

Allman, W. F. (1985, October). Staying alive in the 20th century. *Science 85,* pp. 30–41.

Allman, W. F. (1986, May). Mindworks. *Science 86,* pp. 23–31.

Allport, G. W. (1937). *Personality: A psychological interpretation.* New York: Holt, Rinehart & Winston.

Allport, G. W. (1961). *Pattern and growth in personality.* New York: Holt, Rinehart & Winston.

Allport, G. W., & Odbert, H. S. (1936). Trait-names: A psycho-lexical study. *Psychological Monographs: General and Applied. 47*(1, Whole No. 211).

Alper, J. (1986, July/August). Our dual memory. *Science 86,* pp. 44–49.

Amarilio, J. D. (1979). Insanity- Guilty but mentally ill- Diminished capacity: An aggregate approach to madness. *John Marshall Journal of Practice and Procedure, 12,* 351–381.

American Psychiatric Association. (1993). Practice guideline for major depressive disorder in adults. *American Journal of Psychiatry, 150*(4, whole supplement).

American Psychological Association. (1993). Guidelines for providers of psychological services to ethnic, linguistic, and culturally diverse populations. *American Psychologist, 48,* 45–48.

Anastasi, A. (1979). *Fields of applied psychology* (2nd ed.). New York: McGraw-Hill.

Ancoli-Israel, S., Kripke, D. F., Mason, W., & Kaplan, O. J. (1985). Sleep apnea and periodic movements in an aging sample. *Journal of Gerontology, 40,* 419–425.

Anda, R., Williamson, D., Jones, D., Macera, C., Eaker, E., Glassman, A., & Marks, J. (1993). Depressed affect, hopelessness, and the risk of ischemic heart disease in a cohort of U. S. adults. *Epidemiology, 4,* 285–294.

Anderson, J. R. (1980). *Cognitive psychology and its implications.* New York: W. H. Freeman.

Anderson, J. R. (1983). Retrieval of information from long-term memory. *Science, 220,* 25–30.

Anderson, J. R. (1983). *The architecture of cognition.* Cambridge, Mass.: Harvard University Press.

Anderson, J. R. (1993). Problem solving and learning. *American Psychologist, 48,* 35–44.

Anderson, L. D. (1939). The predictive value of infant tests in relation to intelligence at 5 years. *Child Development, 10,* 203–212.

Andersson, B. (1971). Thirst and brain control of water balance. *American Scientist, 59,* 408–415.

Andreasen, N. C. (1988). Brain imaging: Applications in psychiatry. *Science, 239,* 1381–1388.

Andreasen, N. C., Flaum, M., Swayze, H., O'Leary, D. S., Alliger, R., Cohen, G., Ehrhardt, J., & Yuh, W. T. C. (1993). Intelligence and brain structure in normal individuals. *American Journal of Psychiatry, 150,* 130–134.

APA Task Force on Laboratory Tests in Psychiatry. (1987). The dexamethasone suppression test: An overview of its current status in psychiatry. *American Journal of Psychiatry, 144,* 1253–1262.

Arango, V., Underwood, M. D., & Mann, J. J. (1992). Alterations in monoamine receptors in the brain of suicide victims. *Journal of Clinical Psychopharmacology, 12,* 8s–12s.

Arlin, P. A. (1984). Adolescent and adult thought: A structural interpretation. In M. L. Commons, F. A. Richards, & C. Armon (Eds.), *Beyond formal operations: Late adolescent and adult cognitive development* (pp. 258–271).

Aronson, E. (1969). Some antecedents of interpersonal attraction. In W. J. Arnold & D. Levine (Eds.), *Nebraska symposium on motivation.* Lincoln, Nebraska: Univ. of Nebraska Press.

Aronson, E., & Mills, J. (1959). The effect of severity of initiation on liking for a group. *Journal of Abnormal and Social Psychology, 59,* 177–181.

Arvidson, K., & Friberg, U. (1980). Human taste—response and taste bud number in fugiform papillae. *Science, 209,* 807–808.

Asaad, G., & Shapiro, B. (1986). Hallucinations: theoretical and clinical overview. *American Journal of Psychiatry, 143,* 1088–1089.

Asch, S. E. (1951). Effects of group pressure upon the modification and distortion of judgment. In H. Guetzkow (Ed.), *Groups, leadership, and men.* Pittsburg, PA: Carnegie.

Atkinson, J. W., & Raynor, J. O. (1974). *Motivation and achievement.* New York: Wiley.

Atkinson, R., & Shiffrin, R. (1968). Human memory: A proposed system and its control processes. In K. Spence and J. Spence (Eds.), *The psychology of learning and motivation* (vol. 2). New York: Academic Press.

Au, T. K., & Glusman, M. (1990). The principle of mutual exclusivity in word learning: To honor or not to honor? *Child Development, 61*, 1474–1490.

Austrom, D. R. (1984). *The consequences of being single.* New York: Peter Lang Pub.

Azrin, N. H., & Foxx, R. M. (1974). *Toilet training in less than a day.* New York: Simon & Schuster.

Bachman, J. G., O'Malley, P. M., & Johnston, J. (1978). *Adolescence to adulthood: Change and stability in the lives of young men.* Ann Arbor, MI: Institute for Social Research.

Baddeley, A. (1992). Working memory. *Science, 255*, 556–559.

Bahrick, H. P. (1984). Semantic memory content in permastore: Fifty years of memory for Spanish learned in school. *Journal of Experimental Psychology: General, 113*, 1–29.

Bahrick, H. P., & Hall, L. K. (1991). Lifetime maintenance of high school mathematics content. *Journal of Experimental Psychology: General, 120*, 20–33.

Bahrick, H. P., & Phelps, E. (1987). Retention of Spanish vocabulary over 8 years. *Journal of Experimental Psychology: Learning, Memory, & Cognition, 13*, 344–349.

Bailey, J. M., Pillard, R. C., Neale, M. C., & Agyei, Y. (1993). Heritable factors influence sexual orientation in women. *Archives of General Psychiatry, 50*, 217–223.

Baillargeon, R. (1987). Object permanence in 3 1/2- and 4 1/2-month-old infants. *Developmental Psychology, 23*, 655–664.

Bajwa, W. K., Asnis, G. M., Sanderson, W. C., Irfan, A., and van Praag, H. M. (1992). High cholesterol levels in patients with panic disorder. *American Journal of Psychiatry, 149*, 376–378.

Baker, S. W. (1980). Biological influences on human sex and gender. *Signs: Journal of Women in Culture and Society, 6*, 80–96.

Bales, J. (1986, November). Explaining sexuality? Consider the Sambia. *APA Monitor,* p. 18.

Bales, J. (1987, October). Northwest Airlines sets up walk-in counseling centers. *APA Monitor,* p. 26.

Bales, J. (1988, August). High court: Subjective tests can be validated. *APA Monitor,* p. 5.

Bales, R. F. (1970). *Personality and interpersonal behavior.* New York: Holt, Rinehart & Winston.

Ballenger, J. C. (1986). Biological aspects of panic disorder. *American Journal of Psychiatry, 143*, 516–518.

Balon, R., Jordan, M., Pohl, R., & Yeragani, V. K. (1989). Family history of anxiety disorders in control subjects with lactate-induced panic attacks. *American Journal of Psychiatry, 146*, 1304–1306.

Balster, R. L., & Chait, L. D. (1976). The behavioral pharmacology of phencyclidine. *Clinical Toxicology, 9*, 513–528.

Ban, T. A. (1978). The treatment of depressed geriatric patients. *American Journal of Psychotherapy, 32*, 93–104.

Bandura, A. (1962). Social learning through imitation. In M. R. Jones (Ed.), *Nebraska symposium on motivation: 1962* (pp. 211–269). Lincoln, Nebraska: Univ. of Nebraska Press.

Bandura, A. (1969). *Principles of behavior modification.* New York: Holt, Rinehart, & Winston.

Bandura, A. (1977). *Social learning theory.* Englewood Cliffs NJ: Prentice-Hall.

Bandura, A. (1978). The self system in reciprocal determinism. *American Psychologist, 33*, 344–358.

Bandura, A. (1982). Self-efficacy mechanism in human agency. *American Psychologist, 37*, 122–147.

Bandura, A. (1986). Fearful expectations and avoidant actions as coeffects of perceived self-inefficacy. *American Psychologist, 41*, 1389–1391.

Bandura, A., Ross, D., & Ross, S. A. (1963). A comparative test of the status envy, social power, and secondary reinforcement theories of identificatory learning. *Journal of Abnormal and Social Psychology, 67*, 527–534.

Bandura, A., Ross, D., & Ross, S. A. (1963). Imitation of file-mediated aggressive models. *Journal of Abnormal and Social Psychology, 66*, 3–11.

Barber, T. X. (1969). *Hypnosis: A scientific approach.* New York: Van Nostrand Reinhold.

Barglow, P., Vaughn, B. E., & Molitor, N. (1987). Effects of maternal absence due to employment on the quality of infant-mother attachment in a low-risk sample. *Child Development, 58*, 945–954.

Barinaga, M. (1990). Neuroscience models the brain. *Science, 247*, 524–526.

Barinaga, M. (1991). Monkey see, monkey do. *Science, 251*, 1025.

Barker, R. G. (1968). *Ecological psychology: Concepts and methods for studying the environment of human behavior.* Stanford, Calif.: Stanford Univ. Press.

Barlow, D. H., Blanchard, E. B., Vermilyea, J. A., Vermilyea, B. B., & DiNardo, P. A. (1986). Generalized anxiety and generalized anxiety disorder: Description and reconceptualization. *American Journal of Psychiatry, 143*, 40–44.

Barnes, D. M. (1986). Steroids may influence changes in mood. *Science, 232*, 1344–1345.

Barnes, D. M. (1987a). Neural models yield data on learning. *Science, 236*, 1628–1629.

Barnes, D. M. (1987b). Biological issues in schizophrenia. *Science, 235*, 430–433.

Baron, M., Gruen, R., Kane, J., & Asnis, L. (1985). Modern research criteria and the genetics of schizophrenia. *American Journal of Psychiatry, 142*, 697–701.

Baron, R. A., & Bell, P. A. (1975). Aggression and heat: Mediating effects of prior provocation and exposure to an aggressive model. *Journal of Personality & Social Psychology, 31*, 825–832.

Baron, R. A., & Ransberger, V. M. (1978). Ambient temperature and the occurrence of collective violence: The "long, hot summer" revisited. *Journal of Personality & Social Psychology, 36*, 351–360.

Barsky, A. J. (1993). How does hypochondriasis differ from normal concerns about health? *Harvard Mental Health Letter, 10*(2), 8.

Barsky, A. J., Frank, C. B., Cleary, P. D., Wyshak, G., & Klerman, G. L. (1991). The relation between hypochondriasis and age. *American Journal of Psychiatry, 148*, 923–928.

Barsky, A. J., & Klerman, G. L. (1985, December). Hypochondriasis. *Harvard Medical School Mental Health Letter,* pp. 4–6.

Barton, B. (1980). *Eye movements and advertising effectiveness.* Paper presented at the Annual Colloquium of European Economic Psychology, Leuven, Belgium.

Bartusiak, M. (1980), November). Beeper man. *Discover,* p. 57.

Baruch, G., Barnett, R., & Rivers, C. (1983). *Lifeprints.* New York: McGraw-Hill.

Baruch, G. K., & Barnett, R. C. (1986). Fathers' participation in family work and children's sex-role attitudes. *Child Development, 57*, 1210–1223.

Bashore, T. R., & Rapp, P. E. (1993). Are there alternatives to traditional polygraph procedures? *Psychological Bulletin, 113*, 3–22.

Bass, D., Wells, F., & Ridgeway, R. (1986). *Seven summits.* New York: Warner Books.

Bassuk, E. (1987, January). Mental health needs of homeless persons. *Harvard Medical School Mental Health Letter,* pp. 4–6.

Bassuk, E. L., & Gerson, S. (1978). Deinstitutionalization and mental health services. *Scientific American, 238*(2), 46–53.

Baumrind, D. (1967). Child care practices anteceding three patterns of preschool behavior. *Genetic Psychology Monographs, 75*, 43–88.

Baumrind, D. (1971). Current patterns of parental authority. *Developmental Psychology, 4*(1, pt. 2), 1–103.

Baumrind, D. (1980). New directions in socialization research. *American Psychologist, 35*, 639–652.

Baumrind, D. (1991). The influence of parenting style on adolescent competence and substance use. *Journal of Early Adolescence, 11*, 56–95.

Bavelas, A., Hastorf, A. H., Gross, A. E., & Kite, W. R. (1965). Experiments on the alteration of group structure. *Journal of Experimental Social Psychology, 1*, 55–70.

Baxter, L. R., Jr., Schwartz, J. M., Bergman, K. S., Szuba, M. P., Guze, B. H., Mazziotta, J. C., Alazraki, A., Selin, C. E., Ferng, H. K., & Munford, P. (1992). Caudate glucose metabolic rate changes with both drug and behavior therapy for obsessive-compulsive disorder. *Archives of General Psychiatry, 49*, 681–689.

Bayer, A. E. (1966). Birth order and college attendance. *Journal of Marriage and the Family, 28*, 480–484.

Bayley, N. (1969). *Manual for the Bayley Scales of Infant Development.* New York: Psychological Corporation.

Beach, B. H. (1980, September 8). Blood, sweat and fears. *Time,* p. 44.

Bear, M. F., Cooper, L. N., & Ebner, F. F. (1987). A physiological basis for a theory of synapse modification. *Science, 237*, 42–48.

Beauchamp, G. K., Yamazaki, K., & Boyse, E. A. (1985). The chemosensory recognition of genetic individuality. *Scientific American, 253*(1), 86–92.

Beck, A. T. (1991). Cognitive therapy: A 30-year retrospective. *American Psychologist, 46*, 368–375.

Beck, A. T., Sokol, L., Clark, D. A., Berchick, R., & Wright, F. (1992). A crossover study of focused cognitive therapy for panic disorder. *American Journal of Psychiatry, 149*, 778–783.

Becker, I. M., & Rosenfeld, J. G. (1976). Rational emotive therapy—A study of initial therapy sessions of Albert Ellis. *Journal of Clinical Psychology, 32*, 872–876.

Becker, W. C. (1960). The matching of behavior rating and questionnaire personality factors. *Psychological Bulletin, 57*, 201–212.

Beers, C. (1908). *A mind that found itself.* New York: Longmans, Green & Co.

Beilin, H. (1992). Piaget's enduring contribution to developmental psychology. *Developmental Psychology, 28*, 191–204.

Bekenstein, J. W., & Lothman, E. W. (1993). Dormancy of inhibitory interneurons in a model of temporal lobe epilepsy. *Science, 259*, 97–100.

Bell, A. P., Weinberg, M. S., & Hammersmith, S. K. (1981). *Sexual preference: Its development in men and women.* Bloomington, Ind.: Indiana University Press.

Bell, P. A. (1992). In defense of the negative affect escape model of heat and aggression. *Psychological Bulletin, 111*, 342–346.

Belmont, L., & Marolla, F. A. (1973). Birth order, family size, and intelligence. *Science, 182*, 1096–1101.

Belsky, J. (1986). Infant day care: A cause for concern. *Zero to Three, 7*(1), 1–7.

Belsky, J., & Most, R. K. (1981). From exploration to play: A cross-sectional study of infant free play behavior. *Developmental Psychology, 17,* 630–639.

Bem, D. J., & Allen, A. (1974). On predicting some of the people some of the time: The search for cross-situational consistencies in behavior. *Psychological Review, 81,* 506–520.

Bem, D. J., & Funder, D. C. (1978). Predicting more of the people more of the time: Assessing the personality of situations. *Psychological Review, 85,* 485–501.

Bem, S. L. (1981). Gender schema theory: A cognitive account of sex typing. *Psychological Review, 88,* 354–364.

Bem, S. L. (1989). Genital knowledge and gender constancy in preschool children. *Child Development, 60,* 648–662.

Benbow, C. P., & Stanley, J. C. (1981). Mathematical ability—is sex a factor? *Science, 212,* 118.

Benbow, C. P., & Stanley, J. C. (1983). Sex differences in mathematical reasoning ability: More facts. *Science, 222,* 1028–1031.

Bengtson, V. L., Cuellar, J. B., & Ragan, P. K. (1977). Stratum contrasts and similarities in attitudes toward death. *Journal of Gerontology, 32,* 76–88.

Bennett, W., & Gurin, J. (1982). *The dieter's dilemma.* New York: Basic Books.

Benson, H. (1975). *The relaxation response.* New York: Morrow.

Bentall, R. P. (1990). The illusion of reality: A review and integration of psychological research on hallucinations. *Psychological Bulletin, 107,* 82–95.

Berbaum, M. L., Markus, G. B., & Zajonc, R. B. (1982). A closer look at Galbraith's "closer look". *Developmental Psychology, 18,* 181–191.

Berbaum, M. L., & Moreland, R. L. (1985). Intellectual development within transracial adoptive families: Retesting the confluence model. *Child Development, 56,* 207–216.

Bergin, A. E. (1971). The evaluation of therapeutic outcomes. In A. E. Bergin & S. L. Garfield (Eds.), *Handbook of psychotherapy and behavior change: An empirical analysis.* New York: Wiley.

Berk, L. S. (1981, August 21). Personal communication.

Berko, J. (1958). The child's learning of English morphology. *Word, 14,* 150–177.

Berkowitz, L. (1965). The concept of aggressive drive: Some additional considerations. In L. Berkowitz (Ed.), *Advances in experimental social psychology* (Vol. 2). New York: Academic Press.

Berkowitz, L. (1983). Aversively stimulated aggression: Some parallels and differences in research with animals and humans. *American Psychologist, 38,* 1135–1144.

Berkowitz, L. (1990). On the formation and regulation of anger and aggression: A cognitive-neoassociationistic analysis. *American Psychologist, 45,* 494–503.

Berkowitz, L., Cochran, S. T., & Embree, M. C. (1981). Physical pain and the goal of aversively stimulated aggression. *Journal of Personality & Social Psychology, 40,* 687–700.

Berndt, T. J., Hawkins, J. A., & Hoyle, S. G. (1986). Changes in friendship during a school year: Effects on children's and adolescents' impressions of friendship and sharing with friends. *Child Development, 57,* 1284–1297.

Berndt, T. J., & Perry, T. B. (1986). Children's perceptions of friendships as supportive relationships. *Developmental Psychology, 22,* 640–648.

Berne, E. (1964). *Games people play.* New York: Grove Press.

Bernstein, R. L., & Gaw, A. C. (1990). Koro: Proposed classification for DSM-IV. *American Journal of Psychiatry, 147,* 1670–1674.

Berquier, A., & Ashton, R. (1992). Characteristics of the frequent nightmare sufferer. *Journal of Abnormal Psychology, 101,* 246–250.

Berreby, D. (1992, April). Kids, creoles, and the coconuts. *Discover,* pp. 44–53.

Berridge, K. C., & Fentress, J. C. (1985). Trigeminal-taste interaction in palatability processing. *Science, 228,* 747–750.

Berscheid, E. (1983). Emotion. In H. H. Kelley (Ed.), *Close relationships* (pp. 110–168). New York: W. H. Freeman.

Berscheid, E., & Walster, E. (1974). A little bit about love. In T. L. Huston (Ed.), *Foundations of interpersonal attraction.* New York: Academic Press.

Best, J. B. (1989). *Cognitive psychology* (2nd ed.). St. Paul: West Publishing Company.

Bettman, J. R. (1986). Consumer psychology. *Annual Review of Psychology, 37,* 257–289.

Biddle, W. (1986, March). The deception of detection. *Discover,* pp. 24–33.

Biederman, G. B. (1993). Social learning in invertebrates. *Science, 259,* 1627–1628.

Birch, H. G. (1945). The role of motivational factors in insightful problem-solving. *Journal of Comparative Psychology, 38,* 295–317.

Birnholz, J. C., & Benacerraf, B. R. (1983). The development of human fetal hearing. *Science, 222,* 516–518.

Birns, B., & Sternglanz, S. H. (1983). Sex-role socialization: Looking back and looking ahead. In M. B. Liss (Ed.), *Social and cognitive skills: Sex roles and children's play* (pp. 235–251). New York: Academic Press.

Bitterman, M. E. (1969). Thorndike and the problem of animal intelligence. *American Psychologist, 24,* 444–453.

Blacker, D., & Tsuang, M. T. (1992). Contested boundaries of bipolar disorder and the limits of categorical diagnosis in psychiatry. *American Journal of Psychiatry, 149,* 1473–1483.

Blake, J. (1989). Number of siblings and educational attainment. *Science, 245,* 32–36.

Blazer, D., Hughes, D., & George, L. K. (1987). Stressful life events and the onset of a generalized anxiety syndrome. *American Journal of Psychiatry, 144,* 1178–1183.

Bleda, P. R., & Castore, C. H. (1973). Social comparison, attraction, and choice of a comparison other. *Memory and Cognition, 1,* 420–424.

Block, J. (1961). *The Q-sort method in personality assessment and psychiatric research.* Springfield, Ill.: Charles C. Thomas.

Block, J. (1982). Assimilation accommodation, and the dynamics of personality development. *Child Development, 53,* 281–295.

Bloom, B. S. (1964). *Stability and change in human characteristics.* New York: Wiley.

Bloom, L. (1983). Tensions in psycholinguistics. *Science, 220,* 843–845.

Bloom, L., & Capatides, J. B. (1987). Expression of affect and the emergence of language. *Child Development, 58,* 1513–1522.

Blum, K., Briggs, A. H., Feinglass, S. J., Domey, R., & Wallace, J. E. (1977). Effects of Delta9 tetrahydrocannabinol on amphetamine-aggregate toxicity in mice. *Current Therapeutic Research, 21,* 241–244.

Blumenthal, A. L. (1980). Wilhelm Wundt and early American psychology: A class of cultures. In R. W. Reiber & K. Salzinger (Eds.), *Psychology: Theoretical-historical perspectives* (pp. 25–42). New York: Academic Press.

Bock, K. (1990). Structure in language: Creating form in talk. *American Psychologist, 45,* 1221–1236.

Boggiano, A. K., Klinger, C. A., & Main, D. S. (1986). Enhancing interest in peer interaction: A developmental analysis. *Child Development, 57,* 852–861.

Bolles, R. C., & Fanselow, M. S. (1982). Endorphins and behavior. *Annual Review of Psychology, 33,* 87–101.

Bolter, A., Heminger, A., Martin, G., & Fry, M. (1976). Outpatient clinical experience in a community drug abuse program with phencyclidine abuse. *Clinical Toxicology, 9,* 593–600.

Boon, S., & Draijer, N. (1993). Multiple personality disorder in The Netherlands: A clinical investigation of 71 patients. *American Journal of Psychiatry, 150,* 489–494.

Booth, D. A. (1977). Satiety and appetite are conditioned reactions. *Psychosomatic Medicine, 39,* 76–81.

Borbely, A. (1986). *Secrets of sleep.* New York: Basic Books.

Borg, E., & Counter, S. A. (1989). The middle-ear muscles. *Scientific American, 261*(2), 74–80.

Bornstein, R. F. (1989). Exposure and affect: Overview and meta-analysis of research, 1968–1987. *Psychological Bulletin, 106,* 265–289.

Bouchard, T. J., Jr., Lykken, D. T., McGue, M., Segal, N. L., & Tellegen, A. (1990). Sources of human psychological differences: The Minnesota study of twins reared apart. *Science, 250,* 223–228.

Bouchard, T. J., Jr., & McGue, M. (1981). Familial studies of intelligence: A review. *Science, 212,* 1055–1059.

Boucher, J. D. (1973). *Facial behavior and the perception of emotion: Studies of Malays and Temuan Orang Asli.* Paper presented at the Conference of Psychology and Related Disciplines, Kuala Lumpur.

Bower, B. (1984, October 6). Not popular by reason of insanity. *Science News,* pp. 218–219.

Bower, B. (1987, February 21). Deadly aftermath for Vietnam veterans. *Science News,* p. 117.

Bower, B. (1988, August 27). Retardation: The eyes have it. *Science News,* p. 140.

Bower, B. (1989, August 19). Teenagers reap broad benefits from "authoritative" parents. *Science News,* pp. 117–118.

Bower, B. (1992, July 4). Schizophrenia: Encouraging outlook emerges. *Science News,* p. 6.

Bower, G. H., Karlin, M. B., & Dueck, A. (1975). Comprehension and memory for pictures. *Memory and Cognition, 3,* 216–220.

Bowers, M. (1965). The onset of psychosis—a diary account. *Psychiatry, 28,* 346–358.

Bowlby, J. (1958). The nature of the child's tie to his mother. *International Journal of Psycho-Analysis, 39,* 350–373.

Bowlby, J. (1982a). Attachment and loss: Retrospect and prospect. *American Journal of Orthopsychiatry, 52,* 664–678.

Bowlby, J. (1982b). *Attachment and loss: Vol. 1 Attachment* (2nd ed.). New York: Basic Books.

Boxer, A. M., Gershenson, H. P., & Offer, D. (1984). Historical time and social change in adolescent experience. *New Directions for Mental Health Services,* No. 22, 83–95.

Boyd, J. H. (1986). Use of mental health services for the treatment of panic disorder. *American Journal of Psychiatry, 143,* 1569–1574.

Bozarth, M. A., & Wise, R. A. (1984). Anatomically distinct opiate receptor fields mediate reward and physical dependence. *Science, 224,* 516–517.

Bracha, H. S., Torrey, E. F., Gottesman, I. I., Bigelow, L. B., & Cunniff, C. (1992).

Second-trimester markers of fetal size in schizophrenia: A study of monozygotic twins. *American Journal of Psychiatry, 149,* 1355–1361.

Brackbill, Y. (1958). Extinction of the smiling response in infants as a function of reinforcement schedule. *Child Development, 29,* 115–124.

Braine, M. D. S. (1963). The ontogeny of English phrase structure: The first phase. *Language, 39*(1), 1–13.

Branch, L. G. (1977). *Understanding the health and social service needs of people over age 65.* Boston: Center for Survey Research of the University of Massachusetts and the Joint Center for Urban Studies of MIT and Harvard University.

Brand, C. (1987). Intelligence testing: Bryter still and bryter? *Nature, 328,* 110.

Braver, S. L., Linder, D. E., Corwin, T. T., & Cialdini, R. B. (1977). Some conditions that affect admissions of attitude change. *Journal of Experimental Social Psychology, 13,* 565–576.

Bray, G. A., & York, D. A. (1971). Genetically transmitted obesity in rodents. *Physiological Reviews, 51,* 598–646.

Bray, G. A., & York, D. A. (1971). Genetically transmitted obesity in rodents. *Physiological Reviews, 51,* 598–646.

Brazelton, T. B., Koslowski, B., & Main, H. (1974). The origins of reciprocity: The early infant-mother interaction. In M. Lewis, & L. A. Rosenblum (Eds.) *The effect of the infant on its caregiver* (pp. 49–76). New York: Wiley-Interscience.

Brecher, E. M. (1976). History of human sexual research and study. In B. J. Sadock, H. I. Kaplan, & A. M. Freedman, *The sexual experience* (pp. 71–78). Baltimore MD: Williams & Wilkins.

Breier, A., Albus, M., Pickar, D., Zahn, T. P., Wolkowitz, O. M., & Paul, S. M. (1987). Controllable and uncontrollable stress in humans: Alterations in mood and neuroendocrine and psychophysiolgical function. *American Journal of Psychiatry, 144,* 1419–1425.

Brenner, D., & Howard K. (1976). Clinical judgment as a function of experience and information. *Journal of Clinical Psychology, 32,* 721–728.

Breslau, N., & Davis, G. C. (1987). Posttraumatic stress disorder: the etiologic specificity of wartime stressors. *American Journal of Psychiatry, 144,* 578–583.

Breslau, N., Davis, G. C., Andreski, P., & Peterson, E. (1991). Traumatic events and posttraumatic stress disorder in an urban population of young adults. *Archives of General Psychiatry, 48,* 216–222.

Breslow, M. F., Fankhauser, M. P., Potter, R. L., Meredith, K. E., Misiaszek, J., & Hope, D. G., Jr. (1989). Role of gamma-aminobutyric acid in antipanic drug efficacy. *American Journal of Psychiatry, 146,* 353–356.

Brett, A. S., Phillips, M., & Beary, J. F. (1986). Predictive power of the polygraph: Can the "lie detector" really detect lies? *Lancet, I*(8480), 544–547.

Brett, J. M., Goldberg, S. B., & Ury, W. L. (1990). Designing systems for resolving disputes in organizations. *American Psychologist, 45,* 162–170.

Brobeck, J. R., Tepperman, J., & Long, C. N. H. (1943). Experimental hypothalamic hyperphagia in the albino rat. *Yale Journal of Biology and Medicine, 15,* 831–853.

Brock, T. C. (1965). Communicator-recipient similarity and decision change. *Journal of Personality & Social Psychology, 1,* 650–654.

Bronson, W. C. (1985). Growth in the organization of behavior over the second year of life. *Developmental Psychology, 21,* 108–117.

Brooks, J. (1985). Polygraph testing. *American Psychologist, 40,* 348–354.

Brown, A. S. (1991). A review of the tip-of-the-tongue experience. *Psychological Bulletin, 109,* 204–223.

Brown, B. B. (1980). *Supermind: The ultimate energy.* New York: Harper & Row.

Brown, B. B., Clasen, D. R., & Eicher, S. A. (1986). Perceptions of peer pressure, peer conformity dispositions, and self-reported behavior among adolescents. *Developmental Psychology, 22,* 521–530.

Brown, B. B., Eicher, S. A., & Petrie, S. (1986). The importance of peer group ("crowd") affiliation in adolescence. *Journal of Adolescence, 9,* 73–96.

Brown, B. B., Lohr, M. J., & McClenahan, E. L. (1986). Early adolescents' perceptions of peer pressure. *Journal of Early Adolescence, 6,* 139–154.

Brown, J. B. (1984). Examination of grammatical morphemes in the language of hard-of-hearing children. *Volta Review, 86,* 229–238.

Brown, M. C. (1982). Administrative succession and organizational performance: The succession effect. *Administrative Science Quarterly, 27,* 1–16.

Brown, R. J., & Donderi, D. C. (1986). Dream content and self-reported well-being among recurrent dreamers, past-recurrent dreamers, and nonrecurrent dreamers. *Journal of Personality & Social Psychology, 50,* 612–623.

Browne, M. A., & Mahoney, M. J. (1984). Sport psychology. *Annual Review of Psychology, 35,* 605–625.

Brownlow, S., & Zebrowitz, L. A. (1990). Facial appearance, gender, and credibility in television commercials. *Journal of Nonverbal Behavior, 2,* 51–60.

Brubaker, T. H. (1985). *Later life families.* Beverly Hills, CA: Sage Publications.

Brunner, H. G., Nelen, M. R., van Zandvoort, P., Abeling, N. G., van Gennip, A. H., Wolters, E. C., Kuiper, M. A., Ropers, H. H., & van Oost, B. A. (1992). X-linked borderline mental retardation with prominent behavioral disturbance: Phe-

notype, genetic localization, and evidence for disturbed monoamine metabolism. *American Journal of Human Genetics, 52,* 1032–1039.

Buck, L., & Axel, R. (1991). A novel multigene family may encode odorant receptors: A molecular basis for odor recognition. *Cell, 65,* 175–187.

Buckhout, R. (1974). Eyewitness testimony. *Scientific American, 231*(6), 23–31.

Buhrmester, D., & Furman, W. (1987). The development of companionship and intimacy. *Child Development, 58,* 1101–1113.

Bulcroft, K., & O'Conner-Roden, M. (1986, June). Never too late. *Psychology Today,* pp. 66–69.

Burchinal, M., Lee, M., & Ramey, C. (1989). Type of day-care and preschool intellectual development in disadvantaged children. *Child Development, 60,* 128–137.

Burns, T. L., Moll, P. P., & Lauer, R. M. (1989). The relation between ponderosity and coronary risk factors in children and their relatives. *American Journal of Epidemiology, 129,* 973–987.

Burton, L. M. (1985). *Early and on time grandmotherhood in multigenerational black families.* Unpublished doctoral dissertation, University of Southern California, Los Angeles.

Buss, A. H. (1989). Personality as traits. *American Psychologist, 44,* 1378–1388.

Butler, R. N. (1963). The life review: An interpretation of reminiscence in the aged. *Psychiatry, 26,* 65–76.

Butler, R. N. (1975). Psychiatry and the elderly: An overview. *American Journal of Psychiatry, 132,* 893–900.

Buxton, C. E. (1985). *Points of view in the modern history of psychology.* Orlando, FL: Academic Press.

Byrne, D., & Clore, G. L. (1970). A reinforcement model of evaluative responses. *Personality: An International Journal, 1,* 103–128.

Byrne, D., Ervin, C. R., & Lamberth, J. (1970). Continuity between the experimental study of attraction and real-life computer dating. *Journal of Personality & Social Psychology, 16,* 157–165.

Cadoret, R. J., Cain, C. A., & Grove, W. M. (1980). Development of alcoholism in adoptees raised apart from alcoholic biologic relatives. *Archives of General Psychiatry, 37,* 561–563.

Cahan, S., & Cohen, N. (1989). Age versus schooling effects on intelligence development. *Child Development, 60,* 1239–1249.

Calabrese, J. R., Kling, M. A., & Gold, P. W. (1987). Alterations in immunocompetence during stress, bereavement, and depression: Focus on neuroendocrine regulation. *American Journal of Psychiatry, 144,* 1123–1134.

Caldera, Y. M., Huston, A. C., & O'Brien, M. (1989). Social interactions and play patterns of parents and toddlers with feminine, masculine, and neutral toys. *Child Development, 60,* 70–76.

Calvert-Boyanowsky, J., Boyanowsky, E. O., Atkinson, M., Gaduto, D., & Reeves, J. (1976). Patterns of passion: Temperature and human emotion. In D. Krebs (Ed.), *Readings in social psychology: Contemporary perspectives* (pp. 96–99). New York: Harper & Row.

Campbell, T. (1982). *Formal cues and content difficulty as determinants of children's cognitive processing of televised educational messages.* Unpublished doctoral dissertation, University of Kansas.

Campos, J. J., Barrett, K. G., Lamb, M. E., Stenberg, C., & Goldsmith, H. H. (1983). Socioemotional development. In M. M. Haith & J. J. Campos (Eds.), *Infancy and developmental psychology.* In P. H. Mussen (Gen. Ed.), *Handbook of child psychology.* New York: Wiley.

Campos, J. J., Hiatt, S., Ramsay, D., Henderson, C., & Svejda, M. (1978). The emergence of fear on the visual cliff. In M. Lewis & L. A. Rosenblum (Eds.), *The development of affect* (pp. 149–182). New York: Plenum Press.

Camras, L. A. (1988, April). Darwin revisited. An infant's first emotional facial expressions. In H. Oster (Chair), *Emotional expressions in infants: New perspectives on an old controversy.* International Conference on Infant Studies, Washington, DC.

Cannon, W. B. (1927). The James-Lange theory of emotions: A critical examination and an alternative theory. *American Journal of Psychology, 39,* 106–124.

Cantin, M., & Genest, J. (1986). The heart as an endocrine gland. *Scientific American, 254*(2), 76–81.

Caplan, P. J., MacPherson, G. M., & Tobin, P. (1985). Do sex-related differences in spatial abilities exist? A multilevel critique with new data. *American Psychologist, 40,* 786–799.

Carey, G., Goldsmith, H. H., Tellegen, A., & Gottesman, I. I. (1978). Genetics and personality inventories: The limits of replication with twin data. *Behavior Genetics, 8,* 299–313.

Carli, L. L. (1990). Gender, language, and influence. *Journal of Personality & Social Psychology, 59,* 941–951.

Carlson, N. R. (1977). *Physiology of behavior.* Boston: Allyn and Bacon.

Carpenter, W. T., & Heinrichs, D. W. (1983). Early intervention, time-limited, targeted pharmacotherapy of schizophrenia. *Schizophrenia Bulletin*, 9(4), 533–542.

Carson, R. C. (1989). Personality. *Annual Review of Psychology*, 40, 227–248.

Carter, H., & Glick, P. C. (1976). *Marriage and divorce*. Cambridge, Mass.: Harvard University Press.

Carver, C. S., DeGregorio, E., & Gillis, R. (1980). Ego-defensive bias in attribution among two categories of observers. *Personality and Social Psychology Bulletin*, 6, 44–50.

Case, R. B., Heller, S. S., Case, N. B., & Moss, A. J. (1985). Type A behavior and survival after acute myocardial infarction. *New England Journal of Medicine*, 312, 737–741.

Casto, G., & Mastropieri, M. A. (1986). The efficacy of early intervention programs: A meta-analysis. *Exceptional Children*, 52, 417–424.

Castro, F. G., & Magana, D. (1988). A course in health promotion in ethnic minority populations. In P. Bronstein & K. Quina (Eds.), *Teaching a psychology of people* (pp. 94–101). Washington, DC: American Psychological Association.

Catania, J. A., Coates, T. J., Stall, R., Turner, H., Peterson, J., Hearst, N., Dolcini, M. M., Hudes, E., Gagnon, J., Wiley, J., & Groves, R. (1992). Prevalence of AIDS-related risk factors and condom use in the United States. *Science*, 258, 1101–1106.

Cattell, P. (1966). *The measurement of intelligence of infants and young children*. New York: Psychological Corporation.

Cattell, R. B. (1950). *Personality: A systematic theoretical and factual study*. New York: McGraw-Hill.

Cattell, R. B. (1973, July). Personality pinned down. *Psychology Today*, pp. 40–46.

Cattell, R. B., Saunders, D. R., & Stice, G. F. (1950). *The 16 personality factor questionnaire*. Champaign, Illinois: Institute for Personality and Ability Testing.

Ceci, S. J. (1991). How much does schooling influence general intelligence and its cognitive components? A reassessment of the evidence. *Developmental Psychology*, 27, 703–722.

Centers for Disease Control, The. (1988). Health status of Vietnam veterans. II. Physical health. *Journal of the American Medical Association*, 259, 2708–2714.

Centers for Disease Control, The. (1993a). Quarterly table reporting alcohol involvement in fatal motor-vehicle crashes. *Morbidity and Mortality Weekly Report*, 42(11), 215.

Centers for Disease Control, The. (1993b). Smoking cessation during previous year among adults—United States, 1990 and 1991. *Morbidity and Mortality Weekly Report*, 42(26), 504–507.

Centers for Disease Control, The. (1993c). Years of potential life lost before age 65—United States, 1990 and 1991. *Morbidity and Mortality Weekly Report*, 42(13), 251–253.

Chaiken, S. (1980). Heuristic versus systematic information processing and the use of source versus message cues in persuasion. *Journal of Personality & Social Psychology*, 39, 752–766.

Chance, P. (1986, September). The divided self. *Psychology Today*, p. 72.

Charlesworth, W. R., & Kreutzer, M. A. (1973). Facial expression of infants and children. In P. Ekman (Ed.), *Darwin and facial expression*. New York: Academic Press.

Charney, D. S., Heninger, G. R., & Jatlow, P. I. (1985). Increased anxiogenic effects of caffeine in panic disorders. *Archives of General Psychiatry*, 42, 233–243.

Chase, M. H., & Morales, F. R. (1983). Subthreshold excitatory activity and motoneuron discharge during REM periods of active sleep. *Science*, 221, 1195–1198.

Chase, M. H., & Morales, F. R. (1990). The atonia and myoclonia of active (REM) sleep. *Annual Review of Psychology*, 41, 557–584.

Cherry, F., & Byrne, D. (1976). Authoritarianism. In T. Blass (Ed.), *Personality variables in social behavior*. Hillsdale, NJ: Erlbaum.

Cherry, F., Byrne, D., & Mitchell, H. E. (1976). Clogs in the bogus pipeline: Demand characteristics and social desirability. *Journal of Research in Personality*, 10, 69–75.

Cheyne, J. A., & Rubin, K. H. (1983). Playful precursors of problem solving in preschoolers. *Developmental Psychology*, 19, 577–584.

Childers, J. S., Durham;, T. W., Bolen, L. M., & Taylor, L. H. (1985). A predictive validity study of the Kaufman Assessment Battery for Children with the California Achievment Test. *Psychology in the Schools*, 22, 29–33.

Chinen, A. B. Fairy tales and psychological development in late life: A cross-cultural hermeneutic study. *Gerontologist*, 27, 340–346.

Chodorow, N. (1974). Family structure and feminine personality. In M. Z. Rosaldo & L. Lamphere (Eds.), *Women, culture, and society* (pp. 43–66). Stanford, CA: Stanford University Press.

Chodorow, N. (1978). *The reproduction of mothering*. Berkeley: University of California Press.

Chomsky, N. (1957). *Syntactic structures*. The Hague: Mouton.

Chorover, S. L. (1979). *From genesis to genocide: The meaning of human nature and the power of behavior control*. Cambridge, Mass.: MIT Press.

Chouinard, G., Labonte, A., Fontaine, R., & Annable, L. (1983). New concepts in

benzodiazepine therapy: Rebound anxiety and new indications for the more potent benzodiazepines. *Progress in Neuro-psychopharmacology and Biological Psychiatry*, 7, 669–673.

Chumlea, W. M. (1982). Physical growth in adolescence. In B. B. Wolman (Ed.), *Handbook of developmental psychology* (pp. 471–485). Englewood Cliffs NJ: Prentice-Hall.

Churchland, P. M., & Churchland, P. S. (1990). Could a machine think? *Scientific American*, 262(1), 32–37.

Cialdini, R. B., Levy, A., Herman, C. P., Kozlowski, L. T., & Petty, R. E. (1976). Elastic shifts of opinion: Determinants of direction and durability. *Journal of Personality & Social Psychology*, 34, 663–672.

Cialdini, R. B., Petty, R. E., & Cacioppo, J. T. (1981). Attitude and attitude change. *Annual Review of Psychology*, 32, 357–404.

Cialdini, R. B., & Schroeder, D. A. (1976). Increasing compliance by legitimizing paltry contributions: When even a penny helps. *Journal of Personality & Social Psychology*, 34, 599–604.

Cicirelli, V. G. (1982). Sibling influence throughout the lifespan. In M. E. Lamb & B. Sutton-Smith (Eds.), *Sibling relationships: Their nature and significance across the lifespan* (pp. 267–284). Hillsdale, NJ: Erlbaum.

Cimmerman, A. (1981). The Fay case. *Criminal Defense*, 8, 7.

Clark, K. B., & Clark, M. P. (1947). Racial identification and preference in Negro children. In T. M. Newcomb & E. J. Hartley (Eds.), *Readings in social psychology*. New York: Holt.

Clausen, J. A. (1981). Men's occupational careers in the middle years. In D. H. Eichorn, J. A. Clausen, N. Haan, M. P. Honzik, & P. Mussen (Eds.), *Present and past in middle life* (pp. 321–351). New York: Academic Press.

Clayton, P. J., Grove, W. M., Coryell, W., Keller, M., Hirschfeld, R., & Fawcett, J. (1991). Follow-up and family study of anxious depression. *American Journal of Psychiatry*, 148, 1512–1517.

Clifton, R. K., Gwiazda, J., Bauer, J. A., Clarkson, M. G., & Held, R. M. (1988). Growth in head size during infancy: Implications for sound localization. *Developmental Psychology*, 24, 477–483.

Cloninger, C. R., Martin, R. L., Guze, S. B., & Clayton, P. J. (1986). A prospective follow-up and family study of somatization in men and women. *American Journal of Psychiatry*, 143, 873–878.

Clore, G. L., & Byrne, D. (1974). A reinforcement-affect model of attraction. In T. L. Huston (Ed.), *Foundations of interpersonal attraction*. New York: Academic Press.

Coffey, C. E., Figiel, G. S., Djang, W. T., Sullivan, D. C., Herfkens, R. J., & Weiner, R. D. (1988). Effects of ECT on brain structure: A pilot prospective magnetic resonance imaging study. *American Journal of Psychiatry*, 145, 701–706.

Cohen, J. B., & Chakravarti, D. (1990). Consumer psychology. *Annual Review of Psychology*, 41, 243–288.

Cohen, J. Z., Coburn, K. L., & Pearlman, J. C. (1980). *Hitting our stride: Good news about women in their middle years*. New York: Delacorte Press.

Cohen, N. J., McCloskey, M., & Wible, C. G. (1988). There is still no case for a flashbulb-memory mechanism: Reply to Schmidt and Bohannon. *Journal of Experimental Psychology: General*, 117, 336–338.

Cohen, S., Lichtenstein, E., Prochaska, J. O., Rossi, J. S., Gritz, E. R., Carr, C. R., Orleans, C. T., Schoenbach, V. J., Biener, L., Abrams, D., DiClemente, C., Curry, S., Marlatt, G. A., Cummings, K. M., Emont, S. L., Giovino, G., & Ossip-Klein, D. (1989). Debunking myths about self-quitting: Evidence from 10 prospective studies of persons who attempt to quit smoking by themselves. *American Psychologist*, 44, 1355–1365.

Cohen, S., Tyrrell, D. A., & Smith, A. P. (1991). Psychological stress and susceptibility to the common cold. *New England Journal of Medicine*, 325, 606–612.

Colby, A., Kohlberg, L., Gibbs, J., & Lieberman, M. (1983). A longitudinal study of moral judgment. Monographs of the Society for Research in *Child Development*, 48(1–2, Serial No. 200).

Cole, M. A. (1978–79). Sex and marital status differences in death anxiety. *Omega*, 9, 139–147.

Cole, S. (1979). Age and scientific performance. *American Journal of Sociology*, 84, 958–977.

Coleman, J. S., Campbell, E. Q., Hobson, C. J., McPartland, J., Mood, A. M., Weinfeld, F. D., & York, R. L. (1966). *Equality of educational opportunity*. Report from Office of Education. Washington, DC: U.S. Govt Printing Office.

Coleman, R. M. (1986). *Wide awake at 3:00 a.m.: By choice or by chance?* New York: W. H. Freeman.

Colligan, R. C., Osborne, D., Swenson, W. M., & Offord, K. P. (1983). *The MMPI: A contemporary normative study*. New York: Praeger.

Collins, W. A. (1984). Introduction. In W. A. Collins (Ed.), *Development during middle childhood: The years from six to twelve* (pp. 1–23). Washington, DC: National Academy Press.

Comfort, A. (1976). *A good age*. New York: Crown.

Commons, M. L., Richards, F. A., & Kuhn, D. (1982). Systematic and metasystematic reasoning: A case for levels of reasoning beyond Piaget's stage of formal operations. *Child Development, 53,* 1058–1069.

Condry, J., & Condry, S. (1977). Sex differences: A study of the eye of the beholder. *Annual Progress in Child Psychiatry and Child Development, 1977,* 289–301.

Coplan, J. D., Sharma, T., Rosenblum, L. A., Friedman, S., Bassoff, T. B., Barbour, R. L., & Gorman, J. M. (1992). Effects of sodium lactate infusion on cisternal lactate and carbon dioxide levels in nonhuman primates. *American Journal of Psychiatry, 149,* 1369–1373.

Cordes, C. (1985, September). Chemical cruise steers emotions. *APA Monitor,* p. 18.

Corina, D. P., Vaid, J., & Bellugi, U. (1992). The linguistic basis of left hemisphere specialization. *Science, 255,* 1258–1260.

Cornell-Bell, A. H., Finkbeiner, S. M., Cooper, M. S., & Smith, S. J. (1990). Glutamate induces calcium waves in cultured astrocytes: Long-range glial signaling. *Science, 247,* 470–473.

Coryell, W., Endicott, J., & Winokur, G. (1992). Anxiety syndromes as epiphenomena of primary major depression: Outcome and familial psychopathology. *American Journal of Psychiatry, 149,* 100–107.

Coryell, W., Endicott, J., Keller, M., Andreasen, N., Grove, W., Hirschfeld, R. M. A., & Scheftner, W. (1989). Bipolar affective disorder and high achievement: A familial association. *American Journal of Psychiatry, 146,* 983–988.

Coryell, W., Scheftner, W., Keller, M., Endicott, J., Maser, J., & Klerman, G. L. (1993). The enduring psychosocial consequences of mania and depression. *American Journal of Psychiatry, 150,* 720–727.

Costa, P. T., Jr., & McCrae, R. R. (1980). Still stable after all these years: Personality as a key to some issues in adulthood and old age. In P. B. Baltes, & O. G. Brim (Eds.), *Life-span development and behavior* (Vol. 3, pp. 65–102). New York: Academic Press.

Costello, C. G. (1976). Electroconvulsive therapy: Is further investigation necessary? *Canadian Psychiatric Association Journal, 21,* 61–67.

Cowen, R. (1990, April 14). Cocaine and the nervous system. *Science News,* p. 238.

Cowley, M. (1980). *The view from 80.* New York: The Viking Press.

Crash trauma. (1979, January 8). *Time,* p. 61.

Craske, B. (1977). Perception of impossible limb positions induced by tendon vibration. *Science, 196,* 71–73.

Cravens, H. (1992). A scientific project locked in time: The Terman genetic studies of genius, 1920s-1950s. *American Psychologist, 47,* 183–189.

Crawford, M. H. (1989). How color affects people and work. *Science, 246,* 761.

Crick, F., & Mitchison, G. (1983). The function of dream sleep. *Nature, 304,* 111–114.

Critchlow, B. (1986). The powers of John Barleycorn: Beliefs about the effects of alcohol on social behavior. *American Psychologist, 41,* 751–764.

Crits-Cristoph, P. (1992). The efficacy of brief dynamic psychotherapy: A meta-analysis. *American Journal of Psychiatry, 149,* 151–158.

Cronbach, L. J. (1970). *Essentials of psychological testing.* New York: Harper.

Cronbach, L. J. (1975). Five decades of public controversy over mental testing. *American Psychologist, 30,* 1–14.

Crusco, A. H., & Wetzel, C. G. (1984). The Midas Touch: The effects of interpersonal touch on restaurant tipping. Social *Psychological Bulletin, 10,* 512–517.

Culliton, B. J. (1985). APA issues warning on antipsychotic drugs. *Science, 229,* 1248.

Culliton, B. J. (1987). Take two pets and call me in the morning. *Science, 237,* 1560–1561.

Culotta, E., & Koshland, D. E., Jr. (1992). NO news is good news. *Science, 258,* 1862–1864.

Cummings, L. L. (1982). Organizational behavior. *Annual Review of Psychology, 33,* 541–579.

Cummins, R. C. (1971). Relationship of initiating structure and job performance as moderated by consideration. *Journal of Applied Psychology, 55,* 489–490.

Curcio, C. A., Sloan, K. R., Jr., Packer, O., Hendrickson, A. E., & Kalina, R. E. (1987). Distribution of cones in human and monkey retina: Individual variability and radial asymmetry. *Science, 236,* 579–582.

Curran, J. P., & Lippold, S. (1975). The effects of physical attractiveness and attitude similarity on attraction in dating dyads. *Journal of Personality, 43,* 528–539.

Cusack, J. R. (1993). The wounds of war. *American Journal of Psychiatry, 150,* 997–999.

Czeisler, C. A., Allan, J. S., Strogatz, S. H., Ronda, J. M., Sanchez, R., Rios, C. D., Freitag, W. O., Richardson, G. S., & Kronauer, R. E. (1986). Bright light resets the human circadian pacemaker independent of the timing of the sleep-wake cycle. *Science, 233,* 667–671.

Czeisler, C. A., Kronauer, R. E., Allan, J. S., Duffy, J. F., Jewett, M. E., Brown, E. N., & Ronda, J. M. (1989). Bright light induction of strong (type o) resetting of the human circadian pacemaker. *Science, 244,* 1328–1333.

Czeisler, C. A., Moore-Ede, M. C., & Coleman, R. M. (1982). Rotating shift work schedules that disrupt sleep are improved by applying circadian principles. *Science, 217,* 460–463.

Dajer, T. (1991, November). The lost 24 hours. *Discover,* pp. 80–82.

Damasio, A. R., & Damasio, H. (1992). Brain and language. *Scientific American, 267*(3), 89–95.

Dannemiller, J. L., & Stephens, B. R. (1988). A critical test of infant pattern preference models. *Child Development, 59,* 210–216.

Danziger, C. (1978). *Unmarried heterosexual cohabitation.* San Francisco: R & E Research Associates.

Darwin C. (1967). *The expression of the emotions in man and animals.* Chicago: Univ. of Chicago Press. (Original work published 1872).

Davis, E. A. (1937). *The development of linguistic skills in twins, single twins with siblings, and only children from age 5 to 10 years.* Minneapolis: University of Minnesota Press, Institute of Child Welfare Series, No. 14.

Davis, K. L., Kahn, R. S., Ko, G., & Davidson, M. (1991). Dopamine in schizophrenia: A review and reconceptualization. *American Journal of Psychiatry, 148,* 1474–1486.

Davis, R., & Davis, J. (1985). *TV's image of the elderly.* Lexington, MA: Lexington Books.

Davison, G. C., & Neale, J. M. (1978). *Abnormal psychology* (2nd ed.). New York: Wiley.

Day, G. S. (1976). Assessing the effects of information disclosure requirements. *Journal of Marketing, 40,* 42–52.

de Vries, M. W. (1984). Temperament and infant mortality among the Masai of East Africa. *The American Journal of Psychiatry, 141,* 1189–1194.

DeAngelis, T. (1987, August). Short-term therapy is "magical" choice for many patients. *APA Monitor,* p. 34.

DeAngelis, T. (1990, August). Cognitive dissonance theory alive and well. *APA Monitor,* p. 10.

DeAngelis, T. (1992, October). Not just a good theory: Transference is proven. *APA Monitor,* p. 56.

DeCasper, A. J., & Fifer, W. P. (1980). Of human bonding: Newborns prefer their mothers' voices. *Science, 208,* 1174–1176.

deCharms, R., & Muir, M. S. (1978). Motivation: Social approaches. *Annual Review of Psychology, 29,* 91–113.

Deci, E. L., & Ryan, R. (1980). The empirical exploration of intrinsic motivational processes. *Advances in Experimental Social Psychology, 13,* 39–80.

Dennis, W. (1966). Creative production between the ages of 20 and 80 years. *Journal of Gerontology, 21,* 1–8.

DePiano, F. A., & Salzberg, H. C. (1979). Clinical applications of hypnosis to three psychosomatic disorders. *Psychological Bulletin, 86,* 1223–1235.

Deregowski, J. B. (1972). Pictorial perception and culture. *Scientific American, 227*(5), 82–88.

Dermer, M, & Thiel, D. L. (1975). When beauty may fail. *Journal of Personality & Social Psychology, 31,* 1168–1176.

Derogatis, L. R., Yevzeroff, H., & Wittelsberger, B. (1975). Social class, psychological disorder, and the nature of the psychopathologic indicator. *Journal of Consulting & Clinical Psychology, 43,* 183–191.

Deutsch, M., & Krauss, R. M. (1960). The effect of threat upon interpersonal bargaining. *Journal of Abnormal and Social Psychology, 61,* 181–189.

Devanand, D. P., Verma, A. K., Tirumalasetti, F., & Sackeim, H. A. (1991). Absence of cognitive impairment after more than 100 lifetime ECT treatments. *American Journal of Psychiatry, 148,* 929–932.

Devane, W. A., Hanus, L., Breuer, A., Pertwee, R. G., Stevenson, L. A., Griffin, G., Gibson, D., Mandelbaum, A., Etinger, A., & Mechoulam, R. (1992). Isolation and structure of a brain constituent that binds to the cannabinoid receptor. *Science, 258,* 1946–1949.

deVilliers, J. G., & deVilliers, P. A. (1973). A cross-sectional study of the acquisition of grammatical morphemes in child speech. *Journal of Psycholinguistic Research, 2,* 267–278.

Dewey, J. (1910). *How we think.* Boston: D. C. Heath and Company.

Diaz, R. M., & Berndt, T. J. (1982). Children's knowledge of a best friend: Fact or fancy? *Developmental Psychology, 18,* 787–794.

Dichgans, J., & Brandt, T. (1978). Visual-vestibular interaction: Effects on self-motion perception and posture control. In R. Held, H. W. Leibowitz, & H. L. Teuber, (Eds.), *Handbook of sensory physiology* (pp. 755–804). Berlin: Springer.

Diener, E. (1980). Deindividuation: The absence of self-awareness and self-regulation in group members. In P. B. Paulus (Ed.), *The psychology of group influence.* Hillsdale, NJ: Erlbaum.

DiLalla, L. F., Thompson, L. A., Plomin, R., Phillips, K., Fagan, J. F., III, Haith, M. M., Cyphers, L. H., & Fulker, D. W. (1990). Infant predictors of preschool and adult IQ: A study of infant twins and their parents. *Developmental Psychology, 26,* 759–769.

Dion, K. K. (1977). The incentive value of physical attractiveness for young children. *Personality and Social Psychology Bulletin, 3,* 67–70.

Dion, K. K., & Stein, S. (1978). Physical attractiveness and interpersonal influence. *Journal of Experimental Social Psychology, 14,* 97–108.

Dodd, J., & Jessell, T. M. (1988). Axon guidance and the patterning of neuronal projections in vertebrates. *Science, 242,* 692–699.

Doi, L. T. (1962). Amae: A key concept for understanding Japanese personality structure. In R. Smith & R. Beardsley (Eds.), *Japanese culture: Its development and characteristics.* New York: Wenner Gren Foundation for Anthropological Research.

Dollard, J., Doob, L. W., Miller, N. E., Mowrer, D. H., & Sears, R. R. (1939). *Frustration and aggression.* New Haven, CT: Yale University Press.

Dorow, R., Horowski, R., Paschelke, G, & Amin, M. (1983). Severe anxiety induced by FG 7142, a beta-carboline ligand for benzodiazepine receptors. *Lancet, 2,* 98.

Doty, R. L., Ford, M., Preti, G., & Huggins, G. R. (1975). Changes in the intensity and pleasantness of human vaginal odors during the menstrual cycle. *Science, 190,* 1316–1318.

Dourish, C. T., Rycroft, W., & Iversen, S. D. (1989). Postponement of satiety by blockade of brain cholecystokinin (CCK-B) receptors. *Science, 245,* 1509–1511.

Drake, R. E., & Vaillant, G. E. (1985). A validity study of Axis II of DSM-III. *American Journal of Psychiatry, 142,* 553–558.

Dreverts, W. C., & Raichle, M. E. (1992). Neuroanatomical circuits in depression: Implications for treatment mechanisms. *Psychopharmacology Bulletin, 28,* 261–274.

Drevets, W. C., Videen, T. O., Price, J. L., Preskorn, S. H., Carmichael, S. T., & Raichle, M. E. (1992). A functional anatomical study of unipolar depression. *Journal of Neuroscience, 12,* 3628–3641.

Dudley, R. M. (1991). IQ and heredity. *Science, 252,* 191.

Dunbar, F. (1943). *Psychosomatic diagnosis.* New York: Hoeber.

Duncker, K. (1945). On problem-solving. *Psychological Monographs, 58,* no. 270.

Dunn, G. C., & Gross, D. (1977). Treatment of depression in the medically ill geriatric patient: A case report. *American Journal of Psychiatry, 134,* 448–450.

Dunn, J. (1983). Sibling relationships in early childhood. *Child Development, 54,* 787–811.

Durham v. United States. (1954). *Federal 2nd, 214,* 862.

Dutton, D. G., & Aron, A. P. (1974). Some evidence for heightened sexual attraction under conditions of high anxiety. *Journal of Personality & Social Psychology, 30,* 510–517.

Dywan, J., & Bowers, K. (1983). The use of hypnosis to enhance recall. *Science, 222,* 184–185.

Eagly, A. H. (1983). *Who says so? The processing of communicator cues in persuasion.* Paper presented at the meeting of the Eastern Psychological Association, Philadelphia, Pennsylvania.

Eagly, A. H., Ashmore, R. D., Makhijani, M. G., & Longo, L. C. (1991). What is beautiful is good, but. . .: A meta-analytic review of research on the physical attractiveness stereotype. *Psychological Bulletin, 110,* 109–128.

Eagly, A. H., & Himmelfarb, S. (1978). Attitudes and opinions. *Annual Review of Psychology, 29,* 517–554.

Eaton, W. O., Chipperfield, J. G., & Singbeil, C. E. (1989). Birth order and activity level in children. *Developmental Psychology, 25,* 668–672.

Ebbesen, E. B., Kjos, G. L., & Konecni, V. J. (1976). Spatial ecology: Its effects on the choice of friends and enemies. *Journal of Experimental Social Psychology, 12,* 505–518.

Ebbinghaus, H. (1913). *Memory: A contribution to experimental psychology.* (Translated by H. A. Ruger & C. E. Bussenius.) New York: New York Teacher's College, Columbia University. (Originally published, 1885).

Eccles-Parsons, J. (1982). Biology, experience and sex dimorphic behaviors. In W. Gove & G. R. Carpenter (Eds.), *The fundamental connection between nature and nurture: A review of the evidence.* Lexington, Mass: Lexington Books.

Edwards, A. L. (1961). Social desirability or acquiescence in the MMPI? A case study with the SD scale. *Journal of Abnormal & Social Psychology, 63,* 351–359.

Edwards, D. D. (1986, January 18). Nicotine: A drug of choice? *Science News,* pp. 44–45.

Ehrhardt, A. A., & Meyer-Bahlburg, H. F. L. (1981). Effects of prenatal sex hormones on gender-related behavior. *Science, 211,* 1312–1318.

Eichelman, B. (1985). Hypnotic change in combat dreams of two veterans with post-traumatic stress disorder. *American Journal of Psychiatry, 142,* 112–114.

Eichorn, D. H., Clausen, J. A., Haan, N., Honzik, M. P., & Mussen, P. H. (Eds.). (1981). *Present and past in middle life.* New York: Academic Press.

Eimas, P. D. (1985). The perception of speech in early infancy. *Scientific American, 252*(1), 46–52.

Eisen, S. V. (1979). Actor-observer differences in information inferences and causal attribution. *Journal of Personality & Social Psychology, 37,* 261–272.

Eisenberg, N. (1983). Sex-typed toy choices: What do they signify? In M. B. Liss (Ed.), *Social and cognitive skills: Sex roles and children's play* (pp. 45–70). New York: Academic Press.

Eisenberg, R. B., & Marmarou, A. (1981). Behavioral reactions of newborns to speech-like sounds and their implications for developmental studies. *Infant Mental Health Journal, 2,* 129–138.

Eiser, J. R., & Pancer, S. M. (1979). Attitudinal effects of the use of evaluative biased language. *European Journal of Social Psychology, 9,* 39–47.

Eiser, J. R., & Ross, M. (1977). Partisan language, immediacy, and attitude change. *European Journal of Social Psychology, 7,* 477–489.

Eisert, D. C., & Kahle, L. R. (1982). Self-evaluation and social comparison of physical and role change during adolescence: A longitudinal analysis. *Child Development, 53,* 98–104.

Ekman, P. (1973). Cross cultural studies of facial expression. In P. Ekman (Ed.), *Darwin and facial expression.* New York: Academic Press.

Ekman, P. (1993). Facial expression and emotion. *American Psychologist, 48,* 384–392.

Ekman, P., & Friesen, W. V. (1974). Detecting deception from the body or face. *Journal of Personality & Social Psychology, 29,* 288–298.

Ekman, P., Friesen, W. V., & O'Sullivan, M. (1988). Smiles when lying. *Journal of Personality & Social Psychology, 54,* 414–420.

Ekman, P., Friesen, W. V., O'Sullivan, M., Chan, A., Diacoyanni-Tarlatzis, I., Heider, K., Krause, R., LeCompte, W. A., Pitcairn, T., & Ricci-Bitti, P. E. (1987). Universals and cultural differences in the judgments of facial expressions of emotion. *Journal of Personality & Social Psychology, 53,* 712–717.

Ekman, P., Levenson, R. W., & Friesen, W. V. (1983). Autonomic nervous system activity distinguishes among emotions. *Science, 221,* 1208–1210.

Ekman, P., & Oster, H. (1979). Facial expressions of emotion. *Annual Review of Psychology, 30,* 527–554.

Ekman, P., Sorenson, E. R., & Friesen, W. V. (1969). Pan-cultural elements in facial displays of emotion. *Science, 164,* 86–88.

Ellis, A. (1962). *Reason and emotion in psychotherapy.* New York: Lyle Stuart.

Ellis, A. (1987). The impossibility of achieving consistently good mental health. *American Psychologist, 42,* 364–375.

Ellis, L., & Ames, M. A. (1987). Neurohormonal functioning and sexual orientation: A theory of homosexuality-heterosexuality. *Psychological Bulletin, 101,* 233–258.

Emmerich, W., & Goldman, K. S. (1972). Boy-girl identity task (technical report). In V. Shipman (Ed.), *Disadvantaged children and their first school experiences* (Technical Report PR 72–20). Educational Testing Service.

Emrick, C. D., & Hansen, J. (1983). Assertions regarding effectiveness of treatment for alcoholism. *American Psychologist, 38,* 1078–1088.

Endler, N. S., & Magnusson, D. (1976). Toward an interactional psychology of personality. *Psychological Bulletin, 83,* 956–974.

Epstein, A. W. (1985). The waking event-dream interval. *American Journal of Psychiatry, 142,* 123–124.

Epstein, S., & Fenz, W. D. (1965). Steepness of approach and avoidance gradients in humans as a function of experience. *Journal of Experimental Psychology, 70,* 1–12.

Erikson, E. H. (1950). *Childhood and society.* New York: W. W. Norton.

Erikson, E. H. (1968). *Identity, youth, and crisis.* New York: Norton.

Erikson, E. H., Erikson, J. M., & Kivnick, H. Q. (1986). *Vital involvement in old age.* New York: W. W. Norton & Company.

Ernst, C., & Angst, J. (1983). *Birth order: Its influence on personality.* New York: Springer-Verlag.

Eron, L. D. (1987). The development of aggressive behavior from the perspective of a developing behaviorism. *American Psychologist, 42,* 435–442.

Eron, L. D., Huesmann, L. R., Brice, P., Fischer, P., & Mermelstein, R. (1983). Age trends in the development of aggression, sex typing, and related television habits. *Developmental Psychology, 19,* 71–77.

Eron, L. D., & Peterson, R. A. (1982). Abnormal behavior: Social approaches. *Annual Review of Psychology, 33,* 231–264.

Erwin, E. (1980). Psychoanalytic therapy. *American Psychologist, 35,* 435–443.

Erwin, G., Plomin, R., & Wilson, J. (1984, March 17). Alcohol test may be inaccurate. *Science News,* p. 171.

Eysenck, H. J. (1985). Psychotherapy effects: Real or imaginary? *American Psychologist, 40,* 239–240.

Fagot, B. L., Hagan, R., Leinbach, M. D., & Kronsberg, S. (1985). Differential reactions to assertive and communicative acts of toddler boys and girls. *Child Development, 56,* 1499–1505.

Fagot, B. L., Leinbach, M. D., & O'Boyle, C. (1992). Gender labeling, gender stereotyping, and parenting behaviors. *Developmental Psychology, 28,* 225–230.

Fairchild, L., & Erwin, W. M. (1977). Physical punishment by parent figures as a model of aggressive behavior in children. *Journal of Genetic Psychology, 130,* 279–284.

Falbo, T. (1981). Relationships between birth category, achievement, and interpersonal orientation. *Journal of Personality & Social Psychology, 41,* 121–131.

Falk, J. L. (1971). The nature and determinants of adjunctive behavior. *Physiology and Behavior, 6,* 577–588.

Fantz, R. L. (1961). The origin of form perception. *Scientific American, 204,* 66–72.

Faravelli, C., & Pallanti, S. (1989). Recent life events and panic disorder. *American Journal of Psychiatry, 146,* 622–626.

Faravelli, C., Pallanti, S., Biondi, F., Paterniti, S., & Scarpato, M. A. (1992). Onset of panic disorder. *American Journal of Psychiatry, 149,* 827–828.

Farde, L., Hall, H., Ehrin, E., & Sedvall, G. (1986). Quantitative analysis of D2 dopamine receptor binding in the living human brain by PET. *Science, 231,* 258–261.

Farkas, G. M. (1980). An ontological analysis of behavior therapy. *American Psychologist, 35,* 364–374.

Farley, J., Richards, W. G., Ling, L. J., Liman, E., & Alkon, D. L. (1983). Membrane changes in a single photoreceptor cause associative learning in Hermissenda. *Science, 221,* 1201–1202.

Faulkner, T. W., & Murphy, T. J. (1973). Lighting for difficult visual tasks. *Human Factors, 15,* 149–162.

Fay, R. E., Turner, C. F., Klassen, A. D., & Gagnon, J. H. (1989). Prevalence and patterns of same-gender sexual contact among men. *Science, 243,* 338–348.

Fazio, R. H. (1979). Motives for social comparison: The construction-validation distinction. *Journal of Personality & Social Psychology, 37,* 1683–1698.

Feder, H. H. (1984). Hormones and sexual behavior. *Annual Review of Psychology, 35,* 165–200.

Fein, G. G., Schwartz, P. M., Jacobson, S. W., & Jacobson, J. L. (1983). Environmental toxins and behavioral development. *American Psychologist, 38,* 1188–1197.

Feingold, A. (1988a). Cognitive gender differences are disappearing. *American Psychologist, 43,* 95–103.

Feingold, A. (1988b). Matching for attractiveness in romantic partners and same-sex friends: A meta-analysis and theoretical critique. *Psychological Bulletin, 104,* 226–235.

Feingold, A. (1992). Gender differences in mate selection preferences: A test of the parental investment model. *Psychological Bulletin, 112,* 125–139.

Feingold, A. (1992). Good-looking people are not what we think. *Psychological Bulletin, 111,* 304–341.

Feldman, D. H. (1984). A follow-up of subjects scoring above 180 IQ in Terman's "Genetic Studies of Genius." *Exceptional Children, 50,* 518–523.

Festinger, L., & Carlsmith, J. M. (1959). Cognitive consequences of forced compliance. *Journal of Abnormal and Social Psychology, 58,* 203–210.

Filsinger, E. E., & Anderson, C. C. (1982). Social class and self-esteem in late adolescence: Dissonant context or self-efficacy? *Developmental Psychology, 18,* 380–384.

Fine, A. (1986). Transplantation in the central nervous system. *Scientific American, 255*(2), 52–58B.

Finkelstein, N. W., & Ramey, C. T. (1977). Learning to control the environment in infancy. *Child Development, 48,* 806–819.

Finlayson, D. F., & Loughran, J. L. (1976). Pupils' perceptions in high and low delinquency schools. *Educational Research, 18,* 138–145.

Finn, P. R., & Pihl, R. O. (1987). Men at high risk for alcoholism: The effect of alcohol on cardiovascular response to unavoidable shock. *Journal of Abnormal Psychology, 96,* 230–236.

Fiorito, G., & Scotto, P. (1992). Observational learning in Octopus vulgaris. *Science, 256,* 545–547.

Fischbach, G. D. (1992). Mind and brain. *Scientific American, 267*(3), 48–57.

Fischer, K. W., & Silvern, L. (1985). Stages and individual differences in cognitive development. *Annual Review of Psychology, 36,* 613–648.

Fish, B., Marcus, J., Hans, S.L., Auerbach, J. G., & Perdue, S. (1992). Infants at risk for schizophrenia: Sequelae of a genetic neurointegrative defect. A review and replication analysis of pandysmaturation in the Jerusalem Infant Development Study. *Archives of General Psychiatry, 49,* 221–235.

Fisher, K. (1986, January). Scrutiny attends more public role. *APA Monitor,* pp. 20–21.

Fiske, D. W., Conley, J. J., & Goldberg, L. R. (1987). E. Lowell Kelly (1905–1986). *American Psychologist, 42,* 511–512.

Fiske, S. T. (1993). Controlling other people: The impact of power on stereotyping. *American Psychologist, 48,* 621–628.

Fitzgerald, B. A., & Wells, C. E. (1977). Hallucinations as a conversion reaction. *Diseases of the Nervous System, 38,* 381–383.

Fitzgerald, L. F., & Osipow, S. H. (1986). An occupational analysis of counseling psychology: How special is the specialty? *American Psychologist, 41,* 535–544.

Fitzsimons, J. T. (1973). Some historical perspectives in the physiology of thirst. In A. N. Epstein, H. R. Kissileff, & E. Stellar (Eds.), *The neuropsychology of thirst.* Washington, D.C.: V. H. Winston.

Flach, F. F., & Kaplan, M. (1983). Visual perceptual dysfunction in psychiatric patients. *Comprehensive Psychiatry, 24,* 304–311.

Flood, J. F., Smith, G. E., & Morley, J. E. (1987). Modulation of memory processing by cholecystokinin: Dependence on the vagus nerve. *Science, 236,* 832–834.

Flynn, J. R. (1987). Massive IQ gains in 14 nations: What IQ tests really measure. *Psychological Bulletin, 101,* 171–191.

Ford, D. E., & Kamerow, D. B. (1989). Epidemiologic study of sleep disturbances and psychiatric disorders. An opportunity for prevention? *Journal of the American Medical Association, 262,* 1479–1484.

Foulkes, D., & Fleisher, S. (1975). Mental activity in relaxed wakefulness. *Journal of Abnormal Psychology, 84,* 66–75.

Fox, B. H. (1981). In R. Ader (Ed.), *Psychoneuroimmunology.* New York: Academic Press.

Fox, E. L., & Mathews, D. K. (1981). *The physiological basis of physical education and athletics* (3rd ed.). Philadelphia: Saunders.

Fox, N. A. (1989). Psychophysiological correlates of emotional reactivity during the first year of life. *Developmental Psychology, 25,* 364–372.

Fox, N. A. (1991). If it's not left, it's right: Electroencephalograph asymetry and the development of emotion. *American Psychologist, 46,* 863–872.

Fox, N. A., & Davidson, R. J. (1988). Patterns of brain electrical activity during facial signs of emotion in 10-month-old infants. *Developmental Psychology, 24,* 230–236.

Frank, J. D. (1986, May). Psychotherapy: The transformation of meanings. *Harvard Medical School Mental Health Letter,* pp. 4–6.

Frankel, F. H. (1990). Hypnotizability and dissociation. *American Journal of Psychiatry, 147,* 823–829.

Frankel, F. H. (1993). Adult reconstruction of childhood events in the multiple personality literature. *American Journal of Psychiatry, 150,* 954–958.

Frankenburg, W. K., & Dodds, J. B. (1967). The Denver Developmental Screening Test. *Journal of Pediatrics, 71,* 181–191.

Franklin, N., & Tversky, B. (1990). Searching imagined environments. *Journal of Experimental Psychology: General, 119,* 63–76.

Freud, S. (1885). *Ueber coca.* Vienna: Mortiz Perles.

Freud, S. (1953). The interpretation of dreams. In J. Strachey (Ed.), *The standard edition of the complete psychological works* (Vols. 4 and 5). (Originally published, 1900). London: Hogarth Press.

Freud, S. (1953). Three essays on sexuality. In J. Strachey (Ed.), *The standard edition of the complete psychological works* (Vol. 7). (Originally published, 1905). London: Hogarth Press.

Freud S. (1963). Introductory lectures on psycho-analysis. In J. Strachey (Ed.), *The standard edition of the complete psychological works* (Vols. 15 and 16). (Originally published, 1917). London: Hogarth Press.

Freud, S. (1964). An outline of psychoanalysis. In J. Strachey (Ed.), *The standard edition of the complete psychological works* (Vol. 23). (Originally published, 1940). London: Hogarth Press.

Frey, K. S., & Ruble, D. N. (1992). Gender constancy and the "cost" of sex-typed behavior. *Developmental Psychology, 28,* 714–721.

Frezza, M., di Padova, C., Pozzato, G., Terpin, M., Baraona, E., & Lieber, C. S. (1990). High blood alcohol levels in women. The role of decreased gastric alcohol dehydrogenase activity and first-pass metabolism. *New England Journal of Medicine, 322,* 95–99.

Friedman, H. S., & Booth-Kewley, S. (1987). The "disease-prone personality": A meta-analytic view of the construct. *American Psychologist, 42,* 539–555.

Friedman, H. S., & Booth-Kewley, S. (1988). Validity of the type A construct: A reprise. *Psychological Bulletin, 104,* 381–384.

Friedman, M., & Rosenman, R. H. (1959). Association of specific overt behavior pattern with blood and cardiovascular findings. *Journal of the American Medical Association, 169,* 1286–1296.

Friedman, M. I., & Stricker, E. M. (1976). The physiological psychology of hunger: A physiological perspective. *Psychological Review, 83,* 409–431.

Fries, J. F., & Crapo, L. M. (1981). *Vitality and aging.* San Francisco: W. H. Freeman.

Frijda, N. H. (1988). The laws of emotion. *American Psychologist, 43,* 349–358.

Frodi, A., Bridges, L., & Grolnick, W. (1985). Correlates of mastery-related behavior: A short-term longitudinal study of infants in their second year. *Child Development, 56,* 1291–1298.

Fromm, E. (1970). Age regression with unexpected reappearance of a repressed childhood language. *International Journal of Clinical and Experimental Hypnosis, 18,* 79–88.

Frost, B. J., & Nakayama, K. (1983). Single visual neurons code opposing motion independent of direction. *Science, 220,* 744–745.

Furman, W., & Bierman, K. L. (1983). Developmental changes in young children's conceptions of friendship. *Child Development, 54,* 549–556.

Gaes, G. G., Kalle, R. J., & Tedeschi, J. T. (1978). Impression management in the forced compliance situation. *Journal of Experimental Social Psychology, 14,* 493–510.

Gagne, R. M. (1984). Learning outcomes and their effects: useful categories of human performance. *American Psychologist, 39,* 377–385.

Galbraith, R. C. (1982). Sibling spacing and intellectual development: A closer look at the confluence models. *Developmental Psychology, 18,* 151–173.

Galin, D., Diamond, R., & Braff, D. (1977). Lateralization of conversion symptoms: More frequent on the left. *American Journal of Psychiatry, 134,* 578–580.

Gallup, G. (1975, October 13). The growing acceptance of racial integration. *San Francisco Chronicle.*

Garcia, J., & Koelling, R. A. (1966). Relation of cue to consequence in avoidance learning. *Psychonomic Science, 4,* 123–124.

Gardner, E. P., & Costanzo, R. M. (1981). Properties of kinesthetic neurons in somatosensory cortex of awake monkeys. *Brain Research, 214,* 301–319.

Gardner, H. (1983). *Frames of mind: The theory of multiple intelligences.* New York: Basic Books.

Gardner, M. (1983, August). Illusions of the third dimension. *Psychology Today,* pp. 62–67.

Gardner, R. A., & Gardner, B. T. (1969). Teaching sign language to a chimpanzee. *Science, 165,* 664–672.

Garrison, C. Z., McKeown, R. E., Valois, R. F., & Vincent, M. L. (1993). Aggression, substance use, and suicidal behaviors in high school students. *American Journal of Public Health, 83,* 179–184.

Gartrell, N., Herman, J., Olarte, S., Feldstein, M., & Localio, R. (1986). Psychiatrist-patient sexual contact: Results of a national survey, I: Prevalence. *American Journal of Psychiatry, 143,* 1126–1137.

Garvey, M. J., Wesner, R., & Godes, M. (1988). Comparison of seasonal and non-seasonal affective disorders. *American Journal of Psychiatry, 145,* 100–102.

Gawin, R. H. (1991). Cocaine addiction: Psychology and neurophysiology. *Science, 251,* 1580–1586.

Gazzaniga, M. S. (1983). Right hemisphere language following brain bisection: A 20–year perspective. *American Psychologist, 38,* 525–537.

Gazzaniga, M. S. (1985, November). The social brain. *Psychology Today,* pp. 29–38.

Gazzaniga, M. S. (1989). Organization of the human brain. *Science, 245,* 947–952.

Geldard, F. A., & Sherrick, C. E. (1986). Space, time and touch, *Scientific American, 255*(1), 92–95.

Geller, J. L. (1992). A historical perspective on the role of state hospitals viewed from the era of the "revolving door." *American Journal of Psychiatry, 149,* 1526–1533.

Geracioti, T. D., Jr., Liddle, R. A., Altemus, M., Demitrack, M. A., & Gold, P. W. (1992). Regulation of appetite and cholecystokinin secretion in anorexia nervosa. *American Journal of Psychiatry, 149,* 958–961.

Gerbner, G., Gross, L., Morgan, M., & Signorielli, N. (1980). The "mainstreaming" of America: Violence profile No. 11. *Journal of Communication, 30*(3), 10–29.

Geron, E. (1982). History and recent position of sport psychology. In E. Geron (Ed.), *Handbook of sport psychology* (pp. 25–42). Tel Aviv: Wingate Inst.

Geschwind, N. (1979). Specializations of the human brain. *Scientific American, 241*(3), 180–199.

Geschwind, N., & Behan, P. (1982). Left-handedness: Association with immune disease, migraine, and developmental learning disorder. *Proceedings of the National Academy of Sciences of the United States of America—Biological Sciences, 79,* 5097–5100.

Ghiselli, E. E. (1966). *The validity of occupational aptitude tests.* New York: Wiley.

Gibbons, A. (1991). Deja Vu all over again: Chimp-language wars. *Science, 251,* 1561–1562.

Gibson, E. J., & Walk, R. D. (1960). The "visual cliff." *Scientific American, 202*(4), 64–71.

Gibson, J. J. (1979). *The ecological approach to visual perception.* Boston: Houghton Mifflin.

Gibson, M. J. (1984). Sexuality in later life. *Ageing International, 11,* 8–13.

Gillam, B. (1980). Geometrical illusions. *Scientific American, 242*(1), 102–111.

Gilligan, C. (1982). *In a different voice.* Cambridge, MA: Harvard University Press.

Gillin, J. (1948). Magical fright. *Psychiatry, 11,* 387–400.

Gladue, B. A., Green, R., & Hellman, R. E. (1984). Neuroendocrine response to estrogen and sexual orientation. *Science, 225,* 1496–1498.

Glasser, W. (1976). *Positive addiction.* New York: Harper & Row.

Glassman, J. N., Magulac, M., & Darko, D. F. (1987). Folie a famille: Shared paranoid disorder in a Vietnam veteran and his family. *American Journal of Psychiatry, 144,* 648–660.

Gleitman, L. R., & Wanner, E. (1984). Current issues in language learning. In M. H. Bornstein & M. E. Lamb (Eds.), *Developmental psychology: An advanced textbook* (pp. 181–240). Hillsdale, NJ: Erlbaum.

Glenberg, A. M. (1976). Monotonic and nonmonotonic lag effects in paired-associate and recognition memory paradigms. *Journal of Verbal Learning and Verbal Behavior, 15,* 1–16.

Glenn, N. D., & McLanahan, S. (1981). The effects of offspring on the psychological well-being of older adults. *Journal of Marriage & the Family, 43,* 409–421.

Glick, I. O., Weiss, R. S., & Parkes, C. M. (1974). *The first year of bereavement.* New York: Wiley-Interscience.

Glickstein, M. (1988). The discovery of the visual cortex. *Scientific American, 259*(3), 118–127.

Glucksberg, S., & Danks, J. H. (1968). Effects of discriminative labels and nonsense labels upon the availability of novel function. *Journal of Verbal Learning and Verbal Behavior, 7,* 72–76.

Godden, D. R., & Baddeley, A. D. (1975). Context-dependent memory in two natural environments: On land and underwater. *British Journal of Psychology, 66,* 325–331.

Goeders, N. E., & Smith, J. E. (1983). Cortical dopaminergic involvement in cocaine reinforcement. *Science, 221,* 773–775.

Goisman, R. M. (1985). The psychodynamics of prescribing in behavior therapy. *American Journal of Psychiatry, 142,* 675–679.

Gold, P. W., Goodwin, F. K., & Chrousos, G. P. (1988b). Clinical and biochemical manifestations of depression. Relation to the neurobiology of stress (2). *New England Journal of Medicine, 319,* 413–420.

Gold, P. W., Goodwin, F. K., & Chrousos, G. P. (1988a). Clinical and biochemical manifestations of depression. Relation to the neurobiology of stress (1). *New England Journal of Medicine, 319,* 348–353.

Goldberg, J., True, W. R., Eisen, S. A., & Henderson, W. G. (1990). A twin study of the effects of the Vietnam War on posttraumatic stress disorder. *Journal of the American Medical Association, 263,* 1227–1232.

Goldberg, L. R. & Werts, C. E. (1966). The reliability of clinicians' judgments: A multitrait-multimethod approach. *Journal of Consulting Psychology, 30,* 199–206.

Goldberg, L. W. (1978). Differential attribution of trait-descriptive terms to oneself as compared to well-liked, neutral, and disliked others: A psychometric analysis. *Journal of Personality & Social Psychology, 36,* 1012–1028.

Golden, M. (1964). Some effects of combining psychological tests on clinical inferences. *Journal of Consulting Psychology, 28,* 440–446.

Goldfarb, L. G., Petersen, R. B., Tabaton, M., Brown, P., LeBlanc, A. C., Montagna, P., Cortelli, P., Julien, J., Vital, C., Pendelbury, W. W., Haltia, M., Wills, P. R., Hauw, J. J., McKeever, P. E., Monari, L., Schrank, B., Swergold, G. D., Autilio-Gambetti, L., Gajdusek, D. C., Lugaresi, E., & Gambetti, P. (1992). Fatal familial insomnia and familial Creutzfeldt-Jakob disease: Disease phenotype determined by a DNA polymorphism. *Science, 258,* 806–808.

Goldfried, M. R., Greenberg, L. S., & Marmar, C. (1990). Individual psychotherapy: Process and outcome. *Annual Review of Psychology, 41,* 659–688.

Goldman, W., & Lewis, P. (1977). Beautiful is good: Evidence that the physically attractive are more socially skillful. *Journal of Experimental Social Psychology, 13,* 125–130.

Goldsmith, H. H. (1983). Genetic influences on personality from infancy to adulthood. *Child Development, 54,* 331–355.

Goldsmith, H. H., Buss, A. H., Plomin, R., Rothbart, M. K., Thomas, A., Chess, S., Hinde, R. A., & McCall, R. B. (1987). Roundtable: What is temperament? Four approaches. *Child Development, 58,* 505–529.

Goldstein, A., & Hilgard, E. R. (1975). Lack of influence of the morphine antagonist naloxone on hypnotic analgesia. *Proceedings of the National Academy of Science, 72,* 2041–2043.

Goleman, D. (1980, February). 1,528 little geniuses and how they grew. *Psychology Today,* pp. 28–53.

Gollob, H. F., & Dittes, J. E. (1965). Effects of manipulated self-esteem on persuasibility depending on threat and complexity of communication. *Journal of Personality & Social Psychology, 2,* 195–201.

Gomes-Schwartz, B., Hadley, S. W., & Strupp, H. H. (1978). Individual psychotherapy and behavior therapy. *Annual Review of Psychology, 29,* 435–471.

Goodstein, R. K. (1985). Common clinical problems in the elderly: Camouflaged by ageism and atypical presentation. *Psychiatric Annals, 15,* 299–312.

Gottesman, I. I., & Shields, J. (1972). *Schizophrenia and genetics.* New York: Academic Press.

Gottlieb, D. I. (1988). GABAergic neurons. *Scientific American, 258*(2), 82–89.

Gottman, J. M. (1983). How children become friends. *Monographs of the Society for Research in Child Development, 48*(3, Serial No. 201).

Gould, J. L. (1986) The locale map of honey bees: Do insects have cognitive maps? *Science, 232,* 861–863.

Gould, J. L., & Marler, P. (1987). Learning by instinct. *Scientific American, 256*(1), 74–85.

Gould, S. J. (1981). *The mismeasure of man.* New York: Norton.

Gracely, R. H., Dubner, R., Wolskee, P. J., & Deeter, W. R. (1983). Placebo and naloxone can alter post-surgical pain by separate mechanisms. *Nature, 306,* 264–265.

Graham, C. H., & Hsia, Y. (1958). Color defect and color theory. *Science, 127,* 675–682.

Graham, S. (1990, November). We must deal with the problem of the seriously mentally ill. *APA Monitor,* p. 2.

Gray, S. W., & Ruttle, K. (1980). The family-oriented home visiting program: A longitudinal study. *Genetic Psychology Monographs, 102,* 299–316.

Green, R. (1976). Atypical sex role behavior during childhood. In B. J. Sadock, H. I. Kaplan, & A. M. Freedman (Eds.), *The sexual experience* (pp. 196–205). Baltimore, MD: Williams & Wilkins.

Green, R. (1978). Sexual identity of 37 children raised by homosexual or transsexual parents. *American Journal of Psychiatry, 135,* 692–697.

Green, R. (1987). *The "sissy boy syndrome" and the development of homosexuality.* New Haven, CT: Yale University Press.

Greenberg, J. (1980a, May 10). Ape talk: More than "pigeon" English? *Science News,* pp. 298–300.

Greenberg, J. (1980b, May 24). Stressing the immune system. *Science News,* p. 335.

Greenberg, J. (1981, June/July). An interview with David Rosenhan. *APA Monitor,* pp. 4–5.

Greenberg, J. (1987, February 21). Uncovering amnesiacs' hidden memories. *Science News,* p. 118.

Greenberg, Jerald. (1979). Group vs. individual equity judgments: Is there a polarization effect? *Journal of Experimental Social Psychology, 15,* 504–512.

Greene, D., Sternberg, B., & Lepper, M. R. (1976). Overjustification in a token economy. *Journal of Personality & Social Psychology, 34,* 1219–1234.

Gregory, R. L. (1970). *The intelligent eye.* New York: McGraw-Hill.

Gretarsson, S. J., & Gelfand, D. M. (1988). Mothers' attributions regarding their children's social behavior and personality characteristics. *Developmental Psychology, 24,* 264–269.

Griffiths, R. (1954). *The abilities of babies.* London: University of London Press.

Griffitt, W., & Veitch, R. (1971). Hot and crowded: Influence of population density and temperature on interpersonal affective behavior. *Journal of Personality & Social Psychology, 17,* 92–98.

Grilo, C. M., & Pogue-Greile, M. F. (1991). The nature of environmental influences on weight and obesity: A behavior genetic analysis. *Psychological Bulletin, 110,* 520–537.

Grinspoon, L. (1986, March). Suicide—Part II. *Harvard Medical School Mental Health Letter,* pp. 1–4.

Grob, G. N. (1991). Origins of DSM-I: A study in appearance and reality. *American Journal of Psychiatry, 148,* 421–431.

Gross, A. E., & Crofton, C. (1977). What is good is beautiful. *Sociometry, 40,* 85–90.

Grosskurth, P. (1991). *The secret ring: Freud's inner circle and the politics of psychoanalysis.* Reading, MA: Addison-Wesley.

Grossman, S. P. (1972). Neurophysiologic aspects: Extrahypothalamic factors in the regulation of food intake. *Advances in Psychosomatic Medicine, 7,* 49–72.

Grossman, S. P. (1975). Role of the hypothalamus in the regulation of food and water intake. *Psychological Review, 82,* 200–224.

Grotevant, M. D., Scarr, S., & Weinberg, R. A. (1975, March). *Intellectual development in family constellations with adopted and natural children: A test of the Zajonc and Markus model.* Paper presented at the meeting of the Society for Research in Child Development, New Orleans.

Grush, J. E. (1980). The impact of candidate expenditures, regionality, and prior outcomes on the 1976 Democratic Presidential primaries. *Journal of Personality & Social Psychology, 38,* 337–347.

Guharay, F., & Sachs, F. (1985). Mechanotransducer ion channels in chick skeletal muscle: The effects of extracellular pH. *Journal of Physiology, 363,* 119–134.

Guidotti, A., Baraldi, M., Schwartz, J. P., Toffano, G., & Costa, E. (1979). Molecular mechanism for the action of benzodiazepines on gabaergic transmission. In P. Krogsgaardlarsen, J. Scheelkruger, & H. Kofod (Eds.), *Gaba-neurotransmitters.* New York: Academic Press.

Guilford, J. P. (1982). Cognitive psychology's ambiguities: Some suggested remedies. *Psychological Review, 89,* 48–59.

Guilford, J. P. (1983). Transformation abilities or functions. *Journal of Creative Behavior, 17,* 75–83.

Gulevich, G., Dement, W., & Johnson, L. (1966). Psychiatric and EEG observations on a case of prolonged (264-hour) wakefulness. *Archives of General Psychiatry, 15,* 29–35.

Gur, R. E., Mozley, P. D., Resnick, S. M., Levick, S., Erwin, R., Saykin, A. J., & Gur, R. C. (1991). Relations among clinical scales in schizophrenia. *American Journal of Psychiatry, 148,* 472–478.

Gzesh, S. M., & Surber, C. F. (1985). Visual perspective-taking skills in children. *Child Development, 56,* 1204–1213.

Haan, N., Millsap, R., & Hartka, E. (1986). As time goes by: Change and stability in personality over fifty years. *Psychology and Aging, 1,* 220–232.

Haber, R. N. (1969). Eidetic images. *Scientific American, 220*(4), 36–44.

Haber, R. N. (1985). Perception: A one-hundred-year-perspective. In S. Koch & D. E. Leary, *A century of psychology as science* (pp. 250–281). New York: McGraw-Hill.

Haier, R. J., Siegel, B., Tang, C., Abel, L., et al. (1992). Intelligence and changes in regional cerebral glucose metabolic rate following learning. *Intelligence, 16,* 415–426.

Hall, E. (1984, December). A sense of control. *Psychology Today,* pp. 38–45.

Hall, E. G., & Lee, A. M. (1984). Sex differences in motor performance of young children: Fact or fiction? *Sex Roles, 10,* 217–230.

Hall, R. C. W., Stickney, S. K., LeCann, A. F., & Popkin, M. K. (1980). Physical illness manifesting as psychiatric disease. 2. Analysis of a state-hospital inpatient population. *Archives of General Psychiatry, 37,* 989–995.

Hall, S. S. (1985, May). Aplysia & hermissenda. *Science 85,* pp. 30–39.

Hamer, B. (1982, July/August). All in the family. *Science 82,* pp. 88–89.

Hamer, D. H., Hu, S., Magnuson, V. L., Hu, N., & Pattatucci, A. M. L. (1993). A linkage between DNA markers on the X chromosome and male sexual orientation. *Science, 261,* 321–327.

Hammen, C., Gordon, D., Burge, D., Adrian, C., Jaenicke, C., & Hiroto, D. (1987). Maternal affective disorders, illness, and stress: Risk for children's psychopathology. *American Journal of Psychiatry, 144,* 736–741.

Haney, W. (1981). Validity, vaudeville, and values: A short history of social concerns over standardized testing. *American Psychologist, 36,* 1021–1034.

Hargreaves, W. A., Shumway, M., Knutsen, E. J., Weinstein, A., & Senter, N. (1987). Effects of the Jamison-Farabee consent decree: Due process protection for involuntary psychiatric patients treated with psychoactive medication. *American Journal of Psychiatry, 144,* 188–192.

Harkey, J., Miles, D. L., & Rushing, W. A. (1976). The relation between social class and functional status: A new look at the drift hypothesis. *Journal of Health and Social Behavior, 17,* 194–204.

Harlow, H. F. (1958). The nature of love. *American Psychologist, 13,* 673–685.

Harlow, H. F., & Zimmerman, R. R. (1959). Affectional responses in the infant monkey. *Science, 130,* 421–432.

Harlow, J. M. (1868). Recovery from the passage of an iron bar through the head. *Publ. Mass. Med. Soc., 2,* 327.

Harris, B. (1979). Whatever happened to Little Albert? *American Psychologist, 34,* 151–160.

Harris, J. A., Jackson, C. M., Patterson, D. G., & Scammon, R. E. (Eds.). (1930). *The measurement of man.* Minneapolis: Univ. of Minnesota Press.

Harris, L., & Associates, Inc. (1981). *Aging in the eighties: America in transition.* Washington, DC: National Council on Aging.

Harris, R. L., Ellicott, A. M., & Holmes, D. S. (1986). The timing of psychosocial transitions and changes in women's lives: An examination of women aged 45 to 60. *Journal of Personality and Social Psychology, 51,* 409–416.

Harrow, M., Carone, B. J., & Westermeyer, J. F. (1985). The course of psychosis in early phases of schizophrenia. *American Journal of Psychiatry, 142,* 702–707.

Harrow, M., Goldberg, J. F., Grossman, L. S., & Meltzer, H. Y. (1990). Outcome in manic disorders: A naturalistic follow-up study. *Archives of General Psychiatry, 47,* 665–671.

Harrow, M., & Quinlan, D. (1977). Is disordered thinking unique to schizophrenia? *Archives of General Psychiatry, 34,* 15–21.

Hart, J., Berndt, R. S., & Caramazza, A. (1987). Category-specific naming deficit following cerebral infarction. *Nature, 316,* 439–440.

Hart, L. M., & Goldin-Meadow, S. (1984). The child as a nonegocentric art critic. *Child Development, 55,* 2122–2129.

Hartley, E. L. (1946). *Problems in prejudice.* New York: Kings Crown.

Hartup, W. W. (1983). Peer relations. In P. H. Mussen (Ed.), *Handbook of child psychology* (4th ed., Vol. IV, pp. 103–196). New York: Wiley.

Harvey, J. H., & Weary, G. (1984). Current issues in attribution theory and research. *Annual Review of Psychology, 35,* 427–459.

Hathaway, S. R., & McKinley, J. C. (1940). A multiphasic personality schedule (Minnesota): I. Construction of the schedule. *Journal of Psychology, 10,* 249–254.

Haviland, J. M., & Lelwica, M. (1987). The induced affect response: 10-week-old infants' responses to three emotion expressions. *Developmental Psychology, 23,* 97–104.

Hawkins, D. R. (1986, March). The importance of dreams. *Harvard Medical School Mental Health Letter,* pp. 5–7.

Hayashi, S., & Kimura, T. (1976). Sexual behavior of the naive male mouse as affected by the presence of a male and female performing mating behavior. *Physiology & Behavior, 17,* 807–810.

Hayes, K. J., & Hayes, C. (1952). Imitation in a home-raised chimpanzee. *Journal of Comparative and Physiological Psychology, 45,* 450–459.

Hayflick, L. (1980). The cell biology of human aging. *Scientific American, 242*(1), 58–65.

Hayflick, L. (1985). Theories of biological aging. *Experimental Gerontology, 20,* 145–159.

Hayward, C., Killen, J. D., Hammer, L. D., Litt, I. F., Wilson, D. M., Simmonds, B., & Taylor, C. B. (1992). Pubertal stage and panic attack history in sixth- and seventh-grade girls. *American Journal of Psychiatry, 149,* 1239–1243.

Heath, C. W. (1945). *What people are.* Cambridge, Ma: Harvard University Press.

Hebb, D. O. (1949). *The organization of behavior.* New York: Wiley.

Hechinger, N. (1981, March). Seeing without eyes. *Science 81,* pp. 38–43.

Hefez, A., Metz, L., & Lavie, P. (1987). Long-term effects of extreme situational stress on sleep and dreaming. *American Journal of Psychiatry, 144,* 344–347.

Heider, F. (1958). *The psychology of interpersonal relations.* New York: Wiley.

Heiman, J. R. (1977). A psychophysiological exploration of sexual arousal patterns in females and males. *Psychophysiology, 14,* 266–274.

Heiman, J. R. (1979). Continuing revolutions in sex research. In Z. Rubin & E. B. McNeil, *The psychology of being human* (brief update edition). New York: Harper & Row.

Heinrichs, R. W. (1993). Schizophrenia and the brain. *American Psychologist, 48,* 221–233.

Heit, G., Smith, M. E., & Halgren, E. (1988). Neural encoding of individual words and faces by the human hippocampus and amygdala. *Nature, 333,* 773–775.

Heller, F. A., & Clark, A. W. (1976). Personnel and human resources development. *Annual Review of Psychology, 27,* 405–435.

Helmes, E., & Reddon, J. R. (1993). A perspective on developments in assessing psychopathology: A critical review of the MMPI and MMPI-2. *Psychological Bulletin, 113,* 453–471.

Helmholtz, H. von (1924). *Treatise on physiological optics* (Vol. II) (J. P. Southall, Ed. and trans., from the 3rd German ed.) Rochester, NY: Optical Society of America. (originally published, 1866).

Helson, R., & Crutchfield, R. S. (1970). Mathematicians: The creative researcher and average Ph.D. *Journal of Consulting and Clinical Psychology, 34,* 250–257.

Hemenway, D., Solnick, S. J., & Colditz, G. A. (1993). Smoking and suicide among nurses. *American Journal of Public Health, 83,* 249–251.

Hendricks, J., & Hendricks, C. D. (1979). Concerning old age: Interdisciplinary dimensions. In J. Hendricks & C. D. Hendricks (Eds.), *Dimensions of aging* (pp. 1–7). Cambridge, MA: Winthrop Publishers Inc.

Henn, F. A. (1989). Psychosurgery. In H. I. Kaplan & B. J. Sadock (Eds.), *Comprehensive textbook of psychiatry/v* (pp. 1679–1680). Baltimore, MD: Williams & Wilkins.

Herbert, T. B., & Cohen, S. (1993). Depression and immunity: A meta-analytic review. *Psychological Bulletin, 113,* 472–486.

Herbert, W. (1983a, December 10). Remembrance of things partly. *Science News,* pp. 378–381.

Herbert, W. (1983b, June 25). Schizophrenia clues in angel dust. *Science News,* p. 407.

Herbert, W. (1983c, October 8). MMPI: Redefining normality for modern times. *Science News,* p. 228.

Herbert, W. (1985, March). Cyranoids: Artificial selves. *Psychology Today,* pp. 6–7.

Herbert, W. (1987, April). Science at a snail's pace. *Psychology Today,* p. 80.

Herrnstein, R. J. (1990). Rational choice theory: Necessary but not sufficient. *American Psychologist, 45,* 356–367.

Herz, M. I., Szymanski, H. V., & Simon, J. C. (1982). Intermittent medication for stable schizophrenic outpatients: An alternative to maintenance medication. *American Journal of Psychiatry, 139,* 918–922.

Hess, E. H. (1970). Ethology and developmental psychology. In P. H. Mussen (Ed.), *Carmichael's manual of child psychology* (Vol. 1, 3rd ed.). New York: Wiley.

Hetherington, E. M. (1979). Divorce: A child's perspective. *American Psychologist, 34,* 851–858.

Hilgard, E. R. (1977). *Divided consciousness: Multiple controls in human thought and action.* New York: Wiley-Interscience.

Hilgard, E. R. (1980). Consciousness in contemporary psychology. *Annual Review of Psychology, 31,* 1–26.

Hilgard, E. R., & Hilgard, J. R. (1975). *Hypnosis in the relief of pain.* Los Altos, CA: William Kaufmann.

Hilgard, E. R., & Hilgard, J. R. (1983). *Hypnosis in the relief of pain.* Los Altos, CA: Kaufmann.

Hill, C. T., Rubin, Z., & Peplau, L. A. (1976). Breakups before marriage: The end of 103 affairs. *Journal of Social Issues, 32*(1), 147–168.

Hines, M. (1982). Prenatal gonadal hormones and sex differences in human behavior. *Psychological Bulletin, 92,* 56–80.

Hitchcock, E. R. (1993). Fetal transplant update. *Science, 259,* 442–443.

Hobson, J. A., & McCarley, R. W. (1977). The brain as a dream state generator: An activation-synthesis hypothesis of the dream process. The *American Journal of Psychiatry, 134,* 1335–1348.

Hoffman, M. L. (1979). Development of moral thought, feeling, and behavior. *American Psychologist, 34,* 958–966.

Hogan, R. (1975). Theoretical egocentrism and the problem of compliance. *American Psychologist, 30,* 533–540.

Holden, C. (1986a). Amazing Randi one of 25 MacArthur Genius winners. *Science, 233,* 517.

Holden, C. (1986b). Researchers grapple with problems of updating classic psychological test. *Science, 233,* 1249–1251.

Holden, C. (1986c). Giving mental illness its research due. *Science, 232,* 1084–1085.

Holden, C. (1987a). NIMH finds a case of "serious misconduct." *Science, 235,* 1566–1567.

Holden, C. (1987b). Is alcoholism treatment effective? *Science, 236,* 20–22.

Holden, C. (1991). On the trail of genes for IQ. *Science, 253,* 1352.

Holden, C. (1992). A new discipline probes suicide's multiple causes. *Science, 256,* 1761–1762.

Holden, C. (1993). Wake-up call for sleep research. *Science, 259,* 305.

Hollander, E. P., & Julian, J. W. (1970). Studies in leader legitimacy, influence, and innovation. In L. Berkowitz (Ed.), *Advances in experimental social psychology* (Vol. 5). New York: Academic Press.

Hollander, E. P., & Offerman, L. R. (1990). Power and leadership in organizations: Relationships in transition. *American Psychologist, 45,* 179–189.

Holloway, M. (1991). Rx for addiction. *Scientific American, 264*(3), 95–103.

Holmes, D. S. (1984). Meditation and somatic arousal reduction: A review of the experimental evidence. *American Psychologist, 39,* 1–10.

Holmes, T. H., & Rahe, R. H. (1967). The social readjustment rating scale. *Journal of Psychosomatic Research, 11,* 213–218.

Homans, G. C. (1961). *Social behavior: Its elementary forms.* New York: Harcourt Brace & World.

Hong, L. K. (1978). Risky shift and cautious shift: Some direct evidence on the cultural-value theory. *Social Psychology, 41,* 342–346.

Honts, C. R., Hodes, R. L., & Raskin, D. C. (1985). Effects of physical countermeasures on the physiological detection of deception. *Journal of Applied Psychology, 70,* 177–187.

Hook, S. (Ed.). (1960). *Psychoanalysis, scientific method and philosophy.* New York: Grove.

Hopson, J. L. (1986, June). The unraveling of insomnia. *Psychology Today,* pp. 42–49.

Horn, J. (1986). Intellectual ability concepts. In R. J. Sternberg (Ed.), *Advances in the psychology of human intelligence* (Vol. 3, pp. 35–77). Hillsdale, NJ: Erlbaum.

Horn, J. C. (1985, November). All carrot, no stick. *Psychology Today,* p. 19.

Horn, J. C., & Meer, J. (1987, May). The vintage years. *Psychology Today,* pp. 77–90.

Horn, J. M. (1983). The Texas Adoption Project: Adopted children and their intellectual resemblance to biological and adoptive parents. *Child Development, 54,* 268–275.

Horney, K. (1939). *New ways in psychoanalysis.* New York: Norton.

Horowitz, M. J., Marmar, C., Weiss, D. S., DeWitt, K. N., & Rosenbaum, R. (1984). Brief psychotherapy of bereavement reactions. *Archives of General Psychiatry, 41,* 438–448.

Hosford, D. A., Clark, S., Cao, Z., Wilson, W. A., Lin, F., Morrisett, R. A., & Huin, A. (1992). The role of GABA$_B$ receptor activation in absence seizures of lethargic (Ih/Ih) mice. *Science, 257,* 398–403.

House, J. S., Landis, K. R., & Umberson, D. (1988). Social relationships and health. *Science, 241,* 540–545.

House, R. J., & Singh, J. V. (1987). Organizational behavior: Some new directions for I/O psychology. *Annual Review of Psychology, 38,* 669–718.

Houston, J. P., Schneider, N. G., & Jarvik, M. E. (1978). Effects of smoking on free recall and organization. *American Journal of Psychiatry, 135,* 220–222.

Hovland, C. I., Lumsdaine, A. A., & Sheffield, F. D. (1949). *Experiments on mass communication.* Princeton, NJ: Princeton Univ. Press.

Howes, C. (1987). Peer interaction of young children. *Monographs of the Society for Research in Child Development, 53*(1, Serial No. 217).

Howes, C., & Olenick, M. (1986). Family and child care influences on toddler's compliance. *Child Development, 57,* 202–216.

Hsu, F., Anantharaman, T., Campbell, M., & Nowatzyk, A. (1990). A grandmaster chess machine. *Scientific American, 263*(4), 44–50.

Hubel, D. H. (1979). The brain. *Scientific American, 241*(3), 44–53.

Hudson, A., & Clunies-Ross, G. (1984). A study of the integration of children with intellectual handicaps into regular schools. *Australia & New Zealand Journal of Developmental Disabilities, 10*(3), 165–177.

Huesmann, L. R., Lagerspetz, K., & Eron, L. D. (1984). Intervening variables in the TV violence-aggression relation: Evidence from two countries. *Developmental Psychology, 20,* 746–775.

Hughes, J. R. (1992). Tobacco withdrawal in self-quitters. *Journal of Consulting & Clinical Psychology, 60,* 689–697.

Hughes, J. R., & Hatsukami, D. (1986). Signs and symptoms of tobacco withdrawal. *Archives of General Psychiatry, 43,* 289–294.

Humphreys, L. G., Rich, S. A., & Davey, T. C. (1985). A Piagetian test of general intelligence. *Developmental Psychology, 21,* 872–877.

Huston, A. C. (1983). Sex-typing. In P. H. Mussen (Ed.), *Handbook of child psychology* (4th ed., Vol. 4, pp. 388–467). New York: Wiley.

Hutt, S. J., Hutt, C., Lenard, H. G., Bernuth, H. V., & Muntjewerff, W. J. (1968). Auditory responsivity in the human neonate. *Nature, 218,* 888–890.

Huxley, A. (1954). *The doors of perception.* New York: Harper & Row.

Hyde, J. S., & Linn, M. C. (1988). Are there sex differences in verbal abilities? A meta-analysis. *Psychological Bulletin, 104,* 53–69.

Hyland, M. E. (1987). Control theory interpretation of psychological mechanisms of depression: Comparison and integration of several theories. *Psychological Bulletin, 102,* 109–121.

Iacono, W. G., & Beiser, M. (1992). Are males more likely than females to develop schizophrenia? *American Journal of Psychiatry, 149,* 1070–1074.

Ilgen, D. R., & Klein, H. J. (1989). Organizational behavior. *Annual Review of Psychology, 40,* 327–351.

Inhelder, B., & Piaget, J. (1958). *The growth of logical thinking from childhood to adolescence.* New York: Basic Books.

IQ myth, The (1975). New York: CBS News.

Irwin, M., Daniels, M., Bloom, E. T., Smith, T. L., & Weiner, H. (1987). Life events, depressive symptoms, and immune function. *American Journal of Psychiatry, 144,* 437–441.

Iversen, I. (1992). Skinner's early research: From reflexology to operant conditioning. *American Psychologist, 47,* 1318–1328.

Izard, C. (1971). *The face of emotion.* New York: Appleton Century Crofts.

Jacklin, C. N. (1989). Female and male: Issues of gender. *American Psychologist, 44,* 127–133.

Jacklin, C. N., & Maccoby, E. E. (1983). Issues of gender differentiation in normal development. In M. D. Levine, W. B. Carey, A. C. Crocker, & R. T. Gross (Eds.), *Developmental-behavioral pediatrics.* Philadelphia: W. B. Saunders.

Jackson, C. M. (1929). Some aspects of form and growth. In W. J. Robbins, S. Brody, A. F. Hogan, C. M. Jackson, & C. W. Greed (Eds.), *Growth.* New Haven, CT: Yale University Press.

Jackson, D. N., & Paunonen, S. V. (1980). Personality structure and assessment. *Annual Review of Psychology, 31,* 503–551.

Jackson, P. W., & Messick, D. (1968). Creativity. In P. London & D. Rosenhan (Eds.), *Foundations of abnormal psychology.* New York: Holt.

Jacobs, J. (1971). *Adolescent suicide.* New York: Wiley.

Jacobs, S., & Ostfeld, A. (1977). An epidemiological review of the mortality of bereavement. *Psychosomatic Medicine, 39,* 344–357.

Jacobson, E. (1938). *Progressive relaxation* (2nd ed.). Chicago: Univ. of Chicago Press.

Jacobson, J. L., & Wille, D. E. (1984). Influence of attachment and separation experience on separation distress at 18 months. *Developmental Psychology, 20,* 477–484.

Jaffe, C. M. (1977). First-degree atrioventricular block during lithium carbonate treatment. *American Journal of Psychiatry, 134,* 88–89.

James, W. (1890). *The principles of psychology.* New York: Henry Holt and Company.

Jameson, D., & Hurvich, L. M. (1989). Essay concerning color constancy. *Annual Review of Psychology, 40,* 1–22.

Janicak, P. G., Davis, J. M., Gibbons, R. D., Ericksen, S., Chang, S., & Gallagher, P. (1985). Efficacy of ECT: A meta-analysis. *American Journal of Psychiatry, 142,* 297–302.

Janik, A., & Toulmin, S. (1973). *Wittgenstein's Vienna.* New York: Simon and Schuster.

Janis, I. L., & Feshbach, S. (1953). Effects of fear-arousing communications. *Journal of Abnormal and Social Psychology, 48,* 78–92.

Janowitz, H. D., & Grossman, M. I. (1949). Some factors affecting the food intake of normal dogs and dogs with esophagostomy and gastric fistula. *American Journal of Physiology, 159,* 143–148.

Jeffery, R. W. (1989). Risk behaviors and health: Contrasting individual and population perspectives. *American Psychologist, 44,* 1194–1202.

Jemerin, J. M., & Boyce, W. T. (1990). Psychobiological differences in childhood stress response: II. Cardiovascular markers of vulnerability. *Journal of Developmental & Behavioral Pediatrics, 11,* 140–150.

Jensen, A. R. (1969). How much can we boost IQ and scholastic achievement? *Harvard Educational Review, 39,* 1–123.

Jewett, M. E., Kronauer, R. E., & Czeisler, C. A. (1991). Light-induced suppression of endogenous circadian amplitude in humans. *Nature, 350,* 59–62.

Joffe, L. S. (1980). *The relation between mother-infant attachment and compliance with maternal commands and prohibitions.* Unpublished doctoral dissertation, University of Minnesota.

Johansson, G., von Hofsten, C., & Jansson, G. (1980). Event perception. *Annual Review of Psychology, 31,* 27–63.

Johns, G., & Nicholson, N. (1982). The meaning of absence: New strategies for theory and research. In B. M. Staw & L. L. Cummings (Eds.), *Research in organizational behavior.* Greenwich, Conn.: JAI Press.

Johnson, D. W., & Johnson, R. T. (1975). *Learning together and alone: Cooperation, competition, and individualization.* Englewood Cliffs, NJ: Prentice-Hall.

Johnson, L. C., & MacLeod, W. L. (1973). Sleep and wake behavior during gradual sleep reduction. *Perceptual and Motor Skills, 36,* 87–97.

Jones, E. E., Bell, L., & Aronson, E. (1972). The reciprocation of attraction from similar and dissimilar others. In C. McClintock (Ed.), *Experimental social psychology.* New York: Holt, Rinehart & Winston.

Jones, E. E., & Sigall, H. (1971). The bogus pipeline: A new paradigm for measuring affect and attitude. *Psychological Bulletin, 76,* 349–364.

Jones, H. S., & Oswald, I. (1968). Two cases of healthy insomnia. *Electroencephalography & Clinical Neurophysiology, 24,* 378–380.

Jones, J. W., & Bogat, G. A. (1978). Air pollution and human aggression. *Psychological Reports, 43,* 721–722.

Jones, R. (1978). The third wave. In A. Pines & C. Maslach (Eds.), *Experiencing social psychology.* New York: Knopf.

Jones, S. L., Nation, J. R., & Massad, P. (1977). Immunization against learned helplessness in man. *Journal of Abnormal Psychology, 86,* 75–83.

Jourard, S. M. (1967). Experimenter-subject dialogue: A paradigm for a humanistic science of psychology. In J. Bugental (Ed.), *Challenges of humanistic psychology.* New York: McGraw-Hill.

Judd, L. L., McAdams, L., Budnick, B., & Braff, D. L. (1992). Sensory gating deficits in schizophrenia: New results. *American Journal of Psychiatry, 149,* 488–493.

Jung, C. G. (1933). *Psychological types.* New York: Harcourt Brace & World.

Jung, C. G. (1959). Mandalas. In *Collected works* (Vol. 14). Princeton: Princeton University Press. (Originally published in 1955).

Jung, C. G. (1959). The concept of the collective unconscious. In *Collected works* (Vol. 9, Part I). Princeton: Princeton University Press. (Originally published in 1936).

Kagan, J. (1973). What is intelligence? *Social Policy, 4*(1), 88–94.

Kagan, J., Reznick, J. S., & Gibbons, J. (1989). Inhibited and uninhibited types of children. *Child Development, 60,* 838–845.

Kagan, S., & Madsen, M. C. (1971). Cooperation and competition of Mexican, Mexican-American, and Anglo-American children of two ages and four instructional sets. *Developmental Psychology, 5,* 32–39.

Kahn, R. J., McNair, D. M., Lipman, R. S., Covi, L., Rickles, K., Downing, R., Fisher, S., & Frankenthaler, L. M. (1986). Imipramine and chlordiazepoxide in depressive and anxiety disorders: II. Efficacy in anxious outpatients. *Archives of General Psychiatry, 43,* 79–85.

Kahn, R. S., Davidson, M., Siever, L., Gabriel, S., Apter, S., & Davis, K. L. (1993). Serotonin function and treatment response to clozapine in schizophrenic patients. *American Journal of Psychiatry, 150,* 1337–1342.

Kales, A., Caldwell, A. B., Preston, T. A., Healey, S., & Kales, J. D. (1976). Personality patterns in insomnia: Theoretical implications. *Archives of General Psychiatry, 33,* 1128–1134.

Kales, A., Tan, T. L., Kollar, E. J., Naitoh, P., Preston, T. A., & Malmstrom, E. J. (1970). Sleep patterns following 205 hr of sleep deprivation. *Psychosomatic Medicine, 32,* 189–200.

Kamin, L. J. (1969). Predictability, surprise, attention, and conditioning. In B. A. Campbell & R. M. Church (Eds.), *Punishment and aversive behavior.* New York: Appleton-Century-Crofts.

Kandel, E. R., & Hawkins, R. D. (1992). The biological basis of learning and individuality. *Scientific American, 267*(3), 79–86.

Kanner, A. D., Coyne, J. C., Schaefer, C., & Lazarus, R. S. (1981). Comparison of two modes of stress measurement: Daily hassles and uplifts versus major life events. *Journal of Behavioral Medicine, 4,* 1–39.

Kaplan, M. (1983). A woman's view of DSM III. *American Psychologist, 38,* 786–792.

Kaplan, M. F., & Schwartz, S. (Eds.). (1977). *Judgment and decision processes in applied settings.* New York: Academic Press.

Karlen, N., & Burgower, B. (1985, January 7). Dumping the mentally ill. *Newsweek,* p. 17.

Karnovsky, M. L. (1986). Muramyl peptides in mammalian tissues and their effects at the cellular level. *Federation Proceedings, 45,* 2556–2560.

Kashani, J. H., & Carlson, G. A. (1987). Seriously depressed preschoolers. *American Journal of Psychiatry, 144,* 348–350.

Kassarjian, H. H. (1982). Consumer psychology. *Annual Review of Psychology, 33,* 619–649.

Kassoff, D. B. (1984). Psychotherapeutic approaches and techniques in treatment of the terminally ill patient (1950–1975). In M. Tallmer, E. R. Prichard, A. H.

Kutscher, R. DeBellis, M. S. Hale, & I. K. Goldberg (Eds.), *The life threatened elderly* (pp. 132–145). New York: Columbia University Press.

Katerndahl, D. A., & Realini, J. P. (1993). Lifetime prevalence of panic states. *American Journal of Psychiatry, 150,* 246–247.

Katz, R. (1982). The effects of group longevity on project communication and performance. *Administrative Science Quarterly, 27,* 81–104.

Katzell, R. A., & Thompson, D. E. (1990). Work motivation: Theory and practice. *American Psychologist, 45,* 144–153.

Kaufman, L., & Rock, I. (1962). The moon illusion, I. *Science, 136,* 953–961.

Kaylor, J. A., King, D. W., & King, L. A. (1987). Psychological effects of military service in Vietnam: A meta-analysis. *Psychological Bulletin, 102,* 257–271.

Keck, P. E., Pope, H. G., Jr., & McElroy, S. L. (1991). Declining frequency of neuroleptic malignant syndrome in a hospital population. *American Journal of Psychiatry, 148,* 880–882.

Keller, H., & Scholmerich, A. (1987). Infant vocalizations and parental reactions during the first 4 months of life. *Developmental Psychology, 23,* 62–67.

Kellermann, A. L., & Reay, D. T. (1986). Protection or peril? An analysis of firearm-related deaths in the home. *New England Journal of Medicine, 314,* 1557–1560.

Kellermann, A. L., Rivara, F. P., Somes, G., Reay, D. T., Francisco, J., Banton, J. G., Prodzinski, J., Fligner, C., & Hackman, B. B. (1992). Suicide in relation to gun ownership. *New England Journal of Medicine, 327,* 467–472.

Kelley, H. H. (1983). Love and commitment. In H. H. Kelley (Ed.), *Close relationships* (pp. 265–314). New York: W. H. Freeman.

Kellner, R., Neidhardt, J., Krakow, B., & Pathak, D. (1992). Changes in chronic nightmares after one session of desensitization or rehearsal instructions. *American Journal of Psychiatry, 149,* 659–663.

Kelso, S. R., & Brown, T. H. (1986). Differential conditioning of associative synaptic enhancement in hippocampal brain slices. *Science, 232,* 85–87.

Kenardy, J., Evans, L., & Oei, T. P. S. (1992). The latent structure of anxiety symptoms in anxiety disorders. *American Journal of Psychiatry, 149,* 1058–1061.

Kendell, R. E. (1970). Relationship between aggression and depression. *Archives of General Psychiatry, 22,* 308–318.

Kendler, K. S., Gruenberg, A. M., & Tsuang, M. T. (1985). Subtype stability in schizophrenia. *American Journal of Psychiatry, 142,* 827–832.

Kendler, K. S., Gruenberg, A. M., & Tsuang, M. T. (1988). A family study of the subtypes of schizophrenia. *American Journal of Psychiatry, 145,* 57–62.

Kendler, K. S., Kessler, R. C., Neale, M. C., Heath, A. C., & Eaves, L. J. (1993). The prediction of major depression in women: Toward an integrated etiologic model. *American Journal of Psychiatry, 150,* 1139–1148.

Keniston, K. (1968). *Young radicals: Notes on committed youth.* New York: Harcourt Brace & World.

Keniston, K. (1970). Youth: A "new" stage of life. *The American Scholar, 39,* 631–654.

Keniston, K. (1983, June). Remembering Erikson at Harvard. *Psychology Today,* p. 29.

Kenrick, D. T., & Funder, D. C. (1988). Profiting from controversy: Lessons from the person-situation debate. *American Psychologist, 43,* 23–34.

Kenrick, D. T., Growth, G. E., Trost, M. R., & Sadalla, E. K. (1993). Integrating evolutionary and social exchange perspectives on relationships: Effects of gender, self-appraisal, and involvement level on mate selection criteria. *Journal of Personality & Social Psychology, 64,* 951–969.

Kerckhoff, A. C., & Davis, K. E. (1962). Value consensus and need complementarity in mate selection. *American Sociological Review, 27,* 295–303.

Kessler, R. C., & McRae, J. A. (1984). A note on the relationship of sex and marital status to psychological distress. *Research in Community and Mental Health, 4,* 109–130.

Kety, S. S., Rosenthal, D., Wender, P. H., Schulsinger, F., & Jacobsen, B. (1978). The biologic and adoptive families of adopted individuals who become schizophrenic: Prevalence of mental illness and other characteristics. In L. C. Wynne, R. L. Cromwell, & S. Matthysse (Eds.), *The nature of schizophrenia: New approaches to research and treatment.* New York: Wiley.

Khan, L. M. L., & James, S. L. (1983). Grammatical morpheme development in three language disordered children. *Journal of Childhood Communication Disorders, 6,* 85–100.

Kiesler, C. A. (1982a). Mental hospitals and alternative care: Noninstitutionalization as potential public policy for mental patients. *American Psychologist, 37,* 349–360.

Kiesler, C. A. (1982b). Public and professional myths about mental hospitalization. *American Psychologist, 37,* 1323–1339.

Kiesler, C. A. (1991). Change in general hospital psychiatric care, 1980–1985. *American Psychologist, 46,* 416–421.

Kiesler, S., & Baral, R. (1970). The search for a romantic partner: The effects of self-esteem and physical attractiveness on romantic behavior. In K. Gergen & D. Marlowe (Eds.), *Personality and social behavior.* Reading, Mass.: Addison-Wesley.

Kihlstrom, J. F. (1987). The cognitive unconscious. *Science, 237,* 1445–1452.

Kilham, W., & Mann, L. (1974). Level of destructive obedience as a function of

transmitter and executant roles in the Milgram obedience paradigm. *Journal of Personality & Social Psychology, 29,* 696–702.

Kimchi, R. (1992). Primacy of wholistic processing and global/local paradigm: A critical review. *Psychological Bulletin, 112,* 24–38.

Kimura, D. (1985, November). Male brain, female brain: The hidden difference. *Psychology Today,* pp. 50–58.

Kirk-Smith, M., Booth, D. A., Carroll, D., & Davies, P. (1978). Human social attitudes affected by androstenol. *Research Communications in Psychology, Psychiatry and Behavior, 3,* 379–384.

Kivnick, H. Q. (1981). Grandparenthood and the mental health of grandparents. *Aging & Society, 1*(3), 365–391.

Kivnick, H. Q. (1985). Intergenerational relations: Personal meaning in the life cycle. *Contributions to Human Development, 14,* 93–102.

Klein, D. N., Taylor, E. B., Harding, K., & Dickstein, S. (1988). Double depression and episodic major depression: Demographic, clinical, familial, personality, and socioenvironmental characteristics and short-term outcome. *American Journal of Psychiatry, 145,* 1226–1231.

Kleininna, P. R., Jr., & Kleininna, A. M. (1988). Current trends toward convergence of the behavioristic, functional, and cognitive perspectives in experimental psychology. *The Psychological Record, 38,* 369–392.

Kleinke, C. L. (1977). Effects of dress on compliance to requests in a field setting. *Journal of Social Psychology, 101,* 223–224.

Kleinmuntz, B., & Szucko, J. J. (1984). Lie detection in ancient and modern times: A call for contemporary scientific study. *American Psychologist, 39,* 766–776.

Klinger, E. (1987, October). The power of daydreams. *Psychology Today,* pp. 37–44.

Klinnert, M. D., Emde, R. N., Butterfield, P., & Campos, J. J. (1986). Social referencing: The infant's use of emotional signals from a friendly adult with mother present. *Developmental Psychology, 22,* 427–432.

Kogan, N., & Pankove, E. (1972). Creative ability over a five-year span. *Child Development, 43,* 427–442.

Kohlberg, L. (1963). The development of children's orientations toward a moral order: I. Sequence in the development of moral thought. *Vita Humana, 6,* 11–33.

Kohlberg, L. (1966). A cognitive-developmental analysis of children's sex-role concepts and attitudes. In E. E. Maccoby (Ed.), *The development of sex differences* (pp. 81–173). Stanford, Calif.: Stanford Univ. Press.

Kohlberg, L. (1971). From is to ought: How to commit the naturalistic fallacy and get away with it in the study of moral development. In T. Mischel (Ed.), *Cognitive development and genetic epistemology.* New York: Academic Press.

Kohler, W. (1925). Gestaltprobleme und Anfange einer Gestalttheorie. Jahresbericht u. d. ges. Physiol., 3, 512–539. (Translated in Ellis, W. D., *A source book of gestalt psychology.* New York: Harcourt, Brace, & World, 1938).

Kohler, W. (1927). *The mentality of apes.* London: Routledge & Kegan Paul.

Kolata, G. (1983). Math genius may have hormonal basis. *Science, 222,* 1312.

Kolata, G. (1984). Studying learning in the womb. *Science, 225,* 302–303.

Kolata, G. (1987a). How to ask about sex and get honest answers. *Science, 236,* 382.

Kolata, G. (1987b). Associations or rules in learning language? *Science, 237,* 133–134.

Kolata, G. (1987c). Manic-depression gene tied to chromosome 11. *Science, 235,* 1139–1140.

Kolata, G. (1987d). Panel urges dementia be diagnosed with care. *Science, 237,* 725.

Kolb, B. (1989). Brain development, plasticity, and behavior. *American Psychologist, 44,* 1203–1212.

Kolb, L. C. (1973). *Modern clinical psychiatry* (8th ed.). Philadelphia: W. B. Saunders.

Koller, M. R. (1953). Residential and occupational propinquity. In R. F. Winch & R. McGinnis (Eds.), *Marriage and the family.* New York: Holt, Rinehart & Winston.

Komaki, J., Heinzmann, A. T., & Lawson, L. (1980). Effect of training and feedback: Component analysis of a behavioral safety program. *Journal of Applied Psychology, 65,* 261–270.

Konopasky, R. J., & Telegdy, G. A. (1977). Conformity in the rat: A leader's selection of door color versus a learned door-color discrimination. *Perceptual & Motor Skills, 44,* 31–37.

Korchin, S. J. (1976). *Modern clinical psychology.* New York: Basic Books.

Korner, A. F., Hutchinson, C. A., Koperski, J. A., Kraemer, H. C., & Schneider, P. A. (1981). Stability of individual differences of neonatal motor and crying patterns. *Child Development, 52,* 83–90.

Krantz, D. S., Grunberg, N. E., & Baum, A. (1985). Health psychology. *Annual Review of Psychology, 36,* 349–383.

Krieger, W. G. (1976). Infant influences and the parent sex by child sex interaction in the socialization process. *JSAS Catalogue of Selected Documents in Psychology, 6*(1), 36 (Ms. No. 1234).

Kroger, W. S. (1977). *Clinical and experimental hypnosis* (2nd ed.). Philadelphia: J. B. Lippincott.

Krueger, J. M., Pappenheimer, J. R., & Karnovsky, M. L. (1982). The composition of sleep-promoting factor isolated from human urine. *Journal of Biological Chemistry,*

257, 1664–1669.

Kubler-Ross, E. (1969). *On death and dying*. New York: Macmillan Publishing Co.

Kuhl, P. K., Williams, K. A., Lacerda, F., Stevens, K. N., & Lindblom, B. (1992). Linguistic experience alters phonetic perception in infants by 6 months of age. *Science, 255*, 606–608.

Kurtines, W., & Greif, E. B. (1974). The development of moral thought: Review and evaluation of Kohlberg's approach. *Psychological Bulletin, 81*, 453–470.

LaBerge, S. P. (1981, January). Lucid dreaming. *Psychology Today*, pp. 48–57.

Labouvie-Vief, G. (1985). Intelligence and cognition. In J. E. Birren & K. W. Schaie (Eds.), *Handbook of the psychology of aging* (2nd ed., pp. 500–530). New York: Van Nostrand Reinhold.

Labouvie-Vief, G., & Gonda, J. N. (1976). Cognitive strategy training and intellectual performance in the elderly. *Journal of Gerontology, 31*, 327–332.

Ladd, G. T. (1887). *Elements of physiological psychology*. New York: Scribner's.

Laird, J. D. (1974). Self-attribution of emotion: The effects of expressive behavior on the quality of emotional experience. *Journal of Personality & Social Psychology, 29*, 475–486.

Lakoff, G. (1987). *Women, fire, and dangerous things: What categories reveal about the mind*. Chicago: Univ. of Chicago Press.

Lam, R. W., Beattie, C. W., Buchanan, A., Remick, R. A., & Zis, A. (1991). Low electrooculographic ratios in patients with seasonal affective disorder. *American Journal of Psychiatry, 148*, 1526–1529.

Lamb, M. E. (1978). The father's role in the infant's social world. In J. H. Stevens & M. Mathews (Eds.), *Mother/child, father/child relationships*. Washington, D.C.: National Association for the Education of Young Children.

Lamb, M. E. (1988). Social and emotional development in infancy. In M. H. Bornstein & M. E. Lamb (Eds.), *Developmental psychology: An advanced textbook* (pp. 359–410). Hillsdale, NJ: Lawrence Erlbaum.

Lamb, M. E., & Sternberg, K. J. (1990). Do we really know how day care affects children? *Journal of Applied Developmental Psychology, 11*, 351–379.

Lamper, C., & Eisdorfer, C. (1971). Prestimulus activity level and responsivity in the neonate. *Child Development, 42*, 465–473.

Lampl, M., Veldhuis, J. D., & Johnson, M. L. (1992). Saltation and stasis: A model of human growth. *Science, 258*, 801–803.

Land, E. H. (1977). The retinex theory of color vision. *Scientific American, 237*(6), 108–128.

Landman, J. T., & Dawes, R. M. (1982). Psychotherapy outcome: Smith and Glass' conclusions stand up under scrutiny. *American Psychologist, 37*, 504–516.

Lange, C. G., & James, W. (1922). *The emotions*. Baltimore, MD: Williams & Wilkins.

Langer, E. J., Rodin, J., Beck, P., Weinman, C., & Spitzer, L. (1979). Environmental determinants of memory improvement in late adulthood. *Journal of Personality & Social Psychology, 37*, 2003–2013.

Langlois, J. H., & Downs, A. C. (1980). Mothers, fathers, and peers as socialization agents of sex-typed play behaviors in young children. *Child Development, 51*, 1237–1247.

Langlois, J. H., & Roggman, L. A. (1990). Attractive faces are only average. *Psychological Science, 1*, 115–121.

Langlois, J. H., Ritter, J. M., Roggman, L. A., & Vaughn, L. S. (1991). Facial diversity and infant preferences for attractive faces. *Developmental Psychology, 27*, 79–84.

Lashley, K. S. (1950). In search of the engram. In *Symposium of the Society for Experimental Biology* (Vol. 4). New York: Cambridge Univ. Press.

Lassen, M. K., & McConnell, S. C. (1977). Treatment of a severe bird phobia by participant modeling. *Journal of Behavior Therapy and Experimental Psychiatry, 8*, 165–168.

Latane, B. (1981). The psychology of social impact. *American Psychologist, 36*, 343–356.

Latane, B., & Darley, J. M. (1968). Group inhibition of bystander intervention in emergencies. *Journal of Personality & Social Psychology, 10*, 215–221.

Latane, B., & Darley, J. M. (1970). *The unresponsive bystander: Why doesn't he help?* New York: Appleton-Century-Crofts.

Laumann, E. O. (1969). Friends of urban men: An assessment of accuracy in reporting their socioeconomic attributes, mutual choice, and attitude agreement. *Sociometry, 32*, 54–69.

Laurence, J., & Perry, C. (1983). Hypnotically created memory among highly hypnotizable subjects. *Science, 222*, 523–524.

Lazar, I., & Darlington, R. (1982). Lasting effects of early education: A report from the Consortium for Longitudinal Studies. *Monographs of the Society for Research in Child Development, 47*(2–3, Serial No. 195).

Lazarus, A. A. (1976). *Multimodal behavior therapy*. New York: Springer.

Lazarus, R. S. (1984). On the primacy of cognition. *American Psychologist, 39*, 124–129.

Lazarus, R. S. (1991). Cognition and motivation in emotion. *American Psychologist, 46*, 352–367.

Lazarus, R. S. (1993). From Psychological stress to the emotions: A history of changing outlooks. *Annual Review of Psychology, 44*, 1–21.

Lazarus, R. S., Delongis, A., Folkman, S., & Gruen, R. (1985). Stress and adaptational outcomes: The problem of confounded measures. *American Psychologist, 40*, 770–779.

Leaf, A. (1973). Getting old. *Scientific American, 229*(3), 44–52.

Leary, M. R., & Kowalski, R. M. (1990). Impression management: A literature review and two-component model. *Psychological Bulletin, 107*, 34–47.

Leaton, R. N., & Supple, W. F., Jr. (1986). Cerebellar vermis: Essential for long-term habituation of the acoustic startle response. *Science, 232*, 513–515.

Leavitt, H. J., & Schlosberg, H. (1944). The retention of verbal and motor skills. *Journal of Experimental Psychology, 34*, 404–417.

Lebra, T. S. (1976). *Japanese patterns of behavior*. Honolulu: University of Hawaii Press.

Lee, G. R., & Ellithorpe, E. (1982). Intergenerational exchange and subjective well-being among the elderly. *Journal of Marriage & the Family, 44*, 217–224.

Lee, K., Wells, R. G., & Reed, R. R. (1987). Isolation of an olfactory cDNA: Similarity to retinol-binding protein suggests a role in olfaction. *Science, 235*, 1053–1056.

Lee, V. E., Brooks-Gunn, J., Schnur, E., & Liaw, F. (1990). Are Head Start effects sustained? A longitudinal follow-up comparison of disadvantaged children attending Heart Start, no preschool, and other preschool programs. *Child Development, 61*, 495–507.

Lehman, H. C. (1953). *Age and achievement*. Princeton, NJ: Princeton University Press.

Lehman, H. C. (1954). Men's creative production rate at different ages and in different countries. *Scientific Monthly, 78*, 321–326.

Lehman, H. C. (1958). The influence of longevity upon curves showing man's creative production rate at successive age levels. *Journal of Gerontology, 13*, 187–191.

Lempert, H. (1989). Animacy constraints on preschool children's acquisition of syntax. *Child Development, 60*, 237–245.

Lenneberg, E. H. (1966). The natural history of language. In F. Smith & G. A. Miller (Eds.), *The genesis of language*. Cambridge, Mass.: M.I.T. Press.

Lenneberg, E. H. (1967). *Biological foundations of language*. New York: Wiley.

Lepper, M. R., Greene, D., & Nisbett, R. E. (1973). Undermining children's intrinsic interest with extrinsic reward: A test of the "overjustification" hypothesis. *Journal of Personality & Social Psychology, 28*, 129–137.

Lev-Ran, A. (1974). Sexuality and educational levels of women with the late-treated adrenogenital syndrome. *Archives of Sexual Behavior, 3*, 27–32.

Leventhal, G., & Krate, R. (1977). Physical attractiveness and severity of sentencing. *Psychological Reports, 40*, 315–318.

Leventhal, H. (1970). Findings and theory in the study of fear communications. In L. Berkowitz (Ed.), *Advances in experimental social psychology* (Vol. 5). New York: Academic Press.

Leventhal, H., & Tomarken, A. J. (1986). Emotion: Today's problems. *Annual Review of Psychology, 37*, 565–610.

Levine, J. D., Gordon, N. C., & Fields, H. L. (1978). The mechanism of placebo analgesia. *The Lancet, 2*, 654–657.

Levine, L. E. (1983). Mine: Self-definition in 2–year-old-boys. *Developmental Psychology, 19*, 544–549.

Levinson, D. J. (1986). A conception of adult development. *American Psychologist, 41*, 3–13.

Levinson, D. J., Darrow, C. N., Klein, E. B., Levinson, M. H., & McKee, B. (1978). *The seasons of a man's life*. New York: Knopf.

Leviton, D. (1977). Death education. In H. Feifel (Ed.), *New meanings of death*. New York: McGraw-Hill.

Lewicki, P. (1986). *Nonconscious social information processing*. New York: Academic Press.

Lewin, R. (1984). Practice catches theory in kin recognition. *Science, 223*, 1049–1051.

Lewin, R. (1988). Brain graft puzzles. *Science, 240*, 879.

Lewis, M. I., & Butler, R. N. (1974). Life-review therapy: Putting memories to work in individual and group psychotherapy. *Geriatrics, 29*, 165–174.

Lewis, M., Stanger, C., & Sullivan, M. W. (1989). Deception in 3-year-olds. *Developmental Psychology, 25*, 439–443.

Lewis, Max. (1981, November). Personal communication.

Lewontin, R. C., Rose, S., & Kamin, L. J. (1984). *Not in our genes*. New York: Pantheon Books.

Liberman, R. P., Mueser, K. T., & Wallace, C. J. (1986). Social skills training for schizophrenic individuals at risk for relapse. *American Journal of Psychiatry, 143*, 523–526.

Licht, B. G., & Dweck, C. S. (1984). Determinants of academic achievement: The interaction of children's achievement orientations with skill area. *Developmental Psychology, 20*, 628–636.

Lieberman, J., Bogerts, B., Degreef, G., Ashtari, M., Lantos, G., & Alvir, J. (1992). Qualitative assessment of brain morphology in acute and chronic schizophrenia. *American Journal of Psychiatry, 149*, 784–794.

Liebert, R. M., & Sprafkin, J. (1988). *The early window: Effects of television on children and youth* (3rd ed.). New York: Pergamon Press.

Light, K. C., Koepke, J. P., Obrist, P. A., & Willis, P. W., IV. (1983). Psychological stress induces sodium and fluid retention in men at high risk for hypertension. *Science, 220,* 429–431.

Likert, R. (1961). *New patterns of management.* New York: McGraw-Hill.

Linder, M. E., & Gilman, A. G. (1992). G proteins. *Scientific American, 267*(1), 56–65.

Lindvall, O., Brudin, P., Widner, H., Rehncrona, S., Gustavii, B., Frackowiak, R., Leenders, K. L., Sawle, G., Rothwell, J. C., Marsden, C. D., & Bjorklund, A. (1990). Grafts of fetal dopamine neurons survive and improve motor function in Parkinson's disease. *Science, 247,* 574–577.

Ling, G. S. F., MacLeod, J. M., Lee, S., Lockhart, S. H., & Pasternak, G. W. (1984). Separation of morphine analgesia from physical dependence. *Science, 226,* 462–464.

Linney, J. A., & Seidman, E. (1989). The future of schooling. *American Psychologist, 44,* 336–340.

Linton, H., & Graham, E. (1959). Personality correlates of persuasibility. In C. I. Hovland & I. L. Janis (Eds.), *Personality and persuasibility.* New Haven, Conn.: Yale University Press.

Lipkowitz, M. H., & Idupuganti, S. (1985). Diagnosing schizophrenia in 1982: The effect of DSM-III. *American Journal of Psychiatry, 142,* 634–637.

Lipowski, Z. J. (1988). Somatization: The concept and its clinical application. *American Journal of Psychiatry, 145,* 1358–1368.

Lippitt, R., Polansky, N., & Rosen, S. (1952). The dynamics of power. *Human Relations, 5,* 37–64.

Livingstone, M. S. (1988). Art, illusion and the visual system. *Scientific American, 258*(1), 78–85.

Llinas, R. R. (1988). The intrinsic electrophysiological properties of mammalian neurons: Insights into central nervous system function. *Science, 242,* 1654–1664.

Locke, E. A. (1976). The nature and causes of job satisfaction. In M. Dunnette (Ed.), *Handbook of industrial and organizational psychology.* Chicago: Rand-McNally.

Locke, S. E., Furst, M. W., Heisel, J. S., & Williams, R. M. (1978, April). *The influences of stress on the immune response.* Paper presented at the annual meeting of the American Psychosomatic Society, Washington, D. C.

Locke, S. E., Krause, L., Leserman, J., Hurst, M. W., Heisel, J. S., & Williams, R. M. (1984). Life change stress, psychiatric symptoms, and natural killer cell activity. *Psychosomatic Medicine, 46,* 441–453.

Loeb, G. E. (1985). The functional replacement of the ear. *Scientific American, 252*(2), 104–111.

Loehlin, J. C., Horn, J. M., & Willerman, L. (1989). Modeling IQ change: Evidence from the Texas Adoption Project. *Child Development, 60,* 993–1004.

Loehlin, J. C., Willerman, L., & Horn, J. M. (1988). Human behavior genetics. *Annual Review of Psychology, 39,* 101–133.

Loevinger, J., & Knoll, E. (1983). Personality: Stages, traits, and the self. *Annual Review of Psychology, 34,* 195–222.

Loftus, E. F., & Loftus, G. R. (1980). On the permanence of stored information in the human brain. *American Psychologist, 35,* 409–420.

Logothetis, N. K., & Schall, J. D. (1989). Neuronal correlates of subjective visual perception. *Science, 245,* 761–763.

Logue, A. W. (1991). *The psychology of eating and drinking* (2nd ed.). New York: W. H. Freeman.

Loizos, C. (1967). Play behavior in higher primates: A review. In D. Morris (Ed.), *Primate ethology.* London: Weidenfeld & Nicholson.

Lore, R. K., & Schultz, L. A. (1993). Control of human aggression: A comparative perspective. *American Psychologist, 48,* 16–25.

Lorenz, K. (1937). Uber die Bldung des Instinkbegriffes. *Naturwissenchaften, 25,* 289–300, 307–318, 324–331.

Lorenz, K. (1943). Die angeborenen Formen moglicher Erfahrung. Z. *Tierpsychologie, 5,* 235–409.

Love, D. (1987, November 14). Personal communication.

Lowe, M. G. (1982). The role of anticipated deprivation in overeating. *Addictive Behaviors, 7,* 103–112.

Lubin, B., Larsen, R. M., Matarazzo, J. D., & Seever, M. (1985). Psychological test usage patterns in five professional settings. *American Psychologist, 40,* 857–861.

Luborsky, L., Crits-Cristoph, P., McLellan, A. T., Woody, G., Piper, W., Liberman, B., Imber, S., & Pilkonis, P. (1986). Do therapists vary much in their success? Findings from four outcome studies. *American Journal of Orthopsychiatry, 56,* 501–512.

Luchins, A. S. (1942). Mechanization in problem solving. *Psychological Monographs, 54,* No. 248.

Lucins, D. (1975). The dopamine hypothesis of schizophrenia: A critical analysis. *Neuropsychobiology, 1,* 365–378.

Lugaresi, E., Medori, R., Montagna, P., Baruzzi, A., Corelli, P., Lugaresi, A., Tinuper, P., Zucconi, M., & Gambetti, P. (1986). Fatal familial insomnia and dysautonomia

with selective degeneration of thalamic nuclei. *New England Journal of Medicine, 315,* 997–1003.

Luisada, P. V., & Brown, B. I. (1976). Clinical management of the phencyclidine psychosis. *Clinical Toxicology, 9,* 539–545.

Luria, A. R. (1968). *The mind of a mnemonist.* New York: Basic Books.

Lutz, R. J., & Bettman, J. R. (1977). Multiattribute models in marketing: A bicentennial review. In A. G. Woodside, J. N. Sheth, & P. D. Bennett (Eds.), *Consumer and industrial buying behavior* (pp. 137–149). New York: Evsevier North Holland.

Luxenberg, J. S., Swedo, S. E., Flament, M. F., Friedland, R. P., Rapoport, J., & Rapoport, S. I. (1988). Neuroanatomical abnormalities in obsessive-compulsive disorder detected with quantitative X-ray computed tomography. *American Journal of Psychiatry, 145,* 1089–1093.

Lykken, D. T. (1981). *A tremor in the blood: Uses and abuses of the lie detector.* New York: McGraw-Hill, 1981.

Lykken, D. T. (1981). The lie detector and the law. *Criminal Defense, 8,* 19–27.

Lynn, K. S. (1987). *Hemingway.* New York: Simon & Schuster.

Lynn, S. J., & Rhue, J. W. (1988). Fantasy proneness. *American Psychologist, 43,* 35–44.

Lytton, H., Conway, D., & Suave, R. (1977). The impact of twinship on parent-child interaction. *Journal of Personality & Social Psychology, 35,* 97–107.

M'Naghten's Case. (1843). *English Reports, 8,* 718.

Maccoby, E. E. (1988). Gender as a social category. *Developmental Psychology, 24,* 755–765.

Maccoby, E. E., & Jacklin, C. N. (1974). *The psychology of sex differences.* Stanford, Calif.: Stanford Univ. Press.

MacCoun, R. J. (1989). Experimental research on jury decision-making. *Science, 244,* 1046–1050.

MacKain, K., Studdert-Kennedy, M., Spieker, S., & Stern, D. (1983). Infant intermodal speech perception is a left-hemisphere function. *Science, 219,* 1347–1349.

MacKay, D. M. (1973). Lateral interaction between neural channels sensitive to texture density? *Nature, 245,* 159–161.

MacWhinney, B. (1978). The acquisition of morphophonology. *Monographs of the Society for Research in Child Development, 43*(1–2, Serial No. 174).

Madden, N. A., & Slavin, R. E. (1983). Mainstreaming students with mild handicaps: Academic and social outcomes. *Review of Educational Research, 53,* 519–569.

Madigan, S. A. (1969). Intraserial repetition and coding processes in free recall. *Journal of Verbal Learning and Verbal Behavior, 8,* 828–835.

Madrazo, I., Leon, V., Torres, C., Aguilera, M. C., Varela, G., Alvarez, F., Fraga, A., Drucker-Colin, R., Ostrosky, F., & Skurovich, M. (1988). Transplantation of fetal substantia nigra and adrenal medulla to the caudate nucleus in two patients with Parkinson's disease. *New England Journal of Medicine, 318,* 51.

Madsen, M. C. (1971). Developmental and cross-cultural differences in the cooperative and competitive behavior of young children. *Journal of Cross-Cultural Psychology, 2,* 365–371.

Madsen, M. C., & Shapira, A. (1970). Cooperative and competitive behavior of urban Afro-American, Anglo-American, Mexican-American, and Mexican village children. *Developmental Psychology, 3,* 16–20.

Magnusson, D., & Endler, N. S. (1977). Interactional psychology: Present status and future prospects. In D. Magnusson & N. S. Endler (Eds.), *Personality at the crossroads.* New York: Wiley-Erlbaum.

Mahoney, M. J. (1979). Cognitive skills and athletic performance. In P. C. Kendall & S. D. Hollon (Eds.), *Cognitive-behavioral interventions: Theory, research, and procedures* (pp. 423–443). New York: Academic Press.

Mahoney, M. J. (1989). Scientific psychology and radical behaviorism. *American Psychologist, 44,* 1372–1377.

Mahowald, M. A., & Mead, C. (1991). The silicon retina. *Scientific American, 264*(5), 76–82.

Maier, N. R. F. (1931). Reasoning in humans: II. The solution of a problem and its appearance in consciousness. *Journal of Comparative Psychology, 12,* 181–194.

Malkis, F. S., Kalle, R. J., & Tedeschi, J. T. (1982). Attitudinal politics in the forced compliance situation. *Journal of Social Psychology, 117,* 79–91.

Mancillas, J. R., Siggins, G. R., & Bloom, F. E. (1986). Systemic ethanol: Selective enhancement of responses to acetylcholine and somatostatin in hippocampus. *Science, 231,* 161–163.

Mantell, D. M. (1971). The potential for violence in Germany. *Journal of Social Issues, 27*(4), 101–112.

Manyande, A., Chayen, S., Priyakumar, P., Smith, C. C., Hayes, M., Higgins, D., Kee, S., Phillips, S., & Salmon, P. (1992). Anxiety and endocrine responses to surgery: Paradoxical effects of preoperative relaxation training. *Psychosomatic Medicine, 54,* 275–287.

Maranto, G. (1984, November). Emotions: How they affect your body. *Discover,* pp. 35–38.

Marbach, W. D., Carroll, G., & Miller, M. (1987, April 27). America's big risk. *Newsweek*, pp. 58–60.

Marcos, L. R., Cohen, N. L., Nardacci, D., & Brittain, J. (1990). Psychiatry takes to the streets: The New York City initiative for the homeless mentally ill. *American Journal of Psychiatry, 147*, 1557–1561.

Marcus, E. A., Nolen, T. G., Rankin, C. H., & Carew, T. J. (1988). Behavioral dissociation of dishabituation, sensitization, and inhibition in *Aplysia. Science, 241*, 210–213.

Marder, S. R., Van Putten, T., Mintz, J., Lebell, M., McKenzie, J., & May, P. R. (1987). Low- and conventional-dose maintenance therapy with fluphenazine decanoate. Two-year outcome. *Archives of General Psychiatry, 44*, 518–521.

Marean, G. C., Werner, L. A., & Kuhl, P. K. (1992). Vowel categorization by very young infants. *Developmental Psychology, 28*, 396–405.

Markowitz, J., Brown, R., Sweeney, J., & Mann, J. J. (1987). Reduced length and cost of hospital stay for major depression in patients treated with ECT. *American Journal of Psychiatry, 144*, 1025–1029.

Marks, P. A., & Seeman, W. (1963). *Actuarial description of abnormal personality.* Baltimore: Williams & Wilkins.

Marmor, J. (1985, October). Homosexuality: Nature vs nurture. *Harvard Medical School Mental Health Letter*, pp. 5–6.

Marshall, P. S. (1993). Allergy and depression: A neurochemical threshold model of the relation between the illnesses. *Psychological Bulletin, 113*, 23–43.

Martin, C. L., & Little, J. K. (1990). The relation of gender understanding to children's sex-typed preferences and gender stereotypes. *Child Development, 61*, 1427–1439.

Martin, J., Lobb, B., Chapman, G. C., & Spillane, R. (1976). Obedience under conditions demanding self-immolation. *Human Relations, 29*, 345–356.

Martin, P. J., Hunter, M. L., & Moore, J. E. (1977). Pulling the wool: Impression-management among hospitalized schizophrenics. *Research Communications in Psychology, Psychiatry and Behavior, 2*, 21–26.

Marx, J. (1992). Boring in on Beta-amyloid's role in Alzheimer's. *Science, 255*, 688–689.

Marx, J. (1993). Alzheimer's pathology begins to yield its secrets. *Science, 259*, 457–458.

Marx, J. L. (1985). The immune system "belongs in the body". *Science, 227*, 1190–1192.

Marx, J. L. (1986). Nerve activity alters neurotransmitter synthesis. *Science, 232*, 1500–1501.

Marx, M. H., & Hillix, W. (1963). *Systems and theories in psychology.* New York: McGraw-Hill.

Maslow, A. H. (1954). *Motivation and personality.* New York: Harper & Row.

Maslow, A. H. (1968). *Toward a psychology of being* (2nd ed.). New York: Van Nostrand.

Maslow, A. H. (1970). *Motivation and personality.* New York: Harper & Row.

Mason, W. A. (1965). The social development of monkeys and apes. In I. DeVore (Ed.), *Primate behavior: Field studies of monkeys and apes.* New York: Holt.

Massachusetts Committee on Alzheimer's Disease (1986). *Final report of the special committee established to make an investigation and study relative to "Alzheimer's disease."*

Massion, A. O., Warshaw, M. G., & Keller, M. B. (1993). Quality of life and psychiatric morbidity in panic disorder and generalized anxiety disorder. *American Journal of Psychiatry, 150*, 600–607.

Masters, W. H., & Johnson, V. E. (1970). *Human sexual inadequacy.* Boston: Little, Brown.

Matarazzo, J. D. (1983). Computerized psychological testing. *Science, 221*, 323.

Matheson, J. (1986, February). What is narcolepsy? *Harvard Medical School Mental Health Letter*, p. 8.

Mathews, P. (1993). *The Guinness book of world records.* New York: Bantam Books.

Matthews, K. A. (1988). Coronary heart disease and type A behaviors: Update on and alternative to the Booth-Kewley and Friedman (1987) quantitative review. *Psychological Bulletin, 104*, 373–380.

Mayr, E. (1982). *The growth of biological thought.* Cambridge, MA: Belknap Press.

Mazess, R. B., & Forman, S. H. (1979). Longevity and age exaggeration in Vilcabamba, Ecuador. *Journal of Gerontology, 34*, 94–98.

Mazess, R. B., & Mathisen, R. W. (1982). Lack of unusual longevity in Vilcabamba, Ecuador. *Human Biology, 54*, 517–524.

Maziade, M., Cote, R., Boutin, P., Bernier, H., & Thivierge, J. (1988). Temperament and intellectual development: A longitudinal study from infancy to four years. In S. Chess, A. Thomas, & M. E. Hertzig (Eds.), *Annual progress in child psychiatry and child development* (pp. 335–349). New York: Brunner/Mazel.

Mazur, A., & Rosa, E. (1977). An empirical test of McClelland's "achieving society" theory. *Social Forces, 55*, 769–774.

McCall, J. N., & Johnson, O. G. (1972). The independence of intelligence from family size and birth order. *Journal of Genetic Psychology, 121*, 207–213.

McCall, R. B., & Carriger, M. S. (1993). A meta-analysis of infant habituation and recognition memory performance as predictors of later IQ. *Child Development, 64*, 57–79.

McCarthy, P. (1986, July). Scent: The tie that binds? *Psychology Today*, pp. 6, 10.

McCartney, K., Scarr, S., Phillips, D., & Grajek, S. (1985). Day care as intervention: Comparisons of varying quality programs. Journal of Applied *Developmental Psychology, 6*(2–3), 247–260.

McClelland, D. C. (1961). *The achieving society.* New York: Van Nostrand.

McClelland, D. C. (1973). Testing for competence rather than for "intelligence." *American Psychologist, 28*, 1–14.

McClelland, D. C., Atkinson, J. W., Clark, R. A., & Lowell, E. L. (1953). *The achievement motive.* New York: Appleton-Century-Crofts.

McClements, J. D., & Botterill, C. B. (1980). Goal-setting in shaping of future performance of athletes. In P. Klavora & J. Daniel (Eds.), *Coach, athlete, and the sport psychologist* (pp. 199–210). Toronto: Univ. of Toronto Press.

McClurkin, J. W., Optican, L. M., Richmond, B. J., & Gawne, T. J. (1991). Concurrent processing and complexity of temporally encoded neuronal messages in visual perception. *Science, 253*, 675–677.

McCord, J. (1977, November 26). Thirty year followup: Counseling fails. *Science News*, p. 357.

McCormick, D. A., & Thompson, R. F. (1984). Cerebellum: Essential involvement in the classically conditioned eyelid response. *Science, 223*, 296–299.

McDonough, R. J., Madden, J. J., Falek, A., Shafer, D. A., Pine, M., Gordon, D., Bokos, P., Kuehnle, J. C., & Mendelson, J. (1980). Alteration of T and null lymphocyte frequencies in the peripheral blood of human opiate addicts: In vivo evidence for opiate receptor sites on T lymphocytes. *Journal of Immunology, 125*, 2539–2543.

McGuire, W. J. (1964). Inducing resistance to persuasion: Some contemporary approaches. *Advances in Experimental Social Psychology, 1*, 192–229.

McGowan, R. J., Johnson, D. L., & Maxwell, S. E. (1981). Relations between infant behavior ratings and concurrent and subsequent mental test scores. *Developmental Psychology, 17*, 542–553.

McHale, S. M., & Huston, T. L. (1984). Men and women as parents: Sex role orientations, employment, and parental roles with infants. *Child Development, 55*, 1349–1361.

McHugh, P. R. (1993). Multiple personality disorder. *Harvard Mental Health Letter, 10*(3), 4–6.

McKean, K. (1986, October). Pain. *Discover*, pp. 82–92.

McKinney, J. P., & Moore, D. (1982). Attitudes and values during adolescence. In B. B. Wolman (Ed.), *Handbook of developmental psychology* (pp. 549–558). Englewood Cliffs, NJ: Prentice-Hall.

McLoyd, V. C. (1990). The impact of economic hardship on black families and children: Psychological distress, parenting, and socioemotional development. *Child Development, 61*, 311–346.

McManus, I. C., & Bryden, M. P. (1991). Geschwind's theory of cerebral lateralization: Developing a formal, causal model. *Psychological Bulletin, 110*, 237–253.

McNeil, E. B. (1967). *The quiet furies.* Englewood Cliffs, NJ: Prentice-Hall.

Mead, M. (1963). *Sex and temperament in three primitive societies.* New York: William Morrow. (Original work published 1935).

Meddis, R. (1975). On the function of sleep. *Animal Behaviour, 23*, 676–691.

Meddis, R., Pearson, A. J. D., & Langford, G. (1973). An extreme case of healthy insomnia. *Electroencephalography & Clinical Neurophysiology, 35*, 213–221.

Medin, D. L. (1989). Concepts and conceptual structure. *American Psychologist, 44*, 1469–1481.

Medin, D. L., & Shoben, E. J. (1988). Context and structure in conceptual combination. *Cognitive Psychology, 20*, 158–190.

Meehl, P. E. (1978). Theoretical risks and tabular asterisks: Sir Karl, Sir Ronald, and the slow progress of soft psychology. *Journal of Consulting & Clinical Psychology, 46*, 806–834.

Meer, J. (1985, August). Alone but not neglected. *Psychology Today*, p. 11.

Meer, J. (1985, September). The light torch. *Psychology Today*, pp. 60–67.

Meer, J. (1986, June). The reason of age. *Psychology Today*, pp. 60–64.

Meichenbaum, D. (1977). *Cognitive-behavior modification: An integrative approach.* New York: Plenum Press.

Meiners, M. L., & Sheposh, J. P. (1977). Beauty or brains: Which image for your mate? *Personality and Social Psychology Bulletin, 3*, 262–265.

Meissner, W. W. (1978). *The paranoid process.* New York: Jason Aronson.

Meltzer, H. Y. (1993, August). Clozapine: A major advance in the treatment of schizophrenia. *Harvard Mental Health Letter*, pp. 4–6.

Meltzoff, A. N. (1988). Infant imitation after a 1-week delay: Long-term memory for novel acts and multiple stimuli. *Developmental Psychology, 24*, 470–476.

Mental illness and homelessness: Part I. (1990, July). *The Harvard Mental Health Letter*, pp. 1–4.

Meredith, M. A., & Stein, B. E. (1983). Interactions among converging sensory inputs in the superior colliculus. *Science, 221,* 389–391.

Messer, D. J., McCarthy, M. E., McQuiston, S., MacTurk, R. H., Yarrow, L. J., & Vietze, P. M. (1986). Relation between mastery behavior in infancy and competence in early childhood. *Developmental Psychology, 22,* 366–372.

Meyer, A. (1982, June). Do lie detectors lie? *Science 82,* pp. 24–27.

Meyer, J. P., & Pepper, S. (1977). Need compatibility and marital adjustment in young married couples. *Journal of Personality & Social Psychology, 35,* 331–342.

Michael, R. P., & Bonsall, R. W. (1977). Peri-ovulatory synchronisation of behaviour in male and female rhesus monkeys. *Nature, 265,* 463–465.

Michael, R. P., & Zumpe, D. (1978). Potency in male rhesus monkeys: Effects of continuously receptive females. *Science, 200,* 451–453.

Michael, W. B. (1977). Cognitive and affective components of creativity in mathematics and the physical sciences. In J. C. Stanley, W. C. George, & C. H. Solano (Eds.), *The gifted and creative: A fifty-year perspective.* Baltimore, MD: Johns Hopkins Univ. Press.

Middlebrooks, J. C., & Green, D. M. (1991). Sound localization by human listeners. *Annual Review of Psychology, 42,* 135–159.

Middlemist, R. D., Knowles, E. S., & Matter, C. F. (1976). Personal space invasions in the lavatory: Suggestive evidence for arousal. *Journal of Personality and Social Psychology, 33,* 541–546.

Miles, C. (1935). Sex in social psychology. In C. Murchinson (Ed.), *Handbook of social psychology.* Worcester, Mass.: Clark Univ. Press.

Milgram, S. (1963). Behavioral study of obedience. *Journal of Abnormal and Social Psychology, 67,* 371–378.

Milgram, S. (1965a). Some conditions of obedience and disobedience to authority. *Human Relations, 18,* 57–76.

Milgram, S. (1965b). Liberating effects of group pressure. *Journal of Personality & Social Psychology, 1,* 127–134.

Miller, G. A. (1956). The magical number seven, plus or minus two: Some limits on our capacity for processing information. *Psychological Review, 63,* 81–97.

Miller, G. A., & Buckhout, R. (1973). *Psychology: The science of mental life.* New York: Harper & Row.

Miller, G. A., & Gildea, P. M. (1987). How children learn words. *Scientific American, 257*(3), 94–99.

Miller, I. J., Jr., & Reedy, F. E., Jr. (1990). Variations in human taste bud density and taste intensity perception. *Physiology & Behavior, 47,* 1213–1219.

Miller, I. W., & Norman, W. H. (1979). Learned helplessness in humans: A review and attribution theory model. *Psychological Bulletin, 86,* 93–118.

Miller, J. A. (1984a, August 18). Allergy mechanisms: Learning and itching. *Science News,* p. 102.

Miller, J. A. (1984b, January 28). Mind maps. *Science News,* pp. 62–63.

Miller, J. A. (1985a, November 9). Carving out the nervous system. *Science News,* p. 297.

Miller, J. A. (1985b, November 16). Brain selects among sights and sounds. *Science News,* p. 312.

Miller, J. A. (1985c, November 9). Eye to (third) eye. *Science News,* pp. 298–299.

Miller, J. B. (1976). *Toward a new psychology of women.* Boston: Beacon Press.

Miller, L. B., & Dyer, J. L. (1975). Four preschool programs: Their dimensions and effects. *Monographs of the Society for Research in Child Development, 40*(5–6, Serial No. 162).

Miller, N., Maruyama, G., Beaber, R. J., & Valone, K. (1976). Speed of speech and persuasion. *Journal of Personality & Social Psychology, 34,* 615–624.

Miller, N. E. (1980). Obituary, Walter R. Miles (1885–1978). *American Psychologist, 35,* 595–596.

Miller, R. L., Brickman, P., & Bolen, D. (1975). Attribution versus persuasion as a means for modifying behavior. *Journal of Personality & Social Psychology, 31,* 430–441.

Miller, W. C., Lindeman, A. K., Wallace, J., & Niederpruem, M. (1990). Diet composition, energy intake, and exercise in relation to body fat in men and women. *American Journal of Clinical Nutrition, 52,* 426–430.

Mineka, S., & Hendersen, R. W. (1985). Controllability and predictability in acquired motivation. *Annual Review of Psychology, 36,* 495–529.

Mirsky, A. F., & Orzack, M. H. (1980). Two retrospective studies of psychosurgery. In E. S. Valenstein (Ed.), *The psychosurgery debate.* San Francisco: W. H. Freeman.

Mischel, W. (1974). Process in delay of gratification. In L. Berkowitz (Ed.), *Advances in experimental social psychology* (Vol. 7). New York: Academic Press.

Mishara, B. L. (1975). The extent of adolescent suicidality. *Psychiatric Opinion, 12,* 32–37.

Mishkin, M., & Appenzeller, T. (1987). The anatomy of memory. *Scientific American, 256*(6), 80–89.

Mita, T. H., Dermer, M., & Knight, J. (1977). Reversed facial images and the mere-exposure hypothesis. *Journal of Personality & Social Psychology, 35,* 597–601.

Mittleman, G., & Valenstein, E. S. (1984). Ingestive behavior evoked by hypothalamic stimulation and schedule-induced polydipsia are related. *Science, 224,* 415–417.

Mohs, M. (1982, September). I.Q. *Discover,* pp. 18–24.

Money, J., Berlin, F. S., Falck, A., & Stein, M. (1983). *Antiandrogenic and counseling treatment of sex offenders.* Baltimore: Department of Psychiatry and Behavioral Sciences, Johns Hopkins University School of Medicine.

Money, J., & Ehrhardt, A. A. (1972). *Man and woman, boy and girl.* Baltimore, MD: Johns Hopkins.

Money, J., & Mathews, D. (1982). Prenatal exposure to virilizing progestins: An adult follow-up study of twelve women. *Archives of Sexual Behavior, 11,* 73–83.

Monk, T. H., Weitzman, E. D., Fookson, J. E., Moline, M. L., Kronauer, R. E., & Gander, P. H. (1983). Task variable determines which biological clock controls circadian-rhythms in human performance. *Nature, 304,* 543–545.

Monsaas, J. A., & Engelhard, G., Jr. (1990). Home environment and the competitiveness of highly accomplished individuals in four talent fields. *Developmental Psychology, 26,* 264–268.

Moore, M. (1982). Endorphins and exercise. *The Physician and Sportsmedicine, 10,* 111–119.

Mora, G. (1967). History of psychiatry. In A. M. Freedman & H. I. Kaplan (Eds.), *Psychiatry.* Baltimore: Williams & Wilkins.

Moran, J., & Desimone, R. (1985). Selective attention gates visual processing in the extrastriate cortex. *Science, 229,* 782–784.

Morgan, M., & Gross, L. (1982). Television and educational achievement. In D. Pearl, L. Bouthilet, & J. Lazar (Eds.), *Television and behavior: Ten years of scientific progress and implications for the eighties* (Vol. 2). Washington, DC: U.S. Govt. Printing Office.

Morgan, M. G. (1993). Risk analysis and management. *Scientific American, 269*(1), 32–41.

Morgan, R. E., Palinkas, L. A., Barrett-Connor, E. L., & Wingard, D. L. (1993). Plasma cholesterol and depressive symptoms in older men. *Lancet, 341*(8837), 75–79.

Morgan, W. P. (1980). The trait psychology controversy. *Research Quarterly for Exercise and Sport, 51,* 50–76.

Morongiello, B. A. (1988). Infants' localization of sounds along the horizontal axis: Estimates of minimum audible angle. *Developmental Psychology, 24,* 8–13.

Morrison, A. M., & Von Glinow, M. A. (1990). Women and minorities in management. *American Psychologist, 45,* 200–208.

Morrison, A. R. (1983). A window on the sleeping brain. *Scientific American, 248*(4), 94–102.

Moskowitz, B. A. (1978). The acquisition of language. *Scientific American, 239*(5), 92–108.

Mossler, D. G., Marvin, R. S., & Greenberg, M. T. (1976). Conceptual perspective taking in 2– to 6-year-old children. *Developmental Psychology, 12,* 85–86.

Motley, M. T. (1985). Slips of the tongue. *Scientific American, 253*(3), 116–127.

Mowday, R. T., & Sutton, R. I. (1993). Organizational behavior: Linking individuals and groups to organizational contexts. *Annual Review of Psychology, 44,* 195–229.

Muecke, L. N., & Krueger, D. W. (1981). Physical findings in a psychiatric outpatient clinic. *American Journal of Psychiatry, 138,* 1241–1242.

Mukhametov, L. M. (1984). Sleep in marine mammals. In A. A. Borbely & J. L. Valatx (Eds.), *Sleep mechanisms: Experimental brain research.* Heidelberg, W. Ger.: Springer-Verlag.

Munroe, R. H., Shimmin, H. S., & Munroe, R. L. (1984). Gender understanding and sex role preference in four cultures. *Developmental Psychology, 20,* 673–682.

Murray, C. (1988). *In pursuit of happiness and good government.* New York: Simon & Schuster.

Murray, M. (1986, July 19). Math teachers question role of tests. *Science News,* p. 38.

Myers, J. J. (1984). Right hemisphere language: Science or fiction? *American Psychologist, 39,* 315–320.

Nace, E. P., Davis, C. W., & Gaspari, J. P. (1991). Axis II comorbidity in substance abusers. *American Journal of Psychiatry, 148,* 118–120.

Narayanan, V. K., & Nath, R. (1982). A field test of some attitudinal and behavioral consequences of flextime. *Journal of Applied Psychology, 67,* 214–218.

Nash, J. (1978). *Developmental psychology: A psychobiological approach.* Englewood Cliffs, NJ: Prentice-Hall.

Nash, M. (1987). What, if anything, is regressed about hypnotic age regression? A review of the empirical literature. *Psychological Bulletin, 102,* 42–52.

Nash, M. R., Johnson, L. S., & Tipton, R. D. (1979). Hypnotic age regression and the occurrence of transitional object relationships. *Journal of Abnormal Psychology, 88,* 547–554.

Nathans, J. (1989). The genes for color vision. *Scientific American, 260*(2), 42–49.

National Center for Health Statistics. (1991). Annual summary of births, marriages, divorces, and deaths: United States, 1990. *Monthly Vital Statistics Report, 39*(13). Hyattsville, MD: Public Health Service.

National Clearinghouse for Alcohol and Drug Information. (1985). *Economic costs of alcohol and drug abuse and mental illness.* Rockville, MD: author.

National Council on Aging. (1981). *The myth and reality of aging in America*. Washington, D.C.: Author.

Nauta, W. J. H., & Feirtag, M. (1979). The organization of the brain. *Scientific American, 241*(3), 88–111.

Nauta, W. J. H., & Feirtag, M. (1986). *Fundamental neuroanatomy*. New York: W. H. Freeman.

Neher, E., & Sakmann, B. (1992). The patch clamp technique. *Scientific American, 266*(3), 44–51.

Neiss, R. (1988). Reconceptualizing arousal: Psychobiological states in motor performance. *Psychological Bulletin, 103*, 345–366.

Nell, V. (1990). *Lost in a book: The psychology of reading for pleasure*. New Haven, CT: Yale University Press.

Nelson, J. C., Mazure, C. M., & Jatlow, P. I. (1990). Value of the DST for predicting response of patients with major depression to hospitalization and desipramine. *American Journal of Psychiatry, 147*, 1488–1492.

Nelson, L., & Madsen, M. C. (1969). Cooperation and competition in four-year-olds as a function of reward contingency and subculture. *Developmental Psychology, 1*, 340–344.

Neugarten, B. L. (1968a). The awareness of middle age. In B. L. Neugarten (Ed.), *Middle age and aging* (pp. 93–98). Chicago: University of Chicago Press.

Neugarten, B. L. (1968b). Adult personality: Toward a psychology of the life cycle. In B. L. Neugarten (Ed.), *Middle age and aging: A reader in social psychology*. Chicago: Univ. of Chicago Press.

Neugarten, B. L., & Hall, E. (1980, April). Acting one's age: New rules for old. *Psychology Today*, pp. 66–80.

Nevin, J. A. (1988). Behavioral momentum and the partial reinforcement effect. *Psychological Bulletin*, 44–56.

Newcomb, T. M. (1961). *The acquaintance process*. New York: Holt, Rinehart & Winston.

Newcombe, N., & Dubas, J. S. (1992). A longitudinal study of predictors of spatial ability in adolescent females. *Child Development, 63*, 37–46.

Newell, A., & Simon, H. (1972). *Human problem solving*. Englewood Cliffs, NJ: Prentice-Hall.

Newman, B. M. (1982). Mid-life development. In B. B. Wolman (Ed.), *Handbook of developmental psychology* (pp. 617–635). Englewood Cliffs, NJ: Prentice-Hall.

Newman, P. R. (1982). The peer group. In B. B. Wolman (Ed.), *Handbook of developmental psychology* (pp. 526–536). Englewood Cliffs, NJ: Prentice-Hall.

Nickerson, R. S., & Adams, M. J. (1979). Long-term memory for a common object. *Cognitive Psychology, 11*, 287–307.

Nicoll, R. A. (1988). The coupling of neurotransmitter receptors to ion channels in the brain. *Science, 241*, 545–551.

Normann, R. A., Perlman, I., Kolb, H., Jones, J., & Daly, S. J. (1984). Direct excitatory interactions between cones of different spectral types in the turtle retina. *Science, 224*, 625–627.

Norris, F. H. (1992). Epidemiology of trauma: Frequency and impact of different potentially traumatic events on different demographic groups. *Journal of Consulting & Clinical Psychology, 60*, 409–418.

Novin, D. (1976). Visceral mechanisms in the control of food intake. In D. Novin, W. Wyrwicka, & G. A. Bray (Eds.), *Hunger: Basic mechanisms and clinical implications*. New York: Raven.

Noyes, R., Jr., Clarkson, C., Crowe, R. R., Yates, W. R., & McChesney, C. M. (1987). A family study of generalized anxiety disorder. *American Journal of Psychiatry, 144*, 1019–1024.

Nydegger, R. V. (1975). Information processing complexity and leadership status. *Journal of Experimental Social Psychology, 11*, 317–328.

O'Brien, M., & Huston, A. C. (1985). Development of sex-typed play behavior in toddlers. *Developmental Psychology, 21*, 866–871.

O'Connor, M. J., Cohen, S., & Parmelee, A. H. (1984). Infant auditory discrimination in preterm and full-term infants as a predictor of 5–year intelligence. *Developmental Psychology, 20*, 159–165.

O'Malley, M. N., & Becker, L. A. (1984). Removing the egocentric bias: The relevance of distress cues to evaluation of fairness. *Personality and Social Psychology Bulletin, 10*, 235–242.

O'Malley, S. S., Jaffe, A. J., Chang, G., Schottenfeld, R. S., Meyer, R. E., & Rounsaville, B. (1992). Naltrexone and coping skills therapy for alcohol dependence. A controlled study. *Archives of General Psychiatry, 49*, 881–887.

O'Reilly, C. A., III. (1991). Organizational behavior: Where we've been, where we're going. *Annual Review of Psychology, 42*, 427–458.

Oatley, K., & Jenkins, J. M. (1992). Human emotions: Function and dysfunction. *Annual Review of Psychology, 43*, 55–85.

Oden, G. C. (1987). Concept, knowledge, and thought. *Annual Review of Psychology, 38*, 203–227.

Offer, D., Ostrov, E., & Howard, K. I. (1981). *The adolescent: A psychological self-portrait*. New York: Basic Books.

Offermann, L. R., & Gowing, M. K. (1990). Organizations of the future: Changes and challenges. *American Psychologist, 45*, 95–108.

Olds, J. (1956). Pleasure centers in the brain. *Scientific American, 195*(4), 105–116.

Olds, M. E., & Fobes, J. L. (1981). The central basis of motivation: Intracranial self-stimulation studies. *Annual Review of Psychology, 32*, 523–574.

Oller, D. K., & Eilers, R. E. (1988). The role of audition in infant babbling. *Child Development, 59*, 441–449.

Olney, J. W., Labruyere, J., & Price, M. T. (1989). Pathological changes induced in cerebrocortical neurons by phencyclidine and related drugs. *Science, 244*, 1360–1362.

Olson, D. H., McCubbin, H. I., Barnes, H. L., Larson, A. S., Muxen, M. J., & Wilson, M. A. (1983). *Families: What makes them work*. Beverly Hills: Sage Publications.

Olson, J. M., & Zanna, M. P. (1993). Attitudes and attitude change. *Annual Review of Psychology, 44*, 117–154.

Optican, L. M., & Richmond, B. J. (1987). Temporal encoding of two-dimensional patterns by single units in primate inferior temporal cortex. III. Information theoretic analysis. *Journal of Neurophysiology, 57*, 162–178.

Orne, M. T. (1982, January 16). Hypnosis: Guilty or fraud? *Science News*, p. 42.

Orne, M. T., & Evans, F. J. (1965). Social control in the psychological experiment: Antisocial behavior and hypnosis. *Journal of Personality & Social Psychology, 1*, 189–200.

Orwin, R. G., & Cordray, D. S. (1984). Smith and Glass's psychotherapy conclusions need further probing: On Landman and Dawes' reanalysis. *American Psychologist, 39*, 71–72.

Osherson, D. N., & Markman, E. (1974–75). Language and the ability to evaluate contradictions and tautologies. *Cognition, 3*(3), 213–226.

Oster, H. (1978). Facial expression and affect development. In M. Lewis, & L. A. Rosenblum (Eds.), *The development of affect* (pp. 43–76). New York: Plenum.

Oster, H., & Ekman, P. (1978). Facial behavior in child development. *Minnesota Symposia on Child Psychology, 11*, 231–276.

Ostroff, R. B., Giller, E., Harkness, L., & Mason, J. (1985). The norepinephrine-to-epinephrine ratio in patients with a history of suicide attempts. *American Journal of Psychiatry, 142*, 224–225.

Overton, D. A. (1972). State-dependent learning produced by alcohol and its relevance to alcoholism. In B. Kissin & H. Begleiter (Eds.), *Physiology and behavior* (Vol. 2). New York: Plenum Press.

Owen, D. (1985). *None of the above: Behind the myth of scholastic aptitude*. Boston: Houghton Mifflin.

Palca, J. (1991). Famous monkeys provide surprising results. *Science, 252*, 1789.

Palisin, H. (1986). Preschool temperament and performance on achievement tests. *Developmental Psychology, 22*, 766–770.

Panksepp, J. (1986). The neurochemistry of behavior. *Annual Review of Psychology, 37*, 77–107.

Pantev, C., Hoke, M., Lutkenhoner, B., & Lehnertz, K. (1989). Tonotopic organization of the auditory cortex: Pitch versus frequency representation. *Science, 246*, 486–488.

Parfit, M. (1984, May). Mapmaker who charts our hidden mental demons. *Smithsonian*, pp. 123–131.

Parke, R. D. (1978). Children's home environments: Social and cognitive effects. In I. Altman, & J. F. Wohlwill (Eds.), *Children and the environment*. New York: Plenum.

Parkes, C. M. (1972). *Bereavement*. New York: Int'l Universities Press.

Parnes, H. S., & Less, L. J. (1985a). Shunning retirement: The experience of full-time workers. In H. S. Parnes, J. E. Crowley, R. J. Haurin, L. J. Less, W. R. Morgan, F. L. Mott, & G. Nestel (Eds.), *Retirement among American men*. Lexington, MA: Lexington Books.

Parnes, H. S., & Less, L. J. (1985b). Introduction and overview. In H. S. Parnes, J. E. Crowley, R. J. Haurin, L. J. Less, W. R. Morgan, F. L. Mott, & G. Nestel (Eds.), *Retirement among American men*. Lexington, MA: Lexington Books.

Pascual-Leone, A., Dhuna, A., Altafullah, I., & Anderson, D. C. (1990). Cocaine-induced seizures. *Neurology, 40*, 404–407.

Patrick, G. T. W., & Gilbert, J. A. (1896). On the effects of loss of sleep. *Psychological Review, 3*, 469–483.

Patterson, C. J., Kupersmidt, J. B., & Vaden, N. A. (1990). Income level, gender, ethnicity, and household composition as predictors of chidlren's school-based competence. *Child Development, 61*, 485–494.

Patterson, F. G., Patterson, C. H., & Brentari, D. K. (1987). Language in child, chimp, and gorilla. *American Psychologist, 42*, 270–272.

Pavlides, C., Greenstein, Y. J., & Winson, J. (1988). Comparative extracellular current flow at dendrites and soma of dentate granule cells during long-term potentiation. *Neuroscience Letters, 92,* 177–181.

Pavlov, I. P. (1927). *Conditioned reflexes.* New York: Oxford University Press.

Pearl, D., Bouthilet, L., & Lazar, J. (Eds.). (1982). *Television and behavior: Ten years of scientific progress and implications for the eighties* (Vols. 1 & 2). Washington, DC: U.S. Govt. Printing Office.

Pearson, J. L., Hunter, A. G., Ensminger, M. E., & Kellam, S. G. (1990). Black grandmothers in multigenerational households: Diversity in family structure and parenting involvement in the Woodlawn community. *Child Development, 61,* 434–442.

Pedersen, E., Faucher, T. A., & Eaton, W. W. (1978). A new perspective on the effects of first grade teachers on children's subsequent adult status. *Harvard Educational Review, 48,* 1–31.

Penrose, R. (1989). *The emperor's new mind: Concerning computers, minds & the laws of physics.* New York: Oxford University Press.

Pepler, D., & Rubin, K. H. (Eds.). (1990). *The development and treatment of childhood aggression.* Hillsdale, NJ: Erlbaum.

Pepler, D. J., & Ross, H. S. (1981). The effects of play on convergent and divergent problem solving. *Child Development, 52,* 1202–1210.

Perry, W. G., Jr. (1970). *Forms of intellectual and ethical development in the college years.* New York: Holt, Rinehart & Winston.

Persky, V. W., Kempthorne-Rawson, J., & Shekelle, R. B. (1987). Personality and risk of cancer: 20-year followup of the Western Electric Study. *Psychosomatic Medicine, 49,* 435–449.

Persons, J. B. (1991). Psychotherapy outcome studies do not accurately represent current models of psychotherapy. *American Psychologist, 46,* 99–106.

Pervin, L. A. (1985). Personality: Current controversies, issues, and directions. *Annual Review of Psychology, 36,* 83–114.

Petersen, A. C. (1987, September). Those gangly years. *Psychology Today,* pp. 28–34.

Peterson, C., Seligman, M. E., & Vaillant, G. E. (1988). Pessimistic explanatory style is a risk factor for physical illness: A thirty-five-year longitudinal study. *Journal of Personality & Social Psychology, 55,* 23–27.

Petitto, L. A., & Marentette, P. F. (1991). Babbling in the manual mode: Evidence for the ontogeny of language. *Science, 251,* 1493–1496.

Petty, R. E. (1977). The importance of cognitive responses in persuasion. *Advances in Consumer Research, 4,* 357–362.

Petty, R. E., & Cacioppo, J. T. (1979). Effects of forewarning of persuasive intent and involvement on cognitive responses and persuasion. *Personality and Social Psychology Bulletin, 5,* 173–176.

Phares, E. J., & Lamiell, J. T. (1977). Personality. *Annual Review of Psychology, 28,* 113–140.

Piaget, J. (1967). *Six psychological studies.* New York: Random House.

Piaget, J., & Inhelder, B. (1969). *The psychology of the child.* (H. Weaver, Trans.). New York: Basic Books. (Original work published 1967).

Piccione, C., Hilgard, E. R., & Zimbardo, P. G. (1989). On the degree of stability of measured hypnotizability over a 25-year period. *Journal of Personality & Social Psychology, 56,* 289–295.

Pieterse, M., & Center, Y. (1984). The integration of eight Down's Syndrome children into regular schools. *Australia & New Zealand Journal of Developmental Disabilities, 10*(1), 11–20.

Pihl, R. O., & Parkes, M. (1977). Hair element content in learning disabled children. *Science, 198,* 204–206.

Pilkonis, P. A., Imber, S. D., Lewis, P., & Rubinsky, P. (1984). A comparative outcome study of individual, group, and conjoint psychotherapy. *Archives of General Psychiatry, 41,* 431–437.

Pines, M. (1966). *Revolution in learning: The years from birth to six.* New York: Harper & Row.

Pines, M. (1983, October). Suicide signals. *Science 83,* pp. 55–58.

Pintrich, P. R., Cross, D. R., Kozma, R. B., & McKeachie, W. J. (1986). Instructional psychology. *Annual Review of Psychology, 37,* 611–651.

Pion, G. M. (1991). Psychologists wanted: Employment trends over the past decade. In R. R. Kilburg (Ed.), *How to manage your career in psychology.* Washington, DC: American Psychological Association.

Pittman, T. S., & Heller, J. F. (1987). Social motivation. *Annual Review of Psychology, 38,* 461–489.

Plutchik, R. (1980, February). A language for the emotions. *Psychology Today,* pp. 68–78.

Poizner, H., Klima, E., & Bellugi, U. (1987). *What the hands reveal about the brain.* Cambridge, MA: MIT Press.

Polansky, N., Lippitt, R., & Redl, F. (1950). An investigation of behavioral contagion in groups. *Human Relations, 3,* 319–348.

Pollock, D. A., Rhodes, P., Boyle, C. A., Decoufle, P., & McGee, D. L. (1990). Estimating the number of suicides among Vietnam veterans. *American Journal of Psychiatry, 147,* 772–776.

Pool, R. (1989). Chaos theory: How big an advance? *Science, 245,* 26–28.

Pope, H. G., Jr., Jonas, J. M., & Jones, B. (1982). Factitious psychosis: Phenomenology, family history, and long-term outcome of nine patients. *American Journal of Psychiatry, 139,* 1480–1483.

Pope, H. G., Jr., Keck, P. E., Jr., & McElroy, S. L. (1986). Frequency and presentation of neuroleptic malignant syndrome in a large psychiatric hospital. *American Journal of Psychiatry, 143,* 1227–1233.

Postman, L., & Rau, L. (1957). Retention as a function of the method of measurement. *University of California Publications in Psychology, 8*(3).

Power, T. G. (1981). Sex-typing in infancy: The role of the father. *Infant Mental Health Journal, 2,* 226–240.

Poznanski, E., & Zrull, J. P. (1970). Childhood depression: Clinical characteristics of overtly depressed children. *Archives of General Psychiatry, 23,* 8–15.

Premack, D. (1959). Toward empirical behavior laws: Pt. 1. Positive reinforcement. *Psychological Review, 66,* 219–233.

Press, M. R. (1991). Whatever happened to insomnia (and insomnia research)? *American Journal of Psychiatry, 148,* 419–420.

Pressman, M. D. (1980). Psychological techniques for the advancement of sports potential. In R. M. Suinn (Ed.), *Psychology in sports: Methods and applications* (pp. 291–296). Minneapolis, Minn.: Burgess.

Priest, R. F., & Sawyer, J. (1967). Proximity and peership: Bases of balance in interpersonal attraction. *American Journal of Sociology, 72,* 633–649.

Pritchett, D. B., Luddens, H., & Seeburg, P. H. (1989). Type I and Type II GABA$_A$-benzodiazepine receptors produced in transfected cells. *Science, 245,* 1389–1392.

Pruitt, D. G. (1971). Conclusions: Toward an understanding of choice shifts in group discussion. *Journal of Personality & Social Psychology, 20,* 495–510.

Pryor, J. B., Gibbons, F. X., Wicklund, R. A., Fazio, R. H., & Hood, R. (1977). Self-focused attention and self-report validity. *Journal of Personality, 45,* 513–527.

Psychic Abscam. (1983, March). *Discover,* pp. 10–12.

Purves, D., Voyvodic, J. T., Magrassi, L., & Yawo, H. (1987). Nerve terminal remodeling visualized in living mice by repeated examination of the same neuron. *Science, 238,* 1122–1126.

Quattrochi, J.J., Mamelak, A. N., Madison, R. D., Macklis, J. D., & Hobson, J. A. (1989). Mapping neuronal inputs to REM sleep induction sites with carbachol-fluorescent microspheres. *Science, 245,* 984–986.

Quattrone, G. A. (1982). Overattribution and unit formation: When behavior engulfs the person. *Journal of Personality & Social Psychology, 42,* 593–607.

Quigley-Fernandez, B., & Tedeschi, J. T. (1978). The bogus pipeline as lie detector: Two validity studies. *Journal of Personality & Social Psychology, 36,* 247–256.

Quinn, P. K., & Reznikoff, M. (1985). The relationship between death anxiety and the subjective experience of time in the elderly. *International Journal of Aging and Human Development, 21,* 197–210.

Raaijmakers, J. G. W., & Shiffrin, R. M. (1992). Models for recall and recognition. *Annual Review of Psychology, 43,* 205–234.

Rader, N. (1979, April). *The behavior of pre-crawling infants on the visual cliff with locomotor aids.* Paper presented at the meeting of the Western Psychological Association, San Diego, California.

Raloff, J. (1982, February 6). Childhood lead: Worrisome national levels. *Science News,* p. 88.

Ralph, M. R., & Menaker, M. (1988). A mutation of the circadian system in golden hamsters. *Science, 241,* 1225–1227.

Ralph, M. R., Foster, R. G., Davis, F. C., & Menaker, M. (1990). Transplanted suprachiasmatic nucleus determines circadian period. *Science, 247,* 975–978.

Ramachandran, V. S. (1992). Blind spots. *Scientific American, 266*(5), 86–91.

Ramachandran, V. S., & Anstis, S. M. (1986). The perception of apparent motion. *Scientific American, 254*(66), 102–109.

Ramey, C. (1982). Commentary by Craig T. Ramey. *Monographs of the Society for Research in Child Development, 47*(2–3, Serial No. 195), 142–151.

Ramsay, D. S. (1984). Onset of duplicated syllable babbling and unimanual handedness in infancy: Evidence for developmental change in hemispheric specialization? *Developmental Psychology, 20,* 64–71.

Ransford, C. P. (1982). A role for amines in the antidepressant effect of exercise: A review. *Medicine and Science in Sports and Exercise, 14,* 1–10.

Rapoport, J. L. (1989). The biology of obsessions and compulsions. *Scientific American, 260*(3), 83–89.

Rapoport, J. L., Ryland, D. H., & Kriete, M. (1992). Drug treatment of canine acral lick. An animal model of obsessive-compulsive disorder. *Archives of General Psychiatry, 49,* 517–521.

Ray, W. A., Griffin, M. R., Schaffner, W., Baugh, D. K., & Melton, L. J. (1987). Psychotropic drug use and the risk of hip fracture. *New England Journal of Medicine, 316,* 363–369.

Raz, S., & Raz, N. (1990). Structural brain abnormalities in the major psychoses: A quantiative review of the evidence from computerized imaging. *Psychological Bulletin, 108,* 93–108.

Razran, G. (1961). The observable unconscious and the inferable conscious in current Soviet psychophysiology. *Psychological Review, 68,* 81–147.

Rechtschaffen, A., Gilliland, M. A., Bergmann, B. M., & Winter, J. B. (1983). Physiological correlates of prolonged sleep deprivation in rats. *Science, 221,* 182–184.

Redlich, F., & Kellert, S. R. (1978). Trends in American mental health. *American Journal of Psychiatry, 135,* 22–28.

Regier, D. A., Boyd, J. H., Burke, J. D., Jr., Rae, D. S., Myers, J. K., Kramer, M., Robins, L. N., George, L. K., Karno, M., Locke, B. Z. (1988). One-month prevalence of mental disorders in the United States. *Archives of General Psychiatry, 45,* 977–986.

Regier, D. A., Narrow, W. E., Rae, D. S., Manderscheid, R. W., Locke, B. Z., & Goodwin, F. K. (1993). The de facto US mental and addictive disorders service system. Epidemiologic catchment area prospective 1-year prevalence rates of disorders and services. *Archives of General Psychiatry, 50,* 85–94.

Reiman, E. M., Raichle, M. E., Robins, E., Butler, F. K., Herscovitch, P., Fox, P., & Perlmutter, J. (1986). The application of positron emission tomography to the study of panic disorder. *American Journal of Psychiatry, 143,* 4699–477.

Reinisch, J. M. (1981). Prenatal exposure to synthetic progestins increases potential for aggression in humans. *Science, 211,* 1171–1173.

Reinisch, J. M., & Beasley, R. (Eds.). (1990). *The Kinsey Institute new report on sex: What you must know to be sexually literate.* New York: St. Martin's Press.

Reppert, S. M., Weaver, D. R., Rivkees, S. A., & Stopa, E. G. (1988). Putative melatonin receptors in human biological clock. *Science, 242,* 78–81.

Rescorla, R. A. (1988). Pavlovian conditioning: It's not what you think it is. *American Psychologist, 43,* 151–160.

Resnick, S. M., Berenbaum, S. A., Gottesman, I. I., & Bouchard, T. J., Jr. (1986). Early hormonal influences on cognitive functioning in congenital adrenal hyperplasia. *Developmental Psychology, 22,* 191–198.

Rest, J. (1968). *Developmental hierarchy in preference and comprehension of moral judgment.* Unpublished doctoral dissertation, University of Chicago.

Restak, R. M. (1982, January/February). Newborn knowledge. *Science 82,* pp. 58–65.

Reston, J. (1975, March 14). Proxmire on love. *New York Times.*

Reynolds, B. A., & Weiss, S. (1992). Generation of neurons and astrocytes from isolated cells of the adult mammalian central nervous system. *Science, 255,* 1707–1710.

Reynolds, D., & Murgatroyd, S. (1977). The sociology of schooling and the absent pupil: The school as a factor in the generation of truancy. In H. C. M. Carroll (Ed.), *Absenteeism in South Wales: Studies of pupils, their homes and their secondary schools.* Swansea: Univ. of Swansea, Faculty of Educ.

Rheingold, H. L., & Cook, K. V. (1975). The content of boys' and girls' rooms as an index of parents' behavior. *Child Development, 46,* 459–463.

Rheingold, H. L., Gewirtz, J. L., & Ross, H. W. (1959). Social conditioning of vocalizations in the infant. *Journal of Comparative and Physiological Psychology, 52,* 68–73.

Ricaurte, G., Bryan, G., Strauss, L., Seiden, L., & Schuster, C. (1985). Hallucinogenic amphetamine selectively destroys brain serotonin nerve terminals. *Science, 229,* 986–988.

Rich, C. L., Fowler, R. C., Fogarty, L. A., & Young, D. (1988). San Diego suicide study. III. Relationships between diagnoses and stressors. *Archives of General Psychiatry, 45,* 589–592.

Richards, R., Kinney, D. K., Lunde, I., Benet, M., & Merzel, A. P. C. (1988). Creativity in manic-depressives, cyclothymes, their normal relatives, and control subjects. *Journal of Abnormal Psychology, 97,* 281–288.

Richardson, M. A., Haugland, G., & Craig, T. J. (1991). Neuroleptic use, parkinsonian symptoms, tardive dyskinesia, and associated factors in child and adolescent psychiatric patients. *American Journal of Psychiatry, 148,* 1322–1328.

Roberto, K. A., & Scott, J. P. (1986). Friendships of older men and women: Exchange patterns and satisfaction. *Psychology and Aging, 1,* 103–109.

Roberts, K. (1988). Retrieval of a basic-level category in prelinguistic infants. *Developmental Psychology, 24,* 21–27.

Roberts, L. (1989). Genome mapping goal now in reach. *Science, 244,* 424–425.

Robey, B. (1982). Older Americans. *American Demographics, 4,* 40–41.

Robins, L. N., & Helzer, J. E. (1986). Diagnosis and clinical assessment: The current state of psychiatric diagnosis. *Annual Review of Psychology, 37,* 409–432.

Robinson, L. A., Berman, J. S., & Neimeyer, R. A. (1990). Psychotherapy for the treatment of depression: A comprehensive review of controlled outcome research. *Psychological Bulletin, 108,* 30–49.

Rock, I. (1984). *Perception.* New York: Scientific American Books.

Rock, I., & Palmer, S. (1990). The legacy of Gestalt psychology. *Scientific American, 263*(6), 84–90.

Rodin, J. (1981). Current status of the internal-external hypothesis for obesity: What went wrong? *American Psychologist, 36,* 361–372.

Rodin, J., & Salovey, P. (1989). Health psychology. *Annual Review of Psychology, 40,* 533–579.

Rodin, J., & Stone, G. (1987). Historical highlights in the emergence of the field. In G. C. Stone et al. (Eds.), *Health psychology: A discipline and a profession* (pp. 15–26). Chicago: Univ. of Chicago Press.

Roehrs, T., Timms, V., Zwyghuizen-Doorenbos, A., & Roth, T. (1989). Sleep extension in sleepy and alert normals. *Sleep, 12,* 449–457.

Rogel, M. J. (1978). A critical evaluation of the possibility of higher primate reproductive and sexual pheromones. *Psychological Bulletin, 85,* 810–830.

Rogers, C. R. (1951). *Client-centered therapy: Its current practice, implications, and theory.* Boston: Houghton Mifflin.

Rogers, C. R. (1961). *On becoming a person.* Boston: Houghton Mifflin.

Rogers, M. (1987, February 9). Now, "artificial reality." *Newsweek,* pp. 56–57.

Rogers, R. (1987). APA's position on the insanity defense: Empiricism versus emotionalism. *American Psychologist, 42,* 840–848.

Rohner, R. P., & Rohner, E. C. (1981). Parental acceptance-rejection and parental control: Cross-cultural codes. *Ethnology, 20,* 245–260.

Roitblat, H. L., & von Fersen, L. (1992). Comparative cognition: Representations and processes in learning and memory. *Annual Review of Psychology, 43,* 671–710.

Roopnarine, J. L., & Johnson, J. E. (1984). Socialization in a mixed-age experimental program. *Developmental Psychology, 20,* 828–832.

Roper, S. D. (1989). The cell biology of vertebrate taste receptors. *Annual Review of Neuroscience, 12,* 329–353.

Rorer, L. G., & Widiger, T. A. (1982). *Ascription rules for trait descriptive adjectives.* Paper presented at the annual conference of the Midwestern Psychological Association, Minneapolis, Minnesota.

Rorer, L. G., & Widiger, T. A. (1983). Personality structure and assessment. *Annual Review of Psychology, 34,* 431–463.

Rosch, E. (1973). On the internal structure of perceptual and semantic categories. In T. E. Moore (Ed.), *Cognitive development and the acquisition of language.* New York: Academic Press.

Rosch, E. (1977). Human categorization. In N. Warren (Ed.), *Advances in cross-cultural psychology* (Vol. I). London: Academic Press.

Rose, S. A., Feldman, J. F., & Wallace, I. F. (1988). Individual differences in infants' information processing: Reliability, stability, and prediction. *Child Development, 59,* 1177–1197.

Rosen, D. H. (1976). Suicide survivors: Psychotherapeutic implications of egocide. *Suicide: A Quarterly Journal of Life-Threatening Behavior, 6,* 209–215.

Rosenberg, H. (1993). Prediction of controlled drinking by alcoholics and problem drinkers. *Psychological Bulletin, 113,* 129–139.

Rosenblum, L. A., & Harlow, H. F. (1963). Approach-avoidance conflict in the mother surrogate situation. *Psychological Reports, 12,* 83–85.

Rosenhan, D. L. (1973). *Moral development.* CRM McGraw-Hill Films.

Rosenhan, D. L. (1973). On being sane in insane places. *Science, 179,* 250–258.

Rosenkrantz, A. L. (1978). A note on adolescent suicide: Incidence, dynamics and some suggestions for treatment. *Adolescence, 13,* 109–214.

Rosenthal, D., & Quinn, O. W. (1977). Quadruplet hallucinations: Phenotypic variations of a schizophrenic genotype. *Archives of General Psychiatry, 34,* 817–827.

Rosenthal, M. K. (1982). Vocal dialogues in the neonatal period. *Developmental Psychology, 18,* 17–21.

Rosenzweig, S. (1985). Freud and experimental psychology: The emergence of idiodynamics. In S. Koch & D. E. Leary (Eds.), *A century of psychology as science* (pp. 135–207). New York: McGraw-Hill.

Ross, C. A., Anderson, G., Fleisher, W. P., & Norton, G. R. (1991). The frequency of multiple personality disorder among psychiatric inpatients. *American Journal of Psychiatry, 148,* 1717–1720.

Ross, C. A., Joshi, S., & Currie, R. (1990). Dissociative experiences in the general population. *American Journal of Psychiatry, 147,* 1547–1552.

Ross, H. G., & Milgram, J. I. (1982). Important variables in adult sibling relationships: A qualitative study. In M. E. Lamb & B. Sutton-Smith (Eds.), *Sibling relationships: Their nature and significance across the lifespan* (pp. 225–249). Hillsdale, NJ: Erlbaum.

Roth, M. (1976). The psychiatric disorders of later life. *Psychiatric Annals, 6,* 57–101.

Rotter, J. B. (1972). Beliefs, social attitudes, and behavior: A social learning analysis. In J. B.

Rotter, J. E. Chance, & E. J. Phares (Eds.), *Applications of a social learning theory of personality.* New York: Holt, Rinehart & Winston.

Roueche, B. (1980). *The medical detectives*. New York: Truman Talley Books.

Rousseau, J. J. (1960). *Julie; or, the new Eloise* (R. Porneau, Ed.). Paris: Garnier Freres.

Rowland, K. F. (1977). Environmental events predicting death for the elderly. *Psychological Bulletin, 84*, 349–372.

Roy, A., De Jong, J., & Linnoila, M. (1989). Cerebrospinal fluid monoamine metabolites and suicidal behavior in depressed patients. A 5-year follow-up study. *Archives of General Psychiatry, 46*, 609–612.

Roy-Byrne, P. P., Geraci, M., & Uhde, T. W. (1986). Life events and the onset of panic disorder. *American Journal of Psychiatry, 143*, 1424–1427.

Rubin, J. Z., & Brown, B. R. (1975). *The social psychology of bargaining and negotiation*. New York: Academic Press.

Rubin, L. (1979). *Women of a certain age*. New York: Harper & Row.

Rubin, Z. (1973). *Liking and loving: An invitation to social psychology*. New York: Holt, Rinehart & Winston.

Rubinstein, E. A. (1983). Television and behavior: Research conclusions of the 1982 NIMH report and their policy implications. *American Psychologist, 38*, 820–825.

Ruch, J. C. (1975). Self-hypnosis: The result of heterohypnosis or vice versa? *International Journal of Clinical and Experimental Hypnosis, 23*, 282–304.

Rucker, R. (1981, July/August). Who makes math marvelous, turns magic satin smooth, tends the looking-glass garden, and can make a winner of anyone who plays his games? *Science 81*, pp. 33–37.

Ruff, M. R., Wahl, S. M., Mergenhagen, S., & Pert, C. B. (1985). Opiate receptor-mediated chemotaxis of human monocytes. *Neuropeptides, 5*, 363–366.

Rundus, D. (1971). Analysis of rehearsal processes in free recall. *Journal of Experimental Psychology, 89*, 63–77.

Russell, J. A., & Ward, L. M. (1982). Environmental psychology. *Annual Review of Psychology, 33*, 651–688.

Rusting, R. L. (1992). Why do we age? *Scientific American, 267*(6), 131–141.

Rutter, M. (1983). School effects on pupil progress: Research findings and policy implications. *Child Development, 54*, 1–29.

Rutter, M., Maughan, B., Mortimore, P., Ouston, J., & Smith, A. (1979). *Fifteen thousand hours: Secondary schools and their effects on children*. Cambridge, MA: Harvard University Press.

Ryan, E. D., & Kovacic, C. R. (1966). Pain tolerance and athletic participation. *Perceptual and Motor Skills, 22*, 383–390.

Ryan, M. J. (1980). Psychobiology and consumer research: A problem of construct validity. *Journal of Consumer Research, 7*, 92–96.

Sacks, M., Carpenter, W. T., & Richmond, M. B. (1975). Psychotherapy in hospitalized research patients. *Archives of General Psychiatry, 32*, 581–585.

Sacks, O. (1985). *The man who mistook his wife for a hat*. New York: Summit Books.

Saegert, S., & Winkel, G. H. (1990). Environmental psychology. *Annual Review of Psychology, 41*, 441–477.

Sagi, A., van IJzendoorn, M. H., & Koren-Karie, N. (1991). Primary appraisal of the strange situation: A cross-cultural analysis of preseparation episodes. *Developmental Psychology, 27*, 587–596.

Salit, S. A., & Marcos, L. R. (1991). Have general hospitals become chronic care institutions for the mentally ill? *American Journal of Psychiatry, 148*, 892–897.

Saltz, B. L., Woerner, M. G., Kane, J. M., Lieberman, J. A., Alvir, J. M., Bergmann, K. J., Blank, K., Koblenzer, J., & Kahaner, K. (1991). Prospective study of tardive dyskinesia incidence in the elderly. *Journal of the American Medical Association, 266*, 2402–2406.

Salzman, C. D., Britten, K. H., & Newsome, W. T. (1990). Cortical microstimulation influences perceptual judgments of motion direction. *Nature, 346*, 174–177.

Salzman, C. D., Britten, K. H., & Newsome, W. T. (1990). *Nature, 346*, 174–177.

Samiy, A. H., & Rosnick, P. B. (1987). Early identification of renal problems in patients receiving chronic lithium treatment. *American Journal of Psychiatry, 144*, 670–672.

Sampson, E. E. (1962). Birth order, need achievement, and conformity. *Journal of Abnormal and Social Psychology, 64*, 155–159.

Sampson, E. E. (1978). Scientific paradigms and social values: Wanted—A scientific revolution. *Journal of Personality & Social Psychology, 36*, 1332–1343.

Samson, J. A., Mirin, S. M., Hauser, S. T., Fenton, B. T., & Schildkraut, J. J. (1992). Learned helplessness and urinary MHPG levels in unipolar depression. *American Journal of Psychiatry, 149*, 806–809.

Sandblom, R. E., Matsumoto, A. M., Schoene, R. B., Lee, K. A., Giblin, E. C., Bremner, W. J., & Pierson, D. J. (1983). Sleep apnea induced by testosterone administration. *New England Journal of Medicine, 308*, 508–510.

Sandman, C. A., George, J. M., Nolan, J. D., Van Riezen, H., & Kastin, A. J. (1975). Enhancement of attention in man with ACTH/MSH 4–10. *Physiology and Behavior, 15*, 427–431.

Sapolsky, R. M. (1990). Stress in the wild. *Scientific American, 262*(1), 116–123.

Sarbin, T. R., & Coe, W. C. (1972). *Hypnosis: A social psychological analysis of influence communication*. New York: Holt, Rinehart & Winston.

Savage-Rumbaugh, E. S., Rumbaugh, D. M., & Boysen, S. (1978). Symbolic communication between two chimpanzees. *Science, 201*, 641–644.

Savage-Rumbaugh, E., S. (1987). Communication, symbolic communication, and language: Reply to Seidenberg and Pettito. *Journal of Experimental Psychology: General, 116*, 288–292.

Saxe, L., Dougherty, D., & Cross, T. (1985). The validity of polygraph testing: Scientific analysis and public controversy. *American Psychologist, 40*, 355–366.

Scanlon, J. (1981). Young adulthood. In A. C. Eurich (Ed.), *Major transitions in the human life cycle* (pp. 307–439). Lexington, MA: Lexington Books.

Scarr, S., & McCartney, K. (1988). Far from home: An experimental evaluation of the mother-child home program in Bermuda. *Child Development, 59*, 531–543.

Scarr, S., & Weinberg, R. A. (1976). IQ test performance of black children adopted by white families. *American Psychologist, 31*, 726–739.

Schachter, S. (1977). Studies of the interaction of psychological and pharmacological determinants of smoking: 1. Nicotine regulation in heavy and light smokers. *Journal of Experimental Psychology: General, 106*, 5–12.

Schachter, S. (1982). Recidivism and self-cure of smoking and obesity. *American Psychologist, 37*, 436–444.

Schachter, S., & Singer, J. E. (1962). Cognitive, social, and physiological determinants of emotional state. *Psychological Review, 69*, 379–399.

Schachter, S., Kozlowski, L. T., & Silverstein, B. (1977). Studies of the interaction of psychological and pharmacological determinants of smoking: 2. Effects of urinary pH on cigarette smoking. *Journal of Experimental Psychology: General, 106*, 13–19.

Schachter, S., Silverstein, B., & Perlick, D. (1977). Studies of the interaction of psychological and pharmacological determinants of smoking: 5. Psychological and pharmacological explanations of smoking under stress. *Journal of Experimental Psychology: General, 106*, 31–40.

Schaefer, E. S. (1959). A circumplex model for maternal behavior. *Journal of Abnormal and social Psychology, 59*, 226–235.

Schaffer, H. R., & Emerson, P. E. (1964). The development of social attachments in infancy. Monographs of the Society for Research in *Child Development, 29*(3, Serial No. 94).

Schaie, K. W. (1983). *Longitudinal studies of adult psychological development*. New York: The Guilford Press.

Schatzberg, A. F. (1987, July). New antidepressants. *Harvard Medical School Mental Health Letter*, p. 8.

Scheibel, A. B., & Conrad, A. S. (1993). Hippocampal dysgenesis in mutant mouse and schizophrenic man: Is there a relationship? *Schizophrenia Bulletin, 19*, 21–33.

Scheller, R. H., & Axel, R. (1984). How genes control an innate behavior. *Scientific American, 250*(3), 54–62.

Schiff, M., Duyme, M., Dumaret, A., & Tomkiewicz, S. (1982). How much could we boost scholastic achievement and IQ scores? A direct answer from a French adoption study. *Cognition, 12*, 165–196.

Schiller, P. H. (1957). Innate motor action as a basis of learning. In S. H. Schiller (Ed.), *Instinctive behavior*. New York: Int'l Universities Press.

Schiller, P. H., & Lee, K. (1991). The role of the primate extrastriate area V4 in vision. *Science, 251*, 1251–1253.

Schinnar, A. P., Rothbard, A. B., Kanter, R., & Jung, Y. S. (1990). An empirical literature review of definitions of severe and persistent mental illness. *American Journal of Psychiatry, 147*, 1602–1608.

Schleifer, S. J., Keller, S. E., Camerino, M., Thornton, J. C., & Stein, M. (1983). Suppression of lymphocyte stimulation following bereavement. *Journal of the American Medical Association, 250*, 374–377.

Schlenker, B. R. (1978). Attitudes as actions: Social identity theory and consumer research. *Advances in Consumer Research, 5*, 352–359.

Schlenker, B. R., & Schlenker, P. A. (1975). Reactions following counterattitudinal behavior which produces positive consequences. *Journal of Personality & Social Psychology, 31*, 962–971.

Schnapf, J. L., & Baylor, D. A. (1987). How photoreceptor cells respond to light. *Scientific American, 256*(4), 40–47.

Schneider, B. (1985). Organizational behavior. *Annual Review of Psychology, 36*, 573–611.

Schuckit, M. A., Gold, E., & Risch, C. (1987). Serum prolactin levels in sons of alcoholics and control subjects. *American Journal of Psychiatry, 144*, 854–859.

Schwartz, R. H., Gruenewald, P. J., Klitzner, M., & Fedio, P. (1989). Short-term memory impairment in cannabis-dependent adolescents. *American Journal of Diseases of Children, 143*, 1214–1219.

Schweinhart, L. J., & Weikart, D. P. (1985). Evidence that good early childhood programs work. *Phi Delta Kappan, 66*, 545–551.

Schweinhart, L. J., & Weikart, D. P. (1986). What do we know so far? A review of the Head Start Synthesis Project. *Young Children, 41,* 49–55.

Scott, M. D., & Pelliccioni, L., Jr. (1982). *Don't choke: How athletes can become winners.* Englewood Cliffs, NJ: Prentice-Hall.

Sechenov, I. M. (1965). *Reflexes of the brain.* (Reprint of a 1961 translation by S. Belsky, printed in Moscow, of a work published in Russian in 1863). Cambridge, MA: MIT Press.

Sechrest, L. (1976). Personality. *Annual Review of Psychology, 27,* 1–28.

Seelbach, W. C., & Hansen, C. J. (1980). Satisfaction with family relations among the elderly. *Family Relations, 29,* 91–96.

Segal, M. W. (1974). Alphabet and attraction: An unobtrusive measure of the effect of propinquity in a field setting. *Journal of Personality & Social Psychology, 30,* 654–657.

Segal, N. L. (1985). Monozygotic and dizygotic twins: A comparative analysis of mental ability profiles. *Child Development, 56,* 1051–1058.

Segal, S. P., Cohen, D., & Marder, S. R. (1992). Neuroleptic medication and prescription practices with sheltered-care residents: A 12-year perspective. *American Journal of Public Health, 82,* 846–852.

Seligman, M E. P., & Maier, S. F. (1967). Failure to escape traumatic shock. *Journal of Experimental Psychology, 74,* 1–9.

Seligman, M. E. P. (1970). On the generality of the laws of learning. *Psychological Review, 77,* 406–418.

Seligmann, J., & Gosnell, M. (1986, March 3). Now, the gastric bubble. *Newsweek,* p. 59.

Seligmann, J., & Shapiro, D. (1979, November 12). Saved by lithium. *Newsweek,* p. 102.

Selmi, P. M., Klein, M. H., Greist, J. H., Sorrell, S. P., & Erdman, H. P. (1990). Computer-administered cognitive-behavioral therapy for depression. *American Journal of Psychiatry, 147,* 51–56.

Selye, H. (1976). *The stress of life* (2nd ed.). New York: McGraw-Hill, 1976.

Semmel, M. I., Gottlieb, J., & Robinson, N. M. (1979). Mainstreaming: Perspectives on educating handicapped children in the public schools. In D. C. Berliner (Ed.), *Review of research in education* (Vol. 7, pp. 223–279). Washington, DC: Amer. Educ. Research Ass.

Serbin, L. A., & Sprafkin, C. (1986). The salience of gender and the process of sex typing in three- to seven-year-old children. *Child Development, 57,* 1188–1199.

Shanab, M. E., & Yahya, K. A. (1977). A behavioral study of obedience in children. *Journal of Personality & Social Psychology, 35,* 530–536.

Shanas, E. (1979a). The family as a social support system in old age. *The Gerontologist, 19,* 169–174.

Shanas, E. (1979b). Social myth as hypothesis: The case of the family relations of old people. *The Gerontologist, 19,* 3–9.

Shanas, E. (1980). Older people and their families: The new pioneers. *Journal of Marriage and the Family, 42,* 9–15.

Shapira, A., & Madsen, M. C. (1974). Between- and within-group cooperation and competition among kibbutz and nonkibbutz children. *Developmental Psychology, 10,* 140–145.

Shapiro, A. K., Struening, E., Shapiro, E., & Barten, H. (1976). Prognostic correlates of psychotherapy in psychiatric outpatients. *American Journal of Psychiatry, 133,* 802–808.

Shapiro, D. H., Jr. (1985). Clinical use of meditation as a self-regulation strategy: Comments on Holmes's conclusions and implications. *American Psychologist, 40,* 719–722.

Shatz, M. (1973). *Preschooler's ability to take account of others in a toy selection task.* Unpublished MA thesis, University of Pennsylvania, Philadelphia, Pennsylvania.

Shaver, J. P., & Strong, W. (1976). *Facing value decisions: Rationale-building for teachers.* Belmont, CA: Wadsworth.

Shekelle, R. B., Hulley, S. B., Neaton, J. D., Billings, J. H., Borhani, N. O., Gerace, T. A., Jacobs, D. R., Lasser, N. L., Mittlemark, M. B., & Stamler, J. (1985). The MRFIT behavior pattern study. II. Type A behavior and incidence of coronary heart disease. *American Journal of Epidemiology, 122,* 559–570.

Sheldon, W. H. (1940). *The varieties of human physique: An introduction to constitutional psychology.* New York: Harper.

Sheldon, W. H. (1944). Constitutional factors in personality. In J. McV. Hunt (Ed.), *Personality and the behavior disorders.* New York: Ronald Press.

Shelton, R. C., Karson, C. N., Doran, A. R., Pickar, D., Bigelow, L. B., & Weinberger, D. R. (1988). Cerebral structural pathology in schizophrenia: Evidence for a selective prefrontal cortical defect. *American Journal of Psychiatry, 145,* 154–163.

Shilts, R. (1987). *And the band played on.* New York: St. Martin's Press.

Shock, N. W. (1962). The physiology of aging, *Scientific American, 206*(1), 100–110.

Shore, J. H., Tatum, E. L., & Vollmer, W. M. (1986). Psychiatric reactions to disaster: The Mount St. Helens experience. *American Journal of Psychiatry, 143,* 590–595.

Shotland, R. L. & Heinold, W. D. (1985). Bystander response to arterial bleeding: Helping skills, the decision-making process, and differentiating the helping response.

Journal of Personality & Social Psychology, 49, 347–356.

Shotland, R. L. & Huston, T. L. (1979). Emergencies: What are they and do they influence bystanders to intervene? *Journal of Personality & Social Psychology, 37,* 1822–1834.

Shrauger, J. S. & Osberg, T M. (1981). The relative accuracy of self-predictions and judgments by others in psychological assessment. *Psychological Bulletin, 90,* 322–352.

Shuchter, S. R., Zisook, S., Kirkorowicz, C., & Risch, C. (1986). The dexamethasone suppression test in acute grief. *American Journal of Psychiatry, 143,* 879–881.

Siegel, B. V., Buchsbaum, M. S., Bunney, W. E., Jr., Gottschalk, L. A., Haier, R. J., Lohr, J. B., Lottenberg, S., Najafi, A., Nuechterlein, K. H., Potkin, S. G., & Wu, J. C. (1993). Cortical-striatal-thalamic circuits and brain glucose metabolic activity in 70 unmedicated male schizophrenic patients. *American Journal of Psychiatry, 150,* 1325–1336.

Siegel, S. (1975). Evidence from rats that morphine tolerance is a learned response. *Journal of Comparative and Physiological Psychology, 89,* 498–506.

Siegel, S., Hinson, R. E., Krank, M. D., & McCully, J. (1982). Heroin "overdose" death: Contribution of drug-associated environmental causes. *Science, 216,* 436–437.

Siever, L. J., & Davis, K. L. (1991). A psychobiological perspective on the personality disorders. *American Journal of Psychiatry, 148,* 1647–1658.

Siffre, M. (1975). Six months alone in a cave. *National Geographic, 147,* 426–435.

Sillman, L. R. (1966). Feminity and paranoidism. *The Journal of Nervous and Mental Disease, 143,* 163–170.

Silveira, J. (1971). *Incubation: The effect of interruption timing and length on problem solution and quality of problem processing.* Unpublished doctoral dissertation, University of Oregon.

Silverstein, B., Kozlowski, L. T., & Schachter, S. (1977). Studies of the interaction of psychological and pharmacological determinants of smoking: 3. Social life, cigarette smoking, and urinary pH. *Journal of Experimental Psychology: General, 106,* 20–23.

Simpson, E. L. (1974). Moral development research: A case study of scientific cultural bias. *Human Development, 17,* 81–106.

Simpson, S. G., Folstein, S. E., Meyers, D. A., McMahon, F. J., Brusco, D. M., & DePaulo, J. R., Jr. (193). Bipolar II: The most common bipolar phenotype? *American Journal of Psychiatry, 150,* 901–903.

Singer, J. L., & Kolligan, J., Jr. (1987). Personality: Developments in the study of private experience. *Annual Review of Psychology, 38,* 533–574.

Singer, J. L., & Singer, D. G. (1983a). Psychologists look at television: Cognitive, developmental, personality, and social policy implications. *American Psychologist, 38,* 826–834.

Singer, J. L., & Singer, D. G. (1983b). Implications of childhood television viewing for cognition, imagination, and emotion. In J. Bryant, & D. R. Anderson (Eds.), *Children's understanding of television: Research on attention and comprehension.* New York: Academic Press.

Sinnott, E. W., Dunn, L. C., & Dobzhansky, T. (1958). *Principles of genetics.* New York: McGraw-Hill.

Skinner, B. F. (1953). *Science and human behavior.* New York: Macmillan.

Skinner, B. F. (1969). *Contingencies of reinforcement: A theoretical analysis.* New York: Appleton-Century-Crofts.

Skinner, B. F. (1989). The origins of cognitive thought. *American Psychologist, 44,* 13–18.

Slaughter-Defoe, D. T., Nakagawa, K., Takanishi, R., & Johnson, D. J. (1990). Toward cultural/ecological perspectives on schooling and achievement in African- and Asian-American children.

Sledge, W. H., Moras, K., Hartley, D., & Levine, M. (1990). Effect of time-limited psychotherapy on patient dropout rates. *American Journal of Psychiatry, 147,* 1341–1347.

Slobin, D. I. (1970). Universals of grammatical development in children. In G. B. Flores d'Arcams & W. J. M. Levelt (Eds.), *Advances in psycholinguistics.* New York: American Elsevier.

Sloviter, R. S., Valiquette, G., Abrams, G. M., Ronk, E. C., Sollas, A. L., Paul, L. A., & Neubort, S. (1989). Selective loss of hippocampal granule cells in the mature rat brain after adrenalectomy. *Science, 243,* 535–538.

Smith, C. G., Almirez, R. G., Berenberg, J., & Asch, R. H. (1983). Tolerance develops to the disruptive effects of delta9–tetrahydrocannabinol on primate menstrual cycle. *Science, 219,* 1453–1455.

Smith, F. J. (1977). Work attitudes as predictors of attendance on a specific day. *Journal of Applied Psychology, 62,* 16–19.

Smith, J. (1989). *Senses and sensibilities.* New York: John Wiley & Sons.

Smith, M. B. (1950). The phenomenological approach in personality theory: Some critical remarks. *Journal of Abnormal and Social Psychology, 45,* 516–522.

Smith, M. L., & Glass, G. V. (1977). Meta-analysis of psychotherapy outcome studies. *American Psychologist, 32,* 752–760.

Smith, S. M. (1985). Background music and context-dependent memory. *American*

Journal of Psychology, 98, 591–603.

Smith, S. M., Brown, H. O., Toman, J. E. P., & Goodman, L. S. (1947). The lack of cerebral effects of d-Tubercurarine. *Anesthesiology, 8,* 1–14.

Smith, S. M., Glenberg, A., & Bjork, R. A. (1978). Environmental context and human memory. *Memory and Cognition, 6,* 342–353.

Snow, R. E., & Swanson, J. (1992). Instructional psychology: Aptitude, adaptation, and assessment. *Annual Review of Psychology, 43,* 583–626.

Snyder, C. R., Shenkel, R. J., & Lowery, C. R. (1977). Acceptance of personality interpretations: The "Barnum effect" and beyond. *Journal of Consulting & Clinical Psychology, 45,* 104–114.

Snyder, S. H. (1984). Cholinergic mechanisms in affective disorder. *New England Journal of Medicine, 311,* 254–255.

Snyder, S. H. (1984). Drug and neurotransmitter receptors in the brain. *Science, 224,* 22–31.

Snyder, S. H. (1992). Nitric oxide: First in a new class of neurotransmitters? *Science, 257,* 494–496.

Snyder, S. H., & Bredt, D. S. (1992). Biological roles of nitric oxide. *Scientific American, 266*(5), 68–77.

Snyderman, M., & Rothman, S. (1987). Survey of expert opinion on intelligence and aptitude testing. *American Psychologist, 42,* 137–144.

Sohier, R. (1986). Heterosexual mutuality: Variation on a theme by Erik Erikson. *Journal of Homosexuality, 12,* 25–38.

Solomon, H., & Solomon, L. Z. (1978, March). *Effects of anonymity on helping in emergency situations.* Paper presented at the meeting of the Eastern Psychological Association, Washington, D.C.

Solomon, P. R., & Moore, J. W. (1975). Latent inhibition and stimulus generalization of the classically conditioned nictitating membrane response in rabbits (*Oryctolagus cuniculus*) following dorsal hippocampal ablation. *Journal of Comparative & Physiological Psychology, 89,* 1192–1203.

Solomon, R. L. (1980). The opponent-process theory of acquired motivation: The costs of pleasure and the benefits of pain. *American Psychologist, 35,* 691–712.

Soni, S. D., & Rockley, G. J. (1974). Socio-clinical substrates of folie a deux. *British Journal of Psychiatry, 125,* 230–235.

Sonstroem, R. J. (1981). Exercise and self-esteem: Recommendations for expository research. *Quest, 33,* 124–139.

Sorbera, L. A., & Morad, M. (1990). Atrionatriuretic peptide transforms cardiac sodium channels into calcium-conducting channels. *Science, 247,* 969–973.

Sorce, J. F., Emde, R. N., Campos, J., & Klinnert, M. D. (1985). Maternal emotional signaling: Its effect on the visual cliff behavior of 1–year-olds. *Developmental Psychology, 21,* 195–200.

Soskin, W. F. (1959). Influence of four types of data on diagnostic conceptualization in psychological testing. *Journal of Abnormal and Social Psychology, 58,* 69–78.

Spacapan, S., & Cohen, S. (1977, August). *Density, task load, and helping: Interpreting the aftereffects of stress.* Paper presented at the meeting of the American Psychological Association, San Francisco.

Spanos, N. P., Ansari, F., & Stam, H. J. (1979). Hypnotic age regression and eidetic imagery: A failure to replicate. *Journal of Abnormal Psychology, 88,* 88–91.

Spearman, C. (1927). *The abilities of man.* New York: Macmillan.

Spence, J. T. (1985). Achievement American style. *American Psychologist, 40,* 1285–1295.

Spencer, M. B. (1990). Development of minority children: An introduction. *Child Development, 61,* 267–269.

Spiegel, D., Bierre, P., & Rootenberg, J. (1989). Hypnotic alteration of somatosensory perception. *American Journal of Psychiatry, 146,* 749–754.

Spitz, R. A. (1945). Hospitalism: An inquiry into the genesis of psychiatric conditions in early childhood. *Psychoanalytic Study of the Child, 1,* 53–74.

Spitzer, R. L., & Williams, J. B. W. (Eds.). (1987) *Diagnostic and statistical manual of mental disorders* (3rd rev. ed.). Washington, DC: Am. Psychiatric Assn.

Spring, R. L. (1979). The end of insanity. *Washburn Law Journal, 19,* 23–37.

Squire, L. R. (1986). Mechanisms of memory. *Science, 232,* 1612–1616.

Squire, L. R., Knowlton, B., & Musen, G. (1993). The structure and organization of memory. *Annual Review of Psychology, 44,* 453–495.

Squire, L. R., Ojemann, J. G., Miezin, F. M., Petersen, S. E., Videen, T. O., & Raichle, M. E. (1992). Activation of the hippocampus in normal humans: A functional anatomical study of memory. *Proc. Natl. Acad. Sci. USA, 89,* 1837–1841.

Squire, L. R., & Zouzounis, J. A. (1986). ECT and memory: Brief pulse versus sine wave. *American Journal of Psychiatry, 143,* 596–601.

Sroufe, L. A. (1983). Individual patterns of adaptation from infancy to preschool. In M. Perlmutter (Ed.), *Minnesota Symposium in Child Psychology* (Vol. 16). Hillsdale, NJ: Erlbaum.

Sroufe, R., Chaikin, A., Cook, R., & Freeman, V. (1977). The effects of physical attractiveness on honesty: A socially desirable response. *Personality and Social Psychology Bulletin, 3,* 59–62.

Staats, A. W., & Staats, C. K. (1958). Attitudes established by classical conditioning. *Journal of Abnormal and Social Psychology, 57,* 37–40.

Stallings, J. (1975). Implementation and child effects of teaching practices in Follow Through Classrooms. *Monographs of the Society for Research in Child Development, 40*(5, Serial No. 163).

Stanfiel, J. D. (1981, Spring). The questionable sanity of the insanity defense. *Barrister,* pp. 19–20; 48–51.

Stark, E. (1981, September). Pigeon patrol. *Science 81,* pp. 85–86.

Stark, E. (1984, February). Hypnosis on trial. *Psychology Today,* pp. 34–36.

Starr, M. D. (1978). An opponent-process theory of motivation: VI. Time and intensity variables in the development of separation-induced distress calling in ducklings. *Journal of Experimental Psychology: Animal Behavior Processes, 4,* 338–355.

Staw, B. M. (1984). Organizational behavior: A review and reformulation of the field's outcome variables. *Annual Review of Psychology, 35,* 627–666.

Staw, B. M., & Oldham, G. R. (1978). Reconsidering our dependent variables: A critique and empirical study. *Academy of Management Journal, 21,* 539–559.

Steadman, H. J., Callahan, L. A., Robbins, P. C., & Morrissey, J. P. (1989). Maintenance of an insanity defense under Montana's "abolition" of the insanity defense. *American Journal of Psychiatry, 146,* 357–360.

Steblay, N. M. (1987). Helping behavior in rural and urban environments: A meta-analysis. *Psychological Bulletin, 102,* 346–356.

Steele, C. M. (1986, January). What happens when you drink too much? *Psychology Today,* pp. 48–52.

Stein, M., Miller, A. H., & Trestman, R. L. (1991). Depression, the immune system, and health and illness. Findings in search of meaning. *Archives of General Psychiatry, 48,* 171–177.

Stein, P. J. (1983). Singlehood. In E. D. Macklin & R. H. Rubin (Eds.), *Contemporary families and alternative lifestyles* (pp. 27–47). Beverly Hills: Sage Publications.

Steinberg, L., Elmen, J. D., & Mounts, N. S. (1989). Authoritative parenting, psychosocial maturity, and academic success among adolescents. *Child Development, 60,* 1424–1426.

Stephan, W. G. & Rosenfield, D. (1978). Effects of desegregation on racial attitudes. *Journal of Personality & Social Psychology, 36,* 795–804.

Stern, D. B. (1977). Handedness and the lateral distribution of conversion reactions. *Journal of Nervous & Mental Disease, 164,* 122–128.

Sternberg, D. E. (1986). Neuroleptic malignant syndrome: The pendulum swings. *American Journal of Psychiatry, 143,* 1273–1275.

Sternberg, R. J. (1984). *Beyond IQ: A triarchic theory of human intelligence.* New York: Cambridge Univ. Press.

Sternberg, R. J. (1985). Human intelligence: The model is the message. *Science, 230,* 1111–1118.

Sternberg, R. J. (1987). Liking versus loving: A comparative evaluation of theories. *American Psychologist, 102,* 331–345.

Stevens, C. F. (1979). The neuron. *Scientific American, 241*(3), 54–65.

Stevenson, J. S. (1977). *Issues and crisis during middlescence.* New York: Applton-Century-Crofts.

Stimson, A., Wase, J., & Stimson, J. (1981, June). Sexuality and self-esteem among the aged. *Research on Aging,* pp. 228–239.

Stith, S. M., & Davis, A. J. (1984). Employed mothers and family day-care substitute caregivers: A comparative analysis of infant care. *Child Development, 55,* 1340–1348.

Stocker, C., Dunn, J., & Plomin, R. (1989). Sibling relationships: Links with child temperament, maternal behavior, and family structure. *Child Development, 60,* 715–727.

Stockwell, T. (1986). Cracking an old chestnut: Is controlled drinking possible for the person who has been severely alcohol dependent? *British Journal of Addiction, 81,* 455–456.

Stoel-Gammon, C., & Otomo, K. (1986). Babbling development of hearing-impaired and normally hearing subjects. *Journal of Speech & Hearing Disorders, 51,* 33–41.

Stoll, A. L., Tohen, M., & Baldessarini, R. J. (1992). Increasing frequency of the diagnosis of obsessive-compulsive disorder. *American Journal of Psychiatry, 149,* 638–640.

Stoller, R. J. (1985). *Presentations of gender.* New Haven: Yale Univ. Press.

Strahilevitz, M., Strahilevitz, A., & Miller, J. E. (1979). Air pollutants and the admission rate of psychiatric patients. *American Journal of Psychiatry, 136,* 205–207.

Stunkard, A. J. (1958). The management of obesity. *New York State Journal of Medicine, 58,* 79–87.

Suddath, R. L., Casanova, M. F., Goldberg, T. E., Daniel, D. G., Kelsoe, J. R., Jr., & Weinberger, D. R. (1989). Temporal lobe pathology in schizophrenia: A quantitative magnetic resonance imaging study. *American Journal of Psychiatry, 146,* 464–472.

Suddath, R. L., Christison, G. W., Torrey, E. F., Casanova, M. F., & Weinberger, D. R. (1990). Anatomical abnormalities in the brains of monozygotic twins discordant for schizophrenia. *New England Journal of Medicine, 322,* 789–794.

Suedfeld, P., Ballard, E. J., & Murphy, M. (1983). Water immersion and flotation: From stress experiment to stress treatment. *Journal of Environmental Psychology, 3,* 147–155.

Suedfeld, P., & Coren, S. (1989). Perceptual isolation, sensory deprivation, and rest: Moving introductory psychology texts out of the 1950s. *Canadian Psychology, 30,* 17–29.

Suedfeld, P., & Kristeller, J. L. (1982). Stimulus reduction as a technique in health psychology. *Health Psychology, 1,* 337–357.

Suinn, R. M. (1977). Type A behavior pattern. In R. B. Williams, Jr. & W. D. Gentry (Eds.), *Behavioral approaches to medical treatment* (pp. 55–56). Cambridge, Mass.: Ballinger.

Suler, J. R. (1985). Meditation and somatic arousal: A comment on Holmes's review. *American Psychologist, 40,* 717.

Sulloway, F. J. (1979). *Freud: Biologist of the mind.* New York: Basic Books.

Surrey, J. L. (1985). *Self-in-relation: A theory of women's development.* (Work in Progress, 13). Wellesley College, Wellesley, Massachusetts.

Sussman, N. (1976). Sex and sexuality in history. In B. J. Sadock, H. I. Kaplan, & A. M. Freedman (Eds.), *The sexual experience.* Baltimore, MD: Williams & Wilkins.

Svaetichin, G. (1956). Spectral response curves from single cones. *Acta Physiologica Scandinavica, 39*(Supplementum No. 134), 17–46.

Swap, W. C. (1977). Interpersonal attraction and repeated exposure to rewarders and punishers. *Personality and Social Psychology Bulletin, 3,* 248–251.

Swartz, M., Blazer, D., George, L., & Landerman, R. (1986). Somatization disorder in a community population. *American Journal of Psychiatry, 143,* 1403–1408.

Swift, R. G., Perkins, D. O., Chase, C. L., Sadler, D. B., & Swift, M. (1991). Psychiatric disorders in 36 families with Wolfram syndrome. *American Journal of Psychiatry, 148,* 775–779.

Sylva, K., Bruner, J., & Genova, P. (1976). The role of play in the problem solving of children 3–5 years old. In J. S. Bruner, A. Jolly, & K. Sylva (Eds.), *Play.* New York: Basic Books.

Szapocznik, J., & Kurtines, W. M. (1993). Family psychology and cultural diversity: Opportunities for theory, research, and application. *American Psychologist, 48,* 400–407.

Szasz, T. S. (1961). *The myth of mental illness: Foundations of a theory of personal conduct.* New York: Harper & Row.

Szucko, J. J., & Kleinmuntz, B. (1981). Statistical versus clinical lie detection. *American Psychologist, 36,* 488–496.

Tajfel, H. (1982). Social psychology of intergroup relations. *Annual Review of Psychology, 33,* 1–39.

Takeuchi, A. H., & Hulse, S. H. (1993). Absolute pitch. *Psychological Bulletin, 113,* 345–361.

Talbert, G. B. (1977). Aging of the reproductive system. In C. E. Finch & L. Hayflick (Eds.), *The handbook of the biology of aging.* New York: Van Nostrand Reinhold Co.

Tanner, J. M. (1969). Growth and endocrinology in the adolescent. In L. I. Gardner (Ed.), *Endocrine and genetic diseases of childhood.* Philadelphia, PA: Saunders.

Tauber, E. S. (1974). Phylogeny of sleep. In E. D. Weitzman (Ed.), *Advances in sleep research I.* (pp. 133–172). New York: Spectrum.

Taussig, H. B. (1969). "Death" from lightning and the possibility of living again. *American Scientist, 57,* 306–316.

Taylor, J. R., & Combs-Orme, T. (1985). Alcohol and strokes in young adults. *American Journal of Psychiatry, 142,* 116–120.

Taylor, M., & Gelman, S. A. (1989). Incorporating new words into the lexicon: Preliminary evidence for language hierarchies in two-year-old children. *Child Development, 60,* 625–636.

Taylor, S. E. (1990). Health psychology: The science and the field. *American Psychologist, 45,* 40–50.

Taylor, S. E., & Fiske, S. T. (1978). Salience, attention, and attribution: Top of the head phenomena. In L. Berkowitz (Ed.), *Advances in experimental social psychology* (Vol. 11). New York: Academic Press.

Teborg, R. H. (1968). *Dissipation of functional fixedness by means of conceptual grouping tasks.* Unpublished doctoral dissertation, Michigan State University.

Tedeschi, J. T. (Ed.). (1981). *Impression management theory and social psychological research.* New York: Academic Press.

Tedeschi, J. T., Schlenker, B. R., & Bonoma, T. V. (1971). Cognitive dissonance: Private ratiocination or public spectacle? *American Psychologist, 26,* 685–695.

Tempel, L. W., & Perlmutter, J. S. (1992). Vibration-induced regional cerebral blood flow responses in normal aging. *Journal of Cerebral Blood Flow Metabolism, 12,* 554–561.

Terman, L. M. (1925). Mental and physical traits of a thousand gifted children. In L. M. Terman (Ed.), *Genetic studies of genius.* Stanford: Stanford University Press.

Terman, L. M. (1954). Scientists and nonscientists in a group of 800 gifted men. *Psychological Monographs, 68*(7), 1–44.

Terrace, H. S. (1979). *Nim.* New York: Knopf.

Terrace, H. S. (1987). Chunking by a pigeon in a serial learning task. *Nature, 325,* 149–151.

Tesser, A., & Shaffer, D. R. (1990). Attitudes and attitude change. *Annual Review of Psychology, 41,* 479–523.

Tetrud, J. W., & Langston, J. W. (1989). The effect of deprenyl (selegiline) on the natural history of Parkinson's disease. *Science, 245,* 519–522.

Thomas, A., Chess, S., & Birch, H. (1968). *Temperament and behavior disorders in children.* New York: New York Univ. Press.

Thomas, A., Chess, S., & Birch, H. G. (1970). The origin of personality. *Scientific American, 223*(2), 102–109.

Thompson, J. W., & Blaine, J. D. (1987). Use of ECT in the United States in 1975 and 1980. *American Journal of Psychiatry, 144,* 557–562.

Thompson, L. (1992). Fetal transplants show promise. *Science, 257,* 868–870.

Thompson, L. A., Fagan, J. F., & Fulker, D. W. (1991). Longitudinal prediction of specific cognitive abilities from infant novelty preference. *Child Development, 62,* 530–538.

Thompson, S. K. (1975). Gender labels and early sex role development. *Child Development, 46,* 339–347.

Thorndike, E. L. (1905). *The elements of psychology.* New York: Seiler.

Thurstone, L. L. (1938). Primary mental abilities. *Psychometric Monographs, 1.*

Tiihonen, J., Hari, R., Naukkarinen, H., Rimon, R., Jousmaki, V., & Kajola, M. (1992). Modified activity of the human auditory cortex during auditory hallucinations. *American Journal of Psychiatry, 149,* 255–257.

Timberlake, W., & Allison, J. (1974). An empirical approach to instrumental performance. *Psychological Review, 81,* 146–164.

Timberlake, W., & Farmer-Dougan, V. A. (1991). Reinforcement in applied settings: Figuring out ahead of time what will work. *Psychological Bulletin, 110,* 379–391.

Time. (1986, March 3). Died; Shigechiyo Izumi. P. 79.

Tollefson, D. L. (1984). Personal communication.

Tolman, E. C., Ritchie, B. F., & Kalish, D. (1964). Studies in spatial learning. I. Orientation and the short-cut. *Journal of Experimental Psychology, 36,* 13–24.

Tolson, T. F. J., & Wilson, M. N. (1990). The impact of two- and three-generational black family structure on perceived family climate. *Child Development, 61,* 416–428.

Tomkins, S. S. (1962). *Affect, imagery, consciousness, the positive affects* (Vol. 1). New York: Springer.

Tomkins, S. S. (1963). *Affect, imagery, consciousness, the negative affects* (Vol. 2). New York: Springer.

Tong, Y. C., Dowell, R. C., Blamey, P. J., & Clark, G. M. (1983). Two component hearing sensations produced by two-electrode stimulation in the cochlea of a deaf patient. *Science, 219,* 993–994.

Tordoff, M. G., & Friedman, M. I. (1989). Drinking saccharin increases food intake and preference. *Appetite, 12,* 37–56.

Torrance, E. P., & Wu, T. (1981). A comparative longitudinal study of the adult creative achievements of elementary school children identified as high intelligent and as highly creative. *Creative Child and Adult Quarterly, 6,* 71–76.

Toynbee, A. (1968). Changing attitudes toward death in the modern Western world. In A. Toynbee, A. K. Mant, N. Smart, J. Hinton, S. Yudkin, E. Rhode, R. Haywood, & H. H. Price (Eds.), *Man's concern with death* (pp. 122–132). New York: McGraw-Hill.

Tranel, D., & Damasio, A. R. (1985). Knowledge without awareness: An automatic index of facial recognition by prosopagnosics. *Science, 228,* 1453–1454.

Treatment book is born in controversy. (1989, August). *APA Monitor,* pp. 19–20.

Troll, L. E. (1983). Grandparents: The family watchdogs. In T. A. Brubaker (Ed.), *Family relationships in later life* (pp. 63–74). Beverly Hills: Sage Publishing Co.

Troll, L. E. (1985). The contingencies of grandparenting. In V. L. Bengson & J. F. Robertson (Eds.), *Grandparenthood* (pp. 135–149). Beverly Hills: Sage Publishing Co.

Troll, L. E., Miller, S. J., & Atchley, R. C. (1979). *Families in later life.* Belmont, CA: Wadsworth.

Trotter, R. J. (1987, May). You've come a long way, baby. *Psychology Today,* pp. 34–45.

Trotter, R. J. (1990, June). Chemistry of compulsion. *Discover,* pp. 26–27.

Tseng, W., Ebata, K., Miguchi, M., Egawa, M., & McLaughlin, D. G. (1990). Transethnic adoption and personality traits: A lesson from Japanese orphans returned from China to Japan. *American Journal of Psychiatry, 147,* 330–335.

Tsitouras, P. D., Martin, C. E., & Harman, S. M. (1982). Relationship of serum testosterone to sexual activity in healthy elderly men. *Journal of Gerontology, 37,* 288–293.

Tulving, E., & Schacter, D. L. (1990). Priming and human memory systems. *Science, 247,* 301–306.

Tune, G. S. (1969). Sleep and wakefulness in 509 normal human adults. *British Journal of Medical Psychology, 42,* 75–79.

Turkington, C. (1987, September). Special talents. *Psychology Today,* pp. 42–46.

Turkington, C. (1992, October). Volunteers help ease stress in distress. *APA Monitor,* p. 29.

Tyler, L. E. (1956). *The psychology of human differences.* New York: Appleton.

U. S. Bureau of the Census. (1985). *Statistical abstract of the United States: 1986* (106th ed.). Washington, DC: U.S. Government Printing Office.

Ulrich, R. E., & Azrin, N. H. (1962). Reflexive fighting in response to aversive stimulation. *Journal of the Experimental Analysis of Behavior, 5,* 511–520.

Unestahl, L. E. (1983). *The mental aspects of gymnastics.* Orebro, Sweden: Veje.

Vaillant, G. E. (1977). *Adaptation to life.* Boston: Little, Brown & Company.

Vaillant, G. E. (1979). Natural history of male psychologic health: Effects of mental health on physical health. *New England Journal of Medicine, 301,* 1249–1254.

Vaillant, G. E., & Vaillant, C. O. (1990). Natural history of male psychological health, XII: 45-year study of predictors of successful aging at age 65. *American Journal of Psychiatry, 147,* 31–37.

Valencia, R. R. (1985). Predicting academic achievement in Mexican-American children using the Kaufman Assessment Battery for children. *Educational and Psychological Research, 5,* 11–17.

Valenstein, E. S. (1980a). Causes and treatment of mental disorders. In E. S. Valenstein (Ed.), *The psychosurgery debate.* San Francisco: W. H. Freeman.

Valenstein, E. S. (1980b). Historical perspective. In E. S. Valenstien (Ed.), *The psychosurgery debate.* San Francisco: W. H. Freeman.

Valins, S. (1966). Cognitive effects of false heartrate feedback. *Journal of Personality & Social Psychology, 4,* 400–408.

van Doorninck, W. J., Caldwell, B. M., Wright, C., & Frankenburg, W. K. (1981). The relationship between twelve-month home stimulation and school achievement. *Child Development, 52,* 1080–1083.

van Ijzendoorn, M. H., & Kroonenberg, P. M. (1988). Cross-cultural patterns of attachment: A meta-analysis of the strange situation. *Child Development, 59,* 147–156.

Vandenberg, B. (1978). Play and development from an ethological perspective. *American Psychologist, 33,* 724–738.

Vandenberg, B. (1984). Developmental features of exploration. *Developmental Psychology, 20,* 3–8.

Vanderweele, D. A., & Sanderson, J. D. (1976). Peripheral glucosensitive satiety in the rabbit and the rat. In D. Novin, W. Wyrwicka, & G. A. Bray (Eds.), *Hunger: Basic mechanisms and clinical implications.* New York: Raven.

Verma, A., Hirsch, D. J., Glatt, C. E., Ronnett, G. V., & Snyder, S. H. (1993). Carbon monoxide: A putative neural messenger. *Science, 259,* 381–384.

Vermeulen, A. (1983). Androgen secretion after age 50 in both sexes. *Hormone Research, 18,* 37–42.

Vernon, P. E. (1965). Ability factors and environmental influences. *American Psychologist, 20,* 723–733.

Vinokur, A., & Burnstein, E. (1978). Depolarization of attitudes in groups. *Journal of Personality & Social Psychology, 36,* 872–885.

Volkow, N. D., & Tancredi, L. R. (1991). Biological correlates of mental activity studied with PET. *American Journal of Psychiatry, 148,* 439–443.

Volkow, N. D., Fowler, J. S., Wolf, A. P., Schlyer, D., Shiue, C., Alpert, R., Dewey, S. L., Logan, J., Bendriem, B., Christman, D., Hitzemann, R., & Henn, F. (1990). Effects of chronic cocaine abuse on postsynaptic dopamine receptors. *American Journal of Psychiatry, 147,* 719–724.

Volpicelli, J. R., Alterman, A. L., Hayashida, M., & O'Brien, C. P. Naltrexone in the treatment of alcohol dependence. *Archives of General Psychiatry, 49,* 876–880.

Vondracek, F. W., & Lerner, R. M. (1982). Vocational role development in adolescence. In B. B. Wolman (Ed.), *Handbook of developmental psychology* (pp. 602–614). Englewood Cliffs NJ: Prentice-Hall.

Wafford, K. A., Burnett, D. M., Dunwiddie, T. V., & Harris, R. A. (1990). Genetic differences in the ethanol sensitivity of GABAdn6 A receptors expressed in *xenopus* oocytes. *Science, 249,* 291–293.

Waldhauser, F., Weiszenbacher, G., Frisch, H., Zeitlhuber, U., Waldhauser, M., & Wurtman, R. J. (1984). Fall in nocturnal serum melatonin during prepuberty and pubescence. *Lancet, 1*(8373), 362–365.

Waldrop, M. M. (1984). Natural language understanding. *Science, 224,* 372–374.

Walker, E., & Emory, E. (1985). Commentary: Interpretive bias and behavioral genetic research. *Child Development, 56,* 775–778.

Walker, E., & Lewine, R. J. (1990). Prediction of adult-onset schizophrenia from childhood home movies of the patients. *American Journal of Psychiatry, 147,* 1052–1056.

Walker, J. (1982). "Floaters": Visual artifacts that result from blood cells in front of the retina. *Scientific American, 246*(4), 150–161.

Walker, L. J., de Vries, B., & Bichard, S. L. (1984). The hierarchical nature of stages of moral development. *Developmental Psychology, 20,* 960–966.

Wallace, I., Wallenchinsky, D., Wallace, A., & Wallace, S. (1980). *The book of lists #2.* New York: Bantam Books.

Wallach, M. A. (1970). Creativity. In P. H. Mussen (Ed.), *Carmichael's manual of child psychology* (3rd ed., pp. 1211–1272). New York: Wiley.

Wallach, M. A., & Wing, C. W. (1969). *The talented student: A validation of the creativity-intelligence distinction.* New York: Holt.

Wallis, C., Hull, J. C., Ludke, M., & Taylor, E. (1987, June 22). The child-care dilemma. *Time,* pp. 54–60.

Wandersman, A. H., & Hallman, W. K. (1993). Are people acting irrationally? Understanding public concerns about environmental issues. *American Psychologist, 48,* 681–686.

Wanner, E., & Gleitman, L. R. (Eds.) (1982). *The state of the art.* New York: Cambridge Univ. Press.

Washburn, S. L., & Hamburg, D. A. (1965). The study of primate behavior. In I. DeVore (Ed.), *Primate behavior: Field studies of monkeys and apes.* New York: Holt.

Watson, J. B. (1913). Psychology as the behaviorist views it. *Psychological Review, 20,* 158–177.

Watson, J. B. (1929). *Psychology from the standpoint of a behaviorist* (3rd ed.). Philadelphia: Lippincott.

Watson, J. B. (1930). *Behaviorism.* New York: Norton.

Watson, J. B., & Rayner, R. (1920). Conditioned emotional responses. *Journal of Experimental Psychology, 3,* 1–14.

Watson, J. D., & Crick, F. H. C. (1953). Molecular structure of nucleic acids: A structure for deoxyribose nucleic acid. *Nature, 171,* 737–738.

Watson, J. S., & Ramey, C. T. (1969, March). *Reactions to responsive contingent stimulation in early infancy.* Paper presented at the biennial meeting of the Society for Research in Child Development, Santa Monica, California.

Watson, J. S., & Ramey, C. T. (1972). Reactions to response-contingent stimulation in early infancy. *Merrill-Palmer Quarterly, 18,* 219–227.

Watt, J. A. G. (1985). The relationship of paranoid states to schizophrenia. *American Journal of Psychiatry, 142,* 1456–1458.

Wayner, M. J., Barone, F. C., & Loullis, C. C. (1981). The lateral hypothalamus and adjunctive behavior. In P. J. Morgane & J. Panksepp (Eds.), *Handbook of the hypothalamus* (Vol. 3, Part B, pp. 107–145). New York: Dekker.

Weaver, C. A. (1993). Do you need a "flash" to form a flashbulb memory? *Journal of Experimental Psychology: General, 122,* 39–46.

Webb, W. B. (1974). Sleep as an adaptive response. *Perceptual & Motor Skills, 38,* 1023–1027.

Webb, W. B. (1975). *Sleep the gentle tyrant.* Englewood Cliffs, NJ: Prentice-Hall.

Webb, W. B., & Cartwright, R. D. (1978). Sleep and dreams. *Annual Review of Psychology, 29,* 223–252.

Weber, G. (1971). *Inner city children can be taught to read: Four successful schools.* Washington, D.C.: Council for Basic Education, Occasional Paper no. 18.

Weber, R. J., & Pert, A. (1989). The periaqueductal gray matter mediates opiate-induced immunosuppression. *Science, 245,* 188–190.

Wehr, T. A., Sack, D. A., & Rosenthal, N. E. (1987). Seasonal affective disorder with summer depression and winter hypomania. *American Journal of Psychiatry, 144,* 1602–1603.

Wehren, A., & De Lisi, R. (1983). The development of gender understanding: Judgments and explanations. *Child Development, 54,* 1568–1578.

Weicker, L., Jr. (1987). Federal response to institutional abuse and neglect. *American Psychologist, 42,* 1027–1028.

Weiden, P. J., Mann, J. J., Haas, G., Mattson, M., & Frances, A. (1987). Clinical nonrecognition of neuroleptic-induced movement disorders: A cautionary study. *American Journal of Psychiatry, 144,* 1148–1153.

Weinberg, R. A. (1989). Intelligence and IQ. *American Psychologist, 44,* 98–104.

Weinberg, R. S. (1981). The relationship between mental preparation strategies and motor performance: A review and critique. *Quest, 33,* 195–213.

Weinberger, D. R., Berman, K. F., Suddath, R., & Torrey, E. F. (1992). Evidence of dysfunction of a prefrontal-limbic network in schizophrenia: A magnetic resonance imaging and regional cerebral bllod flow study of discordant monozygotic twins. *American Journal of Psychiatry, 149,* 890–897.

Weinberger, N. M., Gold, P. E., & Sternberg, D. B. (1984). Epinephrine enables Pavlovian fear conditioning under anesthesia. *Science, 223,* 605–607.

Weiner, M. J., & Wright, F. E. (1973). Effects of undergoing arbitrary discrimination upon subsequent attitudes toward a minority group. *Journal of Applied Social Psychology, 3,* 94–102.

Weiner, R. D. (1989). Electroconvulsive therapy. In H. I. Kaplan & B. J. Sadock (Eds.), *Comprehensive textbook of psychiatry/v* (pp. 1670–1678). Baltimore, MD: Williams & Wilkins.

Weingarten, H. P. (1983). Conditioned cues elicit feeding in sated rats: A role for learning in meal initiation. *Science, 220,* 431–433.

Weinstein, N. D. (1989). Optimistic biases about personal risks. *Science, 246,* 1232–1233.

Weintraub, P. (1980, December). Wired for sound. *Discover,* pp. 50–51.

Weisburd, D. E. (1990). Planning a community-based mental health system: Perspective of a family member. *American Psychologist, 45,* 1245–1248.

Weiss, B. (1983). Behavioral toxicology and environmental health science: Opportunity and challenge for psychology. *American Psychologist, 38,* 1174–1187.

Weiss, R. (1988, August 20). Acupuncture: an old debate continues. *Science News,* p. 122.

Weiss, R. (1989, January 21). Safety gets short shrift on long night shift. *Science News,* p. 37.

Weissman, M. M., Wickramaratne, P., Merikangas, K. R., Leckman, J. F., Prusoff, B. A., Caruso, K. A., Kidd, K. K., & Gammon, G. D. (1984). Onset of major depression in early adulthood. Increased familial loading and specificity. *Archives of General Psychiatry, 41,* 1136–1143.

Weitzenhoffer, A. M., & Hilgard, E. R. (1962). *The Stanford Hypnotic Susceptibility Scale, Form C.* Palo Alto, CA: Consulting Psyc. Press.

Weller, A., Smith, G. P., & Gibbs, J. (1990). Endogenous cholecystokinin reduces feeding in young rats. *Science, 247,* 1589–1591.

Wertheimer, M. (1912). Experimentelle Stuidien uber das Sehen von Bewegungen. *Zsch. f. Psychol., 61,* 161–165.

West, M. A. (1985). Meditation and somatic arousal reduction. *American Psychologist, 40,* 717–719.

Wettstein, R. M., Mulvey, E. P., & Rogers, R. (1991). A prospective comparison of four insanity defense standards. *American Journal of Psychiatry, 148,* 21–27.

Whalen, R. E., & Simon, N. G. (1984). Biological motivation. *Annual Review of Psychology, 35,* 257–276.

Wheeler, L., Deci, L., Reis, H., & Zuckerman, M. (1978). *Interpersonal influence* (2nd ed.). Boston: Allyn & Bacon.

White, N. M., & Milner, P. M. (1992). The psychobiology of reinforcers. *Annual Review of Psychology, 43,* 443–471.

Whitehurst, G. J. (1982). Language development. In B. B. Wolman (Ed.), *Handbook of developmental psychology* (pp. 367–386). Englewood Cliffs, NJ: Prentice-Hall.

Whorf, B. L. (1956). *Language, thought, and reality.* Cambridge, Mass.: MIT Press.

Wiens, A. N., & Menustik, C. E. (1983). Treatment outcome and patient characteristics in an aversion therapy program for alcoholism. *American Psychologist, 38,* 1089–1096.

Willerman, L., Schultz, R., Rutledge, J. N., & Bigler, E. D. (1991). In vivo brain size and intelligence. *Intelligence, 15,* 223–228.

Williams, D. A., & King, P. (1980a, December 22). It really is a head start. *Newsweek,* p. 54.

Williams, D. A., & King, P. (1980b, December 15). Do males have a math gene? *Newsweek,* p. 72.

Williams, T. M. (Ed.). (1986). *The impact of television: A natural experiment in three communities.* Orlando, FL: Academic Press, Inc.

Wills, T. A., & Langner, T. S. (1980). Socioeconomic status and stress. In I. L. Kutach, L. B. Schlesinger & Associates (Eds.), *Handbook on stress and anxiety* (pp. 159–173). San Francisco: Jossey Bass.

Wilson, E. O. (1975). *Sociobiology.* Cambridge, Mass.: Belknap Press.

Wilson, R. S. (1983). The Louisville Twin Study: Developmental synchronies in behavior. *Child Development, 54,* 298–316.

Wilson, W. R. (1979). Feeling more than we can know: Exposure effects without learning. *Journal of Personality & Social Psychology, 37,* 811–821.

Winson, J. (1985). *Brain and psyche: The biology of the unconscious.* New York: Anchor Press.

Winson, J. (1990). The meaning of dreams. *Scientific American, 263*(5), 86–96.

Winton, W. M. (1987). Do introductory textbooks present the Yerkes-Dodson Law correctly? *American Psychologist, 42,* 202–203.

Wise, R. A., & Rompre, P. P. (1989). Brain dopamine and reward. *Annual Review of Psychology, 40,* 191–225.

Witt, D. (1977). *Emotional advertising: The relationship between eye-movement patterns and memory-empirical study with the eye-movement monitor.* Ph.D. thesis, University of Saarland, Saarbrucken, West Germany.

Wood, J. M., & Bootzin, R. R. (1990). The prevalence of nightmares and their independence from anxiety. *Journal of Abnormal Psychology, 99,* 64–68.

Woodhead, M. (1988). When psychology informs public policy: The case of early childhood intervention. *American Psychologist, 43,* 443–454.

Woolfolk, R. L., & Lehrer, P. M. (1984). Clinical stress reduction: An overview. In R. L. Woolfolk & P. M. Lehrer (Eds.), *Principles and practice of stress management* (pp. 1–11). New York: Guilford Press.

Wright, A. A., Santiago, H. C., Sands, S. F., Kendrick, D. F., & Cook, R. G. (1985). Memory processing of serial lists by pigeons, monkeys, and people. *Science, 229,* 287–289.

Wu, J. C., & Bunney, W. E. (1990). The biological basis of an antidepressant response to sleep deprivation and relapse: Review and hypothesis. *American Journal of Psychiatry, 147,* 14–21.

Wuethrich, B. (1993, July 3). Evolutionists pick up on one-night stands. *Science News,* p. 6.

Wundt, W. (1862). Die Geschwindigkeit des Gedankens. *Gartenlaube,* 263–265.

Wurtz, R. H., Goldberg, M. E., & Robinson, D. L. (1982). Brain mechanisms of visual attention. *Scientific American, 246*(6), 124–135.

Wynn, K. (1992). Addition and subtraction by human infants. *Nature, 358,* 749–750.

Wynne, L. C., Singer, M. T., Bartko, J., & Toohey, M. L. (1977). Schiaphrenics and their families: Research on parental communication. In J. Tanner (Ed.), *Developments in psychiatric research* (pp. 254–286). London: Hodder & Stoughton.

Yager, T., Laufer, R., & Gallops, M. (1984). Some problems associated with war experience in men of the Vietnam generation. *Archives of General Psychiatry, 41,* 327–333.

Yakimovich, D., & Saltz, E. (1971). Helping behavior: The cry for help. *Psychonomic Science, 23,* 427–428.

Yalom, I. D., Green, R., & Fisk, N. (1973). Prenatal exposure to female hormones: Effect on psychosexual development in boys. *Archives of General Psychiatry, 28,* 554–561.

Yang, K. S. (1986). Chinese personality and its change. In M. H. Bond (Ed.), *The psychology of the Chinese people.* Hong Kong; Oxford University Press.

Yang, R. K., & Douthitt, T. C. (1974). Newborn responses to threshold tactile stimulation. *Child Development, 45,* 237–242.

Yerkes, R. M., & Dodson, J. D. (1908). The relation of strength of stimulus to rapidity of habit formation. *Journal of Comparative Neurology and Psychology, 18,* 459–482.

Yesavage, J. A., & Leirer, V. O. (1986). Hangover effects on aircraft pilots 14 hours after alcohol ingestion: A preliminary report. *American Journal of Psychiatry, 143,* 1546–1550.

Yesavage, J. A., Leirer, V. O., Denari, M., & Hollister, L. E. (1985). Carry-over effects of marijuana intoxication on aircraft pilot performance: A preliminary report. *American Journal of Psychiatry, 142,* 1325–1329.

Yonas, A., Pettersen, L., & Granrud, C. E. (1982). Infants' sensitivity to familiar size as information for distance. *Child Development, 53,* 1285–1290.

Younger, J. C., Walker, L., & Arrowood, A. J. (1977). Postdecision dissonance at the fair. *Personality and Social Psychology Bulletin, 3,* 284–287.

Youngstrom, N. (1992, April). Field of psychoanalysis undergoes resurgence. *APA Monitor,* pp. 24–25.

Zaidel, E. (1983). A response to Gazzaniga. *American Psychologist, 38,* 542–546.

Zajonc, R. (1968). Attitudinal effects of mere exposure. *Journal of Personality & Social Psychology, 9,* 1–27.

Zajonc, R. B. (1984). On the primacy of affect. *American Psychologist, 39,* 117–123.

Zajonc, R. B., & Markus, G. B. (1975). Birth order and intellectual development. *Psychological Review, 82,* 74–88.

Zarbatany, L., Hartmann, D. P., & Rankin, D. B. (1990). The psychological functions of preadolescent peer activities. *Child Development, 61,* 1067–1080.

Zarit, S. H., Cole, K. D., & Guider, R. L. (1981). Memory training strategies and subjective complaints of memory in the aged. *The Gerontologist, 21,* 158–164.

Zarit, S. H., Gallagher, D., & Kramer, N. (1981). Memory training in the community aged: Effects on depression, memory complaint, and memory performance. *Educational Gerontology, 6,* 11–27.

Zeki, S. (1992). The visual image in mind and brain. *Scientific American, 267*(3), 68–76.

Zellner, M. (1970). Self-esteem, reception, and influenceability. *Journal of Personality & Social Psychology, 15,* 87–93.

Zhuo, M., Small, S. A., Kandel, E. R., & Hawkins, R. D. (1993). Nitric oxide and carbon monoxide produce activity-dependent long-term synaptic enhancement in hippocampus. *Science, 260,* 1946–1950.

Zimbardo, P. G. (1979). *Psychology and life* (10th ed.). Glenview, IL: Scott Foresman.

Zinbarg, R. E., Barlow, D. H., Brown, T. A., & Hertz, R. M. (1992). Cognitive-behavioral approaches to the nature and treatment of anxiety disorders. *Annual Review of Psychology, 43,* 235–267.

Zito, J. M., Craig, T. J., & Wanderling, J. (1991). New York under the *Rivers* decision: An epidemiologic study of drug treatment refusal. *American Journal of Psychiatry, 148,* 904–909.

Zucker, L. M., & Zucker, T. F. (1961). Fatty, a new mutation in the rat. *Journal of Heredity, 52,* 275–278.

Zylman, R. (1975). Drinking-driving and fatal crashes: A new perspective. *Journal of Alcohol & Drug Education, 21,* 1–10.

Name Index

Subject Index

Note: Italicized page numbers that appear in this index refer to pages on which a running glossary definition of the particular term can be found.

Acknowledgments

Page 4, cartoon, © Jane Zich, 1986. This cartoon was originally published in the January 1986 edition of the *APA Monitor*; **page 43,** Figure 2.5. From "The Neuron," by Charles F. Stevens. Copyright © 1979 by Scientific American, Inc. All rights reserved; **pages 58–59,** Figures 2.11–2.12. From "The Organization of the Brain," by Walle J. H. Nauta and Michael Feirtag. Copyright © 1979 by Scientific American, Inc. All rights reserved; **page 62,** Figure 2.13. From "The Brain" by David H. Hubel. Copyright © 1979 by Scientific American, Inc. All rights reserved; **page 64,** Figure 2.15, From "Specializations of the Human Brain," by Norman Geschwind. Copyright © 1979 by Scientific American, Inc. All rights reserved; **page 75,** Figure 2.20. REPRINTED FROM PSYCHOLOGY TODAY MAGAZINE. Copyright © 1985. Reprinted by permission of Psychology Today, Inc.; **page 102,** Table 3.4. From "How Children Become Friends," by J. M. Gottman. In *Monographs of the Society for Research in Child Development*, 48, pp. 54–55. © the Society for Research in Child Development, Inc., Reprinted by permission; **page 112,** Figure 3.13. From Tanner, J. M.: Growth and endocrinology of the adolescent. In Gardner, L. In *Endocrine and Genetic Diseases of Childhood*, 2nd edition. Philadelphia, W. B. Saunders Company, 1975; **page 129,** Table 4.1. From Stein, P. J., "Singlehood," in *Contemporary Families and Alternative Lifestyles*, edited by E. D. Macklin and R. H. Rubin. Copyright 1983 by Sage Publications. Reprinted by permission; **page 166,** Figure 5.6. From "Floaters" by Jearl Walker. Copyright © 1982 by Scientific American, Inc. All rights reserved; **page 210,** Figure 6.12. From "Asking the What for Question in Auditory Perception," by A. S. Bregman, 1981, in M. Q. Kubovy & J. Pomeranz (Eds.), *Perceptual Organization*. Copyright 1981 by Lawrence Erlbaum and Associates. Reprinted by permission; **page 219,** Figure 6.19. REPRINTED FROM PSYCHOLOGY TODAY MAGAZINE. Copyright © 1983. Reprinted by permission of Psychology Today, Inc.; **page 245,** Figure 7.5. From "Physiological Correlates of Prolonged Sleep Deprivation in Rats," by A. Rechtschaffen, M. A. Gilliland, B. M. Bergmann, & I. B. Winter. In *Science*, 1983, 221, pp. 182–184. Copyright 1983 by the American Association for the Advancement of Science; **page 248,** Figure 7.7. From WIDE AWAKE AT 3:00 A.M. by Richard M. Coleman. Richard M. Coleman, Ph.D., psychologist, is a former co-director of the Stanford University Sleep Disorders Clinic; serves on the Clinical Faculty of the Stanford University medical School; and is president of Coleman & Associates (since 1980)—an international corporate work/shift scheduling firm in Ross, California; **page 259,** Table 7.2. Copyrighted, Stanford University, 1962, and used by permission; **page 285,** Figure 8.8. From "Thorndike and the Problem of Animal Intelligence," by M. E. Bitterman. In *American Psychologist*, 1969, 24, 444–453. Copyright 1969 by the American Psychological Association. Reprinted by permission of the publisher and author; **page 286,** Figure 8.9. From "Thorndike and the Problem of Animal Intelligence," by M. E. Bitterman. In *American Psychologist*, 1969, 24, 444–453. Copyright 1969 by the American Psychological Association. Reprinted by permission of the publisher and author; **page 297,** quotation. Reprinted from 1962 NEBRASKA SYMPOSIUM ON MOTIVATION, by permission of University of Nebraska Press. Copyright © 1962 by the University of Nebraska Press; **page 303,** Figure 8.13. Map by: Wood Ronsaville Harlin, Inc. Reprinted by permission; **page 313,** Figure 9.1. From "Could a Machine Think?" by Paul M. Churchland and Patricia Smith Churchland. Copyright © 1990 by Scientific American, Inc. All rights reserved; **page 320,** Figure 9.6. From "Retention as a Function of the Method of Measurement," by L. Postman & L. Rau. In *University of California Publications in Psychology*, 1957, 8(3). Reprinted by permission of the University of California Press; **page 336,** Figure 9.16. From "Long-term Memory for a Common Object," by R. S. Nickerson & M. J. Adams. In *Cognitive Psychology*, 1979, 11, 287–306. Reprinted by permission of Academic Press, Inc., and the author; **page 369,** Figure 10.7. From WORD, Fig. 1, p. 154, 1958. By permission of Johnson Reprint Corporation; **page 405,** Figure 11.5. From "Steepness of Approach and Avoidance Gradients in Humans as a Function of Experience," by S. Epstein & W. D. Fenz in *Journal of Experimental Psychology*, 1965, 70, 1–12. Copyright 1967 by the American Psychological Association. Reprinted by permission of the author; **pages 406–407,** Figures 11.6–11.8. From "The Opponent-Process Theory of Acquired Motivation," by R. L. Solomon. In *American Psychologist*, 1980, 35, 691–712. Copyright 1980 by the American Psychological Association. Reprinted by permission of the publisher and author; **page 406,** Table 11.1. From "The Opponent-Process Theory of Acquired Motivation," by R. L. Solomon. In *American Psychologist*, 1980, 35, 691–712. Copyright 1980 by the American Psychological Association. Reprinted by permission of the publisher and author; **page 433,** Figure 12.9. From "Autonomic Nervous System Activity Distinguishes Among Emotions," by P. Ekman, R. W. Levenson, & W. V. Friesen. In *Science*, 1983, 221, pp. 1208–1210. Copyright 1983 by the American Association for the Advancement of Science; **page 435,** Figure 12.11. REPRINTED WITH PERMISSION FROM PSYCHOLOGY TODAY MAGAZINE. © 1980 (Sussex Publishers, Inc.); **page 437,** Figure 12.13. REPRINTED WITH PERMISSION FROM PSYCHOLOGY TODAY MAGAZINE, © 1980 (Sussex Publishers, Inc.); **page 455,** Figure 13.1. Figure A5 from the RAVEN STANDARD PROGRESSIVE MATRICES is reproduced by permission of J. C. Raven, Limited; **page 460,** Figure 13.4. From *Stability and Change in Human Characteristics*, by B. S. Bloom. New York: John Wiley & Sons, 1964; Reprinted by permission of the publisher; **page 476,** Figure 14.3. Taken from the *Handbook for the 16PF*. © 1970 by the Institute for Personality and Ability Testing, Inc. Reproduced by permission; **page 489,** Figure 14.5. Reproduced by permission from the *Minnesota Multiphasic Personality Inventory Manual*. Copyright 1943. Renewed 1970; 1951; 1967 by the University of Missouri. Published by the Psychological Corporation. All rights reserved;

page 493, Figure 14.6. Reprinted by permission of the publishers from Henry A. Murray, THEMATIC APPERCEPTION TEST, Cambridge, Mass.; Harvard University Press. Copyright © 1943 by the President and fellows of Harvard College, © 1971 by Henry A. Murray; **page 507,** Concept Review./© Discover Magazine. Reprinted with permission; **page 510,** Table 15.4. Reprinted with permission from the *Journal of Psychosomatic Research*, 11, by T. H. Holmes and R. H. Rahe, "The Social Readjustment Rating Scale," Copyright 1967, Pergamon Press, Ltd.; **page 514,** Figure 15.1. From "A New Discipline Probes Suicide's Multiple Causes," by C. Holden. In *Science*, 1992, 256, 1761–1762. Copyright 1992 by the American Association for the Advancement of Science; **page 538,** case study. From *Abnormal Psychology*, by G. C. Davison and J. M. Neale. Copyright © 1978. Reprinted by permission of John Wiley & Sons, Inc.; **page 540,** case study. From *Modern Clinical Psychiatry*, by Lawrence C. Kolb. Philadelphia: W. B. Saunders Company, 1973. Reprinted by permission of the publisher; **page 543,** case study. From Elton B. McNeil, THE QUIET FURIES, © 2967, pp. 47–49. Adapted by permission of Prentice-Hall, Inc., Englewood Cliffs, NJ; **page 544,** case study. From THE PEOPLE'S ALMANAC PRESENTS THE BOOK OF LISTS #2 by Irving Wallace, David Wallechinsky, Amy Wallace and Sylvia Wallace. Copyright © 1980 by Irving Wallace, David Wallechinsky, Amy Wallace and Sylvia Wallace. Used by permission of Bantam Books, Inc. All rights reserved; **page 548,** case study. From *Modern Clinical Psychiatry* by Lawrence C. Kolb. Philadelphia: W. B. Saunders Company, 1973. Reprinted by permission of the publisher; **page 549,** Figure 16.3. Reprinted by permission of Elliot Gershon, National Institute of Mental Health; **page 554,** case study. Copyright © 1965 by the William Alanson White Psychiatric Foundation, Inc. PSYCHIATRY (1965) 28: 351; **page 563,** case study. From Elton B. McNeil, THE QUIET FURIES; Man and Disorder, © 1967, pp. 85, 87. Reprinted by permission of Prentice-Hall, Inc. Englewood Cliffs, NJ; **page 623,** Figure 18.4. From "Group Inhibition of Bystander Intervention in Emergencies," by B. Latane & J. M. Darley. In *Journal of Personality & Social Psychology*, 1968, 10, 215–221. Copyright 1968 by the American Psychological Association. Adapted by permission of the author; **page 626,** Figure 18.5. Reprinted from "Developmental and Cross-Cultural Differences in the Cooperative Behavior of Young Children." in *Journal of Cross-Cultural Psychology*, Vol. 2 (1971), pp. 365–371, with permission of the author, M. C. Madsen, and the publisher, Sage Publications, Beverly Hills/London; **page 629,** cartoon. Drawing by Booth; © 1977 The New Yorker Magazine, Inc.; **page 663,** quotation. From *Close Relationships*, edited by Harold H. Kelley. W. H. Freeman and Company. Copyright © 1983; **page 667,** Figure 19.2. From "Sex and Sexuality in History," by N. Sussman. In B. J. Sadock, H. I. Kaplan, & A. M. Freedman (Eds.), *The Sexual Experience*. © 1976 The Williams & Wilkins Co., Baltimore. Reprinted by permission of the publisher and editor; **page A-12,** Table A.1. From "Behavioral Toxicology and Environmental Health Science," in *American Psychologist*, 1983, 38, 1188–1197. Copyright 1983 by the American Psychological Association. Reprinted by permission of the author.

Photo Credits

7 © Brown Brothers; **8** © Brown Brothers; **9** © Brown Brothers; **11** © Brown Brothers; **13** © Ted Polumbaum; **21** © 1979 Joel Gordon; **27** © Sepp Seitz, Woodfin Camp and Associates; **34** Henri Matisse (French, 1869–1954), *Ivy in Flower*, 1953, collage colored paper and pencil, 112" × 112" Dallas Museum of Art, Foundation for the Arts Collection, gift of the Albert and Mary Lasker Foundation; **36** Courtesy Carolina Biological Supply Company; **54** Paul Biddle & Tim Mal Yon/Science Photo Library; **57** (left) Lester V. Bergman and Associates; **57** (right) Lester V. Bergman and Associates; **61** © Susan McCartney, Photo Researchers; **65** © Peter Berndt, M.D., Custom Medical Stock Photo; **66** Courtesy of M.E. Phelps and J.C. Mazziotta, UCLA School of Medicine; **67** Dr. Dean F. Wong, Division of Nuclear Medicine, The Johns Hopkins Medical Institutions; **67** Dr. Dean F. Wong, Division of Nuclear Medicine, The Johns Hopkins Medical Institutions; **78** Kupka, *Disks of Newton*, Georges Pompideu National Art and Culture Center; **80** Photo courtesy of Anthony DeCasper, photographer Walter Salinger; **83** © Dr. Richardson, Custom Medical Stock Photo; **84** CNRI/Phototake; **85** © Ron Chapple, FPG International; **86** © Herb Snitzer, Stock, Boston; **90** © Jon Feingersh, Stock, Boston; **91** University of Wisconsin Primate Laboratory; **95** © Jim Pickerell, Stock, Boston; **96** © Wide World; **97** (both photos) © Doug Goodman, Monkmeyer Press; **99** © Owen Franken, Stock, Boston; **100** (left) © Margaret Miller, Photo Researchers; **100** (right) © Ray Ellis, Photo Researchers; **101** © Mike Mazzaschi, Stock, Boston; **103** © Donald Dietz, Stock, Boston; **104** © John Turner, FPG International; **105** © Richard Hutchings, Photo Researchers; **109** © Cary Wolinsky, Stock, Boston; **113** © J. Berndt, Stock, Boston; **118** Pierre Bonnard, *Dining Room on the Garden*, 1934–35, Solomon R. Guggenheim Museum, New York, Gift, Solomon R. Guggenheim, 1938, photo by Carmelo Guadagno, copyright The Solomon R. Guggenheim Foundation, New York; **121** (top) UPI/Bettmann; **121** (bottom) © Tim Davis, Photo Researchers; **124** © Jim Pickerell, Stock, Boston; **125** © Kent Knudson, FPG International; **126** © William S. Helsel, Tony Stone Worldwide; **127** FPG International; **129** E. Willard Spurr/U.S. Library of Congress/Science Photo Library, Photo Researchers; **130** © Dan Bosler, Tony Stone Worldwide; **131** © Bohdan Hrynewych, Stock, Boston; **133** © Blair Seitz, Photo Researchers; **136** © Michael Krasowitz, FPG International; **143** © Barbara Alper, Stock, Boston; **145** (top) Photo by author; **145** (bottom) © Dr. Dennis J. Selkoe; **146** © Ron Chapple, FPG International; **152** © Dan Bosler, Tony Stone Worldwide; **153** © Bill Losh, FPG International; **158** Josef Albers, *Hommage to the Square: Apparition*, 1959, Solomon R. Guggenheim Museum, New York, photo by